Human Sexuality

From Cells to Society

Martha S. Rosenthal
Florida Gulf Coast University

Australia • Brazil • Japan • Korea • Mexico • Singapore • Spain • United Kingdom • United States

WADSWORTH
CENGAGE Learning·

Human Sexuality: From Cells to Society
Martha S. Rosenthal

Senior Publisher: Linda Ganster

Publisher: Jon-David Hague

Executive Editor: Jaime Perkins

Developmental Editor: Tangelique Williams

Freelance Development Editor: Angela Kao

Assistant Editor: Jessica Alderman

Media Editor: Lauren Keyes

Marketing Manager: Christine Sosa

Marketing Coordinator: Janay Pryor

Marketing Communications Manager: Laura Localio

Senior Content Project Manager: Pat Waldo

Design Director: Rob Hugel

Senior Art Director: Vernon Boes

Senior Manufacturing Planner: Karen Hunt

Rights Acquisitions Specialist: Roberta Broyer

Production Service: Megan Greiner,
    Graphic World Inc.

Text Designer: Jeanne Calabrese

Photo and Text Researcher: Terri Wright

Illustrators: Graphic World Inc. and Argosy

Cover Designer: Jeanne Calabrese

Cover Photo: DOF-PHOTO by Fulvio/Getty Images

Compositor: Graphic World Inc.

For product information and technology assistance, contact us at
Cengage Learning Customer & Sales Support, 1-800-354-9706

For permission to use material from this text or product,
submit all requests online at **www.cengage.com/permissions**
Further permissions questions can be e-mailed to
permissionrequest@cengage.com

Library of Congress Control Number: 2011931456

Student Edition:

ISBN-13: 978-0-618-75571-4

ISBN-10: 0-618-75571-3

Loose-leaf Edition:

ISBN-13: 978-0-8400-2890-7

ISBN-10: 0-8400-2890-3

Wadsworth
20 Davis Drive
Belmont, CA 94002-3098
USA

Cengage Learning is a leading provider of customized learning solutions with office locations around the globe, including Singapore, the United Kingdom, Australia, Mexico, Brazil, and Japan. Locate your local office at
www.cengage.com/global

Cengage Learning products are represented in Canada by Nelson Education, Ltd.

To learn more about Wadsworth, visit **www.cengage.com/wadsworth.com**

Purchase any of our products at your local college store or at our preferred online store **www.CengageBrain.com**

Printed in Canada
1 2 3 4 5 6 7 15 14 13 12 11

This book is for
Barbara Soloff Rosenthal
(June 21, 1936–December 17, 2007)

and

Charles H. Press
(March 20, 1933–February 8, 2010)

about the author

Martha S. Rosenthal began her educational journey studying drugs. She now studies sex and suspects that rock 'n' roll is next. Dr. Rosenthal is a professor of physiology at Florida Gulf Coast University, where she teaches Human Sexuality, Human Physiology, Neuroscience, and Drugs and Society and coteaches Interdisciplinary Issues in Gender. She received her bachelor's degree in biology from the University of Virginia, her master's degree in neuropharmacology from Brown University, and her PhD in neuroscience from UCLA. Dr. Rosenthal taught her first human sexuality class more than 10 years ago and was instantly hooked. Her educational passion is to encourage open and honest communication about sexuality. Dr. Rosenthal also believes that no topic can be understood in a vacuum and that all disciplines influence each other. She has spent a lifetime in multidisciplinary study and identifies with Robert Browning's Last Duchess—"she liked whate'er she looked on, and her looks went everywhere"—(with a different context and hopefully a better outcome). In addition, Dr. Rosenthal guides students to critically analyze and evaluate the information they encounter. Dr. Rosenthal has received several awards, including teacher of the year at both the University of Florida and at Florida Gulf Coast University, and she has been recognized as one of the 20 most influential people on the campus of FGCU. Her mother would like it mentioned that she played violin at Carnegie Hall when she was 9 years old. Dr. Rosenthal is also the coauthor of *Discoveries in Human Systems* (North Carolina: Hunter, 2004). In addition to textbooks, she has written articles on the physiology of sleep and on the use of games in the classroom. Dr. Rosenthal has presented on issues of teaching human sexuality at national and international conferences. When not writing, Dr. Rosenthal enjoys reading, working out, watching movies, and spending time with family and friends.

brief contents

contents

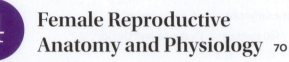

4 Female Reproductive Anatomy and Physiology 70

5 Sex and Gender 100

6 Sexual Response 128

12 Contraceptive Choices and Ending Pregnancy 288

13 Conception, Pregnancy, and Birth 320

14 Sexually Transmitted Infections 354

15 Variations in Sexual Behavior 384

16 Sexual Coercion and Violence 404

17 Sex for Sale 434

preface

Why a book on human sexuality? Although young Americans are bombarded with sexual information, U.S. teen pregnancy rates are among the highest of any industrialized nation, and more than one out of every four Americans will be infected with a sexually transmitted infection during his or her lifetime. American teenagers spend most of their free time watching television, surfing the Internet, playing video games, listening to music, or watching movies, all of which increasingly include sexual content. In fact, for teens aged 13 to 15, much of their information about sexuality comes from entertainment media. Yet only 1 out of every 11 prime-time programs with sexual content presents the risks or responsibilities associated with sex. In addition, our perceptions and knowledge of human sexuality are undergoing widespread changes. New developments in health research, changing laws concerning sexual activity and marriage, and new contraceptive options are only a few of the issues facing us today. Because sexuality has such a momentous impact on our lives, our loves, and our health, open and honest communication about sexuality is essential.

Human Sexuality: From Cells to Society is intended as the primary textbook for a course in human sexuality. The text is appropriate for students with no prior college courses in biology, psychology, or sociology. *Human Sexuality: From Cells to Society* will guide students through the many aspects that encompass human sexuality: biological, psychological, cultural, societal, legal, and religious. It will help students learn to critically evaluate the information about sexuality to which they are exposed and will help students make informed sexual decisions in their own lives.

Why I Wrote This Book

I have been teaching human sexuality for more than a decade, and (shh . . . don't tell my other classes) it is by far my favorite course. Don't get me wrong, I love teaching physiology and neuroscience. Students in these classes will often come show me interesting rashes and the weird ways their appendages bend and ask me for a diagnosis. But when my human sexuality students come to me with questions—about love, relationships, pregnancy, violence, orgasms, or interesting rashes and the weird way their appendages bend—I am so honored that they feel they can trust me with the most intimate aspects of their lives. My desire to reach more students than my classroom could hold was the driving force behind the writing of this book. Facets of sexuality—love, identity, sexual response, gender, parenthood—are among the most essential and defining characteristics of our lives, yet somehow there's still ignorance and embarrassment associated with many of these issues. In this book, I hope to tear off the metaphorical fig leaf and candidly explore these essential and fundamental issues.

Throughout this journey, interested friends and coworkers have asked me which chapter was my favorite. I have to admit, some chapters were more fun than others. Some made me run to my computer to post fun facts to my Facebook wall. Some gave me interesting ideas to try at home. Some chapters made me stomp around the house waving my arms around in frustration. Some chapters made me weep. But what I learned throughout the process is that I am—as I ever was and ever shall be—a teacher, and my greatest joy is helping to guide students on their journeys to become lifelong learners.

The Story of the Book

Human Sexuality: From Cells to Society is designed to help students understand the diverse foundations of human sexuality, as well as provide them with skills to critically evaluate current research and data about sexuality.

The objectives of this text are to

- facilitate the application of **critical thinking skills**.
- present the material in such a way that students can see the varied aspects from **many disciplines** that affect sexuality.
- present the **biological foundations** of human sexuality in an understandable, accessible manner for non-science majors.
- increase awareness and appreciation of **diversity** of views concerning sexuality.
- help students be **more comfortable** in thinking and communicating about sex.
- help students **make informed decisions** regarding sexuality in their own lives.

Critical Thinking

A recent Google search of "contraception" produced 15,000,000 sites, including the Planned Parenthood website, ads from pharmaceutical companies, a Catholic educator's resource on presenting the church's views against contraception, as well as a site explaining how to use a waterproof vibrator in your swimming pool. People today are exposed to more sexual information than ever before, but as with any commodity, as the supply increases, value decreases. We all need to learn to evaluate information to assess its worth. Consequently, *Human Sexuality: From Cells to Society* is intended to help in the development of critical thinking skills so students can evaluate the flood of sexual information they face on a daily basis.

"Critical thinking" involves maintaining a certain degree of skepticism about information, analyzing claims and arguments based on evidence, and recognizing and evaluating the value assumptions that may underlie one's position. As critical thinking is not only a set of skills to be learned but also a way of relating to the world, the text gives exercises designed to help students incorporate these skills and attitudes so they can become intelligent consumers of information. The text will encourage students to examine their own values and the source of data and to consider further questions to more fully discern fact from opinion.

Multidisciplinary Focus

Your author teaches courses in human sexuality, anatomy and physiology, drugs and society, gender, physiological psychology, neuroscience, and other courses that focus on critical thinking and the development of values. My diverse background has made me appreciate a multidisciplinary approach. I believe that no topic can be understood in a vacuum and that all disciplines influence each other.

Human sexuality involves the interaction of body, mind, spirit, and society. It is a tapestry woven from threads of biology, psychology, culture, society, history, language, media, law, and religion. If one were to pull away any one of these threads, the resulting fabric would no longer be whole. *Human Sexuality: From Cells to Society* is therefore designed with a multidisciplinary perspective and will take into account not only the biological and psychological components of sexuality but also the historical, cultural, societal, legal, medical, and religious aspects as well.

Although each topic discussed in this text will cover multidisciplinary aspects, this text is not meant to be the ultimate authority on sex and culture *and* sex and law *and* sex and religion *and* sex and society, etc. That text would be cost-prohibitive, as well as inconveniently long, perhaps approaching the size of Texas. Instead, *Human Sexuality: From Cells to Society* is designed to present background information on each of these areas and to facilitate discussion on the topic. Therefore, each chapter will cover the following:

- *Biology, including anatomy, physiology, technology, and sociobiology.* A biological foundation is key, but it is important to remember that conditions we may have considered to be biological often have a strong societal or cultural influence, while society and culture is likewise strongly influenced by our biology.
- *Psychology.* In some ways, psychology is the "marriage" of nature and nurture, the interaction of biological and societal influences. The brain is the largest sexual organ—emotions, thoughts, and beliefs have a major influence on our sexual behaviors and feelings.
- *Culture, society, and history.* It is easy to forget that aspects of sexuality vary greatly depending on the time and place. Considering each of these gives the students a necessary sense of proportion and reminds them that "there are more things in heaven and earth . . . than are dreamt of in your philosophy."
- *Language.* Language structures thought; it is the use of language that forms our perception of the world and thus guides our thinking and behavior. *Human Sexuality: From Cells to Society* will consider the language used to describe human sexuality and explore the impact this language has on our attitudes.
- *Law.* Because laws change based on societal norms, they give a good illustration of a society's values and expectations. It is also important for students to recognize the legal statuses of many of the issues affecting their lives. As an example, refusal statutes (Chapter 12) and laws on sexting (Chapter 17) are presented in a way to make students recognize the implications these laws have on their own lives.
- *Religion/spirituality.* Religion is a foundation of many people's lives and influences our views, attitudes, and behaviors.
- *Media.* We are inundated with media images of a sexual nature. These images form a backdrop for the development of our views on what is attractive, what is considered appropriate, and what is expected of us. This text will give examples from movies, TV, music, and other sources related to each topic.
- *Health.* Issues related to sexual health encompass all of the above aspects. Health is not only a biological issue but also a psychological issue because the mind has a powerful effect on the body. How society perceives these issues changes over time and in different cultures, as seen by the shifting view of menstruation or pregnancy as a health concern. Finally, societal issues also have a great impact on our health, as illustrated by religious issues (abortion and contraception), legal issues (the legality of anabolic steroids or the legal status of postsurgery transgendered individuals), and the media (the never-ending messages about "male enhancement" or the public perception of HIV/AIDS.)

Increased Emphasis on Biological Foundation of Human Sexuality

Students often consider the biological components of sexuality to be the most difficult (and most boring) part of the course; however, it is the foundation, or the "playing field," upon which all the other forces interact. A biological foundation is crucial for a full understanding of human sexuality. This text offers a biological perspective to topics that may traditionally have been presented with a solely psychological perspective, such as relationships and communication, or love and marriage. The text will by no means dismiss the importance of psychology in the development of our sexuality; rather, it will also highlight the biological foundations of our culture and society. However, the author does have sympathy for the students bemoaning the necessity of understanding the anatomy and physiology, as well as for the faculty who have to listen to all the bemoaning. I hope that I have presented biological topics in an easy-to-understand way.

Contemporary, Inclusive, Accessible Presentation

The concerns and issues facing today's students are very different than they were in the 20th century—sexting, Gardasil, and the legal recognition of same-sex marriage are just a few issues that didn't even exist a decade ago. *Human Sexuality: From Cells to Society* is hot off the press. The research and cultural references are current and relevant.

I tried to write this text as if I were speaking to you individually. I aimed to make the text informal, conversational, and humorous. If you don't get my humor, I apologize; I guess you just had to be there. As I was sitting at my computer, typing away, I cracked myself up. Some examples of humor were deemed a bit too much (my STI greeting cards didn't make the cut—thank goodness for wise editors)—but I hope you enjoy reading this text. I tried to find a way to present not only what students need to know but also what they *want* to know.

In this text, I also tried to show the great diversity of sexuality, such as GLBTQ issues, intersexuality, interracial relationships, and sexuality across the life span. Perspectives and artwork include individuals of all ages, orientations, ethnicities, and physical appearances. Most other texts contain separate chapters on sex throughout the life span. This segregation sets these aspects of sexuality apart and gives the impression that they somehow don't belong with the discussion of "normal" sexuality. In *Human Sexuality: From Cells to Society,* issues of diversity, sexual orientation, and sex across the life span are discussed throughout each chapter.

Organization and Content

Each chapter will begin with an introductory vignette, such as a movie quote, a personal account from the author's files, or a historical anecdote. A chapter outline is then presented. Each section includes learning objectives to help guide students. At the end of each chapter is a chapter summary that maps to the learning objectives and an opportunity for self-evaluation with sample questions and issues for discussion. Each chapter also includes a list of further resources.

The chapter order is designed as a natural progression from topics. If you'll indulge me, it follows the classic story: "Once upon a time there were boys and girls" (Chapters 3–6: what *are* boys and girls, and what do they do?—anatomy, physiology, hormones, gender, sexual response). "They met and fell in love and had sex" (Chapters 7–11: attraction and dating, love and relationships, sexual orientation, consensual sexual behaviors). "Because this is the real world and not a fairy tale, they then had to deal with contraception, pregnancy, and STIs" (Chapters 12–14). "This classic story will be shown on Cinemax" (Chapters 15–17: paraphilias, sexual coercion, sex for sale). The end. It should be noted that the chapter on male anatomy and physiology does not precede the chapter on female A&P for any antiquated reasons of male dominance but rather because most students find the male reproductive system easier to understand than the female system.

Distinctive Content by Chapter

- **Chapter 1: Introduction to Sexuality:** In this chapter, I want to show that human sexuality is ubiquitous, pervasive, and essential to the very core of our most basic characteristics. I show students that the understanding of human sexuality is not limited to one field of study—to truly examine sexuality, one must consider many different disciplines. This chapter also includes the most up-to-date information about abstinence-only education.
- **Chapter 2: Evaluating Studies of Sexuality:** I consider some of the material in this chapter to be among the most important knowledge that a student can learn. In this chapter, I cover the foundations of critical thinking, which is a major focal point of this text. We are all exposed to so much information every day, and it is vital to learn how to evaluate these messages to determine their worth. In this chapter, I guide students through the skills, attitudes, and exercises that can help them become intelligent consumers of information. Also in this chapter, I recognize some of the pioneers who led the way for today's sexuality investigators and discuss many of the factors that scientists must take into consideration when designing their research.

- **Chapters 3 and 4: Male and Female Reproductive Anatomy and Physiology:** These chapters present the biological groundwork for the field of human sexuality: the anatomy, physiology, and hormones. Students often find the biological foundations to be boring or difficult, so I tried to present this information as clearly as possible but also to make it entertaining with some "real-world" tidbits that the students can relate to.
- **Chapter 5: Sex and Gender:** Of all the characteristics a child brings into the world, a person's sex and gender will have the greatest impact—on his or her relationships, personality, skills, grades, career, salary, hobbies, and health. Sex and gender are among the most fascinating, as well as the most controversial aspects of sexuality and identity. What is a man? What is a woman? How different are we, really? In this chapter we discuss how the line between men and women isn't as defined as many think, and we critically evaluate some of the research about sex and gender differences.
- **Chapter 6: Sexual Response:** This chapter covers how our bodies respond sexually, as well as the psychological and physiological factors that affect our responses. As a neuroscientist by training, I tried to include more information than is found in other texts about how the brain and senses influence arousal. I also discuss sexual problems and treatments and critically evaluate the current classification of sexual dysfunction from a feminist perspective.
- **Chapter 7: Attraction, Dating, and Hooking Up:** In my years of teaching, I have found that the material in this chapter is particularly relevant to college students, yet most textbooks don't cover it in much detail. Worrying about how you stack up physically, looking for a partner, hooking up—this is part of the reality of students' lives, but it is given short shrift in most texts. The material in this chapter has led to some of my students' (and my!) favorite lectures. This chapter also includes some biological perspectives that are missing from some other texts, such as the possible role of pheromones and human leukocyte antigens (HLAs) in attraction.
- **Chapter 8: Love:** Ah, love. Love is one of the most basic, universal, and important of human emotions. In this chapter, we talk about what love is; the different types of love; the biological, psychological, and sociological foundations of love; and cultural expressions of love. Students are led through a critical evaluation of the possible gender differences in jealousy. Although many books focus solely on psychological factors, this text also highlights the neuroanatomical, neurochemical, and hormonal foundations of love.
- **Chapter 9: Committed Relationships and Communicating With Your Partner:** In this chapter, I discuss the many different types of adult relationships and the ways that these relationships have changed over the years (for example, marriage is no longer the most common type of relationship among adults in the United States). Another focus of this chapter is the importance of communication with one's partner. Using information from relationship experts such as John Gottman, I give guidelines and suggestions for effective communication and conflict resolution.
- **Chapter 10: Sexual Orientation:** My original plan was to have no separate chapter for sexual orientation, to get away from the idea that it is an "unusual" sexuality that needs to be segregated into its own chapter. However, as I developed the

1 Introduction to Sexuality

"SEX! Now that I have your attention..."

–Bart Simpson's campaign posters

© YURI ARCURS/age fotostock RF

© Image Source/Age fotostock

© Glowimages RM/Age fotostock

Why a Course on Human Sexuality?

After completion of this section, you will be able to . . .

- ○ Recognize that sexuality is ubiquitous and that every person in the world expresses his or her sexuality in his or her own way.

- ○ Reflect on the various emotions that are brought up when you think about sexuality.

- ○ Consider the different sources from which you learn about sexuality.

- ○ Recognize the importance of sexuality education.

- ○ Compare and contrast the different definitions of normality.

Imagine you are standing on a street corner, watching people walk by. A 60-year-old married woman passes in front of you. She is involved in a passionate affair with another man, and she is afraid her husband will find out. Lost in thought, she accidentally brushes against a 20-year-old man. He scowls at her, but his anger is related to his fears that there is something "wrong" with him. He has been dating the woman he loves for 6 months, and now that she has consented to having intercourse, he is having problems maintaining an erection. A 14-year-old girl in low-rider jeans with a distracted look enters the coffee shop next to you. Last night she kissed her best girlfriend and she's starting to fall in love with her. She feels both elated and confused. A mother passes by, holding the hand of her 3-year-old son. He is happy because he has discovered a fun game to play with his penis—bonking it back and forth, which makes it stand up!

Facets of **sexuality**—love, orientation, sexual response, gender, and parenthood—are among the most essential and defining characteristics of our lives. Yet somehow there's still embarrassment associated with many of these issues. Because sexuality and **sexual health** have such a momentous impact on our lives and our loves, open and honest communication about sexuality is vital.

Sexuality is ubiquitous—each day, there are 100 million acts of sexual intercourse, resulting in the birth of more than five babies every second; but sexuality is also unique, as every one of the nearly 7 billion persons on this planet expresses sexuality in his or her own way (World Health Organization, 1992). Sexuality also underlies our most basic identities—whom we love, whether or not we have children, and how we characterize ourselves. The first thing we want to know about a baby is related to sexuality: "Is it a boy or a girl?" And while the ultimate goal of all other bodily functions is the survival of the individual, sex affects no less than the survival of the species. Obvi-

Sexuality A broad term that includes many facets of the way we experience our lives as sexual beings. Sexuality encompasses our sexual behaviors, feelings, gender identities and roles, sexual orientation, and reproduction. It is influenced by physical, psychological, spiritual and cultural factors.

Sexual health The World Health Organization defines sexual health as ". . . a state of physical, emotional, mental, and social well-being related to sexuality . . . [that] requires a positive and respectful approach to sexuality and sexual responses, as well as the possibility of having pleasurable and safe sexual experiences" (World Health Organization, 2006).

ously, sex interests people. But what is sex? The word can describe many things: an act of intercourse, a person's gender, or the exchange of genetic material. Sexuality involves physical, emotional, cognitive, cultural, social, and spiritual components, and we must consider each of these to begin to understand the depth of the human sexual experience.

Here's an exercise to illustrate your feelings about sexuality. First, take out three pieces of paper. On one piece of paper, draw a picture of the human heart. Don't consult any sources or check any diagrams, just draw an accurate image of the human heart as well as you can from memory. When you are done with that, on the back of the page, write down as many words as you can think of, slang or otherwise, to describe the heart (such as pump, ticker, etc.).

Now, on page two, draw an accurate diagram of external male genitalia and on the back of the page write down as many words as you can think of for the male genitalia. On page three, do the same for external female genitalia. Finished?

This exercise may elicit strong emotions, perhaps humor, perhaps embarrassment. You may be tempted to burn the pages so no one can see, or perhaps you will proudly display them on your refrigerator. Were you more comfortable drawing the human heart, or the vulva, or the penis? The odds are low that you have peered into your own chest and observed your heart at work, so how do you explain the relative familiarity you might have with that internal organ, compared to another that is more accessible? On the other hand, you may have found yourself gleefully writing down dozens of creative terms for the genitalia, filling the white space, while the lonely page for cardiac terms stared blankly back at you.

What does this say about the importance we ascribe to our genitalia? Why does the reproductive system evoke such intense feelings? It is, after all, just another organ system like the cardiovascular, digestive, or lymphatic systems. Why are there more taboos related to sexuality than to other human functions? Other animals routinely have sex in public, yet it is a private act in most human societies. We will consider these issues as we progress through the book.

Where Have You Learned About Sex?

Parents often agree that it is important to teach children about fire safety or about the necessity of wearing seat belts, yet many parents are embarrassed to discuss sex with their children. Nevertheless, while 31,000 Americans are injured or killed in a fire each year, it is estimated that 20 times that number of women are victims of rape, attempted rape, or sexual

"Without love and sex—without mating and pair bonding and reproduction—we would feel empty, isolated, and lonely; our societies would wither; and humankind would literally perish" (Regan, 2003, p. xiii).

Thirty percent of the health care costs in the United States are related to sexuality (Elders, 2010).

Sexual Knowledge Test

Take this test from the Alan Guttmacher Institute. Answers are given below, with more information available at www.guttmacher.org/support/quiz.html.

Multiple Choice

1. What percentage of Americans are not virgins when they get married?
   a. 50%
   b. 75%
   c. 95%

2. In Uganda, where abortion is illegal under nearly all circumstances, how does the abortion rate compare to that of the United States?
   a. It is more than twice the U.S. rate
   b. It is less than half the U.S. rate
   c. There are virtually no abortions in Uganda

3. In the United States, from 1995 to 2002, the proportion of teens receiving formal instruction about birth control methods:
   a. increased among both genders
   b. declined among both genders
   c. declined among males but not females

4. In the West African nation of Ghana, what percent of 15- to 19-year-old girls think they cannot get pregnant if they have sex standing up?
   a. 1%
   b. 7%
   c. 21%

5. Among women having an abortion in the United States, what percentage identify themselves with a religion?
   a. 26%
   b. 33%
   c. 78%

6. Which of the following statements about emergency contraception (EC) is true?
   a. In the U.S., EC must be kept behind pharmacy counters
   b. Women under age 17 in the U.S. still need a prescription
   c. The U.S. government does not distribute EC through its foreign aid programs
   d. All of these statements are true

7. For every $1 the U.S. government spends on family planning services under Title X, how much is saved in pregnancy-related health costs?
   a. $1.90 for every $1
   b. $2.60 for every $1
   c. $3.80 for every $1

8. The 24% decline in teen pregnancy in the United States between 1995 and 2002 is mainly the result of:
   a. A sharp decline in adolescent sexual activity
   b. An increase in oral and anal sex and a decrease in vaginal sex
   c. Improved contraceptive use
   d. Widespread fear of HIV/AIDS and other sexually transmitted infections

9. In Sub-Saharan Africa, where the AIDS epidemic has hit hardest, condom supplies amount to about how many condoms per man per year?
   a. 100
   b. 50
   c. 5

True or False

10. Fewer than half of all sexually active adult men in the United States receive any sexual or reproductive health services each year.

11. The hymen is a reliable indicator of whether a woman is a virgin.

12. After a vasectomy, a man can reach orgasm but does not ejaculate.

13. Most women do not show symptoms in the early stages of gonorrhea or chlamydia.

14. Women who masturbated to orgasm during adolescence generally have less difficulty reaching orgasm during intercourse than women who never masturbated.

15. Adult male homosexuals have lower than normal levels of male hormones.

16. A woman's ability to have vaginal orgasms is related to penis size.

17. Less than 10% of American women have had anal intercourse.

18. Sterilization is the most commonly used form of contraception in the United States.

Answers: (1) c; (2) a; (3) b; (4) c; (5) c; (6) d; (7) c; (8) c; (9) c; (10) T; (11) F; (12) F; (13) T; (14) T; (15) F; (16) F; (17) F; (18) T

---

assault (U.S. Fire Administration, 2005; Rape, Abuse, and Incest National Network, 2005). Whereas almost 3 million people are injured or killed in car accidents, approximately 19 million men and women are infected with a **sexually transmitted infection (STI)** each year in the United States, more than 9 million of whom are under age 24 (Weinstock, Berman, & Cates, 2004).

Have you had a serious discussion about sexuality with your parents? Do you think many of your peers have? If you did chat with your parents, was there any discussion beyond the basic facts of intercourse and possibly a mumbled plea to always use condoms? Or perhaps you weren't listening; although 98% of parents surveyed felt that they had communicated with their teens about sex, only 76% of teens said that these discussions took place (SIECUS, 2007). According to the Kaiser Family Foundation, teens

aged 13–15 report that most of their information about sexuality comes from the entertainment media, yet the vast majority of programs do not discuss the risks or responsibilities associated with sex (Kaiser Family Foundation, 2001; Kunkel, Eyal, Finnerty, Biely, & Donnerstein, 2005).

Sexuality education is vitally important. Although young Americans are bombarded with sexual informa-

Sexually transmitted infection (STI) An infection that is most commonly transmitted through sexual contact, such as chlamydia, genital herpes, or HIV.

Sexuality education A broad term to describe education about human sexuality, which may include information about physical, emotional, and social aspects of sexual health and disease; as well as rights and responsibilities; identity; values and attitudes; and many other aspects of sexual behavior.

© Elena Elisseeva/Alamy

tion, U.S. teen pregnancy rates are among the highest of any industrialized nation; each year, around 750,000 teenage women in the United States become pregnant (Alan Guttmacher Institute [AGI], 2010). More than one out of every four Americans will be infected with a sexually transmitted infection (STI) during his or her lifetime; and 25% of sexually active teenagers will contract an STI before they are eighteen (Weinstock et al., 2004). Why are teens in the United States getting pregnant and contracting STIs so much more than teens in other developed countries? Adolescents in the United States don't begin having sex at a significantly earlier age than teens in other **developed countries**, nor do they have significantly more sex. Yet American teens are much *less* likely to use contraceptives and much *more* likely to have more sexual partners and shorter relationships. Also, most other developed countries give their youth clear and unambiguous messages that sex should occur within committed relationships, and that sexually active teens are expected to protect themselves and their partners from pregnancy and STIs (Weinstock et al., 2004). Finally, adolescents in other countries have greater access to reproductive health services, and are taught comprehensive sex education in their schools (AGI, 2006; AGI, 2010).

What Is Normal?

When considering their sexuality, many people wonder, "Am I normal? Does anyone else feel this way?" As you will see, standards of normality are far from universal.

Every person has a different idea of what is "normal." Definitions of normality not only vary from culture to culture, from generation to generation, and from person to person, but also within individuals over the life span: if you were to ask one person her view of sexual normality, it would probably change as her life experience changed.

Historically, religious authorities often mandated sexual norms by declaring some sexual acts to be normal and moral and others to be abnormal and immoral. Many activities designated to be sexually "abnormal" were those that deviated from ancient procreation criteria; in other words, only sexual activities that could result in the birth of a child were considered normal. Hence, masturbation, oral sex, and same-sex activities were considered both abnormal and immoral. Today, many have shifted to a more science-based view of normality. More sexual practices that do not end in procreation are considered normal rather than sinful, and other sexual deviations are defined as disorders rather than abnormalities (Tiefer, 2004). However, the procreation criteria still influence and lurk beneath our views: variations in the ability to maintain an erection, for example, or "how much" sexual desire is normal are subject to the physician's prescription pad.

Developed country A country with financial, educational, and health standards that allow for higher levels of human well-being, as measured by the economic factors, life expectancy, and educational opportunities of the country. Developed countries include the United States, Canada, Australia, the countries of Western Europe, Israel, Kuwait, Japan, Hong Kong, and others.

Although humans experience a wide variety of sexual expression, only a narrow range of behavior falls into some societal views of "normal."

Researcher and educator Leonore Tiefer (2004) points out that there are many different standards of normality, and what is considered common and normal in one situation might be appalling or bizarre in another. The following are some of the ways normality can be defined, as outlined by Tiefer.

- *Subjective normality:* This standard supposes that "I am normal, and so is anyone like me." Most of us consciously or unconsciously subscribe to this point of view.
- *Statistical normality:* In this view, whatever behaviors are most common are normal. Because most Americans are not married, then by this standard marriage is abnormal.
- *Idealistic normality:* This is the pursuit of the ideal as normal, such as the idea that it is typical for women to look like Jennifer Aniston or Beyoncé.
- *Cultural normality:* While it is perfectly acceptable for heterosexual men in Egypt to hold hands, it is not the norm in Western culture. On the other hand, there are some cultures that consider kissing to be abnormal and disgusting.
- *Clinical normality:* Here, scientific data about health and illness is used to assess normality. Although this may seem to be a more subjective measure, clinical standards are not constant. For example, the normal life expectancy of an American in 1900 was 47 years, and physicians periodically reset the clinical standards for measurements such as blood pressure or thyroid hormone level. In addition, quantifiable measures can be difficult to use for nonphysiological matters—what is the "normal" amount of love a person should feel?

Just as there is no single benchmark of normality, there is no single discipline that defines the field of sexuality study. In the next section, we will see that the understanding of human sexuality encompasses many points of view and fields of study.

Perspectives of Sexuality: A Multidisciplinary Approach

After completion of this section, you will be able to . . .

○ Recognize that the understanding of sexuality is not limited to one discipline and that to fully investigate sexuality a person must examine many branches of knowledge.

○ Clarify the roles of biology, psychology, culture and society, anthropology, and language in understanding human sexuality.

○ Note the ways that sexual expression has changed throughout history.

○ Compare and contrast the different attitudes regarding sexuality held by some of the world's major religions.

Although the word *sex* is derived from the Latin word *secare,* meaning "to divide," sexuality is actually just the opposite: it unites and encompasses many fields and worldviews. To best study sexuality, you must therefore consider many disciplines. Human sexuality is a tapestry woven from threads of biology, psychology, culture, society, history, language, media, law, and religion. If you were to pull away any one of these threads, the resulting fabric would no longer be whole.

We often hear of the "nature vs. nurture" debate, although in many ways it is wrong to speak of *any* topic as being solely "biological" or solely "environmental." Most human behaviors are influenced by a combination of nature and nurture. Sexuality is no different. For example, orgasm is not simply a matter of mucous membranes spontaneously charging and discharging; it is dependent on environmental factors ("I can't! My parents are in the next room!"); cultural influences ("Not today, dear, I feel fat"); emotional states ("I don't even want you in my house today, there's no way you're going in *there*"); health status ("I swear, this has never happened to me before"); and others.

There is an old poem about six blind men who encounter an elephant. By feel alone, they try to describe the animal. One of the blind men grabs the elephant's trunk and decides that an elephant resembles a giant snake. One rests his hands upon the great side of the elephant and says that the animal is like a wall. The man who grabs the creature's tail announces that the animal resembles a rope. The poem ends with these lines:

© Ruxana Syed

> And so these men of Indostan
> Disputed loud and long,
> Each in his own opinion
> Exceedingly stiff and strong
> Though each was partly in the right
> And all were in the wrong!
>
> —*John Godfrey Saxe, 1887*

The study of human sexuality is much like those men with the elephant. Imagine a group of people gathered to consider the issue of same-sex attraction. The biologist might compare hormonal or neurological differences in gay and straight people, while a Freudian psychoanalyst may investigate the factors that occurred during the childhood of gay men. The role that lesbians play in different societies could be a topic of interest to a sociologist; a historian might study how the image of homosexuality has changed over the last century. To fully understand sexuality, we must consider many different branches of knowledge: the biological and the psychological, the legal and the religious, as well as the cultural and the historical.

Biology

If you were to ask people to name the sexual organs in males and females, they would most likely say "the penis and the vagina." Well, actually, if you were to ask people to name the sexual organs, they would most likely (a) blush, (b) smack you, or (c) call the cops. If you *were* to get an answer from them, they'd probably say "penis and vagina." But this is not entirely accurate. Although the penis is the primary male sexual organ, its counterpart in the female is the *clitoris,* not the vagina. It is the clitoris that is the seat of sexual pleasure in the female, and the penis and clitoris develop from the same embryological tissue.

Understanding the structure and function of the reproductive anatomy is essential to the understanding of sexuality, as the body is the "playing field" upon which all the other forces interact. Hormones also play a vital role in sexuality. Estrogen and testosterone are the primary hormones that influence sexual functioning; these hormones are responsible for the growth and development of reproductive organs, and also affect our sex drive and behaviors. Other hormones such as oxytocin are involved in maternal behavior and love. (We will explore the anatomy and physiology of the male and female reproductive systems, as well as the hormones that affect these systems, in Chapters 3 and 4.)

What is your largest sexual organ? You may be surprised by the answer to this question, but the brain is the organ that most affects your sexuality. Your brain and your senses play a significant role in your perception and initiation of sexuality. The brain initiates and organizes many sexual behaviors. Certain areas of the brain differ in size in males and females and may even differ in heterosexual males compared to gay males. These **sexually dimorphic** areas of the brain are being investigated regarding their role in some sexual behaviors. The effect of the brain on sexual behavior will be considered throughout the text.

What does the word *sensual* bring to mind? Although it has a sexual connotation, the word *sensual* simply means "relating to the senses." That we associate sensual with sex highlights the fact that our senses are closely related to our sexual behavior: sex is largely experienced through our senses. (We will discuss the role of the senses in sexual response in Chapter 6.)

What role do genes play in love and reproduction? When your partner leaves the dishes piled in the sink, assuming that the magical dish fairy will come to make the kitchen sparkling clean, you may start to appreciate the benefits of asexual reproduction. However, humans would not be here if it were not for sexual reproduction. For some plants and other animals, though, it's a different story. **Asexual reproduction** is the formation of new individuals from the cells of a single parent. It is common in plants, but less so in animals, although jellyfish, bees, and others can reproduce asexually. Asexual reproduction leads to generations of genetically identical individuals. As environments change, these individuals lack the degree of genetic variations that might aid in their survival. **Sexual reproduction** occurs when two sets of genetic information merge to make a new individual with a genetic pattern that is different from that of either parent. One major advantage to sexual reproduction is that it leads to genetic variability and

Biology The science of life and of living organisms.

Sexually dimorphic An anatomical area that has a different form in males and females.

Asexual reproduction A method of reproduction in which a single organism replicates itself.

Sexual reproduction The creation of new generations by the fusion of egg and sperm.

greater survival in changing environments. This drive for genetic variability is hardwired into our brains and behaviors. The incest taboo, one of the oldest and most powerful human proscriptions, prevents the intermingling of genes that are too similar.

Sociobiology/Evolutionary Psychology

Sociobiology is a way of explaining the behavior of humans today, based on evolutionary forces that have been working on us for thousands of years. In each species, some individuals are better adapted to their environment than others. Better-adapted members are more likely to survive to reproduce and pass their genes to the next generation, a phenomenon called **natural selection**. For instance, if 10,000 years ago, a child had a **mutation**—a random genetic change—that caused him or her to be born with legs that were undeveloped and weak, it's likely the child would not have survived long enough to pass the genetic trait for undeveloped legs to his or her offspring. Obviously we don't choose our future partners solely by their genetic structure. But sociobiological theory states that traits such as intelligence and physical health are valued, and these traits correspond to more adaptive genes.

Men and women exhibit different traits or behaviors based on their biology. For instance, who typically seeks out more sexual partners—males or females? According to cross-cultural evidence, males are more sexually promiscuous than females and are more willing to engage in a sexual relationship without an emotional involvement or commitment (Townsend & Levy, 1990). The sociobiological explanation for this is "sperm are cheap." That is to say, males produce hundreds of millions of sperm, and they produce them throughout their lives. A man can (theoretically) deposit his sperm in a different woman every day, and he does not have to stick around to take care of any of the offspring. Imagine the following two men: one has a genetic predisposition to have sex with a different woman every day, and the other is genetically inclined to be sexually faithful. The promiscuous man might produce hundreds of offspring, all with the theoretical gene for promiscuity. Some of these children might not survive, as he has presumably wandered off to impregnate another, but enough will survive for this trait to be passed on. The sexually selective man, however, might only pass on his monogamous genes to a few children. In a short time, the gene for promiscuity in men would become more prevalent.

According to sociobiological theory, different reproductive forces drive females. Females invest more time, energy, and risk with each offspring than males do. In contrast to the billions of sperm produced by males

each month, females are born with all their eggs and release just one egg each month. If that egg is fertilized and she becomes pregnant, her body is vulnerable for the next nine months. After the child is born, like the male, she has the option to abandon the child, but the child's (and the mother's genes') best hope of survival is if she cares for the child. The woman has already made a great investment of time and resources in carrying the child to term. In contrast to promiscuous males, sociobiological theory suggests that it is adaptive for females to be choosy, to wait to have sex with the best male that comes along—the one with the best genes—and the one who is most likely to stick around to help her raise her child, giving the child its best chances for survival (Dawkins, 2006).

It is important to note that there are also nonbiological factors that underlie the fact that heterosexual men report having more sexual partners than heterosexual women do. (These factors will be discussed further in Chapter 11.)

Still, evolutionary psychologists use this model to explain a number of human behaviors. For instance, according to sociobiological theory, men tend to prefer younger women who would be more likely to provide them with more and healthier offspring. Women, on the other hand, theoretically prefer older, richer men, because females are thought to be looking for someone who has the resources to take care of the offspring to insure its survival. John Townsend and Gary Levy (1990a, 1990b) investigated the effects of attractiveness and status (as embodied by clothing) on men and women's willingness to engage in relationships of varying levels of sexual intimacy. The scientists first photographed a group of male subjects who were rated as either handsome or homely. Each subject was photographed three times, in each picture wearing a different outfit. The "high-status" costume consisted of a blazer, shirt, designer tie, and conspicuous Rolex watch. Men wearing this outfit were described as being doctors. Men described as teachers wore a plain white button-down shirt and were rated as "medium status." "Work-

> **Aren't men just programmed to want sex all the time? Isn't it in our genes or something?**

Sociobiology/evolutionary psychology The study of how evolutionary forces affect our behavior.

Natural selection A process by which organisms that are best suited to their environment are most likely to survive. Traits that confer a reproductive advantage tend to be passed on, whereas maladaptive traits are lost.

Mutation A random change in the DNA sequence of a gene.

Who would you rather marry?

ing-class" or "low-status" men were depicted as trainee waiters and photographed wearing fast food restaurant uniforms. Townsend and Levy then asked female students to view the photographs of the men with accompanying descriptions and to state their willingness to engage in relationships with the various men. The study was also performed using male subjects who viewed similarly attired photographs of women.

Male subjects registered significantly more willingness to have sex than did female subjects, regardless of the status of the models, but they were less willing than female subjects to pursue a relationship. For men, the sexual desirability of the models was determined by their physical attractiveness, and it was *that* factor that determined whether the men would be willing to pursue a relationship with the model (Townsend & Levy, 1990b).

Female subjects were significantly more likely than male subjects to consider a relationship with a less attractive, high status model than with an attractive, low status model. For women, the socioeconomic status cues were important in determining the potential partner's suitability for a relationship, and *that* factor determined whether the woman would be willing to consider a sexual relationship with the model.

Critics of sociobiology and evolutionary psychology claim that it is **ethnocentric**, **heterocentric**, and **androcentric**—that it highlights the Western, white, male, heterosexual point of view to the exclusion of others. For instance, when studying nonhuman species, the scientists simply took it for granted that the females were monogamous and they then fit their theories to match this

© Floris Slooff/Shutterstock

idea. More recent studies suggest, however, that many of the females of species previously thought to be sexually faithful were stepping out of the nest unbeknownst to their male partners—more than 10% of offspring of socially monogamous birds are sired by a male other than their social father (Griffith, Owens, & Thuman, 2002). Others feel that sociobiology is reductionist and oversimplifies the foundations of complex human behaviors. Although there may be flaws in its theory or practice, sociobiology still provides an interesting perspective that should not be discounted.

Psychology

Sexuality is much more than just a physical response. Emotions, thoughts, and beliefs have a major influence on our sexual behaviors and feelings. In some ways, psychology is the "marriage" of nature and nurture, the interaction of biological and societal influences. There are various psychological theories of sexuality, which we will now explore briefly—additional coverage of psychological theories is integrated throughout the rest of the book.

We may be most attracted to people whose genetic patterns are unlike our own. The *major histocompatibility complex* (MHC) is a set of genes that produces immune cells to patrol the body and detect foreign cells. When a female mouse is offered a choice between two males, through her sense of smell she chooses the one with an MHC different than her own (Penn & Potts, 1999), thus giving her offspring more variation in their immune factors. A similar finding has been shown in humans (discussed in Chapter 7).

Psychoanalytic Theories

Sigmund Freud was one of the earliest and most influential of sexuality theorists. Freud thought that two forces largely drove human behavior: the death or aggressiveness drive and the more powerful sex drive or **libido**. According to Freud, a person's libido, or sexual energy, is channeled into particular areas of the body at different ages. These **erogenous zones** are the mouth, the anus, and the genitals. For the first year and a half of a baby's life, he or she is in the oral stage, focused on oral pleasures such as breastfeeding. From 18 months to 3 years, the child becomes concerned with toilet training and enters the anal phase. As a child becomes more interested in his or her own genitals and the genitals of others, he or she enters the phallic phase. Freud thought that this stage was particularly critical for male and female development. He believed that it was during this period women develop penis envy; also, it was during the phallic phase that an **Oedipal** or **Electra complex** might develop. Following the phallic phase, the latency period lasts from age 6 until puberty; during this period the sex drive lies relatively dormant. With puberty, the adolescent enters (and remains in) the genital phase, as genitally focused sexual urges again awaken.

Freud also believed that personality was comprised of three different components: the **id**, the **ego**, and the **superego**. The *id* (from the Latin for "it") represents primitive drives such as those related to sex, food, and aggression; it is the part of the unconscious mind that essentially says, "If it feels good, I want it *now!*" The *superego*, on the other hand, is our conscience or sense of morality. It originates in childhood when we acquire our views of right and wrong. Balancing the id and the superego, our primitive desires and our conscience, is the *ego* (from the Latin for "I"). The ego allows us to weigh our physical wants with society's rules so that we can exist in the world.

Many of Freud's theories are based on case studies of his psychiatric patients. Freudian

Ethnocentric The tendency to look at the world from the perspective of one's own ethnic group or culture, which you believe to be superior.

Heterocentric The assumption that everyone is heterosexual and that heterosexuality is the only natural, normal, acceptable, and superior sexual orientation.

Androcentric The emphasis of the male point of view, often to the neglect of the female.

Psychology The science of mind, emotions, and behavior.

Libido (li-BEE-doh) Sexual desire or drive.

Erogenous zones Areas of the body that are particularly sensitive to touch, and that may lead to sexual arousal when stimulated.

Oedipal complex The idea that men unconsciously want to eliminate or replace their fathers and have sex with their mothers.

Electra complex The psychoanalytic term used to describe a girl's romantic or sexual feelings toward her father.

Id The part of the unconscious mind that controls primitive drives such as those related to sex, food, and aggression.

Ego The part of the psyche that mediates the drives of the id and superego.

Superego Our sense of morality, or conscience.

psychoanalysts today might deal with a person's sexual problems by investigating the events of the individual's childhood.

Behavioral Theories

Behavioral psychologists believe that only behaviors can be measured and evaluated, not emotions or feelings. Behaviorists study how people's surroundings influence the way they act and how environmental reinforcements and punishments determine our behaviors. B. F. Skinner was a well-known researcher in this area. His experiments about learning found that reinforcements, or rewards, encourage repetition of an activity because the activity becomes associated with a pleasant stimulus (the reinforcement). Skinner also found that punishment, a negative stimulus, lessens the likelihood of a behavior being repeated. This type of learning is called **operant conditioning**. For instance, if a woman tries a new sexual technique with her husband and it is met with enthusiasm and results in multiple orgasms, the positive results of her behavior make it more likely that she will again be sexually adventurous with her husband. If, however, her efforts are met with derision and indifference, the punishment will make it less likely that she will try new activities with him. Some therapists use **behavior modification**—the use of positive reinforcement and/or punishment—to change a patient's behavior.

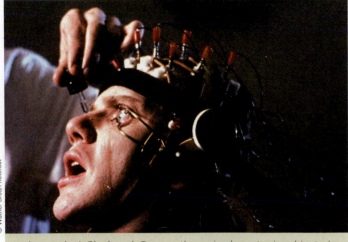

© Warner Bros/Photofest

In the movie *A Clockwork Orange*, the main character is subjected to unpleasant behavioral modification techniques to cure him of his violent tendencies.

Cognitive Learning Theories

Cognitive learning theory asserts that our behaviors are driven by psychological factors—such as the way we perceive and process the world around us—and by the way we cognitively categorize the world. Consequences become rewarding or punishing based on the categories to which they're assigned (Bancroft, 2009). For instance, one man may have an extramarital affair and feel terrific—young, attractive, and happy—so he continues meeting his lover. Another man having an affair might be overcome by guilt and remorse and end the extramarital relationship. In each case, it is not the affair per se that caused the mood, it is how the man *processed* and *perceived* the situation that affected his behavior.

Operant conditioning The use of reinforcement and punishment to increase or decrease the likelihood of certain behaviors.

Behavior modification The psychotherapeutic treatment that uses the theory of operant conditioning to change maladaptive behaviors.

Social Learning Theories

According to social learning theory, behaviors are influenced by a combination of environmental factors (e.g., rewards and punishments) and psychological factors (e.g., feelings, thoughts, and beliefs). Social learning theorists feel that people learn to behave by observing the environment and by modeling the behaviors and attitudes of others by observing outcomes. If someone observes a positive outcome to an action, he or she is more likely to imitate the behavior. If someone observes a behavior being punished, he or she is less likely to repeat that behavior. Our thoughts and feelings also have an important effect on our actions, and factors such as imitation and identification are also important in the development of sexuality. Social learning theorists say that children learn socially appropriate behaviors through peer pressure, parental models, and the media. As an example, a small boy may enjoy dressing up in his mother's clothing, but he eventually learns from peers, parents, or the media that this behavior is not well accepted by society.

Although the empirical evidence for the role of learning in human sexual arousal is meager (Hoffmann, Janssen, & Turner, 2004; O'Donohue & Plaud, 1994), the learning theories discussed above all have some relevance when it comes to sexuality: our sexuality develops in part from behaviors learned in childhood, from rewards and punishments, from imitation and identification, and from our thoughts and perceptions.

Historical Perspectives of Sexuality

Theories of learning help us frame how we look at sexuality today. However, different theorists still have conflicting and unique ideas about sex, as do individuals. Historically, sexual behavior and attitudes have also changed significantly over time.

Prehistory

For most of human history, the male role in reproduction was unclear, largely because of the time gap between intercourse and birth. It was not until perhaps 9,000 years ago that people began to understand the concept of paternity. Once people began to live in agrarian societies, they were able to notice what went on between their black-spotted bull and their cow before the cow gave birth to black-spotted calves, and they eventually made the connection.

Ancient Greece and Rome

Ancient Greece (1000 B.C.–300 B.C.) was truly a man's world. Penises were viewed as the symbol of fertility, and the male body was greatly admired. Men owned all property; women had no legal or political rights. Women were not allowed to read or write and were chaperoned wherever they went. Rape was viewed as a man's right of domination. Women were brought into arranged marriages where they were considered to be the property of men who could divorce them without cause. A woman's only function was to bear children; in fact, the Greek word for woman—*gyne*—means "bearer of children."

Ancient Greek society viewed people as naturally bisexual, and male–male sex was considered normal as long as it did not interfere with the family. Relationships between soldiers or between an older man and an adolescent protégé were considered healthy. Sexual behavior was related to one's social standing. The social superior was the penetrator of the penetrated social inferior, whether he be slave or young boy. In a relationship between the older established man and his younger protégé, sex often occurred face to face, with the older man moving his penis between the young man's thighs (Dover, 1989).

During the Roman Empire (753 B.C.–476 A.D.), life was not much better for women. They were owned by their husbands and forbidden to own property. Ancient Romans did not recognize homosexuality or heterosexuality per se; instead, a man was classified according to whether his sexual behaviors were active or passive. The active penetrator had higher status than the passive penetrated.

Sexual relationships between men were common in ancient Greece.

Middle Ages (476–1450)

Because of the influence of the Church in the Middle Ages, all sex acts that could not lead to procreation were considered evil. People in the Middle Ages held a dichotomous view of women: Madonna and whore. Women were seen as either temptress (Eve) or virtuous (Virgin Mary). To prevent wives or daughters from becoming wanton women while their men were away at the Crusades, women were allegedly fitted with chastity belts that were designed to cover most of the vulva, effectively preventing intercourse or masturbation. However, there is no evidence of the use of chastity belts until the 15th century.

Protestant Reformation (1483–1546)

In the 16th century, Martin Luther, John Calvin, and Protestant leaders organized revolts against the Catholic Church, which many saw as corrupt. One of the many differences between Protestantism and the Catholic Church is each organization's view of sexuality. Both Martin Luther and John Calvin believed sexuality was a natural part of life. They felt that intercourse was for more than just procreation and could deepen the bond between a husband and wife. They further believed that priests should be able to marry and have families.

17th and 18th Centuries

Puritans were followers of the Protestant Reformation. They held a positive view of marital sex but frowned upon sex outside of marriage. To allow intimacy between courting couples, men and women might share a bed, each wrapped in thick blankets to prevent the possibility of sexual intercourse. Nevertheless, the blankets may have been pushed aside, as birth records indicate that many brides of the day were already pregnant. In the 17th century, it is estimated that 10% of women in New England and one third of women in the Chesapeake region were pregnant when they wed (Cate & Lloyd, 1992). A century later, it is estimated that 30% of American children were conceived before marriage (Rothman, 1984). By the 18th century, social acceptance of sexual licentiousness decreased as widespread emphasis on self-control increased. "Normal" women were considered to be sexless and passionless, and premarital sex for women was considered immoral (Cate & Lloyd, 1992).

Victorian Era (1837–1901)

During the Victorian era, sexuality became a target of disapproval like never before. Discourses on prostitution, homosexuality, and masturbation were common and, in fact, these three things were considered threats to social order. During the Victorian era, Freud's theories on sexuality began to achieve their popularity just as sexual repression reached its height. Victorians hid anything that hinted of sex, going so far as to cover piano legs with discreet ruffles so men would not become inflamed upon viewing the naked leg of a piano. When dining in polite society, one would ask for "white meat" or "dark meat" to avoid having to say "breast" or "leg."

For women, sex was considered a marital duty. Women were assumed to be asexual, pure, and passionless. They were told that they would not (and should not) enjoy sex, and if by chance they did, there was something wrong with them. William Acton, a 19th-century physician, said that the idea that women could experience sexual feelings was a "vile aspersion." An encyclopedia of the time stated that it was true that a mucus-like fluid sometimes appeared in the vagina "but this only happens in lascivious women . . ." (Ellis, 2007, p. 224). Victorian men fared little better. It was thought that loss of semen was comparable to loss of blood and that ejaculating more than once a month would greatly weaken a man. Many thought that masturbation led to blindness, insanity, and death (Robinson, 2005).

For all that sexuality was hidden, it still (obviously) existed. Many Victorian women made daily trips to their physicians to get their "wombs aligned," a process involving stimulation of the vulva with a vibrator (discussed further in Chapter 11). Pornography and prostitution flourished, and it is estimated that the city of London had one prostitute for every twelve men (Walkowitz, 1980).

The 20th Century and Beyond

Over the course of the 20th century, sexuality became more accepted and evident in society. The separation of church and state and the rise of scientific thought reduced the power of the Church over sexual mores. For the first time, fears of pregnancy and disease were largely disconnected from sexual activity due to the discovery of penicillin and more efficient methods of contraception. As people moved away from small towns and toward big cities, increased anonymity and independence gave them more sexual freedoms. The media, ever increasing in its pervasiveness through the 20th century, transmitted previously unacceptable images and ideas. The rise of feminism allowed for changes in employment, home life, and sexual standards for women.

In conclusion, the only constant thing about sexual attitudes and behaviors is their variability. Sexual mores can change slowly over thousands of years, or within a generation. Always

You were just given various descriptions and facts about sexuality through history. Did you dutifully drag your highlighter through that section, beginning the process of memorizing facts to be spit out on your test? Sure you did, because you've been rewarded for that behavior for years. But now try to think more deeply. Begin to question the information you are presented. Ask the difficult questions: How do we know about history? Where does the information come from? Who writes history? What factors might affect "which" history becomes acknowledged? So do you now say "Okay, we can never know anything," gleefully throw down your highlighter, and run out into the sunshine to enjoy what's left of your youth? No! Get back to your desk! Although critical evaluation involves a healthy dose of suspicion about information, it does not imply, "Because we're not sure, then all information is equal." In Chapter 2, we will talk more about how to critically evaluate information.

remember that whatever you consider to be sexually normal, there is someone, somewhere, who would be appalled and horrified at your actions.

Religion, Spirituality, and Values

Sex is much less complex for other animals. They engage in intercourse when the female ovulates and is ready to conceive. If dogs feel like licking their testicles, they lick them and are not troubled in the least that your Aunt Mildred is looking on with great consternation. Human sexuality, however, encompasses much more than simple procreation. Religions and morality have a major impact on the expression of sexuality and will be discussed in further detail here and throughout the text. Table 1.1 lists views of sexuality for some of the world's major religions.

Judaism

In general, Judaism holds a positive, natural outlook toward marital sex, which is considered "blessed by God" and pleasurable for both men and women. Sexual connection provides an opportunity for spirituality and transcendence, as well as intimate contact with a partner (Ribner & Kleinplatz, 2007). Sexual activity is considered like food and drink—natural bodily functions that are both necessary and pleasurable but that can cause pain or problems when done improperly. Judaism views sex as an important way to strengthen marital bonds. It is considered wrong for a man to not be concerned with a woman's sexual pleasure, and it is regarded as a *mitzvah*—a commandment and a kindness—to have sex on the Sabbath. In Genesis, the first chapter of the Hebrew Bible, God instructs Jacob to "be fruitful and multiply." This directive is the basis for much of Western society's aversion to non-procreative sexual acts, such as masturbation and oral or anal sex. Childlessness was grounds for divorce in ancient Judaism: a husband could take a handmaiden or a mistress if his wife did not give him a son (although we now know that the man is responsible for the sex of the child!). *Polygyny*, a man having more than one wife at a time, was allowed, although this was more common among the wealthy.

Christianity

Jesus said very little about sexual conduct. Much of Christianity's views on sexuality come from St. Paul and St. Augustine. According to the dualistic philosophy, the spirit is separate from the flesh. In order for the spirit to get to heaven, one must practice self-denial and rid oneself of earthy pleasures, such as wealth, comfort, or sexual pleasure. St. Paul viewed sex as a necessary evil, which should only be partaken in as a means for procreation. It was Paul who said "if they cannot control themselves, let them marry, for it is better to marry than to burn." St. Augustine thought that all sex was sinful and he prayed, "Give me chastity . . . but not yet."

During the Middle Ages, Christianity took a particularly dark view of sexual activity. Sex was only permitted with one's spouse and only for the purposes of procreation. Moreover, sex was prohibited when one's wife was menstruating, pregnant, or nursing. Couples were also forbidden to have sex on Sundays, Wednesdays, Fridays, Saturdays, feast days, and fast days, as well as during Lent, Advent, Whitsun week, and Easter week. Furthermore, it was considered sinful to have sex during daylight or while naked. Erotic fondling, deep kisses, oral sex, and more adventurous positions were also prohibited (Brundage, 1987).

Significant variations in views of sexuality exist today among the various sects of Christianity and Catholicism. There are more than a thousand Christian denominations in North America alone, and there is great disparity in the views of these different sects.

Islam

The prophet Muhammad decreed that the only road to virtue was marriage. In Islam, family is considered of utmost importance, and celibacy within marriage is frowned upon. In some Muslim countries, Muslim men are allowed to have up to four wives, although women can have only one husband. Sex is per-

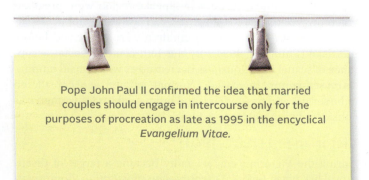

Pope John Paul II confirmed the idea that married couples should engage in intercourse only for the purposes of procreation as late as 1995 in the encyclical *Evangelium Vitae.*

mitted only within marriage; under Islamic law, the penalty for extramarital sex is 100 lashes and/or stoning to death. Within a marriage, however, sex is a good deed, and men are encouraged not to leave the marriage bed until the woman is satisfied. Sex during menstruation is forbidden, as is anal sex. Men and women in Islamic society must abide by *satr al-'awra*—the rules of modesty—and must "lower the gaze," as it is forbidden for a man to look upon women who are strangers to him.

Taoism

According to the Tao, which originated in China, sex is not only natural and healthy, but a sacred union necessary to people's physical, mental, and spiritual well-being. The sexual union of male and female is seen as a way to balance male and female energy. Taoists regard the orgasm as the combined essences of all the body's vital organs; orgasm and ejaculation are not the same thing. Semen is seen as a vital essence, and Taoists believe

Table 1.1 Religious Views on Topics in Human Sexuality

RELIGION	MARRIAGE/ DIVORCE	HOMOSEXUALITY	ASSISTED REPRODUCTIVE TECHNOLOGIES (ART)	CONTRACEPTION/ ABORTION
Christianity * about 2 billion followers * different denominations range from traditional to progressive, conservative to liberal.				
American Baptists	Holds marriage as a sacrament between a man and a woman, so divorce represents the breaking of that sacrament with God. Nonetheless, most modern-day Baptists allow divorce and remarriage.	Views homosexuality as a sin and rejects gay marriage, the ordination of homo-sexual clergy, and the establishment of gay churches.	Accepts all forms of ART as long as there is no embryo wastage.	Supports the use of contraception but opposes abortion.
Mormons or the Church of Latter Day Saints	Believes marriage between a man and a woman is ordained by God, and therefore relatively few divorces are justifiable.	Considers gay and lesbian acts in violation of the moral standards of their church.	Believes that a child's birth into a loving family is central to God's plan and do not oppose the use of ART.	Church members who submit to, perform, encourage, pay for, or arrange for abortions may lose their membership in the Church.
Roman Catholic Church	Believes marriage is purely for intercourse and procreation. Divorce and later remarriage are not allowed unless the marriage is annulled.	Teaches that homosexual *orientation* in itself is not sinful, but homosexual *acts* are immoral and sinful; does not accept gay marriage, and believes it may be necessary to discriminate against homosexuals on issues of adoption, employment, and other arenas.	Does not accept most forms of ART, but gamete intra-fallopian transfer, which is considered to facilitate the conjugal act rather than replace it, may be considered.	Opposes the use of birth control other than natural family planning. Strictly prohibits abortion.
Unitarian Universalist	Supports justice, equality, and acceptance, and therefore allows divorce and remarriage.	Supports equal rights for gays and lesbians; clergy perform same-sex marriages.	Accepts all forms of ART.	Affirms the right of each woman to make decisions concerning her own body.
United Methodist	Considers marriage to be a union between one man and one woman. Considers divorce to be regrettable but allowable; does not preclude a new marriage.	Opposes discrimination based on sexual orienta-tion. Clergy will not perform same-sex marriages.	Accepts all forms of ART as long as there is no embryo wastage.	Believes that abortion is justified in some cases.
Islam * second most common religion in the world * 1.5 billion adherents	Regards marriage as a duty and necessary for the structure and safeguarding of the family. Permits divorce in rare instances. In traditional Islam, only men may choose to terminate a marriage.	Considers homosexuality a moral disorder, sin, and corruption. Many predomi-nately Muslim countries retain the death penalty for homosexuality.	Encourages ART when procreation fails, especially since adoption is not viewed as an acceptable option. The egg and sperm must come from the wife and husband.	Allows contraception, although permanent sterilization is frowned upon. Permits abortion within the first 4 months of pregnancy if there is a threat to the mother's life or future baby's health.

SOURCE: © Cengage Learning 2013. Based on Schenker J.G. (2005). Assisted reproductive practice: Religious perspectives, *Reproductive BioMedicine Online, 10*(3):310-319; Fugeman-Millar A. (2006). Religious perspectives on divorce, *LawNow, 28*:18-19, religioustolerance.org; religiousinstitute.org.
Continued

Table 1.1 Religious Views on Topics in Human Sexuality—cont'd

RELIGION	MARRIAGE/ DIVORCE	HOMOSEXUALITY	ASSISTED REPRODUCTIVE TECHNOLOGIES (ART)	CONTRACEPTION/ ABORTION
Hindu * third most common religion in the world * 900 million adherents	Considers marriage a religious sacrament. Under classic Hindu tradition, divorce is not allowed, but in modern practice, civil divorces do occur.	Considers marriage and bearing children a religious duty which lead to a pro-heterosexual slant.	In vitro fertilization is allowed, but the sperm and egg must come from the husband and wife. Embryos must not be destroyed.	Birth control and abortions are allowed but the latter may create bad karma.
Buddhism 400 million adherents around the world	Considers marriage to be a secular matter, not a religious one. Allows divorce.	No position. Buddha left no teachings on homosexuality. In the West, there tends to be more acceptance of same-sex activity than in the East.	Allows for all forms of ART.	Allows contraception. Traditional Buddhism rejects abortion because it involves the deliberate destruction of life. Modern-day Buddhists believe that exceptions can occur with regard to the health of the mother or unborn child.
Judaism * approximately 15 million Jews around the world * divided into three branches, from most traditional to least: Orthodox, Conservative, and Reform	Involves both a civil divorce procedure as well as a religious procedure called a *get*.	The Orthodox branches consider homosexual behavior a sin, but Reform Judaism and some Conservatives do not. Orthodox rabbis will not perform same-sex marriages, although some Conservative and most Reform rabbis will.	ART technologies are permitted but not obligatory. In more conservative sects, the egg and sperm must originate from wife and husband.	Supports legislation maintaining the legality and accessibility of abortion.

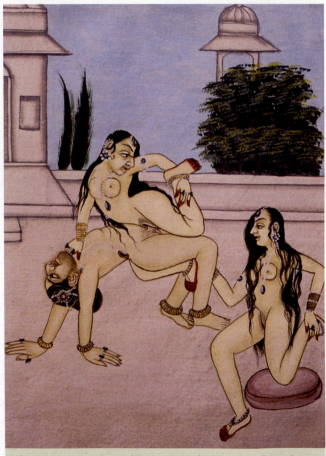

Yin, the female essence, is seen in the principles of earth, moon, and darkness. The male essence of yang is represented by the principles of light, heat, and the sun.

that men should be able to control their ejaculations (Wile, 1992). By not having ejaculation, *ching* (sexual energy) can be retained and redirected through the body into the higher regions of the heart and brain.

Hinduism

Hinduism, the world's third largest religion (after Christianity and Islam), encompasses several ideologies. To the Hindus, physical love is an element of spirituality, necessary to lead to eternal bliss in the next life. *Tantra* is a rigorous spiritual discipline and a vast field of study, not (as we sometimes think of it in the West) merely a sexual practice. Sexuality is seen as a spiritual force, and the act of ritual lovemaking is a means of both celebrating and transcending the physical.

The **Kama Sutra** is an ancient Indian sex manual believed to have been written by Vatsyayana sometime between the 3rd and 5th centuries. The *Kama Sutra* describes 64 different sexual positions, as well as 10 different types of kisses and 8 variations of oral sex. The *Kama Sutra* also gives instructions about relationships and love (Vatsyayana & Dane, 2003).

The *Kama Sutra* gives advice on sexual relations and marriage.

Forming Value Judgments

Religious foundations go deep. No one is asking you to abandon your religion or your values as we explore sexuality throughout this text, but simply that you examine your beliefs. By questioning your values, you understand them more fully; this process often serves to strengthen, rather than weaken, faith.

Values exist at various levels. For example, a **folkway** is a behavior that's commonly accepted by a group of people. A good illustration of how folkways differ among cultures took place in 2005 when then President George W. Bush met with Saudi Crown Prince Abdullah to discuss oil prices. They were photographed holding hands as they walked through Bush's Texas ranch. These images produced a flurry of controversy, because adult men do not customarily hold hands in the 21st-century United States. In the Arab culture, however, handholding is an expression of friendship, respect, and trust between men. When a person disobeys a folkway, he or she may be laughed at, frowned upon, or be the recipient of sarcastic comment. Other examples of folkways are wearing gender-appropriate clothing or maintaining a socially acceptable distance when talking to a stranger.

Mores are the accepted traditional customs that embody the fundamental values or morals of a group. In contrast to folkways, the penalties for disregarding mores may be severe. As an example, in fundamentalist Islamic society it is forbidden for a woman to expose much of her body. The penalty for failing to show proper modesty can be beatings or even death. Rules against incest or rape are mores in American society.

Overlapping the regulatory categories of folkways and mores are **laws**, written collections of rules that can be imposed by authority. Laws regarding sexuality might proscribe rules about adultery, rape, the age of consent, or indecent exposure. Laws may be applied differently, depending on a person's status in society. Until the Supreme Court struck down the laws as unconstitutional in 2003, four states—Texas, Kansas, Oklahoma, and Missouri—had laws against oral and anal sex between same-sex couples, but not between heterosexual couples. In contrast to mores, laws can change very quickly, and may differ from state to state or from city to city.

Although laws change based on societal norms, they give a good illustration of a society's values and expectations. Of course, some laws that remain on the books make us question exactly what values are being sup-

ASK YOURSELF

What three things in your life have most influenced your viewpoints (some answers to consider: religion, friends, family, age, hometown, TV and movies, etc.)? Do you have any prejudices regarding sexuality? Why do you think you have these prejudices? Would you be able to remain friends with someone who held very different values related to sexuality? Why or why not?

ported. For instance, in Connorsville, Wisconsin, it is illegal for a man to shoot off a gun when his female partner has an orgasm. In Florida it is illegal to have sex with a porcupine, presumably unless you yourself are a porcupine. And men who live in Arizona, Florida, Idaho, Indiana, Massachusetts, Mississippi, Nebraska, Nevada, New York, Ohio, Oklahoma, Oregon, South Dakota, Tennessee, Utah, Vermont, Washington, D.C., and Wisconsin should be particularly careful—in these states men are guilty of public indecency if they get an erection that shows through their clothing.

Culture and Society

The opening line of Herman Wouk's novel *Marjorie Morningstar* reads, "Customs of courtship vary greatly in different times and places, but the way the thing happens to be done here and now always seems the only natural way to do it" (Wouk, 1955). People in various times and places have exhibited very different courtship rituals. Imagine that you are snuggling by the fire with your sweetie. Ah, at last you are alone. The moonlight shines in your lover's eyes as you slowly lean forward and . . . bite off his eyebrows. This gesture would be considered perfectly appropriate if you were an Apinayé, a South American Indian tribe studied in the early 20th century. Likewise, if you were an Apinayé and the sentence read, ". . . slowly lean for-

A 2007 Michigan ruling has inadvertently made anyone guilty of adultery also guilty of first-degree criminal sexual conduct, a charge that carries a maximum sentence of life in prison.

Kama Sutra An ancient Indian text, made up of poetry, prose, and illustrations, which contains practical advice for sexual pleasure, love, and marriage.

Folkways Patterns of conventional behavior within a group.

Mores (MORE-ayz) Social norms or customs that embody the fundamental values of a group. Mores are more strongly enforced than folkways.

Laws A written collection of enforceable rules that govern a community.

Culture The set of attitudes, values, goals, and practices that is learned and shared by a relatively large group of people.

Society A group of people that share cultural aspects such as language, dress, and norms of behavior.

Former President George W. Bush and Saudi Crown Prince Abdullah hold hands, a sign of respect and friendship in the Arabic world.

© AP Images/Gerald Herbert

Liminal Experiences

Considered a time of danger and ambiguity, **liminal** experiences describe a period of transition between one stage and another. The term comes from the Latin word *limen*, meaning "threshold." In our discussion of human sexuality, we will investigate a number of liminal experiences, such as birth, menarche or manhood rituals, wedding ceremonies, or sex reassignment transitions. Liminal experiences usually have a ritual or rite of passage associated with them to commemorate the transition. These rituals often involve a separation of participants from the rest of society, the actual time of transition, and finally the reincorporation of the individual back into society.

---

ward and place your lips upon his, letting your tongue dart into his mouth," you'd now be saying, "Eeeeewwwww! Gross! They actually *do* that? Those Americans are messed up!" Until the 20th century, kissing was mostly a Western European phenomenon, unknown in parts of Asia, Africa, and South America (Ellis, 1940).

In response to various social and cultural forces, people show different levels of sex drive and express their sexual desires in different ways. Views of when to start having sex, who to do it with, how to do it, how often you do it, and how much to enjoy it while you're doing it are by no means universal. For example, the **age of consent**—the age at which people can legally have sex—varies not only from country to country, but within the United States from state to state. In fact, what is considered "sex" varies from place to place. In some places, sex is defined as intercourse; in others, sex includes any sexual contact, such as kissing. Age of consent laws may also depend on the age of the teenager's sexual partner. For instance, until 2008, Canada's age of consent was 14, but it has since been raised to 16. However, under certain circumstances, a 12- or 13-year-old can consent to sexual activity with a partner who is less than 2 years older than he or she is. Finally, age of consent laws may differ based on the sex of the two partners; ages and laws vary for sexual activity between a man and a woman, between two males, and between two females. In the United States, the age of sexual consent varies from state to state, and it ranges from 16 to 18.

What is considered attractive also varies over time and culture. In New Guinea, knees are considered erotic. In certain African tribes, the women tie weights to their breasts to help them attain the pendulous shape most admired. Heavy women were long considered the most attractive in Samoa, although the influx of Western television is bringing to the culture an appreciation for the thinner female form, along with an epidemic of eating disorders among the women. Remember, as Shakespeare said: "There are more things in heaven and earth . . . than are dreamt of in your philosophy." What you consider to be abnormal sexual behavior may be quite common and acceptable to others.

Do you think American culture today is sexually permissive or sexually repressive? The answer to that question would depend on a comparison with other cultures. Among the Mangaia of the Cook Islands, sexual activity is encouraged in individuals of all ages. Young people are encouraged to masturbate and are taught how to give and receive sexual pleasure. Compare that to Inis Beag (pronounced *Inis Bay*), the name given to an island off the coast of Ireland, considered to be one of the most sexually repressed societies. In Inis Beag, sex is considered dangerous to one's health. Nudity is never allowed—smocks are worn during intercourse, children wear clothes while being bathed, and although it is a fishing village, the inhabitants don't learn to swim because of the need to take off some clothes in order to do so (Messenger, 1983). In terms of sexual attitudes, as in so many other things, the United States is by no means homogenous; the acceptability of different sexual behaviors varies from state to state, and from community to community (see Figure 1.1). How acceptable is it in the United States to walk down the street holding hands with your partner? Will people shout at you or try to hurt you if you do so? What if your partner is the same sex as you are—how sexually permissive is America then?

In 1998, Eric Widmer and colleagues studied sexual attitudes in 24 countries. The United States was shown to be one of the more sexually repressive Western societies. The countries were classified into four categories: teen permissives (such as West Germany and Sweden), sexual conservatives (represented by Ireland and the United States), homosexual permissives (represented by Canada and Spain), and moderate residuals (Australia and Great Britain). Some countries, such as Japan and the Philippines, did not neatly fit into these categories. People in all 24 countries were questioned about their attitudes about sex outside of marriage. Subjects rated these activities as "always wrong," "almost always wrong," "only sometimes wrong," or "never wrong." Table 1.2 summarizes these findings and includes two representatives of each of the four categories (Widmer, Treas, & Newcomb, 1998).

> **Are Americans more open about sex than people in other countries?**

Liminal The threshold between two different states or stages.

Age of consent The minimum age at which a person can be considered legally competent for consensual sexual relations. This age varies from state to state, and also may depend on other factors.

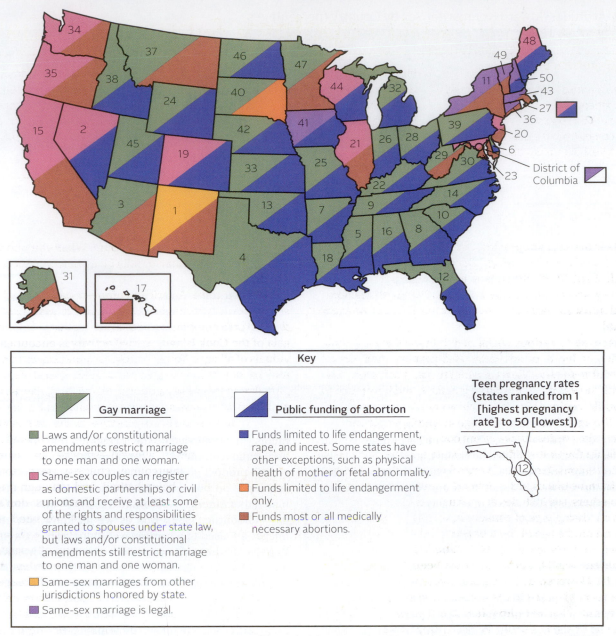

Key

Gay marriage

- Laws and/or constitutional amendments restrict marriage to one man and one woman.
- Same-sex couples can register as domestic partnerships or civil unions and receive at least some of the rights and responsibilities granted to spouses under state law, but laws and/or constitutional amendments still restrict marriage to one man and one woman.
- Same-sex marriages from other jurisdictions honored by state.
- Same-sex marriage is legal.

Public funding of abortion

- Funds limited to life endangerment, rape, and incest. Some states have other exceptions, such as physical health of mother or fetal abnormality.
- Funds limited to life endangerment only.
- Funds most or all medically necessary abortions.

Teen pregnancy rates (states ranked from 1 [highest pregnancy rate] to 50 [lowest])

FIGURE 1.1 Sexuality laws vary from state to state. (Human Rights Campaign, 2011, and Alan Guttmacher Institute, 2009.)

Anthropology

Anthropology is the study of humanity—its origins, customs, and social relationships. Sociocultural anthropologists examine the diverse ways in which different cultures categorize and regard issues such as gender, child rearing, and sexuality. When we consider other cultures, it's important to be wary of and try to avoid ethnocentrism—the belief that your ethnic or cultural group is better or "more normal" than other groups.

Language

What impact does the language used to describe sex have on our attitudes? The linguistic relativity principle suggests that language forms our perception of the world and thus guides our thinking and behavior. A good example of this principle is a 1970s study in which college-age students were asked to pick illustra-

tions for a sociology textbook. Half of the students were told to choose pictures for chapters with titles such as "social man," "industrial man," and "political man." The other half were given the same chapters with different titles: "society," "industrial life," and "political behavior." When presented with the gender-neutral chapter titles, both male and female students were significantly more likely to choose illustrations featuring both males and females. But when the chapters had the more male-directed titles, students were more likely to select pictures of males only (Miller & Swift, 1977).

Use of gender-specific language may even effect how well students recall information. Women better recalled the events of a story when the characters were referred to as "he or she" or "they" rather than by the supposedly gender-neutral "he"

Anthropology The study of the origins, customs, and social relationships of humans.

Table 1.2 Attitudes Toward Nonmarital Sex by Country (percentages)

		AUSTRALIA	CANADA	GREAT BRITAIN	IRELAND	JAPAN	PHILIPPINES	SPAIN	SWEDEN	USA	WEST GERMANY	SUMMARY OF ALL 24 COUNTRIES
Sex before marriage wrong?	Always	13	12	12	35	19	60	20	4	29	5	17
	Not wrong at all	59	69	70	42	15	11	63	89	41	79	61
Sex before 16 wrong?	Always	61	55	67	84	60	77	59	32	71	34	58
	Not wrong at all	9	9	3	1	3	3	14	17	4	13	7
Extramarital sex wrong?	Always	59	68	67	80	58	88	76	68	80	55	66
	Not wrong at all	7	2	2	2	2	1	5	1	2	4	4
Homosexual sex wrong?	Always	55	39	58	71	65	84	45	56	70*	42	59
	Not wrong at all	27	46	26	17	2	3	42	32	19	33	24

*In Chapter 10, note the change in attitudes regarding homosexuality that have occurred since 1998.
SOURCE: © Cengage Learning 2013. Based on Widmer E.D., Treas J., Newcomb R. (1998). Attitudes toward nonmarital sex in 24 countries, *Journal of Sex Research*, *35*(4):349-357.

(Conkright, Flannagan, & Dykes, 2000). Some have suggested that new gender-neutral words should be created, such as "hir" to take the place of "him" and "her," and "sie" instead of "he" and "she." Throughout the text we will discuss how our views are colored by the words used to describe aspects of sexuality.

Media

It is estimated that adolescents in the United States are exposed to some kind of media for 7 to 8 hours per day (Papper, Holmes, & Popovich, 2006; Pardun, L'Engle, & Brown, 2005). In fact, by the time he or she graduates from high school, a typical adolescent will have watched 15,000 hours of television, compared to the 12,000 hours spent in reading and math classes, and only 46 hours in health education classes (American Academy of Pediatrics, 2001).

Many of these media images affect our views of ourselves and of our sexuality. Beautiful, thin, scantily clad actresses wait passively for handsome, buff male action heroes to leap heroically from a rooftop to save them. Five gay men who are extremely concerned with hair products and the right chardonnay help slovenly straight men clean up their act and update their wardrobe. Constantly confronted with images of sexuality, we unconsciously incorporate the ideas they represent into our worldview. These images can significantly impact our self-esteem and body image (discussed further in Chapter 7). Although adolescents acquire much of their information about sexuality from the media, the mass media rarely depict the three C's of responsible sexual behavior: commitment, contraception, and consideration of consequences (Brown, 2002).

Media The tools used to deliver information; often referred to as "mass media" because they are designed to reach a very large audience.

Advertising

Pause for a minute to consider how many advertisements you view in a day. The images include not only television and radio commercials, but also magazine ads, billboards, e-mail, product placement in movies, name brands on T-shirts, and logos on buildings, buses, and bathroom stalls. It is estimated that Americans see more than 3,000 advertisements each day (Kilbourne, 1999). And as we all know, sex sells. Sexual images are used to advertise everything from cigarettes to tires. Women are dressed in provocative clothing—or none at all—in up to 40% of mainstream magazine advertisements and up to 12% of prime-time network TV commercials (Reichert, 2002).

Television

Americans spend about one third of their free time—more hours than are devoted to the next 10 most popular leisure activities combined—watching television, and teens spend more time

Advertisers use sexual images, commonly featuring provocatively dressed female bodies, to sell many products.

The Naming of the Screw

The F bomb. You know what it is. You may even say it sometimes. But the fact that—in a human sexuality text in the 21st century— your author has coyly referred to the word as "the f bomb" underscores our feelings toward this word. In his book The Rape of the A*P*E* (American Puritan Ethic), *the late comedian Allan Sherman wrote about the language we use to describe sex. His essay is reprinted below, with euphemisms inserted in place of* the word.

If you were brought up in America, you no sooner learned *the word* than you learned you were not allowed to use it. Later you discovered there were a hundred more words like that, the most meaningful and to-the-point words you ever heard, but every single one of them was strictly taboo. Eventually, as you grew into adulthood, you found you had to make The Choice: When I want to say *the word*, what word should I use?

Your Choice revealed a lot about you—your social ambitions, your upbringing, your sexual freedom. It also determined some things about your future—for example, the type of sex partners you attracted. (People who say *shtup* wouldn't be caught dead shtupping people who call it consortium. And people who call it consortium would rather remain celibate than consort with people who say shtup.)

It is a paradox. If having sex were some strange esoteric activity—sleepwalking, for example—there would be one or perhaps two or three words for it. But here we are describing the most popular activity on earth, and with all the language of Shakespeare at our disposal we remain mute and tongue-tied. The best we can hope for is a less than satisfactory word, and we must choose it from one of four impoverished sources.

Slang

Get laid: This implies unresponsiveness and dutiful resignation, presumably on the part of the woman, and endows the man with all the passion of a bricklayer.

Screw: The word *screw* conjures up a mind-boggling image: the man, on top, revolving horizontally in a continuous spiral motion, with one Frankensteinian objective—to permanently attach the lady to the bed.

Euphemisms

Sleep with: Since time began, nobody has ever been able to copulate while asleep. Even if it were possible, it would be impolite.

Go all the way: After the first time, why should two people ever see each other again? Having gone all the way, where else have they got to go?

Jargon

Sexual intercourse: It is absolutely impossible for anyone who has ever gotten down and dirty to think of the experience as sexual intercourse. Or, putting it another way, anyone who calls it "sexual intercourse" can't possibly be interested in actually doing it. You might as well announce you're ready for lunch by proclaiming, "I'd like to do some masticating and enzyme secreting."

Sexual congress: I won't even discuss this one. It sounds un-American.

Romanticisms

He ravished her: A horrifying picture. When the ravenous beast had his fill, there was nothing left but a few bones and a chewed-up chastity belt.

He debauched her: Literally, he removed her bauch. Inexcusable.

Modified from Sherman, Allan. (1973). The Rape of the APE: The Official History of the Sexual Revolution 1945-1973, The Obscening of America. Chicago: Playboy Press.

watching television than any one other single activity except sleeping (Teen Health and the Media, 2007).

Television images have greatly changed over time. In the 1960s, censors would not allow Barbara Eden's navel to be visible in the television show *I Dream of Jeannie*, and when Elvis Presley appeared on *The Ed Sullivan Show* in 1957, the camera showed him only from the waist up, so as not to inflame impressionable young girls with his pelvic gyrations. Today, teenagers are exposed to 14,000 sexual references and innuendoes per year on television (Kunkel et al., 1999). *Real Sex,* a magazine-style HBO series, presents segments on sexual fads and fetishes, swingers and orgies, cunnilingus seminars and sex dolls. *Tell Me You Love Me,* a now-cancelled series on HBO, showed explicit and realistic depictions of sexual intercourse, oral sex, and ejaculation.

Scientists working for the Kaiser Family Foundation (KFF), a nonprofit philanthropic organization that focuses on health care issues in the United States, examined thousands of hours of television, including episodes of the 20 programs that teens most frequently watch. The researchers found that 70% of television programs contained some sexual content in the form of talk about sex or sexual behavior (Kunkel et al., 2005). In shows with any sexual content, there was an average of five sex-related scenes per hour and slightly more in shows most watched by teens. When news, sports, and children's program were excluded,

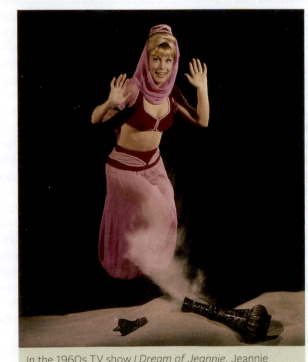

In the 1960s TV show *I Dream of Jeannie*, Jeannie served her "master's" wishes.

11% of television programs depicted or implied intercourse. In these scenes, just under half of the characters did not have an established relationship with their intimate partner, and 15% involved intercourse between characters that had just met (Kunkel et al., 2005).

Although depictions of sexuality are pervasive on television, messages of sexual patience, precaution, risks, or responsibilities are scarce. Only 14% of shows that have any sexual content address risks and responsibilities anywhere in the program. Of shows most watched by teens, only 10% include some message about sexual consequences and responsibilities. One survey of soap operas found that in 50 hours of daytime dramas, there were 156 acts of sexual intercourse and only 5 references to birth control or safe sex (Greenberg & Busselle, 1996).

You may be saying to yourself, "So what if there is sex on television? Television doesn't affect people's views." Most research does not support that opinion. According to the cultivation theory, TV changes our attitudes and behaviors, our ideals and expectations—indeed, our views of reality (Gerbner & Gross, 1976). Men who were exposed to more sexual content on television expected their partners to engage in a broader range of sexual activities, and women exposed to lots of sex on television expected sex to occur earlier in a relationship (Aubrey, Harrison, Kramer, & Yellin, 2003). Teens who had just viewed television dramas with a large amount of sexual content were less likely to rate casual sexual encounters as negative (Bryant & Rockwell, 1994). Including safe sex messages in programs with sexual content could influence attitudes about condoms. When subjects viewed programs in which the show included a discussion of sexual risks and responsibilities along with the sexual activity, subjects were more likely to view condom use as a positive thing compared to those who watched sexual content with no safe sex messages (Kunkel et al., 2005).

Viewing sex on TV may also affect our sexual behaviors. Heavier viewing of sexual content on TV has been found to be associated with earlier sexual intercourse and progression to more advanced noncoital sexual activities (Collins et al., 2004; Pardun et al., 2005). It is hard to determine whether watching more sex on TV actually *causes* an increase in sexual behavior or if those who have earlier intercourse—and are perhaps more interested in sex—are therefore more likely to seek out television shows with sexual content. In their study, Collins and colleagues controlled for these factors by performing a longitudinal study—monitoring the television viewing habits of teenagers when they were virgins and then comparing their later sexual activity to their television viewing habits. The researchers also controlled for amount of parental supervision, religiosity, sensation-seeking behaviors, deviant behaviors, and other factors. The study results do appear to confirm that the amount of sexual content viewed does decrease the age at which viewers first have sexual intercourse. Teens exposed to high levels of television sexual content are also twice as

"The TV's busted - we'll have to do our own sex and violence tonight."

www.CartoonStock.com

likely to either get pregnant or be responsible for a pregnancy before the age of 20 (Chandra et al., 2008).

Other Media

Media is more than television; it includes the Internet, movies, magazines, newspapers, video games, and music. The average Internet user spends 13 hours online each week—not counting e-mail (Harris Interactive, 2009). The Internet has become an important method for social networking. In February of 2009, Twitter had more than 7 million unique visitors and almost 55 million monthly visits, and people checked in onto Facebook pages more than 1 billion times (Compete, 2009; Nielsen Online, 2009). But the Internet is used for more than updating your status and forwarding videos of cats swinging from ceiling fans. In the Broadway show *Avenue Q,* happy little puppets sing "the Internet is for porn," and there is some truth to this line. Sex is one of the most frequently searched for topics on the Internet (Freeman-Longo and Blanchard, 1998). Interested parties can get information about sexual positions and contraception, or, with a couple of clicks, you can view live sex acts.

Other media contain their share of sex. Two thirds of all Hollywood movies made each year are rated R, and 17% of all magazine ads in 1993 that pictured at least one man and one woman depicted or implied intercourse (Brown, 2002). Of video games, 27% of teen-rated and 36% of mature-rated games contain sexual themes or content, although most do not indicate that they include this content (Haninger & Thompson, 2004; Thompson, Tepichin, & Haninger, 2006).

Through music we learn about our role in society and expected behaviors. Music is a way to express one's identity. A fan of the Black Eyed Peas and a polka aficionado are going to have a hard time compromising on what music to listen to on

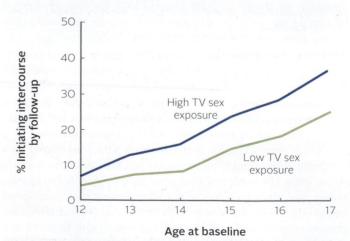

FIGURE 1.2 The effect of watching sex on TV with age of initiation of intercourse in teens (© Cengage Learning 2013, from Collins et al., watching sex on television predicts adolescent initiation of sexual behavior, *Pediatrics, 114*(3), 2004).

> We have come a long way from the early days of Hollywood. From 1930 until 1966, the Hays Code dictated what was considered morally fit for the American film-going public. The following were forbidden due to immoral content: "Excessive and lustful kissing, lustful embraces, suggestive postures and gestures . . . sex relationships between the white and black races . . . and pointed profanity (this includes the words hell, S.O.B., damn)" (ArtsReformation.com, 2006).

_____

_____

_____

_____

road trips. Not including music videos, the average American youth listens to music 1.5–2.5 hours per day (Martino et al., 2006; Pardun et al., 2005). Music and music videos contain more sexual content (up to 50%) than any other media, including TV and movies (Pardun et al., 2005; Brown, 2002; Lowry & Shidler, 1993). Research suggests that young people who listen to music in which women are valued solely for their appearance and men for their ability to be sexually voracious were more likely to engage in sexual intercourse and to progress to more advanced levels of noncoital sexual activity (Martino et al., 2006).

Clearly, we are inundated with messages about sex and sexuality every day of our lives, and these media messages play a powerful role in how we think about sexuality. In the next section we will consider some of the more formal systems of sex education.

Sex Education

Imagine how you would feel if playing gin rummy, and playing it well, were considered a major component of happiness and a major sign of maturity, but no one ever told you how to play, you never saw anyone play, and everything you ever read implied that normal and healthy people just somehow "know" how to play and really enjoy playing the very first time they try! (Tiefer, 2004, p. 8)

We don't teach math by giving one lecture a year. You have to do it all the time and keep reinforcing it.

—*Joycelyn Elders, former U.S. Surgeon General, on comprehensive sex education*

After completion of this section, you will be able to . . .

O Discuss age-appropriate sexuality education.

O Consider effective and appropriate ways for parents to communicate with their children about sex.

O Define *abstinence-only education* and *comprehensive sex education*.

O Evaluate pros and cons of abstinence-only education and comprehensive sex education.

As occurs when discussing any kind of education, talk of sex education usually raises more questions than it answers. A few of the most common: What should people be taught about sexuality? At what

age? Should sexuality be taught at home or in the schools? Should sexually explicit materials be available at the public library? And finally, who decides these matters?

What Should Be Taught?

If you were to ask any 10 people what they learned about sex while they were growing up, you would most likely get 10 very different responses. One person may have learned only about menstruation and pregnancy, while another may have focused on the emotional aspects of relationships. One woman may never have discussed anything sexual at all, even as another may have had candid discussions with her parents about orgasms and three-ways. Although many people are taught about how babies are born and what sexually transmitted infections they can catch, human sexuality encompasses much more than that. A discussion about sex can (and should!) include many aspects, such as:

• What are the proper names for the genitals, and how do they work?

• What happens at puberty? What changes occur and what does this mean physically and emotionally?

• Are there differences between boys and girls? How can society's expectations for the genders affect our lives?

• What is love? How do you know when you're in love?

• How do you know if someone is interested in you in "that" way? How do you know if he or she really likes you or is just using you? What is a healthy relationship?

• How do you say "no" to activities that make you uncomfortable?

• How are babies born? What methods prevent conception? How do you choose a contraceptive that is best for your lifestyle?

• What are some of the ways that people behave sexually?

• What are some risks—both physical and emotional—to sexual activity? What about the pleasures? How can you minimize your risks and maximize your pleasure?

Obviously, these topics cannot all be covered in one afternoon. Instead, information about sexuality can be imparted in everyday discussions, at appropriate times and appropriate ages. Parents can look for "teachable moments," such as something on a TV show or when seeing a pregnant woman. Sex education encompasses more than facts—it is also about feeling at ease when communicating about sexuality. Frequent, casual discussions also set the tone that it's okay for children to ask questions and that sex is normal and natural. Teaching young children openly and honestly about sexuality makes them more likely to be comfortable with their bodies and feel good about themselves.

When Should Sex Education Begin?

Obviously, the age of a child will greatly influence what they can be told about sexuality. When your 4-year-old asks where babies come from, now is not the time to discuss the formation of the corpus luteum (which will be discussed in Chapter 4). On the other hand, a 15-year-old should not be put off with "when a man and a woman love each other very much, they hug in a special way and make a baby."

Barbara Huberman, national director of Training and Sexuality Education for Advocates for Youth, has some suggestions for age-appropriate sexuality education (Huberman, 2007). She suggests that children below the age of 5 should be taught the correct terms for the parts of the body. Just as you wouldn't teach your child that their lungs are called puff-puffs, you shouldn't teach your child to call her vulva a "hoo hoo." Using silly words teaches children that these parts are somehow different, perhaps shameful or mysterious, than the rest of their bodies. Also remember that one person's "hoo hoo" is another person's "pee pee," a situation bound to lead to later confusion. Young children should also be taught about privacy and respect. They should know that no one has the right to touch them in any way that makes them uncomfortable and that they should tell a familiar adult if such an event occurs. Because children are naturally curious and even very young children may masturbate, young people can be taught that while it is alright to touch themselves, these things are done in private. Starting sex education at a young age gives children the tools and information to make appropriate choices later in life.

Children between the ages of 5 and 8 are more curious about how the body works. They might want to know how babies get into and out of the mother. They are also very interested in gender roles: What do boys do? What do girls do? How are mommies different than daddies (Huberman, 2007)? Parents can let children know that their options are not limited to traditional gender roles—that women can be firefighters and men can stay home with the children. As children enter school and meet other children with different family dynamics, parents can let their children know that families come in many varieties, and it is love that makes a family. They can also discuss how love comes in many forms, and not everyone falls in love with someone of the other sex.

Young people are maturing sexually at younger ages than ever before. It is important that preadolescents know about the future changes to their bodies *before* they occur. Girls should learn about menstruation and boys should learn of nocturnal emissions (wet dreams) and ejaculation before puberty. Preadolescents may ask more in-depth questions about masturbation, menstruation, and nocturnal emissions, as well as intercourse, birth control, and sexually transmitted infections (STIs). At this point, parents should begin to talk about the responsibilities and consequences of sex.

With the onset of puberty, adolescents will have more and more

© Comstock/Getty Images RF

questions about sex, although they may not share their curiosity with their parents. Adolescents will question how they stack up physically against others and will begin to ask about relationships and love, as well as the realities of sexual intercourse and oral sex.

Who Should Be Responsible for Sex Education?

Young people will receive sex education, even if their parents never broach the subject of sex. Children will learn about sex from TV and the Internet, from peers, and from other sources. In a perfect world, all parents would be very comfortable having discussions with their children about all aspects of sexuality. This just isn't the case, however. In many cases, parents (or children) are too uncomfortable to discuss intimate issues with their families. Sometimes parents believe that they have communicated with their children about sex, but their children don't always agree (Brody, 2009; SIECUS, 2007).

The sexual education programs of different countries vary, based on that culture's values, needs, and attitudes. Much of Western Europe has mandatory, comprehensive sex education that covers many subjects. In the United Kingdom, a formalized program of sexual education is not compulsory, but a group is seeking to require it for children as young as 4. Information about reproductive health is presented in schools in Japan and some other Asian countries. In Africa, a number of programs are beginning to focus their efforts on halting the growing HIV/AIDS epidemic. Iran provides accurate and age-appropriate information about family planning and maternal health. Although most public school students in the United States receive some sort of sex education, there is little consistency in the ages at which it's taught and the scope of what is covered. There are no federal requirements that standardize sexuality education, so each individual state and local jurisdiction can teach very different types and amounts of material to different ages. It is important that public school sexual education programs address the concerns and issues facing all students, regardless of race, socioeconomic class, or sexual orientation. In later chapters, we will discuss how attitudes regarding sex education affect the information we receive about menstruation, the effectiveness of condoms and birth control pills, modes of transmission of HIV and other STIs, sexual response and behavior, and other topics.

Advice for Parents in Talking with Their Children About Sex

Parents may be uncomfortable when discussing sex with their children. Here are some suggestions to make it easier.

Be willing to answer questions simply, honestly, and openly. "Why is the sky blue?" "Why is that man so fat?" Children ask questions about everything, and although their questions are sometimes embarrassing or inopportune, parents usually respond to their queries openly and honestly. If, however, a child's questions about their bodies and where babies come from elicit a sharp "why do you want to know that?" or "we'll talk about it when you're older," then they quickly get the signal that sex is shameful or should not be discussed. Parents are often uncomfortable when discussing sexuality with their children, but if they establish open lines of communication from an early age, children will feel more comfortable in discussing sexuality with their parents. It's all right for parents to admit to their children that they are uncomfortable, but they should let their kids know that it's all right to ask questions.

Give accurate information. Parents may not always have correct information. For example, a survey of more than 1,000 parents of teenaged kids found many parents to be misinformed about the realities of contraceptives (Eisenberg, Bearinger, Sieving, Swain, & Resnick, 2004). More than half of the parents falsely believed that condoms were not very effective at preventing STIs or pregnancy and did not think that birth control pills safely prevented pregnancy almost all of the time. In reality, when used consistently and correctly, condoms prevent pregnancy 97% of the time and prevent HIV transmission in 98–100% of high-risk sexual encounters, and birth control pills prevent pregnancy in 99% of cases (Warner, Hatcher, & Steiner, 2004). If parents don't know an answer to a child's question, they can research the information from reputable sources (who knows, it may even spice up their own sex lives!). Parents should educate themselves about the realities of their children's lives, peer pressure, and what is considered "normal" in their world.

Sex is about more than biology. Discussions about sexuality are incomplete if they simply cover the mechanics of body parts. Sexuality is about emotions and values, and parents should share their expectations, standards, and beliefs with their children. Although most parents want their children to share their values, conversations about sex will be less effective when parents "lay down the law" to impose their views on their children, rather than presenting their values and giving information to their children to support their opinions.

Pick the appropriate time and place. Have enough time to discuss any questions that might arise, and choose a setting in which neither you nor your child is likely to be more embarrassed or distracted. Don't overwhelm your child with more information than his or her age and situation can handle.

Listen. Encourage your child to talk about sex and to ask questions. Ask your children questions about their views on sexuality, what their friends say, and what their concerns are. Listen to what they have to say—listen without judgment, without criticism, and without fear.

It's not just what you say . . . Education isn't just about what you say to your children; how you act is also important. Children are always learning, even if we're not aware that we're teaching. The way you talk about your body, the way you interact with men and women, and your relationship dynamics are all important, because children observe and incorporate your beliefs and actions into their worldview.

Abstinence-Only Education

During much of George W. Bush's administration, abstinence-only education (AOE) was the only federally supported type of sex education in the United States. According to section 510 of title V of the Social Security Act, which established the requirements and appropriations for AOE, the program had ". . . as its exclusive purpose, teaching the social, psychological, and health gains to be realized by abstaining from sexual activity" (Section 510, 42 U.S.C. § 710). It taught that sexual activity outside of marriage was physically and psychologically harmful for people of any age. Under AOE, all unmarried people were discouraged from engaging in any sexual behavior, including kissing, and those teaching these programs were forbidden to mention contraception, except to discuss its failure rates. Sex Respect, advertised as "the world's leading abstinence education program," taught "if premarital sex came in a bottle, it would probably have to carry a Surgeon General's warning. . . . There's no way to have premarital sex without hurting someone" (Simson & Sussman, 2000). In part due to the AOE policy, by 2002, one third of teens in the United States had not received any formal instruction about contraception (Lindberg, 2006).

In comparison, comprehensive sex education (CSE) "takes a broad and multi-faceted approach" to human sexuality and "seeks to provide students with a broad range of pertinent and factually accurate information" (Simson & Sussman, 2000). CSE teaches adolescents the benefits of abstinence but also provides them with information about birth control and prevention of STIs, as well as helping people develop their communication and decision-making skills. Evidence has shown that CSE programs help delay the onset of sexual activity in teens and make them more likely to use contraception when they become sexually active (Dailard, 2002).

To be eligible for federal aid as a comprehensive sexuality program, the curriculum must be an effective, **evidence-based** program that has been proven on the basis of rigorous scientific research to change behavior—which means it will delay sexual activity, increase condom

Evidence-based An approach to decision-making that is based on data and scientific studies to determine the best practices.

From Section 510, 42 U.S.C. § 710: Abstinence-only education . . .

- "Teaches that abstinence from sexual activity is the only certain way to avoid out-of-wedlock pregnancy, sexually transmitted diseases, and other associated health problems."

- "Teaches that a mutually faithful monogamous relationship in context of marriage is the expected standard of human sexual activity."

- "Teaches that sexual activity outside of the context of marriage is likely to have harmful psychological and physical effects."

or contraceptive use for sexually active youths, or reduce pregnancy among those who complete the course. The program must be medically accurate and complete, provide age-appropriate information and activities, and include activities to educate youths who are sexually active regarding responsible sexual behavior with respect to both abstinence and contraceptive use.

Problems With Abstinence-Only Education

Most people agree that adolescents should wait to have sex until they are physically and emotionally ready, so what is the problem with abstinence-only education? Many consider AOE to be unrealistic, ineffective, and discriminatory. In addition, under the federal AOE program, the sexual education presented to our youth often contained false information. Finally, many believe that the government should not dictate morality for its citizens.

Unrealistic. According to AOE programs, men and women should remain abstinent until marriage. But what is the definition of abstinence? Not having vaginal intercourse or not partaking in any sexual activity whatsoever? In order for the AOE statement that "the only completely reliable way to protect yourself against pregnancy and sexually transmitted diseases is to remain abstinent" to be true, abstinence must mean a total abstention from all sexual activity. After all, ejaculation during mutual masturbation can lead to pregnancy, and engaging in unprotected oral or anal sex still exposes people to a risk of sexually transmitted infections.

In recent years, puberty is occurring earlier, but people are delaying marriage and spending more time on their education and careers. The median age for first intercourse today is about 17.4 for women and 17.7 for men (Santelli et al., 2006). The median age for first marriage in 2009 was 25.9 for women and 28.1 for men (U.S. Census, 2009b). Therefore, the average length of time between first sex and first marriage is 8.5 years for women and 10.4 years for men. In 1970, when many of the politicians who voted for AOE were young, the median age at first intercourse was 19.2 years, and first marriage was 20.8, a gap of only 19 months (Santelli, 2008; Santelli, Ott, Lyon, Rogers, & Summers, 2006). So at a time when sexual maturity occurs earlier than ever and marriage occurs later than ever, the federal government, through AOE, had basically decreed that adults should spend many years of their life celibate. (See Figure 1.3 for median ages for intercourse and marriage in 1970 and 2009.)

The reality is that most people don't remain completely abstinent until they marry in their late 20s. Approximately 50% of males and females between ages 15 and 19 have had vaginal intercourse and 63% have had some form of sexual contact such as oral and anal intercourse (Mosher, Chandra, & Jones, 2005).

Ineffective. While the federal government's support of AOE grew in the early part of the 21st century, a long-term national study found that these programs did not increase abstinence, delay first intercourse, or reduce the number of sexual partners or STI rates (Trenholm et al., 2007). Although the Bush administration reported that AOE was successful, program outcomes were measured by students' attitudes, not behaviors. For instance, if students answered "yes" on a test that asked if abstinence could bring "social, psychological and health gains," the pro-

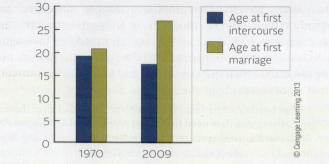

FIGURE 1.3 Median ages for intercourse and marriage, 1970 and 2009.

gram was reported to be a success. In fact, teen pregnancy rates rose in 2005–2006 for the first time in more than a decade; it is thought that one of the factors related to this rise may be the lack of information about contraception in AOE programs (AGI, 2010). On the other hand, comprehensive sex education programs that provide information about both abstinence and contraception have been shown to delay sexual activity in teens (Kirby, 2001; Santelli et al., 2006). Teens who have gone through comprehensive sex education are more likely to use contraception and have fewer sexual partners once they do become sexually active, compared to teens taught only AOE. In the face of these findings, proponents of AOE claimed that it was the values that were taught, not the effectiveness of the program, that was important. "Whether or not these programs work is a bogus issue," said Robert Rector, abstinence-only advocate (SIECUS, 2007).

Discriminatory. Abstinence-only education teaches teens that the "expected standard of human sexual activity is in the context of marriage." What about those teens who are already sexually active? AOE does not provide them with the information that could help them to make wiser sexual choices. And what of those who choose not to marry—or are not always allowed to marry, such as gays and lesbians? The administration's policy for them is lifelong celibacy.

False information. In 2004, the U.S. House of Representatives Committee on Government Reform reported that 11 of the 13 commonly used AOE curricula under review contained false, misleading, or distorted information about contraception, abortion, or reproductive health (Santelli et al., 2006). Many AOE programs grossly underestimated the effectiveness of condoms and other contraceptives in preventing STIs and pregnancy and gave false information about the physical and psychological risks of abortion. Some federally funded programs even got basic reproductive information wrong; one curriculum reported that a fetus contains 24 (rather than the actual 23) chromosomes from each parent. AOE programs also perpetuate sexist and harmful gender stereotypes: These programs often portray girls and women as sexually passive and submissive and emphasize the idea that it is their responsibility to help curb boys' unbridled sexual impulses (Valenti, 2006).

Whose morality? Whose rights? Section 510 teaches that marital monogamy is the expected standard of human sexuality. Whose standard? Is it the role of the U.S. government to dictate morality to its citizens? And whose rights are being considered in the development of these programs?

ASK YOURSELF

The U.S. government spends a lot of money on anti-drug campaigns to educate kids about the dangers of drugs so they will avoid them. Why is sex treated differently?

State laws generally allow mature minors to make decisions regarding birth control, treatment of STIs, prenatal care, and adoption (Beh & Diamond, 2006), yet the underlying message of AOE is that while adolescents have the right to make their own decisions about sexual issues, they have no right to information about these issues.

"Teens need a comprehensive sexuality program that gives them all the information they need to become empowered and responsible for preventing pregnancy and disease. We have to stop trying to legislate morals and instead teach responsibility."

—*Joycelyn Elders, former U.S. Surgeon General*

Under President George W. Bush, funding for AOE increased every year, from $60 million in 1998 to $191 million in 2008. Between 1996 and 2006, the federal government spent more than $1.3 billion on programs whose sole purpose was to teach the benefits of sexual abstention. No federal money was spent for any education program that discussed the effectiveness of condoms to reduce the risks of infection or pregnancy. States had the choice to accept millions of dollars of abstinence-only funding from the federal government or to refuse the funds and have the option to teach comprehensive sex education. From 1996 to 2006, teen pregnancy rates in California, which taught CSE, dropped more than 40%. Texas, which spent more on AOE than any other state, had more sexually active students than other states, and one of the highest teen pregnancy rates in the United States (AGI, 2010).

The vast majority of parents believe their adolescents should receive comprehensive sex education and be provided with information on topics such as contraception, how to make responsible sexual choices, abortion, masturbation, and homosexuality; only 15% of parents want abstinence-only education taught in the schools (Santelli et al., 2006). Groups that support comprehensive sex education programs include (among others): the American Medical Association, the American Academy of Pediatrics, the American Nurses Association, the American Public Health Association, the American College of Obstetricians and Gynecologists, the American Psychological Association, the Society for Adolescent Medicine, the National Education Association, the American School Health Association, and the American Association of University Women (Beh & Diamond, 2006). From 1996 to 2006, there was a disparity between what Americans wanted and what the federal government supported with regard to sex education. Teachers, parents, students, and health organizations wanted young people to receive comprehensive sex education, whereas conservative groups, evangelical Christians, and politicians promoted AOE (National Public Radio [NPR], 2004).

President Barack Obama's proposed 2010–2015 fiscal budget cut the funding for AOE programs to $50 million per year and

Although evangelical Christian groups seem to wield enormous political power, these groups often have beliefs that differ from those of most Americans. For example, 81% of evangelical or born-again Christians surveyed believe it is morally wrong for unmarried adults to engage in sexual intercourse, compared with 33% of other Americans (born-again Christians and Evangelicals represented 39% of this sample) (NPR, 2004). Most evangelical and born-again Christians polled believe that unmarried people should abstain from passionate kissing, and they are 3 times as likely as non-evangelicals to believe that sex education should not be taught in schools (NPR, 2004).

allocated $185 million per year for more comprehensive sexuality education programs that focus on both abstinence and the use of contraceptives to prevent STIs and pregnancy.

It is clear that politics has a direct effect on our sexual lives. For a decade, abstinence-only education was the policy, receiving hundreds of millions of tax dollars, regardless of the fact that most people were against it, and evidence showed it didn't work. It took a change in the presidential administration to reduce its scope. No matter how you feel regarding sex education, if you have an opinion, it is important to remember to vote for the government representative that agrees with your stance. Whom you vote for, and what they stand for, can influence your life at its deepest core.

Sexuality Education Across the Life Span

Education about sexuality should not stop with the onset of sexual intercourse. Indeed, when it comes to sexuality, as with most intriguing topics, we should strive to educate ourselves as much as possible. New developments in health research, changing laws concerning sexual activity and marriage, and new contraceptive options are only a few of the issues facing people today. Obviously, we all need to learn the skills necessary to evaluate information so we can make intelligent decisions regarding our sexual lives. As our sexual needs and realities change, we need to learn about contraception, giving and receiving sexual pleasure, pregnancy and infertility, same-sex relationships, fetishes, and sexual dysfunctions, topics rarely covered in formal sex education courses. Hopefully, by taking this course on human sexuality, you will continue your journey as a lifelong learner of sexuality.

Chapter Summary

Why a Course on Human Sexuality?

- Sexuality is ubiquitous and every person in the world expresses his or her sexuality in his or her own way. Thinking about or talking about sexuality often brings up strong emotions.
- Teenagers get most of their information about sexuality from the media, which does not adequately discuss the risks and responsibilities of sex. Sexuality education is vitally important on many levels.
- What is considered "normal" differs from person to person, from time to time, and from culture to culture. There are many different standards of normality, including subjective normality, statistical normality, idealistic normality, cultural normality, and clinical normality.

Perspectives of Sexuality: A Multidisciplinary Approach

- To best understand human sexuality, one must consider many disciplines, including biology, psychology, history, religion, culture and society, language, media, and law.
- Biological aspects of sexuality include anatomy and physiology, hormones, and genetics. Sociobiology investigates the ways that social behaviors are influenced by biological factors.
- Sexuality is more than just a physical response. Emotions, thoughts, and beliefs have a powerful influence on sexual behaviors and feelings. Various psychological theories—including psychoanalytic, behavioral, cognitive learning, and social learning—address issues of sexuality.
- Sexual behavior and attitudes change significantly over time. Ancient Greece and ancient Rome were male-dominated societies in which male–male sex was

accepted as long as it did not interfere with the family. During the Middle Ages, the Catholic Church's position that intercourse was only for procreation influenced sexual behaviors. The Protestant Reformation changed some of those views. During the Victorian era, people focused on sexuality like never before, although it was also a time of sexual repression. Over the course of the 20th century, sexuality became more accepted and evident in society.

- Religions have a huge impact on sexual beliefs and expression. The Judeo-Christian tradition is founded on the dictum to "be fruitful and multiply." Judaism generally holds a positive, natural outlook toward marital sex. Significant variations exist today between different sects of Christianity and Catholicism and their views of sexuality. In Islam, marriage and family are of utmost importance. Other religions celebrate sexuality as a sacred union necessary to a person's well-being.
- Sexual attitudes and behavior are strongly influenced by social and cultural forces. Compared to other Western countries, the United States is one of the more sexually repressive societies. Language forms our perception of the world and thus guides our thinking and behavior.
- The media strongly affects our sexual thoughts and behaviors. Americans are exposed to hundreds (or even thousands) of hours of television each year, most of it containing some sexual content. Most of the programs with sexual content do not include messages related to sexual risks and responsibilities. Advertising, the Internet, and music also are rife with sexual content.

Sex Education

- Sexuality education should begin early in a person's life, but should be presented in an age-appropriate manner. Children below the age of 5 should be taught about privacy and respect, and the correct terms for body parts. Children between 5 and 8 are more curious about how the body works and about gender roles. Children should be taught about future changes to their bodies before they occur. Adolescents may want to know about relationships, masturbation, menstruation, and nocturnal emissions, as well as intercourse, birth control, and STIs.
- Parents should be open and honest with their children, should provide accurate information, and should listen to their children's questions.
- Abstinence-only education (AOE) teaches that abstinence is the only certain way to avoid pregnancy, STIs, and other health problems. AOE programs are forbidden to mention contraception, except to discuss its failures, and they teach that any sexual activity (including kissing) outside of marriage is likely to have harmful effects. Comprehensive sex education (CSE) provides students with a broader range of information, including information about contraception as well as abstinence. Many studies have found AOE to be unrealistic, ineffective, discriminatory, and to provide false information to its students.

Additional Resources

Log in to CengageBrain to access the resources your instructor requires. For this book, you can access:

 **CourseMate** brings course concepts to life with interactive learning, study, and exam preparation tools that support the printed textbook. A textbook-specific website, Psychology CourseMate, includes an integrated interactive eBook and other interactive learning tools including quizzes, flashcards, videos, and more.

CENGAGENOW **CengageNOW** is an easy-to-use online resource that helps you study in less time to get the grade you want—NOW. Take a pre-test for this chapter and receive a personalized study plan based on your results that will identify the topics you need to review and direct you to online resources to help you master those topics. Then take a post-test to help you determine the concepts you have mastered and what you will need to work on. If your textbook does not include an access code card, go to CengageBrain.com to gain access. Visit www.cengagebrain.com anytime to access your account and purchase materials.

Web Resources

The American Association of Sexuality Educators, Counselors, and Therapists
The American Association of Sexuality Educators, Counselors, and Therapists (AASECT) is an interdisciplinary professional organization whose members are committed to promoting the understanding of human sexuality and healthy sexual behavior.

Advocates for Youth
Founded on the view that young people have the right to accurate and complete sexual health information, Advocates for Youth provides information on STIs, violence and

harassment, contraception, gay and lesbian issues, and many other related topics.

The Guttmacher Institute
The Guttmacher Institute advances sexual and reproductive health in the United States and worldwide through an interrelated program of social science research, policy analysis, and public education.

The Kaiser Family Foundation
The Kaiser Family Foundation produces and disseminates information on many sexuality and health-related topics.

The Kinsey Institute for Research in Sex, Gender, and Reproduction
The Kinsey Institute for Research in Sex, Gender, and Reproduction was founded by Alfred Kinsey in 1947. Since then, the Kinsey Institute has supported interdisciplinary research into sexuality.

Planned Parenthood
Planned Parenthood provides information and services related to reproductive health. They are strong advocates for pro-choice legislation and comprehensive sex education.

The Religious Institute
This database includes statements from 28 religious denominations on issues such as contraception, abortion, assisted reproductive technology, sexual orientation, marriage, sexual education, and adolescent sexuality.

The Society for the Scientific Study of Sexuality
The Society for the Scientific Study of Sexuality (SSSS) is the oldest professional society dedicated to the advancement of knowledge about sexuality. "Quad S" has members who represent a wide range of disciplines.

The Sexuality Information and Education Council of the United States
The Sexuality Information and Education Council of the United States (SIECUS) was founded to provide comprehensive education and accurate information about sexuality and sexual and reproductive health. SIECUS "affirms that sexuality is a fundamental part of being human, one that is worthy of dignity and respect."

The World Association for Sexual Health
The World Association for Sexual Health (WAS) is committed to promoting sexual health for all, and supports the creation of knowledge through research, which can help people to attain and maintain sexual health.

2

Evaluating Studies of Sexuality

"We are the recorders and reporters of facts—not the judges of the behaviors we describe."

—Alfred Kinsey

"Thinking is skilled work. It is not true that we are naturally endowed with the ability to think clearly and logically—without learning how, or without practicing."

—Author Alfred Mander

©Steve Hix/Somos Image/age fotostock

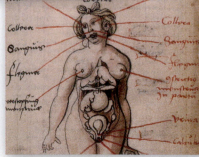
Wellcome Library, London

© Adrian Neal/Getty Images

How Do We Know What We Know About Sex?

After completion of this section, you will be able to . . .

○ Identify important sex researchers through history.

○ Recognize that society and politics influence sex research.

From the first human who ever wondered how babies were made to today's scientists analyzing the neurological foundations of desire, curiosity about sex has driven people to look for answers, and sexual research has profoundly affected society. Not only does our sexual knowledge influence people's opinions and behaviors, but the attitudes, customs, and mores of a culture have an impact on scientific investigations. Many courageous men and women throughout the years have worked—often at the risk of personal harm and social censure—to improve our understanding of sexuality.

Sex Researchers Through History

Havelock Ellis (1859–1939) was a British physician and social reformer who felt that human sexuality was a normal and natural expression of love. A pioneer in the field of human sexuality, Ellis's major work was the seven-volume *Studies in the Psychology of Sex,* an encyclopedia of sex. Ellis wrote that sexual feelings in women were ordinary and healthy, homosexuality occurred naturally, and masturbation was normal, ideas that were shocking during the Victorian era. A British court found the first volume of Ellis's encyclopedia to be obscene; later volumes were published only in the United States. Until 1935, only medical professionals were allowed to read the series. Ellis's work had an important influence on changing public perception of sexuality, and it promoted the view that sexuality is not just a biological process but a psychological process as well.

In 1886, German psychologist **Richard von Krafft-Ebing** (1840–1902) wrote *Psychopathia Sexualis,* in which he described various sexual deviations and cataloged sexual positions and non-procreative sexual acts. Krafft-Ebing coined the terms *sadism* (after the Marquis de Sade) and *masochism* (after author Sacher-Masoch, who wrote of a man's desire to be whipped and enslaved by the woman he desired). Because *Psychopathia* was written for legal and medical professionals, Krafft-Ebing chose a scientific-sounding title and wrote some sections in Latin to discourage lay readers. Despite his efforts, the general public clamored for the book, which went through many printings and translations.

Magnus Hirschfeld (1868–1935) was a gay German–Jewish physician dedicated to treating sexual problems, educat-

Havelock Ellis was a pioneer of sexuality research.

In Victorian times, physicians told their patients that nocturnal emissions (wet dreams) would lead to gonorrhea, blindness, and death. A story about Ellis (perhaps apocryphal) says that in his younger years he thought about committing suicide to avoid this grisly end but instead chose to keep a journal of his impending ejaculation-related doom. When death did not immediately follow his nocturnal emissions, he became angry over the misinformation provided by physicians and eventually committed his life to sexuality research.

_____

_____

ing the public about sexuality, and eradicating discriminatory policies. He fought to repeal paragraph 175, the section of the German penal code that criminalized homosexuality. In 1896, he wrote a paper in which he argued that genetic factors influenced sexual orientation. Hirschfeld also fought for employment opportunities for women and worked to decriminalize abortion. In 1919, he opened the Magnus Hirschfeld Foundation, an institute for sexology (the study of sex), which contained laboratories, lecture halls, and a library. The Nazis destroyed years of data, as well as the institute itself, in 1933. Today, the German Society for Social–Scientific Sexuality Research awards the Magnus Hirschfeld medal for outstanding service to sexual science.

Sigmund Freud (1856–1939) had a powerful effect on Western views of sexuality. Freud believed that sexuality was the basis of almost every human action and that the libido was a principal motivating force in the development of personality. He felt that children go through different psychosexual stages of development—such as the oral, anal, and phallic stages—and the differences in satisfying biological or sexual urges at these stages significantly shape one's adult personality. Freud's ideas gained popularity in America in the early 20th century, at a time when ideas of free love and social reform were beginning to take hold. Since then, his theories have had an enormous effect on the modern world. His ideas about the unconscious mind, the meaning of dreams, and the Oedipal complex have entered the vernacular, as have the concepts of the "Freudian slip," "penis envy," and "anal person-

Magnus Hirschfeld published the first journal of sexology, created the first gay rights organization, organized the first international sexology congress, and opened the first institute for sexology.

Sigmund Freud was one of the most influential psychologists of the 20th century.

Alfred Kinsey's research led to the development of the modern field of sexology.

people, and Catholics and Jews, were underrepresented in Kinsey's sample. Still, these interviews led to the publication of *Sexual Behavior in the Human Male* in 1948 and *Sexual Behavior in the Human Female* in 1953, both of which shot to the top of the best-seller lists despite their dry, scientific tone (Kinsey, Pomeroy, Martin, & Gebhard, 1948, 1953). Kinsey's findings scandalized mid-20th century America; he reported that American men and women participated in masturbation, premarital sex, same-sex experiences, and adultery. The government was not amused, and Kinsey's work was branded immoral and obscene. Kinsey died in 1956.

alities." Freudian ideas and images abound in popular culture: Alfred Hitchcock's *Spellbound,* Woody Allen's *Oedipus Wrecks,* and Roman Polanski's *Chinatown* all show overt Freudian influences.

A biologist by training, **Alfred Kinsey** (1894–1956) became one of the premier sex researchers of the 20th century and greatly influenced society's knowledge of and views about human sexuality. Kinsey began his career by collecting and studying gall wasps. In 1938, he was asked to teach the "marriage course" for seniors at Indiana University, perhaps because university administrators thought an entomologist would be a "safe" choice. Dismayed by the widespread ignorance and dishonesty regarding sexual matters, Kinsey wanted to approach the study of sexuality as systematically and scientifically as he studied his wasps. Students in his course first completed questionnaires about their sexual behavior. Then, frustrated by the limitations of these written questionnaires, Kinsey began conducting face-to-face interviews, and started traveling out of town to carry out interviews with more subjects. Over the years, he and three colleagues conducted face-to-face interviews with almost 12,000 men and women in the United States. Hoping to persuade the world that sexuality was natural, Kinsey founded the Institute for Research in Sex, Gender, and Reproduction at Indiana University in 1947.

Kinsey knew it would be nearly impossible to interview a cross-section of the American public because many people would refuse to discuss such intimate topics, so he used group sampling, in which he encouraged all the members of specific groups (such as students in a college class, fraternities, or prisons) to participate in his study. Some groups, including people of color, elderly

Although Kinsey has been celebrated in books and film (one of the latest film adaptations starred Liam Neeson as Alfred Kinsey), physician **Clelia Mosher** (1863–1940), who studied the sexual habits of American women half a century before Kinsey published his work, did not attract as much attention; her results went unpublished until 1980. Contrary to the beliefs of the day, most of the married Victorian women interviewed by Mosher said that they experienced sexual desire and orgasm. One of the first to study female physiology, Mosher challenged the stereotype of the physically weak woman (Jacob, 1981).

The husband-and-wife team **William Masters** (1915–2001) and **Virginia Johnson** (b. 1925) directly observed and recorded the physiological responses of men and women during sexual activity. From 1957 to 1965, Masters and Johnson monitored more than 10,000 acts of sexual activity in adults ranging in age from 18 to 89. Their subsequent books explained the cycle of physical response to sexual stimulation and described the phenomenon of female multiple orgasm, male refractory period, and the myth of the vaginal versus clitoral orgasm (Masters &

Physician Clelia Mosher studied the sexual habits of Victorian women and challenged the widely held stereotypes about women's physical limitations.

In their laboratory, William Masters and Virginia Johnson observed the sexual responses of hundreds of volunteers.

Psychologist Evelyn Hooker showed that there is no difference in psychological adjustment between heterosexuals and homosexuals.

Dr. Ruth Westheimer has written several books on human sexuality and is a widely known sex educator. Born to Jewish parents in Germany in 1928, Dr. Ruth was sent to Switzerland in 1938 to escape the Nazis. After learning that her parents died in Auschwitz, she immigrated to Israel, where she trained as a sniper in the Israeli army, and was wounded in the war for Israeli independence. Dr. Ruth moved to the United States in 1956 and completed her doctorate in education. Her television show *Sexually Speaking* first aired in 1980 and Dr. Ruth's ability to put others at ease while speaking honestly yet humorously about intimate matters endeared her to audiences.

Johnson, 1966). Their work focused on physical arousal rather than on the connection of sexual response to emotional states.

At the request of Alfred Kinsey, endocrinologist **Harry Benjamin** (1885–1986) first consulted on the case of a boy who wanted to become a girl. At the time, this condition was almost unheard of and there was no consensus as to how to treat this phenomenon. Benjamin first introduced the term *transsexuals* and published the first book on the subject, which described the treatment path he developed. Dr. Benjamin was considered a very kind and caring man, especially to a group of people who were often treated with scorn or even violence. His work provided the basis for the Standards of Care for Gender Identity Disorders, a protocol that outlines the typical treatment for transsexuals.

Evelyn Hooker (1907–1996) was an American psychologist who published the first empirical research that disputed the belief that homosexuality was a mental illness. Dr. Hooker performed many psychological tests on heterosexual and homosexual males and found no psychological differences between them. Her work was the foundation that ultimately influenced the American Psychiatric Association to remove homosexuality from the *Diagnostic and Statistical Manual of Mental Disorders* in 1973.

Sexologists Today

We are lucky to live in a time in which so many talented scientists are discovering the mysteries of human sexuality; the work of many of these researchers will be described throughout this book. Well-known people in the field today and their areas of interest include the following: Sexologist Beverly Whipple studies women's health issues and the sexual physiology of women. Pepper Schwartz explores the dynamics of interpersonal relationships. Lisa Diamond is changing the way we look at sexual orientation. Past president of the Society for the Scientific Study of Sexuality, Milton Diamond investigates aspects of

Sexologist One who studies human sexuality. Sexologists may come from various disciplines, including biology, medicine, psychology, sociology, anthropology, and criminology. Many sexologists are also therapists or educators.

intersexuality and gender identity. Ira Reiss, a prominent sexuality researcher for more than 40 years, has worked to reverse society's double standard in sexuality for men and women, and feels that sexuality is a natural and healthy outlet. Edward Laumann examines the sociology of sexuality and codirected (along with John Gagnon) the 1992 National Health and Social Life Survey, a comprehensive survey of sex in America. Other sexologists are media figures, better known for their efforts to increase public awareness of sexual issues. Ruth Westheimer (Dr. Ruth) is a sex therapist, author, and media personality. Former porn star Annie Sprinkle now educates the public about sexuality. Dan Savage is an openly gay author and playwright whose humorous and irreverent syndicated sex advice column runs in newspapers around the world.

Political Issues in Sex Research

As discussed in Chapter 1, in 2004 the U.S. Congress voted to appropriate $131 million for Abstinence-Only Sex Education (AOE). When confronted with data from the National Campaign to Prevent Teen and Unplanned Pregnancy that showed that the only programs proven to lower teen pregnancy rates included information about both contraception and abstinence, an adviser to President Bush told reporters that the AOE program would continue nonetheless, saying "values trump data."

In addition to influencing what kind of sex education programs are taught, political agendas influence the type and scope of research that is performed. In 1953, Alfred Kinsey published *Sexual Behavior in the Human Female,* which horrified McCarthy-era Americans with its finding that females were just as capable of sexual response as males. A Congressional committee in the 1950s claimed that Kinsey's work "undermined the moral fiber of the nation," contributed to the rise of juvenile delinquency, and left the country vulnerable to a Communist takeover. Kinsey lost a major source of his funding a year later. In 1988, Edward Laumann and colleagues received a federal grant to conduct the National Health and Social Life Survey (NHSLS), which was designed to question 20,000 people about their sexual attitudes and behaviors. Unfortunately, the NHSLS lost its funding in 1991 by a vote in the U.S. Senate on the grounds that it was inappropriate for the government to support sex research and that the real purpose of the study was "to legitimize the homosexual lifestyle" (Bancroft, 2008). Laumann and colleagues later received enough financial support from private foundations to study 3,400 subjects (Bancroft, 2004) (see the Sex Actually feature on page 36). The ideological agenda of a political administration can influence what scientific studies get funded, the format through which sexuality education is disseminated, and even the type of sexuality information available on government web pages.

ASK YOURSELF
Who decides which research and educational programs get funded? Who decides what is "obscene" or what is necessary? Whose values should be represented?

Investigating Human Sexuality

After completion of this section, you will be able to . . .

- List the important considerations in producing high-quality research.

- Define and understand the terms *population, sample, representative sample, convenience sample, sampling bias, volunteer bias,* and *observer effects.*

- Compare and contrast surveys, case studies, observations, and experiments.

- Define and understand the terms *hypothesis, independent variable, dependent variable, control, placebo,* and *blind study.*

- Recognize the importance of cross-cultural research studies in helping us avoid ethnocentrism and heterocentrism.

- Explain what institutional review boards (IRBs) are and how they protect human subjects.

We are born with an innate curiosity about the world and our place in it. To function properly in and adapt to our surroundings, we make observations, create a theory, test our premise, and draw conclusions. This is the scientific method in its simplest form. Every day, researchers explore the mysteries of human sexuality to discover our beliefs, behaviors, and attitudes about sex. To conduct high-quality research, scientists acquire important skills, as well as the ability to critically evaluate information (Figure 2.1). Scholars refine these skills through many years of work. In designing research, scientists must carefully consider what and whom they are studying, the methods by which they will find their answer, and how to ensure the **validity** of their findings.

What Exactly Are You Investigating?

In order to perform reputable research, you will need to clearly define what you are studying.

Use precise and unambiguous language. Consider the statement, "I fooled around with Chris." The possible meanings of this remark could vary greatly depending on the speaker. To a 9-year-old boy, it might mean that he and Chris went out and rode bikes and hit things with sticks. A 14-year-old might mean that she and her best friend Chris French-kissed. To a 37-year-old desperate housewife it might indicate that she had a sexual affair with Chris, the lawn boy.

High-quality research depends on precise language. Using accurate language can be particularly difficult in sex research; for instance, how would you clearly and universally define "attractive" or "love"? Even the word "sex" has many interpretations. In 1999, after President Clinton engaged in oral sex with Monica Lewinsky and passionately averred "I did not have sex with that woman," Stephanie Sanders and June Reinisch distributed a questionnaire asking students to determine which interactions individuals would consider as having "had sex." Although some of the respondents considered kissing to be "having sex," others didn't agree that oral or anal sex was sex (Sanders & Reinisch, 1999). When this study (discussed at greater length in Chapter 11) was repeated with a more representative sample, there was even less consensus regarding which behaviors constituted "having sex" (Sanders et al., 2010). Given sexuality's inherent emotional, political, and legal ramifications, it is particularly important that researchers in this area clearly define their terms.

Use valid and specific measurements. Imagine you want to gauge the effect of a person's appearance on the success of their relationship. How would you measure a person's relative appearance? By whose standards? How would you quantify the success of a relationship? By the number of years a couple spends together or by how many fights they have? By their self-assessments or based on others' observations of them? Each of these standards will give you a different perspective; you need to choose which will best answer your question. Your means of measurement needs to be **reliable**, meaning it is accurate, stable, and consistent over repeated tests of the same subject. You will also need to make sure that your project is designed to measure only the issues in which you are interested. For instance, in studying the effect of appearance on relationships, you would need to control for other factors that might influence a couple's rapport, such as education, alcohol use, or psychological issues. Regardless of the techniques chosen, you will have to clearly describe your methods so your study can be replicated by an independent source.

Who Are You Studying?

You will need to consider which group of people you're interested in, as well as how you will select the subjects who will take part in your study.

Carefully consider your subject pool. To study human sexuality, you first need to choose your **population**, or the group you want to investigate, such as the inhabitants of the United States, postmenopausal women, or the students at your university. It is usually impossible to obtain information from everyone in your population, so scientists get data from a **sample**, or subset of individuals in the target population. The sample you use greatly influences the outcome of your research.

Validity The extent to which findings accurately reflect the concept that they are intended to measure.

Reliability The extent to which the measurement of a test is consistent and accurate over time.

Population The group of individuals being studied.

Sample A subset of individuals in the population.

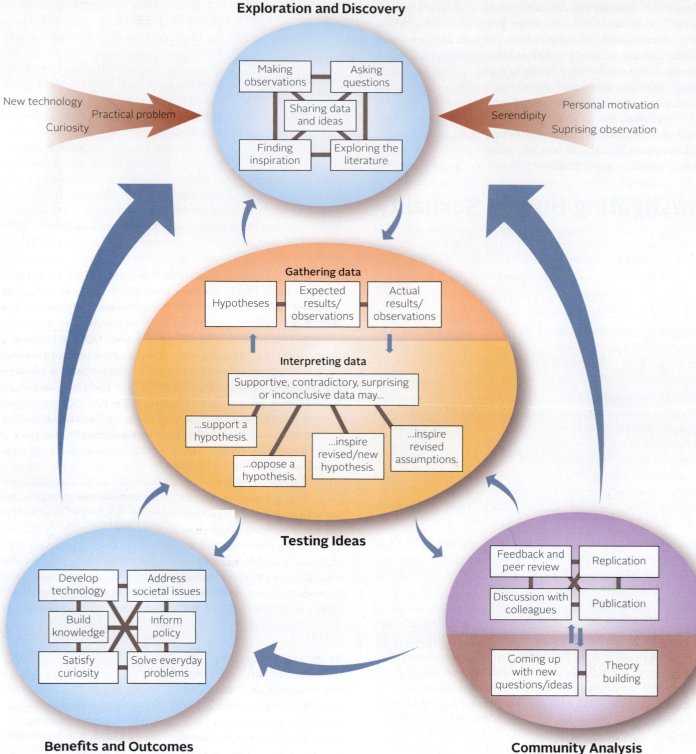

Exploration and Discovery

Making observations

Asking questions

Sharing data and ideas

Finding inspiration

Exploring the literature

New technology

Practical problem

Curiosity

Personal motivation

Serendipity

Suprising observation

Gathering data

Hypotheses

Expected results/observations

Actual results/observations

Interpreting data

Supportive, contradictory, surprising or inconclusive data may...

...support a hypothesis.

...oppose a hypothesis.

...inspire revised/new hypothesis.

...inspire revised assumptions.

Testing Ideas

Feedback and peer review

Replication

Discussion with colleagues

Publication

Coming up with new questions/ideas

Theory building

Community Analysis and Feedback

Develop technology

Address societal issues

Build knowledge

Inform policy

Satisfy curiosity

Solve everyday problems

Benefits and Outcomes

FIGURE 2.1 How science works: The process by which scientists develop ideas, gather information, and interpret and disseminate data. (© Cengage Learning 2013. Adapted with permission from *Understanding Science,* 2011. University of California Museum of Paleontology, http://www.understandingscience.org)

A **random sample** (also called **probability sample**) is a sample in which each member of the population has an equal probability of being selected. At best, this results in a **representative sample**, in which the characteristics of your sample with regard to age, race, sex, religion, etc., match that of the population you are studying. For example, a representative sample of the United States population would be 51% female, 13% African American, and 16% Hispanic. Thirty-nine percent would have an associate's or bachelor's degree, and the members of your sample would be of an age, religious identity, and otherwise have characteristics that represented the greater U.S. population. Larger samples tend to give more accurate results than smaller samples, but using a large sample does not necessarily mean that the group of subjects you are studying is representative of the larger population. Researchers often use **convenience samples**—those subjects who are easily accessible for participation. An example is a professor who uses her students as subjects in research studies. Using convenience samples can lead to **sampling bias**, because some members of a population may be over-represented and others excluded. The groups that are most often available to researchers in an academic environment are middle-class North American college students of European descent. Thus, many sex studies are lacking information on elderly people, certain minority groups, and people with disabilities. Consider your own classroom population: how closely do you and your classmates conform to a representative sample of the population of the United States?

People who are willing to volunteer for sex studies (or for any experimental studies for that matter) do not necessarily represent the attitudes, behaviors, and beliefs of the general population, a phenomenon known as **volunteer bias**. To get an idea of what volunteer bias entails, consider whether you would take part in any of the following studies:

- Fill out an anonymous survey about your personal sexual attitudes and experiences.
- Undergo a 30-minute face-to-face interview, during which the researcher will ask you questions about your sexual attitudes and experiences.
- Watch a sexually explicit video and later describe your reactions to the film to the researcher.
- Watch a sexually explicit video with measurement equipment attached to your genitals, to assess your degree of arousal to the film.
- Watch a sexually explicit video and then masturbate to orgasm while being observed in the laboratory by the researcher.
- Consume a specified amount of alcohol prior to masturbating to orgasm in the laboratory.
- Engage in sexual intercourse in the laboratory while being observed by researchers.

As the research design became more intimate, it is likely that fewer of you would have considered participating. The attitudes and behaviors of subjects who take part in more physical experiments might not accurately represent the attitudes and behaviors of the rest of the population. People who volunteer for sexuality studies are more likely to be male, to have had sexual intercourse, to have performed oral sex, to hold more positive attitudes about sexuality, to be more interested in sexual variety, and to have less sexual anxiety and guilt than those who would not volunteer (Wiederman, 1999).

How Will You Find Your Answer?

Scientists can pursue many approaches to answer their questions. The research method you choose can influence the type of answer you receive.

ASK YOURSELF

Imagine you want to conduct a magazine survey on how common same-sex activity is. What magazine would you use? How might your results differ if your sample is made up of readers of *Playboy* or of *The Ladies' Home Journal?* If you send your questionnaire through *Out* or through *Christianity Today?*

Choose an appropriate method of investigation. How would *you* learn about sex? If you were given the assignment to find out about sex in this country—who is doing what, with whom, how often they're doing it, and if they mind if we watch—how would you conduct your research? Would you ask your friends? Listen to a story about "my cousin's friend's sister who got pregnant without having sex"? Tell your best friend that there's a guy in class who likes her and watch how her behavior changes? Hide in a closet and watch the mayor having sex? Congratulations! You're on your way to being a sex researcher (except for that last option—if you do that, you're on your way to jail). The major **research methods** employed by those who investigate sexuality are *surveys, case studies, observations,* and *controlled experiments.* Different questions call for different means of study. Scientists need to assess which method best serves their purpose, weigh the advantages and disadvantages, and evaluate the practicality and ethical concerns of each of these methods.

Surveys

Surveys are a way to study the attitudes, opinions, and behaviors of individuals. Data can be gathered through written questionnaires or interviews. Survey subjects are presented with a number of questions. In written surveys, subjects are given a list of responses from which to choose, whereas interview questions are often open-ended. Written surveys are frequently sent through the mail or administered through a magazine, and responses are kept anonymous. Magazines such as *Glamour* or *Playboy* have the ability to reach millions of readers each month,

Random sample (also called a **probability sample**) A sample in which each member of the population has an equal probability of participating.

Representative sample A sample that has similar characteristics (such as age, sex, ethnicity, education) as the population from which it was drawn.

Convenience sample A sample that is not necessarily representative of the population, but that is easily accessible to the researcher.

Sampling bias The tendency for some members of the population to be over-represented and others to be excluded from a sample.

Volunteer bias The tendency for those who volunteer for research to be different in some way from those who refuse to participate.

Research methods A systematic approach to gathering information and evaluating the findings.

Surveys A scientific collection of data from people regarding their attitudes, beliefs, and behaviors.

sexactually

Research and Human Sexuality

In the 1990s, the National Health and Social Life Survey (NHSLS) was published (Laumann et al., 1994). For the study, 3,432 people, aged 18 to 59, completed written questionnaires and met with 220 professional interviewers who questioned them about their sexual practices and beliefs. The authors tried to accurately represent the U.S. population, and more African Americans and Latinos took part in this study than in other studies, although Jews, Asian Americans, Native Americans, and the elderly were still underrepresented. The authors had an exceptional completion rate for their survey—79%. The participants were reassured that their responses were anonymous and confidential and that by sharing their experiences they would provide a social benefit and broaden the knowledge base in this important area. The NHSLS is one of the most comprehensive and accurate surveys available today, and we will discuss many of its findings in later chapters.

In 2010 the National Survey of Sexual Health and Behavior (NSSHB) was released. The NSSHB is the largest nationally representative study of sexual behaviors ever performed. Including data from 5,865 adolescents and adults aged 14 to 94, the NSSHB is one of the most comprehensive sexual studies done in nearly 20 years, and provides us with information about American's sexual and sexual-health behaviors. Whereas the Laumann study (the NHSLS) was limited to adults aged 18 to 59, the NSSHB includes data from men and women across the life span. Another advantage to the NSSHB is that it is the most current of all major surveys. The world has changed significantly since the NHSLS was performed in 1992. Oral and anal sex are more widely practiced. The Internet has influenced sexual knowledge, norms, and behaviors. Attitudes about same-sex relationships have changed, and same-sex marriages are legal in some states. Since 1997, more than $1.5 billion of federal funding has been spent on abstinence-only education. The development of a vaccine to prevent cancers associated with the sexually transmitted human papilloma virus and the extensive marketing of Viagra and other medications to treat erectile dysfunction have also influenced the national outlook on sex (Herbenick et al., 2010). Findings from this survey will be discussed throughout the textbook.

enter their responses on the keyboard. This technology allows the scientists to reach those who cannot read or—because questions are prerecorded—those who speak languages other than English.

Sometimes researchers get their information by interviewing subjects, either in person or over the telephone. Personal interviews give scientists the flexibility to pursue certain questions and omit others. They may establish rapport with their subjects and get information that might not be included on a written questionnaire. However, interviews can be a more time-consuming and expensive means of gathering data than written questionnaires. Subjects may also be more reticent in a face-to-face interview than in an anonymous written survey. Finally, scientists may filter the subjects' responses through their own biases and personal interpretations.

© Regis Vincent/Getty Images

Surveys—both written and oral—are a fairly easy and inexpensive way to get information from large groups of people. Scientists hoping to learn about sexual attitudes or behaviors from either questionnaires or interviews should, however, be aware of the weaknesses of this method of investigation. Most sexuality surveys have a low rate of response (Turner, 1999). Because only a very small percentage of a population usually returns surveys, you must consider the effects of volunteer bias on your results. Veracity is also a major concern in survey studies. Although you might think that people would be honest in an anonymous survey, the fact is that people don't always tell the truth when asked about sexuality. It may not always be intentional; people may forget or misunderstand the question, or they may give the answer that they think the researcher wants to hear. Scientists Michele Alexander and Terri Fisher found a particularly ingenious way to discover how honest their survey participants were being. In their study, college students completed questionnaires regarding their sexual attitudes and behaviors under three conditions. The researchers were looking for sex differences in self-reported sexual behavior. When male and female subjects thought their responses were anonymous, there was a moderate difference in reported behaviors between the sexes. When they believed that others would observe their responses, however, the women reported less permissive attitudes and behaviors than men did, as both genders tended to give socially expected answers. The researchers also had some subjects answer the questionnaire while attached to what they thought was a lie detector. In these subjects, sex differences in self-reported sexual behavior were negligible (Alexander & Fisher, 2003). This study will be discussed further in Chapters 5 and 11.

Case Studies

Case studies are a biographical account of an individual or a small group. Information may come from public records or from interviews with the subject or with individuals who have known

but their readers are not a representative sample of the general population.

Internet surveys are becoming more common. They save both time and money because the researchers don't have to print out questionnaires, mail them, and sort the responses (Fenton, Johnson, McManus, & Erens, 2001; Rhodes, Bowie, & Hergenrather, 2003). Internet surveys have fewer errors and unanswered questions, as menus and prompts can guide participants through the process and ensure that they answer all questions. Not everyone is on the Internet, however, so Internet surveys may be particularly prone to sampling bias (Turner, 1999). However, as time passes and more people use the Internet, this effect will diminish. The use of computer-assisted self-interviews is gaining popularity. Rather than pencil and paper questionnaires, subjects can listen to questions through headphones and

Case study An in-depth study of an individual or individuals, rather than a study that looks at a sample of the population.

the subject. Freud used many individual case studies to form his theories of psychological development. Later in the century, anecdotal studies gave us information about the G-spot. Case studies are not commonly used in sexuality research. People may be able to generate ideas or hypotheses from case studies, but because the sample size is very small, case studies give only limited information. The investigator's personal biases may also color the interpretation of the data, so a case study's findings should not be **overgeneralized**.

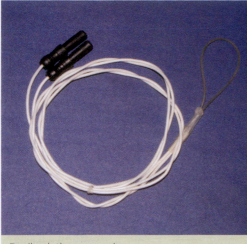
Penile plethysmograph.

Vaginal photoplethysmograph.

Both photos © Behavioral Technology, Inc.

Observational Methods

Empiricism is the view that knowledge comes from what we can experience, observe, and measure. In **direct observation**, researchers observe their subjects, usually in a laboratory, and record their responses. This type of research is fairly rare in sexuality, because most people are unwilling to be observed and measured during intimate acts. Nevertheless, hundreds of male and female volunteers, heterosexual and homosexual, reported to the laboratories of William Masters and Virginia Johnson to be observed while involved in various sexual activities, either alone or with a partner. As mentioned earlier, Masters and Johnson's data provided the world with some of the first empirical data on the physiological responses of the body that occur during sexual arousal (Masters & Johnson, 1966, 1979).

Two devices used to measure sexual arousal are the penile plethysmograph and the vaginal photoplethysmograph. The **penile plethysmograph** is a gauge that indirectly measures the changes in blood flow to the penis when a man is exposed to sexual stimuli. A stretchable band with mercury in it is fitted around the subject's penis. The device measures any changes in the circumference of the penis, even those not detected by the subject. This machine was first developed by Kurt Freund in Czechoslovakia to prevent draft dodgers from claiming they were homosexual in order to avoid military duty. The **vaginal photoplethysmograph** is a tampon-shaped cylinder with a light source and a light detector. The device is inserted into the vagina where it emits light. When a woman is sexually aroused, the vaginal walls engorge with blood, which affects the amount of light that is backscattered to the photoplethysmograph, thus giving an indirect measure of sexual arousal.

Investigators can also learn about sexual behavior by interacting with subjects in a more natural environment, a process called **participant observation**. In this case, researchers put themselves into the environment they are studying. Some are surreptitious; others reveal their identity. An example of participant observation is a scientist who dances at a strip club and records her observations of the interactions between the dancers and the club patrons (Frank, 2003). Another example would be if you went to fraternity parties and observed the interactions of the guests. While there, holding a red plastic cup containing your beverage of choice, you might notice the ways in which party-goers interact, flirt, or hook up.

Observational studies, like all other types of studies, have advantages and disadvantages. An advantage to observational studies is that they are based on firsthand scrutiny rather than on a subject's sometimes-faulty memories and misrepresentations. In direct observational studies, researchers can carefully control the environment to eliminate confounding factors. Unfortunately, observational studies can be expensive and susceptible to volunteer bias; as mentioned, subjects who are willing to be observed in sexuality studies are not representative of the general population. **Observer effects** are another confounding factor: If your subjects are aware they are being observed, it may affect their behavior. If you were being videotaped while having intercourse, how closely would your actions match your typical behaviors in bed? Finally, observations are subject to the witness's interpretation—what one scientist views as an attempt to hook up might be seen by another as a casual conversation. Clear guidelines and definitions need to be established before the observations begin.

The Experimental Method

It is only through the experimental method that researchers can identify cause-and-effect relationships. An **experiment** begins with a **hypothesis**, which is a prediction about the world based on observations. Each experiment has at least two

Generalization To suppose that a specific example applies to the general public.

Empiricism (em-PEER-uh-sizm) The view that knowledge comes through experience and observation.

Direct observation A study in which the investigators do not manipulate the conditions, but only observe subjects in a particular situation and record and interpret the outcome.

Participant observation The researcher participates in the events being studied.

Penile plethysmograph (pluh-THIZ-moh-graf) A device that indirectly measures blood flow in the penis.

Vaginal photoplethysmograph A device that uses light to indirectly measure blood flow to the vagina.

Observer effects The effect that the presence of the observer has on a subject's behavior.

Experiment A controlled test or investigation, designed to examine the validity of a hypothesis. Also, the act of conducting an investigation. An experiment is the only way in which a cause-and-effect relationship can be determined.

Hypothesis (high-PAH-thi-sis) A proposed explanation for facts or observations.

variables. A variable is anything that can vary or change, such as an attitude or a behavior. The **independent variable** is a factor that is controlled and manipulated by the researcher, whereas the **dependent variable** is observed and measured. What happens to the dependent variable *depends* on what your independent variable is. You might say that the independent variable is the presumed cause, and the dependent variable is the presumed effect; when you change the independent variable (the cause), you observe the effect on the dependent variable. For example, imagine you have developed a cream to treat erectile dysfunction. To test your discovery, you instruct a group of impotent men to rub the medicinal ointment onto their penises for 10 minutes. The independent variable is the medicinal ointment. The dependent variable is whether the subject gets an erection.

Subjects are randomly assigned to either the control group or the experimental group. The **control group** is treated identically to the experimental group in every way, except the control group is not exposed to the independent variable. The use of a control group allows researchers to determine the actual effects of the independent variable. For example, what if 62% of your subjects get an erection after rubbing on the cream that you have developed? Do you immediately run out and buy a boat to celebrate your success? Not so fast. You neglected to use a control group of men who rub a **placebo** cream—one that looks and feels identical but has no medicine—onto their penises for 10 minutes. If you had done that, you would have found that many of the men got erections from the simple act of massaging their penis for 10 minutes, and your medicine had no significant effect.

Let's use another example to illustrate the terms we have learned. Suppose you want to study the effect alcohol has on the ease of reaching orgasm in females. Your hypothesis may read: *All else being equal, alcohol increases the time it takes for a woman to have an orgasm.* One hundred fifty female volunteer subjects come to the laboratory. Half of them consume a drink of vodka and club soda and the other half drinks club soda only. Subjects don't know which they are drinking

CONTROL GROUP   OUT OF CONTROL GROUP
MUELLER

because the soda masks the taste of the vodka. Twenty minutes later they are brought into a room and are told to masturbate to orgasm.

In this study, the independent variable (the cause) is the alcohol. It is this variable that is manipulated: The test subjects will drink alcohol and those in the control group will drink only club soda. The dependent variable is the effect: how long it takes a woman to have an orgasm. If you find that the group of women who consumed alcohol took significantly longer to achieve orgasm than did the control group, you can say that your results are consistent with the hypothesis.

Although they can be time-consuming and expensive, experiments are the best method for identifying causal relationships. They also give us the opportunity to control for unwanted variables. However, one must remember that not all findings can be generalized to the "real world." The artificiality of the surroundings may influence your results. Perhaps some of your subjects, who normally can stimulate themselves to orgasm, cannot when told to do so in a lab. Also, your results are subject to volunteer bias. The women who agree to masturbate in a laboratory may not be representative of women in the general population.

The best research method to use depends on the nature of the study. Each method has pros and cons, which are summarized in Table 2.1.

Studying Sexuality Across the Life Span

Humans are sexual throughout their lives, from before birth (in Chapter 11 we will learn that fetuses masturbate) to old age. How one's sexuality is expressed, however, changes over the course of a person's life. Throughout the book, we will consider how various aspects of sexuality are expressed at different stages of life.

Because it is more convenient, most sexuality inquiries study adults between the ages of 18 and 60. However, there are studies that have explored the sexual attitudes and behaviors of people outside of this age range.

Some studies have widened their scope to survey teens and adolescents about their sexual attitudes and behaviors. For example, the 2010 National Survey of Sexual Health and Behavior questioned 820 young men and women between the ages of 14 and 17 and found, among other things, that condom use among adolescents has become a commonplace behavior (Fortenberry et al., 2010). In the mid-1990s, the National **Longitudinal Study** of Adolescent Health questioned more than 125,000 U.S. students in grades 7 through 12 (ADD Health, 2002). Using a combination of surveys and interviews, scientists questioned adolescents about their physical and psychological health, substance abuse, sexual behavior, as well as relationships with family, friends, and roman-

---

So what's the best method to use to do research?

Variable Anything that can vary or change, such as an attitude or a behavior.

Independent variable The variable that is manipulated in an experiment.

Dependent variable The variable that is observed and measured and that may change as a result of manipulations to the independent variable.

Control group The group of subjects who are not exposed to the independent variable.

Placebo (plu-SEE-bo) An inactive substance that resembles the treatment you are testing.

Longitudinal study A research study that involves repeated observations of the same group of subjects over a long period of time. This usually involves surveys or observations rather than experiments that determine causal relationships.

Table 2.1 Summary of Research Methods

	STRENGTHS	WEAKNESSES
Surveys	• Effective means of measuring the attitudes, opinions, and behaviors of many people. • Allows a wide range of responses. • Follow-up questions are possible during interviews. • Less expensive and time-consuming than other methods.	• Susceptible to sampling bias and volunteer bias. • Self-reports may be inaccurate or biased so reliability is difficult to determine. • Inability to draw conclusions about causal relationships. • Interviews are time-consuming.
Case study	• Extensive, in-depth evidence gathered on a single person or small group. • Data may be gathered in a number of different ways.	• Limited generalizability. • Being observed may change the subject's behavior. • Won't provide the information needed for many types of questions. • Inability to draw conclusions about causal relationships.
Observational methods	• Data are more reliable and less likely to be misrepresented. • Researchers can sometimes control the environment.	• Time-consuming and expensive. • Susceptible to volunteer bias and difficulty in obtaining study population. • Observer effects. • Inability to draw conclusions about causal relationships.
Controlled experiments	• Best method for identifying causal relationships. • Researcher can carefully control the environment.	• Artificial environment limits generalizability, and may affect subjects' responses. • Usually a smaller sample size than in surveys. • Susceptible to volunteer bias. • Time-consuming and expensive. • Manipulation of some variables unethical or impractical.

© Cengage Learning 2013

tic partners. This study found that students who feel connected to their parents—who feel their parents are caring, warm, and supportive—delay sexual activity and have a lower incidence of pregnancy compared to their peers. A recent Canadian survey of more than 1,200 adolescents found that there is a disconnect between what teenagers in Toronto have learned about—HIV/AIDS, STIs, and pregnancy—and what they *want* to learn about: healthy relationships and sexual pleasure (Flicker et al., 2009). Other findings about teen sexuality will be discussed throughout the text.

American seniors say "yes!" to sex. The National Council of Aging (NCOA) led a nationwide survey of 1,300 subjects aged 60 and over (Dunn & Cutler, 2000). This survey found that 48% of older Americans were sexually active—defined as engaging in one or more of five sexual acts—vaginal intercourse, giving or receiving oral sex, anal intercourse, or masturbation—at least once a month. In fact, 71% of men and 51% of women in their 60s reported that they were still sexually active. Another survey of more than 3,000 adults over the age of 57 showed that sexual activity did decrease with age, and this decrease was related to the subject's overall health (Lindau et al., 2007).

Studying Cross-Cultural Sexuality

Cultural forces—such as a person's country, religion, race, and ethnicity—greatly influence sexual behavior, expression, and attitudes. It is important that research studies be conducted cross-culturally to help us avoid ethnocentrism (judging other cultures by the standards of one's own culture). People naturally feel pride in the culture in which they've been raised; however, problems arise when we view other cultures not just as different

Do old people still want to have sex?

but as inferior or wrong. This attitude can drive a wedge between people and cause us to misjudge others based on false assumptions. Examples of ethnocentrism might include the following: thinking that British people drive on the "wrong" side of the road or believing that the lack of sexual restrictions in Mangaian culture demonstrates that Mangaians are immoral. We also should be careful to steer clear of heterocentrism, the assumptions that all people are heterosexual and heterosexuality is better than other orientations. Heterocentrism is evident in the United States in the language we use, the assumptions we make, and the laws we live under. We think nothing of it when we see a man and woman holding hands as they walk down the street, but people may stop and stare, laugh, or think "why do they have to rub it in our faces" when they see two women or two men do the same. As we learned in Chapter 1, abstinence-only education programs are heterocentric when they teach that the expected standard of human sexual activity is only found in the context of marriage. Learning about other cultures and groups can help us to stop judging others according to our own limited experiences.

The Pfizer pharmaceutical company, the makers of Viagra, performed a global sexuality study in which 27,500 men and women aged 40 to 80 from 29 countries were questioned about their sexual attitudes, behavior, and beliefs (Laumann et al., 2005; Laumann et al., 2006). More than 80% of men and 60% of women in this study said that sex was an important part of their lives. South Korea had the highest combined percentage of men and women who rated sex as important (87%) and Hong Kong had the lowest (37%). The United States and Canada came in at 73% and 76%, respectively. The researchers' questions about sexual satisfaction in relationships found varied ratings from coun-

Cross-Cultural Studies of Adolescent Sexuality

Almost 34,000 15-year-olds in 22 countries in Europe as well as Israel and Canada took a survey of their general health, relationships, substance use, and sexual behavior (Godeau et al., 2008). This study showed that a substantial minority of 15-year-olds has had vaginal intercourse: the numbers ranged from a low of 14% in Croatia to a high of 38% in England. Encouragingly, more than 82% of sexually active students reported that they or their partners used condoms or hormonal contraceptives during their most recent intercourse, although students in Central and Eastern Europe were less protected, perhaps because of less access to affordable contraception and reproductive health services, as well as the influence of traditional and religious values. Contraceptive use was highest in countries such as the Netherlands, where people are "strongly accepting of teenage contraceptive use and are insuring adolescent access to contraception and sex education" (Santelli, Sandfort, & Orr, 2008). U.S. teens were less likely than Western European teens to use effective methods of birth control.

---

try to country, with the highest ratings of both physical and emotional satisfaction coming from people who were enjoying better health. Sexual satisfaction was also related to social factors such as gender equality: couples in Western countries reported more satisfaction with their sex lives than did couples who lived in cultures in which women have a more submissive role (Laumann et al., 2006).

In 2005, almost 1,600 black, Hispanic, and white youths between the ages of 15 and 25 from around the United States were interviewed about, among other things, their sexual attitudes and behavior (Cohen, Celestine-Michener, Holmes, Merseth, & Ralph, 2007). Some of these findings are summarized in Figures 2.2 and 2.3.

How Will You Guarantee That Your Study Is Safe and Ethical?

All researchers are required to protect the rights and safety of their human subjects. To maintain ethical standards, an independent institutional review board (IRB) reviews research projects. These committees evaluate and monitor research proposals to determine the potential value of the research and weigh it against any possible risk to the participants; they ensure that the studies are scientifically sound, ethical, and safe. IRBs exist almost everywhere scientific research is conducted in the United States, including universities and research institutes. For an IRB to approve a proposal, researchers must not expose the participants in the study to harm or ask participants to undergo undue stress. Subjects must give their **informed consent**, a process by which a subject confirms his or her willingness to participate after being told what to expect from the procedure, how the information will be used, how anonymity or

confidentiality will be assured, and to whom they might address questions. The identities of the participants and their responses are to be confidential. Subjects must not be compelled in any way to participate in the study; for example, college students should not be required to take part in any one specific experiment in order to receive course credit. Subjects also have the right to withdraw from a study at any time. Yet, to avoid influencing results, it is sometimes necessary for researchers to deceive

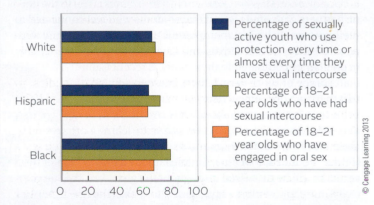

FIGURE 2.2 Sexual behavior of black, Hispanic, and white youth. (Based on Cohen et al., 2007.)

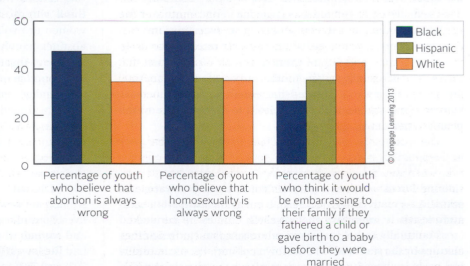

FIGURE 2.3 Social attitudes of black, Hispanic, and white youth. (Based on Cohen et al., 2007.)

Informed consent A process by which a subject confirms his or her willingness to participate in a study after having been informed about potential risks and benefits.

Confidentiality Discretion in keeping information secret.

subjects about the actual nature of the study. When subjects are deceived, they must be debriefed after the study and told about the true purpose of the experiment.

How Will You Ensure the Validity of Your Results?

Even after you have carefully chosen your sample and research design, you have to be conscientious when interpreting and presenting your research, in order to ensure that your findings are valid.

Maintain objectivity. Science may be objective, but all scientists are not. Every person involved in a scientific study, both as participant and investigator, comes into the study with his or her own experiences and values that may affect the design or interpretation of the work. To illustrate, if a scientist truly believes that abortion is psychologically devastating to women, when interviewing women who have had abortions, he or she may unconsciously look for evidence to support that point of view and interpret a subject's answers based on this presumption.

Subjects are also susceptible to suggestion; their preconceived notions and desire to please the researcher can influence the results of a study. For this reason, researchers often deceive subjects about the true purpose of the research. The deception may be benign—for example, if subjects are made to think they are rating the attractiveness of people in photos, when the researcher is actually interested in determining if the names given to the people in the photos affects the ratings—or more extreme—for example, in one study subjects were falsely led to believe that they were administering an electrical shock to others (see the Sex Actually feature on page 42).

Another way to reduce bias is to design blind studies, in which the investigator or participant (or both) is unaware if the subject is in the experimental group or the control group. In a **single blind study**, subjects do not know if they are receiving the treatment, but the researchers do. For instance, if you were testing the efficacy of a new method of vasectomy, the patient could be unaware of the method of surgery, but the surgeon clearly needs to know which procedure to perform. If neither the subject nor the investigator is aware of who is in the control group and who is in the experimental group, it is called a **double blind** study. As an example, imagine your company has designed a drug to reduce social anxiety. You administer the drug to a number of subjects and then observe their interactions at a party. If you knew which subjects received the drug, you might rate their social interactions as more successful. Likewise, if subjects knew they had received the drug, they may feel more confident and less apprehensive with other people. Double blind studies are used to reduce the influence of the placebo effect and of observer bias.

Don't overgeneralize. It's important to remember that your findings don't apply to everyone! There will always be exceptions, even when your results are very strong. This is especially true considering that most research in the United States is done on heterosexual, Caucasian college students, a group that does not necessarily represent the behaviors and beliefs of the rest of the world.

The importance of not overgeneralizing research findings also applies in terms of "real world" applications. As an example, early studies showed that spermicide inactivated the HIV virus. People made decisions regarding their sexual behavior

Institutional review boards evaluate research proposals to ensure that the studies will be safe and ethical.

based on this information. Later studies showed that this was not the case; in fact, the use of a spermicide may actually *increase* HIV transmission between individuals. How did this error occur? Initial studies showed that spermicide damages the HIV virus in a laboratory setting; when nonoxynol-9 is applied to the HIV virus in a petrie dish, the virus is inactivated (Malkovsky, Newell, & Dalgleish, 1988). But when actual people use spermicide, HIV transmission can be increased because the spermicide disrupts the walls of vagina and cervix to make the environment more prone to transmission of the virus. It should be noted that HIV transmission rates are dependent on the amount of spermicide use; professional sex workers who applied the spermicide four times daily were most prone to increased HIV transmission (Kreiss et al., 1992). (This specific study will be discussed further in Chapter 12.)

Don't confuse **correlation** *and* **causation**. Just because two factors occur together does not mean that one *causes* the other. If it were to be discovered that obese people are more likely to get divorced, it would not necessarily mean that being overweight is bad for a relationship; it may be that being unhappy causes people to gain weight! Or perhaps both weight and marital status are related to a third factor, such as finances or education. Here are more examples in which correlation is confused with causality:

- "My boyfriend and I went to see Bowling for Soup in concert. Then we had lots of unprotected sex and I got pregnant. So you should be careful listening to Bowling for Soup, because you might get pregnant."
- Eighty-seven percent of heroin addicts were breastfed. Therefore, breast milk is a gateway drug that leads to heroin.

Single blind study An experimental procedure in which the subjects do not know if they have received the treatment being tested.

Double blind study An experimental procedure in which neither the investigator nor the subjects know who is in the experimental group and who is in the control group.

Correlation A causal, complementary, parallel, or reciprocal relationship between two variables.

Causation When one variable causes the other.

© Kristopher Grunert/Photolibrary

Stanley Milgram's Study on Obedience

The controversial "Milgram" experiments were performed in 1961 at Yale University, 3 months after the start of the trial of Nazi war criminal Adolf Eichmann (Milgram, 1963). Psychologist Stanley Milgram was interested in the psychological forces that could allow everyday citizens to carry out such atrocities as were committed in Nazi Germany. How could people "follow orders" that violated their most deeply held moral and ethical beliefs? This classic study investigated the effect of authority on obedience.

The study involved three participants: the experimenter (the researcher leading the study), the learner (the victim), and the teacher (the subject of the experiment). Only the teacher was an actual subject, the learner was an actor who pretended to be a subject but was actually working for the researcher. Although the subjects believed they had an equal chance of being chosen to be the learner or the teacher, the process was rigged so that the subject was always assigned the role of teacher, and the actor was always assigned the role of the learner. The learner and teacher were told that they were going to participate in a study designed to investigate the effects of punishment on learning and memory.

The teacher and learner were then put into separate rooms where they could communicate but not see each other (Figure 2.4). The teacher was instructed to teach a list of word pairs to the learner. When the learner made a mistake, the teacher was told to administer a shock to the learner. (The teacher—i.e., the study subject—was given a single 45-volt shock so he could experience what the jolt was like.) The teacher was told that the voltage of the shock given to the learner would start at 15 volts and increase with each wrong answer, up to a maximum of 450 volts. Shock levels were labeled for their intensity, from slight shock, to moderate and strong shock, to intense and extremely intense shock, and finally to fatally high levels that were marked "XXX." Although the teacher believed that he was actually administering painful stimuli to the learner, there was no actual shock—the learner (really an actor) was instructed to shout in pain and bang on the wall as the intensity of the shocks supposedly increased. At 330 volts, as the voltage reached a dangerous level, the teacher heard only silence from the learner. At this point, many of the teachers indicated their desire to stop the experiment. The experimenter told the teachers that they could not stop and that the experiment required that they continue. None of the participants stopped administering the jolt at a level below "intense shock," and most of the participants—65%—administered the maximum voltage to the learners. Most subjects were very upset and uncomfortable in doing so, yet they administered the shock anyway, because they were instructed by the authority figure to do so.

At the end of the experiment, Dr. Milgrim debriefed his subjects and had them meet and shake hands with learners so they could see that they were unharmed. A year after the study, the subjects were interviewed by a psychiatrist and they were found to have experienced no long-term distress. Most of the former participants who were surveyed later said they were glad to have participated. Nevertheless, this study raised questions about ethics in scientific experimentation. Concern over the possibility that psychological experiments such as these could traumatize some of its participants led to discussion about the rights of research subjects. IRBs will not approve research that is distressing to subjects. Milgrim's study probably could not be performed today.

> **ASK YOURSELF**
>
> Does the search for knowledge justify emotional distress to subjects? How do you decide?

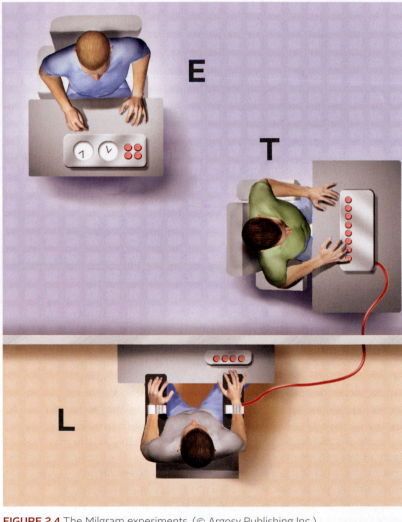

FIGURE 2.4 The Milgram experiments. (© Argosy Publishing Inc.)

Let's choose one finding—the prevalence of homosexuality in America—from two surveys: the National Health and Social Life Survey (NHSLS; Laumann, Gagnon, Michael, & Michaels, 1994), and the Kinsey surveys (Kinsey et al., 1948, 1953). According to Kinsey, 37% of American males and 13% of American females had at least one same-sex experience. In the NHSLS study, however, 9% of men and 4% of women reported having engaged in at least one same-gender sexual activity since puberty. What are some reasons you can think of to explain the discrepancies?

> **What was the population studied?** Kinsey used group sampling rather than repre-

sentative sampling. He also interviewed a proportionately large number of institutionalized males. In contrast, the NHSLS study excluded prisoners, as well as those living in barracks or college dormitories. What effect might this have on the results?

Kinsey and his colleagues personally interviewed almost 12,000 individuals, compared to 3,432 interviews done by the NHSLS researchers. How does this affect your view of the findings?

> **When were the surveys done?** More than 40 years separate the two surveys. How might the different time frames influence responses? Was there a difference in the acceptance of same-sex

behaviors in the 1940s and in the 1990s? Was there a different "ease of access" for males and females in the 1940s and the 1990s that might influence same-sex activities?

> **How was "homosexuality" defined?** How did the researchers define homosexuality for purposes of their surveys? Kinsey's considered any experience over the entire lifetime, and allowed for fantasy as well as sexual activity with same-sex partners in the definition. Laumann and colleagues defined three categories of homosexuality—same-gender sexual behavior, same-gender desire and sexual attraction, and self-identity as homo-

sexual. How might these different definitions affect the results?

> **What questions were asked?** Julia Ericksen (1999) suggests that the questions asked in sexuality surveys shape our opinions more than the answers given, and that "the assumptions driving the research helped create the sexuality the research revealed" (Ericksen, p. 11). How did the questions asked in each survey show the views and possible biases of the researchers?

Critically evaluate information in *this* text. Why did the author choose the surveys she did? What influence will the information in this book have on your developing view of sexuality?

Critically Evaluating Studies of Sexuality

After completion of this section, you will be able to . . .

- Identify important components of critical thinking.
- Define and understand *peer-review process*.
- Learn to evaluate the strength of an argument.
- Recognize fallacies of relevance and fallacies of insufficient evidence.

People today are exposed to more information about sex than ever before, but as with any commodity, as the supply increases, value decreases. To become an intelligent consumer of information, you must learn to think critically. Critical thinkers don't just accept what they are told; they maintain a healthy degree of skepticism about information. They are aware of their own and others' biases and assumptions. Critical thinkers are able to analyze arguments and statements by looking at evidence, as well as by recognizing the difference between "good" evidence and "weak" evidence. This is difficult, especially when you are asked to critically evaluate a position with which you agree. People who hold strong opinions on a topic are likely to accept evidence that supports their position at face value and make a case against opposing views (Lord, Ross, & Lepper, 1979). As you can see, critical thinking entails both a set of skills and a mind-set. In this section, we will lay out some of the skills you should acquire to evaluate the barrage of sexual information to which you are constantly exposed (Bassham, Irwin, Nardone, & Wallace, 2002; Browne & Keeley, 2000; Lee, 2000).

Consider the Quality of the Research

When evaluating studies of sexuality—or any studies—you need to consider the project design and approach. Did the research use a suitable method to achieve its goals? Was the sample appropriate and the **methodology** clear? Has the study been replicated? You should also consider the quality of the source and the proper use of statistics.

Were the data published in a respected, peer-reviewed journal such as *The Journal of Sex Research* or *The Lancet,* or was it published in *Joe Bob's Journal of Sciencey Things?* High-quality research goes through the **peer review process**, by which a scholar's work is subjected to the scrutiny of others who are experts in the field. Independent reviewers assess the value of the work and check for inconsistencies.

Many people get important health information from magazines and newspapers. However, when research is presented in the popular media, the press may distort or simplify its meaning. One study compared newspaper and magazine articles about breast cancer and mammograms with the research on which the articles were based. The study found 42 content-based inaccuracies in the 60 articles that contained traceable references to the original research (Moyer, Greener, Beauvais, & Salovey, 1995). In fact, 88% of articles about breast cancer and mammography (with traceable citations) that were printed in women's magazines were found to contain inaccuracies (Moyer et al., 1995). Whenever possible, seek the **primary sources** of the information.

The Internet is a convenient source of information for many people. However, most sites on the Internet do not undergo peer review. For example, Wikipedia (a highly used reference source) can be amended by almost anyone who chooses to do so. In 2009 when the French composer Maurice Jarre died, a student at Dublin University posted a fraudulent quote on Jarre's Wikipedia page. The news organizations picked up the phony quote and published it, falsely attributing it to Jarre. As you encounter information, be sure to check out the sources and verify the data.

Nineteenth-century British Prime Minister Benjamin Disraeli said, "There are three kinds of lies—lies, damned lies, and statistics" (a quote commonly misattributed to Mark Twain). Indeed, there are many ways to lie with statistics. You might make a conclusion not supported by the data: "Only 5% of buyers complained about this product. Therefore, 95% of people were satisfied." Statistics might omit necessary information: "Bayer aspirin works 50% faster." Faster than what? A kick in the head? When faced with statistics, ask yourself what further

© Digital Vision/Getty Images

information you need before you can judge the impact of the statistics. And finally, remember: 98% of statistics are made up (that's a made-up statistic).

Recognize Underlying Value Assumptions

Everyone has views about the way the world should be. Usually, a value assumption is not clearly stated in an argument; rather, it is a position so taken for granted by the author that he or she does not feel the need to articulate it. So how can you discover an author's value assumption if it is not stated in his or her argument? Let's give an example.

- "Condoms should be distributed to all students in junior high schools because they will prevent disease and teen pregnancy."

The conclusion of the author is that condoms should be distributed to all junior high students. The reason is the prevention of disease and pregnancy. But the unspoken value assumption is that *concerns over public health are more important than a parent's right to decide if and when they want their children to have free access to condoms.* You may or may not agree with the conclusion, but if you can identify the author's value assumption, you can better evaluate the argument. Using the example above, if you *do not* feel that public health is more important than a parent's autonomy, then the author's rationale is not valid for you, regardless of your feelings about condom distribution.

Evaluate the Strength of the Argument
Fallacies of Relevance

When an argument doesn't address the facts and instead focuses on irrelevant and unrelated matters, it is a **fallacy of relevance**. Examples of these include *ad hominem* and *ad populum* argu-

Brian: "Look. You've got it all wrong. You don't need to follow me. You don't need to follow anybody! You've got to think for yourselves! You're all individuals!"
Followers: "Yes, we're all individuals."
Brian: "You're all different!"
Followers: "Yes, we're all different."
Dennis: "I'm not."
—Monty Python's *Life of Brian*

Methodology The methods, procedures, and techniques used to gather information.

Peer review process The means by which experts in the field check the quality of a research study.

Primary source The original publication of a scientist's data, results, and theories.

ments, appeals to emotion, tautologies, red herrings, and searches for perfect solutions.

In an *ad hominem* argument, the author attacks the background or the motives of a person rather than addressing the facts of the issue.

- "Senator Wilson is in favor of stem cell research, but he had an affair with his secretary, so why should I listen to him?"
- "My mother said I should wait till I get married to have sex, but she didn't, so why should I?"

An *ad populum* argument does not address the facts of an argument; it instead simply gives the popular opinion. Just because "most people agree" doesn't mean that they're right.

- "Most college students don't think oral sex is sex, so therefore it isn't."

An *appeal to emotion* also does not present any concrete evidence; instead, the author hopes to persuade by presenting the issue in an emotionally charged way.

- "Little Angela White is struggling for breath. She has been fighting for life since she entered this world, one week ago. Angela's mother did not take prenatal vitamins during her pregnancy. Please help punish other evil mothers who do not care about their babies by making it illegal not to take prenatal vitamins."

When a conclusion is supported only by itself, the argument is *circular reasoning,* or a *tautology.* When this author was a little girl, she was in the car one night while her dad was driving. She saw the red lights of a radio tower in the sky. "Dad, what are the lights for?" she asked. He replied, "So planes don't crash into the poles." "Well, what are the poles for?" "To hold up the lights." The author now realizes that her dad was not just being a smart ass; he was actually imparting an important message about the nature of a tautology. The following is another example of circular reasoning:

- "Abortion is wrong because the Bible is against it. The Bible is against it because it's wrong."

A *red herring* diverts the reader's attention to another issue, and doesn't address the facts at hand.

- "People may claim that condoms reduce the spread of sexually transmitted infections, but what they don't realize is that the packaging from one of the major brands is made of nonrecyclable material and is hurting our environment."

When one assumes that a resolution to a problem does not deserve our support unless it solves the problem completely, he is said to be *searching for a perfect solution.*

- "We should get rid of marriage since almost half of marriages end in divorce."

Fallacies of Insufficient Evidence

When an argument does address the facts, but doesn't provide sufficient evidence to support the conclusion, this is a **fallacy of insufficient evidence**. Examples include appeals to inappropriate authority, appeals to ignorance, false dilemmas, hasty generalizations, and slippery slope arguments.

Some sources of information are more reliable than others. For instance, if you were hoping to get information about the spread of sexually transmitted diseases, the Centers for Disease Control would be a better source than, say, Paris Hilton. Arguments that are based on the statements of "experts" who are not qualified to make reliable claims are *appeals to inappropriate authority.*

- "Tom Cruise said that there's no such thing as postpartum depression, so all those scientists must be wrong."

An *appeal to ignorance* assumes that if we haven't proven that something is true, then it must be false (or vice versa). Remember, an absence of evidence is not the same as evidence of absence.

- "There is nothing in Mr. Vogel's personnel file that says he is not from Pluto. Therefore, I can only assume that he comes from Pluto."

If the argument is designed such that there are only two possible outcomes: *either* this *or* that will happen, then the author has created a *false dilemma* or *either/or* fallacy.

- "If we don't distribute condoms in our high schools, then all the girls will get pregnant."

A *hasty generalization* is one of the most common types of fallacies in reasoning that people make. We often give more credence to personal experiences than to data and evidence. When people make generalizations, they may be guilty of **egocentrism**, the practice of regarding one's own opinions as most important. Some examples of hasty generalizations include:

- "I had had terrible side effects while taking birth control pills. So the pill is really dangerous and should be banned."
- "Men are not as affectionate as women."

In 2003, then-Senator Rick Santorum made the following statement against a Supreme Court ruling that said homosexual practices are constitutionally protected: "If the Supreme Court says that you have the right to consensual (gay) sex within your home, then you have the right to bigamy, you have the right to polygamy, you have the right to incest, you have the right to adultery. You have the right to anything." This is a classic example of a *slippery slope* argument, in which one small step leads to an ever-intensifying chain of events, culminating in a catastrophic result. We can only hope that ex-Senator Santorum takes a refresher course in critical thinking. Another example of a slippery slope argument is as follows:

- "If a woman uses cocaine while she is pregnant, she can be held accountable for endangering her unborn child. What's next? Will we punish women for drinking caffeine, or not getting enough exercise? Will pregnant women go to jail if they don't eat enough calcium?"

Fallacy of relevance An argument that focuses on matters unrelated to the facts of the issue.

Fallacy of insufficient evidence An argument that doesn't provide sufficient evidence to support its conclusion.

Egocentrism The practice of regarding one's own experiences or opinions as most important.

sexactually

Critical Thinking Quiz

Match the statement to the type of fallacy:

1. I know you don't really like me, but you should go out with me because I had a really hard day. First, my pet boa constrictor died. Then my father told me he's having a sex change operation. With all I went through, don't make it worse by turning me down for a date.

2. Condoms should not be used because they don't completely protect against every sexually transmitted infection.

3. If we allow porn on the Internet, then everyone will just stay home and masturbate all day, marriages will fail, and society as we know it will be destroyed.

4. My aunt got pregnant on the pill, so I know it doesn't work.

5. My mother says I should use a condom, but she got pregnant when she was 16, so why should I listen to her?

6. Gay men are more likely than straight men to have a college education. Therefore college causes people to be gay.

7. If we don't give Gardasil to all preteen girls, then they will all get cervical cancer.

8. Most Americans are against gay marriage. Therefore gay marriage is wrong.

9. Many people criticize Rush Limbaugh for being homophobic and anti-women. But he's very nice to his dog, so I think they're being too hard on him.

10. My hairdresser says you can't get pregnant when you have your period, so I'm not going to use a condom this week.

11. My last three girlfriends have all wanted to be taken out for expensive dinners and get fancy jewelry. Women sure are shallow.

A. *Ad hominem*
B. *Ad populum*
C. Appeals to emotion
D. Red herring
E. Confusing correlation with causality
F. False dilemma
G. Slippery slope
H. Searching for perfect solutions
I. Inappropriate appeals to authority
J. Hasty generalization

Answers: (1) C; (2) H; (3) G; (4) J; (5) A; (6) E; (7) F; (8) B; (9) D; (10) I; (11) J

Using Your Critical Thinking Skills

After completion of this section, you will be able to . . .

O Apply critical thinking skills to evaluate the strength of arguments.

Use your critical thinking skills to evaluate the following studies and statements:

- Last year, a study was done in which the students in a math class at MIT were surveyed regarding their alcohol use. By the standards of the survey, 95% of the students were considered heavy drinkers. Therefore, this study proves that the level of alcohol use in America is at its highest ever.

- A study was performed in which 50 men rubbed Rogaine on their heads each day for 3 months. At the end of 3 months, 54% of the men had increased hair growth. Therefore, Rogaine causes hair growth.

- Everyone knows that people are either born gay or born straight.

- More educated people tend to have more liberal attitudes toward sex. This means that going to college makes you more prone to sexual experimentation.

- A study is done in which 15 20-year-old male college students are shown a 2-minute pornographic video in which a male and female have sexual intercourse. Ten of the participants got erections while watching the video, the other five did not. The conclusion of the researcher is that one third of the male population must be gay.

- "An enemy of babies and mothers everywhere, Dr. Cavanaugh is in favor of stem cell research, a procedure that will cause the death of millions of unborn children. . . . These stem cells will supposedly be used to find miraculous cures for diseases, although thus far not one Alzheimer's patient has been cured of his disease by the use of stem cells" (from Cadwallader & Rosenthal, 2003).

Critical thinking skills are useful not only in evaluating the material in the rest of this textbook; these skills will also help you evaluate the information and arguments you will be presented with for the rest of your life. In subsequent chapters, we will explore real examples of current research related to human sexuality, which you will be encouraged to critically examine using the skills described in this chapter.

Chapter Summary

How Do We Know What We Know About Sex?

- Sexologists study human sexuality. Sexologists come from various fields, including biology, medicine, psychology, sociology, anthropology, and criminology. In addition to doing sexuality research, many sexologists are also therapists or educators.
- Many men and women through history have worked to improve our understanding of sexuality. Some of the important sex researchers throughout history were Havelock Ellis, Richard von Krafft-Ebing, Magnus Hirschfeld, Sigmund Freud, Alfred Kinsey, Clelia Mosher, William Masters and Virginia Johnson, Harry Benjamin, and Evelyn Hooker. Many of those who studied sexuality have suffered personal and professional harm due to political or social mores.
- Society and politics influences sex research. Many sexologists have lost their funding or experienced social censure because of the prevailing political feelings of their day.

Investigating Human Sexuality

- To produce top-rate research, scientists must rigorously follow certain procedures. They must use precise language, specific measurements, and an appropriate sample. They need to maintain objectivity, not overgeneralize, and be careful to not confuse correlation and causation.
- The *population* is the group a scientist wants to investigate. It is usually impossible to obtain information from everyone in the population, so scientists usually get data from a *sample*, which is a subset of individuals in the target population. A *representative sample* is a group in which the characteristics of the sample match that of the population. A *convenience sample* is one that is easy for the scientist to reach. Use of a convenience sample can lead to

sampling bias, which occurs when some members of a population are overrepresented and others are excluded.

- People who are willing to volunteer for sex studies are not representative of the general population, a phenomenon known as *volunteer bias*.
- Scientists need to evaluate which method of investigation—survey, case study, observation, or experiment—will best serve their purpose. *Surveys* study the attitudes, opinions, and behaviors of individuals. Information can be gathered through written questionnaires, interviews, or on the Internet. A *case study* is an in-depth investigation of an individual or individuals, rather than on a sample of the population. In *observational studies*, researchers observe their subjects, usually in a laboratory but sometimes in a more natural environment. If subjects are aware they are being observed, it may affect their behavior, a phenomenon known as *observer effects*. An *experiment* can determine cause-and-effect relationships. There are advantages and disadvantages to each of these methods.
- A *hypothesis* is a prediction about the world based on observations. Each experiment has at least two variables. The *independent variable*—the presumed cause—is a factor that is controlled and manipulated by the researcher, while the *dependent variable*—the presumed effect—is observed and measured. A *control group* is the group of subjects who are not exposed to the independent variable. They may be exposed to a *placebo*, which is an inactive substance that resembles the treatment being tested. *Blind studies* are a way to try to reduce bias in research designs.
- Cross-cultural studies are important to help us avoid ethnocentrism and heterocentrism.

- Subjects must be protected from harm, and researchers should maintain objectivity and avoid overgeneralization. Institutional review boards review research project proposals to weigh the potential value of the research against any possible risk to the participants. Subjects in a research study must give informed consent.

Critically Evaluating Studies of Sexuality

- To become an intelligent consumer of information, you must learn to think critically. When evaluating studies of sexuality, you should consider the quality of the research. The *peer review process* is a method by which experts in the field check the quality of a research study.
- Critical thinkers maintain a healthy degree of skepticism about information. By learning to evaluate the strength of an argument, you will be able to analyze arguments based on evidence, and to recognize the difference between good evidence and weak evidence.
- In order to critically evaluate a position, it is important to recognize fallacies of relevance—such as *ad hominem* and *ad populum* arguments, appeals to emotion, tautologies, red herrings, and searches for perfect solutions—and fallacies of insufficient evidence—such as appeals to inappropriate authority, appeals to ignorance, false dilemmas, hasty generalizations, and slippery slope arguments.

Additional Resources

Log in to CengageBrain to access the resources your instructor requires. For this book, you can access:

 **CourseMate** brings course concepts to life with interactive learning, study, and exam preparation tools that support the printed textbook. A textbook-specific website, Psychology CourseMate includes an integrated interactive eBook and other interactive learning tools including quizzes, flashcards, videos, and more.

CENGAGENOW **CengageNOW** is an easy-to-use online resource that helps you study in less time to get the grade you

want—NOW. Take a pre-test for this chapter and receive a personalized study plan based on your results that will identify the topics you need to review and direct you to online resources to help you master those topics. Then take a post-test to help you determine the concepts you have mastered and what you will need to work on. If your textbook does not include an access code card, go to CengageBrain.com to gain access. Visit www.cengagebrain.com anytime to access your account and purchase materials.

Web Resources

Austhink
This page, titled "Critical Thinking on the Web," lists resources to help you nurture your critical thinking skills.

Fallacy Files
A discussion of common fallacies of reasoning.

The Magnus Hirschfeld Archive for Sexology
Contains information about the history of sexology as well as other topics.

Print Resources

Bassham, G., Irwin, W., Nardone, H., Wallace, J.M. (2002). *Critical thinking: A student's introduction.* New York, NY: McGraw-Hill.

Browne, M.N., & Keeley, S. (2000). *Asking the right questions: A guide to critical thinking* (6th ed.). Saddle River, New Jersey: Prentice Hall.

Bullough, V.L. (1994). *Science in the bedroom: A history of sex research.* New York, NY: Basic Books.

Roach, M. (2008). *Bonk: The curious coupling of science and sex.* New York, NY: W.W. Norton & Co.

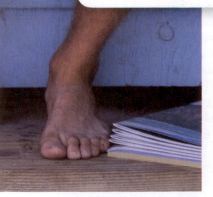

3 Male Reproductive Anatomy and Physiology

"We are right to note the license and disobedience of this member, which thrusts itself forward too inopportunely when we do not want it to, and which so inopportunely lets us down when we most need it; it impenously contests for authority with our will: it stubbonly and proudly refuses all our incitements, both of the mind and hand."

—**Michel de Montaigne**

"If the world were a logical place, men would ride side saddle."

—**Rita Mae Brown**

© Gabriela Medina/ Getty Images

© Digital Vision/ Getty Images   © Peter Cade/ Getty Images

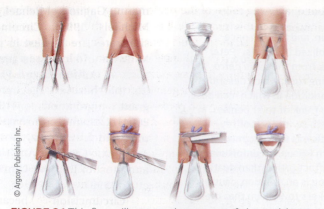

FIGURE 3.1 This figure illustrates the process of circumcision.

that have been removed from infants are used to grow artificial skin for burn victims and in the manufacture of insulin (Zhang, Ma, Wang, & Zhang, 2002).

Circum(de)cision: To snip or not to snip? Circumcision is a very prickly subject. Arguments in favor of circumcision include health concerns, religious reasons, social incentives, and motives related to sexual satisfaction. Anti-circumcision arguments include issues of autonomy, as well as health and sexual satisfaction. Although many people seem to feel either passionately for or passionately against circumcision, the research on this issue is incomplete, as well as contradictory. As one physicians group advises its doctors: "Newborn circumcision has potential medical benefits and advantages as well as disadvantages and risks. When circumcision is being considered, the benefits and risks should be explained to the parents and informed consent obtained" (American Academy of Pediatrics, 1989, p. 390). Table 3.1 summarizes the views of pro-circumcision and anti-circumcision positions, and includes some questions that will help you fully consider the issue.

The shaft. The shaft, or body of the penis, consists of three cylinders of erectile tissue that fill with blood and stiffen during sexual arousal (Figure 3.2). The two **corpora cavernosa** run dorsally along the upper portion of the penis. The **corpus spongiosum** is the third cylindrical mass that runs along the lower surface of the penis; it surrounds the **urethra**, which carries both urine and semen through the penis (although not at the same time!).

The root. The inner ends of the corpora cavernosa are called the **crura**. They are covered by muscle and attach to the pubic bone inside the pelvic cavity, which helps to support the penis during erection. The base of the penis contains an extensive network of muscles that help control urination and ejaculation. By squeez-

Corpora cavernosa Two cylinders of erectile tissue that run along the upper part of the penis.

Corpus spongiosum Erectile tissue that runs along the underside of the penis and encloses the urethra.

Urethra (you-REE-thra) Tubular structure that serves as a passageway for both urine and semen.

Crura The inner branches of the penile shaft.

Kegel (KAY-gill) exercises Exercises that involve clenching and unclenching of the muscles of the pelvic floor.

ing and relaxing the muscles that stop the flow of urine (a process known as **Kegel exercises**), men may get stronger orgasms and better ejaculatory control.

Penis Size

It was once thought that the length of the typical erect penis of American males was 6.2 inches (Kinsey, Pomeroy, Martin, & Gebhard, 1948), although current studies suggest that the average length is just over 5 inches (Wessells, Lue, & McAninch, 1996). Why the discrepancy? When Kinsey gathered information, subjects sent in *self-measurements* of their penis, allowing for the strong possibility of mismeasurement and exaggeration. Also, due to self-selection bias, men who volunteered to send in their measurements to Kinsey were more likely to possess organs larger than average.

Penis size is largely determined by hereditary factors. There is no evidence that penis size is related to the size of any other body part such as the hand or foot, although it does seem to be correlated positively with overall height and negatively with body fat level (Lever, Frederick, & Peplau, 2006). One study found that gay men have larger penises than straight men (Bogaert & Hershberger, 1999), but contrary to a popular stereotype, there is no evidence that black men have larger penises than white men. There is, however, a difference in males' *perception* of their size. In one survey, 80% of black respondents stated that they were "well endowed," and fewer than 20% of the white participants rated themselves so (Edwards, 1998). Perception is all!

Although men may think a large penis is a necessary component of sexual satisfaction, partners rarely mention penis size as important in sexual fulfillment. Factors such as a man's per-

> The largest medically verified penis on record was 13.5 inches long and 6.25 inches around (Dickinson, 1949).

> **ASK YOURSELF**
>
> How would you determine the size of the average penis? By reading scientific articles? By studying a condom company's web page? By accosting men, ruler in hand, in the restroom of the local mall? What are some problems with trying to find the average penis size?

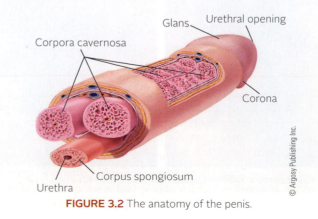

FIGURE 3.2 The anatomy of the penis.

Glans, Urethral opening, Corpora cavernosa, Corona, Corpus spongiosum, Urethra

sonality and grooming rate much higher on a partner's lists of priorities (Wylie & Eardley, 2007). In a survey of heterosexual men and women, although 84% of women said that they were satisfied with the size of their partner's penis, only 55% of men were satisfied with their own size (Lever et al., 2006). It is important to remember that smaller penises grow proportionately more when erect than larger penises, causing Masters and Johnson to call erections "the great equalizer."

The *Kama Sutra,* an ancient Sanskrit text that gives instructions on the art of lovemaking, ranks men by their penis size, describing them as horses, bulls, or hares. Females are similarly ranked (by the depth of the vagina) as elephants, mares, and deer (Vatsyayana & Dane, 2003); sexual satisfaction is said to be more likely if a man and woman are comparatively endowed. During the reign of Pope Innocent III (1198–1216), marriages could legally be annulled if the genitals of a husband and wife didn't fit properly.

> "There's such a thing as *too* big. My ex-husband was enormous. When I first saw it, I laughed, and said 'and what do you think you're going to do with that?' He was very proud of his penis, but unfortunately he thought that since he had a big penis, all he had to do was show up."
>
> —*From the author's files*

Penis enlargement techniques.

Men have been trying to enlarge their penises for millennia. Sadhus, the holy men of Northern India, reject all earthly desires in their quest for enlightenment. They consequently damage their penises so that they may no longer be used for pleasure. The Sadhus may hang weights or wear tight metal rings on their penises. After the nerves are dead, the Sadhus can then lift large weights with their penises (see photo). The Topinama Indians of Brazil encouraged poisonous snakes to bite their penis, causing enormous swelling. Although we in Western culture may consider these practices to be barbaric, American men also will go to great lengths to achieve the goal of a larger penis: doctors slice open the abdomen to remove adipose, slit open the skin of the penis, and wrap the belly fat around the penis to artificially enlarge it. Hooray for modern medicine!

Surgical procedures to enhance the size of the penis are usually one of two types: one increases the length of the penis, the other increases the girth. To lengthen the appearance of the penis, a surgeon cuts the ligaments that attach the shaft of the penis to the pubic

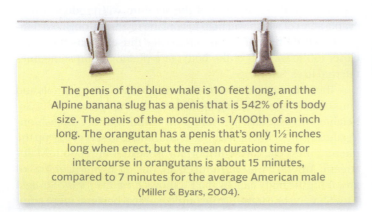

The penis of the blue whale is 10 feet long, and the Alpine banana slug has a penis that is 542% of its body size. The penis of the mosquito is 1/100th of an inch long. The orangutan has a penis that's only 1½ inches long when erect, but the mean duration time for intercourse in orangutans is about 15 minutes, compared to 7 minutes for the average American male (Miller & Byars, 2004).

Do women like big penises better?

bone, allowing more of the penis to hang outside of the body. A drawback of this surgery is that because the penis is no longer anchored to the pubic bone, it may flap around loosely and have a reduced angle of erection. To increase a penis's girth, a doctor can implant fat or skin cells around the shaft. The negative side of this surgery is that it can cause the penis to feel somewhat soft, and as fat cells are reabsorbed back into the body, the penis can take on an uneven and lumpy appearance. Serious complications may result from penile enhancement surgery, including decreased sensitivity, pain during sexual activity, scarring, hair growth, and infection (Wessells et al., 1996).

Fifty-eight men who had undergone at least one penile augmentation surgery were surveyed regarding their procedure (Klein, 1999). Some findings from this study include the following:

- Average length of erect penis before surgery: 5.4 inches
- Average length of erect penis after surgery: 5.7 inches
- Average length of an erect penis the men seeking the surgery said is ideal: 7.9 inches
- Percentage of men dissatisfied with their surgical results: 68%

The average cost of penile augmentation surgery is between $5,000 and $17,000. Penis enlargement surgeries are not endorsed by the American Urological Association or by the American Society of Plastic and Reconstructive Surgeons.

Penis piercings.

Men pierce their penises for various reasons: they like the way it looks, they hope it will increase sexual stimulation for themselves or their partners, or they find the process of piercing erotic. Piercing can take anywhere from 4 weeks to 6 months to heal. During this time, it is important to use latex barriers for any sexual contact. Risks of genital piercing include allergic reactions, infections, and scarring.

The Scrotum

Below the penis hangs the pigmented pouch of skin called the **scrotum**, which holds the **testes**, or male reproductive organs. It seems to be bad planning (or just malicious) on the part of Mother Nature for the testes to be located outside the body where they are vulnerable to injury, but there is a reason for it: the testicles hang away from the body in the scrotum because the optimal temperature for sperm production and viability is slightly below body temperature, about 93°F. Vigorous exercise,

A Sadhu with a weight attached to his penis.

Table 3.1 Arguments For and Against Circumcision

	ISSUES	PRO-CIRCUMCISION ARGUMENT
Health	**Hygiene**	Circumcision enhances hygiene by preventing the accumulation of smegma.
	Urinary tract infections (UTI)	Uncircumcised boys have significantly more UTIs in the first year of life than circumcised boys do (American Academy of Pediatrics, 1999; Wiswell & Hachey, 1993; Wiswell & Roscelli, 1986).
	Scar tissue	The slight scar tissue produces little harmful effect.
	Balanitis and phimosis	Circumcised boys cannot get inflammation of the glans (balanitis) or phimosis (a tight, nonretractable foreskin).
	Pain	Many painful procedures are medically necessary, and many infants don't appear to respond with particular pain to the procedure.
	Human papillomavirus (HPV) and HIV	Circumcision reduces both the rate of HPV transmission (Castellsague et al., 2002) and the rate of HIV transmission (Auvert et al., 2001; Bailey, Muga, Poulusse, & Abicht, 2002; Patterson et al., 2002).
	Penile cancer	Circumcised men have lower rates of penile cancer (Schoen, Wiswell, & Moses, 2000).
	Health risks involved in the procedure	The health risks associated with circumcision are lower than the risks associated with not circumcising.
Social	**Social pressure**	A boy should look like his father and like the other boys in the locker room.
	Sexual sensitivity	When glans sensitivity was tested in sexually aroused men, no differences were found (Payne et al., 2007).
	Sexual practices	Circumcised men report more varied sexual practices and less sexual dysfunction as adults (Laumann et al., 1997).
	Sexual pleasure of the woman	Some studies suggest that women who have had sexual experience with both circumcised and uncircumcised men prefer a circumcised penis (Williamson & Williamson, 1988). The loss of sensitivity allows the male to delay orgasm longer, increasing his partner's pleasure.
	Informed consent and personal choice	It is the responsibility of the parents to care for and make decisions about the child's health.
	Religious reasons	It is religious tradition to circumcise Jewish and Muslim males.

© Cengage Learning 2013

immersion in a hot tub, or the use of a laptop computer (on one's lap) has been found to raise scrotal temperatures enough to inhibit sperm production (Sheynkin, Jung, Yoo, Schulsinger, & Komaroff, 2004). Despite the commonly held belief that switching from briefs to boxers will help increase a man's sperm count, underwear selection has been shown to have no significant effect on fertility (Munkelwitz & Gilbert, 1998). The scrotum can rise or fall, depending on temperature and sexual activity. When temperature is high, the scrotum will lower and

Perineum (per-ih-NEE-um)
The sensitive skin between the genitals and the anus.

Pubic hair (PYOO-bic hair) The hair, often somewhat coarse and stiff, that grows in the pubic region just above the external genitals.

expand. Glands in the skin of the scrotum will produce sweat, evaporation of which will help to cool the testes. During cold temperatures, contraction of the cremaster muscle pulls the testes closer to the warmth of the body, in a phenomenon sometimes referred to as "shrinkage."

The **perineum** is the sensitive area between the genitals and anus of both sexes. Massaging this area during sexual activity can heighten orgasm and pleasure. **Pubic hair** may act as cushioning during intercourse, as a visual cue, and also serves to trap the pheromones, chemicals important in sexual attraction. Mainstream America was introduced to the term *manscaping*, or grooming the body hair, by the TV show *Queer Eye for the Straight Guy.* Shaving or trimming the pubic hair has become more com-

ANTI-CIRCUMCISION ARGUMENT	CONSIDERATIONS
". . . there is little evidence to affirm the association between circumcision status and optimal penile hygiene" (The American Academy of Pediatrics, 1999).	Is removal of the foreskin necessary, or can proper hygiene eliminate the smegma? If we severed every organ that produced nasty secretions, none of us would have ears.
Although circumcision may decrease the incidence of UTIs, there is only a low incidence of UTIs during the first year of life (Wiswell & Roscelli, 1986).	What other factors might "cause" higher UTI rates in uncircumcised boys? How might you weigh the risks of UTI vs. the risks of circumcision?
The foreskin protects the glans from friction and infection; its removal causes scar tissue to grow.	To what degree does this scar tissue affect sexual functioning?
The incidences of balanitis and phimosis are rare and the conditions' effects are minor.	Weigh the risks and incidence of these conditions.
There is some evidence that boys who are circumcised without anesthesia will be sensitized to pain later in life (Payne, Thaler, Kukkonen, Carrier, & Binik, 2007; Taddio, Katz, Ilersich, & Koren, 1997).	Does the amount of pain felt by the infant affect your decision? Does it matter if the pain is short term, or if it has long-term consequences?
The foreskin doesn't cause HIV or HPV.	Consider other factors that are related to circumcision, such as education levels, race, or sexual practices.
Penile cancer is very rare and does not justify routine circumcision.	Penile cancer rates are relatively low, but the effects can be physically and emotionally devastating. How do you assess the risks and benefits of routine circumcision in boys to prevent a rare yet terrible illness?
Health risks associated with circumcision include pain, bleeding, infection, the chance of amputation, and death.	There is a large variation in the reported health risks. You need to consider if these reports are from in-hospital or at-home procedures, and whether local anesthesia was used.
If the other boys in the locker room jumped off the Brooklyn Bridge, would you?	How might you assess the relative value of social pressures and health issues?
The glans of the uncircumcised penis is more sensitive to touch than the circumcised glans (Sorrells et al., 2007).	How could you best compare the sensations of two men, one who is circumcised and one who is not?
Circumcision causes a loss of tactile sensitivity and sexual sensations (Liptak, 2003), which may cause the need for more varied sexual practices, such as oral sex.	Does this mean the foreskin causes sexual problems? Is inhibition located in the foreskin? What other factors might be related to this?
Some studies suggest that women who have had sexual experience with both prefer an uncircumcised penis (O'Hara & O'Hara, 1999).	Clearly, it is necessary to evaluate these studies. How would you design a study to discover how circumcision affects the sexual pleasure of the woman? What factors would you need to control for?
There is a lack of informed consent when this is done on infants; men are not given a choice regarding their own circumcision. Only 2 of every 1,000 men who are not circumcised at birth choose to have the procedure done at a later date.	Just because a man doesn't choose to be circumcised as an adult, does this necessarily mean that these men prefer to be uncircumcised? What other reasons might there be for not getting circumcised as an adult? How much relative value do you place on autonomy?
	Do parents have the right to impose their religious beliefs upon a child?

sexactually

Penis Piercings

There are several types of penis piercings. Some men pierce through the glans and urethra vertically; this kind of piercing is called an *apadravya* (pictured on the left). A horizontal piercing through the glans and urethra is called an *ampallang*. A *dydoe* passes through the ridge of the glans. Some men pierce the perineum (a *guiche*), or the loose flesh on the underside of the penis (a *frenum*). A pierced scrotum is called a *hafada* (pictured on right). One of the most popular penis piercings is the *Prince Albert* (pictured at right) in which a ring goes through the urethra at the base of the glans. This was very popular during Victorian times to secure the penis to the pant leg and to prevent unseemly bulges.

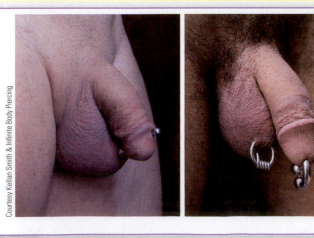

Courtesy Kellan Smith & Infinite Body Piercing

© Joel Gordon

mon in males. An advantage to this procedure is that it can make the penis appear larger. Also, some people prefer performing oral sex on a partner who has shaved his pubic hair. Disadvantages to shaving this area are the itching that occurs when the hair grows back, as well as the frightening proximity of the razor to the testicles.

Internal Anatomy

After completion of this section, you will be able to . . .

○ Identify the forms and functions of the *testes, seminiferous tubules, Sertoli cells, cells of Leydig, epididymis, vas deferens,* and *ejaculatory duct.*

○ List some of the components of semen.

○ Compare and contrast the locations and secretions of the *seminal vesicles, prostate gland,* and *Cowper's gland.*

○ Label the male internal reproductive anatomy.

The internal reproductive anatomy of the male includes the testes, the ejaculatory pathway, and a number of glands. The **testes**, also called the **gonads**, are the primary reproductive organs. Their main function is to produce **gametes** (in this case, sperm) and testosterone.

Each testis measures about 1½–2 inches long by 1 inch wide. There appears to be a close correlation between testicle size and promiscuous social structure. One study of non-human primates confirmed this correlation: The researchers found that female gorillas in heat will mate with only one male, but female chimpanzees in heat will mate with many males. Relative to body size, the testicles of male gorillas are small, but the more promiscuous chimpanzees have large testicles, owing to their need to produce the copious sperm necessary to "compete" with other chimpanzees' sperm in the female reproductive tract (Margulis & Sagan, 1991). The relative size of human testes falls somewhere between that of the monogamous gorilla and the promiscuous chimp.

Each testicle is suspended in the scrotum by the **spermatic cord**—a cylindrical casing that contains nerves, muscles, blood vessels, and the vas deferens—that is anchored in the abdominal area. The pain from an injury to the testicles can radiate up into the abdomen. Due to the unequal length of the left and right spermatic cords, one testicle often hangs slightly below the other. In 85% of men it is the left testicle that hangs lower. This may be related to the fact that 85% of men are right-handed; in left-handed men the right testicle often hangs lower. Early anatomists thought that the left testicle created seed that would result in the birth of a girl, while the right testicle produced boys. They believed it was therefore proper that the right testicle should be higher, as accorded the higher status of "boy seed."

Testicles begin their prenatal development in the abdominal cavity. They start to descend toward the developing scrotum during the last 2 to 3 months before birth. In about 3–4% of male infants, one or both of the testes fail to descend, a condition called **cryptorchidism**. Undescended testes can result in infertility and also increase the risk of testicular cancer. This condition is generally corrected with surgery, usually during infancy.

Components of the Testes

Each testicle contains seminiferous tubules, Sertoli cells, the interstitial cells of Leydig, and spermatogonia. **Seminiferous tubules** are tiny tubes where sperm are produced. Eighty to 90% of the testicular mass consists of these tubules. Each testis contains between 250 and 1,000 seminiferous tubules, and each tubule measures 1 to 3 feet in length. This means that if a man were able to lay his seminiferous tubules end to end, they could stretch across as many as six football fields.

Each seminiferous tubule is lined with two types of cells: spermatogonia and Sertoli cells. Spermatogonia are primordial germ cells. These will eventually develop into mature sperm. **Sertoli cells** nurture and facilitate spermatogenesis. These cells are joined tightly to one another, preventing antibodies and other substances in the blood from accessing the developing sperm, in a structure called the "blood–testes barrier." Sertoli cells also secrete anti-Müllerian hormone, which is important in the prenatal sexual differentiation of males.

Testes (TEST-ease, singular: testis or testicle) The male gonad that produces sperm and testosterone.

Gonad The reproductive organ that produces gametes.

Gamete The male or female reproductive cell—the sperm or egg.

Spermatic cord The cord-like structure containing blood vessels, nerves, and the vas deferens that runs from the abdomen down to each testicle.

Cryptorchidism (kript-OR-kid-izm) Undescended testes.

Seminiferous tubules (sem-ih-NIFF-er-us—from Latin roots meaning "seed bearing") Long, convoluted tubes in the testes where sperm is produced.

Sertoli cells (sir-TOLE-ee) Supportive cells that secrete hormones, nurture developing sperm, and form the blood–testes barrier.

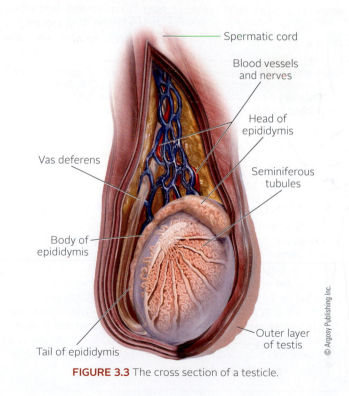

Spermatic cord

Blood vessels and nerves

Head of epididymis

Vas deferens

Seminiferous tubules

Body of epididymis

Tail of epididymis

Outer layer of testis

© Argosy Publishing Inc.

FIGURE 3.3 The cross section of a testicle.

The **cells of Leydig** lie in the small connective tissue spaces between the tubules (not *in* the seminiferous tubules). These cells synthesize and secrete testosterone and other androgens necessary for sperm production and the development of stereotypically male physical characteristics such as broad shoulders and a deep voice.

The Ejaculatory Pathway

Sperm travel from the seminiferous tubules to the epididymis to the vas deferens. From there they move to the ejaculatory duct, eventually leaving the body through the urethra. Cilia and smooth muscle in the pathway propel sperm toward the urethra.

Sperm are first produced in the seminiferous tubules of the testes. From the testes they travel to the **epididymis**, a comma-shaped space about 2 inches long that lies on top of and in back of each testis. The epididymis contains a tightly coiled tube that, if straightened, would measure about 20 feet long. Sperm spend up to 3 weeks in the epididymis, during which time they mature. When sperm first leave the testes, they are unable to fertilize an egg and can only swim in circles. The epididymis secretes the aptly named *sperm forward-mobility protein,* which helps the sperm swim in a forward direction rather than in a circle. During their time in the epididymis, some of the abnormal sperm are destroyed.

The **vas deferens** serve as a pathway to carry mature sperm from the epididymis to the ejaculatory duct. The vas deferens pathway lies near the surface of the skin of the scrotum. Each vas deferens is a tube of smooth muscle about 18 inches long. The end of each vas deferens widens into an **ampulla**, a sac-like swelling in which sperm may be stored for varying periods of time depending on the frequency of ejaculation. A **vasectomy** is a procedure in which the two vas deferentia are severed. This prevents sperm from reaching the ejaculatory duct and being expelled from the body. (This procedure will be described in Chapter 12.)

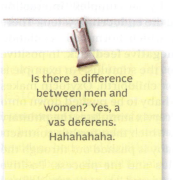

Is there a difference between men and women? Yes, a vas deferens. Hahahahaha.

From the vas deferens, the **ejaculate** passes on to the **ejaculatory ducts**, which are two short (about 1-inch) tubes that pass through the prostate gland to terminate in the urethra. It is the urethra, a hollow tube of smooth muscle that collapses when not in use, that carries both sperm and urine to the outside world.

The Seminal Glands

Only about 1% of the fluid that is ejaculated from the penis is sperm. The rest is **seminal fluid**. **Semen** contains both sperm and seminal fluid. The sperm is produced in the testicles, and the seminal fluid comes from three glands: the seminal vesicles, the prostate gland, and Cowper's gland. Seminal fluid contains water, mucus, enzymes, minerals, sugars, acids and bases, and other substances. Its purpose is to provide nutrition and protection for the sperm during their arduous journey through the female reproductive tract. A man typically ejaculates about one to two teaspoons of semen (containing around 300 million sperm), although this can decrease with age and frequency of ejaculation.

About two-thirds of the total volume of seminal fluid is produced by the two **seminal vesicles**. These are pouch-like glands, about 2 inches long, located behind the bladder, that empty into the ejaculatory duct. The fluid from the seminal vesicles is alkaline, which helps the sperm survive longer in the acidic vagina. Seminal vesicle secretions contain fructose and vitamins, to nourish the sperm and provide energy for their passage through the female reproductive tract. The secretions also contain prostaglandins, which cause contractions of the cervix and uterus, presumably to help the mobility of the sperm once they are deposited.

The **prostate gland** is a doughnut-shaped gland, about the size of a walnut, that encircles the urethra. There is a muscle at the bottom of the prostate

Interstitial cells of Leydig (LIE-dig) Cells that synthesize and secrete testosterone and other androgens. "Interstitial" is a medical term that means "to stand between"; interstitial cells of Leydig are found between the seminiferous tubules of the testes.

Epididymis (ep-uh-DID-ih-mus) The portion of the ejaculatory pathway where sperm mature and learn to swim.

Vas deferens (Vas DEAF-er-enz, plural: vas deferentia) The tube that carries sperm from each epididymis to the ejaculatory duct.

Ampulla The sac-like swelling at the end of each vas deferens.

Vasectomy The cutting of the vas deferentia to prevent sperm from entering the ejaculate.

Ejaculate When used as a noun, it is another word for semen.

Ejaculatory duct The part of the ejaculatory pathway that passes through the prostate and connects the vas deferens and the urethra.

Seminal fluid The white milky substance produced by the seminal vesicles, prostate gland, and Cowper's gland that provides nutrition and protection for the sperm.

Semen (SEE-men) The fluid released during ejaculation, which is made up of sperm and seminal fluid.

Seminal vesicles Two glands that produce a thick, alkaline secretion that makes up most of semen.

Prostate gland A gland that surrounds the urethra, which produces a fluid that is added to semen.

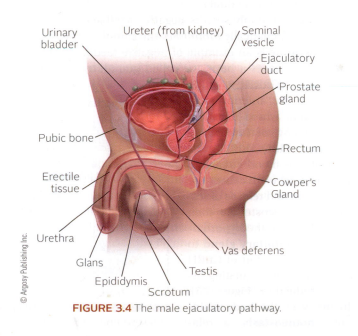

Urinary bladder

Ureter (from kidney)

Seminal vesicle

Ejaculatory duct

Prostate gland

Pubic bone

Rectum

Erectile tissue

Cowper's Gland

Urethra

Vas deferens

Glans

Testis

Epididymis

Scrotum

© Argosy Publishing Inc.

FIGURE 3.4 The male ejaculatory pathway.

4 Female Reproductive Anatomy and Physiology

"Bob loved vaginas. . . . He loved the way they felt, the way they tasted, the way they smelled, but most importantly he loved the way they looked. . . . I held my breath. He looked and looked. He gasped and smiled and stared and groaned. He got breathy and his face changed. 'You're so beautiful,' he said. 'You're elegant and deep and innocent and wild.'"

—Eve Ensler (2000), The Vagina Monologues. New York: Villard, pp. 53–37.

© Image Source/Getty Images

© Blend Images Photography/Veer   © PhotoEdit/Alamy

For thousands of years, the female body has been both intensely scrutinized and utterly ignored. It has been worshipped as a giver of life and scorned for its limitations. It has been feared for its mysteries and restrained as an unruly entity. In this chapter, we will study the female body and the processes that have so frightened and captivated people through the ages.

External Anatomy

After completion of this section, you will be able to . . .

- ○ Identify the form and functions of the *vulva, mons pubis, perineum, labia majora, labia minora, clitoris, vestibule, greater and lesser vestibular glands,* and *pubococcygeus muscle.*

- ○ Define *labiaplasty* and *clitoridectomy.*

- ○ Label the external female anatomy.

- ○ Compare and contrast the clitoris to the penis.

- ○ Assess the risks of and the reasons for clitoridectomy.

Women: look at your genitals. No, not if you're in class or the library or a coffee shop. Later. Get a mirror and a spotlight and really examine yourself. Many of you are probably cringing at the thought of looking at your own bodies. Although men treat their genitalia as old friends, giving them names and frequently taking them out to play, many women have a much less familiar relationship with their genitals. Even to women themselves, the female anatomy is often mysterious. This air of mystery regarding female anatomy, not to mention downright fear and stigma, is not new. Until the Renaissance, virtually no accurate knowledge of female reproductive anatomy existed.

The external female genitalia, or **vulva**, include the mons pubis, labia, clitoris, and the urethral and vaginal openings. The secretion of a protective, waxy substance called **sebum** helps to waterproof the vulva and to repel urine, menstrual blood, and bacteria. Thousands of nerves carry sensation from the area, making the vulva a major source of sexual stimulation.

Components of the Vulva

The **mons pubis** is the pad of fat that covers, cushions, and protects the joint between the left and right pubic bones. This is a delicate joint, a fact painfully remembered by any woman who has taken a hard jolt on a bicycle. At puberty, rising levels of androgens promote the growth of pubic hair over the mons pubis, which may serve to trap *pheromones*, chemical secretions that influence one's physiology or behavior. The amount of pubic hair is in part determined by genetics. It has become fashionable in Western society for women to trim or shave their pubic hair. In a bikini wax, a woman trims the sides of the pubic triangle so hair is not visible while she is wearing a bathing suit. In a "landing strip" type of waxing, more hair is removed from the sides so there is a strip of hair over the center of the mons pubis. When a woman gets a full Brazilian wax (also called a *sphinx*), all pubic hair is removed.

The perineum is the skin between the vagina and the

Vulva (VUL-vah) The external female genitalia. Another word for vulva is *pudendum*, which regrettably derives from the Latin word meaning "something to be ashamed of."

Sebum A waxy secretion that helps to protect the vulva.

Mons pubis (mahns PYOO-bis) The pad of fat that covers, cushions, and protects the pubic joint. It is also called the *mons veneris* ("mound of Venus"), named for the Roman goddess of love.

Labia majora (LAY-bee-ah ma-JORE-ah) Large outer folds of skin on both sides of the vulva.

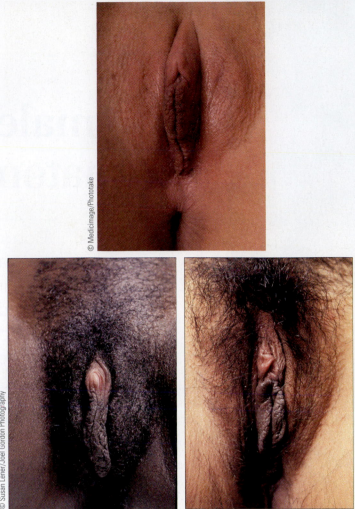

A woman viewing photographs in a magazine like *Playboy* or *Penthouse* might look at those images and think, "I don't look like that; there must be something wrong with me." In reality, vulvas vary greatly in appearance.

anus. Laden with nerves, it is a very sensitive part of the anatomy.

Labia

The two large folds of skin called the **labia majora** ("large lips") surround, protect, and cover the inner genitals. The darker outer skin is covered with hair, while the hairless inner surface contains sweat glands and oil-secreting sebaceous glands. The amount of fat in the labia differs from woman to woman and can

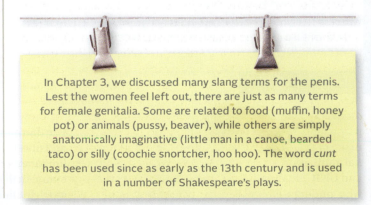

In Chapter 3, we discussed many slang terms for the penis. Lest the women feel left out, there are just as many terms for female genitalia. Some are related to food (muffin, honey pot) or animals (pussy, beaver), while others are simply anatomically imaginative (little man in a canoe, bearded taco) or silly (coochie snortcher, hoo hoo). The word *cunt* has been used since as early as the 13th century and is used in a number of Shakespeare's plays.

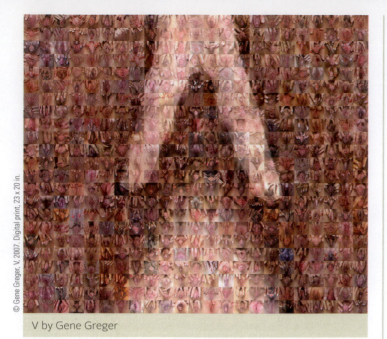

V by Gene Greger

© Gene Greger, V, 2007. Digital print, 23 x 20 in.

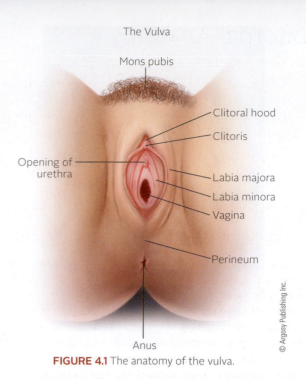

The Vulva

Mons pubis

Clitoral hood

Clitoris

Opening of urethra

Labia majora

Labia minora

Vagina

Perineum

Anus

© Argosy Publishing Inc.

FIGURE 4.1 The anatomy of the vulva.

change depending on estrogen levels, enlarging during pregnancy and decreasing after menopause. The labia majora, which are **homologous** to the male scrotum, are well-supplied with nerves and respond to sexual stimulation.

The smaller, hairless **labia minora** nestle between the labia majora. These inner lips run from the hood of the clitoris down either side of the urethral and vaginal openings. The color and appearance of the labia minora vary enormously from woman to woman, even from one labium to its partner. The labia minora contain oil glands to lubricate the skin around the genitals.

In recent years, **labiaplasty**—the use of lasers to reduce or reshape the inner or outer labia—has become increasingly popular. This surgery involves the removal of very sensitive tissue, so women who have labiaplasty will lose some sexual sensitivity. Some women choose to undergo this procedure, which can cost up to $12,000 or more, for various reasons: to more easily wear tight or revealing clothing, to more comfortably participate in activities such as bicycling or horseback riding, or to improve their self-confidence. Other women have seen pornographic images of women whose labia have been digitally and surgically altered and feel that they need surgery to look "normal" (Liao & Creighton, 2007). It is interesting that when men choose elective reconstructive surgery on their genitals, they enlarge their penises, whereas women usually reduce their labia. According to the American College of Obstetricians and Gynecologists (ACOG), labiaplasty, as well as other cosmetic vaginal rejuvenation procedures such as hymen restoration, G-spot amplification, and clitoral hood removal, are not medically indicated, and the safety and effectiveness of these procedures has not been documented (ACOG, 2007). In fact, many of these surgeries fall within the definition of female genital mutilation as defined by the World Health Organization and UNICEF, although it is important to note that most women who undergo labiaplasty are consenting adults, whereas the

A person who has a preference for hairless genitals is known as an *acomoclitic*.

majority of clitoridectomies are performed on young children who are unable to give consent.

A study of 258 women who had undergone a variety of vulvovaginal procedures showed that most women were satisfied with their results (Goodman et al., 2010). There are some caveats, however. Professional labiaplasty surgeons, who gathered data on patients from their own clinics, performed this study, and their analysis made no distinction between surgeries done to correct functional impairment and surgeries done for purely aesthetic reasons. When evaluating the results, it is important to characterize what determines "success." Many of the women had the procedure to increase their partner's sexual pleasure. Also, women reporting satisfaction may be experiencing *effort justification*, a psychological concept which says that people tend to attribute a greater value to outcomes into which they put a great deal of effort, time, or expense. Of course, many of these women do experience increased sexual satisfaction—as we'll see in Chapter 6, sexual arousal is greatly affected by a woman's mood, attitude, and self-image.

Clitoris

The **clitoris** is the small sensitive sexual organ located just behind the junction of the labia minora. Like the penis, the clitoris consists of erectile tissue with a foreskin, glans, shaft, and crura. A protective hood, similar to the foreskin of

Homologous/Analogous Homologous structures have the same evolutionary origin, but may have a different function. Analogous structures have the same function, but evolved independently.

Labia minora The inner hairless lips that surround the vaginal opening.

Labiaplasty A surgical alteration in the size and/or appearance of the labia.

Clitoris (CLIT–or-us, clit-ORE-us) The very sensitive bit of erectile tissue located in the front of the vulva.

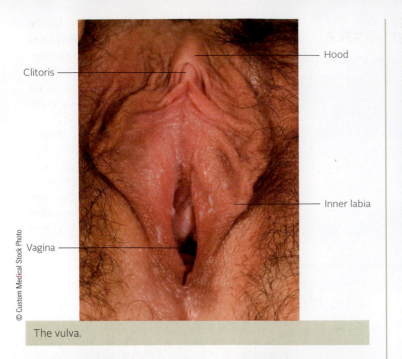

Clitoris — Hood

Inner labia

Vagina

© Custom Medical Stock Photo

The vulva.

the penis, covers the clitoris. Smegma can accumulate under the hood, causing pain and an unpleasant odor. Women can prevent its formation by drawing back the foreskin to clean underneath. Every woman's clitoris is a different size; the glans is usually a bit smaller than a pencil eraser, and the average length of both the glans and the shaft is just under 1 inch (Lloyd, Crouch, Minto, Liao, & Creighton, 2005). The shaft is made up of erectile tissue that fills with blood when a woman is aroused. The shaft swells and hardens, although it does not get as rigid as the penis when erect. As the shaft progresses deeper into the woman's body it splits into two forks, called crura, which extend along either side of the vaginal opening and attach to the pelvic bones. The shaft of the clitoris is shorter than the shaft of the penis, but the clitoral crura are longer than the crura of the penis (about 3 inches long) and more spread out. Neither pleasure nor sex drive are related to the size of the clitoris, which, while smaller than the average penis, contains twice as many nerve endings.

Both the penis and the clitoris are important for sexual sensations. But unlike the penis, which serves other functions such as urination and sexual reproduction, the clitoris has only one purpose: pleasure. Given that females are the ones with an organ whose one and only use is for sexual pleasure, it is ironic that many believe that men are more easily aroused than women. It is also interesting that there is comparatively little research into the clitoris. A search of the PsychINFO database for the years from 1887 to 2000 listed 1,482 sources containing the term "penis" but only 83 sources containing the term "clitoris" (Ogletree & Ginsburg, 2000). Your author believes that if *males* had an organ that existed solely for sexual pleasure, not only would this organ be considered proof of the superiority of men and their right to orgasms-on-demand, but mil-

Clitoridectomy Surgical removal of all or part of the clitoris. Also called **female genital mutilation (FGM).**

Infibulation The complete removal of the clitoris and labia minora, as well as parts of the labia majora.

lions of dollars would be provided to fund research into this fascinating organ.

To some cultures, this organ of pleasure is considered so dangerous that it must be removed. In some African countries and parts of the Middle East, the clitoris is surgically excised for social conventions or so the girl will meet the cultural ideals of femininity and modesty. This procedure is known as **clitoridectomy**, but is perhaps most accurately called **female genital mutilation (FGM)** and is condemned by nearly all proponents of universal human rights. The less severe forms of the procedure involve the removal of the clitoral hood (hoodectomy) or of the glans of the clitoris itself. The most radical form of female genital mutilation is called an **infibulation**, which involves the complete removal of the clitoris and labia minora as well as parts of the labia majora. The edges of the labia majora are then sewn together to cover the vagina, leaving a small hole to allow for the flow of urine and menstrual blood. The scarred tissue must be cut or ripped open for intercourse or childbirth. Perhaps 15% of all clitoridectomies performed in Africa are infibulations (World Health Organization, 2000).

Clitoridectomies are often performed in primitive and unsanitary conditions with no anesthesia, using an unsterilized knife, razor blade, or a shard of glass. These procedures can lead to pain, scarring, infection, transmission of the HIV virus, shock, hemorrhage, and even death. The loss of her clitoris can adversely affect a woman's sexual pleasure, and genital scarring can make intercourse very painful. Clitoridectomies make childbirth a riskier event for both the mother and her baby; in fact, FGM increases the likelihood of death of the mother or baby during childbirth by 50% (Banks et al., 2006).

Female genital mutilation is most common across central Africa and parts of the Middle East, where as many as 99% of the women have undergone the procedure (Toubia, 1994). Amnesty International estimates that every day 6,000 girls and women around the world experience FGM. Although not accepted by the

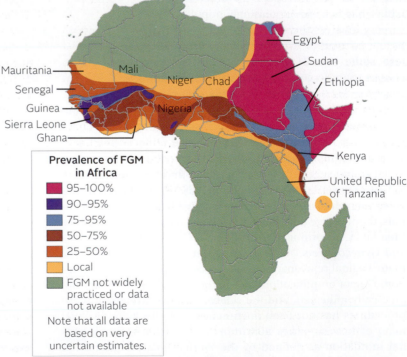

Prevalence of FGM in Africa

- 95–100%
- 90–95%
- 75–95%
- 50–75%
- 25–50%
- Local
- FGM not widely practiced or data not available

Note that all data are based on very uncertain estimates.

FIGURE 4.2 Prevalence of female genital mutilation (FGM) in Africa. Based on UN agencies, Amnesty, US Government, and afrol archives, www.afrol.com. By permission.

dominant culture here, clitoridectomies are nonetheless also performed in the United States. An estimated 228,000 American girls have been cut or are at risk of undergoing the procedure because they come from an ethnic community that practices female genital cutting (African Women's Health Center, 2010). This figure does not include the thousands of babies each year who have had their clitorises removed or reduced if a pediatric surgeon considers it to be "abnormally large" (discussed further in Chapter 5).

Women undergo ritual clitoridectomies for a number of reasons, primarily because it is an expected social custom. In these cultures, a woman is not considered a true, marriageable woman unless she has had her clitoris removed. FGM is thought to ensure a girl's chastity by diminishing her ability to experience sexual pleasure. Although many Muslims believe that female circumcision is required by the Islam religion, except for one disputed *hadith,* there is in fact no mention of genital modification or mutilation mentioned in the Qur'an. The prophet Muhammad himself never allowed his daughters to undergo the procedure.

Vestibule, Glands, and Other Underlying Structures

The cavity between the labia minora is called the **vestibule**, and it contains the openings to the urethra and vagina, as well as ducts of the greater vestibular glands. The tubular **urethra** carries urine from the bladder. The urethra is shorter and straighter in women than it is in men. This, as well as its proximity to the vaginal opening, makes women more susceptible to urinary tract infections (UTIs) such as cystitis. Cystitis can be prevented by maintaining cleanliness around the urethral opening, as well as by drinking cranberry juice, which prevents the bacteria from adhering to the bladder walls.

Posterior to the urethra is the larger vaginal opening, which may be covered by a fold of tissue called the **hymen**. The presence or absence of the hymen does not indicate whether a woman is a virgin, as the hymen can be torn by many activities other than intercourse, including horseback riding, gymnastics, or insertion of a tampon.

The **greater vestibular glands**, which are homologous to the male's Cowper's glands, lie just inside the labia minora on each side of the vaginal opening. They secrete mucus into the vestibule during sexual arousal, although the major source of vaginal lubrication is fluid from blood vessels that cross the vaginal walls. Located on the upper wall of the vagina, the **lesser vestibular glands** (also called

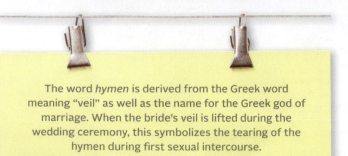

The word *hymen* is derived from the Greek word meaning "veil" as well as the name for the Greek god of marriage. When the bride's veil is lifted during the wedding ceremony, this symbolizes the tearing of the hymen during first sexual intercourse.

ASK YOURSELF

Is it ever right to impose one society's values on another society? Can one society insist that another society stop a traditional practice? In what situations? Can you think of a comparable situation of an unnecessary surgery performed in America, and the response that might be made by other countries with different values?

Skene's glands) are considered to be the female equivalent of the prostate gland and may be involved in the somewhat controversial phenomenon of female ejaculation (discussed in the next section). These glands vary greatly in size from woman to woman, and in some cases, are absent entirely.

The **pubococcygeus (PC)** muscle stretches from pubic bone to coccyx, surrounding the urethral, vaginal, and anal openings, and supporting a number of pelvic organs. Rhythmic clenching and unclenching of the PC muscles are called Kegel exercises, and can be done to help prevent incontinence and perhaps to increase the strength of orgasm.

Internal Anatomy

After completion of this section, you will be able to . . .

○ Identify the form and functions of the *vagina, uterus, fallopian tubes,* and *ovaries.*

○ Define *lactobacteria.*

○ Label the internal female anatomy.

○ Evaluate the arguments for and against the existence of the G-spot and female ejaculation.

○ Compare the homologous reproductive structures in females and males.

The Vagina

Deer, mares, and elephants. In increasing order of size, these are the three classifications of women described in the Kama Sutra, based on the depth of the vagina. The **vagina**, located between the rectum and the urethra, is a collapsible tube of smooth muscle, 3 to 5 inches long. When unaroused, the walls of the vagina touch. The inner lining of the walls is a mucous membrane containing ridges that stimulate the penis during intercourse. The middle layer of the walls is composed of smooth muscle. Although smooth muscles are capable of great strength, they are not subject to voluntary control; it is the pubococcygeus muscle that can be contracted. When a woman is aroused, blood rushes to the vagina. Fluid

Vestibule The cavity between the labia minora that contains the openings of the urethra and vagina.

Urethra Tube that carries urine from the bladder.

Hymen The fold of tissue that may cover the vaginal opening.

Greater vestibular glands Also called **Bartholin's glands (BART-linz)**, these glands secrete mucus during sexual arousal.

Lesser vestibular glands Also called **Skene's glands (SKEENZ)** or the **female prostate**, these glands may be involved with female ejaculation.

Pubococcygeus (PU-bo-coc-see-GEE-us; PC) muscles The sling of muscles that form the pelvic floor.

Vagina From the Latin word meaning "sheath" or "scabbard," the vagina is the muscular passage into which the penis is inserted during heterosexual intercourse and through which the baby passes during birth.

critical evaluation

Whether the G-spot and female ejaculation even exist is a subject of controversy. There are a number of issues to consider when evaluating the data.

> **What was the research design?** While many anecdotal reports, case studies, and questionnaire studies support the existence of the Gräfenberg area (Darling, Davidson, & Conway-Welch, 1990; Davidson, Darling, & Conway-Welch, 1989; Santamaria, 1997), there is little actual experimental research into the specific stimulation of the area (Hines, 2001; Levin, 2003). What is the relative value of case studies and anecdotal information versus clinical studies? How might the existence of a G-spot best be determined?

> **Were the subjects aware of the nature of the study?** In one of the few published studies about the effects of specific stimulation of the area, both the women in the study and the physician examining them were told that a highly sensitive spot existed and that the physician was looking for it (Goldberg et al., 1983). What effects do mental imagery and expectations have on sexual arousal?

> **Is there an *ad populum* fallacy in effect?** Most women believe that the G-spot exists (Davidson et al., 1989). But just because people believe that something exists, does that mean that it necessarily does?

> **Is there a searching for perfect solutions fallacy in effect?** Although stimulation of the G-spot is thought to excite the female prostate to cause female ejaculation, these glands vary in size and may not even be present in every woman. Some scientists have used this inconsistency as an argument against the existence of the G-spot and female ejaculation (Hines, 2001). But do the glands need to be present and uniform in all women to prove the existence of the G-spot and female ejaculation?

It is clear that further research is needed. Physical examination of subjects who are not aware of the specific research goals, as well as chemical analysis of female ejaculate, could give us more understanding as to the nature of the G-spot.

(not blood) from the capillaries crosses the vaginal walls, protecting the vagina. In parts of Africa, some men consider a lubricated vagina to be not only disgusting, but a sign that their partners have been unfaithful (Braunstein & van de Wijgert, 2003). Women in these countries dry their vaginas, which promotes vaginal tearing during intercourse, increasing a woman's chance of infection with the HIV virus.

Some parts of the vagina are fairly insensitive; in fact, it is possible to do surgery on the upper part of the vagina without anesthesia. At first it seems unfortunate that there are few nerve endings in the vagina, but it is important to remember that the vagina is the birth canal through which the baby enters the world from the uterus. If you were to ask a woman in the midst of childbirth about vaginal sensitivity, she would strongly declare that the vagina did not need to be any more sensitive than it already is. The vagina also functions as a repository for sperm and as a passageway for menstrual flow.

The **G-spot** is thought to be an area of the vagina that, when stimulated, produces powerful orgasms and female ejaculation. Gynecologist Ernst Gräfenberg first described the G-spot in 1950. His finding was largely ignored until 1982 when sex researchers again described the area, leading to its renewed popularity as a subject of research and discussion (Ladas, Whipple, & Perry, 1982).

A healthy vagina contains **lactobacteria**, which prevent the growth of yeast infections, harmful bacteria, or even sexually transmitted infections (STIs) including HIV (Klebanoff, Hillier, Eschenbach, & Waltersdorph, 1991). Lactobacteria increase the acidity of the vagina, killing most of the sperm deposited during sexual intercourse. When lactobacteria fail, other bacteria flourish, which can lead to the common vaginal infection vaginosis. The discharge associated with vaginosis contains trimethylamine, the substance responsible for the characteristic odor of spoiling fish (Brand & Galask, 1986). The chemical compounds putrescene and cadaverine may also be produced. You can tell just from their names that these are substances you don't want anywhere near your vagina.

A number of things destroy the helpful lactobacteria and disturb the vaginal flora. **Douching**, antibiotics, hormones, stress, STIs, poor hygiene, and a change in sexual partners can all upset the delicate balance of organisms in the vagina (Cleveland, 2000). Even sexual intercourse can disturb the vaginal ecosystem. For a few hours after intercourse, the alkalinity of semen can support the growth of "bad" bacteria.

G-spot A reportedly highly sensitive area on the anterior (front) wall of the vagina.

Lactobacteria Beneficial bacteria that help prevent the growth of harmful microorganisms in the vagina.

Douche (DOOSH) A device or procedure in which water, vinegar, or other solutions are gently sprayed into the vagina.

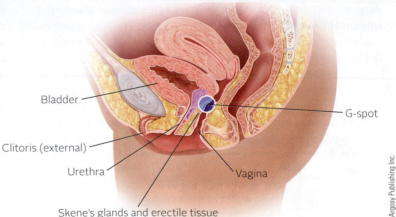

© Argosy Publishing Inc.

FIGURE 4.3 How to find your (or your partner's) G-spot: The putative G-spot is located about 1 to 2 inches up from the vaginal opening, near the front wall of the vagina. While facing your partner, insert one or two fingers in her vagina with your palm facing her pubic bone. Gently bend your fingers toward your palm so that they stroke the front wall of the vagina. The G-spot sometimes feels like a series of ridges, or it may feel spongy. When the area is stimulated, a woman may feel pleasure, an urge to urinate, or both.

Labels in figure: Bladder; G-spot; Clitoris (external); Vagina; Urethra; Skene's glands and erectile tissue

The Uterus

The **uterus** stands alone. Ovaries are homologous with testes, the clitoris compares to the penis, but males have no anatomical equivalent to the uterus. (See Table 4.1 for a list of homologous structures of the male and female.) The uterus, or womb, is a pear-shaped organ that holds the developing fetus. It is located in the pelvic cavity between the bladder and rectum, and connects to the inner part of the vagina. The uterus is held in place by six ligaments and moves inside the body depending on the woman's position or the fullness of her bladder. The uterus of a woman who has never been pregnant is about the size of a small fist, and weighs about 2 ounces. During pregnancy, the weight of a woman's uterus increases to about 2 pounds, and the volume of the uterus can increase about 1,000-fold.

The **cervix** is the lower end of the uterus that leads into the vagina. The opening of the cervix, called the **os**, is about the width of a drinking straw and is normally covered by a mucous plug. During childbirth, the os will expand to 10 centimeters (about 4 inches) and the mucous plug will be released.

The inner lining of the uterus is called the **endometrium**. This lining will thicken and renew each month in anticipation of conception. If a fertilized egg is not deposited in the endometrium, the lining is shed as menstrual flow. Three layers of smooth muscle make up the thick middle layer called the **myometrium**. The outermost **perimetrium** is a membrane that covers the body of the uterus, but not the cervix. It helps to keep the uterus lubricated and cushioned.

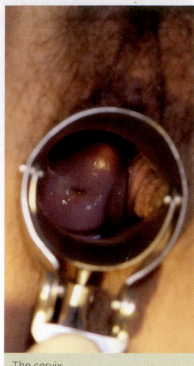

The cervix.

The uterus is home to the developing fetus. If fertilization occurs, the fertilized egg implants in the endometrial lining, where it continues its development. During labor, strong contractions of the myometrial layer expel the fetus through the vaginal birth canal and out of the body. The uterus secretes many substances, including proteins, sugars, and fats, which will help to maintain the developing fetus. The uterus also makes *prostaglandins,* which contract the uterus and widen the cervix during labor. Furthermore, the uterus synthesizes and secretes a number of substances that aid in pain relief. *Beta-endorphins* are produced in and released from the uterus, as is *anandamide,* which is the body's natural form of THC, the active ingredient in marijuana. Anandamide may also help regulate the early stages of pregnancy by helping the embryo to cling to the endometrial wall (Schmid, Paria, Krebsbach, Schmid, & Dey, 1997).

The Fallopian Tubes

Fallopian tubes, also called **uterine tubes** or **oviducts**, connect the upper end of the uterus to the ovaries. Each fallopian tube is about 4 inches long. Fallopian tubes are not directly attached to the ovaries; rather, they open into the abdominal cavity very close to each ovary. Long, finger-like projections called **fimbriae** extend toward the ovary without actually touching it.

After an ovum, or egg, is released from the ovary during ovulation, it enters and travels through the fallopian tube where it may be fertilized by sperm. The tubes help to nourish and conduct the ova on their journey to the uterus. An **ectopic pregnancy** occurs when the ferti-

Uterus The pear-shaped organ in which a fertilized egg is implanted and a fetus develops.

Cervix The lower part of the uterus that leads into the vagina and dilates during childbirth.

Os (ahss) The opening of the cervix.

Endometrium (end-oh-MEE-tree-um) The inner lining of the uterus, consisting of epithelial cells, blood vessels, and glands.

Myometrium The thick middle layer of the uterus, made up of smooth muscle.

Perimetrium The outermost layer of the uterus.

Fallopian tubes These tubes lead from the ovaries to the uterus, and carry the egg on its way to the uterus. Also called **uterine tubes** or **oviducts**.

Fimbriae (FIM-bree-ah) Finger-like projections of the fallopian tube.

Ectopic pregnancy When the fertilized egg implants outside of the uterus.

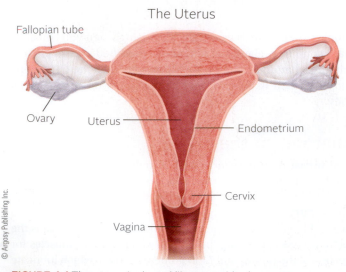

The Uterus

Fallopian tube

Ovary

Uterus

Endometrium

Cervix

Vagina

FIGURE 4.4 The uterus is shaped like an upside-down pear.

lized egg implants outside of the uterus, most often in the fallopian tubes. This is an extremely dangerous condition that can lead to hemorrhage and death.

The Ovaries

Gray, lumpy, and pitted, the **ovaries** lie below and behind the fallopian tubes, anchored to each side of the uterus by a ligament. Each almond-sized ovary is essentially a seedpod, releasing an egg each month. Like the testes, ovaries contain the gametes necessary for fertilization. Unlike testes, however, ovaries contain all the potential eggs a woman will have throughout her life. Ovaries not only produce and release the ovum, but they are also endocrine organs, secreting the hormones estrogen and progesterone.

Breasts

After completion of this section, you will be able to . . .

- Explain some of the factors that cause changes in the size of the breasts.

- Identify the components and functions of the breast.

- Evaluate the risks and benefits of breast augmentation and reduction surgery.

- Explain the value of breastfeeding.

Humans, dogs, cats, cows, apes, rats, elephants, and dolphins—what do they all have in common? All are mammals, a class of animals whose name derives from the breast. Carl Linnaeus, an 18th-century botanist who organized all of life into a taxonomic scheme, decided that the mammary gland, or breast, was what best characterized mammals. Although the primary function of breasts is to feed the young, this purpose is often forgotten amid the sexualized images of breasts we encounter daily.

On February 1, 2004, during the Super Bowl halftime show, Justin Timberlake pulled off a leather patch on Janet Jackson's top, briefly exposing her breast (Janet's nipple was conveniently decorated and covered). CBS was fined more than half a million dollars for airing the event. On that same night on television, an average 1-hour prime time show exhibited five acts of murder or violence. Hysteria abounded as America viewed a woman's breast, yet the homicidal body count on other stations was considered business as usual. It's also interesting to note that it was Ms. Jackson who was excoriated for possessing the breast rather than Mr. Timberlake for tearing off her clothing. The sight of a breast does not cause such consternation in other countries. In Africa, parts of China, and the beaches of Europe, women can expose their breasts and it is not seen as a sexualized act. The

Ovaries The female gonads that produce eggs, estrogen, and progesterone.

Breast Containing skin, fat, connective tissue, and mammary glands, breasts produce milk for the young. Breasts are also a secondary sexual characteristic.

Nipple The pigmented erectile tissue in the center of the surface of the breast from which milk is secreted.

Areola (air-ee-OH-la) The colored area around the nipple.

Table 4.1 Homologous Structures of the Male and Female

FEMALE	MALE
Ovaries	Testes
Labia	Scrotum
Clitoris	Penis
Clitoral hood	Foreskin
Uterus, fallopian tubes, and vagina	—
—	Epididymis, vas deferens, and seminal vesicles
Bartholin's glands	Cowper's glands
Lesser vestibular glands/Skene's glands	Prostate gland
Breasts	Breasts

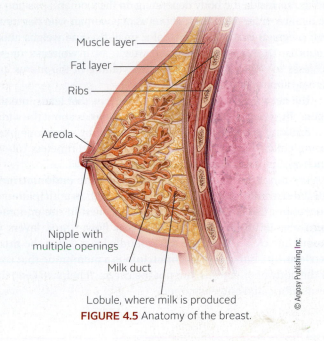

FIGURE 4.5 Anatomy of the breast.

© Argosy Publishing Inc.

hoopla over breasts is especially surprising when you consider that mammary glands are actually modified sweat glands. Primitive mammals don't have nipples; instead the milk seeps out of the skin like sweat, and babies lick it off the mother's body.

Anatomy of the Breast

Each **breast** has between 15 and 20 milk-producing mammary glands, separated by fatty tissue. Milk is produced in lobes, of which there are between five and nine per breast. A duct travels from each lobe to carry milk to the **nipple**. Each lobe is further divided into about 24 lobules, spread throughout the nipple. The **areola** is the colored ring surrounding the nipple, which contain muscles for erection of the nipple, and Montgomery's glands, which lubricate the nipple to prevent cracking during breastfeeding.

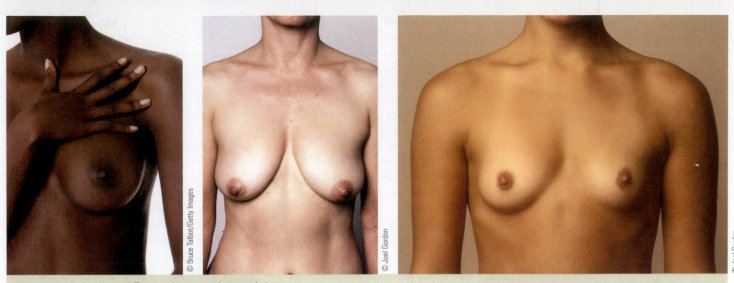

Breasts come in many different shapes, colors, and sizes.

Breast Size

No other body part (except for the uterus) changes so dramatically in size, shape, and function as does the breast. The breast will change size over the course of a woman's lifetime, during pregnancy, even during a woman's monthly menstrual cycle. In other organs, genes that control growth are shut off once a certain age is reached, but because the breast needs to be poised for constant change, these growth-controlling genes are not as active in breast tissue. Unfortunately, this makes breast tissue particularly vulnerable to the genetic changes associated with cancer.

It is during **puberty** that a girl's breasts first begin to grow. The size of the breast in a nonpregnant woman is related to the amount of fat and connective tissue (or the size of the implants). Breast size increases during pregnancy, due to proliferation of cells of ducts and lobules, increased blood flow, water retention, and milk. Contrary to some outdated beliefs, small-breasted women produce as much milk as large-breasted women.

Estrogen allows fat deposition in the breast. This does not necessarily mean that women with large breasts have more estrogen than women with small breasts; rather, breast size depends on how responsive a woman is to the estrogen her body secretes, a factor that is genetically determined. Androgens inhibit the growth of breast fat, so women with low levels of testosterone or who are unresponsive to testosterone develop larger than normal breasts. Other hormones, including growth hormone, thyroid hormone, insulin, and cortisol also affect breast growth.

Breast Augmentation and Reduction Surgeries

In 2010, about 318,000 American women had their breasts surgically enlarged. Just over 1% of the surgeries were performed on girls aged 18 and under (American Society for Aesthetic Plastic Surgery, 2010). Breast augmentation surgery is one of the most commonly performed plastic surgeries in the United States. The surgery is usually done for cosmetic reasons, after mastectomy, or in sex reassignment surgery. Although many people feel that breast implants represent women's subjugation to society's artificial standards of beauty, others feel that breast implants are a source of female empowerment. The finding that women who undergo breast augmentation surgery are 3 times more likely to commit suicide in the first years after surgery than women in the general population suggests that women who look to improve their sense of self-worth through breast enhancement surgery might better explore other options (Lipworth et al., 2007; Pukkala et al., 2003).

Implants are inserted under the breast tissue through an incision where the breast meets the chest wall, around the areola, or in the armpit. The average cost of breast augmentation surgery is between $5,000 and $6,000 (but can cost as much as $10,000 or more) and is not covered by health insurance. In fact, in some cases, health insurance providers may refuse to insure women who currently have breast implants, because implants can make mammograms more difficult to perform and accurately read.

Justin Timberlake and Janet Jackson at the 2004 Super Bowl.

Puberty The stage of life during which physical growth and sexual maturation occur.

Will I be able to breast-feed if I have breast implants?

In most cases, yes; women with breast implants usually are able to breast-feed. But any breast surgery makes a woman 3 times more likely to have an inadequate milk supply (Bondurant, Ernster, & Herdman, 1999). With silicone breast implants, there is a slight chance that a leak or rupture can allow silicone into the milk.

More than 50% of patients experience some problems with implants, including asymmetry, deflation, visibility, rupture, scarring, hardening, over- or under-sensitivity of the nipple, and infection (Zuckerman, Santoro, & Hudek, 2003). Of people with implants, 25% to 40% will need another operation to correct problems, and most, if not all, implants will need to be removed or replaced within 7 to 10 years (Zuckerman et al., 2003). Although previously banned because of safety concerns, the Food and Drug Administration has again allowed the use of silicon breast implants. Previous studies found a statistically significant link between ruptured or leaking silicone implants and fibromyalgia and other connective tissue diseases (Brown, Pennello, Berg, Soo, & Middleton, 2001), although the newer forms of silicon implant may be safer and have less risk of leakage.

The average bra size in the United States has recently increased from 34B to 36C. This corresponds with the overall increase in the size of American women.

Some women choose to undergo *breast reduction surgery* because of physical discomfort in the neck, back, and shoulders or because they are self-conscious about what they perceive as overly large breasts. In this procedure, an incision is made around the areola and down the breast. Skin, fat, and glandular tissues are cut away. The nipple and areola may be removed and repositioned, and skin is reattached. Women who undergo this surgery will have noticeable scarring and may have a loss of sensation in the nipples. They will be unable to breast-feed, and breasts may be mismatched or the nipples unevenly positioned. A less invasive procedure involving liposuction of the breast is being tested (Mellul, Dryden, Remigio, & Wulc, 2006).

Lactation

When the August 2006 cover of *Baby Talk* magazine featured a mother breastfeeding her baby, the magazine received more than 700 letters, many from readers who were "shocked," "offended," and "embarrassed." Others called the cover "gross" or "inappropriate," because "a breast is . . . a sexual thing." Apparently, even nursing mothers can forget that breasts are not simply an attractive fashion accessory to liven up your little

Lactation (lack-TAY-shun) The secretion of milk from the breast.

ASK YOURSELF
Why are women's breasts considered beautiful to look at except when fulfilling the purpose for which they are designed?

black dress or an interesting bauble to flash to your *Girls Gone Wild* cameraman. But the fact nevertheless remains: the major function of breasts is to feed and nourish newborn infants. This function is accomplished through **lactation**, which is the secretion of milk from the breast. During lactation, breasts may gain as much as a pound. The areola will darken and spread and the glands around the areola develop to lubricate the nipple. After weaning (when a child no longer feeds on mother's milk), the glands and lobules atrophy. Fat can take their place in the breast, but doesn't always, so breasts may be more saggy than they were before pregnancy.

Breast milk is the perfect food for an infant. It contains the ideal proportions of proteins, fats, carbohydrates, calcium, and other nutrients needed by the developing body. Through breast milk, the mother can pass immune factors on to her baby, factors that are unavailable from any other means (discussed further in Chapter 13).

Hormones

After completion of this section, you will be able to . . .

○ Chart the feedback regulation of estrogen and progesterone.

○ List the effects of estrogen, progesterone, and testosterone on the female body.

Female anatomy and physiology are controlled by a number of hormones, including estrogen and progesterone. Like testosterone, these hormones are regulated by a complex interaction between the brain and the endocrine system. (Refer back to Table 3.2 for a summary of hormone effects in men and women.)

© Wolfgang Weinhaupl/Westend61/Corbis

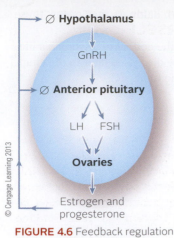

∅ **Hypothalamus**

GnRH

∅ **Anterior pituitary**

LH   FSH

Ovaries

Estrogen and progesterone

FIGURE 4.6 Feedback regulation of estrogen and progesterone.

In brief, a woman's biology is driven by the following hormonal process. The hypothalamus releases GnRH, which travels to the anterior pituitary gland, causing the secretion of two hormones: **luteinizing hormone (LH)**, which causes the egg to be released from the ovary during ovulation, and the aptly named **follicle-stimulating hormone (FSH)**, which stimulates the follicles, or developing eggs. These hormones travel through the bloodstream to the ovaries, where they promote the production and release of **estrogen** and **progesterone.** The estrogen and progesterone then signal the hypothalamus and pituitary gland to temporarily halt production of GnRH, FSH, and LH, thus regulating their own production; this "feedback regulation" process is illustrated in Figure 4.6.

Hormones That Affect the Female Body

Estrogen

Estrogen is the umbrella term used to refer to several steroid hormones that promote the development of female sex characteristics and regulate the menstrual cycle. The most potent form of estrogen is produced in the ovaries. Other forms are produced in the placenta, liver, and adipose tissue (fat). Both men and women have estrogen, although during their childbearing ages women have 3 to 10 times more estrogen than men do.

Estrogen has widespread effects on the body, brain, and behavior. These effects are summarized in Figure 4.7.

Estrogen increases body fat. When a girl reaches puberty, elevated estrogen secretion causes her body to increase its adipose levels, especially in the belly, buttocks, and thighs. Yet the media barrage of images of slim-hipped, flat-bellied women bombards women with the message that their bodies are wrong—not only the shape but also by the very fact of its womanness. Interestingly, males are also presented with unrealistic media images, yet these figures (enormous muscles, huge penis) are of a *hyper*-masculinity.

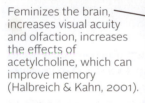

The average body fat percentage for females is 27%; for males, it's 15%. For a woman to lose enough body fat to show a "six-pack"—visible abdominal muscles—she often has to get below 10% body fat, a level at which she will often stop menstruating.

Progesterone

Progesterone is a steroid hormone that is secreted from the ovary during the premenstrual phase. Its major function is to prepare for and maintain pregnancy. Progesterone supports the implantation and survival of the fertilized egg by causing the endometrial glands to secrete proteins and sugars. Because it would be maladaptive for a second egg to be fertilized and implanted in an already pregnant woman, progesterone also inhibits the development of new follicles, decreases motility of the fallopian tubes, and thickens cervical mucus. Finally, progesterone inhibits uterine contractions until the onset of labor.

Progesterone serves several other functions in the body as well. It may improve memory and cognitive development, because it helps protect neurons and helps to form *myelin,* the fatty insulation that covers the axon of the neuron (Schumacher et al., 2004). Scientists are investigating progesterone as a treatment for multiple sclerosis, a disease characterized by a deterioration of myelin (Confavreux, Hutchinson, Hours,

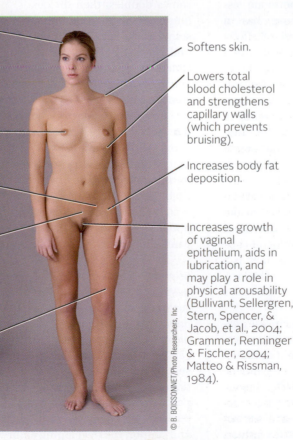

Feminizes the brain, increases visual acuity and olfaction, increases the effects of acetylcholine, which can improve memory (Halbreich & Kahn, 2001).

Stimulates growth and development of breast tissue

Stimulates development of the fallopian tube and aids in ovum transport.

In the uterus, estrogen increases growth of endometrial cells, causes smooth muscle contractions, and promotes cervical secretions.

Promotes bone growth at puberty, stops growth at certain point, enhances calcium deposit into bone and prevents its breakdown. Widens the pelvis to allow for childbirth.

Softens skin.

Lowers total blood cholesterol and strengthens capillary walls (which prevents bruising).

Increases body fat deposition.

Increases growth of vaginal epithelium, aids in lubrication, and may play a role in physical arousability (Bullivant, Sellergren, Stern, Spencer, & Jacob, et al., 2004; Grammer, Renninger & Fischer, 2004; Matteo & Rissman, 1984).

FIGURE 4.7 The effects of estrogen on the female body.

Luteinizing hormone (LH) A hormone that stimulates ovulation in females.

Follicle-stimulating hormone (FSH) A hormone that stimulates the development of eggs during a woman's ovulatory cycle.

Estrogen A generic term for a group of female sex hormones that affect secondary sexual characteristics and regulate the menstrual cycle.

Progesterone Secreted by the ovaries, progesterone is very important in the maintenance of pregnancy.

Table **4.2** Spermatogenesis vs. Oogenesis

	SPERMATOGENESIS	OOGENESIS
How many gametes produced at a time	Hundreds of millions of sperm	One egg
Time for gamete formation	Sperm produced every 100 days, from puberty onward	A human female is born with all the primary oocytes she will ever have
Number of functional gametes from one stem cell	Four	One
Size	Sperm are among the smallest cells in the body	The egg is one of the largest cells in the body

© Cengage Learning 2013

Anabolic/androgenic steroids like synthetic testosterone masculinize a woman's body.

Oogenesis (OH-uh-GEN-ih-sis) The production of eggs.

Oogonia (OH-uh-GO-nee-ah) A stem cell that will become a primary oocyte.

Primary oocyte (OH-uh-site) An immature female germ cell containing 46 chromosomes.

Follicles Fluid-filled sacs in the ovaries that contain the primary oocytes and hormone-secreting cells.

Secondary oocyte Also called the **ovum**, this is a female germ cell containing 23 chromosomes that is released from the ovary during ovulation.

Polar body A by-product of meiosis, this cell contains 23 chromosomes but is nonfunctional.

Cortinovis-Tourni-aire, & Moreau, 1998). Progesterone also raises the core body temperature, normalizes blood clotting and thyroid function, helps build bone, and acts as an anti-inflammatory.

Testosterone

The hormone testosterone has a number of effects on the body (for a more complete review, see Chapter 3). There is a correlation between a woman's testosterone levels and her sexual responsiveness (Tuiten et al., 2000), but this does not mean that a woman with normal hormone levels will be turned into a voracious sexual dynamo if you slip some steroids into her. Sexual arousal in women is a complex interaction of biology, psychology, culture, as well as hormones.

When women are exposed to *large* amounts of testosterone (as might occur if a woman were to take synthetic testosterone), both physical and behavioral changes occur. The clitoris of a woman on high doses of synthetic testosterone may enlarge, her

voice will deepen, and male pattern baldness may occur. These effects are permanent.

Hormone levels change over the course of a woman's lifetime. Some of these changes will be discussed later in the chapter, when we look at puberty and menopause.

Oogenesis

After completion of this section, you will be able to . . .

○ Define the terms *oogenesis, oogonia, mitosis, meiosis, follicles, primary oocytes, secondary oocytes, polar bodies,* and *ovulation.*

○ Explain the process of oogenesis from oogonia to ovulation.

○ Compare and contrast oogenesis and spermatogenesis.

Oogenesis is the production of eggs. This process is more complex than spermatogenesis in males (see Table 4.2). As we discussed in Chapter 3, every cell in the body except for the egg and the sperm has 46 chromosomes in its nucleus. Each egg and each sperm must therefore have *half* the number of chromosomes in them, so that when they meet, the newly fertilized egg will then have the requisite 46 chromosomes. To reproduce, most cells of the body undergo a process called *mitosis,* in which a cell with 46 chromosomes doubles, then divides into two cells of 46 chromosomes each. Eggs and sperm undergo *meiosis,* a process by which an immature germ cell with 46 chromosomes doubles and then splits *twice* to make four mature gametes of 23 chromosomes each.

The human ovum—90,000 times the size of the sperm—is about the diameter of a human hair (Tallack, 2006).

By the third month of prenatal development, a female fetus has approximately 6 million to 7 million **oogonia**, or primitive germ cells. Oogonia have 46 chromosomes, and multiply by mitosis until the fourth or fifth fetal month. Oogonia develop into **primary oocytes**, which also contain 46 chromosomes each. Before birth, primary oocytes begin the process of meiosis, but don't finish, entering a stage of *meiotic arrest* until puberty. When a girl is born, she has between 500,000 and 2 million primary oocytes, held in mid-division.

Once a girl reaches puberty, she is left with about 400,000 primary oocytes (the rest have degenerated). Oocytes develop in structures called **follicles**, which are oocyte-containing sacs surrounded by hormone-secreting cells. Each month after puberty, the hormone FSH causes a primary oocyte to complete the first stage of meiotic division, producing two unequal cells with 23 chromosomes each. The larger of these is called a **secondary oocyte**, the smaller is a **polar body**. The nonfunctional polar body cannot be fertilized and consists of almost nothing except 23 chromosomes. The secondary oocyte has received almost all the cellular material necessary to produce and support the developing embryo. In a way, the polar body is simply discarded genetic material; it allows for the oocytes to

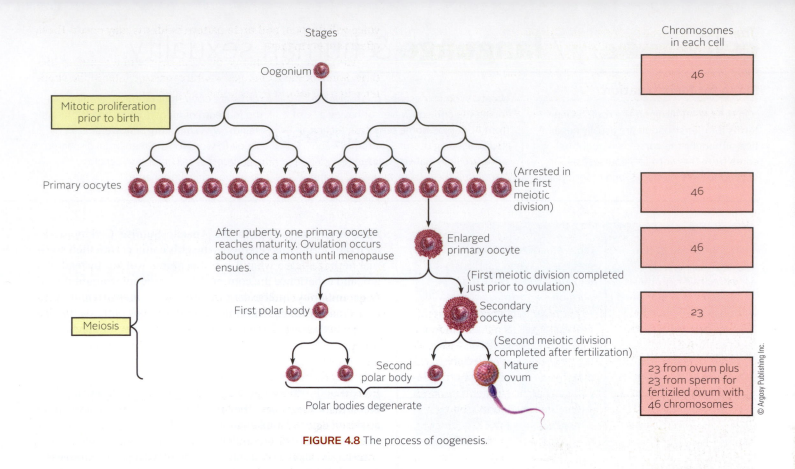

Stages

Oogonium

Mitotic proliferation prior to birth

Primary oocytes

(Arrested in the first meiotic division)

After puberty, one primary oocyte reaches maturity. Ovulation occurs about once a month until menopause ensues.

Enlarged primary oocyte

(First meiotic division completed just prior to ovulation)

Meiosis

First polar body

Secondary oocyte

(Second meiotic division completed after fertilization)

Second polar body

Mature ovum

Polar bodies degenerate

Chromosomes in each cell

46

46

46

23

23 from ovum plus 23 from sperm for fertiziled ovum with 46 chromosomes

© Argosy Publishing Inc.

FIGURE 4.8 The process of oogenesis.

be divided down to the necessary 23 chromosomes, without also dividing the necessary cytoplasmic material.

The secondary oocyte, or ovum, then begins the second stage of meiosis, but doesn't finish the process. It is released into the fallopian tube in a process called **ovulation**, leaving behind the hormone-secreting cells of the follicle. If sperm fertilizes the secondary oocyte, the ovum then completes meiosis in the fallopian tube. If the secondary oocyte is not fertilized, the ovum degenerates and the process of menstruation will occur later in the cycle. The process of oogenesis is summarized in Figure 4.8.

Menstrual Cycle

After completion of this section, you will be able to . . .

○ Define and understand the terms *menarche, menstruation,* and *corpus luteum.*

○ Identify factors involved in early menarche.

○ Explain the events that occur during the *follicular phase, ovulation, luteal phase,* and *menstrual phase.*

○ Recognize that reactions to menstruation are culturally determined.

Menstruation is a woman's monthly flow of blood, endometrial tissue, and mucus. It is perhaps most accurately called the "ovulatory cycle," but because we can see the flow of blood, and not the release of the egg, it is named after the menstrual stage of the cycle. An average American woman will get her period between 450 and 480 times, losing more than 40 quarts of blood and fluid over the course of her lifetime. In the past, women probably did not experience as many cycles over the course of their lives as women do today. Women began their periods at a later age and entered menopause earlier. Also, women used to have more children, began having children at an earlier age, and breastfed longer than we do today, all of which reduce the number of menstrual periods a woman would have in her lifetime.

Changes Across the Life Span: Puberty and Menarche

Puberty involves three stages: First, increased levels of estrogen initiate breast development; androgens released from the adrenal glands result in pubic hair growth; and finally, menstruation begins. The beginning of a girl's first menstrual flow is called **menarche**. The average age for the onset of puberty has been dropping, and today many girls begin puberty earlier than had been the norm in the past. Twenty-seven percent of African American girls and 7% of white girls have breast or pubic hair development by age 7; by age 9, almost half of African American girls and 15% of white girls show signs of puberty (Herman-Giddens et al., 1997). The average age

Ovulation Release of the ovum into the fallopian tube.

Menstruation The shedding of the uterine lining that occurs approximately once a month.

Menarche (MEN-are-key) A woman's first menstrual cycle.

Slang for Menstruation

"On the rag." "Falling off the roof." Slang terms for menstruation are usually negative, although "the curse" is thought to come from the word for "courses," as applied to rivers, seasons, and other cyclical events. Women describe themselves as "riding the crimson wave," or having a "visit from Aunt Flo." Some terms are technical— "BUS: bleeding uterus syndrome"—and some are imaginatively amusing— "attracting the lesbian vampires." Some terms are downright poetic: according to the Museum of Menstruation and Women's Health (www.mum.org), "flowers" is an obsolete word for the menstrual discharge, and "fluor" is still used in gynecology to describe vaginal discharge.

Twinkies lead to tampons? Perhaps. The "critical fat hypothesis" suggests that girls need to reach a certain body mass before menarche begins. A 100-pound girl has, on average, 25 pounds of fat, which represents a store of 87,000 calories, just over the body's caloric requirement to maintain a pregnancy. When a girl has enough adipose (fat), the hormone leptin may travel to her brain to begin the process of sexual maturity. The fact that children today are heavier than ever before may be one factor driving early menarche (Angier, 1999; Chehab, Mounzih, Lu, & Lim, 1997).

of menarche has also dropped over the past 2 centuries. In 1830, the typical girl began her period by age 17; today, the average age at which a girl begins to menstruate is 12.4 (Chumlea et al., 2003). Early onset of menarche may be related to higher body weight (Anderson, Dullal, & Must, 2003), plastic by-products called phthalates, or environmental estrogens (Tiwary, 1998). Many correlational studies also suggest that there is an association between an absent father and early pubertal development in daughters. The earlier the family disruption, the earlier puberty occurs (Tither & Ellis, 2008). The evolutionary explanation for this phenomenon is that a girl growing up in an unstable and potentially risky environment—one without a father—may benefit by entering puberty earlier and thus having more opportunity to reproduce. A link has been found between early menarche and an increased risk of breast cancer (Steingraber, 2007).

Menarche is a liminal experience—a time of transition when a girl is considered to have become a woman—and is recognized in different ways throughout the world. In Japan, the family celebrates it as an important and happy occasion. Although not officially a part of Jewish law, it is customary for many Jewish mothers to lightly slap their daughter's face when the girl first starts menstruating. Soon after her first period, an Apache girl takes part in the Apache Sunrise Ceremony, or *na'ii'ees*. During this ceremony, the girls connect with their spiritual heritage, learn what it is to become a woman instead of a girl, and experience the communal meanings of womanhood in her community. In 21st-century America, is menstruation celebrated as a woman's monthly reminder of her potential to give life, or is it looked as a shameful secret to be kept hidden?

Phases of the Menstrual Cycle

Every month between puberty and menopause, a woman's body prepares for pregnancy. The inner lining of the uterus develops to accommodate the implantation of a fertilized egg. If the ovum has not been fertilized, the endometrial lining is shed. This cyclical shedding is called menstruation, the **menstrual phase**, or **menses**. An average cycle is about 28 days, although this can vary greatly (generally from 21 to 40 days) from woman to woman, and in the same woman from month to month. A woman's physical health, drugs taken, and even mood can affect her cycle. Most variation is seen in the days between menstruation and ovulation; the cycle is more predictable in the postovulatory phase. The menstrual cycle is divided into four phases: the follicular phase, ovulation, the luteal phase, and the menstrual phase. For ease of counting, day 1 of the cycle is considered the first day of the menstrual period. We shall begin our discussion, however, with the follicular phase.

During the **follicular phase**, which typically lasts from days 6 through 13, the endometrial lining of the uterus begins to thicken, cervical mucus begins to thin, and oocytes mature within their follicles. These changes are caused by rising levels of the hormones FSH and estrogen. On approximately day 14 of the cycle, the hormone LH causes the follicle containing the secondary oocyte to rupture and release its oocyte from the ovary near the fallopian tube in a process called **ovulation**. Once released, the secondary oocyte is called an ovum. The follicular cells are left behind in the ovary, and become the **corpus luteum**. Ovulation may not occur

Menstrual phase (also called **menses**) The shedding of the endometrium on days 1 through 5 of the cycle.

Follicular (fuh-LICK-you-lar) phase The stage when the endometrium begins to thicken and develop, typically around days 6 through 13 of the cycle.

Ovulation The release of the secondary oocyte, usually around day 14 of the cycle.

Corpus luteum (COR-pus LOO-tee-um) The hormone-releasing cells left behind in the ovary after the ovum has been released.

> **ASK YOURSELF**
> - Women: How did you feel about getting your period for the first time? What was your expectation of menstruation before you first got your period? What was the reaction of your family and friends?
> - Men: What were you told about menstruation? When? By whom? How do you think the women in your life experience menstruation?

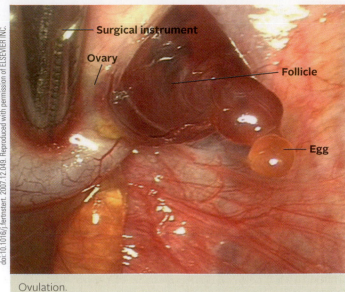

Laparoscopic observation of spontaneous human ovulation, Jean-Christophe Lousse, M.D., Jacques Donnez, M.D., Ph.D. Fertility and Sterility, published online 28 April 2008, doi:10.1016/j.fertnstert.2007.12.049. Reproduced with permission of ELSEVIER INC.

Surgical instrument

Ovary

Follicle

Egg

Ovulation.

Why do we menstruate? It seems inefficient for the body to take the energy to build up the endometrial layer, only to shed it each month. However, it appears that this process is actually more energy efficient than permanently maintaining a fully developed endometrium. The endometrial lining ready for implantation is thick with hormones, proteins, fats, and sugars, and uses 7 times more oxygen than an endometrium after menstruation; this thickened endometrial lining increases the overall metabolic demands of the body (Strassman, 1996). It is estimated that in 4 months of cycles, a woman saves an amount of energy equal to 6 days worth of food over what she would have needed to keep a perpetually active endometrium (Angier, 1999).

in every menstrual cycle; anovulatory cycles are most common in the years just after menarche.

Other female mammals are sexually receptive to males only when they are ovulating, when they physically and behaviorally display their reproductive availability. Humans, however, can and do have sex at any time during a woman's reproductive cycle and are the only animals that do not advertise their reproductively fertile times.

The **luteal phase** begins after ovulation and lasts until the final day of the cycle. During this phase, the corpus luteum secretes both progesterone and estrogen, which prepares the body to support an embryo if fertilization occurs. If fertilization does occur, the embryo gives a signal that helps to maintain the corpus luteum. The hormones from the corpus luteum then support the fetus for the first 6 weeks of growth, until the placenta develops. If the egg is not fertilized, the corpus luteum degenerates, progesterone and estrogen levels fall, and the endometrium is shed during the menstrual phase. Menstrual flow contains blood and cervical and vaginal mucus, as well as endometrial tissue, which some women call "clots." On average, a woman loses only 6 tablespoons (3 ounces) of fluid—half blood, half endometrial tissue—during a menstrual cycle. While most blood is designed to clot, menstrual blood, which contains very few platelets, does not clot. What stops menstrual blood from flowing is the constriction of the specialized spiral arteries that feed the endometrium. During the menstrual phase, estrogen and progesterone levels are low, which releases the hypothalamus and ante-

Can I have sex during my period?

Some women experience *mittelschmerz*, an ache or twinge in their ovary when they release the egg during ovulation.

rior pituitary from feedback inhibition. FSH levels begin to rise, and the cycle begins anew. This process is summarized in Figure 4.9.

In 1971, Martha McClintock, then a graduate student at Harvard University, noticed that the women in her dorm eventually ended up having their periods at the same time. McClintock took swabs from the armpits of some women at different points in their cycles. When other women were exposed to these swabs, their menstrual cycles changed (McClintock, 1971). Although this **menstrual synchrony** often occurs, it does not happen in every situation, and some believe the phenomenon doesn't exist at all (Weller & Weller, 1993; Yang & Schank, 2006). Synchrony may depend upon the amount of time the women spend together, or the phase a woman is in when she contacts others. There is a popular myth that all women will entrain to one "alpha" female's cycle, but there is no evidence that this is true (McClintock, 1998). It is difficult to say exactly what effect one woman's menstrual cycle might have on another; what is important to recognize is that social interactions can influence ovulatory cycles.

People may engage in sex at any time during a woman's cycle. Orgasm during menstruation may even help relieve the discomfort of menstrual cramps. However, some couples are less likely to initiate sexual activity during menstruation, perhaps because of religious prohibitions, or to avoid the "mess" of the menstrual flow.

Attitudes About Menstruation

Blood is kinda like snot. How come it's not treated that way? People with runny noses do not hide their tissues from colleagues and family members. They do not die of embarrassment when they sneeze in public. Young girls do not cringe if a boy spies them buying a box of Kleenex. Caught without a hanky on a cold

Luteal (LOO-tee-al) phase Typically from days 15 to 28; during this stage the hormones released from the corpus luteum prepare the body for possible pregnancy.

Menstrual synchrony The theory that the menstrual cycles of women who live together tend to become synchronized over time.

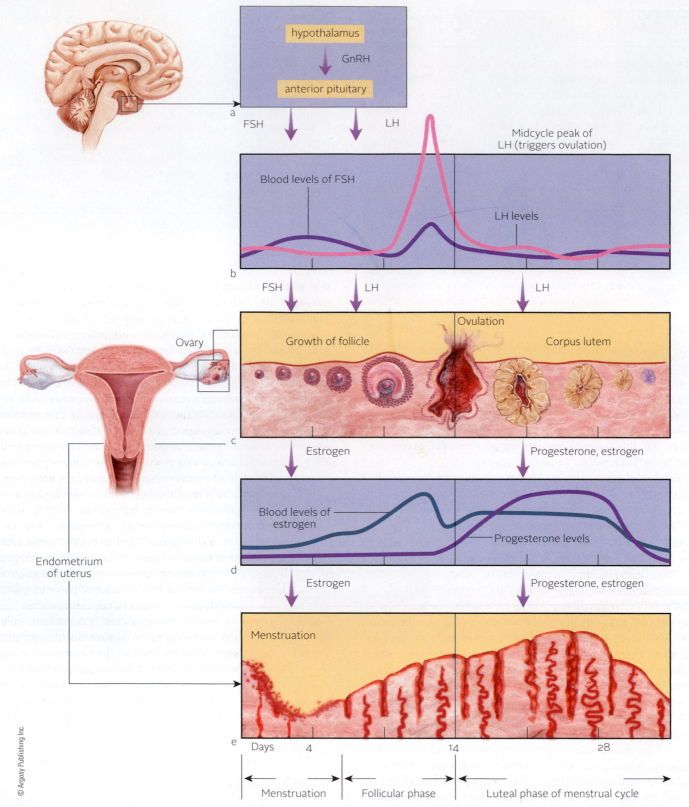

FIGURE 4.9 Summary of hormonal events of the menstrual cycle. After the menstrual phase, estrogen levels are low. This signals the hypothalamus to secrete GnRH, stimulating the release of FSH from the anterior pituitary, and causing maturation and growth of up to 20 follicles. By day 10, a single follicle will continue to develop and grow while the others will deteriorate. This follicle produces estrogen, which thickens the endometrium. On day 13, the high estrogen levels lead to a surge of LH, causing the secondary oocyte to be released from the ovary. The follicular cells that are left behind in the ovary become the corpus luteum, which secretes progesterone and estrogen; these hormones prepare the body for pregnancy. Progesterone and estrogen also feed back to the brain to inhibit FSH and LH levels to prevent further oocytes from maturing. If no fertilization occurs, the corpus luteum degenerates, estrogen and progesterone levels fall, and the endometrium, no longer supported, is shed. Estrogen and progesterone levels are now low, releasing FSH and LH from feedback inhibition, and the cycle resumes.

According to feminist icon Gloria Steinem, if men got their periods, menstruation would become "an enviable, boast-worthy, masculine event: Men would brag about how long and how much. Boys would mark the onset of menses, that longed-for proof of manhood, with religious ritual and stag parties. Congress would fund a National Institute of Dysmenorrhea to help stamp out monthly discomforts. Sanitary supplies would be federally funded and free. . . . Military men, right-wing politicians, and religious fundamentalists would cite menstruation ("men-struation") as proof that only men could serve in the Army ("you have to give blood to take blood"), occupy political office ("can women be aggressive without that steadfast cycle governed by the planet Mars?"), be priests and ministers ("how could a woman give her blood for our sins?") or rabbis ("without the monthly loss of impurities, women remain unclean")."

From Steinem, G. (1978, October). If Men Could Menstruate. Ms. Magazine. p. 110.

day, people sometimes use their sleeves; they are sheepish but not humiliated. They do not blush or stammer or hide the evidence. No one celebrates congestion. It is inconvenient and occasionally, when accompanied by a cold, decidedly unpleasant. But those who suffer publicly—*ah choo!*—are casually blessed. It is, in essence, no big deal. The same is not true of periods. (Houppert, 1999, p. 4)

Many Americans still view menstruation as embarrassing, annoying, or disabling. Some still accept taboos against sexual activity during menstruation, or believe that women are particularly moody, unpredictable, or susceptible to illness during particular times in their cycle. Western attitudes about menstruation are pervasively negative.

Nope, not true; hair treatments are not affected by where a woman is in her menstrual cycle. Nor is it true, as was believed in the past, that menstruating women cause meat to spoil, wilt flowers, turn sharp knives dull, or make wine sour. In some places, menstruating women have been confined to huts during their period. It's not all bad though: In some cultures, menstrual blood is considered powerful. Moroccans used menstrual blood to dress wounds, and menstrual blood has been suggested as a treatment for gout, goiter, and other conditions.

When an orthodox Jewish woman starts her period, she and her husband begin a state of marital separation. They are not allowed to have sexual contact while she has her period, and for 7 days afterward. Upon completion of this time, the woman takes a *mikvah,* or a ritual bath, to ensure her cleanliness. After she has completed the *mikvah,* the husband and wife can be reunited sexually. Biologically, this may increase the chances of conception, as he will be rejoining his wife with an abstinence-induced heightened sperm count, which corresponds to her likely time of ovulation.

What are the media images of menstruation? How is it portrayed in movies, TV, and advertisements? *Seinfeld, Sex and the City,* and *Nip/Tuck* have aired entire episodes on the topics of masturbation, oral sex, and group sex, yet the subject of menstruation is barely mentioned. And the only non-negative factor that is shown related to a woman's period is the relief expressed when she finds she isn't pregnant. Ads for enigmatically named "feminine hygiene products" show confident women in white pants playing volleyball, yet make no mention as to what the advertized product's actual purpose is. Instead, a mysterious blue liquid is shown filling tampons and pads. Magazines aimed at teenage girls, such as *Teen Vogue* and *Seventeen,* are full of stories on how embarrassing it is to have your period and ads for tampons that push the message that menstruation is a secret to be hidden at all costs. A recent study found that young women who have higher levels of shame regarding menstruation report less sexual assertiveness and higher levels of sexual risk (Schooler, Ward, Merriwether, & Caruthers, 2005). It appears that menstrual shame is related to body shame, which affects sexual decision-making. Given this correlation, it can only benefit society if women are taught to regard the cycles of their body as natural and empowering, rather than as a source of embarrassment. Typical questionnaires about menstruation ask women about their cyclic changes and emphasize negative and unpleasant symptoms. But when women are asked to complete a menstrual joy questionnaire—which focuses on positive symptoms such as high spirits, a feeling of power, or a sense of creativity—women report more positive symptoms and attitudes about menstruation (Chrisler, Johnson, Champagne, & Preston, 1994).

> I've been told that I shouldn't get my hair colored or treated during my period because it won't "take." Is this true?

Menopause

After completion of this section, you will be able to . . .

O Define the terms *climacteric, perimenopause,* and *menopause.*

O List the physical and psychological effects of perimenopause.

O Evaluate the risks and benefits of hormone replacement therapy.

Over time, both men and women have a decline in their fertility; this period of transition is called the **climacteric** stage. By the time she's in her 40s, a woman's ovaries begin to lose their capacity to respond to FSH and LH. Therefore, fewer eggs develop, and the production of estrogen and progesterone gradually diminishes. The woman may begin to experience **perimenopause**, the onset of menopausal symptoms and menstrual irregularity. This generally lasts for about 4 years, but a woman can be perimenopausal for anywhere from a few months to 10 years. In women, this transitional period ends with **menopause**, the cessation of menstruation. A woman is considered to have gone through menopause (also called "the change of life") when she has had no menstrual periods for 12 consecutive months, with no other biological or physical cause (such as pregnancy or disease). Menopause can occur naturally with age or because of ovarian loss due to surgery, drugs, or radiation.

The average age for menopause in the United States ranges from 45 to 55, with a mean age of 51. Various factors, the most important of which is genetics, determine when a woman goes through menopause. Smoking cigarettes can lower the age of onset, as can poor nutrition and certain diseases such as diabetes, autoimmune disorders, or infection with HIV (Jones, 1997). Women who have experienced more ovulatory cycles, such as those who have had fewer pregnancies, shorter cycle lengths, or less oral contraceptive use, may enter menopause at an earlier age (Cramer, Xu, & Harlow, 1995). Even a woman's birth month may influence when she goes through menopause: in a study of nearly 3,000 women, those born in the spring entered menopause earlier than those born in the autumn (Cognacci et al., 2005).

Headaches and hot flashes

Teeth loosen and gums recede

Risk of cardiovascular disease

Backaches

Body and pubic hair becomes thicker and darker

Bones lose mass and become more fragile

Hair becomes thinner and loses luster

Breasts droop and flatten

Nipples become smaller and flatten

Skin and mucous membranes become drier, skin develops a rougher texture

Abdomen loses some muscle tone

Stress or urge incontinence

Vaginal dryness, itching and shrinking

© David J. Green

Physical symptoms of menopause.

Physical and Psychological Effects of Perimenopause

Perimenopausal symptoms are different in all women—some women have many indications, some have none. About 85% of women have some perimenopausal symptoms, both physical and psychological.

A perimenopausal woman may see changes in her body shape. Certain parts of the body, such as the labia majora, breasts, and uterus are normally maintained by estrogen. As estrogen levels decrease, these tissues may shrink. A woman's body fat can redistribute from the thighs and buttocks to the abdomen. Some women experience night sweats and **hot flashes**, which are intense feelings of warmth, especially in the upper body. After menopause, women can have bone loss, dry skin, and an increased risk of cardiovascular disease. These symptoms are summarized in the photo above.

Climacteric (climb-ACK-ter-ic) The gradual transitional period between one's reproductive and post-reproductive years.

Perimenopause The time from the onset of menopausal symptoms until 1 year after a woman's last period.

Menopause (MEN-oh-paws) The time of life when a woman's menstrual cycles permanently end, usually around age 51.

Hot flash Sudden, temporary feeling of warmth, flushing, and sweating, often associated with menopause.

Hormone replacement therapy (HRT) The replacement of naturally occurring estrogen and progesterone with (usually) synthetic equivalents to treat the symptoms of menopause.

A woman going through menopause may experience depression, anxiety, forgetfulness, irritability, or mood swings. Although estrogen can have a direct effect on mood, it is important to consider that a menopausal woman's moods and feelings may be related to society's view of postmenopausal women. The Hmong women of Laos view menopause as a welcome stage in their lives, a time when they will be freed from the burden of menstruation and achieve a higher status in society. The Hmong women report no negative physical or psychological symptoms associated with the change of life (Rice, 1995). Because women in the United States are often appreciated for their appearance rather than for their years of accumulated wisdom, it is natural for some older women to feel depressed, marginalized, or ignored by society. Other women feel that menopause gives them a new lease on life and are excited to be free from concerns about pregnancy or PMS.

Just like menarche, menopause is a liminal experience; the transition, in menopause, is from fertile woman to one past her reproductive life. Given the average life span in the Western world, a woman will spend one third of her life after menopause. But whereas other liminal experiences are often recognized and celebrated, menopause is usually ignored or considered a shameful period; it may even be pharmacologically prevented through hormone replacement therapy.

Hormone Replacement Therapy

Some people view menopause as an endocrine deficiency disease rather than as a normal stage of life. If menopause is defined this way, it is not surprising that physicians would want to "treat" it with hormone replacement therapy. **Hormone replacement therapy** (**HRT**) is the replacement of naturally occurring estrogen and progesterone with (usually) synthetic equivalents. The use of HRT has a long and complex history, and the precise effects of replacement hormones are not clear even today.

For decades, scientists observed that postmenopausal women and women whose ovaries had been removed were more likely to have coronary heart disease, so researchers in the 1960s did a large, randomized clinical trial on the effects of estrogen on heart disease—by studying men! These estrogen therapy trials were abandoned, as the men were found to have increased rates of heart attacks, blood clots, and cancer (Barrett-Connor & Grady, 1998). Somehow, these lessons from the past were forgotten. In the following decades, some observational studies suggested that HRT for postmenopausal women was beneficial for the heart.

Like patent medicines of the past, HRT was considered a miracle cure for the widely disparate conditions that occur in middle age. Hormone replacement therapy was thought to reduce a woman's chance of getting heart disease, osteoporosis, colon cancer, and Alzheimer's disease, and to reduce the unpleasant symptoms of menopause (Fackelmann, 1995; Paganini-Hill & Henderson, 1996; Zandi et al., 2002). In 1992, more than 31 million prescriptions were written for postmenopausal estrogen (Barrett-Connor & Grady, 1998). It is estimated that 16% to 25% of American women over the age of 50—about 6 million women—took estrogen or progesterone for menopausal symptoms (Wysowski, Golden, & Burke, 1995).

Because so many women were routinely using hormone replacement therapy, researchers began to investigate the long-term risks and benefits of HRT. The Women's Health Initiative (WHI), sponsored by the National Institutes of Health and the National Heart, Lung, and Blood Institute, was launched in 1991 and followed a total of 161,808 postmenopausal women aged 50–79 in both clinical and observational trials. In different clinical trials, women were put on either estrogen plus **progestin,** on estrogen alone, or on a placebo.

HRT was found to reduce a woman's risk of colorectal cancer and **osteoporosis.** HRT also helped decrease menopausal symptoms such as hot flashes and night sweats. Other results, however, were disturbing. The WHI found that women who received the HRT had an increased risk of breast cancer, stroke, heart attack, blood clots, and dementia (Espeland et al., 2004; Rapp et al., 2003). Results from other countries showed similar findings (Banks et al., 2003; Holmberg & Anderson, 2004). The WHI study was prematurely cancelled in 2002, 3 years before its scheduled conclusion, as it became clear that the risks of HRT outweighed the benefits (Rossouw et al., 2002). As word got out about the dangers of HRT, about half of the women who had been taking hormones stopped, a factor cited in the dramatic fall in breast cancer rates since 2003 (Ravdin et al., 2007).

The story doesn't end there, however. Recent reevaluation of the data in the WHI showed that a woman's age has a dramatic effect on the risks and benefits of HRT. Whereas women who began hormone replacement many years after menopause did increase their risk of death, women who started HRT in their 50s actually had a 7% *lower* risk of heart attack and a 30% lower risk of dying from any cause than women who did not take hormones (Rossouw et al., 2007). When started early, HRT may also decrease the risk of dementia and boost libido in postmenopausal women (Kelly, 2007; Maki, Gast, Vieweg, Burriss, & Yaffee, 2007).

Based on these findings, it is clear that the question of whether women should or should not use HRT is a complicated issue. Women should consider the risks and benefits of HRT in consultation with their physicians. The American College of Obstetricians and Gynecologists (ACOG) recommends that women who take HRT for the management of menopausal symptoms should be encouraged to take the lowest effective dose for as short a time as possible (ACOG, 2007).

There are other ways women can address the symptoms of menopause: Some alternate therapies have been found to be helpful, and some form of exercise should be incorporated into everyone's life, young or old. Exercise will not only protect the heart, it will increase bone density, improve mood, and reduce stress. A healthy diet will also protect against many health problems. Foods (such as soy) that contain natural forms of estrogen may help symptoms of menopause. Women concerned about preventing osteoporosis should speak with their physicians about drugs to increase bone density. Over-the-counter lubricants can battle vaginal dryness. It has been found that avoiding spicy foods and caffeine can help limit hot flashes, as can incorporating stress-relieving activities into the day. Finally, every woman over 40, whether she has yet to begin, is in the midst of, or concluded this transitional phase of menopause, should get regular mammograms.

Premarin, the most commonly prescribed form of conjugated estrogens, is named for its source: PREgnant MARe urINe.

Progestin A synthetic or externally derived form of progesterone.

Osteoporosis A disease in which bones become porous and easily fractured. This can often occur in postmenopausal women.

Pelvic inflammatory disease (PID) An infection of the upper reproductive system in women that can lead to scarring and infertility if untreated.

Female Reproductive Health Issues

After completion of this section, you will be able to . . .

○ Define the conditions *pelvic inflammatory disease, endometriosis,* and *fibroid tumors.*

○ Explain what is involved in a *hysterectomy, Pap smear,* and *mammogram.*

○ Compare the cancers of the breast and female reproductive system.

○ Understand how to perform a breast self-examination.

○ Define *PMS, PMDD, dysmenorrhea, amenorrhea,* and *toxic shock syndrome.*

○ List the physical and psychological symptoms of PMS.

A number of conditions can affect the female reproductive system. These conditions may be benign or grave, rare or common. We discuss a few of these issues in this section.

Pelvic inflammatory disease (PID) is an infection of the upper reproductive system in women, including the uterus, fallopian tubes, and ovaries. It is thought that more than a million women each year in the United States experience an episode of PID (Centers for Disease Control and Prevention [CDC], 2008). PID is often a complication of STIs such as gonorrhea and chlamydia, but not all cases are sexually transmitted. Most women have no physical signs of PID, but some women exhibit severe symptoms such as pain in the lower abdomen, unusual vaginal discharge or bleeding, nausea, vomiting, and fever.

Sexually active women are most at risk, especially those under age 25. The cervix in younger women is not yet fully developed, which allows the spread of bacteria into the uterus and beyond. Douching also increases the risk of PID. This disease is diagnosed with a physical pelvic exam. If necessary, a physician may perform an ultrasound to confirm the diagnosis. PID is treated with antibiotics, although these can't reverse the damage that may have already been done to the reproductive tract. Without treatment, PID can lead to permanent scarring of the reproductive tract, which can lead to ectopic pregnancies or infertility. The CDC estimates that more than 75,000 U.S. women each year become infertile as a result of PID (CDC, 2010).

Endometriosis occurs when tissue from the inner lining of the uterus detaches and lodges in other regions of the body, including the ovaries, fallopian tubes, bladder, or even (rarely) the intestines or brain. This misplaced tissue responds to the hormonal signals that travel through the bloodstream and will bleed with each menstrual cycle. About 10–15% of women are affected by endometriosis sometime in their life. The incidence of endometriosis has soared over the last century. In 1920, there were 21 cases reported worldwide; in 1996, 6 million women in the United States alone were diagnosed with endometriosis. Part of the increase is certainly a result of increased awareness and diagnosis, but other factors such as environmental pollutants are probably increasing the incidence of the condition. Endometriosis is more common in women who don't become pregnant early in their reproductive life. It is often treated surgically, or with progestins or GnRH blockers.

Fibroid tumors grow in the smooth muscle of the uterus. They are not cancerous, but they can cause pain, bleeding, infertility, and complications during pregnancy. Fibroids are very common; it is thought that by age 50, more than 80% of black women and nearly 70% of white women have fibroid tumors (Day Baird, Dunson, Hill, Cousins, & Schectman, 2003). Fibroids are the leading cause of hysterectomy in the United States (Farquahar & Steiner, 2000).

Hysterectomy—the surgical removal of the uterus—is one of the most commonly performed surgical procedures in the United States, where 600,000 hysterectomies are performed each year; this works out to more than one such operation every minute of every hour of every day. One third of American women have had their uterus removed by the time they are 60 years old. Hysterectomies are much more common in the United States than they are in Canada or Europe. Only about 10% of hysterectomies are performed because of cancer (Keshavarz, Hillis, Kieke, & Marchbanks, 2002). Hysterectomies are most often performed for uterine fibroids, endometriosis, and uterine prolapse (when the uterus slips down into the vagina), conditions for which alternate treatments exist.

ASK YOURSELF

There are between 2 and 6 times as many hysterectomies performed in the United States as in Europe (Broder, Kanouse, Mittman, & Bernstein, 2000). Why do you think there is such a high incidence of hysterectomies in the United States? What questions should a woman ask before she gets a hysterectomy?

Cancers of the Breast and Female Reproductive System

Perhaps because of their capacity to change in size, the breast and uterus are especially prone to cancer. Breast cancer is the most common cancer in women; one in every eight women will develop breast cancer sometime in her life. According to the American Cancer Society, the rate of new cases of breast cancer has increased by more than 1% each year since the 1940s, although the overall breast cancer death rate in the United States has dropped steadily in the past decade, due to early detection and advances in treatments. Even though the incidence of breast cancer in African American women is lower than in white women, African American women have a 30% higher death rate than white women (American Cancer Society, 2010). This may be related to disparities in treatment or diagnosis, or to differences in the tumor cells themselves. Four hundred men also die each year of breast cancer (American Cancer Society, 2010).

Lesbians are at a slightly greater risk of developing breast cancer than are heterosexual women (Dibble, Roberts, & Nussey, 2004). Obviously, this is not directly due to a woman's sexual orientation, but rather correlated with other factors. Some reasons for this higher risk include the facts that lesbians have fewer pregnancies, are less likely to take hormonal contraceptives, and are less likely to breast-feed, all of which may protect against breast cancer. Other contributing factors are that lesbians report greater past cigarette use and have a higher average body mass index (BMI) than heterosexual women (Dibble et al., 2004). It also seems as though lesbians are less likely to perform breast self-exams and are more likely to delay treatment when a problem is found (White & Dull, 1997).

Death from breast cancer occurs if the cancer metastasizes to other parts of the body, which is why early detection is key for survival. Awareness of any changes in the breast, as well as mammograms for women over the age of 40, greatly increases early detection and survival rates. It should be noted that the American Cancer Society no longer recommends that women perform monthly breast self-exams (BSE), as one study showed that BSEs do not increase survival rate and may actually be harmful because they can lead to increased anxiety and unnecessary biopsies (Kösters & Gøtzsche, 2007). However, others believe that regular self-exams may help young women who are not yet receiving annual mammograms to detect potentially harmful changes in their breasts. Women should talk to their doctors to develop an appropriate breast cancer screening regimen based on their individual medical situations. Other reproductive cancers include endometrial, cervical,

Endometriosis (END-oh-me-tree-OH-sis) The presence of endometrial tissue outside of the uterus.

Fibroid tumors A benign tumor that commonly grows in the uterus.

Hysterectomy (hiss-ter-EK-toe-mee) The surgical removal of the uterus. Sometimes the cervix, fallopian tubes, and ovaries are removed as well.

Self Breast Exam

Women should get into the habit of regularly examining their breasts, so as to best detect any changes. A breast exam can be done lying down, but some women prefer to examine their breasts in the shower. It is best to wait about a week after the end of the period to perform this exam. First, visually inspect the breasts for skin puckering, discharge, or any other changes. Put your right arm behind your head, and then inspect your right breast using your left hand. Start at the outer edge of your breast. Using the pads of your fingers, press firmly in a spiral motion toward the nipple, feeling for any lumps. Don't forget to check your armpit. Gently squeeze your nipple for signs of discharge. Then put your left arm behind your head and use your right hand to inspect your left breast. If you find any lumps, discharge, or changes in your breast, tell your doctor right away. Most lumps are not cancer, but early detection is your best chance of survival.

© Joel Gordon

Table 4.3 Cancers of the Breast and Female Reproductive System

TYPE OF CANCER	SYMPTOMS	RISK FACTORS	DIAGNOSIS/DEATHS EACH YEAR IN U.S.*
Endometrial (uterine)	Pelvic pain, unusual bleeding (especially after menopause).	Older age, obesity, high-fat diet, polycystic ovarian disease. Prolonged exposure to estrogens, such as early menarche, late menopause, estrogen-only HRT, and never giving birth can increase risk.	43,470 new cases, 7,950 deaths. 4th most common cancer, 8th most deadly cancer in women. Death rate higher in African American women.
Cervical	Abnormal bleeding, pelvic discharge, pelvic pain. This is a slow-growing cancer: symptoms may not appear until late in the disease.	Risk increased in women who had sex at an early age, and increasing number of sexual partners. Most cases are due to the HPV virus. Smoking also increases risk, as does multiple pregnancies and a family history.	12,200 new cases, 4,210 deaths. Cervical cancer rates have decreased by more than 50% in the past 30 years due to wide-spread screening (ACOG, 2009).
Ovarian	Enlarged abdomen; pelvic, abdominal, or back pain; vaginal bleeding; persistent GI distress. Difficult to diagnose in early stages.	High-fat diet, obesity, diabetes, family history of ovarian or breast cancer, cigarette smoking. Prolonged exposure to estrogens can increase risk.	21,880 new cases, 13,850 deaths. 9th most common cancer, 5th most deadly cancer in women.
Breast	A lump in the breast, change in size or shape of the breast, discharge from the nipple, changes in the skin over the breast, swelling in the armpit.	Family history, increased age, obesity, a diet that includes lots of red meat, and high alcohol consumption (Cho et al., 2006). Prolonged exposure to estrogens can increase risk. Abortion and birth control pills do not increase risk of breast cancer (Marchbanks et al., 2002; Melbye et al., 1997).	207,090 new cases in women, 39,840 deaths. Most common cancer, second most deadly cancer in women. African American women have a higher death rate than white women.

*These are estimated numbers from the American Cancer Society, 2010.
© Cengage Learning 2013

and ovarian cancer. Cancers of the breast and female reproductive system are summarized in Table 4.3.

Sex After Cancer

Treatments for cancer, such as radiation, chemotherapy, surgery, or hormones may cause sexual side effects, including a loss of desire for sex, pain during intercourse, or a change in the size or lubrication of the vagina. Women undergoing these side effects are encouraged to speak to their health care provider, their partner, and/or other cancer survivors. Women can consider other means of intimacy, or use lubricants or experiment with other positions that may increase their comfort.

Diagnosis and Treatments

By the time a woman reaches age 21 (or earlier, if she is sexually active), she should start having an annual pelvic exam. The **gynecologist** performs this physical exam to look for

Gynecologist A physician who specializes in the health of the female reproductive system.

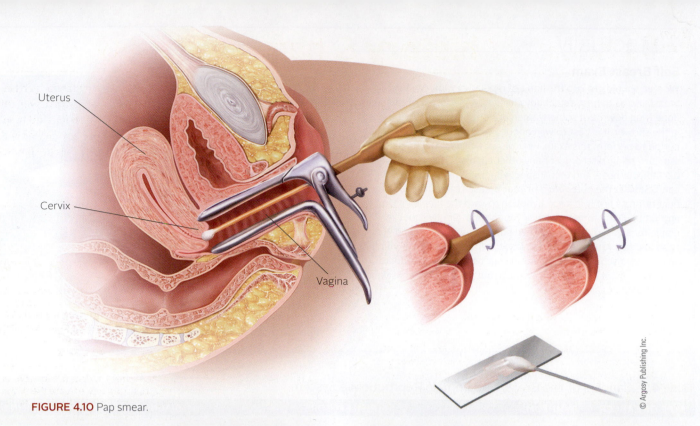

Uterus

Cervix

Vagina

FIGURE 4.10 Pap smear.

© Argosy Publishing Inc.

Breast cancer survivors Melissa Etheridge and Richard Roundtree

© AP Images/Kevork Djansezian

© Getty Images

Mammogram.

© Keith Brofsky/Getty Images

Pap smear Developed by Dr. George Papanicolaou, this procedure involves a physician taking a sample of cells from the cervix to test for cellular changes that may indicate infection or cancer.

Mammogram An X-ray of the soft tissue of the breast, used to detect abnormalities such as tumors.

Premenstrual syndrome (PMS) The physical and/or emotional difficulties that some women experience in the days before menstruation.

irritation, discharge, or abnormalities. Using a speculum, the physician can inspect the size and shape of the cervix and vaginal walls. He or she will remove cells from the cervix and examine them under a microscope, a procedure called a **Pap smear** (Figure 4.10). This test can detect abnormal cells that may indicate cervical cancer or other cervical problems. Biennial (every other year) gynecological examinations with a Pap

smear are vital for early detection of problems and to ensure continued health.

Mammograms are an imaging technique employing low-dose X-rays that detect cysts, tumors, or cancerous masses in the breast, up to 2 years earlier than would be detected by a patient or a physician. A woman with no family history of breast cancer should get a mammogram every year or two beginning at age 40 and every year after 50. If a woman has a high risk for breast cancer, she might want to consider annual mammograms at an earlier age.

Menstrual Problems

PMS/PMDD

Premenstrual syndrome (PMS) describes the physical and/or emotional difficulties that some women experience in the days before menstruation. The exact nature of PMS is unknown. There

In the 1950s, women were encouraged to leave the workforce and become full-time homemakers. It was during this era that Katharina Dalton first published her work on PMS, suggesting that for at least one week out of every month, women were both physically and emotionally ill and were a risk to themselves and others (Greene & Dalton, 1953). During the 1980s, a time of cultural backlash against feminism, PMS became an accepted "fact" in the minds of men and women in Western society. In the words of Chrisler and Caplan (2002), "Each time women make substantial gains in political, economic, or social power, medical or scientific experts step forward to warn that women cannot go any farther without risking damage to their delicate physical and mental health."

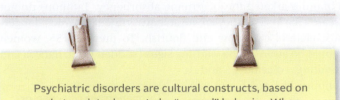

> Psychiatric disorders are cultural constructs, based on what society deems to be "normal" behavior. When students read a description of PMDD with all references of menstruation removed, they named both male and female friends and relatives as possible sufferers for what was called "episodic dysphoric disorder"
> (Nash & Chrisler, 1997).

Table 4.4 Causes of PMS Symptoms

SYMPTOM	CAUSE
Bloating	Normally, progesterone competes with aldosterone, a hormone that causes reabsorption of sodium (and hence water) into the body. When progesterone levels fall prior to menstruation, aldosterone increases the reabsorption of water and salt, which leads to bloating.
Cramping	Progesterone normally inhibits uterine contractions, and prostaglandins increase them. During menstruation, progesterone levels are low and prostaglandin levels are high.
Impaired concentration	Estrogen, which is low during menstruation, increases levels of the neurotransmitter acetylcholine, necessary for cognition and memory (Halbreich & Kahn, 2001).
Migraines	Women were found to be 71% more likely to have a migraine in the two days preceding the start of their menstrual period (MacGregor, 1997). Low estrogen increases the response of the blood vessels to serotonin.
Mood changes	Estrogen blocks an enzyme that degrades serotonin, which results in an elevation of mood (Halbreich & Kahn, 2001). Progestins increase the concentration of this enzyme, leading to depression and irritability. The orbitofrontal cortex and reward centers of the brain are also involved in mediated mood across the menstrual cycle (Dreher et al., 2007; Protopopescu et al., 2005).

© Cengage Learning 2013

is no agreement in the literature as to the number or severity of its symptoms, the time frame the "premenstrual" period actually encompasses, or what percentage of the female population actually experiences PMS. The American College of Obstetrics and Gynecology reports the incidence at 40%, and the American Psychiatric Association reports that up to 75% of American women report minor or isolated symptoms. About 5–8% of women have PMS symptoms that are severe and debilitating enough to interfere with their ability to function. The *Diagnostic and Statistical Manual of Mental Disorders (DSM-IV),* which provides diagnostic criteria for psychological disorders, categorizes this extreme form of PMS as **premenstrual dysphoric disorder (PMDD)**. There are pros and cons to having PMDD considered as a psychological illness. Because it is listed in the *DSM,* PMDD can be covered by health insurance, and its greater visibility may translate to more money spent on research into its causes and the development of new treatments. However, its inclusion may pathologize the normal female reproductive process.

Premenstrual symptoms usually begin three to six days before the start of the period. More than 200 different changes have been associated with the premenstrual phase (Campagne & Campagne, 2007). The most frequently reported physical change is fluid retention. Other common complaints include acne, muscle pain, insomnia, and changes in energy level and sex drive. Some behavioral changes include mood swings, cravings for sweet or salty foods, irritability, anxiety, sadness, tension, and feeling out of control. Not all women experience negative premenstrual effects; some women feel energized, happy and clear, and have increased sex drive, creativity, and sense of personal power (Chrisler & Caplan, 2002; Parlee, 1982).

Premenstrual dysphoric disorder (PMDD) A severe and debilitating form of PMS.

Although there is no denying that physical changes can occur in the days before menstruation, our beliefs and perceptions have a powerful effect on our brain and body. If you expect to have PMS, it is likely that you will. A woman is more likely to remember feelings of irritability or anger that occur during the premenstrual phase; also, if these emotions occur, she is more likely to remember them as having occurred during the premenstrual phase, even if they did not (Campagne & Campagne, 2007; McFarland, Ross, & DeCourville, 1989). The perception of being premenstrual can affect both physical and emotional states. Women who believed that they were premenstrual reported more pain, water retention, and a change in eating habits even though they were *not* in fact premenstrual, but simply told that they were (Ruble, 1977).

Cultural expectations also influence our perceptions. Women in our society are expected to be calm, happy, kind, nurturing, soft-spoken, and think of others more than themselves. Obviously, if a woman expresses anger, exhaustion, or the desire to put her own needs ahead of others, she must have a disorder! Quick—give her drugs! The wide acceptance of the "premenstrual syndrome" doesn't allow women to "own" their emotions—if she's feeling negative, it's just the hormones talking. PMS may be the only time that some women feel "allowed" to express anger or other negative emotions, and only then by blaming it on hormones, rather than on any justified sense of frustration.

> "Women complain about premenstrual syndrome, but I think of it as the only time of the month that I can be myself."
>
> —*Roseanne Barr*

Whether it's because of hormonal shifts or cultural expectations, many women *do* experience physical and emotional changes in the days before their period. Some of these women will seek hormonal or psychiatric medications, although one study suggested that approximately 20% of patients with severe PMS showed a sustained improvement in their symptoms when treated with a placebo (Freeman & Rickels, 1999). Other treatments for the symptoms of PMS include dietary changes, exercise, aspirin or ibuprofen, getting enough sleep, and stress management.

Dysmenorrhea/Amenorrhea

Many women experience **dysmenorrhea**—pain or discomfort during menstruation. Menstrual pain may include cramps, lower back pain, headache, and bloating. **Amenorrhea** is the absence of menstruation. Amenorrhea can occur with emotional stress, illness, anorexia, low body fat, or excessive exercise. Generally, a woman needs to have at least 18% to 22% body fat for menstrual cycles to continue normally (Frisch, 1987). Injections of **leptin**, a hormone that is stored in fat and tells the brain how much energy is available, restored menstruation in female athletes who had stopped menstruating because of intense exercise or dieting regimens (Welt et al., 2004).

Toxic Shock Syndrome

In the late 1970s and early 1980s, there was a surge in **toxic shock syndrome (TSS)**, a serious and sometimes fatal disease caused by the presence of the *Staphylococcus* bacteria. It was discovered that a significant percentage of TSS sufferers used Rely tampons, a brand marketed for its extreme absorbency. Tampons do not create TSS; instead they create an environment in which dangerous bacteria can grow and flourish. To prevent TSS, women should be aware of the warning signs (sudden fever, nausea and vomiting, dizziness, and a sunburn-like rash), use tampons with the lowest absorbency possible to control the flow, and change tampons frequently.

• • •

Reproductive anatomy and physiology are significant in creating the reality of "male" and "female." However, in our next chapter, we'll see that issues of sex and gender are not as straightforward as we have been led to believe.

Dysmenorrhea (dis-men-or-REE-ah) Pain or discomfort during menstruation.

Amenorrhea The absence of menstruation, usually caused by disease, stress, low body fat, or excessive exercise.

Leptin A hormone that plays a key role in appetite regulation and fat metabolism.

Toxic shock syndrome (TSS) A rare but potentially fatal pattern of symptoms caused by bacteria. The use of very absorbent tampons can increase the risk of TSS.

Chapter Summary

External Anatomy

- The vulva is for protection and sexual excitement. Every vulva is very different in appearance.
- The mons pubis and the labia majora are fatty tissues covered in pubic hair that cushion and protect underlying structures. The perineum is the skin between the vagina and the anus.
- The sensitive labia minora run from the hood of the clitoris to the vaginal opening. In recent years, labiaplasty has become increasingly popular. This surgery involves the removal of very sensitive tissue, so women who have labiaplasty will lose some sexual sensitivity.
- The clitoris has a similar structure and embryological origin to the penis, but it contains twice as many nerve endings, and its only function is for sexual pleasure. In some cultures, the clitoris is cut away in a procedure called a clitoridectomy. This surgery, performed primarily due to social custom, can lead to pain, scarring, infection, increased risk of HIV transmission, shock, hemorrhage, and even death.
- The cavity between the labia minora is called the vestibule, which contains the openings to the urethra and vagina. The greater vestibular glands aid in vaginal lubrication, while the lesser vestibular glands may be involved in female ejaculation. The pubococcygeus (PC) muscles support a number of pelvic organs.

Internal Anatomy

- The vagina is a fairly insensitive, collapsible tube of smooth muscle into which the penis is inserted during intercourse, and through which the baby passes during childbirth. A healthy vagina contains lactobacteria, which prevents the growth of harmful substances.
- The G-spot is reputed to give powerful orgasms and female ejaculation when stimulated. Its existence is controversial, but it is thought to be the area near the front wall of the vagina, about an inch and a half up from the vaginal opening.
- The uterus is where the fertilized egg implants and a fetus develops. Its inner layer, the endometrium, builds up each month in anticipation of pregnancy and is shed during menstruation. The middle myometrial layer contains strong muscles for contraction during labor. The cervix is the lower part of the uterus that leads into the vagina and that dilates during childbirth.
- During a woman's reproductive years, the ovaries produce eggs and hormones. Each month, they release an egg into the fallopian tubes, which lead from the ovaries to the uterus. The fallopian tubes are the normal site of fertilization.
- Several anatomical structures in males are homologous to structures in women. Ovaries are comparable to the testes, labia to the scrotum, and the clitoris to the penis.

Breasts

- Breasts change dramatically in size, shape, and function over the course of a lifetime. They first begin to grow as a result of the influence of estrogens during puberty. Pregnancy also increases the size of the breasts. Most of their size is due to fat.
- Breasts are composed of milk-producing mammary glands, separated by fatty tissue. Milk is produced in lobes and travels to the nipple. The areola surrounds the nipple and contains muscles for nipple erection, and glands for lubrication of the nipple.
- Breast augmentation surgery is very popular in the United States but does carry with it certain risks. More than 50% of patients experience some problems with implants.
- Lactation is the secretion of milk, which is the major function of the breast. Breast milk contains the ideal proportion of nutrients needed by the baby.

Hormones

- Follicle-stimulating hormone (FSH), luteinizing hormone (LH), estrogen, and progesterone are regulated by a complex interaction between the brain and the endocrine system.
- Estrogen and progesterone have a number of effects on the brain, body, and behavior of women.

Oogenesis

- The production of eggs is more complex than the production of sperm.
- Oogonia are stem cells with 46 chromosomes. They reproduce by mitosis before a girl is born, becoming primary oocytes. Primary oocytes begin meiosis before birth, but don't finish, entering meiotic arrest until once each month, when one primary oocyte becomes two cells, a small polar body and a secondary oocyte. The 23-chromosome secondary oocyte is released into the fallopian tube during ovulation. If a sperm fertilizes it, it will complete meiosis.

Menstrual Cycle

- Each month, a woman's body prepares for pregnancy by building up the endometrial lining of the uterus. When an egg is not fertilized, the lining sheds in a process called menstruation.
- The beginning of a woman's first menstrual flow is called menarche. The permanent end of her menstrual cycles is called menopause. Girls sometimes enter puberty early; this may be related to environmental pollutants, hormones, or excess body weight.
- The menstrual cycle is divided into four phases. During the follicular phase, the follicles grow and the endometrial lining builds up. The secondary oocyte is released during ovulation. During the luteal phase, the corpus luteum, which are the follicular cells that are left in the ovary after the release of the oocyte, release progesterone and estrogen to maintain the embryo in case fertilization occurs. If the egg is not fertilized, then the lining is no longer maintained and it is shed during menstruation.
- There are varying cultural reactions to menstruation. Many Americans still view menstruation as embarrassing, annoying, or disabling. Some still accept taboos against sexual activity during menstruation, or believe that women are particularly moody, unpredictable, or susceptible to illness during particular times in their cycle. Menstruation is usually ignored by the media, or presented in a negative light.

Menopause

- Both men and women gradually undergo a decline in fertility. In women, levels of estrogen slowly decline and fewer eggs develop. Perimenopause is the term that describes the time from the onset of menopausal symptoms until one year after a woman's final period.
- Menopause is associated with a number of physical and psychological indications. Some women take hormone replacement therapy to prevent these changes, but HRT is associated with risks as well as benefits.

Female Reproductive Health Issues

- Women may contract a number of reproductive health issues, including PID, endometriosis, fibroid tumors, and cancer.
- A hysterectomy is the surgical removal of the uterus. There are 2 to 6 times as many hysterectomies performed in the United States as in Europe.
- Breast cancer is the most common cancer in women. Early detection is key for survival.
- Regular breast self-exams, Pap smears, and mammograms can greatly improve a woman's long-term health. A Pap smear is a procedure in which cervical cells are examined under a microscope. A mammogram is an imaging technique to detect changes in the breast.
- Many women experience symptoms of premenstrual syndrome (PMS). These symptoms may be due to physical changes, as well as societal expectations.

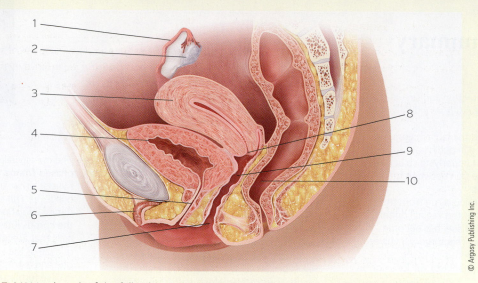

FIGURE 4.11 Match each of the following parts of the female reproductive system with its corresponding number in the diagram: cervix, clitoris, fallopian tube, ovary, rectum, urethra, urinary bladder, uterus, vagina, vaginal orifice.

Answers: 1. fallopian tube; 2. ovary; 3. uterus; 4. urinary bladder; 5. urethra; 6. clitoris; 7. vaginal orifice; 8. cervix; 9. vagina; 10. rectum

MAKING INFORMED DECISIONS

Over the course of a lifetime, a woman may choose to make use of various surgical and pharmaceutical procedures to alter her body and/or biology in the hopes of conforming to society's current view of the ideal woman. In the following scenarios, what are the issues surrounding the decisions?

evaluate and *decide*

Imagine the following conditions:

> Dolie lives in Somalia. Her little girl Aman is 7 years old, and it is time for her to undergo *halalays,* or ritual clitoridectomy. Dolie also had the surgery done when she was 7 years old and knows the pain and fear associated with it. If Aman does not undergo *halalays,* she will be unable to marry and will be a social outcast.

> Shannon is a 25-year-old woman who wants to get breast augmentation surgery. Her fiancé wishes she had larger breasts, and Shannon has been feeling insecure lately.

> Margaret is 52. She is entering menopause and has been very bothered by hot flashes. She is depressed by the idea of no longer being considered young and sexy and wants a miracle cure.

What factors will you consider in advising these women? Consider the issues and questions below to make your decision.

>>

PROCEDURE	ISSUES TO CONSIDER
CLITORIDECTOMY	Why are you considering clitoridectomy? What are the values underlying your decision: Social acceptance? Religious tradition? A logical evaluation of risks and benefits? How do you assess the relative importance of these values?
	Clitoridectomy is associated with many serious health problems, some life threatening. Yet to not perform the surgery can lead to social shunning, a societal death, if you will. To what degree does social acceptance trump biological health in making a decision?
	Parents obviously make decisions for their children every day—that is the role of a parent. At what point does this interfere with the personal choice of the woman-to-be?
	Who has the right to decide what ranks as aesthetically acceptable genitalia? Society? Physicians? Parents? The individual? Why?
BREAST AUGMENTATION SURGERY	What are the risks and benefits involved? It is easy to see the risks that can affect the individual, but can you see any risks to society?
	What effect should societal pressure have on one's decision to surgically change one's body? How is Shannon's desire to change her body to conform to cultural standards different than Dolie's decision regarding the clitoridectomy?
	To what degree should we change ourselves to please our partners?
	How much have you incorporated societal standards of beauty?
HORMONE REPLACEMENT THERAPY	What are the risks and benefits to hormone replacement therapy? What biological factors (predisposition to diseases, age, etc.) should Margaret take into consideration?
	What effect does HRT have on mood? What other factors could improve possible mood changes associated with menopause?
	What is society's view of HRT? Why does society have this view—what values does it espouse?
	What values underlie the desire to take synthetic hormones at menopause?

Additional Resources

Log in to CengageBrain to access the resources your instructor requires. For this book, you can access:

 **CourseMate** CourseMate brings course concepts to life with interactive learning, study, and exam preparation tools that support the printed textbook. A textbook-specific website, Psychology CourseMate includes an integrated interactive eBook and other interactive learning tools including quizzes, flashcards, videos, and more.

CENGAGENOW **CengageNOW** is an easy-to-use online resource that helps you study in less time to get the grade you want—NOW. Take a pre-test for this chapter and receive a personalized study plan based on your results that will identify the topics you need to review and direct you to online resources to help you master those topics. Then take a post-test to help you determine the concepts you have mastered and what you will need to work on. If your textbook does not include an access code card, go to CengageBrain.com to gain access. Visit www.cengagebrain.com anytime to access your account and purchase materials.

Web Resources

Current links to all of the following websites and videos can be found on the Psychology CourseMate for this text at www.cengage-brain.com/.

The National Women's Health Information Center

The National Women's Health Information Center is a one-stop gateway for women seeking health information. It provides information and resources on women's health issues designed for consumers, health care professionals, researchers, educators, and students.

American Breast Cancer Foundation

This site, presented by the American Breast Cancer Foundation, offers general information about breast cancer.

The Breast Cancer Site

If you visit http://www.thebreastcancersite.com, you can click on a site that will provide a free mammogram to a woman who could not otherwise afford one.

Feminist Women's Health Center

Established in 1980, Feminist Women's Health Center (FWHC) is a nonprofit organization that promotes and protects a woman's right to choose and receive reproductive health care.

Susan Komen Breast Cancer Foundation

Information on breast cancer, support, resources, and references.

The North American Menopause Society

This organization is devoted to promoting understanding of menopause and midlife issues.

Relevant and Fun YouTube Vidoes

Uby Kotex "Reality check" and "So obnoxious" videos. These clips are of Kotex ads that make fun of the stereotypical ads for "feminine hygiene products."

Storm Large's song "Eight Miles Wide." Just watch it. Trust me.

Print Resources

Angier, N. (2000). *Woman: An Intimate Geography.* New York: Houghton Mifflin.

Boston Women's Health Book Collective. (2005). *Our Bodies, Ourselves: A New Edition for a New Era.* New York: Touchstone.

Ensler, E. (1998). *The Vagina Monologues.* New York: Villard Publishing Company.

Kaysen, S. (2001) *The Camera My Mother Gave Me.* New York: Knopf.
Yalom, M. (1998). *A History of the Breast.* New York: Ballantine Books.

Video Resources

Breast Men. (1997). 95 minutes. Based on actual facts of the Texan surgeons who invented silicon breast implants. From HBO Video.

Busting Out. (2005). 57 minutes. An exploration of the history and politics of breast obsession in America, and its connection with breast cancer, breastfeeding, and body image. Bullfrog Films.

Period Piece. (1998). 30 minutes. A documentary about girls' first menstrual periods. Women of different ages talk candidly about their first experience. Women's feelings and society's complicated attitude toward menstruation are presented. It includes a historical and humorous look at old educational films. From Jay Rosenblatt Film Library.

The Vagina Monologues. (2002). 76 minutes. Based on the play by Eve Ensler. HBO Video.

5 Sex and Gender

As soon as you're born, grownups check where you pee
And then they decide just how you're s'posed to be
Girls pink and quiet, boys noisy and blue
Seems like a dumb way to choose what you'll do

Well it's only a wee wee, so what's the big deal?
It's only a wee wee, so what's all the fuss?
It's only a wee wee and everyone's got one
There's better things to discuss

Now girls must use makeup, girl's names and girl's clothes
And boys must use sneakers, but not pantyhose
The grownups will teach you the rules to their dance
And if you get confused, they'll say "Look in your pants"

If I live to be nine, I won't understand
Why grownups are totally obsessed with their glands
If I touch myself, "Don't do that," I'm told
And they treat me like I might explode

Now grownups watch closely each move that we make
Boys must not cry, and girls must make cake
It's all very formal and I think it smells
Let's all be abnormal and act like ourselves

—"It's Only a Wee Wee" by Peter Alsop

Copyright 1981 Moose School Music (BMI)

For more of Peter's songs, go to peteralsop.com

© mark downey/Alamy

© Fine Art Commercial/Alamy   © Bob Thomas/Getty Images

Introduction

After completion of this section, you will be able to . . .

○ Define and distinguish between the terms *gender*, *sex*, and *gender roles*.

"Is it a boy or a girl?" When a new human being enters the world, the first thing that others want to know is the baby's sex. Of all the characteristics a child brings into the world, his or her sex and gender will have the greatest impact—on relationships, personality, skills, grades, career, salary, hobbies, and health (Eliot, 2009).

So, how do you know if a person is a man or a woman? *Saturday Night Live* used to have a popular series of sketches about an androgynous person named Pat. It was impossible to determine Pat's gender, and people would go to great lengths to try to determine if Pat was a man or a woman. In fact, the entire premise of the sketch was how uncomfortable people were when they couldn't determine someone's gender. Take a minute to consider the cues that help you in your identification. Obviously, we use physical cues, such as body shape, hair, clothing, and movements. But there are many other signals, such as the way a person communicates, gestures, shakes hands, or interacts with others. We get gender information based on life histories, relationships, and even make assumptions (sometimes erroneously) based on the person's partner.

The term **gender** is often used synonymously with **sex**, although "gender" is a social construct that includes the behavioral, social, and legal status of an individual, whereas "sex" better describes the biological aspects of being male and female, such as chromosomes and anatomy. For example, the effectiveness of a drug might depend on the *sex* of an individual (but not the gender), and the relative scarcity of male nurses is related to *gender roles* (but not sex differences). *Male* and *female* are considered to be biological terms; *man* and *woman* are social or gender-related terms (Diamond, 2005).

Society expects men and women to exhibit gender-appropriate attitudes and behaviors, called the **gender role**. These socially stipulated expectations about gender are usually based on the notion of opposites; anyone who moves away from one extreme must by definition move toward the other. Thus a woman who acts in a way that is considered not traditionally feminine is considered to be acting more masculine.

Gender The classification of an individual as a man or woman, based on behavioral, psychological, and cultural traits.

Sex The classification of an individual as male or female, based on a biological foundation.

Gender role The cultural expectation of behavior for each gender.

The term "opposite" establishes permanent polarity, with no room to move between genders, to adopt characteristics of both male and female genders, or to identify as something else entirely. There's little room to maneuver in such a state of opposites . . . people often have trouble subscribing to all the roles and expectations that are assigned to their gender." (Kailey, 2005, p. 5–6)

In this chapter, we will examine the biological and social forces that affect sex and gender, as well as consider what makes a man a man, a woman a woman, and why many people have characteristics of both.

What Makes Someone Male or Female?

After completion of this section, you will be able to . . .

○ Recognize the varied ways in which sex can be classified.

It seems as though it's the simplest thing in the world—you're either a woman or a man, end of story. But take a minute to consider what exactly it is that ultimately determines a person's sex. Is the classification made according to genitalia? Chromosomes? Identity?

How strongly do chromosomes influence our behavior? As an example, there is a genetic factor that is strongly correlated with violence. A person who has this factor is more than 5 times as likely to commit a violent crime as someone without the genetic factor. In fact, 93% of prisoners in the United States share this genetic trait (Harrison & Beck, 2002), which can be easily identified with a simple test. So what should we do with these potentially violent criminals? Should we treat this condition with pharmaceuticals or therapy? Or should we just lock these people up to protect society from their violent tendencies? Put down the torches and pitchforks, folks—the genetic factor we are talking about is the Y chromosome. Obviously, just because men are more likely to commit crimes does not mean that all men will commit a crime! It also does not mean that the Y chromosome *causes* crime. We are more than the sum of our chromosomes. Our genes have a significant effect on our appearance and behavior, but they are not the *only* influence. And, as we will learn, a person's sex chromosomes do not always correspond to his or her external genitalia or gender identity.

Perhaps you feel the gonads determine sex. If so, would a female who has her ovaries removed become a male? Would a castrated male now be female? Maybe you feel it is the presence of a penis or a vagina that determines a person's sex. When children are born, physicians do not do a chromosome check; instead, they take a quick glance down and proclaim, "You have a boy/girl!" depending on what

Pat from *Saturday Night Live*.

© Buena Vista/Photofest

ASK YOURSELF

How do you feel if you meet someone of indeterminate gender? Does your manner of interaction change? How do you interact differently with men and women? How do your own expectations, conversational style, or physical mannerisms change?

they see. However, in many cases, the external genitalia are not clearly a penis or a vulva. If a penis is less than 1 inch long, does that mean the owner is not a male? If the clitoris is enlarged, does that mean the possessor is not a female?

"Well, okay then," you huff. "How about this? You are whatever sex the doctors declare you to be when you're born, and that's it." Consider this: there is a condition in which children are born with what appears to be a vagina and are raised as females. Once puberty hits, however, with its concurrent flood of hormones, testosterone causes a penis to develop, and the person that was thought to be a female is discovered to be a genetic and anatomical male.

Maybe you believe that our gender is determined by how we're brought up; if you raise a child of either sex as a boy, the child would then incorporate the behaviors, abilities, and identity of a boy. Proponents of this idea, such as the late Dr. John Money, believed that children were a blank slate and biology had little to no effect on their behavior (Money & Ehrhardt, 1972). In the 1960s, Dr. Money had a "real world" opportunity to present his theory, when a small boy who had his penis removed in a circumcision that went horribly awry was raised as a girl. We will discuss this case later in the chapter (see the Sex Actually feature on page 118). Finally, perhaps you feel that genetics, anatomy, and social forces are irrelevant and it is one's gender identity—a person's own sense of being male or female—that determines sex.

As you can see, trying to define these terms is not easy. Sex and gender aren't as straightforward as we once thought they were; there is no single clear-cut definition that you can highlight and memorize for the test. As we progress through this chapter, you will be encouraged to critically evaluate the factors that contribute to our understanding of these concepts.

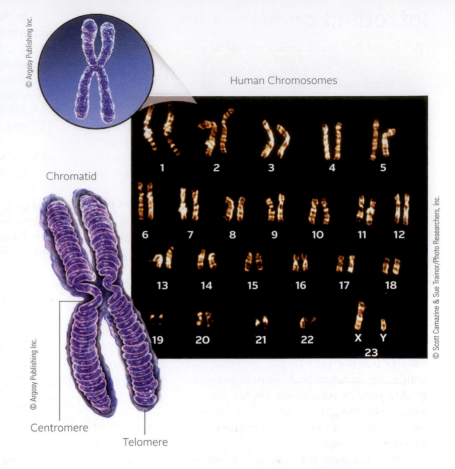

Human Chromosomes

Chromatid

Centromere

Telomere

Development of Biological Sex

After completion of this section, you will be able to . . .

○ Define the terms *Müllerian system* and *Wolffian system*.

○ Explain the difference between the X and Y chromosomes.

○ Distinguish between male and female prenatal sex determination.

○ Describe the process by which an XY individual develops male reproductive anatomy.

Prenatal Sex Differentiation

During fertilization, each parent donates one copy of each of his or her 22 autosomes, as well as one sex chromosome. Males donate either an X or a Y sex chromosome; females give an X sex chromosome. Although there are exceptions, usually an individual with two X chromosomes is anatomically female, and a person with an X and a Y is anatomically male.

The Y chromosome—the smallest of all the chromosomes in the human body—is thought to have fewer than 100 genes. Because more than half of the human population does not have a Y chromosome, this chromosome cannot carry instructions for any traits that are necessary for a person's survival. Many of the genes carried on the Y chromosome control sperm production and the capability to grow testes, an admirable ability certainly, but not essential for life. The X chromosome *is* indispensable, however, and contains more than 1,000 genes, including those for color vision and blood clotting. Because only one copy of most of these genes is necessary, one X chromosome in most cells of a female is inactivated. This inactivated chromosome becomes a dot of condensed material called the **Barr body**, the presence of which is used during amniocentesis to identify a fetus as female. Because one X chromosome in each cell is randomly inactivated, in some regions of the body the X chromosome from the

This woman has a condition called AIS; she has a clitoris, a vagina, and a Y chromosome.

Barr body The inactivated X chromosome in female mammals.

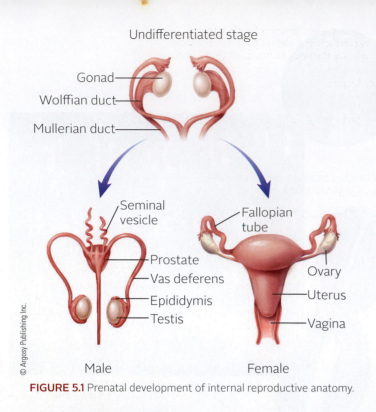

Undifferentiated stage

Gonad
Wolffian duct
Mullerian duct

Seminal vesicle
Prostate
Vas deferens
Epididymis
Testis

Male

Fallopian tube
Ovary
Uterus
Vagina

Female

© Argosy Publishing Inc.

FIGURE 5.1 Prenatal development of internal reproductive anatomy.

Some lizards, turtles, and all species of crocodiles have no sex chromosomes. They become males or females depending on the temperature of the water in which the eggs are incubated (Eliot, 2009)

mother might be active, whereas the father's X chromosome might be active in other regions.

During the first 6 weeks of prenatal development, the gonads and genitalia of embryos are identical and undifferentiated. Embryos have two duct systems—the **Müllerian**, which will become the female reproductive anatomy, and the **Wolffian**, or male system. By the 8th week of prenatal development, the sex chromosomes will start to influence the anatomical and hormonal development of the embryo. Unless acted upon by the Y chromosome, the Müllerian system becomes the "default," and the fetus will develop female reproductive anatomy (Figure 5.1).

The Y chromosome contains a region called the sex determining region of the Y chromosome (SRY). Along with another gene called *Sox9*, the SRY aids in the development of the testes. In the growing testes, Leydig cells begin production of testosterone, which will cause the Wolffian duct system to develop into the epididymis, vas deferens, and seminal vesicles. Some testosterone is converted into dihydro-testosterone (DHT), which leads to the growth of the penis and scrotal sac. Remember, however, that the embryo has an undeveloped version of both male and female internal anatomy. The

Müllerian duct system The prenatal duct system that will become the female uterus, fallopian tubes, and upper vagina.

Wolffian duct system The prenatal duct system that will become the male epididymis, vas deferens, and seminal vesicles.

Anti-Müllerian hormone A hormone, secreted from the testes, that prevents the development of the female reproductive duct system.

Sertoli cells of the testes produce **anti-Müllerian hormone (AMH)**, which prevents development of the female duct system (Figure 5.2).

As far as we know, there is no special hormone necessary for a fetus to develop a female reproductive anatomy. If there is no Y chromosome, the Müllerian duct system will develop into the uterus, fallopian tubes, and upper portion of the vagina. Low levels of androgens will lead to the degeneration of the Wolffian system. The *Dax1* gene may also play a role in development of the female anatomy (Goodfellow, 1999).

By the end of the 12th week, genitalia have been differentiated and are usually identifiable as male or female.

Sex and Gender Differences— How Significant Are They?

After completion of this section, you will be able to . . .

O List some physiological differences between males and females and identify the health consequences of these differences.

O Define the terms *stereotypes* and *sexism*.

O List some behavioral differences between men and women.

O Recognize that experience and learning can cause small, innate gender differences to become larger.

O Compare and contrast the biological and social foundations of possible sex and gender differences.

O Evaluate the current research regarding the differences between men and women.

One of the liveliest debates among those who study human sexuality concerns the differences between men and women. Male and female physiological variations might best be described as differences in sex, whereas behavioral dissimilarities are better described as gender differences. However, biological factors may influence behaviors, and social situations can affect our physiology. Also, those looking for an answer to the "nature–nurture" debate will be disappointed; few, if any, human behaviors can be explained by a solely biological or an exclusively cultural basis. Nature and nurture interact; biological differences may influence men and women's abilities, and different societal opportunities dictate the activities men and women perform, thus changing their brains and bodies. As an example: males may be born with a small, innate advantage over females in their ability to visualize objects rotated in space. But the toys, sports, and games that boys are exposed to enhance this natural ability and widen the gap between males and females by the time a boy grows to be a man (Eliot, 2009).

Due to X inactivation in females, sons are actually genetically closer to their mothers than daughters are. A daughter expresses only half of her mother's X chromosomes (and half of her father's), whereas a son expresses all of the genes on his mother's X chromosome. Also, males are more closely related genetically to their mothers than to their fathers, because the X chromosome is larger than the Y, so males have more of their mother's than their father's genes operating in them.

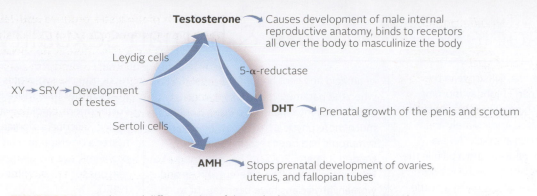

Testosterone → Causes development of male internal reproductive anatomy, binds to receptors all over the body to masculinize the body

Leydig cells

5-α-reductase

XY → SRY → Development of testes

DHT → Prenatal growth of the penis and scrotum

Sertoli cells

AMH → Stops prenatal development of ovaries, uterus, and fallopian tubes

FIGURE 5.2 Prenatal sexual differentiation of the male. (© Cengage Learning 2013)

Brain: Many areas of the brain are **sexually dimorphic**, meaning they differ in size in men and women. Parts of the frontal cortex (involved in reasoning and decision making) and the hippocampus (important in memory) are larger in women, while males in general have larger parietal lobes (involved in spatial perception) and amygdalae, which are important in anger, fear, and sex drive (Goldstein, Seidman, Horton, Makris, & Kennedy, et al., 2001; Gur, Turetsky, Matsuui, Yan, & Bilker, et al., 1999).

Blood: Males are able to carry more oxygen in their blood than women due to their higher blood volume and hemoglobin count.

Pulmonary: Men have greater lung capacity and take fewer breaths per minute than women.

Basal metabolism and weight: Men have a higher metabolic rate than women, in part due to their higher percentage of skeletal muscle. After weight loss, men have higher levels of leptin, a hormone that causes the body to feel full (Nicklas, Katzel, Ryan, Dennis & Goldberg, 1997). This may partially explain why women are more likely to gain weight back after dieting.

Senses: Females have a slightly stronger sense of hearing than males (Cassidy & Ditty, 2001) and have a greater sensitivity to odors (Doty, Shaman, Applebaum, Giberson, & Sikorski, et al., 1984). Overall, males have sharper vision than females; they are especially better at detecting slight motions within the visual field. Most of these sensory differences are small.

Skin: Women have thinner skin and are less prone to acne than males. Women have more adipose (fat). They sweat less copiously but more effectively than males, and their sweat is more alkaline than males'.

Cardiovascular: Women have a faster heart beat and lower blood pressure than males.

Digestive: Food moves through a woman's body more slowly than through a man's. Men secrete more stomach acid while women have more cholesterol in their bile and are more prone to gall bladder disease.

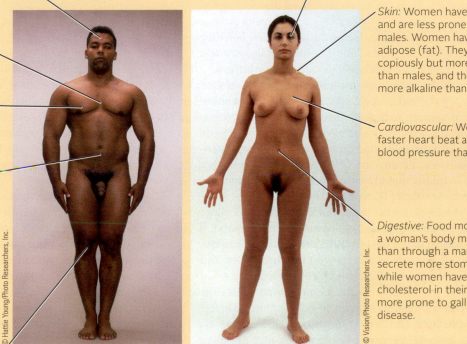

© Hattie Young/Photo Researchers, Inc.

© Vision/Photo Researchers, Inc.

Bones and joints: The higher density of bones in men makes them less likely to have osteoporosis. Female athletes are more likely to have knee injuries than are male athletes due to a woman's wider pelvis, weaker musculature, and joints.

Drug metabolism: Women have much less of the enzyme that breaks down alcohol and will consequently become more intoxicated on the same amount of alcohol than will a man. On the other hand, amphetamines seem to show a more powerful effect on males, increasing more of the pleasure-causing neurotransmitter dopamine into their brains (Munro, McCaul, Wong, Oswald, & Zhou, et al., 2006). Cigarette smoking is more dangerous for women than for men. Controlling for the number of cigarettes smoked, female smokers are 20%-72% more likely than male smokers to develop lung cancer (Legato, 2002).

FIGURE 5.3 Physiological differences between males and females.

Physiological Differences Between Males and Females

Some physical differences between the sexes are obvious, and some are not so obvious; scientists now know that adult males and females vary in almost every organ of the body (Figure 5.3).

Regardless of the fact that women are not simply "little men," historically, most medical research has been done on males (Legato, 2002). This may be because when designing a research study, scientists try to eliminate as many confounding factors as possible; for example, where a female is in her menstrual cycle could affect

James, 65, and Teresa, 64, arrive in the emergency room early Monday morning. James feels a crushing pain in his chest and left arm. He is treated immediately and aggressively for a heart attack. Teresa reports heartburn, nausea, and a pain in the jaw and shoulders. Although she is also having a heart attack, she is given a bottle of antacid and sent home. Later that day, when the paramedics wheel her unconscious body into the ER, Teresa will suffer much more physical harm than if her early symptoms had been recognized and treated (Legato, 2002). The symptoms of a heart attack are often different in men and women; physicians have been taught to recognize the symptoms typically felt by males rather than those felt by females. Furthermore, cardiologists are twice as likely to ascribe a woman's symptoms to hysteria or emotion than to physical problems, even when tests show physical reasons for the symptoms (Tobin et al., 1987).

a study's results. Also, scientists want to avoid potential dangers of testing drugs on females who may be or may become pregnant. Nevertheless, health professionals and scientists must consider the wide array of physical differences between the male and female body to best treat all people.

Male mortality is greater than female mortality at every stage of life. Although more males are conceived than females—about 120 males for every 100 females—male fetuses have a higher mortality rate and there are about 105 males *born* for every 100 females (Martin et al., 2009). At birth, males are at a greater risk than females for cerebral palsy, premature birth, and stillbirth, although the exact reason for this is unknown (Johnston & Hagberg, 2007; Zeitlan et al., 2002). Males also have more developmental disorders such as autism, Tourette's syndrome, and hyperactivity disorder; they also have more X-linked genetic disorders such as hemophilia and Duchenne muscular dystrophy. Rates of diabetes, alcoholism, ulcers, and lung cancers are more common in males, and males are more likely than females to die of accidents or suicide (Kraemer, 2000).

The same medication may have a different effect on males and females. For example, a daily low dose of aspirin reduces the risk of heart attacks in males but lowers the incidence of stroke in females (Berger et al., 2006). This may be because males and females metabolize the drug differently.

Females have a lower threshold for pain than males do. Women report pain with milder stimuli, describe it more fully, feel it longer, and tolerate it less well (Fillingim, 2000; Mogil et al., 2003). Although women feel more pain than men, men are more likely to ask for and receive medications such as morphine to relieve their postsurgical pain; women are more likely to be thought to be complaining unnecessarily. In addition to genetic, cellular, anatomical, and hormonal differences in pain perception in males and females, cultural conditioning is also at work. After experiencing an injury, boys are much more likely to be told to "take it like a man" and "work through the pain" than are girls, who are more likely to be coddled. Pain sensitivity is also dependent on environmental factors: men report less pain if they are observed by an attractive female scientist than if they are observed by a male (Fillingim & Maixner, 1995).

When they are being treated in a health care setting, males and females may be affected differently by similar behaviors. For example, female hospital patients responded positively when touched by a health care practitioner, whereas male patients reacted negatively (Whitcher & Fisher, 1979). Finally, women are more likely to seek health care, and men are more likely to ignore problems that could be treated; this in part contributes to the longer life expectancy of women.

Behavioral Differences Between Men and Women

Alex and Chris have been dating for 6 months. A talented athlete, Alex is decisive, independent, and competitive. Chris is gentle, kind, and tries to be patient and helpful. Chris has the tendency to let Alex take charge.

Did you unconsciously decide that Chris is female and Alex is male? Disregarding (for now) your probable built-in view that a couple consists of a male and a female, how did you come to your gender assumptions?

Gender roles are the gender-specific behaviors and personalities that are expected in our culture. Often, people hold gender role **stereotypes**, which are oversimplified, preconceived ideas about the way men and women "should" act in society. **Sexism**, an inflexible and often negative view of a person based on his or her sex, can lead to discrimination against one sex. It is a sad fact that women in the United States still earn less than men who work in the same profession: a full-time female worker in the United States earns about 78% of what the average full-time male worker makes, even though the average female full-time employee actually has more education than the male (Cloud, 2008). Conservatives claim the wage discrepancy exists because women choose careers in which they don't have to work long hours so they can take time for their families. Liberals claim the gap is due to sex discrimination. It's hard to determine which viewpoint is correct, but a recent study took an innovative approach. What if you could construct an experiment in which employees changed their sex before work one day, and then observed the effect it had on their salary (Cloud, 2008)? Researchers Kristen Schilt and Matthew Wiswall looked at salaries of transsexuals, before and after their transition to the other sex. They found that men who became women earned almost 12% less after transitioning, whereas women who became men earned 7.5% more. Schilt tells the story of Susan, a lawyer who remained at the same law firm after transitioning to a man and becoming Thomas. A colleague at the firm mistakenly thought that Susan had been fired and Thomas had taken her place. This

Stereotype An oversimplified, preconceived idea about a group of individuals.

Sexism A belief that one sex is inferior to the other, often characterized by discriminatory or abusive behavior toward the other sex.

Boys and girls often act out their aggression in different ways. Studies have shown that boys may be more physically aggressive, but girls are socially aggressive. The movie *Mean Girls* shows the way that female aggression affects relationships.

attorney commended the head of the firm for the replacement, saying that Susan had been incompetent, but the "new guy" was "just delightful" (Schilt, 2006, p. 476).

How much have the stereotypical images of men and women affected your worldview? Imagine a different person that typifies each of the following characteristics: aggressive, risk-taker, empathetic, emotional, good at math, highly sexed. For which of these did you visualize a male and for which a female?

Beyond the physiological, are men and women more alike or more different? Conventional wisdom says that the two sexes differ in ways other than the physiological, although much research contradicts this. Professor Janet Shibley Hyde suggests that males and females are actually much more alike than they are different (Hyde, 2005; Petersen & Hyde, 2010). Dr. Hyde performed a **meta-analysis** on the studies of psychological gender differences. She found that while there are gender differences in many psychological variables, for the vast majority of factors, the *degree* of these differences is so small as to be negligible. When differences do exist, it is hard to determine if the disparity is primarily biological or societal. Any innate differences that may exist are surely influenced by society, which exaggerates these differences. The human brain shows remarkable **plasticity**, which means that it changes and adapts to experiences. Every action, task, and memory reinforces certain brain circuits at the expense of other circuits. So while the brains of infant boys and girls may be quite similar, over the course of a lifetime, social interactions and experiences will encourage some neural patterns and inhibit others, exaggerating what may have been small or nonexistent innate differences.

In this section, we'll consider some behavioral differences between males and females, and the biological and societal causes for these ostensible disparities.

> "... an individual's capacities emerge from a web of interactions between the biological being and the social environment. Within this web, connecting threads move in both directions."
> (Anne Fausto-Sterling, 1992, p. 8)

Aggression

Most people consider males to be more aggressive than females.

In reality, both males and females are aggressive, but may exhibit their aggression in different ways. Physical aggression involves physically hurting or threatening another, whereas **social aggression** refers to hurting others by damaging their relationships. Social aggression may include friendship manipulation, social exclusion, sending harassing text messages, and spreading malicious gossip. It can also refer to nonverbal acts such as eye rolling and looks of disdain. Although research has consistently shown that males are more physically aggressive, both males and females report being victims of social aggression, usually by peers of the same gender (Carlo et al., 1999; Paquette & Underwood, 1999). However, social aggression seems to be more upsetting to girls than to boys (Paquette & Underwood, 1999).

Why are males more physically aggressive? Although most people believe that testosterone causes violent behavior, as we learned in Chapter 3, testosterone's effect on human aggression is not clear (Archer, 2006; Simpson, 2001). Males are also considered more aggressive than females because most studies of human aggression have been performed on men, by men. When researchers have studied women, they often measured women's aggression by incidents of male-typical physical aggression, and have therefore reported women as being less aggressive. Women have the potential to be as aggressive as men, but women may be under more social restrictions in the expression of their aggression (Richardson & Hammock, 2007). When subjects were asked to play a video game in which they could drop bombs on an opponent, females dropped fewer bombs. However, when subjects' identities were hidden and they were aware that their actions were anonymous, females actually dropped more bombs than males did (Lightdale & Prentice, 1994). It is worth noting that while women describe aggression as a loss of self-control, men view it as a way

Meta-analysis A statistical method of combining and evaluating a large body of research on a related issue.

Plasticity The characteristic of the brain that allows it to change and reorganize with experience.

Social aggression Also called *relational aggression*, this type of aggression involves the causing of harm by intentionally damaging one's relationship with others.

of imposing control over others (Astin, Redston, & Campbell, 2003).

Risk Taking

The "Darwin Awards" are given to people who "improve the human genome by removing themselves from it in a spectacularly stupid manner." Past winners have met their demise through perilous pursuits such as playing catch with rattlesnakes or using a lighter to examine the inside of a fuel tank. The vast majority of Darwin Award winners are male.

Males are more likely than females to engage in risky behaviors, even if there is no apparent gain to the action. In one study, college-aged men and women were asked to toss a ring onto a pole from any distance they chose. On average, the women stood only 1 to 2 feet away, which increased their chances of success. Men, however, took a riskier position and stood 5 to 10 feet from the pole. When these males were observed by other males, they stepped back even farther, heightening the risk of failure still more (Sorentino, Hewitt, & Raso-Knott, 1992). This risk-taking phenomenon is observed in our closest evolutionary cousins; it is the male monkey that chatters to his buddies, "hey, watch me leap from this branch to that one on the other side of the jungle," while the female monkeys shake their heads as his poor monkey body goes crashing to the ground.

So, why are males greater risk-takers than females? Some suggest that evolutionary factors underlie these behaviors. Males may need to make themselves stand out in order to win the (reproductive) favor of the female. Due to evolutionary forces, women are twice as likely to reproduce as men are. So while a female can play it safe and be reasonably assured that she will pass on her genes, a male has to make a splash and get noticed in order to reproduce. The *type* of risky behavior men participate in may be important: A man who leaps heroically into a river to save a drowning child will win more favor with women than a man who runs up and pokes a grizzly bear with a stick just to see what will happen. Farthing (2005) found that although both men and women considered those who took "heroic" risks to be more attractive than heroic-risk avoiders, men also preferred friends who took nonheroic or pointless risks, while women did not. However, taking nonheroic physical risks may raise a man's status in his peer group, which would indirectly make him more attractive to women.

Testosterone may also increase risk-taking behavior. Men who have been exposed to more testosterone in the womb earn more as financial traders and make the most money on days when the market is particularly volatile, requiring quick decisions and the ability to take risks (Coates, Gurnell, & Rustichini, 2009). Testosterone doesn't seem to affect women's risky behaviors in the same way (Zethraeus et al., 2009).

Social factors also affect daring behavior. Women are more likely to underestimate their abilities; men tend to overestimate their abilities (Visser, Ashton, & Vernon, 2008; Blanch et al., 2008). In movies, men are shown making gravity-defying leaps across rooftops in order to get the bad guys and save the girl, while women are more often portrayed as helpless ninnies who won't even get out of the street when a bus is zooming at them. Daily stereotypical images will feed into and influence our view of "appropriate" behaviors.

Navigation

It is a well-known stereotype that men in our society won't ask for directions. This may or may not be accurate, but it *is* true that males and females navigate differently. Males navigate with vectors ("Go three miles north, then turn west"), whereas females use landmarks ("Go straight through five stoplights, then turn left at the green house"). When navigating, females are more likely to use the more advanced cortex; men rely on more primitive areas of the brain such as the hippocampus (Maguire, Burgess, & O'Keefe, 1999; Sax, 2005).

Response to Stress

Males respond to stressful situations with a mechanism known as **"fight or flight"**; females respond differently to stress, using a response that's been called **"tend and befriend"** by Shelley Taylor and colleagues (Taylor et al., 2000). The **sympathetic nervous system's** fight-or-flight response has long been considered

"Fight or flight" Long considered to be the instinctual response of humans when survival is threatened, this is now thought to better characterize a male's behavioral response to danger.

"Tend and befriend" A behavioral pattern in response to stress that involves tending offspring and seeking out others for joint protection. This better characterizes the female response to stress or threat.

Sympathetic nervous system The branch of the autonomic nervous system that prepares the body for emergency, stress, activity, and excitement.

> "The secret of realizing the greatest fruitfulness and the greatest enjoyment of existence is to live dangerously! Build your cities on the slopes of Vesuvius! Send your ships out into uncharted seas! Live in conflict with your equals and with yourselves!"
> —Friedrich Nietzsche (a male), 1887

Lost, but too embarrassed to stop and ask for directions. Another sufferer of directile dysfunction.

the way a human body responds to stress. However, almost all research done on this system has been performed on males. Fight-or-flight may be an adaptive response to dangerous situations for males, but perhaps not for females. For most of human history, females have spent much of their adult lives either pregnant or caring for young. Fleeing from an attacker may not make adaptive sense, requiring as it might the abandonment of their young. Fighting an attacker might also be inappropriate, given a female's lesser physical strength and aggression compared to males. Instead, women may respond to stress by nurturing themselves and their offspring, and by creating and maintaining social networks. The hormone oxytocin, known to lower blood pressure, fear, and anxiety, and to enhance relaxation and bonding behaviors, may be at the core of this tending response. The effects of oxytocin are decreased by testosterone and maintained by estrogen (Taylor et al., 2000).

Emotional Expression

Although there is a perception that females experience more emotions than males, this has not been confirmed by research, although men and women may differ in the frequency in which they report certain emotions (Simon & Nath, 2004). Men report more frequent positive emotions than women, while women report more frequent negative feelings than men (Simon & Nath, 2004). Women also report that they *express* emotions more than men; societal and physiological influences may limit men's verbalization of their emotions. Think of the cold, impassive images of males presented to boys as the ideal to which they should aspire. Keanu Reeves seems barely able to register concern as he fights for the future of the world in the *Matrix*. Arnold Schwarzenegger in the Terminator movies was, quite literally, a machine. A small boy is told to "man up and stop crying," but a small girl may be gathered in her daddy's arms and comforted while she cries.

Actually, infant boys tend to be fussier and more emotionally expressive than young girls, but they are socialized throughout their lives to show less emotion (Eliot, 2009). This does not mean that men don't experience emotions, just that their expression may be more internalized. Compared to women, men undergo greater increases in heart rate, blood pressure, and sweating when confronted with highly emotional situations. Physiologically, some studies suggest that emotions may be processed differently in the brains of male and female adolescents

(Sax, 2005; Schneider, Habel, Kessler, Salloum, & Posse, 2000), but much more research needs to be done before we make any generalizations.

American women are 2 to 3 times more likely to be diagnosed with depression than American men. Again, both cultural and biological factors may underlie this finding. Women in our society are more encouraged to express emotions and will seek health care and treatment more than men, perhaps accounting for this higher *diagnosis* of depression in women. Biologically, depression is associated with low levels of a neurotransmitter called serotonin. It appears that men synthesize serotonin at a rate 52% higher than that of women, which may lower their risk of depression (Nishizawa et al., 1997).

Social Interactions

Social scientists often use the phrase "face to face" to describe friendships in girls and women, while "shoulder to shoulder" better describes the friendships of boys and men. What this means is that women's relationships are likely to involve conversations and personal self-disclosure. For girls and women, a game or activity is simply an excuse to get together; for boys and men the game or activity is central to the relationship. Men are more likely to be friends with others who share their interest in some activity, and their gatherings will focus on their shared interests rather than on the conversation. In addition, women are more likely to maintain a small number of intimate relationships; men are more likely to have wider, but more shallow, social circles (Baumeister, 2007). You can even see this on the playground: girls are more likely to play one-on-one and less likely to let others into their small social circles, while boys play in groups.

Communication

© Blend Images/Alamy

© Dan Kenyon/Getty Images

In 1991 Deborah Tannen published *You Just Don't Understand*, which illustrated how males and females have different communication styles. In her book Tannen describes a man and woman having a conversation as they drive along in a car. The woman asks, "Do you want to stop and get a drink?" The man, not being thirsty, says "no" and drives on. The woman, who actually meant, "I'm thirsty. Let's stop and get a drink," seethes silently about her inconsiderate partner (Tannen, 1991).

One generally accepted stereotype concerning conversational differences between Western men and women is the idea that women are more likely to ask questions to ensure the flow of conversation, and men are more likely to make direct statements of fact. Deborah Tannen called this "rapport talk and report talk," and suggested that while women see conversation as a means of sharing and connecting, men are more likely to see it as a means to transmit information and be seen as an expert. Other conversational stereotypes include the assumption that men interrupt more than women, that women are more likely to nod or say "mm hmm" to indicate that they are listening, and that men are more likely to challenge or dispute their conversational partner's statements. Men and women may also process nonverbal communication signals differently; women are thought to be better than men at interpreting facial expressions and more likely to respond to nonverbal cues such as tone of voice or facial expression (McClure, 2000). Differences in conversational styles between men and women can lead to misinterpretations of meaning.

However, many people argue that there are no conclusive gender differences in communication (Canary & Hause, 1993), and that any perceived differences either are small, due solely to social role expectations, or are methodological artifacts. For example, when males and females were put into a group, stereotypical gender patterns of communication existed for the first 30–60 minutes (a typical length of time for communication studies). But when group interaction continued for more than an hour, these stereotypical sex differences vanished (Wheelan & Verdi, 1992).

Cognitive Differences

In 2005 Lawrence Summers, then president of Harvard University, angered many people when he suggested that women have less innate mathematical and scientific ability than men. His statement produced a storm of controversy regarding the cognitive abilities of women and men. Some studies have showed women to be superior in verbal abilities such as reading comprehension and spelling, and men to excel in spatial relationships and the manipulation of visual images (Halpern & LaMay, 2000; Kimura, 1992). Although there may be some small, inborn differences in biological factors that affect academic achievement, societal factors such as one's learning environment, income level, or encouragement by others play a much larger role in students' school performance.

Testosterone may improve performance on spatial tasks and hinder verbal abilities. Men perform more poorly on tests of spatial relations during the spring, when testosterone levels are lowest (Kimura, 2002). Women's spatial test scores vary with their menstrual cycles, and are best at times of lowest estrogen and highest testosterone (Hausmann, Slabbehoorn, Van Goozen,

Stereotype threat The fear that one will perform negatively on a task and that this will confirm an existing stereotype of a group with which one identifies.

Although it is a cultural stereotype that women speak more than men, a recent study found no significant difference between the sexes in the number of words spoken each day (Mehl, Vazire, Ramirez-Esparza, Slatcher, & Pennebaker, 2007). In mixed-gender groups, men actually talk more than women (Caspi, Chajut, & Saporta, 2008).

Everyone says that boys are better in math and girls are better in English. But in my high school, our Advanced Placement calculus class was mostly girls. What's really going on?

Cohen-Kettenis, & Gunturkun, 2000). Testosterone has been shown to increase the growth of the right hemisphere of the brain, which is more efficient at processing spatial relationships, and slow the development of the left hemisphere, which is dominant for language. When male subjects were asked to list as many words as possible that began with a certain letter, those subjects with highest testosterone levels listed the fewest, and their lower testosterone peers were able to list more (Lamoureaux & Boucher, 2006). Language may also be processed differently in boys and girls. While girls process both written and spoken language in the same part of the brain, boys showed greater brain activity in specific brain areas—auditory or visual—depending on the way the word was presented (Burman, Bitan, & Booth, 2008). This could account for quicker processing of language in adolescent girls, although there is no evidence that this difference persists into adulthood.

In the past, boys were thought to be better than girls in math, outscoring them on school and standardized tests; in the 1980s, thirteen times more boys than girls scored over 700 on the math portion of the SAT. That number has dropped steadily and is now about three to one (Halpern et al., 2007), and there is no longer any significant difference in boys' and girls' scores on math tests in grades 2–11 (Hyde, Lindberg, Linn, Ellis, & Williams, 2008). Such a rapid change is powerful support *against* a theory of biological difference in male and female math ability. Academic achievement in any subject is strongly influenced by social factors such as variations in training and experience, self-confidence, motivation, and gender-role socialization. How your teacher feels about math may even influence your achievement. The math anxiety of first- and second-grade female teachers from one school district was assessed. At the beginning of the school year, there was no relation between a teacher's math anxiety and her students' math achievement. But by the end of year, the more anxious female teachers were about their own math skills, the more likely that their female students (but not male students) agreed that "boys are good at math and girls are good at reading." Girls who accepted that belief scored lower on math tests than those who had not developed the stereotype (Beilock, Gunderson, & Levine, 2010).

Luigi Guiso and colleagues examined the math and reading test scores in 40 countries, and found that in more gender-equal countries, the gender gap in math scores has disappeared. Interestingly, in these countries, the girls' reading scores also improved, *increasing* the gender gap for reading (Guiso, Monte, Sapienza, & Zingales, 2008).

Societal perceptions can influence a person's performance. In the United States, women are generally perceived to be weaker in math than men; this **stereotype threat** often becomes a self-fulfilling prophecy. A number of studies have supported the influence of stereotype threat. College-aged students who had similar backgrounds in math were asked to take a math test. One group of students was told that in the past, men had scored higher on the test than women did; the other group was told that men and women performed equally well on the test. Male and female students who believed that the test was gender-fair scored equally well on the test, but the females who believed that they would score lower than males on the test did, in fact, do just that (Spencer, Steele, & Quinn, 1999). A recent study found that if test takers were asked "what is your sex?" at the *end* of the Advanced Placement calculus exam rather than at the beginning, 4,700 more girls could qualify for AP calculus credit each year (Danaher & Crandall, 2008).

Sexuality

Pornography and romance novels are billion dollar industries. Males are the primary consumers of pornography, and most romance novels are read by women. Both porn and romance novels contain a lot of sex; however, the context differs. Pornography is usually characterized by impersonal, casual sexual encounters outside of the context of a relationship (Typical dialogue: "Ding dong! The pizza's here! Oh, aren't you a handsome pizza delivery man. Let's have sex right now.'") Romance novels also contain their share of sex, but it is in the context of a loving romantic relationship (Typical dialogue: "Tristan's throbbing manhood was evidence of his passionate devotion for Bethany. Try as he might, he could never forget her milky mounds of desire. He would scale the highest mountain, if only she would belong to him forever.")

The dominant cultural stereotype is that men are more likely to initiate sex and be more sexually aggressive. Once a male hits puberty, society expects him to be almost perpetually aroused, and to seek out as many sexual partners as possible. Although there is no biological evidence that women are less arousable, a common perception is that women are not as highly sexed as men.

Compared with women, men report having more frequent sexual fantasies and feelings. Men are more likely than women to masturbate, and men report desiring sex more often than their female partners (Lippa, 2006). Gay men admit having sex more often than do lesbians (Bryant & Demian, 1994). Men also desire a larger number of sexual partners than women do; this phenomenon has been observed in 52 countries around the world (Schmitt et al., 2003).

Who is smarter, men or women? In early versions of the Stanford-Binet IQ test, women had a slight tendency to score higher than men. The questions that caused this discrepancy were identified and removed (Rose, 2009). Today, both males and females perform similarly on general intelligence tests, although males routinely overestimate and women underestimate their own intelligence (Furnham, 2001).

_____
_____
_____
_____
_____

A committed relationship seems to be a more important foundation for sexuality for women than for men. "Women's sexuality tends to be strongly linked to a close relationship. For women, an important goal of sex is intimacy; the best context for pleasurable sex is a committed relationship. This is less true for men" (Peplau, 2003, p. 38). Some suggest that the sexual act in and of itself is what is important for adolescent boys, while the outcomes and consequences of sex, such as relationships or social standing, are more important to teenage girls (Eyre & Millstein, 1999).

There are both biological and cultural explanations for these findings. Different regions of the brain may be stimulated when males and females view erotic materials. When watching erotic film clips, men showed increased activity in the more primitive hypothalamus and thalamus; women did not (Karama et al., 2002). Sociobiological theory suggests that it is most adaptive for males to desire and have sex with a larger number of partners. A male who slept with 100 females in a year would have the potential for 100 offspring to carry on his genes. A monogamous male would at most have one child in that same time. Sexual strategies theory states that it is not adaptive, however, for females to be promiscuous (Schmitt et al., 2003). A woman who slept with 100 men and a woman who slept with one man would still have the potential to carry only one child. However, the likelihood of the single partner helping the monogamous woman raise her child is theoretically higher than the likelihood of one of the scores of men who slept with the promiscuous woman helping her raise what is most likely not his child.

Social expectations also play a strong role in sexual desire. In most cultures, males are expected to be more sexually aggressive and promiscuous than females, and to be the initiator in sexual encounters. Penalties for women who are demonstrative in their sexuality may range from mild social censure to death. Female sexuality tends to be more easily changed by cultural and situational factors than male sexuality (Diamond, 2008; Peplau, 2003). The possibility also exists that some of the sex differences in self-reports of sexuality may not be due to actual differences in behavior, but rather to men's and women's different reporting of their behaviors.

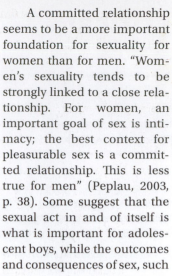

"Women need a reason to have sex. Men just need a place."
—Billy Crystal

critical evaluation

Are gender differences biologically or socially constructed? Are they innate, preprogrammed traits, or are they the result of cultural expectations and the environment in which we are raised? The following considerations should be kept in mind when evaluating gender research.

> **Research design** Are the subjects aware of being observed? Are their responses anonymous? When subjects are assured of their anonymity, their responses are much less likely to conform to expectations related to stereotypical gender roles. As we've seen, women act less aggressively when they think they are being observed than when their behaviors are anonymous (Lightdale & Prentice, 1994). In a study of college students, when female subjects thought others would see their responses, they reported fewer sexual partners than males did. But when female subjects were attached to alleged lie detectors, the women actually reported more partners than the men did (Alexander & Fisher, 2003).

Also, the sex of the investigator can affect the results; subjects may give different responses to the same question depending on whether the investigator is a man or a woman (Fisher, 2007).

> **The subjects** The age of the subjects may influence the results. Brain regions associated with language and fine motor skills develop up to 6 years earlier in girls than in boys, and brain areas related to visual targeting and spatial memory develop earlier in boys (Hanlon, Thatcher & Cline, 1999). Some cognitive differences between males and females are most strongly seen in children, and may diminish with age. Other cognitive differences may increase with age, as societal forces influence males' and females' interests and achievements.

Most gender and sexuality studies are conducted with white, middle-class college students as subjects. Scientists must be careful not to overgeneralize results. Results are most likely to be overgeneralized (be attributable to "all men" or "all women") when they conform to stereotypically expected behaviors.

> **Data analysis** Some differences in behavior may be more related to factors such as the relative status of the subjects, rather than to their gender. Therefore, the stereotypically confident, assertive male and the passive, pleasing female may be playing out their roles as supervisor and subordinate rather than displaying a true difference in the sexes.

With most gender differences, there is much more variation within groups than between groups. That means there is a wider range of math abilities between the highest and lowest scoring males than between the average male and average female. This is seen in many behaviors, including aggression, empathy, and cognition (Petersen & Hyde, 2010; Hyde, 1984, 2005).

How significant is the finding? If statistical differences are found in certain behaviors, does this have any practical meaning in the real world? Many gender differences show only a small effect size; although there may be statistical disparities between men and women, there is much more overlap and similarity in their behaviors than there are differences (Hyde, 2005). As an example, Figure 5.4 shows the distribution for a sex difference that would be considered moderately strong. Of the many psychological sex differences that have been measured, 77% are *smaller* than the difference represented by the curves in Figure 5.4.

> **Correlation and causation** These are not the same thing and it's important to be careful about the difference between the two. Let's say that someone

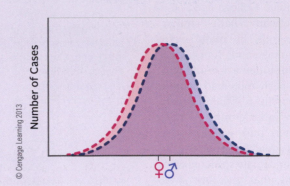

FIGURE 5.4 This graph shows the distribution for a gender difference that would be considered moderately strong. You can see that there is a great deal of overlap, and that even though this difference would be considered statistically significant, the actual discrepancy between the average male and the average female is much smaller than the range within each sex.

exposed prenatally to high amounts of testosterone is more likely to become an engineer (i.e., there is a *correlation* between high prenatal testosterone and becoming an engineer). That doesn't mean that testosterone *causes* technological abilities; after all, there is a correlation between fetal testosterone levels and who's wearing pink or blue pampers, but that doesn't mean the relationship is causal (Eliot, 2009).

> **The bias of the researcher** The way a question is worded can show a researcher's preconceptions. Simon Baron-Cohen (2003) found that males were more likely than females to agree with the question "If I were buying a car, I would want to obtain specific information about its engine capacity." From this, he concluded that men are more likely than women to systemize information. But perhaps such a question better measures the interest of the subject toward the information, rather than the way the subject sorts out data. Would he have obtained the same result if the question was, "When I purchase sheets, I want specific information about the material and thread count"?

The behavior that is studied and the way the behavior is defined can reveal a scientist's preconceived notions about gender. For example, the phrase "maternal deprivation" may be used when discussing children of mothers who work outside the home, but the similar phrase "paternal deprivation" is not used to describe children of employed fathers. What does this different use of language tell you about the scientist's opinions about working mothers and working fathers?

Also, scientists may expect to see gender-specific behaviors, and be more likely to notice and report these characteristics than characteristics that don't meet their expectations.

> **Reporting of the data** Which book sounds more interesting: *Men Are from Mars, Women Are from Venus* or *Humans Are from Earth?* Researchers tend to look for differences rather than similarities, and if a scientist were to find a *lack* of difference in a characteristic (such as math ability), this finding is less likely to be published than if he or she found a difference.

> Scientist Simon Baron-Cohen is the first cousin of Sacha Baron-Cohen, better known by his alter egos Borat, Ali G, and Brüno.

> "The fact is that human behavior is an extremely complex mix of genes, hormones, environments, relationships, situations, drives, motivations—a vast, churning stew . . . We are all products of both nature and nurture, constantly interacting." —Caryl Rivers, Journalism Professor, 2006

Development of Gender Roles Across the Life Span

After completion of this section, you will be able to . . .

- ○ Define the term *gender schema*.
- ○ Catalogue the ways in which gender roles are reinforced.
- ○ Recognize that views of masculinity and femininity are culturally constructed and subject to change.

FIGURE 5.5 Clothing color worn by infants, by percentage (Shakin, Shakin, and Sternglanz, 1985).

Jason and Heather Cooper are playing in the Springfield Elementary dodgeball tournament. Jason whips the ball at the other team, bashing an opponent in the head. "Way to go, Jason!" calls his dad. His mother proudly turns to a neighbor on the bleachers and says, "He's so active. He's quite a competitor." Heather catches a ball thrown at her by the other team and hurls it back, knocking down a member of the other team. Heather's mom turns to her husband, horrified. "Why is she so aggressive?" With the opposing team's return rally, a ball smashes Jason in the face, and his dad calls out, "Suck it up. Walk it off, boy!" When Heather is then hit in the back with the ball, Heather's mother runs onto the court. "Stop the game! Heather, are you hurt? You shouldn't play this any game anymore. Come home, I bought you an Easy-Bake oven."

Of course, this is an extreme example, but almost from the moment of birth, a child's sex determines how he or she will be treated, including the way he or she is spoken to, the toys he or she is given, the chores he or she is assigned, and even the color of his or her clothing (Figure 5.5).

> "I was at a party and a woman there had a new baby. 'Oh, what a pretty baby,' I exclaimed. The mother scowled a bit, and then I noticed the blue cap on the baby. 'He's so handsome!' I amended, and the mother smiled." —Author's files

From an early age, children learn that men and women are "supposed to" act in certain ways. How do children acquire these stereotypes? Sandra Bem (1981) suggests that we develop **gender schemas**, an understanding of what it means to be male or female, from our interactions with others in our society. From the day we are born, we compartmentalize information about gender into a set of beliefs about men and women. For instance, one young child may learn that "Women are soft. They stay at home and take care of children. Men are strong and have jobs and yell at the TV." Through observation, a child learns that certain careers, behaviors, physical characteristics, and even objects are "appropriate" for one gender or another. In one study, 8- and 9-year-old children watched as adult role models chose one item each from 16 pairs of objects. When the children were then asked their own preference for items in the set, the boys chose the items that were selected by the adult men significantly more than the girls did (Perry & Bussey, 1979). As a child's worldview enlarges, more information broadens his or her gender schema, and many experiences are viewed through the "lens" of gender. Gender-appropriate behaviors are reinforced and encouraged, and gender-inappropriate actions are condemned. Children begin to judge themselves according to their view of gender-appropriate characteristics; children whose self-concept is consistent with the prevailing societal gender schema are likely to have higher self-esteem than children whose characteristics don't match society's views.

Reinforcement of gender roles comes from various sources. Parents, peers, teachers, the media, as well as religious and ethnic group identity all give signals for how we are expected to behave, and help to socialize us into accepted gender roles.

Very few parents sit down with their children and say, "Jason, boys are loud and boisterous and play with trucks. Stop being gentle and kind to your sister. And no more expressions of emotion! Heather, you should start feeling more anxious over your appearance. You need to help me out some more in the kitchen and stop expressing your desires. And I don't like this early aptitude for math that you appear to be showing. Cut it out and go write some poetry or something." Rather, **socialization** into gender roles is more subtle. Parents tend to treat girls more tenderly, and speak more harshly to boys. They are more likely to treat girls as if they were fragile—to play less roughly with them and to coddle them more when hurt. Parents may be more restrictive of girls and allow boys to have more freedom (Morrongiello & Dawber, 2000). Fathers are more likely than mothers to pressure their children into gender roles, especially their sons (Lytton & Romney, 1991).

Children are given toys or activities that are considered gender appropriate (Lytton & Romney, 1991). Both societal and biological forces may underlie the choice of certain toys and games for boys and girls. Adults and peers will reinforce the toy choice, and will be supportive of children when they play with toys stereotypically considered appropriate for their gender. Females who enjoy "masculine" activities are more tolerated than are boys who participate in "feminine" activities. It may not just be society that influences gender stereotyping of toys. Studies suggest that children choose gender-traditional toys by the age of 9 months, *before* they have a sense of what gender they actually are, and that even primates show this sex-type preference for toys (Alexander & Hines, 2002; Campbell, Shirley, Heywood, & Crook, 2000; Hassett, Siebert, & Wallen, 2008). One study suggests that gendered toy preference may occur as early as 3–4 months, and that the strength of these preferences correlates with prenatal hormone exposure (Alexander, Wilcox, & Farmer, 2009). Regardless of whether there are biological or societal explanations for toy preference, one study suggests that giving gender-

---

Gender schema Children learn how their culture defines the roles of men and women, and then internalize this knowledge and act accordingly.

Socialization The way people learn and adopt the behavior patterns of their culture.

neutral toys to children doesn't affect their behavior later in life; for example, giving dolls to boys does not turn them into more nurturing men (Lytton & Romney, 1991).

"I believe in gender neutral toys for children. When my children were small I had both 'boy toys' and 'girl toys' available to them. And they played with all of them! But my son would take Barbie and pretend she was a gun and make 'ratatatatat' noises when he aimed her at people, and my daughter would tuck the trucks into a carriage and wheel them around." —Author's files

Conventional wisdom holds that girls are shortchanged in school. It is thought that teachers call on boys more than girls, and that boys receive more help, praise, and attention (Sadker & Sadker, 1994). It is often the case that teachers are likely to assign different tasks and have different expectations for boys and girls in math and English. However, some refute the idea that schools are hurting our girls (Kleinfeld, 1998). Judith Kleinfeld claims that the literature shows no consistent pattern in whether boys or girls receive more attention and that when boys receive more attention it is often of a disciplinary, rather than academic, nature. In fact, men today are more likely to be diagnosed with learning disabilities, more likely to drop out of high school, and less likely to graduate from college than women.

Ethnicity A group of people with common racial, national, religious, or cultural ties.

Race A group of people who are believed to have the same genetic background based on physical characteristics.

Feminine Qualities and behaviors judged by a particular culture to be ideally associated with or especially appropriate to women and girls.

Masculine Qualities and behaviors judged by a particular culture to be ideally associated with or especially appropriate to men and boys.

Androgyny Having both masculine and feminine traits, feelings, and qualities.

Film and television are rife with stereotypical gender roles. Men are shown to be authoritative, active figures, while women appear passive and less capable. Although there are more women than men in the world, more men than women are seen on television overall. Furthermore, women who are shown are limited to a few stereotypical roles (housewife, mother, and receptionist), and when female TV characters are shown to be successful in their careers, they are often depicted as having an unhappy personal life. Although there are more female lawyers and police officers shown on TV than ever before, there is a difference in how they are portrayed; female TV police officers are less likely to be involved in action sequences than their male counterparts. TV representations of male roles are also restricted: Although TV shows us that women can be police officers, firefighters, or doctors, men are rarely shown as nurturers or caretakers. The lack of visibility of these "female" pursuits discourages men from expressing these parts of their personalities, and affords an even lower status to what might be considered "women's work."

In American television commercials, females are depicted as the users of products, whereas males are the professionals and authority figures demonstrating products. Women are more often shown at home with domestic products; men are outdoors with automobiles and sports products. Finally, products that yield social or self-enhancement are aimed at and shown by women, while products that give pleasurable rewards are aimed at and shown by men (Furnham & Mak, 1999). These commercials do more than influence what products we may buy. Consider this study: Male and female college students were shown either several gender-stereotyped commercials—such as a woman who was so excited about a new acne medicine that she bounced on her bed with joy—or gender-neutral commercials for insurance companies or cell phones that had no humans in them. These commercials had nothing to do with math ability, but the women who watched ditzy females in commercials were less likely to express interest in careers such as engineering and computer sciences and more likely to express interest in verbal-related fields such as communications. Women who watched the gender-neutral commercials expressed the opposite preference (Davies, Spencer, & Steele, 2005; Davies et al., 2002).

Religious doctrine is another societal factor that influences our views of males and females. Judaism, Christianity, and Islam all have a tradition of male dominance. In these religions, God himself is considered to be masculine, so in many conservative branches women are banned from becoming rabbis or priests. This is changing in some religious traditions, such as Reform and Conservative Judaism, and many sects of Protestantism. The Latter Day Saints' (Mormon) position on women has changed little in the past two centuries: a woman's place is deemed to be in the home, taking care of husband and children. A Hindu woman is considered to be the property and responsibility of her husband, and she is to act as his servant, mother to his children, his minister in decision-making, and his lover in bed. As the deity in Buddhism is less identified with a particular sex, the role of women in Buddhism is more equal than in many other religions.

Our **ethnicity** may affect the development of gender roles. Although the terms *race* and *ethnicity* are often used interchangeably, there is a difference. **Race** is more related to one's biological descent and physical characteristics, whereas ethnicity describes a group with common racial, national, religious, or cultural ties. For example, if an Asian baby was adopted and raised in Italy, his race

Forty-three percent of undergraduate college students in the United States are male, down from 58% thirty years ago.

ASK YOURSELF

Here are some characteristics associated with the word "female"—loyal, affectionate, compassionate, gentle, understanding—and some characteristics that fit in with society's view of "male"—ambitious, self-sufficient, athletic, independent (Auster & Ohm, 2000). Do any of the characteristics listed for the other gender apply to you?

would be Asian, but his ethnicity Italian, as he would share a language and culture with his adopted country. Based on this definition, gender role development is affected by a person's ethnicity rather than by his or her race.

Stereotypical gender roles are often particularly encouraged in Hispanic American culture. Women are expected to be chaste and selfless, as well as faithful, passive, and subordinate to men. Men are expected to be strong, sexually aggressive, brave, and responsible. Achievement and education are important for both Asian American men and women, but an Asian woman is expected to place family as a higher priority than her own ambitions. Gender roles for African American men and women can be more fluid and egalitarian. The stereotype is that the strength of African American women is key in holding together the family and community (Hill, 2002). The economic relationship between African American men and women is more equal than other ethnic groups (Hill, 2002). This may be in part because under slavery, African American women were not economically dependent on their husbands. Also, unemployment rates for African American men are more than twice that of Caucasian men (Bureau of Labor Statistics, 2007).

Changing Views of Masculinity and Femininity

The notion of what is considered **"masculine"** or **"feminine"** is culturally constructed. In 1974 Sandra Bem devised an **androgyny** scale, composed of traits described as masculine or feminine (Bem, 1974). The world has changed since the 1970s; more women work outside of the home, and more men participate in traditionally female fields. So in 2000 Carol Auster and Susan Ohm reevaluated the Bem scale. They found that 18 out of 20 feminine traits still qualified as "feminine," but only 8 out of 20 male traits still qualified as "masculine" (Auster & Ohm, 2000). Society has changed, and masculine traits are becoming more desirable for both men and women. Traits such as "assertive," "analytical," "athletic," "self-sufficient," and "willing to take a stand" are no longer considered to be the sole province of the male gender. When asked to rate characteristics that they would themselves ideally wish to have, both males and females gave a list that included both stereotypically "masculine" and "feminine" traits. Psychologically androgynous people can exhibit both masculine and feminine traits, and may be able to use a wider range of traits to meet the demands of various situations (Bem, 1974).

What Does It Mean to Be a Man?

According to sociologist Michael Kimmel (2001), the traditional Western ideology of masculinity includes four main points:

- No Sissy Stuff: Household duties, nurturing others, and child rearing are women's work.
- Be a Big Wheel: Strive for wealth, power, status, and sexual success.
- Be a Sturdy Oak: Hide your emotions and be reliable in a crisis. Emulate inanimate objects such as trees, rocks, and pillars.
- Give 'em Hell: Be aggressive, take risks, live life on the edge, and go for it!

As you peruse typical men's magazines like *Maxim* and *FHM* you can certainly see these messages reiterated. Men who read these magazines get the following messages about masculinity: Women are there for your pleasure—score with as many big-breasted beautiful women as you can. Buy the latest electronic gadgets and expensive clothes so you'll look rich and cool. Drink until you get wasted. And above all, take nothing seriously. Maintain a cool and ironic distance at all times (Wisneski, 2007).

Is this what it means to be a man? How do men characterize male identity? Almost 28,000 randomly selected men, ages 20–75, from eight countries around the world were asked to rate nine attributes for their importance to the male identity (Sand, Fisher, Rosen, Heiman, & Eardley, 2008). Having frequent sex, being attractive to women, and being financially stable were rated as important, but by no means did they head the list. The number one attribute to the male identity was being seen as a man of honor, followed closely by being in control of one's own life and having the respect of friends. These findings were consistent across all nationalities and all age groups studied.

Transgender/Transsexuality

After completion of this section, you will be able to . . .

○ Define the terms *gender identity*, *transsexual/transgendered*, *gender identity disorder*, *transwoman*, *transman*, *FTM*, and *MTF*.

○ Identify the possible biological causes of transsexuality.

○ Describe the process by which one undergoes sex reassignment.

○ Compare the acceptance of transgendered individuals in Western society with Native American or Eastern society.

○ List some of the ways transgendered individuals experience discrimination in the United States.

○ Analyze your beliefs regarding a case study of transsexuality and marriage.

The most beautiful thing about being a transsexual person is being able to experience the world in two genders. . . . We have all faced the world in two genders, and we have the gift of being able to share our experiences and the insight that we've gained simply from living our lives. Those of us who embody both genders, who have taken the masculine and feminine parts of ourselves and put them together, can be especially helpful in teaching others, both transsexual and nontranssexual, to accept, integrate, and cherish both the masculine and feminine in people and in the universe. (Kailey, 2005, p. 140)

Gender identity is a person's subjective sense of being a man or a woman. This usually develops by age 3. In some people, there is an incongruity between their biological sex and their gender identity. These people are called either **transsexual** or **transgendered**. This is not to be confused with a **transvestite**, someone who is sexually aroused by dressing in the clothing of the opposite sex (discussed in Chapter 15). A transsexual is usually considered to have **gender identity disorder** (also called **gender dysphoria**), a psychological condition characterized by the feeling of being at odds with one's body, genitalia, and/or birth sex, although many in the transgendered community take issue with the inclusion of gender identity disorder in the diagnostic manual of mental illness. It is difficult to know the prevalence of transsexuality. Most of our estimates come from surgeons, physicians, and psychologists, from whom transgendered people seek medical help in order to transition. But those who change their physical bodies are only a small percentage of the transgendered population. The fourth edition of the *Diagnostic and Statistical Manual of Mental Disorders (DSM-IV)* estimates that the prevalence of male-to-female (MTF) transsexuality is one in 12,000–40,000; the prevalence of female-to-male (FTM) transsexuality is lower, perhaps because transmen are less likely to surgically transition and physicians are therefore less aware of the prevalence of FTM.

In the situation presented in the question above, the person's orientation didn't change, the label did. In this case, it's because the label was not based on whom you may be attracted to, but instead on the gender of the person feeling the attraction. Milton Diamond proposes the terms **gynecophilic**, **androphilic**, and **ambiphilic** rather than homosexual, heterosexual, and bisexual. These terms refer to the type of partner one prefers rather than to one's sex (Diamond, 2005).

Possible Origins of Transsexuality

We don't know why biological sex and gender identity don't match in some people. It was once thought that gender identity was shaped solely by how a person was raised, and that biological males could assume a female gender identity if they were raised as females. What

Say you're a woman who loves men, but then you change into a man, but you still love men. If sexual orientation doesn't change, how can you go from being straight to being gay?

happened to Bruce Reimer (see the Sex Actually feature on page 118) provided one instance in which that belief was demonstrated to be false. Genetic males born with testicles but without penises fare better psychologically when they are not reassigned as female (Reiner & Gearhart, 2004). Scientists now recognize that many critical processes affecting gender identity occur before birth.

Gender identity may be influenced by brain anatomy, genetic variations, or other physiological factors. The bed nucleus of the stria terminalis, a structure in the limbic system that may play a role in sexual behavior, may be related to sexual identity. This area is larger in males, both gay and straight, than it is in females. However, in MTF transsexuals, the nucleus is as small as it is in biological females (Kruijver et al., 2000; Zhou, Hofman, Gooren, & Swaab, 1995). Transsexuals may have genetic variations in the genes that code for androgen and estrogen receptors (Hare et al., 2009; Henningsson et al., 2005). Others suggest that transsexuality may be due to prenatal hormone imbalance (Green & Young, 2001) or prenatal exposure to drugs (Cohen-Kettenis, Mellenberg, Poll, Koppe, & Boer, 1999).

Sex Reassignment

If a transsexual wishes to live as the opposite gender, he or she may choose to undergo **sex reassignment**. The process of sex reassignment usually takes years. Before surgery, transsexuals are psychologically screened and undergo therapy. They then live for 1 to 2 years as the other gender, as a "real life test." During this time, transsexuals usually change their legal names and sex designations. Following these changes, they can begin hormone therapy to promote the development of the secondary sexual characteristics of the other gender. Some transsexuals then have sexual reassignment surgery, in which the surgeon creates the external genitalia. Medical science cannot yet construct testes or ovaries. The MTF surgery is less complicated and usually more successful than a phalloplasty (the surgery a FTM transsexual may undergo). Not all transsexuals choose to have surgery. The multiple surgical procedures are painful, costly, and often not covered by insurance. Also, some people feel that the reproductive anatomy is only one small part of what makes them men or women, and that by changing their social interactions, physical appearance, and behaviors, their

Gender identity One's subjective sense of being a man or woman.

Transgendered A general term for variations of gender expression, including female and male impersonators, transsexuals, and drag kings and queens.

Transsexual A more specific term, referring to people who feel that their biological sex doesn't represent their true identity.

Drag kings, drag queens A person who dresses (often flamboyantly) as the opposite sex for the purpose of entertainment or performance. Gender stereotypes are often exaggerated in drag performances.

Transman and transwoman A person who is born male but identifies as female can be called male-to-female (MTF) or a transwoman. One who is born female but identifies as male is called female-to-male (FTM) or transman.

"I remember being 3½ years old. I sat up in bed and my pajama bottoms came off and I remember looking down between my legs and saying to my mother 'There's a mistake! I'm a girl!' When I was a teenager and all the hormones hit, I 'transitioned' from a child to a man. I felt like, 'I've got this body; I may as well do the best I can with it.' I tried to be the best man I could. This was in the fifties and sixties and I perceived anything else as tantamount to suicide. I was an extremely skilled actress and I learned to be quintessentially male. Eventually I got to the point where I was able to drop the façade and be a woman full time. I've had a wonderful, successful life and a wide circle of friends." —Deena, a transsexual (from the author's files)

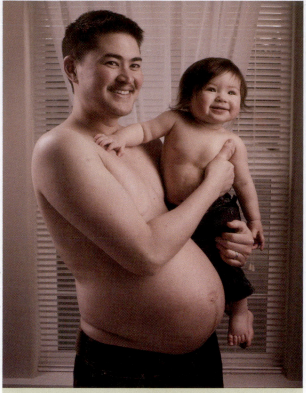

Thomas Beatie was born a woman but had chest reconstructive surgery and testosterone therapy to become a man. Thomas's wife is infertile, so the couple decided that Thomas, who didn't have his reproductive organs removed when he transitioned, would stop taking testosterone so he could get pregnant. Thomas successfully gave birth to the couple's little girl in 2008, to a little boy in 2009, and to another boy in 2010. In his words, "Wanting to have a biological child is neither a male nor female desire, but a human desire" (cited in Bone, 2008).

physical manifestation of gender matches their identity to a satisfactory degree.

Cultural, Social, and Legal Issues of Sex Reassignment

Some societies tolerate or even embrace different forms of gender expression, while in others, acceptance of differences comes harder. Many Native American tribes believe there are three genders: female, male, and "two-spirit." Two-spirit individuals have both masculine and feminine spirits in the same body (Goulet, 1996). They may be biologically of one sex and have androgynous characteristics, or they may be intersexed. Two-spirits have a special status in Native American society and are thought to be lucky. The *hijras* of India are born biologically male or intersex, but they have a non-male gender

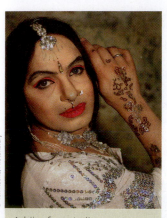

A *hijra* from India.

Victims of Discrimination Against Transsexuals

Brandon Teena (pictured) was a transman who was raped and murdered at the age of 21 when others learned of his biological sex.

Many transsexuals have been victims of discrimination. In 1995, Tyra Hunter, a transwoman, was injured in a car accident. Paramedics arrived on the scene and began to administer life support, but after discovering that Tyra had a penis, chose to stop treatment and instead laugh and make jokes, while onlookers begged them to help her. Tyra died later that day in the emergency room. In 1999, a fellow soldier beat PFC Barry Winchell to death because Winchell was dating FTM transsexual Calpernia Addams.

identity and are considered a third gender. *Hijras* live in communes that worship the mother goddess *Bahuchara Mata*. As *hijras* transition in their commune from student to teacher, they gradually assume more feminine characteristics. Their transition may end with castration, referred to as *nirvana*, or rebirth. To earn money, *hijras* may perform at marriage and birth ceremonies, or they may live as beggars or prostitutes.

The acceptance of transsexuals is less likely in the United States, where they face discrimination in many situations. In 2007 Susan Stanton (formerly Steve Stanton) was fired as city manager for Largo, Florida, when she revealed that she was a transsexual (she was later hired by the city of Lake Worth, Florida). Transsexuals are often denied appropriate health care. Because most transsexuals—even those who have undergone sex reassignment surgery— still have the internal reproductive anatomy of their birth sex, transwomen still need to have prostate exams, and transmen still need to go to the gynecologist. In 1999 Robert Eads, a transman, died of ovarian cancer after more than 20 gynecologists refused to see him. Transsexuals face not only the danger of losing their jobs, homes, and families, but their very lives. Transgendered people have a 1-in-12 chance of being murdered, compared to the 1-in-18,000

Transvestite A person, usually male, who derives sexual gratification from dressing in the clothing of the opposite sex.

Gender identity disorder Also called **gender dysphoria**, this is a psychological condition in which there is an incongruity between one's physical sex and one's gender identity, which causes clinically significant distress or impairment in social or occupational functioning.

Gynecophilic One who prefers a female partner.

Androphilic One who prefers a male partner.

Ambiphilic One who likes both female and male partners.

Sex reassignment The process by which transsexuals change their physical and legal status to better align with their gender identity. This process may include psychological counseling, hormone therapy, and surgery.

The Reimer Twins

Bruce Reimer and his identical twin brother, Brian, were born in Canada in 1965. After being diagnosed with phimosis, a condition where the foreskin cannot be fully retracted over the head of the penis, the 8-month-old boys were brought in to be circumcised. The doctor attempted a new circumcision technique, which went horribly awry, and Bruce's penis was burned off. Unsurprisingly, the twins' mother then decided to cancel Brian's circumcision.

A physician who examined Bruce wrote, "one can predict that he will be unable to live a normal sexual life from the time of adolescence: that he will be unable to consummate marriage or have normal heterosexual relations, in that he will have to recognize that he is incomplete, physically defective, and that he must live apart" (Colapinto, 2001, p. 16). Justifiably horrified when presented with such a future, Bruce's parents looked for help. The twins were brought to Dr. John Money, a psychologist at Johns Hopkins Medical Center in Baltimore. Dr. Money was a renowned proponent of the theory that gender identity was entirely a function of social learning rather than biological forces—of "nurture" over "nature." Dr. Money met with the Reimers and recommended that Bruce be castrated and raised as a girl. At the age of 22 months, Bruce, renamed "Brenda," underwent surgery to construct a vagina.

"Brenda's" mother began to raise a little girl. Brenda wore frilly dresses and received dolls and toy sewing machines. When describing her children, Mrs. Reimer made sure to accentuate incidents in which Brenda followed prescribed gender roles, and downplay the many incidents that demonstrated a less successful transition. As Brenda aged, however, more and more evidence suggested that Brenda was not comfortable in a female role. For reasons of his own, Dr. Money chose to ignore the abundant evidence that the gender reassignment was not entirely successful. In writing of the twins, he extolled how happy Brenda was, and how well she had adapted to the role of a little girl. Brenda and Brian made numerous trips to Baltimore to meet with Dr. Money, where he observed their behavior, questioned them regarding their gender identity, and had them participate in "sex play," in which the twins were instructed to assume copulatory positions and mimic the actions of intercourse.

As time went by, Brenda became more and more opposed to meeting with Dr. Money, finally declaring that she would commit suicide if forced to see him again. At the age of 14, Brenda was finally told that she had been born a boy, and about the accident that led to the loss of the penis. Brenda immediately decided to switch back to a male identity, and renamed himself "David." He began testosterone injections, underwent a mastectomy, and had penis construction surgery. David eventually married a woman and adopted her children.

Unfortunately, this true story does not have a happy ending. In 2002 David's twin Brian died of an overdose of antidepressants. By 2004 David was beset by financial and marital problems. Two days after his wife of 14 years requested a separation, David Reimer died of a self-inflicted gunshot wound.

Courtesy of Ron Reimer. Used with permission. Stills from CBC TV Archive Sales

"Brenda" as a child

Courtesy of Ron Reimer. Used with permission. Stills from CBC TV Archive Sales

David as a teen after reverting back to a male identity

© Winnipeg Free Press/The Canadian Press

David as an adult

What if I meet a transgendered person? How do I refer to him or her? How should I act?

- Use the pronoun of the gender the person is presenting.

- To be supportive, don't go overboard by winking or gushing, just treat them with normal respect and acceptance.

- Don't "out" them to other people by telling others about their transgendered status without their permission.

- Don't ask if they're "done." They are not dinner.

- Don't ask if they've had "the operation" unless you routinely question friends and strangers about their genitalia.

chance faced by average Americans (Human Rights Campaign, 2009).

Transgender issues lead to many legal questions. When considering these emotionally charged matters, try to critically evaluate the issues involved. Imagine that Liz has been married to her husband Mike for 14 years and loves him deeply. Four years ago, Mike revealed that he has always considered himself to be a woman, and he began his transition the following year. Mike (now Michelle) has since undergone surgical reassignment surgery. Liz and Michelle live together and love each other.

Interview with Jenn, a 25-Year-Old Transwoman

Q: When did you know that you wanted to be female?

A: As long as I can remember. It never felt right to be a boy. I was always fascinated by girls. When I was seven I told my dad that I didn't feel like a boy and I wanted to be a girl. On every star and birthday candle, I always wished to be a girl.

Q: How do you feel about how transsexualism is portrayed in the media?

A: It doesn't seem to deal with it much, but when it does, it shows it like a mental disorder. I remember seeing this show once with a transwoman on it, and they kept saying "What makes this man want to be a woman?" They focused on the male part and always referred to her as male. Also, they seem to always show MTF transsexuals—it's as if FTM don't exist.

Q: What is the biggest misconception about transsexuals?

A: That all transsexuals are just gay men who want to dress up—that is so untrue! Or that dressing and acting as a woman is just a fetish or a way to get off. (*Author's note*: Some experts do believe that transgendered MTF individuals are either "extremely" gay men, or are sexually aroused by the thought of themselves as women.)

Q: What do you want people to know about transsexuals?

A: I think people should be themselves and not be afraid. Be accepting and give them respect. If someone wants to be called Mary instead of Jonathan, then call them Mary. It's common courtesy. It won't turn you into a Satanist or anything.

ASK YOURSELF

- Liz still loves the person she married. Is Liz now a lesbian? Bisexual? What do you think?

- Liz and Michelle live in Texas, a state that does not recognize same-sex marriage. Is their marriage still legal? Why do you feel the way you do—for legal reasons? Biological reasons? Emotional reasons? Explain your rationale.

- Would you feel differently about this situation if Liz transitioned to Larry, and Mike remained married to him? Why or why not? Do you think that Michelle and Liz's or Mike and Larry's relationship would be more likely to survive? Why?

Intersexuality

After completion of this section, you will be able to . . .

○ Define the terms *intersex* and *disorder of sex development*.

○ List examples of intersexuality and describe the biological foundation of these disorders.

○ Think critically about the current treatment of intersexed individuals.

According to Greek mythology, the god Hermes and the goddess Aphrodite created a son, Hermaphroditus, who was said to be unusually beautiful. One day, the nymph, Salmacis, saw Hermaphroditus bathing in a pool and was so besotted that she flung herself at him, clinging so tightly that their bodies fused into one. Forever joined, both male and female, s/he was then called Hermaphroditus for the rest of his/her life. This story tells us the origins of the word *hermaphrodite;* the term, now considered to be obsolete, was once used to describe people who possess characteristics of both sexes. **True hermaphro-**

dites are people who have ambiguous genitals as well as both male and female gonads (such as an ovary and fallopian tube on one side of the body, and testicles and a vas deferens on the other side). True hermaphroditism is rare. The more common occurrence is when people have the gonads of their chromosomal sex and ambiguous or opposite external genitalia—a condition that used to be called **pseudohermaphroditism**. The more accurate term that is used today is **disorders of sex development (DSD)**, or **intersex**. An intersexed person is "one in whom sexually dimorphic characters are mixed so that he or she carries both male and female biologic features not usually occurring in the same individual" (Diamond, 2005). A DSD birth is estimated to occur between 0.02% and 1.7% of the time (Blackless et al., 2000; Sax, 2002). The wide variation in this range of incidence is because of differing definitions of intersexuality. Perhaps 1 in every 2,000 people are born with atypical genitalia; in about 1 in 4,500 births the genitalia is ambiguous enough that a doctor is unable to definitively determine the baby's sex (Diamond, 2005).

Examples of Intersexuality

The human body develops in varied and sometimes unforeseen ways. Just as our genes affect our height and eye color, so do they affect our sexual organs. Guevedoces, androgen insensitivity syndrome, Klinefelter's syndrome, and congenital adrenal hyperplasia are just a few of the examples of the diverse sexual expression of the human form. (A review of Figure 5.2, about prenatal sexual differentiation, might help your understanding of the following discussion.)

True hermaphrodite An obsolete term describing a congenital condition in which a person has both testes and ovaries.

Pseudohermaphrodite An obsolete term describing an individual whose internal reproductive organs are of one sex, and whose external genitalia resemble that of the other sex, or are ambiguous.

Disorders of sex development Congenital conditions in which development of chromosomal, gonadal, or anatomic sex is atypical.

Intersex Those with mixed male and female reproductive anatomy. This term is preferred by those who feel that "disorder" is demeaning.

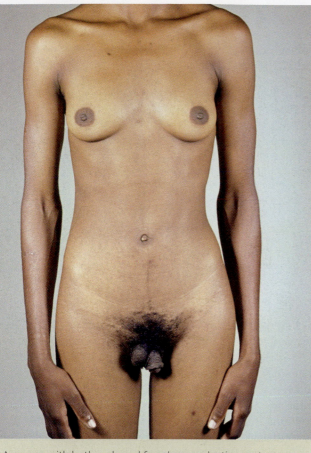

A person with both male and female reproductive anatomy.

Guevedoces

A child is born in a village in the Dominican Republic. Upon seeing the baby's vulva, the doctor tells the proud parents that they have a little girl. They name her Luisa. At puberty, however, some changes begin to occur. Luisa's body changes shape and her voice deepens. Her labia majora begin to fuse into a scrotum, testes descend, and her clitoris enlarges into a penis. Luisa has **guevedoces**.

Guevedoces is a rare autosomal recessive genetic condition that is common in areas of the Dominican Republic and Turkey. Those with guevedoces (also called "5-alpha-reductase deficiency") are missing the enzyme that converts testosterone to dihydrotestosterone (DHT). They have a Y chromosome, and therefore develop testes and testosterone, which leads to the development of the male internal reproductive tract. The testes also produce anti-Müllerian hormone, to prevent the growth of the ovaries and uterus. It is DHT, however, that causes descent of the testes, and pre-natal growth of the penis and scrotal sac; the lack of this hormone gives these children a female or ambiguous appearance at birth. Once puberty hits, the undescended testes produce enough testosterone to cause what appeared to be a clitoris to grow into a penis, and

Guevedoces (Gway-veh-DOH-chays) An autosomal recessive disorder of sex development in which the baby is born with apparently female genitalia, but the penis and scrotum develop at puberty.

Androgen insensitivity syndrome (AIS) An intersex condition in which the body is insensitive to the effects of testosterone.

"'Men' and 'women' are social categories. We have the freedom to decide who counts as a man and who counts as a woman. The criteria change from time to time."
(Roughgarden, 2004, p. 23)

the labia majora to completely fuse into a scrotum (Imperato-McGinley, Guerrero, Gautier, & Peterson, 1974). In the Dominican Republic, where this condition is more common (and more accepted), these children generally grow up to adopt a male gender identity; in the United States, they often receive feminizing surgery and hormones and are raised as girls.

Androgen Insensitivity Syndrome

Approximately once in every 13,000 births, a child is born with a defective gene on the X chromosome that prevents the formation of functional androgen receptors. People with **androgen insensitivity syndrome (AIS)** have a Y chromosome, which causes testes to form. The testes produce anti-Müllerian hormone (which prevents the development of the uterus and ovaries), as well as testosterone. The testosterone, however, has no functional receptors to bind to. It floats through the bloodstream unable to "dock" and exert its masculinizing effects on the body. Therefore, female external genitalia develop, and these children are raised as girls. This condition is often not detected until puberty, when the girl goes to her physician because she has not begun to menstruate. Upon examination, the doctor may then discover the undescended (and infertile) testes, and a genetic test can reveal the Y chromosome. The testes are usually removed surgically, as undescended testes are more likely to become cancerous.

AIS may be "complete" or "partial." Those with complete AIS have labia majora, a functional clitoris, and a short vagina that ends in a membrane instead of a cervix. They do not have a uterus and will not menstruate. Those with complete AIS usually appear very feminine. They have no acne, little to no armpit or body hair, and large breasts. They identify as female, and usually have romantic relationships with men rather than women (Zucker, 1999).

Klinefelter's Syndrome

In **Klinefelter's syndrome**, a Y sperm fertilizes an ovum that has an extra X chromosome, and the boys end up with

Hermaphroditism is common in the ocean; many invertebrates and fish switch genders depending on the situation. The Bluehead Wrasse fish switches between male and female based on social cues. The largest fish becomes male. If something happens to that fish, then the next-largest female becomes male. In some mammals also, including deer, kangaroos, pigs, bears, and hyenas, certain individuals have both male and female characteristics.

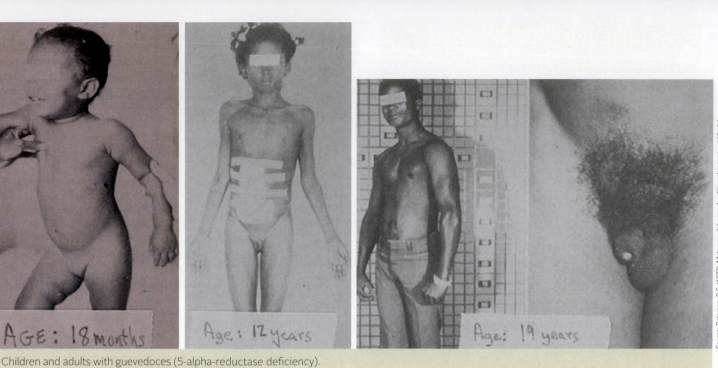

Children and adults with guevedoces (5-alpha-reductase deficiency).

Source: Peterson, R.E. (1977). Male pseudohermaphroditism due to steroid 5 alpha reductase deficiency. American Journal of Medicine, 62(2): 170-91.

ASK YOURSELF

People with complete AIS have the chromosomes and gonads of a male, and the external anatomy and gender identity of a female. Should someone with AIS be legally able to marry a man? Able to marry a woman? Allowed to marry any adult they choose? Why or why not?

an extra X chromosome in each cell in their body—XXY. This occurs once in every 500–1,000 births. Due to the influence of the extra X chromosome, males with Klinefelter's syndrome have what may be considered a more feminine body shape, including some breast development, narrow shoulders, wide hips, decreased muscle mass, and sparse facial and body hair (Figure 5.6). These males have small and underdeveloped genitalia, reduced sex drive, erection difficulties, and infertility problems. Klinefelter's syndrome is associated with a greater likelihood of problems with reading, writing, speech, and problem solving. There is controversy as to whether Klinefelter's syndrome should be considered an intersex condition (Blackless et al., 2000; Sax, 2002), because a person with this disorder has male chromosomes as well as internal and external male anatomy. However, Klinefelter's males are more likely to have gender identity disorder than males in the general population (Mandoki, Summer, Hoffman, & Riconda, 1991).

Congenital Adrenal Hyperplasia (CAH)

In some children, an autosomal recessive gene leads to an increase in androgen levels. When this happens in boys, there are few gender-related symptoms. In girls, however, the high levels of prenatal androgens can have both behavioral and physical effects. Many studies suggest that girls with con-

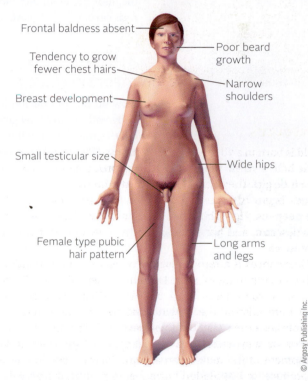

Frontal baldness absent
Poor beard growth
Tendency to grow fewer chest hairs
Narrow shoulders
Breast development
Small testicular size
Wide hips
Female type pubic hair pattern
Long arms and legs

© Argosy Publishing Inc.

FIGURE 5.6 Klinefelter's syndrome.

genital adrenal hyperplasia (CAH) may exhibit more "boyish" conduct and CAH women are more likely to be lesbians, although some of these studies lack a clear definition or proper controls (Dittman, Kappes, & Kappes, 1992; Fausto-Sterling, 2000). Physically, the excess androgens masculinize the external genitalia, causing the clitoris to enlarge and the labia to fuse partially, so it looks more like a scrotum.

Klinefelter's syndrome A condition in which males have an extra X chromosome.

Intersexuality and the Olympics

Female Olympic athletes were once forced to undergo physical examinations and/or gynecological exams to prevent males from trying to participate in female events. Actually, the only known case of a male trying to infiltrate the women's events was in 1936 when Hermann Ratgen, a Nazi youth, disguised himself as "Dora" in the women's high jump event. Three women out jumped him; he came in fourth. Gender testing was dropped in 2000.

> **ASK YOURSELF**
>
> What do you think determines gender? Is it chromosomes? Gonads? Hormones? Genitalia? Identity? How would you decide whether a person should be allowed to compete in men's or women's events? Consider the following situations.

- In 1988 Maria Patiño, a hurdler on the Spanish Olympic team, was shocked to discover that according to genetic tests, she had a Y chromosome and was not allowed to compete as a female. She was stripped of her past titles, and barred from further competition. Maria had androgen insensitivity syndrome. Should an XY individual with androgen insensitivity syndrome be allowed to compete as a woman? Why or why not?
- Due to her greatly enlarged clitoris, a woman with congenital adrenal hyperplasia (CAH) was banned from competing in the Olympic games as a woman. Do you agree with this decision?
- Joan is an XY individual whose penis was accidentally severed during a freak gardening accident in infancy. She has undergone reconstructive surgery and has been raised as a girl. She identifies as a woman and is in love with a man. Should Joan be allowed to compete as a woman? Why or why not?

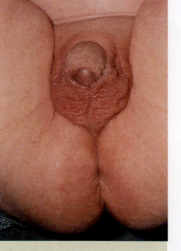

© National Medical Slide Bank/Custom Medical Stock Photo, Inc.

A small child with congenital adrenal hyperplasia (CAH).

Congenital adrenal hyperplasia (CAH) An autosomal recessive disorder wherein excessive prenatal exposure to androgens causes masculinization of the female genitals.

Women with CAH are fertile, and the enlarged clitoris is sexually responsive.

Treatment of Intersexuality

How do doctors decide if a baby with ambiguous genitalia is male or female? In about 90% of these cases, intersex infants—whether they have male or female internal anatomy—undergo genital surgery to make them appear as anatomical females. One surgeon explained: "You can make a hole, but you can't build a pole" (Hendricks, 1993). If an attending physician considers a baby girl's clitoris to be "too large," he or she may recommend shortening it. There are, however, numerous problems that occur with genital surgery, including extensive scarring, the need for multiple surgeries, and sexual difficulties (Minto, Liao, Woodhouse, Ransley, & Creighton, 2003). These procedures often diminish or eliminate the ability to orgasm, and there is no guarantee that feminizing genital surgery leads to an improvement in psychological or social health (Slijper, Drop, Molenaar, & de Muinck Keizer-Schrama, 1998). Many in the intersex community decry this practice and call for a stop of the practice of amputating healthy tissue to conform to societal standards.

Suzanne Kessler (1995) asked college women, "Suppose you had been born with a larger than normal clitoris and it would remain larger than

Transsexuals want their anatomy to coincide with their psyche, and will sometimes make necessary changes, even if it means losing sexual function. Intersexed people usually want sexual function, even if the anatomy does not appear as the "norm."

normal as you grew to adulthood. Assuming that the physicians recommended surgically reducing your clitoris, under what circumstances would you have wanted your parents to give them permission to do it?" The results are seen in Figure 5.7.

The question of how physicians should handle the birth of an intersexed child has been addressed by a variety of experts. The widely respected sex researcher Milton Diamond, members of the Intersex Society of North America, and others have a number of suggestions. Medicine's primary dictum, "First, do no harm," as always, is of utmost consideration: surgery is appropriate to save a life or significantly improve a child's physical well-being, but most experts believe

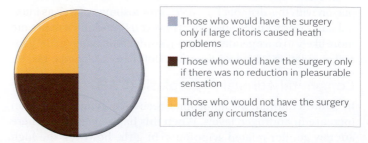

- Those who would have the surgery only if large clitoris caused heath problems
- Those who would have the surgery only if there was no reduction in pleasurable sensation
- Those who would not have the surgery under any circumstances

FIGURE 5.7 College women's wishes regarding clitoral reduction surgery. (© Cengage Learning 2013.)

that unnecessary surgery should not be performed on intersexed infants simply to achieve a social result. Children with DSD should be assigned a provisional sex based on the probability of gender identity, but surgeons need not act with undue haste (Diamond, 1997). Parents should consult with geneticists, endocrinologists, psychologists, and other intersexed individuals to determine the best solution for the child.

Imagine a baby born with an oddly shaped but functional arm. Would one choose an invasive, traumatizing pediatric surgery that almost inevitably produces scarring and loss of sensation, just to make the arm conform more closely to the standard shape? (Bloom, 2002)

ASK YOURSELF

In parts of Africa and the Middle East, girls undergo ritual clitoridectomies. In the United States, infants with an abnormally large clitoris may have it surgically reduced or removed. What are the differences between "their" ritual clitoridectomy and "our" clitoridectomy? What are the similarities?

"While nature generally favors variety, society usually doesn't" (Diamond, 2005). Although people may be uncomfortable with the fact that gender is not absolute, the reality is that there are many happy, healthy people who do not fit neatly into the categories of male and female. Throughout history, the faction in power has set standards that define "us" and "them": Aryan and Jew, black and white, gay and straight. Such rigid classifications lend themselves to supporting discrimination. The reality is that in life's spectrum, most people fall into the middle of experience rather than its outer extremes. There is black and white and a rainbow of colors in between, gay and straight and every combination imaginable. Why are we reluctant to recognize a continuum of gender?

Chapter Summary

Introduction

- The term *gender* is often used synonymously with *sex*, although gender is a social construct that includes the behavioral, social, and legal status of an individual, whereas sex better describes the biological aspects of being male and female, such as chromosomes and anatomy.

What Makes Someone Male or Female?

- Biological sex is not a clear-cut concept, and is influenced by genetics, anatomy, hormones, and identity.

Development of Biological Sex

- The father, who can contribute either an X chromosome or a Y chromosome to the mother's X chromosome, determines the sex of the baby. If the baby has an X and a Y chromosome it will be a boy, and if it has two X chromosomes it will be a girl.
- For the first 6 weeks of prenatal development, the gonads and genitalia of embryos are identical and undifferentiated. Embryos have two duct systems—the Müllerian system, which will become the female reproductive anatomy, and the Wolffian, or male system. By the 8th week, the sex chromosomes will start to influence the anatomical and hormonal development of the embryo.
- The sex-determining region of the Y chromosome causes development of the testes, which secrete testosterone, thus causing the Wolffian duct system to develop into the epididymis, vas deferens, and seminal vesicles. Some testosterone is converted into DHT, which leads to the growth of the penis and scrotal sac. The testes also produce AMH, which prevents development of the Müllerian duct system.

Sex and Gender Differences

- Males and females differ in almost every organ system of the body. These dissimilarities have important consequences for clinical research and medical treatment.
- Gender roles are the gender-specific behaviors and personalities that are expected by our culture. Stereotypes are oversimplified, preconceived ideas about the way men and women "should" act in society. Sexism—inflexible and often negative views of a person based on his or her sex—can lead to discrimination.

- Men and women may exhibit differences in their activities, social interactions, emotional responses, cognitive abilities, and sexual behaviors. The degree of these differences, as well as their foundation (whether biological or societal) is very controversial. Though there may be some innate biological differences between men and women, these differences are greatly influenced by learning and society.
- When evaluating the current research on gender differences, be sure to consider the research design, the ways in which the data was analyzed, and other factors that can influence the conclusions drawn.

Development of Gender Roles

- From an early age, children learn that men and women are "supposed to" act in certain ways. From observations and interactions with others, children develop gender schemas, an understanding of what it means to be male or female, based on interactions with others in society.
- Parents, teachers, the media, as well as religious and ethnic group identities reinforce gender role expectations. Expectations of "masculine" and "feminine" behavior are culturally determined and subject to change.

Transgender/Transsexuality

- Gender identity is a person's subjective sense of being a man or a woman. *Transgendered* is a general term for variations of gender expression, including female and male impersonators, transsexuals, and drag kings and queens. *Transsexual* is a more specific term. Transsexual individuals have a discrepancy between their biological sex and their subjective sense of being a man or a woman. A transman, or FTM, is a person who was born female but identifies as male; a transwoman, or MTF, was born male and identifies as female.
- Gender identity disorder is a psychological condition in which there is an incongruity between one's physical sex and one's gender identity, which causes clinically significant distress or impairment in social or occupational functioning. Some people feel that this should not be considered a psychological disorder.

- Transsexuality may have a biological basis and may be influenced by brain anatomy, genetic variations, or other physiological factors.
- Sex reassignment involves psychotherapy, hormonal treatments, and living as the other gender. Not all transsexuals undergo sex reassignment surgery.
- Transsexuals face many forms of discrimination in the United States. In some Native American tribes, those who have both masculine and feminine spirits in the same body are thought to be lucky.

Intersexuality

- Many children are born with a condition in which their external genitalia are ambiguous or do not correspond to their chromosomal and gonadal sex. Disorders of sex development are congenital conditions in which development of chromosomal, gonadal, or anatomic sex is atypical. Some feel that use of the term *disorders* is demeaning, and prefer the term *intersex*. Some types of intersexuality include guevedoces, androgen insensitivity syndrome (AIS), Klinefelter's syndrome, and congenital adrenal hyperplasia (CAH).
- In guevedoces, a chromosomal male is missing an enzyme that converts testosterone to DHT, and thus appears as anatomically female when born. He grows male anatomy at puberty. In AIS, a chromosomal male lacks receptors for testosterone and is impervious to its effects. A Klinefelter's male has an extra X chromosome. Women with CAH are exposed to high prenatal levels of androgens and their genitals are masculinized.
- Physicians and parents dealing with the birth of an intersexed child should be sure to carefully consider all options to determine the best solution for the child.

Some people have the perception that the more feminine a person is, the less masculine he must be; that a man who exhibits "feminine" characteristics of compassion or cooperation is less manly.

evaluate and *decide*

Imagine the following situations, which are all based on actual events:

> You are a young woman, working on your Ph.D. in physics. You have worked hard to develop your thesis, and your research is coming along nicely. You have a preliminary meeting with your defense committee to discuss your findings and progress. You dress carefully for your presentation and clearly discuss your research. After your presentation, you meet with your (all male) committee to hear their feedback. They tell you that you "act like a girl" and that you "smile too much." Your voice inflections "aren't professional" and you phrase too many points as questions. No comment is made about your research or data.

> You and your partner have just had a baby who has ambiguous genitalia. Upon further examination, the baby is found to have XY chromosomes, small testes, low testosterone levels, and a micropenis (a penis that is less than 1.7 cm in length when stretched). Your physician tells you that it is unlikely that your son's penis will ever grow enough to permit satisfactory penetration of a female.

> Your neighbors are the parents of Zachary, who is 6 years old. When Zachary was 2, he asked his parents to call him "Aurora," because he knew that he was a girl. Zachary/Aurora has maintained this identity for the past 4 years, and will only play with dolls and wear dresses. Zachary/Aurora was eventually diagnosed with gender identity disorder. Two weeks after Zachary/Aurora was enrolled in the school system, child services took him/her from your neighbors due to concerns about the parents' refusal to raise the child with a traditional gender role. You know that in every other way they are loving and devoted parents.

What factors would you consider when advising these people or experiencing these situations?

SITUATION	ISSUES TO CONSIDER
FEMALE IN MALE-DOMINATED FIELD	How would you respond to your committee's comments?
	Do you think it's necessary for people working in gender-nontraditional fields to change their behavior to conform to the norm? What are the ramifications (both positive and negative) for doing so?
	What is the value of "acting like a lady" or "acting like a man"? How often do you ignore your instincts and act in a "gender-appropriate" way (e.g., males not showing weakness or fear, females not showing anger)? What are the ramifications of this? How can you evaluate the consequences of your behaviors for your well-being?
INTERSEXED CHILD	What makes a person a male or female? Is it the chromosomes? The gonads? The genitalia? Gender identity? Something else?
	Do you think this child should undergo castration and be raised as a girl? Why or why not? What are the risks and benefits of changing the gender of the child?
	How accepted do you think a male with a micropenis is in society? How much do people care about the size of the penis? Do men or women care more? List both negative and positive ramifications of having a micropenis.
	Who has the most right to make the decision about possible treatments? The parents? The physician? The child? Why do you think so?
ZACHARY/AURORA	Should the state be allowed to remove a child from its home if the parents do not raise it to adopt gender stereotypes? Why or why not?
	At what age should a person be able to declare his/her gender identity?
	How would it affect the other children in class if the child dressed and identified as female?
	What are some of the risks ahead for Zachary/Aurora if she is raised as a girl? Some benefits? What are the risks and benefits if Z/A is raised as a boy?

Additional Resources

Log in to CengageBrain to access the resources your instructor requires. For this book, you can access:

 **CourseMate** brings course concepts to life with interactive learning, study, and exam preparation tools that support the printed textbook. A textbook-specific website, Psychology CourseMate includes an integrated interactive eBook and other interactive learning tools including quizzes, flashcards, videos, and more.

CENGAGENOW **CengageNOW** is an easy-to-use online resource that helps you study in less time to get the grade you want—NOW. Take a pre-test for this chapter and receive a personalized study plan based on your results that will identify the topics you need to review and direct you to online resources to help you master those topics. Then take a post-test to help you determine the concepts you have mastered and what you will need to work on. If your textbook does not include an access code card, go to CengageBrain.com to gain access. Visit www.cengagebrain.com anytime to access your account and purchase materials.

Web Resources
Accord Alliance

Accord Alliance is an organization set up to promote comprehensive and integrated approaches to care that enhance the health and well-being of people and families affected by disorders of sex development (also called "intersex"), by promoting interaction between patients, families, scientists, and health care providers.

Biological and Sociocultural Views and Consequences of Gender Stereotyping

Discusses biological and sociocultural views and consequences of gender stereotyping.

Ingersoll Gender Center

The Ingersoll Gender Center supports transgendered people toward growth and well-being. They provide support, education, advocacy, and information resources for people interested in gender identity issues, and for service providers, employers, families, and friends to promote understanding, awareness, and acceptance of gender diversity.

Prenatal Genital Development

Photos of the external genital development changes in the embryo and fetus.

Print Resources

Bornstein, K. (1995). *Gender outlaw: On men, women, and the rest of us.* New York, NY: Vintage Books.

Eugenides, J. (2002) *Middlesex: A novel.* New York, NY: Farrar, Straus and Giroux.

Kailey, M. (2005). *Just add hormones: An insider's guide to the transsexual experience.* Boston, MA: Beacon Press.

Levant, R., and Pollack, W. (eds.) (2003). *A new psychology of men.* New York, NY: Basic Books.

Petersen, J.L. & Hyde, J.S. (2010). A meta-analytic review of research on gender differences in sexuality, 1993-2007. *Psychological Bulletin, 136*(1): 21–38.

Tannen, D. (1991). *You just don't understand: Men and women in conversation.* New York, NY: Ballantine Books.

Travis, C. (1992). *The mismeasure of woman.* New York, NY: Simon and Schuster.

Video Resources

Boys Don't Cry (1999). 118 minutes. Rated R. The story of Brandon Teena, a transgendered youth who was murdered.

Hedwig and the Angry Inch (2001). 93 minutes. Rated R. Raises interesting questions regarding gender, identity, and love. And it has great music.

Science of the Sexes: Growing Up and *Different by Design* (2002). 51 minutes each. Why do humans have two different sexes if other species have survived with just one? These programs look at the hormonal cascade that happens in adulthood, culminating in sexual reproduction, and the many advantages conferred by the resulting genetic variety. The effects of estrogen and testosterone and the physiology of sex are seen through a number of fascinating experiments and examples. Experts featured include psychiatrist Sebastian Kraemer, anthropologist Helen Fisher, and neuroscientists Raquel and Ruben Gur. A Discovery Channel production.

TransAmerica (2005). 103 minutes. Rated R. The story of a presurgical transsexual woman who discovers she has a son, now a teenage runaway. The two embark on a cross-country road trip and grow to understand each other.

The Third Sex (1997). 53 minutes. Two sexes drive the reproductive cycle. Yet for some, the fundamental physiology of male or female is not readily apparent. This program examines intersexuality through four case studies: ambiguous genitalia deriving from a missing sex chromosome, androgen insensitivity syndrome, 5-alpha-reductase deficiency in an insular Caribbean community, and hermaphroditism in South Africa. The issue of societal acceptance is addressed as well, along with the vital importance of emotional support and counseling. Contains nudity. A Discovery Channel production.

6 Sexual Response

i like my body when it is with your
body. It is so quite a new thing.
Muscles better and nerves more.
i like your body. i like what it does,
i like its hows. i like to feel the spine
of your body and its bones, and the trembling
-firm-smooth ness and which i will
again and again and again
kiss, i like kissing this and that of you,
i like, slowly stroking the, shocking fuzz
of your electric fur, and what-is-it comes
over parting flesh . . . . And eyes big love-crumbs,

and possibly i like the thrill

of under me you quite so new

—e.e. cummings "i like my body when it is with your." Copyright 1923, 1925, 1951, 1953, © 1991 by the Trustees for the E.E. Cummings Trust. Copyright © 1976 by George James Firmage, from COMPLETE POEMS: 1904-1962 by E.E. Cummings, edited by George J. Firmage. Used by permission of Liveright Publishing Corporation.

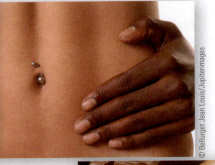
© Bellurget Jean Louis/Jupiterimages

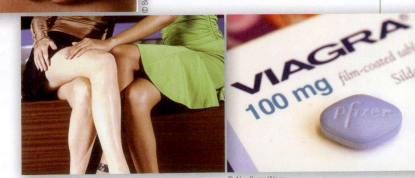
© Ben Edwards/GettyImages   © Alex Segre/Alamy

Sexual Response

After completion of this section, you will be able to . . .

○ Describe what occurs in men and women during *desire, excitement, plateau, orgasm,* and *resolution.*

○ Compare male and female orgasms.

○ Name other models of sexual response.

○ Evaluate the universality of Masters and Johnson's human sexual response cycle.

○ Recognize how sexual expression may change across the life span.

○ Consider the effect of disease or injury on sexual response.

From 1957 to 1965, 694 men and women, aged 18 to 89, arrived at the laboratory of William Masters and Virginia Johnson to do their part for science. Fitted with electrodes and implants, researchers' stopwatches at the ready, these volunteers masturbated and copulated more than 10,000 times under the watchful eyes of scientists. Using data from these observations, Masters and Johnson categorized **erotic** response into four stages, christened the **human sexual response cycle (HSRC)**. It is important to note that **sexual response** does not actually occur in distinct unconnected phases; rather, these stages are abstractions to organize the events of sexual arousal. Masters and Johnson's stages include *excitement,* the beginning of physical sexual response; *plateau,* when erotic arousal intensifies; *orgasm,* the intensely pleasurable climax of sexual excitement; and *resolution,* when the sexual tension dissipates and arousal reduces. We will also consider the mental state of *desire,* although this is not included in Masters and Johnson's HSRC.

Desire

When a person wants sexual stimulation or intimacy, he or she is feeling **desire**. Many things can stimulate desire—a sensual touch, a lascivious glance, an erotic thought, fantasy, or memory. Desire can last for a fleeting moment or persist for a lifetime. Desire is harder to define than other stages of sexual arousal, because it exists in the mind rather than the body (although the mind and body are intricately intertwined).

Researchers do not agree about desire's place in the sexual response cycle described above. Masters and Johnson did not include desire at all, as they measured only quantifiable physiological responses. Psychotherapist Helen Singer Kaplan modified Masters and Johnson's sexual response cycle by adding sexual desire

Erotic Relating to or tending to arouse sexual desire or excitement.

Human sexual response cycle (HSRC) Masters and Johnson's four-stage model of physiological responses that occur during sexual stimulation.

Sexual response The physical and emotional ways a person may respond to sexual stimulation.

Desire A drive or motivation to seek out sexual objects or to engage in sexual activities.

Proceptivity An automatic, hormonally driven, situation-independent sexual response.

Arousability A person's ability to become sexually aroused once certain triggers or situations are encountered.

© Fancy (RF)/jupiterimages

as an early stage. Sexologists make distinctions between types of desire. **Proceptivity** is best described as lust or libido. It is automatic, intense, hormone-driven, and independent of the situation. Proceptivity is related more to male sexual desire, whereas **arousability**—a person's capacity to become aroused once certain triggers, cues, or situations are encountered—may best describe female sexual desire (Diamond, 2008). In sexologist Rosemary Basson's circular model of female sexual response, desire can both initiate sexual stimulation and follow stimulation (Basson, 2000). For example, a woman may take part in sexual activity without initially feeling desire—if her partner wishes to, if they are trying to get pregnant, or because she wants emotional intimacy—but once the intimacy begins, her desire may increase. In this case, the sexual desire may *follow* the initiation of sexual activity rather than precede it.

The idea of desire is further complicated because, especially in women, desire and physical arousal are not always connected. When it comes to sexual arousal, men's minds are more in synch with what their bodies are doing than women's are. A review of studies involving more than 2,500 women and 1,900 men showed that men's subjective ratings of arousal more closely matched their body's responses (Chivers, Seto, Lalumire, Laan, & Grimbos, 2010). By scientific or clinical standards, a woman's sexual arousal is often measured by vaginal lubrication or by increased blood flow to the genitals. However, a woman may feel desire without being lubricated, and she may experience increased genital blood flow without feeling desire. In their lab, Meredith Chivers and colleagues fitted gay and straight men with penile strain gauges, and lesbians and straight women with vaginal photoplethysmographs (discussed in Chapter 2). She then showed the subjects films of nude exercise, solitary masturbation, male–male and female–female same-sex intercourse, male–female copulation, and even bonobo chimpanzees copulating. The researchers measured the subjects' physical arousal during the films and asked the subjects to self-report their degree of sexual arousal. The study found two interesting results: (1) that men and women were aroused by different films, and (2) that there was a discrepancy between what women reported being aroused by and what their measured physical arousal was. The men's arousal (both reported and measured) was gender specific—straight men were aroused by images of heterosexual or lesbian sex and of women masturbating or exercising in the nude. Films of gay male intercourse, male masturbation, or nude male exercise aroused the gay men. It was a different story for the women. Any images of sex—homosexual, heterosexual, or bonobo—physically aroused the women, but naked men or women exercising did not arouse them. When asked, though, the women *reported* that they felt no sexual arousal to the images of monkey sex or gay male intercourse. Chivers theorized that women experience lubrication at any sexual image, even if they are not consciously aroused, due to evolutionary forces. Why? A lubricated woman is at lower risk for vaginal tearing and infection if intercourse is nonconsensual.

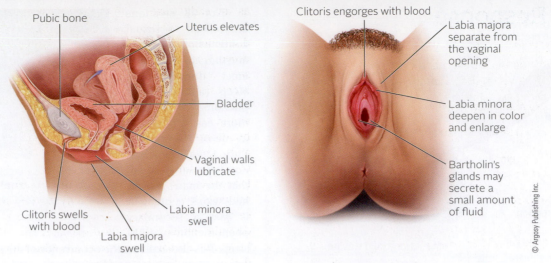

FIGURE 6.1 Physical changes in the female during the excitement phase.

Excitement

Excitement—the first phase of Masters and Johnson's sexual response cycle—is the body's initial response to feelings of sexual desire. It can last anywhere from a few minutes to several hours. Excitement can be initiated by an erotic touch, the sight of an attractive person, a suggestive whisper, or by a sexually arousing thought. As mortified adolescent males realize during math class, sexual excitement can occur without any noticeable sexual stimulation at all.

Excitement in both males and females is characterized by an increase in heart rate and blood pressure, as well as heightened muscle tone. Blood rushes to the vessels of the genitalia (an occurrence called **vasocongestion**), which then enlarge and deepen in color. Both males and females may also show a **sex flush**, a rash-like reddening of the skin of the upper abdomen and chest caused by dilating capillaries.

Women

When a woman becomes sexually excited, the shaft of the clitoris increases in size and becomes erect, though not as firm as an erect penis. The labia majora spread and separate, and the labia minora increase in size and darken in color. The uterus lifts and enlarges, and the size and shape of the vagina changes. The upper two-thirds of the vagina gets both wider and longer, while the outer one-third narrows, allowing it to better grip the penis (or finger or cucumber or whatever). The vagina will lubricate as fluid (not blood) leaks out of the blood vessels near the surface of the vaginal walls.

In some African societies, vaginal lubrication is looked upon with disgust. Not surprisingly, female orgasm is often not considered important in these societies and occurs much more rarely than in Western societies, if at all. During excitement, a

> As with any aspect of the human body that is involved with sex, the erection has inspired the invention of many euphemistic slang terms. Among them: boner, woody, chubby, hard-on, rod, schwing, skin flute, pitching a tent, kickstand, heat-seeking moisture missile, and one-eyed trousersnake.

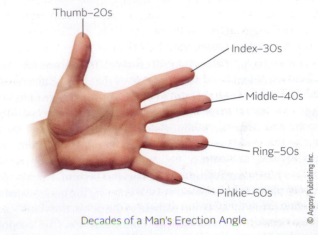

Decades of a Man's Erection Angle

FIGURE 6.2 The angle of a man's erection decreases as he ages.

woman's nipples become erect, the areolae darken, and her breasts may increase in size up to 25% as a result of fluid accumulation. Women generally reach the excitement stage more slowly than men. The physical changes that occur in the female during the excitement phase are illustrated in Figure 6.1.

Men

When a man becomes sexually excited, blood rushes into the genital tissues, causing an **erection**, as the penis becomes stiff, hard, and larger in length and diameter. The angle of the penis changes—while relaxed, the penis can point down toward the floor, but with erection it can be horizontal to the floor or almost vertical, depending on the man's age or health (Figure 6.2). The urethral opening in the glans widens, scrotal skin thickens and constricts, and the testes elevate and enlarge. In most men, nipples will become erect (Figure 6.3).

Excitement The body's initial physical response to sexual arousal.

Vasocongestion Accumulation of blood in the genitals caused by sexual excitement.

Sex flush A reddening of the skin of the chest and upper abdomen that can spread to other parts of the body.

Erection The enlarged and firm state of the penis, clitoris, or nipple.

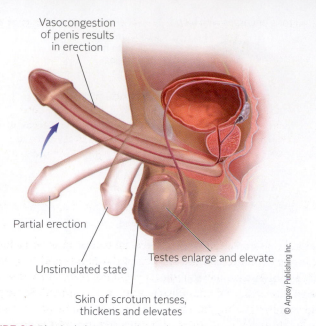

Vasocongestion of penis results in erection

Partial erection

Unstimulated state

Testes enlarge and elevate

Skin of scrotum tenses, thickens and elevates

© Argosy Publishing Inc.

FIGURE 6.3 Physical changes in the male during the excitement phase.

Autonomic processes control erection. The **autonomic nervous system (ANS)** is a series of nerves that carry information from the brain and spinal cord to the heart, smooth muscle, and glands. It is divided into the sympathetic and parasympathetic nervous systems. The **sympathetic nervous system** controls "fight or flight" responses—it mobilizes your body to act in case of emergency. In contrast, "business as usual" responses are mediated by the **parasympathetic nervous system**. Parasympathetic nerves will dilate blood vessels entering the penis, causing the inflow of blood. As blood gathers in the penis, the veins leading out become constricted, preventing outflow. The corpora cavernosa and corpus spongiosum fill with blood and an erection occurs. The sympathetic nervous system diminishes an erection. Remember that the sympathetic nervous system is associated with stressful occasions, when an erection may be inconvenient. If you are running away from a pack of wild dogs, you don't want an erection banging back and forth as you run; the blood engorging your penis could better be used to power your legs to run away.

Nitric oxide is also involved in the process of erection. Nitric oxide (NO) is not to be confused with nitrous oxide, also known as laughing gas. A sexual stimulus causes the release of NO from the corpus cavernosa, which leads to relaxation of smooth muscle in the penis, allowing blood to flow in.

Autonomic nervous system (ANS) A series of nerves that carry information from the brain and spinal cord to the heart, smooth muscle, and glands, the ANS includes the sympathetic and parasympathetic nervous systems.

Sympathetic nervous system A series of nerves that are involved with "fight or flight" responses, the sympathetic nervous system also diminishes erection and is more active during orgasm.

Parasympathetic nervous system Nerve pathways involved with maintaining "business as usual" processes in the body, as well as erections.

REM sleep The stage of sleep associated with rapid eye movements, dreams, erections, and a lack of skeletal muscle tone.

Plateau The period of sexual excitement prior to orgasm, characterized by intensification of the changes begun during excitement.

Not all erections are related to sexual content. Both the penis and the clitoris become erect during **REM sleep** (although this phenomenon is much more easily observed in men!). An erection during REM sleep does not necessarily mean that the man's dream had sexual content; it is just a secondary phenomenon of REM sleep. This also explains the occurrence of the erection that often occurs upon awakening (sometimes called "morning wood"): REM sleep occurs more often at the end of sleep, toward morning; in fact, we often wake up directly from a dream.

© STOCK4B-RF/Jupiter Images

Men often have erections upon waking in the morning; these erections are associated with REM sleep.

Can a man fake an erection? When men in a research study were told to "fake" sexual arousal, they had very limited success. Men were more successful at suppressing sexual arousal (Mahoney & Strassberg, 1991).

Plateau

In most circumstances, the word **plateau** is used to describe a relatively stable period of leveling off. Not so in sexual arousal. During the plateau phase, sexual arousal grows as a precursor to orgasm. The physical changes begun during excitement continue. Both men and women will experience increases in their heart rate, respiratory rate, blood pressure, and muscle tension. The genitalia will deepen in color and the sex flush may further spread across the chest. The plateau generally lasts anywhere from a few seconds to a few minutes; prolonging the length of the plateau period can result in more intense orgasms.

Women

During the plateau (Figure 6.4), the labia minora swell and deepen in color, the uterus elevates further, and Bartholin's glands may produce lubrication. Nipples become more erect

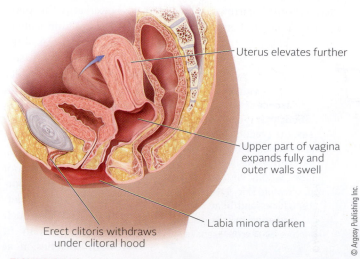

Uterus elevates further

Upper part of vagina expands fully and outer walls swell

Labia minora darken

Erect clitoris withdraws under clitoral hood

© Argosy Publishing Inc.

FIGURE 6.4 Physical changes in the female during the plateau phase.

and the areolae may increase in size. The lower third of the vagina swells as it engorges with blood, creating what is called the **orgasmic platform**. As it fills with blood during arousal, the engorged clitoris shortens and withdraws beneath the clitoral hood, so it is pulled up and out of the way of a thrusting penis.

Men

The coronal ridge and glans of the penis increase in size and deepen in color during the plateau (Figure 6.5). The prostate gland enlarges and the testes elevate and rotate slightly, so that they lie closer to the groin. Cowper's gland may release a bit of clear, alkaline fluid, which protects sperm by neutralizing any urine remaining in the urethra. This fluid also lubricates the glans.

Orgasm

"The grasp divine, th' emphatic, thrilling squeeze.
The throbbing, panting breasts and trembling knees.
The tickling motion, the enlivening flow,
The rapturous shiver and dissolving—Oh!"

—*John Wilkes, 18th-century English political leader*

The word **orgasm** derives from the Greek word *orgasmos*, meaning "excitement" or "swelling." Orgasm is considered to be one of the most pleasurable physical events that humans can experience. Every orgasm is different—it may be an intense shrieking affair with a loss of consciousness, or a subtle relaxation accompanied by a smile and a sigh. Some people can achieve orgasm through fantasy alone, but most people need direct physical stimulation.

Though intense, orgasm typically lasts less than a minute. In both males and females, it is characterized by a feeling of euphoria, along with a series of rhythmic contractions of the

> In French, the term for orgasm is "le petit mort," which literally translates to "the little death."

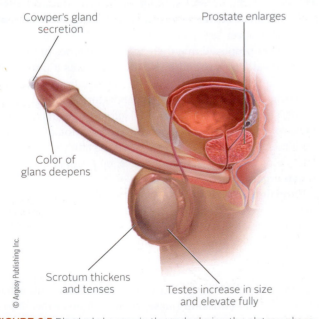

Cowper's gland secretion

Prostate enlarges

Color of glans deepens

Scrotum thickens and tenses

Testes increase in size and elevate fully

© Argosy Publishing Inc.

FIGURE 6.5 Physical changes in the male during the plateau phase.

> "Electric flesh-arrows, a second wave of pleasure falls over the first, a third which touches every nerve end, and now the third like an electric current traversing the body. A rainbow of color strikes the eyelids. A foam of music falls over the ears. It is the gong of the orgasm."
> —Anaïs Nin

genital region. People may show facial contortions and a loss of voluntary muscle control, spasms of the hands and feet, and a release of muscle tension. Blood pressure, respiratory rate, and heart rate peak, and a sex flush may appear or spread. Some people vocalize during this stage, and orgasm can be accompanied by laughter, tears, moaning, shouting, sighing, or silence.

During orgasm, brain areas related to reward are activated, while the amygdala, the seat of fear and rage, shuts down (Holstege et al., 2003). Both men and women increase secretion of the hormones prolactin, oxytocin, vasopressin, and endorphins. Prolactin is released after orgasm, and it may be related to the time that needs to pass after a man has had an ejaculation before another can occur (called the refractory period, discussed below). Prolactin may also contribute to the sleepy feeling that men experience after orgasm. Oxytocin, which is involved in sexual bonding, causes uterine contractions in women and aids in emptying the semen-producing ducts in men. Vasopressin may also affect uterine contractions, and endorphins, which are structurally and functionally related to morphine, may contribute to the sensation of pleasure and well-being felt with orgasm.

Women

During sexual arousal, muscles surrounding the clitoris contract, compressing the vein that drains blood from the clitoris. Blood enters and engorges the clitoris with blood. At a certain point, vasocongestion sets off a muscular reflex, expelling the blood that was trapped in surrounding tissues, and leading to an orgasm (Figure 6.6).

When a woman has an orgasm, she may experience strong muscular contractions of the vagina, uterus, and anus. Women typically experience between three and fifteen of these rhythmic contractions, which occur at 0.8-second intervals. Not all women report contractions upon orgasm, and for those who do, it is not clear if the contractions occur before, during, or after the perceived beginning of the orgasm. Some women may expel a small amount of fluid from the prostate-like Skene's glands during orgasm. (Recall the more detailed discussion of female ejaculation in Chapter 4.)

A **multiple orgasm** occurs when a person has an or-

Orgasmic platform The swelling of the walls of the outer third of the vagina, which occurs during the plateau stage.

Orgasm Waves of intense pleasure, often associated with vaginal contractions in females and ejaculation in males.

Multiple orgasm When a person has an orgasm, and then has one or more additional orgasms without his or her body first going through resolution.

Table 6.1 Factors That Influence Orgasm in Women

Biological Factors	• Hormonal changes seen with aging may decrease a woman's likelihood and intensity of orgasm. • 34–45% of a woman's ability to orgasm may be related to genes that code for factors such as androgen levels, the angle of the vagina, the size of the clitoris, the presence of Skene's glands, or levels of chemical substances (Dunn, Cherkas, & Spector, 2005; Ben Zion et al., 2006).
Sexual Activity	• Less than 25% of women always have an orgasm during vaginal intercourse, although 95% of women can orgasm through masturbation (Lloyd, 2005). • Sexual encounters that include cunnilingus and manual stimulation rather than just vaginal intercourse increase the likelihood of orgasm (Richters, de Visser, Rissel, & Smith, 2006).
Marital Status	• Married women are less likely to report an inability to orgasm (Laumann et al., 1999). • A women may be less likely to have an orgasm if she is with her non-regular sexual partner (Richters et al., 2006).
Education	• 87% of women with an advanced degree report "always" or "usually" attaining orgasm during masturbation compared to 42% of women with only a high school education (Laumann et al., 1994).
Religion	• 79% of women without a religious affiliation report having orgasms during masturbation, but only 53–67% of women who report a religious affiliation do (Laumann et al., 1994).
Ethnicity/Race	• African American women were more likely than white or Hispanic women to report that they always had an orgasm during sexual activity with their partner (Laumann et al., 1994).
Age	• In a survey of women aged 16–59, a woman was less likely to have achieved orgasm in her most recent sexual encounter if she was aged 16–19 or 50–59 (Richters et al., 2006).
Psychological Influences	• Women who lost their fathers in childhood or whose fathers were emotionally unavailable report less orgasmic experience (Laumann et al., 1994).
Cultural Influences	• Women who live in cultures that downplay or degrade female sexuality are much less likely to report achieving orgasm (Meston, Levin, Sipski, Hull, & Heiman, 2004).

© Cengage Learning 2013

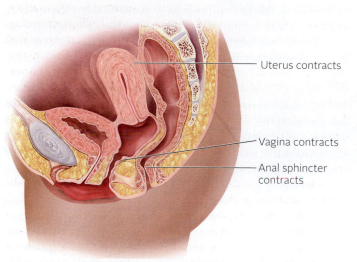

© Argosy Publishing Inc.

Uterus contracts

Vagina contracts

Anal sphincter contracts

FIGURE 6.6 Physical changes in the female during orgasm.

gasm, and then goes on to have one or more additional orgasms within a short period before the body returns to a pre-plateau level of excitement. Physiologically, women are capable of multiple orgasms, although not all women report or desire them, as the clitoris may be too sensitive for further stimulation.

Female orgasm is capricious. According to the Global Study of Sexual Attitudes and Behaviors (Laumann, Paik, & Rosen, 1999), 25% of women

Emission The first stage of male orgasm, when seminal fluids move into the upper urethra.

Ejaculatory inevitability The feeling of a "point of no return" when an orgasm is coming and it can't be prevented.

between the ages of 18 and 59 reported that they had not had an orgasm for at least several months, compared to 2.5% of men. For most women, the ability to orgasm depends on many variables, including physical, psychological, and societal factors (see Table 6.1).

Although there is no significant exploration into the different type of orgasms that *men* may have, the question of the "right type" of female orgasm has persisted for years. The idea that there are two kinds of female orgasm—an "immature" orgasm obtained through clitoral stimulation and a "mature" vaginal orgasm achieved through intercourse—is attributed to Sigmund Freud, who never actually wrote of this distinction. In 1973, Irving Singer proposed that there were three types of female orgasms: vulval, uterine, and blended. Singer was a philosopher, however, and these categories were generated from descriptions of orgasms in literature rather than laboratory studies.

Masters and Johnson felt that all female orgasms were physiologically identical and occurred with stimulation of the clitoris. To put this into context, remember that the clitoris is the female analogue of the penis. Although it can be *possible* for a man to have an orgasm without stimulation of the penis, it is more difficult and unusual. It is the same with the clitoris. Also remember that the clitoris is not only the tiny nubbin above the surface. Like an iceberg, much of the clitoris lies below the surface and can be stimulated during vaginal intercourse.

Men

Orgasm in males consists of two stages: emission and ejaculation. During the **emission** phase, seminal fluids move into the upper urethra, giving men a feeling of **ejaculatory inevitability**

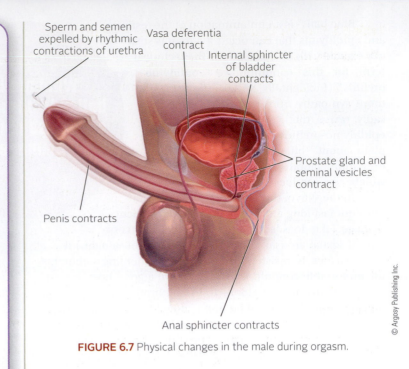

FIGURE 6.7 Physical changes in the male during orgasm.

Sperm and semen expelled by rhythmic contractions of urethra

Vasa deferentia contract

Internal sphincter of bladder contracts

Prostate gland and seminal vesicles contract

Penis contracts

Anal sphincter contracts

© Argosy Publishing Inc.

muscles, as well as in the ducts and glands, causing semen to be ejected from the body. The muscles surrounding the urethra and base of the penis contract three to six times at 0.8-second intervals, which is associated with feelings of intense pleasure. On average, 2 to 6 milliliters of fluid is ejaculated, and the ejaculate can be expelled up to 2 feet. Orgasms occurring in conjunction with stimulation of the prostate gland can result in orgasms perceived as "deeper," more widespread, intense, and longer lasting.

Ejaculation occurs in spurts: the first contains sperm as well as fluid from the prostate; later spurts come from the seminal vesicles. Paradoxically, it seems that secretions from the seminal vesicles are spermicidal. Why should this fluid actually be detrimental to the sperm it is designed to carry? Roy Levin (2005) postulates that because the seminal vesicle fluid is ejaculated last and is therefore deposited in the outer portion of the vagina, it has little effect on the previously deposited sperm, and may serve to hinder the sperm deposited from any subsequent sexual partners.

Some men can experience multiple orgasms. During a laboratory study, one man had six ejaculatory orgasms within 36 minutes with no refractory period (Whipple, Myers, & Komisaruk, 1998). However, this is fairly rare. Unlike women, most men experience a **refractory period** after orgasm—a period of time during which they are physiologically incapable of having another orgasm or ejaculation. This may last for a few minutes to more than 24 hours, depending on age and the frequency of sexual activity. The refractory period might be related to the release of the hormone prolactin: In one study, a healthy young male with a very short refractory period was found to have no increase in prolactin secretion after orgasm (Haake et al., 2002).

(also called "the point of no return")—the sense that an orgasm is coming and can't be prevented. Smooth muscle in the walls of the vasa deferentia, ejaculatory ducts, seminal vesicles, and prostate glands contract, causing seminal fluid to collect in the urethra at the base of the penis (Figure 6.7). The muscular sphincter around the urethra closes, preventing semen from entering the bladder and urine from joining the ejaculate. In cases of **retrograde ejaculation** some or all of the semen goes into the bladder. Although relatively uncommon, this can occur in men with diabetes, after prostate surgery, or with the use of some drugs that treat high blood pressure or with some mood-altering drugs. The semen does not hurt the bladder and is eliminated from the body with urine.

For most men, orgasm and ejaculation are linked, but they can be experienced separately; men may have orgasms without ejaculation, and ejaculations without orgasm. During **ejaculation**, reflex centers in the spinal cord send signals down sympathetic nerves, causing rhythmic contractions of the penis, anus, and pelvic

On average, 2 to 5 minutes of penile thrusting, or 100–500 thrusts at a maximum rate of 2 per second, will result in emission prior to orgasm (Levin, 2005).

Retrograde ejaculation   When ejaculated fluid enters a man's bladder rather than leaving the body.

Ejaculation   The ejection of sperm and semen from the penis, usually accompanied by orgasm.

Refractory period   The period after an orgasm during which a male is physiologically incapable of having another orgasm.

"Blue balls" is an inflammation of the testicles and epididymis that can occur if a man is sexually excited with no ejaculation. The technical term for this condition is "epididymo-orchitis." (Incidentally, you might get a lot more sympathy from your partner if you sadly reveal that you are suffering from epididymo-orchitis than if you sulkily complain about "blue balls.") During sexual excitation, blood collects in the testicles, which can produce an ache and a bluish tinge in the skin of the scrotum. This condition does not last long and will not cause permanent damage. (If it does last for hours or days after cessation of sexual arousal, medical help should be sought.) If your partner is insistent that you do something about his uncomfortable condition, you should be a good host or hostess, and show him the door—to the bathroom to take care of himself, or to the street if he prefers to address the situation at home. Women may experience a similar sensation if they do not reach orgasm, although "blue vulva" has not become a common part of the vernacular—use that phrase, and people are likely to think you're referring to a car.

Female orgasms versus male orgasms. When men and women were asked to write descriptions of their orgasms, readers were not able to differentiate between the descriptions of men's orgasms and women's orgasms (Vance & Wagner, 1976). However, some differences in male and female orgasms have been observed. In a survey of more than 19,000 Australians aged 16–59, men had orgasms in 95% of sexual encounters, whereas women did 69% of the time (Richters, de Visser, Rissel, & Smith, 2006). Females don't have a refractory period and are more likely to have multiple orgasms; females can have extended orgasms which last for a long time; and men reach a "point of no return"—in other words, once a man's orgasm begins, it will continue automatically even if the stimulus stops. If sexual stimulation is discontinued in the middle of a female orgasm, the orgasm can end. Women also tend to have more contractions, and a wider area of tissue undergoes contractions. There may also be differences in how men and women perceive the importance of orgasm during sex (Figure 6.8).

Faking orgasm. Question: Why do so many women fake orgasm? Answer: Because so many men fake foreplay.

Both men and women fake orgasm. In one online survey of more than 16,000 men and women aged 14–74, 72% of women and 26% of men admitted to faking an orgasm in their current or most recent relationship, and 55% of men believe they could tell if their partners faked an orgasm (Mialon, 2005). Of those who fake orgasm, most pretend during penile–vaginal intercourse (Muehlenhard & Shippee, 2009). People may fake orgasm by making sounds—moans, shrieks, or words—that lead their partners to believe they are climaxing (Brewer & Hendrie, 2011). In women, these copulatory vocalizations do not typically occur during foreplay, when women are most likely to orgasm, but before and simultaneously with male ejaculation.

People may fake orgasm for many reasons. Perhaps they are feeling too tired or distracted to enjoy sex, and they feel that faking orgasm will end it sooner. Images from the media feed into some people's unrealistically high expectations for sex—that sex always involves simultaneous orgasm, screaming, clawing, and the knocking over of lamps, rather than a sensual, intimate expression of love. A man who is losing his erection during intercourse may fake orgasm to end the encounter without embarrassment. Some women try to be "polite" to their partners to encourage their "hard work." The danger in this is that when you fake orgasm you are encouraging your partner to continue performing in a way that doesn't lead to orgasm. So your partner is thinking, "When I make little twirly motions she whips her head around and screams 'yes yes yes!' I must remember this maneuver and use it again!" while you are mentally yawning and thinking, "I hate that little twirly motion. Why is my partner doing it so often?"

Resolution

During the **resolution** phase of the sexual response cycle, the body returns to its nonexcited state. Heart rate, blood pressure, and respiratory rate first dip below normal, then return to their normal, prearoused levels. There is a general loss of muscle tension and a feeling of relaxation. The release of prolactin and other substances during orgasm may even cause people to fall asleep.

What are blue balls? Is it true that it can cause permanent damage?

Female brown trout fake orgasms in order to dupe their partner into ejaculating prematurely. They then find a genetically superior male to actually fertilize their eggs (Petersson & Jarvi, 2001).

FIGURE 6.8 The perceived importance of orgasm during sex. (Data from Levin, 2004a.)

© Cengage Learning 2013

Resolution The last stage in Masters and Johnson's sexual response cycle, when the body returns to its nonexcited state.

In the famous "deli scene" from the film *When Harry Met Sally*, Meg Ryan's character shows how a woman could fake an orgasm. Director Rob Reiner considered Meg Ryan's first efforts in performing this scene too mild, and instructed her to pound on the table and scream. Thus, the female actress's depiction of a female orgasm is based on the male director's demonstration of what he felt a female orgasm should be like.

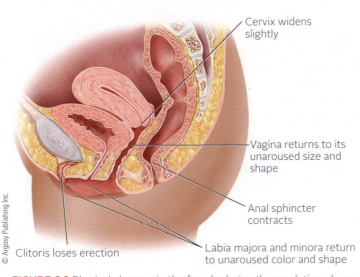

Cervix widens slightly

Vagina returns to its unaroused size and shape

Anal sphincter contracts

Labia majora and minora return to unaroused color and shape

Clitoris loses erection

FIGURE 6.9 Physical changes in the female during the resolution phase.

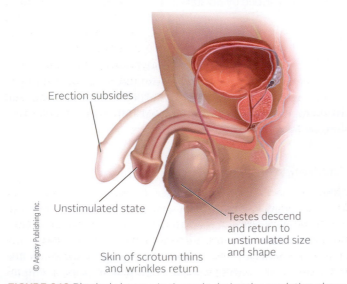

Erection subsides

Unstimulated state

Skin of scrotum thins and wrinkles return

Testes descend and return to unstimulated size and shape

FIGURE 6.10 Physical changes in the male during the resolution phase.

© Argosy Publishing Inc.

<u>**sex**actually</u>

Why Do Women Have Orgasms?

Are female orgasms necessary? Whereas the purpose of the male orgasm seems to be more straightforward—to rapidly propel the sperm into the female reproductive tract to support fertilization—the female orgasm serves no obvious adaptive purpose. Technically, the species could survive without female orgasm. (Although this doesn't consider the prospect of hordes of grumpy and frustrated women descending upon the post-orgasmic satisfied men and wreaking havoc in ways too terrible to consider.)

So why do women have orgasms? There are a number of theories. Perhaps when a woman has an orgasm, she feels more intimately bound to her partner, thus better ensuring the continued existence of the pair bond. Others think that sexual arousal in a woman may delay the time with which sperm reach the fallopian tubes, which may actually *increase* the possibility of fertilization. Freshly ejaculated sperm cannot fertilize an egg. They must first be functionally reprogrammed, a process that requires interaction with factors secreted from the female (Levin, 2005). When a woman is aroused, the uterus and cervix are raised up away from the vagina, increasing the time it takes for sperm to enter the uterus from the vagina. This gives sperm time to be "reprogrammed" and better able to fertilize an egg.

Still others, such as Elisabeth Lloyd, believe that the female orgasm has no evolutionary purpose; instead it is a "happy accident." After all, many things exist without clear evolutionary purpose—men's nipples, for example. Lloyd asserts that because most women do not always have orgasms through intercourse alone, it is not an effective adaptation for pair bonding.

> "Women's orgasms are Mother Nature's way of conning heterosexual women into bedding down with men, thereby risking disease, pregnancy and conversations about pro sports."
>
> —*Dan Savage, American journalist*

Within minutes, the woman's body returns to its prearousal state (Figure 6.9). The vagina, clitoris, uterus, labia, and breasts go back to their normal size and color. The os of the cervix dilates, which allows semen to travel up into the uterus. In men, the stimulation from sympathetic nerves constricts the blood vessels leading into the penis and erection subsides rapidly. About 50% of the size of the erection is lost within a few seconds, and the remaining erection slowly subsides over the course of a few minutes. The scrotum relaxes, and the testes drop further from the body (Figure 6.10).

Other Models of Sexual Response

Masters and Johnson's HSRC is not the only description of human sexual response. Dr. Helen Singer Kaplan's **triphasic model** includes only sexual desire, excitement, and orgasm. She felt that the plateau phase was redundant and could better be considered the latter part of the excitement phase. David Reed's

Triphasic model Helen Singer Kaplan's model of sexual response that includes desire, excitement, and orgasm.

Table 6.2 Summary of the Human Sexual Response Cycle

STAGE	EFFECTS IN THE FEMALE	EFFECTS IN THE MALE	EFFECTS IN BOTH
Excitement	• Vagina lubricates and changes shape—upper $2/3$ widens, outer $1/3$ narrows • Uterus lifts and enlarges • Clitoris increases in diameter • Labia majora flatten, spread, and separate • Labia minora increase in size • Nipples become erect, areolae darken, size of breasts increases	• Penis becomes erect • Urethral opening widens • Scrotal skin constricts • Testes elevate • Nipples become erect (60% of men)	• Increase in muscle tone, heart rate, blood pressure, and respiration • Sex flush occurs in perhaps 25% of men and women
Plateau	• Vagina swells and produces orgasmic platform • Labia minora become red and engorged • Clitoris glans retracts under its hood and decreases in size by 50% • Nipples become more erect	• Glans of penis increases in size and darkens in color • May be preorgasmic emission from Cowper's glands • Testes elevate more, rotate slightly, and lie closer to the groin • Prostate gland enlarges	• Heart rate, blood pressure, respiration increase • Increase in muscle tension • Sex flush
Orgasm	• Rhythmic contractions of vagina, uterus, rectum • May be ejaculation from Skene's glands	• Emission: Contraction of the seminal vesicles, prostate, and Cowper's gland to give the feeling of inevitability • Rhythmic contractions of penis and bulbocavernosus muscle • Ejaculation: Reproductive ducts and accessory glands contract, emptying contents into urethra • Refractory period after orgasm	• Rhythmic contractions • Increase in heart rate, blood pressure, respiration • Release of muscular tension • Sex flush • Involuntary contractions of hands and feet
Resolution	• Vaginal contractions cease within about 10 seconds • Clitoris leaves retracted position • Labia minora lighten in color • Breasts decrease in size	• Erection diminishes • Arterioles to the penis constrict and lose about 50% of size of erection	• Heart rate, blood pressure, respiration, muscle tension return to normal

© Cengage Learning 2013

erotic stimulus pathway theory focuses less on the physical changes and more on the psychosocial aspects of sexual response. His theory includes four stages: *seduction, sensation, surrender,* and *reflection.* Seduction includes all the actions that enhance attractiveness, such as what we wear and how we act. Sensations such as sound, touch, and smell affect our arousal; how we interpret these sensations is influenced by our past experiences. Physically, Reed felt that we surrender to orgasm, because it's necessary to give up control and take our mind off our performance in order to experience it. Finally, our reflections on the sexual experience will affect our future sexual patterns. Building on Reed's linear pathway, Beverly Whipple and Karen Brash-McGreer proposed a circular model for female sexual response (1997), suggesting that as a woman reflects on a satisfying sexual experience, it can increase her desire, leading to the seduction phase of the next sexual experience.

Erotic response is more than the physical changes that occur; it is a complex interplay of physiological and psychological factors that are highly susceptible to familial,

Erotic stimulus pathway theory David Reed's model of sexual arousal that includes seduction, sensation, surrender, and reflection.

religious, and cultural attitudes (Haroian, 2000). Sexual response varies from person to person, and from one incident to the next, and sexual fulfillment can occur without the completion of all phases as described by Masters and Johnson.

Sexual Response Across the Life Span

Humans are sexual beings throughout their entire lives (DeLamater & Friedrich, 2002). Sexuality is expressed in different ways at different points in life, depending on biological, psychological, societal, and cultural influences. In this section, we focus on children, adolescents, teenagers, and adults over 50.

Children, Adolescents, and Teenagers

Although the thought of children as sexual beings can make adults uncomfortable, human sexuality begins very early in life. Male infants get erections, and the vaginas of female infants lubricate. Infants as young as 5 months can have orgasms and children may masturbate at a very young age. During the first few years of life, a child's physical body is of primary importance. Sexual interests, curiosity, arousal, and sexual behaviors

critical evaluation

Masters and Johnson's human sexual response cycle may be widely accepted as "the" model of sexual response in both men and women, but how universal is it? What flaws exist in the model?

> **What was the sample?**
Masters and Johnson's subjects were not representative of the average American population of the time. Not only did the researchers specifically choose subjects with a higher than average intelligence, but these subjects volunteered to be observed having sex in a laboratory. Because most people would not volunteer for such a study, volunteer bias may have played a part. In addition, to participate in the study, all subjects were required to be orgasmic. However, in the real world, not all people—especially not all women—experience orgasm as easily or as frequently as Masters and Johnson's subjects did. Does this mean that non-orgasmic people have no sexual response, or that they necessarily have dysfunctional responses? Must an orgasm occur with every act of sexual intimacy in order for it to be considered normal?

> **Was there experimenter bias?** Masters and Johnson guided their subjects as to the response they considered "correct." When sexual encounters occurred without orgasm, the researchers immediately spoke with the subjects about these "failures" and made suggestions for "improvement of future performance" (Masters & Johnson, 1966, p. 314). Subjects quickly learned what their response "should" be, and tried to give it to the researchers.

> **How universal is the model?**
The HSRC has been interpreted as the "proper" or "normal" sexual response in humans. Although humans had been happily fornicating for 100,000 years, with the publication of Masters and Johnson's Human Sexual Response, they learned how they had apparently been doing it wrong.

> **Is the model appropriate for both men and women?** Men and women don't have identical physical or emotional responses to sexual intimacy. For example, men tend to be more genitally focused, whereas sexual arousal in women may be more subjective and mental. Women may not be aware of genital vasocongestion, and may be more focused on emotional intimacy. Finally, women rate orgasm to be less important than affection and emotional communication in a sexual relationship. Orgasmic release may not always occur for women, and it can occur in many different ways.

> **Is all sexual response created equal?** Different sexual experiences may produce different sexual response cycles. Consider a young couple, newly married, flush with the fervor of new love and passion. Now fast-forward 25 years to the couple, still in love, and still engaged in satisfying sex. Would it be surprising if their sexual arousal and patterns changed over the years? Is their response wrong at one point and right at the other? Might not sexual response change depending on whether your partner is new and novel or long-term and familiar?

> **What comes first?** According to the HSRC, sexual arousal springs forth unbidden and unannounced. How did the excitement occur? Should the model consider desire, passion, fantasy, or sexual drive?

> **Is sexual response strictly physical?** The HSRC model focuses mostly on physical changes, and places orgasm as the goal of sex. ("The cycle of sexual response, with orgasm as the ultimate point in progression . . ." Masters & Johnson, 1966, p. 127.) This mechanistic model considers successful sex to be an erect penis, inserted into a lubricated vagina, resulting in orgasm. In addition to being heterocentric, this model ignores the emotional and spiritual aspects of sexual intimacy, and does not address how intimacy and emotions, as well as social and cultural factors, can influence the sexual experience. Author Paul Joannides (2006) compares this physical model of sexual arousal to "showing the genitals on the statue of David while covering the rest of him with duct tape or a gunny sack" (p. 49).

Although the HSRC is not perfect, Masters and Johnson's pioneering efforts provided us with a valuable tool with which we can study the body's responses during sexual arousal.

---

may be spontaneously expressed unless or until the child is taught to repress or inhibit these behaviors (Haroian, 2000). Children can be very sexually curious, and may "play doctor" with other young children, or touch their own sexual organs. Friedrich and colleagues (1998) interviewed mothers regarding the sexual behavior of their children, aged 2–12. Many children were observed touching their genitals at home (Figure 6.11). This becomes less common as the children age, most likely because older children become more private in their sexual expression.

If a young boy has an erection, a small girl masturbates to orgasm, or children investigate each other's genitals, it is important that we not ascribe adult meanings to the child's sexual response. As professor Ken Plummer says,

> Sexuality certainly has its physiological and behavioral base: but amongst humans it has an essentially symbolic, socially constructed meaning. Nothing automatically translates itself for the child into sexual meaning—this, like everything else, has to be learned and is culture specific. So although a baby may experience a physiological change called orgasm, meaning has to be given to it. . . . The simple imposition of adult sexual meanings (in all their diverse forms) onto the child's experiences (in all their diverse forms) is a gross error. (Plummer, 1991)

A young child's hypothalamus is very active, secreting a burst of GnRH every 90 minutes. This hormonal pulse stops at about age 4. At about age 10, the adrenal glands release a bit of sex hormones; sexual fantasies and masturbation often begin around this age (DeLamater & Friedrich, 2002). From age 6 to 12, physical aspects are not as much in the forefront. Although the desire for sexual

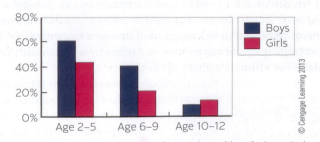
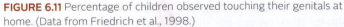

FIGURE 6.11 Percentage of children observed touching their genitals at home. (Data from Friedrich et al., 1998.)

pleasure continues, children may be more thoughtful, private, and discriminating in how they express these desires. By age 12 or so, the pulse generator in the hypothalamus has been turned back on (perhaps as a result of a signal from body fat), and steroid hormones are again released, leading to puberty.

Adolescence is a time of physical changes and sexual curiosity. With the hormonal and physical changes come an increased preoccupation with sex—fantasies, masturbation, and sexual experimentation with others. From age 13 to 15, adolescents experience many physical changes. Their sexual behaviors increase and may become a preoccupation. Sexual desires in adolescents can lead to poor social judgments, high-risk behaviors, and a lack of discrimination (Haroian, 2000). By mid to late adolescence—age 16 and up—there are fewer physical changes and the hormonal storm has calmed. Teenagers often seek sexual gratification through masturbation and in the context of a relationship.

Adults Over 50

Sexual function normally changes with age. In general, the sexual arousal cycle slows down. The stages may take longer to achieve and may be less intense. During excitement, diminished blood flow to the genitalia may result in reduced lubrication in women and delayed and less firm erections in men. Muscle tension may not be as strong during the plateau phase, and a man's testes may not elevate as much as when he was young. In addition, many men lose the sensation of ejaculatory inevitability. Both men and women may experience fewer contractions during orgasm, and men may have a reduction in the volume and force of ejaculation, and a longer refractory period. For both men and women resolution, the return to the prearoused state, occurs more quickly than in the young.

Women. By 2020, there will be as many menopausal women in the United States as there will be women in their childbearing years. As women age, they may notice changes in their sexual response. Some women have increased sexual response in midlife, due to freedom from the fears of pregnancy, satisfaction in their relationships, or improved self-esteem. Other women may notice a decrease in sexual response and activity as a result of the hormonal changes associated with menopause. Changes in an older woman's sexual response may also be caused by societal factors—Western society doesn't generally view older women as sexually attractive. In many cases, a reduction in sexual desire in older women may be related to her perception of her own attractiveness. The greater extent to which a woman perceives herself as less attractive than she was a decade earlier, the more likely she was to report a decline in sexual desire (Koch, Mansfield, Thurau, & Carey, 2005).

As women age, their metabolic rate slows, body fat percentage increases, and the distribution of fat changes, settling more around the abdomen. In the media, photos of older women are routinely altered to make the women appear younger and thinner. An older woman may look at these unrealistic images and think, "she's my age but she doesn't have any wrinkles," which can adversely affect her self-esteem. However, while many

ASK YOURSELF

Did you receive any information about sexual response in your high school sex education classes? From your parents? From your friends or the media? If so, how accurate was the information you received?

midlife women want to weigh less, they are also more realistic in their desired body image than younger women, and report less difference in their actual weight and their desired weight.

As always with sexual response, the context is of utmost importance. A woman's sexual arousal will depend not only on her hormonal status, but on her physical health, relationship status, partner availability, life stressors, and mental health as well. The best predictor of sexual satisfaction for midlife women are those factors associated with her quality of life and relationship status—communication, emotional intimacy, companionship, and respect (Koch et al., 2005).

Men. Although men over 50 report more sexual problems, they may actually have more satisfying sex lives than men in their 30s (Figure 6.12; Mykletun, Dahl, O'Leary, & Fossa, 2006). In a survey of 1,185 men between the ages of 20 and 79, researchers asked the men about sexual functioning and satisfaction. Although men in their 50s reported being less satisfied with their sexual drive, erections, and ejaculations, their overall level of sexual satisfaction was high. This may be because while men in their 30s and 40s are stressed about their careers and busy raising children, men in their 50s are more adjusted to what they want out of life, less concerned with career stress, and more confident and comfortable in who they are.

Aging/Elderly

As life expectancy rises, the number of older Americans will greatly increase. By the year 2030, almost 20% of Americans—some 72 million people—will be 65 years or older (U.S. Census Bureau, 2005). Our culture doesn't usually acknowledge the sexuality of older adults. Media images of sexually active older adults are few and far between and are often viewed with humor or even disgust. Even health care professionals can disregard an older person's sexual life. Physicians may neglect to deal with issues related to sexually transmitted infections (STIs) or sexual function in older people.

Although old age is often associated with a decrease in sexual activity and interest, many older men and women remain sexual throughout their lives. A representative national survey of more than 2,200 older men and women in Finland found that age was a predictor of a person's sexual behavior, but not of sexual desire (Kontula & Haavio-Mannila, 2009). Older men and women who

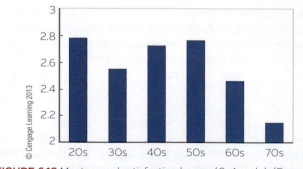

© Cengage Learning 2013

FIGURE 6.12 Men's sexual satisfaction by age (0–4 scale). (From Mykletun et al., 2006.)

were in good health and who had positive self-esteem and a sexually skillful partner were more likely to report sexual desire. Sexual desire and activity depends on physical factors, such as hormone levels, illness, and medication; psychological factors, such as sexual attitudes, body image, and mental health; and social factors, including availability of partners, the communication and quality of the relationship, and income (DeLamater & Sill, 2005).

Though there may be some physical and mental changes, both men and women can feel sexual desire and arousal throughout their lives. Those who have been sexually active throughout their adult lives, and who value and enjoy sex, tend to remain active as they age. Remember also that one's outlook greatly influences his or her sexual response, and people's comfort with their body or their relationship significantly affects sexual functioning, especially in women. Physiological changes may not be as strong, but older adults still desire sex and can still experience intense and pleasurable sexual relationships.

Effect of Disease or Injury on Sexual Response

Many medical conditions negatively affect sexual functioning. When a person is in pain, or experiencing depression, sexual response is often compromised. **Cardiovascular disease**—which affects more than 70 million Americans—may impair sexual functioning. Reduced blood flow associated with heart disease can hinder blood flow to the genitalia, resulting in difficulties with erection and lubrication. Although the risk of death during sexual activity is very low, those with cardiovascular disease may also experience anxiety regarding the physical exertion that sexual activity puts on the heart, which can hamper their performance or enjoyment of the sexual act (Jackson, 2009).

Diabetes can also affect sexual function. More than 8% of the U.S. population—more than 25 million people—has diabetes, and the number is increasing daily (American Diabetes Association, 2011). Poor diet and a lack of exercise greatly contribute to a person's risk of contracting type 2 diabetes. Aside from its devastating effects on the body's metabolic system, diabetes is a leading cause of kidney failure, blindness, and heart disease. Most diabetics have impaired blood flow and/or some degree of nerve damage, two factors that underlie erectile dysfunction and problems with vaginal lubrication. In addition, the high blood glucose predisposes diabetic women to yeast infections.

In some cases, it is the *treatment* of conditions that can impair sexual functioning. Pain-relieving narcotics reduce a person's orgasmic potential, and many antidepressants reduce sexual desire and functioning. Pharmacological treatment of benign prostatic hyperplasia (BPH) can lead to erectile dysfunction and reduced sexual desire, and surgical treatment of BPH can also cause impotence or retrograde ejaculation.

Men and women with spinal cord injuries can and do experience desire, arousal, and orgasm. Even some women who have suffered complete spinal cord injuries still experience sensations during intercourse and can experience orgasm; it is thought that signals travel to the brain on a different nerve pathway than normal in these women (Komisaruk & Whipple, 2005).

Though the frequency of sexual activity, degree of erection or lubrication, and overall sexual satisfaction is usually decreased after spinal cord injury (Yang, 2000), it may be that sexual satisfaction in those with spinal cord injury is not related to physical function or orgasmic capacity. Instead, it may depend on factors such as self-image, problems with immobility or incontinence, partner satisfaction, and relationship quality (Phelps, Albo, Dunn, & Joseph, 2001).

Psychological Control of Sexual Arousal

After completion of this section, you will be able to . . .

○ Consider the role of *spectatoring* in sexual arousal.

○ List the effect of external factors, emotions, and physical concerns on sexual arousal.

"The largest sexual organ is the brain."

Masters and Johnson called it **spectatoring**—mentally stepping outside of oneself during sexual activity with a partner and monitoring the experience. When people do this, they are not "in the moment," and not paying attention to the physical and sensory events going on. Spectatoring hinders sexual arousal and can even lead to sexual problems; persistent worry about performance can lead to inhibited sexual functioning. After all, the word "ecstasy" is derived from Greek, meaning "out of consciousness" (or out of one's mind)—thinking during sex would subtract from the experience.

External factors may affect sexual arousal. Stimuli from the outside world can enhance sexual response, as with mood lighting or erotic music, or diminish it, as with a smoke alarm or a crying baby. A partner's excitement (or lack thereof) can also influence sexual response. Often, visual or verbal evidence of a partner's sexual excitement enhances a person's sexual experience, but some may interpret this as a threat or demand for sexual activity, which can diminish response. Perception of external consequences—such as pregnancy, STIs, or getting caught or interrupted—or even distracting thoughts about school or work can take away from the sexual experience.

Emotions also influence sexual response. Feelings of guilt or regret, or thoughts of past negative sexual experience, may slow or prevent a person from responding to a sexual situation, as can relationship discord or distrust. Although anxiety may lessen a woman's sexual response, in some cases it may actually increase erections in men. When male subjects were first shown an anxiety-producing film they showed increased sexual arousal upon viewing an erotic film (Purdon & Holdaway,

Can paralyzed people have orgasms?

Cardiovascular disease A disease of the heart or blood vessels, cardiovascular disease is the number one cause of death and disability in the United States.

Diabetes A metabolic disease in which the body is unable to produce or is resistant to insulin, leading to abnormally high levels of blood sugar.

Spectatoring Mentally stepping outside of oneself during sexual activity with a partner and monitoring the experience.

2006). Thoughts of others can enhance or lessen one's sexual arousal. It is not uncommon for people to fantasize about others or about past sexual experiences. Thinking of *your partner's* other partners, though, can have a negative impact on your sexual encounter.

Sexual response is also affected by physical concerns. Performance anxiety can occur when a person stops focusing on the erotic sensations and emotional connections of the sexual act, and becomes overly concerned with his or her physical performance. A person may question if he or she is "doing it right," or mentally compare himself to others. Men are more likely to have concerns regarding sexual performance, whereas women are more likely to be anxious about their body—usually its appearance or odor (Meana & Nunnink, 2006). A survey of 14- to 74-year-old women found that those who were more satisfied with their body image reported more sexual activity and orgasm, were more likely to initiate sex and more comfortable in trying new sexual behaviors, and had more comfort in undressing in front of their partner or leaving lights on during sexual activity (Ackard, Kearney-Crooke, & Peterson, 2000).

Physiological Factors That Control Sexual Response

After completion of this section, you will be able to . . .

○ Describe the role of the central nervous system, hormones, and the senses in sexual response.

○ Define *primary* and *secondary erogenous zones,* and *pheromones.*

Central Nervous System

Humans and other animals have evolved to find sex pleasurable—the continuation of the species depends upon it! Therefore, it is not surprising that so many of our bodily systems are involved with relaying sexual pleasure. In this section, we will talk about the role of the brain, spinal cord, neurotransmitters, hormones, and senses in sexual response.

Many areas of the **central nervous system** (the brain and spinal cord) play an essential role in sexual response (Figure 6.13). Nerves of the spinal cord carry important signals to and from the genitals and the brain. The brain's **cerebral cortex** processes thoughts, memories, and fantasies; receives sensory signals; and sends out voluntary motor responses. The cortex also gives you an idea of what behaviors are appropriate, and makes conscious decisions for your actions. The temporal lobe of the cortex, which contains the amygdala and the hypothalamus, is particularly important for sexual response. The **hypothalamus** is vital for sexual arousal and functioning. In addition to controlling hormone release, biological rhythms, and sex drive, the hypothalamus regulates emotions and the behaviors that accompany them. One region in particular—the medial preoptic area of the hypothalamus (MPOA)—has been associated with sexual arousal and behavior. Electrical stimulation of this area produces sexual behaviors, and damage to the area eliminates these responses.

Neurotransmitters are chemicals released from neurons; they relay information between one neuron and another. Many neurotransmitters influence sexual functioning. *Dopamine,* which is involved in mood, reward, and attention and is stimulated by such drugs as cocaine and amphetamines, stimulates the hypothalamus and may facilitate sexual arousal (although use of these drugs ultimately hurts sexual functioning by creating problems achieving erections and orgasms). On the other hand, the neurotransmitters *serotonin* and *melatonin* may inhibit sexual activity. *Nitric oxide,* another neurotransmitter, is important in the mechanism of erection, whereas *phenylethylamine* may be important in infatuation.

Hormonal Control of Sexual Response

Hormones are chemicals secreted into the blood that regulate many bodily functions, including growth, metabolism, and reproduction. Both men and women produce testosterone (the purported "male" sex hormone) and estrogen (the "female" sex hormone), although in differing amounts. Before puberty, both boys and girls secrete low levels of sex hormones from the adrenal glands. At puberty, the gonads take over most production; in men, the testes produce testosterone (and a little estrogen), and in women, the ovaries produce estrogen (and a little testosterone). These hormones are important in reproductive function, as well as in the development of secondary sexual characteristics—the physical traits that differentiate males from females.

Estrogen's role in sexual arousal is unclear. Women need a certain level of estrogen for vaginal lubrication and blood flow to the genitalia. In addition, women feel sexier and flirt more in the days before ovulation, when estrogen levels are highest (Durante & Li, 2009). Women are more likely to have sex during their most fertile days—ovulation and the five days preceding ovulation (Wilcox et al., 2004). However, females are sexually responsive even when estrogen levels are low, and there is little evidence that estrogen facilitates orgasmic function.

Testosterone is necessary for normal sexual functioning in males. Men who have **hypogonadism** produce abnormally low levels of testosterone and generally experience less sexual desire and activity. **Castration** is the use of surgical or chemical techniques whereby a biological male loses use of the testes, thus drastically reducing his testosterone levels. Castration leads to a reduction of sperm production, as well as a decrease in sex drive and erectile and ejaculatory abilities. In some states, convicted sex offenders may be required to receive weekly injections of progesterone in the form of Depo-Provera, which reduces testosterone, sex drive, and sexual function. Although testosterone is involved in the sex drive, it does not appear that taking more testosterone will heighten a person's sex drive; in fact, when men increase their testosterone levels through the use of anabolic/androgenic steroids, negative feedback to the anterior pituitary will inhibit hormone release, ultimately decreasing sex drive and leading to shrinkage of the testicles.

Central nervous system
The brain and spinal cord.

Cerebral cortex   From the Latin for "bark," the cerebral cortex is the outermost layer of the brain, important in sensation, voluntary movement, memory, awareness, language, reasoning, and higher thought.

Hypothalamus   A part of the brain involved in hormone release, biological rhythms, emotions, and sex drive.

Neurotransmitter   A chemical substance released from a nerve cell that carries signals between the neuron and other cells.

Hypogonadism   Low functioning of the ovaries or testes.

Castration   Surgical or chemical disabling of the testes so as to drastically reduce a male's testosterone levels.

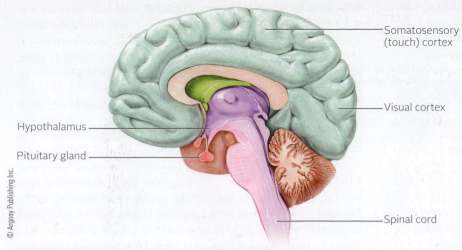

Erogenous zones are areas of the body that are particularly sensitive to touch, and that lead to sexual arousal when stimulated. **Primary erogenous zones** are very sensitive areas with many nerve endings. Most are located around body openings, such as the genitals, mouth, ear, and anus, but also include the breast and fingers. **Secondary erogenous zones** become sensitized through experience, and are specific for each person. For one person, a partner's stroke at the back of the knee may cause sexual arousal; for another, the same behavior may arouse nothing more than giggles.

FIGURE 6.13 Many parts of the central nervous system play an essential role in sexual response.

Testosterone is also important in women's sexual functioning. When women's androgen levels diminish, as with surgical or natural menopause, women may gradually lose sexual desire. In women whose ovaries have been removed, hormonal supplements of both estrogen and androgens together improve sexual desire more than estrogen replacement alone. Some physicians recommend a testosterone patch to treat low sex drive in women. However, the patch was found to produce only a slight increase in sexual satisfaction—women who wore the patch twice weekly had one more "satisfying sexual event" per month than women on placebo. In addition, increased levels of testosterone in women may increase their risk of heart attack and stroke. An advisory committee to the Food and Drug Administration (FDA) unanimously decided that more research was necessary before the testosterone patch would be endorsed. Of course, it is important to remember that sexual arousal is a complex interaction of biology, psychology, culture, as well as hormones.

Senses

Touch

Skin—the gateway between the outside world and ourselves—is the largest organ in the body. The sense of touch most directly affects our response to sexual stimuli. The metaphor of touch infuses our emotional world; as naturalist and poet Diane Ackerman points out in *A Natural History of the Senses* (1990), we call our emotions "feelings," and when something affects us deeply it "touches" us. Touch is necessary for more than sexual arousal; it is necessary for life itself. When young animals are given food and water but deprived of physical contact, they develop abnormal cognitive and behavioral functions as adults. Premature infants who are massaged regularly gain weight significantly faster than unmassaged babies: they are more alert, active, and responsive, and have fewer physical problems later in life. In a classic study, psychologist Harry Harlow offered baby rhesus monkeys a choice between two artificial surrogate "mothers": one was made of wire and fed them, and one was made of terrycloth and did not feed them. Babies spent significantly more time with the non-feeding terrycloth "mother," suggesting that they preferred touch to food.

> "Love is blind; that is why it always proceeds by the sense of touch."
> —French proverb

Vision

Vision is second only to touch in its importance for sexual arousal. Both men and women can be sexually aroused by visual cues, such as an attractive person or erotic artwork, and these arousing images produce a strong response in the brain; in fact, the responses occur even before the brain is able to classify the content of a picture (Anokhin et al., 2006).

Both genders respond to visual stimuli, although men report more sexual arousal when viewing visual erotica, and some women do not recognize their body's physical response to the images.

Men and women showed similar brain activity upon viewing visual erotica, except men had more activity in their hypothalamus, which correlated with their increased reports of sexual arousal (Karama et al., 2002).

Taste

Whereas all other senses can be experienced from a distance, taste must be experienced intimately; to taste an object, the object must be taken into the body through the mouth. Many bodily secretions may be tasted during sexual activity; in addition to saliva, semen, and vaginal fluid, the tongue may encounter earwax, urine, menstrual blood, or breast milk. Sexual partners often have strong preferences in relation to what substances they will allow to come in contact with their mouths. These preferences depend not only on the specific secretion, but on the state of arousal. For example, although 78% of males said it would be acceptable to taste a partner's blood (from a small cut), only 39% said they would taste menstrual blood; and though 81% of males would allow their mouths to come in contact with earwax during sexual arousal, only 36% said they would taste their partners earwax when they were not sexually excited (Levin, 2004b).

Hearing

Sounds have the potential to both enhance and lessen a person's sexual arousal. A partner's sounds of delight may heighten the erotic potential of an encounter, whereas the sounds of a roommate's

Primary erogenous zones Sensitive areas of the body, often located around body openings, that lead to sexual arousal when stimulated.

Secondary erogenous zones Areas of the body that become sensitized through personal experience.

conversation in the next room may stifle the mood. Many people consider music—whether the pounding of the drums or an erotic lyric that perfectly expresses a moment—to be an integral component of sex.

Olfaction and Pheromones

"Smell is 80% of love."
—Author *Tom Robbins*

Each day we breathe in approximately 23,040 times, moving 438 cubic feet of air, which all passes over our olfactory receptors and carries information about odor. Smell was probably the first sense to develop, and more primitive species depend on this sense to find food, detect danger, and sniff out mates. Signals from the olfactory system in humans travel directly to the **limbic system**, an area of the brain containing structures that are involved in motivation, memory, and emotional response.

In other species, olfaction plays a direct role in governing sexual arousal; in humans, the effect is subconscious and subtle. Body odor can signal physical and immunological health and as such can be an important component in mate selection. Herz and Cahill (1997) reported that whereas men primarily consider a woman's appearance, women rank a man's body odor as the most important characteristic in choosing a sexual partner; however, these preferences may pertain only to Western society, in which people are expected to be minty-clean and April-fresh. Many Westerners would be stymied if they visited the tribe in New Guinea in which people say good-bye to each other by putting a hand in each other's armpit and stroking it over themselves, so that their departing friend's odor will remain with them.

Some find the odor of genital secretions to be very sexually arousing; others are turned off by the smell. There is a legend that Napoleon loved Josephine's natural smell. During one of his absences he sent her a note that read, "I return in three days; don't bathe." In the 1990s, vending machines in Japan offered panties supposedly worn by schoolgirls. These soiled panties could be purchased for the equivalent of about $50 (Mizuguchi, 1994).

Men can smell when women are at the most fertile times of their cycle. When asked to smell T-shirts worn by women during fertile and infertile times of their cycles, men rated the smell of the T-shirts worn by women in their fertile phase as more pleasant and sexier (Singh & Bronstad, 2001).

Sometimes we have a powerful and instant response to others. "It's chemical," we claim, as we declare love at first sight. It just might be. Human pheromones may play a role in attraction and arousal, mood, reproductive cycles, and other forms of subconscious sexual communication. **Pheromones** are colorless,

In rural Austria, a girl would keep an apple slice under her armpit while dancing. At the end of the dance, she would offer the sweat-soaked slice to the man of her choice, who would eat the apple (Levin, 2004b).

odorless, airborne chemical signals given off by the body, which are thought to affect behavior in animals; whether they also affect human behavior is a controversial question.

Some evidence supports the existence of such chemosensory communication in humans. As we discussed in Chapter 4, women who live together may show some synchronization of their menstrual cycles (McClintock, 1971). When women dabbed on a synthetic substance thought to be a possible pheromone, their sexual behavior with men was 3 times more frequent than in women who received a placebo (McCoy & Pitino, 2002). The substance was thought to act by influencing men's attraction to the women, not by increasing the women's sexual drive, because the incidences of sexual intercourse and sleeping next to a partner increased, but the incidence of masturbation did not. Another study using a putative male pheromone showed a similar phenomenon in male subjects (Cutler, Friedmann, & McCoy, 1998). The effect of these chemical signals may depend on one's sexual orientation: exposure to male pheromones produced the same brain excitation in gay men as it did in heterosexual women (Savic, Berglund, & Lindström, 2005). Some pheromones may *decrease* libido; a recent study found that when a woman cries, her tears contain a pheromone that may reduce a man's sexual arousal. Men who unknowingly smelled the pheromone in a woman's tears had lower salivary levels of testosterone, rated photos of women to be less attractive, and showed reduced neuronal activity in brain areas that had previously reacted to erotic images (Gelstein et al., 2011).

However, the exact role of human pheromones has not been determined. It is unclear whether human pheromones act by means of the **vomeronasal organ (VNO)** (Figure 6.14), the organ in other species that perceives pheromones, or through the olfactory epithelium (Grosser, Monti-Block, Jennings-White, & Berliner, 2000; Yoon, Enquist, & Dulac, 2005). Scientists do not even agree whether human pheromones exist at all. Regardless of the exact role that pheromones play in human interactions, those who expect a magic elixir that, once applied to the body, will make the other sex fall willingly at their feet, will be disap-

Limbic system A set of structures in the brain that controls emotions, instinctive behavior, and motivation. The hypothalamus is part of the limbic system.

Pheromones (FAIR-uh-mone) A chemical released by one individual that changes the physiology or behavior of another individual of the same species.

Vomeronasal organ (VNO) The organ that detects pheromones in many species. Its function in humans is controversial.

If you want to arouse a man, try sticking a pumpkin pie under each armpit. That's the finding from the labs of Alan Hirsch and Jason Gruss. They measured penile blood flow when men were exposed to different smells. The winner was a combination of the smell of pumpkin pie and lavender, which increased blood flow by 40%, with doughnuts and licorice coming in second. The aroma of baked cinnamon buns was found to increase blood flow to the penis more than perfume did (Hirsch & Gruss, 1999).

_____

_____

_____

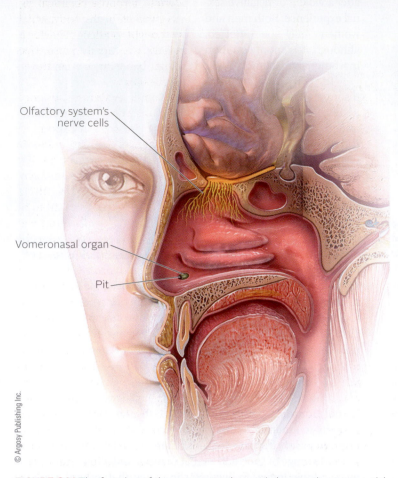

Olfactory system's nerve cells

Vomeronasal organ

Pit

© Argosy Publishing Inc.

FIGURE 6.14 The function of the vomeronasal organ in humans is controversial.

pointed. Very few human behaviors are triggered and expressed in such a stereotyped way. Human behaviors are complex and dependent on learning, the physical environment, the social context, as well as the free will of the individual (Jacob & McClintock, 2000).

Sexual Problems and Treatments

After completion of this section, you will be able to . . .

O Describe the symptoms, etiologies, and treatment of sexual desire disorders, sexual arousal disorders, orgasmic disorders, and sexual pain disorders.

O Define *erectile dysfunction, premature ejaculation, dyspareunia,* and *vaginismus.*

O Explain the mechanism of action of Viagra, and explain why it is not generally effective in women.

O Compare the incidence of sexual dysfunctions in heterosexuals and gays and lesbians.

O Consider the incidence of sexual dysfunction in the United States.

O Evaluate the current means of classifying sexual problems.

No one has "perfect" sex each and every time; variations in desire, arousal, and orgasm are normal. But when a problem with any of these aspects persists and causes personal distress or problems in a relationship, it might be considered a sexual dysfunction. Sexual dysfunction is complicated—it is usually multicausal and multidimensional, and has multiple effects on the person, the partner, and their relationship (Metz & McCarthy, 2007). Sexual problems are quite common, although their exact incidence is difficult to assess. The 4th edition of the *Diagnostic and Statistical Manual of Mental Disorders (DSM-IV-TR)* characterizes **sexual disorders** as disorders of desire, arousal, orgasm, or sexual pain.

Sexual Desire Disorders

Hypoactive sexual desire (HSD) is the persistent or recurrent absence of sexual thoughts, fantasies, desire for, or initiation of sexual activity, either alone or with a partner. HSD is thought to be the most common sexual problem in the United States, affecting women more than men. But how much desire is "normal"? Women in general may be less interested in sex than men are, although women are more likely than men to view an absence of sexual desire in a relationship as problematic (Rosen & Leiblum, 1987). Also, women may experience desire in a different way than men do. There is a danger in applying male standards of "normalcy" to women, who may be pathologized as having low sexual desire compared to a male benchmark. Physical, psychological, and social factors all affect a person's sexual desire. Overall, sexual desire tends to diminish as we age. This may be related to hormonal changes or to the increased incidence of health issues and illness in later life. Depression or guilt may negatively impact sexual desire, as can relationship problems or a lack of attraction to one's partner. The psychological stresses of daily life may also have an effect on a person's erotic mood. The treatment for some of these issues—antidepressant drugs—also tends to reduce sexual desire. Finally, societal standards also affect sexual desire. Attitudes that negate female sexuality, holding oneself or one's partner to impossible physical standards of beauty, or a fear of loss of control can diminish desire.

According to the *DSM-IV-TR,* hypoactive sexual desire becomes a diagnosable disorder when this absence of desire causes personal distress or problems in the relationship. Perhaps, then, hyposexual sexual desire might best be reconsidered as a **discrepancy in desire** between partners. Low sexual desire may also be a normal by-product of a long-term relationship. As therapist Esther Perel (2009) states,

Part of why it is difficult to sustain desire in long-term relationships is because what fuels desire is sometimes going in a different direction than what fuels long-term relationships. What makes [for healthy] long-term relationships is predictability, stability and reliability. All these things

Sexual disorder An inability to react physically or emotionally to sexual stimulation compared to an average healthy person or according to one's own standards.

Hypoactive sexual desire (HSD) Absent or deficient desire for sexual activity.

Discrepancy in desire When partners routinely experience different levels of sexual desire to the point where it has a negative impact on their relationship.

In 2006 the mayor of Novo Santo Antonio, a small town in Brazil, gave out free Viagra to men over the age of 60. This program, approved by the town's legislature, was dubbed *pinto allegre*, which means "happy penis" in Portuguese. After an initial unforeseen problem—the incidence of extramarital affairs multiplied—the program was changed so that the Viagra is now distributed to the wives of the men who sign up for the program.

that create security and safety are not the same ingredients as the ones that fuel desire. So we're trying to integrate two very different contradictory human needs in one relationship and for a multitude of years. And that is a paradox. We've never, in the history of human kind, tried to integrate these two sets of opposing needs in one place. (p. 3)

There is a push to treat hyposexuality pharmaceutically, although there is often no physical origin for this complaint. Testosterone patches are being developed, although most women with HSD have normal testosterone levels. **Cognitive-behavioral therapy (CBT)** seems to be most successful in treating disorders of low sexual desire. CBT focuses on how a person thinks and how these thoughts affect his or her attitudes and behavior. Sex therapists suggest that those who wish to increase their sexual desire try to create a sexual environment, both externally and mentally. Men and women trying to increase their sexual desire can focus on sensual physical feelings or fantasies, rather than trying to will themselves into sexual arousal. Couples may strive to make intimacy a priority, to link this intimacy to sex, and to appreciate that intercourse is not the only way that sexual intimacy can be expressed.

Cognitive-behavioral therapy (CBT) A form of therapy that seeks to modify fixed patterns of negative thoughts and behaviors.

Sexual aversion disorder Aversion to or avoidance of sexual activity.

Sensate focus Designed to reduce anxiety, these exercises help participants focus on the sensory experience, rather than viewing orgasm as the sole goal of sex.

Sexual arousal disorders The persistent or recurrent inability to attain or maintain sufficient sexual excitement necessary for satisfactory sexual encounters.

Impotence (IM-puh-tense) A failure to achieve or maintain an erection sufficient for sexual activity; from the Latin, meaning "loss of power."

Erectile dysfunction The persistent inability of a man to obtain or sustain an erection.

Older couples should also remember that the priapic excesses of their youth might no longer be a reality; ordinary adults in a long-term relationship aren't in a constant frenzy of sexual desire. It may also be that neither partner necessarily has an "abnormal" sex drive; they simply have different levels of desire.

Sexual Aversion Disorders

A person with a **sexual aversion disorder** reacts to sexual contact or activity with extreme discomfort, disgust, or fear. Women with sexual aversion disorder may even avoid gynecological exams. Some people experience distress during all sexual encounters, whereas others develop the aversion

after a violent or negative sexual experience. Both men and women may be affected, although it is more common in women than in men.

To treat sexual aversion disorder, it is necessary to identify and resolve the underlying conflicts that contribute to the negative sexual response. This may include cognitive-behavioral exercises to understand and overcome the underlying sexual issues; couples therapy to deal with subsequent relationship issues; and pharmacological treatments and **sensate focus** exercises to reduce anxiety. Sensate focus exercises are a series of body touching techniques, which begin with nonsexual touch and slowly move toward more sexual contact. These exercises can increase a person's awareness of sensation and encourage him or her to focus on the feeling in a nonthreatening way.

Sexual Arousal Disorders

Sexual arousal disorders are defined as the persistent or recurrent inability to attain or maintain sufficient sexual excitement—be it erection or lubrication—for satisfactory sexual encounters. There is a wide range of "normal" sexual arousal, and it may simply take some people longer to become stimulated than others. The idea that there is a "right" and "wrong" way for arousal to occur can cause anxiety, which can exacerbate the situation. Males typically take longer to become erect as they age, and women are often not aware of their lubrication and often do not equate lubrication with sexual arousal (Chivers, 2005).

Men

Impotence is a failure to achieve or maintain an erection sufficient for sexual activity. Most men experience this at least once in their lives. When impotence becomes persistent, it may be classified as **erectile dysfunction (ED)**. As many as 30 million men in the United States between the ages of 40 and 70 experience some degree of erectile dysfunction; the incidence increases with age (Laumann et al., 1999; Rowland & Burnett, 2000). ED can be caused by physiological conditions, such as problems with the blood vessels, nerves, or erectile tissue; psychological or situational conditions, such as depression, fatigue, alcohol, fear of failure, or anxiety; or a combination of both.

Erectile dysfunction can hurt a man's self-esteem and damage his relationship with his partner. Female partners of men who have developed ED report engaging in less frequent sexual activity, and fewer of these women report being sexually satisfied with their partners compared to before they developed ED (Fisher, Rosen, Eardley, Sand, & Goldstein, 2005).

Various tests are used to determine whether ED is primarily of physiological or psychological origin, including nerve function, ultrasound, and *nocturnal penile tumescence (NPT)*. An NPT test involves checking to see if the penis becomes erect during sleep. Over the course of a normal night's sleep, people cycle

© Krumina/ Shutterstock

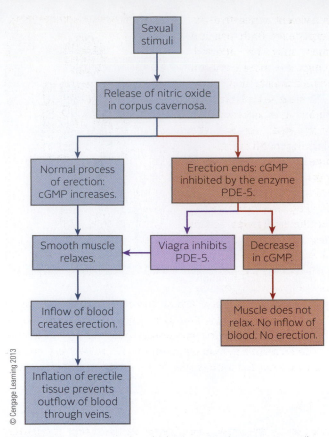

FIGURE 6.15 The process by which Viagra works to treat erectile dysfunction.

ASK YOURSELF

In their book *Human Sexual Inadequacy*, Masters and Johnson (1970) asserted that 90% of impotency cases were psychological in origin. Today, 90% of impotency cases are thought to be physical in origin. To what factors do you account this change? Has there been a change in men's bodies so that more cases are a result of physical causes? Are we more able to diagnose medical causes? Is it related to the fact that a drug exists that *treats* physical causes?

sexactually

The Top 10 Possible Marketing Slogans for Viagra

Suggested generic names: Mycoxafailin, Mycoxafloppin, Mydixadrupin, Mydixarizen.

1. The quicker dicker upper
2. One-a-day, like iron
3. Reach out and touch someone
4. Be all that you can be
5. We bring good things to life
6. When it absolutely, positively has to be there tonight
7. Home of the whopper
8. Like a rock!
9. Strong enough for a man, but made for a woman
10. This is your penis. This is your penis on drugs. Any questions?

in and out of REM sleep. During REM, the penis (and the clitoris) normally becomes erect. If a man has normal erections during his sleeping REM stages, it is evidence that his ED may be of a psychological rather than physical origin.

There are more treatments for erectile dysfunction than for any other type of sexual problem. Treatments include cognitive-behavioral therapy and a range of pharmacological, surgical, or mechanical approaches. Because of their ease and familiar route of administration, oral medications are the most popular treatment for erectile dysfunction in the United States; in fact, sales of drugs to treat ED were thought to account for $6 billion in 2006. The most well known of these drugs is **Viagra**. Originally developed as a drug to treat blood pressure and cardiovascular ailments, Viagra's effectiveness in promoting erections was discovered during drug testing after the male subjects did not want to return their drug samples after the study was completed. Viagra was released in the United States on March 27, 1998, and within 3 months more than 3 million prescriptions had been issued, making it the fastest-selling drug in history.

The ED drugs Viagra (sildenafil citrate), Cialis (tadalafil), and Levitra (vardenafil) all work by inhibiting the enzyme **phosphodiesterase-5 (PDE-5)**. During an erection, release of nitric oxide in the corpus cavernosa of the penis causes an elevation of a substance called cyclic GMP (cGMP), which relaxes the smooth muscle of the penis, allowing blood to flow in. Cyclic GMP is broken down by the enzyme phosphodiesterase 5 (PDE-5). Viagra and other drugs inhibit PDE-5, thus facilitating cGMP's effect on erection (Figure 6.15). It is important to note that PDE-5 inhibitors do not produce a spontaneous erection; they only prolong an erection that occurs due to sexual stimula-

tion. These drugs are most effective in men whose impotence is caused by hormonal or physiological issues; their overall success rate is approximately 70%.

Phosphodiesterase-5 inhibiting drugs have minor differences in their potency, duration of action, and side effects (Kim, 2003). Common side effects include headache, facial flushing, nasal congestion, and digestive problems. In about 2–3% of men taking Viagra, visual disturbances occur, including temporary increased brightness, or a blue haze. These effects, which may last for a few minutes to a few hours, occur because PDE-6, an enzyme in the retina, is also partially inhibited by sildenafil. Men who take Viagra may also double their chances of hearing impairment (McGwin, 2010). Priapism, a sustained, painful, and unwanted erection, is rare, but more common in young men with normal erectile function who take these drugs. Not everyone can take PDE-5 inhibitors. They are never to be taken in conjunction with nitrate drugs, because the combination may cause a severe and potentially fatal reduction in blood pressure. Men with hypotension or who are at significant cardiovascular risk may not want to take Viagra.

Men who take the rave drug Ecstasy (MDMA) may experience increased sexual desire but also impairment in their ability to maintain an erection. Because of this, some men take "sextacy," a dangerous combination of MDMA and

Viagra One of a number of drugs used to treat erectile dysfunction.

Phosphodiesterase-5 (PDE-5) The enzyme inhibited by Viagra.

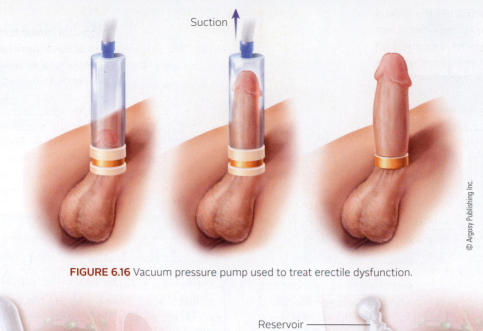

Suction ↑

FIGURE 6.16 Vacuum pressure pump used to treat erectile dysfunction.

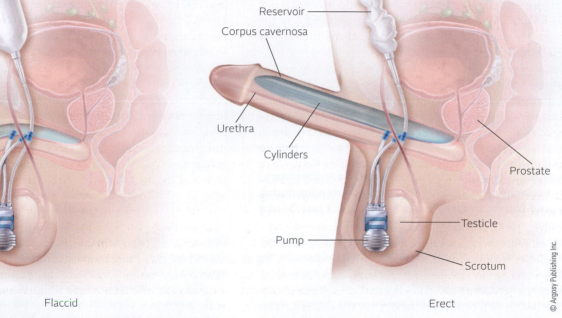

Reservoir

Corpus cavernosa

Urethra

Cylinders

Prostate

Testicle

Pump

Scrotum

Flaccid

Erect

© Argosy Publishing Inc.

FIGURE 6.17 A penile implant creates an artificial erection.

Viagra. The combination of these two drugs significantly raises a man's risk of heart attack and other cardiovascular dangers.

Other medications are also being investigated for the treatment of ED. *Apomorphine* works in the brain to affect perceptions of arousal and pleasure. *Vasomax* and *yohimbine* increase blood flow to the penis. Because these drugs may cause serious side effects, men should consult their physicians before trying any new medication.

Viagra and other drugs are now the treatment of choice, but those who cannot take them, or who don't have satisfactory results, can pursue options such as injectibles, vacuum pumps, or penile prostheses, as well as cognitive-behavioral therapy.

Through its effects on prostaglandins, the drug *Alprostadil* dilates the vessels leading into the penis, causing an erection. Unfortunately, until recently, the only way for men to take this drug was by a suppository inserted into the urethra, or through an injection into the penis. Many men were understandably hesitant to try this drug. Aprostadil is now available as a topical cream (Alprox), which may cause mild pain and burning at the application site.

Vacuum pressure pumps can be used to increase blood flow to the penis to help men achieve erections (Figure 6.16). The pump is a plastic cylinder placed on the penis, with a vacuum-like pump to pull the air out of the cylinder and pull blood into the penis. While a penis pump may cause a temporary increase in the size of the penis, it can also cause nerve and skin damage, as well as severe embarrassment, if the penis gets stuck in the pump.

If penile blood vessels are blocked or damaged, **vascular surgery** may reverse the problem. When all else fails in treatment of erectile dysfunction, a **penile implant** may be used (Figure 6.17). These surgically implanted penile prostheses are inflatable or partially rigid at all times.

Vacuum pressure pumps A manual or battery-operated pump that draws blood into the penis to create an erection.

Vascular surgery An operation to improve blood flow to the penis to improve erection.

Penile implant A surgical implant that creates an artificial erection.

In regard to psychologically based erectile dysfunction, men may work on reducing their feelings of anxiety and improving sexual communication with their partners. Couples experiencing ED can also appreciate the fact that sexual expression takes many varied forms and explore other options, such as manual or oral sex. In the words of one man with ED, "Even if you don't have a knife, you can still lick the jar."

Women

Women may also encounter problems with sexual arousal. They may be slow to lubricate or have trouble becoming sexually excited in response to sexual stimulation. These problems may have physical causes, such as neurological, vascular, or hormonal factors, but they are more frequently related to psychological issues. Women's sexual arousal is not as closely tied to their physical responses as it is in men. Instead, anxiety, fatigue, negative imagery, or relationship issues are more likely to underlie a woman's lack of sexual arousal.

Because women's levels of desire are less closely tied to their physical responses, medical science has not had as much success in treating women's sexual arousal disorders. There are currently no FDA-approved drugs available for any form of female sexual dysfunction. For men, arousal almost always leads to sexual desire. In women, however, arousal and desire may be disconnected. Although PDE-5 inhibitors such as Viagra may increase a woman's vaginal blood flow, they do not necessarily affect her desire to have sex. These drugs would probably be most effective in women with hormonal or physiologically based arousal problems, rather than emotionally or lifestyle-based issues. In other cases, behavioral or psychological treatments might be most effective. For instance, sex play can be slowed down. A woman's partner may focus on foreplay and intimacy until she is aroused. Couples can also address issues outside of the bedroom that affect sexual arousal, such as fatigue related to work and childcare responsibilities, negative imagery or feelings about sex, or possible problems in the relationship.

But perhaps the reason for the unavailability of products that enhance female sexual arousal has less to do with the way women's bodies work and more to do with the way society views women's sexuality. Commercials for erectile dysfunction or male enhancement creams are common, but ads for products that aim to improve women's sexual function are largely absent from the airways. Zestra, a botanical massage oil designed to enhance female sexual pleasure, has been found to improve women's sexual arousal and desire (Ferguson, Hosmane, & Heiman, 2010). Nevertheless, Zestra has had a difficult time getting its ads approved to run on TV, radio, or websites, although these ads are tame compared to similar products aimed at male sexual arousal (Ellin, 2010). This may be because our culture is largely uncomfortable with women's sexuality, especially older women's sexuality.

Orgasmic disorder When there is a delay in or absence of orgasm following sexual stimulation, or if orgasm occurs more quickly than desired.

Premature ejaculation Ejaculation that occurs too rapidly for one's partner to fully enjoy sexual relations.

Premature ejaculation can lead to difficulties in one's relationship.

© wavebreakmedia ltd/Shutterstock

Orgasmic Disorders

Orgasmic disorders are characterized by one of the following two conditions: (1) a persistent or recurrent delay in or absence of orgasm following sexual stimulation, or (2) the occurrence of orgasm more quickly than desired. Orgasmic disorders are most commonly manifested in males as early ejaculation, and in females as a delay in orgasm. The incidence of "too rapid" female orgasm is rarely recognized and not classified as a sexual dysfunction in the *DSM-IV-TR*.

Men

When talking about ejaculation, how early is "premature"? Many men ejaculate before a woman reaches orgasm—do they all suffer from premature ejaculation? There is no universally accepted definition or diagnostic criteria for **premature ejaculation (PE)** (Perelman, 2006). In general, men with PE ejaculate too rapidly—either with minimal sexual stimulation or shortly after penetration—for their partners to fully enjoy sexual relations, and this condition affects sexual satisfaction, psychological well-being, and relationship contentment. These men often have decreased self-confidence, and may have difficulties in their relationships over real or perceived problems in satisfying their partners. Women whose partners have PE report lower sexual satisfaction and more interpersonal problems in the relationship. The men themselves also report less sexual satisfaction, because they are anxious and preoccupied with ejaculatory control during sex. PE may be a lifelong problem, or it may develop after a period of normal ejaculatory function. It can occur in all situations, or only with certain partners. Up to 25–30% of men are reported to suffer from PE at some point in their lives (Perelman, 2006; Laumann et al., 1999; Rowland & Burnett, 2000). Men who have graduated from college are only two thirds as likely to report climaxing too early as men who do not have a high school diploma (Laumann et al., 1999).

Both physiological and psychosocial issues underlie premature ejaculation. Physically, men with PE may have abnormal responses of the sympathetic nervous system early in the sexual response cycle, which slows erections and prematurely triggers the ejaculatory reflex (Rowland & Burnett, 2000). Anxiety about intercourse will enhance this sympathetic reaction and exacerbate the condition.

Premature ejaculation is treated with a combination of cognitive-behavioral strategies plus pharmaceutical interventions. Although no medications are currently indicated specifically for PE, doctors can prescribe antidepressants, which have been found to have a side effect of delaying ejaculation, or erection enhancers like Viagra. Topical anesthetics may be used on the penis, although in this case the man should use a condom so as not to anesthetize his partner's genitalia. The injection of vasoactive substances such as Alprostadil into the penis may allow men to maintain an erection after ejaculation has occurred, to better satisfy his partner. Sex therapy can help men and their partners deal with performance anxiety and self-confidence, discuss optimal positions for intercourse, and improve communication. To help a man better recognize and control his ejaculatory inevitability, there are a number of techniques he can employ to lengthen intercourse, such as squeezing the glans, or the "**stop-start technique**," in which he learns to temporarily halt sexual stimulation right before ejaculation. Heterosexual couples are also encouraged to recognize that sexual expression does not begin and end with vaginal intercourse and ejaculation.

At the other end of the spectrum, **delayed ejaculation** occurs when a man is unable to reach orgasm, or reaches orgasm only after prolonged stimulation, for example, intercourse that lasts for 30–45 minutes or more. Men with this relatively infrequent condition may have difficulty ejaculating during vaginal intercourse, although they may be able to during masturbation or oral sex. Delayed ejaculation may be caused by certain drugs, such as antidepressants, alcohol, or Viagra, or with diseases such as leukemia, syphilis, or multiple sclerosis. More commonly, psychological factors such as performance anxiety, fear of loss of control, sexual guilt, or underlying hostility toward their partners plays a role.

If a man has *never* ejaculated, even by masturbation or nocturnal emissions, he should consult a urologist to determine if there is an underlying physical cause. If delayed ejaculation occurs only in certain situations, he would be better served by seeking the help of a sex therapist. Typical treatment of delayed ejaculation involves behavior modification, in which the couple goes through a period of time during which they can cuddle, but intercourse is off limits. They slowly work up to penetrative intercourse. The man will often be given "homework," such as sensate focus exercises, to help him deal with the problem. The therapist will often work with the couple to deal with sexual communication issues and to help them find techniques to provide ideal stimulation.

Women

Failure to achieve orgasm with intercourse is more common for women than erectile difficulties are for men. However, medical science has not poured millions of dollars into the development of new drugs to address this problem, as it has for ED. Orgasmic disorders are the second most frequently reported sexual problem by women after hypoactive sexual desire. In the National Social and Health Life Survey conducted in the early 1990s (Laumann, Gagnon, Michael, & Michaels, 1994), 24% of women reported that they had not had an orgasm for at least several months. Women with orgasmic disorder may be unable to reach orgasm (**anorgasmia**) or have difficulty in reaching orgasm after what would usually be an adequate amount of sexual stimulation. In many cases, women have difficulty in reaching orgasm during vaginal intercourse, which might not stimulate the clitoris sufficiently, but are able to through masturbation or oral sex.

Orgasmic disorder may have a physical origin, such as diabetes, neurological problems, chronic illness, or hormonal deficiencies, or may be related to drugs such as antidepressants or opiates. More commonly, however, there are psychosocial foundations. Women with orgasmic disorders are less likely to be educated about sex, less comfortable in communicating their desire for clitoral stimulation to their partners, more likely to have negative attitudes about masturbation, and more likely to have psychological problems (Kelly, Strassberg, & Kirchner, 1990).

Women who have difficulty reaching orgasm may try using medications or devices to improve blood flow to the vagina, but behavioral or psychological techniques are more effective. Women can work with their partners to improve sexual communication and technique. They can practice sensate focus exercises. A woman may also be encouraged to learn about her body's sexual response through masturbation, which allows her to experience sexual pleasure by controlling the degree of stimulation without any real or perceived pressure from a partner.

Sexual Pain Disorders

Dyspareunia is difficult or painful sexual intercourse. Women are more often affected by this problem, although it may affect men as well. Sexual pain occurs in women across the globe. In a survey of more than 6,500 women aged 18–65 from 11 countries, the percentage of women who reported that they "always or usually" experienced pain during intercourse ranged from a low of 3.6% in Australia to a high of 18.6% in Brazil. In the United States, a survey of more than 1,400 women aged 18–59 found that 15.5% of them had ever experienced pain during intercourse during the past 12 months (Laumann et al., 1999). Another U.S. survey of more than 1,000 postmenopausal women found that about 25% reported sometimes or frequently experiencing pain during intercourse. Of those, more than a third said that their pain during sex was so extreme that it interrupted or halted intercourse (Kellog, Kingsberg, & Krychman, 2009). Nevertheless, fewer than half of these older women had initiated a conversation with their health care professional about their vaginal pain. Dyspareunia can result from both physical factors—such as infection, endometriosis, vaginal dryness, or phimosis—and emotional factors—such as inhibitions or abuse. Dyspareunia is most often treated by dealing with the underlying medical problem. The use of personal lubricants or estrogen creams can also help to decrease dryness, itching, and pain.

Vaginismus is a painful, involuntary spasm of the pubococcygeus (PC) muscles of the outer third of the vagina, making penetration difficult or impossible. Vaginismus may have physical causes, such as infection or injury during childbirth, but it most often has psychological origins, such as sexual trauma or abuse, or being taught that intercourse is dirty or wrong. Vaginismus is most often treated with education, counseling, and behavioral exercises. Women may slowly insert vaginal dilators of increasing size to help relax the muscles of the vagina. It also helps to address any underlying psychological fears or issues.

Stop-start technique   A method of overcoming premature ejaculation in which a man and his partner learn to recognize when he is approaching orgasm, temporarily stop sexual stimulation, and restart when he has regained some control.

Delayed ejaculation   When a man is unable to reach orgasm within a satisfactory amount of time.

Anorgasmia   An inability to reach orgasm, even with "adequate" stimulation.

Dyspareunia (dis-puh-ROO-nee-ah)   Difficult or painful sexual intercourse.

Vaginismus   A painful involuntary spasm of the muscles of the vagina.

Penis captivus, not to be confused with vaginismus, is the term used to describe an occurrence that is theoretically possible—a man becomes stuck in a woman after her vaginal muscles clamp down on his penis—but whether the phenomenon has ever actually happened is a matter of some dispute. One medical report of an occurrence has since been found to be a hoax, although other sources claim this can occur, albeit extremely rarely.

In dealing with sexual problems, couples should have realistic physical, psychological, and relationship expectations (Metz & McCarthy, 2007). They should recognize that just as there are many purposes for sex, there are also many styles of arousal and sexual satisfaction. The "good enough sex" model encourages couples to focus on intimacy and pleasure, and to be open and flexible in their definition of sex. Couples can work as an "intimate team" to integrate sex into their daily lives, and integrate their daily lives into sex.

Sexual Issues in Gay and Lesbian Relationships

It is important to consider the sexual issues of people in same-sex relationships on their own terms rather than evaluating them according to what is deemed "standard" or "normal" for heterosexual relationships. Such heterocentricity can lead to a misunderstanding about the realities of sexuality—not only of those in same-sex relationships, but also of those in mixed-sex (heterosexual) relationships. For instance, many studies have shown that lesbians have less sex than heterosexual women, and books and articles have been written about the apparent problem of diminished sexual interest in lesbians (this will be discussed further below). However, what if it was found that women in mixed-sex relationships had as much *desire* for sexual activity as women in same-sex relationships? Then the "problem" might not be that lesbians don't have enough sex, but that women in mixed-sex relationships are, perhaps at the instigation of their male partners, having *more* sex than they would ideally like (Holmberg & Blair, 2009).

Overall, when comparing men and women in heterosexual relationships with those in same-sex relationships, there are more similarities than differences (Holmberg & Blair, 2009). Men and women in mixed- and same-sex relationships report similar levels of sexual satisfaction and sexual communication, although gays and lesbians reported slightly higher levels of sexual desire than those in heterosexual relationships.

Gay men have many of the same sexual concerns as heterosexual or bisexual men, such as erectile dysfunction and desire discrepancy between partners. Some sexual issues are more commonly seen in men who have sex with men, such as pain during receptive anal intercourse, and the need to negotiate relationship openness agreements, whereas other issues occur less frequently: delayed ejaculation is not a common problem among gay men (Nichols, 2004). In general, women who have sex with women report fewer sexual problems than women who have sex with men. Vaginismus and dyspareunia are almost unknown in the lesbian community, and women who have sex with women are less likely than heterosexuals to have trouble

Has a man's penis ever gotten stuck in a woman's vagina?

lubricating or achieving orgasm during sex (Nicols, 2005). Just as with straight women, sexual desire discrepancy between partners is the most common sexual problem lesbians face.

Let's revisit the idea that lesbians have less sex. An influential book written in 1983 by Philip Blumstein and Pepper Schwartz reported that lesbian couples had less frequent sexual contact than gay or heterosexual couples, a phenomenon termed **lesbian bed death**, or **LBD**. Since then, this phenomenon has been reevaluated. Is sexual frequency the only or best indication of a healthy sex life? Lesbians spend more time on a typical sexual encounter than do heterosexuals, and they are more likely to orgasm during sex than are women who have sex with men. If the measure of one's sexual health was not how many times per week an encounter occurred, but the length of time spent during an encounter or the percentage of time orgasm occurred, then lesbians could be considered sexually "healthier" than heterosexual couples (Iasenza, 2002). Another consideration: some say that one of the functions of sex is to improve intimacy and communication between partners. Women who have sex with women tend to have more egalitarian relationships and a higher degree of intimacy, so perhaps their relationships don't "need" as much sex (Nichols, 2004). Finally, when considering the frequency of sexual encounters, perhaps men (gay and straight) and women define "sexual relations" differently, and lesbians define this ambiguous term more narrowly than do gay men or heterosexual men and women. These points illustrate that we should remember that heterosexual relationships are not the standard by which all human activity is to be measured.

U.S. Incidence of Sexual Dysfunctions

A nationwide, representative survey of women and men aged 18–59 showed that 43% of women and 31% of men have some form of sexual dysfunction, and that the incidence of sexual problems is associated with variables including gender, age, education, marital status, and physical and emotional health (Table 6.3; Laumann et al., 1999).

Men experience more sexual problems as they age, which can be attributed to erectile dysfunction and a decrease in sexual desire. Women, on the other hand, experience fewer problems as they mature, except for difficulties associated with lubrication. Young women are more likely to be single and therefore more likely to have a higher partner turnover, interspersed with times of sexual inactivity. This sexual instability in conjunction with inexperience may lead to more stressful and less satisfying sexual encounters. Higher educational attainment was associated with fewer sexual problems. Overall, men and women with less education report more sexual anxiety and less pleasurable sexual experiences. Poor physical and emotional health is also associated with sexual problems, as are negative sexual experiences, such as rape or sexual victimization during childhood. Married people generally show the lowest rates of sexual difficulties. It is important not to confuse correlation with causation—although

Lesbian bed death (LBD) The slang term for the diminishment of sexual activity between two long-term lesbian partners.

(Weatherby et al., 1992). Marijuana may enhance and prolong orgasm, although its effects are most likely the result of increased awareness of bodily sensations and diminished time perception.

Anaphrodisiacs

Some substances, called **anaphrodisiacs**, inhibit sexual response. *Antidepressants* such as Prozac work by affecting serotonin levels, a substance involved in modulating sexual desire. These antidepressants may delay or increase the difficulty in achieving erection and orgasm. *Opioids* such as codeine, heroin, oxycontin, and the cough suppressant dextromethorphan also diminish sexual function and make it more difficult to achieve orgasm. *Nicotine,* the active ingredient in cigarettes, constricts blood vessels, which can impair the ability of the genitals to become engorged with blood during excitement. Your sex drive may

Anaphrodisiac   A substance that diminishes sexual desire.

even be affected by drugs your mother took before you were born: When baby male mice were exposed to low doses of aspirin—which blocks prostaglandin production, thought to be necessary to masculinize the brain—either through the womb or through nursing, they showed lower than normal sex drives as adults (Amateau & McCarthy, 2004).

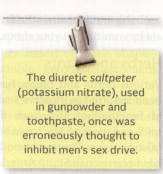

The diuretic *saltpeter* (potassium nitrate), used in gunpowder and toothpaste, once was erroneously thought to inhibit men's sex drive.

Sexual response is a complex and multilayered phenomenon, encompassing biological, psychological, social, and cultural factors. In the next chapters, we will discuss how people become attracted to and begin relationships with others, fall in love, and have relationships.

Chapter Summary

Sexual Response

- The Masters and Johnson human sexual response cycle (HSRC) encompasses four stages: excitement, plateau, orgasm, and resolution. Some people believe that the mental state of desire should also be included in a measure of sexual response. During excitement, men and women experience an increase in heart rate and blood pressure. Blood rushes to the vessels of the genitalia, causing an erection in males and lubrication in females. During plateau, sexual arousal grows as a precursor to orgasm. Orgasm is characterized by a feeling of euphoria, along with a series of rhythmic contractions of the genital region. During resolution, the body returns to its nonexcited state.

- While pleasurable for both, there are some differences in male and female orgasm. Females don't have a refractory period and are more likely to have multiple orgasms. Women also tend to have more contractions, and a wider area of tissue is involved.

- Other models of sexual response include Helen Kaplan's triphasic model and David Reed's erotic stimulus pathway theory. These models include aspects other than the physical changes that the HSRC focuses on.

- There are questions about the universality of the HSRC. The model focuses solely on the physical changes of sexual response, and the research design lends itself to volunteer bias. In addition, the model may overgeneralize and may not be applicable for all men and women.

- People of all ages experience sexual arousal. Not only does one's physical response to sexual arousal change over time, but society's views of arousal change, depending on the age and physical status of the aroused.

- Disease and injury affect sexual response. Cardiovascular disease and diabetes may both impair sexual functioning. Men and women with spinal cord injuries can and do experience desire, arousal, and orgasm.

Psychological Control of Sexual Arousal

- "Spectatoring" is mentally stepping outside of oneself during sexual activity with a partner and monitoring the experience.

This can hurt sexual arousal and can even lead to sexual problems.

- Sexual arousal is affected by many factors, including external stimuli such as lighting, music, or voices; emotions such as guilt, regret, or love; and physical concerns such as performance anxiety or self-consciousness.

Physiological Factors That Control Sexual Response

- Many areas of the brain and spinal cord are essential for sexual response. The neurotransmitters serotonin and dopamine and hormones such as estrogen and testosterone are also important.

- The senses play a key role in sexual arousal. Touch is particularly important. Erogenous zones are areas of the body that lead to sexual arousal when stimulated. Both men and women can be sexually aroused by visual cues. Taste and hearing also play a role, and may enhance or lessen sexual response. Olfaction's role is important, although it may be subconscious and subtle. The role of pheromones in human sexual response is controversial.

Sexual Problems and Treatments

- Sexual disorders are characterized as disorders of desire, arousal, orgasm, or sexual pain. There may be physical, psychological, environmental, or even cultural factors underlying these disorders.

- Women are more likely than men to suffer from hypoactive sexual desire, although a "normal" amount of desire differs from person to person and is influenced by life events.

- Erectile dysfunction—a persistent inability to achieve or maintain an erection—is the most commonly diagnosed sexual arousal disorder. It is often treated with Viagra or other drugs that enhance erection. Viagra and other PDE-5 inhibitors do not cause a spontaneous erection; they prolong an erection that occurs as a result of sexual stimulation. These drugs are most effective in men whose impotence is due to hormonal or physiological issues. Viagra is probably not effective in women, because women's levels of desire are not as closely tied to their physical responses.

- Although many women don't have regular orgasms, premature ejaculation (PE) is the most commonly discussed orgasmic disorder. An ejaculation is generally considered premature when ejaculation occurs too rapidly for a man's partner to fully enjoy sexual relations. PE is often treated with a combination of cognitive-behavioral strategies and pharmaceutical interventions.

- Dyspareunia is a sexual pain disorder most commonly experienced by women. Vaginismus is a painful, involuntary spasm of the pubococcygeus muscles, making penetration difficult or impossible.

- Overall, when comparing men and women in mixed-sex relationships with those in same-sex relationships, there are more similarities than differences.

- A nationwide survey found that 43% of women and 31% of men in the United States have some form of sexual dysfunction, although this number depends on one's definition of sexual dysfunction, and on the survey methods used.

- Many people find fault with the current classifications of sexual dysfunction. It is thought that these classifications lead to a medicalization of sexuality, ignore the context in which sexual problems occur, and serve women particularly poorly.

The Effects of External Substances on Sexual Arousal

- An aphrodisiac is a substance that is thought to arouse or increase sexual response. Many substances are reported to work as aphrodisiacs, although there is no clear definition of what exactly an aphrodisiac does. Some purported aphrodisiacs may cause erection, improve overall health, or reduce inhibitions. As sexual response is much more complex than a simple physiological reflex, people should not expect to find sexual ecstasy in a magic pill.

- Anaphrodisiacs inhibit sexual response. Drugs such as antidepressants, opioids, and nicotine can act as anaphrodisiacs.

evaluate and *decide*

We are inundated with opinions about "normal" sexual response, although these responses vary depending on an individual's age, physical health, emotional state, relationship status, and many other factors.

Imagine the following situations:

> John is the owner of a small business, employing about 50 people. He is in the process of choosing an insurance policy for his company, and needs to decide what treatments and procedures should be included in the coverage. He is considering whether or not Viagra and other treatments for erectile dysfunction should be covered.

> Melinda doesn't always have an orgasm with her husband, although she is satisfied in general with their sex life. Does she have a sexual dysfunction? Should she seek counseling or pharmacological treatments?

What factors would you consider when advising these people?

SITUATION	ISSUES TO CONSIDER
SHOULD VIAGRA BE COVERED BY INSURANCE?	How do the benefits of ED drugs compare to the risks?
	When considering benefits, should John consider the benefits to the individual? To the company? To society in general?
	What determines "need" of a drug or treatment? How devastating is ED to a person's well-being?
	If John were to also consider covering contraception and infertility treatments, how would you compare those treatments to treatments for ED? What are some reasons for your answers?
	Does the gender and age composition of his employees matter? Why? If there are only a few older males working for John, would their need or desire for ED treatment be less than if there were many employees desiring the drug?
IS AN OCCASIONAL INABILITY TO ORGASM A SEXUAL DYSFUNCTION THAT SHOULD BE TREATED?	Is an inability to have an orgasm a sexual dysfunction? How often would the anorgasmia have to occur—once? A majority of the time? Always?
	Can Melinda have orgasm by masturbation? Is this a physical or psychological issue?
	How is Melinda's relationship with her spouse? What is his response to her anorgasmia?
	Is this affecting her relationship with her husband?
	Can sex be satisfying without an orgasm? Always? Never? Does it matter if you are a man or woman? Why or why not? What is the "goal" of sexual activity?
	If neither Melinda nor her husband consider Melinda's inability to have an orgasm during intercourse a problem, does that mean it is not a problem? Why or why not?

Additional Resources

Log in to CengageBrain to access the resources your instructor requires. For this book, you can access:

 **CourseMate** brings course concepts to life with interactive learning, study, and exam preparation tools that support the printed textbook. A textbook-specific website, Psychology CourseMate includes an integrated interactive eBook and other interactive learning tools including quizzes, flashcards, videos, and more.

CENGAGENOW **CengageNOW** is an easy-to-use online resource that helps you study in less time to get the grade you want—NOW. Take a pre-test for this chapter and receive a personalized study plan based on your results that will identify the topics you need to review and direct you to online resources to help you master those topics. Then take a post-test to help you determine the concepts you have mastered and what you will need to work on. If your textbook does not include an access code card, go to CengageBrain.com to gain access. Visit www.cengagebrain.com anytime to access your account and purchase materials.

Web Resources

Current links to all of the following websites and videos can be found on the Psychology CourseMate for this text at www.cengage-brain.com/.

Sexual Health.
An index of pages related to sexual health, including sexual response and aphrodisiacs.

The Guide to Getting It On.
A rich source of information about sexuality, including links to information about sexuality and traumatic brain injury, as well as other physical and mental disorders

Sex and Intimacy in MS.
Links regarding sexuality for those who are living with traumatic brain injury, multiple sclerosis, and other disabilities.

Jon Lajoie sings "Too Fast," a song about premature ejaculation.

Print Resources

Ackerman, D. (1990). *A Natural History of the Senses.* New York: Random House.

Masters, W., & Johnson, V. E. (1966). *Human Sexual Response.* Boston: Little, Brown.

Tiefer, L. (2008) *Sex Is Not a Natural Act, and Other Essays* (2nd ed.). Boulder, CO: Westview Press.

Video Resources

The Anatomy of Sex. (2005). 50 minutes. This video explores the biological forces that underlie sex drive. Why are people attracted to each other? What happens during orgasm? Why do humans mate front to front? All of these questions and more are discussed in this Discovery Channel production.

(Sex)abled: Disability Uncensored. (2009). 15 minutes. Celebrates people with disabilities as sexual beings. Available at http://www.sexsmartfilms.com/free-videos/sex-abled-disability-uncensored.

Orgasm, Inc. (2009). 73 minutes. A documentary about the pharmaceutical industry and the marketing campaigns that are centered on issues of female desire and sexual dysfunction.

Portraits in Human Sexuality: Sexual Dysfunction and Therapy. (2006). 39 minutes. This program introduces the most common dysfunctions while dispelling myths about female sexuality, stressing the importance of good communication and offering advice on improving sexual technique. Common sexual disorders are commented upon as well. In addition, a case study of a couple with psychogenically induced low sex drive provides an opportunity for viewers to learn what it is like to participate in sex therapy. Contains clinically explicit language and illustrations. Produced by FilmsMedia Group: Films for the Humanities & Sciences.

7 Attraction, Dating, and Hooking Up

There are lots of ways to ruin a date. Here are a few things NOT to say on a date.

- I didn't say you NEEDED a boob job, I just said it wouldn't hurt to consider it.
- I know you don't eat meat, but I wanted to use this two-for-one McDonald's coupon before it expired.
- You don't sweat much for a fat girl.
- I have 37 cats. Here, let me show you pictures of all of them.
- How do you feel about hairy backs?
- I'm not drinking tonight; it interferes with the herpes medication.
- Let me tell you about the time that I was anally probed by aliens.
- I believe that Pauly Shore is a misunderstood genius.
- You remind me of my ex.
- I just finished 6 weeks at an ex-gay conversion camp, and I'm ready to dive into heterosexuality!
- Oh, you like my tattoo? My cellmate at Sing Sing did it for me.

© Radius Images/Corbis

©LWA-Dann Tardif/Corbis

© Rolf Bruderer/Corbis

Attraction

After completion of this section, you will be able to . . .

○ Recognize the role that beauty plays in choosing partners.

○ Compare universal and subjective standards of beauty.

○ Catalogue what is considered attractive with regard to symmetry, skin, hair, eyes, height, weight, and age.

○ Consider the efforts that people make to improve their appearance.

ASK YOURSELF

How much are your beauty ideals influenced by your culture?

You've probably heard it said, "beauty is only skin deep." However, most societies greatly value physical beauty. What is beauty? Why do we seek it so?

A desire for beauty may be hardwired into our brains: even infants, not yet exposed to cultural standards of beauty, will show a preference for beautiful faces. When 2- to 8-month-old infants were shown pictures of women's faces that had been previously rated for their attractiveness, the infants spent more time looking at the faces rated more attractive (Langlois et al., 1987). In another study, researchers asked adult subjects to rate the attractiveness of flashed images of faces. The images were shown so quickly—13 milliseconds—that subjects reported they could not see the faces and were simply guessing in their assessments. Nevertheless, subjects accurately rated the attractiveness of the faces, suggesting that images of beauty are processed automatically in the brain (Olson & Marshuetz, 2005).

Is beauty a universal standard or does every society differ in what its people consider to be beautiful? Darwin imagined that standards of beauty would vary greatly in different societies.

Although it's true that many criteria of beauty are subjective and vary over time and in different cultures (as shown in the photos below), studies have shown that when people of different ethnicities, cultures, and sexual orientations rate the attractiveness of others, there is a high degree of agreement in their assessments (Kranz & Ishai, 2006; Langlois et al., 2000). This is thought to be because attractive features and youth signal physical and reproductive fitness: people may seek attractive partners because of the genetic advantages that will be passed on to their children.

Universal Signs of Beauty

Evolutionary theory suggests that universal ideals of beauty are related to attributes that will impart the greatest reproductive advantages. Signs of female beauty are often correlated with youth and fertility. Female facial attractiveness is universally associated with a blend of some young features (large eyes, a small nose, and a small chin), some mature features (prominent cheekbones and narrow cheeks), and some expressive features (high eyebrows, large pupils, and a large smile) (Cunningham, 1986). Women's hormone levels may influence their perceived beauty: when women are ovulating and their estrogen levels are higher, subjects rate them to be more visually appealing.

A man's attractiveness is related to the degree to which his face gives the impression of dominance, assertiveness, or leadership (Mazur & Mueller, 1996). Dominant faces have an oval or rectangular shape, deep-set eyes with heavy brow ridges, and

Many beauty standards are subjective and vary in different cultures.

Girls of the Kayan tribe on the border of Burma and Thailand wear brass rings around their necks as a sign of elegance and status. As the girls grow, more rings are added, elongating their necks

Women of the Maori tribe of New Zealand tattoo their lips and chin. A woman with full, blue lips is considered the most beautiful and desirable.

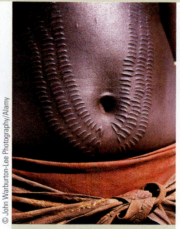

Scars are beautiful to the Karo tribe of southwestern Ethiopia. Knives cut scars into the chest and torso of the women, and ash is rubbed into the scars to produce a raised welt.

In Mauritania, a country on the northwest coast of Africa, heavier is better. Thick ankles, plump arms, stretch marks, and large buttocks are considered among the most beautiful parts of the body.

prominent chins. They may, like Brad Pitt or Robert Pattinson, have a larger jaw muscle. Testosterone enhances the growth of these "masculine" features. Male teenagers with dominant looking features have sex at a younger age than those with less dominant features (Mazur, Hapler, & Udry, 1994). Women are often attracted to typically masculine (dominant) faces, but with some atypically masculine features like large eyes or wide smiles. Over-exaggerating the dominant features in a face has been shown to *decrease* a male's attractiveness, making him appear as less warm, honest, cooperative, and perhaps to have a lower potential as a parent (Cunningham, Barbee, & Pike, 1990).

Not only do hormones shape our beauty, but they may also affect how we rate beauty in others. When a woman is at the most fertile point in her cycle, her body changes as well as her partner preferences. Additionally, men respond differently to ovulating women than to women at other phases of their menstrual cycle. These effects are summarized in Table 7.1.

Symmetry

Physical symmetry is thought to be a sign of attractiveness and reproductive health, and an appreciation for symmetry seems to exist across cultures (Little, Apicella, & Marlowe, 2007; Perrett, May, & Yoshikawa, 1999; Rhodes et al., 2001). Factors such as mutations, toxins, and poor nutrition can alter a person's development and decrease the symmetry of their bilateral traits, which scientists call **fluctuating asymmetry**. Bilateral symmetry may be correlated to a person's overall reproductive fitness. For example, women with asymmetrical breasts may be less fertile and more prone to breast cancer (Møller, Soler, & Thornhill, 1995; Scutt, Lancaster, & Manning, 2006). Men with more symmetrical bodies are considered more attractive and masculine looking, have higher social status, and have 2 to 3 times as many sex partners. Although their partners have more orgasms, these men have been found to be more prone to infidelities and dishonest behavior in relationships (Thornhill, Gangestad, & Comer, 1995). Studies suggest that women selectively prefer more symmetrical and masculine-appearing men near ovulation, but not at other times; perhaps the women are uncon-

The faces of Beyoncé and Colin Farrell illustrate some of the universally accepted differences in the male and female ideals of beauty. Note the size and shape of the eyes, the height of eyebrows over the eye socket, and the shape of the jaw.

Table 7.1 Changes That Occur During Ovulation

Physical changes in the woman	Decrease in waist-to-hip ratio (Kirchengast & Gartner, 2002)
	Lightened skin color (Van den Barghe & Frost, 1986)
	More symmetrical breasts (Roberts et al., 2004)
Heterosexual women's preferences in a male partner	Prefer taller men (Pawlowski & Jasienska, 2005)
	Prefer men with more masculine bodies and facial features, such as brow ridges and a strong jaw line (Little, Jones, & Burriss, 2007; Penton-Voak, Perrett, Castles, Kobayashi, & Burt, et al., 1999)
	Prefer more masculine voices (Feinberg et al., 2006)
	Prefer more dominant-appearing men with more symmetrical features (Gangestad & Cousins, 2001)
	Assess other females' (but not males') attractiveness lower than they do during other points in their cycle (Fisher, 2004)
Actions of ovulating women	More likely to respond to pickup lines from men (Gueguen, 2009)
	More likely to wear more revealing clothing (Durante, Li, & Haselton, 2008)
Response of men to ovulating women (compared to non-ovulating women)	More likely to find their faces attractive (Roberts et al., 2004)
	More likely to consider their scent attractive (Havlicek, Dvorakova, Bartos, & Flegr, 2006)
	More likely to guard ovulating women, to be more attentive, and to call their cell phone randomly more often to check up on them (Gangestad, Thornhill, & Garver, 2002)
	Female lap dancers earn higher tips during their most fertile times (Miller, Tybur, & Jordan, 2007)

© Cengage Learning 2013

sciously reaping the benefits of the men's genetic fitness but not choosing them for long-term partners (reviewed in Gangestad & Cousins, 2001).

Most people's facial features are not truly symmetrical. The right hemisphere of the brain, which is more involved with emotions and facial feature recognition, controls the left side of the face, while the left hemisphere, involved in speech and language, controls the right side of the face. When speaking, most people therefore make larger movements on the right side of their face, and the left side of the face is more involved when making facial expressions (Graves, Goodglass, & Landis, 1982; Skinner & Mullen, 1991).

Averageness

Judith Langlois and Lori Roggman digitally produced a series of composite faces. They found that the computerized images, each of which represented an averaged representation of a face, were rated more attractive than almost all of the individual faces that were combined

Attraction A characteristic that causes pleasure or interest by appealing to a person's desires or tastes, and causes one to be drawn to the other.

Fluctuating asymmetry Small, subtle differences in the size of one of a bilateral feature, such as arms, legs, or breasts.

Phi (φ; pronounced "fee") is a fixed mathematical proportion: 1 to 1.618033988749895 to be precise. Named after the Greek sculptor Phidias, phi (also called the "divine" or "golden" proportion) represents the division of a line or a figure in which the ratio of the smaller section to the larger one is the same as the ratio of the larger to the whole (Green, 1995). For example, each finger has three sections separated by a joint. The ratio of the size of the first joint closest to the hand to the next two joints is approximately 1:1.618, as is the ratio of the distal two joints to the entire finger. Each joint is 1.6 times the length of the next.

Phi is a proportion that can be seen in a number of cases—in nature, art, architecture, music, and in the human body. It is thought that the degree to which the proportions of facial features conform to the golden ratio in part determines how beautiful the face is.

to produce the composite image. They hypothesized that the average of a population represents the optimal design of physical traits (Langlois & Roggman, 1990; Rhodes & Tremewan, 1996). As researcher Lisa DeBruine says, "there are more ways to be nonaverage and ugly than there are ways to be nonaverage and beautiful" (Quill, 2009). Indeed, if you look at plastic surgery trends, they seem to represent a shift toward today's more racially blended society—a move toward the average, as it were. Fuller lips and a wider bridge of the nose are some of the more requested surgical reconstructions performed. On the other hand, if beauty is average, why aren't average people considered beautiful? Other studies show faces are judged more attractive when certain features were exaggerated beyond the mean (Perrett et al., 1994). Johnston and Franklin (1993) used a computer program to allow subjects to manipulate faces until they designed "the most beautiful" female face. The resulting faces differed from those of the average population in that they had fuller lips and a smaller lower jaw, which they suggest are signs of increased fertility related to hormonal levels.

Skin

Smooth, clear skin is a visible sign of health and youth. From smallpox to acne, many diseases and infections first show themselves in the skin. When we are young, a new layer of skin appears every 2 weeks, but as we age we no longer replace dead cells as rapidly. Oil glands become less active, skin sags as fat deposits are lost, and collagen and elastin breakdown allows for wrinkles to develop. Women may show wrinkles earlier than men, due to their thinner skin and greater facial expressivity.

The color of our skin varies with age and sex, as well as race. Women tend to be paler and to have lighter skin than men, due to lower levels of hemoglobin in the blood and melanin in the skin. Most people in the world have brown skin, but Western images of beauty are often light skinned: "fair" is even a synonym for beauty. There may be a sociobiological rationale underlying this preference—a woman's skin color may broadcast her fertility because it lightens during ovulation and becomes darker when she is pregnant or on birth control pills (Van den Barghe & Frost, 1986). Fair skin also better shows when someone is blushing. Although a blush may be embarrassing to the one whose discomfiture is brightly exhibited, a blush ac-

Ultraviolet (UV) light A component of sunlight that is beneficial in small amounts, but can damage the skin cells and cause premature aging and skin cancer.

Collagen and **elastin** Connective tissues that provide strength and elasticity to the skin.

tually helps strengthen social bonds and soften judgments. People are more likely to forgive social blunders in people who show their embarrassment with a blush (Dijk, de Jong, & Peters, 2009). Fairer skin is often valued even among the African American population, even though darker skin has more melanin, which protects against **ultraviolet (UV) light** damage and skin cancer (Bond & Cash, 1992; Hunter, 2002). People with darker skin have fewer wrinkles and get them 10 to 20 years later than those with lighter skin. They are also less prone to acne and skin cancer, less likely to go gray or bald, and have less body hair. It seems as though a preference for lighter skin may be related to a desire for the rights and privileges afforded to those with lighter skin, rather than objective standards of beauty.

A number of environmental factors have an adverse effect on one's skin. Cigarette smoke constricts the blood vessels and increases breakdown of **collagen** and **elastin**, producing more wrinkles, earlier gray hair, and more baldness (Grady & Ernster, 1992). Tanning also damages the skin. When exposed to UV rays, the skin tries to shield itself by producing more melanin. Unfortunately, this newly formed melanin does not protect the skin from cancer, but it does cause the skin to thicken. UV rays also help break down collagen and elastin fibers, leading to more wrinkles.

Hair

Healthy hair has long been considered a sign of female beauty and male power. Judges 16:19 of the Bible tells of how Samson lost his strength when Delilah cut his hair. Ancient Jewish law states that a man may divorce his wife if she leaves the home without covering her hair. Tribesmen in the highlands of New Guinea believe that

Most people's faces are not truly symmetrical. These three images show a woman's actual face (b), an image showing a left-left mirror image composite (c), as well as an image in which the right side of her face is reproduced (a). Note how different these images appear.

ghosts of their ancestors live in the hair. A bald man is therefore feared: his ancestors have obviously abandoned him (Etcoff, 1999). Healthy hair can give information about reproductive fitness because genetics, diet, health, and age affect the color, thickness, and health of our hair.

There is a perception in Western society that "gentlemen prefer blondes," and men should be "tall, dark, and handsome." Various theories have been suggested to explain why blond hair is popular for American women. Infants and children often have lighter skin and hair; perhaps blond hair in adults gives the impression of youth and the increased fertility associated with it. It may be that blondes' lighter skin makes it easier for others to detect a number of medical conditions, such as anemia and cyanosis; therefore blondes clearly advertise their health and fertility (Ramachandran, 1997).

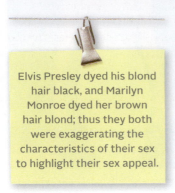

Elvis Presley dyed his blond hair black, and Marilyn Monroe dyed her brown hair blond; thus they both were exaggerating the characteristics of their sex to highlight their sex appeal.

Eyes

Ralph Waldo Emerson said that "Eyes . . . speak all languages. . . . What inundation of life and thought is discharged from one soul into another through them! The glance is natural magic" (Emerson, p 172). A person's eyes clearly signal interest in others—when a person is sexually aroused, his or her pupils enlarge. Studies have shown that when a photo is retouched to increase the size of the pupils, subjects rate the photo as more attractive (Cunningham, 1986). Large, clear, widely spaced eyes with arched eyebrows are thought to be attractive in women; in a man, more deeply set eyes and flat, lower set eyebrows are considered handsome.

Height

In Western culture, women prefer men that are taller than them, and men prefer women that are shorter than them. In one study, only 0.3% of women were found to be taller than their husbands, less than what would occur by chance (Gillis & Avis, 1980). Noticeably shorter husbands are often rich and/or powerful. In a study of more than 23,000 online daters, women were surveyed about the men they might consider dating (Hitsch, Hortasçsu, & Airely, 2005). The researchers questioned the women about vari-

Your first name may affect how attractive you are perceived to be. Women named Heather or Ashley are perceived as being more attractive than women named Ethel or Gertrude. When shown photographs of faces that were labeled with names that were considered to be either attractive or unattractive, faces labeled with the more popular names were rated as more attractive (Erwin, 1993).

_____

_____

_____

ous desired characteristics, including appearance, height, and salary. They found that compared to a man who is 5 inches taller than a woman and earns $50,000 per year, a man who is 5 inches shorter than a woman would have to earn over half a million dollars per year to make up for his "shortcomings."

A man's height can impact his earning potential. Whereas the average height for men in the United States is 5 feet 9 inches, more than 50% of Fortune 500 Company CEOs are over 6 feet tall. One study showed that men over 6 feet tall earned $4,000 more than men who were 5 feet 5 inches (Frieze, Olson, & Good, 1990). In the 1988 presidential election, 5-foot-8-inch Michael Dukakis carried only 10 states, giving 6-foot-2-inch George Bush the victory. In 2008, 6-foot-1-inch Barack Obama handily won over the 5-foot-8-inch John McCain. The taller candidate has won in 68% of presidential elections since 1900.

Weight

Although Western society holds slenderness in highest regard, this is not true of all cultures. Many societies revere a plumper female form. A cross-cultural analysis found that in places where food is scarce, heavier women are thought to be more beautiful, because body fat is an indication of wealth and prosperity (Anderson, Crawford, Nadeau, & Lindberg, 1992). In the United States, where high-calorie food is abundant and supersized portions are the norm, the slim female body is considered most attractive. There is evidence that males prefer women to have a **body mass index (BMI)** of approximately 19.4 (Thornhill & Grammer, 1999; Tovee & Cornelison, 2001). A BMI of 19.4 corresponds to a weight of 113 for a 5-foot-4-inch woman and 131 for a 5-foot-9-inch man.

Although some think that overall BMI is most important in determining a woman's physical attractiveness (Tovee & Cornelissen, 2001), Devendra Singh claims that, barring

Body mass index (BMI) A measure of a person's weight in relation to his or her height.

Such disparate models of beauty as Sophia Loren, Twiggy, and Kate Moss all have a waist-to-hip ratio of between 0.68 and 0.69.

extremes, the **waist-to-hip ratio (WHR)** may be more important to men than breast size or weight. If a woman's waist measured 26 inches and her hips were 38 inches, her WHR would be 26/38, or 0.68 (Singh, 1993).

The WHR in a healthy premenopausal woman typically ranges from 0.67–0.8, compared to 0.85–0.95 for a man. Singh's studies show that men of different cultures judge a WHR of approximately 0.7 to be the most appealing proportion for women (Singh, 1993, 2004), a ratio shared by icons such as Beyoncé, Audrey Hepburn, Elle Macpherson, and most *Playboy* centerfolds (Barbie dolls are an anomaly, having a scant 0.54 ratio). One study found that lesbian and bisexual women also considered women with a 0.7 WHR to be the most sexually attractive, although they were particularly attracted to heavier women with a 0.7 WHR (Cohen & Tannenbaum, 2001).

An hourglass shape in women may be a sign of health and fertility because hormones play an important role in determining the waist-to-hip ratio. Estrogen decreases the WHR, and testosterone increases the ratio. In fact, women may have a higher WHR ratio in the autumn, when testosterone levels are at their peak, and an hourglass figure in the spring, when testosterone levels decline (Van Anders, Hampson, & Watson, 2006). Estrogen increases the deposition of fat around the buttocks and thighs, which is very difficult to lose. Nature has designed it so that fat remains there as a potential energy store for pregnancy and lactation. Women with a WHR below 0.8 are twice as likely to become pregnant via in vitro fertilization as women with a higher WHR (Wass, Waldenstrom, Rossner, & Hellberg, 1997). Testosterone, on the other hand, increases the accumulation of fat around the waist and decreases its deposit on the hips. Postmenopausal women and women with polycystic ovarian disease have proportionately higher testosterone levels and generally have WHRs more like males. Belly fat, while easier to lose, may be the most damaging to the health. A high WHR is associated with an increased incidence of type 2 diabetes; gallbladder disease; carcinomas of the breast, ovary, and endometrium; and heart disease and stroke (Johnston & Franklin, 1993).

The ideal of a slender waist in women is not a new one. Researchers surveyed 345,000 works of British and American literature to assess how various features of female beauty were rated. They found that although some texts praised large breasts and others admired small, and some extolled the virtues of slim women and (many more) praised the plump, *all* romantic references to the female waist described a narrow or slender waist as a necessary component of beauty. Similar results were found when ancient Chinese and Indian texts were surveyed (Singh, Renn, & Singh, 2007).

Age

Youth is considered more of a premium for women, perhaps because a woman's reproductive ability ends decades before a man's. Males in 37 cultures showed a preference for females with a mean age of 24.8, which corresponds to a woman's most fertile age (Buss, 1989). It is common for women to be in relationships with men who are older. For a first marriage, brides are an average of 2 to 3 years younger than grooms. For a second marriage, that age span increases to 5 years and to 8 years for a third marriage. Media images of older men with younger women are common, although the reverse is treated as big news. When there is a great discrepancy in age between partners, the older partner (usually male) often brings wealth and/or power to the relationship, while the younger brings youth and beauty. When Anna Nicole Smith married J. Howard Marshall, there was a 63-year difference in their ages.

Sexualization Across the Life Span

Sexualization occurs when any of the following is present: a person's value comes only from his or her sex appeal; a person is portrayed as an object for other's sexual pleasure, rather than as

"Cougar": A woman over 40 who seeks out younger men for romantic or sexual encounters.

Waist-to-hip ratio (WHR) The ratio of a person's waist measurement to his or her hip measurement. Someone with a 28-inch waist and 40-inch hips would have a WHR of 0.7.

Sexualization To make sexual (usually inappropriately), or to hold a person to a standard that equates a narrowly defined physical attractiveness with being sexy.

Although a desire for a small waist has stayed relatively constant, the "ideal" female form has changed over the years. In the late 19th century, women's roles were primarily as wives and mothers, and plumpness was considered most attractive. Women would wear bustles to accentuate the size of their buttocks (a). American women got the vote in the 1920s and with this newfound freedom came a new image of beauty—the flapper. Thin was in, and women would bind their breasts to achieve the slim, boyish shape considered most attractive (b). In the 1950s, the hourglass shape was popular once again (c), and women were expected to be happy housewives who vacuumed while wearing high heels and pearls. During the "women's lib" era of the 1960s, images of female beauty changed once again, as 91-pound Twiggy was the most popular model of her era. Today, the image of the size 0 model permeates the fashion magazines (d). In her groundbreaking work *The Beauty Myth*, Naomi Wolf (1991) suggests that images of beauty change with the expected role in society. As women achieve more political freedoms, they are more imprisoned by unrealistic expectations of their appearance. Western women today have more personal, economic, and political freedom than ever before, yet are held by what is perhaps the most unrealistic image ever—a boy's small hips and thighs coupled with large, gravity-defying breasts, an appearance that is almost impossible to achieve without surgery.

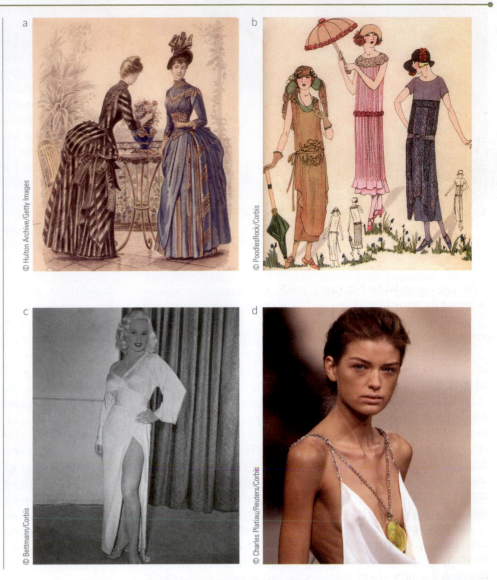

a © Hulton Archive/Getty Images

b © PoodlesRock/Corbis

c © Bettmann/Corbis

d © Charles Platiau/Reuters/Corbis

a self-governing individual; a person is held to a narrowly defined (and often unrealistic) standard of physical attractiveness; or sexuality is inappropriately imposed upon a person (APA, 2007). Even very young girls are sexualized in our society. Sexualized images of young girls occur in all media: TV, movies, music videos, video games, advertising, and magazines. Researchers evaluated the advertisements in five popular magazines over a 40-year period. Although only 1.5% of ads portrayed children in a sexualized manner, of those, 85% sexualized girls rather than boys (O'Donohue, Gold, & McKay, 1997). This sexualization trend may be increasing slightly over time. Even girls' dolls are sexualized. The very popular Bratz dolls wear miniskirts, fishnet stockings, and high-heeled boots more appropriate for a dominatrix than for a child's toy.

Sexualization has negative effects on a person's academic achievement, physical health, and emotional well-being. Girls who are frequently exposed to sexualized images of women and young girls begin to think of and treat their bodies as objects of others' desire (APA, 2007), a process called **self-objectification**. This detracts from a girl's ability to concentrate and focus attention, and may result in impaired performance in school. Researchers had male and female college students put on either a sweater or a bathing suit, fill out a questionnaire that measured body shame, and take a math test. The men wearing the bathing suit reported feeling "silly," but the women felt shame. The women wearing the bathing suits also scored much lower on the math test than did the women wearing sweaters, presumably due to either stereotype threat or because these women were so overwhelmed by their insecurity and shame related to body image that they could not concentrate on the test (Fredrickson, Roberts, Noll, Quinn, & Twenge, 1998). In a recent study, when a man simply gazed at a woman in an objectifying way, her performance on a math test suffered (Gervais, Vescio, & Allen, 2011). Constant exposure to sexualized images may actually put women at greater physical risk as self-objectification has been

Strawberry Shortcake was a popular icon for girls in the 1980s. Today, Bratz dolls capture almost half of the fashion doll market.

linked to decreased condom use, diminished sexual assertiveness, and eating disorders (Harrison, 2000; Impett, Schooler, & Toman, 2006). Sexualization is also associated with low self-esteem and depression (APA, 2007).

Awareness and education may help reduce the prevalence of these images. Critically evaluate the media you consume, and make your feelings about these images known to the companies that produce them.

Even as suggestive images of girls and young women abound, older women are rarely depicted as sexual beings. In fact, older women are rarely seen at all in television and movies. Although women older than 60 make up 22% of the U.S. population, they account for only 8% of the characters in film (Lauzen & Dozier, 2005). Men older than 60 don't fare much better: 18% of the U.S. population comprised 8% of characters in film. In addition, "older females were cast in a particularly negative light. As compared to males, older females were perceived as 'less friendly, less intelligent, less good, possessing less wealth, and being less attractive'" (Bazzini, McIntosh, Smith, Cook, & Harris, 1997, p. 541). They also are shown to wield little occupational power or leadership compared to older men (Lauzen & Dozier, 2005).

Pheromones

At some level, we may all be looking for someone whose pheromones click with ours. Men who were previously exposed to female pheromones rated women as more attractive compared to men who were not exposed to the chemical (Kirk-Smith, Booth, Caroll, & Davies, 1978).

The **human leukocyte antigen (HLA)** genes (called the **major histocompatibility complex [MHC]** in animals) are a series of genes that help an organism recognize its own healthy cells and reject invading parasitic organisms;

Self-objectification The process by which people regard themselves superficially, by their physical appearance, measurements, or weight, rather than by their health, character, or intelligence.

Human leukocyte antigens/ major histocompatibility complex (HLA/MHC) The human leukocyte antigens (also called the major histocompatibility complex [MHC]) are a series of genes that play an important role in the immune system, by coding for proteins that differentiate self from non-self.

as such, it is important to have a mix of HLA types, so a body is able to fight different diseases. Because there are so many HLA proteins, no individual carries a complete set, and it is advantageous to pick a partner with different HLA genes, so as to give your offspring the ability to recognize and destroy a wide variety of invading organisms. The HLA also influences both body odors and body odor perception. Males were asked to wear a plain T-shirt for two nights, and to avoid scented soaps and colognes. Women then smelled the T-shirts and rated their odor. Women rated body odors from men who differed from them in their HLA as more pleasant than the odors of men with similar HLAs. When women were on oral contraceptives, however, they thought that men with similar HLAs smelled more pleasant (Wedekind, Seebeck, Bettens, & Paepke, 1995). It is thought that by preferring the odors of HLA-dissimilar men, women help to ensure their offspring have more effective immune systems. As oral contraceptives make the body act as if it is already pregnant, women may subconsciously prefer the safety of those who are perceived as carrying similar genetic traits. A recent study found that the more similar the HLA between men and women in a heterosexual couple, the less sexually satisfied the woman was with her partner, and the more affairs she had (Garver-Apgar, Gangestad, Thornhill, Miller, & Olp, 2006). Choosing a partner with different HLA genes may also affect your fertility. A study of the Hutterites, a religious farming community who don't believe in contraception and who tend to marry within the community, showed that partners with more similar HLAs had higher miscarriage rates and overall lower fertility (Weitkamp & Ober, 1999).

An individual's gender and sexual orientation may affect his or her body odor preferences. For example, when asked to choose, heterosexual men, heterosexual women, and lesbians all preferred the odor of heterosexual men over that of gay men; gay men, however, preferred the odor of other gay men (Martin et al., 2005). Gay men also preferred the odor of heterosexual women to that of lesbians. It may be that gay and straight men respond differently to female pheromones. Scientists had heterosexual and homosexual subjects inhale steroidal substances, which they claim may act as pheromones. They found that gay men responded to steroids in a way similar to heterosexual women, and lesbians responded to steroids in a way similar to heterosexual men (Berglund, Lindstrom, & Savic, 2006; Savic, Berglund, & Lindström, 2005). Others, though, criticize these studies, and claim that the substances used are not proven to be pheromones.

The Pursuit of Beauty

We live in a democracy, under the principle that all are created equal. The American dream is that anyone can achieve anything through hard work. This belief leads to the idea that if we just try hard enough, we can look like the beautiful celebrities we see every day. Laws of physics be damned; *this* diet will be the one to change our Rosie O'Donnell reality into our Cameron Diaz dreams. Given this version of the American "dream," it should come as no surprise that more money is spent in pursuit of beauty in the United States than on education or social services (Etcoff, 1999).

If one's only knowledge of American society came from media images, one would assume this nation is peopled with beautiful thin women and buff handsome men. Observe the people in your local mall and consider how closely their appearance match-

ASK YOURSELF

What measures do you take to attain your personal standards of beauty? How many of these may be harmful or dangerous?

es that of the characters of most TV shows or movies. Our nation's economy depends on our pursuit of the impossible dream of youth and beauty—those who are insecure about their weight, their appearance, and their desirability are more likely to purchase diet aids and beauty products.

Media images affect not only our self-esteem, they may also affect our relationships. Average-looking people were judged less attractive if both male and female subjects had previously viewed centerfolds from *Playboy* or *Playgirl* rather than abstract art slides (Kenrick, Gutierres, & Goldberg, 1989). More disturbingly, this study also found that after viewing centerfolds, men rated themselves as less in love with their wives. In a more recent study, men watched mock video interviews of an opposite-sex stranger. Mated men's ratings of their partners were lower if the interviewee smiled and acted warmly (Mishra, Clark, & Daly, 2007).

Diets

Market research firm MarketData estimates that more than $60 billion per year is spent on the weight-loss industry. There are currently more than 17,000 diet plans, products, and programs that aim to help people achieve their dream body. But here's the bad news: most diets fail. There are a number of reasons for this. First, it is a rare and recent occurrence in the human experience that we have too much food; the human body has evolved to keep weight on, not to lose it. Also, yoyo dieting predisposes your body to gain weight—with each diet you go on, you raise your levels of **ghrelin**, a hormone that increases your appetite and makes your body retain fat. Finally, any change you make must be a permanent lifestyle change—you must learn to make healthy food choices and to incorporate exercise into your life *for the rest of your life.* Any temporary changes in your diet or lifestyle will produce temporary changes in your weight.

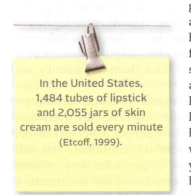

In the United States, 1,484 tubes of lipstick and 2,055 jars of skin cream are sold every minute (Etcoff, 1999).

Cosmetics

Keats was not talking about makeup when he said, "beauty is truth, and truth beauty." Makeup, implants, and hair dyes are at their core deceitful, as they are designed to amplify signals of fertility such as youth or health. (The word "pretty" actually originates from Old English terms meaning "crafty" or "deceitful.") For example, women tend to blush more, have higher eyebrows, and have fuller lips than men; eye makeup, blush, and lipstick enhance these attributes. Mascara and eye makeup increase the appearance of the size of the eyes, a sign of youth. Foundation helps to

A beautiful model becomes such only through the efforts of many styling professionals and the use of computer software such as Photoshop.

project a universal characteristic of good health—smooth skin. As we try to put our "best face forward," the cosmetics industry reaps the benefits, to the tune of $280 billion in annual global sales.

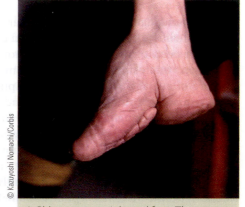

A Chinese woman's bound foot. The practice of foot binding was outlawed in 1911.

More Extreme Measures

Many of the artifices women attempt in the name of beauty are actually damaging to their health. Until it was outlawed in 1911, some young Chinese girls' feet were tightly wrapped to prevent them from growing. Small feet were seen as feminine, so girls had their toes and heels bent under their soles. The bones would break, and the foot would not grow. These women could only hobble a few steps, and were supported by and dependent on men throughout their lives. In 18th- and 19th-century England and the United States, women wore tight stays or corsets to make their waists as small as possible. The fact that they could barely breathe made them much more dependent and submissive. Constant wearing of a tight corset would distort the rib cage and other internal organs, causing complications and even death.

Women today still undergo dangerous procedures in the pursuit of beauty. Women inject **Botox** into their faces, permanently damage their feet by wearing spiked heels, and risk cancer by lying out in the

Ghrelin A hormone produced in the stomach that increases appetite and decreases fat loss. Dieting and lack of sleep increase ghrelin levels.

Botox A medication injected into the face to paralyze the muscles and prevent wrinkles. Botox is a neurotoxin produced by the bacterium *Clostridium botulinum* (which causes botulism). Botulinum is one of the most toxic naturally-occurring substances known to man.

eating behavior (Hudson, Eva, Pope, & Kessler, 2007). Many college women control their weight with vomiting, diuretics, and laxatives (Levenkron, 1983). The onslaught of idealized images may increase a woman's likelihood of having an eating disorder. In one study, the more media exposure a woman had, the more likely she was to have eating disorder symptoms (Stice, Schupak-Neuberg, Shaw, & Stein, 1994), and the more likely she was to believe that women must be thin to be attractive.

Although disordered eating behaviors are more common in women, men are not immune to this problem. Over the last few years, the rate of eating disorders in men has risen. This may be because of the proliferation of unrealistic media images of well-sculpted and heavily muscled male bodies (Chao et al., 2008). Men with eating disorders are more likely to focus on their body shape and type rather than on their weight.

Despite the barrage of media images, both men and women should remember that beauty is more than skin deep. Although we may be initially attracted to someone's appearance, we spend time with a person because of who they are, their intelligence and integrity and character, not because of a random arrangement of skin and bone and muscle.

Although attraction is a very individual phenomenon, the steps people take to attract a mate are fairly universal. Even though we may believe that the beautiful people of the world draw all the attention, it takes more than just physical beauty to attract others. In fact, women who are approached most often may be those who send the most signals—those who are most adept at flirting (Moore, 1985).

How to Flirt

After completion of this section, you will be able to . . .

O Describe the universal components of flirting for men and for women.

O Clarify the factors that make for successful conversation.

"There are times not to flirt. When you're sick. When you're with children. When you're on the witness stand."

—*Author Joyce Jillson*

Some facial expressions—such as those indicating happiness, anger, and sadness—are universal and appear to be hardwired into the human brain. Similarly, the expressions and movements associated with flirting are recognized by people of all cultures, so while you may not speak the language, your flirtatious intentions will be recognized as clearly in a marketplace in Mozambique or a gay bar in Greenland as in your own local dance club.

Flirtation paves the way for sexual interactions that can propagate the species. However, flirtation is not solely the province of heterosexuals; gays and lesbians flirt in much the same way that straight people do, although there is fairly little research about homosexual flirting styles. One study showed that when courting, lesbians are less constrained by traditional gender roles and enter into relationships more quickly than heterosexual couples (Rose & Zand, 2002).

There are many reasons that people flirt (Henningsen, 2004). People flirt to increase intimacy in an existing relationship, to see if someone is interested in beginning a romantic relationship, or just for the fun of it. Some may flirt to build their self-esteem, or to gain a reward from another, such as bigger tips or a better evaluation. Many scientists have studied courtship rituals and have described some of the universal features of flirting (Givens 2005; Moore, 1985, 2010; Perper, 1985).

To meet someone, you must first attract his or her attention by advertising your physical presence, gender, and willingness to be approached. If you don't present one of the three, you may have more difficulty in attracting the kind of attention you want. Men will often exaggerate their body movements, such as shaking their whole arm to extinguish a match. They may thrust out their chest or roll their shoulders. Men may use objects such as expensive watches, cell phones, or cars to advertise their availability and status (Givens, 2005). Women from all over the world have a consistent flirting expression. The woman smiles at her admirer and lifts her eyebrows, opening her eyes wide. After a few seconds, her eyelids drop, and she tilts her head down and looks away to the side. She may cover her face with her hands and giggle, or toss her head and flip her hair. A woman may stretch in a way that shows off her breasts, and walk with an exaggerated sway to her hips. She may be more facially expressive than normal; people pay more attention to the face when it is active; a deadpan face is perceived as unfriendly and unapproachable.

Men may think that because they often approach the woman and speak first, they are initiating the flirtation, but in reality, two-thirds of the time it is the woman who gives the nonverbal go-ahead that gets the flirtation rolling in heterosexual encounters, usually by catching and holding the eye of the man in whom she is interested (Perper, 1985). Eye contact is a powerful, emotionally loaded way to communicate. Prolonged eye contact usually only occurs with intense emotion, such as love or anger. Most eye contact between strangers usually lasts only a fraction of a second; if held for a second or longer it's often a sign of interest (Moore, 2010). A flirtatious glance is usually held for less than 3 seconds; much longer than that, and the glance may seem threatening. An **eyebrow flash**, a very brief lift of the eyebrows, often accompanies the quick gaze. While in most cultures this signifies recognition, in Japan it has clear sexual connotations.

Approaching someone you're interested in is risky because you don't always know if the other person is interested. You can gather a lot of information by nonverbal signs. Despite the fact that we can consciously control our facial expressions to look on politely, even when someone is boring us to tears, our body language usually shows what we're really feeling. Psychologists call this "**nonverbal leakage**." If your conversation partner's head is turned toward you, but the rest of the body is turned away, this may be a sign that he or she would rather be somewhere else. If the person's arms and legs are folded, this can show that he or she is not open to your advances. However, if his or her body posture mimics yours, this can be a sign of rapport (Perper, 1985).

Flirtation Behaviors meant to arouse romantic or sexual interest. In the 16th century, the word "flirt" meant "to sneer or scoff at" (Morris, 2004).

Eyebrow flash A very brief lift of the eyebrows that designates recognition or an invitation for interaction.

Nonverbal leakage Cues in a person's body language that indicate their true emotional state or intentions.

In heterosexual encounters, women tend to control the pace of the flirtation (Moore, 2010). A woman can slow down the pace by not making eye contact or by crossing her arms across her chest, or she can stop the interaction entirely by sneering, yawning, or flirting with others. Ideally, neither partner entirely controls the interaction. Successful flirtation is like a dance, a playful give and take in which both partners eventually synchronize their actions.

What to Talk About

As soon as you open your mouth, you will be giving the object of your attention information about your education, background, and social class. The game may be over with your first sentence.

Some suggest that what you say is not as important as how you say it. When people are courting, their voices get higher, softer, and singsongy, the same tones used for children and to show concern: flirters say "hiiii!" instead of "hi"—short, clipped, monosyllabic answers can be a sign of disinterest. When speaking, you may want to speak into your partner's left ear—sounds from the left ear go to the more emotional right hemisphere of the brain.

The purpose of successful flirting is not to show off, not to be overtly sexual, but just to show someone that that you are interested in him or her and want to start a conversation. A cute or flippant opening line works less well than a simple straightforward statement. The best opening lines are either compliments or questions that require a response. David Givens, the director of the Center for Nonverbal Studies, suggests using an opening line that involves a **shared focus** (Givens, 2005). For instance, consider these opening lines:

- Do you live around here?
- Baby, I'm no Fred Flintstone, but I can make your Bedrock.
- I like your MP3 player—what kind is it?

Line #1 seems innocuous, but it may be seen as invasive, and it focuses only on one person. Line #2 is just cheesy. But line #3 opens up a safe dialogue about a similar object to which both people can relate but which is external to them.

Once you've broken the ice, you can start a conversation. When talking, keep your partner in mind. You don't know them

> Once I've gotten someone's attention, what am I supposed to say? Is there some great opening line I should use?

Pickup lines that don't work:
"Pardon me, miss. I seem to have lost my phone number. May I borrow yours?"
"If I said you had a beautiful body, would you hold it against me?"
"I hope you know CPR, because you take my breath away."
"I've just moved you to the top of my 'to do' list."
"Is that a mirror in your pocket? Because I can really see myself in your pants!"
"That's a nice set of legs. What time do they open?"

yet and don't know how they'll respond to emotionally charged topics such as politics, religion, sex, or amusing bodily functions. Keep the conversation general—you might think that anyone would be fascinated by an in-depth account of your recent barium enema, or would chortle with delight at your philosophy professor's latest witticism about dialectical materialism, but you would be wrong. Although it can be detrimental to share too much personal information too quickly, people can also be turned off if you do not share any intimate details about yourself. Usually, men are less willing to disclose personal details about their feelings. Try to draw your partner out to discover his or her interests and things that you might have in common.

During initial conversation, people often search for common interests and establish compatibility. If the exchange is going well, partners may nod and laugh. The conversation has a well coordinated back and forth rhythm, without too much silence or interruption, although people in Asian cultures tend to be more tolerant of conversational silences than we are in the West (Givens, 2005). While speaking, women hold eye contact longer than men do, and adopt a more intimate conversational distance. This is not necessarily a sign of interest, however, and men may misinterpret their actions.

Can Flirting Be Misconstrued?

The place it occurs, the type of comment, and the effort expended can all affect the perception of flirtation. Downey and Damhave (1991) found that a comment was more likely to be perceived as flirtatious if it occurred in a bar rather than in a school hallway, if someone went out of their way to approach the person rather than making inadvertent eye contact, and if they paid a compliment rather than asking for the time. In other words, if you catch someone's eye in the hallway and ask for the time, it is not likely to be considered flirtatious, but if you go out of your way to compliment someone in a bar, then they will most likely consider that you are flirting with them.

Men are more likely to misconstrue women's actions, such as smiling or complimenting him, as flirtations (Henningsen, 2004; Kowalski, 1992). According to Haselton and Buss's **error management theory** (2000), it is genetically advantageous for men to do so. A man who has to decide if a woman is sexually interested in him can make two mistakes: he can assume that a woman who is not interested in him is in fact interested and try to pursue a sexual relationship with her, at the risk of rejection and hurt feelings. Conversely, he may falsely believe that a woman is not interested in him, and therefore not bother trying to have a sexual relationship with her. According to Haselton and Buss, the genetically advantageous error is for men to risk rejection rather than to risk missing the chance to spread their genes around.

Shared focus An external subject that both participants can see, hear, or experience.

Error management theory The theory that suggests that when making a decision, a subject can make two types of errors, a false positive or a false negative. It is more adaptive to err on the side that is less evolutionarily risky or that allows for a possible sexual encounter.

Well, you've attracted his or her attention—the next step is for the two of you to interact socially, perhaps even to go on a date.

Dating and Hooking Up

After completion of this section, you will be able to . . .

- ○ Define *courtship, sexual script, dating,* and *hooking up.*
- ○ List some universal components of a date.
- ○ Compare and contrast dating in the 20th century with dating today.
- ○ Consider the issues involved with dating later in life, same-sex dating, interracial dating, and dating challenges experienced by disabled people.
- ○ List characteristics of students who hook up and of those who don't.
- ○ Consider the reasons why people have hookups.
- ○ Identify some of the things that people look for when choosing a partner.
- ○ List some of the places that people go to meet a partner.

Although the term seems innocently old-fashioned, every culture has formalized processes of **courtship**, the manner in which men and women meet and move toward marriage. Sociologists believe that how a person acts in a given social setting can resemble an actor following a script. Even sexual behavior is socially learned—a **sexual script**, if you will—and these scripts can differ for men and women. There is a saying, commonly attributed to Judith Martin (aka Miss Manners), that suggests "there are three possible parts to a date, of which at least two must be offered: entertainment, food, and affection. It is customary to begin a series of dates with a great deal of entertainment, a moderate amount of food, and the merest suggestion of affection. As the amount of affection increases, the entertainment can be reduced proportionally. When the affection *is* the entertainment, we no longer call it dating. Under no circumstances can the food be omitted." It is true that most courtship rituals involve food and some form of entertainment.

Universal Elements of Courtship

Courtship From the Indo-European root *gher,* meaning "to grasp or enclose," courtship is the sequence of interactive behaviors by which men and women choose a mate.

Sexual script The socially learned idea of "proper" sexual behavior. Men and women often have different sexual scripts; traditionally, men are seen as the sexual initiators, and women as the "gatekeepers" who decide how much sexual activity will occur.

We've all heard that "the way to a man's heart is through his stomach." Although this is anatomically inaccurate, it may be sociologically correct. Sharing food is a universal element of courtship. A man may provide food to his intended to show that he can provide for her and any possible offspring, whereas a woman may illustrate her nurturance and caring by cooking for her partner.

Excitement often heightens sexual arousal.

Music is another common component of dating. When bodies move in synchrony with each other, it is a sign of compatibility and interest. Music encourages a couple to move together, to show that they follow the beat of the same drummer, as it were. The type of music played can influence our emotions. Women evaluating photos of men rated them more attractive when listening to soft rock compared to when they were listening to *avant garde* jazz (May & Hamilton, 1980).

In *The Art of Love,* written in the 1st century, Ovid advises men who want to seduce a woman to first bring her to a gladiatorial tournament, which would cause her to be more easily aroused. Ovid may have been on to something. Individuals who have been physiologically stimulated will show heightened sexual arousal. According to Schachter and Singer's two-factor theory of emotion (1962), our bodies produce a physiological response, but it is up to our cortex to interpret the situation and assign an appropriate emotion to what we are experiencing. College-aged heterosexual males who were physiologically excited by a number of (nonsexual) means, such as running in place or listening to a comedy routine, were more erotically responsive to images of attractive women, compared to men who had not been physically stimulated (White, Fishbein, & Rutstein, 1981).

Courtship Today

While there may be some universal components of courtship, these rituals vary from culture to culture and also can change very quickly within cultures. Before the 20th century, a young person's family and community closely supervised his or her search for a suitable mate. Among the middle and upper classes, a young woman and her family would invite a young man to call on her in her home. The young woman had the power, as she and her family controlled the length of time and the environment of the visit (Bogle, 2008). Any form of sexual contact in these visits

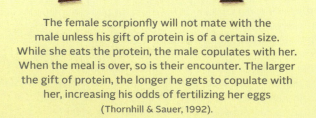

The female scorpionfly will not mate with the male unless his gift of protein is of a certain size. While she eats the protein, the male copulates with her. When the meal is over, so is their encounter. The larger the gift of protein, the longer he gets to copulate with her, increasing his odds of fertilizing her eggs (Thornhill & Sauer, 1992).

was extremely rare. In the early to mid-20th century, there was a change in dating styles. As a result of economic and societal changes, the power in the dating relationship shifted to the men, who controlled the interaction. In most cases, the man initiated the **date**, calling enough in advance so as not to be insulting. He picked the woman up and paid for any expenses. There was no expectation of any physical or emotional commitment after a date, and it was accepted that both men and women might date several persons at a time until the time when it was determined that they were **going steady**. Courtship then went through a profound transformation in the 1960s. The sexual revolution loosened the restrictions and made premarital intercourse acceptable. Feminism and the availability of oral contraceptives changed the sexual script and opened up options for women.

Today, college students find themselves in an atmosphere conducive to indiscriminate sexual interactions rather than formalized courtship. Young college-aged men—who may have more desire for casual sexual encounters than women do—are outnumbered by women: there are 100 women for every 72 men in college (National Center for Education Statistics, 2009). As a scarce commodity, men have more power and are better able to determine the sexual script. In addition, in college, many students are for the first time living in close proximity to a large group of like-minded people their own age and have access to large amounts of alcohol. The culture has changed significantly since the 1950s; it is not surprising that the sexual script has also changed.

The term "dating" is more ambiguous today. Glenn and Marquardt (2001) described different types of dating. The most commonly used definition is when a couple "hang out," perhaps by studying or watching TV together. This can lead to confusion in which the parties don't know if they are a couple or if they are "just friends." "Going out" doesn't mean that anyone actually goes anywhere; instead it indicates that a couple are linked. "Dating" can also describe a fast-moving, highly committed relationship (i.e., joined at the hip), when two people quickly form a serious and intense bond, spending most of their time together, or when, less commonly, couples have a committed exclusive relationship but only see each other a few nights a week.

Although male initiative was a key marker of the traditional form of dating, men today are less likely to take the initiative to ask out college women. Traditional dates are much more rare today. In one study, only 37% of the women reported having been on more than six dates of this kind (Glenn & Marquardt, 2001). These traditional dates most often occur on events such as Valentine's Day or the high school prom. It may also be the fear of rejection that prevents men from asking women out on a traditional date. When

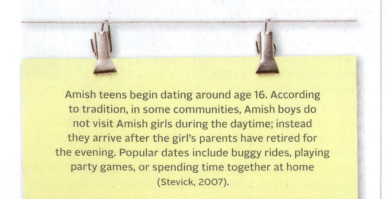

Amish teens begin dating around age 16. According to tradition, in some communities, Amish boys do not visit Amish girls during the daytime; instead they arrive after the girl's parents have retired for the evening. Popular dates include buggy rides, playing party games, or spending time together at home (Stevick, 2007).

asked to imagine a hypothetical situation in which they and another person were attracted to each other at a party, but neither asked the other out, students attributed their own lack of initiative as stemming from a fear of rejection but ascribed the other's failure to make the first move to a lack of interest (Vorauer & Ratner, 1996).

Dating Across the Life Span

After students leave college, traditional dating becomes more of the norm in social interactions. Young adults lead more regimented lives and are around people of all ages, most of them strangers. Hooking up and having random sexual encounters no longer represents the lifestyle and goals of most adults.

Most Americans eventually cohabitate or marry (discussed in Chapter 9). But all relationships eventually end, whether through breakup, death, or divorce. At the end of a long-term relationship, it can be hard to get back into the dating scene. Older men and women may find that the dating world has changed significantly since they were single, and they now have to deal with sexual mores and sexually transmitted infections (STIs) that were unheard of when they were young. However, older daters have the advantage of experience: they often have a better idea of what they want, as well as what they won't tolerate in a potential partner.

Unwanted Sexual Activity

Unwanted sexual activity on a date is more common than you might think. In one study of college students, 97.5% of women and 93.5% of men reported some unwanted sexual activity, including kissing, petting, or intercourse (Muehlenhard & Cook, 1988). In a more recent study of mostly African American teenaged women, unwanted sex was reported by 41% of participants (Blythe, Fortenberry, Temkit, Tu, & Orr, 2006). The most prevalent reason was the fear that her partner would get angry if denied sex. It is important to differentiate between **unwanted sex** and **nonconsensual sex**. Willing participation in unwanted sex is different than forced sex. It is not uncommon for people to engage in sexual activities that they are not in the mood for. Women most often do this to satisfy a partner's needs or to promote intimacy, even as men will have unwanted sex to avoid tension in the relationship (O'Sullivan & Allgeier, 1998).

Men and women use different coercive tactics to get their dates to engage in unwanted sexual activity. Males are more likely to succumb to psychological pressure (blackmail and cajolery), peer pressure, and surrender to society's sexual expectations for men; women are more likely to fall victim to the greater physical force or persistent arguments of their dates (Muehlenhard & Cook, 1988; Struckman-Johnson, 1988). Coercive and nonconsensual sexual activity will be further discussed in Chapter 16.

Same-Sex Dating

Same-sex and opposite-sex relationships have more

Date An appointment to go out socially with another person, often out of romantic interest. The word today has a more formal connotation, in which an event is planned ahead of time, and often includes food and/or entertainment.

Going steady The dating period before engagement and marriage, when a couple is exclusive and not dating others.

Unwanted sex Sex that is willingly consented to, although at least one participant may have no sexual interest or motivation to take part in the sexual activity.

Nonconsensual sex Also called "non-con," nonconsensual sex involves sexual acts that occur without mutual consent and against the will of one participant.

similarities than differences (Means-Christensen, Snyder, & Negy, 2003). Like most people, gays and lesbians want to find a partner with whom they can share their feelings, mutual interests, and physical intimacy. In addition to the challenges that all people face when trying to find a partner, gays and lesbians have to deal with other difficulties, including a smaller pool of potential companions and issues related to where they can go to safely meet other gays and lesbians. Those under 21, or who don't like the bar scene, don't have access to gay bars at which to find a partner. Gays and lesbians who aren't yet "out" and who hide their orientation from others have an extra burden placed on their dating life. Another potential difficulty is that people can't always tell someone else's orientation—there is no secret handshake that gays and lesbians can use to determine if the person they are interested in is gay. When dating, it is a sad fact that gays and lesbians often have to consider their personal safety when showing affection in public. Gay and lesbian relationships will be discussed further in Chapter 10.

Singer Seal and model Heidi Klum married in 2005.

Interracial Dating

Fifty years ago, a mixed-race couple holding hands on the street might have elicited shock or even violence. Today, due to an increasingly diverse population, changes in the law, and shifting attitudes, **interracial** dating is much more common and accepted. One hundred years ago, 86% of immigrants entering the United States were European. By 1999, more than half came from Latin America, 27% from Asia, and only 16% from Europe (Long, 2003). Until 1967, interracial marriage was illegal in 16 states. Since **miscegenation** laws were struck down as unconstitutional, there has been a huge increase in interracial marriage and dating. In a recent survey, more than 24% of college students said they had been in an interracial relationship, and almost 50% said they would consider the possibility (Knox, Zusman, Buffington, & Hemphill, 2000). The best predictors of interracial dating are being young, a male of color, college-educated, and from a more racially tolerant town (Fisman, Iyengar, Kamenica, & Simonson, 2008; Tubbs & Rosenblatt, 2003). People who grow up in an area with a larger fraction of inhabitants of a particular race are actually *less* likely to date someone from this racial group (Fisman et al., 2008).

As with any relationship, there are both benefits and difficulties to dating someone of another race. A survey of college students in both interracial and intraracial relationships found that couples in interracial relationships reported significantly *higher* relationship satisfaction than same-race couples. There were no significant differences in their conflict or attachment styles compared to intraracial couples (Troy, Lewis-Smith, & Laurenceau, 2006). People dating someone of another background can also get a deeper understanding of and

Interracial An interracial couple includes partners who are members of different races.

Miscegenation Marrying, cohabiting, or having sexual relations with a partner of a different race.

appreciation for their partner's culture. A difficulty is that those in interracial relationships may face opposition from others. Black-white partnerships are generally less accepted than other interracial relationships, such as an Asian or Latino with a white partner (Tubbs & Rosenblatt, 2003).

Gays and lesbians also meet and enter into relationships with those of different races, ethnicities, and classes than themselves. Gay and lesbian interracial couples may face even more opposition than straight mixed-race couples. Interracial lesbian couples can face a triple whammy—discrimination for their gender, their race, and their orientation (Long, 2003).

Dating and Disability

In a society that denies their sexuality, dating may be more difficult for people with disabilities. There may also be a concern, often unspoken and almost always incorrect, that people with disabilities will be unable to be parents or that their children might inherit their disability. Able-bodied men and women may be unwilling to pursue a relationship with a disabled person due to the (often incorrect) assumption that they are unable to have sex. Perhaps fears of "not knowing what to do if something goes wrong," or of "not knowing what to say," may prevent a person from dating a disabled man or woman.

One study of 102 adolescents between the ages of 12 and 22 with spina bifida and 60 with cerebral palsy found that only 15% of those with spina bifida and 28% of those with cerebral palsy had ever been on a date (Blum, Resnick, Nelson, & St. Germaine, 1991). In those whose disability began earlier in life, dating may be hampered by such barriers as social isolation, a difficulty in finding partners, or lack of sexual knowledge. They may have been more sheltered as children and adolescents and less adept at social skills. Their images of dating may come from the media, and an idealized image of romance and relationships can give unrealistic expectations.

Communication is important in any relationship but may be especially so in a relationship with a disabled person; if both partners honestly address their thoughts and concerns and openly deal with the issues facing them, they can have a mutually satisfactory relationship.

Table 7.2 Hooking up and Dating: A Comparison

	TRADITIONAL DATING	HOOKING UP	THINGS TO CONSIDER
Description	Clearly defined Traditionally, the man initiates, contacts the woman in advance, plans the activity, picks the woman up, and pays for the date. Date occurs out in the open. One partner asks the other out.	Ambiguous term Either the man or woman may initiate, usually with nonverbal cues. No real expenses. More private and spur of the moment. Often occurs at the end of the night, after drinking.	Perceptions affect behavior: if people assume that a hookup means intercourse, they may believe that intercourse is more common on campus than it actually is, which can affect their behavior. Men may hope that when they say, "I hooked up," listeners will assume that more happened than actually did. Women may want others to assume that less happened.
Physical intimacy and relationship status	Sex may occur after a number of dates, after the partners have gotten to know each other. As dating progresses, sexual intimacy increases.	Sex comes first, and then dates may occur if a relationship follows, although this is uncommon. Sexual intimacy is not related to the degree of emotional connection or to the level of commitment. In fact, sexual intimacy may be *less* likely if one partner really likes the other.	In dating, you go on dates in hopes of having a sexual relationship. In hooking up, women may have sex in hopes of a relationship developing so they can go on a date. In the dating era, sex was a rarer "commodity," and relationships had to develop and build up to sex. Today, sex is more common and emotional intimacy and commitment are rarer on college campuses, and they often occur only after a sexual encounter.
Alcohol	Not a major focus of typical date.	Alcohol makes people hook up with someone they wouldn't otherwise be attracted to, and go farther than they otherwise would go sexually.	Drinking increases hooking up, and hooking up increases drinking, as people often drink in anticipation of a hookup later in the night.
Goal	Find a partner and get married.	Sexual gratification without the commitment. Women are more likely to want a hookup to become a relationship; men are more likely to want it to remain as just sex.	Traditional dates are no longer the mechanism by which college students find partners. Dates may occur *after* they're already in an exclusive relationship.
Battle of the sexes	Traditionally, men held most power—they initiated the date, and decided where to go.	Men hold most power. Both can initiate, but hooking up is more skewed to what men traditionally want (casual sexual encounters) than what women want (relationships and emotional connection).	Men generally control the intensity of relationship and how emotional it gets. According to the "principle of least interest," the person with the least interest in continuing the relationship holds all or most of the power.

© Cengage Learning 2013. SOURCE: Bogle, 2008.

Hooking Up

Over the years, casual sexual encounters have been given lots of names: one-night stands, casual sex, friends with benefits, hooking up, booty calls, and chance encounters (Grello, Welsh, & Harper, 2006). All are sexual relationships in which the partners do not define the relationship as romantic or their partner as a boyfriend or girlfriend. The phenomenon is not new, but the frequency with which it occurs, and its acknowledgment as the current sexual norm, is. According to Paul, McManus, and Hayes (2000, p. 76), **hookups** are defined as "a sexual encounter, which may or may not include sexual intercourse, usually occurring on only one occasion between two people who are strangers or brief acquaintances." Hookups are generally assumed to be spontaneous, short-term, based on sexual desire or physical attraction, and may include experiences from kissing to intercourse, and anything in between.

However, people often broaden the definition to encompass their own personal experiences, and to include emotional and relational interactions (Epstein, Calzo, Smiler, & Ward, 2009). Many hookups occur not with a stranger, but with a friend or an ex-girlfriend or boyfriend (Manning, Giordana, & Longmore, 2006). Hooking up and dating may be continuous rather than discrete; the term is sometimes used to describe the beginning of the dating experience (Epstein et al., 2009). African American students in particular are more likely to view hooking up as a step in the development of a romantic relationship rather than as an isolated sexual experience (Paul et al., 2000). Using the

Hookup A term with many interpretations, it is most commonly defined as a one-time sexual encounter between two people who are strangers or brief acquaintances. A hookup can include any physical intimacy from kissing to intercourse.

Table 7.3 College Students and Hooking Up

Percentage of students who had ever "hooked up"	78%
The average number of times a person hooks up in college	10.8
Percentage of males who said their hookups included sexual intercourse	47.5%
Percentage of females who said their hookups included sexual intercourse	33.3%
Percentage of hookups (without sexual intercourse) when the hookup partner is never seen again	28%
Percentage of hookups (with sexual intercourse) when the hookup partner is never seen again	49%

© Cengage Learning 2013. SOURCE: Paul et al., 2000.

Alcohol use increases the frequency of hookups.

description of "hooking up" may be one way of dealing with the uncertainty that exists in the first stages of dating, and men and women may use this term to downplay romantic setbacks. (Differences between traditional [heterosexual] dating and hooking up are summarized in Table 7.2.) Moreover, a hookup is defined as a sexual encounter that occurs with no expectation of a future romantic relationship, but this is also not always the case. A third of 7th-, 9th-, and 11th-grade students in one survey wanted their hookup partner to become their boyfriend or girlfriend afterward (Manning et al., 2006).

African Americans may use the expression "hooking up" differently (Paul et al., 2000). The phrase is more likely to be used to describe meeting up with people, as in "we hooked up in the produce section"—a phrase that takes on an entirely different meaning if one assumes that hooking up necessarily includes a sexual encounter. Obviously, the ambiguous nature of the phrase can lead to confusion and miscommunication!

Incidence of Hookups

Perhaps due to the indefinable nature of hookups, there is some question as to how frequently the phenomenon actually occurs. In a survey of 1,000 college women, Glenn and Marquardt (2001) found that 91% of the respondents said hooking up occurred "very often" or "fairly often" at their schools, and 40% of the respondents had themselves experienced a hookup. Fifty-three percent of undergraduate students in another survey reported engaging in sex with a non-dating partner (Grello et al., 2006). In their survey of 555 undergraduates, Elizabeth Paul and colleagues (2000) found that hooking up was even more widespread. The results from that survey are summarized in Table 7.3.

Students who had never hooked up were found to differ significantly from students who had experienced at least one hookup that included sexual intercourse. Students who had never had a hookup were more likely to be in a current romantic relationship and had longer romantic relationships than people who had

Friends with benefits (FWB) More than a hookup but less than a relationship, "friends with benefits" describes two friends who have sex without any exclusive romantic commitment. The phrase was popularized in Alanis Morissette's 1995 song "Head Over Feet."

experienced a sexual hookup. These students were less likely to report game-playing attitudes about love, in which relationships are seen as "scoring." Racial minorities and students who defined themselves as "very religious" were less likely to hook up (Bogle, 2008; Owen, Rhoades, Stanley, & Fincham, 2010). Finally, students who had never hooked up were less exhibitionistic and had higher self-esteem. In contrast, students who had had intercourse during hookups were more impulsive, risky, and rebellious. They had more fear of intimacy than other students, and a more passionate and/or game-playing style of love. Interestingly, women who engaged in sexual intercourse during hookups showed a more altruistic love style than males who hook up. This may reflect their false view that women "owe" men sexual gratification, and they will end an evening with sex even if they don't want to (Paul et al., 2000).

Hookups frequently involve drugs or alcohol (Grello et al., 2006; Owen et al., 2010). Alcohol use was highest among those who had hookups that included sexual intercourse, next highest among those who had non-intercourse hookups, and lowest among those who had not experienced a hookup. The *frequency* of intoxication was not predictive of hookup experience, but the *degree* of intoxication was—those who had had sexual intercourse during a hookup reported being more drunk than other students. In fact, 14% of these students were impaired enough that they relied on friends' stories the next day to let them know what happened (Paul et al., 2000). It's possible that some people use alcohol to loosen their inhibitions; or some may drink preemptively so they can later use alcohol as an excuse for their behavior.

Hookups are not always with strangers or brief acquaintances. "**Friends with benefits**" (FWB) describes the relationship between friends who are physically intimate with each other. The relationship combines the psychological intimacy of friendship with the physical intimacy of lovers, without the responsibility of a commitment, as both parties are free to date and engage in a physical relationship with others. In a survey of college students, 60% of individuals reported that they had had this type of relationship (Bisson & Levine, 2009). Friends with benefits relationships are not limited to young adults; the National Survey of Sexual Health and Behavior found that a sizable minority of women and men of all ages reported that their most re-

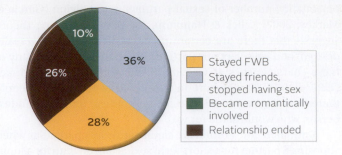

FIGURE 7.1 Outcomes of "friends with benefits" relationships. (© Cengage Learning 2013. Data from Bisson & Levine, 2009.)

Legend:
- Stayed FWB
- Stayed friends, stopped having sex
- Became romantically involved
- Relationship ended

Pie chart values: 36%, 28%, 26%, 10%

cent sexual event occurred with a friend (Herbenick et al., 2010). Some advantages in the FWB relationship include the ability to have sex with a trusted friend but without the commitment. Disadvantages are that the sex might complicate the friendship, or increase the chance that unreciprocated feelings could develop in one participant. The fact that most of the time no ground rules are established exacerbates this risk. Outcomes of this type of relationship are shown in Figure 7.1.

Why Do People Have Hookups?

The most commonly cited reasons for hooking up include a fear of intimacy, time constraints, and reluctance to open one's self up to getting hurt. People may try to avoid "catching feelings," or becoming emotionally involved. When talking about their reasons for hooking up, many women described it as a way to avoid the hurt and rejection that can come from being open to emotion (Glenn & Marquardt, 2001). A small but significant number of subjects agreed with the statement, "Sometimes it is easier to have sex with a guy than to talk to him."

Students are under great pressure to succeed in school and work. Competition for grades may leave little time for romance. Relationships, especially those of the joined-at-the-hip variety, are seen as time consuming and more of a commitment than students want to make. Hooking up is considered a way to have sexual release without the commitment of a relationship. Coed dorms make hookups easy, as a steady supply of (often intoxicated) men and women are available 24 hours a day. Some may hook up with others out of a desire for a connection, no matter how temporary, while others are simply bored and looking for something (or someone) to do on a Saturday night. Others hook up in order to avoid the pain of a

> **I think I'm about the only person in school who doesn't hook up all the time. Is there something wrong with me?**

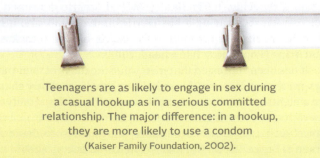

Teenagers are as likely to engage in sex during a casual hookup as in a serious committed relationship. The major difference: in a hookup, they are more likely to use a condom (Kaiser Family Foundation, 2002).

breakup. Finally, women may also take part in hookups because it is the currently accepted sexual script on campus, and they have little choice (Bogle, 2008).

College students hook up almost twice as often as they go on dates (Bradshaw, Kahn, & Saville, 2010). But given the choice, 95% of women and 78% of men said they would choose traditional dating over hooking up. So why don't they? Young adults may hook up because they act according to what they believe is the norm, rather than their own convictions, a concept called **pluralistic ignorance**. Pluralistic ignorance occurs when an individual believes that his or her private attitudes are unusual, based on the public behavior of others. Therefore, each group member publicly conforms to the norm, while believing that he or she is the only one in the group that privately disagrees with the prevailing attitudes. In one survey, both men and women reported being less comfortable with hooking up than they believed their peers were (Lambert, Kahn, & Apple, 2003). The ambiguous nature of the term "hooking up" may lead people to believe that there is more intercourse going on in hookups than there actually is, and may even cause them to partake in activities they are not comfortable with, because they think that "everyone is doing it." On college campuses today, students underestimate the number of students who are virgins, and overestimate the number of hookups that involve intercourse (Bogle, 2008).

Ramifications of Modern Dating and Hooking Up

In one study of heterosexual college students, nearly half of both men and women reported having had a "really terrible hooking up experience" (Kahn et al., 2000). Men generally found the hookups terrible because the woman wanted a relationship or because of the

Pluralistic ignorance A situation in which most members of a group privately reject a norm, but secretly and incorrectly assume that most others accept it.

overuse of drugs or alcohol. Hooking up may put women in a particularly vulnerable position, both physically and emotionally. Physically, the alcohol—as well as the atmosphere of a casual sexual encounter—increases a woman's chance of being involved in a sexual encounter not of her choosing; nearly half of women who reported having had a terrible hooking-up experience reported that they were pressured into sexual acts against their will. Emotionally, hooking up may put women in the position of allowing the man to define the status of the relationship. In addition, any unprotected sex carries the risk of unwanted pregnancy or STIs.

Between random hookups and instant joined-at-the-hip mini-marriages, how are people supposed to learn how to be in a mature relationship? Glenn and Marquardt (2001) note, "It is difficult to explain how . . . trying to separate sex from feeling, as in hooking up—is good preparation for a trusting and happy marriage later on." Joined-at-the-hip relationships are also problematic. In these, the couple has formed an exclusive and intense bond quickly, before they have the opportunity to explore alternatives to the relationship or to understand fully if it is mutually fulfilling.

Who Are We Looking For?

What exactly are people looking for when choosing a mate? Many believe that people choose partners who are similar to themselves in key dimensions such as attractiveness, education,

personality, number of sexual partners, and religion (Garcia & Markey, 2007; Kalick & Hamilton, 1986). A contrasting theory suggests that there are certain preferences that are universally desired, and we select our partners based on getting as many of these characteristics as we can; in the words of Steven Pinker (1997, p. 417), "Somewhere in this world of five billion people there lives the best-looking, richest, smartest, funniest, kindest person who would settle for you."

Both men and women are significantly less particular when choosing a partner for a short-term sexual liaison than for a long-term mate. In the short term, both men and women indicate that although they are not willing to compromise on physical attractiveness, they are willing to compromise on intellect or social status (Regan, 1998). Things change when choosing a long-term partner, however. In this case, both men and women require their partner to be not only attractive, funny, socially adept, and attentive to others' needs (Regan, 1998), but they also prefer a partner who is kind, intelligent, honest, and has an exciting personality (Buss, 1989; Regan & Berscheid, 1997). Women may also prefer men who are perceived to like children (Roney, Hanson, Durante, & Maestripieri, 2006).

When people describe traits they value in a partner, both men and women put "sense of humor" high on the list. However, the trait may be valued differently by men and women. Women prefer men who were funny, as well as those who appreciated the woman's sense of humor. But men did not rate funny women as more desirable; instead, her ability to laugh at his jokes was more important (Bressler, Martin, & Balshine, 2006).

Do males and females look for different characteristics in a mate? When David Buss questioned men and women in 37 different cultures about what is important in a long-term partner, he found that when choosing a woman, men considered good looks to be the most important characteristic, whereas women wanted men to have good financial prospects (Buss, 1989). Susan Sprecher and colleagues (1994) surveyed more than 13,000 adults in the United States to determine their willingness to marry under different situations. They found that although women were more likely than men to marry someone who was not good looking, women were less likely than men to marry someone who was not likely to hold a steady job. This may be changing—in a more recent survey, Pamela Regan and Ellen Berscheid (1997) found that women did *not* preferentially rate social or financial power as a more desirable trait in a prospective spouse, although education was rated as important in a potential partner. Moore and colleagues suggest that as women have more control over their fiscal futures, the financial status of their partner becomes less important (Moore, Cassidy, Smith, & Perrett, 2006). Still, compared to men, women are more likely to value emotional expressiveness in their partners (Regan & Sprecher, 1995). In fact, 80% of American women in their 20s felt that having a husband who could talk about his feelings was more important than having one who makes a good living (Popenoe & Whitehead, 2001).

It has been suggested that men value the looks of their partners more than women do. Facial attractiveness, body shape, and weight were more important in determining desirability for males than for females; for women, kindness, empathy, career choice, and intelligence were more important considerations (Braun & Bryan, 2006). But males' interest in beauty should not

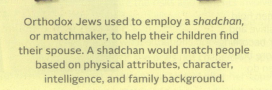

Orthodox Jews used to employ a *shadchan*, or matchmaker, to help their children find their spouse. A shadchan would match people based on physical attributes, character, intelligence, and family background.

be looked at as an objectification of women only; indeed, they objectify whoever they're in a relationship with. Personal ads of those trying to attract men (i.e., straight women or gay men) are more likely to mention looks, while ads of those seeking women (gay women and straight men) are more likely to refer to sincerity, friendship, and financial security. In their personal ads, women emphasize psychological characteristics and men focus on the physical (Deaux & Hanna 1984; Groom & Pennebaker, 2005). Whereas lesbians devoted little ad space to body shape, gay men were more interested in physical attractiveness (Hatala & Prehodka, 1996).

Where Do You Go to Meet Someone?

People are most likely to date the people they know or encounter on a regular basis—in classes, work, bars, or religious organizations. Internet dating sites such as Match.com may change this, and give people the opportunity to interact safely with others outside of their usual environment. When communicating online, people may be more open and emotionally forthcoming than they are in person (Ben-Ze'ev, 2003). People don't have to worry about the way they look or act and instead can focus on what they're saying. When meeting someone online, you can learn about their values and personality before being distracted by their appearance. Online interactions, however, also give people the opportunity to misrepresent themselves. It is important

to be safe and not expose yourself to physically, financially, or emotionally dangerous situations. People use the Internet for dating in ways other than visiting dating sites—40% of Internet users report flirting with someone online, and 21% report having been introduced to a potential date by a third party using e-mail or instant messaging (Madden & Lenhart, 2005).

Speed dating is becoming a popular way for people of all ages, religions, and orientations to meet a potential mate. People gather at an event and spend an allotted amount of time (usually between 3 and 8 minutes) in conversation with one other person. At the end of each cycle, they mark down their interest in having a further meeting with their partner, and then move on to the next interaction. If both partners respond that they would like to see each other again, speed date organizers send the participants the information on those they are interested in.

Even though speed dating gives people the opportunity to meet a large number of singles, it may highlight superficial traits. When data from more than 10,000 participants in a speed dating service were examined, scientists found that the most desirable features in a mate were almost exclusively physical traits, such as attractiveness, BMI, and weight. Factors such as education, religion, income, and personality had little effect on a person's choices (Kurzban & Weeden, 2005; Todd, Penke, Fasolo, & Lenton, 2007).

> I'm dating this woman, and I'd really like it to be more serious. What should I do?

How Does a Romantic Relationship Grow from a Date?

There are a number of factors that increase the intensity of a relationship. A person might try to increase the frequency and duration of contact, or be more emotionally forthcoming. One could demonstrate his or her feelings by giving more verbal expressions or tokens of affection.

Or, people might directly discuss their desire for a more serious relationship with their partner. Committed relationships will be discussed in Chapter 9.

Speed dating A dating event in which people meet a large number of people through a series of short one-on-one encounters.

8 Love

"One word frees us of all the weight and pain of life: That word is love."

—**Sophocles**

"Love is the immortal flow of energy that nourishes, extends, and preserves. Its eternal goal is life."

—**Smiley Blanton, American psychoanalyst**

"Love stinks."

—**J. Geils Band**

© iceteaimages RF/Age fotostock

© Blend Images/Masterfile

© Paper Boat Creative/Getty Images

What Is Love?

After completion of this section, you will be able to . . .

○ Distinguish between the three phases of romantic love.

○ List and describe the six Lee "love styles."

○ Illustrate Sternberg's triangular theory of love.

○ Clarify the six different types of love described by the Sternberg theory.

○ Compare and contrast "like," "love," and "in love."

○ Describe what it feels like to fall in love.

Love is one of the most basic, universal human emotions, but it is difficult to explain exactly what love is. Love is the driving force behind the most selfless acts of charity and the basest acts of violence. Although you may use the word *love* when talking about any number of things—a food you enjoy, a principle you value, or a person with whom you want to spend your life—for the purposes of this discussion, we shall limit our definition of love to the interpersonal. Therefore, love is a feeling of pleasure in another's happiness and pain in that person's harm.

According to Zick Rubin (1973), love is characterized by concern for the other's well-being, a desire for their physical presence and emotional support, and a longing for intimate, confidential communication with the beloved. This depiction may be used to describe the bond one has with close friends; in fact, many components of friendship are similar to those of a loving, intimate relationship, including trust, tolerance of the person's faults, respect, enjoying each other's company, confiding in each other, and providing assistance in times of need. But as we all know, friendship and love are different. Some characteristics that are unique to romantic relationships include exclusiveness and sexual desire. Although sex is an important component of romantic love, 95% of women and 91% of male respondents did *not* agree with the statement "the best thing about love is sex" (Tennov, 1979).

Three phases of romantic love, each with characteristic feelings and distinct physiological processes, are described by Helen Fisher and colleagues (Fisher, 1998; Fisher, Aron, Mashek, Haifang, & Brown, 2002). These three phases, lust, attraction, and attachment, are summarized in Table 8.1.

The lust phase An intense craving for sexual contact.

The attraction phase The period of time during which couples are infatuated and pursue a relationship.

The attachment phase A long-term bond between partners.

fMRI (functional magnetic resonance imaging) A specialized form of MRI, fMRI is a medical imaging technique that shows the neural activity of the brain.

Described by poet W. H. Auden as "an intolerable neural itch," **lust** is the passionate sexual instinct, evolved to allow humans to initiate the mating process with any available partner. During the **attraction** phase, couples become infatuated and pursue a relationship. This stage usually lasts between 6 and 18 months and is characterized by feelings of exhilaration, a craving for the union, and intrusive

© moonsabuy/Shutterstock

thinking about the love interest. During this stage, hormonal and physiological changes occur that heighten the attention toward our partner and deflect attention away from other potential partners, thus decreasing the threat of someone breaking the partnership. **Attachment**, or companionate love, is thought to have evolved to allow cooperation for parental duties. It is associated with feelings of closeness, peace, comfort, as well as mild euphoria when in contact with one's partner and anxiety when apart for long periods.

Is Love an Emotion or a Drive?

The underlying drive of romantic love may be related to mating and pair bonding—and what a strong drive it is. People live for love, die for love, and kill for love. When Arthur Aron and colleagues studied the brain activity of people in the early stages of passionate love, **fMRI scans** showed increased activity in the areas related to reward and motivational drives (Aron, Fisher, Mashek, Strong, & Li, 2005). As the length of the subjects' relationship increased, different areas of the brain became involved, including areas that are involved with emotions. Aron and colleagues suggest that early passionate love is not an emotion in and of itself; rather, it is probably best characterized as "a motivation or goal-oriented state that *leads to* various specific emotions, such as euphoria or anxiety" (p. 335). Unlike many emotions, love is not associated with any specific facial expression, and it is focused on a single reward. The emotions associated with love—elation, anxiety, joy, fear—may come and go, but the motivation—to be with your beloved—remains.

Different Types of Love

How many people or things do you love? I love my spouse, my family, my pets, my friends, the movie *Harold and Maude,* and chocolate. I love all of these, but my actual feelings for each are quite different. (Thank goodness. My spouse would be very upset if this were not the case. The pets would probably be a bit disturbed, too.) Despite these differences, the primary word we use to describe these feelings is "love."

The John Lee "Love Styles"

John Lee was a sociologist who compiled statements about love from hundreds of works of fiction and nonfiction, which were evaluated by writers, psychologists, philosophers, and other professionals. From this he identified six styles of love—what he called the "colors" of love. Lee suggests that people with compatible styles of love will probably be more content with each other than people with incompatible love styles.

According to Lee, just as red, yellow, and blue are three primary colors, from which all other colors are formed, there are three primary love styles that can produce other forms of love.

Table 8.1 Characteristics of the Stages of Love

Stage	Characteristics	Hormones and Neural Pathways Involved	Biological Foundations
Lust	Craving for sexual gratification with any appropriate partner	Androgens and estrogens, pheromones, and the senses	To initiate the mating process
Attraction	Energy and attention focused on one particular person; decreased attention on other potential partners	High dopamine and norepinephrine; low serotonin	Allows both parties to keep focused on each other in order to choose and pursue a partner, and to maintain a relationship
Attachment	Feelings of security, comfort, and emotional union	Oxytocin, vasopressin	To sustain the relationship long enough to complete parental duties

© Cengage Learning 2013

Mania, or manic love, is a combination of eros and ludus. It is obsessive, possessive and jealous love. It is characterized by roller coaster highs and lows. Manic lovers may sit by the phone for hours waiting for that call. Like an erotic lover, a manic lover wants an intense, physically stimulating relationship, but usually chooses inappropriate partners.

Eros (EH-ros) refers to romantic or passionate love. It emphasizes physical attraction and sexual desire. Erotic love is highly idealized, which is why purely romantic love cannot last forever. Flaws and shortcomings exist, and erotic lovers are quick to fall in and out of love, although erotic lovers are more likely than other types of lovers to be highly satisfied with their relationships (Meeks, Hendrick & Hendrick, 1998).

Agape ("AH-gah-pay") is altruistic and selfless love. It is a combination of eros and storge. In agapic love, nothing is expected in return, and the other's wishes are considered more important than your own. An agapic lover may not try to find a perfect partner for him or herself but instead submit to the will of God or to try to support all those who need their love. This sort of love is considered more socially acceptable in women than in men.

Ludus (LOO-dus), or ludic love, involves game playing and "scoring." Ludic lovers enjoy the game of seduction, and do not necessarily value commitment or intimacy. For a ludic lover, sex is for fun, not for expressing emotion or commitment, and a game player may juggle several relationships at once. This sort of love is more common in college-aged men and in women whose parents are divorced (Dion & Dion 1993; Paul, McManus, & Hayes, 2000).

Storge ("Store-gay") is a deep companionate attachment, deep friendship or nonsexual affection. This is the sort of love that binds parents and children, close friends, as well as couples whose quiet calm love has built over time. Storgic lovers don't suddenly fall in love with an idealized lover; they instead develop feelings of affection for their partner through pleasurable activities. Commitment, stability, and comfort are the goals. Women often score higher than men on storgic scales.

Pragma (PRAG-ma) or pragmatic love, combines the cold, conscious elements of ludic love with the nonsexual affection of storgic love. It is practical and business-like. Partners tend to balance the negative with the positives to get the best relationship "deal" that they feel they can. Pragmatic lovers may plan the best time to get married, have children, or get divorced based on financial or social factors. Pragmatic love is more often seen in women than men (Dion & Dion 1993).

FIGURE 8.1 John Lee's "love styles."

© Cengage Learning 2013

The three primary styles of love are **eros**, **storge**, and **ludus** (Lee, 1977), and the other forms are **mania**, **agape**, and **pragma** (Figure 8.1). There may be a genetic basis underlying these "colors" of love. Scientists have found associations between gene markers and Lee's love styles. There was a significant association between dopamine receptors and the eros loving style, as well as between the mania style of love and serotonin (Emanuele, Brondino, Pesenti, Re, & Geroldi, 2007).

Eros Romantic or passionate love.

Storge Companionate attachment or nonsexual affection.

Ludus A game-playing style of love.

Mania Obsessive jealous love that combines eros and ludus.

Agape Altrustic love that combines eros and storge.

Pragma Pragmatic love that combines storge and ludus.

The Triangular Theory of Love

Psychologist Robert Sternberg (1986) suggests that love is made up of three components—intimacy, passion, and commitment—that combine to form various kinds of love.

Intimacy involves emotional closeness, caring, and sharing. It includes the desire to give and receive emotional support, the feelings of warmth toward another person, and the wish to share one's innermost thoughts with the other.

Passion describes an intense romantic or sexual desire for another person and is usually accompanied by physical attraction and physiological arousal. It involves a deep desire to form a union with the object of your affection. Other needs, such as those for self-esteem, nurturance, or self-actualization, may contribute to the experience of passion. This "hot component" of love is often the first element in a romantic relationship, as well as the first to end.

Commitment is called the "cold," conscious component of love. It involves both a short-term and a long-term decision: the decision that one loves another and the decision to maintain that love. Commitment is a dedication to maintaining the relationship through good times and bad and can alone sustain a relationship if both intimacy and passion are gone.

These three components make up the Sternberg love triangle (Figure 8.2). According to the theory, the *amount* of love depends on the absolute strength of each of the components and the *kind* of love depends on the strengths of the three components relative to each other. Couples are well-matched if their triangles are roughly the same shape and size (i.e., if they have approximately the same levels of passion and commitment and intimacy). Sternberg has described several types of love based on these components:

- *Liking* involves only emotional intimacy. This may describe our relationships with friends, which have no (sexual) passion or long-term commitment.
- When there is only passion without intimacy or commitment, such as with "love at first sight," this is called *infatuation*. Infatuation is associated with a high degree of physiological arousal. It is often one-sided, and it may fade quickly.
- *Empty love* involves only commitment, such as a couple whose relationship has long since lost any intimacy or passion but who stay together "for the children," social appearance, or other reasons.
- *Romantic* love combines both passion and intimacy. This may be present in the first phase of a relationship, or in a summer fling. Romantic love is characterized by emotional intensity, fragility, and sexual excitement. The intense emotions experienced during passionate love may be both positive (joy, elation, ecstasy) and negative (despair, emptiness, jealousy), although when people recall a past passionate love, they recall the positive emotions more than the negative. Romantic love may be short-lived, because it lacks commitment.
- Both intimacy and commitment are components of *companionate* love. Examples of companionate love might be a marriage in which the passion has faded, or a long-term,

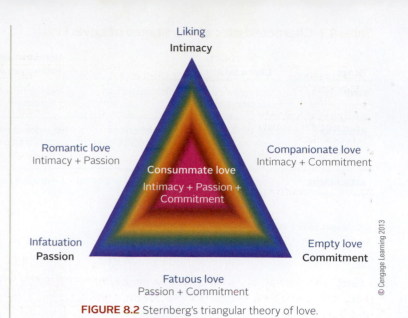

FIGURE 8.2 Sternberg's triangular theory of love.

© Cengage Learning 2013

deeply committed friendship. Companionate love usually causes fewer emotional ups and downs than passionate love, but is associated with such positive emotions as joy, comfort, trust, contentment, and respect (Sprecher & Regan, 1998). Companionate love is more durable than romantic love, and may even grow over time.

- In *fatuous* love, you do not really know the person to whom you're making a commitment. Fatuous love combines passion and commitment, without intimacy. An example of this type of love is a whirlwind courtship, in which two people meet and decide to get married after spending a weekend together.
- If a couple is lucky enough to have all passion, intimacy, and commitment in balance, they share *consummate* love. This is the type of relationship most of us are seeking.

> There's a girl I like, and she says she *loves* me but she's not *in love* with me. Is she just blowing me off?

Is There a Difference Between "Love" and "In Love"?

A number of studies have tried to differentiate among "liking someone," "loving" someone, and being "in love" with someone. Although various factors are common to all three—a positive mood, a desire for the other's presence, and a desire to know the other— there are a number of characteristics that differentiate the emotions. The most distinctive characteristic of "liking someone" was a desire for an interaction with him or her; "love" was especially characterized by trust; and "in love" was distinguished by a feeling of arousal (Lamm & Wiesmann 1997; Regan, Kocan, & Whitlock, 1998). Like and love actually have more in common than do love and "in love" (Lamm & Wiesmann 1997). Lamm and Wiesmann's findings regarding the differences among liking, loving, and being in love are summarized in Table 8.2.

Table 8.2 Characteristics of Liking, Love, and In Love

	Liking	Love	In Love
Most common characteristic	Positive mood when thinking about or being with the other	Positive mood when thinking about or being with the other	Arousal when thinking about or with the other
Distinctive characteristics that differentiate the emotions	Desire for interaction with the other Attribution of positive characteristics to the other Perception of similarities with the other	Trust Tolerance and altruistic behavior toward the other Calmness due to the other's presence	Arousal Thinking about the other Behavior toward the other is inhibited

SOURCE: Lamm & Wiesmann, 1997

What Does It Feel Like to Fall in Love?

Falling in love involves a complex amalgam of emotions. At any one time, you can experience euphoria or torment, sleepless nights or restless days, hope or uncertainty. A person in love may alternate between soaring ecstasy and crushing fear, between feeling invincible and feeling helpless. The lover can experience a longing for emotional reciprocity along with a fear of rejection.

Fisher (2000) has described of the following characteristics associated with passionate love:

- The other person begins to take on "special meaning," seeming unique from all others in the world.
- You might feel a sense of responsibility and might reorder your daily priorities to become available to the beloved. Lovers may feel emotionally dependent on the relationship.
- Thoughts of the beloved intrude on your thoughts constantly. When you're in love you might ask yourself, "What would he/she think of this?" Past conversations may be replayed in order to analyze every single syllable uttered.
- Romantic love involves idealization of another. A person in love often focuses on trivial (or even annoying) aspects of the adored and considers these characteristics to be wonderful. MRI scans of people in love show that brain areas involved with social judgments are shut off, meaning that when we deeply love another, we are blind to his or her faults (Bartels & Zeki, 2004).

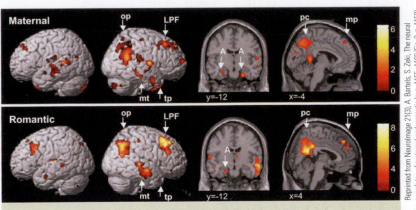

fMRI scans of people in love.

Reprinted from NeuroImage 21(3), A. Bartels, S. Zeki; The neural correlates of maternal and romantic love, 1155–1166 (Fig. 2, p. 1158) with permission from Elsevier.

The Origins of Love

After completion of this section, you will be able to . . .

- ○ List the areas of the brain that correspond to the emotion of love.
- ○ Identify the role that specific neurotransmitters play in the expression of love.
- ○ Describe the psychological theories that explain why people fall in love.
- ○ Recognize the psychological and physiological benefits that love and friendship bestow.

In his *Symposium,* Plato describes the origin of love. He tells us that humans were originally two-sided creatures with four legs, four arms, two faces, and two sets of genitals. There were three sexes: "children of the sun" were two men joined together; two coupled women were called "children of the earth"; and when a man and a woman were connected they were called "children of the moon." Zeus feared their strength, and punished them for their pride by cutting them in two, forever separating them from their other half. Humans now spend their lives searching for their other halves, and making love is our effort to join back together and become one. The way we speak of love references Plato's beliefs. We often speak of "our better half" or say that "we are one" when describing our partners.

The Biology of Love

Although the organ most commonly associated with love is the heart, it is actually the brain and the senses that most strongly influence our perceptions of love.

The Brain

Scientists have observed brain activity in subjects who describe themselves as being "truly, deeply and madly in love" (Bartels & Zeki, 2000, p. 3829; Aron et al., 2005). These subjects looked at pictures of their true love and at pictures of friends. When gazing upon the photos of their beloved, areas of the brain related to positive emotions, motivational drives, and reward increased their activity; brain areas that slowed down were those related to negative emotions, fear, aggression, as well as the part of the brain that makes social judgments about people. The same

Are You Passionately in Love?

Here is the Passionate Love Scale, designed by Elaine Hatfield and Susan Sprecher (Hatfield & Sprecher, 1986, p. 391.)

Please think of the person whom you love most passionately *right now*. If you are not in love, please think of the last person you loved. If you have never been in love, think of the person you came closest to caring for in that way.

Try to describe the way you felt when your feelings were most intense. Answers range from (1) Not at all true to (9) Definitely true.

I would feel deep despair if _____ left me.	1 2 3 4 5 6 7 8 9
Sometimes I feel I can't control my thoughts; they are obsessively on _____.	1 2 3 4 5 6 7 8 9
I feel happy when I am doing something to make _____ happy.	1 2 3 4 5 6 7 8 9
I would rather be with _____ than anyone else.	1 2 3 4 5 6 7 8 9
I'd get jealous if I thought _____ was falling in love with someone else.	1 2 3 4 5 6 7 8 9
I yearn to know all about _____.	1 2 3 4 5 6 7 8 9
I have an endless appetite for affection from _____.	1 2 3 4 5 6 7 8 9
For me, _____ is the perfect romantic partner.	1 2 3 4 5 6 7 8 9
I sense my body responding when _____ touches me.	1 2 3 4 5 6 7 8 9
_____ always seems to be on my mind.	1 2 3 4 5 6 7 8 9
I want _____ to know me—my thoughts, my fears, and my hopes.	1 2 3 4 5 6 7 8 9
I eagerly look for signs indicating _____'s desire for me.	1 2 3 4 5 6 7 8 9
I possess a powerful attraction for _____.	1 2 3 4 5 6 7 8 9
I get extremely depressed when things don't go right in my relationship with _____.	1 2 3 4 5 6 7 8 9
Add up the numbers to get your passionate love scale score.	Total _____

The Meaning of Various PLS Scores:

- **Extremely passionate = 99–120 points.** You are wildly in love, and can't stop thinking about the object of your affections. Your heart pounds, your pulse races, and you find it impossible to keep away from the object of your desire—even when pursuit is dangerous or foolish.
- **Passionate = 79–98 points.** You often feel passion, but not with such unrelenting intensity.
- **Average = 61–78 points.** On occasion, you experience such bursts of passionate feeling.
- **Cool = 42–60 points.** You feel only tepid passion and then only infrequently.
- **Extremely cool = 14–41 points.** The thrill is gone.

Adapted from Journal of Adolescence, Vol 9(4), Hatfield & Sprecher, "Measuring passionate love in intimate relationships," p. 391, © 1986 with permission from Elsevier.

---

reward areas light up in couples who have been in love for 20 years, although these couples also have increased activity in regions of the brain that produce oxytocin (Acevedo, Aron, Fisher, & Brown, 2011; Acevedo, Aron, Fisher, & Brown, 2008).

In 2004 Bartels and Zeki investigated the pathways of maternal love. They found that whether romantic or maternal, love and attachment stimulate similar neuronal pathways in the brain. These pathways respond to oxytocin and vasopressin (discussed below), which are necessary for the formation of a bond between couples and between a mother and her child. There are some differences in neural activity for romantic and maternal love. Romantic love stimulates the hypothalamus, which controls, among other things, sexual arousal. Maternal love stimulates the *periaqueductal gray*, a brain area high in oxytocin and endorphins thought to be involved in maternal behaviors and pain reduction during childbirth (Bartels & Zeki, 2004).

Dopamine (DOH-pah-mean; DA), serotonin (ser-oh-TOE-nin), and norepinephrine (nor-ep-ih-NEF-rine; NE) Substances released from neurons that affect mood, motivation, and excitement.

The Senses

When we are in a romantic relationship, physiological changes occur that cause us to focus on our partner and disregard potential rivals for our affection. People in love pay less visual attention to attractive people of the opposite sex. Students involved in heterosexual relationships were instructed to write descriptions of times they felt extreme love for their partner, while control subjects wrote of times that they felt extreme happiness. Subjects then took a visual attention test. Although there was no overall reduction in the subjects' visual attention, subjects who were thinking of their beloved showed reduced attention times when exposed to pictures of attractive people of the opposite sex (Maner, Rouby, & Gonzaga, 2008).

Our sense of smell also adjusts to help us focus on our romantic partners: heterosexual female subjects who were highly in love were less able to identify an opposite-sex friend (a potential partner and thus a threat to the relationship) by his smell but were not inhibited in their ability to identify the scent of a same-sex friend (Lundström & Jones-Gotman, 2009). The more in love the subjects were, the worse they performed in identifying the odor of an opposite-sex friend.

The Chemistry of Love

Several chemical substances have been found to influence the experience of love. **Dopamine (DA)** and **norepinephrine (NE)** are neurotransmitters that are involved in mood, motivation, attention, and excitement. Drugs such as cocaine, amphetamines, and Ritalin raise DA levels, and lead to physiological actions such as increased attention, exhilaration, pounding heart, loss of sleep and appetite, and anxiety. It is thought that the attraction phase of love is associated with physiological arousal as well as an almost obsessive focus on one's beloved—effects that are related to an increased activity of both DA and NE (Fisher et al., 2002). Brain areas that fire when people view a picture of their romantic partner are pathways that are rich in dopamine (Aron et al., 2005; Bartels & Zeki, 2004).

Serotonin is a neurotransmitter that has been linked to mood, obsession, sex, and sleep. Disorders such as depression and obsessive-compulsive disorder (OCD) are associated with low levels of serotonin. Serotonin levels decrease during infatuation, which may cause the obsession one often feels during this early phase of love. Serotonin transporters are low in patients with OCD, as well as in people who have recently fallen in love. When infatuated subjects were retested 12–18 months after the start of the romance, serotonin levels were indistinguishable from controls (Marazziti, Akiskal, Rossi, & Cassano, 2000). This supports the idea that passionate romantic love generally lasts 6–18 months.

> "It is remarkable how similar the pattern of love is to the pattern of insanity."
>
> —Merovingian, character in *The Matrix Revolutions*

Phenylethylamine, or PEA, is a neurochemical that can increase levels of DA and NE, especially the DA pathways involved with mood and pleasure. PEA has been called the "love drug" because high levels of this substance have been associated with love and orgasm. Amphetamine-like PEA may be partially responsible for the feelings of euphoria and exhilaration experienced during infatuation. PEA metabolites are high in people who are happy in their relationship; PEA levels are low during the breakup. PEA levels do not stay high indefinitely; some studies suggest that levels decrease within 18 months to 3 years.

In 1985 Robert Palmer sang, "You might as well face it, you're addicted to love." We all know romance junkies, people who crave relationships, jump in quickly, then end the relationships and immediately search for a new love. Some evidence suggests that these people may suffer from a craving for PEA. When they are given a drug that prevents the normal breakdown of PEA, romance junkies choose partners more carefully and are more comfortable not having a mate (Liebowitz & Klein, 1979) (Figure 8.3).

When scientists investigated the hormonal changes of men and women who had recently fallen in love, they found that men experienced a fall in testosterone, while women's levels rose (Marazziti & Canale, 2004). When the men and women were

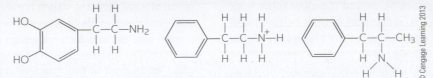

FIGURE 8.3 The chemical structures of, left to right, dopamine, phenylethylamine, and amphetamine. Notice how similar they are.

© Cengage Learning 2013

retested 12–24 months later, after the initial flush of infatuation was over, these hormonal differences disappeared. Evolutionary theory suggests that a man's testosterone levels decrease to ensure that he devotes his energies to his partner rather than looking for other women, whereas a woman's testosterone levels rise to increase her sex drive to ensure mating.

Oxytocin and vasopressin are neuropeptides released from the pituitary gland. **Oxytocin** causes the uterus to contract during labor (the word *oxytocin* is derived originally from the Greek for "swift birth") and allows for the release of breast milk. Oxytocin also seems to be important in trust, empathy, emotional accessibility, and pair bonding. When subjects played the role of "investors" in a game, almost half of the subjects would hand all their money over to unknown trustees if they were previously exposed to oxytocin (Kosfeld, Henrihs, Zak, Fischbacher, & Fehr, 2005). Oxytocin calms those who are exposed to it. It dampens activity in the amygdala, which processes fear and rage, and decreases secretion of the stress hormone **cortisol**. Oxytocin promotes positive judgments: compared to subjects exposed to a placebo, those exposed to oxytocin rated both male and female strangers as more attractive and more trustworthy (Theodoridou, Rowe, Penton-Voak, & Rogers, 2009).

Oxytocin also facilitates pair bonding and close relationships. When married couples received a nasal spray with either oxytocin or placebo and then participated in a videotaped conflict discussion, those who got oxytocin showed more positive communication behavior (Ditzen et al., 2009). When the brains of couples who said they were still in love after 20 years of marriage were scanned, areas rich in oxytocin showed increased activity (Acevedo et al., 2008; 2011).

Orgasm increases levels of oxytocin, perhaps promoting a desire to be with your partner, increasing the likelihood that you will have sex, and thus releasing more oxytocin and enhancing the pair bonding process. **Vasopressin** is also important in pair bonding and social behavior, memory formation, as well as with blood pressure and fluid regulation. The effects of oxytocin and vasopressin on pair bonding are seen in small mouse-like rodents called voles.

Chocolate has high levels of PEA, causing some to theorize that chocolate is a popular gift during courtship because it elevates levels of our "love drug." Nice theory, but in reality most of the PEA in chocolate is broken down by the body before it reaches our brain. Also, sauerkraut has higher levels of PEA than does chocolate, although giving beribboned boxes of shredded cabbage fermented in brine for Valentine's Day doesn't seem to have caught on.

© Elina Manninen/Shutterstock

Phenylethylamine (FEN-el-ETH-el-a-mean; PEA) A neurochemical released during infatuation and excitement.

Oxytocin (ox-ee-TOE-sin) Hormone involved in uterine contractions, love, and bonding.

Cortisol (CORE-tiz-all) A corticosteroid hormone produced by the adrenal gland, cortisol is released during times of stress and affects blood pressure, blood sugar, and immune responses.

Vasopressin (vay-zo-PRESS-in) Hormone that affects water levels in the body, as well as bonding and parenting behaviors.

Two species of voles, prairie voles and meadow voles, have been extensively studied due to differences in their behavior and what these differences can teach us about the physiology of pair bonding. Prairie voles form lifelong bonds with their partner. These voles spend hours together and are affectionate and attentive parents. On the other hand, meadow voles show no monogamous behavior. They are sexually promiscuous and do not form pair bonds, even for parenting. Despite these behavioral differences, these two species are more than 99% genetically alike. One of the differences in their genetic makeup: oxytocin and vasopressin receptors. Monogamous prairie voles have oxytocin and vasopressin receptors located in brain regions that are associated with reward and reinforcement, while the meadow voles do not. When prairie voles copulate, oxytocin levels rise in females, and vasopressin levels rise in males (Insel & Hulihan, 1995). If oxytocin levels are blocked, females won't bond with their partner; similarly, vasopressin antagonists prevent pair bonding in males.

Endorphins were named for "endogenous morphine"—they are our body's natural form of opiates, similar to the man-made drugs morphine or heroin. While the beginning of a relationship is associated with a rise in PEA, DA, and NE, giving us the cocaine-like euphoria, the level of these substances drop over time, and people lose the feeling of exhilaration associated with early love. Fortunately, after the infatuation ends, if a long-term relationship continues, endorphin levels may increase. Endorphins give us feelings of security, euphoria, and peace. Being separated from your beloved for unusual periods can literally make you lovesick, like an addict not getting his or her fix.

The Psychology of Love: Why Do We Fall in Love?

Psychologists have come up with numerous theories to explain why people fall in love. But as with any time we try to analyze a complex human behavior, when we look at the psychology of love, no single theory can adequately address all aspects of the behavior. Thus, a range of theories can be helpful.

Behavioral Reinforcement Theories

Behavior reinforcement theories suggest that we like or love people because we associate good feelings with them. For example, if you took a bus to work, and the bus driver gave you a free ride every day, you would be more prone to like your bus-mates, even if they had nothing to do with your reward. On the other hand, Griffitt and Veitch (1971) showed that if you were to meet someone in a hot crowded room, you would be more likely to dislike them. According to behavioral reinforcement theories, the better the feelings we associate with a person, the stronger the feeling (i.e., we like a person that we associate with good feelings, and love a person we associate with *very* good feelings).

Physiological Arousal Theories

"I found it hard to breathe and hard to concentrate. My throat closed up and I had trouble speaking. I was sweating and tingling all over." Is that a description of someone in love, or someone having a heart attack? The most commonly described feelings associated with love and infatuation are very similar to our body's stress reaction. According to physio-

Endorphins (en-DORE-fins)
Chemicals released in the brain that reduce pain and promote feelings of well-being.

logical arousal theories, which are the most widely accepted psychological theories about emotion, our bodies experience a physiological change, and *then* we assign an emotion to that physical sensation. For instance, if you were walking along and a big hairy spider fell in front of you, you would probably experience a stress reaction: you might gasp, your heart would pound, and your breathing would quicken. Your brain would assign an emotion to that physical response. "There is a big hairy spider in my way. I am feeling fear." However, if you were walking along and a beautiful naked man or woman were to drop in front of you, you would probably gasp and your heart and respiratory rate would elevate. In this case, your brain would say, "There is a beautiful naked person in front of me. I am feeling lust." The physical response was the same, but your brain interpreted the response and assigned it an emotion based on the stimulus. This theory is based on studies done in the 1960s and 1970s (Dutton & Aron, 1974; Schacter & Singer, 1962), and was supported by a later study: male college students were told to rate the attractiveness of females after exposure to a nonsexual physiological stimulus such as exercise or listening to a comedy routine. After the stimulus, males rated attractive females as more attractive compared to subjects who did not exercise or listen to the comedy routine (White, Fishbein, & Rutstein, 1981).

Evolutionary Theories

According to evolutionary theory, love arose due to some basic sociobiological needs: the drive to protect offspring, the need to be protected from outside threats, and the sexual drive. The feeling of love allows us to form the bonds we need to achieve these goals and to successfully pass on our genes. There are a number of behaviors that support evolutionary theory. For instance, heterosexual males tend to look for young, healthy female mates—those who are most likely to successfully carry their offspring—whereas heterosexual females prefer males who have the resources to support them and their offspring. The development of love would make males and females more likely to stay together long enough to successfully reproduce and to help each other raise the young.

sexactually

Who Says Scientists Aren't Romantic: A Possible Love Letter from a Scientist

To my limerent:
From the first time I saw you, I felt both physiological and psychological modifications to my psyche that will likely endure throughout my remaining life span. Not only do you occupy my diurnal cognitions, but of late you also evince increased visibility in my nightly REM sleep activity.

The proportions of your facial features perfectly demonstrate the ratio of phi, and your waist-to-hip quotient seems to advertise a maximally adaptive breeding potential.

Thoughts of you increase the activity of my caudate nucleus and insula with a concurrent deactivation of amygdaloid regions. Your presence augments the activity of dopaminergic pathways, leading to a generalized increase in sympathetic action, as indicated by tachycardia, dyspnea and hyperhidrosis.

My every thought is of you, as evidenced by a reduction in serotonin transporter molecules. Some day I hope to form a stable dyad with you and cooperate in parental duties.

Yours,
Snooky bear

Love: Who Needs It? Health Benefits of Love

Who needs love? We all do. Not only for that dizzy golden dancing feeling described in some love songs, but because our very lives depend on it. We identify the heart as the organ with which we feel love, and this may be more than a random association. People who feel loved and who share close, loving relationships with others show lower rates of health problems, including heart disease and cancer. In his best-selling book, Dean Ornish (1999) gives examples of studies that show the importance of love:

- In one study, researchers studied 4,700 people in California over a 10-year period. The people who reported the least social contact died at nearly 3 times the rate of those reporting the most. Another study of almost 1,500 Australians over the age of 70 found that those in regular personal or close contact with five or more friends at the beginning of the study were less likely to die 10 years later (Mendes de Leon, 2005).
- College students who report "strained and cold" relationships with their parents have significantly higher rates of hypertension and heart disease years later.
- Women who say they feel isolated die of breast and ovarian cancer at several times the expected rate.

> "Love and intimacy are at the root of what makes us sick and what makes us well. I am not aware of any other factor in medicine—not diet, not smoking, not exercise—that has a greater impact."
>
> —*Dr. Dean Ornish*

Social support helps regulate our behavior. Those with commitments to and relationships with other people tend to eat better and take fewer risks. Companionship can affect the way our bodies respond to stress. When college women were asked to quickly count backwards by seventeens from a number in the thousands, their heart rate and blood pressure increased. When these women had a friend with them, their stress response was cut in half (Kamarck, 1990).

Gustav Klimt's *The Kiss*.

© Erich Lessing / Art Resource, NY

The presence of a loved one—or even a photograph of our beloved—can decrease the perception of pain. Heterosexual women involved in a long-term relationship were given a series of painful stimuli. Their perception of that pain was diminished when holding the hand of their partners, and diminished even more when viewing a photo of their loved one (Master et al., 2009).

Being in love may even make us more creative. Subjects were asked to imagine one of two situations—a long walk with their beloved, or casual sex with a person to whom they were attracted but not in love. (A control group imagined a nice walk on their own.) Subjects then tried to solve creative insight prob-

from cells to society / **politics** & human sexuality

In 1975, Elaine Hatfield and Ellen Berscheid received a small grant from the National Science Foundation (NSF) to study the importance of social justice and equity in romantic exchanges (Hatfield, 2006). William Proxmire, a senator from Wisconsin, bestowed the "golden fleece" award to Dr. Hatfield, for "fleecing" the taxpayers for what he deemed to be frivolous and wasteful research. Senator Proxmire said, "I believe that 200 million Americans want to leave some things in life a mystery, and right on top of the things we don't want to know is why a man falls in love with a

woman" (cited in Blitstein, 2008). The *Chicago Daily News* ran a call-in poll, and 87.5% of the public agreed with Senator Proxmire. Hatfield and Berscheid received hate mail, their funding was revoked, and the NSF decreed that studies of romantic love would no longer be funded. Dr. Hatfield persevered (although she has never again applied for government funding for her research). Today, she is one of the premier scholars in the scientific study of passionate love, and has received a number of professional awards and accolades.

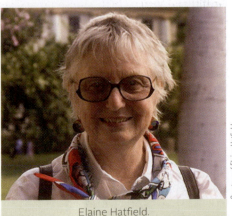

Elaine Hatfield.

Courtesy of Elaine Hatfield

lems and analytical logic problems. Those who were thinking of romantic love solved more creativity problems and fewer analytic problems than those in the control group, while those imagining sex solved more analytic problems and fewer creative problems than controls (Förster, Epstude, & Özelsel, 2009).

> "Love takes off masks that we fear we cannot live without and know we cannot live within."
>
> —*James Baldwin, American writer*

With Whom Do We Fall in Love?

After completion of this section, you will be able to . . .

O Understand the factors that affect whom we fall in love with.

O Recognize that love occurs at all stages of the life span.

Various factors come into play to determine with whom we will fall in love; these include physical attractiveness, another's feelings toward us, proximity, and shared traits and values.

Physical Attractiveness

When given a choice of more than one potential partner, individuals will prefer the one who is more physically attractive. This statement probably did not elicit great surprise; you probably muttered "well, duh" as you read the preceding sentence. Although we have grown up with the maxims: "Beauty is only skin deep," "Never judge a book by its cover," and "Beauty is in the eye of the beholder," it appears as though these sentiments are not an accurate assessment of the ways people truly judge others.

There may be truth to the old saying "Men fall in love with those they consider beautiful; while women find beautiful those that they love." Males place a higher value on physical attractiveness in selecting a partner for a relationship than do women. Women place more value on such traits as ambition, status, and personality. This has been shown not only in American cultures (Townsend & Wasserman, 1998), but in other cultures as well (Buss, 1994).

What if we all only have one true love and my true love is some guy over in China or something? How will I ever meet him?

Matching hypothesis The idea that people are most likely to form long-term relationships with those who are equally as attractive as they are.

Reciprocity A mutual give and take, generally used to describe the idea that we like someone better if they like us.

Mere exposure effect The phenomenon in which people prefer things they are familiar with.

Proximity Being around another person frequently.

According to the **matching hypothesis**, people are more likely to form long-term relationships with partners who match them in physical attractiveness. This may be due to the tendency of people to avoid being rejected by someone more attractive than themselves. When we see couples in which the man is significantly less attractive than the female, we tend to assume that the man is wealthy, intelligent, and/or successful.

Why is physical beauty so valued? Evolutionary forces may in part explain the human desire for beauty. As we discussed in Chapter 7, characteristics such as clear skin or symmetrical features, which are considered universally beautiful, might be related to health and hence to reproductive potential.

People often pair up with someone who is about as attractive as they are.

Reciprocity

Hundreds of years ago, Italian women used to put drops of belladonna (also known as deadly nightshade) in their eyes to dilate the pupils. Dilated pupils are considered attractive because the pupil normally dilates when a person is aroused. And what, I ask you, is more attractive than someone who is attracted to you?

Reciprocity means that we like people who like us. If we discover that someone likes us, we appreciate their good taste and give them a second look. Reciprocity may set up a sort of positive feedback loop—if someone is complimentary and warm toward us, we are more likely to feel warmly toward them, which can increase our self-esteem, as well as make us more likely to express our positive feelings toward them. Relationships in which only one person is expressive and complimentary are unlikely to last.

Proximity

Robert Zajonc (1968) showed subjects a series of unfamiliar words in Turkish and then asked them to rate how "good" they believed the meaning of the unknown words to be. The more the subjects were exposed to a particular word, the more positive their attitude was toward that word. This phenomenon is called the **mere exposure effect**.

Right now you may be asking yourself why your author is blathering on about Turkish words when this poor girl wants to know how to find her true love. The mere exposure effect shows how **proximity** to potential partners affects us, in that the more we're exposed to something, the more we like it. Most of us find love from the people we are around every day—people at school, work, or in our neighborhood. It is also likely that people who go to the same university, or who attend the same church, may have similar values and interests. Laumann and colleagues (1994) considered this when they asked their subjects where they met romantic partners. Locations in which people gather who share common interests—such as university classes or health clubs—are called "high preselection locales." A low preselection locale is one in which people probably don't share common interests, such as a bar. Laumann found that high preselection locales were more likely to yield sex partner connections than were low preselection locales.

Similarities

Although we've all heard the axiom "opposites attract," this refers to opposing charges of magnets or ions. When dealing with the complexities involved with human love, it is much more likely that "birds of a feather flock together." Most married couples in the United States share the same race and religion, and are similar in terms of age, socioeconomic class, intelligence, education, and physical attractiveness (Feingold, 1988). A recent study by Luo and Klohnen (2005) of 291 newlyweds showed that people tend to marry those with similar attitudes, religion, and values. Interestingly, these factors did not correlate with satisfaction in marriage; rather, it is similarities in personality that appear to be more important in marital happiness. So we are more likely to marry those with similar attitudes and values, but we are more likely to be happy in the marriage if our personalities are similar. (This will be discussed further in Chapter 9.)

Falling in Love Beyond Cultural Expectations

Society often disapproves of romantic relationships between people of differing ages, races, or who are the same gender.

Is love colorblind, or does race affect who we fall in love with? Interracial dating is much more common today than in the past, and young people are more open to the possibility of

In the movie *Harold and Maude*, 20-year-old Harold fell in love with 79-year-old Maude.

© Paramount Pictures/Photofest

ASK YOURSELF

For what reasons are people discouraged from loving someone much older or much younger than themselves? Does it matter if the older person is male or female? Why? For what reasons does society discourage interracial love? What about same-sex love?

entering into an interracial relationship than people were in the past. Yet we are most likely to fall in love with those who share similar values and backgrounds, as well as those who we come in contact with frequently, so this may in part explain why interracial couplings are not very common in the United States. (We will consider interracial rates of cohabitation and marriage in Chapter 9.)

As discussed, we tend to fall in love with partners who are similar to us in many areas, such as age, race, education, and religion. The clear exception is that most people fall in love with someone of a different sex. Even though men and women are not actually from other planets, they do exhibit a number of differences in communication styles and personality traits. We could in good faith ask why some people fall in love with members of the *opposite* sex. We don't know why some people are romantically attracted to the other sex and some people to the same sex, but there are several theories (discussed in Chapter 10). It is simplistic to expect that any one reason will explain sexual orientation; the interactions among a number of factors probably influence our sexual and romantic inclinations. What is clear is that love is love: gays, lesbians, and bisexuals do not love any more or less or differently than heterosexuals (Peplau, 1993).

Love Across the Life Span

Our parents are our first teachers about love and intimacy, and an infant's relationship with his or her primary caregiver can influence attachment styles later in life. Mary Ainsworth did studies with infants and their mothers—1-year-old infants were put into an unfamiliar environment. The baby's behavior was assessed in four situations—with the mother present, with the mother and a stranger present, with only a stranger present, and when totally alone. Based on these studies, Ainsworth described three types of attachment styles.

Securely attached infants happily explored the new environment while using mom as a "home base." They engaged with strangers and appeared to feel safe. They showed some distress when their mother left. When reunited, these infants sought contact, but then continued to explore their environment. Not all infants are securely attached, however. Insecurely attached babies are classified as either anxious–ambivalent or avoidant. **Anxious–ambivalent** infants are less likely to disengage from their mothers to explore the room. They were fearful of strangers and very distressed when their mothers left the room. Upon her return, these infants often responded to her with rage or indifference. Infants with an **avoidant** attachment may show little emotion to the mother or the stranger, and may not react when the mother leaves the room or upon her return.

Secure attachment Infants show some distress upon caregiver's departure, and are comforted by his or her return.

Anxious–ambivalent attachment Infants show sadness or distress upon departure of the caregiver, and anger or ambivalence upon his or her return.

Avoidant attachment Infants show little to no distress upon caregiver's departure, and little to no response to his or her return.

These styles can have ramifications in our adult behaviors. Securely attached adults find it relatively easy to get close to others and have others get close to them, without smothering their partner. They don't overly worry about emotional intimacy or about being abandoned. Those with an anxious–ambivalent style of attachment are often more insecure in relationships, and they may want to merge completely in efforts to become close to their partner. Avoidant adults may find it difficult to trust their partners, to depend on others, and to share intimacy. In the United States, about 56% of subjects classified themselves as securely attached, 19% as anxious ambivalent, and 25% as avoidant (Hazan & Shaver, 1987).

Divorce may influence the way a child views and expresses love. Researchers investigated the love styles of men and women whose parents divorced when they were young (Sprecher, Cate, & Levin, 1998). Women whose parents were divorced showed more avoidant and less secure attachments as adults. They scored higher on ludic styles of love, while women from attached families scored higher on pragma, mania, and agape. The authors suggest that women from divorced families may have let go of the fairy tale view of marriage. Males from divorced homes scored higher on eros or romantic love scales, and men who grew up in families in which the parents remained married but were unhappy scored the lowest on eros scales. There is evidence that it might not be the *divorce* per se, but rather the quality of relationship a person has with his or her parents that affects the person's intimate relationships.

In Shakespeare's classic play, Romeo and Juliet were adolescents—Juliet was a mere 13 years old. Adolescence is a time during which we first learn how to be in love and how to be loved, and how to safely ride the roller coaster of emotions associated with infatuation. Adolescence may be the time when we have our first lesson that love is not a fairy tale, that it can be painful and unrequited, and how to deal with this pain better than Romeo and Juliet did. Young people will often have their first crushes on unattainable figures such as movie stars and teachers, which provides a safe outlet to first experience these feelings.

As young adults, people try to find the balance between intimacy and isolation—to be able to be vulnerable and depend on one another while still maintaining autonomy and a sense of individuality. People need to find the delicate balance between dedication to relationship and family, and building a career.

Although many of us imagine love to be a condition of youth, there is no age limit on love. Older partners have shared a lifetime of joy and sadness, and their connection often deepens with the passing years. As author Lawrence Durrell says, "The richest love is that which submits to the arbitration of time" (Durrell, 1991, p 257). Falling in love at 60 is as exciting as falling in love at 16, although there are some differences. Older people often are surer of who they are and what they want in a partner. They have already achieved success in their lives, and have the confidence that comes with age and experience. They may feel less pressure to score, and focus more on being with a partner with whom they can be themselves. Older people searching for a new love may carry baggage from past relationships—memories of past spouses, sexual expectations, or chil-

Unrequited love (un-ree-KWHY-ted) Love that is not reciprocated.

© Hill Street Studios/ Age fotostock

dren and grandchildren who can't accept their parents or grandparents looking for a new relationship.

> "Age does not protect you from love. But love, to some extent, protects you from age."
>
> —*Jeanne Moreau, French actress*

When Love Goes Bad

After completion of this section, you will be able to . . .

O Define *unrequited love* and recognize its relationship to obsessive or even violent behaviors.

O Evaluate the findings regarding gender differences in jealousy.

Although love can be one of the best of all human experiences, it can also be responsible for some of the worst pain and heartache. People do horrific things in the name of love—about 15–25% of all homicides in the United States involve intimate partners (Wilson & Daly, 1998). Approximately 1,000 women are killed each year by current or ex-husbands, down from more than 1,400 annual deaths in the early 1980s. The decreased incidence of spousal murder may be due to the increased availability of abused women's shelters. Interestingly, there has been an even larger drop in the number of American men killed by their spouses, a fact that is also attributed to the increased accessibility of women's shelters; it appears that when women have options for escaping their abusive spouses, they are less likely to kill them (Daly & Wilson, 2006).

Unrequited Love

Even when it doesn't result in violence, **unrequited love** is associated with negative emotions such as pain, suffering, jealousy, disappointment, anger, and frustration. Positive emotions also come into play, such as happiness upon viewing the beloved, and joy for being in love. When unrequited lovers look back upon the relationships, most remember the positive emotions. Those who were the object of desire don't feel as positively. Some felt flattered, although most thought the unwanted advances

© Todd Warnock/Getty Images

were annoying, and were uncomfortable with having to reject the pursuing partner (Baumeister, Wotman, & Stillwell, 1993).

Unrequited love can become **obsessive relational intrusion**, which often takes the form of stalking—one person attempting an intimate relationship with another who either doesn't want the same type of relationship, or wants none at all. Each year, 1 million American women and 370,000 American men are followed and harassed by rejected lovers (National Criminal Justice Reference Service, 2001). Ten percent of men and 23.5% of women report having experienced intrusional behavior, including receiving unwanted letters, e-mails, notes, phone calls, visits, or gifts; being followed or monitored; or having friends or family pursued about the relationship (Spitzberg & Rhea, 1999). Relational stalking can also become more serious, when one makes verbal or physical threats against the target or his/her loved ones, damages the target's property, or invades the target's personal or work space (Regan, 2003).

Jealousy

Falling in love goes hand in hand with vulnerability—to love someone means you open yourself up to him or her, and forsake other opportunities. But sometimes one partner may perceive a threat to that connection through an outside person. **Jealousy** is defined as an emotional state "that is aroused by a perceived threat to a valued relationship or position and motivates behavior aimed at countering the threat" (Daly, Wilson, & Weghorst, 1982). It produces feel-

critical evaluation

Do you think that men are more jealous of a physical infidelity and women are more bothered by emotional faithlessness? How might these studies on gender differences in jealousy be evaluated?

> **What was the research design?** The way a question is worded often affects the result. Is this gender difference in jealousy an actual evolutionary mechanism or an artifact of the research design? In Buss's design, subjects were asked to choose between the worst of two bad situations—emotional or physical infidelity. When David DeSteno and colleagues repeated this experiment, they allowed subjects to rate their *relative feelings* of anger, jealousy, and hurt in both situations, and the gender differences disappeared (DeSteno, Bartlett, Braverman, & Salovey, 2002).

> **Were any ambiguous terms used in the studies?** Could research participants interpret the word "upset" differently? What about "emotional attachment"?

> **How does the subject pool affect the findings?** These subjects were mostly heterosexual Caucasian college students. Would the findings be different if the students were of another race? If they were older? Married? Of a different socioeconomic class? What about jealousy in gay and lesbian relationships? Are there gender differences in jealousy when both partners are male or both female?

> **How precise are the measurements of jealousy?** People often imagine they would respond in a certain way to a situation, but when faced with the actuality, they respond differently. In this study, subjects were asked to imagine situations of jealousy and rate their feelings. Might actual events produce a different result? How *generalizable* are these results to the real world?

> **What are the potential biases and assumptions?** Are there any other explanations that could justify the findings? Christine Harris and Nicolas Christenfeld (1996) suggest that these findings may exist due to reasonable differences between the sexes in how they interpret evidence of infidelity. They found that men are more likely to believe that a woman will have sex only when she's in love. So evidence of a sexual infidelity might suggest to a man that his partner has fallen in love with another. Women, however, are more likely than men to believe that men can have sex without being in love, so a sexual infidelity might not bother her as much, because it's not as likely to imply to her that he has fallen in love as well.

Jealousy and obsession can sometimes have horrible repercussions. Violence in relationships will be explored further in Chapter 16.

ings of anxiety and insecurity, mistrust and rejection. Although jealousy can hurt a relationship—it is one of the most commonly mentioned reasons why a relationship fails—it can also be a sign of how important a person's partner is to him or her. The underlying causes of an infidelity may affect one's degree of jealousy. Jealousy was higher when a partner's (hypothetical) infidelity was perceived to be due to internal, controllable, or intentional factors, rather than external causes such as alcohol or social pressure (Bauerle, Amirhkan, & Hupka, 2002).

Obsessive relational intrusion Similar to stalking, it is the willful and continued intrusion into the personal life of a former partner.

Jealousy A state of envy, fear, or suspicion caused by a real or imagined threat to an existing situation or relationship.

Students' Thoughts on Emotional and Physical Infidelity

Students in a Human Sexuality class were asked, "Which would bother you more: if your long-term partner still loved you but was sexually unfaithful, or if he or she was faithful but in love with someone else? Why?" Here are some of their responses.

- "I would be bothered more if my partner in a long-term relationship still loved me but was sexually unfaithful. Although my partner loved me, the fact that they were unfaithful would make it impossible for me to trust them again and therefore I could not be with them anymore. Because I feel that one of the most important things to a relationship is trust." (Brendan, male student)

- "It would personally bother me more if my long-term partner was faithful to me, but in love with someone else. I feel this way because I do not think that you can control who you love most of the time, but you can control who you have sex with. My partner could realize it was a mistake and stop being sexually unfaithful. Whereas, if his heart was somewhere else, that is not as easy to change." (Allison, female student)

- "If my long-term partner tells me he loves me and is sexually unfaithful, then he really does not love me nor care for me. When you love somebody you don't do things that will hurt them." (Priscila, female student)

- "The one that would bother me more is if my partner was faithful but in love with someone else. This will bother me more because she is not just being untruthful, but because we will be living a lie. But knowing that all this time she was just lying about our relationship and that I was just a cover will bother me much more. Being sexually unfaithful is more like an impulse or something more carnal. You could forgive if someone cheats, but there is nothing to do when you know that nothing of the relationship was real." (Sebastian, male student)

- "I think it would bother me more if my long-term partner still loved me but was sexually unfaithful. I would want to know what I wasn't providing for her sexually." (Michael, male student)

- "It would bother me more to have a long-term partner that was faithful but in love with someone else. There would be no point to the relationship if his feelings were toward someone else. I believe that feelings come before sex." (Emma, female student)

- "If I had to choose it would be a partner that was sexually faithful, and not in love with me. I would choose this because I know that I could not get any STIs, and if it was a kid the kid would be from me." (Justin, male student)

- "It would bother me more if my long-term partner was faithful but in love with someone else. I don't find faithfulness to be as important as love. It is much more important to me that the person I'm with loves me, as opposed to just being faithful to me. If my wife was in love with another person but was staying faithful to me, I would take it as an insult—a kind of pity faithfulness." (Brent, male student)

- "It would bother me more if they were faithful but in love with someone else. As unbelievable as it may seem, I do think it is not only possible but inherent that we are sexually attracted to more than one person. I think it is primarily our egos that can't handle the idea of polygamy. I think it would be unnatural to have a set of sexual blinders when you're in a relationship." (Katie, female student)

Would you be more upset if your partner cheated on you sexually, or if he or she fell in love with someone else? Male and female college students were asked to think of a serious past, present, or desired committed romantic relationship. They were then told to imagine that their partner became involved with someone else, and were asked which would upset them more: to imagine their partner forming a deep emotional attachment to the other person, or to imagine their partner enjoying passionate sexual intercourse with the other (Buss, Larsen, Westen, & Semmelroth, 1992; Sagarin, Becker, Guadagno, Nicasle, & Millevoi, 2003). It was found that men said they would be more upset when imagining their partner having sex with someone else, while women were more upset at emotional infidelity; physiological measurements of skin activity and pulse rate confirmed this difference. Sociobiological theory supports this finding—if a man's wife has sex with another, he may unwittingly end up supporting another man's child; if a woman's husband falls in love with someone else, her child's may suffer from the loss of his resources. Sagarin and colleagues (2003) showed that these gender differences disappeared when a partner has an affair with someone of the same sex. Both men and women reported significantly less jealousy in response to a same-sex infidelity than to an opposite-sex infidelity. This may be because the evolutionary threat of impregnation is removed, or because the injured party consoles him or herself with the idea that they aren't competing on the same playing field.

Cultural Expressions of Love

After completion of this section, you will be able to . . .

- ○ Understand that love is universal.

- ○ Consider how love is expressed differently by disparate groups of people.

- ○ Analyze the messages about love that are disseminated by the media.

Gender Differences

Passionate love is a universal human trait. William Jankowiak and Edward Fischer (1992) examined 166 tribal cultures and found that passionate love existed in at least 147 of them. The lack of romantic love in the other cultures was thought to arise from ethnographic oversight—the anthropologists failed to ask the right questions—rather than from a deficiency of passionate love in those societies. Love may be universal, but there are differences in the way men and women of different cultures value or express their love.

Who is more romantic, men or women? Most people think women are the dreamy impractical lovers, but in reality, men fall in love faster and take longer to give up at the end of a relationship. Men are more likely to have a ludic, or game playing style of love, while storgic, agapic, or pragmatic love styles are more characteristic of women (Hendrick & Hendrick, 1986b). Men are more likely than women to correlate the degree to which they consider themselves to be in love with their sexual satisfaction in the relationship (McCabe, 1999). Aron and colleagues (2005) looked at brain areas active during early passionate love and found that women in love had more activity in areas of the brain related to memory, but the visual areas of men's brains were more active. Although there are differences, both men and women value communication, commitment, and intimacy in loving relationships.

Cultural Differences

The expression or style of love may differ depending on our cultural background. Asian women were found to be less likely to have a ludic style of love, and more likely to have a storgic or agapic style of love than women of Anglo or European descent (Dion & Dion, 1993). Latinos scored higher on pragma than mania (Leon, Parra, Cheng, & Flores, 1995), and African Americans were less likely than whites or Hispanics to show agapic love styles (Hendrick & Hendrick, 1986b).

Different cultures may view the experience of love in diverse ways. Although American and Italian subjects tend to view love as a positive experience, Chinese students associated love with sadness, pain, and heartache (Wu & Shaver, 1992). In India,

The Language of Love:

English......I Love You	Spanish......Te Amo
French......Je T'aime	German......Ich Liebe Dich
Japanese......Kimi o ai shiteru	Italian......Ti Amo
Mandarin......Wo Ai Ni	Swedish......Jag Alskar Dig
Eskimo......Nagligivaget	Greek......S'Agapo
Hawaiian......Aloha Wau la Oe	Irish......Taim I'ngra Leat
Hebrew......Ani Ohev Otakh	Russian......Ya Lyublyu Tyebya
Albanian......Une Te Dua	Finnish......Mina Rakkastan Sinua
Turkish......Seni Seviyorum	Hungarian......Szeretlek
Persian......Du Stet Daram	Maltese......Ien Inhobbok
Catalan......T'estimo	

romantic love and intense emotional attachments are often seen as a disruptive threat to the family structure (Levine, Sato, Hashimot, & Verma, 1995).

Throughout history, those in political and religious power have viewed passionate lovers' powerful feelings as a threat to the social order (Hatfield & Rapson, 1993); in fact, for 1,500 years the Catholic Church proclaimed passionate love and sex for any purpose other than procreation to be a mortal sin. The idea of an ardent, all-encompassing romantic love as a prerequisite for marriage is a relatively recent Western concept. Differences in basic defining characteristics between Western and other cultures may in part determine variations in how we view love. Cultures such as those in the United States, Canada, and Western Europe are individualistic, in which individual goals are emphasized over group goals. The self is viewed as independent and unique, defined by individual attitudes. In these cultures, it is not only acceptable but often encouraged to deviate and identify one's self outside of the group identity. American society values passionate love as a basis for marriage. We choose partners based on physical attractiveness, compatibility, intimacy, and wealth. Collectivist cultures such as those in China, Africa, and Southeast Asia emphasize collective goals and duties over individual rights. The self is defined by group membership and by one's relationship with others. In these cultures, conformity and harmony are valued. In collectivist cultures, a person is encouraged to choose partners

sexactually

Romantic-Comedy Behavior Gets Real-Life Man Arrested

(From *The Onion*, April 7, 1999)

TORRANCE, CA—Denny Marzano, a 28-year-old Torrance man, was arrested Monday for engaging in the type of behavior found in romantic comedies.

Police officers take Denny Marzano into custody following his latest romantic-comedy-like crime.

Marzano was taken into custody after violating a restraining order filed against him by Kellie Hamilton, 25, an attractive, unmarried kindergarten teacher who is new to the L.A. area. According to Hamilton, Marzano has stalked her for the past two months, spying on her, tapping her phone, serenading her with The Carpenters' "Close To You" at her place of employment, and tricking her into boarding Caribbean-bound jets.

Hamilton made the call to police at approximately 7:30 p.m., when she discovered that the bearded cable repairman she had let into her apartment was actually Marzano in disguise.

"Thank God he's in custody, and this nightmarish ordeal is finally over," said Hamilton, a single mother struggling to raise an adorable, towheaded boy all alone in the big city. "I repeatedly told him I wasn't interested, but he just kept resorting to crazier and crazier schemes to make me fall in love with him."

Marzano, who broke his leg last week falling off a ladder leaning against Hamilton's second-story bedroom window, said he was "extremely surprised" that his plan to woo Hamilton had failed.

"She was supposed to hate me at first but gradually be won over by my incredible persistence, telling me that no one has ever gone to such wild lengths to win her love," Marzano said. "But for some reason, her irritation never turned to affection."

In addition to the stalking charges, Marzano is accused of framing Stuart Polian, a handsome Pasadena attorney and chief competitor for Hamilton's hand, for arson. Marzano denied the charge.

"While it is true that I would love to have seen my main romantic rival out of the picture, I did not burn down that animal shelter and try to pin it on Mr. Polian," Marzano said. "I believe and have always believed I can win Kellie's love without resorting to such illegalities."

Marzano had been arrested for engaging in romantic-comedy behavior on five previous occasions. The most recent arrest came in May 1998, when he pretended to be a confession-booth priest in the hopes of manipulating a Fresno, CA, woman into unwittingly revealing her love for him.

The movie *An Officer and a Gentleman* portrayed many of the myths of love.

based on the family's wishes. Companionate, respectful, friendly partnerships are valued over passionate ones. In one survey, men and women from 11 different cultures were asked, "If a man (woman) had all the other qualities you desired, would you marry this person if you were not in love with him (her)?" In an individualistic society such as the United States, only 3.5% of participants said yes, while 49% of respondents from India answered in the affirmative (Levine et al., 1995).

The Language of Love

Consider the expressions we use to describe the act of falling in love: "swept off your feet," "lovesick," and "head over heels." Even the expression "falling in love"—it seems to suggest that we are walking along, minding our own business, and we unexpectedly plunge into a big puddle of passion. These terms give the impression that we have no control over love—that love is something that happens to you, despite the fact that it actually takes commitment and work. Many metaphors are commonly used to describe love, including images of love as a disease ("He was lovesick but now the relationship is dead"), love as fire ("She's his latest flame, I hope she doesn't get burned"), love as a physical force ("There were sparks when I saw her and I was magnetically drawn to her"), love as union ("We were made for each other—he's my other half"), and love as a natural force ("She swept me off my feet with waves of passion") (Kovecses, 1988; Lingual Links Library, 2006).

Images of Love in Literature and Media

Adora is a beautiful young girl. She is poor but works hard to support herself and her widowed father. Regardless of hard times, she is always kind and selfless. She dreams of a strong man who will come and rescue her. Gallant is just such a man. Handsome, tall, and successful, he comes from a far off land, determined to win fair Adora's heart. But fate contrives to keep the lovers apart. Due to her naïveté, Adora becomes trapped and is unable to free herself. Luckily, Gallant is resourceful and overcomes many obstacles in order to win fair Adora. His perseverance pays off and Adora and Gallant find true love. And they lived happily ever after.

This scenario forms the basis for many love stories, from *Cinderella* to *Pretty Woman*, from *Snow White* to *An Officer and a Gentleman*. Unfortunately, most of these messages we receive about love are myths. Mary-Lou Galician (2004) evaluates the ideas of romance we get from the media and discusses the common myths of love we incorporate through these messages, including the following:

- Your soul mate is cosmically predestined, so nothing and no one can ultimately separate you.
- There is such a thing as "love at first sight."
- Your perfect partner should know what you're thinking or feeling without your having to tell them.
- To attract and keep a man, a woman should look like a model, while the man must be taller, stronger, older, and richer than the woman.
- Bickering and fighting a lot is a sign that a man and woman really love each other passionately.
- All you need is love, so it doesn't matter if you and your love have very different values.

Dr. Galician reminds her readers that the media model of love is quite unrealistic, and she gives a number of "prescriptions" for a healthy relationship, meant to help us to overcome these deep-seated beliefs about love.

There is one final myth about love not mentioned by Dr. Galician:

- And they lived happily ever after.

Relationships may start as romantic love, with its attendant giddiness and glee. But although we all grew up learning that "they lived happily ever after," in real life the fairy tale eventually ends. That weird snorty laugh that seemed so cute when you first met starts to get really annoying. And there's only so much time a couple can spend in bed—eventually the checkbook needs to be balanced and the dog needs to be walked. If the relationship is to continue, a couple must develop feelings of intimacy, commitment, affection, trust, and loyalty. In the next chapter, we explore more of what goes into these committed relationships.

Chapter Summary

What Is Love?

- Love is one of the most basic human emotions, yet it is difficult to describe. The word "love" is used to describe many different feelings. Romantic love has been described as encompassing three phases: *lust,* which initiates the mating process; *attraction,* which allows couples to pursue a relationship; and *attachment,* which sustains the relationship long enough to complete parental duties.
- John Lee described six "colors" of love, including eros, storge, ludus, agape, pragma, and mania. Eros is romantic love, storge is companionate attachment, and ludus is a game playing style of love. Agape is a mixture of eros and storge, and is altruistic and selfless. Eros and ludic love combine to make mania, which is obsessive and jealous. Pragma, or pragmatic love, combines the cold elements of ludus with the nonsexual affection of storge.
- Robert Sternberg's triangular theory of love suggests that love is made up of intimacy, passion, and commitment, and different combinations of these components can describe various types of love. Liking involves only intimacy, infatuation only passion, and empty love involves only commitment. Romantic love combines both passion and intimacy. Both intimacy and commitment are components of companionate love. Fatuous love combines passion and commitment. If a couple is lucky enough to have all passion, intimacy, and commitment in balance, they share consummate love.
- "Liking," "love," and "in love" are different emotions, with distinct characteristics.
- Falling in love involves a complex combination of emotions. There are some characteristics associated with passionate love: The other person begins to take on special meaning and thoughts of your beloved intrude on your thoughts incessantly; you may idealize your beloved; and, you may feel a sense of responsibility toward him or her.

The Origins of Love

- The areas of the brain involved in positive emotions, motivational drives, and reward are particularly active when one is in love. During love, areas related to fear, aggression, and social judgments decrease in activity.
- The neurotransmitters dopamine, norepinephrine, serotonin, phenylethylamine, and endorphins, and the hormones testosterone, oxytocin, and vasopressin are involved with the different emotions experienced during love.
- There are many theories as to why humans fall in love. There are biological, evolutionary, and psychological foundations for this phenomenon.
- Love and friendship bestow both psychological and physiological benefits. People who feel they are loved and who share close, loving relationships with others show lower rates of health problems, including heart disease and cancer.

With Whom Do We Fall in Love?

- There are a number of factors that affect with whom we fall in love. People tend to fall in love with physically attractive partners, but we are most likely to form long-term relationships with partners who match us in physical attractiveness.
- We are most likely to fall in love with people who are attracted to us, and who we encounter in our everyday lives. Most married couples in the United States share the same race and religion, and are similar in terms of age, socioeconomic class, intelligence, and education. We tend to marry those who share our values and attitudes.
- The way infants attach with their mothers can affect relationships throughout life. Love is a lifelong process; people love others from infancy until old age.

When Love Goes Bad

- Love has been used as the justification for horrific crimes of violence. Unrequited love is most associated with feelings of jealousy, disappointment, anger, and frustration, but can also cause feelings of joy for being in love. Ten percent of men and almost 25% of women report that a rejected lover has intruded on their lives in an unwanted way.
- It is thought by some that men become more upset if their partners cheat on them sexually, while women become more upset if their partners fall in love with another. This finding may be due to research design flaws.

Cultural Expressions of Love

- Although love is a basic, universal emotion, there are gender and cultural differences in the way it is expressed. Men fall in love faster than women, and are more likely to have a ludic love style. Storgic, agapic, or pragmatic love styles are more characteristic of women. People from individualistic societies such as the United States, Canada, and Western Europe are more likely to value passionate love as a basis for marriage. People from collectivist cultures such as China and Southeast Asia emphasize collective goals and duties over individual rights, and a person is encouraged to choose a partner based on the family's wishes.
- The media present us with a number of myths about love, which we incorporate into our expectations. Some of these myths include the idea that your soul mate is predestined, that there is such a thing as love at first sight, and that all you need is love, so it doesn't matter if you and your love have very different values.

Match each description of love to the corresponding type of love from Sternberg's theory (not all choices will be used):

1. Lamar and Cherise stay together for the sake of the children. Though their marriage no longer has intimacy or passion, they feel a deep sense of commitment to raising their children in a two-parent home.

2. Betty and Barney met in Las Vegas and fell "in love at first sight." They spent 24 hours a day together for a week, eating, laughing, gambling, and having amazing sex. At the end of the week, they go to the Graceland chapel where they are legally married by an Elvis impersonator.

3. Tom and Mark have been together for 40 years. They are open and loving but no longer have sex.

4. Shane and Carson met while they were on a service learning trip to the Dominican Republic. While there, they shared a passionate connection, both emotional and physical. When the trip was over, both went back to their partners in the states.

A. Companionate love

B. Consummate love

C. Empty love

D. Fatuous love

E. Infatuation

F. Liking

G. Romantic love

Answers: (1) C; (2) D; (3) A; (4) G

9 Committed Relationships and Communicating With Your Partner

"Two are better than one, because they have a good return for their toil. For if they fall, one will lift up his fellow; but woe to him who is alone when he falls and has not another to lift him up. Again, if two lie together, they are warm; but how can one be warm alone? And though a man might prevail against one who is alone, two will withstand him."

—Ecclesiastes 4:9-12

Marriage is an institution that brings together two people "under the influence of the most violent, most insane, most delusive and most transient of passions. They are required to swear that they will remain in that excited, abnormal and exhausting condition continuously until death do them part."

—George Bernard Shaw, 1908

"Marriage means commitment. Of course, so does insanity."

—Author Unknown

© Rubberball RF/Age fotostock

© Christian Ammering/Age fotostock

© Tetra Images RF/Corbis

Communication and Building a Relationship

After completion of this section, you will be able to . . .

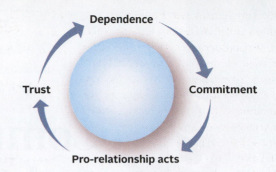

FIGURE 9.1 The interaction of trust, dependence, and commitment. (© Cengage Learning 2013)

Attraction, dating, and love . . . these lead us to bond with one another and form intimate relationships, some short-lived, some which last a lifetime. If you are in a relationship, how do you know if it is "right"? Although you can never know what life will bring, you can determine some basic characteristics about your relationship that will help you decide whether you and your partner are a good match. First, do you like your partner? Would you choose to be friends with him or her? How about your family and friends—do they like your partner and think he or she is right for you? How well do you know your partner? Do you trust him/her? Finally, how do you like yourself when you are with your partner? Do you feel strong and attractive and confident when you're together, or do you doubt yourself more? If you have found someone to build a relationship with, intimacy, trust, commitment, and communication are factors that help a relationship to grow.

Intimacy involves emotional closeness, caring, and self-disclosure of feelings, hopes, dreams, and fears. Intimacy often increases as couples learn to trust each other. In the early stages of a relationship, a couple may talk about superficial things such as movies or academic majors. As their relationship progresses, one partner may venture to share more personal issues. If the other partner doesn't reciprocate, or if he or she dismisses or denigrates, then intimacy may diminish and the relationship may stall (Regan, 2003). However, if partners learn to trust each other, the emotional and physical intimacy can develop and blossom. As the relationship builds, each person can strive to balance their individuality with their couple-hood—to balance the "we" with the "I."

Certain skills help develop intimacy. First of all, you must know and love yourself before you are able to be emotionally intimate with others. Low self-esteem and self-doubts can hurt the development of an intimate, trusting relationship with another. Intimacy is more likely to develop if you are approachable and honest, listen openly and respectfully to others, and are discreet with information that has been shared with you.

Although both males and females equally value and

Intimacy From the Latin *intimus*, meaning "inner" or "innermost," intimacy involves emotional closeness and self-disclosure, and may include a physical familiarity.

desire intimacy, heterosexual males may have been raised with cultural inhibitions against expressing intimacy or showing vulnerability. Gay males are more likely than heterosexual males to agree with the statement "you should share your most intimate thoughts and feelings with the person you love" (Engel & Saracino, 1986, p. 242). Perhaps this is because gay men are less likely than heterosexual men to adopt stereotyped beliefs about gender roles.

Intimacy, trust, and commitment interact in the development of a relationship (Wieselquist, Rusbult, Foster, & Agnew, 1999). When couples begin to count on each other's presence and to depend on each other for happiness, commitment to the relationship grows. Commitment to the relationship will make you more likely to show caring behaviors that support the relationship, such as accommodating your partner's needs. These pro-relationship acts tend to increase your partner's trust, which increases his or her willingness to become dependent on the relationship, which further increases commitment (Figure 9.1).

Communication is vital to the long-term health of a romance. Couples need to discuss their feelings about the relationship, celebrate their joys, and air their grievances. Couples that are able to communicate with each other are happier and more satisfied than those who do not (Hahlweg, Kaiser, Christensen, Fehm-Wolfsdorf, & Grother, 2000). Bottling up your feelings during a fight may actually be detrimental to your health, especially for women. In a study of nearly 4,000 men and women, women who didn't speak their minds during an argument were 4 times as likely to die during the 10-year study period (Eaker, Sullivan, Kelly-Hayes, D'Agostino, & Benjamin, 2007).

Skills for Effective Communication

In any relationship, there comes a time when you must discuss emotional issues with your partner. The issue that sets it off may be as trivial as control of the TV remote or as serious as an infidelity. The following skills can help you communicate effectively with your partner:

- **Plan the proper time and place.** If you have something important to discuss, choose an occasion when you are alone, relaxed, and have plenty of time. You should both be undistracted and calm; don't wait until the day your partner's puppy dies or after he or she gets news of a promotion at work.
- **Leveling and editing.** State your thoughts and feelings clearly, simply, and honestly, without sarcasm or judgments. Try to focus on the positive. That can be difficult when you're angry with your partner, but try not to say things that will deliber-

ately hurt him or her. Remember that cartoon image of a man with an angel on one shoulder and a devil on the other, each telling him what to say or do? Don't listen to your inner devil; wrap its impish little mouth with duct tape and let your inner angel guide the discussion. Let your partner know when he or she does something that pleases you. Instead of saying, "Can't you just leave me alone for an hour, is that too much to ask?" say, "I really appreciate when you take telephone calls in the other room while I'm watching TV."

- **Be specific with examples and requests.** Asking your partner to "be more considerate" may not give him or her enough information. Give your partner concrete examples of things he or she has done that have hurt you, and behaviors you would like to see.
- **One issue at a time.** Oftentimes in a relationship, couples won't bring up issues that bother them, thinking they're too insignificant to discuss. These annoyances can build, however, and come rushing out during an unrelated discussion. "Dear, I wish you would remember to take out the garbage." "Yeah?! Well your mother was rude to me at our wedding, and you didn't fill my car up with gas last November." Try to address one issue at a time, without bringing up past offenses.
- **Don't assume.** You can only know someone's behavior, not the intention or emotion behind it. Don't assign an intention to your partner's behavior. Ask your partner questions to make sure you understand what he or she is trying to say.
- **Complain, don't criticize.** A complaint is a healthy way to vent your anger about something you wish were otherwise, whereas a criticism attacks or blames another. An easy way to remember the difference is that criticisms often begin with "you," while complaints can begin with "I." In other words, you are more likely to get a positive response from your partner if you were to say, "I'm hurt when you don't call when you say you will," rather than, "You selfish jerk, was it too much for your tiny pea brain to remember to call me?"
- **Maintain your independence.** Speak for yourself. Don't say what your friends think, or what you read in a book. Also, beware of the dreaded *they:* "They say that it's bad for couples to disagree," or "Everyone knows that men aren't emotional." Your relationship should be a *we,* not a *they.*
- **Validation.** Demonstrate to your partner that you can understand his or her feelings. This does not mean you should ignore or downplay your own opinions, but you should always show respect to theirs. Remember that your view is not the only view—be open to your partner's interpretation.
- **Respect your partner.** Listen respectfully and fully, without interrupting. Try to tolerate your differences. Couples cannot always compromise. Although you should try to negotiate your differences, sometimes you may have to agree to disagree.
- **Handling impasses.** Couples cannot always resolve their differences. Sometimes stepping away from the discussion for at least 20 minutes can help each partner more clearly see the other's perspective, to help you both come to an understanding and resolution of the conflict. Be sure to schedule a "time-in" after your "time-out" so you will both know when the issue will be readdressed.

ASK YOURSELF

Which signals give more information: verbal or nonverbal? Which are more likely to convey how a person is actually feeling? What examples support your position?

Communication should certainly not be limited to discussions of the "state of their union"; couples should converse about opinions, worldviews, and daily experiences. These academic exchanges not only give us a sounding board and a chance to flex our intellectual muscle, but they increase the intimacy we share with our partners.

Gender Differences in Communication

"My wife says I never listen to her. At least I think that's what she said."

—*Author Unknown*

Tricia and Aidan have been together for 4 years. Tricia has been having trouble at work and vents to Aidan about her problems. Aidan listens, considers the situation, and tells Tricia what she could do to help fix the situation at work. Tricia dismisses each of his suggestions, and both Tricia and Aidan leave the conversation feeling frustrated. Tricia just wanted to express her feelings about her work situation and wanted Aidan to listen and commiserate, without trying to fix things. Aidan felt that Tricia obviously didn't want to solve her problem because she didn't take any of his suggestions, so she should just stop complaining.

Men and women often have different communication styles and goals, which can lead to miscommunication and frustration. Men tend to use language to inform, to negotiate, or to gain status (Tannen, 1991). Men might therefore be less likely to ask for advice (or driving directions!) or to admit insecurities, as this puts them in a "one-down" position. On the other hand, women are more likely to use language to connect and create rapport with others. They are consequently more likely to respond to others in a way that shows that they understand others' positions and feelings. Whereas men listen for the "bottom line," for a decision that needs to be made or an action that has to be taken, women listen for details to fill in the big picture. When a spouse is silent, men are prone to assume all is well, but women are more likely to presume that something is wrong. Finally, women ask more questions, are quicker to self-disclose emotional information, and are more likely to discuss the emotional undercurrents of daily interactions (DeLange, 1995). Being aware of these differences can help men and women communicate more effectively.

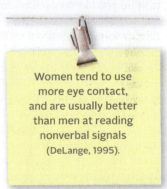

Women tend to use more eye contact, and are usually better than men at reading nonverbal signals (DeLange, 1995).

Nonverbal Communication

When communicating with your partner, the message you intend might not be the message he or she receives. In fact, most of our communication with others is actually nonverbal. Your tone of voice, body language, and facial expressions can all influence the impact of your message.

Here's a good example of the importance of nonverbal communication: Imagine that you and your partner have just argued, and your partner says, "You're always right." If he or she says it with a smile, while edging closer to you and holding your hand, you might rightly perceive that the fight is over. However, if a sneer and a roll of the eyes accompany the statement, it's probably meant sarcastically, and the battle begins anew.

What Makes a Successful Long-Term Relationship?

If you find a long-term, happy couple and ask them how they've maintained their love over the years, most often they will tell you that you have to work at a relationship. This is not the answer we want to hear so we nod patronizingly and think, "Well, if they have to work at it, then maybe they're not as happy as I thought." We then continue waiting for what the media have taught us will happen: We will be walking down the street and the "perfect person" will fall into our lives. After some entertaining misunderstandings, we will discover what is so obvious to everyone around us: that we have found "the one." We declare our true love and live happily ever after. Because we have now found our perfect partner, we will agree on everything, perfectly understand each other at all times, and be in such a constant state of passion that we have spontaneous sex on the kitchen table at least three times a week. None of this "work on a relationship" stuff for us!

Unfortunately, we are forced to live in the real world, and in the real world it really does take effort and commitment to keep a relationship alive. Most relationships do not end because the couple fell out of love, but because they stopped working on the relationship. Happy relationships are based on deep friendship, affection, mutual respect, and caring for one's partner. Satisfied couples enjoy each other's company and know each other well. People in successful long-term relationships do not live in a constant state of soaring passion; rather, they work with the little mundane details of life—making your partner's coffee just the way she likes it, or bringing home dinner when you know he's had a hard day—to build a strong partnership.

According to the Enrich Couple Inventory, designed by David Olson, David Fournier, and Joan Druckman (1983), a few factors are common to happy couples. More than 21,000 American couples completed a questionnaire, and key differences were found between the happiest and the unhappiest pairs. Happy couples felt that their partners were good listeners who understood their feelings and opinions. They felt that there was a good balance in the amount of leisure time spent together and separately. Money and sex are common causes of difficulties in relationships—happy couples were able to make financial decisions together, and reported having satisfying and fulfilling sexual relationships. Finally, in happy couples, both members were equally willing to make adjustments in the relationship. John Gottman (1994b), an expert on relationships, feels that long-term happiness in a relationship is more dependent on both people having compatible views on how to work through disagreements, rather than if the couple agrees on details like cleaning or balancing the checkbook.

Every couple will have disagreements. In fact, Gott-

Magic ratio A relationship is more likely to be successful if there are at least five positive interactions for each negative interaction.

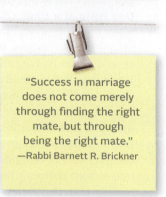

Dr. John Gottman is world-renowned for his work on marriage, relationships, and communication.

man suggests that couples who do not argue in their first 3 years have a higher rate of divorce than couples who do (Gottman, 1994a). Ideally, of course, couples want a relationship with high rewards (good sex, emotional support) and low costs (few arguments and conflicts). Gottman (1994b) proposes the **magic ratio**: in a successful relationship, there needs to be at least five positive interactions for each negative interaction. A couple can have a volatile relationship and argue frequently, and still have a successful marriage, as long as there is five times as much laughter, fun, and love to counterbalance the arguments.

Dr. Gottman suggests the following ways to increase the positive interactions in a relationship (Gottman 1994b; Gottman & Silver, 1999):

- **Know your partner.** Learn each other's likes and dislikes, stressors and delights. Be familiar with little details of their lives—their favorite salad dressing or their least favorite aspect of their job, as well as the major events in their lives—their wishes, hopes, fears, and dreams.

- **Like your partner.** Nurture your fondness and admiration for him or her. Focus on each other's favorable qualities and the positive feelings you have for each other, and remember good times you've shared. Enjoy each other's company—joke around and share your joy.

- **Interact frequently.** Tell each other about your day, your thoughts, and your experiences. When your partner mentions something, even if it is mundane or insignificant, don't ignore or insult them. Marital happiness is associated with the frequency of shared pleasurable experiences (for women, especially experiences that focus on emotional closeness).

- **Care for your partner.** Be affectionate and appreciative. Show your interest in and concern for your partner.

> "Success in marriage does not come merely through finding the right mate, but through being the right mate."
> —Rabbi Barnett R. Brickner

- **Respect your partner.** Be tolerant of both your own and your partner's faults. Learn to complain about a behavior without criticizing your partner. Be empathic and accepting of the qualities you do not always admire.
- **Let your partner influence you.** Honor and respect his or her opinions, beliefs, and views. Share your power—let your partner help you to solve problems.
- **Solve your solvable problems.** Bring up problems gently, soothe yourself, your partner, and learn to communicate and compromise.
- **Be committed to your relationship and your partner.** Have a positive attitude about your relationship, and focus on building your bond. Create shared meaning with your partner by sharing your values, attitudes, goals, interests, and traditions.

ASK YOURSELF

As a student, you know you have taken classes on every subject under the sun, from physics to philosophy. Yet most people are never taught anything about how to communicate with their partners or deal with problems in a relationship. Do you think relationship issues should be covered in sex education classes?

To Marry, or Not to Marry

After completion of this section, you will be able to . . .

O Define *cohabitation.*

O List the reasons for and ramifications of cohabitation.

"I think, therefore I'm single."

—*Anonymous*

If you were to make assumptions about Western society based on the media, you might think that the primary focus of all adults is to get married. Bridget Jones bemoans her "singleton" status, and the image of the "old maid" is one of an unattractive, grumpy woman. Yet, as of the beginning of the 21st century, the most common type of American household—almost one in three—consists of a person living alone (Hobbs, 2005). Although there are 25 million American households that consist of a husband, wife, and children, there are 27 million homes in which a single adult lives alone.

In 1960, 72% of all adults were married. By 2008, that percentage had fallen to 52% (Pew Social Trends, 2010). Over the past few decades, it has become much more common for an American adult to be single. People are waiting until later in life to marry, and many are choosing to live together rather than to legally wed. Others haven't yet found Mr. or Ms. Right, or consider their current educational or career paths to be a priority over marriage. Being single is much less stigmatized today than in the past. A 1957 survey of Americans showed that 80% of people believed that anyone who preferred to remain single was "sick," "neurotic," or "immoral." A great change occurred in the 20 years that followed that survey. By 1979, 75% of the population thought it was morally acceptable to be single and have children (Coontz, 2005).

Although some single people are lonely, others are very happy with their single status. In fact, one survey of 52- and 53-year-old men and women found that single women scored higher on some tests of psychological well-being than did married women (Marks, 1996). Single men, however, didn't fare as well as their married counterparts.

Cohabitation

Cohabitation is when a couple lives together in a consensual union that has not been legally formalized or religiously sanctioned. Many people view cohabitation as a *precursor* to marriage; about 75% of cohabitors say they plan to marry their partners (Smock, 2000). Some, such as same-sex partners who are legally forbidden to marry, consider living together as an *alternative* to marriage. Like married couples, cohabitors share a residence and resources, and coordinate their economic, social, and sexual activities. Cohabitation usually comes with an understanding of sexual fidelity. Unlike married couples, there are few legal or religious sanctions to regulate the lives of cohabitors. Compared to legally wed spouses, cohabitors are less likely to hold traditional ideas about the family and gender roles, and are more likely to share equally in household tasks. Cohabitors are also more likely than married couples to join with a partner of a different race or educational level (Blackwell & Lichter, 2000).

Incidence of Cohabitation

Between 1960 and 2004, the number of cohabiting couples in the United States rose nearly 1,200% (Popenoe & Whitehead, 2005a). Of Americans born between 1933 and 1942, only 16% of males and 6% of females cohabited before marriage; today, most couples who marry lived together first (Michael, Gagnon, Laumann, & Kolata, 1994; Pew Social Trends, 2010). Close to half (44%) of all adults in the United States have cohabited at some point in their lives (Pew Social Trends, 2010). According to the U.S. Census Bureau (2001), there are currently about 9.7 million Americans living with an unmarried opposite-sex partner, and 1.2 million Americans living with a same-sex partner. In fact, cohabiting unions have become the most prevalent type of relationship among men and women in their 20s (Scott, Schelar, Manlove, & Cui, 2009). Most young adults believe that cohabitation is acceptable, even if marriage is not being considered (see Figure 9.2). Within 5 to 7 years of living together, about 40% of cohabiting couples have married, while 39% have broken up and 21% are still cohabiting (Caspar & Bianchi, 2002).

Cohabitation is more common among those with lower educational and socioeconomic status—60% of women who drop out of high school have lived with a partner, compared to 37% of women who graduate from college (Bumpass & Lu, 2000). Cohabitation is also more common in people who are less religious, those who have

Cohabitation Living together and having an emotionally and physically intimate relationship without being married.

There are 100 million unmarried adults in the United States.

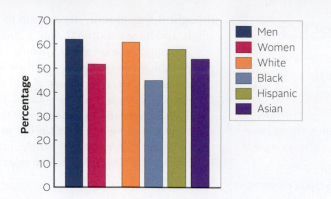

FIGURE 9.2 Percentage of young adults who agree that cohabitation is an acceptable lifestyle choice, by gender and race/ethnicity. (From Scott et al., 2009. CHILD TRENDS. ONLINE Copyright 2009 by CHILD TRENDS INCORPORATED. Reproduced with permission of CHILD TRENDS INCORPORATED via Copyright Clearance Center.)

been divorced or whose parents were divorced, those who hold less traditional views of marriage and gender roles, and people who are more sexually liberal (Bumpass & Lu, 2000).

More and more children live in homes with cohabiting couples. In 1984, 6% of children were born to parents who lived together; by 1994, that number had almost doubled, to 11% (Bumpass & Lu, 2000). By 2000, 41% of the households of cohabiting couples included a child—either as a product of the cohabiting union or from a previous relationship—under the age of 18 (Popenoe & Whitehead, 2005a).

Reasons for and Ramifications of Cohabitation

Not everyone marries. Due to personal choice, financial concerns, or (in the case of same-sex couples) legal restrictions, many partners have committed, exclusive relationships without being legally wed. Why do people choose to live together rather than getting married?

It may be because people are marrying at a later age than ever before. During these potentially sexually active years before marriage, people may consider living with someone a way to battle loneliness, save on financial costs, and provide a steady, safe sexual partner. Changes in the way we view marriage and divorce may also account for the rising rates of cohabitation. Because of escalating divorce rates, people are more aware of the fragility of marriage and the costs of divorce. They may enter into cohabiting unions to avoid the emotional and financial devastation that can occur with legal divorce. Many couples believe that cohabitation will give them a chance to test their compatibility and evaluate their relationship. A national survey of American high school seniors showed that 66% of boys and 61% of girls agreed or mostly agreed with the statement "it is usually a good idea for a couple to live together before getting married in order to find out whether they really get along" (Bachman, Johnston, & O'Malley, 2000).

Contrary to the belief that cohabitation diminishes the risk of divorce, there is no evidence to suggest that living together before marriage strengthens marriage. In fact, those who live together before marriage have a *greater* chance of divorcing in later marriages (DeMaris & Rao, 1992; Kamp Dush, Cohan, & Amato, 2003). (One bit of good news is that when a couple cohabits as a *precursor* to marriage—when a woman's cohabitation is limited to her future husband—it does not raise her risk of divorce (Teachman, 2003)). Cohabiting couples also have lower levels of relationship happiness and well-being, as well as lower lev-

els of commitment than married couples (Brown & Booth, 1996; Nock, 1995). Couples who live together disagree more often with their partners and report more fights or violence than married couples (Brown & Booth, 1996); this difference was not related to race, age, or education levels.

These facts may lead you to ask: Is it cohabitation itself that can hurt relationships, weaken marriages, and lead to divorce? Does cohabitation predispose people to divorce, perhaps by changing their views of marriage? If a person has had a number of relationships and breakups, he or she may learn to deal with the end of a relationship and develop a lower tolerance for unhappiness in a relationship. When men and women between the ages of 18 and 23 live with a partner of the other sex, their attitudes toward marriage and divorce change, in a way that may make them more prone to divorce (Axinn & Thornton, 1992).

But perhaps cohabitation itself is not harmful to romantic partnerships. It may be that those with stronger relationships go on to marry and that cohabitation serves to "winnow out" the weaker relationships. Or perhaps married and cohabiting couples have similar difficulties, but married people are less likely to report problems. Selection factors may also influence the association between cohabitation and later divorce. Maybe people who choose to live with a partner have different characteristics than non-cohabitors, and it is these characteristics that predispose someone to divorce. After all, cohabitors are more likely to have a lower socioeconomic and educational level; maybe it is these factors that lead to the dissolution of a relationship rather than the cohabitation itself. As another example, more independent people who are less committed to the institution of marriage may be more likely to cohabit, and also more likely to end a subsequent marriage when problems arise. Studies have shown support for this position, in that those who live together have been found to hold more unconventional attitudes and behaviors about marriage and divorce than those who marry, and are more autonomous, less traditional, and less religious (Axinn & Thornton, 1992; DeMaris & MacDonald, 1993). As cohabitation becomes more commonplace, the self-selection forces may decrease. A large survey of couples in Australia found that the higher risk of divorce among those who cohabited before marriage declined substantially in the 1990s (DeVaus, Qu, & Weston, 2005). In several European nations where cohabitation is much more common than in the United States, the effect of premarital cohabitation on later divorce has diminished or even reversed (Liefbroer & Dourleijn, 2006; Popenoe, 2008).

Children who grow up in households with cohabiting couples tend to have worse life outcomes than children who grow up with married couples. Because it is estimated that 40% of all children will one day live in a cohabiting household (Bumpass & Lu, 2000), this may have significant consequences. Before they are 5 years old, 50% of children born to a couple who are living together but unmarried will see their parents break up, compared to 15% of children born to married couples (Manning, Smock, & Majumdar, 2004). Cohabitation is also associated with higher rates of child abuse and domestic violence (Margolin, 1992). However, this may be because married women are less likely than cohabiting women to report domestic violence, or because a woman is less likely to marry a man who is violent. Or it may be that social pressures and marital commitment make a married man less likely to abuse his family.

Although couples who live together have more egalitarian attitudes about gender, cohabiting men are about as unlikely to help with the housework as married men: cohabiting men performed 19 hours of work per week for every 37 hours done by a woman (married men performed 18 hours per week) (South & Spitze, 1994). When single men—who previously undertook cooking and cleaning for themselves—enter into cohabitation, they decrease their time doing housework; women entering into cohabitation increase their time doing housework (Gupta, 1999). Because cohabitating couples are less likely to pool income than married couples, the greater household responsibilities for cohabiting women represent a decrease in their standard of living.

Finally, rates of depression among cohabiting couples are more than 3 times those of married couples (Brown, 2000). It may be that the greater level of depression is related to higher relationship instability relative to married couples. When biological or stepchildren are present, cohabiters' depression scores are even higher (Brown, 2000).

Marriage

After completion of this section, you will be able to . . .

○ Compare and contrast the reasons for marriage in the past and today.

○ Define *traditional marriage* and *egalitarian marriage.*

○ Assess the amount of housework done by men and by women.

○ Recognize the diminishing social role that marriage plays in our society today.

○ Identify the factors that influence who a person is likely to marry.

○ List the benefits of marriage.

○ Evaluate the relationship between marriage and psychological well-being.

Marriage is considered one of the most important institutions of society, serving familial, economic, social, spiritual, and personal functions. Most young people expect to marry at some point in their lives and consider a happy marriage to be one of their most important goals.

Why Do People Get Married—Yesterday and Today

Why do people get married? Is it for love? Family? Children? Financial considerations? Companionship? A green card? Until quite recently, marriages were a practical matter. While it was hoped that feelings of respect and companionship would develop over the course of the relationship, neither passion nor romantic love were the basis of wedlock. Instead, marriage created extensive ties between groups, through which families could accumulate wealth and power.

> In Brazil in 1996, Hedir Antonio de Brito, a paraplegic, applied for a marriage certificate to marry Elzimar Serafim, the love of his life. The Roman Catholic Church denied his marriage application on the grounds that, as a paraplegic, he could not consummate the marriage.

Even today, most societies of the world see marriage as a way of producing extended familial connections, which increase a group's power, wealth, and influence. In the Bella Cool and Kwakiutl societies of the Pacific Northwest, the desire for family connections was so strong that if one family wished to trade with another, and there was no available pair to wed, the member of one family could undergo a marriage contract with a dog belonging to the family of the other tribe (Coontz, 2005).

In earlier times, producing children to carry on the family line was of paramount importance and a major motivation to marry. Today, nearly 70% of Americans disagree with the statement "the main purpose of marriage is having children"; in fact, whereas in 1960 the average American woman had 3.6 children, in 2003 the average was only 2.04 (Smith, 1999). The introduction of oral contraceptives did much to change the face of modern relationships. With accessible, effective birth control, women can better plan their families and have the freedom to focus on their own needs and interests. Americans today are more likely to see child rearing and marriage as separate pursuits, and out-of-wedlock births are becoming much more accepted. Fifty years ago, only 5% of children were born to unmarried mothers; by 2008, that number soared to 41% (Pew Social Trends, 2010). Twenty-nine percent of white women, 53% of Hispanic women, and 72% of black women giving birth in 2008 were unmarried (Pew Social Trends, 2010). And while in 1960, 87% of children lived with two married parents, today, that number has fallen to 64% (Figure 9.3).

Historically, many marriages formed because of financial necessity. Through marriage, families could manage tasks that one

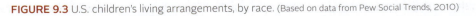

FIGURE 9.3 U.S. children's living arrangements, by race. (Based on data from Pew Social Trends, 2010)

Table 9.1 Percentage of College Students in the United States Answering "No" to the Question: If a Boy (Girl) Had All the Other Qualities You Desired, Would You Marry This Person if You Were Not in Love with Him (Her)?

	1967	1984	1995
Men	64.6%	85.6%	79.2%
Women	24.3%	84.9%	80%

SOURCE: Levine et al., 1995; Simpson, Campbell, & Berscheid, 1986.

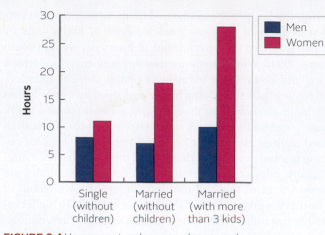

FIGURE 9.4 Hours spent on housework per week. (Based on data from Achen & Stafford, 2005.)

person couldn't perform alone. While one partner worked in the fields, the other could keep the home and raise the children. With the industrial revolution, more work moved outside of the house, and spouses were less dependent on each other, allowing for love to take on more importance in choosing a partner. In the past, a woman's financial security depended on her finding a husband. Women today have greater educational and financial opportunities. In fact, more than 80% of women feel that it is more important to have a husband who can communicate his deepest feelings than to have a husband who makes a good living (Popenoe & Whitehead, 2001).

Today, love is considered of utmost importance in marriage. As the song tells us, "love and marriage go together like a horse and carriage . . . you can't have one without the other." Love has become much more significant in the process of choosing a mate than it was in the past. In 1956, women rated "love and mutual attraction" only sixth in importance out of eighteen possible characteristics for their future husband, but by 2001 it was the most important criteria for both men and women (Buss, Shackelford, Kirkpatrick, & Larsen, 2001; Pew Social Trends, 2010). Perhaps increasing opportunities and status for women have diminished the necessity of women to marry for reasons other than love, or it may also be that most American college students now view love as a necessary precondition for marriage (Table 9.1). When asked, "If a partner had all the other qualities you desired, would you marry this person if you were not in love with him or her?" participants from collectivist countries such as India, Pakistan, and Thailand were most likely to say they would marry without love.

Young people today expect that their future marriages will "last a lifetime and . . . fulfill their deepest emotional and spiritual needs" (Popenoe & Whitehead, 2000). People want to marry a best friend who will share and understand their deepest feelings, needs, and desires; in fact, 94% of never-married singles agreed with the statement "When you marry, you want your spouse to be your soul mate, first and foremost" (Popenoe & Whitehead, 2001).

Traditional Versus Egalitarian Marriage

In **traditional marriages**, spouses allocate roles and responsibilities based on sex, women being responsible for domestic duties

Traditional marriage A marriage in which spouses assume traditional gender roles.

Egalitarian marriage A marriage characterized by shared roles and responsibilities, regardless of gender.

and children, while men take financial responsibility and make family decisions. **Egalitarian marriages** are characterized by more shared roles and responsibilities in all aspects of married life.

Even in this "enlightened" age, married women spend more time doing housework than married men. In fact, having a husband adds an extra 7 hours per week of housework to a woman's load, while having a wife saves a man an hour of housework each week (Figure 9.4). When men leave a union to live on their own, they increase the time spent on household chores by 61%; becoming single *decreases* a woman's load by 16% (Gupta, 1999).

Both men and women overestimate the time they spend doing housework, although while women overreport the time by 68%, men overestimate by 148% (Achen & Stafford, 2005; Press & Townsley, 1998).

Traditional gender roles in housework still stand in most American homes. Wives assume most responsibility for what are deemed "female tasks," and males perform "male tasks." What is the difference? Traditional male tasks, such as household repairs, lawn work, or snow shoveling, usually have the following qualities: a well-defined start and finish, personal discretion as to when the task should be performed, and a leisure component within the task. In comparison, traditionally female tasks, such as cooking, cleaning, and child care, must be performed daily, at set times, with little discretion as to when the task should be done (Blair & Johnson, 1992). Wives perceive the division of household labor to be fairer when their husbands help out with the "female" chores, and when they perceive that their husbands appreciate their household labors. Wives who feel that household labors are fairly divided may be more happy and satisfied with their marriage (Blair & Johnson, 1992; Wilcox & Nock, 2006; Yogev & Brett, 1985).

Although the amount of housework performed seems to correlate with a woman's outside employment, women perform more housework than men regardless of whether they work outside of the home or not (Blair & Johnson, 1992). As a woman's outside earnings increase from none to about half of the total household income, the division of housework becomes more equitable. However, in households where the wives are the primary breadwinners, they also perform the vast majority of household chores (Cooke, 2006). In other words, the more a husband is economically dependent on his wife, the *less* housework he does (Brines, 1994).

Many today bemoan the changes in marriage; in fact, people have *always* thought marriage was better in the past. Ancient Greeks complained about the declining morals of their wives, while ancient Romans decried the high divorce rates of their society.

Some things that are thought to be "the way it's always been" are a fairly new development in marriage. For instance, monogamous relationships are not the norm, and the type of marriage mentioned most often in the first five books of the Bible is polygamy (Coontz, 2007). (In fact, the Bible *never* explicitly defines marriage as between one man and one woman). Also, it is a fairly recent development that marriages need to be licensed by the state or sanctified by the Church. In the past, two people could simply declare their intentions, without any witnesses, and in the eyes of the Church they were married. Arranged marriages were also common in the past, and the husband and wife had little choice over whom they would be bound to for life. Some examples of traditional marriage are better left to the past. For example:

- In the past, marriages were often nullified if the union didn't produce a child.
- Men owned not only all the property accrued in the marriage, but also the wife and her children.

- Under the system of *coverture,* upon marriage a woman's existence was incorporated into that of her husband. A wife therefore had no legal rights to any wages she earned; nor did she have the right to own property or to enter into contracts.
- Until the end of the 19th century, men had the legal right to beat or imprison their wives.
- It was legal in the United States for a man to demand that his wife have sex with him whenever he wanted it—it wasn't until 1993 that marital rape became a crime in every state.

Marriage Demographics

Marriage today plays a less dominant role in American society than it did in the past. In 2006, for the first time, fewer than half of households in the United States were made up of married couples. Those who are single, divorced or widowed, cohabitating, or living with a same-sex partner head a growing number of households. Although the social reasons for marriage (family and social ties, legitimacy for children, and parental partnerships) are becoming less of a motivation to marry, the personal aspects of marriage, such as love and emotional intimacy, are gaining importance.

The U.S. marriage rate has dropped by nearly 50% since 1970 (Popenoe & Whitehead, 2005b), due in part to high divorce and cohabitation rates. Today there are fewer stigmas against remaining single or having children out of wedlock. Women are less dependent on men for financial support, and family pressures to marry are no longer paramount.

Through the Life Span: Young Adult Attitudes About Relationships and Marriage

In 1960, 68% of adults in their 20s were married; today, 26% of 20- to 29-year-olds are married, 20% are cohabiting, 35% are in a nonresidential romantic relationship, and 24% are not currently in a romantic relationship (Pew Social Trends, 2010; Scott et al., 2009). Of those in their 20s, men, blacks, and Asians are less likely to be married than are women, whites, and Hispanics.

Although marriage is less common today than it was in the past, most young adults expect to marry some day (although only 26% wish they were currently married) (Scott et al., 2009). Among adults aged 20–24, love, fidelity, and a lifelong commitment are considered very important for a successful relationship, whereas having enough money is considered significantly less important. Young adult men are more likely than women to regard having enough money as very important for a successful relationship (Figure 9.5). Asians are less likely to regard love as very important compared to white and Hispanic young adults, and blacks are more likely than other groups to consider money very important for a successful relationship (Scott et al., 2009).

Whom Do We Marry?

Married couples tend to be similar concerning race, religion, age, socioeconomic class, appearance, and education, and may even have similar genes (Rushton & Bons, 2005). We tend to marry those with comparable attitudes and values, although similarities in personality may be more important to marital happiness (Luo & Klohnen, 2005). Married couples also tend to be alike with regard to physical attractiveness (Feingold, 1988). It

> The composition of households varies by location. The proportion of married couples ranged from a high of 69% in Utah County, Utah, to a low of 26% in Manhattan (Roberts, 2006).

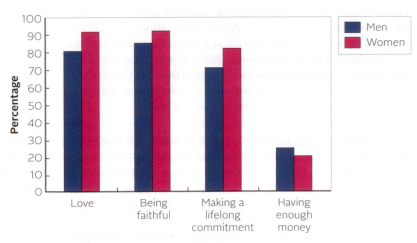

FIGURE 9.5 Very important elements of a successful relationship, by gender. (From Scott et al., 2009.)

Cultural Perspectives of Marriage

After completion of this section, you will be able to . . .

○ Define the terms *monogamy, polygamy, open marriage, polyamory, swinging,* and *common-law marriage.*

○ Identify the phases of the marriage ceremony as a liminal experience.

○ Compare the position that marriage holds in different religions.

○ Consider the incidence of interracial marriage by racial group.

○ Compare miscegenation laws with today's laws against same-sex marriage.

A Jewish couple under the chuppah.

Marriage exists in every culture of the world, yet its expression varies greatly. There are different forms, traditions, and expectations of marriage throughout the world.

The term **monogamy** does not, as people assume, refer to sexual fidelity. Instead, monogamy refers to having one spouse at a time. Because bigamy is against the law in the United States, all married couples are technically monogamous. The fact that a number of them are *adulterous* is another matter. The term **polygamy** refers to having many spouses at a time. It is more common for a man to have many wives—**polygyny**—than for a woman to have many husbands—**polyandry**. Although 84% of traditional cultures permit a man to take more than one wife at once, no more than 10% of men in those cultures engage in polygyny at some point during their lives. Only one half of one percent of human cultures have polyandry as a marital system (Fisher, 1998). We may think of monogamy as the natural order, yet only 16% of world societies stipulate that a man should take only one wife at a time.

In an **open marriage**, partners have consensual comarital sex—**comarital** as opposed to **extramarital** because the couple have sexual relations with others with the consent of their spouse. Partners in an open marriage are emotionally faithful to their spouses, but open to sexual encounters with others.

Monogamy From the Greek words *monos,* meaning "one," and *gamos,* meaning "marriage," monogamy is the practice of having one spouse at a time.

Polygamy The practice of having more than one spouse at a time.

Polygyny The system in which one man has more than one wife.

Polyandry The system in which one woman has more than one husband.

Open marriage A marriage in which partners, with each other's permission and without guilt or jealousy, have intimate relationships with others outside the primary relationship.

Comarital Extramarital sexual relations with the consent of one's spouse.

Extramarital A sexual relationship outside of marriage without the consent of one's spouse.

Polyamory The practice, desire, or acceptance of having more than one loving and sexual relationship at a time, in a context of honesty, openness, and negotiation.

Swinging Non-monogamous, consensual sexual activity that is experienced together as a couple.

Relationship ground rules about the type of comarital relationships allowed and where and when they can be entered into are established, which helps to manage the jealousy that may arise.

The extramarital relationship may involve love and emotional involvement with others or may focus on the sexual. **Polyamory** is the love of many people at once. The love may be emotional, sexual, spiritual, or any combination thereof. **Swinging** is consensual, non-monogamous sexual activity, and swingers treat the extramarital sex as any other social activity that can be experienced as a couple. The couple remain committed to their relationship, and together attend private parties, clubs, or conventions for swingers. Happy swingers say their comarital sexual activities add variety to their sex life and actually strengthen the marital bond; indeed, swingers generally rate the happiness of their marriage and of their lives higher than the non-swinging population do (Bergstrand & Williams, 2000). There are perhaps 3 million swingers in the United States. Most are white, middle-aged, middle-class churchgoers (Bergstrand & Williams, 2000).

Obviously, the polyamorous lifestyle won't work for everyone. It can be a recipe for jealousy, hurt, and disappointment. Without ground rules about safe sex, an open marriage can lead to one partner infecting the other with an STI. In any relationship, it is important that the partners are open and honest about their needs and desires.

The marriage ceremony is a liminal experience—a rite of passage recognizing the transition from one state to another. There are generally three phases to liminal experiences: **separation**, **transition**, and **incorporation** back into the community. Separation occurs when the individual is removed from his or her previous state of singlehood. In Western weddings, the bride-to-be may wear an engagement ring to show her new status. The outrageous behavior of some "bridezillas" shows that the normal rules of behavior may not apply to those in this phase. During transition, participants engage in specialized rituals. The wedding couple, often dressed in clothing specific for the event, walks down an aisle. In Jewish weddings, the event actually takes place under a symbolic threshold, a canopy called a *chuppah.* Many couples light unity candles to represent their transition from two families into one. The couple's kiss symbolizes their union. The couple is then incorporated back into the community, but with a different status—a mar-

Different Types of Marriage

In the Dieri tribe of Australia, a man may only marry his mother's mother's brother's daughter's daughter or his mother's father's sister's daughter's daughter.

Among ancient Peruvians, virginity was considered repulsive. If a groom found out his bride was a virgin, he felt cheated.

The Nayars of Tibet had a custom whereby a girl, upon reaching puberty, had intercourse with a "stand-in husband." They have sex until he is satisfied that the marriage is consummated, at which time she returns to her family. She may then marry anyone she chooses, except for the stand-in.

Each of the male wedding guests at a Nasamonian wedding must have intercourse with the bride before leaving. Not to do so is rude.

SOURCE: Sherman, 1973.

---

ried couple—with rights, benefits, and responsibilities they didn't previously have. The bride tosses her bouquet, symbolizing her break with her old identity.

Religion and Marriage

Christian faiths believe that God created the institution of marriage as a lifelong commitment that should not be entered into lightly. According to the Roman Catholic Church, "what God has joined together, let no man put asunder"; therefore, no divorce is allowed. Members of the Church of Latter Day Saints, also called Mormons, may choose to "seal" their marriage not just until "death do you part," but "for time and for all eternity." A marriage between already deceased ancestors can be sealed, if living persons act as their proxies; the deceased individuals may then accept or reject this sealing in the spirit world.

Are most Mormons polygamous?

Early in its history, the Church of Latter Day Saints (LDS) allowed for "plural marriages," until polygamy was declared illegal in 1878. The head of the Church of LDS issued a manifesto against polygamy in 1904; nevertheless, some Mormons continued to secretly practice polygamy. It is now Church of LDS policy to excommunicate any Mormon who practices or openly advocates polygamy. A splinter group of Mormon fundamentalists has broken with the Church of LDS and practices polygamy, although the Mormon Church has disassociated itself from these groups.

In Judaism, after the wedding ceremony takes place under a *chuppah,* the groom smashes a glass with his foot, which symbolizes the Jewish people's mourning for the destruction of the Temple in Jerusalem. Before the ceremony, a Jewish bride and groom sign a *ketubah,* or marriage contract, which describes the obligations of the husband and the rights of the wife.

Islam considers marriage a sacred obligation: a contract between a man, a woman, and Allah. Given family's utmost importance in Islam, the saying that "marriage is half of religion" highlights its central role in social and spiritual life. During the *Nikah* ceremony, the *mahr,* or marriage contract, is signed. Among other things, the *mahr* describes the **dower** that a groom pays to his bride, both before marriage is consummated and throughout her life. Muslims are allowed to divorce, although it is not encouraged. *Talaq ahsan* is the traditional Islamic form of divorce. A man simply has to state, "I divorce thee, I divorce thee, I divorce thee" to his nonmenstruating wife and abstain from sexual intercourse with her for 3 months, and they are divorced.

The Hindu religion sees marriage as a sacred duty and a means for spiritual growth. Hindus believe that people are not complete without marriage, and the joining of a man and wife is important for maintaining social traditions.

© Harry Hu/Shutterstock

A couple lighting a unity candle during their wedding ceremony.

Separation In a liminal experience, the stage where a person is separated from his or her previous situation in anticipation of taking on a new role or identity.

Transition The actual liminal stage, when the person is not in one state or another, but is "betwixt and between."

Incorporation After a liminal experience, the stage where a person is reintegrated back into society, but in a transformed state.

Dower The money or property that a man brings to his bride at marriage. A *dowry* is the money or property that a woman brings to her husband at marriage.

A *ketubah* is a Jewish marriage contract that traditionally includes the text that specifies the couple's biblical obligations to each other. One such obligation is the minimum frequency with which the man must have sex with his wife. Men who have no occupation are required to have sex with their wives every day, while sailors must have sex with their wives at least once every 6 months. If the husband does not fulfill his obligation, he must divorce his wife.

During the wedding ceremony, a Hindu couple circles a sacred fire seven times, which forever binds the man and woman together. To Buddhists, marriage is a personal concern and social convention, not a religious duty. Teachings of the Buddha, however, do encourage faithfulness and respect for one's partner. For a comparison of marriage and divorce rates based on religious affiliation in the United States, see Figure 9.7.

Common-Law Marriage

Legal in 11 states and the District of Columbia, a **common-law marriage** usually entails that a couple cohabit, are free to enter into contracts, and present themselves as husband and wife. Common-law marriages are legally binding in some states, although they are not licensed nor blessed by a religious ceremony. There is no such thing as "common-law

Common-law marriage A marriage without license or ceremony that is legally binding in some states.

Miscegenation Marriage, cohabitation, or sexual relations involving individuals of different races.

divorce"; a couple must go through the state to legally dissolve their common-law marriage.

Interracial Marriage

If all people in the United States were randomly paired with each other, 44% of all marriages would be interracial; in reality, only 5–8% of marriages in the United States are between partners of different races, although one in every seven new marriages involves a mixed-race couple (Fisman et al., 2008; Pew Social Trends, 2010; Rosenfeld, 2007). Whites are least likely to wed interracially, but due to their demographic majority, are involved in more interracial marriages than any other group. Almost three-quarters of all interracial couples involve a white person with a non-black partner, and just under 25% of all mixed marriages are black/white. Of these, nearly three-quarters are between a black husband and a white wife. This gender pattern is reversed with Asians: it is much more common for an Asian woman to be married to a non-Asian man than for an Asian man to have a non-Asian wife. The least common coupling is a black woman married to an Asian man (Mills, 2003; U.S. Census Bureau, 2008). "Hispanic" is considered an ethnic group, which may include people of all races. Therefore, if a Hispanic person marries a non-Hispanic person of the same race, the coupling is not registered with the U.S. Census Bureau as interracial. Hispanics are more likely to intermarry than are whites or blacks (Laumann, Gagnon, Michael, & Michaels, 1994).

Same-race and interracial couples are similar in attachment and conflict management styles, although mixed-race couples actually report higher satisfaction levels in their relationship than do same-race couples (Troy, Lewis-Smith, & Laurenceau, 2006). As with any marriage, mixed-race couples have their problems, and in addition to working through these day-to-day struggles, interracial couples may have to deal with cultural differences and society's bigotry and fear of the unfamiliar. Society is thankfully becoming more accepting of mixed-race relationships. At one time, 42 states had **miscegenation** laws, which prohibited Americans of European descent from marrying African Americans, Indians, Mongolians, Hindus, Japanese, or Chinese. These laws were gradually repealed until 1965; at that point, they continued to remain on the books only in the South. In 1967, the Supreme Court lifted the ban on miscegenation. At that time, 72% of Americans were opposed to interracial marriage, and

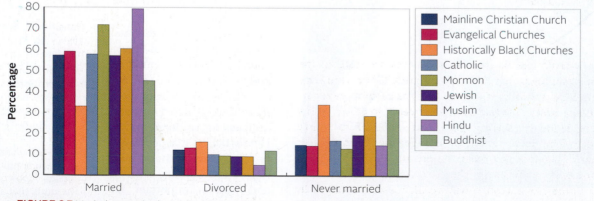

FIGURE 9.7 Marital status in the United States, based on religious affiliation. (Based on data from Pew Social Trends, 2008.)

Mildred Jeter and Richard Loving.

In 1958 Mildred Jeter, a black woman, and Richard Loving, a white man, fell in love. Although they lived in Virginia, they married in Washington, D.C., because Virginia laws prohibited the marriage of different races. Upon their return to Virginia, they were arrested, found guilty, and sentenced to prison. The sentence was suspended if they agreed to leave the state of Virginia. In giving his judgment, the trial judge proclaimed, "Almighty God created the races white, black, yellow, Malay and red, and he placed them on separate continents. And but for the interference with his arrangement there would be no cause for such marriages. The fact that he separated the races shows that he did not intend for the races to mix." Having no choice, the couple returned to D.C., where they worked to fight the law. In 1967 the U.S. Supreme Court struck down Virginia's Racial Integrity Act of 1924, thus ending miscegenation laws in the United States.

> "The freedom to marry has long been recognized as one of the vital personal rights essential to the orderly pursuit of happiness of free men. . . . Marriage is one of the 'basic civil rights of man,' fundamental to our very existence and survival. To deny this fundamental freedom on so unsupportable a basis as the racial classifications embodied in these statutes, classifications so directly subversive of the principle of equality at the heart of the Fourteenth Amendment, is surely to deprive all the State's citizens of liberty without due process of law. . . . These convictions must be reversed. It is so ordered." —From the U.S. Supreme Court decision on *Loving v. Virginia* (388 U.S. 1, 12 (1967))

only 1 out of every 1,000 marriages was interracial (Troy et al., 2006). It wasn't until the year 2000 that laws against interracial marriage were removed from Alabama's state constitution—and 40% of voters wanted to keep the law on the books. Even today, 14% of all adults in the United States (30% of those over age 65), think that interracial marriage is bad for society (Pew Social Trends, 2010). Since 1 out of every 19 children born today is of mixed race, interracial marriages should only become more accepted as time goes on.

Prejudice against interracial couples still exists. In 2009 Keith Bardwell, a white Louisiana Justice of the Peace, refused to issue a marriage license to an interracial couple. He claimed to be concerned for the welfare of the children the couple might someday have. "I'm not a racist. I just don't believe in mixing the races that way," Bardwell said. "I have piles and piles of black friends. They come to my home . . . they use my bathroom. I treat them just like everyone else" (Foster, 2009). Bardwell did refer the couple to another Justice of the Peace, who performed the wedding. After widespread criticism from this incident, Bardwell resigned from his post.

Same-Sex Marriage

Same-sex marriage is banned in almost every state in the union. The laws regarding marriage equality differ from state to state, and from year to year. One thing is certain: gay marriage will be a hotly contested issue for years to come. Many people are against allowing gays and lesbians to marry the person they love. Some of the reasons people use when arguing against gay marriage are discussed in a very tongue-in-cheek manner in the Sex Actually feature on page 220. Same-sex marriage will be discussed at length in Chapter 10.

When couples marry, federal laws award them more than 1,000 benefits and protections, including tax benefits, hospital visitation, Social Security survivor settlements, health insurance allowances, and family leave allowances. Because same-sex partners are barred from marrying, gays and lesbians are denied many of these benefits. Marriage equality advocates argue that such a denial affords these Americans second-class citizen status, as the Constitution guarantees justice and freedom for all Americans, not just the majority.

Del Martin, 87, and Phyllis Lyon, 83, were the first couple to marry in San Francisco city hall when same-sex marriage became legal in California. They had been a couple for more than 55 years, and worked for women's rights and gay rights throughout their lives.

Why Gay Marriage Is Wrong

- Because the Bible says it's an abomination. In America we are required to live by all the words in the Bible, which is why it's illegal to eat shellfish and why we jail people who work on the Sabbath.
- Because marriage is for procreation. This is why we don't allow menopausal women or sterile men to be married and why childless couples are required to divorce.
- Because it validates the gay lifestyle. As we all know, the gay lifestyle is about promiscuity. So we should not allow these promiscuous people to pledge monogamy to each other.
- Because it's unnatural. Clearly all those animals that form stable same-sex unions got that way because same-sex marriage is legal in a few states. Also, we never do "unnatural" things. This is why we never take antibiotics or use electronic appliances and why airplanes fall from the sky.
- Because gay marriage will destroy the sanctity of marriage. In fact, the only thing keeping most heterosexual couples married is that fact that two women can't marry each other. If they did, everyone else would be compelled to get divorced.
- Because heterosexual marriage is an unchanging institution and the cornerstone of our society. This is why divorce is forbidden, interracial marriage is illegal, men keep concubines, and married women are not allowed to work.
- Because gay people already have the right to marry: they have the right to marry someone of the opposite sex. Who cares about compatibility or sex or love?
- Because gay marriage will change society, and our society has never changed. I believe it was George Washington who posted on his Facebook page that "A woman or a black man will never run for president of the United States."
- Because it imposes its acceptance on all of society. How dare we force people to respect and accept others?

© Cengage Learning 2013

Conflict

After completion of this section, you will be able to . . .

○ Recognize how different attributional styles can affect the relationship of both happy and unhappy couples.

○ List the four warning signs of a relationship in trouble.

○ Define *criticism, contempt, defensiveness,* and *stonewalling.*

○ List some strategies for dealing with conflict in a relationship.

Newly engaged couples don't lack for information—there are dozens of magazines, books, and websites, all guiding new lovers through every step of the wedding-planning process, from what kind of stamps to use for the invitations, to how to incorporate stepparents into the processional. But once couples are married, the checklists and instruction manuals disappear. Many couples find themselves married, but without any idea of what to expect from marriage or how to increase the chances that theirs will last (McCarthy, 2010).

Criticism An expression of a person's shortcomings or an attack on his or her character.

Conflicts are inevitable in any relationship—it is estimated that married couples have between one and three disagreements each month (McGonagle, Kessler, & Schilling, 1992). Conflicts can even help a relationship by allowing couples to air unresolved issues. It's *how* you resolve the conflict that's important.

When a conflict occurs, partners look for explanations for their spouse's behaviors. The types of explanations or attributions we make strongly influence the happiness of our relationships. Bradbury and Fincham (1990) found significant differences in the attributions made in stressed and nonstressed relationships. When presented with a positive event or occurrence, happy couples credit their partner's basic positive characteristics, and are confident that positive occurrences will usually occur. Stressed or unhappy couples, on the other hand, will claim that their partner performed a positive act due to external or accidental forces, and assume that the action is unusual and probably won't be repeated. When a negative event occurs, happy couples assume that external forces must be responsible for the lapse, and assume it probably won't happen again, whereas unhappy couples believe that it is the shortcomings of their partner that are responsible for the negative event, and it is one in a series of negative occurrences that are sure to take place again. These findings are summarized in Table 9.3.

Relationships in Trouble

"What counts in making a happy marriage is not so much how compatible you are, but how you deal with incompatibility."

—*Professor George Levinger*

John Gottman (1994b) describes the warning signs that a relationship is in trouble. He writes that the "four horsemen of the apocalypse" are criticism, contempt, defensiveness, and stonewalling.

Criticism is "attacking someone's personality or character—rather than a specific behavior—usually with blame." Remember that criticism is different than complaining—while a complaint addresses a behavior you wish were different, a criticism assails or blames another, often attacking the person's character. A criticism often overgeneralizes ("you always do this," "you never do this"). See the difference in the following sentences, which both address the same issue but in a different way: "I was upset when I came home and found that you hadn't gone to the store after we agreed that you would shop and make dinner tonight." "You didn't go shopping again, even though you

© killerb10/iStockphoto

Table 9.3 The Effect of Different Attributional Styles in Happy and Unhappy Couples

EVENT	RELATIONSHIP	ATTRIBUTIONAL STYLES			OUTCOME
		INTERNAL/EXTERNAL	STABLE/UNSTABLE	GLOBAL/SPECIFIC	
Positive: You remembered our anniversary	Happy relationship	Internal: You are a good person.	Stable: You are always so thoughtful.	Global: You are thoughtful in so many ways.	Well-being
	Unhappy relationship	External: Your secretary must have reminded you.	Unstable: This is unusual. You'll probably forget next time.	Specific: You never remember other important events.	Distress
Negative: You forgot our anniversary	Happy relationship	External: You've been so busy at work.	Unstable: This probably won't happen again.	Specific: You remember other events.	Well-being
	Unhappy relationship	Internal: You are inconsiderate.	Stable: You never remember important events.	Global: This is yet another example of your inconsideration.	Distress

SOURCE: Adapted from Regan, 2003.

John Gottman (1994b) suggests that a therapist can deduce a couple's chance of divorce by listening to them describe the history of their relationship. If their relationship story is one of chaos, disappointment, and separate lives, then they may be more likely to separate.

promised me you would. I just can't trust you—you never do what you say you'll do."

When you constantly criticize and intentionally insult your partner, **contempt** has entered the relationship. As contempt grows, respect, admiration, and affection diminish. Some signs of contempt include insulting and name calling, mockery, or sarcasm. There are a number of nonverbal signs of contempt, including rolling your eyes, sneering, or curling your upper lip.

A steady barrage of contempt often leads to **defensiveness**, as your partner tries to protect him or herself. Defensiveness, while a natural response to criticisms, can damage a relationship. When you are being defensive you are not addressing the concerns of your partner or the underlying issues of the conflict. Denying responsibility, making excuses, or "yeah, but"-ing your partner are all examples of defensiveness. Pasting on a fake smile and folding your arms across your chest are nonverbal signs of defensiveness, as is playing with your neck or shifting from side to side.

Stonewalling involves removing yourself, emotionally or physically, from the conflict by not responding to your partner. The stonewaller may think he's trying to be neutral, but his actions convey disapproval, distance, and smugness. More men than women stonewall. Habitual stonewalling can signal a serious problem in a relationship—if one partner refuses to communicate, it can be hard to heal a marriage.

Successful couples use **conciliatory gestures** during an argument to deescalate the conflict. These gestures include reminding your partner what you admire about them, empathizing with their position, keeping the conversation on track, and hearing the conciliatory messages behind the angry tone of voice.

Couples deal with conflicts in many ways—some more successful than others. Successful conflict management strategies (adapted from Regan, 2003, and Gottman & Silver, 1999) include the following:

Do:

- Try to solve your problems reasonably and rationally.
- Communicate openly and honestly.
- Keep a positive mind-set about your spouse.
- Clearly state your opinions and desires. Remain focused on the issue.
- Understand and support your partner, and acknowledge his or her views.
- Compromise.
- Calm down. Recognize when you're feeling overwhelmed, and make a deliberate effort to relax. This may mean taking a 20-minute break from the discussion.
- Try and try again.

Don't:

- Seek control through threats, sarcasm, or verbal or physical aggression.
- Manipulate your partner by faking an emotion or trying to instill guilt.
- Avoid the issue, change the subject, or try to joke it away.

Sometimes, problems in the home escalate to the point of violence. More than 10% of the U.S. population—more than 30 million men, women, and children—are physically and emotionally hurt in the place where they should be safest: the home (Tjaden & Thoennes, 2000). The problem of domestic abuse will be discussed in Chapter 16.

Contempt An intense feeling regarding someone as inferior or worthless.

Defensiveness A psychological strategy to deal with negative characterizations of one's self, often putting the blame on others rather than on yourself.

Stonewalling Emotionally or physically removing yourself from the conflict by not responding to your partner.

Conciliatory gestures Behaviors to make peace in a conflict, such as apologizing, taking responsibility, or compromising.

Ending a Relationship

After completion of this section, you will be able to . . .

- ○ Consider the factors that underlie the prevalence of divorce.

- ○ Describe some of the reasons that couples divorce.

- ○ Define *adultery* and identify some of the reasons that people commit adultery.

- ○ Evaluate studies that attempt to determine the incidence of infidelity.

- ○ List the factors that affect one's risk of divorce.

- ○ Identify the financial, physical, emotional, and social costs of divorce.

- ○ Describe the four tasks by which one might start to heal from the death of a spouse.

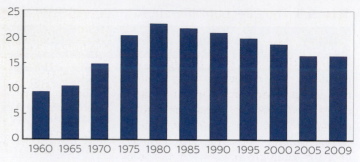

FIGURE 9.8 The number of divorces per 1,000 married women age 15 and older, by year, in the United States. (Adapted from Wilcox, 2010.)

"Three rings of marriage are the engagement ring, the wedding ring, and the suffering."

—*Author Unknown*

Relationships may end when the benefits of a relationship no longer outweigh the costs. John Gottman (1994a) describes the steps that couples go through when withdrawing from a relationship. First, the problems in the relationship are seen as severe, and talking things over with one's partner seems useless. Each person begins leading a separate life, and feelings of loneliness set in.

People disengage from a relationship in different ways. Some are direct and explicitly tell their partner that the relationship is over, while others indirectly withdraw or simply fade away. Some are concerned with protecting their partner's self-esteem; others are self-oriented. People also respond differently to the end of a relationship. Those who felt that they lost more with the end of the relationship—those who were more satisfied with the relationship, were closer to their partner, or believe it would be more difficult to find someone new—experience greater distress at the relationship's dissolution. Although the end of a relationship can be painful, it can offer each partner a new chance of happiness.

The word **divorce** comes from the Latin *divertium* meaning "separation" or "dissolution of marriage." The lifetime probability of divorce for a recently married couple is estimated to be between 40% and 60%. Approximately 14% of the U.S. population is currently divorced or separated (Pew Social Trends, 2010).

The American divorce rate rose fairly steadily from 1860 to 1950, when it reversed temporarily. After 1960 there was a sharp increase and the divorce rate peaked in 1979. Since then, however, divorce rates have steadily declined (Figure 9.8), although most Americans believe the rates have gone up in the last few decades (Pew Social Trends, 2010). Prior to the end of the 20th century, a spouse seeking a divorce had to plead causes such as adultery, cruelty, or mental illness. Today, "no fault" divorces exist, in which both spouses agree that the dissolution of

Divorce The legal dissolution of a marriage.

the marriage was due to irreconcilable differences, and do not (legally) blame the other for the breakdown of the marriage. This change in the law has made it easier to get divorced. Changing attitudes about divorce may also partially explain its greater incidence than in the past. Divorce has become less stigmatized. Gove and colleagues (1990) suggest that as divorce becomes more common, it will cause even more divorce, as people will no longer view marriage as a long-enduring state. Children of divorce may hold diminished expectations of the permanence of marriage—92% of women from intact families strongly agreed with the statement "If I marry, I expect my marriage to last for life," compared to 82% of women from families in which the parents had divorced. Women from families affected by divorce were also much less likely to have a relationship in their family that they admired (Glenn & Marquardt, 2001).

Attitudes about marriage have also changed. People today hold higher expectations about marriage than previous generations did. They place increased importance on love and emotional intimacy, and less importance on extended family ties and legitimacy for children. In fact, the view that your spouse must first and foremost be your soul mate may be one of the reasons for the breakdown of marriages. When the "perfect" love we have been led to expect breaks down, and parental or financial pressures get in the way, some people assume the relationship is over and they end the union. In one study, only 15% of the population agreed that "When there are children in the family, parents should stay together even if they don't get along" (Popenoe & Whitehead, 2001).

Economic changes may also have contributed to the rise in divorce rates. Divorce and remarriage are more common in societies in which both men and women are economically autonomous, and less common when spouses are dependent on each other to make ends meet. As women become more educated and independent, equity issues and unhappiness with the perceived fairness of responsibilities may influence marital dissolution.

As a gay American and not having the same rights as my heterosexual peers, I most definitely believe that it should be much more difficult to get divorced. If the sanctity of marriage consists of not allowing gays to marry, then I believe the sanctity of marriage is most certainly threatened by the outrageously high divorce rates. There is definitely hypocrisy present and it is completely contradictory. Therefore, I believe that obtaining a divorce should be made much more difficult.

—*Author's files*

Why Do Couples Divorce?

Although changes in laws, attitudes, and economic realities may partially explain the rise in divorce rates in the United States, these changes do not completely answer the question of why individual couples split up. Most marriages experience the same pressures—why do some succeed and some fail? Divorcing couples frequently report that their partner did not meet their emotional needs, or that they simply grew apart (Gigy & Kelly, 1992). Lack of communication, boredom, and physical or emotional abuse terminate a number of relationships. Some marriages end due to external forces, such as infidelity or drug addiction, while others succumb to personality conflicts or the couple falling out of love. Money and sex are common stressors. Couples with financial problems are twice as susceptible to divorce (Gottman 1994b). Of course, it may be that already existing problems are exaggerated by personal financial distress or societal economic downturns. Some people may think that the more often a couple has intercourse, the happier they are. Actually, the amount of sex is unimportant—how the couple handles conflict is more indicative of marital success. Some of the factors underlying divorce are discussed below.

This billboard advertised a divorce law firm in Chicago.

The intensity of a person's smile in a yearbook or other early photograph predicts the likelihood of whether or not the individual will later divorce. Scientists rated the intensity of the participants' smiles in old photographs. The top 10% of smilers had a divorce rate of about 5%, while the bottom 10% of smilers were 5 times more likely to divorce (Hertenstein, Hansel, Butts, & Hile, 2009). This may be because smiling is indicative of underlying emotional dispositions that have direct and indirect consequences on a person's life and relationships.

Falling Out of Love

There are cultural differences in how people view the effect of falling out of love on a marriage. Brazilians were most likely to agree with the statement "If love has completely disappeared from a marriage, I think it is probably best for the couple to make a clean break and start new lives." Pakistanis and those from the Philippines were most likely to disagree with the statement (Levine, Sato, Hashimot, & Verma, 1995). It is interesting to note that while students in the United States were highest in their ratings of the importance of love in getting married, they were relatively low in their assessment of the importance of love in *remaining* married.

Adultery

What exactly is **adultery**? The *American Heritage Dictionary* describes adultery as "voluntary sexual intercourse between a married person and a partner other than the lawful spouse." Adultery is also called "infidelity" or "cheating." An affair can occur once, or it can last for years. (Note: Although we use the term *extramarital sex* in this section, we are referring to sexual encounters that occur outside of any committed relationship, not just marriage.) Does intercourse have to occur for adultery to take place? Some consider an interaction to be adultery even if there is no intercourse. Among the Lozi people of Africa, a man has committed adultery if he gives a woman a beer. An American wife today might similarly feel betrayed if her spouse engaged in oral sex with another. Others don't believe that an infidelity has taken place even when sexual intercourse has occurred. Some Inuit people loan their wives to visitors (with her permission) as a sign of hospitality. In other cultures, only women are capable of committing adultery—a man can have intercourse with a woman who is not his wife and it is accepted.

The definition of adultery is further muddied by what's come to be known as **Internet infidelity**, which is a computer interaction that takes energy of any sort (thoughts, feelings, and behaviors) outside of the committed relationship in a way that damages the interactions of the couple (Atwood, 2005). Different people have different definitions of what an infidelity entails, but two major components of Internet infidelity include secrecy and sexual chemistry (Hertlein & Piercy, 2006). Is it considered cheating if the parties never actually meet? Most people consider infidelities to encompass not just physical components, but emotional components as well. Compared to men, women tend to view a wider range of activities as cheating (Whitty, 2005). The Internet can make it easy to engage in problematic behavior due to its "seven A's": anonymity, accessibility, affordability, approximation (how the Internet mimics real world communication), acceptability (that online communication is increasingly the social norm), ambiguity (in what is acceptable and unacceptable behavior), and accommodation (the difference between one's real and ideal self) (Hertlein & Stevenson, 2010). Although the Internet can make it easy to pursue secretive relationships, these relationships are

In the New Testament, remarriage after divorce is considered adultery: "Whoever divorces his wife and marries another, commits adultery against her; and if she divorces her husband and marries another, she commits adultery" (Mark 10:11-12).

Adultery Voluntary extramarital sexual intercourse (from the Latin root *adulterare*, meaning to corrupt or to spoil).

Internet infidelity An extramarital relationship that begins on the Internet; it can involve flirting, emotional intimacy, sexual talk, or other events, which take energy away from the primary relationship and hurt it in some way.

also easy to discover. Deleted e-mails are never truly deleted, and suspicious partners can purchase software that gives a history of all the keystrokes made on the computer.

Although every infidelity is different, affairs have been classified in three ways: as emotional without a sexual component, sexual without an emotional component, and those that involve both love and sexual contact (Thompson, 1984). Women are more likely than men to have affairs that have an emotional component without a sexual one, and men are more likely to have a sexual affair without the love.

Why do people cheat? People engage in extramarital sex for a number of reasons. Some may be seeking love or attention, or may act out of lust, a need to feel desired, or a longing for excitement. People may have an affair as a way to express hostility toward their spouse, or as an excuse to leave them.

Others may desire variety, or succumb to curiosity. Women may be more likely to seek emotional closeness—looking for their "soul mate"—while men desire sexual excitement. In general, those with stronger sexual interests, those with more permissive sexual values, those who are less satisfied with their relationship, and those who have greater sexual opportunities are more likely to engage in sexual infidelities (Treas & Giesen, 2000). Hormone levels may also influence monogamy. Men with higher levels of testosterone are more likely to engage in extramarital affairs, and more likely to get divorced (Booth & Dabbs, 1993). When a woman's estrogen levels are higher, she (and others) rate her as more attractive, and she is more likely to flirt with other men and to cheat on her partner (Durante & Li, 2009).

People cheat on their spouses—even when the penalty is death (or impeachment). There must be very strong biological drives underlying infidelity. Estimates of non-paternity rates in humans range from 0.8% to 30%, with an average rate of 3.3% (Alvergne, Faurie, & Raymond, 2009). This could mean that about 1 in every 30 children is not the biological offspring of his or her supposed father. Sociobiological theory says that sexual variety helps survival. According to theory, it is adaptive for males to "spread their seed" far and wide, to leave as many offspring as possible. Females are theorized to engage in extramarital sex to get better or more varied DNA for her offspring, or to have "spare" men available to provide her with resources. The theory says that because males don't want to get "stuck" providing resources for offspring that are not theirs, men should provide more care to children who more closely resemble them. In the Sine Saloum region

A number of species are thought to "mate for life"; individuals in about 90% of bird species form lifelong partnerships. However, it is estimated that only 10% of individuals thought to be monogamous are sexually faithful. When males in a pair bond were vasectomized, the females still laid eggs. In one study of Eastern Bluebirds, 15–20% of chicks were sired by a male outside of the partnership (Morell, 1998). The only truly monogamous creature is the flatworm *Diplozoon paradoxum*. When the male and female meet as adolescents, their bodies literally fuse together, and they remain monogamous until death (Angier, 2008).

of Senegal, polygyny is common, and the assumption is that women may be sneaking out to improve their lot. In a recent study, researchers got information about how much time and resources fathers spent on their children, and created a paternal-investment index—the higher the score, the more time and resources the father spent on the child. They also took photos of children and their presumed fathers (Alvergne et al., 2009). More than 100 judges from distant villages looked at photos of individual children along with photos of three adult men, and were asked to decide which man was the child's father. Investigators found that compared to children who did not resemble their fathers, children who looked like their fathers got more paternal care and resources and had a higher and healthier body mass index (BMI).

A recent study has found that a gene variation may in part determine a man's likelihood of infidelity. Remember the prairie voles from Chapter 8? Prairie voles are monogamous, and when they copulate, vasopressin levels rise in males; it is thought that this hormone is related to pair bonding in males. Scientists have found that variations of the gene that codes for vasopressin affect how men bond to their partners (Walum et al., 2008). Men can have none, one, or two copies of this gene. The more copies, the worse men scored on an assessment of pair bonding. Men with two copies of the gene were less likely to be married, and if they were married, they were more than twice as likely to have had a recent marital crisis compared to men without the gene. Now remember, genes are not destiny. Just because a man has the gene doesn't mean he will cheat, and men without the gene are not guaranteed to be faithful. But this does give us interesting information about the biological foundations of monogamy.

Is forbidden fruit sweeter? In a phenomenon called "the wedding ring effect," single women seem to be more interested in pursuing a man who's already taken. In a recent study, men and women who were either single or in a relationship viewed information about an opposite-sex person and indicated their interest in pursuing this target. Half the subjects were told that the target was single and half were told that he or she was currently in a relationship. Fifty-nine percent of single women were interested in pursuing a relationship with a single man, but when told he was in a relationship, 90% wanted to pursue him. Only single women were more interested in pursuing an attached target rather than a single target (Parker & Burkley, 2009). The theory is that these men were "pre-screened," and already proven to be satisfactory as a mate.

Regardless of the reason it occurs, extramarital sex can have a devastating effect on a relationship, leading to feelings of anger,

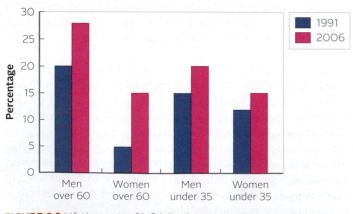

FIGURE 9.9 Lifetime rate of infidelity, by percentage. (From Whisman & Snyder, 2007.)

Cross-Cultural Views on Extramarital Relations

Russia may have the highest rate of adultery in the world, with perhaps 50% of men and 25% of women admitting to having sex with a partner other than their spouse.

Men in poor countries tend to cheat the most. In economically struggling countries, men tend to have high rates of infidelity and women have low rates. In richer countries, the rates are more similar, although in all countries, men report cheating more than women do.

Despite our stereotypical view, men in Italy and France have similar or lesser rates of adultery compared to men in the United States.

In China, slang for adultery is: "A man trying to stand in two boats at the same time." Swedes call it "Sneaking off to the left."

In Indonesia, the punishment for extramarital sex is up to 7 years in prison. In a number of countries in the Middle East, a man is exempted from any penalty for murdering his wife if he catches her committing adultery.

Although one in every five adults in South Africa has HIV, the infidelity rate is still very high.

According to Jewish law, adultery occurs when a married woman has sex with a man other than her husband. A married man who has sex with another woman commits a lesser sin.

In Japan, it doesn't legally count as infidelity if one pays for it.

SOURCE: Druckerman, 2007.

---

jealousy, and betrayal as well as increasing the risk of depression, anxiety, and other mental health problems. Couples therapists consider extramarital affairs to be one of the most damaging events to a relationship (Whisman & Snyder, 2007). Adultery is one of the most commonly cited causes of divorce in the United States and other countries (Amato & Rogers, 1997). But does having an affair increase the chance of divorce, or does being in an already disintegrating marriage increase the likelihood of someone having an affair? Or perhaps a third factor, such as a lack of communication in a marriage, contributes to both.

Attitudes about adultery. Although adultery occurs everywhere, its acceptability varies widely from culture to culture. Some societies freely allow adultery in all cases, in others it's fine as long as you don't discuss it. In some cultures, marital infidelity is acceptable under certain conditions (only on certain holidays, or with a certain person). Penalties for extramarital sex range from mild social disapproval to death. For more cross-cultural views on extramarital relations, see the From Cells to Society feature on this page.

Most Americans disapprove of adultery; in fact, about half of the states still have laws on the books forbidding adultery, which, if they were enforced, would deny adulterers the right to vote, serve alcohol, practice law, adopt children, or raise their own children (Treas & Giesen, 2000). In a survey of 1,447 men and women, 80% of Americans said that extramarital sex was "always wrong"; only 2% said it was "not wrong at all" (Widmer, Treas, & Newcomb, 1998). Unsurprisingly, men and women who had had an extramarital affair were less likely to disapprove of extramarital sex than those who had never had an affair (Wiederman, 1997). Men report more extramarital sex than women, and are more accepting of it; people over 65 report less extramarital sex and are less accepting of it.

Predictors of adultery. It can be difficult to determine factors that may increase the likelihood that a person will commit adultery. Most models of extramarital sex are formulated after the fact; in other words, married individuals are asked whether they have ever engaged in extramarital sex, and the occurrence of adultery is then "predicted" based on characteristics of those subjects who answered in the affirmative. But a causal relationship is very diffi-

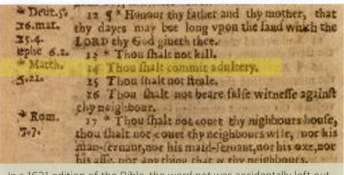

In a 1631 edition of the Bible, the word *not* was accidentally left out of the seventh commandment, thus instructing its readers, "Thou shalt commit adultery." Dubbed "The Wicked Bible," most copies were recalled immediately.

cult to determine from this method. One recent study, however, did not use retrospective data; instead, it followed 1,270 married subjects with no prior history of adultery who completed subsequent surveys over a 20-year period (DeMaris, 2009). This study found that the risk of extramarital sex is greater in males, in African Americans and Hispanics, and in those who were less religious, had ever experienced a divorce, or were the child of a divorce. Those who spent more time away from their spouse, lived in a large urban area, or had more education were also more likely to have an extramarital sexual experience.

Although the incidence of extramarital sex increases with a man's age, a woman is most likely to engage in extramarital sex between the ages of 30 and 50 (Wiederman, 1997).

Incidence of adultery. Obviously, it is difficult to get an accurate assessment of the incidence of infidelity. The National Health and Social Life Survey found that 24.5% of men and 15% of women admitted to having engaged in extramarital intercourse at some point in their lives (Laumann et al., 1994); other studies suggest that around one third of men and one quarter of women engage in extramarital sexual relationships at least once in their lives (Mark, Janssen, & Milhausen, 2011). In a recent study, 23.2% of men and 19.2% of women indicated they had cheated on their partner during their current relationship (Mark, et al., 2011). When extramarital activities other than intercourse (such as kissing or emotional

How many people in America cheat on their spouses? How would you go about determining the rate of infidelity in the United States? Estimates of the incidence of marital infidelity range from 20% to as high as 70%. What questions should you ask when considering the incidence of adultery?

> **What was the research design?** How was the information gathered? Anonymous surveys? Face-to-face interviews? Magazine questionnaires? DNA testing? What would be the most accurate assessment? A nationwide survey used both face-to-face interviews as well as anonymous computer questionnaires to gather information about American women. In this study, 1% of the women interviewed said they'd been unfaithful to their husbands in the past year, but more than 6% of those who filled out the anonymous computer survey reported an infidelity (Whisman & Snyder, 2007). On the other hand, magazine surveys may overestimate the adultery rate, as women who are particularly interested in infidelity may be more likely to respond to these surveys. Currently, most infidelity research is based on questionnaires and surveys.

> **What time frame is considered in the study?** A survey that asked about extramarital sex "in the past year" would show a lower incidence than one that asked if the subjects had "ever" had an infidelity.

> **How does the subject pool affect the findings?** The demographics of your subjects can change your results. From where is your sample pool gathered? Is this a representative sample of subjects?

  • The incidence of extramarital sex differs based on the age of the subject, so it is important to consider the age range of subjects in the study (see Figure 9.9). How might a survey of 22-year-old men differ from a study of 65-year-old women in incidence and acceptance of extramarital sex?

  • Fifteen percent of the women polled by the Sunday supplement *Parade Magazine* admitted to ever having an affair (Clements, 1994), whereas 54% of *Cosmopolitan* readers reported extramarital sex (cited in Fisher, 1992).

> **Were any ambiguous terms used in the studies?** Does the survey explicitly define the term *sex* or *sex partner*? Does it clearly characterize what is considered an *infidelity* or *cheating*?

> **Are the subjects telling the truth?** Because Americans so greatly disapprove of extramarital sex, it is probably true that some people lie about their experiences, and the incidence of extramarital sex may be higher than has been reported. In Laumann's study, 21% of the participants were interviewed while a child, spouse, or other person was in the room with them. This may certainly affect the veracity of the report—when interviewed alone, 17% of the respondents reported having two or more sex partners in the past year; only 5% said so when their spouses were present in the interview room with them (Laumann et al., 1994 p. 568).

divorces involve couples who have two children, and 7% of divorces involve people who have three dependent children (Fisher, 1992). Although couples with children have lower divorce rates, the arrival of the first baby often strains the relationship between the mother and father; parents report lower marital satisfaction than childless couples (Kurdek, 2001). Remember that a low divorce rate does not necessarily mean the relationship is happier.

Length of marriage. Divorce generally occurs between 2 and 4 years after the wedding (Fisher, 1992). It is remarkable that this pattern appears, considering there is such a variation in the amount of time that couples are together before they wed. The median age at first divorce is 30.5 for males and 29 for females (U.S. Census Bureau, 2001).

Age, education, and race. People who marry in their teens are 2 to 3 times more likely to divorce than people who marry at an older age. Fifty-nine percent of women who married under the age of 18 got divorced or separated within 15 years, compared to 36% of those married at age 20 or older (National Center for Health Statistics, 2002). Couples who have either very low or very high levels of education, or who come from a family with divorced parents, have a higher risk of divorce as well. African Americans also are more at risk for divorce than are whites or Hispanics (Regan, 2003)—9.1% of African American males and 12.9% of African American females are divorced, compared to 8.3% of white males and 10.9% of white females (U.S. Census Bureau, 2004). There are more divorced single women in this country than divorced single men. At first, that seems counterintuitive, but it is because more men are likely to remarry after a divorce, and to remarry sooner than women do.

Although these are depressing statistics, don't despair! Although the divorce rate in the United States is almost twice what it was in 1960, it is currently down from its high point in the late 1970s. A number of factors decrease your odds of divorce in the first 10 years of marriage. Some of these factors are listed in Table 9.4. As you can see, if you are a reasonably well educated person who makes a decent income, who waits until after age 25 to marry, and does not have a baby before marriage, your risk of divorce falls precipitously. Of course, communication between partners will greatly increase your chances of a satisfying union.

The Costs of Divorce

Divorce is usually associated with financial problems, more so for women than for men. According to Long Island University's National Center for Women and Retirement Research, the average woman sees a 27% drop in her standard of living after divorce, while the average man improves his standard of living by 10% (Peterson, 1996). Women are more likely to have custody of the children, which, aside from being an economic burden in itself, reduces their ability to pursue well-paying employment. Although men are required to pay child support, some are unable or unwilling to assume their responsibility.

Divorce can also be physically and emotionally difficult. Divorce increases a person's risk for physical illness and mortality from disease, perhaps by suppression of the immune system or other physical stressors. Compared to those who had been continuously married, men and women who had been through a divorce had about 20% more chronic health problems like diabetes, cancer, and heart disease (Hughes & Waite, 2009). And even if they remarry,

connections) are taken into account, women report as many acts of infidelity as men (Mark et al., 2011).

Other Factors that Influence the Risk of Divorce

A number of factors influence a couple's risk of divorce, including number of children, the length of the marriage, and the spouses' age, education level, family history, and race.

Number of children. The more children a couple bears, the less likely they are to divorce. According to data collected each decade by the United Nations, 39% of divorces occur among couples with no dependent children, 26% among couples with one child, 19% of

Table 9.4 Factors That Decrease the Risk of Divorce

FACTOR	PERCENT DECREASE IN RISK OF DIVORCE
Annual income over $50,000 (vs. under $25,000)	–30%
Having a baby 7 months or more after marriage (vs. before marriage)	–24%
Marrying after age 25 (vs. under age 18)	–24%
Own family of origin is intact (vs. having divorced parents)	–14%
Religious affiliation (vs. having none)	–14%
Some college (vs. high school dropout)	–13%

© Cengage Learning 2013. SOURCE: Popenoe & Whitehead, 2005a.

they may never recover their previous level of health: people who remarry have more chronic health problems than those who have remained continuously married, although they have better overall health than those who have not remarried (Hughes & Waite, 2009). Divorce raises a person's risk of automobile accident, suicide, violence, and homicide (Gottman, 1998). Divorce may cause feelings of loneliness, fear of the future, and depression. In other cases, divorce can enhance a person's autonomy and personal growth. In fact, 50% of men and 60% of women report being happier 1 year after their divorce than they were during their marriage (Faludi, 1991).

What are the effects of divorce on children? Those who grow up in households where parents are divorced are nearly 3 times more likely to get divorced themselves than someone who comes from an intact home. Women whose parents have divorced report less trust and satisfaction, and more ambivalence and conflict in their intimate relationships. Children of divorce have higher rates of physical illness, depression, and drug and alcohol problems, as well as academic, social, and behavioral problems (Gottman, 1998). However, it is important to consider what the studies are actually examining. Children of divorce are from unhappy families; they are being compared with children from intact families, some of which are happy, some unhappy. It would be more revealing to compare the physical and psychological well-being of children of divorce with children in intact but unhappy families. Otherwise, the studies simply show that it is better to be in a happy family than in an unhappy family. Chronic marital conflict—regardless of whether it ends in divorce or not—has been connected with emotional distress in children.

Remarriage

Most divorced people eventually remarry although men are more likely to remarry than women are; the likelihood that a divorced woman will remarry has been declining since the 1950s (CDC, 2004). Unfortunately, remarriages have a higher divorce rate than first marriages, perhaps because of the selection factor—those who have already divorced may be less likely to stay in a troubled marriage.

Death of a Spouse

The death of a spouse is considered to be the most stressful event of adulthood, which can cause intense suffering and long-lasting physical and emotional pain (Holmes & Rahe, 1967; Stroebe, Schut, & Stroebe, 2007). Nevertheless, losing a spouse is also a normal and natural human experience, as 45% of women and 15% of men over the age of 65 become widowed. The loss of a spouse is associated with psychological pain, such as grief, sadness, loneliness, and suicidal thoughts, as well as physical ailments such as headache, chest pain, insomnia, and gastrointestinal distress. There are also secondary consequences of the loss, including changes in one's social life, eating habits, living arrangements, and financial support. The death of a spouse at a young age may be particularly devastating to the partner left behind, as it is perhaps more unexpected than later in life, and there are fewer peer models and support for the widow or widower's grief.

Even when we control for socioeconomic and lifestyle factors, it appears that **widows** and **widowers** have an increased risk of mortality (Stroebe et al., 2007). Death may be due to many causes, including accidents, health problems, or suicide. Suicide is especially seen in widowers and in those who lose their spouse at a young age. Being widowed before the age of 34 increases the chance of suicide by 17 times for white men and by 9 times for African American men (rates were significantly lower for women). As many as 1 in every 400 widowed men under age 35 will commit suicide each year, compared to 1 in 9,000 married men (Luoma & Pearson, 2002). Although the death of a spouse does raise one's mortality, it is important to remember that the overall risk of death is still low. For instance, in men over age 55, 5% of widowers die in the first 6 months of bereavement, compared to 3% of married men.

Men and women who are dealing with the death of a partner can focus on four tasks to deal with their grief (Worden, 2001). First, the bereaved should recognize and accept the reality of his or her loss, without denying or minimizing it. Second, he or she should experience and express the emotions that occur, including loneliness, grief, despair, anger, and fear. The one left behind needs to adjust to their environment without their loved one. He or she will need to develop new skills, make new friends, and find a support network. Finally, the bereaved will need to withdraw emotional energy from the deceased spouse and reinvest their energy in the present and move on. Humans are amazingly resilient. Most bereaved people eventually recover from their loss and go on to live fulfilling lives.

People have so many choices in how they live their lives. They may remain single, live with a partner, get married, or get divorced. They can have emotional and physical intimacy with one person or many people. Regardless of the types of connections that people choose to make, the act of connecting with others is the foundation of what makes us human.

> My grandmother died of cancer and my grandfather died just 3 weeks later. Can a person die of a broken heart?

Widow A woman whose partner has died.

Widower A man whose partner has died.

© Joel Gordon

10 Sexual Orientation

"When a twelve-year-old boy matter-of-factly tells his parents—or a school counselor—that he likes girls, their reaction tends not to be one of disbelief, dismissal or rejection. 'No one says to them: "Are you sure? You're too young to know if you like girls. It's probably just a phase,"' says Eileen Ross, the director of the Outlet Program, a support service for gay youth in Mountain View, California. 'But that's what we say too often to gay youth. We deny them their feelings and truth in a way we would never do with a heterosexual young person.'"

—Denizet-Lewis, 2009

"The white light streams down to be broken up by those human prisms into all the colors of the rainbow. Take your own color in the pattern and be just that."

—Charles R. Brown

© Joel Gordon

© govicinity/ Shutterstock   © Joel Gordon

A discussion of all sexual orientations is incorporated throughout this text because homosexual activities are not some deviant condition separate from "normal" sexuality. However, the scope of research, body of knowledge, and cultural practices specific to bisexual and homosexual communities warrants a broader discussion. This chapter addresses a range of psychological, sociological, and biological issues related to sexual orientation.

Introduction

After completion of this section, you will be able to . . .

○ Define the terms *sexual orientation, homosexual, heterosexual, bisexual, gay,* and *lesbian.*

Take a moment and imagine your parents having sex. *Eeeewwwwwwww!* But wait a minute. In most cases we're talking about a man and a woman who, in an act of love, gave you life. Why is that icky to consider? For whatever reason, sometimes we get uncomfortable imagining people having sex. Perhaps this is why some people get uncomfortable when considering homosexuality. But being gay or lesbian isn't just about having sex, which represents only a tiny proportion of a couple's lives together. Being gay or lesbian is also about love, attraction, and relationships.

Are you confused about the proper language to describe same-sex attraction? Are you unsure as to whether you should call someone *gay* or *homosexual,* or if the expression should be *sexual preference* or *sexual orientation?* If you are, don't feel bad—even researchers of human sexuality don't agree about these terms. Generally speaking, though, here are some guidelines: **Sexual orientation** refers to one's attractions: emotional, romantic, and physical. The term "sexual orientation" is recommended over "sexual preference," which implies a conscious or deliberate choice. The term **homosexual** refers to someone whose sexual orientation is toward others of the same sex, whereas **heterosexuals** are attracted to the other sex, and **bisexuals** to either sex. The terms "**gay**" and "**lesbian**" are used to refer to homosexual men and women, respectively, although the term "gay" can also be used to describe both men and women. Many people today use the acronym **GLBTQQ**, which refers to those who are gay, lesbian, bisexual, transgendered, **queer**, and/or questioning.

The word *homosexual,* which dates back to the 19th century, is dissatisfying in several ways. Not only does it discount emotional attachments while focusing on the sexual, but it is often used as a noun— "you are a homosexual"—as if a person could be defined solely by his or her sexual identity. Not only the term but also the idea of homosexuality is a Western concept. "No previous human cultures have defined sexual orientation as a type of *person* for whom a specific

Sexual orientation A person's predisposition or inclination regarding sexual behavior, emotional attachment, or physical attraction to one or both sexes.

Homosexual A person whose sexual orientation is toward others of the same sex.

Heterosexual A person whose sexual orientation is toward others of the opposite sex.

Bisexual A person who may be sexually oriented to both men and women.

Gay A man whose sexual and romantic attractions are toward other men. The term can be generalized to include lesbians. "Gay" is also used to describe the people, practices, and culture associated with homosexuality.

form of attraction is central to their personality, cognitions, gender role, and sexual behavior" (Kauth, 2002, p. 3). Most other societies view people not in terms of same-sex or other-sex behaviors, but by social sex roles or participation in specific sexual acts, such as playing a passive role rather than an active one (Gonsiorek, Sell, & Weinrich, 1995).

Models and Measures of Sexual Orientation

After completion of this section, you will be able to . . .

○ Compare and contrast the Kinsey scale with the Klein sexual orientation grid.

○ Define *sexual fluidity.*

○ Clarify the differences between male and female bisexuality.

Sexual orientation was once considered to be an "all or none" phenomenon: you were either **straight** or gay. Alfred Kinsey broke with tradition and believed that sexual orientation existed on a continuum:

> The world is not to be divided into sheep and goats. Not all things are black nor all things are white. It is a fundamental of taxonomy that nature rarely deals with discrete categories. Only the human mind invents categories and tries to force facts into separated pigeonholes. The living world is a continuum in each and every one of its aspects. The sooner we learn this concerning human sexual behavior the sooner we shall reach a sound understanding of the realities of sex." (Kinsey, Pomeroy, Martin, & Gebhard, 1948, p. 639)

Sex researchers have used Kinsey's orientation scale for more than half a century. The **Kinsey scale** (Figure 10.1) arranges sexual behavior on a continuum, with "0" representing exclusively heterosexual behavior, "3" representing behavior that is equally heterosexual and homosexual, and "6" representing exclusively homosexual behavior.

Kinsey's scale is not perfect. The categories are ambiguous and open to interpretation, and the scale focuses on sexual behaviors rather than on a person's emotions or sexual identity

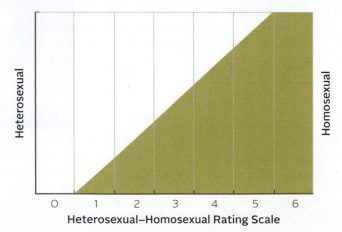

FIGURE 10.1 The Kinsey scale: "0" represents exclusively heterosexual behavior, "3" represents behavior that is equally heterosexual and homosexual, and "6" represents exclusively homosexual behavior. (© Cengage Learning 2013)

The word *gay* used to mean merry, carefree, or uninhibited, often with a sexual connotation. It is thought that the first use of the word *gay* to mean homosexual started in the 1920s. The word *lesbian* is derived from Lesbos, the home of the Greek poet Sappho, whose love poems are addressed to both men and women. *Dyke*—a slang word for lesbian—is thought to date back to 1710, when British newspapers referred to the cross-dressing female pirates Anne Bonny and Mary Read by using the French word "dike," which refers to a manner of dress. The slang term *faggot* may be derived from a contemptuous word for a woman dating back to the 16th century.

(Coleman, 1987). Kinsey also failed to account for specific life situations (such as prison) and didn't consider changes that may occur in one's orientation over time.

Because of problems with Kinsey's scale, others have developed measurements to assess sexual orientation. The multidimensional **Klein sexual orientation grid (KSOG)** (Klein, 1990; Klein, Sepekoff, & Wolf, 1985) considers the following:

- *Sexual behavior*—with whom have you had sex?
- *Sexual fantasies*—about whom are your sexual fantasies?
- *Sexual attraction*—to whom are you sexually attracted?
- *Social preference*—with members of which sex do you socialize?
- *Emotional preference*—do you love and like only members of the same sex, only members of the other sex, or members of both sexes?
- *Lifestyle preference*—what is the sexual identity of the people with whom you socialize?
- *Self-identity*—how do you identify yourself sexually?

According to the KSOG, both women and men have an emotional preference for women as close friends and show a social preference for members of the same sex.

The KSOG also questions subjects about their sexual behavior in the past, present, and in an ideal future. Subjects' responses are recorded on a 1–7 scale—similar to Kinsey's, but with less emotionally loaded reference point descriptions (e.g., the KSOG uses the phrase "same-sex only" rather than Kinsey's "exclusively homosexual"). Klein found that for some people, sexual behavior can change from one period of their life to another, and sexual identity sometimes has little to do with a person's sexual behavior. Some people feel the Klein grid is too complex for easy use, and not everyone agrees that the seven parameters measured by Klein and colleagues are necessary or important in sexuality (Coleman, 1987).

Bisexuality

A bisexual person is sexually and emotionally attracted to both sexes to varying degrees. He or she may be attracted to men and women in different ways or for different reasons or may feel that gender isn't an important consideration. Some people believe that bisexuality should be considered a separate orientation; others feel it is a point along the continuum of heterosexuality and homosexuality. Because bisexuality does not fit neatly into the binary model often used by researchers, bisexual responses are often either ignored or lumped into the homosexual category for interpretation. Although bisexuality is not well-represented in the research (only 16% of journal articles on same-sex activity have "bisexuality" in their title), people with bisexual attractions outnumber those with same-sex attractions, especially among women (Diamond, 2008).

According to Kinsey's scale, as people become more attracted to their same sex, they become less attracted to the other sex. However, Michael Storms (1980) developed his two-dimensional model of sexual orientation based on his finding that bisexuals were as likely to report same-sex fantasies as were homosexuals, and as likely to report other-sex fantasies as were heterosexuals.

Many feel that bisexuality is more common in women than in men, and that women are more "fluid" in their sexuality (Bailey, Pillard, Neale, & Agyei, 1993; Chandra, Mosher, Copen, & Sionean, 2011; Diamond, 2008; Kinnish, Strassberg, & Turner, 2005; Laumann, Gagnon, Michael, & Michaels, 1994). A recent national survey found that nearly 3 times as many women as men reported having any same-sex partners in the past 12 months (Chandra et al, 2011). Meredith Chivers and colleagues (2004) found that women—regardless of their sexual orientation—experienced strong genital arousal to both male and female sexual stimuli. In fact, many women who do not identify themselves as bisexual have same-sex fantasies or attractions (Nichols, 1990; Vrangalova & Savin-Williams, 2010). Male and female bisexuality may be different in other ways as well. A study by Richard Lippa (2006) found that for men, a high sex drive was associated with increased sexual attraction to one sex or the other—to males if the man identifies as gay, and to females if the man identifies as heterosexual. For most women, however, as Storms's model suggests, a high sex drive is associated with increased sexual attraction to *both* men and women. This is supported by a recent survey of more than 13,000 men and women that found that women who report more opposite sex partners in their lifetimes were also more likely to report any same-sex experience. Among men, the percentage who had engaged in same-sex behavior did not vary by the number of female partners (Chandra, et al., 2011).

Lesbian A term used to describe a woman whose sexual and romantic attractions are toward women.

GLBTQQ Gay, lesbian, bisexual, transgender, queer, and/or questioning.

Queer An umbrella term to describe people with a sexual orientation or gender expression that does not conform to heteronormative society.

Straight A slang term for a heterosexual.

Kinsey scale A classification system to gauge a person's sexual orientation at a given time.

Klein sexual orientation grid (KSOG) A multidimensional measurement of sexual orientation.

Sexual Fluidity

Current conventional wisdom states that sexual orientation is fixed and early developing, and not likely to change throughout life. Yet that description better describes the sexual orientation of males, probably because most research is done on men, by men (Mustanski, Chivers, & Bailey, 2002). Whereas men are more likely to view their sexuality as fixed and innate, women are more likely to see it as subject to change based on specific relationships, choices, and circumstances (Diamond, 2008; Rosenbluth, 1997). Men who were in heterosexual marriages or relationships and then come out as gay describe themselves as having finally found their true orientation. Women in that same situation are more likely to validate both relationships: "That's who I was then, this is who I am now."

The fact that sexuality, especially women's sexuality, is **fluid** does not mean that sexual orientation is all about choice. When a woman "switches" preferred sexes, she usually says the attraction was unexpected and beyond her control: a person does not sit down at the kitchen table with a pad and paper and make a list of pros and cons and decide upon her orientation. Just because something changes doesn't mean you can control it. When you went through puberty, you went through a number of changes. Did you choose those transformations? Could you change back if you really wanted to? Women are born with a sexual orientation, but it's not the last word in their sexual expression. Many women have a capacity for fluidity and may change their orientation over time. The reasons for the switch are not always sexual—chance, opportunity, practical necessity, political values, or emotional considerations can all influence a woman's sexual expression (Diamond, 2008). It is an old saying that "women become attracted to those they love, and men fall in love with those they are sexually attracted to." Sexuality science supports this axiom. Love and sexual desire are independent processes, so a woman may be sexually oriented toward men, but still fall in love with a woman (Diamond, 2003a). Additionally, not all women are equally fluid; some may be more sensitive to situations and relationships that facilitate erotic feelings.

Many people are aware of the potentially harmful political ramifications of the idea that a person may "switch" sexual orientation, given that those who believe that homosexuality is not biologically determined are less accepting of gays and lesbians, and less likely to feel that homosexuals deserve equal rights. However, in the words of Daryl Bem:

> "Most civil rights statutes protect against discrimination on the basis of race, creed, color, and sex. But if race, color, and sex are protected because they are based in biology—and, hence, not freely—then what is the rationale for including creed? Surely Jews, Catholics, Jehovah's Witnesses, Seventh-Day Adventists, and Mormons—to mention some who have historically sought protection under this provision—have never had to argue that their religious beliefs were biologically determined before earning the right to be protected against arbitrary discrimination." (Bem, 1996b)

Lisa Diamond adds, "Perhaps instead of arguing that gay, lesbian, and bisexual individuals deserve civil rights because they are powerless to their behavior, we should affirm the fundamental rights of all people to determine their own emotional and sexual lives." (Diamond, 2008, p. 138)

The mounting evidence that male and female sexualities are profoundly different highlights the need for more studies on female sexuality. Also, it should not be assumed that studies of males always apply to females.

Sexual fluidity The idea that a person may change from other-sex attractions to same-sex attractions throughout his or her life.

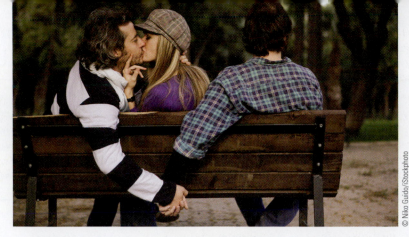

If there were a "Bisexual Pride" parade, would it go both ways?

The Prevalence of Homosexuality

After completion of this section, you will be able to . . .

○ Recognize the difficulties in accurately assessing the incidence of homosexuality.

○ Critically evaluate the measurement methods used.

What percentage of the population is gay? There seem to be political agendas behind both exaggerating and minimizing the incidence of homosexuality. Arguments have been made that the numbers of gays and lesbians are swelling as part of some insidious recruitment plot. On the other hand, some underestimate the number of gays and lesbians, perhaps to trivialize or pathologize their existence. There is a perception that 10% of the population is gay, but this number is not based on any research. It may have been extrapolated from Kinsey's data, which was based on non-random samples. See the Critical Evaluation feature on pages 238 to 239 to consider the difficulties involved in estimating the prevalence of homosexuality.

What Determines a Person's Sexual Orientation?

After completion of this section, you will be able to . . .

○ Identify and evaluate a number of purported causes of homosexuality.

○ Appraise the success of conversion therapy programs.

The question "what causes homosexuality?" is both politically suspect and scientifically misconceived. Politically suspect because it is so frequently motivated by an agenda of prevention and cure.

Scientifically misconceived because it presumes that heterosexuality is so well understood, so obviously the "natural" evolutionary consequence of reproductive advantage, that only deviations from it are theoretically problematic. Freud himself did not so presume: "[Heterosexuality] is also a problem that needs elucidation and is not a self-evident fact based upon an attraction that is ultimately of a chemical nature." (Bem, 1996a, p. 320)

Most researchers believe that a complex combination of forces—biological and social—determines a person's sexual orientation. It is important to again emphasize that almost all efforts of explaining the causes of homosexuality are based on studies of men, even though evidence suggests that the phenomenology of sexual orientation is different for women and men (Peplau, Spalding, Conley, & Veniegas, 1999). We will now explore some of the most prominent theories of sexual orientation.

Psychosocial Theories of Homosexuality

Psychosocial theories of sexual orientation suggest that sexual orientation is learned. Psychoanalytic theory and learning theory are two psychosocial theories that are commonly used when addressing questions related to how sexual orientation takes shape within an individual.

Psychoanalytic Theory

Psychoanalytic theory suggests that development of a gay identity might result from parental behaviors. Freud was one of the first proponents of this idea, hypothesizing that men become gay due to interactions with emotionally distant fathers and overbearing mothers. No research has supported this belief.

Learning Theory

Freud thought an infant's sexuality was undifferentiated and could be directed at males or females. *Learning theory* suggests that early experiences are important in the development of our sexual orientation. We repeat activities that give us pleasure, and avoid those that are painful. According to this theory, bad heterosexual experiences cause a person to become gay. But consider that if every straight person who ever had a bad experience with the opposite sex were to become gay, there might be very few straight people left. Also false is the belief that women become lesbians due to sexual abuse by men (Peters & Cantrell, 1991). The fact is, many people have pleasurable sexual experimentation with same-sex partners during adolescence, and these experiences do not usually lead to a later homosexual identity. Despite years of looking, no one has ever found a social factor that is completely responsible for same-sex attraction.

Further evidence against the theory that same-sex attraction is due solely to learned or environmental factors comes from descriptions of same-sex sexual behaviors—including courtship, pair bonding, and copulation—that have been observed in 450 animal species (Bailey & Zuk, 2009). Female bonobo chimpanzee spend a considerable amount of time in same-sex sexual behavior, including genital-to-genital rubbing that can culminate in orgasm. Bottlenose dolphins show one of the highest rates of same-sex sexual behavior of any animal: about half of male sexual interactions are with other males (Bailey & Zuk, 2009). Penguins in captivity and Hawaiian albatrosses can form long-lasting same-sex pair bonds and also engage in same-sex copu-

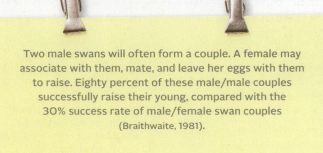

Two male swans will often form a couple. A female may associate with them, mate, and leave her eggs with them to raise. Eighty percent of these male/male couples successfully raise their young, compared with the 30% success rate of male/female swan couples (Braithwaite, 1981).

Table 10.1 Concordance of Sexual Orientation Between Siblings

	GAY	LESBIAN	PERCENTAGE OF SHARED GENES BETWEEN THE SIBLINGS
Identical twin	52%	48%	100%
Fraternal twin	22%	16%	50%
Non-twin sibling	9.2%	14%	50%
Adoptive sibling	11%	6%	0%

SOURCE: Bailey & Pillard, 1991; Bailey et al., 1993.

lation. It is estimated that 8% of rams show exclusive same-sex behaviors (Roselli, Larkin, Schrunk, & Stormshak, 2004)—scientists have practically dangled negligee-clad ewes in heat in front of these rams, yet the males insist on running over and mounting other males.

Biological Factors Underlying Homosexuality

The theory of *direct biological causation* suggests that genes and hormones work on the developing brain and directly affect sexual orientation. When considering this evidence, keep in mind that correlation does not prove causation—the existence of a biological difference in gay and straight men does not necessarily mean that the biological factor *caused* them to become gay.

Genetic Influences

A number of scientists (Bailey & Pillard, 1991; Bailey, Dunne, & Martin, 2000; Bailey, Pillard, Neale, & Agyei, 1993; Langstrom, Rahman, Carlstrom, & Lichtenstein, 2010) have surveyed gay men and lesbians about their siblings to discover the **concordance rate** of homosexuality. The researchers tried to determine how often the sibling of a gay man was also gay. They then repeated the study to see how often lesbians had sisters who were gay. Table 10.1 summarizes these findings.

This study suggests that there is probably a genetic component to homosexuality, but that same-sex attrac-

Concordance rate The extent to which two individuals (usually twins) share similar characteristics such as height, weight, or sexual orientation.

critical evaluation

Ascertaining the rate of homosexuality has presented challenges to researchers. What are some issues to consider when estimating what percentage of the population is gay?

> **What is the definition of homosexuality?** There is no unified definition of homosexuality. When researchers investigate the rate of homosexuality, they often use different conceptual measures, or fail to define their criteria at all. Three main components have traditionally been used to measure sexual orientation: sexual behavior, attraction, and identity (Savin-Williams, 2006). Based on those definitions, the prevalence of homosexuality varies. In general, polling subjects about their same-sex attraction yields the highest incidence of homosexuality, 2 to 5 times above that of same-sex behavior or identity (Savin-Williams, 2006). In fact, in a recent survey of college students, 79% of women and 43% of men reported "at least some same-sex attraction" (Vrangalova & Savin-Williams, 2010). Using sexual identity as the measurement scale yields the lowest numbers of homosexuality, as most individuals who are attracted to their own sex or who participate in same-sex behaviors do not identify as gay or lesbian (Diamond, 2008; Reece et al., 2010a). According to the National Health and Social Life Survey (Laumann et al., 1994), while only 1.4% of women and 2.8% of men self-identify as lesbian or gay, 7.5% of women and 7.7% of men admit to same-sex desires. Just over 4% of women and almost 5% of men report same-sex sexual behavior since turning 18, although that percentage jumps to over 9% for males if you consider sexual activity since puberty. There are further questions about sexual behavior to consider:

• **What constitutes sexual behavior?** The frequency of sexual acts? The number of partners? If a person's orientation is determined by his or her sexual behavior, then gay virgins are not counted as gay, nor are those who are attracted to the same sex but only have heterosexual sex. On the other hand, heterosexuals who have same-sex encounters for reasons other than arousal (such as rape) would be counted as gay.

> **Should both physical and psychological factors be considered?** Many studies of sexual orientation only consider sexual acts, rather than arousal or emotional attachment (Diamond, 1993). Sexual attraction and being in love do not always occur together. A person may be sexually attracted to another, yet not be in love with him, or he or she may love him, but not feel sexual desire for him. Why is sexual orientation so often classified as sexual desire rather than affection? There may be gender differences underlying this perception—lesbians appear to perceive affection and political perspectives as central to their self-definition, while gay men's identity is more related to sexual behavior and fantasy (Gonsiorek et al., 1995). As most research is done on gay men rather than lesbians, perhaps this contributes to the perception.

> **What time frame should be considered?** Many studies of homosexuality ask people about their sexual experiences in the past year. Yet "only one-quarter to one-half of the U.S. men who report male-male contacts in adulthood also report having had such contacts during the preceding twelve months" (Rogers & Turner, 1991). Lisa Diamond (2003b) found that during a 7-year period, nearly two-thirds of women changed their sexual identity at least once, often because the limited labels offered in surveys did not adequately describe their experiences or feelings.

> **What about sexual fantasies?** Masters and Johnson (1979) found cross-preference sexual fantasies to be common for all their subjects: lesbian fantasies were the fifth most common fantasies for heterosexual women, and heterosexual fantasies were the third most commonly reported fantasies for women who identified as lesbians. In a more recent survey of college students, 52% of women and 22% of men reported "at least some same-sex fantasy" (Vrangalova & Savin-Williams, 2010).

> **What other factors should be considered?** A person's age? Intentions? Do adolescent experimentations or prison experiences "count?" What do *you* think characterizes homosexuality?

> **How did the researchers measure sexual orientation?**

• **What scale did the researchers use?** Chung and Katayama (1996) analyzed 144 studies in the *Journal of Homosexuality* from 1974 to 1993. They found that only 10% of these used a multidimensional scale to assess homosexuality, 12.5% used a single scale (similar to Kinsey's), 33% of these studies used subject self-identification as the determination of homosexuality, and 31% never even described how the subjects' sexual orientation was determined. Another analysis found that 25% of studies fail to define sexual orientation at all (Shively, Jones, & DeCecco, 1984).

• **How were the questions worded?** Sometimes, sexual behavior of men and women may be reported differently. In a nationwide survey, males were asked specifically about oral and anal sex with another male, but females were asked about "any sexual contact with another female," which would yield more responses (Mosher, Chandra, & Jones, 2005).

> **Who were the subjects?** Many of the gay subjects in today's studies of sexual orientation are recruited from "gay-oriented" magazines or organizations, a group of people that may not be a representative sample of the average gay American. Also, many studies of gays and lesbians only include those who *identify* as such, thus disregarding the responses of many people who are attracted to the same sex or who have same-sex relationships but don't identify as gay.

> **What are the researchers' assumptions about sexuality and orientation?** These are often unstated views about sex and gender. For instance, many researchers look for cross-gendered traits in people with same-sex attraction; the underlying assumption is that males act one way and females act another, and if you act like the "other" gender in one way, you are more likely to be attracted to the "wrong" gender. Researchers may misinterpret their data, ignore contradictions, or manipulate statistics, in order to get the result that fits with their conceptual model. In addition, conceptually or scientifically flawed research may be published and accepted because its conclusions are consistent with social prejudices (Kauth, 2005).

> **How was the study conducted?** Was physical arousal measured in a laboratory setting? If so, consider how the presence of stopwatches, strain gauges, and a bevy of white-coated scientists taking notes might affect a subject's sexual arousal. Also, were subjects asked to fill out an anonymous questionnaire, or did they answer questions face to face?

> **Were the subjects honest?** Subjects don't always tell the truth, especially regarding sexuality. In the United States today, gay people face the risk of discrimination and violence—it is no wonder that some people will not admit their homosexuality, even if assured of a study's confidentiality. Also, sometimes subjects choose not to answer questions about homosexual behavior. Statistical analyses of these studies suggest that those who refuse to respond to questions about homosexuality may be disproportionately more likely to have had homosexual experiences (Fay, Turner, Klassen, & Gagnon,

1989). Sometimes subjects might not understand the question, or the questions may be too limited. When asked whether their identity was "heterosexual, homosexual, bisexual or something else," 3.9% of males and 3.8% of females in a nationwide survey answered "something else" (Mosher et al., 2005), but it is unclear what the subjects meant by this choice. Because of these facts, Rogers and Turner (1991) argue that currently accepted estimates of homosexuality are minimums because many gay or bisexual people don't tell the truth about their same-sex activities due to fear. Even observational results can be hidden (e.g., men can sometimes suppress their erections on penile plethysmographs).

> **Have the findings been overgeneralized?** The gay people in these studies are often Caucasian college students in the United States, and information from this pool of subjects is often generalized to all gay people. Also, as mentioned, most studies on homosexuality are done on men. Lesbians and bisexuals are much less studied than gay men (Chung & Katayama, 1996), although reports on gay male behavior may be generalized to lesbians. Recent advances suggest that gay men and lesbians may exhibit very different behaviors.

> **What were the control groups?** Not all studies on homosexuality include heterosexuals as a comparative control: an analysis of 144 scientific articles about homosexuality found that only 43% of these studies included heterosexuals (Chung & Katamaya, 1996). In about one quarter of the studies examined, the heterosexuality of subjects was simply assumed (e.g., a survey was taken of college students, and all college students were assumed to be heterosexual.) From this exhaustive analysis, the challenges in ascertaining the incidence of homosexuality are clear. Thus, it is important when hearing results of studies conducted regarding homosexuality to first understand how the research was conducted.

tion is not entirely genetic. There are a few compelling questions raised from this study. Fraternal twins share 50% of their genes, as do non-twin brothers; however, the concordance rate for gay fraternal twins was more than twice as high as seen in non-twin brothers. This suggests that some environmental factor, perhaps in the womb, influences male sexual orientation. Adoptive brothers, who share no genes, were 11% concordant for homosexuality, which is higher than would be expected by chance, an effect which may be due to sampling error. This study did not include a random sample of gay men: these men were recruited through advertisements in gay magazines, a nonrepresentative sample. In some cases, the ratings of the sibling's orientation came from the gay subject *speculating* as to his brother's sexual orientation. Subsequent studies that better controlled for sampling bias showed lower levels of concordance (Bailey et al., 2000).

The largest twin study to date suggests that for men, genetic factors control between 34% and 39% of their sexual orientation; an individual's unique environment (including circumstances during pregnancy, physical and psychological traumas, peer groups, and sexual experiences) explained 61–66% of one's orientation; and shared environmental influences had no effect on sexual orientation (Langstrom et al., 2010). Genetics seemed to be less of a factor in female sexual orientation, controlling 18–19% of a woman's sexual orientation (Langstrom et al., 2010). It is also important to consider that even if male homosexuality runs in families, that fact does not prove that homosexuality is genetic. Many traits—such as religious affiliation and the language one speaks—run in families, but for environmental rather than genetic reasons (Peplau et al., 1999). However, the data seem to suggest that sexual orientation is at least partly controlled by genetic factors.

At one time not too long ago the media had announced the discovery of the "gay gene" on the X chromosome. Not only was this an overgeneralization of the data by the media, but the original finding by Dean Hamer and colleagues (Hamer, Hu, Magnuson, Hu, & Pattatucci, 1993) has not been replicated (Rice, Anderson, Risch, & Ebers, 1999). To date, no distinct gay gene has been identified, although other studies have suggested the involvement of other chromosomes (Mustanski et al., 2005). A recent study suggests that there may be two genes that influence male homosexual orientation, with at least one of them located on the X chromosome (Camperio-Ciani, Cermelli, & Zanzotto, 2008).

Although a single "gay gene" hasn't been found, that doesn't mean that genetic factors don't underlie sexual orientation. After all, there is no single gene for height, skin color, handedness, or other traits that have a large inherited component. It is unlikely that a single gene would control such a complex interaction of physical, psychological, and sociological factors as sexual orientation.

Gay people are not infertile and are just as able to reproduce as straight people. Many gay people get married and have children. Some may do so to avoid the social stigma of coming out as gay; others may have done so early in life before realizing their orientation. And some gay people get married and have children for the same reason heterosexual people do: because having children is a basic human desire! Perhaps biological factors that predispose someone to a same-sex orientation give adaptive benefits that better allow those genes to be passed down. As an example, it is hypothesized that gay men may be predisposed to nurture nieces and nephews, who share some of their genetic code, which can ensure that their own genes get passed down. The fa'afafine are a group of effeminate, same-sex attracted men in Samoa. It has been found that fa'afafine are more likely to be altruistic toward nieces and nephews than either single men or women or mothers or fathers. They are more willing to babysit, help with homework, and pay medical expenses or school fees (Vasey & VanderLaan, 2010). It has also been shown that mothers and maternal aunts of gay men had more offspring than did the female relatives of straight men (Camperio-Ciani, Corna, & Capiluppi, 2004; Camperio-Ciani et al., 2008); it may be that "gay genes," if they exist, may act to increase how attracted both men and women are to men, perhaps increasing the number of offspring who share that gene, and keeping the "gay genes" in the pool.

How would gay people keep their genes around? If they're not able to reproduce, why are there still gay people?

Prenatal Influences

The more older brothers a man has, the greater his chances of being gay. With each older brother, a man's probability of being gay increases by about 33% (Blanchard & Bogaert, 1996; Blanchard, Cantor, Bogaert, Breedlove, & Ellis, 2006). The number of sisters, younger brothers, or adoptive siblings does not seem to affect the incidence of homosexuality (Bogaert, 2005). The **maternal immune hypothesis** suggests that when a woman is pregnant with a male fetus, her immune system becomes sensitized to proteins that only males possess, and her immune system may affect the prenatal brain development of subsequent male fetuses.

Hormonal Influences

Although hormonal manipulations can change reproductive behaviors in animals (Phoenix, Goy, Gerall, & Young, 1959), hormone levels in adult humans do not influence sexual orientation. Gay men and straight men have no difference in their levels of circulating androgens. Furthermore, alteration in hormone levels in adults by surgical removal of the gonads or hormone injections will not change sexual orientation.

Exposure to *prenatal* hormones, however, may be a different story. Prenatal hormones affect many anatomical factors, including bone growth. In women the index finger (2D) and ring finger (4D) are roughly the same length; in men the index finger is shorter than the ring finger (a low **2D:4D ratio**); it is thought that higher prenatal androgen exposure reduces the 2D:4D ratio (Manning, Scutt, Wilson, & Lewis-Jones, 1998; Figure 10.2). Girls with congenital adrenal hyperplasia (CAH), who have been exposed to high levels of prenatal androgens, have an index finger to ring finger ratio more like that of boys (Brown, Hines, Fane, & Breedlove, 2002). The right hand 2D:4D ratio of lesbians is also more like that of males (Williams et al., 2000).

Neuroanatomical Influences

In searching for differences in the brains of heterosexual and homosexuals, Simon LeVay looked at the brains of 41 cadavers: 19 gay men, 16 presumed heterosexual men, and 6 presumed heterosexual women. LeVay found that one area of the hypothalamus (INAH-3) was twice as large in volume in heterosexual men than in women and gay men (LeVay, 1991). This suggests that there may be a biological foundation to male sexual orientation.

This study should be interpreted with caution. First of all, the heterosexuals were *presumed* to be heterosexual; there was no specific information about their sexual behavior. Also, it is important not to confuse correlation with causation. Just because the gay men had a smaller INAH-3 than the straight men does not mean that this area controls sexual orientation. Perhaps their sexual behavior, possible drug use, or other factors changed the size of their hypothalamuses. It is noteworthy, however, that similar differences in the hypothalamuses of "homosexual" and "heterosexual" rams have been found (Roselli, Larkin, Resko, Stellflug, & Stormshak, 2004).

There are other possible brain differences between gay and straight men, including differences in the suprachiasmatic nucleus (Swaab & Hofman, 1990), the anterior commissure (Allen & Gorski, 1992), the corpus callosum (Witelson et al., 2007), and in brain symmetry (Savic & Lindstrom, 2008). The fact that every human's brain is unique and ever-changing makes it difficult to generalize about the relationship between brain anatomy and sexual orientation.

As with almost all human behavior, it is most likely that both biological and environmental factors interact to influence a person's sexual expression. As Lisa Diamond states, "Sociocultural factors interact with real bodies in real time to generate different forms of erotic experience" (2008, p. 22).

Some people believe that they have **gaydar**—the ability to tell if someone is gay or lesbian by the way they look, move, or act

---

> Can a person tell someone is gay just by looking at them?

Maternal immune hypothesis The theory that a man's sexual orientation is related to the number of older brothers he has; prenatal factors in the mother's womb play a role.

2D:4D ratio The ratio of length of the pointer finger compared to the ring finger. This tends to be lower in men and lesbians than in heterosexual women.

Gaydar The ability to intuitively know if someone is gay or straight.

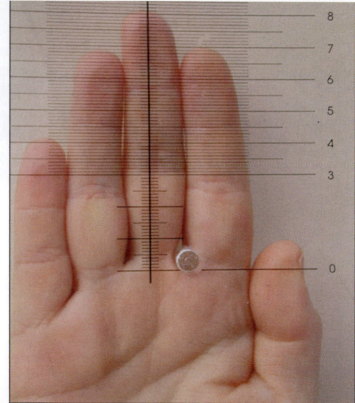

FIGURE 10.2 Finger length in males and females.

Dr. Marc Breedlove/Breedlove-Jordan Lab

(Ambady, Hallahan, & Conner, 1999). There may be some truth to this, as some physical and behavioral differences between gay and straight men have been proposed. Gay men may be more likely than straight men to have hair that whorls counterclockwise, and they may have more dense fingerprint ridges in the thumb and pinkie of the left hand. One study of 5,122 men suggested that gay men have larger penises than straight men (Bogaert & Hershberger, 1999). When shown male and female faces, some of whom were gay and some were straight, participants correctly guessed the sexual orientation at a rate significantly better than chance. Their accuracy was as good when they were exposed to images for only 50 milliseconds. Participants were even able to guess the orientation of the person in the images when shown just the eyes (Rule, Ambady, Adams, & Macrae, 2008; Rule, Ambady, & Hallett, 2009). Heterosexual women's ability to judge men's sexual orientation is better the closer the women are to ovulation; their accuracy is not affected by their fertility when judging the sexual orientations of other women (Rule, Rosen, Slepian, & Ambady, 2011). In some cases, listeners could correctly identify if a male speaker is gay or straight; differences in pitch variation, tonal quality, and word emphasis are given as identifying tools (Gaudio, 1994; Smyth, Jacobs, & Rogers, 2003). However, these studies had very small populations, and in the Smyth and colleagues study, the subjects—all self-identified and out gay males—were specifically chosen because the researchers thought their voices "sounded gay"; these findings are not generalizable to all gay men. There may also be a signal picked up by the olfactory sense—when asked to choose the odor they preferred, gay men preferred the odor of other gay men over that of straight men or women (Martin et al., 2005). However, it is important not to confuse sexual orientation with gender roles. Just as the vast majority of gays and lesbians do not fit the stereotypes, some heterosexuals do match them. There is no way to precisely deduce someone's sexual orientation. Overall, the magnitude of similarities between heterosexuals and homosexuals most likely outweighs the differences (Kauth, 2002).

Can Orientation Be Changed?

"When was the last time you heard anyone ask 'What causes heterosexuality?' Implicit is the assumption that since the majority of people are heterosexual, heterosexuality is normal (and in no need of explanation), while any deviation from the norm is not. It is not unlike asserting that since most people are right-handed, left-handed people must be abnormal. In fact, until the end of the 1950s, left-handedness was considered immoral and wicked in Catholic schools and left-handed students were forced to write with their right hands. But writing with your right hand when you are really left-handed, like trying to love someone of the opposite gender if you are really gay, is forced and artificial behavior."

—*Psychologist Jeff Lutes, 2008*

Exodus International and Love Won Out are both Christian "exgay" **conversion therapy groups**. Although the American Psychiatric Association removed homosexuality from its list of mental illnesses decades ago, these groups, along with NARTH, the National Association for the Research and Therapy of Homosexuality, believe that homosexuality is a mental illness, primarily caused by parenting styles. Their methods of converting someone who is currently gay include psychotherapy, aversion therapy, and, of course, Gatorade. Joseph Nicolosi, past president of

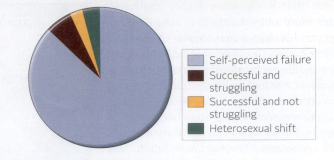

FIGURE 10.3 Self-perceived success and failure from reparative therapy. (From Shidlo & Schroder, 2002.)

NARTH, tells fathers that to prevent their sons from becoming gay, they should bond with them through rough horseplay, such as tossing them in the air. "Even if (the dad) drops the kid and he cracks his head, at least he'll be heterosexual," Nicolosi said. "A small price to pay" (Simon, 2006). He further recommends that men who are trying not to be gay drink Gatorade and call their friends "dude" (Besen, 2006).

Robert Spitzer interviewed 200 men and women over the telephone regarding their sexual attractions and history prior to and subsequent to conversion therapy (Spitzer, 2003). In his study, 11% of men and 37% of women reported they had completely changed their sexual orientation. Yet Spitzer's study has been criticized for many reasons. Success was based on self-reports from the subjects, and there were no physical measurements or verification. The subjects in this study were self-selected—which means they wanted to take part in the study. Perhaps those who consider themselves a "success" regarding treatment would be more likely to volunteer for such a study. The subjects were also not representative of the population. Largely Caucasian and middle-aged, 93% reported that their religion was extremely or very important to them. In fact, greater than two-thirds of the subjects were provided by professional ex-gay organizations or by NARTH, and 78% spoke publicly about the success of the ex-gay movement. Spitzer failed to ask about the sexual orientation of the respondents prior to therapy—were some of them bisexual?—or about any negative effects they may have experienced as a result of the treatment.

Shidlo and Schroeder (2002) considered some of these factors in a better-designed study, which surveyed 202 individuals who had been through conversion therapy. Eighty-seven percent of their subjects felt that conversion therapy failed, and 88% of this group felt that they had suffered long-term harm from the therapy. Of the 13% who felt the therapy was a success, 46% occasionally slipped back into same-sex behavior and 12% controlled their sexuality by remaining celibate (Figure 10.3). Of the eight individuals who reported that they had successfully shifted to heterosexuality, seven had paid positions as ex-gay counselors.

So, can people successfully change their sexual orientation? It depends on what you mean by "success." Does it mean not *acting on* one's desires, or not *experiencing* same-sex desire? For some, sexuality may be fluid throughout their lifetimes, and same-sex desires may indeed discontinue. For others, however, it seems

Conversion or reparative therapy A type of therapy, condemned by the American Psychological Association, that seeks to convert a gay person into a heterosexual.

clear that while some highly motivated individuals may change their sexual *behavior,* sexual attraction usually cannot be altered. Even the director of NARTH admits that, while a minority of clients refrain from same-sex sexual behavior, all clients still retain same-sex desires (Boodman, 2005).

Conversion therapy has been rejected by the American Psychological Association, the American Medical Association, the National Association of Social Workers, the National Association of School Psychologists, the National Education Association, the American Psychiatric Association, and the American Academy of Pediatrics, which states, "Therapy directed specifically at changing sexual orientation is contraindicated, since it can provoke guilt and anxiety while having little or no potential for achieving changes in sexual orientation" (American Academy of Pediatrics, 1993). In addition, there are a number of ethical concerns over how conversion therapy is carried out. Most programs are offered by religious ministries and are therefore not subject to oversight by professional associations, licensing boards, or health departments. False information may be provided to clients, who may not be informed about possible negative effects of the treatment. Harm suffered by those who go through conversion therapy may include psychological harm—depression, lowered self-esteem, and sexual dysfunction; social harm—damaged relationships with family, friends and partners; and spiritual harm—a negative impact on their religious beliefs or excommunication from their church.

When Evangelical preacher Ted Haggard's homosexual activities were exposed, he wrote a letter stating, "I've been warring against it all of my adult life . . . through the years I've sought assistance in a variety of ways, with none of them proving to be effective." Although he had everything to lose, and believed with all of his heart that his desires were wrong, he still needed to express those desires. The founders of ex-gay groups Exodus International, Love Won Out, and Love in Action have all left their programs because of their same-sex behaviors.

Living and Loving as a Gay Man or Lesbian

After completion of this section, you will be able to . . .

○ Consider the challenges faced by those who grow up with the knowledge that they are gay.

○ Define *coming out.*

○ Recognize some of the factors that influence when someone comes out.

○ Compare and contrast same-sex and other-sex relationships.

○ Define *civil marriage, religious marriage, civil union,* and *domestic partnership.*

○ Identify the advantages and disadvantages for children raised by same-sex parents.

○ List some of the rights and benefits denied to children of same-sex partners.

○ Describe some of the challenges experienced by gay and lesbian seniors.

What is the "gay lifestyle"? Many believe that the "gay lifestyle" is a nonstop party of promiscuous sex and drug use. This image was formed during the 1970s when, before the advent of AIDS, some people (gay and straight) were freer in their sexual expression. The idea of the freewheeling gay lifestyle does not represent the lives of gays and lesbians today. Society can no more generalize a *gay lifestyle* than it can proclaim that there is a single, identifiable *heterosexual lifestyle.* There are some preconceptions about the lives led by gays and lesbians. Society presents the image of the limp-wristed, promiscuous, gay florist, and the short-haired, flannel-wearing, truck-driving lesbian. How realistic are these portrayals? There are some careers that do seem to be stereotypically gay. Perhaps some gay people feel they will never be accepted by mainstream society and enter fields that are traditionally or stereotypically gay-friendly. Nearly half of gays and lesbians involved in one study said that their orientation influenced their career choice (Ryan & Futterman, 2001). However, gays and lesbians are found in all occupations, cultures, religions, races, and socioeconomic classes.

Growing Up Gay

From the day we are born, the standard-issue message we receive is clear: We will grow up, become attracted to a person of the opposite sex, get married, and have children. We are inundated with this idea—parents, teachers and friends, movies, TV, music, and advertisements all model for us that we need to make ourselves attractive for the opposite sex so we can fall in love and raise a family. Everyone around us takes it for granted that this is what we want, what everyone wants. But what if this is not your dream? What if you are attracted to those of your own sex (in which case, in most states of our nation, marriage is not an option for you)? What if you received the message that homosexuality was wrong? While many gays and lesbians first knew they were "different" as children, they were understandably hesitant to speak of it, or hoped they would "grow out of it."

Gay and lesbian youth who are also members of an ethnic minority face double or triple discrimination in society. Most children growing up as a racial or religious minority are able to model their behavior and find support against discrimination from their family. Lesbian and gay adolescents, however, "must learn to manage a stigmatized identity without active support and modeling from parents and family" (Ryan & Futterman, 2001). More than a third of gay, lesbian, and bisexual respondents in one survey said that at least one family member had refused to accept them because of their sexual orientation (Herek, 2006).

Luckily, homosexuality is becoming much more mainstream and accepted than it was in the past. In 1997 there were approximately 100 GSA (gay-straight alliance) organizations in U.S. high schools; as of 2006 there were more than 3,000—nearly 10% of U.S. high schools had a GSA (GLSEN.org, 2008). Books and websites aimed at gay and lesbian teenagers may help young people deal with and accept their sexuality.

Coming Out

"**Coming out**" means to acknowledge, accept, and openly express one's sexual orientation. The expression comes from the phrase "coming out of the closet." The idea of coming out was first introduced in the 19th century, by Karl Ulrichs, an advocate of homosexual rights who felt that by becoming visible in society, homosexuals might change public opinion.

Being "out" has both benefits and risks. The major benefit is that the individual can live openly and honestly, without screening conversations or denying his or her identity. This is psychologically beneficial; in a sample of lesbian and bisexual women, the more "out" the women were, the less psychological distress they reported (Morris, Waldo, & Rothblum, 2001). Lesbians and gays who are "out" also have higher satisfaction in same-sex relationships, better job attitudes, and even show slower progression of HIV infection (Legate, Ryan, & Weinstein, 2011). There are, however, potential risks. When a person comes out, he or she risks losing friends, family, and jobs. In an older study, 46% of gay and lesbian teens reported losing at least one friend after coming out (D'Augelli & Hershberger, 1993), and 26% of gay youth are forced to leave home because of their sexual identity (Edwards, 1997). Those whose parents reject them for being gay are more likely to be depressed, lonely, and feel isolated. Gays and lesbians may choose to be out in some situations and not others, based on their assessment of the possible dangers of a situation. And danger does exist. In 1998 college student Matthew Shepard was murdered for being gay. About 18% of hate crimes are motivated by sexual orientation. Given that about 3% of the American population identifies as homosexual, gays and lesbians are victimized at 6 times the overall rate (Southern Poverty Law Center, 2005). Antigay hate crimes will be discussed later in the chapter.

While coming out is not a linear and orderly sequence of events with predicted outcomes, in many cases there is a progression—from self-awareness to self-acceptance to disclosure—although there may be a wide variability in the timing and outcome of these events (Parks, 1999).

> I don't understand why gay people have to make a big deal about it. I didn't "come out" as a straight person and have a big party to announce it.

Disclosure

Here's something to try: For a week, change or obscure the pronoun when talking about your significant other. Don't touch each other in public, and don't give any outward sign that you have a romantic or emotional relationship to anyone. The effort to constantly hide who you are would eventually become very stressful. When gays and lesbians disclose their sexual orientation, it does not necessarily mean they make a big public announcement regarding their orientation; rather, it can be as simple as referring to their partner without changing pronouns, or by holding hands in public. How "out" a person is can differ depending on the situation—a person may be out to his or her friends, but not at work, or they may hide their sexual orientation in potentially dangerous situations. Gays and lesbians typically first come out to trusted friends, then siblings or their mother. The father is usually the last to be told (Green, 2000).

Age. People come out at different stages in their life: some when they are young, others when they are grandparents. When a person comes out depends on personal, social, and historical factors (Parks, 1999). Gays and lesbians today first recall desiring a member of the same sex at age 10 for gay men, and 12 for lesbians, significantly younger compared to gays and lesbians in the past (Grov, Bimbi, Nanin, & Parsons, 2006). This may be because of increased awareness and acceptance.

Race. Gay and lesbian African Americans, Hispanics, and Asian Americans are less likely than Caucasians to be out to their parents, perhaps due to familial disapproval or more negative attitudes regarding homosexuality (Green, 2000; Kennamer, Honnold, Bradford, & Hendricks, 2000). In a recent survey of gay, lesbian, and bisexual young adults, Latino men reported the highest number of negative family reactions to their sexual orientation in adolescence (Ryan, Huebner, Diaz, & Sanchez, 2009).

Education. More-educated white gay men are more likely to be out than less-educated white gay men; in African American gay men, however, as education increases, the likelihood of being out decreases. This may be because of their fear of a "double whammy" of discrimination due to race and sexual orientation (Kennamer et al., 2000).

Occupation. Gay men in higher income brackets were

When Ellen DeGeneres (right) first came out on her sitcom in 1997, it brought the show its highest ratings, as well as a great deal of controversy. DeGeneres went on to host a successful talk show. Rosie O'Donnell, Neil Patrick Harris, Jane Lynch, and T. R. Knight are other celebrities who have since come out of the closet.

© Jeff Kravitz/FilmMagic/Getty Images

Coming out Acknowledging to oneself and others that one is gay or lesbian.

less likely to be out; presumably as they feel they have more to lose. The most closeted professions include schoolteachers, physicians, attorneys, and ministers; those in the entertainment, artistic, or food-service fields are most likely to be out (Harry, 1993).

Response to Coming Out

It can be particularly difficult for some gay people to disclose their orientation to their family, who may respond with anger, shock, or rejection. Parents may also worry about the lives their gay children have, or even worry that they did something to cause their children to be gay or lesbian. Parents may be disappointed and may need to go through their own adjustment—to change their expectations of the future, of the possibility of grandchildren, or what they should tell friends and neighbors. **PFLAG (Parents and Friends of Lesbians and Gays)** is an organization that helps parents come to terms with their child's sexual orientation, and gain support from other families in similar situation.

Gay and Lesbian Relationships

In 2009 there were more than 580,000 same-sex households in the United States (U.S. Census Bureau, 2009a). Gays and lesbians meet their partners in much the same way that straight people do—through friends, social clubs, church, bars, or online. How do gay and lesbian relationships compare with heterosexual relationships?

Same-sex and other-sex relationships have more similarities than differences (Kurdek, 1998; Means-Christensen, Snyder, & Negy, 2003). Like heterosexuals, most gay men and lesbians want to form stable, long-lasting, committed relationships (Herek, 2006). They want to share intimate feelings with a partner, and balance independence with togetherness.

It is a myth that in gay and lesbian relationships, one partner plays the "man's role" and one plays the "woman's role." In reality, same-sex relationships tend to be more egalitarian than straight relationships, which are more likely to adhere to traditional gender roles. Same-sex couples are more likely to evenly divide child care and housework (Johnson & O'Connor, 2002; Rosenbluth, 1997). Same-sex relationships are also described as being more like best-friendships combined with romantic and erotic attraction (Peplau, 1981).

Lesbians may actually have higher relationship satisfaction than other couples. Lesbian couples show very high levels of equality in the relationship. Household tasks are distributed fairly, and equal independence is considered to be very important (Herek, 2006). Lesbian couples are described as more emotionally nurturing and they spend more leisure time together (Rosenbluth, 1997). Kurdek (2001) hypothesizes that this may be because women are "relationship experts," and focus on social and relational connections, communication, and problem solving. Gays and lesbians are also nicer to each other during arguments than straight couples are, and use more humor and less belligerence during disagreements (Gottman, Levenson, Gross, et al., 2003; Gottman, Levenson, Swanson, et al., 2003).

PFLAG (Parents and Friends of Lesbians and Gays) A support group for gays, lesbians, bisexuals, as well as transgendered and intersex individuals and their friends and family.

ASK YOURSELF

What would you do if you found out your child were gay?

Some people believe that same-sex couples have lower levels of commitment than married couples. It is important to properly evaluate this idea. Although most heterosexual couples have the option to marry, most same-sex couples do not. Studies on the stability of gay relationships should compare gay couples with *cohabiting* straight couples, rather than with married couples because the social and financial ramifications of legal divorce are more prohibitive than those of simply "breaking up" (Kurdek, 2004). Also, the population of gay and lesbian couples in these studies includes those who *would* marry if allowed alongside those who *would not* marry their partners, who might be said to hold lower levels of relationship commitment. Finally, same-sex couples get less social support from family members, which can lead to relationship instability. One comparison of childless, cohabiting same-sex couples with married heterosexual couples found that for 50% of the comparisons, gay and lesbian partners did not differ from heterosexual partners; in 78% of the comparisons in which there was a difference, same-sex partners functioned better than their heterosexual counterparts. The only area in which gay and lesbian partners fared worse than heterosexual partners who were parents was in the area of social support (Kurdek, 2004).

Sexual Activity

There is an old joke in the gay community that goes like this: "What does a lesbian bring on her second date?" "A U-Haul." "What does a gay man bring on his second date?" "What second date?" This joke plays upon the stereotype of the commitment-prone lesbian and the promiscuous gay male. Is there any truth to these labels? It is true that when comparing men and women, men in general are more likely to report more sexual partners and to engage in casual sex. With same-sex couples, those characteristics may be doubled. In other words, when two men are in a relationship, the lack of female influence may lead to the sexual extremes of male behavior. Lesbians, on the other hand, tend to form instant intense emotional bonds and build long-term relationships. Lesbians are likely to have had fewer sexual partners and are more likely to be monogamous (Nichols, 1990). The fact is that behavior differences between male gay couples and female gay couples, if any, are probably related more to dissimilarities in the genders than to anything having to do with sexual orientation.

Frequency of sexual activity is thought to be highest in gay male couples, followed by heterosexual couples, with lesbians having the lowest frequency of sexual activity (Peplau & Ghavami, 2009). In other words, the more males there are in a relationship, the more often a couple has sex. Gay male couples are more likely than heterosexual couples or than lesbians to discuss whether the relationship will be sexually exclusive. But remember—gay male couples are usually not married. Just as with heterosexual couples, there is a lower expectation of sexual monogamy with cohabitation than with marriage.

Just like heterosexuals, gays and lesbians express themselves sexually in a variety of ways, and for a variety of reasons. Most straight people do not limit their sexual expression to vaginal intercourse; instead, they touch, caress, explore, and taste their partner's body. One difference is that same-sex partners tend to be less "goal-driven" than heterosexual

But what do they *do?*

Table 10.2 Types of Legally Binding Relationships in the U.S.

TYPE OF RELATIONSHIP	DEFINITION	AVAILABILITY	PORTABILITY	BENEFITS PROVIDED
Civil marriage	A legal status established through a state government–issued license.	• Available in all states to heterosexual couples. • Available to same-sex couples only in Connecticut, Iowa, Massachusetts, New Hampshire, New York, Vermont, and the District of Columbia.	• Heterosexual persons married in one state are considered married in all other states. • Same-sex marriages are not recognized in most states.	• Heterosexual couples receive 1,138 federal benefits in the areas of Social Security, employment, health care, taxation, family leave, the judicial system, and others. • There are no federal benefits for same-sex couples.
Civil union	A legal mechanism by which same-sex partners can have a legal status somewhat similar to civil marriage.	Delaware, Hawaii, Illinois, New Jersey, Rhode Island	Not recognized in most states.	Varying subsets of rights, dependent on the state. No federal benefits available for same-sex couples.
Domestic partnership	A relationship between two individuals who live together and mutually support one another as spouses, but who are not legally joined in civil marriage or civil union.	California, Colorado, Maine, Nevada, Oregon, Washington, Wisconsin	State-, community-, or employer-specific, so not portable	• Domestic partnership laws grant some or most state spousal rights afforded to married couples. • There are no federal benefits available to those in a domestic partnership.

SOURCE: Pawelski et al., 2006.

partners, to be more aware of their partner's subjective state, and to spend more time caressing and teasing each other sexually before beginning direct genital stimulation. Sexual practices of both heterosexuals and homosexuals will be discussed more fully in Chapter 11.

Marriage Equality

In February of 2000, the Fox TV network aired a show called *Who Wants to Marry a Multi-Millionaire?* in which 50 women competed in a "pageant," wearing bathing suits and evening gowns, hoping to be chosen to be the bride of Rick Rockwell, a self-described millionaire whom they had never met. At the end of the program, Rick chose Darva Conger as his bride, and they were immediately married on national TV. As of that moment, due to the "sanctity" of their marriage, Darva and Rick received more than 1,000 legal rights and benefits that are not available to same-sex couples who have been in loving, committed relationships for decades.

While the U.S. federal government does not recognize any form of gay marriage, some states have allowed different types of unions between same-sex partners. A *civil marriage* is one in which two people have all the rights and obligations of marriage, via a license issued by the state government. At the time this book was printed, same-sex couples could obtain civil marriages only in Connecticut, Iowa, Massachusetts, New Hampshire, New York, Vermont, and the District of Columbia, although the union is not recognized in most other states; only Maryland and Rhode Island recognize legal same-sex marriages from other states. Same-sex marriages were legal in California from June 16, 2008, to November 5, 2008, until the passage of Proposition 8. After its passage, same-sex marriage licenses were no longer granted in California. In 2010 a federal judge overturned the law as unconstitutional. This ruling is currently being appealed.

A **religious marriage** may be a rite, sacrament, or solemnization of the union of two people (Pawelski et al., 2006). Religious

Cartoon by Mike Luckovich

officials in the United States have the authority to also establish civil marriages. **Civil unions** give same-gender couples a legal status similar to civil marriage. Finally, a **domestic partnership** is a relationship between two people, sometimes of the same gender, who live together and mutually support one another as spouses (Pawelski et al., 2006). They receive some state rights, but none of the federal rights or benefits of civil marriage. These types of relationships are summarized in Table 10.2.

The Same-Sex Marriage Debate

Americans are divided on whether gay people should be allowed to legally marry.

Religious marriage A religious rite, sacrament, or solemnization of the union of two people.

Civil unions A legal contract between partners that confers all or some of the rights of marriage but without the historical and religious meaning.

Domestic partnership A relationship between two people, sometimes of the same gender, who live together and mutually support each other as spouses.

When the Gallup organization surveyed Americans regarding a "nontraditional" marriage, 94% disapproved. Reasons given included the idea that there is a need to preserve the integrity of marriage, and children of such a union would suffer.

Americans also believed that a state may refuse to recognize any marriage that offends it, and that most people would be offended by such a union. Finally, it was agreed that such a marriage went against

the teachings of the Bible. While you may assume that this poll was regarding same-sex marriage, it was actually done in 1958, to determine American's views on interracial marriage.

Opposition to same-sex marriage has consistently fallen over the years, and by 2010, a slight majority of Americans believed that same-sex couples deserve the same legal benefits as other-sex couples. The support for gay marriage varies greatly according to age, gender, and political party affiliation, and has undergone significant changes in a relatively short time (see Table 10.3).

Opponents of legal recognition of same-sex marriages appeal to tradition and religious teachings to support their position. Some believe, as does former Pennsylvania senator Rick Santorum, that marriage is primarily about procreation, and "not about affirming somebody's love for somebody else," although no laws have been suggested to prevent sterile or post-menopausal people from marrying. Supporters of gay marriage cite human rights, as well as evidence that same-sex and heterosexual relationships do not differ in their basic dimensions (Herek, 2006).

Current Laws Regarding Same-Sex Marriage

In 1996 President Bill Clinton signed the **Defense of Marriage Act (DOMA)**, which allows each state to deny any same-sex marriage or civil union that has been recognized in another state, and which asserts that federal law recognizes that *marriage* is "a legal union of one man and one woman" and that *spouse* "refers only to a person of the opposite sex who is a husband or a wife." Because of DOMA, same-sex couples that are married or in a civil union are not granted any federal benefits.

Although same-sex marriage is not legal in the United States, many countries around the world recognize gay marriages or civil unions, including Andorra, Argentina, parts of Australia, Belgium, Brazil, Canada, Croatia, the Czech Republic, Denmark, Finland, France, Germany, Iceland, Israel, Luxembourg, the Netherlands, New Zealand, Norway, Portugal, Slovenia, South Africa, Spain, Sweden, Switzerland, and the United Kingdom.

"For a prime minister to use the powers of his office to explicitly deny rather than affirm a right . . . would serve as a signal to all minorities that no longer can they look to the nation's leader and to the nation's Constitution for protection, for security, for the guarantee of their freedoms. We would risk becoming a country in which the defense of rights is weighed, calculated, and debated based on electoral or other considerations. That would set us back decades as a nation. It would be wrong for the minorities of this country. It would be wrong for Canada."

—*Canadian Prime Minister Paul Martin discussing the Civil Marriage Act, February 2005*

DOMA (Defense of Marriage Act) A U.S. law, passed in 1996, that limits the federal government's definition of marriage as a legal union between one man and one woman.

economic, health, and social—upon those who enter into it. Married people are better off physically, psychologically, and financially. The U.S. General Accounting Office has identified 1,138 rights and protections awarded to married couples that are denied to same-sex couples. Some of these rights include the ability to make medical decisions for partners; family leave to care for a seriously ill partner; and inheritance, veterans', tax, and Social Security benefits. In 2004 the American Psychological Association issued a statement supporting the legalization of same-sex marriages. They state that denying gays and lesbians legal access to civil marriage is discriminatory and harmful to their psychological, social, financial, and physical well-being. Denying marriage rights to same-sex couples may even hurt the financial well-being of the nation. In 2004 the Congressional Budget Office determined that allowing civil marriage for same-sex couples would *increase* federal income tax revenues by $400 million each year, as well as decreasing Medicaid payouts. The net result would be savings of nearly $1 billion per year (Pawelski et al., 2006).

In July of 2004 Virginia banned civil unions between same-sex partners. Apparently, though, there was the lingering fear that sneaky gay people would find a way to enter into contracts with each other in order to leave their long-term partners property, to give them power of attorney, or to make health care deci-

Table 10.3 Support for Legal Recognition of Same-Sex Marriage

	2006	2010
Self-described conservative	18%	30%
Self-described moderate or liberal	73%	63%
Republican	19%	32%
Democrat	53%	67%
Males aged 18-49	31%	37%
Females aged 18-49	55%	67%
People age 50 and older	32%	41%
People under age 50	44%	61%
First-time college students	61%	65%
Overall	39%	52%

SOURCE: Information from Gallup poll, May 2006; CNN poll, 2010, Vara-Orta, 2007; (Pryor, Hurtado, DeAngelo, Blake, & Tran, 2010) .

Marriage bestows considerable benefits—psychological,

© 2011 Bruce F. Press Photography

sions for them. So Virginia voters passed the Marshall-Newman amendment, which prohibits any contracts between people of the same sex that might allow for any of the rights of marriage. Until the passing of this law, all mentally competent adults in the United States were able to enter into contracts. The passing of this law serves to treat gays and lesbians as subcitizens, deprived of a basic right of all other American adults (Rauch, 2004).

Gay Parenting

The American Academy of Pediatrics estimates that between 1 million and 10 million children in the United States are being raised by at least one parent who is gay or lesbian (Pawelski et al., 2006). By the year 2000, 34% of female couples and 22% of male couples were raising children, the highest proportion of which live in the South (Bennett & Gates, 2004). Many same-sex couples have children from previous heterosexual relationships; others were artificially inseminated or used a surrogate mother, and others adopt.

Some people have concerns about children who are raised by gays and lesbians. Some believe that these children will have a higher incidence of gender-identity confusion or be more likely to identify as gay when they grow up, although studies have found this not to be true—the vast majority of children raised by lesbians and gay men grow up to be heterosexual (Patterson, 1992). Some fear same-sex parents because they believe that same-sex relationships are more unstable, although gay or lesbian unmarried parents are more than twice as likely as heterosexual unmarried parents to be in long-term relationships (Bennett & Gates, 2004).

Finally, some are concerned that children raised by same-sex couples will suffer due to the stigma of having gay parents. Unfortunately, there is still discrimination against gays and lesbians in this country. Children raised in these households may have a "coming out" process of their own as they decide when and how much to share about their family. Homophobia and discrimination can negatively impact a child's life; children raised by lesbians who reported homophobic encounters showed more psychological distress than children who had not been harassed (Gartrell, Rodas, Deck, Peyser, & Banks, 2005). However, the fact that a group is discriminated against cannot be justification against their rights as parents. Imagine if someone said, "Jewish people are discriminated against in our society.

Therefore it is harmful for children to be raised in Jewish households." What uproar there would be! It is ironic that, in general, many of the same people who stigmatize gay couples are the ones who feel that children shouldn't be raised by gays and lesbians due to bias against homosexuals. Stop the prejudice, and the stigma is gone!

There are a number of cases in which gays and lesbians have lost custody of their biological children simply because of their sexual orientation. In the Virginia case of *Bottoms v. Bottoms,* a grandmother sued for and won custody of her grandchild because the boy's mother was a lesbian. In 1995 a lesbian mother in Florida lost custody of her 11-year-old daughter to the girl's father, who had served 8 years in prison for murdering his first wife, and who had been accused of child molestation by another daughter. The man's attorney said that this was in the best interest of the child, who "should have the opportunity to live in . . . a traditional family setting with traditional family values" (Lectaw, 1996; Navarro, 1996).

Outcomes for Children

Many studies have found that all else being equal, children raised in a household with two happy parents do better than those raised by a single parent. When investigating the outcomes of children raised by same-sex parents, it is important to compare children with two other-sex parents to children of two same-sex parents.

Children of same-sex parents are at least as well adjusted as children raised by heterosexual parents (Farr, Forssell, & Patterson, 2010; Gartrell & Bos, 2010; Herek, 2006; Patterson, 1992, 2006; Wainright, Russell, & Patterson, 2004). In fact, in 2004 the American Psychological Association issued this statement:

> The results of some studies suggest that lesbian mothers' and gay fathers' parenting skills may be superior to those of matched heterosexual parents. There is no scientific basis for concluding that lesbian mothers or gay fathers are unfit parents on the basis of their sexual orientation. . . . On the contrary, results of research suggest that lesbian and gay parents are as likely as heterosexual parents to provide supportive and healthy environments for their children.

The American Psychological Association, American Academy of Pediatrics, National Association of Social Workers, the American Medical Association, and the American Bar Association have all released statements supporting same-sex parenting.

Because same-sex couples cannot accidentally get pregnant, they often have to undergo rigorous and expensive procedures to have children, insuring that every child of a same-sex couple is greatly wanted and loved. A long-term study of children raised by lesbians found that these children were less likely to suffer from physical and sexual abuse than were their peers who were raised by heterosexuals. This is thought to be due to the absence of adult heterosexual men in the households (Gartrell, Bos, & Goldberg, 2010; Gartrell et al., 2005). Girls raised by lesbians tend to have higher self-esteem, show more maturity and tolerance than their peers, and are older when they have their first heterosexual contact (Gartrell et al., 2005, 2010). Children raised by same-sex parents seem to be less constrained by traditional gender roles; boys are less aggressive, and girls are more inclined to consider nontraditional careers, such as doctor, lawyer, or engineer (Gartrell et al., 2005; Stacey & Biblarz, 2001). Over the course of more than 20 years, scientists studied the psychological adjustment of 78 teenagers who were raised by

lesbian mothers. Compared to age-matched counterparts raised by heterosexual parents, these adolescents were rated higher in social, academic, and total competence, and lower in social problems, rule-breaking, aggression, and externalizing problem behavior (Gartrell & Bos, 2010).

There are fewer studies of children raised by two men, but gay fathers are more likely than straight fathers to put their children before their career, to make big changes in their lives to accommodate a child, and to strengthen bonds with their extended families after becoming fathers (Bergman, Rubio, Green, & Padrone, 2010). It is important for all children to have both male and female role models; lesbian mothers are more concerned with providing male role models for their children than are single heterosexual mothers (Kirkpatrick, Smith, & Roy, 1981). Children raised by lesbians or gay parents may be more likely to consider having a same-sex relationship, and girls raised by lesbian mothers may be more likely to have same-sex contact and to identify as bisexual compared to their peers (Gartrell et al., 2010; Stacey & Biblarz, 2001). However, there is no evidence that children raised by gay or lesbian parents are more likely to identify as gay, lesbian, or bisexual as adults (Stacey & Biblarz, 2001). Overall, though, there are more similarities than differences in the parenting styles of heterosexual and homosexual parents.

Children raised by lesbians and gays may have some different outcomes than those raised by straights just as there may be differences in children raised by Christians and by Jews, by athletes and couch potatoes, or by New Englanders and Midwesterners. Parents instill their values, experiences, and behaviors in their children, and no child has the exact same experience as any other child. What is important is that a child is raised by a person or persons who love and care for him or her.

Because the federal government does not legally recognize same-sex marriages, none of the federal protections that come with marriage will be granted to same-sex couples, or their children. While denying gays and lesbians the right to marry does not prevent them from becoming parents, it does prevent their children from receiving the financial, social, and medical benefits allowed to other children of heterosexual couples. Some of the rights and protections denied to children of same-sex parents include the following:

Medical

- The nonbiological parent may be powerless to authorize medical treatments or make medical decisions for a child in case of an emergency.

- Same-sex couples are less likely to have access to family health insurance.

Security

- Children are denied the right of a legal relationship with their nonbiological parent.
- If a same-sex couple separates, the child is not eligible for child support from the nonbiological parent.
- If the biological parent dies, the nonbiological parent may not be awarded custody of the child they have raised (Gilgoff, 2004).

Financial

- There are more than 1 million gay or lesbian veterans in the United States. Spouses and nonbiological children of these veterans are denied the benefits awarded to legally married military personnel.
- If a gay or lesbian parent dies, the family is denied access to hundreds of thousands of dollars in survivor benefits that children of legally married couples receive.

Gays and lesbians have been raising children as long as there have been parents and children, and they will continue to do so in the future. The issue at hand is whether the children of these unions will be raised with legal and financial benefits automatically conferred upon children of heterosexual (or closeted homosexual) parents.

Adoption Laws

There are currently more than half a million children in foster care and more than 100,000 children awaiting adoption in the United States (Farr et al., 2010). However, same-sex couples are forbidden to adopt children in Mississippi (Florida repealed their ban on gay adoption in 2010); Utah and Arkansas have made same-sex adoption technically impossible by limiting adoption to couples who are legally married. Only 10 states plus the District of Columbia give the opportunity for same-sex couples raising a child to jointly establish themselves as the legal parents of the child.

Gay and Lesbian Seniors

It is estimated there are as many as 3 million gay and lesbian seniors in the United States; by 2030 that number will nearly double (Knauer, 2009). Almost 25% of same-sex couples include one partner over the age of 55. In addition to the difficulties faced by all seniors, gay and lesbian seniors must contend with additional financial, health, and accommodation problems. Because there is no legal federal recognition of same sex-relationships, when one partner dies, the other is denied thousands of dollars in benefits, including Social Security benefits. Unlike heterosexual married couples, same-sex couples are taxed on their retirement plans and on the inheritance of a shared home. Because women earn less than men, elderly lesbians are particularly vulnerable to financial woes. Older gay, lesbian, and bisexual adults are more likely to suffer from chronic physical health problems such as diabetes or hypertension and more likely to report symptoms of psychological distress than their heterosexual counterparts. Gay and lesbian seniors are also less likely to have a live-in partner or adult children to help care for them (Wallace, Cochran, Durazo, & Ford, 2011). Older homosexuals may also have problems finding a place to live when they can no longer care for themselves; almost half of nursing homes report intolerance from the staff toward same-sex residents (Cahill, South, & Spade, 2000). Recently, though, some retirement communities have been established that cater primarily to elderly gays and lesbians.

Like heterosexuals, same-sex couples form deep emotional connections and want to celebrate their commitment in front of their family, friends, and community. Denying same-sex couples and their children the right to legally wed hurts them physically, emotionally, and economically.

Societal Attitudes

After completion of this section, you will be able to . . .

- Assess the effect of a person's age, sex, religious views, race, and political perspective on his or her views of homosexuality.

- Appreciate the changing view of homosexuality over time.

- Consider the accuracy of the media images of gays and lesbians.

Many people feel very strongly about the issue of gay rights. There has been a flurry of legal activity regarding same-sex marriage and workplace discrimination, and the country is polarized regarding these issues.

A Gallup poll of 1,002 adults conducted in May 2006 showed that 89% of Americans believed that gays should have equal job opportunities and 54% viewed homosexuality as an acceptable lifestyle (see Figure 10.4). Americans are more intolerant about same-sex relationships than most other Western countries; a study in 2002 found that while 42% of Americans felt that homosexuality was morally wrong, only 16% of Italians, 13% of French, 9% of Dutch, and 5% of Spaniards felt similar antipathy (Fetto, 2002).

A person's age, sex, religious views, race, and political perspective are often correlated with their views on homosexuality. When Americans were questioned on their attitudes about homosexuality, those who worship weekly, self-described conservatives, and seniors were least tolerant of homosexuality, whereas younger people and self-described liberals were most tolerant. Figure 10.5 illustrates these differences.

Males tend to be more intolerant than women, especially toward gay men, and homophobia may be more common among some minority cultures in the United States although clear empirical evidence supporting racial differences in homophobia are limited (Jenkins, Lambert, & Baker, 2009). When considering this, it is important to note that attitudes about sexuality, gender roles, and family responsibilities vary among cultural and ethnic groups (Ryan & Futterman, 2001). In other words, antipathy toward homosexuality in the minority cultures may not necessarily be related to the same-sex interaction per se, but due to the flouting of traditional gender roles, religious beliefs, or failure to carry on the family line (Herek & Gonzalez-Rivera, 2006). The greater intol-

"Why is it that, as a culture, we are more comfortable seeing two men holding guns than holding hands?"
—Ernest Gaines, author

Percentage who consider homosexuality acceptable:

- **By year**

1982	34%
1992	38%
1997	42%
2002	51%
2006	54%

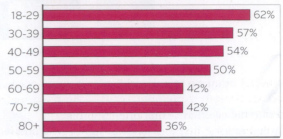

- **By age group**

18–29	62%
30–39	57%
40–49	54%
50–59	50%
60–69	42%
70–79	42%
80+	36%

- **By region**

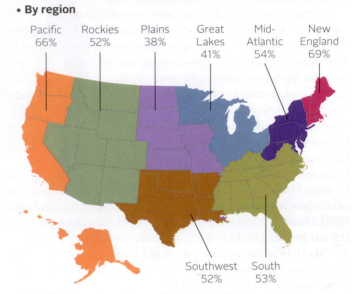

Pacific 66%   Rockies 52%   Plains 38%   Great Lakes 41%   Mid-Atlantic 54%   New England 69%

Southwest 52%   South 53%

FIGURE 10.4 Americans' views of homosexuality. (© USA Today, 1997. Adapted with permission.)

As every student who has ever taken a test knows, the way a question is worded may affect the responses received. In a recent poll, half of the respondents were asked if they favored letting "gay men and lesbians" serve in the military, and the other half were asked if they were in favor of letting "homosexuals" serve. Those who got the "gay men and lesbians" question were 11 percentage points more in favor compared to those who got the "homosexuals" question (New York Times/CBS News Poll, 2010).

erance toward homosexuality in black and Latino cultures may be one of the factors leading to the skyrocketing rates of HIV infection among gay black and Latino men. When minority men are "**on the down-low**"—hiding their gay identity—they are less aware of and less likely to disclose their HIV status.

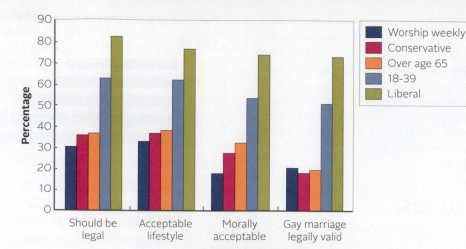

FIGURE 10.5 Attitudes about homosexuality. (© Cengage Learning 2013. Based on data from Gallup Poll, May 2006.)

Those who believe that sexual orientation is biologically determined are more likely to support gay and lesbian civil rights than those who believe homosexuality is a result of environmental influences (Armesto & Weisman, 2001; Tygart, 2000; Whitley, 1990). This may be due to attributional theory—people who are perceived to have caused their stigma will be judged more harshly than if their position is perceived to be caused by an accident or others' actions.

For so many years, gays and lesbians were made to feel ashamed of their sexual orientation. It is very difficult to accept who you are, and live as you are, meant to be, when most of the world disapproves of you. The decision to be who you are and to live your life regardless of what others think of you is something to be proud of indeed.

Cross-Cultural Perspectives of Homosexuality

If you travel the world, you will see wildly divergent views regarding same-sex behavior. Some consider male same-sex behavior a necessity for initiation into manhood, while others punish such behaviors with death. Most European nations are accepting of homosexuality; the United States is one of the most intolerant Western countries on this subject (Widmer, Treas, & Newcomb, 1998).

In other parts of the world, sexuality is not viewed as a dichotomy of homosexuality or heterosexuality, but by the gender role assumed—masculine or feminine—or by the particular sexual act—active or passive. In many Latin American cultures, a man is not considered to be homosexual if he plays the active (masculine) role of penetrator, rather than the passive (feminine) role of the penetrated. In Nicaragua, for example, a man who anally penetrates another man is called *hombre-hombre,* which translates to "manly man" (Lancaster, 1988). With its emphasis on family and on traditional gender roles, Hispanic culture can take a par-

> **What's up with "gay pride"? There aren't any "straight pride" parades.**

ticularly dim view of lesbians, who may flout the expected woman's role of mother and supportive wife.

As a rite of manhood in the Sambia tribe of Papua New Guinea, young boys are required to fellate older boys and swallow the sperm to acquire strength and virility. From the time they are 7 until their early teens, the boys engage exclusively in homosexual activities; during this time, it is taboo to touch or look at females. Once a boy reaches puberty, he is in turn fellated by the younger boys. These young men generally get married in their early 20s, and then never again engage in homosexual activity; it is thought that contact with a woman's vagina has made his penis unclean, and dangerous for another man to touch (Herdt, 1981).

In certain parts of the Middle East, homosexual acts are punishable by death. Many in the Arab world believe that homosexual behavior is either a willful choice or a symptom of psychiatric illness. Marriage and family obligations are paramount; to reject these is to reject the most basic foundations of Arab society. Iranian law states that any penetrative sexual act between adult men is punishable by death.

Attitudes About Same-Sex Relationships Through History

Throughout human history, same-sex activity has been variously viewed as a superior expression of love, a terrible sin, and a non-issue. In Ancient Greece, marriage was for procreation and financial benefits, and love was discouraged between spouses. It was considered manly to have same-sex desires, and intimate relationships between men were exalted—physically, intellectually, and spiritually. Adolescent boys often had a sexual relationship with an older mentor. The Ancient Greeks did not have a word or concept like today's homosexual/heterosexual dichotomy; they believed that people could respond erotically to both male and female beauty.

Homosexual behavior was legal and generally accepted until the end of the 12th century, when the persecution of "sodomites" intensified. It is important to note that it was the *act* of **sodomy** (which included oral or anal sex) that was considered heretical, not the person. Many people were put to death for the

On the down-low An African American slang phrase often used to describe men who have sex with men but who identify as heterosexual.

Sodomy Any sexual act that is not penile-vaginal penetration although it usually refers to oral or anal intercourse.

The Heterosexual Questionnaire

One way to detect unspoken prejudice—be it racial, religious, or homophobia—is to turn the situation around, and substitute "white," "Christian," or "heterosexual" into the situation. To illustrate, here are some questions typically posed to gays and lesbians. What are your feelings after reading the heterosexual questionnaire?

- What do you think caused your heterosexuality? Is it possible that your heterosexuality is just a phase you may grow out of?
- If you have never slept with a person of the same sex, is it possible that all you need is a good gay lover?
- Why do you insist on flaunting your heterosexuality? Can't you just be who you are and keep it quiet?
- A disproportionate majority of child molesters are heterosexual. Do you consider it safe to expose children to heterosexual teachers?
- Just what do men and women do in bed together? How can they truly know how to please each other, being so anatomically different?
- With all the societal support marriage receives, the divorce rate is spiraling. Why are there so few stable relationships among heterosexuals?
- Statistics show that lesbians have the lowest incidence of sexually transmitted diseases. Is it really safe for a woman to maintain a heterosexual lifestyle and run the risk of disease and pregnancy?
- There seem to be very few happy heterosexuals. Techniques have been developed that might enable you to change if you really want to. Have you considered trying aversion therapy?

act of sodomy, whether the act was committed with a person of the same sex or a person of the opposite sex.

Early American views on homosexuality reflect our Puritan roots. All of the 13 original colonies had laws against sodomy, which made the act punishable by death in some cases. Until 1961, all 50 states had laws on the books against sodomy. These laws were declared unconstitutional in 2003.

The 20th century saw a renewal of antigay violence. In Nazi Germany, homosexuality was seen to be part of a Jewish plot that would emasculate German men and diminish the perpetuation of the Aryan race. Nazis declared gay men enemies of the state and forced them to wear a pink triangle on their clothing. About 100,000 men were arrested as homosexuals, and as many as 15,000 were sent to the concentration camps, where 60% died (U.S. Holocaust Memorial Museum, 2011). They also forced lesbians to wear a black triangle, but persecuted women less harshly because they were seen to be easier to persuade to switch, or force to comply.

The United States has its own dark history of discrimination. In the late 19th century, New York State had laws against "disorderly conduct" or any solicitation for a "crime against nature or other lewdness" (McGarry & Wasserman, 1998). These laws came to be used as justification to criminalize any public gathering of gay people; their mere presence made the gathering disorderly and against nature. Taverns had their liquor licenses revoked if they allowed gays to congregate, and gay bars were routinely raided and their patrons arrested. Senator McCarthy's "witch hunts" of the 1950s were not only aimed at eliminating Communists but homosexuals as well. In 1953 President Dwight D. Eisenhower signed an order making "sexual perversion" (widely interpreted to mean homosexuality) grounds for exclusion from federal employment (D'Emilio, 1983). In the 1960s homosexuals were rated as the third most dangerous people, outranked only by Communists and atheists. In 1974 most people did not feel that gays and lesbians had the right to be in same-sex relationships (Aguero, Block, & Byrne, 1984).

Religious Perspectives of Homosexuality

Although many use the Bible as a weapon against gays and lesbians, the Judeo-Christian Bible contains few explicit statements about homosexuality: in Leviticus 18:22 and 20:13, and in Romans 1:26-27. Some religious scholars disagree about what these passages actually mean. It is unclear who the verses address, the specific type of forbidden behavior, or the type of sin committed. Some think the passages condemn pagan rituals or proscribe the place that intercourse occurs. Also, almost no one today, no matter how religious, follows all of the actual laws of the Bible (see the From Cells to Society feature on page 252). In addition, different parts of the Bible were written in Hebrew, Aramaic, and Greek, and translations may change the meanings of the passages. For example, some modern translations include the word "homosexuality," although this term was first invented

The Stonewall Inn was a gay bar in Greenwich Village. Early on June 28, 1969, police began a routine raid of the bar; this time, however, patrons fought back. The raid became a riot that lasted for several days. The Stonewall riot became a catalyst for gays and lesbians to begin to demand their rights, and has been hailed as the birth of the gay liberation movement.

© Fred W. McDarrah/Getty Images

The Bible and Homosexuality

Some people cite the Bible as their justification for homophobic policies. For example, Leviticus 18:22 states, "Thou shalt not lay with man as with woman; it is an abomination." But let's face it, the world has changed since the Bible was written, and how many of us truly follow all of its laws today? The Bible states that other modern-day activities are also abominations, including eating pork and shellfish (Leviticus 11:7, 11:10), wearing the clothing of the other gender (i.e., woman in pants) (Deuteronomy 22:5), and having sex during a woman's period. In fact, Leviticus 15:19–25 and 20:18 state that couples who engage in sex during menstruation are to be exiled and cut off from among their people. The Bible also forbids divorce (Mark 10:1–12), gossiping (Leviticus 19:16), and wearing clothes made of more than one

fabric or planting more than one type of seed in a field (Leviticus 19:19).

Additionally, the Bible decrees you should be put to death if you work on the Sabbath (Exodus 35:2), curse your father or mother (Leviticus 20:9), or commit adultery (Leviticus 20:10, Deuteronomy 22:22). If it is discovered that a bride is not a virgin, Deuteronomy 22:13-21 states that she should be stoned to death as quickly as possible. If your child is disrespectful, or a glutton or a drunkard, then "all the men in the city shall stone him to death" (Leviticus 21:18–21). Harry Potter would be out of luck because Leviticus 20:27 orders that a man who is a wizard should be put to death. The Bible also states that if anyone, even someone in your own family, worships another God or follows another religion, they should be killed (Deuteronomy 13:6–10, Deuteronomy 17:2–7). In fact, if

you find a city that worships another God, the Bible decrees that you should destroy the city and all its inhabitants, including the animals (Deuteronomy 13:12–15).

On the other hand, according to the Bible, it was acceptable to own slaves (Leviticus 25:44–46), to sell one's daughter into slavery (Exodus 21:7), and to rape women who were captured during wartime (Deuteronomy 21:10–14). There are a number of passages that endorse cannibalism (2 Kings 6:26–29, Jeremiah 19:9) and baby killing, as Psalm 137 reads, "Happy is the one who seizes your infants and dashes them against the rocks."

Although there are many rules in the Bible that may no longer be relevant today, there is one that we should always try to live by, Matthew 7:1: Judge not, lest ye be judged.

---

in the late 19th century and there was no comparable term in Biblical times. Neither Jesus nor Saint Paul explicitly condemned homosexuality. Early Christianity indicated that non-procreational sex was unnatural, but it was the *act* that was forbidden rather than the feelings. Nevertheless, the more conservative branches of both Christianity and Judaism condemn homosexual behavior. Less conservative branches, such as Reform Judaism, Unitarian Universalism, and the United Church of Christ permit same-sex marriages. (See Table 1.1 for a review of religious beliefs about homosexuality.)

Under Catholicism, homosexual acts are seen as a sin, and gay men and lesbians are instructed to embrace chastity so as not to sin. Only heterosexual acts within a marriage for procreative purposes are seen as acceptable. Muslims believe that while homosexual sexual desires may be seen as natural, these desires are not to be acted upon because they are a threat to the family and to procreation.

The position of the Hindu religion on homosexuality is complex. Hindus consider love to be an eternal force, and erotic desire is one of the most legitimate pleasures on earth; indeed, the *Kama Sutra* states that homosexual sex "is to be engaged in and enjoyed for its own sake." Nowhere in Hindu sacred texts does it say that romantic love is limited to a man and a woman. However, some Hindus look upon all non-procreative sexual acts as negative, and homosexuality was illegal in India until 2009, when the Delhi high court decriminalized homosexual acts between consenting adults. Buddhism is largely concerned with whether an action is helpful, harmless, and based on good intentions. Therefore, sexual acts are generally acceptable when they are mutually consensual and don't physically or emotionally harm others. According to the historical record, Buddha's sayings include no explicit references to homosexuality, and homosexuality is not considered a barrier to one's spiritual development.

Same-Sex Portrayals in the Media

Gays and lesbians are more visible in the media than ever before. In the past, gays and lesbians in films did not fare very well. If shown at all, they were depicted as objects of derision or disgust. In the 1961 movie *The Children's Hour,* the character played by Shirley MacLaine hangs herself in anguish over her lesbian tendencies. In 1959's *Suddenly, Last Summer,* the gay character is actually *eaten* by men who are upset by his sexual come-on.

Gays and lesbians became more visible in the 1990s, and for the most part, avoided being eaten (or at least, cannibalized). In some films, such as *The Birdcage,* stereotypical images of gays abound, whereas in more recent films, such as *Brokeback Mountain* and *But I'm a Cheerleader,* gays and lesbians are more likely to be portrayed as people from a number of walks of life.

It is thought that the first openly gay character to appear as a regular on an American TV show was in the 1970s. During the filming of the Loud family in the 1973 PBS documentary *An American Family,* son Lance Loud came out on national television to the dismay of his family and the delight of the producers. In 1989 *Thirtysomething* was the first primetime drama to show two men in bed together. Because of the scene, corporate sponsors boycotted the show, resulting in a loss of $1 million to the network. The two gay characters were promptly written off the show. *Ellen,* a 1990s sitcom starring Ellen DeGeneres, was the first TV show starring an openly gay person, about a gay person. The Showtime series *Queer as Folk* and *The L Word* focused on the lives of gays and lesbians, respectively.

In the 21st century, gays and lesbians are much more visible on TV, although many of their portrayals are of stereotypical images. *Will and Grace,* which ran from 1998 to 2005 and was the most popular TV show to focus on homosexuality, featured two gay men—Will, an attorney who spent most of the series without

The movies *The Birdcage*, *Brokeback Mountain*, and *But I'm a Cheerleader* portrayed gay issues with varying degrees of realism.

ASK YOURSELF

How realistic are the images of gays and lesbians on TV? How have these shows advanced the acceptance of gays and lesbians? How have they hurt?

controversy when it was discovered that one character, Billy, would approach another male character with flowers, and the two would make out. Many people were upset by this discovery. As one gamer wrote, "This is morally reprehensible. *GTA* is a real man's game, *Bully* is a disgrace" (Baertlein & Dabrowski, 2006). (For the record, *GTA (Grand Theft Auto)* is a game in which a player takes on the role of a criminal, committing robberies and murders in order to earn points.)

Perhaps because popular music often represents rebellion, and the flouting of conventional mores, gays and lesbians thrive in the music industry. The Indigo Girls are a folk rock duo known for their sweet harmonies and political activism. Elton John, k.d. lang, and Melissa Etheridge are award-winning musicians who have sold hundreds of millions of albums among them.

Discrimination and Antigay Prejudice

After completion of this section, you will be able to . . .

○ Identify sources of discrimination against gays and lesbians.

○ Recognize some health issues of particular concern to gays and lesbians.

○ Define *homophobia* and *hate crimes*.

○ List some possible reasons for homophobia.

Intolerance against gays and lesbians can lead to discrimination and homophobia.

Discrimination

Although society is much more accepting of same-sex relationships than it was in the past, discrimination still exists in employment, health, family matters, and in the military. The psychological, physical, and financial disadvantages of discrimination may lead to stress, depression, and anxiety in those who are subjected to it.

Employment

Title VII of the Civil Rights Act guarantees protection against discrimination in employment on the basis of race, religion, gender, national origin, and disability. Because sexual orientation is not included, in 29 states it is legal to fire an employee based solely on his or her sexual orientation. In 2006 the European Union unanimously approved a resolution banning discrimination against gays and lesbians in the workplace. A similar law in the United States—the Employment Nondiscrimination Act (ENDA)—has not been passed by Congress.

Still, things are improving. Eighty-six percent of Fortune 500 companies include sexual orientation in their nondiscrimination policy. A majority of the nation's largest corporations offer

a partner, and Jack, effeminate, flamboyant, and promiscuous. On *Queer Eye for the Straight Guy*, five stereotypically gay men, who were into fashion, design, and hair products, showed a messy straight man how to decorate and choose wine. Today, the Logo network is the first network specifically marketed to the gay, lesbian, bisexual, and transgendered community. Savvy corporations can benefit by aiming their advertising at same-sex couples. Subaru, Travelocity, and MasterCard are some of the companies that have had pro-gay marketing strategies.

The Advocate, a magazine first published in 1967, is the oldest continuing gay publication in the United States. Other publications aimed at the GLBTQ audience include *Out* and *Curve.* Websites featuring news relevant to the GLBTQ community include gay.com and 365gay.com, whereas sites such as AfterEllen.com and AfterElton.com feature news regarding gays and lesbians in media and entertainment. Gay and lesbian singles looking for romance can access gaysingles.com as well as match.com. Gay and lesbian gamers can go to gaygamer.net to communicate with others about video games. Some games, such as *SaGa Frontier*, include GLBTQ characters. The videogame *Bully* generated some

domestic partnership benefits, although unlike their heterosexual counterparts, gay and lesbian employees will be taxed on these benefits.

Gays in the Military

Prior to World War I, there was no formal mechanism for the exclusion of gays and lesbians from military service. Following WWI, the army began to implement processes to identify and disqualify potential homosexuals, including those with a "degenerate physique," such as sloping shoulders and an absence of body hair (Center for the Study of Sexual Minorities in the Military [CSSMM], 2001).

In 1993, what's come to be known as **"Don't ask, don't tell"** became the military policy toward homosexuality. Crafted by Colin Powell and presented as a compromise measure by President Bill Clinton, the policy barred anyone who had romantic or sexual contact with members of the same sex from serving in the armed forces of the United States, and forbade disclosure of one's sexual orientation, or speaking about any homosexual relationships. The policy further stated that as long as service men and women hid their sexual orientation, their commanding officers were not allowed to scrutinize their sexuality, although if homosexual behavior was even suspected, an officer could initiate an investigation. After the passage of "Don't ask, don't tell," there was an increase in violence against gays in the military, and dismissals of gay and lesbian service people rose by 73% (CSSMM, 2001). By 2006 more than 11,000 service men and women had been dismissed under this policy, many of whom had skills critical for national security (Associated Press, 2010). It is estimated that discharging and replacing these personnel cost the U.S. government $369 million (CSSMM, 2001). "Don't ask, don't tell" was repealed in 2010.

Health Issues

Lesbians are more at risk of breast and endometrial cancers than are heterosexual women. This may be because oral contraceptives and childbirth lessen a woman's risk of these cancers, as well as because lesbians are more likely to smoke cigarettes. Unfortunately, lesbians are also less likely to have had a Pap smear in the past year (Marrazzo, Koutsky, Kiviat, Kuypers, & Stine, 2001). Lesbians have the lowest rates of STIs, but are certainly not immune to them. Unprotected anal intercourse predisposes people to a number of risks, and men who have unprotected anal sex with men are at a higher risk of acquiring a number of sexually transmitted infections, as well as anal cancer.

Men who have sex with men and women who have sex with women have higher rates of depression, anxiety, and **post-traumatic stress disorder (PTSD)**, which are often correlated with discrimination and homophobia. Gay men are also more likely than straight men to have an eating disorder (Yelland & Tiggemann, 2003). Gays and lesbians are also more likely to experience violence and hate crimes. Some lesbians and gays are rejected by their family of origin and thrown out of their Church because of their sexual orientation, which can raise their risk of depression and anxiety. A survey of self-identified lesbi-

Don't ask, don't tell The policy that prohibited anyone who "demonstrates a propensity or intent to engage in homosexual acts" from serving in the U.S. military.

PTSD (post-traumatic stress disorder) An anxiety disorder that occurs in reaction to a traumatic event. Sufferers can experience flashbacks, emotional numbness, and physical symptoms.

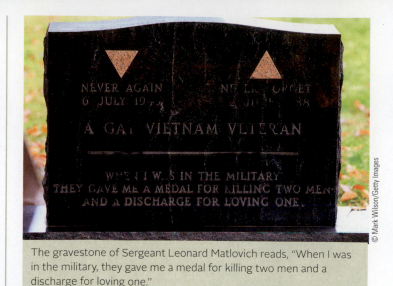

The gravestone of Sergeant Leonard Matlovich reads, "When I was in the military, they gave me a medal for killing two men and a discharge for loving one."

an, gay, and bisexual young adults found that those who reported higher levels of family rejection during adolescence were more likely to report depression, illegal drug use, and attempted suicide (Ryan et al., 2009). Everyone needs a source of emotional support; those who are rejected from their families may find support from friends, GLBTQ organizations, and coworkers.

In a national survey, 90% of gay and lesbian physicians reported observing antigay bias in patient care (Schatz & O'Hanlan, 1994). According to the same survey, more than two-thirds knew of lesbians or gays who were denied care or who received substandard care because of their sexual orientation, and more than half of the gay physicians themselves reported being discriminated against by their medical peers. Gay men are barred from donating blood. The Food and Drug Administration has also advised sperm banks to ban gay men from donating sperm, although all donors are screened extensively for HIV and other STIs, and other high-risk donors—such as intravenous drug users or men who have sex with prostitutes—are not banned (Stimola, 2005).

Perhaps due to fear of discrimination, more than a third of men who have sex with men do not disclose their sexual behaviors to their physicians. This is especially true of black, Hispanic, and Asian men (Bernstein et al., 2008).

Homophobia/Homonegativism/ Antigay Prejudice

A negative emotional response—such as fear, anger, anxiety, or discomfort—to gays and lesbians is called **homophobia**. Homophobia may not be the best term because phobia comprises only a tiny portion of antigay responses. Antigay feelings are usually multidimensional and encompass actions, attitudes, beliefs, and judgments against gay people. Many things that are labeled "homophobia" are better described as **homonegativism**, prejudice, or **heterosexism**. **Prejudice** is "a hostile or negative attitude toward a distinguishable group" (Aronson, 2003). Homonegativism or antigay prejudice exists in the classroom, workplace, and community.

The National School Climate Survey (Kosciw, Diaz, & Greytak, 2008) of 6,209 students aged 13 to 21 found that homophobia was fairly common in schools in the United States. More than 90% of students frequently heard the word "gay" being used in a negative way ("that's so gay"), and almost three-quarters of students often or frequently heard homophobic words such as "faggot" or "dyke." When school staff were present, the use of derogatory language by students remained largely unchallenged. School staff were much more likely to intervene when students used sexist or racist language, thus sending the message that homophobic language was tolerated. In fact, nearly two-thirds of students reported hearing homophobic remarks *from teachers or other school employees.* Harassment doesn't stop with words—44% of GLBT students experienced physical harassment, and 25% were physically assaulted while at school—punched, kicked, or injured with a weapon. Excessive abuse has a deleterious effect on gay and bisexual youth, who are significantly more likely to think about, attempt, and commit suicide than their straight counterparts.

About 60% of GLBT students reported feeling unsafe in their schools because of their sexual orientation. Students who experienced higher frequency of harassment because of their sexual orientation were more likely to miss school, and less likely to say they would go on to college. However, in schools with gay-straight alliances, or where educators were supportive, students heard fewer homophobic remarks, experienced less harassment and assault, were less likely to feel unsafe, less likely to miss school due to safety concerns, and had a greater sense of belonging to the school community.

Homophobia does not exist only in the United States. Although in 2006 the European Parliament passed a resolution condemning homophobia in the European Union, homonegativity still exists in Europe. Gays and lesbians are well accepted in Western and Northern European countries, but not as well accepted in Central and Eastern European countries (Stulhofer & Rimac, 2009). Countries in which Roman Catholic, Eastern Orthodox, or Muslim values have a stronghold are more homonegative. In most Islamic countries, homosexual activity is forbidden, and same-sex intercourse can be punished by the death penalty in Iran, Saudi Arabia, Sudan, Pakistan, and others. Before Columbus encountered the Caribbean, sexual freedom was the norm, including the full acceptance of homosexuality (Burns, 1988). Now the area is largely homophobic, and homosexual acts are illegal in many Caribbean islands, including Barbados, Jamaica, and Trinidad.

Biphobia

Unfortunately, bisexuals experience distrust not only from heterosexuals, but also from the lesbian/gay community (Rust, 2002). Many people hold a monosexist belief—that the only legitimate forms of sexuality are heterosexuality and homosexuality. Some feel that bisexuality threatens the hard-won political identity of those in the gay community, or that bisexuals are "traitors" that move back and forth from the world of the "oppressor" to the

Fred Phelps, pastor of the Westboro Baptist Church, is virulently homophobic. He and his followers (mostly members of his family) picket at 15 church services per week, as well as at the funerals of military personnel.

© Chip Somodevilla/Getty Images

world of the "oppressed." Others feel that bisexuals are responsible for transmitting the HIV virus to the "straight world," or that a relationship with a bisexual is doomed because he or she would always be dissatisfied with the current relationship. When Michele Eliason (1997) administered the Beliefs About Sexual Minorities Scale to heterosexual college students, she found that subjects were more likely to rate bisexual men and women (compared to gay men or lesbians) somewhat or very unacceptable.

Why Does Homophobia Occur?

There are several possible reasons for homophobia, including religious beliefs, insecurity about one's own orientation, and ignorance.

- *Religious reasons.* Those who hold more fundamentalist or conservative religious beliefs may have more negative attitudes toward homosexuality.
- *Traditional gender-role stereotypes.* Those who embrace more traditional beliefs about the "proper" role of men and women in society are more likely to hold negative feelings about gays and lesbians. In our society, men are more subject to rigid gender-role mores than are women, and men tend to hold more negative feelings about homosexuality than women do (Herek & Gonzalez-Rivera, 2006).
- *Latent homosexuality.* Henry Adams and his colleagues at the University of Georgia performed a study that suggests that at least some homophobia might be the result of anxiety about one's own sexual orientation (Ad-

Homophobia Although it literally means a fear of homosexuals and homosexuality, it has come to mean negative attitudes and actions toward homosexuals.

Homonegativism Negative actions, attitudes, beliefs, and judgments toward homosexuals or homosexuality.

Heterosexism Discrimination in favor of heterosexuals and against GLBTQ individuals.

Prejudice A hostile or negative attitude toward a distinguishable group.

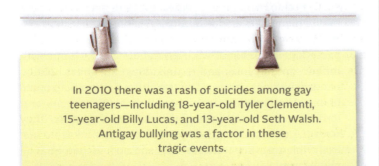

In 2010 there was a rash of suicides among gay teenagers—including 18-year-old Tyler Clementi, 15-year-old Billy Lucas, and 13-year-old Seth Walsh. Antigay bullying was a factor in these tragic events.

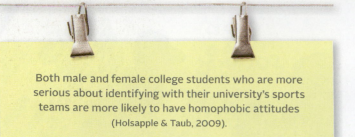

Both male and female college students who are more serious about identifying with their university's sports teams are more likely to have homophobic attitudes (Holsapple & Taub, 2009).

ams, Wright, & Lohr, 1996). White male college students were assessed using the Kinsey scale, and participants who reported exclusively heterosexual arousal and experiences were chosen. These men were screened to determine their degree of homophobia, and brought into the laboratory where they were hooked up to penile plethysmographs, which measured their degree of erectile responses. The men were then shown 4-minute segments of erotic videotapes depicting explicit consensual sexual activity between a man and a woman, between two women, and between two men. While all of the men exhibited penile erections when watching the heterosexual and lesbian videos, 80% of the homophobic males had moderate or definite tumescence while watching two men have sex (compared to 34% of non-homophobic men); these men reported, however, that they were not aroused by the video. It is theorized that some men who have strongly homophobic feelings toward gay men may be denying their own erotic feelings toward other men.

- *Ignorance.* Some people may be uncomfortable with gays and lesbians due to minimal personal interactions with them. Knowing a gay or lesbian person decreases one's intolerance toward gays and lesbians in general. Others may be homophobic because of incorrect ideas, such as the false belief that gay men are more likely to sexually abuse children.

- *Fears of society upheaval.* Same-sex couples threaten the social status quo, "not only because their behavior necessitates a critique of gender roles, but because the questioning of one social norm frequently leads to the questioning of others" (Rosenbluth, 1997, p. 607).

As with any prejudice, homophobia occurs when a person is judged solely by one characteristic. When we begin to learn more about each other, and focus on our similarities rather than our differences, it is much more difficult to hate and fear each other.

Hate Crimes

A **hate crime** is violence or crimes committed because the victim belongs to a certain race, religion, ethnicity, or sexual orientation. According to the Department of Justice, in 2009 hate crimes based on sexual orientation made up approximately 18.5% of all reported hate crimes. Of those, more than 55% resulted from bias specifically against gay males and 15% from bias against lesbians. In a recent study of hate crimes in the Los Angeles area, 35.8% were motivated by sexual orientation (Dunbar, 2006), and violent crimes based on sexual orientation were more severe than were those based on race or religion. More than one-third of gay men and lesbians have

Hate crime A crime committed against a person because of his or her perceived membership in a certain social group.

been victims of interpersonal violence. Between 1998 and 1999, many U.S. cities observed 40% increases in violent incidents against gays. During the same time period, despite the decline in the nation's murder rate, there was a 13% rise in antigay murders (Parrott & Zeichner, 2005).

Many hate crimes go unreported. In the Los Angeles study, white gay men were most likely to report their victimization, and lesbians of color were least likely to report. More than 20 states have either no hate crime laws, or hate crime laws that don't include sexual orientation. In 2009 President Barack Obama signed the Matthew Shepard and James Byrd, Jr., Hate Crimes Prevention Act, which expanded hate crimes legislation to include sexual orientation and gender identity.

Dispelling the Myths

Some homophobia occurs because of false beliefs about the lives of gays and lesbians. Here we will dispel some of these myths.

- **Myth:** If someone is or has been married, he or she can't be gay.
- **Fact:** Up to 25% of gay men and a third of lesbians have been in heterosexual marriages. These marriages might occur before they recognize that they are gay or because they may be trying to fulfill society's expectations.
- **Myth:** Gays and lesbians have psychological problems.
- **Fact:** In the first half of the 20th century, homosexuality was viewed as a sickness to be cured. Past conversion therapies for gays and lesbians included severe exercise, aversion therapy, electroconvulsive shock, lobotomies, hysterectomies, castration, and exorcisms. In 1973 the American Psychiatric Association deleted homosexuality as a disease from the *Diagnostic and Statistical Manual of Mental Disorders (DSM)*, largely based on the efforts of Dr. Evelyn Hooker. Dr. Hooker showed that gay and straight men did not differ in their psychological adjustment (Hooker, 1957), a finding that has been replicated many times over the years. Today, gay adults are just as happy with their quality of life as are straight adults. Although gay people face discrimination, data compiled from more than 11,000 interviews found little evidence that sexual orientation directly affected quality of life or health (Horowitz, Weis, & Laflin, 2001). This does not mean that all gays and lesbians are free from emotional problems. Those who are subject to homophobia and harassment may be at higher risk for depression and anxiety (Mays & Cochran, 2001).
- **Myth:** Gay people want special rights.
- **Fact:** Gays and lesbians want the right to make a home with the person they love, and to walk down the street holding hands with their partner. They want the right to help make financial and medical decisions with their life partners, and to have a part in the lives of the children they raise. They want the right to keep their jobs and home and to be free from violence. They want no more and no less than what all people want.

ASK YOURSELF

How would you respond to an undesired sexual approach from someone of the same sex? Would it be different from a "come on" from a person of the opposite sex? Why?

Chapter Summary

Introduction

- A person's *sexual orientation* is his or her predisposition toward sexual and emotional attachments toward men, women, or both. A homosexual is physically and emotionally attracted to those of the same sex, heterosexuals toward the other sex, and bisexuals toward both sexes to varying degrees. The terms "gay" and "lesbian" are preferred over homosexual because "homosexuality" focuses on the sexual rather than emotional aspects of the relationship.

Models and Measures of Sexual Orientation

- The Kinsey scale arranges sexual behavior on a continuum from exclusively heterosexual to exclusively homosexual behavior. Other scales, such as the Klein sexual orientation grid, include factors other than sexual behaviors, such as attraction, fantasy, and emotional connection, and take past, present, and future events into consideration as well.
- Some studies suggest that compared to men, women's sexual expression is more bisexual and fluid. Women are more likely than men to change between other-sex and same-sex attractions throughout their life.

The Prevalence of Homosexuality

- It is very difficult to determine the incidence of homosexuality in a population. Some of the reasons for this difficulty include the lack of a consistent definition of homosexuality, disagreement as to what factors should be considered, inconsistencies in research methods, and the honesty of subjects.

What Determines a Person's Sexual Orientation?

- There is no one single cause of same-sex behaviors, any more than there is one single factor underlying heterosexual behavior. Genetic influences, prenatal factors, hormonal effects, and neuroanatomical differences have all been considered, as have psychosocial influences.
- Although some gays and lesbians can choose to change their *behavior,* homosexual desires and attraction cannot be changed. Conversion "therapy" often causes psychological, social, and spiritual harm to those who undergo it.

Living and Loving as a Gay Man or Lesbian

- The stereotypical "gay lifestyle" does not represent the lives of gays and lesbians today (if, indeed, it ever did). Just as there is no single, identifiable heterosexual lifestyle, all gays and lesbians do not live the same way.
- Gay and lesbian youth undergo unique problems while growing up, although things may be easier than in the past. Gays and lesbians come out—acknowledge their sexual orientation to themselves and others—at different times and in different ways. When a GLBT individual comes out may depend on his or her age, race, religion, or other factors. Coming out is psychologically beneficial, as one can live openly and honestly, but openly gay individuals also face the risk of rejection and even outright violence.
- Same-sex and other-sex relationships have more similarities than differences. There is evidence, however, that same-sex couples have more equality, honesty, and openness in their relationships.
- A religious marriage is a rite or sacrament solemnizing the union of two people. A civil marriage is conferred by the state government and gives two people all the rights and obligations of marriage. Civil unions give same-sex couples a legal status similar to civil marriage. A domestic partnership is a relationship between two people who live together and mutually support one another as spouses.
- The federal government does not recognize any form of gay marriage, although in some states same-sex couples can get married or obtain civil unions. The lack of federal recognition, however, means that these couples are denied 1,138 benefits and rights granted to heterosexual couples.
- Children being raised by gay and lesbian couples are also denied benefits received by children of heterosexual couples. Children of gay and lesbian parents are as psychologically well-adjusted—if not more so—as children of straight parents.
- In addition to the difficulties faced by all seniors, gay and lesbian seniors must contend with additional financial and accommodation problems. Because there is no legal federal recognition of same-sex relationships, when one partner dies, the other is denied thousands of dollars in benefits, including Social Security benefits.

Societal Attitudes

- Americans today are more intolerant about same-sex relationships than most other Western countries, although the situation is improving. More Americans consider homosexuality acceptable than in the past, and the younger generations are most accepting of rights for gays and lesbians. Americans who worship weekly, self-described conservatives, minorities, and seniors are least tolerant of homosexuality, while younger people, self-described liberals, and those who believe that sexual orientation is biologically determined are most tolerant.
- Throughout history, same-sex activity has been viewed as a superior expression of love, as a terrible sin, and as a non-issue.
- Gays and lesbians are more visible in the media than ever before, although many portrayals are of stereotypical images.

Discrimination and Antigay Prejudice

- Society is much more accepting of same-sex relationships than it was in the past, but there is still much discrimination, in employment, health, family matters, and in the military. The psychological, physical, and financial disadvantages of discrimination may lead to stress, depression, and anxiety.
- Although it literally means a fear of homosexuals and homosexuality, homophobia has come to mean negative attitudes and hostility toward homosexuals. Homophobia may be due to fundamentalist religious views, fear, ignorance, or insecurity over one's own sexual orientation. Hate crimes based on sexual orientation make up more than 15% of all reported hate crimes.
- There are many myths about gays and lesbians. Education and understanding will help society become more tolerant.

11 Consensual Sexual Behavior

"Sex embellishes most of life. It sells everything from newspapers to toothpaste. The pursuit of it has humbled heads of state, terminated promising careers, and brought fame and shame to lots of ordinary people."

—John Robinson & Geoffrey Godbey (1998, p. 18)

"Without fantasy, sex is not much more than friction."

—Erica Jong (2006, p.70)

"I used to think masturbation was not really sex because it only involved me. That's a very limited view of human sexuality, and it isn't going to work for women."

—Author Betty Dodson

© Image Source RF/Getty Images

© Full House Images/Getty Images

© STOCK4B-RF/Getty Images

Introduction

After completion of this section, you will be able to . . .

○ Understand that humans have sex for many varied reasons.

The World Health Organization estimates that 100 million acts of sexual intercourse occur every day around the world (WHO, 1992). Over the hundreds of thousands of years that human beings have been participating in procreative intercourse, it is estimated that they have had sex 1,200 trillion times.

Why Do People Have Sex?

Unlike humans, most other species have sex only for reproduction. In fact, most animals—dolphins and bonobo chimpanzees are the exception—are unable to mate if they are not in heat. Only humans—who hide their fertility—can and do have intercourse at all times. And although humans, like other species, are driven to react to fertility signals, we are able to choose to override our reproductive cycles and not reproduce.

So why do people have sexual intercourse? The question at first seems laughingly obvious, until you begin to tally the reasons and realize how many motives there actually are. Some people have intercourse to procreate; others do so for physical pleasure. Some sleep with others for financial gain, or to assert their power. Humans have intercourse to express emotion, relieve stress, or burn calories. People may have sex for social reasons, such as cementing relationships between families, or antisocial reasons, such as rejecting parental or societal values (Coleman, 1987; Hill, 1997). By surveying nearly 2,000 people, Cindy Meston and David Buss compiled 237 reasons why people have sex, ranging from the obvious—"I wanted to experience physical pleasure"—to the unusual—"I wanted to get rid of a headache" (Meston & Buss, 2007). Meston and Buss classified the reasons into four main categories: physical, goal attainment, emotional, and insecurity (see the Sex Actually feature on this page). According to the researchers, the most common reasons included being attracted to the other person, wanting to experience physical pleasure or to express love, marking a special occasion, or because the opportunity arose. Reasons such as wanting to harm another person by giving them a sexually transmitted infection or wanting to achieve a promotion were among the least common. However, what may be a rare reason in the general population may be a frequent motivator for an individual. For example, although most people are not motivated to have sex to humiliate another, for some individuals, that may be their principal sexual expression.

Men and women listed similar reasons for having sex: 20 of the top 25 reasons given were identical for both men and women. However, men were more likely to say they had sex for physical reasons such as a partner's appearance or desirability, whereas women were more likely to say they had sex as a way of expressing love for a person. Men were also more likely to list utilitarian reasons—such as wanting to improve their sexual skills, taking advantage of the opportunity, or the baffling "I wanted to change the topic of conversation." In contrast to the stereotypical idea that says women are more likely to use sex to gain resources, it was the men who were more likely to say they had sex to gain status, resources, or advancement at work.

It is important to remember that the Meston–Buss study included only college students. People at different times in their lives will give different reasons for sex—a sense of duty to a partner or the desire to procreate may be more powerful motivators later in life. Also, this study measured only the reasons that people were aware of and admitted to. There may be other factors—innumerable and mysterious—driving human beings to engage in intercourse.

Sexual expression is influenced by biological, psychological, religious, cultural, and societal factors. Physical fitness, hormones, or gender may shape a person's sexual attitudes and behaviors. For example, women are described as being more **erotically plastic** than men. Over time, individual women show greater variation in sexual behavior than men, and women are more responsive than men to cultural factors, such as the permissiveness or restraint encouraged by a society. Society also exerts a powerful influence on sexual expression. Americans of the 1960s and 1970s were more likely to engage in (or admit to!) casual sex than were men and women in the Victorian age. A person's religious views may also affect his or her sex life. Some fundamentalist sects of Christianity view all non-marital, non-procreative sexual activities as sinful. Some religions forbid sex at certain times, such as during menstruation, and some prohibit any sexual intercourse for certain adherents, such as Roman Catholic priests or Buddhist priests in monasteries. The Shaker religion required *all* of its followers to remain celibate throughout their lives (not surprisingly, there are almost none of these practitioners left!). In this chapter, we will explore the myriad ways that humans express themselves sexually.

Erotic plasticity The degree to which a person's sexual expression can change as a result of social, cultural, and situational forces.

---

sexactually

Reasons People Give for Having Sex

- Physical
  - "I wanted to achieve orgasm."
  - "The person's appearance turned me on."
  - "It feels good!"
  - "I wanted to relieve stress."
  - "It seemed like good exercise."
- Goal attainment
  - "I wanted to be popular."
  - "I wanted to break up a rival's relationship."
  - "I wanted to make money."
  - "I wanted to feel closer to God."
- Emotional
  - "I realized I was in love."
  - "I wanted to express my love for the person."
  - "I wanted to say 'Thank you.'"
  - "I wanted to lift my partner's spirits."
- Insecurity
  - "I felt it was my duty."
  - "I didn't know how to say no."
  - "I was feeling lonely."
  - "I wanted to keep my partner from straying."

SOURCE: Meston & Buss, 2007.

Maybe because it is so widely practiced, or perhaps due to the societal shame that still colors the activity, there are literally hundreds of slang terms associated with self-pleasure. Some of the terms that have entered the vernacular for male masturbation include *jerking off, beating your meat, choking the chicken,* and *spanking the*

monkey (this author notes the violence inherent in these expressions and hopes that men are more gentle with themselves than it sounds). Other terms include *buttering your corn, a date with Rosie Palm and her five sisters, keeping the census down,* and *wanking.* There are fewer terms

for female masturbation, but some are positively poetic, such as *polishing the pearl, tiptoeing through the two lips,* and *exploring the Deep South.* Other slang includes *let your fingers do the walking, flicking the bean, diddling, jill off, mistress-bate, she bop,* and *making kitty purr.*

How Do You Learn About Sexual Practices?

Many of you probably learned about "the birds and the bees" from your parents. They may have also told you about pregnancy, contraception, and sexually transmitted infections (STIs). But how many of you talked with your parents about orgasms? Masturbation? About the emotional aspects of relationships? One survey of more than a thousand 15- to 21-year-old girls and their mothers found that although 75% of mothers talk to their daughters about abstinence, only 35% discuss sexual pleasure with them (Brody, 2009). But sex is not just about "don'ts"—it is about pleasure and connection and emotions. These are some of the topics we will touch on in this chapter.

Solitary Sexual Practices

After completion of this section, you will be able to . . .

- Define *masturbation, dildo, vibrator, sexual fantasies,* and *nocturnal emissions.*
- Identify the factors that make a person more or less likely to masturbate.
- List the various reasons that people masturbate.
- Describe the health benefits of masturbation and sexual fantasy.
- Consider historical, religious, and cultural aspects of masturbation.
- Describe common characteristics of fantasies for men and women.

"No other form of sexual activity has been more frequently discussed, more roundly condemned, and more universally practiced than masturbation."

—*Lester Dearborn, marriage counselor*

"Don't knock masturbation—it's sex with someone I love."

—*Woody Allen*

Masturbation

Masturbation is the stimulation of one's own genitals, which produces feelings of pleasure and often results in orgasm. Men and women of all ages masturbate, with their hands, objects, or

(for the especially limber) their mouths. There is even evidence that fetuses masturbate (Giorgi & Siccardi, 1996; Meizner, 1987).

People masturbate for many reasons, including pleasure, relaxation, and to relieve sexual tension. Some masturbate because they are bored or as a sleep aid. Some masturbate to preserve their virginity or to avoid sexually transmitted infections. Masturbation allows both men and women to learn about their bodies and their sexual response. In fact, women who masturbate as adolescents are more likely to find sexual gratification with a partner. This doesn't necessarily mean that adolescent masturbation *causes* sexual satisfaction in adulthood; it may be that women who masturbate as adolescents are more open to exploring their sexuality, or better learn how their bodies function sexually.

Factors That Affect the Frequency of Masturbation

Masturbation is the most prevalent sexual behavior (Herbenick et al., 2010a). Kinsey and colleagues found that 92% of males and 62% of females said they had masturbated at some point in their lives (Kinsey, Pomeroy, Martin, & Gebhard, 1948, 1953). Current rates are similar or slightly higher (Herbenick et al., 2010a; Pinkerton, Bogart, Cecil, & Abramson, 2002). The 1994 National Health and Social Life Survey (NHSLS) found that 60% of males and 40% of females reported masturbating sometime in the past year (Laumann, Gagnon, Michael, & Michaels, 1994), and the more recent National Survey of Sexual Health and Behavior (NSSHB) survey showed that 74% of adult men and 58% of adult women masturbated in the past year (Herbenick et al., 2010a). Most people have masturbated at some time in their lives, but the frequency depends on a person's sex, age, health, and sexual habits.

Men are more likely than women to masturbate, and among those who do masturbate, men do so more frequently than women (Leitenberg, Detzer, & Srebnik, 1993; Pinkerton et al., 2002). In fact, when comparing many possible gender differences between men and women, researchers found that one of the largest differences between the sexes was the incidence of masturbation (Oliver & Hyde, 1995; Petersen & Hyde, 2010). Biological, social, or psychological factors may support this disparity. Men's greater exposure to testosterone may enhance their sex drive. In addition, men have easy access to and may touch

Masturbation The stimulation of one's own genitals, which produces feelings of pleasure and often results in orgasm.

their penis many times a day when urinating. The clitoris, however, is not as readily accessible. Socially, women are taught to associate sexual pleasure with romance and emotional intimacy, not only with physical pleasure. Women are less likely to admit masturbating and more likely to feel guilty about doing it. Perhaps their guilt is in part associated with the perception that women don't masturbate, causing fewer women to admit it, thus further supporting the fallacy.

Teens and college students report the highest frequency of masturbation, averaging two to three times per week (Cornog, 2003; Pinkerton et al., 2002). This incidence decreases as we age; only about 28% of men and 8% of women in their 40s masturbate at least once a week (Laumann et al., 1994). A survey of adults aged 57 to 85 found that half the men and more than a quarter of the women reported masturbating in the past 12 months (Lindau et al., 2007).

Other factors associated with frequency of masturbation include race, education, and religion. Whites and those with more education are more likely to report masturbating (Dodge et al., 2010; Gerressu, Mercer, Graham, Wellings, & Johnson, 2008; Herbenick et al., 2010a; Laumann et al., 1994). Masturbation is not associated with certain religious affiliations, rather with a person's level of commitment to his or her religious beliefs: people who are more devout are less likely to report masturbating, or start masturbating at a later age (Cornog, 2003).

It is a fallacy that people masturbate only when they are not involved in a sexual relationship. Eighty-five percent of men and 45% of women who were living with a sexual partner reported masturbating in the past year (Laumann et al., 1994). Some studies even suggest that the frequency of masturbation *increases* with a person's frequency of intercourse. Gerressu and colleagues (2007) found that women who report more oral and anal sex, and more sexual partners, were *more* likely to report masturbating.

Vibrator A dildo powered by batteries or electricity to vibrate, thus intensifying genital stimulation.

Dildo A penis-shaped object, usually made of rubber, silicone, or plastic, that is inserted into the vagina or anus for sexual pleasure.

How to Masturbate

People usually masturbate by stimulating the genitals, either manually or with a

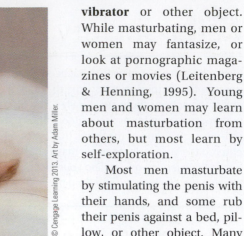

A man masturbating.

A woman masturbating.

vibrator or other object. While masturbating, men or women may fantasize, or look at pornographic magazines or movies (Leitenberg & Henning, 1995). Young men and women may learn about masturbation from others, but most learn by self-exploration.

Most men masturbate by stimulating the penis with their hands, and some rub their penis against a bed, pillow, or other object. Many men lie on their back or stand in the shower while making a fist around their penis, stroking up and down. Some men put both hands on the penis; others use their free hand to stimulate the testicles or nipples. Some find it pleasurable to insert a finger or an object into the anus to stimulate the prostate gland. Sometimes men use a lubricant or soapsuds to reduce friction. The speed and force used differ from person to person. Men sometimes begin with a gentle rubbing, and lightly stroke the head of the penis. Others enjoy more intense stimulation and use a vibrator (Reece et al., 2009). As orgasm nears, men may more vigorously stroke the penis. Most men have an orgasm from masturbating in less than 3 minutes (Kinsey et al., 1948).

Women use a broader range of behaviors to masturbate than men. Women may manually stimulate the vulva or breasts, insert objects such as a penis-shaped **dildo** into the vagina, or squeeze their thighs together rhythmically. Most women rub the clitoris and labia minora in a circular or back-and-forth motion. More than half of women polled in a recent survey have used a vibrator to stimulate the area, although some women find constant direct contact of the clitoral glans too intense (Herbenick et al., 2009). Vibrator use is common in the United States—approximately 53% of women and 45% of men ages 18 to 60 have used a vibrator. Vibrator use is associated with improved sexual function and better sexual health (Herbenick et al., 2009; Reece et al., 2009). Some women use lubricants such as Astroglide or K-Y Jelly, whereas others rely on their natural lubrication. The average speed for a masturbating woman to achieve orgasm is 4 minutes (Cornog, 2003).

Although women in pornographic movies often masturbate by inserting a dildo into the vagina, most women do not masturbate only in this way because the inner vagina contains relatively few nerve endings. If a dildo is used, it is important to be sure that the object is clean, smooth, and unbreakable.

The History of the Vibrator

Women in the Victorian age were thought to suffer from a condition known as "hysteria," symptoms of which included anxiety, sleeplessness, irritability, erotic fantasy, vaginal lubrication, and sensations of heaviness in the abdomen and lower pelvic area (Maines, 1999). Doctors thought this dangerous condition was caused by the uterus wandering upward inside the body, until it threatened to choke its host. To treat hysteria, doctors would manually stimulate the vulva, thus producing a "hysterical paroxysm." When the patient would thrust her pelvis and utter cries of pleasure, the doctor would know that her womb had returned to its rightful place. It would often take many weeks of daily treatment until the woman was "cured." Typically, male physicians found "gynecological massage" difficult to learn and too time-consuming, so the electric vibrator was developed. Eventually, women purchased home vibrators from catalogues, so they could align their wombs in the privacy of their own home. Devices that today would be considered sexual aids were marketed as health-promoting, anti-aging medical devices. By 1917, there were more vibrators than toasters in American homes (Maines, 1999).

A vibrator for home use, circa 1902.

© Kurt Rogers/San Francisco Chronicle/Corbis

Masturbation and Health

It is ironic that masturbation, arguably the safest sexual act, has over the years been thought to lead to horrible physical and mental consequences. In fact, not only is masturbation physically and psychologically harmless, there are a number of therapeutic benefits to self-stimulation. Aside from producing sexual pleasure, masturbation relieves stress and lowers blood pressure, and can be enjoyed by couples or by those not in a relationship. Some feel that masturbation may improve a man's fertility because ejaculation flushes out the old, less motile sperm left behind in the urethra. Masturbation may even lower a man's chance of getting prostate cancer; men who ejaculated five times or more a week, especially while in their 20s, were found to be less likely to develop the disease (Giles et al., 2003). It may be that frequent ejaculation prevents carcinogenic substances from building up in the prostate gland. (It is important to note that frequent ejaculation through intercourse with a large number of sexual partners is not medically beneficial because of the increased risk of contracting an STI; infection with certain STIs such as trichomoniasis and gonorrhea may even raise a man's risk of prostate cancer.) Finally, masturbation presents no risk of pregnancy or transmission of STIs. It may even lower a woman's chance of getting an STI because orgasm increases the acidity of the vagina and protects against infection.

> "If God had intended us not to masturbate, He would have made our arms shorter."
>
> —*George Carlin*

Is there such a thing as "too much" masturbation? Usually, the only problem that frequent masturbation causes is chafing. A person can use lubricants like K-Y Jelly or Astroglide to cut down on friction. Pain or injury can occur when objects are used for masturbation. A man can get his penis trapped in a vacuum cleaner or tub faucet, and objects inserted into the vagina or anus can break off or get stuck. Objects inserted into the anus should have a base that flares outward, as a trip to the emergency room to retrieve an umbrella or a gerbil lost in the rectum is not conducive to good sex. You should also be careful where and when you masturbate, as it can be dangerous if done while driving or operating heavy machinery. In particular, **autoerotic asphyxiation**—masturbation while hanging or strangling oneself—is a potentially life-threatening activity (discussed further in Chapter 15). As with any habit, if masturbation begins to interfere with your

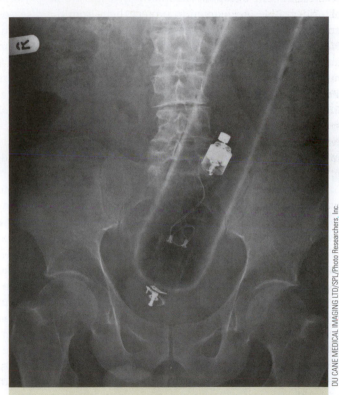

An X-ray of a vibrator in a person's large intestine. Wonder how it got there? Hint: not by being swallowed.

DU CANE MEDICAL IMAGING LTD/SPL/Photo Researchers, Inc.

Autoerotic asphyxiation
Masturbation while hanging or strangling oneself.

life—for instance, if you are frequently missing work or social engagements—that is a sign that you may have a problem. Also, if you can only experience sexual pleasure when alone, you should open the lines of communication with your partner, or consider talking to a trained psychologist or sex therapist.

Historical Perspectives of Masturbation

Four-thousand-year-old hieroglyphics tell the story of how the Egyptian god Atum is said to have created the world through an act of sacred masturbation, as he "copulated with [his] hand and his ejaculate became all life" (Friedman, 2001). Society's perception of masturbation was all downhill from there; throughout most of human history, masturbation has been considered dangerous and sinful. Masturbation was once thought to lead to impaired morals, depression, social failure, epilepsy, tuberculosis, blindness, insanity, sterility, and early death (Shannon, 1913).

Because masturbation was thought to be so dangerous, many "cures" were developed to eliminate the practice of the "secret sin." For decades, Victorian physicians would perform clitoridectomies on women to protect them from the diseases and death they thought were certain to follow masturbation. Men were encouraged to wear straitjacket pajamas or erection alerts to discourage handling of the penis. Some would wear a little suit of armor that fit over the penis and testicles. Others wore a *spermatorrhea ring.* Available from the Sears catalogue, these rings fit along the base of the penis and had sharp metal spikes on their inner lining that would pierce the penis when a man started to get an erection. As a last resort, some chronic masturbators had their foreskin stapled shut, or were castrated. In the 19th century, John Kellogg invented cornflakes as one part of a diet that he felt would lessen the sex drive and diminish the practice of masturbation, which he called a "crime doubly abominable." Dr. Graham invented the graham cracker for the same reasons (Carnes, 1994).

Attitudes began to change in the early 20th century when Havelock Ellis published his work, questioning the conventional wisdom regarding masturbation. Kinsey's studies, which demonstrated how widespread the activity was, helped to bring it into the mainstream. During the sexual revolution of the 1960s, masturbation began to be more accepted. Today, more people accept masturbation to some extent than ever before.

© Mary Evans Picture Library/Alamy

A spermatorrhea ring.

Religious Perspectives of Masturbation

There is no single unanimous position on masturbation in the Christian, Jewish, Islamic, Buddhist, or Hindu scrip-

A 1640 legal code in Connecticut allowed for the death penalty for "blasphemers, homosexuals and masturbators."

ture (Cornog, 2003). In the Judeo-Christian tradition, masturbation generally has been condemned as sinful, mostly because of the mandate to "be fruitful and multiply." In fact, Catholic theologian St. Thomas Aquinas believed that masturbation was a worse sin than rape, incest, and adultery because in these other sins, procreation was a possibility. Many people believe that the biblical story of Onan—who "spilled his seed on the ground"—refers to masturbation. However, Onan was not punished for masturbating; he was punished because he didn't follow the Jewish custom in which a man was obligated to impregnate his brother's widow in order to continue the family line. His sin referred to *coitus interruptus,* not masturbation.

Cultural Perspectives of Masturbation

Masturbation is treated differently in different cultures. It is often reviled, sometimes treated with amusement or contempt, and at times even encouraged. Society's response to masturbation may vary depending on the age or sex of the participant, and where or when it occurs.

In 1991 Pee-wee Herman was arrested for allegedly masturbating in an X-rated movie theater. The object of numerous jokes, his show was pulled off the air, and his handprints and star were taken off the sidewalk of Hollywood Boulevard. His career has since had a comeback, although not to his previous level of success.

When former U.S. Surgeon General Joycelyn Elders stated that because masturbation was safe and healthy, it should be mentioned in school health curricula, people misinterpreted her statements to mean that she thought students should be taught how to masturbate. As a result of the ensuing public outcry, President Clinton fired her in 1994.

In an October 1993 column, Ann Landers endorsed masturbation as a safe, realistic alternative to abstinence for everyone from teens to the elderly. Although she expected to be attacked for her column, she received an avalanche of letters thanking her for her honesty and courage.

What explains the different responses to these events? Was it the time and place the event occurred? The position the individual held in the public eye and the responsibilities inherent in those positions? The difference between doing it and talking about it? What do you think?

Masturbation has come a long way from its identity as the "secret sin." In fact, nowadays the behavior is openly talked about, chuckled about, and even praised in many popular movies, TV shows, and songs. One character's emis-

© AP Images/Danny Johnston

Former U.S. Surgeon General Joycelyn Elders.

sions played a seminal role in the movie *There's Something about Mary,* and a young teen's close relationship with an apple pie is one of the most memorable scenes in *American Pie.* On TV's *Seinfeld,* Jerry, George, Elaine, and Kramer held a contest to see who could go the longest without masturbating, thus proving themselves to be "master of their domain." Self-pleasure is the main theme in songs such as the Divinyls' "I Touch Myself" and Cindy Lauper's "She Bop."

Masturbation was the core of a joke in the movie *There's Something about Mary.*

negatively correlated with sexual guilt and anxiety (Pelletier & Herold, 1988).

Fantasies provide many benefits (Maltz & Boss, 1997). They may enhance one's self-esteem and sexual interest. They can satisfy a person's curiosity about sexual activities, preserve a pleasant memory, or allow him or her to rehearse for future possibilities. Erotic thoughts can facilitate orgasm and relieve stress and tension. During fantasy, a person can try on other roles and explore situations he or she would never want to actually experience in real life. As one woman explained, "In my life, I run the show. I talk the most. I'm the loudest. In fantasy, I can shut up, lie back, and be submissive. Fantasy gives wings to my shadow self" (Maltz & Boss, 1997, p. 24). On the other hand, fantasies don't necessarily make us happy or improve our relationships; they may even get in the way of intimacy with a partner. If a person were to pursue a dangerous fantasy in actuality, he or she may be put in a risky situation.

So what do people fantasize about? The most common fantasies of both men and women involve intimate sexual imagery with past, present, or imaginary lovers (Leitenberg & Henning, 1995). Scenes of sexual power and irresistibility, varied or forbidden sexual images, and submission or dominance involving some physical force are also common. Gays and lesbians have similar fantasies as heterosexuals, except for the gender of the imagined partner. It is normal to fantasize about people other than your partner during intercourse. In one study, 98% of men and 80% of women reported sexual fantasies about someone other than their sex partner (Hicks & Leitenberg, 2001). There doesn't seem to be a connection between fantasies and sexual dissatisfaction with one's partner.

Erotic Dreams and Fantasy

The brain is often described as the largest sexual organ. Our thoughts can greatly enhance or diminish our sexual arousal and activity during masturbation or intercourse (or during a boring lecture). **Sexual fantasies** are almost any mental images that are sexually arousing to the individual (Leitenberg & Henning, 1995). These images may be stories, fleeting thoughts, bizarre or realistic images, memories of past events, or hopes for future events. Erotic images can occur spontaneously or intentionally, while the person is awake or asleep.

Erotic dreams are (usually) involuntary images that occur when we're asleep. Most females and almost all males report having erotic dreams at some time in their lives. These images alone can result in vaginal lubrication, clitoral and penile erection, and orgasm. Both males and females can have erotic dreams that result in orgasm. In males, these are called **nocturnal emissions** or **wet dreams**; however, not all erotic dreams are wet dreams, and not all wet dreams are erotic. Nocturnal emissions are most likely to occur during teenage and early adult years, but they can occur throughout one's life. Eighty-three percent of men report experiencing a wet dream at some time in their lives (Kinsey et al., 1948). In general, the less often a man masturbates, the more nocturnal emissions he will have.

Most men and women fantasize—while daydreaming, while masturbating, and during intercourse (Leitenberg & Henning, 1995). In fact, sexual fantasies are probably the most common form of human sexual expression (Ellis & Symons, 1990). The National Health and Social Life Survey found that 54% of men and 19% of women have sexual thoughts at least once a day (Laumann et al., 1994). Sexual fantasies are the most private form of sexual expression and are therefore less constrained by social pressures than other means of sexual activity (Ellis & Symons, 1990). During fantasy, people can imagine anything they want, privately, however unrealistic or socially unacceptable.

Sigmund Freud felt that "a happy person never phantasizes [sic], only an unsatisfied one" (cited in Leitenberg & Henning, 1995, p. 476.) In this case, however, Dr. Freud got it wrong because those who don't fantasize are *more* likely to experience sexual dissatisfaction and sexual dysfunction (Cado & Leitenberg, 1990). Fantasy is positively correlated with sexual arousability, orgasm frequency, and sexual satisfaction (Shulman & Horne, 2006), and

Male and Female Fantasies

In general, men are more likely to fantasize about doing something sexual to a partner, whereas women are more likely to imagine something sexual being done to them (Leitenberg & Henning, 1995). Women's fantasies tend to be more passive and romantic than men's fantasies, and focus more on the emotional aspects of the encounter such as affection and commitment (Zurbriggen & Yost, 2004). Story and context play a more central role in female fantasies, as do the setting, mood, and ambience (Ellis & Symons, 1990; Leitenberg & Henning, 1995). Women are more likely than men to fantasize about familiar partners, or about same-sex sexual activities (Sue, 1979). Women are also more likely to imagine themselves as the objects of other's sexual desire and the recipients of

Sexual fantasies Mental imagery that is sexually arousing to the individual.

Erotic dreams Dreams with an erotic content.

Nocturnal emissions Also called a "**wet dream,**" this is an ejaculation that occurs during sleep, usually during a dream.

sexual activity (Ellis & Symons, 1990; Leitenberg & Henning 1995; Maltz & Boss, 1997).

Rape fantasies are fairly common in women; more than 60% of women have had a rape fantasy (Bivona & Critelli, 2009; Pelletier & Herold, 1988; Sue, 1979). This does *not* mean that women really want to be raped! A rape fantasy is very different than an actual rape. In a fantasy, the woman is in total control of the experience. Her sexual partner is usually someone she finds sexually attractive and all his actions are done to enhance her pleasure. She is in no danger and won't experience physical harm.

Why would a woman fantasize that she is being forced to have sex? A theory from the 1970s posited that because society tells women that their sexual feelings are wrong, a rape fantasy would absolve women of responsibility in a sexual encounter (Moreault & Follingstad, 1978). This theory has not been supported because women who have sexual force fantasies generally have lower levels of sexual guilt and more positive attitudes toward sexuality (Pelletier & Herold, 1988; Shulman & Horne, 2006; Strassberg & Lockerd, 1998). Rape fantasies may actually be a fantasy of sexual power, in which the woman is so sexually desirable that men must take her (Strassberg & Lockerd, 1998).

Men fantasize more frequently than women do, and their fantasies are more active, visual, and sexually explicit (Ellis & Symons, 1990; Leitenberg & Henning, 1995; Zurbriggen & Yost, 2004). Men fantasize about having a variety of sexual experiences with attractive, eager, and willing partners. Their fantasies are more likely to involve strangers, imaginary lovers, or multiple partners (Sue, 1979). Men are more likely to view women as the objects of their sexual desire—to fantasize about a woman's body and what he wants to do to it (Ellis & Symons, 1990; Leitenberg & Henning, 1995). When fantasizing, men focus on the sexual desire and pleasure of their partner more than women do (Zurbriggen & Yost, 2004). Finally, while women are more likely to fantasize about being dominated during sex, men are more likely to fantasize about forcing someone else into various sexual activities (Leitenberg & Henning, 1995). Men who show greater acceptance of rape myths (discussed in Chapter 16) have a higher incidence of sexual dominance fantasies (Zurbriggen & Yost, 2004).

Is it normal to have a fantasy about something that you'd never ever want to happen in real life?

Sexual Practices with a Partner

After completion of this section, you will be able to . . .

○ Recognize that people define "having sex" in many ways, and that personal reasons often influence their definitions.

○ Define *foreplay, frottage, cunnilingus, fellatio, sixty-nine,* and *anilingus.*

○ Give examples of sex toys.

○ Compare and contrast some of the most commonly performed positions for vaginal intercourse.

○ Consider ways to make anal sex as safe and comfortable as possible.

What is sex? The answer is not as obvious as it may seem; in fact, there are widely divergent opinions as to which activities constitute a person having had sex. In 1991 Stephanie Sanders and June Reinisch asked 599 students what behaviors they defined as sex. Subjects were asked "would you say you 'had sex' with someone if the most intimate behavior you engaged in was . . . ?" In this study, 59% of subjects said that oral sex did not constitute having had sex with a partner; 19% responded similarly regarding anal sex. One half of 1% of the subjects did not consider vaginal intercourse to be sex, even as 2% of subjects considered deep kissing to be sex (Sanders & Reinisch, 1999). Attitudes have changed somewhat in the two decades since this survey was first performed. College students today are significantly less likely to think that oral sex and manual-genital contact count as sex. They are also slightly less likely to consider penile-vaginal intercourse to be sex, and more likely to consider deep kissing to be sex (Hans, Gillen & Akande, 2010). These differences are summarized in Figure 11.1.

The surveys referred to above and in Figure 11.1 were performed on college students. Recently, scientists repeated the

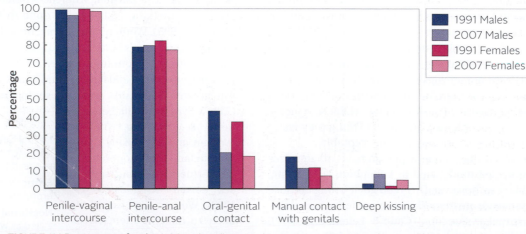

FIGURE 11.1 Percentage of male and female college students who consider that they would have "had sex" if they engaged in the listed behaviors, by year. (© Cengage Learning 2013. SOURCE: Hans et al., 2010; Sanders & Reinisch, 1999.)

survey using a representative sample. The survey respondents were 486 men and women, aged 18 to 96; responses indicated that there is no universal consensus as to which behaviors constitute "having sex" (Sanders et al., 2010). The age of the participant had a significant effect on his or her views regarding sexual behaviors. As seen in the earlier study, compared to those aged 30 to 64, 18- to 29-year-old men were less likely to consider manual and oral sex to be sex. In addition, men over 65 were less likely to regard certain sexual behaviors as sex. They were less likely to think that anal sex was sex, and less likely to think that penile-vaginal contact was sex if there was no ejaculation, if a condom was used, or if the encounter was brief. The authors of the study hypothesize that older men may view sex with an eye toward procreation, so behaviors that are less likely to result in pregnancy are not as commonly regarded as sex.

Other studies support the finding that definitions of sex vary, and that many people hold an ambiguous definition of sex (Peterson & Muehlenhard, 2007). One hundred students were asked to describe experiences that were "almost but not quite sex" or "just barely sex." Many subjects expressed ambiguity about their definitions of sex. Even when subjects were able to define sex, there were often inconsistencies between their definition of sex and their descriptions of their own behavior as sex or not sex. For example, some students who defined sex as penile-vaginal penetration and who say they had experienced that, still classified themselves as virgins. It appears

that a person's definition of sex changes based on the consequences of applying this label. For example, if the perceived outcome of having sex is negative, such as hurting one's self-image, having gone against one's religious beliefs, or having hurt a relationship, subjects will describe the activity as "not sex." If the perceived outcome is positive, such as enhanced social status, subjects may "count" an activity as sex, even if it doesn't fit in their previous definition of sex. However, while inconsistent and motivated definitions for sex can allow a person to keep his or her illusions and help his or her self-image, a person cannot "define away" risks—just because someone chooses to think that anal sex "doesn't count" as sex, the risk of STIs still exists (Peterson & Muehlenhard, 2007).

What sort of sexual activities do people experience? The possibilities are as variable as the people who partake in them. In a recent national survey, 97% of men and 98% of women between the ages of 25 and 44 reported ever having vaginal intercourse. Ninety percent of men and 89% of women reported ever having had oral sex, and 44% of men and 36% of women reported ever having experienced anal sex (Chandra, Mosher, Copen, & Sionean, 2011). Men typically have an orgasm in 85–95% of their sexual encounters, whereas women report experiencing orgasm in only 64–69% of encounters, although men and women are not always accurate in their assumption of whether their partner had an orgasm (Figures 11.2a and 11.2b). Women are more likely to reach orgasm if a sexual encounter includes manual or oral stimulation of genitals rather than just vaginal intercourse (Herbenick et al., 2010b; Richters, de Visser, Rissel, & Smith, 2006; Schick et al., 2010). In general, the more sexual practices engaged in during an encounter, the more likely it was for orgasm to occur, especially for women (Herbenick et al., 2010b).

FIGURE 11.2 Orgasm: actual occurrence and perception by partners (**a** refers to female orgasm, and **b** refers to male orgasm). (© Cengage Learning 2013. SOURCE: Schick et al., 2010; Herbenick et al., 2010.)

Foreplay

Foreplay is sexual activity including touching, cuddling, kissing, and manual- and oral-genital contact that can occur before or without intercourse. These activities are often enjoyed as ends in themselves. Some consider the word "foreplay" to be problematic because it implies that all sexual activities other than vaginal intercourse are somehow simply a prelude to "real" sex. This would lead to the misguided conclusion that gays and lesbians never have "real" sex and only experience foreplay.

People can choose to enjoy a variety of sexual activities that don't involve vaginal, oral, or anal penetration. **Outercourse**, sexual activity that does not include penetration, can include mutual masturbation, erotic massage, and **frottage** (also known as **dry humping**).

While both men and women enjoy foreplay before intercourse, the duration of and activities enjoyed during foreplay vary greatly. When Kinsey and colleagues questioned Americans of the mid-20th century about their sexual habits, the average time for foreplay was reported to be 12 minutes (Kinsey et al., 1953). As foreplay duration increased, so did the percentage of women who experienced orgasm during the encounter. Although studies in the 1970s found that couples were spending more time on foreplay, a recent study by Andrea Miller and Sandra Byers shows the duration of foreplay to be remarkably close to that of Kinsey's day (Miller & Byers, 2004). One hundred and fifty-two heterosexual couples reported both their actual and their ideal duration of foreplay and intercourse, as well as how long they thought most men and women would like foreplay to last. Men estimated the actual duration of foreplay to be longer than women did, although both men and women ideally wanted more foreplay than they actually got. When asked how long they thought most men and women would like foreplay to last, both men and women in the Miller and Byers study thought that men would want less foreplay than they actually do.

About two-thirds of people turn their heads to the right when they kiss.

Kissing

The English word *kiss* is at least 1,200 years old. It is thought that the name arose as an imitation of the sound of the kiss itself (Morris, 2004). The *Kama Sutra*—the ancient Indian treatise on the art of love—described 17 different types of kisses. The Romans characterized kisses into three different types: *oscula*, which were friendly kisses, romantic *basia* kisses, and the passionate deep *savia*. Others categorize kisses differently: by their meaning, by the part of the body kissed, or even by the sound made. Kisses are given for many reasons: One may kiss the flag or a religious relic to show respect, a mother may kiss her child's boo-boo to make it better, or a mafia don may kiss another to indicate that he has ordered his assassination.

Although any part of the body can be kissed, the mouth is the most commonly kissed part. Lips are one of the most sensitive parts of the human body, containing many nerve endings. Typically, a closed-mouth kiss can show greeting, respect, or affection, while a **French kiss**, in which the mouth is open and tongues intertwine, shows passion.

Although kissing is almost universal in Western cultures, in other cultures it is considered dangerous and disgusting. Until Western occupation after World War II, there was no Japanese word for "kissing." They have since borrowed from the English to make the word *kissu*. Sexual kissing is unknown among the Balinese, Manus, Oceania, the Thonga tribe of Africa, the Siriono of South America, and the Lepcha of Eurasia (Tiefer, 1995).

Kissing is not only fun—it may also enhance your physical and emotional health. Romantic kissing can improve your relationship satisfaction, lower blood pressure, alleviate stress, reduce levels of the stress hormone cortisol, and even decrease total blood cholesterol (Floyd et al., 2009). Remember, though, that some viral infections such as herpes and mononucleosis can be transmitted through kissing.

Manual Stimulation of the Genitals and Breasts

"Sex is not a soccer game. The use of hands is permitted."

—*Professor Carole Wade*

Touch is extremely important. When babies are given food and nourishment but aren't touched, they often become ill; some even die (Stack, 2004). Harry Harlow did a series of experiments in which baby monkeys were given a choice between two mother substitutes: a soft terrycloth "mother" that didn't provide food, and a metal one that did provide food. The baby monkeys would choose the soft terrycloth mother, and would only go to the wire monkey when they needed food. Monkeys raised with only the wire mother did not digest food as easily and had dysfunctional behaviors later in life (Harlow, Dodsworth, & Harlow, 1965). Research has shown that touch is critical for growth, development, and health in humans (Field, 2001).

Touch, of course, plays a primary role in sexuality. Areas such as the breast, vagina, clitoris, and penis that are particularly sensitive to sexual stimulation are known as *primary erogenous zones*

© David Young-Wolff/Getty Images

Foreplay Kissing, snuggling, and manual- and oral-genital contact.

Outercourse Sexual activity without penetration of the penis into the vagina, mouth, or anus.

Frottage Also known as **dry humping**, frottage involves the rubbing of your body parts against someone else's for sexual stimulation. This can be done dressed or undressed.

French kiss An open-mouthed kiss that involves the touching of both people's tongues.

Tribadism.

squeeze the testicles too hard. Some men enjoy a finger or a dildo inserted into the anus, which can stimulate the prostate gland and intensify orgasm. Friction can irritate the penis; a lubricant or a lotion can reduce chafing, but it's important to use a water-based lubricant if using a latex condom because oil-based lubricants can cause the condom to weaken and tear. During orgasm, don't push too hard on the underside of the penis because this can put pressure on the urethra, causing discomfort during ejaculation.

Sex Toys

Sex toys are devices that are used to enhance a person's sexual pleasure during masturbation or with a partner. People of all ages and orientations use sex toys, although many of these devices are illegal in some states, including Georgia, Mississippi, Alabama, and Texas. (Incidentally, the possession of firearms in these states is allowed. In fact, it is a law that all inhabitants of Kennesaw, Georgia, *must* own a gun.) It is important that sex toys be kept scrupulously clean because they can transmit STIs. Be sure to use sex toys that won't break or shatter. The safest materials are silicone, Pyrex, and stainless steel. Following are some examples of sex toys:

Manual genital stimulation.

(see Chapter 6). Stimulation of the breasts can be a source of great sexual pleasure; some women can orgasm from breast stimulation alone. Others find stimulation of the nipples uncomfortable or unsatisfying. Although men's nipples are sensitive, men are more likely to stimulate a woman's breasts than to have their own nipples touched.

Manual stimulation of the genitals can be highly arousing. Everyone differs in the way he or she likes to be touched. Some learn how to best stimulate their partner by watching him or her masturbate. Be open with your partner and communicate—either verbally or nonverbally—your likes and dislikes.

Touch doesn't need to be on the genitals to be erotic. Many people find areas such as the shoulder, neck, or knee to be very arousing. Women generally prefer that their partners caress their entire body before focusing on the genitals. Most women enjoy it when their partner strokes or rubs the labia and the clitoris. Sometimes, direct contact with the clitoral glans is too intense. The clitoris doesn't produce its own lubrication and it should not be stroked if it is dry, so make sure the area is lubricated with vaginal secretions or with a lubricant. Some women enjoy the feeling of vaginal penetration during manual stimulation (fingers should be clean and the fingernails trimmed). And some women enjoy **fisting**, the insertion of the entire hand into the vagina or rectum.

Manual stimulation is the most common sexual practice among lesbians, followed by oral sex and **tribadism**, where women rub their genitals together (although tribadism, also called "dry humping," is not exclusive to lesbians). Two women generally spend more time caressing each other's bodies before focusing on the breasts or genitals than heterosexual couples do.

Men often enjoy it when their partners caress their genitals early on in the sexual encounter. Like lesbians, gay male couples are more likely to spend more time touching their partner's entire body before stimulating the penis. Some men like their partner to use two hands: one to stroke the penis, and the other to stimulate the scrotum. Keep in mind that the glans of the penis is more sensitive than the base, and care should be taken to not

- **Dildos** are penis-shaped objects that penetrate the vagina or rectum. They can have a single or a double head.
- **Ben Wa balls** are hollow metal balls that are inserted into the vagina. As they roll around, they enhance sexual arousal and orgasm.
- **Vibrators** come in all shapes and sizes. Some are designed to arouse the clitoris and vagina, others are angled to best stimulate the G-spot, and others are inserted into the anus. The "jack rabbit," which has a separate stimulator for the clitoris, is a popular model of vibrator. It is designed to vaguely resemble a rabbit so it may be sold as an "entertainment device" rather than a sex toy.
- Shaped like a vagina or anus, and made of a soft silicone gel, **pocket pussies** are designed for a man to masturbate into them.

Fisting The insertion of the fist or hand into the rectum or vagina. Typically, the clenched fist is not inserted; instead, the fingers are kept flat and as close together as possible. This is more often practiced among lesbians and gay male couples.

Tribadism A form of non-penetrative sex in which two women rub their vulvas together.

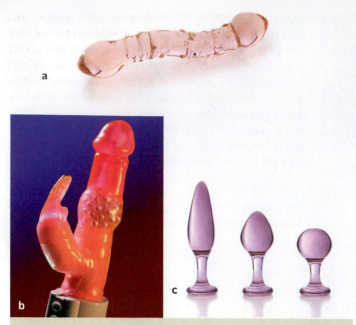

Some common sex toys: (a) a double-headed dildo, (b) a vibrator, and (c) butt plugs. (© maxstock2/Alamy; © Steve Allen/Alamy; © maxstock/Alamy)

- **Cock rings** are placed on the base of the penis. In some cases, the testicles can be restrained as well. The tight ring prevents the blood from leaving the penis, thus helping to maintain erection.
- **Nipple clamps** fasten tightly to the nipples, and are often used in bondage and domination activities.
- A **butt plug** is a short dildo that is inserted into the anus. The base is flared to keep it from becoming lodged in the rectum.

Oral Sex

Cunnilingus is the term that describes oral stimulation of the female genitals, and **fellatio** is oral stimulation of the penis. Cunnilingus is sometimes called "going down" on a woman; slang terms for fellatio include "giving head" and "blow job." Oral sex can be performed on one person at a time, or two people can simultaneously orally stimulate each other's genitals, in an activity called "**sixty-nine**." Sixty-nine can be

Cunnilingus Oral stimulation of the female genitals.

Fellatio Oral stimulation of the male genitals.

Sixty-nine Simultaneous oral-genital stimulation.

Anilingus Oral stimulation of the anus, also known as "rimming."

a challenging sexual position: both participants must be of a similar height and fairly flexible. Simultaneous oral-genital contact may not be as sexually stimulating due to the inherent physical challenges and because one must focus on giving pleasure rather than solely on receiving it. **Anilingus**, also known as "rimming," is oral stimulation of the anus. When performing anilingus, hygiene is very important in order to prevent the transmission of intestinal infections or hepatitis. HIV and other STIs can be transmitted through oral contact with the genitals or anus.

The rates of oral sex have increased over the years. In Kinsey's study, 60% of married, college-educated couples reported that they had ever engaged in oral sex. Today, 81% of males and 80% of females between the ages of 15 and 44 have engaged in oral-genital contact (Chandra et al., 2011). Men and women are more likely to say that they have ever received oral sex than have given oral sex (Herbenick et al., 2010a; Laumann et al., 1994).

Caucasian men and women are significantly more likely to report having given or received oral sex than are blacks or Hispanics (Laumann et al., 1994; Mosher, Chandra, & Jones, 2005). In a survey of more than 12,000 Americans aged 15 to 44, 88% of whites, 75% of blacks, and 68% of Hispanics said that they had ever engaged in oral sex (Mosher et al., 2005). However, in the recent NSSHB survey (Dodge et al., 2010), Hispanic men and women were more likely to report giving and receiving oral sex in the past year than blacks or Caucasians were.

The incidence of oral sex increases with a person's education level. Other factors that are positively correlated with oral sex are higher self-esteem, ever having masturbated, emotional involvement with a partner, and frequency of church attendance (Herold & Way, 1983; Mahoney, 1980).

When performing cunnilingus, it is best to start slow and don't immediately stimulate the clitoris. Licking or sucking the labia minora and the vestibule can be highly arousing. When the

A painting by Édouard-Henri Avril depicting the life of Sappho.

Ancient Times, plate XIII from 'De Figuris Veneris' by F.K Forberg, engraved by the artist, 1900 (litho) by Avril, Edouard-Henri (Paul) (1849–1928) Private Collection/The Stapleton Collection/The Bridgeman Art Library

woman is aroused, use circular or back-and-forth movements on or around the clitoris. The tongue can be firm and pointed to arouse a precise area, or wider to softly stimulate a larger area. Some women like a finger or tongue inserted into the vagina during cunnilingus.

When performing fellatio, one can lick or suck the glans or shaft of the penis either gently or vigorously. It is not necessary to perform deep throat—taking the entire penis into the mouth. Instead, a person can use one hand on the lower part of the shaft while stimulating the glans and upper part of the penis. Some men also like their scrotum to be stimulated, either with the mouth or the hands. While performing oral sex, teeth should be covered because the penis and testicles are very sensitive! Men, do not hold down your partner's head while he or she is performing oral sex on you. The lack of control can not only be frightening for them, but may stimulate their gag reflex, which would certainly dampen the sexual excitement of the moment. It is a personal decision whether to spit out or swallow the semen after the man ejaculates, or to remove one's mouth before he has an orgasm. Swallowing semen isn't harmful if your partner is free from STIs and is HIV negative. Some foods change the taste of the ejaculate. Coffee and alcohol can make it bitter, fruits can make semen taste sweet, and red meat and dairy can make the ejaculate more sour and acidic tasting.

Not everyone is comfortable receiving or performing oral sex. Some do not like the smell or taste of the genitals, or are afraid that their partner would be offended by their odor. Many women are uncomfortable about their vaginas and may feel their partner shares their discomfort and doesn't want to "go down on them." Their anxiety may decrease their sexual enjoyment of the act. Men may be afraid that their partner does not like the taste of their semen. However, many men and women enjoy performing cunnilingus and fellatio and find the taste and smell and appearance of the vulva and penis to be erotic.

Fellatio.

The missionary position.

feeling in the vagina. The penis should not be inserted until the vagina is lubricated, either by natural or applied lubrication, or coitus can be uncomfortable for both the man and the woman. While some prefer hard fast thrusting, others prefer slow and intimate intercourse—communicate your desires to your partner, either verbally or nonverbally. Most women don't achieve orgasm from vaginal penetration alone because the vagina is fairly insensitive and it is the clitoris that contains most of the nerve endings in the vulva. Most women need clitoral stimulation for orgasm during sexual contact.

Positions

Sexual positions are limited only by one's imagination and flexibility. The *Kama Sutra* describes dozens of sexual stances, and *The New Joy of Sex* lists 112 different positions for vaginal intercourse. We will describe some of the more commonly performed positions.

Male on top, woman supine. The **missionary position** is the most commonly used position in the United States (Dizon, Partridge, Amsterdam, & Krychman, 2009). In the missionary position, the woman lies on her back with her knees bent and legs spread while the man enters her from above. The man usually supports himself on his hands and knees, and the woman may wrap her legs around the man's waist or put them over his shoulders. The man generally controls the speed and depth of penile thrusts. The man-on-top position allows the woman to stroke her partner's body, and allows the participants to face each other. This position may be particularly effective for those couples hoping to get pregnant because the semen doesn't leak out of the woman's vagina as easily. A disadvantage to the missionary position is that it may be harder for a woman to have an orgasm because her clitoris is not always stimulated, and she has less control over the angle and depth of penetration. The man may be less able to control his ejaculation, and may become fatigued after supporting his body weight on his arms. This position may also be difficult if one partner is obese or pregnant, or if the man has a particularly large penis.

Female on top, man supine.
In this position, the man lies on his back while the woman sits or lies on top of him, facing either his head or his feet. In this way, the woman has more control over the angle, depth, and speed of penile

According to an old law that is still on the books, sexual positions other than the missionary position are illegal in Washington, D.C.

Vaginal Intercourse

Vaginal intercourse, or **coitus**, is sexual activity in which the erect penis is inserted into the vagina. One or both partners move their hips, which thrusts the penis partially in and out of the vagina, causing friction on the penis and a pleasurable

Coitus (CO-ih-tus) Another word for vaginal intercourse, where the penis is inserted into the vagina.

Missionary position Vaginal intercourse with the man on top and the woman lying on her back.

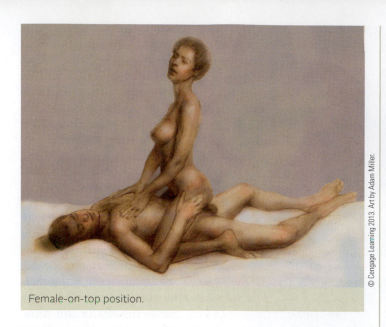

Female-on-top position.

Rear-entry position, also known as "doggie style."

thrusting and the man's hands are free to caress the woman's body and clitoris, making it more likely for a woman to achieve orgasm. In the female-superior position, the man doesn't have to support his weight, and it's easier for him to control ejaculation. Some women are uncomfortable with this position because their bodies are more visible to the man, or because of the depth of penetration. Some people also find that this position makes it more difficult to keep the penis in the vagina during thrusting.

Side by side. When engaging in sexual intercourse, a man and woman may lie side by side and face each other. This position gives less physical strain because both partners are lying down and neither has to support their own weight for long periods of time. Both partners can control the thrusting motions, and hands are free to caress each other. However, penetration can be awkward and not as deep.

Side-by-side position.

Rear entry. In the "doggie style" position, the woman kneels on her hands and knees while the man enters her vagina from behind. The woman can also lie on her belly and arch her back as the man enters her from the rear. This position allows for deep penetration and more direct stimulation of the clitoris and G-spot. The man can caress the woman's body and clitoris as he thrusts. The rear-entry position is also good when the woman is obese or in the later stages of pregnancy. It can, however, be hard to maintain the angle of insertion and the penis can be more easily dislodged from the vagina. Sexual partners don't face each other in the rear-entry position, which may lead to a sense of

emotional distance. The position can also produce some fairly strange and sometimes embarrassing noises.

Other positions. Participants need to have both good balance and flexibility to have sex while standing up. Some find this position erotic, although others find it difficult to keep the penis in the vagina and maintain deep thrusting. When both partners are seated, the man may sit on a chair or bed while the woman sits on his erect penis with her legs either on the floor or around his waist. Two people may have intercourse as the woman reclines on a bed or chair with her feet on the floor, as the man enters her while standing or kneeling.

Anal Sex and Other Forms of Intercourse

People may engage in intercourse in which the penis is not inserted into the vagina. In **femoral coitus** the man thrusts his

Variations in sexual positions are limited only by one's imagination and flexibility.

penis between his partner's thighs, or in **mammary coitus**, between a woman's breasts. **Anal intercourse** is when the penis is inserted into a man's or a woman's anus and rectum, an area highly innervated with nerve endings. Although there is a perception that anal sex is a gay male activity, not all gay men engage in anal sex. Anal sex is less common among gay men than oral and manual sex, and 20% of gay men report not practicing anal sex at all (Laumann et al., 1994). In fact, in a recent national survey, anal sex was significantly more likely to be reported by heterosexual men than by gay or bisexual men (Chandra et al., 2011). Anal sex is becoming more common than in the past; in the 1990s, fewer than 10% of adult men and women reported having engaged in anal intercourse in the past year (Laumann et al., 1994), but recent studies show that greater than 20% of men and women in their 20s and 30s have had anal sex at least once in the past year (Herbenick et al., 2010a). Recent reports suggest that up to 44% of heterosexual men report ever having had anal sex with their female partners (Chandra et al., 2011; Herbenick et al., 2010a; McBride & Fortenberry, 2010).

"Queef": A slang term describing the flatulent sound caused by the release of air from the vagina.

Anal sex is one of the riskiest of all sexual behaviors, as the rectal tissues are easily torn. HIV and STIs are more easily transmitted through anal intercourse than through oral or vaginal sex. However, condom use during anal sex is actually less likely than during vaginal intercourse (McBride & Fortenberry, 2010). During anal sex, it is also important to use an external lubricant to prevent tissue tearing because the anus doesn't produce its own lubrication. After anal intercourse, you should wash the penis (or remove and change condoms) before having vaginal or oral sex.

Sexual Activity Across the Life Span

After completion of this section, you will be able to . . .

O Understand that people of all ages express themselves sexually.

O Differentiate between normal and potentially problematic sexual expression during childhood.

O List the factors that influence the age at which a person first has intercourse.

O Recognize the changing perceptions of oral and anal sex among teens.

O Identify the factors that are correlated with a person's frequency of sexual activity.

O Evaluate the discrepancy between the number of partners reported by heterosexual males and females.

O Explain some of the physical changes that occur sexually as people age.

O Describe some of the specific sexual challenges faced by those with physical and mental disabilities.

Sexual Activity in Childhood

Although many people think of childhood as a time of "innocence," children show a broad range of sexual behaviors. According to parents' reports, 2- to 5-year-olds frequently masturbate and touch their genitals in public and at home, touch their mother's breasts, try to look at people when they're nude, and expose their sex parts to adults (Friedrich, Fisher, Broughton, Houston, & Shafran, 1998). Parents report fewer observations of these behaviors as children age; this is in part due to the fact that parents have less ability to observe their children as they get older, and also because as children learn modesty, they hide their sexual activities more. Children between the ages of 6 and 9 exhibit fewer sexual behaviors than younger children, but still touch their genitals at home, and try to look at people when they are nude or undressing. Sexual activity increases again once children turn 11 or 12, as their interest in the opposite sex and their attempts to view naked people increase (Friedrich et al., 1998).

We are all born with the biological foundations of sexuality, but our social environment largely influences how it's expressed. Context is very important. Imagine two 4-year-old boys, Luis and Leon. Luis is found masturbating by his mother, who slaps his hand and shrieks, "Bad, bad, bad!" When Leon is discovered masturbating, his mother sits down with him and says, "That feels good, doesn't it? But that's something that people do in private." Luis and Leon will have learned a very different lesson about sexuality. In both cases, the action was the same, but the feelings, associations, and expression that will result may be very different.

It is important to remember that what may be considered a sexual act among adults may not be sexual for children. When a small boy and girl "play doctor" and take off each other's clothes, although their parents may impart a sexual context to the action, perhaps the children were simply curious about the differences between a boy's body and a girl's body. Many sexual behaviors in children are often more closely linked to sensuality and attachment, rather than to passion and eroticism (Thanasiu, 2004).

There is, however, a correlation between the frequency of childhood sexual behaviors and sexual abuse (Kendall-Tackett, Williams, & Finkelhor, 1993). So how can a parent determine if a child's sexual behavior is normal or problematic? Sexual play in children who have been abused tends to be more sophisticated and compulsive. Children who have been sexually abused may show sexual knowledge or act in ways that are more consistent with adult sexual behavior (Thanasiu, 2004). They may experiment sexually with children who are not their normal playmates, or who are not within a year of their developmental or chronological age. Also, normal sexual behaviors don't typically cause emotional or physical discomfort to the child, so if the young person is showing guilt, anxiety, or shame of his or her sexuality, this may be a cause for alarm (Thanasiu, 2004).

Age at First Intercourse

The median age for first intercourse in the United States is 17.7 years for boys and 17.4 years for girls (Santelli et al., 2006). On average, African

Femoral coitus When the penis is thrust between a partner's thighs.

Mammary coitus The man rubs his penis between his partner's breasts.

Anal intercourse The insertion of the penis into the anus.

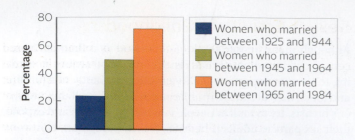

FIGURE 11.3 Percentage of women in the United States who lost their virginity before marriage. (© Cengage Learning 2013. SOURCE: Whyte, 1990.)

American teenagers have intercourse for the first time by age 15.8, whites by 16.6, Hispanics by age 17, and Asian Americans by 18.1 (Upchurch, Levy-Storms, Sucoff, & Aneshensel, 1998). By age 20, 66% of men and 62% of women have had vaginal intercourse (Chandra et al., 2011). Surveys suggest that teenagers are waiting longer to have intercourse than in the past, although the decline in sexual experience may be greater for teenage boys than for teenage girls. This may be due to increased abstinence, or because teens today are less likely to admit to intercourse.

A **purity pledge** is an oral or written promise to refrain from sexual activity, usually until marriage. This vow is often taken as part of a religious youth group event. By 1995, 12% of all teenagers (an estimated 2.2 million people) had taken a vow to abstain from sex until marriage (Bruckner & Bearman, 2005). However, 88% of those who promised to remain virginal until marriage broke that vow and had premarital intercourse (Bruckner & Bearman, 2005).

A 2005 study suggested that teens that take a purity pledge have fewer sex partners than those who do not vow abstinence (Bruckner & Bearman, 2005). But this study compared those who took a purity pledge with *all* non-pledgers. Pledgers tend to be more religious, more conservative, and have more negative attitudes about sex and birth control. When the activity of adolescent purity pledgers was compared with non-pledgers who matched them in these characteristics, it was found that pledgers were just as likely to have premarital sex as non-pledgers, and didn't differ in age of first intercourse (Rosenbaum, 2009).

Those who had taken a virginity pledge also were less likely to use a condom than those who had not taken a vow. It may be that those who make a public promise to remain virgins until marriage are less educated in the realities of condom use, or that using a condom would show premeditation to the sexual act. Pledgers were 4 times more likely to partake in anal sex and 6 times more likely to partake in oral sex compared to all non-pledgers, but showed no significant differences in these activities when compared to matched controls (Bruckner & Bearman, 2005; Rosenbaum, 2009). In one recent study, 6% of teens who said they had never had penile-vaginal intercourse tested positive for a sexually transmitted infection (DiClemente, Sales, Danner, & Crosby, 2011). Unfortunately, those who had taken a purity pledge were less likely to obtain STI-related health care, and were less likely to be aware of their STI-positive status. It may be unsurprising to note that when questioned 5 years after pledging, 82% of pledgers denied ever having made a purity vow (Rosenbaum, 2009).

In the past, most women waited until marriage to have intercourse. Today, premari-

Purity pledge A promise to refrain from sexual activity until marriage.

tal sex is the norm rather than the exception (Figure 11.3; Finer, 2007; Whyte, 1990).

Compared to past generations, teenagers today are more likely to report using contraceptives during their first intercourse. Unfortunately, 26% of females and 18% of males aged 15 to 19 use no contraception at their first intercourse (Abma, Martinez, Mosher, & Dawson, 2004). The older a person is the first time they have intercourse, the more likely they are to use contraception at first intercourse. A media survey of television shows that depicted scenes of first-time sex found that in the 20 scenes of first-time sex, only in 1 was there mention of any risks or responsibilities in the same scene (Kunkel, Eyal, Finnerty, Biely, & Donnerstein, 2005).

Although more teens are waiting longer to have sex, some are engaging in coitus at an earlier age. In 2002, 13% of girls aged 14 and younger had reported having had intercourse (Abma et al., 2004). Sadly, between 10% and 13% of these girls are forced into intercourse their first time (Abma et al., 2004; Mosher et al., 2005). Coercive sex will be further explored in Chapter 16.

Society views first intercourse differently for males and females. Most describe a woman's first time as a loss—"losing her virginity"—while men are described as having gained something—having "gotten some." Former Surgeon General Joycelyn Elders said, "We train our girls to be virgins, but we want our young men to be studs. And I wonder whom we think our studs are having sex with" (Elders, 1998, p. 15).

What Factors Influence Someone to Initiate Intercourse?

Factors that are associated with initiation of intercourse among virgins include having older friends, getting low grades, engaging in deviant behaviors such as cheating on tests or breaking into homes or businesses, and sensation-seeking behaviors. Teens who are more religious, live with both parents, and who have parents who would disapprove if their teen had sex have a lower probability of intercourse initiation (Collins et al., 2004). Parental monitoring also lowers a teen's probability of first-time sex, although parents aren't always as aware as they think they are about the activities of their children (Young & Zimmerman, 1998). A group of 140 seventh- and eighth-grade boys and girls and their parents were asked whether the children had ever used tobacco, smoked pot, used alcohol, or had intercourse; the percentages of parents and children responding "yes" are shown in Figure 11.4.

Even the type of music you listen to may influence your sexual behavior. Steven Martino and colleagues surveyed 1,461 teenaged boys and girls over a 3-year period. When first surveyed, most of the subjects were virgins. Upon follow-up interviews 1 and 3 years later, the teens who had listened to more music with a sexually degrading message were more likely to have had intercourse and to have participated in non-coital sexual activities. The study controlled for factors such as race, religion, and parental involvement. Sexually degrading content included explicit references to sexual acts in which women were valued merely for their appearance and men for their ability as sexual machines (Martino et al., 2006).

Some factors, such as self-esteem and sports participation, influence male and female adolescents differently. Adolescent boys with high self-esteem are more likely to have

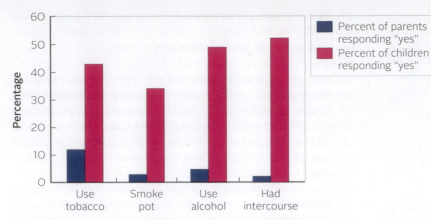

FIGURE 11.4 Parents' awareness of sex and drug use in their children. (© Cengage Learning 2013. SOURCE: Young & Zimmerman, 1998.)

Sexual Activity in Teens

Masturbation, not intercourse or other partnered sexual behaviors, is the most characteristic sexual behavior of adolescents (Fortenberry et al., 2010; Figure 11.5). In a recent survey, 46% of all high school students had ever had sex, a decrease since 1991, when 54% of high school students reported having had sex (Eaton et al., 2010). Most of this decline occurred between 1991 and 2001; in fact, rates have increased slightly since then (see Table 11.1), a rise that corresponds with the increase in federal support of abstinence-only education (Eaton et al., 2006; Eaton et al., 2010). The rates of intercourse in teens are highly dependent on age: while 53–66% of 18- and 19-year-olds have had sex, only 30-33% of 16- and 17-year-olds and about 10% of those aged 14 and 15 have had vaginal intercourse (Chandra et al., 2011; Fortenberry et al., 2010).

sex, but teenage girls with *low* self-esteem are more likely to have sex. Participation in competitive sports makes teenage boys more likely to be sexually active, while sporty adolescent girls are *less* likely to be sexually active and less likely to have unwanted pregnancies (Sabo, Miller, Farrell, Melnick, & Barnes, 1999).

As the rates of vaginal intercourse have decreased, more students are having oral and anal sex (see Table 11.2). Although in the past oral sex was viewed as a more intimate experience than vaginal sex, today many teens view it as no big deal.

Forty-seven percent of 15- to 19-year-olds have had oral sex with someone of the opposite sex (Chandra et al., 2011) and 11% of teens have had anal sex (Lindberg, Jones, & Santelli, 2008). Adolescents also experience oral sex at an earlier age than in the past. In a survey of ninth-graders, almost 20% had had oral sex, and 13.5% had experienced vaginal intercourse (Halpern-Felsher, Cornell, Kropp, & Tschann, 2005). These adolescents perceived oral sex to be less risky, more prevalent, and more socially acceptable than vaginal sex. Although oral sex does provide a lower risk of infection, STIs such herpes, gonorrhea, syphilis, and

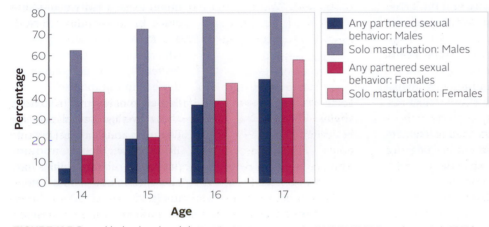

FIGURE 11.5 Sexual behaviors in adolescents. (© Cengage Learning 2013. SOURCE: Fortenberry et al., 2010.)

Table 11.1 Changing Trends in Sexual Activity of High School Students in the United States

		1991	2001	2005	2009
Percentage of high school students who have ever had intercourse	**All**	54.1%	45.6%	46.8%	46%
	Female	50.8%	42.9%	45.7%	45.7%
	Male	57.4%	48.5%	47.9%	46.1%
Percentage of high school students who had intercourse with more than four people	**All**	18.7%	14.2	14.3%	13.8%
	Female	13.8%	11.4%	12%	11.2%
	Male	23.4%	17.2%	16.5%	16.2%
Percentage of high school students who used a condom at last intercourse	**All**	46.2%	57.9%	62.8%	61%
	Female	38%	51.3%	55.9%	53.9%
	Male	54.5%	65.1%	70%	68.6%

© Cengage Learning 2013. SOURCE: Eaton et al., 2006, 2010.

Table 11.2 Sexual Activity of Teens in the United States

	15- TO 17-YEAR-OLDS		18- TO 19-YEAR-OLDS	
	MALES	**FEMALES**	**MALES**	**FEMALES**
Vaginal intercourse	31.8%	33%	65.6%	61.7%
Gave oral sex	22.5%	25.1%	54.8%	53.2%
Received oral sex	33.4%	26.8%	67.9%	58.2%
Had anal sex	6.2%	7.0%	16.6%	14.9%
No sexual contact	52.6%	58.2%	22.9%	28.0%

© Cengage Learning 2013. SOURCE: Chandra et al., 2005.

HIV can still be transmitted through oral-genital contact. Among adolescents, there are fewer who recognize that they are at risk of STI and HIV transmission through oral sex than those who recognize vaginal sex infection risk: in one study, only 68% of adolescents thought they could get HIV from oral sex, and in another study, 14% of students estimated their risk factor for getting HIV or chlamydia through oral sex as zero (Boekeloo & Howard, 2002).

Oral sex and anal sex were more common among white teens and in households with a higher socioeconomic status (SES). Vaginal sex was more common among nonwhite teens and among those from lower SES households (Lindberg et al., 2008).

Fortunately, high school students are increasingly likely to use contraception (Eaton et al., 2010; Terry & Manlove, 2001). In 1991, 46% of students reported using a condom the last time they had intercourse; in 2009, that number increased to 61%; and by 2010, 80% of males reported using a condom during their last intercourse (Fortenberry et al., 2010). Still, condom use is not as common or regular as it should be: only 25–33% of college students report consistent condom use (Desiderato & Crawford, 1995; Eisenberg, 2001).

Sexual Activity in Adults

How often? How long? How many? Men and women often wonder how their sexual behaviors compare to others.

How Often Do People Have Sex?

In the early 1990s the World Health Organization estimated that intercourse occurred about 42,000 million times per year, which breaks down to about 1,300 ejaculations per second (WHO, 1992). However, like money, sex is not equally distributed across the population! About 15% of adults engage in half of all sexual activity, and 20% of adults in the United States report having had no sex at all in the previous year (Robinson & Godbey, 1998). About one-third of Americans have intercourse at least twice a week, one-third have sex a few times a month, and one-third have sex a few times a year or not at all (Laumann et al., 1994); the national average is about once a week (Robinson & Godbey, 1998).

Many factors are correlated with a person's frequency of sexual activity, including age, marital status, education, political leanings, and even music preferences.

- *Age:* Kinsey's surveys showed an inverse relationship between age and the frequency of sexual intercourse. That finding is still true today. Men and women between the ages of 18 and 29 reported having sex 84 times per year; 40- to 49-year-olds just over 63 times a year; and by the time a person reaches his or her 60s, the frequency of sex falls to 27 times per year (Smith, 1998).
- *Marital status:* Though there may be a perception that many married people never have sex, married people actually have more sex than single people.
- *Education:* Those with some college education have the highest frequency of sex, while those who have advanced degrees report less sexual activity. So as not to discourage students from attending graduate school due to fears of future celibacy, it may be that those with advanced degrees are more honest in reporting their sexual activity, or more rigorous in defining what "counts" as sex (Robinson & Godbey, 1998).

Jazz enthusiasts are 30% more sexually active than the average person (Robinson & Godbey, 1998).

- *Politics:* Those who define themselves as liberal engage in more sexual activity than moderates or conservatives. Sexual activity is highest among those who characterize themselves as "extremely liberal," although those who call themselves "extremely conservative" also have above average sexual activity. Robinson and Godbey (1998, p. 19) propose, "People who are passionate about politics are also passionate about other things."
- *Sexual orientation:* Lesbians in long-term relationships have sex less frequently than gay male or heterosexual couples (Nichols, 1990). However, as mentioned in previous chapters, many studies show that lesbians have greater sexual satisfaction in their intimate relationships than heterosexuals do. Lesbians and gay men tend to take more time and have more non-genital contact than heterosexual couples. Compared to heterosexual women, lesbians are more likely to orgasm, to receive oral sex, and to have sex that lasts more than an hour (Lever, 1995).
- *Religion:* Jews and agnostics report more sex than Catholics. Protestants report the lowest levels of sexual activity (Robinson & Godbey, 1998).
- *Free time:* Those who work 60 hours a week or more are *more* sexually active than other workers (Robinson & Godbey, 1998). Those who watch more TV, especially PBS, are also more sexually active.

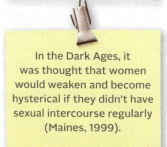

In the Dark Ages, it was thought that women would weaken and become hysterical if they didn't have sexual intercourse regularly (Maines, 1999).

critical
evaluation

Why do heterosexual men report more sexual partners than heterosexual women?

> **What was the sample population?** This information comes from national surveys of thousands of Americans. However, not only is not every person questioned about their sexual activities, entire groups of people such as prisoners, the institutionalized population, and the homeless are typically left out. Also, men may be underreporting their visits to prostitutes, who are not covered by national surveys (Brewer et al., 2000).

> **What was the research design?** The format of the survey could influence subjects' responses. Are the surveys anonymous? Are subjects interviewed, or do they write their answers on a computer? Do subjects understand what they are being asked? Subjects' responses can be influenced by something as seemingly

innocuous as the sex of the researcher. When questioned by female research assistants (but not by male assistants), some men reported more sexual partners when they were told that women are now more sexually permissive than men. This was mostly seen in men who scored high in hypermasculinity and ambivalent sexism (Fisher, 2007).

> **What is the definition of "sex"?** It may be that men and women differ in who they consider to be a sexual partner. Perhaps women only count sexual experiences that include vaginal intercourse, and men use a broader definition of sex when counting their partners.

> **How honest are the responses?** Many think that men over-report and women under-report their sexual activity in order to fulfill

societal expectations. Alexander and Fisher (2003) gave written sexual surveys to their subjects under three conditions. In one, subjects were alone in a room taking an anonymous survey. In another, subjects took their survey while a student worker was nearby and potentially able to see their answers. In the last condition, subjects were attached to a (fake) lie detector, which they thought would detect any false answers. When female subjects thought that others would see their answers, they reported fewer sexual partners than males. However, when they thought they were hooked up to lie detectors, females actually reported more partners than the men.

> **How do men and women arrive at their answers?** Perhaps men and women

estimate their number of partners differently. Brown and Sinclair (1999) suggest that women are more likely to think about the individual incidents of sex, a method that leads to underestimation because relevant instances may be forgotten. Men, however, are more likely to give a rough approximation of partners, which tends to lead to overestimation.

Although most scientists recognize that projections concerning the number of partners of men and women are problematic at best, and false at worst, research on the topic continues to be published and promoted, thereby reinforcing the stereotype of the promiscuous male and the chaste female (Kolata, 2007).

Length of Intercourse

Seventy-five percent of the men in Kinsey's study reported that sexual intercourse lasted less than 2 minutes (Kinsey et al., 1948). Since Kinsey's day, the reported duration of intercourse has increased. In a study of 152 heterosexual couples who described their actual and ideal duration of foreplay and intercourse, the average duration of intercourse was approximately 7 minutes (Miller & Byers, 2004). Both men and women wanted intercourse to last at least twice as long as it actually did. Although some people may think that a quick orgasm is the goal of sexual interactions, adherents of Hinduism, Buddhism, and Taoism believe that sexual energy should be prolonged and couples should maintain their sacred communion as long as possible.

Number of Partners

With how many people has the average American had sexual intercourse? Recent large-scale surveys show that adult men report an average of 5.1–8.0 female partners over the course of a lifetime, and adult women report an average of 3.2–4.0 (Chandra et al., 2011; Fryar et al., 2007; Mosher et al., 2004). About 3% of both men and women report no sexual partners since the age of 18 (Laumann et al., 1994), and about 21% of all men and 8% of all women say that they have had more than 15 other-sex sex partners (Chandra et al., 2011). Black men and women were most likely to have had more than 15 sexual partners, followed by whites, and then by Hispanics (Chandra et al., 2011; Fryar et al., 2007).

Astute readers will have noticed a problem in the preceding paragraph: it is logically impossible for heterosexual men to have more female partners on average than heterosexual women

have male partners. When a heterosexual man is having sex with a woman, a heterosexual woman is having sex with a man, so the averages should be the same. What factors explain this discrepancy? See the Critical Evaluation box for some possible answers to this question.

Sexual Activity Later in Life

Over the course of the 20th–21st centuries, the rate of growth of the elderly population (people 65 years old and older) has exceeded the growth rate of the rest of the population. Although the total population tripled between 1900 and 1994, the elderly population increased by a factor of 11. Whereas in 1994 12% of Americans were elderly, the U.S. Census Bureau projects that by the year 2030, about 20% of the U.S. population will be over age 65 (Vincent & Velkoff, 2010).

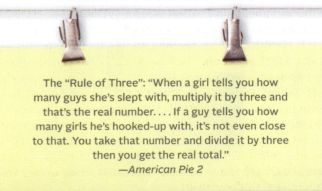

The "Rule of Three": "When a girl tells you how many guys she's slept with, multiply it by three and that's the real number. . . . If a guy tells you how many girls he's hooked-up with, it's not even close to that. You take that number and divide it by three then you get the real total."
—*American Pie 2*

Our bodies change as we age. After a woman goes through menopause, her levels of estrogen decrease, causing her vagina to shorten and narrow. The vaginal walls will thin, become less elastic, and lose some lubrication. Age-related changes occur more gradually in males, but after about age 50, men experience more erectile dysfunction and impotence. Erections may be less firm and take longer to occur. Men may produce less sperm and less semen and have a longer refractory period between orgasms. In both men and women, orgasm spasms become less powerful and fewer in number. However, the experience of orgasm remains pleasurable.

Aging does not mean the end of one's sexual life. As people get older, some become less interested in sex or less sexually active or responsive, but others enjoy sex more because they have a deeper understanding of their partner and of themselves, and no more fears of pregnancy. A survey of more 3,000 adults between the ages of 57 and 85 showed that sexual activity did decline with age, but that this was more a factor of overall health than of age itself (Figure 11.6; Lindau et al., 2007). For all subjects aged 57 to 85, the women were less sexually active than men, perhaps because women were more likely to be without a partner, or to have a partner (usually older than they are) who was in poor health. About half of the sexually active couples under 75 reported that they had oral sex (Lindau et al., 2007). Among those who were still sexually active, about half the subjects reported at least one sexual problem. The most common problems among women in the Lindau study included low desire, difficulty with vaginal lubrication, and an inability to orgasm. More than a third of the men had erectile difficulties. However, few of these people (38% of men and 22% of women) reported having discussed sex with a phy-

Older sexually active individuals must remember that they are not immune from STIs—1 in every 10 people diagnosed with AIDS in the United States is over 50.

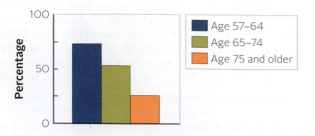

FIGURE 11.6 Percentage of older Americans who are still sexually active, by age. (© Cengage Learning 2013. SOURCE: Lindau et al, 2007.)

sician since the age of 50. Elderly people who live in nursing homes or assisted living facilities may have an additional burden placed on their sex lives. The lack of privacy and stringent rules about "appropriate" behavior between residents can make sexual expression particularly complicated. A 2009 survey of 81 nursing homes found that one-third of the staff reacted with disgust to residents' sexual expressions (Melby, 2010).

But it's not all bad news! Peggy Kleinplatz and colleagues interviewed men and women over 60 who had been in relationships of 25 years or longer, and who self-reported experiencing optimal sexuality (Kleinplatz et al., 2009a). Although many people don't think of the elderly as sexual sages, couples who have made good sex last a lifetime are a valuable resource. The men and women in this study reported that their perceptions of optimal sexuality have changed over time. They found that sex got better with time, and that it became greater as it became slower, less goal-directed, and less orgasm-focused. As one subject said, "The great relief of sexual urges is not the same as great sex." About half of couples interviewed were openly non-monogamous, and some degree of consensual polyamory was built into their primary partnerships.

Sexuality and Disability

Imagine that it was decreed that only people who looked like Brad Pitt and Angelina Jolie could be considered sexual; anyone younger or older, fatter or thinner, or more or less attractive was regarded as asexual. Most of us would take issue with that—just because we don't look like a celebrity does not mean that we don't have sexual needs and desires. The same is true of people with disabilities. Most people with physical or mental disabilities have sexual feelings, yet are often treated as though they do not. Disabled adults express their sexuality in as many diverse ways as those without disabilities.

Disabled people may face psychological, physical, and social obstacles in achieving a satisfying sex life. Not only are there almost no images in the media of disabled people being sexual, but society's ideas of beauty can negatively impact disabled people's body image and self-esteem. Physical challenges may limit their mobility or sexual functioning. Some of those who have lived with a disability since a young age may have been socially isolated during their formative years, when young people are first establishing their sexual identity and learning how to flirt and date (Shuttleworth, 2000). Also, parents can unconsciously send negative messages about the possibility of a sex life and romance in their disabled children's future, and physicians aren't always forthcoming with sexual advice. Over the course of their training, most medical students receive fewer than 10 hours of sexuality education, the majority of it concerned with erectile dysfunction (Solursh et al., 2003). Consequently, doctors are often more comfortable discussing death and disease than their patients' sex lives. Patients—disabled or otherwise—may need to initiate discussions with their physician about any sexual concerns, or seek alternate sources of information.

Spinal Cord Injuries

The spinal cord carries signals between the brain and the rest of the body. When the spinal cord is damaged or severed, a person may lose voluntary control or sensation. The extent of the damage depends on the site and severity of the injury. There are approximately 250,000 people in the United States with spinal cord injuries (SCI); 10,000 people each year in the United States survive a spinal injury, most of whom are males under the age of 25 (DeForge et al., 2004). In addition to paralysis, SCI also leads to loss of sensation, bladder and bowel control problems, and alterations in sexual functioning.

Men and women with spinal cord injury often have a decreased desire for and frequency of sexual activity. They may experience fewer opportunities for sex, and have more difficulty in initiating intercourse. Men may have problems with erection and ejaculation. There are two erection centers in the spinal cord. The higher center in the upper lumbar cord controls psychogenic erections—those due to mental stimuli. The lower center in the sacral region of the spinal cord controls reflexive erections—those due to direct stimulation. Men with spinal injuries above the lumbar region can have reflexive erections but not psychogenic erections (Benevento & Sipski, 2002). They can't feel sensations from the genitals because fibers that carry sensation to the brain have been severed. Men with damage to the sacral region of the spinal cord usually won't have reflexive erections but may have erections due to mental stimulation and erotic thoughts (Benevento & Sipski, 2002). Overall, 54–87% of men with SCI can still achieve erections (Alexander, Sipski, & Findley, 1994). Erectile problems can be treated with penile prostheses, vacuum erection devices, injectible vasoactive drugs, or with drugs such as Viagra. Ejaculation, however, is a more complicated neurologic process, and is more affected by SCI. Most men with SCI are unable to ejaculate naturally (Benevento & Sipski, 2002). Spinal cord injury affects not only ejaculation, but also the quality of sperm, making infertility a particular problem in these men.

Most women with SCI can still have intercourse, get pregnant, and deliver vaginally, although they may have problems getting comfortable during intercourse, and they have a diminished ability to reach orgasm (Sipski, Alexander, & Rosen, 2001). Only about half of women with SCI can achieve orgasm, and the sexual dysfunction is more severe in women with damage to the lower spinal cord (Sipski et al., 2001).

It is important to remember that there is not a "right way" and a "wrong way" to have sex. If you or your partner has an SCI, you may need to change your definition of sexual expression and explore different physical, emotional, and sensual experiences. For example, although 99% of men reported penile-vaginal intercourse to be their favorite sexual activity before injury, only 16% of men felt the same after SCI; most preferred oral sex, kissing, and hugging (Benevento & Sipski, 2002).

ASK YOURSELF

Can you think of a film in which a disabled person is a major character? How is the sexuality of the disabled person portrayed?

Sex and Cancer

It is common for cancer patients to lose some sexual desire. Chemotherapy and radiation quite literally poison the body and make patients feel tired and ill. Patients are often in pain and afraid for their very survival. In addition, cancer patients often feel as if they don't own their bodies. In teaching hospitals, medical teams and students may come in and poke and prod and peer at a patient's most intimate anatomy. Therefore, patients get used to separating themselves from their bodies, a habit that can be difficult to reverse when they are with their partner (Katz, 2007). Also, the loss of a breast or a testicle to cancer can greatly affect one's body image. Because we are inundated with media images of beauty and virility, it can be hard for cancer survivors to tell prospective partners about their medical past.

Sex and Mental Disability

People with mental disabilities have sexual feelings, although they are often treated as asexual, or as if their normal, human sexual drives are something to be discouraged (Aunos & Feldman, 2002). Too often, group homes or institutions disregard or discourage expression of sexuality in those who are mentally or developmentally disabled. But if the goal is for mentally disabled to have as normal a life as possible, then sexuality is a part of that. Some group homes offer classes in birth control, STI, and sexual abuse, as well as dating and pleasuring their partners. Most mentally disabled people are able to have rewarding, responsible, and loving relationships.

Communicating with Your Partner About Sex

After completion of this section, you will be able to . . .

○ List some suggestions for successful sexual communication and apply these strategies to your own life.

"People who videotape their sex are doing it for only one of two reasons. Maybe they're doing it because they are so egotistical that they love nothing more than watching themselves . . . . Or maybe people tape themselves so they can watch the playback together like football players looking for ways to improve their performance the next time. 'All right. Let's take a look right here, shall we? Okay. Here is what I'm talking about. See how your elbow is up so high and your back is arched right there? Not the best time to do that. I think I'd hold out on that until . . . there. That is when you should do it—right . . . *there*. And what is going on right here? What is happening? I'll tell you. Nothing. A lot of energy. . . . Look at my face. Nothing. Nothing going on. . . . You might want to kick in once in a while. You know what I'm saying. Now I know I'm biting my lip. That's to keep from laughing. Where did you come up with *that* little technique? Did you make that up? I thought so. Don't do it. Okay? Don't cry . . . . Come on! This is how we learn! Let's get back in there and try it again. Come on. What do you mean, you're not in the mood?"

—Ellen DeGeneres (2003, pp. 166–7)

"Great sex" is a goal for many couples. But what is great sex? Does it have to involve intercourse? Is it more about sensuality or sexuality? Is it related to orgasm? Connection? Performance? As we know, the media not only often portrays sex unrealistically, it can also marginalize people who don't fit into a narrow spectrum—those whose age, size, shape, or sexual orientation doesn't conform to the portrayed ideal. Peggy Kleinplatz and colleagues interviewed a number of people, of varying ages and orientations, who said they had experienced great sex. The subjects shared their view of optimal sexuality (Kleinplatz et al., 2009b). The results were surprising.

Although magazines and movies promise great sex when you learn the "10 secret techniques that will drive your partner crazy," and the mainstream media often portray simultaneous orgasm as the ultimate goal of sex, in reality people see things differently. When real people were questioned about sex and what made it good, lust, desire, and orgasm were rated as only minor components of optimal sexuality. In reality, it's not about the physiology and mechanics of sex, it's about the connection with your partner (Kleinplatz et al., 2009b).

According to the interviewees, great sex is mostly related to connection and intimacy. The best sex can happen when you are totally focused and absorbed in the moment. Sharing a deep sexual and erotic intimacy with your partner, and being in a caring, accepting, and mutually respectful relationship are also important. In fact, according to the study, the depth of connection with your partner is one of the most critical elements of great sex. It is important to be genuine and express yourself with honesty, to open yourself up, and to surrender to your partner and to the moment. Sex can be enhanced when you look at it as a discovery process to learn things about yourself. Finally, communication and empathy are key.

Sexual communication is the best predictor of sexual satisfaction (Areton, 2002). Couples who show greater sexual self-disclosure and communication about sexual preferences report higher sexual satisfaction in long-term relationships (MacNeil & Byers, 2009). However, it is not always as easy as we would like. Most people don't take Ellen DeGeneres's tongue-in-cheek suggestion and record their partners during sex so they can critique their performance. In the real world, people have to find a way to let their partners know about their sexual satisfaction. For some, nonverbal signals such as moaning or moving a certain way can feel like an easier way to give feedback to a partner. We also need to convey our sexual likes and dislikes. If only it were as easy as wearing a sign. In the gay community, the "bandana code" signals to potential partners what one's preferences and interests are. Different colored bandanas indicate different sexual practices; the side in which the bandana is worn indicates whether one is an active or passive partner (see Table 11.3; Tikkanen & Ross, 2000).

Many consider it very awkward to openly discuss their sexual needs and desires. Some feel that discussing sex is embarrassing or even improper. Others believe that if the relationship were "right" then there would never be any sexual problems. For some couples,

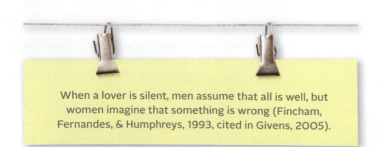

When a lover is silent, men assume that all is well, but women imagine that something is wrong (Fincham, Fernandes, & Humphreys, 1993, cited in Givens, 2005).

Table 11.3 Bandana Code

BANDANA WORN ON LEFT SIDE	COLOR	BANDANA WORN ON RIGHT SIDE
Anal sex, top	Dark blue	Anal sex, bottom
Oral sex, top	Light blue	Oral sex, bottom
Likes to tie up partner	Gray	Likes to be tied up
Likes to spank partner	Fuchsia	Likes to be spanked
Likes to take videos of partners	Black velvet	Will perform for the camera

© Cengage Learning 2013. SOURCE: Tikkanen & Ross, 2000.

it is hard to find the time to discuss their sexual issues. Often, sexual problems stem from the fact that there is not enough time for sex, so for them it may feel particularly daunting to find time to talk about the problems in their sex life (Raykeil, 2006). Although it is difficult to communicate about sex, silence opens the door for misunderstanding. When considering sexual histories and STI status, it is particularly important to communicate—your very life may depend on it! Below are some successful communication strategies (Gottman & Silver, 1999; Raykeil, 2006; Regan, 2003).

Do:

- *Choose the right time and place.* Turn off the TV and the phone, and wait until the kids or friends or parents are gone.
- *Communicate openly, honestly, and respectfully.* Clearly state your opinions and desires and remain focused on the issue at hand. Stay reasonable and rational, and don't manipulate your partner or try to control him or her through guilt, threats, sarcasm, or verbal or physical aggression. Don't rely solely on nonverbal cues; these may be misinterpreted.
- *Keep calm.* Recognize when you're feeling overwhelmed and make a deliberate effort to relax. This may mean taking a 20-minute break from the discussion.
- *Keep a positive mind-set about your partner.* Know that your difficulties are ultimately coming from a place of frustration because you aren't physically expressing the love you and your partner feel for each other in a way you would like.
- *Consider seeing a sex therapist.* Sex counselors and therapists help people who are concerned about their sexual arousal, performance, or satisfaction. People of all ages, orientations, religions, ethnicities, and relationship status seek help from certified sex therapists. A listing of certified counselors and therapists in your area can be found at the American Association of Sexuality Educators, Counselors and Therapists website: www.aasect.org.
- *Try and try again.* Don't expect huge changes to occur overnight. Celebrate your successes and build on them. Let your partner know when he or she is doing something right!

Don't:

- *Don't wait too long.* Don't let things build until they are at a danger point.
- *Don't avoid the issue, change the subject, or try to joke it away.* Sometimes acknowledging the problem is the hardest

part. You may be afraid of what your partner will feel. But he or she may be having similar frustrations and it will help if one of you finally articulates the issue.

- *Don't let anger get in the way.* However, anger is not the most toxic emotion to relationships—contempt is, as well as criticism, defensiveness, and stonewalling (Gottman, 1994).
- *Don't compare yourselves to others.* Don't even compare yourselves to your past selves. Relationships change and you probably won't have the same number or type of sexual encounters you had in the early stages of your relationship.
- *Don't limit yourselves.* Sex doesn't have to be vaginal intercourse. Physical intimacy can come in a number of different ways. It can also help to vary your routine in activities that lead up to lovemaking. Take a long walk together, or watch an erotic film. Take time to remind each other why you chose each other.

Human beings have found countless ways to express themselves sexually. There is no right or wrong way, but each activity has its own risks and benefits. In the next few chapters we will explore some of the consequences of sexual contact, as we discuss contraception, pregnancy and childbirth, and sexually transmitted infections.

Chapter Summary

Introduction

- Humans have sex for many varied reasons. A recent survey found 237 separate reasons why people engage in intercourse, including physical motives, emotional incentives, goal attainment, and insecurity.

Solitary Sexual Practices

- Masturbation is the stimulation of one's own genitals, which produces feelings of pleasure and often results in orgasm. Men and women of all ages masturbate. People may use a dildo (a penis-shaped object) or a vibrator (a battery-powered dildo) to masturbate.
- Men are more likely than women to masturbate. Teens and college students, whites, and those with more education are also more likely to report masturbating.
- Masturbation, arguably the safest sexual act, provides many therapeutic benefits, although in the past, it was falsely believed to lead to dire consequences. People masturbate for many reasons, including pleasure, relaxation, boredom, to relieve sexual tension, and to preserve their virginity or to avoid sexually transmitted infections. Masturbation allows both men and women to learn about their bodies and their sexual response.
- Masturbation has been treated differently in different times and cultures. It often has been reviled, sometimes treated with amusement or contempt, and at times even encouraged.
- Sexual fantasies—arousing mental images—may be the most common form of human sexual expression. Most men and women fantasize, while daydreaming, masturbating, and/or during intercourse. Orgasms may occur during erotic dreams. Fantasy is positively correlated with sexual arousability, orgasm frequency, and sexual satisfaction.
- In general, men are more likely to fantasize about doing something sexual to a partner, while women are more likely to imagine something sexual being done to them. Men's fantasies tend to be more visual and focus on the sexual act, while women's fantasies are more romantic, and focus on the context of the act.

Sexual Practices with a Partner

- People's definition of what constitutes having "had sex" differs. A person's gender, age, or personal beliefs may influence his or her definition of "having sex."
- People experience a wide array of sexual practices. Open communication with one's partner helps determine one's likes and dislikes.
- Foreplay is sexual activity including touching, cuddling, kissing, and manual- and oral-genital contact that can occur before or without intercourse. As the length of time of foreplay increases, so does the likelihood of a woman experiencing orgasm.
- Touch is very important in sexual arousal. Touch doesn't need to be on the genitals to be erotic. Frottage involves the rubbing of one's body parts against someone else's for sexual stimulation.
- Sex toys are devices that are used to enhance a person's sexual pleasure during masturbation or with a partner. People of all ages and orientations use sex toys. Some sex toys include dildos, vibrators, cock rings, pocket pussies, and butt plugs.
- Oral contact with the genitals can be very sexually stimulating. Oral stimulation of the female genitals is called cunnilingus, with the male genitals is fellatio, and with the anus is anilingus. Simultaneous oral-genital stimulation is called "sixty-nine." The rate of oral sex has increased over the years.
- During vaginal intercourse, the erect penis is inserted into the vagina. There are many different positions in which people have intercourse. The missionary position is the most commonly used position in the United States, although woman-on-top, rear-entry, and side-entry positions are also common.
- Anal intercourse is when the penis is inserted into a man's or woman's anus and rectum. Anal sex is one of the riskiest of all sexual behaviors. During anal sex, using a condom, an external lubricant, and washing the penis (or removing and changing condoms) before having vaginal or oral sex can reduce STI risk.

Sexual Activity Across the Life Span

- Sexual expression is normal in people of all ages. Children show a broad range of sexual behaviors. Two- to five-year-olds frequently touch their genitals in public and at home, try to look at people when they're nude, and expose their sex parts to adults. Sexual play in children who have been abused tends to be more sophisticated and compulsive, and to occur with children who are not within a year of their age.
- The average age for first intercourse in the United States is 17.7 years for boys and 17.4 years for girls. Age of teens' friends, their success in school, self-esteem, participation in sports, and parental involvement in their lives all influence the likelihood of participating in sexual activity. Abstinence-only education programs have not been shown to decrease teen sexual activity. In fact, more high school students are having oral sex and anal sex than in the past, and young people are less likely to consider these behaviors as "having sex" than did young people in the past.
- A number of factors are correlated with a person's frequency of sexual activity, including age, marital status, education, and even political leanings and music preferences. About 15% of adults engage in half of all sexual activity, while 20% of all adults in the United States report having had no sex at all in the past year. The average duration of intercourse among U.S. couples is about 7 minutes.
- Over the course of a lifetime, adult men in the United States report an average of five to eight female partners, while women report three to four male partners. It is statistically illogical for heterosexual men to have more female partners on average than heterosexual women have male partners. The discrepancy may come from sampling errors or research design, ambiguously worded questions, or dishonest survey participants.
- Aging does not mean the end of one's sexual life. As people get older, some become less interested in sex or less sexually active or responsive, but others enjoy sex more because they have a deeper understanding of their partner and of themselves, and no more fears of pregnancy.
- Physically and emotionally disabled individuals have sexual needs and desires, although they are often treated as asexual.

Communicating with Your Partner About Sex

- It may be difficult or embarrassing, but communicating with your partner about your sexual needs and desires is the best way to ensure sexual satisfaction. Some successful communication strategies include choosing the right place and time, communicating honestly and respectfully, and keeping a positive mind-set. Don't let anger get in the way, and don't try to avoid the issue.

MAKING INFORMED DECISIONS

Sexuality—when to do it, how to do it, and what exactly "it" is—is one of the preeminent preoccupations of humanity. Every sexual decision you make is based on many factors.

evaluate and *decide*

Imagine the following situations:

> Kaden is considering having sex for the first time.

> Tashika defines herself as a virgin, and has taken a pledge to remain abstinent until marriage. In her mind, "sex" is defined as being penetrated by a penis, whether vaginally, anally, or orally. Last month, Tashika had too much to drink at a party and ended up performing oral sex on a boy she barely knows. She decided this "doesn't count" as sex.

What factors would you consider in advising these people? Consider the issues and questions below to make your decision.

SITUATION	ISSUES TO CONSIDER
FIRST-TIME SEX	What are the risks and benefits of Kaden's decision? What changes might occur to Kaden's health, emotions, or social standing?
	What are the values that underlie Kaden's decision? Religious? Emotional? Health? How should a person weigh these values?
	What factors may influence Kaden's decision, including sexual desire, love, peer pressure, alcohol, or drugs? What are "good" reasons to lose one's virginity? "Bad" reasons?
	Context is very important. Many factors may affect a person's decision. Does Kaden's gender matter in this case? What if Kaden was a 16-year-old boy, and the gorgeous 21-year-old woman next door wanted to have casual sex with him? What would your answer be? Would your feelings change if Kaden was a 16-year-old girl, and the gorgeous 21-year-old man next door wanted to have casual sex with her? Why does gender affect your decision?
THE DEFINITION OF SEX	By changing her definition of sex in this situation, what are the risks and benefits for Tashika?
	Why do you think there are such widely disparate definitions of "having sex"?
	What do you imagine the underlying assumptions are of one who feels that deep kissing is having sex, compared to someone who feels that anal intercourse is not having sex?
	What is your definition of "having sex"? Can you think of any circumstances under which you would make exceptions to your definition? Does it matter if force is involved? If alcohol is involved? If love is involved? Why or why not?

Additional Resources

Log in to CengageBrain to access the resources your instructor requires. For this book, you can access:

 **CourseMate** CourseMate brings course concepts to life with interactive learning, study, and exam preparation tools that support the printed textbook. A textbook-specific website, Psychology CourseMate includes an integrated interactive eBook and other interactive learning tools including quizzes, flashcards, videos, and more.

CENGAGENOW CengageNOW is an easy-to-use online resource that helps you study in less time to get the grade you want—NOW. Take a pre-test for this chapter and receive a personalized study plan based on your results that will identify the topics you need to review and direct you to online resources to help you master those topics. Then take a post-test to help you determine the concepts you have mastered and what you will need to work on. If your textbook does

not include an access code card, go to CengageBrain.com to gain access. Visit www.cengagebrain.com anytime to access your account and purchase materials.

Current links to all of the following websites and videos can be found on the Psychology CourseMate for this text at www.cengagebrain.com/.

Web Resources

Good Vibrations
Provides a wealth of information, books, discussion, and links related to healthy sexuality.

Mark Twain on Masturbation
Mark Twain's comments on masturbation, given in a speech delivered to the Stomach Club, a society of American writers and artists, in Paris in 1879.

Society for Human Sexuality
The Society for Human Sexuality is a social and educational organization whose purpose is to promote understanding and appreciation for the many forms of adult intimate relationships and consensual sexual expression.

Print Resources

Cornog, M. (2003). *The Big Book of Masturbation: From Angst to Zeal.* San Francisco, CA: Down There Press.

Laqueur, C. (2003) *Solitary Sex: A Cultural History of Masturbation.* Cambridge, MA: Zone Books.

Love, P. (1994). *Hot Monogamy.* New York: Dutton.

Maines, R. (1999). *The Technology of Orgasm: "Hysteria," the Vibrator, and Women's Sexual Satisfaction.* Baltimore, MD: Johns Hopkins University Press.

Maltz, W. and Boss, S. (1997). *In the Garden of Desire: The Intimate World of Women's Sexual Fantasies.* New York: Broadway Books.

Video Resources

The Art of Love. (1996). 108 minutes. Exercises that couples can engage in to explore every part of their bodies and bring high levels of pleasure to each other. Goes beyond sexuality and moves into a world of sensuality by helping couples enrich their sexual lives, through an enhanced communication. From Wishing Well Video Distributing.

Embracing Our Sexuality: Women Talk About Sex. (1994). 45 minutes. This video contains the conversations of nine women who gather together for a weekend retreat to talk about sexuality. The women range in age from their 20s to their 70s and come from different racial/ethnic backgrounds and sexual orientations. The women talk frankly about sexual orientation, menstruation, masturbation, sexual fantasies, orgasms, and the effect of AIDS and sexual abuse on their lives. From New Day Films.

Finding Our Way: Men Talk About Their Sexuality. (1998). 38 minutes. What do men really want sexually? How did they learn about sex? How does sexual expression change with age? This video follows the discussion of 10 men who meet at a weekend retreat. They range in age from 27 to 71 and come from a variety of backgrounds and sexual orientations. From New Day Films.

Sexual Pleasure Education Series: Couples Who Want a Better Sex Life, Oral Sex and Sexual Fantasies and Sex Aids and Sexual Approaches. (1991). 60 minutes each. (Explicit.) Persons who know more about sex have the best sex lives, have more sex, enjoy it more, manage it better. This series by the Institute for Advanced Study of Human Sexuality combines accurate information about sex with explicit and erotic scenes using real people, not actors and actresses. From Multi-Focus.

Sexual Secrets: A Sex Surrogate's Guide to Great Lovemaking. (1993). 60 minutes. Mar Simone, a sexual surrogate partner, shares her techniques to heighten sexual pleasure. Includes communication skills, sensual and sexual caress, manual and oral lovemaking, intercourse and afterplay. From Multi-Focus.

First: Perspectives on Sexual Awakening and Identity. (2008). 40 minutes. This program collects stories and reflections on that very subject from 10 women, all of whom speak candidly about their backgrounds, their expectations prior to having sex, and how they have learned to define themselves sexually. Heterosexual and gay issues are both addressed in detail. From Films for the Humanities and Sciences.

Sexuality Reborn. (2006). 48 minutes. The physical and emotional effects of spinal cord injury are frankly discussed by four couples. These couples demonstrate and share their personal experiences concerning self-esteem, dating, bowel and bladder function, sexual response, and varying types of sexual activities. Kessler Institute for Rehabilitation.

Still Doing It: The Intimate Lives of Women over 65. (2007). 54 minutes. Explores the lives of older women. Partnered, single, straight, gay, black and white; nine extraordinary women, age 67–87, express with startling honesty and humor how they feel about themselves, sex and love in later life, and the poignant realities of aging. New Day Films.

12 Contraceptive Choices and Ending Pregnancy

A typical woman is fertile for almost 39 years of her life. For a woman to only give birth to two children, she would need to spend 89% of her fertile life—about three decades—using contraception.

—Trussell, 2004a

In 2008 Americans spent $3.5 billion on prescription birth control pills and $263 million on condoms.

—Singer, 2009

© Fabio Cardoso/Corbis

© Joel Gordon

© Robert Ginn/Age fotostock

Introduction to Contraceptive Methods

After completion of this section, you will be able to . . .

○ List some methods of contraception used throughout history as well as methods used today.

○ Identify the roles played by Anthony Comstock and Margaret Sanger in the history of contraception.

○ Define *effectiveness* of contraception and differentiate between "perfect" and "typical" use.

When college students were asked their reasons for having sex, they listed "having a baby" last (Hill, 1997). Throughout history, humans have looked for means to separate the pleasurable act of intercourse from its sometimes inconvenient consequence: childbirth.

The History of Contraception

Humans did not always know what caused pregnancy. It was thought that conception might occur because of contact with the spirits, by eating fruit, or by exposure to certain animals or birds. The Japanese believed that pregnancy was related to butterflies, and ancient Teutons believed that storks brought babies, a folktale that lives on today (Connell, 2002).

In part due to the Biblical command to "be fruitful and multiply," contraception was discouraged by all Christian faiths for many years. It wasn't until 1930 that the first mainstream Christian sect—the Anglican Church—officially permitted certain forms of birth control (Campbell, 1960). Today, some religions, including the Roman Catholic Church, a few Protestant denominations, and many Hindus condemn the use of contraception.

The earliest oral contraceptives came from fruits and plants, including pennyroyal, willow, Queen Anne's lace, juniper, and others. Pomegranates and yams are high in natural plant estrogens and may prevent conception. Unripe or semi-ripe papaya contain high levels of papain, which increase uterine contractions (Adebiyi, Adaikan, & Prasad, 2002). Although some natural substances do provide some protection against pregnancy, others used by women in the past—such as a mixture of alcohol infused with dried beaver testicles—were not as effective in preventing conception. A few such substances were even dangerous

The oldest known guide to contraception was the *Petrie Papyrus*, an Egyptian document from 1850 B.C. The Bible also contains references to contraception, including withdrawal and vaginal sponges. The Persian physician Avicenna, considered to be the father of modern medicine, recommended that after intercourse, a woman jump backward seven times while sneezing, in order to dislodge the sperm (Connell, 2002).

or lethal: women ingested mercury, strychnine, and lead to prevent or end unwanted pregnancies. Before modern methods of contraception were available, women inserted any number of substances, including crocodile dung, mule earwax, and weasel testicles into their nether regions in their efforts to avoid pregnancy (Skuy, 1995). Half a lemon could act as a primitive diaphragm, and the acidity had a spermicidal action (Connell, 2002). Although these options do have some biological basis, they are not reliable forms of birth control.

Anthony Comstock.

Douching involves flushing the vagina with mixtures of water and other substances such as vinegar, baking soda, or iodine. For centuries, women have (ineffectively) attempted to flush the semen away after intercourse; in fact, the most popular contraceptive used during the Depression was a Lysol douche (Tone, 2001). In the past, many also believed that shaking up a warm Coca-Cola and allowing it to explode into the vagina would effectively wash away the semen. Not only is this ineffective as a contraceptive, it may actually force the semen further into the uterus.

Early American women learned about contraception from family, friends, physicians, and through advertisements in newspapers and pamphlets. This access to information fell sharply in the late 19th century largely due to the efforts of one man: Anthony Comstock.

Anthony Comstock was born in Connecticut in 1844 to devout Congregationalist parents. In the 1860s he moved to New York and was shocked by the easily accessible sex he saw. Anthony Comstock became a one-man purity campaign, crusading against tobacco, alcohol, gambling, atheism, and pornography. The Comstock Act of 1873 allowed for the confiscation and destruction of any material that was considered obscene, including contraceptive devices. The act banned the dissemination through mail or across state lines of any "article of an immoral nature, or any drug or medicine, or any article whatever for the prevention of conception." Physicians were not allowed to provide their patients with any information that might aid in the prevention of pregnancy or sexually transmitted diseases. Once they were made illegal, availability of contraceptive items moved underground into a flourishing black market.

In the early 20th century Margaret Sanger, while working as an obstetric nurse in some of the poorest neighborhoods of New York City, was moved by the difficult conditions and suffering of women who had no power to control their fertility. Women at the time were expected to have as many children as possible, even if it killed them. Sanger—whose mother died at age 50 after 18 pregnancies—believed that a woman had the right to control her own body, that every person should be able to decide whether to have a child, and

© Bettmann/CORBIS

Margaret Sanger.

that every child should be wanted and loved. She led the movement for the distribution of information about sexuality and contraception, and in 1914 Margaret Sanger established the National Birth Control League, which later became the Planned Parenthood Federation of America. Challenging the view that information about contraception was obscene, Sanger opened the first birth control clinic in America in 1916. As a result of her work, she was arrested less than a month later and spent 30 days in prison, where she taught birth control techniques to the other inmates. Over the decades, she fought for open access to information about contraception, and her efforts led to the eventual weakening of the Comstock laws.

Criminalization of the use of contraceptives in the United States would not be overturned until 1965, when the Supreme Court reversed the law in the case of *Griswold v. Connecticut,* stating that married couples' access to contraception was protected by their constitutional right to marital privacy. Unmarried couples would be awarded the same right seven years later with the passage of *Eisenstadt v. Baird.* Today, although contraception is legal, there are a number of state and federal policies that limit women's access to contraceptive information and services (Alan Guttmacher Institute [AGI], 2005).

Contraceptive Options

Ninety-nine percent of women in the United States who have ever had sexual intercourse with a male have used at least one contraceptive method (Mosher & Jones, 2010). Sixty-two percent of the 62 million American women between the ages of 15 and 44 currently use some form of birth control; 38% do not use birth control. Some women don't use contraception because they are trying to get pregnant, because they are sterile, or because they are not currently having heterosexual intercourse.

Sexually active fertile women who don't use contraception are at particular risk of getting pregnant; 52% of unplanned pregnancies each year occur to the 11% of women who did not use a contraceptive during the month they became pregnant. The other 48% of unplanned pregnancies occur to the 89% of sexually active women who did use a contraceptive (Boonstra, Gold, Richards, & Finer, 2006). For the average fertile woman, with each act of unprotected intercourse there is a 2–4% chance of pregnancy, which leads to an 85–90% chance of pregnancy over the course of a year (Trussell, 2004b).

Awareness of the importance of contraception has increased: In 1980, only 43% of women or their partners used a contraceptive the first time they had sex; by 2008, 84% of women reported that they used some method of birth control at first intercourse (Mosher & Jones, 2010). Teenagers who don't use a contraceptive the first time they have sex are twice as likely to become teen mothers as are those who use contraception the first time; they also have higher rates of sexually transmitted infections (Moore, Driscoll, & Lindberg, 1998; Shafii, Stovel, & Holmes, 2007).

Men and women looking to control their fertility have many options. Hormonal methods—including oral contraceptives, the patch, the ring, injectables, and implants—reduce fertility by their effect on a woman's hormonal cycle. Condoms, cervical caps, sponges, and spermicides present a physical barrier that

> "Contraceptives should be used on every conceivable occasion."
> —Spike Milligan, comedian and writer

Table 12.1 Most Popular Methods of Contraception in the United States

METHOD OF CONTRACEPTION (IN ORDER OF PREVALENCE OF USE)	PERCENTAGE OF USE, BY WOMEN WHO CURRENTLY USE BIRTH CONTROL	NUMBER OF USERS (IN THOUSANDS)
Birth control pill	28.0%	10,700
Tubal sterilization	27.1%	10,356
Male partner use of condom	16.1%	6,152
Male partner's vasectomy	9.9%	3,783
Depo-Provera	3.2%	1,223
Withdrawal	5.2%	1,987
IUD	5.5%	2,102
Fertility awareness–based methods	1.1%	420
Implant, patch, ring, or Lunelle	3.5%	1,338
Cervical cap, contraceptive sponge, female condom, or other methods	0.4%	153
Total	**100%**	**38,214**

Note: Percents may not add up to 100% due to rounding.
© Cengage Learning 2013. SOURCE: Mosher & Jones, 2010.

unplanned pregnancy, and you may have to re-experience unpleasant side effects that can be associated with the first few months of pill use.

Reversibility

Oral contraceptives are easy to discontinue—you only have to stop taking them! Just be sure to immediately use another form of contraception if you do not plan on becoming pregnant. Fertility may be temporarily reduced but usually returns to normal levels within 1 to 3 months; for the average woman, ovulation returns within 2 weeks.

> I've heard that I shouldn't take the pill continuously for more than a couple of years.

Other Forms of Hormonal Contraceptives

The patch and the ring are two forms of hormonal contraception that don't need to be taken daily. **Ortho Evra** is a matchbook-sized patch that is placed on the skin of the butt, stomach, upper outer arm, or upper torso; it protects a woman from pregnancy for a week at a time. **NuvaRing** is a small, flexible ring that is inserted into the vagina once a month. Both of these contraceptives release both estrogen and progestin and protect a woman from pregnancy by preventing ovulation and thickening the cervical mucus. These methods may have less chance of user error than daily oral contraceptives. The failure rate increases if the woman doesn't use as directed, or if the ring slips out of the vagina or the patch falls off the skin and they are not replaced in a timely manner. Advantages and disadvantages of these methods are similar to those of oral contraceptives, although the patch and the ring don't seem to increase formation of SHBG, which may mean they are less likely to decrease sex drive. Women on the Ortho-Evra patch should be aware that they may be exposed to as much as 60% more estrogen than they would be exposed to with oral contraceptives, which can increase the risk of blood clots.

Implanon, a small progestin-containing rod that is inserted on the inside of a woman's upper arm, gives continuous contraceptive protection for up to 3 years. Approved by the FDA in 2006, Implanon works by thickening cervical mucus and preventing ovulation. In one 3-year study of more than 2,300 women, not one pregnancy was reported to have occurred in more than 73,000 monthly cycles (Croxatto et al., 1999; Ismail, Mansour, & Singh, 2006). Overall, Implanon's failure rate is 0.05%, meaning that only 1 in 2,000 women using Implanon will become pregnant over the course of a year.

Insertion and removal of Implanon is easier than with the previous contraceptive implant (Norplant); insertion takes just over 1 minute and removal takes about 2.6 minutes. Side effects are similar to those of oral contraceptives, although women with high blood pressure should visit their physician twice a year. Since Implanon contains only progestin, women can use it while breastfeeding. About 30% of European and Canadian women who have used Implanon discontinued its use within 2 years, primarily due to

complaints about irregularities in their menstrual cycle (Affandi, 1998). Fertility returns within 1 month after the rod is removed.

Depo-Provera (depot medroxyprogesterone acetate, or DMPA) is an injection given every 3 months into the arm or buttock. DMPA contains only progestin, and prevents pregnancy by thickening cervical mucus, and by preventing ovulation and implantation. It is a very effective reversible method of birth control; fewer than three women in a thousand will become pregnant while using Depo-Provera (Hatcher, 2004). Unlike other forms of birth control, perfect-use and typical-use failure rates are almost identical. This is because the progestin provides protection against pregnancy for up to 4 months, so women who are 2 or even 4 weeks late in getting their next injection are still protected.

Depo-Provera has advantages similar to those of oral contraceptives. Because it contains no estrogen, women who can't take combination oral contraceptives can use it, and it may be used while breastfeeding. Irregular bleeding is the most common side effect associated with Depo-Provera. In most women, periods become fewer and lighter; in fact, 50% of women will stop having their periods entirely after a year of use, and 80% will stop after 5 years of use (Knowles & Ringel, 1998). Some women using DMPA gain 4 to 5 pounds per year for about 3 years, although any changes in weight may of course be due to unrelated factors, such as poor dietary habits or a lack of exercise (Connell, 2002). Other side effects are similar to those of oral contraceptives, although a woman experiencing negative side effects cannot immediately discontinue Depo-Provera, as the drug remains in her system for up to 16 weeks. Forty-three percent of women who had ever used Depo-Provera discontinued its use, usually because of its side effects (Mosher & Jones, 2010). In addition, it may take as long as 18 months for fertility to return after discontinuing DMPA, although the median time for conception in women choosing to become pregnant after getting off Depo-Provera is 10 months (Connell, 2002). Like the other hormonal contraceptives, this method offers no protection against STIs. Women who have diabetes, migraines, major depression, high cholesterol, or high blood pressure should carefully consider their use of Depo-Provera, as should women who have ever had breast cancer, a heart attack, stroke, Cushing's syndrome, blood clots, or liver disease. New injectable contraceptives that have fewer side effects than Depo-Provera are being developed.

Ortho Evra The hormonal contraceptive patch.

NuvaRing The hormonal contraceptive ring.

Implanon A contraceptive rod inserted on the inside of a woman's upper arm.

Depo-Provera The hormonal contraceptive injection, given every 3 months.

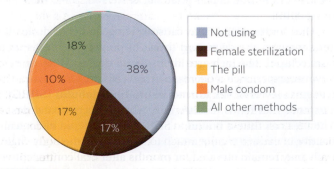

- Not using — 38%
- Female sterilization — 17%
- The pill — 17%
- Male condom — 10%
- All other methods — 18%

FIGURE 12.3 Percentage distribution of U.S. women aged 15–44, by current contraceptive status. (From Mosher & Jones, 2010.)

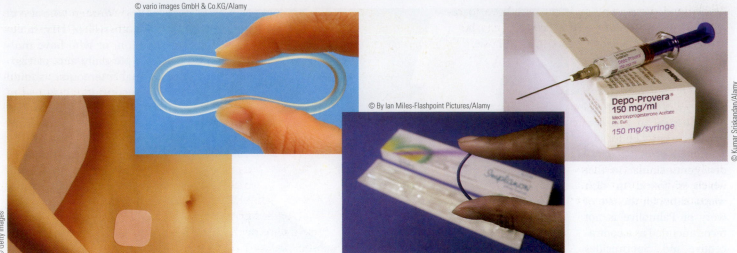

© vario images GmbH & Co.KG/Alamy

© By Ian Miles-Flashpoint Pictures/Alamy

© Kumar Sriskandan/Alamy

© Getty Images

Left to right: the Ortho Evra patch, the NuvaRing, Implanon, and Depo-Provera.

Other hormonal contraceptives are also under development. Most promising is a vaccine that would cause the body's immune system to attack hCG (human chorionic gonadotropin), which is necessary for the establishment and maintenance of early pregnancy. Preliminary tests have shown this to be effective in preventing pregnancy, but there are safety concerns over possible side effects related to the immune system.

Barrier Methods

After completion of this section, you will be able to . . .

O Compare and contrast the use, efficacy, and advantages and disadvantages of different forms of barrier contraceptives.

Devices that physically prevent the egg and sperm from meeting are some of the oldest forms of birth control in the world. Women may use diaphragms, cervical caps, and contraceptive sponges, whereas both men and women may use spermicide or condoms to prevent fertilization.

Barriers Worn by the Woman

Diaphragms and Cervical Caps

Diaphragms and **cervical caps** are latex rubber barriers that cover the cervix to prevent sperm from entering the uterus. First introduced in the United States by Margaret Sanger in 1916, the diaphragm was once the most commonly used form of medical contraceptive in the United States (Connell, 2002). Today, less than a fifth of a percent of women who use contraception use a diaphragm (Mosher & Jones, 2010). Both the diaphragm and cap are meant to be used with a spermicide applied to the inner dome. Both may be inserted up to 2 hours before intercourse, and must be left in place for at least 8 hours afterward (but not more than 24 hours). Diaphragms and cervical caps need to be fit by a physician, and refitted if a woman changes her weight by more than 10 pounds. Approved in 2002, **Lea's Shield** is a one-size-fits-most reusable silicone barrier, about the size of a diaphragm. It is held in place by the vaginal walls and therefore does not need to be individually fitted to each woman, and it is less easily dislodged than diaphragms or cervical caps. Because it is made of silicone, latex allergies are not a concern.

Studies have shown it to be slightly more effective than the diaphragm or cervical cap.

Contraceptive Sponge

Ancient Egyptian women would gather sponges from the ocean and insert them into their vaginas to help prevent pregnancy. The concept is still alive "Today." Approved in 1983, the **Today contraceptive sponge** was the most popular over-the-counter female contraceptive and was used by more than 115,000 women (Connell, 2002). It was taken off the market in 1995, not because of safety or reliability issues, but because the FDA increased the stringency of its guidelines for the air and water supply of the factory that made the sponge, and the company could not afford to upgrade the factory. The Today sponge was reapproved by the FDA in 2005 and is back on the market. Other contraceptive sponges include Pharmatex and Protectaid.

Soft and disposable, the contraceptive sponge provides a physical barrier to sperm entering the uterus, as well as the spermicide Nonoxynol-9. To use, a woman moistens the sponge with water, squeezing it to produce suds. She folds the sponge and inserts it deep into the vagina to cover the cervix. It can be put in place up to 24 hours before intercourse, and must be left in for 6 hours after intercourse. It is removed by pulling on the attached loop, and then discarded.

© Gary Parker / Photo Researchers, Inc.

The contraceptive sponge. On the TV show *Seinfeld*, the Elaine character was dismayed when the contraceptive sponge was taken off the market. She bought as many cases of sponges as she could and would use them only when she met a man she deemed "spongeworthy," or worth the cost of using one of her limited number of sponges.

Diaphragm, cervical cap, Lea's Shield, and **Today contraceptive sponge** Contraceptive devices that cover the cervix and act as a barrier to prevent sperm from entering the uterus.

Barriers Used by Either the Woman or the Man

Spermicides

Spermicides are agents that kill sperm. Chemically, spermicides are surfactant detergents similar to that which is found in dish soaps, although the use of Ivory or Palmolive is not recommended as a contraceptive aid. Spermicides come in the form of contraceptive foams, jellies, creams, tablets, vaginal suppositories, or on a film,

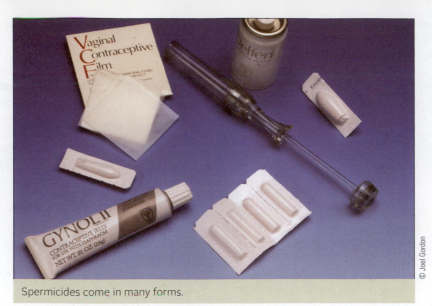

Spermicides come in many forms.

and they are available without a prescription. Be sure to follow directions for use because they all differ in their application. For maximum effectiveness, the spermicide should be applied no more than 60 minutes before intercourse, and left in place for 6 to 8 hours afterward. Although they may be used alone, they are often used in conjunction with contraceptive barriers such as diaphragms, cervical caps, and condoms.

The active ingredient in all spermicides available in the United States is Nonoxynol-9 (N-9), which prevents pregnancy by chemically disrupting the head of the sperm, affecting its mobility (Cates & Raymond, 2004). The sperm then becomes unable to fertilize an egg.

It was once thought that spermicides protected against bacterial infections or HIV. Recent studies, however, have found that not only is this incorrect, but Nonoxynol-9 may even *increase* a woman's risk of contracting the HIV virus by causing irritation of the cervix and vagina, which may make it easier for viruses to enter into the bloodstream (Kreiss et al., 1992; Roddy, Zekeng, Ryan, Tamoufe, & Tweedy, 2002).

How is it possible that for years health care professionals advised people that the use of Nonoxynol-9 would protect them from sexually transmitted infections when the opposite may actually be true? Preliminary studies showed that Nonoxynol-9 did in fact damage the HIV virus. However, these studies were done in a petri dish in a laboratory. When actual people used N-9, the spermicide irritated the vaginal walls and enhanced the likelihood of HIV transmission. The effect of N-9 may also depend on who is using it, and how often it is applied. Women may experience vaginal irritation with N-9 use, especially women who may have a pre-existing STI. Also, STI transmission rates go up significantly with increased spermicide use. Lesions of the cells of the vagina (which could lead to increased entry of STIs into the bloodstream) were found in 15% of placebo users, 18% of women who used a spermicide every other day, 24% of those who used it daily, and up to 53% of women who used the spermicide four times daily (Roddy, Cordero, Cordero, & Fortney, 1993).

Spermicide A contraceptive agent that kills sperm.

Condom A device, worn by a male or female, designed to prevent sperm from entering the vagina.

Women who are at high risk of HIV infection, or who have multiple daily acts of vaginal intercourse, should reconsider their use of Nonoxynol-9. Also, N-9 should not be used for anal sex because it damages the lining of the rectum, increasing the risk of HIV transmission.

Male Condoms

The word condom is thought to be from the Latin *condon,* meaning "receptacle," or from the Italian *guantone,* meaning "glove." Condoms are one of the world's oldest contraceptive devices. Although it is a common belief that "Dr. Condom," a physician for the amorous King Charles II, invented the condom, a 12,000-year-old drawing of a man with a sheath over his penis during sexual intercourse has been found in a cave in France (Parisot, 1987). Gabriele Falloppio, a 16th-century physician who first described the fallopian tubes, may have performed the first clinical trial testing the condom, in order to prevent the spread of syphilis. Rubber condoms became available in the 19th century, providing protection against pregnancy and disease.

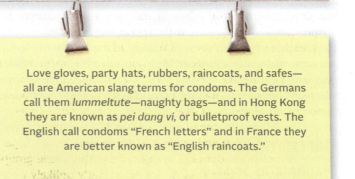

Love gloves, party hats, rubbers, raincoats, and safes—all are American slang terms for condoms. The Germans call them *lummeltute*—naughty bags—and in Hong Kong they are known as *pei dang vi,* or bulletproof vests. The English call condoms "French letters" and in France they are better known as "English raincoats."

Condoms are available in various sizes, colors, and designs.

Soldiers in WWI were denied condoms because it was believed that anyone who engaged in the risky behaviors that led to a "venereal disease" deserved to suffer the consequences. Soldiers did indeed suffer the consequences; between April 1917 and December 1919, one in every eleven U.S. soldiers was diagnosed with a venereal disease, treatment of which cost the government more than $50 million (Tone, 2001). Although the secretary of the navy felt condoms were immoral and "un-Christian," the assistant secretary of the navy—Franklin Delano Roosevelt—waited until his boss was away from the office to order the distribution of condoms to sailors (Brandt, 1985).

Usually made of latex, polyurethane, or the intestinal membrane of lambs, a condom is a sheath that fits over the penis to physically prevent the sperm (or microorganisms) from entering the vagina or anus. Condoms are the only easily reversible contraception method that is available to men, other than withdrawal. In part due to their effectiveness in protecting against STIs, the percentage of women who have had a partner who used a condom increased from 52% in 1982 to 93% in 2008 (Mosher & Jones, 2010). Today, condoms are available in a wide variety of colors, sizes, shapes, and designs. Some have textured surfaces to enhance sensation, and others are flavored. Some condoms have enlarged tips to serve as a receptacle for semen, and many condoms have a spermicidal lubricant added, although there is no evidence that condoms with spermicide are more effective. In fact, one of the world's largest condom manufacturers has stopped making condoms with Nonoxynol-9 because of this spermicide's irritant effect on the lining of the vagina.

Even though condoms are the most effective method (other than complete abstinence) to prevent becoming infected with an STI, many people do not use them. Males reported using a condom in 21.5% of their past 10 acts of vaginal intercourse (Reece et al., 2010b). In women, the percentage was 18.4%. Condom use is highest in adolescents and unmarried adults; blacks and Hispanics report higher condom use compared to other racial groups. Men and women older than 50 are particularly unlikely to use condoms—two-thirds of those over fifty did not use a condom

It is estimated that more than 5 billion condoms are used annually worldwide (The Male Condom, 2006). The condom is very popular in Japan, used by 75% of couples who use contraception. Rigid restrictions against oral contraceptives may contribute to the condom's popularity.

during their last sexual encounter (Reece et al., 2010b).

Although latex condoms provide the best protection against STIs, up to 7% of the population is allergic to latex; people with this allergy experience symptoms such as skin rash, hives, eye infections, runny nose, wheezing, and difficulty breathing when exposed to latex (Knowles & Ringel, 1998). Polyurethane condoms are suitable for those with an allergy to latex. Thinner than latex condoms, they conduct heat better, have a longer shelf life, and don't degrade in oil-based lubricants. The new "baggy" polyurethane condoms are reported to provide a more natural feeling during intercourse. Unfortunately, polyurethane condoms are more expensive, 10 times more prone to breakage, and may not be as effective as latex in protecting against STIs. Condoms made from natural materials, such as lamb's intestines, allow for a greater ability to transmit sensation and warmth, but they are not as effective in preventing STIs or pregnancy.

How to use a condom. Condoms are inexpensive, costing as little as 25 cents each (or they can often be obtained free from Planned Parenthood centers or clinics). Condoms should be stored in a cool, dry place. Be sure to check the expiration date on the package—latex condoms deteriorate with age. Handle condoms carefully and never use a sharp object to open the package. You may choose to apply a few drops of water-based lubricant (lube) inside and outside of the condom, to prevent tears and increase sensitivity. Never use oil-based lube as this can damage latex condoms. Spermicide can also be placed inside the tip of the condom.

Once a man gets an erection, but before there is contact between the penis and vulva or anus, he (or his partner) rolls the condom onto the penis. Uncircumcised men should pull back their foreskin before putting on the condom. If the condom does not have a reservoir tip, be sure to leave about half an inch at the top to hold the semen. Unroll the condom all the way down, smoothing out any air bubbles along the way. For anal intercourse, men should use thicker condoms, or two at once, along with the appropriate lubricant to reduce the risk of breakage. After intercourse, the man should withdraw before the penis is completely soft. Holding the rim of the condom against the base of the penis prevents semen from spilling from the condom. Be sure to throw away the condom—never use the same condom twice. Never date anyone who would consider using the same condom twice.

Errors associated with condom use are not uncommon. Men may have trouble with the fit and feel of the condom, or with its slippage during withdrawal or during sex (Crosby, Yarber, Sanders, Graham, & Arno, 2008). About 1–2% of condoms slip off or break. Every condom made in the United States is tested electronically for holes and weak spots, so it may be that the characteristics and experience of the user better determine breakage and slippage of the condom, rather than product design flaws (Macaluso et al., 1999). If a condom breaks during intercourse, don't panic! The man should pull out quickly and put on a new condom, preferably with spermicide. Women part-

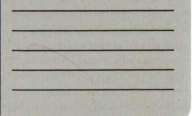

World War II pilots in toilet-less long-distance bombers used condoms to collect urine. The urine-filled condoms would often be thrown from the plane over enemy territory. Today, drug smugglers fill condoms with cocaine or heroin; the condoms are then swallowed by human "mules" who transport the drug internally. If the condom breaks, the results can be fatal.

ners can apply spermicidal foam, and consider using emergency contraception. Also, try to figure out why the condom broke so you can avoid that problem in the future.

Men sometimes lose their erections when wearing a condom; in one study, 37% of men reported condom-associated erection loss on at least one occasion (Graham et al., 2006). Another problem with condom use is if people don't like them, they are less likely to use them. More than three-quarters of men and nearly 40% of women reported that condoms decreased their sexual pleasure (Crosby, Milhausen, Yarber, Sanders, & Graham, 2008). Forty-three percent of men and 30% of women said putting on the condom spoiled the mood (Crosby et al., 2008). Those who complain that condoms reduce sexual sensation should best remember that it is better than the complete lack of sexual sensation they will experience when their partner won't have sex without a condom. A few drops of a water-based lubricant inside the condom can increase sensation.

Not only do condoms come in many sizes, but the average condom can expand to fit over someone's head. If his penis is larger than his skull, he's probably not someone you want to have sex with anyway.

Condoms and STIs. Condoms are the only form of contraception (other than abstinence) that can protect against HIV and other STIs transmitted through genital secretions, such as gonorrhea, chlamydia, trichomoniasis, and hepatitis B (Davis & Weller, 1999). Consistent condom use decreases the risk of HIV transmission by 90% (Warner et al., 2004). Condoms do not provide 100% protection against all sexually transmitted infections—only total abstinence does. Condoms may not physically cover the lesions associated with herpes simplex II, chancroid, or syphilis. Although it was previously thought that condoms would not protect against the HPV virus, in a recent study, women who reported that their partners always used a condom were 70% less likely to be diagnosed with HPV than women whose partners used a condom less than 5% of the time (Winer et al., 2006).

Condom availability in school. Almost half of students in grades nine through twelve report having had sexual intercourse, and more than one-sixth of high school males and one-ninth of high school females have had sex with four or more partners (Eaton et al., 2010). Although condom use is increasing among teens—80% of males and 69% of females said they used a condom during their most recent act of penile-vaginal intercourse (Fortenberry et al., 2010)—condom use is by no means consistent or universal, which may be one reason why each year approximately 3 million adolescents become infected with STIs and approximately 750,000 teenage girls become pregnant (Yang & Gaydos, 2010).

Most high schools teach students about safe sex, yet many don't provide the tools needed to practice it. High school students can find condoms difficult to obtain. They may be stymied by the cost, embarrassment, lack of confidentiality, or access to condoms. Some schools make condoms available for sexually active students. One study estimated that 4.7% of middle schools and 8.4% of high schools in the United States have condoms available

for their students (Small et al., 1995). Student counseling is available at 98% of these schools and mandatory in 49% of schools that distribute condoms (Kirby & Brown, 1996). Counseling often includes information about abstinence and instructions on proper use of condoms (Kirby & Brown, 1996).

Some fear that providing condoms to students will encourage sexual activity. However, studies have shown that in schools where condoms are provided, students are not more likely to have intercourse than students at schools where condoms are not made available. There was no difference in the age at first sexual intercourse, incidence of sexual activity, or number of recent sexual partners between students at schools that did and did not distribute condoms. In fact, in one representative sample of 4,166 high school students, teens in schools where condoms were available were *less* likely to report ever having had intercourse or having engaged in recent sexual intercourse (Blake et al., 2003). However, students at these schools where condoms are available are significantly more likely to use a condom when they do have intercourse (Blake et al., 2003; Guttmacher et al., 1997).

Some think that providing condoms to students disregards the religious beliefs or wishes of parents, or that it violates a statute that requires school systems to obtain parental consent before administering health services to children. In 81% of schools that supply condoms, some type of parental consent is required (Kirby & Brown, 1996). Still others feel that it is cost-prohibitive to provide condoms in schools, although it is cheaper than supporting unplanned teen pregnancies, paying for abortions, or treating STIs.

School condom availability programs have stimulated strong support as well as strong opposition (Kirby & Brown, 1996). The American College of Obstetricians and Gynecologists, the American Academy of Pediatrics, and the American Medical Association have all adopted policies recommending that comprehensive school health programs provide condoms to adolescents; the conservative groups The Family Research Council and Focus on the Family strongly oppose the availability of condoms in schools.

Female Condoms

The female condom is a sheath, closed at one end, with flexible rings at both ends, that fits in the woman from the cervix to the labia.

> **My boyfriend says he can't wear a condom because he is too big. What should he do?**

---

sexactually

Factors associated with condom use among sexually active youth include:

- Attending a school in which condoms are made available
- Positive attitudes toward condoms, including a belief that they do not reduce sexual pleasure
- Communicating with one's parents about condom use
- Perceptions that peers use condoms
- Confidence of proper condom usage
- Belief in condoms' effectiveness against pregnancy and STI
- Not using alcohol or drugs during the sexual encounter
- Engaging in a short-term or casual sexual experience rather than longer term or steady relationship

SOURCE: Blake et al., 2003.

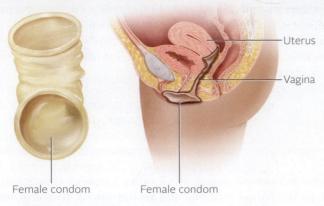

FIGURE 12.4 The female condom. (© Argosy Publishing Inc.)

Not as popular as male condoms, female condoms have been used by only 1.9% of women aged 15 to 44 (Mosher & Jones, 2010).

The female condom can be inserted up to 8 hours before intercourse. A lubricant can be applied to both the inside and outside of the condom. Squeeze the inner ring shut and push it into the vagina, up against the cervix. Male and female condoms should not be used at the same time, as friction may cause breakage. The condom has an outer ring that remains outside of the vagina and through which the penis is guided. After intercourse, remove the condom immediately. Preferably while still lying down, squeeze and twist the outer ring so semen does not leak out of the pouch. Pull the condom out and discard after a single use.

Polyurethane female condoms are more expensive than male condoms, and are not as effective as male condoms in preventing pregnancy. Female condoms made of nitrile rubber or of latex are less expensive and as effective in preventing pregnancy and STIs as male condoms. Other models in development will use a sponge rather than an inner ring, to improve comfort and stability.

Behavioral Methods

After completion of this section, you will be able to . . .

O Define, compare, and contrast the practice, efficacy, and advantages and disadvantages of different forms of behavioral methods of contraceptives, including *abstinence, outercourse, withdrawal,* and *fertility awareness–based methods.*

Abstinence

The avoidance of sexual intercourse is called **abstinence**, or celibacy, and it is the most effective way to avoid unplanned pregnancy and sexually transmitted infections. It is best to remain abstinent until you are physically and emotionally mature enough to handle the responsibilities of a sexual relationship.

Primary abstinence is when a person has never had sexual intercourse with another. Some people choose abstinence after having had previous sexual experience. Abstinence can be voluntary or involuntary—some people choose to be celibate, whereas others are abstinent because they currently have no relationship, are in poor health, or their life situation precludes a sexual relationship.

There is little consensus as to what exactly abstinence entails. Some consider abstinence to mean no sexual behavior whatsoever, including masturbation; others regard abstinence to mean no vaginal intercourse. In fact, in a survey of college students, almost 81% felt that oral-genital contact didn't count as "having sex," and almost 22% felt that penile-anal intercourse wasn't sex (Hans, Gillen, Akande, 2010).

Complete abstinence from any genital sexual activity between a man and a woman is 100% effective in preventing pregnancies and STIs. Abstinence has no hormonal side effects, it is immediately reversible, and it costs nothing. Many people may find it difficult to abstain from sexual activity for long periods.

By 1995, 12% of all teenagers (an estimated 2.2 million people) had taken a vow to abstain from sex until marriage (Bruckner & Bearman, 2005). However, most pledgers don't keep their promises; pledgers are just as likely to have premarital sex as non-pledgers, and don't differ in their rates of STIs, oral sex, or anal sex (Rosenbaum, 2009). You will be more likely to remain abstinent if you plan ahead, and make your decision while you are clearheaded, sober, and not in the throes of passion. Decide what your boundaries are, what activities you will participate in, and clearly inform your partner ahead of time what you will and won't do.

"The vows of abstinence break far more easily than latex condoms."
—Joycelyn Elders, former U.S. Surgeon General

Outercourse

Sexual activity that does not include the insertion of the penis into the vagina, mouth, or anus is called **outercourse**. It may include masturbation, body rubbing (also called frottage or dry humping), fantasy, erotica, and sex toys.

Participating in outercourse, an important part of foreplay, allows a person to enjoy sexual activity with less fear of pregnancy or infection with sexually transmitted diseases. There are no hormonal side effects, fertility is not diminished, and except for the cost of whatever props, jellies, or devices that strike your fancy, it is free. An added benefit is that those who explore sexual options outside of intercourse learn many ways to pleasure their partners and themselves, which can improve later sexual enjoyment. Some people, however, find it difficult to abstain from vaginal intercourse for prolonged periods, and may find themselves tempted to have intercourse without being prepared to protect themselves from pregnancy or STIs (Knowles & Ringel, 1998). In addition, you should be aware that herpes, genital warts, and syphilis may still be transmitted by skin-to-skin contact. What's more, if sperm is ejaculated near the vulva, it may enter the uterus and fertilize an egg.

Withdrawal

Coitus interruptus is the Latin name for withdrawal—when a man removes his penis from the vagina and ejaculates outside of the woman's body.

Abstinence Refraining from sexual intercourse. To best prevent pregnancy and STIs, a person must abstain from all genital sexual contact.

Outercourse Sexual activity that does not include the insertion of the penis into the vagina, mouth, or anus.

Coitus interruptus, also called the **withdrawal method** of contraception When a man removes his penis from the vagina and ejaculates outside of the woman's body.

Perhaps the world's oldest form of birth control, withdrawal is described in Genesis 38, when Onan "spilled his seed upon the ground" rather than impregnating his dead brother's wife. In 2008, 59% of women surveyed had ever used withdrawal as a method of birth control, compared to 25% in 1982 (Mosher & Jones, 2010). Withdrawal is the third most commonly used method of contraception used by college students during last intercourse, after condoms and the pill (American College Health Association–National College Health Assessment II, 2010). About 6% of sexually active unmarried women use withdrawal as their contraceptive method of choice (Knowles & Ringel, 1998). Withdrawal is generally about as effective as some barrier methods of contraception; failure rate is perhaps 4% with perfect use, and 18% with typical use (Jones, Fennell, Higgins, & Blanchard, 2009). To be most effective, the man must withdraw in time, ejaculate away from the vaginal opening, and there needs to be no sperm present in the pre-ejaculatory fluid.

Withdrawal is one of the few methods that obligates the male to be responsible for birth control. Some men find withdrawal difficult or frustrating; a man has to rely on his own sensations to know when he is about to reach the "point of no return" and to withdraw. This may be more difficult for younger men who don't yet have the knowledge or control that aids in effective withdrawal, or for men who have premature ejaculation. Also, while withdrawal offers a slight protection against STIs, pre-ejaculatory fluid may still contain infected cells.

"Family planning has many misconceptions."
—Anonymous

Fertility awareness–based methods (FABM) A set of practices used to determine the most fertile times of a woman's cycle. Abstinence or barrier methods of contraception may be used during these fertile times.

Natural family planning Avoidance of sex during a woman's fertile time of her cycle, without the use of any other contraceptive method.

Basal body temperature (BBT) method A method of determining a woman's fertility by charting changes in her body temperature.

Cervical mucus method A technique of fertility awareness–based contraception that determines fertility through changes in the cervical mucus.

Rhythm method Also known as the **calendar method**, this is a way to determine a woman's most fertile times by charting her menstrual cycle.

Ovulation predictor kits Allow a woman to test her urine daily for the presence of luteinizing hormone (LH), which increases prior to ovulation.

Symptothermal method A combination of fertility awareness based methods used to determine a woman's most fertile time.

Fertility Awareness–Based Methods

Couples who practice **fertility awareness–based methods (FABM)** of contraception use the physical signs of a woman's hormonal fluctuations to predict her fertility. A woman can then reduce her chances of getting pregnant by being aware of her fertile times and abstaining from sex or using a barrier method of contraception during these times (Pallone & Bergus, 2009). **Natural family planning** methods

"It is now quite lawful for a Catholic woman to avoid pregnancy by a resort to mathematics, though she is still forbidden to resort to physics or chemistry."
—H. L. Mencken, Notebooks, 1956.

exclude concurrent use of all other forms of contraception, including barrier methods, and are the only birth control methods approved by the Catholic Church.

Forms of FABM

Regardless of whether she plans to use it to control pregnancy, every woman should be aware of her fertile times. Typically, a woman's fertile days are four to five days before ovulation and two days after ovulation, usually between days ten and seventeen of her cycle, but this varies from woman to woman, and from month to month.

A woman using the **basal body temperature (BBT) method** of contraception takes her temperature (with a specially designed thermometer) each morning immediately upon awakening. Prior to ovulation, there may be a slight dip in her temperature; then, on the day of ovulation, her body temperature generally rises between 0.4 and 0.8 degrees Fahrenheit. It will remain elevated until her period, due to the presence of progesterone. After mapping her temperature for at least three months, the woman becomes aware of her cycle and plans accordingly. It is best, though, for a woman to continue tracking her temperature throughout the time she uses the BBT method. She should also be aware that several factors can influence her body temperature, including illness, time of day, lack of sleep, and drug and alcohol use.

The **cervical mucus method** of birth control involves noting changes in color, consistency, and pH of cervical fluid and cervical mucus during ovulation. Right after menstruation, the vagina feels dry. In the days before ovulation, the mucus will be cloudy, thick, and sticky. At ovulation, the thinning of the mucus—which becomes clear and slippery, and will stretch between the fingers—indicates enhanced fertility.

The **calendar** (or **rhythm**) **method** of birth control relies on the consistency of ovulation during a woman's cycle. If her periods occur regularly each month, a woman can determine the times of the month when ovulation is most likely to occur. For this method, a woman uses a calendar to chart the length of her menstrual cycles. Based on her 12 previous menstrual cycles, she subtracts 18 days from her shortest menstrual cycle to determine her first fertile day, and 11 days from her longest menstrual cycle to determine her last fertile day. She would then remain abstinent during her most fertile time. This method is less effective for women with irregular cycles, or for women whose cycles are always less than 27 days long. An easier, yet more expensive, way involves the use of **ovulation predictor kits**, which allow a woman to test her urine daily for the presence of luteinizing hormone (LH), which increases 12 to 24 hours prior to ovulation. To get the best results from natural family planning, a woman should use the calendar method together with BBT and mucus tests; used together, these are called the **symptothermal method**.

Effectiveness of FABM

"When I got pregnant with my third, it was a total surprise. I was 42, using a diaphragm appropriately, my husband had been told he had a low sperm count, and it was just a few days before my period was due! So much for 'safe days' and 'unsafe days.'"

—*Author's files*

Traditionally, women have been told that their most fertile window is between days 10 and 17 of the menstrual cycle. This assumes that ovulation occurs exactly 14 days before the onset of the menstrual period, although this is usually not the case. Women should be aware that the timing of this fertile window could be highly unpredictable, even if their cycles are usually regular. In fact, more than 70% of women are in their fertile window before day 10 or after day 17 of their menstrual cycle, and there are actually few days of the cycle during which a woman is *not* potentially fertile, including during menstruation (Wilcox, Dunson, & Baird, 2000).

Intrauterine Devices (IUDs)

After completion of this section, you will be able to . . .

○ Describe the mechanism of action, efficacy, and advantages and disadvantages of IUDs.

An **intrauterine device (IUD)** is a small device made of flexible plastic that is placed in the uterus. Legend has it that the concept of the IUD stems from Arabian camel drivers, who would insert small stones into the uterus of each female camel to prevent pregnancy on their long journeys. Both Hippocrates and the 11th-century Persian physician Avicenna described the use of a form of primitive IUDs. In 1926 Ernst Grafenberg developed the "G ring," a circular IUD wrapped in silver wire, which had a 98.4% success rate in preventing pregnancy. The silver used in the G-ring was contaminated with copper, which probably increased the ring's efficacy (copper use in IUDs is discussed below).

Today, IUDs are the world's most popular form of reversible birth control used by women, utilized by nearly 128 million women worldwide (Connell, 2002). Forty-five percent of married women in China use IUDs (World Health Organization [WHO], 2002). They are much less widely used in the United States, although they are becoming more popular. In 1995 less than 1% of American women who used contraception had an IUD; by 2002 that percentage had risen to 2%, and by 2008, 5.5% of women in the United States using contraception chose the IUD as their method (Mosher & Jones, 2010). Although IUDs are recognized as one of the safest and most effective forms of reversible birth control available, there is a perception in the United

States that IUDs are not safe. This is probably a result of bad publicity caused by the Dalkon Shield, a faulty IUD used in the 1970s. The Dalkon Shield was pulled from the market after being linked with pelvic inflammatory diseases, second trimester miscarriages, and deaths. This defective device eventually led to more than 11,000 lawsuits and the removal of some safe IUDs from the American market.

IUDs come in several sizes, shapes, and types. The basic form is of a T-shaped frame. The arms of the frame hold the IUD in place near the top of the uterus. The two types of IUDs currently available in the United States are the copper-containing ParaGard Copper T 380A, which can be left in place for up to 10 years, and Mirena, which slowly releases a small amount of progestin.

IUDs work by preventing fertilization. The presence of the IUD in the uterus causes low-grade inflammation and prompts the release of white blood cells, which are toxic to both sperm and egg. The copper in the ParaGard hinders fertilization by inhibiting the transport of the sperm though the fallopian tubes, diminishing their ability to penetrate the egg, and may itself be toxic to the sperm and egg. The progestin in Mirena thickens cervical mucus, thins the endometrial lining, and prevents ovulation. There is a slight chance that IUDs may also inhibit the implantation of fertilized eggs, but most scientists believe this probably does not occur. Whereas fertilized eggs are recovered in the fallopian tubes of about half of women using no contraception, in women using IUDs no fertilized eggs were found in the fallopian tubes (Grimes, 2004).

One of the most effective methods available, IUDs offer long-term, immediate protection against pregnancy. Once in place, IUDs do not require any further action by the woman, except for a quick check each month to make sure the device is still in place. Fertility returns as soon as the IUD is removed. Women who use the IUD report the highest user satisfaction of any contraceptive method besides sterilization (Society of Family Planning, 2010). The IUD is available by prescription only, and it must be inserted and removed by a clinician.

Failure rates associated with IUDs are generally less than 1% per year (Grimes, 2004). Most failures occur within the first 3 months of insertion, and drugs such as aspirin and antibiotics may increase the failure rate. Although it was previously thought that IUDs were more effective for women who had already given birth than for women who had not, recent studies suggest that the IUD is equally effective in both sets of women (Society of Family Planning, 2010). IUDs are not recommended for women who are anemic or who already have heavy cycles or extreme cramping; who have multiple fibroids, abnormally large or small uterine cavities, or preexisting infections of the uterus, cervix,

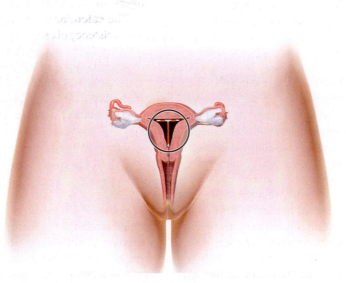

FIGURE 12.5 The IUD is placed in the uterus. (© Argosy Publishing Inc.)

Intrauterine device (IUD) A small device that is placed in the uterus to prevent pregnancy.

The Rule of 120

According to the "rule of 120," which was observed by doctors as late as 1969, a woman would be granted a voluntary sterilization only if her age, multiplied by the number of her children, equaled no less than 120. Therefore, a 20-year-old would be allowed to undergo the procedure only if she had already had six children. A 30-year-old could be voluntarily sterilized only if she had at least four children. A woman with one child had to wait until she was 120 years old until a physician would perform the procedure on her. SOURCE: Arnold, 1978.

or vagina; or in women who have valvular heart disease, or who are on anticoagulants. IUDs are not recommended for women with active STIs or a history of pelvic infection, or women with multiple sex partners, as they are more at risk for pelvic inflammatory disease (PID). Women who are pregnant or who have given birth within the last 4 weeks should not use an IUD.

A string that hangs from the IUD through the cervix lets the woman know her IUD is in the correct position. Approximately 4–5% of IUDs are partially or completely expelled during the first year, which increases a woman's chance of pregnancy. Expulsion rates for copper IUDs may be higher in younger women who have not had children (Society of Family Planning, 2010). Expulsion of the device is most likely during menstruation, so a woman using an IUD should check the string after each menstrual period to make sure it's still in place (Knowles & Ringel, 1998). If the string becomes lost, an ultrasound or X-ray can help to determine the location of the IUD. The progestin in some brands of IUD may help reduce uterine contractions that can lead to expulsions.

In the unlikely case that a woman does become pregnant while using an IUD, she stands a 50% greater chance of miscarriage or premature birth, which is reduced if she has the IUD removed as soon as she knows she's pregnant (Sivin, 1989). Also, although a woman using an IUD has a lower chance of having an ectopic pregnancy—a fertilized egg that implants somewhere other than the inner lining of the uterus—than a woman who uses no contraception, if she does become pregnant while using an IUD, she has an increased risk of ectopic pregnancy compared to if she had been using oral contraceptives (Spinnato, 1997).

Sterilization

After completion of this section, you will be able to . . .

○ Describe the mechanism of action, efficacy, and advantages and disadvantages of tubal sterilization and vasectomies.

Sterilization is the most popular method of contraception in the United States, currently used by more than 13 million American men and women. Sterilization refers to procedures that make an individual permanently incapable of conceiving or of fertilizing a partner. Sterilization is usually chosen by married people over 30 who already have all the children they want, by younger people who know they never want to have children, or by people with a hereditary condition who do not want to pass on the condition to another generation. The sterilization procedure for a woman is called **tubal sterilization**; for a man, **vasectomy**. Vasectomies, though less popular, are simpler, faster, more effective, less expensive, and safer than tubal sterilizations.

Tubal Sterilization

The first tubal sterilization was performed in 1880 during a Cesarean section to prevent the woman from undergoing additional high-risk pregnancies. It is estimated that more than 10 million women in the United States have undergone tubal sterilization. This procedure involves cutting or blocking the fallopian tubes, thus preventing the egg and sperm from meeting. Eggs are still produced, but they dissolve and are reabsorbed back into the body. Tubal sterilization does not affect a woman's hormones—she will still experience monthly periods, and her sexual desire will not be affected.

The tubal sterilization procedure is performed in various ways. In a laparoscopy, an outpatient procedure that generally takes 20 to 30 minutes and produces very little scarring, the surgeon makes a tiny incision underneath the navel, through which he or she inserts a laparoscope, a long thin hollow instrument with a tiny camera on the end. Other instruments are inserted, one of which is a tube that pumps a harmless gas into the abdominal cavity, inflating it for better visibility and room for the surgeon to work. The surgeon then cuts and closes off the fallopian tubes, either by clamps, clips, or cauterization. He or she then releases the gas from the abdomen. The incision is closed with a few stitches. After the procedure, a woman will likely feel bloated,

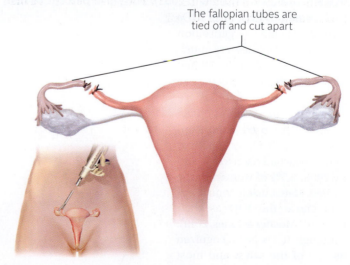

The fallopian tubes are tied off and cut apart

FIGURE 12.6 During a tubal sterilization, the fallopian tubes are cut, preventing fertilization of the egg. (© Argosy Publishing Inc.)

gassy, nauseated, and dizzy. Her shoulder may feel sore as the gas migrates up her body. If she has received general anesthesia, a woman should remain in the hospital for a number of hours, but regardless of the anesthesia, a woman should take it easy for up to a week after the procedure.

A new method of tubal ligation, *Essure,* is performed without abdominal incision or anesthesia. A spiral-like device made of polyester fibers and metals is inserted up through the vagina into each fallopian tube. Within a few months, the body creates scar tissue around the device, which blocks the passage of egg and sperm through the tube. The procedure takes about 35 minutes, is very effective, and is safer than tubal sterilization surgery (Duffy et al., 2005).

Although extremely effective, sterilization is not 100% effective in preventing pregnancy; typically, 4 to 5 out of every 1,000 women who have been sterilized may get pregnant, probably because of a failed or ineffective surgical procedure (Pollack, Carignan, & Jacobstein, 2004). Although the tiny sperm may be able to jump the gap in the fallopian tube to fertilize an egg, the egg, if it becomes fertilized, is too large to cross the site where the tube has been severed and will most likely implant in the fallopian tube, leading to an ectopic pregnancy, a life-threatening complication.

Vasectomy

Currently, approximately 42 million to 60 million men worldwide have had a vasectomy. About 500,000 vasectomies are performed on American men each year, and more than 3.7 million American women rely on their partner's vasectomy for contraception (Mosher & Jones, 2010). During a vasectomy, the vas deferentia—the tubes that carry the sperm out of the testes—are cut. A man with a vasectomy will still produce sperm, but they are harmlessly reabsorbed into the man's body. He will still have erections and orgasms and will ejaculate, but the sperm won't be added to the semen. Because sperm contributes only about 1–5% of the volume of semen, there is no noticeable difference in the amount of ejaculate. Vasectomy is one of the few methods available that allows a man to be responsible for birth control.

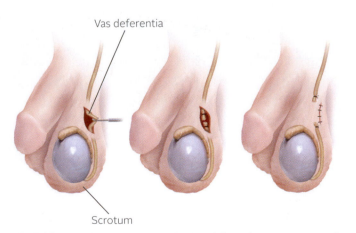

Vas deferentia

Scrotum

FIGURE 12.7 During a vasectomy, the vas deferentia are cut, preventing the sperm from leaving the body. (© Argosy Publishing Inc.)

The vasectomy is completed in a simple outpatient procedure that usually takes 15 to 20 minutes. A local anesthetic is applied. Traditionally, the surgeon uses a scalpel to make two small incisions in the skin on each side of the scrotum, to expose each vas deferens. The vas deferentia are lifted, cut and tied, and often cauterized; then they are returned to the scrotal sac. The incision site is closed with three or four stitches. A different vasectomy procedure doesn't involve a scalpel; instead, a tiny puncture is made in the scrotum. This procedure takes about 10 minutes, creates a much smaller incision site that may not require any stitches, and has a faster recovery time. After the procedure, the man should rest and put ice on the incision site for at least 4 hours. It is recommended that the man relax for a few days after the procedure. After resuming normal activity, it is suggested that men wear scrotal supports such as jock straps or briefs rather than boxers for a week.

Vasectomies are about 99.9% successful, which means that 1 woman out of 1,000 whose partner has had a vasectomy may become pregnant. The few failures usually occur if a couple has sex too soon after the procedure, when sperm remaining in the man's reproductive tract can be released in the semen. Men are advised to wait either 12 weeks, or until the man has had between 15 and 20 ejaculations for all the sperm to leave the system (Connell, 2002).

Some men and women regret being sterilized. Reversal is a complicated and costly procedure, and its success depends on the method of sterilization, the length of time since the procedure, and the health and age of the man or woman involved. Reversal may be particularly difficult for vasectomies because surgeons must try to reconnect channels that are only 1/100th of an inch in diameter.

New Forms of Contraception Under Development

After completion of this section, you will be able to . . .

○ Describe some new forms of contraception under development.

Short answer to why women are so often in charge of birth control: life isn't fair. The relative lack of male-oriented chemical contraception (in other words, a "male pill") may be due to the nature of male and female gametogenesis, as well as difficulties in designing a drug that is reversible (a bigger challenge in the male). Contraception in men involves completely suppressing production of the millions of sperm that are produced daily, whereas in women, it involves preventing the development or fertilization of (usually) one egg per month. Of course, it may also be due to the un-ignorable fact that women are the

Sterilization The act of making a man or woman unable to reproduce.

Tubal sterilization A procedure in which the fallopian tubes are cut or blocked, thus preventing the egg and sperm from meeting.

Vasectomy A method of sterilization in which the vas deferentia are cut, preventing sperm from being added to the ejaculate.

ASK YOURSELF

Why is it that practically all forms of reversible birth control involve the woman having to take charge? Why isn't there more birth control for men?

Table 12.2 Summary of Contraceptive Methods

TYPE OF CONTRACEPTIVE	MECHANISM OF ACTION	RISK OF PREGNANCY IN 1 YEAR:		OTHER (NON-CONTRACEPTIVE) RISKS	NON-CONTRACEPTIVE BENEFITS
		TYPICAL USE	PERFECT USE		
Total abstinence	Prevents the sperm from entering the vagina.	NA	0%	Frustration. Difficult to maintain. Many are unprepared for safe sex if intercourse does occur.	Protection against STI. Acceptable to those who don't believe in premarital sex.
Hormonal	Oral contraceptives — Prevents ovulation, thickens cervical mucus, may decrease mobility of fallopian tubes.	8.0%	0.3%	Menstrual irregularities; breast tenderness; minor depression; loss of sexual desire; slight increased risk of blood clots, stroke, and heart attack.	Diminished heavy flow and risk of anemia; protection against PID, ovarian cysts, and some forms of cancer; can be used as emergency contraception.
	Patch, ring	8.0%	0.3%		Same as above, plus less risk of forgetting.
	Depo-Provera	0.3%[a]	0.3%	Same as OC, plus weight gain (4–5 lbs over 3 yrs) and breakthrough bleeding.	Same as above, plus longer protection against pregnancy, and it contains progesterone only.
	Implanon	0.05% (higher in women >154 lbs.)	0.3%	Same as OC. Must be implanted by doctor.	
Condoms	Male — Prevent the sperm from entering the vagina.	13–17%	2%	May give false sense of security, as they don't provide 100% protection against STIs; latex allergies.	Currently the most effective protection (other than total abstinence) against STIs.
	Female	15–21%	5%		The only contraceptive that allows women to take responsibility for STI prevention.
IUD	Copper-T — Prevents fertilization.	0.8%	0.6%	Heavy or irregular flow, cramps, slight risk of uterine perforation. May increase risk of PID, especially in first 20 days of use.	May decrease risk of endometrial cancer; can be used as emergency contraception.
	Mirena	0.1%	0.1%		
Fertility awareness	Basal body temperature, calendar, mucus — Times intercourse to avoid most fertile days.	20–25%	9%	No protection against STIs during sexually active times.	
Withdrawal	Keeps sperm from entering the vagina.	18%	4%[b]	Risk of exposure to STI.	
Sterilization	Tubal sterilization	0.5%	0.5%	Risks of surgery; regret after procedure.	
	Vasectomy	0.15%	0.1%		May protect against ovarian cancer.
Spermicides	Chemically destroys sperm.	26–29%	18%	Repeated exposure may increase risk of STI transmission. May increase risk of yeast infections in women.	
Female barriers	Diaphragm — Prevent the sperm from entering the uterus.	16%	6%	Slight increased risk of UTI; latex allergies.	Diaphragm may reduce risk of PID by 50% (Connell, 2002). May give slight protection against some forms of STI (Moench et al., 2001).
	Cap	16–32%	9–26%[c]		
	Sponge	13.3–15.5%	9.2–11%[d]		
	Lea's Shield	15%	NA		
No method	Allows millions of sperm to make a mad dash toward the egg.	85%	85%	Risk of exposure to STI.	You can meet exciting new friends in the STI clinic.

© Cengage Learning 2013. [a]Trussell et al., 1990. [b]Kowal, 2004. [c]The lower number is for women who have never had a child; the upper for women who have had a child. [d]Edelman & North, 1987. SOURCES: Information from Mosher & Jones, 2010; Trussell, 2004b.

ones who get pregnant. Political realities factor in as well—because of some well-publicized drug recalls and our litigious society, pharmaceutical companies and the FDA are more risk-averse than they were in the past, and may be less likely to develop and approve new drugs that are designed to be used by basically healthy individuals. In addition, a contraceptive that only prevents pregnancy must still be used in combination with a condom in order to block transmission of STIs (Hoffer, 2010).

A third of couples rely on the three methods generally identified as "male methods": male condoms, withdrawal, and vasectomy (Stewart & Gabelnick, 2004). In one survey, more than 90% of women thought that a male pill would be a good idea and a majority thought they would use it if it were available, and only 2% of the women said they would not trust their partners to use it (Glasier et al., 2000). Another survey found that men were open to the idea of a hormonal method of contraception for men (Martin et al., 2000).

Gossypol, extracted from cottonseed oil, is an oral contraceptive designed to be taken by men. Gossypol stops the production of sperm without affecting hormone levels or sex drive. Unfortunately, it may lead to sterility—approximately 20–25% of men who used this product for an extended period of time remained infertile (Stewart & Gabelnick, 2004).

Other potential contraceptives designed to be used by men include hormonal injections, microbicides, ultrasound waves, and antibodies to sperm. Weekly injections of testosterone were found to reduce the production of sperm, although it can take a number of weeks for enough sperm to be eliminated from the semen to be effective, and androgen-related side effects were bothersome, although these can be reduced if progestin is added to the injection. Sperm are able to swim toward the egg due to progesterone's response on calcium channels in the sperm cell. An exciting new avenue of research involves inhibiting these calcium channels, thus preventing sperm's ability to reach the egg (Lishko, Botchkina, & Kirichock, 2011). In animal studies, the microbicide PRO 2000 has been found to be an effective contraceptive, as well as being active against HIV, the herpes virus, and the bacteria that cause chlamydia and gonorrhea (Schwartz & Gabelnick, 2002). Brief exposure to ultrasound waves—very short, inaudible sound waves—may produce months of sterility, and chemicals are under development that would induce men to produce antibodies to sperm.

Emergency Contraception

After completion of this section, you will be able to . . .

○ Define *emergency contraception.*

○ Describe the mechanism of action, effectiveness, side effects, and advantages and disadvantages of emergency contraception.

○ Evaluate the ethical issues involved in refusal statutes.

No contraceptive method is perfect; about half of unintended pregnancies occur among women who are using contraception (Henshaw, 1998). Even with perfect use, diaphragms and cervical caps may be dislodged, and up to 2% of condoms slip off or break. Seventy-two percent of women do not use birth control pills perfectly, and many women who believe they take their birth control pill every day actually do not (Potter, Oakley, de Leon-Wong, & Cañamar, 1996). Finally, women may be forced into having unprotected sexual intercourse—many American women are raped, most often by someone they know, resulting in an estimated 32,000 unintended pregnancies each year (Holmes, Resnick, Kilpatrick, & Best, 1996). Emergency contraception is designed to prevent a pregnancy after unprotected vaginal intercourse has already occurred (Knowles & Ringel, 1998). Researchers estimate that up to 50% of unintended pregnancies and abortions in this country could be prevented by the use of emergency contraception (Stewart, Trussell, Van Look, 2004).

Emergency contraception (EC) is provided either hormonally or by the insertion of an IUD. Insertion of a copper IUD is 99% effective in preventing a pregnancy if it is inserted within five to seven days after unprotected intercourse. The IUD can then be left in place for many years of effective contraception, or it can be removed after the next menstrual period. As previously stated, IUDs are not recommended for women at risk for STI at time of insertion or for rape victims because they are at increased STI risk.

Emergency contraceptive pills (ECP) contain higher doses of the same hormones found in birth control pills. Combination pills contain both estrogen and progesterone, whereas others, such as Plan B, contain only progestin. Ella, approved by the FDA in 2010, contains ulipristal acetate, which acts on progesterone receptors. Plan B emergency contraception pills are most effective in preventing fertilization if taken within 72 hours of unprotected intercourse. And although Ella can be taken within five days, it is important to note that all forms of emergency contraception are more effective if taken sooner rather than later because these drugs are not effective if ovulation has already occurred (Glasier et al., 2010). ECPs do not provide long-term contraception; a woman must be sure to use another form of birth control if she has vaginal intercourse before she gets her next period.

Isn't emergency contraception the same thing as an abortion?

Mechanism of Action

Emergency contraceptive pills are essentially high-dose birth control pills, and as such, work in a similar way. ECPs' main method in preventing fertilization is by inhibiting ovulation, but they may also thicken the cervical mucus, alter the transport of sperm through the fallopian tubes, or directly affect the ability of the sperm to fertilize the egg (Croxatto et al., 2004). It was once thought that ECPs impaired the implantation of a fertilized egg in the uterus, but recent studies have shown that they probably do not (Croxatto et al., 2004).

When taken after fertilization has already occurred, ECPs do not interfere with implantation of the egg in the uterus (Noe et al., 2010). In fact, if a woman is already pregnant when she takes an ECP (which is not recommended), her fetus will not be harmed (Trussell, Steward, & Raymond, 2006). Studies of women who have become pregnant after taking ECPs have found no increased risk of miscarriage or birth defects (Zhang, Chen, Wang, Ren, Yu, &

Emergency contraception
Measures that protect against pregnancy after unprotected sex has already occurred.

Table 12.3 Advantages and Disadvantages of Contraceptive Methods

Type of contraceptive		No effect on hormones	Extremely effective in preventing pregnancy	Easy to use immediately	Available without prescription	Ok for spontaneous sex	Doesn't affect sexual sensation	Use only as needed	Reversibility	Protects against STIs	Ok for breastfeeding or those who cannot take estrogen
Total Abstinence		X	X		X			X	Immediate	X	X
Hormonal	Oral contraceptives		X	X		X	X		1-3 months		
	Patch and ring		X	X		X	X				
	Depo-Provera		X	X		X	X		Up to 18 months		X
	Implanon		X	NA		X	X		1 month		X
Condoms	Male	X		X	X			X	Immediate	X	X
	Female	X			X			X	Immediate	X	X
IUD	Copper-T	X	X	NA		X	X		Immediate		X
	Mirena		X	NA		X	X		Immediate		X
Fertility awareness	Basal body temperature, rhythm, mucus	X			X		X		Immediate		X
Withdrawal		X			X	X	X	X	Immediate		X
Sterilization	Tubal sterilization	X	X	NA		X	X		Should be considered irreversible		X
	Vasectomy	X	X	NA		X	X				X
Spermicides		X		X	X		X	X	Immediate	May actually ↑ risk of HIV transmission	X
Female barriers	Diaphragm, cervical cap, Lea's Shield	X					X	X	Immediate	Some slight protection	X
	Sponge	X		X	X		X	X	Immediate		

© Cengage Learning 2013.

Cheng, 2009). More than 85% of obstetrician/gynecologists who refuse to perform abortions for personal or religious reasons say they *would* prescribe EC for their patients (Knowles & Ringel, 1998). Susan Wood, former assistant commissioner of women's health at the FDA, said, "the only connection this pill has with abortion is that it has the potential to prevent the need for one" (Wood, 2006).

Effectiveness

Combination ECPs reduce the risk of pregnancy by 75%, and progestin-only pills such as Plan B reduce the risk of pregnancy by up to 89% (Stewart, Trussell, & Van Look, 2004). Ella may be more effective than Plan B (Glasier et al., 2010). This does not mean that 25% of women who use ECPs will get pregnant after using them. On average, 8% of women who have unprotected sex will get preg-

The History of Plan B

In the early 1970s women were instructed to take higher than normal doses of oral contraceptives up to 72 hours after intercourse to prevent pregnancy (Yuzpe, Thurlow, Ramzy, & Leyshon, 1974). Because this entailed taking up to 40 progestin-only birth control pills at one time, a simpler solution was sought.

In 1999 the FDA approved Plan B, a progestin-only emergency contraceptive pill. The American Medical Association, the American College of Obstetricians and Gynecologists, the American Public Health Association, the Society for Adolescent Medicine, as well as other respected medical professionals supported making Plan B available over the counter (OTC). In 2003 two advisory committees to the FDA voted overwhelmingly in favor of this switch, describing the drug as "safer than aspirin."

In 2002 Dr. W. David Hager, a physician whose recommended treatment to women suffering from PMS is for them to read the Bible and pray, was appointed to the FDA's reproductive health drugs advisory committee by President George W. Bush. Dr. Hager expressed fears that freely available ECPs would cause a frenzy of sexual promiscuity in teenagers. Janet Woodcock, deputy commissioner for operations, added her fears that OTC availability of emergency contraception would lead to "sex-based cults centered around the use of Plan B" (Shorto, 2006).

FDA scientists were presented with numerous scientific studies that showed that availability of Plan B in no way increased sexual activity; that women who received ECP supplies were more likely to use these supplies when needed, but not more likely to have unprotected sex; and that availability of ECPs didn't decrease women's use of condoms or other contraceptive methods (Gold, Wolford, Smith, & Parker, 2004; Graham, Moore, Sharp, & Diamond, 2002; Raine et al., 2005). Nonetheless, in 2005 the FDA rejected the switch to OTC. Susan Wood, who was the director of the FDA's Office of Women's Health and assistant commissioner for Women's Health, resigned her position in protest to this decision. It was later discovered that the Bush administration was involved in the decision to reduce availability of ECPs, a highly unusual event, as the FDA usually has the last word on drug decisions.

Today, Plan B is available without a doctor's prescription for those aged 17 and older, although there is no medical or scientific basis for this age cutoff. There are both advantages and disadvantages to ECPs being available over the counter. The earlier a woman uses emergency contraception, the more effective it is—requiring a doctor's prescription delays the time until a woman can take the medication. However, if no prescription is required, women are less likely to be counseled by a physician as to its proper use, and to get information about more effective longer-term methods of contraception (Trussell & Raymond, 2009). Also, OTC drugs are usually not covered by insurance.

---

nant, but only 2% of women who use combination ECPs and 1% of women who use progestin-only ECPs will get pregnant (Stewart, Trussell, & Van Look, 2004). ECPs are more effective the sooner after sex the pills are taken (Trussell et al., 2006). Because ECPs are essentially high-dose birth control pills, the same drug interactions may occur. Emergency IUD insertion is more effective, reducing the risk of pregnancy by 99.9% (Stewart, Trussell, & Van Look, 2004).

Emergency contraception is safe—no deaths or serious complications have been linked to its use (Trussell et al., 2006). Given the short duration of exposure, ECPs can be used even by women who have been advised not to use oral contraceptives as their method of birth control (although, to be safe, these women may choose progestin-only ECPs or insertion of a copper IUD if they needed emergency contraception). Nausea and vomiting occur in some women, although these are less likely to occur with Plan B. A woman can take anti-nausea medications 30 minutes before taking the pills to reduce this side effect. Some women experience breast tenderness or headache, or a change in the timing or flow of their next menstrual period.

Although emergency contraception is safe, effective, easy to use, and reduces a woman's chance of pregnancy and possible need for an abortion, doctors rarely provide information about emergency contraception; in fact, only 20% of women treated in hospital emergency departments after sexual assaults are provided with EC (Amey & Bishai, 2002). Since Plan B became available over the counter, more women have access to emergency contraception; in 2002, 4% of sexually active women in the United States had ever used EC, but by 2008, 10% of American women had used emergency contraception at least once (Mosher & Jones, 2010). However, refusal statutes (see the From Cells to Society feature on page 310) may still prevent women from receiving EC.

Abortion

After completion of this section, you will be able to . . .

- Define *abortion*.

- Consider the reasons that women may choose to have an abortion.

- Compare the mechanism of action, side effects, and advantages and disadvantages of medication and surgical abortion procedures.

- Evaluate the existence of post-abortion syndrome.

- Describe the legal history of abortion in America.

- Consider the effect of the legality of abortion on its incidence worldwide.

Refusal Statutes

In 2004 Amanda Phiede, a college student at the University of Wisconsin, brought her doctor's prescription for a refill of her birth control pills to her Kmart Pharmacy. Pharmacist Neil Noesen refused to fill her prescription because he didn't want to "commit a sin." Nor would he return Amanda's prescription form so she could go elsewhere to fill it. Amanda eventually got her prescription filled at another pharmacy but missed a dose of her pill due to the delay. Noesen received a reprimand and a limit on his license that requires him to prepare a written notice specifying which of his professional duties he chooses not to perform.

After *Roe v. Wade,* most states passed laws protecting medical professionals who choose not to perform abortions based on their religious, moral, or personal values. These *refusal statutes* have been expanded to include many other medical procedures, such as physician-assisted suicide, which is legal in Oregon, and *in vitro* fertilization procedures. The more than 12 million women in the United States who use prescription methods of birth control should be aware that in 13 states, pharmacists can refuse to fill those prescriptions if they don't personally believe in the use of contraceptives.

Recently, there have been a number of other rights-of-refusal cases in the country.

In Texas, a woman was not allowed to fill her prescription for emergency contraception after being raped. In California, a gay woman was refused treatment at a fertility clinic because of her sexual orientation. (In 2008 the California Supreme Court declared that physicians may not discriminate against gays and lesbians in medical treatment.)

In other cases, doctors would not prescribe Viagra to unmarried men or assist in sterilization procedures (Stein, 2006). In a recent survey, 8% of physicians in the United States felt they were under no obligation to present information about medically available treatments they may consider objectionable—this translates to at least 40 million Americans who are under the care of physicians who won't disclose all medical options (Curlin, Lawrence, Chin, & Lantos, 2007).

What do you think? Should health care workers who refuse to participate in activities they find morally objectionable be required to refer patients elsewhere for the procedure? Physician William Toffler does not think so. "Think about slavery. I am a blacksmith and a slave owner asks me to repair the shackles of a slave. Should I have to say, 'I can't do it but there's a blacksmith down the road who will'?" (Stein, 2006). Alternatively, what options does this leave the patient?

What are the limits of the rights of refusal? If you will allow a bit of slippery slope speculation, consider the following scenarios.

- A physician who is a Jehovah's Witness could refuse to give a patient a blood transfusion.
- A Scientologist pharmacist could refuse to fill a prescription for antidepressants.

Are there any ethical differences between these situations? Why or why not?

Medical professional refusal rights lead to thorny ethical dilemmas. Do medical professionals have a responsibility to impose their views on their patients? On one hand, by entering the field, they have consented to abide by the professional standards established by the boards under which they are licensed. On the other hand, do people lose the right to act on their moral and religious beliefs when they enter health care? Where do their rights end and patient rights begin? Whose well-being comes first—the patient's or the health care provider's? Should health-related decisions be left up to a patient, or to others? Should scientific factors be considered in this decision, or the moral or religious beliefs of the caregivers? In other words, who should choose what's right for the patient, and what factors should be considered?

An **abortion** is the medical termination of a pregnancy before the embryo or fetus has developed enough to survive outside of the womb. Throughout her lifetime, a typical woman in the United States spends 5 years pregnant, postpartum, or trying to become pregnant, and 30 years trying to avoid pregnancy. The odds of using contraceptives flawlessly for 30 years are slim. Each year, more than 3 million women in the United States have an unplanned pregnancy; 48% of these unintended conceptions occurred in a month during which contraception was used (Finer & Henshaw, 2006). Fewer than half—1.2 million—of these unintended pregnancies end in abortion. (Some unplanned pregnancies end in adoption, which will be discussed in the next chapter.) It is estimated that at least a third of all women in the United States will have an abortion at some time in their lives (AGI, 2003; Stewart, Ellertson, & Cates, 2004). A woman is most likely to choose an abortion if she is young, poor, or unmarried. Women of color, those who become pregnant over the age of 40, and women who have had three or more previous live births are also more likely to choose to end a pregnancy (Stewart, Ellertson, & Cates, 2004).

Abortion The medical termination of a pregnancy before the embryo or fetus has developed enough to survive outside of the womb.

Of women in the United States aged 15 to 44:

- The 16% who are poor account for 42% of abortions.
- The 61.5% who are white account for 36% of abortions.
- The 14.4% who are black account for 30% of abortions.
- The 17% who are Hispanic account for 25% of abortions.
- The 17% who are teenagers account for 17.6% of abortions.
- The 56% who are unmarried account for 85% of abortions (Jones, Finer, & Singh, 2010).

In 2006 teenagers in the United States had more than 750,000 pregnancies. Of these, 27.3% ended in abortion, 14.3% ended in miscarriage, and 58.3% resulted in a birth. The abortion rate in 2006 was one of the lowest in the last 30 years (Kost, Henshaw, & Carlin, 2010).

There are several reasons why a woman might choose to have an abortion. It may be that she feels she is too young (or too old) to be able to raise a child or that having a child would interfere with her education or career goals. A woman may find herself suddenly single or unable to afford a child. Her physical health—or psychological health, in the case of a pregnancy due to rape or incest—may be at risk, or the fetus may be found to have a severe medical disorder that would negatively impact his or her quality of life. Usually, a woman chooses abortion to reduce the risk of physical, psychological, social, or economic harm for herself or for any present or future children.

Societal Views on Abortion

Do you want to pick a fight with someone? Discuss abortion. Abortion is one of the most controversial issues in contemporary society. "Pro-life" proponents feel that human life begins at conception and abortion represents the murder of an unborn child. Members of the "pro-choice" movement feel that a woman has the right to control her body and choose whether she wants to become a parent and that the government has no right to interfere with her choice.

National public opinion polls show that a majority of Americans support some form of legalized abortion. In a recent CBS News poll, 36% felt that abortion should be generally available, 39% felt that abortion should be available with stricter limits than it has now, 23% felt that abortion should not be permitted, and 2% were unsure (CBS, 2010). Reduced support for legal abortion is often correlated with one's political party and residence: Republicans and those who live in the South or Midwest are less likely to support abortion, as are African Americans, those with more conservative attitudes on premarital sex, and people with lower levels of education. A higher commitment to traditional religion is associated with stronger disapproval of abortion, although the Bible does not specifically prohibit the act.

Abortion in the Media

Although about half of unwanted pregnancies end in abortion in the real world, abortion is often not even discussed as an option in movies and TV. Instead, women in this situation usually either keep the baby or lose it to miscarriage. When abortion is depicted in films, the movie usually takes place in the past, and the woman often suffers negative consequences from her decision (Navarro, 2007).

Violence Against Abortion Providers

Anti-abortion activists employ numerous tactics to prevent women from getting legal abortions. Activists may block the clinic entrance, shout insults at the woman, or otherwise intimidate or even assault her. They also target abortion providers. Fifty-six percent of all abortion providers and 82% of large providers experienced some kind of harassment in 2000, including picketing of clinics and staff members' homes, physical interference with patients, vandalism, and threats of violence (Boonstra, Gold, Richards, & Finer, 2006).

Methods of Abortion

In the United States almost 90% of abortions are performed within the first trimester (Stewart, Ellertson, & Cates, 2004). First-trimester methods of abortion include medication abortions, aspiration, and dilation and curettage (or D&C). Abortions performed after the first trimester use the methods of dilation and evacuation, and instillation. Medication abortions account for 13% of all abortions, and 22% of abortions performed before 9 weeks gestation (Jones, Zolna, Henshaw, & Finer, 2008).

Medication Abortions

The French company Roussel Uclaf developed **mifepristone** in the early 1980s. Originally called RU-486 (for the company that developed it and the catalog number assigned to it), mifepristone was approved by the FDA in 2000. Taken up to 56 days after the first day of the last menstrual period, mifepristone terminates a pregnancy by blocking the actions of progesterone, a hormone that helps maintain pregnancy, and by increasing the effects of prostaglandins in the body. Two days after taking mifepristone, a woman takes the prostaglandin analog **misoprostol**, which softens and dilates the cervix and causes uterine contractions, which leads to the expulsion of the embryo. The patient then returns to her doctor 12 days later to ensure she is no lon-

Mifepristone (mih-FEH-prih-stone) Also called RU-486, this drug ends a pregnancy by blocking the actions of progesterone.

Misoprostol (mye-so-PRAH-stole) Aids mifepristone by increasing the effects of prostaglandins.

© Universal Studios/Photofest

© Fox Searchlight/Photofest

In the movie *Knocked Up* (above) a woman, newly promoted to her dream job as an on-camera TV personality, decides to have the baby that results from a one-night stand. In *Juno* (right) a pregnant teen decides to go through with the pregnancy and give up the baby for adoption.

© MIKE HUTMACHER/MCT /Landov

Dr. George Tiller was the medical director of a clinic in Kansas, one of only three in the nation that would perform abortions after the 21st week of pregnancy. Anti-abortion groups protested outside the clinic every day for years; right-wing pundits repeatedly called Dr. Tiller a mass murderer and compared his actions to those of Nazis. In 2009 Dr. Tiller was murdered, gunned down in his church by an anti-abortion activist. His clinic is now closed.

ger pregnant. Mifepristone is 92–96% effective in ending a pregnancy (Wiebe, Dunn, Guilbert, Jacot, & Lugtig, 2002).

Methotrexate is another drug used to terminate pregnancy. It works by halting cell division, thus interfering with the implantation of the embryo. An injection of methotrexate can be given up to 49 days after the first day of the last menstrual period, and is followed 5 days later by misoprostol. Methotrexate is not as effective an abortifacient as mifepristone.

Side effects of medication abortions are similar to those of miscarriage: abdominal pain, cramping, dizziness, fatigue, nausea, vomiting, and diarrhea. Heavy bleeding can also occur and can continue for up to 2 weeks after mifepristone and for up to 4 weeks following methotrexate. In very rare cases, women have died after medication abortions, although the exact cause of death in these cases is unknown.

Medication abortions are less invasive and painful than surgical abortions, and they don't cause injury to the cervix or uterus. They don't require the use of anesthesia, and they are less expensive than surgical procedures. However, medication abortions are not as safe as surgical abortions and may require an extra clinic visit. Waiting and uncertainty are a major disadvantage to medication abortions. In these abortions, the termination of pregnancy is not complete immediately. In most women who take mifepristone/misoprostol, abortion begins about four hours after taking miso-

---

Methotrexate (meth-oh-TREKS-ate) Ends a pregnancy by stopping cell division and interfering with the implantation of the embryo.

Vacuum aspiration A surgical method of abortion, in which the uterine contents are removed by suction.

Dilation and curettage (D&C) An abortion method in which the uterine contents are scraped out with a metal loop.

Dilation and evacuation (D&E) A method of surgical abortion most commonly used during the second trimester, which combines vacuum aspiration with forceps and a curette.

---

prostol and is complete within three to four days. Methotrexate/misoprostol take longer; on average, it takes about a week for abortion to be completed, although in 15–20% of women it may take up to four weeks to successfully terminate pregnancy (Wiebe et al., 2002). About 8% of the time, surgery is needed to complete the abortion.

Surgical Abortions

Vacuum aspiration is the safest and most common form of abortion in the United States. It can be performed during the first trimester. In this method, the cervix is gradually dilated by the insertion of increasingly thick rods, or by laminaria, an absorbent seaweed stick, which slowly expands as it absorbs fluid. Misoprostol is sometimes used to soften and dilate the cervix. An angled tube attached to an aspirator is inserted into the uterus and empties the uterine contents by suction. The procedure takes about 10 minutes. Compared to medication abortion, surgical vacuum aspiration is quicker and more certain. It is fairly safe and simple; when performed during the first trimester it poses no long-term risk to future fertility. However, it is more invasive and painful than medication abortions, it and carries a small risk of injury or infection.

Dilation and curettage (D&C) is usually performed in a hospital, under heavy sedation or general anesthesia. In this surgical abortion method, the cervix is dilated and the uterine contents are scraped from the uterine lining with a metal loop. A D&C is not as safe as vacuum aspiration and carries a higher risk of hemorrhage, infection, and perforation of the uterus.

© Yelena Kovalenko/Alamy

A curette is used to perform a D&C.

Dilation and evacuation (D&E), which combines vacuum aspiration with forceps and a curette, is most commonly used during the second trimester, when simple vacuum aspiration would be too risky. Often performed in conjunction with a sedative, painkiller, or general anesthesia, the cervix is dilated, albeit more fully than it is during a first trimester abortion to accommodate the larger products of conception. Some of the uterine contents are removed via vacuum aspiration, and the remaining contents are removed with a curette and forceps. A D&E is a riskier procedure because it is performed later in pregnancy.

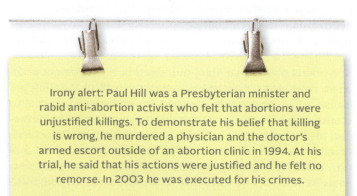

Irony alert: Paul Hill was a Presbyterian minister and rabid anti-abortion activist who felt that abortions were unjustified killings. To demonstrate his belief that killing is wrong, he murdered a physician and the doctor's armed escort outside of an abortion clinic in 1994. At his trial, he said that his actions were justified and he felt no remorse. In 2003 he was executed for his crimes.

Intact dilation and extraction is a late-term abortion (performed between weeks 20 and 24) in which an intact fetus is surgically removed from the uterus through the cervix. Also called **partial birth abortion,** the fetus is pulled out feet first, and then the skull is punctured and compressed so it can fit through the dilated cervix. This procedure is very rarely performed—only 0.17% of abortions are intact D&E—and may be done in cases in which severe fetal deformities or fetal death is discovered, or if the mother's life is in danger (Finer & Henshaw, 2003). In 2003 Congress passed a ban on partial birth abortions, which allows for fine or imprisonment for physicians who perform this procedure. In 2007 the U.S. Supreme Court upheld a nationwide ban on partial birth abortions.

Safety of Abortion

When performed by trained professionals in a hygienic setting, abortion is a safe procedure. Fewer than 1% of women who receive a legal abortion in the United States experience a major complication (AGI, 2003). Risks associated with surgical abortion are rare but include perforation of the uterus, bowel, or bladder; shock; sterility; or death. The risks associated with medication abortions include heavy bleeding and infection. The chance of death from a legal abortion today is 0.6 per 100,000 procedures, which falls to 1 in 1 million when performed at or before 8 weeks of pregnancy (Boonstra et al., 2006). In comparison, the risk associated with childbirth is about 11 times as high as that associated with all abortion. In countries where abortion is illegal, it is estimated that 68,000 women die each year from abortion complications (Ahman & Shah, 2004).

Psychological Consequences of Abortion

Women who choose to terminate a pregnancy may experience positive as well as negative emotions. After abortion, the most widely experienced emotion is relief (Armsworth, 1991); rates of psychological distress following abortion are actually lower than those felt by the women before their abortions (Adler, Ozer, & Tschann, 2003; Pope, Adler, & Tschann, 2001). Adolescents or adult women who have an abortion do not appear to be at elevated risk of depression or low self-esteem after the procedure (Warren, Harvey, & Henderson, 2010). However, some women may feel guilt, anger, or ambivalence after the procedure. Up to 20% of women may experience mild, temporary depression following the abortion, which can linger in up to 10% of women. Most women are psychologically well-adjusted 2 years after the procedure.

A woman's emotional response to abortion depends on a number of factors, including her relationship with her partner, the support (or lack thereof) she receives from others, and the counseling or information about abortion she receives beforehand. A woman's age, religion, and the length of gestation will also affect her response to abortion. A woman with pre-existing mental health problems is more likely to experience emotional and psychological problems following her abortion. In general, in adult women who have an unplanned pregnancy, the risk of mental health problems is no greater if they have a single, elective, first-trimester abortion than if they delivered that pregnancy (Major et al., 2008).

Many pro-life groups claim that a large percentage of women who have undergone an abortion are suffering from post-abortion syndrome (PAS), a condition similar to post-traumatic stress disorder and characterized by guilt, depression, lowered self-esteem, and flashbacks. PAS is not recognized as a psychological disorder by the American Psychiatric Association or by the American Psychological Association, whose expert panel studied the evidence and decided "legal abortion of an unwanted pregnancy . . . does not pose a psychological hazard for most women" (Adler et al., 1990, p. 41). Still others feel that PAS may exist, but that it is rare.

Legal Status of Abortion

Women have always found ways to end unwanted pregnancies; abortions were not invented in 1973 with the passage of *Roe v. Wade*. In ancient times, women would terminate pregnancies with abortifacient herbs, the use of sharpened tools, or other techniques. What has changed is that in the United States women can now terminate pregnancies safely and legally.

For much of our nation's history, abortion was permitted. Abortion began to be criminalized in the mid-19th century because of a national desire to increase the population and to protect women from substandard procedures; before that, it is estimated that up to a quarter of all conceptions were terminated by abortion (McLaren, 1990). By the beginning of the 20th century, every state in the union had laws banning abortion. Approximately 200,000 to 1.2 million illegal abortions were performed in the United States each year in the 1950s and 1960s, before the passage of *Roe v. Wade* (Cates, Grimes, & Schulz, 2003).

The court case that has become practically synonymous with abortion rights originated in 1970 in Texas. Norma McCorvey, a poor, uneducated, alcoholic, drug-using young woman, who had already given up two children for adoption, became pregnant again. Under Texas law, abortions were prohibited except in cases in which the woman's life was in danger. McCorvey's name was disguised as "Jane Roe," and she was made the lead plaintiff in a class action suit seeking to legalize abortion (Levitt & Dubner, 2005). Dallas district attorney Henry Wade defended the Texas law. The case made it to the highest court in the land, where, in 1973, the Supreme Court struck down Texas's law as unconstitutional. Passage of the law happened too late for Norma McCorvey, who gave birth and again put the child up for adoption.

Roe v. Wade decreed that a woman's right to a safe, legal abortion was protected under her constitutionally guaranteed right to privacy. The court decision stated that during the first trimester, the decision about abortion was left to the judgment of the woman and her physician, and states have little right to interfere. After the first trimester, each state could regulate abortion procedures in ways reasonably related to the woman's health. In 1992, in the case of *Planned Parenthood of Southeastern Pennsylvania v. Casey,* the law was modified so that the trimester system

Partial birth abortion A rarely performed procedure in which an intact fetus is removed from the uterus during the second trimester. Also called **intact dilation and extraction**.

Roe v. Wade The 1973 U.S. Supreme Court decision that stated that most laws against abortion violated a woman's constitutional right to privacy, thus overturning many laws that restricted abortion.

Does post-abortion syndrome (PAS) exist? Is it common or rare? Why do some studies support its existence and others do not? Consider the following issues:

> **Are women more depressed after abortion?** How was the emotional condition of the women measured? By psychological tests? Questionnaires? Interviews? "Depression" can be an ambiguous term if it is not related to a specific set of psychological guidelines. The wording of a questionnaire can also affect the results. Asking a woman "Do you feel guilty that you murdered your unborn child?" compared to "After the procedure, did you experience relief?" could certainly affect the psychological findings.

> **If there is depression, what is causing it?** Have factors related to the unplanned pregnancy rather than the abortion been considered? An unwanted pregnancy is difficult in all instances; it is upsetting to have an unwanted child, upsetting to have an abortion, and upsetting to give up a child for adoption. (Consistent and conscientious use of contraceptives is always recommended!) Whereas as many as 20% of women may show signs of depression after abortion, post-partum depression affects as many as 70% of women after childbirth, and as many as 95% of birth mothers report grief and loss after giving up a child for adoption, the majority of whom continue to experience these feelings many years later (Sachdev, 1989).

What was the woman's experience at the abortion clinic? Did she encounter anti-abortion activists who blocked her way or shouted at her? Women may experience emotional fallout from this harassment. Sadness after an abortion is correlated to perceptions of stigma and low social support for the abortion decision (Major et al., 2008).

> **Is it significant that the American Psychological Association does not recognize PAS as a mental illness?** Just because the American Psychological Association (APA) doesn't recognize PAS does not mean it doesn't exist. The APA is made up of people—educated, intelligent people—but people who are subject to the cultural viewpoints of the time. Just because a professional body doesn't currently recognize a disorder does not necessarily mean that the disorder doesn't exist. However, one should also consider that the APA is a trusted psychological association without a specific religious, political, or ideological agenda.

> **What was the research design?** When and how were these studies performed?

Were the women questioned days, months, or years after the procedure? How might the timing of the study affect the results? Many of these studies used a questionnaire to ascertain women's emotional states. What were the controls to assure that women answered truthfully and did not either deny or exaggerate problems?

What was the population studied? A study done by David Reardon found that a whopping 94% of respondents experienced negative psychological effects after abortion. However, all of Dr. Reardon's subjects were recruited from a group called Women Exploited by Abortion, so they were self-selected as already experiencing negative effects. On the other hand, in studies that found no evidence of PAS, some of the women in the survey population did not agree to be interviewed after their abortions. The feelings of those non-participators could skew the findings; for instance, if most of the non-responders felt traumatized by their abortion and did not want to talk about it, their non-inclusion in the survey would make abortion appear to be less emotionally difficult than previously presented.

> **Did the study use appropriate controls?** What was the baseline health of the women before the procedure? Did they have any pre-existing psychological conditions? Perhaps a woman who is more likely to have an unplanned pregnancy is more likely to suffer from psychological problems.

What were the reasons given for the abortion? A woman ending a wanted pregnancy due to medical necessity might react with more grief than a woman ending an unwanted pregnancy. The APA task force on mental health and abortion found that women who have abortion due to fetal abnormality have negative psychological associations equivalent to those experienced by women who experience a miscarriage or stillbirth, but less than women who deliver a child with life-threatening abnormalities (Major et al., 2008).

Women who choose abortion are more likely to be young, poor, and uneducated, characteristics that may affect a woman's emotional state. Was the psychological health of women post-abortion compared with *all* women, or with those of a similar demographic?

> "The ability of women to participate equally in the economic and social life of the nation has been facilitated by their ability to control their reproductive lives."
> —Supreme Court Justice Sandra Day O'Connor, 1992

was replaced with consideration about fetal viability. After viability—when the fetus is capable of sustained survival outside the woman's body—the state may choose to regulate or even prohibit abortion but can't impose restrictions that interfere with the life or health of the pregnant woman. In general, states with the strongest anti-abortion laws are those in which women suffer from higher levels of poverty, lower levels of education, and a lower ratio of female-to-male earnings (Schroedel, 2000). In these states, far less money is spent per child on foster care, education, and child welfare.

The *Casey* decision also made it easier for states to add restrictions for women seeking abortions. Since 1973 there have been more than 20 major opinions handed down by the Supreme Court regarding a woman's access to abortion. Most states have enacted laws that modify *Roe v. Wade,* and many restrictions on abortion have been added, including parental notification or consent for minors, mandatory ultrasounds, and obligatory waiting periods. In 2005, 52 state laws were passed restricting abortion, and more than 100 more are being considered to further limit the procedure.

There is no universally agreed upon answer to when life begins. Some believe life begins at the moment of conception, whereas some believe life begins at birth. Some believe that a fetus is alive when it attains a certain degree of brain activity or when it can survive outside of the womb. Since abortion has been legalized, it is

The real "Jane Roe," Norma McCorvey, has converted to Christianity and become a member of the anti-abortion movement, working to make abortion illegal.

As of 2005, only 13% of the counties in the United States have an abortion provider; a third of American women of reproductive age live in a county without an abortion provider (Jones et al., 2008). In fact, there are a number of states, including Kansas, Mississippi, North Dakota, and South Dakota, that have only one clinic in the entire state in which abortions are performed.

_____

_____

_____

_____

_____

more likely for a woman to obtain an abortion earlier in pregnancy. In 1970 only 20% of abortions were performed at or before 8 weeks of pregnancy; today 60% of abortions occur within the first 8 weeks, and 88% occur within the first trimester (Boonstra et al., 2006; CDC, 2004). As we will learn in Chapter 13, a 12-week fetus cannot experience pain. At that stage of development, the fetal nervous system and brain are quite immature, and the cortex—where sensations are processed—has not yet developed. Furthermore, the chemicals involved in the transmission of pain don't begin to develop until the third trimester.

Abortion Around the World

There are perhaps 42 million abortions performed worldwide each year (Shah & Ahman, 2009). Legal restrictions on abortion don't affect its incidence, and in fact abortion rates are often highest in countries where abortion is highly restricted (this is probably mostly due to the state of women's rights and the availability of safe contraceptives). In contrast, abortion levels are low in western European countries where abortion is legal and covered by national health insurance, and there are fewer unintended pregnancies (Figure 12.8; Henshaw, Singh, & Haas, 1999). When abortions are restricted or illegal, women will still get abortions, but under clandestine or dangerous conditions. Worldwide, almost half of all abortions are unsafe; in developing regions, 92% are unsafe (Shah & Ahman, 2009).

• • •

The average woman in the United States is fertile for almost four decades; sexually active heterosexual women therefore need to spend most of their lives using contraception. In fact, 99% of women in the United States who have ever had sexual intercourse with a male have used at least one contraceptive method (Mosher & Jones, 2010). Different forms of contraception will address the varying needs of different couples; it is up to individual women and men to educate themselves as to what method best suits their lifestyle.

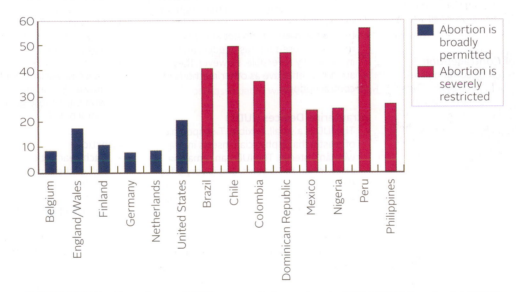

FIGURE 12.8 Abortion rates per 1,000 women. (© Cengage Learning 2013. SOURCE: Boonstra et al., 2006.)

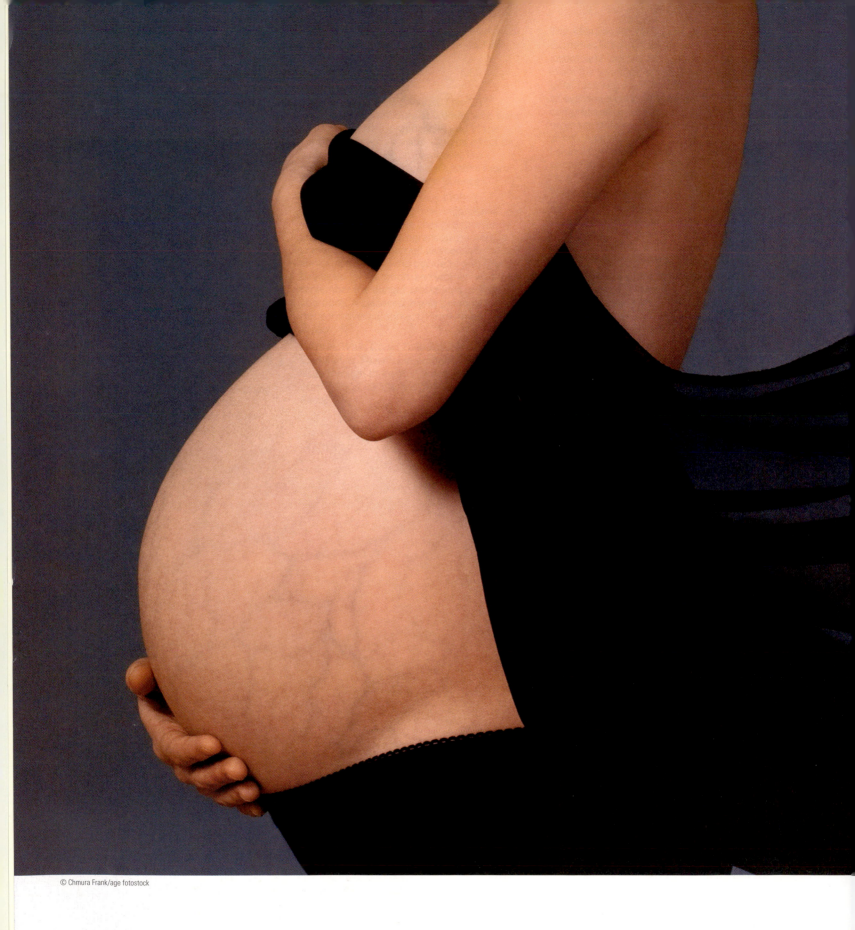

Conception, Pregnancy, and Birth

"Imagine yourself as the world's tallest skyscraper, built in nine months and germinating from a single brick. As that 'seed' brick divides, it gives rise to every other type of material needed to construct and operate the finished tower—a million tons of steel, concrete, mortar, insulation, tile, wood, granite, solvents, carpet, cable, pipe and glass as well as all furniture, phone systems, heating and cooling units, plumbing, electrical wiring, artwork and computer networks, including software. This brick and its daughter bricks also know exactly how much of each to make, where to send them, and when and how to piece it all together. Now imagine further that when the building is done it has the capacity to love, hate, converse, do calculus, compose symphonies, and have rapturous physical relations with other towers, a prime result of which is to create new buildings even more elaborate than itself."

—Tsiaras & Werth, 2002, p. 5

© Chad Riley RF/Age fotostock

© Frank and Helena/cultura/Corbis

© Mauro Fermariello/Photo Researchers, Inc.

Even though there are 7 billion people on earth, successful fertilization and birth is not simple. Most conceptions either fail to implant or are miscarried before birth. In this chapter, we will discuss what happens when a sperm fertilizes an egg and begins the process by which a new life is created.

The Process of Conception

After completion of this section, you will be able to . . .

○ Define the terms *fertilization* and *zygote*.

○ Identify some of the challenges of fertilization.

○ Describe ways by which a couple may increase their chance of conception.

○ List and describe the methods used for sex selection.

Fertilization, or **conception**, occurs when the nucleus of one of the smallest cells of the body—the sperm—fuses with the nucleus of one of the largest, the egg. This typically occurs in the fallopian tube. During intercourse, sperm are ejaculated into the vagina, cross the cervix into the uterus, and swim into the fallopian tube, where they meet the recently ovulated secondary oocyte (egg cell) (Figure 13.1).

Fertilization or **conception**
The joining of the nucleus of the egg with the nucleus of the sperm.

Although only one sperm actually penetrates the egg, a fertile man produces many millions of sperm. This is because many barriers confront a sperm on its journey to the egg. Although the alkalinity of semen offers some protection, many sperm instantly die when confronted with the inhospitable acidity of the vagina. In addition, the woman's body may selectively kill off less-suitable sperm, as well as any sperm from a partner whom she has not been previously exposed to for at least 3 months (Robertson, 2010). Other sperm never reach their goal because they flow out of the vagina. Fibrinogen from the prostate gland helps prevent this sperm loss by thickening the semen. Surviving sperm travel through the cervix, which is usually blocked by mucus. Fortunately, this mucus thins out during ovulation to ease the passage. Once the sperm traverse the uterus, they enter the fallopian tube. Half of the sperm refuse to stop and ask for directions, and pick the fallopian tube into which the egg has *not* been ovulated that month. Out of the several hundred million sperm that were deposited into the vagina, fewer than 200 typically reach the correct fallopian tube, and even fewer make it to the egg. Sperm locate the egg in part by using odor receptors, similar to those in the nose, which "sniff out" the sperm-attracting chemical secreted by the egg (Spehr et al., 2003).

A sperm has to travel 2,000 times its own length (at a speed of about 0.12 inch per minute) before it arrives at the fallopian tube. This distance would be comparable to a 2.25-mile swim for a 6-foot man. It is advantageous that sperm don't immediately reach the fallopian tube because a freshly ejaculated sperm

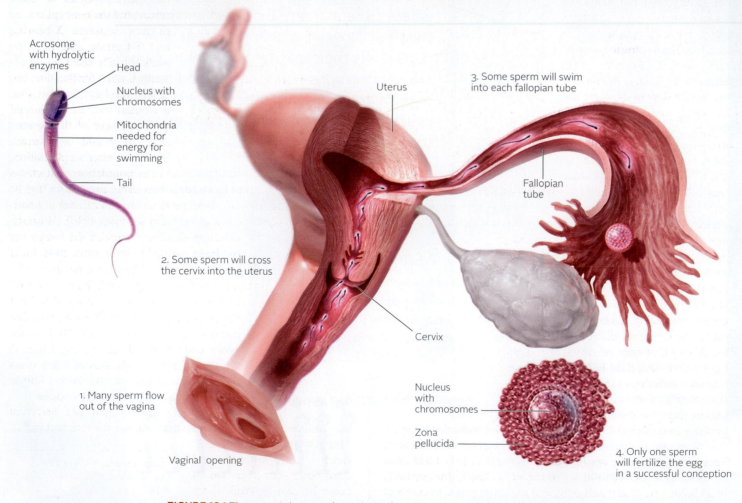

Acrosome with hydrolytic enzymes

Head

Nucleus with chromosomes

Mitochondria needed for energy for swimming

Tail

3. Some sperm will swim into each fallopian tube

Uterus

Fallopian tube

2. Some sperm will cross the cervix into the uterus

Cervix

1. Many sperm flow out of the vagina

Vaginal opening

Nucleus with chromosomes

Zona pellucida

4. Only one sperm will fertilize the egg in a successful conception

FIGURE 13.1 The sperm's journey through the female anatomy. (© Argosy Publishing Inc.)

cannot fertilize an egg. The digestive enzymes in the acrosome on the head of the sperm need time to mature in the female reproductive tract so they can penetrate the **zona pellucida**, the jelly-like coat surrounding the egg. It takes the digestive enzymes from many sperm to break through the zona pellucida, although only one sperm actually penetrates the egg. Once one sperm enters the egg, the electrical and chemical properties of the ovum change, and the egg secretes a chemical that hardens the zona pellucida and destroys the surface receptors that bind sperm, preventing any other sperm from penetrating. An egg fertilized by more than one sperm is incompatible with life, and would be spontaneously aborted. Perhaps one-fifth of all miscarriages occur because two sperm penetrate the egg (Tallack, 2006). Once the successful sperm enters the egg, its body and tail detach and its nucleus is drawn toward the nucleus of the egg, where the chromosomes combine. Fertilization causes the secondary oocyte to finish meiosis II and produce a **zygote**, a fertilized egg.

The best way for a couple to increase the chance of conception is, not surprisingly, to have sex—every day if the male has a normal sperm count, and every other day if his sperm count is low. Couples hoping to conceive can further improve their chances by having intercourse on certain days of the cycle and in certain positions. Biological factors may predispose women to desire intercourse during her most fertile days (Wilcox et al., 2004). The man-on-top position may be optimal for conception, especially if the woman keeps her knees elevated afterward to prevent the loss of sperm through the vagina. The chance of conception is greatest within a 6-day window that includes ovulation and the 5 days preceding it (Wilcox, Weinberg, & Baird, 1995). There are a number of ways a woman can detect when she's ovulating, including store-bought ovulation indicators, which detect luteinizing hormone (LH) levels in the urine or saliva; charting the woman's basal body temperature, which dips slightly right before ovulation; and tracking cervical mucus, which thins a few days before ovulation. Finally, men and women who would like to conceive should not wait too long because women over 35 and men over 40 have reduced fertility.

Normally, 1,200 males are conceived for every 1,000 females. Because male fetuses are less likely to survive, only 1,049 boys are born for every 1,000 girls (Martin et al., 2009). Incidentally, male babies are also less hearty, and are more prone to cerebral palsy, premature birth, and stillbirth. Over the past few years, the

> I've heard that there are things you can do if you want to make sure you have a baby boy. What can parents do to select the sex of their child?

male birthrate has been steadily decreasing (see the From Cells to Society feature on page 324).

There are various reasons why some people may want to select the sex of their child. Medically, many human diseases disproportionately affect boys, including hemophilia and Duchenne muscular dystrophy. Culturally, males are more valued in some societies, such as India and China. When parents in these countries are strongly encouraged to have only one or two children, they are more likely to want boys. Traditionally, the fetus's sex has been identified after the first trimester through amniocentesis or (less accurately) through ultrasound, but recently a procedure has been developed which may be able to detect the sex of the embryo through a simple blood test (Scheffer et al., 2010).

It is thought that having sex at certain times in the ovulatory cycle will make it more likely to conceive either a boy or a girl, although Wilcox and colleagues (1995) found that the timing of sexual intercourse had no influence on the sex of the baby. Sex-selective assisted reproductive techniques can be employed at three times: before conception, as doctors separate X-bearing and Y-bearing sperm to be preferentially used for fertilization; after fertilization but before implantation because a woman may be implanted with embryos of the desired sex (Bjorndahl & Barratt, 2002); or after implantation. When population restrictions are placed on families in cultures that value men more highly, some couples choose to abort the fetus or even murder or abandon the live baby if it is a girl (Sudha & Rajan, 1999). Although selective abortion based on the baby's sex has been banned in India since 1994, India is experiencing a significant decline in female births (George, 2006; Jha et al., 2006). China's one-child policy, designed to limit the population, has produced a great disparity in the sex ratio: 847 girls are born for every 1,000 boys (Chan, Yip, Ng, Chan, & Au, 2002). It is thought that in a few years there may be as many as 40 million Chinese men who will be unable to find brides.

Culturally encouraged sex selection may also occur in the United States. Chinese, Korean, and Indian American parents have significantly more second- and third-born sons than would occur by chance. While there are usually 105 boys born for

A sperm penetrating an egg.

© 3D4Medical / Photo Researchers, Inc.

ASK YOURSELF

If a sex-selection method that was absolutely accurate were developed, would you use it? If you were allowed to have only one child, would you prefer to have a boy or a girl? Why?

Zona pellucida The thick protective coating around the egg.

Zygote A fertilized egg.

The drop in the male birthrate may be due to a number of factors, including environmental pollutants, diet, and stress.

Environmental pollutants. Dioxins are a family of carcinogenic compounds found in herbicides, waste incineration, and plastics, which can mimic the effects of estrogen in the body. One native community in Ontario, located near a number of chemical refineries and exposed to high amounts of dioxins, has had twice as many girls born than boys between 1999 and 2003 (MacKenzie, Lockridge, & Keith, 2005).

Diet can also influence the sex ratio. Pregnant women who ingest fewer calories or who are more likely to skip meals are less likely to produce boys (Mathews, Johnson, & Neil, 2008).

Stress can lower a woman's probability of giving birth to a boy. After the terrorist attacks of September 11, 2001, there were more male fetuses miscarried and fewer boys born (Catalano, Bruckner, Marks, & Eskenazi, 2006). Other stressful factors can lower a woman's probability of giving birth to a boy, including living through a

strong earthquake around the time of conception (Fukuda, Fukuda, Shimizu, & Moller, 1998), experiencing political and social upheavals (Catalano, 2003), and not cohabiting with a partner at the time of birth (Norberg, 2004). It is theorized that mothers are less likely to give birth to boys during times of stress because weaker males are less likely to survive to reproductive age, and in an uncertain environment, girls have a better chance of passing their genes on to the next generation (Catalano & Bruckner, 2006).

every 100 girls, among these parents, if their first child is a girl, there are 117 second-born sons for every 100 girls, and if their first two children are girls, that number leaps to 151 third-born sons for every 100 girls (Eliot, 2009). This suggests that these parents may be using techniques to control the sex of their unborn children.

Infertility

After completion of this section, you will be able to . . .

○ Define the terms *infertility* and *sterility.*

○ Identify the typical causes of male and female infertility.

○ Compare and contrast the processes of *assisted reproductive technologies (ART), artificial insemination, in vitro fertilization, gamete intrafallopian transfer (GIFT),* and *intracytoplasmic sperm injection.*

○ Explain the process of surrogate motherhood and adoption.

Although at this point in your life you may be more concerned with preventing pregnancy, there are millions of people in the United States who are desperately trying to have a child. **Infertility** is a reduced ability to conceive a child; **sterility** is a complete inability to reproduce. In the past, fertility doctors might declare couples to be infertile if they failed to conceive a child on their own after 5 years of unprotected intercourse; the length of time was first lowered to 2 years, and now couples are routinely declared infertile after 1 year of failing to conceive on their own. Couples older than age 35 are encouraged to seek fertility treatments after 6 months of unprotected intercourse because they face a time constraint in seeking medical intervention. In couples who are having trouble conceiving, the problem typically lies with the man about 40% of the time, 40% of the time it is the woman who is infertile, and in 20% of cases the problem is with both partners (Nelson & Marshall, 2004). If a couple is having trouble getting pregnant, it is recommended that

Infertility Failure to conceive after a year of unprotected intercourse.

Sterility The complete inability to conceive.

the man be assessed for infertility first because his test is easier, less invasive, and even somewhat enjoyable compared to a woman's examination.

More than 6 million American women and their partners (about 10–15% of couples) have problems getting pregnant, although about half of these couples will eventually conceive a child (Nelson & Marshall, 2004). Infertility can be emotionally devastating. Infertile couples can experience disappointment and frustration as each month passes without a pregnancy. Infertile men and women may feel as if they are failing their partners or their families. They may feel the injustice of their inability to have children while many unfit parents are able to give birth. Those who are troubled by infertility can seek both medical and psychological counseling to deal with their struggle.

Male Infertility

Male fertility depends on the size, shape, and motility of ejaculated sperm. A man may be considered infertile if he has fewer than 20 million sperm per each milliliter of semen; less than 5 million sperm per milliliter of semen, and he is considered sterile. In addition, the sperm must be able to swim for at least 2 hours after ejaculation and have the proper shape so they can penetrate the egg. Over the past 40 years, the average volume of ejaculate has decreased 20%, the average sperm count has decreased 40%, and the sperm that are produced have poorer motility and more abnormal shape (Auger, Kuntsmann, Czyglik, & Jouannet, 1995; Carlsen, Giwercman, Keiding, & Skakkebaek, 1992; Travison, Araujo, O'Donnell, Kupelian, & McKinlay, 2007).

Several factors can cause male infertility, including structural abnormalities, environmental factors and diet, behavioral practices, and advanced age.

- *Structural abnormalities.* Men may have diminished sperm count or impaired motility if they have undescended testes or varicocele. Infections such as mumps or sexually transmitted infections can hinder sperm production or block the passage of sperm through the ejaculatory pathway. Men can even form antibodies against their own sperm and destroy them.

- *Environmental factors and diet.* Exposure to radiation and pollutants may decrease sperm count. Chemicals in car exhaust, insecticides, and plastics are broken down to estrogen-like substances that disrupt a man's normal hormonal functions. Eating beef may hurt a man's fertility because cattle in North America routinely are given various hormones, including testosterone and progesterone, to increase growth and development of the animals. These steroids are present in the meat we consume. Fertility may even be affected if a man's *mother* ate beef while she was pregnant. Sons whose mothers ate a lot of beef had lower sperm concentrations (Swan, Liu, Overstreet, Brazil, & Skakkebaek, 2007). When their mother ate more than seven beef meals a week, the son's sperm concentration was 24% lower than in men whose mothers ate less beef. But vegetarians should not be complacent—a higher intake of foods that contain soy may also decrease a man's sperm concentration because soy contains isoflavones, which have estrogenic activity in the body (Chavarro, Toth, Sadio, & Hauser, 2008).

- *Behavioral practices.* Stress and extreme physical exercise can cause the release of cortisol, which may inhibit the production of testosterone. Drugs can also impair fertility by altering hormones or by affecting sperm directly (Nudell, Monoski, & Lipshultz, 2002). Long-term, heavy alcohol use reduces testosterone production and can lead to impotence. Marijuana changes the pH of sperm, which makes them swim too fast and tire themselves out too early, making them less likely to reach the egg (Lishko, Botchkina, Fedorenko, & Kirichok, 2010). Marijuana also makes sperm less able to break down the egg's protective coat. Smoking cigarettes has negative effects on sperm production, motility, and morphology. Also, the antidepressant Paxil can damage the DNA of sperm (Tanrikut, Feldman, Alternus, Raduch, & Schlegel, 2009). Anabolic steroids impair fertility in a number of ways: they reduce production of follicle-stimulating hormone (FSH) and LH, they lead to erectile dysfunction, and they increase the morphological abnormalities in sperm.

- *Advanced age.* Women aren't the only ones with a biological clock. As men age, their testosterone levels decrease, leading to

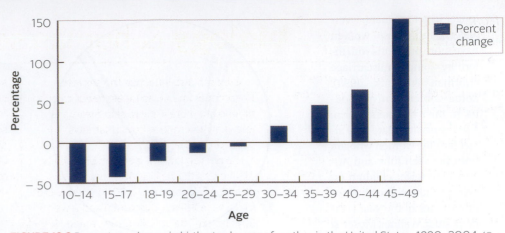

FIGURE 13.2 Percentage change in birthrates by age of mother in the United States, 1990–2004. (© Cengage Learning 2013. SOURCE: Martin et al., 2006.)

diminished sperm count and motility. For a woman under 30, having a male partner over 40 decreases her chance of conceiving by about 25%. If a woman is between 35 and 37 and her male partner is over 40, the chances of conception fall to one in three (de La Rochebrochard, de Mouzon, Thepot, & Thonneau, 2006). In the last few decades, the numbers of older fathers trying to conceive has increased dramatically (Raeburn, 2009).

Female Infertility

Female infertility may be due to ovulatory irregularities, structural problems, advanced age, or other issues.

- *Irregular ovulation.* Many factors can affect normal ovulation. Hormonal imbalances, stress, and chronic disease can impair ovulation, as can both obesity and low body weight.
- *Structural problems.* An abnormally shaped uterus can impair fertility, as can uterine growths such as fibroid tumors. Obstructions of the fallopian tubes caused by infections or endometriosis can make it difficult to get pregnant. A **hysterosalpingogram** is a procedure in which dye is injected into a woman's uterus and fallopian tubes to locate any blockages or tumors.
- *Advanced age.* As a woman ages, her hormone levels decline and she stops producing eggs. While a woman in her mid-20s has an 85% chance of getting pregnant in 1 year, that falls to less than 50% for a woman in her mid-30s, to 10–20% for a 40-year-old woman, and to less than 10% for a woman over 45. Regardless, more women are waiting longer to get pregnant. Between 1990 and 2004 fewer younger women gave birth, the percentage of women aged 35–39 who gave birth rose 43%, and the birthrate for women aged 45–49 jumped by 150% (Figure 13.2; Martin et al., 2006). However, age is not the only factor influencing infertility: women under 25 make up the fastest growing segment of U.S. women with impaired fertility (Chandra, Martinez, Mosher, Abma, & Jones, 2005).
- *Other causes.* Many other factors may influence **fecundity**. Women who smoke cigarettes may take

Do you have an older brother? You may have a decreased chance of having children. Whereas people who have an older sister have a 67% chance of having future children, those with an older brother have only a 62% chance. It is thought that the environment in the womb of a woman who previously carried a son may affect the fertility of her future children (Rickard, Lummaa, & Russell, 2009).

Hysterosalpingogram A procedure in which dye is injected into a woman's uterus and fallopian tubes to locate any blockages or tumors.

Fecundity The state of being fertile; the ability to produce offspring.

longer to get pregnant. Overweight and obese women
have more problems with infertility and miscarriage
(Norman & Clark, 1998).
Some women form antibod-
ies to their partner's sperm.
Even your birth date may affect fertility; women who are
born between June and Au-
gust have fewer children on
average than women born at
other times of the year (Hu-
ber, Fieder, Wallner, Moser, &
Arnold, 2004).

Assisted Reproductive Technologies (ART)

While once considered the realm
of science fiction, today about
1% of babies in the Western
world are born with **assisted
reproductive technology** (CDC,
2009).

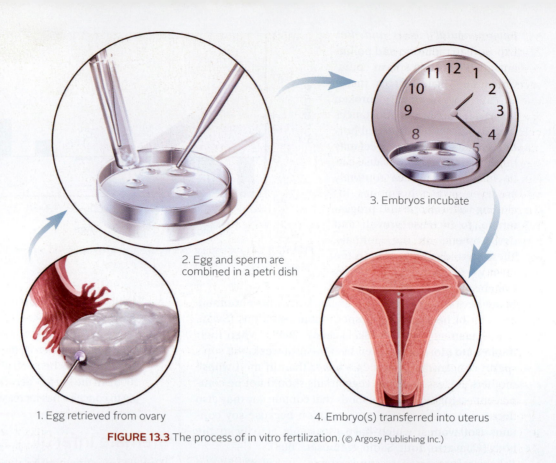

2. Egg and sperm are combined in a petri dish

3. Embryos incubate

1. Egg retrieved from ovary

4. Embryo(s) transferred into uterus

FIGURE 13.3 The process of in vitro fertilization. (© Argosy Publishing Inc.)

In **artificial insemination**, sperm, either from the woman's partner or from a donor, is inserted into the woman's vagina or uterus. This can be done at home or with a doctor's assistance. It is most effective when the sperm is first "**washed**" and concentrated, then put directly into the uterus. Donor sperm is used in 80,000 to 100,000 inseminations a year in the United States (Mundy, 2006). Women may choose to use donated sperm if their partner is infertile or if they don't have a male partner. A man may donate his sperm directly to a woman he knows or anonymously to a sperm bank. Sperm banks have large catalogues of sperm samples, and women can read about the donors' appearance, medical history, likes and dislikes, even SAT scores. They can often see handwriting samples and hear taped interviews with the donor. Sperm purchased from a sperm bank costs about $700 per sample; donors in the United States receive about $50 for each "donation."

Assisted reproductive technologies A group of therapies used to establish pregnancy.

Artificial insemination Impregnating a woman with semen through methods other than intercourse.

Sperm washing A procedure in which sperm cells are separated from semen, to facilitate the removal of dead or slow moving sperm, as well as prostaglandins, which might impair fertilization.

In vitro fertilization (IVF) The joining of an egg and sperm outside of the body, to be implanted in the uterus.

Clomid A fertility drug that stimulates FSH and LH secretion.

Embryo A fertilized egg before it becomes a fetus, from conception to 8 weeks of pregnancy.

Gamete intrafallopian transfer (GIFT) An in vitro fertilization procedure in which the egg and sperm are individually put into the fallopian tube, where they can join.

In England in 1978, Louise Brown, the world's first "test tube baby," was conceived through in vitro fertilization. **In vitro fertilization (IVF)** literally means "fertilization in glass." The general procedure is as follows: On the third day of her cycle, the woman takes a fertility drug such as **Clomid**, which blocks estrogen receptors in the hypothalamus. The brain senses a drop in estrogen and boosts secretion of gonadotropin-releasing hormone (GnRH), leading to an increase in FSH and LH release. This stimulates multiple oocyte production. When the follicles have matured enough, the woman receives an injection of a hormone called human chorionic gonadotropin (hCG), which causes ovulation within 36 hours. Before the oocytes are released, however, the doctor retrieves the mature eggs from the ovary. The eggs and sperm are prepared for fertilization and placed together in a petri dish. After two to four days, many **embryos** have begun to grow. The embryos are put into the uterus via a catheter through the cervix. Usually no more than three or four embryos are placed in the uterus (the rest are cryo-preserved for later transfer) to prevent multiple births. The woman then receives injections of progesterone to keep her uterus thickened and suitable for implantation.

In **gamete intrafallopian transfer (GIFT)**, the only method of IVF approved by the Catholic Church, mature oocytes are removed from the ovary and placed directly in the fallopian tube, along with washed and concentrated sperm. The hope is that the sperm will fertilize the egg in the fallopian tube. Because fertilization occurs in the body and not a laboratory, this is technically *in vivo* fertilization, not in vitro. Although it is more invasive, GIFT may have a slightly higher implantation rate than IVF.

In general, IVF has a 23–40% success rate, and costs $12,000–$15,000 for each attempt. The success rate of IVF depends on the age of the woman, her overall health, the causes of her infertility, and on other factors. Forty percent of transfers in women under 35 will lead to a live birth. For women over 44, only 2% of IVF attempts will lead to a birth (CDC/American Society for Reproductive Medicine, 2009). Other health factors such as smoking or weight also influence the success of the procedure. Overweight women are one-third less likely to have a successful IVF birth. Cigarette smoking reduces a woman's chance of having live birth by 28%; smoking is like adding 10 years to a woman's reproductive age (Lintsen et al., 2005).

The major complications associated with IVF are multiple births and low birth weight babies. Because of the financial and time requirements of IVF, more than one oocyte is fertilized, leading to many embryos. A number of these are usually implanted at one time in order to raise the odds of a successful pregnancy. However, this often leads to multiple births, with its concurrent risks of miscarriage, premature birth, and low birth weight. Some have found that assisted reproductive techniques are associated with an increased risk of **preeclampsia**, placental abnormalities, and Cesarean sections (Shevell et al., 2005). Others suggest that ARTs are associated with a 30–40% increased risk in birth defects (Hansen, Bower, Milne, de Klerk & Kurinczuk, 2005), although it is important to remember that those who are more likely to use assisted reproductive techniques—older mothers and couples who can't conceive naturally—may be more prone to genetic or other abnormalities.

In IVF, the egg may come from the woman who wants the child or from a donor egg. Donor eggs are used in 12% of all IVF attempts, and more in older women; 91% of women aged 47 and older used donor eggs for their IVF attempts (Orenstein, 2007). In 2004, 15,175 donor eggs were implanted leading to the birth of 5,449 babies, and this number grows by 20% each year (Orenstein, 2007). A woman who decides to donate her eggs must first go through psychological and physical tests and must stay celibate for 2 months. She is then injected with hormones for 10 days, which stimulates her ovaries to produce many eggs; the eggs are retrieved from the ovaries through the vaginal wall. A "donor" egg is actually a misnomer because women in the United States get paid an average of $5,000 for their eggs.

In 2009 Nadya Suleman (known as "Octomom" in the media) gave birth to octuplets, which were conceived through in vitro fertilization. Her story elicited strong feelings because this unemployed single mother was on public assistance programs and already had six other young children at home.

© Jeff Steinberg/Matt Smith, PacificCoastNews/Newscom

ASK YOURSELF

What does it mean to be a mother? Donating an egg? Carrying a baby to term? Raising a child?

Although only one sperm penetrates an egg, men with fewer than 20 million sperm per milliliter are considered infertile. With the use of **intracytoplasmic sperm injection (ICSI)**, these men can father a child. Mature oocytes are removed from the ovary, and a single sperm is removed surgically from the epididymis. The sperm is washed and introduced into the cytoplasm of the egg. When the fertilized egg has between 16 and 64 cells, the embryo is transferred to either the uterus or the fallopian tube. Some studies have found that babies born as a result of ICSI have a higher rate of birth defects, possibly because men with greatly reduced sperm have an increased prevalence of chromosomal abnormalities. Others have found no heightened risk with ICSI (Shevell et al., 2005).

Although most cases of infertility are resolved with low-tech solutions and cost less than $2,000, in some cases infertility treatments can cost far more (Aronson, 2006). The typical total cost of in vitro fertilization leading to a live birth is estimated to be more than $41,000 (Chambers et al., 2009). Most employers do not provide infertility insurance.

In the mid-1980s, Mary Beth Whitehead agreed to be inseminated by William Stern's sperm, carry the baby to term, and then return the baby to Mr. Stern and his wife. After giving birth, Ms. Whitehead changed her mind and refused to give up the baby to the Sterns. After a number of highly publicized trials, the Sterns were eventually awarded custody of "Baby M." **Surrogate mothers** (or "gestational carriers") are artificially inseminated by either the male partner's sperm or donor sperm, and carry the baby to term for the couple. Sometimes a donor egg is used. Surrogate mothers are usually paid for their services—about $20,000 in the United States although some couples "outsource" this service to India, where surrogate mothers typically receive only about $5,000. Gestational carriers sign legal documents requiring them to surrender the newborn. Some docu-

Preeclampsia A complication of pregnancy characterized by hypertension, protein in the urine, and fluid retention, which, if untreated, can lead to organ failure, seizures, coma, and death.

Intracytoplasmic sperm injection (ICSI) An in vitro fertilization procedure in which a single sperm is injected directly into an egg for fertilization.

Surrogate mother A woman who is artificially inseminated and carries a baby to term for another woman or couple.

> How do we classify infertility? Is infertility a disease or simply a disappointing personal situation? According to the Americans with Disabilities Act, a person is disabled if he or she has an impairment that limits one or more major life activities, including reproduction. Infertility has been shown to cause depression and anxiety similar to that of women with cancer and heart disease (Domar, Zuttermeister, & Friedman, 1993). On the other hand, infertility is not life-threatening and does not interfere with a person's ability to physically function from day to day.

> What factors should be considered?

- **Cost**

  IVF can be prohibitively expensive; the high cost may prevent some couples from having a family. Should money be the criterion that determines whether a couple can reproduce?

  It is estimated that mandated infertility insurance would cost insured members between 40 and 50 cents per month, although some estimate the cost as high as $2 per month (Blackwell, 2000; Griffin & Panak, 1998). Does the cost matter? How would one determine what is an unacceptable financial burden for the insured to pay for others' misfortunes?

- **The effect on society**

  In vitro fertilization increases the incidence of multiple births, which is associated with an increased risk to both mother and child. Some suggest that if infertility were covered by insurance, couples might not need to implant as many embryos in each cycle. In states with mandated infertility insurance coverage, fewer embryos were transferred and multiple birth rates were lower (Frankfurter, 2003).

  On the other hand, perhaps those who would not consider treatment might attempt IVF if the cost were lower, increasing the world's already burgeoning population, and lowering the adoption rate.

> How much should individual circumstances be considered in the decision? For many couples, IVF is not their only means of having a family. Some infertile couples may already have children. And although adoption is not an alternative for everyone (gays and lesbians are not allowed to adopt children in some states), most infertile couples can adopt children. Should this be taken into consideration when evaluating the issue? Should different rules apply for couples who already have children or who could adopt? Should limits be set regarding what procedures are covered, how many attempts, and the characteristics of the people involved? If so, who sets these limits and how?

> Will insuring couples against infertility lead down a slippery slope? Is there a limit to what insurance should cover? What is that limit?

> What are the value assumptions underlying the IVF issue? Does a person have the right to have a family? Do their rights impinge on others who must shoulder the costs?

ASK YOURSELF

How "far" should a couple go to reproduce? When is it not "meant to be"? At a certain age? After a certain number of procedures? When is it financially prohibitive?

ments also specify the types of behaviors that the woman can and cannot do while pregnant.

Adoption

As mentioned, most people who want children also have the option of adopting. Legally and emotionally, there is no difference between an adopted child and a biological child, and adoptive parents assume all responsibilities toward their child. Parents may adopt children for many reasons. They may be infertile, or they may have a medical condition that would make childbirth difficult. Some parents want to care for a child in need or avoid further overpopulating the world.

Adoptions can be open or closed. In a closed adoption, no identifying information about the birth parents is provided to the adoptive parents and the child. In open adoptions, the biological parents and children have information about each other and may sometimes have a relationship with each other. There are fewer children available for adoption in the United States than in the past, for several reasons: the availability of legal abortions, the increased use of contraception, and the greater acceptance of single parenthood. Some adoptive parents travel to other countries such as China or Korea for their children. Regardless of where the adoptive child is from, all prospective adoptive parents in the United States are first evaluated by a home study to determine their emotional and financial stability before being granted adoption rights.

Pregnancy

After completion of this section, you will be able to . . .

O Estimate the average length of pregnancy.

O Identify the tests used to confirm pregnancy.

O Recognize the different divisions of a woman's pregnancy.

O Define the germinal stage, the embryonic stage, and the fetal stage of pregnancy.

O Define the term *ectopic pregnancy*.

O Explain the differences between dizygotic and monozygotic twins.

O Understand the functions of the placenta, umbilical cord, and amniotic sac.

O Identify the changes in both the embryo/fetus and the mother during each trimester.

Pregnancy and childbirth are organized into groups of three. There are three stages of prenatal development: germinal, embryonic, and fetal. Also, there are three trimesters, each about three months long. Even childbirth is divided into three stages.

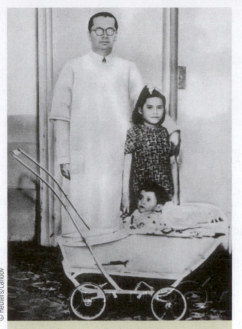

Lina Medina, reported to be the youngest ever to give birth, with her son.

sexactually

The World Records of Birth

- The oldest woman to give birth was Spain's Maria del Carmen Bousada, who delivered twins (with the assistance of IVF) when she was one week shy of her 67th birthday. Maria died of cancer less than 3 years later (Jones & Higgs, 2010).
- Australian Les Colley became the world's oldest father with the birth of his 9th child. He was 92 at the time (Page, 2007).
- The youngest mother was Peruvian Lina Medina (pictured), who had a son in 1939 when she was 5 years old. Lina started her period at 8 months of age and developed breasts when she was 4 (Escomel, 1939).
- The record for the most children ever born to one mother is held by a Russian woman from the 18th century, who had 69 children: 16 pairs of twins, 7 sets of triplets, and 4 sets of quadruplets.
- Elizabeth Ann Buttle of Wales holds the record for the longest interval between children. She had her first child in 1956 when she was 19 and her last in 1997 when she was 60, an interval of more than 41 years.
- The heaviest baby (that survived) was born in 1955 to Carmelina Fedele of Italy, whose son weighed in at a whopping 22 pounds, 8 ounces.

Changes in the Woman's Body

While pregnant, a woman's body will undergo enormous changes. Obviously, her hormonal system is altered during pregnancy, as progesterone and estrogen levels rise. Her breasts enlarge, as does her uterus, which grows from 2 ounces to 2 pounds, increasing in size up to 1,000-fold. Other organs move around in the body. Her pubic bones shift alignment, and her ligaments weaken. A pregnant woman's heart beats more strongly, and her heart rate increases. Her blood volume increases up to 50% because it needs to help feed the embryo and fetus. This thinner blood more easily passes the placenta. Fluid volume increases throughout the body, even in the cornea, so some pregnant women can no longer wear contact lenses while pregnant. A pregnant woman moves up to 50% more air in and out of her lungs with each breath. Late in pregnancy, the uterus may interfere with the contraction of the diaphragm, and breathing may be more difficult.

A pregnant woman needs about 60,000 to 100,000 extra calories during the course of her pregnancy. As the saying goes, she is "eating for two." On average, a woman will gain 25 to 35 pounds with a pregnancy, although underweight women should gain more and overweight women should gain less; even obese women should gain at least 15 pounds. Of the approximately 30 pounds gained, only 7 are fat tissue. Apart from the weight of the baby, women gain a few pounds in breast and uterine tissue, as well as around 10 pounds in blood and other fluids (Institute of Medicine, 1990). It is essential that a pregnant woman maintain a healthy diet for optimum development of the baby. If her weight is too high or too low, it can lead to problems during pregnancy or birth.

Average Length of Pregnancy

Pregnancy, also called **gestation**, lasts for approximately 9 calendar months, or 38 to 40 weeks. Physicians typically start counting a woman's pregnancy from the first day of a woman's last menstrual period before conception. By this count, the egg is actually fertilized during week 3, meaning that a woman's pregnancy could technically be considered to start while she was still a virgin.

So when exactly does pregnancy begin? According to the American College of Obstetricians and Gynecologists, pregnancy does not begin until a fertilized egg implants in the lining of the uterus, a process that takes up to 10 days to complete. Some individuals think pregnancy begins when a sperm first penetrates the egg. The medical community starts counting from the first day of the woman's last menstrual period, and the general public usually considers a woman pregnant from the time of her first missed period.

In China, Korea, and Vietnam, a baby's age is counted from the time of conception. Thus, when babies are born, they are considered to be 1 year old.

Tests to Confirm Pregnancy

More than 3,000 years ago, a woman would mix her urine into barley seed. If the barley grew faster with the urine, it meant that she was pregnant. It is thought that the elevated level of estrogen in her urine was responsible for the accelerated plant growth. In the early 20th century, it was discovered that a woman produces a hormone called **human chorionic gonadotropin (hCG)** when a fertilized egg implants in her uterus. Similar in structure to LH, hCG is produced by the embryo and placenta early in pregnancy and helps to maintain the corpus luteum's production of progesterone. It was found that hCG also

Gestation The state of being pregnant.

Human chorionic gonadotropin (hCG) A hormone produced early in pregnancy.

causes changes in the ovaries of rabbits. In the so-called *rabbit test,* a woman's urine was injected into a rabbit, which was killed and dissected a few days later to see if its ovaries were enlarged. If so, the pregnancy test was positive.

Determining pregnancy today is convenient, simple, anonymous, and no bunnies need to die. Home pregnancy tests determine the hCG level in a woman's urine. Levels of hCG start to rise 7 to 9 days after fertilization; it can first be detected by a blood test about 11 days after conception, and by a urine test about 12 to 14 days after conception. Levels of hCG reach a peak 60 to 70 days after fertilization, then decrease (Stewart, 2004). Home pregnancy tests are not perfectly accurate. False negatives can occur if the test is done too early, before hCG levels are high enough, or with an ectopic pregnancy. False positives are rarer and can be indicative of certain diseases. Other signs of pregnancy include **Hegar's sign**, a softening of the cervix around the 6th week of pregnancy, and **Chadwick's sign**, the darkening of the cervix and vagina.

The First Trimester

Momentous changes occur in the embryo and fetus during the first 3 months of pregnancy. This first trimester encompasses the germinal stage (the first 2 weeks of development), the embryonic stage (from implantation until week 8), as well as the first month of fetal development.

The Germinal Stage

The first 2 weeks of prenatal development are called the **germinal stage**, which is divided into three phases: conception, cleavage, and implantation. At **conception**—when the sperm penetrates the egg—the union creates a zygote, or a fertilized egg. During **cleavage**, the zygote will begin to divide, from one cell to two, from two to four, from four to eight, and so on. Doubling occurs rapidly; it takes only 42 sets of mitotic cell divisions to produce what eventually becomes a newborn baby with trillions of cells. The zygote divides by mitosis into a **morula**, a solid ball of 16 to 64 cells. The morula, still surrounded by the zona pellucida, enters the uterus 3 to 4 days after conception, where it rests in the uterine cavity for 2 to 3 days, getting nutrients from the uterine glands. By day 6, the morula has become a **blastocyst**, a hollow ball of cells with a fluid-filled center. The blastocyst is comprised of an inner cell mass, which will become the embryo, and an outer layer of cells, which will become the placenta. Because the zona pellucida impedes the growth and implantation of the blastocyst, the uterus secretes an enzyme to dissolve it. By days 7 to 10, the blastocyst begins to **implant** in the uterine wall; this process takes about a week. Once implanted, the blastocyst is called an embryo. Around day 12, the embryo secretes hCG, which travels through the blood to the ovary and prolongs the life of the corpus luteum, ensuring that it continues to secrete progesterone and estrogen to maintain the uterine lining. Progesterone also inhibits uterine contractions.

In about 1–2% of pregnancies, the fertilized egg implants outside of the uterus, a condition called **ectopic pregnancy**. Most often, ectopic pregnancies implant in the fallopian tube, but they can implant in the abdomen, ovaries, cervix, or other areas. Since 1970, the rate of ectopic pregnancies has risen by 600% (Fylstra, 1998). Scarring in the fallopian tubes caused by pelvic inflammatory disease or tubal surgery can increase a woman's risk of ectopic pregnancy, as can endometriosis, advanced age, and smoking. With very rare exceptions, implantation outside of the uterus always results in the loss of the embryo or fetus. In the mother, ectopic pregnancy causes 10–15% of all pregnancy-related deaths, and is the leading cause of first trimester maternal death (Tenore, 2000). Symptoms include cramps, pain on one side of the lower abdomen, nausea, vomiting, and vaginal bleeding.

Multiple pregnancies. When a woman is pregnant with more than one fetus, it is a **multiple pregnancy**. The most common of these are twins (two fetuses) and triplets (three fetuses). One hundred years ago, the birth of twins was a fairly rare occurrence, accounting for perhaps 1 out of every 80 births. Today in the United States, 1 out of every 33 children born is a twin. Since 1980, the birthrate for triplets and other multiples has risen by 423% (Martin et al., 2009). The increase in multiple pregnancies may be due to the use of fertility drugs, which cause the release of multiple eggs, and due to the implantation of multiple embryos during IVF. The chance of multiple pregnancy also increases with maternal age because ovulation is more erratic in older women, and more than one egg may be released. Finally, more women are taking folic acid before conception, which may increase the chance of multiple pregnancy.

Twins may be dizygotic or monozygotic. **Dizygotic twins**—better known as fraternal twins—occur when two eggs are fertilized at the same time, each by a different sperm. Although they share a womb, dizygotic twins are only as genetically similar as any other brothers and sisters. Most twins—about two-thirds—

Anandamide, a naturally occurring neurotransmitter that binds to cannabinoid receptors (the same receptors that bind marijuana), is involved in the process of implantation (Schmid, Paria, Krebsbach, Schmid, & Dey, 1997). Anandamide is a key chemical messenger between the embryo and the uterus; smoking pot at the time of conception may interfere with the process of implantation (Schuel, 2006).

Hegar's sign A softening of the cervix that can indicate pregnancy.

Chadwick's sign A sign of pregnancy in which the cervix and vagina darken.

Germinal stage The first 2 weeks of prenatal development.

Conception The fertilization of an egg by a sperm.

Cleavage The division of the fertilized egg.

Morula A solid mass of 16 to 64 cells.

Blastocyst A hollow, fluid-filled ball of cells.

Implantation The process by which a fertilized egg implants in the lining of the uterus.

Ectopic pregnancy When the fertilized egg implants outside of the uterus, usually in the fallopian tube.

Multiple pregnancy When a woman is pregnant with more than one fetus.

Dizygotic twins Twins that result from the fertilization of two separate eggs from two separate sperm.

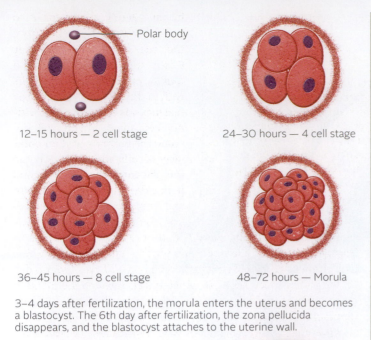

12–15 hours — 2 cell stage

Polar body

24–30 hours — 4 cell stage

36–45 hours — 8 cell stage

48–72 hours — Morula

3–4 days after fertilization, the morula enters the uterus and becomes a blastocyst. The 6th day after fertilization, the zona pellucida disappears, and the blastocyst attaches to the uterine wall.

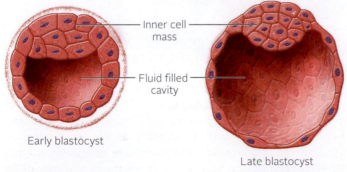

Inner cell mass

Fluid filled cavity

Early blastocyst

Late blastocyst

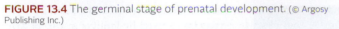

FIGURE 13.4 The germinal stage of prenatal development. (© Argosy Publishing Inc.)

are dizygotic. Twins tend to run in families, usually through the mother's line (it may be related to the likelihood of multiple ovulation). If there is one set of twins in your family, you're 3 times more likely than the general population to have twins yourself. In the past, twins were most common in African populations and least common in Asians, although these differences are disappearing with the advent of IVF (Martin et al., 2010). Triplets and other multiple births are usually dizygotic.

In **monozygotic**, or identical, twins, one egg is fertilized by one sperm, but the fertilized egg splits in two early in development, producing genetically identical twins. This occurs once in every 250 births. If the embryo divides 1 to 2 days after fertilization, each embryo has its own placenta and amniotic sac. Most of the time, division occurs between 3 and 8 days after fertilization, and each embryo has its own amniotic sac, but they share one placenta. It is rare for an embryo to divide as late as 12 days after conception; this may result in **conjoined twins** who share a placenta and an amniotic sac.

The Embryonic Stage

From the time it implants in the uterus, until 8 weeks after conception, the fertilized egg is considered an embryo. During the embryonic stage, the major organs begin to develop and grow, so

the embryo may be most vulnerable to drugs and viruses during this stage. At the beginning of the 3rd week, the placenta begins to develop.

Maternal and embryonic structures interlock to form the **placenta**, the life-support system for the embryo and fetus. The pancake-shaped placenta attaches inside the uterus, and is connected to the fetus by the **umbilical cord**. The placenta contains many blood vessels, across which nutrients, gases, and wastes are exchanged between maternal and fetal blood. Each day, about 75 gallons of blood pass through the placenta—approximately 10% of the mother's total blood flow. The placenta also secretes hCG, estrogen, and progesterone, which help to maintain pregnancy.

The mother's and fetus's blood supply do not actually mix. There is a membrane in the placenta that allows certain substances through and prevents the passage of others. Water, oxygen, carbon dioxide, glucose, and other nutrients can cross, as can viruses and maternal antibodies. Most drugs taken by a woman, including alcohol, cocaine, and steroid hormones, cross into the fetus's blood supply. This is particularly damaging because a developing fetus does not have a fully developed liver to effectively process and metabolize these drugs. Large molecules and bacteria cannot cross the placenta to enter the fetus's bloodstream.

The **amniotic sac** is the fluid-filled pouch that lines the uterus, in which the embryo (and fetus) develops. **Amniotic fluid** comes from the placenta, and contains water, salts, glucose, urea, and cell debris. The fluid is replaced every 3 hours. Toward the end of the pregnancy, the fetus swallows about half a liter of amniotic fluid a day. The fluid helps to cushion and protect the fetus, and to maintain a constant temperature. Because the fetus is floating in the fluid, it can exercise its muscles and develop symmetrically.

The Development of the Embryo and Fetus During the First Trimester

After 1 month, the embryo is about the size of the head of a match, but it is already beginning to develop most of the major organ systems. The neural tube—which will become the brain and spinal cord—has begun to form, and the embryo has the beginnings of arm and leg buds, as well as a tail. The heart is one of the first systems to develop because it is needed to carry oxygen and nutrients to the rapidly growing tissues. In

Identical triplets can occur when a single fertilized egg splits in two, and then one of the resulting two eggs divides again. This is extremely rare.

Monozygotic twins Genetically identical twins derived from a single fertilized egg.

Conjoined twins Twins whose bodies are joined together *in utero*.

Placenta The organ that supplies the developing fetus with nutrients and oxygen.

Umbilical cord The cord that connects the placenta to the fetus.

Amniotic sac The fluid-containing sac that contains the fetus and the placenta during development.

Amniotic fluid The fluid that nourishes and protects the developing fetus.

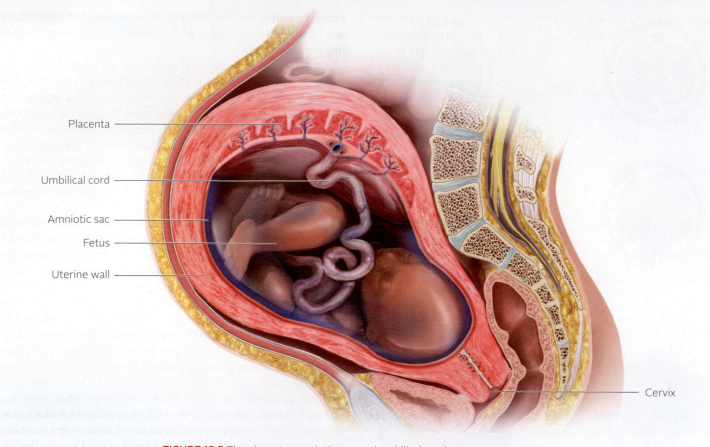

Placenta

Umbilical cord

Amniotic sac

Fetus

Uterine wall

Cervix

FIGURE 13.5 The placenta, amniotic sac, and umbilical cord. (© Argosy Publishing Inc.)

proportion to the rest of the body, the embryo's heart is 9 times as large as an adult's. It needs extra power to get the blood not only to the developing organs, but around the umbilical cord and placenta as well.

In its 2nd month, most of the embryo's major organ systems are forming. Cartilage is beginning to grow in the limbs, fingers, and toes, and the tongue and taste buds have begun to form. The eyes, brain, and spinal cord begin to develop, and the embryo produces at least 50,000 neurons each second throughout most of its development. The embryo goes through two pairs of rudimentary kidneys before it gets its final set in the 3rd month. Beginning in the 8th week, sexual differentiation begins in what was a sexually neutral fetus; testes form in XY fetuses and ovaries in XX fetuses. By the end of the 8th week, the developing being is now called a **fetus**.

In its 9th through 12th weeks, the fetus is 2½ to 3½ inches long and weighs about an ounce and a half. Most major organ systems are present and the appendages are fully formed, with fingerprints and the beginnings of fingernails. The external geni-

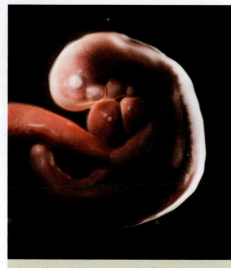

An embryo in its 1st month of development.

© Science Picture Co/Getty Images

talia begin to develop, and the fetus's body may be covered by lanugo, a soft, downy hair. The fetus has a large head and a well-formed face, with fused eyelids and external ears. At this point, a heartbeat can be detected, and the fetus may begin to suck its thumb. The kidneys are working, and the fetus's bladder fills twice an hour, excreting urine directly into the amniotic fluid, where it is swallowed and reabsorbed into the fetus's blood. From there, it travels to the placenta, to the mother's blood supply, and to her kidneys for excretion.

Changes in the Mother During the First Trimester

Women may start to experience some physical changes within a couple weeks of conception. Early signs of pregnancy include swelling and tenderness of the breasts, fatigue, and of course, a missed period. HCG levels increase, which can often be detected by home pregnancy tests within 2 weeks of conception. As the pregnancy progresses, she may begin to notice both physical and emotional changes, including water retention, frequent urination, heartburn, constipation, and headaches. Rising levels of estrogen and progesterone may cause her areola and labia to darken.

Fetus The unborn offspring from the end of the 8th week after conception until it is born.

Throughout the first trimester, many pregnant women experience food cravings and aversions. Mothers-to-be often desire healthier fare than they may be used to, and load up on dairy and fruits. Pregnant women typically gain 3 to 4 pounds during the first trimester. They may crave sweets because the sugar gives their fatigued bodies a burst of energy, and may combat the low blood sugar that can exacerbate morning sickness. Pregnant women also crave salt, which their bodies need to restore the fluid balance after their blood volume has increased.

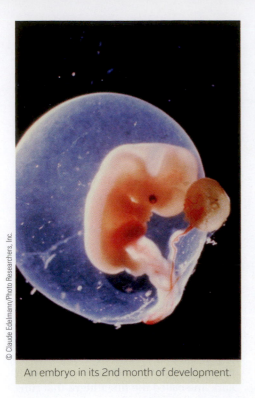

An embryo in its 2nd month of development.

About two-thirds to three-quarters of women experience **morning sickness**—nausea, vomiting, and food aversions that occur mostly in the first trimester, but in some women can continue throughout pregnancy. The term "morning sickness" is actually a misnomer because symptoms are not limited to mornings and can occur throughout the day, and because it is not a sickness; indeed, it may be an adaptation that helps the embryo survive. In fact, women who have morning sickness in their first trimester are less likely to miscarry than women who don't. The theory is that morning sickness causes pregnant women to expel and avoid substances that may be toxic to the developing embryo, especially at a time when fetal organ development is at its peak (Flaxman & Sherman, 2000). Pregnant women have the strongest aversions to strong-tasting vegetables, caffeine, alcohol, and meats, fish, and eggs—foods that are more likely to spoil or be a source of parasites than plants or grains. Indeed, morning sickness is more common in societies with an animal-based diet than in cultures with a plant-based diet (Flaxman & Sherman, 2000).

A woman's emotional response to her pregnancy may depend on several factors, including her relationship status, her own relationship with her parents, the state of her career, her self-image, her socioeconomic standing, the number of previous births, and other life situations. Her response will also depend on whether the pregnancy was planned or unplanned. She will also need to come to terms with being pregnant; while some women are overjoyed, others may be shocked and frightened. In the first trimester, a woman may experience a wide variety of emotions, including nervousness, excitement, anxiety, joy, and anticipation. Her emotional response often depends on her physical symptoms, such as nausea, vomiting, and morning sickness (Rofe, Littner & Lewin, 1993). Emotional support from the woman's partner can help her through a psychologically stressful time (Somers-Smith, 1999). An expectant father also experiences a variety of emotions—from joy, to fear, to ambivalence—depending on the situation. The expectant father's partner should be aware of and sensitive to his emotional needs as well (Finnbogadottir, Svalenius, & Persson, 2003). Pregnancy can be a time of bonding and intimacy for a couple, or it can be a difficult time that weakens an already troubled relationship. Maintaining your bond and remembering that you were partners and lovers before you were expectant parents can help your evolving relationship.

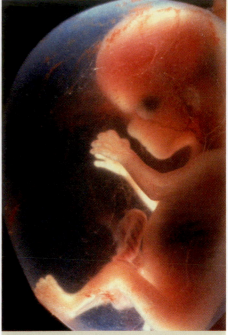

A fetus in the 3rd month of development (the end of the first trimester).

It is thought that Charlotte Brontë, author of *Jane Eyre*, died of excessive vomiting caused by morning sickness.

The Second Trimester

The Development of the Fetus During the Second Trimester

During the second trimester, the fetus greatly increases in size, until it is about a foot long and weighs 2 pounds by the end of the 6th month. Its physical features mature so the unborn baby looks more recognizably human. Bones develop and harden, although the bones are not yet connected at the joints by tendons. The developing fetus begins to kick and move in its now-functional placenta. By the middle of the second trimester, the fetus has a sleep/wake cycle and responds to sound. It is covered by **vernix**, a greasy waxy substance that protects the fetus from its constant immersion in amniotic fluid and lubricates the way when it is time for delivery. There is a chance that a premature baby born at the end of the second trimester could survive.

Changes in the Mother During the Second Trimester

In many women, the second trimester is the most enjoyable time of pregnancy. The nausea and vomiting of morning sickness may have passed, and the fetus is not

Morning sickness Nausea, vomiting, and food aversions associated with pregnancy, perhaps related to high hCG levels.

yet large enough to cause too much discomfort and inconvenience. Women usually gain about a pound a week during the second trimester. The mother usually feels the first fetal movements during the 4th month; this is called **quickening**. During the second trimester, some women experience heartburn, bloating, constipation, and hemorrhoids. A woman's pelvis may begin to widen as the placenta produces a hormone that makes the ligaments and joints in the pelvis more flexible. Women may be tired and have an increased appetite. **Braxton-Hicks contractions** may begin during the second trimester. These usually painless contractions don't widen the cervix as birthing contractions do; instead, they prepare the uterus for childbirth.

The Third Trimester

The Development of the Fetus During the Third Trimester

During the last 3 months of pregnancy, the fetus greatly increases in size. Its organ systems continue to develop and enlarge. During the 7th month, the head and body become more proportionate, and the baby's lungs, though still immature, are beginning to function. During the 8th month, the fetus gains about half an ounce a day, and will weigh about 5 or 6 pounds by the end of the 8th month. The bones of the baby's head are soft because the brain is growing rapidly and needs room for enlargement. At 8 months, the fetus may respond to familiar sounds; it has been shown that babies who had been exposed to a soap opera theme song during pregnancy relaxed and stopped crying when they heard the same theme music, while babies who hadn't been exposed to the song in the womb didn't change their behavior (Hepper, 1991). By their 9th month in the womb, babies

Vernix A white waxy substance that coats and protects the skin of the fetus.

Quickening The initial movements of the fetus as felt by the pregnant woman.

Braxton-Hicks contractions Uterine contractions that may help prepare for childbirth, but which don't dilate the cervix.

Linea nigra The dark vertical line that runs down the belly button to the pubic area during pregnancy.

Gestational diabetes A type of diabetes that can occur in pregnant women.

may not move as much—they are simply out of room! During this last month before birth, babies continue to grow, reaching an average size of 20 inches and 7½ pounds. The downy hair covering their body is often shed, and they turn in the uterus, preparing for birth.

In 9 months, the fetus has undergone quite a journey. From one fertilized egg, the baby has grown into an organism with 75 trillion cells, each with its own specialized func-

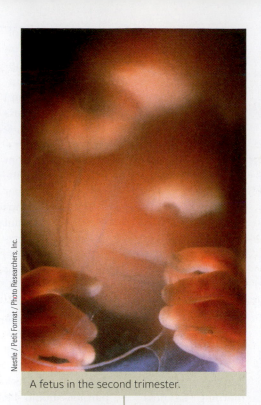

A fetus in the second trimester.

> My girlfriend is pregnant. Is it all right that we have sex? I don't want to poke the baby, or give him a complex or anything.

tion. Although at birth the baby's brain contains 100 billion neurons, with 100 trillion connections—more than the stars in the galaxy—it is not done developing. In fact, the brain will not complete development for about 20 more years.

Changes in the Mother During the Third Trimester

As the unborn baby continues to grow, the mother may become more and more uncomfortable, until even everyday activities such as walking, sitting, breathing, and sleeping become difficult. The woman continues to gain about a pound a week in her 7th and 8th month, although weight gain slows down in the final month of pregnancy. In their third trimester, expectant mothers may experience heartburn, indigestion, hemorrhoids, and constipation, as well as headaches, leg cramps, and back pain. Ankles and feet may swell, and the woman may develop a dark line called the **linea nigra** that runs from her navel to her pubis. About 4–7% of women develop **gestational diabetes**, a temporary form of diabetes. Around week 28, the placenta starts producing high levels of hormones that can cause insulin resistance. This is a common complication of pregnancy, but is easily managed and almost always temporary. During the third trimester, women may experience a number of emotions, including joyful expectation of the birth of their child, fear of the pain of childbirth, anxiety for the health of the unborn baby, and concern about the changes that their life will undergo (Rofe et al., 1993).

For men who are worried about having sex with their partners during the later stages of pregnancy, it is impossible to poke the baby with your penis during sex, unless you are attempting intercourse while your partner is actually giving birth. Unless there are mitigating

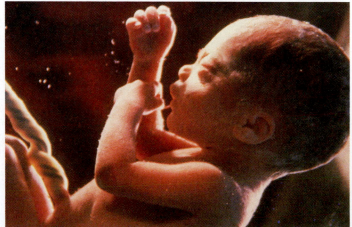

A fetus in the third trimester.

The Couvade Syndrome

A significant number of fathers-to-be have pregnancy symptoms, too. In the phenomenon known as *couvade,* males experience many of the symptoms that their pregnant partners are undergoing, including insomnia, fatigue, weight gain, irritability, cravings, and nausea. The cause of this phenomenon is unknown. It may be that men are showing empathy to their partners, or they may be jealous and want attention. There may be a hormonal explanation: testosterone levels fall and estrogen and prolactin

rise in expectant fathers (Berg & Wynne-Edwards, 2001). This phenomenon is even seen in marmosets. Among these monogamous monkeys, fathers gained as much as 20% of their original body weight when their mates were pregnant (Ziegler, Prudom, Schultz-Darken, Kurian, & Snowdon, 2006). Couvade may help monkeys (and men) get through the grueling weeks to come with a newborn, or it may be a case of monkey-see, monkey-do, in which the males mirror the behavior of their partners by eating and resting more.

ASK YOURSELF

Imagine that tomorrow, suddenly, men as well as women were able to give birth and breast-feed. When a couple engaged in intercourse, the male and female would have an equal chance of getting pregnant. What changes would there be in the world? How might such things as abortion laws, contraceptive availability, and beauty standards for men and women change?

circumstances, it is safe for you and your partner to have intercourse throughout her pregnancy. If the woman is healthy, having an orgasm won't bring on early labor, although the contractions may lull the fetus to sleep. Although some women may be less interested in sex during the first trimester due to nausea and fatigue and during the last trimester due to physical discomfort, some women enjoy sexual relations throughout their pregnancy and may even have an increased sex drive. Later in the pregnancy, couples may need to try positions other than the missionary position to accommodate the woman's belly.

Problems That Can Occur During Pregnancy

After completion of this section, you will be able to . . .

- ⚪ Define the terms *miscarriage* and *stillbirth.*
- ⚪ Identify the typical causes of miscarriages and birth defects.
- ⚪ Distinguish between fetal evaluation technologies.
- ⚪ Consider factors that affect the rates of unplanned pregnancy.
- ⚪ Compare the teen pregnancy rates in the United States with those in other countries

The time a baby spends in the womb greatly influences the rest of its life. Hormone levels, infections, nutrition, and even the mother's mood or lifestyle can affect the baby's future intelligence,

weight, and sexual orientation, as well as its likelihood of having high blood pressure, diabetes, and coronary heart disease (Leon, Johansson, & Rasmussen, 2000). Even if the mother is healthy, a pregnancy is considered high-risk if the mother is over 35, obese, or has had a previous Cesarean section.

Problems in the Pregnancy

A **miscarriage** is the spontaneous expulsion of the embryo or fetus from the uterus before it's able to live outside of the womb. Most miscarriages occur during the first trimester and are often caused by a chromosomal abnormality that is incompatible with life. Miscarriages during the second trimester are usually a result of the mother's poor health; her exposure to drugs or toxic substances; or the condition of her cervix, her uterus, or the placenta. Even extreme stress can increase the risk of a miscarriage because high levels of cortisol (a "stress" hormone) may suppress progesterone (Arck et al., 2001). If the fetus is delivered dead after 20 weeks of gestation, it is usually called a **stillbirth**.

Although the physical effects of a miscarriage are not usually overwhelming, the experience can be emotionally devastating. Even if the miscarriage occurs early in the pregnancy, parents often feel a strong loss, as their plans and dreams for the child die. Well-meaning friends may make it worse by making insensitive comments or by not acknowledging that the parents endured a loss. Women who have lost a pregnancy may experience grief, depression, anger, anxiety, and even post-traumatic stress disorder (Swanson, Karmali, Powell, & Pulvermakher, 2003). Miscarriage can also be hard on a relationship. Often, the baby isn't quite "real" to first-time fathers until the first time he holds the baby in his arms, but the mother often begins to bond with her unborn child very early in the pregnancy. After miscarriage, fathers are more likely to keep to themselves, deny their own loss, and avoid dealing with the emotional aspects. This discrepancy can lead to stress in a relationship; almost one-third of women said their interpersonal relationship with their partner was more distant 1 year after miscarriage and almost 40% said their sexual relationship had suffered (Swanson et al., 2003). However, when mothers feel that their partners share their feelings and experiences, their relationship may be even stronger after their loss.

Miscarriage A pregnancy that terminates on its own before the embryo or fetus can survive outside of the womb.

Stillbirth The death of a fetus more than 20 weeks after conception but before birth.

The Causes of Birth Defects

Within 38 weeks, a single cell becomes a human being. When you consider the innumerable opportunities for missteps and mutations along the way, it is surprising that any of us are born healthy. Some babies are not so lucky. There are many factors that can lead to birth defects, including genetic abnormalities, teratogenic agents, and infectious diseases. Common causes of birth defects are summarized in Table 13.1.

Genetic abnormalities, teratogenic agents, and infectious diseases.

About 4,000 human diseases are of genetic origin. Some are mild, such as color blindness, and some are so severe that they are incompatible with life. Genetic counselors can help parents assess their risks for these diseases. **Teratogens** are agents that can harm the developing embryo or fetus. Exposure to these substances within the first 8 weeks of development is usually most damaging. Drugs such as alcohol, nicotine, cocaine, and even aspirin can harm the fetus and lead to long-term problems. Babies are also susceptible to infection (usually during childbirth) from the mother's viral or bacterial infections, such as HIV, herpes, or German measles (rubella).

A child with fetal alcohol syndrome has certain facial characteristics as well as developmental problems.

Fasstar Enterprises www.fasstar.com

A child whose mother took thalidomide while she was pregnant.

© Bettmann/CORBIS

Teratogen An agent that can cause physical defects in the developing embryo or fetus.

Rh factor An antigen found on the surface of the red blood cells of most people.

Fetal alcohol syndrome A medical condition that causes developmental problems in an unborn child; it results from excessive alcohol consumption by the mother during pregnancy.

Bilirubin A pigment in the bile that is a breakdown product of hemoglobin; excessive amounts in the blood produce a yellowish appearance of the skin.

RhoGAM A drug that can prevent an Rh-negative mother's antibodies from reacting to the fetus's Rh-positive cells.

Toxemia A potentially dangerous condition of pregnancy characterized by hypertension, edema, and protein in the urine.

Ultrasound A procedure in which sound waves are bounced off internal tissues in order to visualize the fetus.

Rh incompatibility.

Eighty-five percent of people have a protein on the surface of their blood cells called the **Rh factor**—those who are Rh-positive have the protein and those who are Rh-negative do not have the protein. If the mother and the baby both have the Rh factor, or if they both do not, there is no problem. But in 8% of pregnancies, the mother is Rh-negative and the baby is Rh-positive (this occurs if the father is Rh-positive). During labor and delivery, fetal blood cells can enter the Rh-negative mother's tissues, causing her to form antibodies against fetal Rh-positive cells. This isn't a problem for the first Rh-positive baby, but if she becomes pregnant with a *second* Rh-positive baby, these antibodies enter the fetus and destroy its mature red blood cells. The fetus develops jaundice because of an accumulation of **bilirubin**, which is toxic and can cause brain damage. Luckily, there is an easy treatment. An Rh-negative mother is given a drug called **RhoGAM** at 28 weeks into her first pregnancy and again within two to three days of the delivery of her first infant. This destroys all Rh-positive fetal cells, so the mother doesn't form antibodies against future babies.

Toxemia.

Six to seven percent of women in their last trimester develop **toxemia**, which is characterized by an increase in blood pressure, sudden weight gain, severe swelling of the ankles and face, and protein in the urine. If untreated, toxemia can lead to eclampsia, which can cause seizures, coma, and even death.

Advanced age.

Both men and women are waiting longer to have children. Advancing age increases the risk of miscarriage and some birth defects. Because a woman's eggs begin to develop before she is born, as she ages, the older eggs are less viable and more prone to mutation. As men age, their sperm are constantly dividing. With each replication and division, there are more chances of mutation. Children of older mothers are more prone to chromosomal anomalies such as Down syndrome. The children of older fathers are at higher risk for achondroplasia (a type of dwarfism), schizophrenia, bipolar depression, and autism (Malaspina et al., 2001; Reichenberg et al., 2006; Wyrobek et al., 2006).

Fetal Evaluation

Several tests have been developed to monitor the baby's development and to identify possible problems. An **ultrasound** uses high frequency sound waves to provide a picture of the fetus. Sound waves penetrate the mother's body. They pass through fluid-filled tissues and bounce off solid tissues. The reflected sound waves are collected and an image is pro-

Table 13.1 Common Causes of Birth Defects

CAUSE	EXAMPLE	EFFECT	MISCELLANEOUS
Genetic Diseases	Down syndrome	Having three copies of chromosome 21 causes characteristic facial features and mental retardation.	Risk increases with mother's age, from 1/1,000 for a 30-year-old, to 1/100 at age 40.
	Sickle cell anemia	Blood cells are deformed and unable to properly carry oxygen, which leads to systemic problems.	Most prevalent in African Americans.
	Tay-Sachs disease	In this fatal neurological condition, babies usually die by age 5.	Common in Jews of Eastern European descent.
Drugs	Alcohol	More than 3 ounces of alcohol per day may cause **fetal alcohol syndrome**, characterized by undersized babies with multiple deformities, learning problems, and poor coordination.	"The hangover that lasts a lifetime."
	Tobacco	Nicotine restricts blood vessels to fetus. This results in pregnancy complications, miscarriages, low birth weight, and increased incidence of sudden infant death syndrome (SIDS).	More than 13% of pregnant women smoke (Martin et al., 2009). Smoking has been linked to 115,000 miscarriages and 5,600 infant deaths a year (Murkoff, Eisenberg & Hathaway, 2002).
	Cocaine	Cocaine damages the placenta; restricts blood flow to the fetus; and increases miscarriage, premature labor, and stillbirth. It causes long-term physical and behavioral problems for the child.	Approximately 45,000 women in the United States used cocaine during pregnancy in 1992 (NIDA Notes, 1995).
	Caffeine	High amounts may increase the risk of miscarriage and low birth weight. Moderate amounts may increase teratogenic effects of other drugs like alcohol and tobacco (Nehlig & Debry, 1994).	Caffeine is found in coffee, tea, and soft drinks. Small amounts are also found in chocolate.
	Thalidomide	Fetuses develop hands and feet but not arms or legs.	Thalidomide was a tranquilizer and morning sickness drug used in the 1950s and 1960s.
	Pseudoephedrine	Babies can be born with a hole in the abdominal wall through which intestines hang.	Found in decongestants.
	Aspirin	Can harm fetal heart.	Other nonsteroidal anti-inflammatory drugs (NSAIDs) such as ibuprofen may also affect the fetus's heart.
Viruses and bacteria	Rubella	Can lead to heart defects, blindness, deafness, and other problems.	Most damaging to the embryo or fetus during weeks 3–12.
	Gonorrhea, chlamydia	Can cause blindness.	Chlamydia is the most common infection passed from mother to fetus.
	HIV	The virus that causes AIDS	20–65% chance of being passed on to child.
	Herpes	Can cause neurological damage or death if baby is exposed to active virus.	Almost 25% of pregnant women have genital herpes.

(© Cengage Learning 2013)

duced. Ultrasound images may indicate the sex of the child, help estimate the due date, and identify possible structural irregularities, such as **hydrocephalus** or heart abnormalities. Ultrasounds are often performed during the 4th month of pregnancy. High definition and "real time" ultrasounds are now available.

Amniocentesis, usually performed between 14 and 18 weeks, can identify genetic defects and conclusively determine the chromosomal sex of the fetus. During this procedure, the fetus is located via ultrasound, and a needle is inserted through the mother's abdominal and uterine wall and into the amniotic sac. Fluid is withdrawn from the sac and the chromosomes of the fetal cells in the fluid are analyzed for genetic abnormalities. This procedure is usually performed when the mother has some reason to fear for the presence of genetic abnormalities, such as Down syndrome. Results may take several weeks.

To get quicker results than with an amniocentesis, a woman may choose to get **chorionic villus sampling (CVS)**. In this

Hydrocephalus A condition in which cerebrospinal fluid builds up in the brain, enlarging the head and potentially causing brain damage.

Amniocentesis A prenatal diagnostic procedure in which a small amount of amniotic fluid is withdrawn to detect genetic abnormalities of the fetus.

Chorionic villus sampling (CVS) A prenatal test used to determine chromosomal disorders in the embryo or fetus.

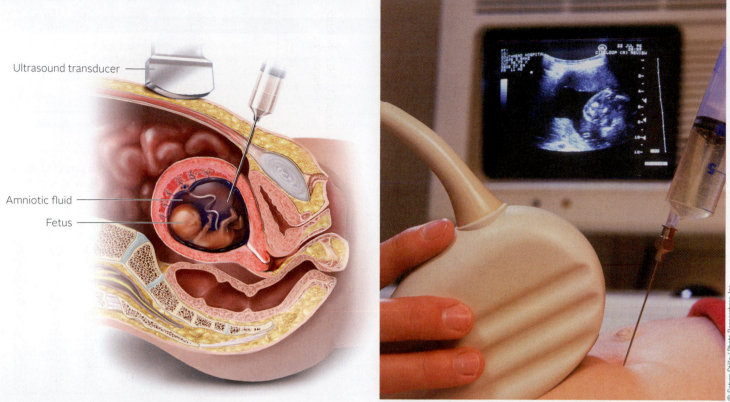

Ultrasound transducer

Amniotic fluid

Fetus

FIGURE 13.6 Diagram and photo of amniocentesis. (© Argosy Publishing Inc.)

procedure, a thin tube is guided in through the cervix, and a small portion of the **chorion**—the fetal side of the placenta—is removed. CVS is usually performed between the 9th and 14th weeks, and results are available in less than a week. CVS can determine genetic abnormalities such as Down syndrome, cystic fibrosis, Tay-Sachs disease, or sickle cell anemia. Unfortunately, CVS increases the risk of miscarriage; up to 2% of women who undergo this procedure will spontaneously abort (Sundberg et al., 1997; Tabor, Vestergaard, & Lidegaard, 2009).

Alpha fetoprotein is normally produced by the baby's liver; high levels, however, may indicate neural tube defects such as **spina bifida** or **anencephaly**. Spina bifida is a birth defect in which the spinal cord is exposed and imperfectly fused. In anencephaly, a major portion of the brain is small or absent. Taking folic acid before and during early pregnancy greatly reduces risks of having a baby with neural tube defects. It is recommended that women start taking folic acid before they get pregnant because it takes a while for adequate levels to build. The alpha fetoprotein test is imperfect, and is associated with a fairly high number of both false positives and false negatives.

Chorion One of the membranes of the placenta.

Alpha fetoprotein A protein normally produced by the fetus. High levels can indicate a developmental defect.

Spina bifida A congenital defect in which the spinal cord is exposed and imperfectly fused.

Anencephaly A birth defect in which parts or most of the brain are small or missing.

Unplanned Pregnancy

A woman's response to pregnancy will vary greatly depending on whether it is a wanted or planned pregnancy or an undesired pregnancy. Her response may differ based on her age, marital status, financial situation, or number of children.

In 2001 there were 6.4 million pregnancies in the United States. Almost half of those pregnancies were unintended (Finer & Henshaw, 2006). About 5% of all women of reproductive age have an unplanned pregnancy (Mosher & Jones, 2010). According to data from the National Survey of Family Growth (NSFG), of the 3.1 million unintended pregnancies in the United States in 2001, 44% led to birth, 42% were aborted, and 14% were lost to miscarriage (Finer & Henshaw, 2006). The same study found that unintended pregnancy rates were highest among women under age 24, women who cohabit with a male partner, minority women (especially black women), and low-income women of all races. The unplanned pregnancy rate among women 18 to 24 was more than twice the rate for women overall—1 in 10 women under age 24 had an unintended pregnancy in 2001. Women who live with a male partner were

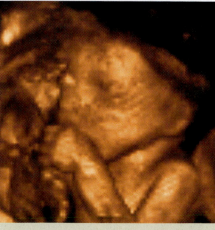

A 3-D ultrasound image. The fetus can be seen sucking its thumb.

more than twice as likely to have an unplanned birth compared to married women or unmarried women who were not cohabiting. The NSFG study found that while 40% of pregnancies in white women are unplanned, 54% of pregnancies in Hispanic women and 69% of pregnancies in black women are unintentional. Finally, women living in poverty are almost 4 times more likely to have an unplanned pregnancy than women of higher socioeconomic status (Finer & Henshaw, 2006). This increase corresponds with cuts in state and federal reproductive health programs for low-income women.

Teen Pregnancy

By the end of the 20th century, about 1 out of every 9 girls aged 15 to 19 in the United States became pregnant, accounting for almost 500,000 births (Trussell, Brown, & Rowland Hogue, 2004). Pregnancy rates are almost 3 times higher in Hispanic teenagers than among whites (Figure 13.7; Gavin et al., 2009). With an incidence of teen pregnancy more than twice as high as in Canada, 5 times the rates seen in France, and greater than 14 times as high as in Japan, the United States has the highest rate of teen pregnancy among developed countries (Figure 13.8; Singh & Darroch, 2000; Unicef, 2001). Between 1991 and 2005, teen pregnancy rates dropped by one third (Martin et al., 2006). It is thought that this decline was due to both decreased sexual experience and improved contraceptive use (Santelli et al., 2004), although the decreased fertility of males may also be a factor (Skakkebaek et al., 2006). However, pregnancy rates in American girls aged 15 to 19 increased in 2006 and again in 2007. Both social and demographic conditions, such as a population's socioeconomic status, religious beliefs, and racial differences, as well as state policies, such as Medicaid availability and abstinence-only education programs, can affect teen pregnancy and birthrate (Santelli & Kirby, 2010; Yang & Gaydos, 2010).

Why is the teen pregnancy rate so high in America? It's not that U.S. teens are the most sexually active—that distinction belongs to Denmark—but our teen birthrate is 6 times the teen birthrate in Denmark (Blow, 2008). Girls in many other countries have easy access to legal contraception and abortion, and receive mandatory, medically accurate sexuality education. In comparison, between the years 1994 and 2001, two thirds of the states in America cut funding for family planning, made birth control less accessible, and put tighter controls on sex education (Connolly, 2006).

Teenaged mothers are more likely to live in poverty and go on welfare; in fact, nearly 8% of teen mothers eventually require financial assistance from the government. Teen pregnancies cost an estimated $7 billion per year in the United States. Teen mothers are less likely to graduate from high school, and fewer than 2% will graduate from college. Because teenaged girls who get pregnant are less likely to receive adequate prenatal care, their babies are more likely to be low birth weight and have health and developmental problems throughout their lives. They are more likely to be abused or neglected, less likely to graduate from high school, and more likely to become teenaged parents themselves.

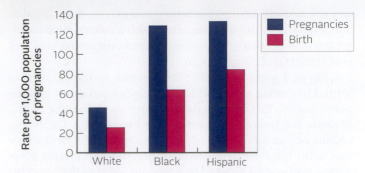

FIGURE 13.7 Teenage pregnancies and births in the United States, by race and ethnicity. (© Cengage Learning 2013. SOURCE: Gavin et al., 2009.)

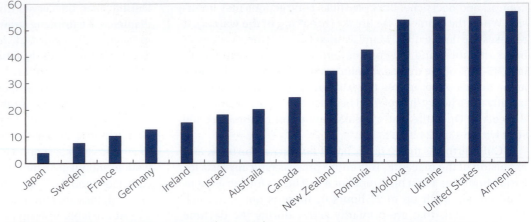

FIGURE 13.8 Births per 1,000 women aged 15 to 19, by country. (© Cengage Learning 2013. SOURCE: Singh & Darroch, 2000.)

Childbirth

After completion of this section, you will be able to . . .

O Recognize the symptoms of impending birth.

O Define the terms *lightening, bloody show, breaking the waters,* and *episiotomy.*

O Explain what occurs during labor, delivery of the baby, and delivery of the placenta.

O Compare and contrast a head-first birth with a breech delivery and a transverse delivery.

The fetus plays an important role in determining the length of the pregnancy. As the fetus matures, its cortisol levels increase, which raises the placenta's production of estrogen (Nathanielsz, 1996). The change in the estrogen-to-progesterone ratio increases uterine contractions and leads to increased levels of prolactin, a hormone involved in milk production. The mother's oxytocin levels also rise, causing uterine contractions and milk let-down. In addition, oxytocin also inhibits memory, which may help mothers forget the pain of childbirth, perhaps a significant reason why they may agree to go through it again.

Physical symptoms alert the woman to the impending birth. **Lightening** occurs when the baby's head drops into the pelvic cavity. This relieves the pressure on the mother's diaphragm, but intensifies the strain on her bladder. Lightening usually occurs 2 to 4 weeks before a woman gives birth to her first baby, but later in subsequent pregnancies. During pregnancy, the cervix is blocked by a mucous plug. As the cervix **dilates**, the plug may be released. In addition, capillaries may rupture, causing the cervical mucus to appear pink or brownish, a condition called the **bloody show**. Other signs that childbirth is approaching include indigestion, diarrhea, abdominal cramps, and backache. Braxton-Hicks contractions may intensify. When the amniotic sac breaks (**breaking of the waters**), it releases the fluid within. Many women fear that their water will break in public, and the gush of fluid will embarrass them. In fact, 85–90% of the time, a woman's water doesn't break before labor begins. Also, unless the woman is lying down, there is usually not a heavy flow of fluid because the baby's head blocks the cervix. Once the water breaks, labor contractions usually start within 12 to 24 hours.

Childbirth has three stages: labor, delivery of the baby, and expulsion of the placenta. This entire process typically lasts for 8 to 14 hours for a first birth, and for 4 to 9 hours for subsequent children, although up to 24 hours or more is not abnormal. Most mammals that are primarily active during the daytime (including humans) labor through the night, so the young are delivered by daytime (Cassidy, 2006). Babies born between 1 a.m. and 6 a.m. have up to a 16% greater chance of dying than babies born during the day (Gould, Qin, & Chavez, 2005). This may be due to the availability, alertness, and quality of physicians and medical personnel.

Throughout most of the 20th century, American women gave birth lying down in a hospital bed, legs spread and strapped into stirrups, wrists restrained by their sides. This was for the ease of the doctors, not the laboring women. Women will more naturally squat or crawl while laboring. French obstetrician Frederick LeBoyer encouraged women to deliver their babies in a warm bath in a dimly lit room, to ease the transition for the baby.

Labor

During labor, the cervix, which begins as an opening about the diameter of a drinking straw, will widen enough to allow a baby to fit through. Labor is divided into three phases: early, active, and transitional. **Early labor** is the longest and least intense phase of labor. It can last 4 to 24 hours. During early labor, the cervix thins and softens (effaces) and dilates to about 3 centimeters. Early **effacement**, or the softening and thinning of the cervix, occurs slowly without noticeable contractions, but once a woman is in labor, mild to moderate contractions usually occur 5 to 20 minutes apart and last 30 to 45 seconds each. A laboring woman should go to the hospital somewhere between the end of early labor and the beginning of **active labor**, when contractions are 5 minutes apart or less.

Active labor lasts up to 5 hours. Its intense and regular contractions dilate the cervix to 7 centimeters. **Transitional labor**

Lightening When the baby drops into the pelvic cavity in preparation for delivery.

Dilation When the diameter of the cervix widens.

Bloody show The discharge of blood and mucus early in labor.

Breaking of the waters The breaking of the amniotic sac and release of amniotic fluid before childbirth.

Early labor The first, longest, and least intense phase of labor.

Effacement Softening and thinning of the cervix.

Active labor The middle stage of labor.

Transitional labor The shortest and hardest stage of labor, during which the cervix dilates to its full 10 centimeters and the head of the fetus moves into the birth canal.

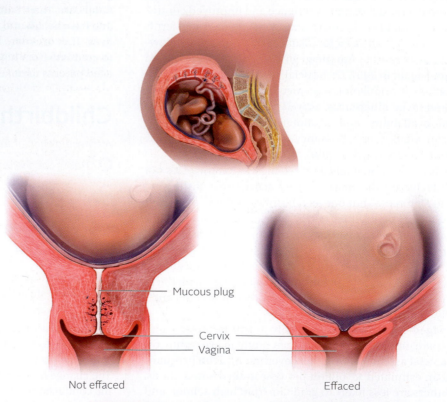

Mucous plug

Cervix
Vagina

Not effaced

Effaced

FIGURE 13.9 Cervical effacement. (© Argosy Publishing Inc.)

is the shortest, but hardest and most painful stage of labor, with very strong contractions, each lasting 60 to 90 seconds and occurring 2 to 3 minutes apart. During this stage, which lasts up to 60 minutes or more, the cervix dilates to its full 10 centimeters and the head of the fetus moves into the birth canal.

Expulsion of the Fetus

During this stage, the mother feels an overwhelming urge to push, as increased oxytocin levels cause strong uterine contractions of about a minute in duration and thrust the baby out through the birth canal. This stage usually lasts 30 to 60 minutes, but can take as little as 10 minutes or as long as 4 hours in first-time mothers. During its passage down the birth canal, the fetus rotates and turns its head (Figure 13.10). The baby usually comes out facing down, which puts less pressure on the mother's back. **Crowning** is when the baby's head appears in the external opening of the vagina. This stage ends with the birth of the baby.

Ninety-five percent of the time, the fetus presents head down, which is easiest on both the mother and the baby. About 4% of babies are in the **breech** position during birth, in which their feet, buttocks, or knees rest against the cervix. Breech births (Figure 13.11) have a higher mortality rate and are harder to deliver vaginally. The baby's head is best at dilating the cervix; if the cervix is not completely open, it can strangle the child as it passes into the birth canal. Today, almost all breech babies are delivered by Cesarean section (discussed in further detail later). Breech births are more common when the fetus is premature or smaller than average, when the uterus is unusually shaped or has fibroids, or when the placenta partly covers the cervical opening. **Transverse deliveries**—in which the baby's shoulders or arms are presented first—are fairly rare and always require a Cesarean delivery.

This sentence is written inside a circle that represents the diameter of a fully dilated cervix.

Uncomfortable mothers-to-be should be glad they're not an Australian Stumpy, a lizard that gives birth to a single infant that weighs one-third of the mother's body weight; this would be equivalent to a woman giving birth to a 7-year-old child (Munns & Daniels, 2007).

An **episiotomy** is a procedure in which a surgical incision is made between the vagina and the anus to prevent the tearing of the perineal tissues and to relieve pressure on the baby's head. Although episiotomy is performed in 80% of births in the United States, it is a controversial procedure. The American College of Obstetricians and Gynecologists currently recommends that an episiotomy *not* be routinely performed, as infants do just as well without, and mothers may actually do better because torn tissue heals faster than incised tissue. Women who don't get an episiotomy have less blood loss, less infection, less incontinence, and less postpartum pain. An episiotomy may be necessary if the baby's head is particularly large, or if its shoulder is stuck in the birth canal.

Expulsion of the Placenta

The third stage—when the placenta is expelled through the vagina—is the shortest stage, typically lasting 30 minutes or less, but might be the most dangerous for the mother due to the possibility of excessive bleeding. While the mother is delivering the

Crowning The appearance of the baby's head at the vaginal opening.

Breech The birth position in which the baby's feet, buttocks, or knees are against the cervix.

Transverse The birth position in which the baby's shoulders or arms are presented first.

Episiotomy An incision made to the perineum during childbirth.

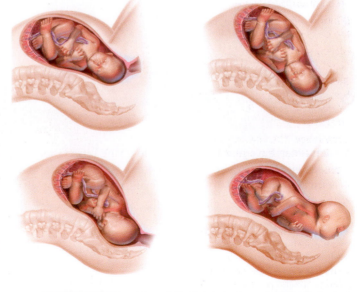

FIGURE 13.10 Expulsion of the fetus. (© Argosy Publishing Inc.)

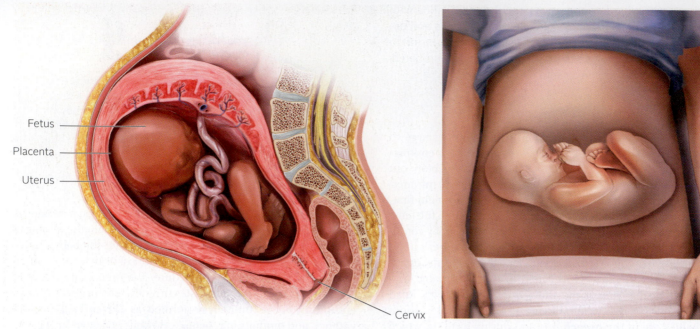

Labels on left illustration: Fetus, Placenta, Uterus, Cervix

FIGURE 13.11 A baby in the breech position, left, and in the transverse position, right. (© Argosy Publishing Inc.)

placenta, the baby is being tended to. He or she is cleaned of mucus, and silver nitrate is put in the baby's eyes to prevent bacterial infection. The umbilical cord is clamped in two places and cut off between the clamps about 3 inches from the baby's abdomen. This doesn't hurt because there are no nerve endings in the cord.

Variations in Birthing Situations

After completion of this section, you will be able to . . .

○ Define the terms *midwife, doula,* and *epidural.*

○ Describe the different ways by which pain may be reduced during childbirth.

○ Describe what is involved in prepared childbirth and Cesarean sections.

○ Explain why human birth is particularly difficult.

○ Catalogue the challenges involved with multiple births and with premature and low birth weight babies.

○ Compare the maternal and infant mortality rates in the United States with those of other countries.

Women today have many choices when giving birth. They may choose to give birth in a hospital or at home, with a midwife or an obstetrician, with the use of pain-relieving medications or without. Some women deliver vaginally; others need surgical intervention.

Ninety-eight percent of births in the United States, Canada, and England occur in a hospital, where women have immediate access to

Midwife A professional trained to assist in normal labor and birth.

Doula An experienced labor companion who provides physical and emotional support to laboring women.

necessary resources should an emergency occur. Some women give birth in a birthing center. In many of these centers, labor, delivery, and postpartum recovery all occur in one comfortable and homey room. Some of these centers are in a hospital, whereas others are separate. Less than 1% of births take place at home (Martin et al., 2009). Some doctors won't attend a home birth due to fears of legal reprisals, but low-risk, midwife-assisted home births have outcomes as safe as those in hospitals (Declercq, Paine, & Winter, 1995; Durand, 1992).

Midwives and Doulas

It is only recently in the course of human experience that (mostly male) doctors help a woman give birth. Women have always assisted other women during labor and delivery. **Midwives** (the vast majority of whom are female) attend about 8% of all vaginal births in the United States (Martin et al., 2010). Women attended by midwives have lower Cesarean section rates, fewer interventions such as labor induction or episiotomies, and lower infant mortality rates than those attended by doctors. This may be because women with high-risk pregnancies are less likely to use a midwife. A pregnant woman may also decide to use a **doula** to assist in her pregnancy. Although not medical professionals, doulas offer physical and emotional support to laboring women, and can provide experience, information, and insight. Pregnant women with doulas have lower rates of perinatal problems, fewer Cesarean sections, shorter delivery times, and fewer interventions and complications (Sosa, Kennell, Klaus, Robertson, & Urrutia, 1980).

Pain Reduction

> "Natural child birth means no drugs will be administered into the female's body during the delivery. The father can have all he wants."
>
> —*Bill Cosby*

Pain is a fact of childbirth. In describing the experience of childbirth, the comedian Carol Burnett said, "Take your lower lip, and

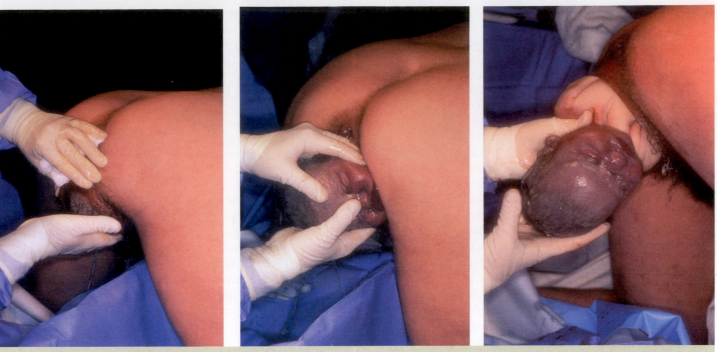

Vaginal childbirth.

Photos © Scott Camazine/Phototake

pull it over your head." Although each woman experiences child-birth differently, in general, pain seems to be more intense in first-time mothers, younger women, women with a history of menstrual problems, those delivering bigger babies, and those who are more afraid or less prepared. Various methods are used to ease the pain of childbirth.

It is thought that the myrrh brought by the three wise men may not have been just a gift for the baby Jesus but may have been a salve to help ease Mary's labor pains. The first recorded use of general anesthesia during childbirth was in 1847 when chloroform was used to ease the pain of a laboring woman (Cassidy, 2006). General anesthetics are not largely used today, except in some cases of surgical deliveries. Local anesthetics such as epidurals are much more common.

An **epidural** is a local anesthetic, which is injected through the lower back into the membranes surrounding the spinal cord. This numbs the woman to pain but still allows her to use her muscles to push the baby out. Although most women in the United States get an epidural when giving birth, this procedure is not without its risks. Women may find it harder to push, and they may be more likely to need external stimulation to get contractions going. However, an epidural doesn't increase the chance of Cesarean section, and may actually shorten labor (Wong et al., 2005).

Most anesthesiologists will give an epidural to women with a lower back tattoo. They usually choose an area of non-tattooed skin through which to insert the needle. If the tattoo is exceptionally large or relatively fresh, some physicians won't perform the procedure.

Many women successfully reduce their pain with nonpharmaceutical methods, such as hypnosis, transcutaneous electrical nerve stimulation (TENS), acupuncture, or hydrotherapy. Preparation, knowledge, and distraction may also alleviate labor pains.

In **prepared childbirth**, the mother and her birth partner are taught about labor and delivery, and practice breathing and relaxation techniques. There are many benefits to prepared childbirth. Parents learn what goes on during birth, what the hospital visit may entail, possible complications, and medical interventions available. The fear of the unknown can intensify pain, so knowledge of the process may lessen the woman's discomfort. Prepared childbirth increases the involvement of the partner. In some childbirth classes, pregnant women learn breathing patterns to increase oxygen delivery to the muscles, and relaxation techniques to decrease muscle tension, techniques developed by Dr. Fernand Lamaze. In childbirth classes, parents have the opportunity to meet with other pregnant couples and share their experiences, and develop friendships with others who will have children of the same age.

Pregnant couples are encouraged to make a birth plan, which is a list of their wishes for the birth process. These plans may include who should be in the delivery room, what procedures the parents wish or do not wish, what methods should be used for pain relief, if the mother wants an episiotomy, and who cuts the cord. Parents may also consider whether they want to bank the blood from the umbilical cord, a process gaining popularity because cord blood contains stem cells that can be used for future organ transplants. Couples who do not have a medical condition that may require future stem cell transplant are encouraged to use public storage rather than the more expensive private storage banks.

Can you get an epidural if you have a tattoo on your lower back?

Epidural Injection of an anesthetic into the space of the spinal cord where spinal fluid circulates, resulting in decreased sensation from the waist down.

Prepared childbirth The mother and her birth partner learn what occurs during labor and delivery, and practice breathing and relaxation techniques.

Surgical Deliveries

A **Cesarean section (C-section)** occurs when the baby is delivered through an incision in the abdominal wall and uterus, rather than passing through the vagina. In this procedure, the woman will receive either a local or general anesthetic. The physician cuts through the abdomen and uterus to remove the baby. Usually, the incision is a horizontal cut below the bikini line. A Cesarean section is recommended when the mother has a particularly small pelvis or the baby has a very large head; when the baby is in a breech or transverse presentation; or if the baby is in fetal distress. C-section risks include those posed by any surgical procedure, including pain, blood loss, or infection. During childbirth, the scalpel could accidentally nick the baby's head, and babies born by Cesarean are more prone to breathing difficulties in their first few days of life. Babies born via C-section are more likely to develop allergies, asthma, and other immune system–related troubles, perhaps because of the different bacteria to which they are exposed during surgical delivery (Dominguez-Bello et al., 2010). The recovery time and maternal mortality rate for surgical births are higher than for vaginal deliveries. Finally, after a woman has a C-section, subsequent pregnancies have an increased risk of miscarriage, ectopic pregnancy, and placenta abnormalities (Ecker & Frigoletto, 2007). Perhaps for these reasons, as well as others, women who deliver their first baby by C-section are 12% less likely to have another child compared to women who gave birth vaginally (Tollånes, Melve, Irgens, & Skjærven, 2007).

In 1970, 5.5% of babies delivered in the United States were delivered surgically; today, almost 32% of deliveries are by Cesarean section (Hamilton, Martin, & Ventura, 2009). This rise can be attributed to a number of factors. Babies are larger today than in the past due to better nutrition and larger mothers. Some women prefer the convenience of scheduling the birth of their child. In addition, there are more high-risk pregnancies—older mothers and multiple births—which are more likely to require surgical births. The increased use of fetal monitors makes doctors quicker to consider that a baby is in distress even though these monitors are not entirely accurate. Many women are told that if they have ever had a C-section, all subsequent births need to be surgical due to the risk of uterine rupture. In fact, most women who have had a Cesarean section are able to deliver vaginally in subsequent births although risk factors must be considered. Finally, as vaginal births can provide a wider possibility of problems, physicians who fear malpractice suits may be more prone to suggest Cesarean sections.

Cross-Cultural Perspectives of Childbirth

Birth reflects the culture in which it takes place (Cassidy, 2006). In patriarchal societies where conditions are poor, many women die giving birth; in places where motherhood and fertility are esteemed, new mothers are pampered. From the Victorian age and through the 1940s, women were thought to be frail and feminine. It wasn't polite to speak of pregnancy and childbirth in public, and many women used drugs to sleep through the entire labor. The influence of women's liberation in the United

Cesarean section (C-section)
The delivery of a fetus by a surgical incision in the abdominal wall and uterus.

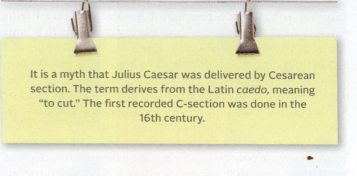

It is a myth that Julius Caesar was delivered by Cesarean section. The term derives from the Latin *caedo*, meaning "to cut." The first recorded C-section was done in the 16th century.

States in the 1970s changed this view. Empowered women embraced their feminine strengths and delivered their children without aid of drugs. Although pain during labor is common to all women, how pain is perceived and expressed differs from culture to culture. In some societies, women are free to shout out in pain; in others, women are encouraged to demonstrate a quiet, stoic endurance (Callister, Khalaf, Semenic, Kartchner, & Vehvilainen-Julkunen, 2003).

Difficult Birth Situations

Human birth is particularly difficult; in fact, humans take 3 to 4 times longer to deliver their babies than other primates. This is largely because of two facts: humans walk upright, which narrows the pelvis, and human newborns (and their heads) are proportionately bigger than other mammals. Polar bears, which weigh more than 500 pounds, give birth to cubs whose heads are smaller than a human baby's head (Cassidy, 2006). Yet even though a human baby's head is proportionately bigger than that of other mammals, the newborn's head size is nevertheless too small. Humans are born relatively immature and require prolonged parental care. Compared to newborn calves or lambs, which can walk and feed immediately upon birth, human babies are helpless—much of our brain development happens outside of the womb after birth. However, if the baby finished its development while still in the womb, its head would not fit through the birth canal. This is one of the reasons that human infants and fetuses spend so much time in REM sleep, which helps brain development (Roffwarg, Muzio & Dement, 1966). This of course raises the compelling question: what do infants and fetuses dream of?

In 2000, Ines Ramirez, a 40-year-old woman in Mexico, performed a Cesarean section on herself to deliver her child. After laboring unsuccessfully for hours in her remote cabin, Ines drank three shots of alcohol, cut her own abdomen with a kitchen knife, and successfully delivered her ninth child. Both mother and baby survived. (Cassidy, 2006; Molina-Sosa et al., 2004).

_____
_____
_____
_____
_____

Preterm Births

Each year in the United States more than 400,000 babies are born too early. A baby is considered **preterm** or **premature** if it is born between 20 and 37 weeks. Approximately 12.5% of all births and 50% of twins are preterm (Martin et al., 2006). A chance of a premature delivery is increased if the mother is under 18 or over 40, if she has received inadequate prenatal care, if she takes drugs or smokes during pregnancy, or if she has a malformed uterus or incompetent cervix. African American women are also more likely to deliver premature babies (Martin et al., 2010). Boys are more likely to be born prematurely and premature baby boys are less likely to survive than premature girls; in fact, of all the influences on preterm babies' health and survival, the greatest risk factor is the male sex (Eliot, 2009).

Premature babies—or "preemies" as they are called—face many challenges; in fact, prematurity is the most common cause of infant mortality in the United States. Premature babies often have respiratory problems. **Surfactant** is a substance normally produced during the last weeks of pregnancy that keeps the lungs slightly inflated and that eases respiration. Babies born too early do not make surfactant, so inflating their lungs is like blowing up a completely flat balloon, compared to inflating one that is already halfway inflated. Premature babies' underdeveloped chest muscles compound their breathing difficulties. These babies can be treated with oxygen as well as administration of a synthetic surfactant until they eventually develop their own surfactant. Premature babies may also have anemia because of a relative deficiency of oxygen-carrying red blood cells. They face an increased risk of bleeding in the brain due to immature blood vessels. Babies born too early are also more prone to infection, have trouble maintaining body heat, and may have jaundice, a temporary yellowing of the skin caused by a buildup of bilirubin. Premature babies may face some developmental problems as they grow up.

Low Birth Weight

Of newborns in the United States, 8% have low birth weight (less than 5 pounds, 8 ounces), and 1.5% have very low birth weight (less than 3 pounds, 5 ounces). Low birth weight can occur if the mother used drugs, alcohol, or tobacco during her pregnancy; if she received inadequate prenatal care or had poor nutrition; or if she has a chronic illness. Low birth weight babies may have respiratory problems later in life, as well as a higher risk of type II diabetes, high blood pressure, and heart disease. Very low birth weight infants often suffer many complications, including cerebral palsy, blindness, and learning disabilities. Infants usually don't survive when they weigh less than 1 pound.

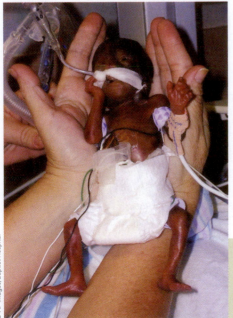

© AP Images/Baptist Hospital

Multiple Births

Multiple births are risky—twins have 6 times the neonatal mortality rate than singletons. Sixty percent of twins, 90% of triplets, and almost all quadruplets and quintuplets are born before 35 weeks, and with a low birth weight.

Mother and Infant Mortality

Death in childbirth used to be common. As recently as 100 years ago, 1 in every 100 women died while giving birth (Mintz, 2007). Doctors—who did not know of the existence of germs—would routinely go directly from working with cadavers to delivering children, thus spreading *puerperal fever*, a form of blood poisoning, and endangering the lives of women. Even today, around 350,000 women die each year during pregnancy or childbirth (Moyer, 2010). Most of these are in developing countries, although 25 countries have lower maternal death rates than the United States (Table 13.2).

Maternal deaths are most commonly caused by hemorrhage, followed by infection, eclampsia, and obstructed labor (Trussell, 2004). Women who have had a clitoridectomy are at higher risk of death during childbirth (Banks et al., 2006). The maternal death rate for black women in the United States is 3 to 4 times greater than for white women, possibly due to higher blood pressure or less prenatal care (Chang et al., 2003).

As difficult as birth is for the mother, it is 100 times more deadly for the baby. Before 1850, **infant deaths** were a commonly accepted part of everyday life (Brosco, 1999). Things have improved today. Singapore, Sweden, and Japan

Premature birth Also called preterm, a baby is premature if it is born between 20 and 37 weeks. Babies born at less than 32 weeks of gestation are "very preterm."

Surfactant A substance that prevents the collapse of the lungs.

Infant death The death of a baby before his or her first birthday.

Amillia Taylor was born in 2006 at just under 22 weeks, weighing less than 10 ounces. She suffered respiratory problems and a brain hemorrhage. She is often cited as the most premature baby to survive. The survival rates for premature infants continue to improve: 99% of infants delivered at 38 weeks survive, 82–85% delivered at 25 weeks survive, and 53–66% delivered at 23 weeks survive (The Express Group, 2010; Hoekstra, Ferrara, Couser, Payne, & Connett, 2004).

Table 13.2 Maternal Deaths

COUNTRY	NUMBER OF MATERNAL DEATHS IN 2000	LIFETIME RISK OF MATERNAL DEATH: 1 IN:	MATERNAL MORTALITY RATIO (MATERNAL DEATHS PER 100,000 LIVE BIRTHS)
Sweden	2	29,800	2
Ireland	3	8,300	5
Canada	20	8,700	6
Germany	55	8,000	8
United Kingdom	85	3,800	13
Israel	20	1,800	17
United States	660	2,500	17
Cuba	45	1,600	33
Iraq	2,000	65	250
Sudan	6,400	30	590
Nigeria	37,000	18	800
Afghanistan	20,000	6	1,900

© Cengage Learning 2013. SOURCE: Cassidy, 2006.

have the lowest infant mortality rates in the world, with 2.3–2.7 infant deaths for every 1,000 births, while Angola is the worst, with 18.4% of infants dying before they are 1 year old (CIA World Factbook, 2007). Just under 7 of every 1,000 babies die before their first birthday in the United States, a rate comparable to that of Poland and Slovakia (MacDorman & Mathews, 2008). The relatively high rate of infant death in America is most likely due to the frequency of high-risk pregnancies, older mothers, and premature and multiple births. The infant mortality rate in African Americans is double that of the rest of the U.S. population and is higher than that seen in women who live in Saudi Arabia and Serbia (MacDorman & Mathews, 2008). This may be because of maternal health issues, high-risk pregnancies, or less access to prenatal care.

The Postpartum Period

After completion of this section, you will be able to . . .

○ Define *Apgar score* and *colostrum.*

○ Describe the differences between newborns and adults.

○ List the physical and emotional changes the mother undergoes postpartum.

○ Evaluate the benefits and disadvantages of breastfeeding.

Hours before birth, the baby floats gently in a safe and familiar environment. It is dark and quiet, and food and oxygen are delivered directly through the bloodstream. Then, they are suddenly pushed rudely out through a very small passageway into a cold, bright, loud place. They must suddenly breathe, eat,

Apgar score A method to quickly assess the health of a newborn.

urinate, fight infection, and control their own body temperature. No wonder so many babies enter the world crying.

The **Apgar score** was developed by anesthesiologist Virginia Apgar to assess the newborn's health 1 minute and 5 minutes after childbirth. Babies receive a score of 0–10 for five different measurements, which can be conveniently remembered with the acronym APGAR: Appearance (color), Pulse (heart rate), Grimace (reflex irritability), Activity (muscle tone), and Respiration. A score of 7–10 is normal, 4–6 suggests some possible problem, and a score of 0–3 is critically low. Infants with low Apgar scores are more likely to have neurological disabilities and low IQ scores later in life (Odd, Rasmussen, Gunnell, Lewis, & Whitelaw, 2008).

What Babies Look Like

Bill Cosby's thoughts in the hospital room after the birth of their first baby:

> . . . and I looked at it . . . and it wasn't getting any better. So I went over to my wife, and kissed her ever so gently on the lips, and I said "I love you very very much dear. You just . . . had . . . a lizard." I mean, because the thing changed colors, like, five times! And I said to the doctor, "Can you put this back? 'Cause it isn't finished cooking! It needs to cook two, three months!" But the hospital made us take it home. (Cosby, 1983)

When a baby is first born, he or she doesn't immediately resemble the adorable, apple-cheeked angels of the diaper commercials. Because the bones in the baby's head haven't fused yet, the heads of babies who have been delivered vaginally are often misshapen and pointed from the tight journey down the birth canal. Their bodies may be coated in cheesy vernix or still covered in downy hair. The baby's skin may be blotchy with birthmarks or acne. Many babies have a yellow tinge to their skin due to excessive bilirubin. Many Caucasian babies are born with blue eyes because they have not yet produced the pigment that will darken their eyes later. They cannot focus well yet and may appear cross-eyed, and pus may leak from the eyes. The passage of maternal hormones into the baby's bloodstream before birth can cause the baby's breasts to enlarge and even vaginal bleeding in females. So there you have it: a pointy-headed, cheesy-coated, cross-eyed, blotchy baby with breasts and acne. Congratulations!

To add insult to injury to the fathers, mothers most often describe the baby as most resembling the dad (Daly & Wilson, 1982). This is thought to be an adaptation to reassure fathers that the child is theirs. In one study, mothers and fathers were asked to evaluate how much their newborn baby boys looked liked themselves. Independent judges then evaluated the babies. All mothers in the study said that newborn boys most resembled dad, whereas only 83% of the fathers agreed. Even fewer of independent raters—40%—thought the baby looked like the father (Alvergne, Faurie, & Raymond, 2007).

ASK YOURSELF

What are your views on breast-feeding in public? Is it always appropriate or only under certain circumstances? Given that the function of breasts *is* to feed children, why do many people get squeamish at the sight of a woman breastfeeding?

Adaptations of the Newborn

Newborns are not just smaller people; many of their organ systems are significantly different than those of adults. In an adult, blood travels from the right side of the heart to the lungs to be oxygenated. It then returns to the heart's left side, which sends oxygenated blood to the body. A fetus, however, receives its oxygen from the placenta, so the fetus's heart has two shunts that allow blood to bypass the pulmonary circulation. Once the baby is born, though, the heart must suddenly shift and send blood to the lungs. When the baby breathes his or her first breath, the blood pressure in the right side of the heart falls and shuts a flap over these shunts, forcing blood to flow through the lungs. Over the next few weeks, fibers grow over the flaps to seal the shunts.

An infant's nervous system is also different from that of an adult. Newborns have a number of reflexes, such as the grasp reflex, the sucking reflex, and the plantar reflex (an extension of the toes in response to stimulation on the ball of the foot). Although normal in infants, these indicate brain damage in adults. Infants also have a different kind of fat than adults, called brown fat, which generates body heat. A newborn's digestive system also functions differently than an adult's because the heart and liver release glucose for energy a few hours after birth.

Changes in the Mother

Within 6 weeks of giving birth, the mother's uterus shrinks from 2 pounds to 3 ounces. She may have lochia, a bloody vaginal discharge that lasts for up to 10 days after giving birth. Soon after birth, women are usually tired and emotional. They may be healing from episiotomies or other procedures. Women may sweat more than usual, as the body eliminates the extra pregnancy fluids. Unsurprisingly, soon after giving birth, a woman's level of sexual interest may not immediately return to prepregnancy levels. Women can resume sexual activity when they feel ready: obstetricians usually advise a 4- to 6-week waiting period.

As many as 85% of women experience minor postpartum depression, sometimes referred to as **baby blues**. This weepiness and irritability may be a result of fatigue, stress, and the realization of changes in their lives. The sudden drop in progesterone and estrogen can also lead to moodiness and sadness. Baby blues usually last for only a few days. In perhaps 10–15% of women, however, **postpartum depression** can last from a few weeks to a year or longer (Epperson, 1999). These women experience extreme sadness, sleep and appetite changes, and apathy about themselves and their new child. Women with postpartum depression can be treated with psychotherapy and antidepressant drugs. Support and understanding from family is also important in their treatment. Perhaps 1 or 2 women out of every 1,000 who have given birth can experience **postpartum psychosis**, a break from reality that includes hallucinations and delusions (Epperson, 1999). In 2001, Andrea Yates drowned her five children in the bathtub while suffering from postpartum psychosis. She was found not guilty by reason of insanity.

Breastfeeding

Women don't produce breast milk continuously. It takes a lot of energy—about 600 calories a day—to lactate, so breast milk is produced only when it's needed. During pregnancy, the ducts of the breast involved with lactation develop, and levels of the hormone prolactin, which stimulates milk production, begin to rise. However, during pregnancy, the high levels of estrogen and progesterone inhibit prolactin's effects. After delivery, levels of estrogen and progesterone decrease, so circulating prolactin can be incorporated into the breast lobules to produce milk. Suckling further stimulates **lactation** by increasing prolactin and oxytocin levels. Oxytocin will cause contraction of the muscles around the breast lobules, forcing milk out through the nipple.

Milk is not produced immediately after delivery. During the first three to four days, the mother produces **colostrum**, a thin, yellowish secretion that contains more protein and less fat and milk sugar than regular breast milk, as well as white blood cells and antibodies. Only a very small amount is pro-

Baby blues A common, fairly mild, and short-lived period of crying, moodiness, and irritability that many women experience shortly after childbirth.

Postpartum depression A form of clinical depression that can affect women after childbirth. Symptoms can be moderate or severe enough to require hospitalization.

Postpartum psychosis A serious mental illness that affects new mothers. It can include severe anxiety, hallucinations, and delusions.

Lactation The production and secretion of milk by the mammary glands.

Colostrum The thin, yellowish secretion of the breast that is produced late in pregnancy and for a few days after birth, until the breast milk comes in.

duced, but the baby requires only about a teaspoon in the first few days of life. After a few days, about 2½ to 3 cups of breast milk is produced a day.

Lactation consultants can show new mothers how to nurse. New mothers usually need to breast-feed or pump milk from their breasts every 2 to 3 hours. Some recommend that the mother use one breast per feeding because breast milk changes through the course of the "meal." As physician Leonard Sax (2005) describes it, the first milk that comes down is the appetizer, thin and watery, low in fat and calories. The regular breast milk is the entrée, followed by the dense high-fat, high-calorie hindmilk, which he compares to dessert, and which may help promote satiety and sleep in the nursing infant. If the mother switches breasts during a feeding, the baby consumes more milk but is less satisfied.

Sweeter and waterier than cow's milk, breast milk contains everything an infant needs to survive. Breast milk contains the perfect proportions of water, lactose, fats, and proteins, as well as more than 100 ingredients that are not found in cow's milk and that can't be exactly duplicated in commercial formula. Breast milk also contains important immune factors and antibodies and reduces the risk of infection and incidence of allergies in babies. Finally, breast milk is individually made for each baby and changes from day to day as the baby grows and changes.

The American Academy of Pediatrics strongly recommends that new mothers exclusively breast-feed their babies for the first 6 months, and support breastfeeding for the first year and beyond as mutually desired by the mother and child. "Extensive research, especially in recent years, documents diverse and compelling advantages to infants, mothers, families, and society from breastfeeding and the use of human milk for infant feeding. These include health, nutritional, immunologic, developmental, psychological, social, economic, and environmental benefits" (American Academy of Pediatrics, 1997).

There are other advantages to breastfeeding. Breast milk is safe and uncontaminated. It is free and convenient—all the supplies a mother needs are always available. Breastfeeding helps the uterus shrink back to its prepregnancy size and may suppress ovulation and menstruation. It also burns calories and may help a

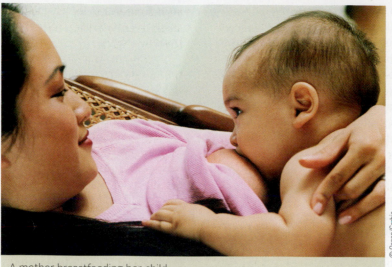
A mother breastfeeding her child.
© Ocean/Corbis

mother lose some of her pregnancy weight. Breastfeeding may also provide long-term benefits for both mother and baby: Breastfeeding for at least 2 years may reduce a woman's risk of uterine and breast cancers (Newcomb et al., 1994). Babies who are breast-fed have lower rates of obesity later in life. Breastfeeding may even raise a baby's intelligence. After controlling for the mother's age, education, weight, and drug use, and for the baby's birth weight and size, babies that were breast-fed for 9 months or longer had higher IQs than those who were breast-fed for a month or less (Mortensen, Michaelsen, Sanders, & Reinisch, 2002). Finally, breastfeeding is an opportunity for mothers to bond with their child. Fathers can also participate—the mom can use a breast pump to store the milk and the partner can bottle-feed using the breast milk.

Despite the many benefits of breastfeeding, about 30% of the population is bottle-fed from birth. Although almost 70% of mothers breast-feed their children (more so in highly educated women), fewer than one-third of babies are still breast-fed at 6 months of age, and only 10% of babies after 1 year (Cassidy, 2006). Many women consider breastfeeding inconvenient, especially when returning to work. Women may be dismayed to discover that their breasts may leak milk when they hear a baby cry. Also, breastfeeding women need to watch their dietary intake, and alcohol, drugs, and strong foods will be passed on to the baby through the milk, as can the HIV virus.

A woman can breast-feed a child she did not carry, but it requires patience, determination, perseverance, and luck. Weeks to months before she plans to begin breastfeeding, the woman should use a breast pump to stimulate the nipples and induce a milk supply. Oxytocin nasal spray may promote milk letdown. The newborn baby should be put to suckle as soon as possible. Fifty-four percent of mothers who nurse babies they didn't give birth to have to give supplementary nutrients to their children (Waterston, 1995). Lact-aid is a device that supplies formula milk through a feeding tube placed next to the nipple. The baby suckles the breast nipple and tube together. The supplemental formula can be reduced gradually as the mother's own milk supply increases. Even if the adoptive mother's milk supply doesn't reach levels of those of women who had carried a child, both mother and baby can benefit from the emotional bonding of breastfeeding.

My partner and I will be having a child in 3 months (I'm the one who's pregnant). Both she and I would like to breast-feed. I've read that it is possible for a woman who did not carry the child to breast-feed. Is this true?

Lactation consultant A health care professional who provides support and information about breastfeeding to new mothers.

Parenting

Once the parents arrive home with their child, their lives will change forever. Along with the joy and satisfaction of raising a child come challenges and frustrations. This is compounded by the fact that the United States—along with Swaziland and Papua New Guinea—is one of only 3 countries out of 168 studied that doesn't guarantee paid leave for new mothers (Heymann, Earle, Simmons, Breslow, & Kuehnhoff, 2004). In fact, new mothers in the United States fare far worse concerning lactation and sick leave than new mothers in most other industrialized nations.

The stereotypical image of a husband and wife caring for their children together is becoming less common. Out-of-wedlock births are becoming more accepted, and more single parents are raising their children alone. Since 1960 the percentage of women having children out of wedlock has increased more than sixfold. In 2003 more than one third of white births and more than two thirds of African American births were to unwed mothers (Besharov & West, 2001). Only 63% of children in the United States under the age of 18 live with both biological parents, which constitutes the lowest rate of all industrialized Western nations (Popenoe & Whitehead, 2005). Unfortunately, being raised by single parents may be detrimental to children. Scientists investigated more than 65,000 children with single parents and more than 920,000 children with two parents. After adjusting for socioeconomic factors and causes that might select people into single parenthood, they found that children of single parents showed an increased risk of psychiatric disease, suicide attempts, and alcohol- and narcotic-related illnesses (Weitoft, Hjern, Haglund & Rosen, 2003).

More people today are choosing to remain child-free (Longman, 2006). Women today are twice as likely to be child-free as they were 30 years ago (Dye, 2008). This is especially true among the educated and liberal; in the United States, the fertility rates in states that voted for George W. Bush in 2004 were 12% higher than in states that voted for John Kerry (Longman, 2006). In Germany, 30% of women (and 40% of women who are college graduates) are child-free by choice. It used to be that having children raised a couple's economic outlook: kids could help in the fields and assist in the raising of the younger children. Children today are more likely to be an economic burden, what with the cost of text-messaging bills and college tuition. Children may be more than an economic burden; as a group, parents report higher levels of depression than non-parents, after controlling for socioeconomic status and other characteristics (Evenson & Simon, 2005). However, while children may be economically "worthless," they are emotionally "priceless" (Zelizer, 2000); the love and affection they can add to their parents' lives is immeasurable.

• • •

From the joining of the egg with the sperm, to the delivery of the baby, the process of conception, pregnancy, and birth is one of the most miraculous events on earth.

Chapter Summary

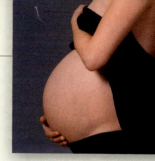

The Process of Conception

- Fertilization occurs when the nucleus of a sperm fuses with the nucleus of an egg, producing a zygote. Although only one sperm penetrates the egg, many sperm are needed because most never make it to the fallopian tube, and the hydrolytic enzymes from many sperm are needed to break through the egg. Conception is most likely if intercourse occurs on the day of ovulation or on the two to three days preceding it.
- Techniques exist for couples that want to select the sex of their child. Sex-selective assisted reproductive techniques can be employed at three times: before conception, as doctors separate X-bearing and Y-bearing sperm to be preferentially used for fertilization; after fertilization but before implantation, as a woman may be implanted with embryos of the desired sex; or after implantation, through selective abortion.

Infertility

- Infertility is a reduced ability to conceive a child, and sterility is a complete inability to reproduce. Male infertility is often due to environmental agents, infections, or drugs that impair sperm count or motility. Female infertility may be caused by irregular ovulation or structural problems. Advancing age in both men and women impairs fertility.
- Assisted reproductive techniques include artificial insemination—whereby sperm, either from the woman's partner or from a donor, is inserted into the woman's vagina or uterus—and in vitro fertilization, in which the egg is fertilized by the sperm outside of the woman's body and implanted in the uterus. Some couples choose gamete intrafallopian transfer (GIFT), in which oocytes are placed in the fallopian tube, along with sperm. In intracytoplasmic sperm injection (ICSI), a single sperm is injected directly into an egg.
- Infertile couples may also consider using a surrogate mother or adopting a child. A surrogate mother is a woman who is artificially inseminated and carries a baby to term for another woman. Adoptions can be open or closed, depending on the amount of contact the adoptive parents and the birth parents would like to have with the child and with each other.

Pregnancy

- The average pregnancy lasts for 38 to 40 weeks, depending on when one starts counting. Pregnancy is usually confirmed by a physical exam and elevated hCG levels.
- Pregnancy is split into three stages—germinal, embryonic, and fetal—as well as three trimesters of three months each. During the germinal stage, the fertilized egg divides and implants in the uterus. The embryonic period lasts from implantation until 8 weeks after conception. The fetal stage is the 3rd through 9th months of development.
- An ectopic pregnancy occurs when the zygote implants outside of the uterus. Except in extremely rare cases, this will always result in the loss of the embryo.
- When a woman is pregnant with more than one fetus, it is a multiple pregnancy. Dizygotic twins occur when two eggs are fertilized at the same time, each by a different sperm. Monozygotic twins occur when one egg is fertilized by one sperm, but the fertilized egg splits in two early in development, producing genetically identical twins.
- The placenta, which attaches inside the uterus, is the organ that supplies the developing fetus with nutrients and oxygen. It is connected to the fetus by the umbilical cord. The amniotic sac is the fluid-filled pouch that lines the uterus, in which the fetus develops.
- Most of the major organs begin to develop and grow in the embryo and fetus during the first trimester. During the second and third trimesters, organ systems continue to develop and the fetus increases in size. The mother experiences many physical and emotional changes throughout the pregnancy.

Problems That Can Occur During Pregnancy

- A miscarriage is the spontaneous expulsion of the embryo or fetus from the uterus before it's able to live outside of the womb. A stillbirth occurs if the fetus is delivered dead after 20 weeks of gestation.
- Miscarriages and birth defects can occur due to genetic factors, drug use, and viruses and bacteria. The mother's blood type and age also influence the baby's development.
- Tests to monitor the fetus's development and potential problems include ultrasound, amniocentesis, and chorionic villus sampling.
- Almost half of the pregnancies in the United States are unplanned. Unintended pregnancy rates are highest among young women, poor women, and minorities.
- The United States has the highest rate of teen pregnancy among developed countries, which has potential negative effects for the mothers, the offspring, and for society. Teen pregnancy rates may be related to social factors, such as a population's socioeconomic status, religious beliefs, and racial differences; as well as state policies, such as Medicaid policies and abstinence-only education programs.

Childbirth

- Physical symptoms such as lightening (when the baby's head drops into the pelvic cavity), the blood show (a discharge of blood and mucus), and the breaking of the amniotic sac alert the pregnant woman to impending birth.
- Childbirth has three stages: labor, during which the cervix dilates to 10 centimeters, delivery of the baby through the birth canal, and expulsion of the placenta.
- Most of the time, the fetus is born head first. Sometimes the baby is in the breech position, in which the baby's feet, buttocks, or knees rest against the cervix. Rarely, a baby presents transversely, shoulders or arms first. An episiotomy is a procedure in which a surgical incision is made between the vagina and the anus to prevent the tearing of the perineal tissues and to relieve pressure on the baby's head.

Variations in Birthing Situations

- Women have many birthing options, including where to give birth, who will oversee the delivery, whether to use pain-relieving medications, and whether to deliver vaginally or surgically. A midwife is a professional who is trained to assist in normal labor and birth. A doula is a labor companion who provides physical and emotional support to laboring women.
- Human birth is particularly difficult, due to our narrow pelvis and a newborn baby's proportionately large head. During labor, pain may be reduced through the use of an epidural, which is the administration of a local anesthetic, or with nonpharmacological means. In prepared childbirth, the mother and her birth partner are taught about labor and delivery, and practice breathing and relaxation techniques.
- A Cesarean section occurs when the baby is delivered through an incision in the abdominal wall and uterus, rather than passing through the vagina. C-sections have become very common, and today almost 32% of deliveries in the United States are by C-section.
- Some situations, including premature delivery, low birth weight, and multiple births, make childbirth even riskier. Babies born prematurely, or at low birth weight, may face a number of physical challenges. While maternal and infant mortality are much lower than in the past, the United States still has a high mortality rate compared to other developed nations.

The Postpartum Period

- Immediately after birth, a baby's health is assessed with the Apgar test. Many of their organ systems, including their respiratory system, nervous system, and digestive

- system, do not at this point resemble those of adults.
- After giving birth, women undergo both physical and emotional changes. Many women experience minor postpartum depression, although this may be more severe in 10–20% of women.
- Breast milk is not produced immediately after delivery. Colostrum is a thin, yellowish secretion that is produced within the first few days. Breast milk is perfectly designed to give the baby all the nutrients and immune factors it needs for at least the first year of its life. Although some women find it inconvenient, breastfeeding bestows many short- and long-term advantages on both baby and mother.
- Many children today are not raised in traditional two-parent heterosexual households, and more couples are choosing to remain child-free than in the past.

MAKING INFORMED DECISIONS

The meeting of an egg and a sperm can be much more than the simple joining of two cells. Conception has enormous biological, psychological, religious, philosophical, and legal ramifications.

evaluate and decide

Imagine the following situations:

> Senator Taylor is proposing a bill by which pregnant women would be subject to fines or prison sentences if they drink alcohol or smoke cigarettes while pregnant.

> Malik and Diane are planning their family and feel very strongly that they would like to have a girl. Technology exists to allow them to choose the sex of their baby.

What factors will you consider in advising these people? Consider the issues and questions below to make your decision.

SITUATION	ISSUES TO CONSIDER
DRUG USE WHILE PREGNANT	Should a woman be punished for drinking alcohol and smoking cigarettes while pregnant? Whose rights come first—the baby's or the mother's? Why? What are the values underlying your decision? How do you decide if health or freedom is most important?
	Should the government have a role in regulating healthy behaviors for pregnant women? If so, should the government regulate healthy behaviors for *all* people?
	Do you feel that a woman gives up her own freedoms when she is pregnant?
	Because drug use by males could potentially affect their sperm and the health of future children, should men be penalized for using drugs if they happen to get a woman pregnant? Why or why not?
	What if the mother is an alcoholic? Withdrawal could be more dangerous for both the woman and the baby, so should different rules apply?
	If a woman has the right to abort her child, why wouldn't she have the right to potentially endanger her unborn child?
	Should women be penalized for not taking prenatal vitamins? For taking an aspirin? At what point (if any) should a pregnant woman be punished for her behavior? Why?
CHOOSING THE SEX OF THE UNBORN BABY	What are the risks and benefits of sex selection? What are the values underlying your decision?
	Does it matter by which method gender selection is done? For instance, is there a difference if a couple employs techniques before conception or after fertilization? Why or why not?
	What are the future ramifications for societies in which the men greatly outnumber the women?
	Should gender selection technology be available to anyone who desires it? To those who can afford it? Only to those who have a "good reason" for using it?
	What reasons would you find "acceptable" for sex selection of a baby? If the parents have the genes for a sex-linked genetic disorder? If the parents already have five girls and want a boy? If the husband is the only male in his generation and wants a boy to "carry on the family name?" If in their culture males are considered more valuable? Who gets to decide what an "acceptable" reason is?

Additional Resources

Log in to CengageBrain to access the resources your instructor requires. For this book, you can access:

 **CourseMate** brings course concepts to life with interactive learning, study, and exam preparation tools that support the printed textbook. A textbook-specific website, Psychology CourseMate includes an integrated interactive eBook and other interactive learning tools including quizzes, flashcards, videos, and more.

CENGAGENOW **CengageNOW** is an easy-to-use online resource that helps you study in less time to get the grade you want—NOW. Take a pre-test for this chapter and receive a personalized study plan based on your results that will identify the topics you need to review and direct you to online resources to help you master those topics. Then take a post-test to help you determine the concepts you have mastered and what you will need to work on. If your textbook does not include an access code card, go to CengageBrain.com to gain access. Visit www.cengagebrain.com anytime to access your account and purchase materials.

Current links to all of the following websites and videos can be found on the Psychology CourseMate for this text at www.cengage-brain.com/.

Web Resources

Realityworks

Realityworks provides innovative, hands-on teaching tools that engage students in the learning process. They design products and programs that help students feel the reality of life's decisions. Products include the award-winning Baby Think It Over program.

RESOLVE

The mission of RESOLVE, a nonprofit organization founded in 1974 by Barbara Eck Menning, is to provide timely, compassionate support and information to people who are experiencing infertility and to increase awareness of infertility issues through public education and advocacy.

Reproductive Science Center

Provides information on assisted reproductive technologies (IVF, GIFT, and frozen embryos).

Our Bodies, Ourselves

Information about pregnancy, labor, and birth from Boston Women's Health Book Collective.

Print Resources

Iovine, V. (1997). *The Girlfriends' Guide to Pregnancy.* New York: Perigee Books.

Kane, E. (1988). *Birth Mother: The Story of America's First Legal Surrogate Mother.* San Diego, CA: Harcourt Brace Jovanovich.

Murkoff, H., Eisenberg, A., & Hathaway, S. (2002). *What to Expect When You're Expecting* (3rd ed.). New York: Workman Publishing Company.

Reynolds, K. (1997). *Pregnancy and Birth: Your Questions Answered.* New York: DK Publishing.

Rosenthal, S. (1996). *The Fertility Sourcebook.* New York: McGraw-Hill.

Tsiaras, A., & Werth, B. (2002) *From Conception to Birth: A Life Unfolds.* New York: Doubleday.

Video Resources

Bill Cosby: Himself. (1983). 105 minutes. Includes a hilarious riff on childbirth and parenting.

Birth Stories. (1995). 30 minutes. This series of funny and frank interviews, in which women tell their personal stories of pregnancy and birth, is interspersed with black and white footage of actual birth. The video captures the full range of women's emotional reactions, from amazement to resentment, providing amusing but illuminating insights into a common experience that is still poorly understood or appreciated. From Cinema Guild.

The Business of Being Born. (2008). 87 minutes. This film interlaces intimate birth stories with historical, political, and scientific insights about the current maternity care system.

Drinking for Two: Fetal Alcohol Syndrome. (2000). 30 minutes. The story of a young pregnant woman who continues drinking and smoking during her pregnancy and of her son, an innocent victim of fetal alcohol syndrome. From NIMCO Inc.

Gattaca. (1997). 101 minutes. Story about the new future when genetic testing controls our destiny.

Giving Birth. (2007). 35 minutes. Contrasts the medical model of birth with the midwifery model. Obstetricians, nurses, mothers, and doulas speak about natural birth and their experiences. The film shows two births, including a water birth. Video can be found at http://www.suzannearms.com/OurStore/videos.

The Intimate Universe: The Human Body—An everyday miracle. (1998). 51 minutes. This episode celebrates the miracle of birth. Beautiful photography follows the process from the sperm meeting the egg, the growth of the embryo, and the delivery of the fetus. From Discover Channel Films. Can be found at http://school.discovery.com/lessonplans/programs/buildingababy/q.html.

Life's Greatest Miracle. (2001). 60 minutes. This special on birth from the *Nova* TV series features fantastic footage.

Ultimate Guide: Pregnancy. (2002). 51 minutes. This visually stunning program takes viewers from the moment of conception to the moment of birth. Photographic and computer images capture every stage of embryonic and fetal development as well as the changes experienced by the expectant mothers during pregnancy. The program culminates with the filming of two births, one with and one without surgical intervention. A Discovery Channel production, available through Films for the Humanities and Sciences.

We Are Dad. (2005). 71 minutes. The story of Steven Lofton and Roger Croteau, pediatric AIDS nurses who become foster parents to HIV-positive infants, and decided to challenge Florida's law banning adoption by gay people.

14 Sexually Transmitted Infections

True or false? (answers at the bottom of the page)

1. Teenagers and young adults account for most cases of sexually transmitted infections (STIs). _____
2. All STIs except HIV can be cured. _____
3. The symptoms of STIs are often unnoticed. _____
4. When the symptoms of an STI disappear, you no longer have an infection. _____
5. Untreated STIs can cause sterility in both males and females. _____
6. If you use a condom, you can't get an STI. _____
7. In general, women are at a greater risk for most STIs than men. _____
8. If a woman has a yearly Pap test, she will know if she has any STIs. _____

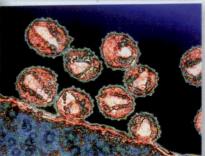

© CAVALLINI JAMES/Age fotostock

True or False Answers: All odd-numbered questions are true; all even-numbered questions are false.

© Lee Snider/Photo Images/CORBIS

© Karin Kohlberg/ Getty Images

Introduction

After completion of this section, you will be able to . . .

○ Classify the differences between some of the organisms that cause STIs, including bacteria, viruses, parasites, and other organisms.

○ Differentiate between the terms *incidence* and *prevalence*.

○ Compare the incidence of STIs in the United States to that of other countries.

○ Identify the groups who are most susceptible to infection with sexually transmitted diseases.

Since the time that plants and animals first began sexual reproduction, infections have been passed through sexual contact; all plants and animals that reproduce sexually develop sexually transmitted infections (STIs) (Baskin, 1999). Once called venereal diseases (from Venus, the Roman goddess of love) or social diseases, STIs affect hundreds of millions of people worldwide.

When diagnosed early, most STIs can be successfully treated. However, many have no symptoms, especially in women, causing those who are infected to unknowingly pass on the infection to others. When left untreated, STIs can cause severe health problems, including pelvic inflammatory disease, infertility, cancer, and even death.

Throughout this chapter we will refer to "sexually transmitted infections" rather than "sexually transmitted diseases." An "infection" means that bacteria, viruses, or other organisms that could possibly cause a disease are present in a person's body. "Disease" means that the infection is causing symptoms. As we will see, most STIs can occur with no symptoms. Also, some of the conditions discussed in this chapter, such as scabies and pubic lice, are not diseases. For these reasons, STI is a more accurate term than STD.

These infections are most commonly transmitted through sexual contact, be it oral, anal, or vaginal intercourse; or skin-to-skin contact with the genitalia. Many of them can also be passed through childbirth or by exposure to contaminated blood—by sharing infected needles, transfusions with contaminated blood, or by needle sticks in a health care setting. But because the most common means of transmission is through sexual contact, these are referred to as sexually transmitted infections.

Sexually transmitted infections come from bacteria, viruses, parasites, and other organisms. **Bacteria** are tiny, single-celled microorganisms that can cause infections in animals and humans. Examples of bacterial STIs include chlamydia, gonorrhea, and syphilis. Bacterial STIs can be cured with antibiotics, although once you are cured, you can be reinfected. **Viruses** are submicroscopic infectious agents that need a host to grow and reproduce. Viruses invade a host cell and cause the cell to produce new viral particles that spread to other cells. Simple organisms, viruses are composed of just genetic material (DNA or RNA) plus a protein coat. Human papillomavirus, herpes, hepatitis, and HIV are all viruses that can be sexually transmitted. Viral infections cannot be cured, although in some cases your body can clear the infection on its own. Once you have been infected with a virus, immunity develops so you cannot be reinfected. **Parasitic insects** such as pubic lice or scabies need a host to survive. They feed off the blood of their human host and can be spread by close contact with an infected individual. Trichomoniasis is a common sexually transmitted infection caused by **protozoa**, one-celled animals that are larger and more complex than bacteria.

Incidence/Prevalence

It is important to differentiate between the terms "incidence" and "prevalence." **Incidence** refers to the number of new cases that occur within a specified time (usually within a year), whereas **prevalence** is the percentage of people who currently have the condition.

Bacteria Single-celled microorganisms that can cause infection in humans.

Viruses Submicroscopic infectious agents that need a host to grow and reproduce.

Parasites Creatures that depend upon a host organism to survive.

Protozoa Single-celled animals that are more complex than bacteria.

Incidence The number of new cases that occur in a population during a specified time period.

Prevalence The number or percentage of people in a group that have a particular condition.

A healthy White Campion flower, left, and a White Campion with a sexually transmitted fungus, right.

© Alistair Laming/Alamy
© Nigel Cattlin/Alamy

> More than 20 STIs have been identified. The three most common are HPV, trichomoniasis, and chlamydia. These account for 88% of all new STIs in 15- to 24-year-olds (Weinstock et al., 2004).

> The term "men who have sex with men" is more appropriate than "gay or bisexual men" because many men who have sex with other men self-identify as hetero-sexual. In a sample of more than 4,000 New Yorkers, 12% of men said they had sex only with men in the past year, yet 72% of these men identified themselves as heterosexual (Pathela et al., 2006).
> _____
> _____
> _____
> _____

Sexually transmitted infections affect men and women of all ages, races, education, and economic levels, although they are most common in people under the age of 25. Worldwide, it is estimated that more than 400 million people each year are infected with an STI—that's more than 1 million new infections every day. Most of these are curable bacterial or protozoal infections. It is hard to know exactly how many people have STIs. Most cases are not reported because many STIs are **asymptomatic** and undiagnosed. It is clear, however, that the incidence of sexually transmitted infections is rising. Sexual activity begins at an earlier age, and marriage occurs later than in the past. During these sexually active years, teens and young adults are more likely to be exposed to these infections.

The United States has the highest rate of sexually transmitted infection in the industrialized world; up to 19 million new STIs occur each year in the United States, almost half in those aged 15 to 24 (Weinstock, Berman, & Cates, 2004). Rates of syphilis in the United States are 10 times greater than those in Canada, and 32 times greater than those in the United Kingdom (Darroch et al., 2001). U.S. gonorrhea rates are more than 8 times higher than those in England, 9 times higher than Canadian rates, and 74 times greater than those seen in the Netherlands or France (Darroch et al., 2001; Panchaud, Singh, Feivelson, & Darroch, 2000). Compared to teens in France, 20 times more teens in the United States are infected with chlamydia (Darroch et al., 2001; Panchaud et al., 2000). STIs cost the United States as much as $15 billion each year, and this does not include indirect costs of lost work or reduced productivity (Chesson, Blandford, Gift, Tao, & Irwin, 2004).

Many factors, both biomedical and behavioral, influence the spread of STIs. Some infections are more communicable than others—for instance, you have a much greater chance of contracting gonorrhea from a partner than HIV. The site of the infection; the health, age, genetics, and sex practices of the individual; and the prevalence of the STI in different groups also affect transmission rate (Bosarge, 2006).

> African Americans represent 12.6% of the U.S. population but 49% of all reported cases of chlamydia, syphilis, and HIV and 71% of all cases of gonorrhea (CDC, 2009a).

Minorities, women, men who have sex with men, and young adults are particularly affected by sexually transmitted infections. Minorities, especially African Americans, are more likely to be infected with gonorrhea, chlamydia, HIV, and other sexually transmitted infections. This may be due to poverty, lack of accurate information, or living in communities with a higher incidence of infection. Reported rates may be higher because minorities are more likely to seek health care in clinics, where incidence is reported, rather than at private providers, who do not always report STIs.

Women are twice as likely as men to acquire an STI during unprotected sex. Women are also more often asymptomatic, and therefore less likely to seek treatment for their infections. Consequently, women suffer more long-term consequences from STIs, including pelvic inflammatory disease, infertility, and cervical cancer. Women may be more prone to infection because the vagina is susceptible to small tears, through which organisms can enter the bloodstream. The greater surface area of the mucosal membranes in the vagina may also be more conducive to the growth of organisms. Finally, women don't always have control over a man's condom use, and using a condom is one way to prevent infection.

Men who have sex with men have a particularly high risk of becoming infected with an STI: 53% of all new HIV infections and almost two-thirds of syphilis cases occur in men who have sex with men (Centers for Disease Control and Prevention [CDC], 2008a). Lesbians, on the other hand, have low rates of gonorrhea, syphilis, HIV, hepatitis B, and other STIs compared to heterosexual or bisexual women (Nichols, 2005). However, lesbians are not completely safe from infection—STIs can be spread from woman to woman through unprotected vaginal contact.

Sexually active teens and young adults have a particularly high risk of acquiring an STI. Those aged 15 to 24 represent 35% of the sexually experienced population, but almost half of all STI cases (Weinstock et al., 2004). In fact, more than one out of every four teenaged girls in the United States has an STI (Forhan et al., 2009). This rate is even higher among black teenaged girls, of whom nearly half have had at least one STI (Forhan et al., 2009).

There may be behavioral, biological, and cultural reasons underlying the high rate of infection among teens. Teens and young adults are more likely to have multiple partners and less likely to practice safe sex than older adults. Biologically, a young woman's cervix is not fully matured and is more susceptible to infection. A young woman's vaginal flora is less acidic, and therefore less able to protect against the growth of harmful bacteria. Finally, younger people may have less access to condoms and health care.

Teens and adults are not the only ones who have STIs. Each year, thousands of children are infected, usually through child sexual abuse. In 2007 there were 13,629 reported cases of chlamydia and almost 4,000 cases of gonorrhea in children

Asymptomatic When a person has a disease or infection but experiences no symptoms.

critical evaluation

The efficacy of condoms in preventing sexually transmitted infections is a subject of heated debate. Critically evaluate some of the issues at hand.

> ### What are the difficulties inherent in the research?

Scientists rely on self-reports, and it is difficult, if not impossible, to perfectly determine the consistency or correctness of condom use (Steiner & Cates, 2006). STI transmission depends on many factors other than condom use, such as circumcision, the type and stage of the infection, the type of sex, and presence of other infections. Confounding factors can make it difficult to accurately gauge the effect of condoms. Mutually monogamous couples are less likely to use condoms because they have less need. Those who have multiple partners or who

engage in risky sexual behaviors may be more likely to use condoms. It is therefore hard to truly understand the effectiveness of condoms in preventing STIs because those who engage in risky behaviors use more condoms. This may negatively affect measurements of their efficacy.

> ### Is there a "searching for perfect solutions" fallacy occurring?

Although condoms greatly decrease the transmission of many STIs, including gonorrhea, chlamydia, and HIV, they don't give 100% protection from all sexually transmitted infections. STIs such as herpes and genital

warts may be transmitted through skin-to-skin contact by areas not covered by a condom. Some claim that because condoms are not perfectly effective in all cases, their use should not be encouraged.

> ### Is there an "appeal to ignorance" fallacy occurring?

In June 2000, the National Institutes of Health (NIH) organized a review of scientific evidence on the effectiveness of condoms in preventing STIs. The review found that although the evidence existed to show that condoms reduced transmission of HIV to men and women and gonorrhea to men, the evidence that condoms

prevented other STIs was insufficient. The NIH made this statement because it is difficult to precisely quantify the degree to which condom use offers protection against STI transmission. Social conservatives leapt on this finding and decried the promotion of condom use. Remember, though, "absence of proof is not proof of absence": just because the evidence was not all in does not mean that condoms didn't work, just that the full story was unknown. Incidentally, more recent studies have found condoms to statistically reduce transmission of many other sexually transmitted infections.

sexual events and partners (Smoak, Scott-Sheldon, Johnson, Carey, 2006).

Unfortunately, sexually transmitted infections are common, and although some are easily treated, others can have devastating

consequences. The good news is that with a little common sense and forethought, you can greatly reduce your risk of becoming infected.

Table 14.1 STI Facts

STI	TYPE	SYMPTOMS	TRANSMISSION	IF LEFT UNTREATED?
Chlamydia	**Bacterial**	• Symptoms show up 5–21 days after exposure • Most women and some men have no symptoms **Women:** • Vaginal discharge and bleeding; pain or burning with urination, more frequent urination; pain in abdomen or lower back; fever, nausea, and vomiting **Men:** • Watery, white drip from penis; pain or burning with urination, more frequent urination; swollen or tender testicles	• Spread during vaginal, anal, or oral sex with someone who has chlamydia • Can be transmitted during childbirth	• Can transmit chlamydia to sexual partner or fetus • Can lead to more serious infections of the eye and joints, damage to the reproductive organs, ectopic pregnancy, infertility, and increased susceptibility to HIV • Long-term damage is more severe in women
Gonorrhea	**Bacterial**	• Most symptoms show up 2–21 days after exposure • Most women and some men have no symptoms **Women:** • Thick yellow-green vaginal discharge; vaginal bleeding; pain or burning with urination or bowel movement; cramps or pain in abdomen **Men:** • Thick yellow or white discharge from penis; more frequent urination; pain or burning with urination or bowel movement	• Gonorrhea is very contagious and is easily spread during vaginal, anal, or oral sex with an infected partner • Can be transmitted during childbirth	• Can transmit gonorrhea to sexual partner • Can lead to serious consequences, including infertility, PID, heart trouble, skin disease, arthritis, blindness, and increased susceptibility to HIV

© Cengage Learning 2013. SOURCE: Hiatt, Clark, & Nelson, 2002.

Table 14.1 STI Facts—cont'd

STI	TYPE	SYMPTOMS	TRANSMISSION	IF LEFT UNTREATED?
Syphilis	**Bacterial**	• Symptoms are indistinguishable from many other diseases **Primary syphilis:** • Symptoms first appear 2–4 weeks after infection; painless, reddish-brown sore or sores on the mouth, genitals, breasts, anus, fingers; sore lasts 2–6 weeks, then goes away, but the infection persists **Secondary syphilis:** • Symptoms show up 2 weeks to 6 months after primary sore heals, followed by a rash anywhere on the body, even palms and soles of feet; flu-like symptoms; eventually, rash and flu-like feelings go away, but syphilis remains **Tertiary syphilis:** • Bacteria spreads through body and damages brain, nerves, eyes, bones, joints, and heart	• Spread during vaginal, anal, or oral sex with someone who has syphilis • Can be spread during pregnancy and childbirth	• Can transmit syphilis to sexual partner • Can cause heart disease, brain damage, increased susceptibility to HIV infection, blindness, or death • Increases miscarriage and stillbirth, and causes physical complications in babies born with syphilis
Bacterial vaginosis	**Bacterial**	• Slight grayish vaginal discharge; fishy odor; some women have no symptoms	• Not transmitted sexually, but sexually active women are at higher risk	• Increased risk of PID, miscarriage, premature delivery, and low-birth-weight babies • Increased susceptibility to chlamydia, gonorrhea, and HIV
Genital warts	**Viral**	• Symptoms show up 1–6 months after contact with HPV types 6 and 11 • Small bumpy warts on genitalia, anus, abdomen, upper thighs • Itching, burning around genitalia	• Very contagious • Spread during vaginal, anal, manual, or oral sex with someone who has genital warts • Can be transmitted during childbirth	• Can transmit genital warts to sexual partner • There is no cure. Warts may go away on their own, remain unchanged, or grow and spread
Hepatitis B	**Viral**	• Many people have no symptoms or mild symptoms • Most symptoms show up 1–4 months after contact with the hepatitis B virus • Flu-like feelings that don't go away • Fatigue, jaundice (yellow skin), dark urine, light-colored bowel movements	• Spread by contact with body fluids, such as blood, semen, vaginal secretions, or saliva • Spread during vaginal, anal, or oral sex with someone who has hepatitis B • Spread by sharing needles • Can be passed from mother to child during childbirth	• Can transmit hepatitis B to sexual partner or to someone you share a needle with • Some people recover completely, some cannot be cured • Symptoms may go away, but can still give hepatitis B to others • Can cause permanent liver damage and increase risk of liver cancer
Herpes	**Viral**	• Most symptoms show up 1–30 days or longer after having sex • Some people have no symptoms **First outbreak:** • Flu-like feelings; small, itchy, painful blisters on genitals or mouth. Blisters burst and become open sores that last 1–4 weeks. Blisters scab over and go away, but you still have herpes **Recurrences:** • Itching or burning before sores appear	• Spread during vaginal, anal, manual or oral sex with someone who has herpes • Can be spread even when there are no visible symptoms of infection • Can be transmitted during pregnancy or childbirth	• Can transmit herpes to sexual partner • A baby who was infected during pregnancy or childbirth may experience mild infections or permanent neurological damage • Increases risk of HIV transmission • Herpes cannot be cured

Continued

Table 14.1 STI Facts—cont'd

STI	TYPE	SYMPTOMS	TRANSMISSION	IF LEFT UNTREATED?
HIV/AIDS	**Viral**	• Most symptoms show up several months to years after contact; can be present for many years with no symptoms • Flu-like feelings that don't go away • Unexplained weight loss or tiredness, diarrhea, white spots in mouth • In women, yeast infections that don't go away • Opportunistic infections	• Spread by contact with infected body fluids, such as blood, semen, vaginal secretions, or breast milk • Spread during vaginal, anal, or oral sex with someone who has HIV • Spread by sharing needles • Can be transmitted during pregnancy, childbirth, or through breastfeeding	• HIV cannot be cured; eventually leads to AIDS, which causes illness and death
Pubic lice	**Parasite**	• Itching • Presence of thin white specks at the base of the pubic hair	• Can be transmitted sexually by skin-to-skin contact • Can be passed through non-sexual means, by contact with infested clothing, towels, or bedding	• Treated with over-the-counter cream
Scabies	**Parasite**	• Itching • Itchy bumps and small lines in genitals, around waist, and on hands, wrist, and fingers	• Can be transmitted sexually by skin-to-skin contact • Can be passed through non-sexual means, by contact with infested clothing, towels, or bedding	• Treated with prescription cream
Trichomoniasis	**Protozoa**	• Some women have no symptoms—most men have no symptoms; symptoms occur 1–2 weeks after exposure • Itching, burning, or pain in the vagina • Vaginal discharge smells and/or looks different. May be a yellow-green, frothy discharge • Fishy odor	• Spread during vaginal, anal or oral sex • Can transmitted during childbirth	• Can transmit to your sexual partners • Increased susceptibility to HIV and increased risk of HIV transmission • Pregnant women may have increased risk of premature delivery and low-birth-weight babies • Men can get infections in the urethra or prostate gland

Chapter Summary

Introduction

- All plants and animals that reproduce sexually develop sexually transmitted infections (STIs). When detected early, most STIs can be successfully treated. When left untreated, some STIs can lead to severe health problems.
- Sexually transmitted infections come from bacteria, viruses, parasites, and other organisms.
- *Incidence* refers to the number of new cases that occur within a specified time, whereas *prevalence* is the percentage of people who currently have the condition.
- Sexually transmitted infections affect men and women of all ages, races, education, and economic levels, although they are most common in people under the age of 25. The United States has the highest rate of STIs in the industrialized world. Women, young people, and minorities are most likely to be infected.

Bacterial Infections

- Sexually transmitted bacterial infections include gonorrhea, syphilis, chlamydia, and bacterial vaginosis. They are most commonly transmitted by oral, anal, and vaginal sexual contact. Bacterial STIs can be treated and cured with antibiotics.
- Many bacterial infections produce no symptoms. When symptoms do appear, they often include pain or burning with urination, lower back pain, redness or itching, and vaginal or penile discharge.
- Chlamydia is the most commonly reported bacterial infection in the United States. Usually asymptomatic, untreated chlamydia can lead to PID and other infections. PID can lead to chronic pain, ectopic pregnancies, and infertility.
- Gonorrhea may produce no symptoms. Untreated gonorrhea can lead to epididymitis in men and PID in women.
- The first stage of syphilis is characterized by the appearance of a small, round sore or sores on the genitals, anus, mouth, breasts, or fingers. The sore disappears, and weeks to months later, the bacteria spreads throughout the body, causing a rash and flu-like symptoms. These symptoms eventually disappear as the bacteria lies dormant. After many years, syphilis may invade many tissues of the body and cause widespread damage.
- Bacterial vaginosis is the most common infection of the vagina. It is not transmitted sexually, although sexually active women are at greater risk. Bacterial vaginosis occurs when antibiotics, douching, or disease disrupt the normal bacterial flora of the vagina.

Viral Infections

- Sexually transmitted viral infections include HPV, herpes, hepatitis, and HIV/AIDS. There is no cure for viral infections. Some clear on their own; others infect the person for life.
- Human papillomavirus (HPV) is the world's most common sexually transmitted virus. There are more than 100 strains of HPV, some of which are harmless, some of which cause normal warts, and about 30 of which are sexually transmitted. Low-risk sexually transmitted HPV can lead to genital warts, while high-risk forms of the virus can cause changes that may predispose a person to the development of cervical, penile, and oropharyngeal cancers. HPV is transmitted by oral, anal, and vaginal sex, as well as through skin-to-skin contact with an infected person.
- The vaccine Gardasil protects against the forms of HPV that cause 90% of genital warts and 70% of cervical cancers. It is approved for use in those aged 9 to 26, and does not protect a person if he or she is already infected with HPV.
- Two viruses, HSV-1 and HSV-2, cause herpes. Genital herpes is usually caused by infection with HSV-2. Herpes is transmitted through skin-to-skin contact with an infected person. The mucous membranes are most prone to infection.
- The first outbreak of herpes is characterized by the presence of a small painful blister, which eventually bursts and heals. Itching or pain in the area, before the appearance of sores or blisters, may indicate later outbreaks. Those with herpes are most contagious when in the midst of an outbreak, but can shed virus at any time, even when asymptomatic.
- There are many forms of viral hepatitis. Hepatitis B is transmitted by contact with blood, semen, vaginal secretions, and saliva, and is most often passed by sexual contact, sharing needles, during childbirth, or in a health care setting. Symptoms include flu-like feelings, as well as jaundice, dark urine, and light-colored stools, although many people have no symptoms. Most people clear the infection on their own and suffer no lasting ill effects. About 5–10% become chronic carriers and can transmit the infection throughout life. Of these, some experience serious health consequences, including liver cancer. There is a vaccine against the HBV virus.
- More than 33 million people around the world are living with HIV/AIDS. Since the human immunodeficiency virus (HIV) was first described in 1981, more than 25 million men, women, and children have died of AIDS. HIV is transmitted through contact with infected blood, semen, vaginal secretions, and breast milk. In the United States, minorities are particularly affected by HIV/AIDS. Around the world, no other area has been as hard-hit as sub-Saharan Africa, where AIDS is the number one cause of death.
- HIV works by destroying cells' helper-T cells (also called CD4 cells). These cells of the immune system coordinate the body's immune response to foreign invaders. Without these cells, diseases that would normally be destroyed are able to run rampant in the body.
- You can reduce your risk of contracting HIV by practicing safer sex, avoiding contact with body fluids that may contain the virus, and being educated about risk factors.
- Although not a cure, the development of highly active anti-retroviral therapy (HAART) has greatly expanded the life expectancy of those infected with HIV.

Other Sexually Transmitted Infections

- Pubic lice ("crabs") are parasitic organisms that attach to pubic hair and burrow into the host's skin, causing itching and redness. Scabies burrow into skin and deposit eggs, usually around the genitals, waist, or hands, leaving an itchy, red rash. These parasites are treated with over-the-counter cream. Pubic lice and scabies can be transmitted through sexual contact, or by contact with infested clothing, towels, or bedding.
- Yeast infections are not sexually transmitted. They occur because of an imbalance of the normal flora of the vagina. The itching and irritation can be easily treated with a prescription cream.
- Trichomoniasis is the most common curable STI in the world, infecting more than 180 million people each year. Trichomoniasis is caused by a protozoan parasite. It is passed sexually or during childbirth. Symptoms include redness, burning, itching, as well as vaginal discharge and a fishy odor. It can be cured with a single dose of metronidazole.

Dealing With Sexually Transmitted Infections

- During an STI examination, you will be asked about your medical and sexual history. You will then be given a physical exam. Be sure to ask any and all questions of your health care provider.
- You can prevent infection with an STI. Be knowledgeable about STIs, and aware of their modes of transmission and common symptoms. Be honest with your partner and communicate about your past and present sexual life. Don't take risks that could increase your chance of being infected. Correct and consistent use of condoms and dental dams greatly lowers your chances of being infected with an STI.

MAKING INFORMED DECISIONS

In 2007 Texas Governor Rick Perry issued an executive order making it mandatory for all girls entering sixth grade in 2008 to be vaccinated against the HPV virus (this order was later overturned by the Texas legislature). Should a vaccine against HPV be required?

evaluate and*decide*

Consider the following situations:

> How safe is Gardasil?
> How would mandatory HPV vaccination affect society?
> Should the vaccine be mandatory or voluntary?

What factors will you consider when making your decision?

SITUATION	ISSUES TO CONSIDER
RISKS AND BENEFITS	The long-term safety of Gardasil is unknown. The virus won't give indefinite protection, so girls will probably need a booster shot after a number of years. The exact number of years is unknown.
	Gardasil was mandated for girls aged 9 through 11, although only 5% of the test subjects were preteen girls. Some suggest that giving the vaccine to young girls may be detrimental, and younger women tend to have a shorter duration of HPV positivity, which is correlated with a lower likelihood of developing precancerous lesions. If girls are vaccinated at a young age, this may postpone their exposure to the virus, which may actually heighten their risk. However, if you give it to girls too late, they may already be sexually active and infected with HPV, so the vaccine will be ineffective.
	How much importance should be given to the cost of the vaccine? The full course of Gardasil costs approximately $360 plus the cost of office visits, and may not be covered by insurance.
	Gardasil does not protect against all high-risk forms of HPV; HPV viruses other than 16 and 18 cause about 30% of cervical cancers. But should a vaccine be discarded just because it is not 100% effective in all cases?
	How do you weigh the risks of Gardasil and the social implications of mandatory vaccination against the benefit of reducing the incidence of a life-threatening cancer? What issues are of greatest importance? What value assumptions underlie your position?
SOCIAL ISSUES	Do you think that a vaccine against HPV will lead to risky sexual behaviors? Consider that the hepatitis B vaccine has not led to increased drug use.
	Might those who are vaccinated neglect their annual gynecological exams based on a false sense of protection? The vaccine does not protect a woman against all forms of cervical cancer. Also, while Gardasil is one causal factor of cervical cancer, it is not the only one: smoking, drinking, the presence of other STIs, genetics, and other factors are related to cancer rates.
MANDATORY VS. VOLUNTARY VACCINATION	What value assumptions underlie the decision to make a vaccine mandatory? How do you personally rate the importance of personal freedom versus public safety?
	If the vaccine is mandatory, women of a lower socioeconomic status (SES) will be vaccinated for free. These women are most likely to *not* have a yearly Pap test, and a vaccine may therefore be particularly helpful for them.
	Other vaccines such as meningitis and whooping cough were not mandated in Texas. Mandatory use for vaccines against measles, mumps, and diphtheria are endorsed only after several years of experience. Why do you think the governor considered the HPV vaccine to be different? HPV is the only vaccine against a disease that is sexually transmitted—do you think the mode of transmission matters when considering mandatory vaccinations?
OTHER ISSUES	Governor Perry has several personal and financial ties to Merck, the corporation that produces Gardasil. Should these links be considered, or should the issue be considered solely on the scientific facts?
	What other options exist? Could the money that would be used to vaccinate the girls be used to increase screening against cervical cancer? African American and lower SES women are most likely to die of cervical cancer because they are least likely to get regular Pap tests. Because cervical cancer is slow growing, increased screening could greatly reduce the incidence and fatality of this cancer.

Additional Resources

Log in to CengageBrain to access the resources your instructor requires. For this book, you can access:

 **CourseMate** CourseMate brings course concepts to life with interactive learning, study, and exam preparation tools that support the printed textbook. A textbook-specific website, Psychology CourseMate includes an integrated interactive eBook and other interactive learning tools including quizzes, flashcards, videos, and more.

CENGAGENOW **CengageNOW** is an easy-to-use online resource that helps you study in less time to get the grade you want—NOW. Take a pre-test for this chapter and receive a personalized study plan based on your results that will identify the topics you need to review and direct you to online resources to help you master those topics. Then take a post-test to help you determine the concepts you have mastered and what you will need to work on. If your textbook does not include an access code card, go to CengageBrain.com to gain access. Visit www.cengagebrain.com anytime to access your account and purchase materials.

Current links to all of the following websites and videos can be found on the Psychology CourseMate for this text at www.cengagebrain.com/

Web Resources

Afraid to Ask?
Detailed photographs and education on sexually transmitted diseases (STDs), including herpes, chlamydia, gonorrhea, trichomoniasis, vaginal warts (genital HPV), HIV and AIDS, and much more.

American Social Health Association
General information about STIs

AIDS and HIV Information from AVERT
This website contains HIV and AIDS statistics, information for young people, personal stories, a history section, information on becoming infected, a young and gay section, and lots more.

Sex Education Links
Provides information and additional links about STIs.

Centers for Disease Control and Prevention
The Centers for Disease Control and Prevention is a government agency that works to protect public health and safety. The CDC is a source for information, statistics, and treatment guidelines for STIs.

Hans Rosling on HIV
Hans Rosling unveils new data visuals that untangle the complex risk factors for HIV. He argues that preventing transmissions—not drug treatments—is the key to ending the epidemic.

Print Resources

Cates, W. (2004). Reproductive Tract Infections. In R.A. Hatcher et al. (Eds.), *Contraceptive Technology* (18th ed.). New York: Ardent Media.

Daniel E.L., Levine C. (Eds.). (2001). Should Cases of HIV Infection Be Reported By Name? In *Taking Sides: Clashing Views of Controversial Issues in Health and Society* (5th ed.). Dubuque, Iowa: McGraw-Hill/Dushkin.

Shilts, R. (1987). *And the Band Played On: Politics, People and the AIDS Epidemic.* New York: St. Martin's Press.

Taverner, W.J. (2002) Should Schools Make Condoms Available to Students? In *Taking Sides: Clashing Views on Controversial Issues in Human Sexuality* (8th ed.). Dubuque, Iowa: McGraw-Hill/Dushkin.

Video Resources

And the Band Played On. (1993). 141 minutes. Award-winning HBO production based on the book by Randy Shilts about the discovery of the AIDS virus.

The Age of AIDS. (2005). 240 minutes. A chronicle of HIV/AIDS, one of the worst pandemics ever known. Through interviews with researchers, activists, and patients, Frontline investigates the science, politics, and human cost of this disease, and asks: what has been learned, and what must be done to stop AIDS?

Angels in America. (2003). 352 minutes. Based on Tony Kushner's award-winning play. Illustrates the sexual, racial, religious, political, and social issues confronting the country in the early years of the AIDS epidemic. From HBO Films.

Bad Blood: The Tuskegee Syphilis Experiment. (1992). 60 minutes. This documentary portrays the history of this experiment that used African American men as guinea pigs. Could also be used to illustrate ethical issues in research.

The Lost Children of Rockdale County. (1999). 90 minutes. A syphilis outbreak in an affluent community uncovers the hidden lives of troubled teenagers. Frontline documentary by PBS Video.

Miss Evers' Boys. (1997). 118 minutes. Award-winning film by HBO. The true story of the U.S. government's 1932 Tuskegee syphilis experiments, in which a group of black test subjects were allowed to die, despite a cure having been developed.

Sexually Transmitted Diseases. (2000). 19 minutes. This examination of the STI epidemic focuses on chlamydia, herpes, and genital warts as well as AIDS, strongly emphasizing prevention and early detection. The program explains the complications from infection. From Films for the Humanities and Sciences.

15 Variations in Sexual Behavior

"Today's unspeakable perversion is tomorrow's kink is next week's good clean fun."

—**Columnist and author Dan Savage**

"There is hardly anyone whose sexual life, if it were broadcast, would not fill the world at large with surprise and horror."

—**W. Somerset Maugham**

"I was really into bestiality, sadomasochism, and necrophilia, but then I realized I was just beating a dead horse."

—**Anonymous**

"The only unnatural sex act is that which you cannot perform."

—**Alfred Kinsey**

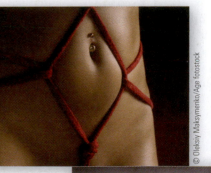

© Oleksiy Maksymenko/Age fotostock

© Radius Images/Corbis

© Joel Gordon

Introduction

After completion of this section, you will be able to . . .

○ Recognize the influence of society and culture on standards of normalcy and deviance.

○ Define *paraphilia*.

○ Identify common characteristics of those who have paraphilias.

○ Describe some of the proposed causes of paraphilic behavior.

ASK YOURSELF

How would *you* define which sexual activities are considered "normal" and which are "deviant"? What standards would you use? By statistical frequency of sexual acts? By sociocultural norms? By the effect the acts have on a person's life?

There is an old joke that goes, "What is the difference between 'kinky' and 'perverted'?" The answer is: "Kinky uses a feather. With perverted you use the whole chicken." Sexual behaviors are limited only by one's imagination, and in this chapter we will explore many variations of erotic expression. Paraphilias are a group of behaviors that involve repeated and intense sexual arousal to atypical and sometimes socially deviant stimuli. Some of the behaviors discussed in this chapter may make you feel uncomfortable, frightened, aroused, or even disgusted.

As we've learned, human sexuality has a rich variety of expression. But what is "normal" sexual behavior? *Psychopathia Sexualis,* written by 19th-century sexologist Richard von Krafft-Ebing, gave one of the first detailed descriptions of paraphilic behavior. This book contained case studies of sadism, masochism, fetishes, pedophilia, exhibitionism, and frotteurism, among others. Krafft-Ebing wrote that sexual deviance was "every expression of (the sexual instinct) that does not correspond with the purpose of nature—i.e., propagation" (Brown, 1983, p. 277). Although a few people may still agree with this designation, it is clear that standards of sexual "normalcy" change over time. Sexual relationships between adult males and adolescent boys were accepted and encouraged in Ancient Greece. Ancient Hindu culture saw the sex act as a refined form of combat in which the male attacks and the female resists; what would today be considered sadomasochistic behaviors were seen as normal actions meant to enhance passion (Bhugra, 2000). Homosexuality, masturbation, and anal sex were once considered mental disorders or symptoms of mental disorders but are now considered part of the spectrum of healthy sexual expression. Other behaviors, such as hypoactive sexual desire or sexual aversion disorder, which were once considered normal, are now classified as mental ailments (Moser & Kleinplatz, 2005).

In general, our views of whether a behavior is sexually aberrant are based on societal norms rather than on fixed medical criteria (Brown, 1983). The concept of "sexual deviance" is influenced by many factors, including religion, attitudes about sex, and how individualistic or collectivist a culture is (Bhugra, Popelyuk, & McMullen, 2010). A behavior that is considered "normal" in one culture may be frowned upon or even illegal in another. For example, topless sunbathing among women at public beaches is accepted in Western Europe, but in the United States it is condemned and illegal. On the other hand, nonmarital sex is mostly accepted in the Western world but is stigmatized harshly in many Moslem countries (Moser & Kleinplatz, 2005). Cross-dressing has occurred in most societies; in China it is common and accepted for male actors to perform in female clothing (Bhugra, 2000).

Published by the American Psychiatric Association, the ***Diagnostic and Statistical Manual of Mental Disorders (DSM)*** is the handbook that describes the diagnostic criteria for all formally recognized mental disorders. Counselors, therapists, health care workers, academics, and even those in the legal profession use the *DSM*. According to the *DSM*, **paraphilias** are "recurrent, intense sexually arousing fantasies, sexual urges, or behaviors, generally involving 1) nonhuman objects, 2) the suffering or humiliation of oneself or one's partner, or 3) children or other non-consenting persons." Further, these behaviors occur over a period of at least 6 months and cause "clinically significant distress or impairment in social, occupational, or other important areas of functioning" (American Psychiatric Association, 2000, p. 566).

To be classified as a paraphilia, the fantasy or behavior must be for the purpose of sexual arousal. It is not a paraphilia for a man to dress as a woman for Halloween, or for a nude model to get undressed in a life-drawing class, if this behavior is not related to sexual arousal. Also, if a man becomes aroused when his girlfriend wears high heels in bed, it doesn't mean he has a paraphilia, unless his sexual desire doesn't depend on the girlfriend—only the shoes—for 6 months or more, and if his fantasies or behavior causes him distress or interferes with his life, his work, or the law. Paraphilic behaviors also tend to be compulsive; the person would like to stop but feels powerless and controlled by his urges.

Just as with almost all sexual phenomena, paraphilias exist on a continuum. Some are as harmless and benign as fantasizing about silky lingerie, whereas others may be as severe as sexually victimizing children. Some people can function sexually without the paraphilic stimuli and use the object or behavior as an alternate route to sexual arousal; for others, their sole means of sexual excitement is with the paraphilic behavior.

Paraphilias can be conceptualized in terms of unusual objects of attraction, such as inanimate objects, children, or nonconsenting persons; or unusual sexual activities, such as a desire for pain or humiliation (Lawrence, 2009). In this chapter, we will categorize paraphilias as coercive or noncoercive. Individuals practice noncoercive paraphilias privately or with amenable adult partners. Noncoercive paraphilias include fetishism, transvestism, sadism, and masochism. Coercive paraphilias, including exhibitionism, voyeurism, frotteurism, and pedo-

Diagnostic and Statistical Manual of Mental Disorders (DSM) The manual that describes mental health disorders in children and adults.

Paraphilia (pair-uh-FILL-ee-uh) From the Greek words *para*, meaning "deviation," and *philia*, meaning "love or attraction," a paraphilia is a persistent and atypical sexual interest in nonhuman objects, physically or emotionally painful experiences, or nonconsenting or sexually immature individuals.

philia, involve the unwilling participation of others.

The inclusion of paraphilias in the *DSM* is controversial. Paraphilias may not meet the definition of a mental illness. Because the *DSM* does not define healthy sexuality, the characterization of disordered sexuality becomes particularly problematic. Additionally, in the *DSM*'s definition of a paraphilia, the behavior itself indicates a diagnosis (Moser & Kleinplatz, 2005). But a behavior alone may not be a reliable indicator of an underlying paraphilic focus of sexual arousal (First, 2010). Someone who takes off his clothing in public might meet the diagnostic criteria for exhibitionism, but he might just be drunk. Or have Alzheimer's disease. Or poor impulse control. One would need to know the underlying motivation behind the exhibitionism before assuming a behavior is indicative of a diagnosis (First, 2010). Some of the definitional criteria for paraphilias are also questionable. Many people who exhibit what would be classified as paraphilic behaviors don't experience distress or psychosocial impairment (Långström, 2010). Others may experience distress with actions that society would consider normal; psychological distress may be due to the imposition of society's views on one's sexual outlook. A Victorian woman who experienced lust or sexual arousal may well have wondered if she was abnormal, when in fact she was responding as a sexually healthy woman. Many sexologists debate whether the continued inclusion of paraphilias in the mental health handbook simply represents a value judgment that crosses the line into "policing the bedroom."

Prevalence of Paraphilias

It is almost impossible to determine how many people have paraphilias. Most of the people with noncoercive paraphilias don't feel their behaviors are problematic and consequently don't seek help. Social mores or laws against these sexual variations make self-reports unreliable. Much of our information about paraphilias comes either indirectly, from the few victims of coercive paraphilias who report the crime, or from those whose actions got them in trouble with their spouses or with the law, and which necessitated psychological intervention. It is most likely that the prevalence of paraphilias is much greater than imagined. In 1986 the U.S. Commission on Pornography found that almost one fourth of the more than 3,000 magazine and book titles sold in "adults only" outlets could be considered paraphilic (Lebegue, 1991). The large commercial market for paraphilic paraphernalia, books, magazines, and websites suggests that the prevalence of paraphilias is high (Aggrawal, 2009).

So who is the "typical" person with a paraphilia? Paraphilias usually begin during early puberty, and most people who seek treatment for a paraphilia are between ages 15 and 25 (Aggrawal, 2009). Paraphilias are much more rare in men over age 50. People

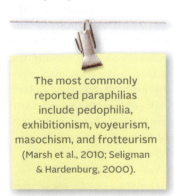

The most commonly reported paraphilias include pedophilia, exhibitionism, voyeurism, masochism, and frotteurism (Marsh et al., 2010; Seligman & Hardenburg, 2000).

ASK YOURSELF

Do you think paraphilias are a sign of mental illness, or just an extreme on the continuum of human sexual expression? Why do you think so?

meeting the criteria for a paraphilia come from all religions, races, orientations, occupations, and education levels. There is no specific personality type that is prone to paraphilic behavior. However, there is one overwhelmingly common characteristic: almost all people with a paraphilia are men. For this reason, throughout most of the chapter, those with paraphilias will usually be described as "he" rather than as "he or she." Some men with paraphilias have emotional problems, including depression, anxiety, and poor self-esteem. Some theorize that pedophiles or other men with paraphilic behavior were more likely to have experienced physical or sexual abuse as children (Marsh et al., 2010; Seligman & Hardenburg, 2000). This does not necessarily mean that childhood sexual abuse *causes* paraphilias. Those with paraphilias may have intimacy problems and fear rejection; although about half of all men with paraphilias are married, most report sexual dysfunctions in their marriages. Many people meeting the criteria for a paraphilia have impulse control disorders, or other compulsive behaviors, such as problems with alcohol or other substance abuse (Krueger & Kaplan, 2001; Marsh et al., 2010). People with paraphilias may also have other disorders, such as temporal lobe epilepsy, Tourette's syndrome, Huntington's disease, and multiple sclerosis, or have experienced a traumatic brain injury.

The most common paraphilias in women are pedophilia, sadomasochism, and exhibitionism. The only paraphilia more common in females than in males is hybristophilia—being sexually aroused by criminals (Aggrawal, 2009).

It is unusual for a man to have just one paraphilia; most who meet the criteria for paraphilic behavior have two to five paraphilias (fetishism, transvestism, and S&M is one common combination), and they may exhibit different paraphilias at different times in their lives (Abel & Osborn, 1992; Abel, Becker, Cunningham-Rathner, Mittelman, & Rouleau, 1988; Krueger & Kaplan, 2001; Seligman & Hardenburg, 2000). This may be because men who have engaged in one paraphilia are less inhibited about trying others, or it may be that an underlying cause—be it biological or psychological—predisposes a person to paraphilic behaviors. Sometimes people escalate from one harmless behavior such as masturbating while fantasizing about rubber, to observing others without their knowledge, to more aggressive sexual behaviors (Seligman & Hardenburg, 2000).

Causes of Paraphilias

Just as more mainstream sexual desires do not have a simple, single foundation, we don't know why some people develop paraphilias. Most likely, it is a combination of factors—developmental, psychological, biological, and sociological—that predispose someone to alternate sexual expressions.

Developmental Theories

Developmental theories suggest that a person may develop a paraphilia due to childhood traumas or events that permanently alter his sexual expression.

Table 15.1 Courtship Disorder Theory

NORMAL COURTSHIP STAGE	NORMAL BEHAVIOR	ABNORMAL (PARAPHILIC) BEHAVIOR
Search for a partner	A suitable partner is searched for and selected by viewing a number of prospective partners.	A *voyeur* spends all his energies and attains orgasm by simply looking at and masturbating to the image of a prospective partner.
Pretactile interaction	Looking, smiling, posturing, and talking to a prospective partner.	An *exhibitionist* masturbates while showing his genitals. An *obscene phone caller* masturbates while talking to a prospective partner. All sexual energy is spent in the pretactile stage of interaction.
Tactile interaction	Petting, touching, kissing a prospective partner.	A *toucher* grabs intimate parts of his prospective partner, and a *frotteur* rubs his penis against buttocks while achieving orgasm. Sexual satisfaction depends solely on touching a partner and other stages are passed over.
Genital union	Penile-vaginal copulation.	A *biastophile*, or preferential rapist, skips the previous stages of courtship and prefers to rape his prospective partner.

© Cengage Learning 2013. SOURCES: Aggrawal, 2009; Freund et al., 1983.

Psychoanalytic theory. According to psychoanalytic theory, which is largely based on the theories of Sigmund Freud, paraphilias are manifestations of unresolved inner conflicts caused by traumatic events during childhood; specifically, an unresolved Oedipus complex and its associated castration anxiety. Freud held that boys have unconscious sexual feelings for their mothers and subconsciously want to kill their fathers, who are the rivals for their mothers' attention. Further, he theorized that boys believe that if they were to act on these feelings, their fathers would castrate them. According to Freud, adult paraphilias are attempts to deal with this perceived threat; for example, a man may expose himself as reassurance of the presence of his genitals. Although most psychologists today find little validity in Freud's ideas of the Oedipal or castration complex, it is true that childhood experiences can influence adult behaviors.

Lovemaps. Psychologist John Money believed that every person develops a **lovemap**—a template of his or her ideal romantic partner and lover. According to this theory, the basic pattern for our perfect mate is formed during childhood and is modified over the years by our experiences and environment. For example, if a child's normal sexual play is hampered by too much punishment or prohibition, he or she may grow up to have difficulties with sexual arousal or orgasm. On the other hand, a person may develop compulsive sexual behaviors if as a child he or she overly resisted sexual punishments or prohibitions. According to Money's theory, a person may develop paraphilias if specific childhood encounters redesign the lovemap, such that the erotic energy is redirected to objects or otherwise inappropriate sexual outlets (Money, 1984).

Lovemap A theory developed by psychologist John Money that describes a person's template for his or her ideal romantic partner.

Courtship disorder theory The theory that paraphilias are due to a disturbed courtship cycle.

Classical conditioning A learning process that occurs when a previously neutral stimulus is paired with another stimulus that produces a naturally occurring response. Eventually, the previously neutral stimulus comes to evoke the response without the presence of the other stimulus.

Courtship disorder theory. The **courtship disorder theory** of development (Freund, Scher, & Hucker, 1983) posits an explanation for a number of paraphilias, including voyeurism, exhibitionism, telephone scatologia, frotteurism, and biastophilia. Two or more of these paraphilias often occur together in many offenders. The theory suggests that in some people, the normal cycle of courtship becomes short-circuited because all the paraphiliac's energy is spent in one stage of courtship (Table 15.1).

Behavioral Theories

Our childhood experiences influence our sexual expressions. As a result of **classical conditioning**, an otherwise nonsexual object or behavior may take on erotic undertones through its association with sexual pleasure. Imagine a boy who gets an erection while touching women's silky lingerie. He may learn to associate his sexual pleasure with the panties, and he may begin to masturbate thinking of or using the undergarments. In time, the learned association between sexual arousal and the object or behavior becomes more strongly connected and eventually sexual satisfaction depends on the conditioned stimulus. The consequences of our actions also modify the occurrence and form of our behaviors, a psychological phenomenon known as *operant conditioning*, wherein the behavior is reinforced by the rewarding consequences. As an example, as the boy masturbates while fantasizing about lingerie, his subsequent orgasm reinforces the fetish.

Biological Theories

Neural and hormonal abnormalities may exist in some men with paraphilias. Some men with paraphilic sexual interests may show different brain activity during sexual excitement. In men without paraphilias, sexual arousal is associated with EEG activation in the right parietal lobe, whereas in paraphiliacs, the left frontal lobe is more active (Waismann, Fenwick, Wilson, Hewett, & Lumsden, 2003). Some paraphiliacs have been found to have anatomical differences in parts of their frontal and temporal lobes (Bhugra, Popelyuk, & McMullen, 2010). Alterations in dopamine, serotonin, or testosterone levels may also be related to abnormal sexual behaviors. Lowering testosterone with Depo-Provera or raising serotonin levels with **selective serotonin reuptake inhibitors (SSRIs)** such as Prozac decreases sexual desires and behaviors.

Additionally, there may be similarities between obsessive-compulsive disorders (OCD) and the paraphilias and disorders of sexual frequency (Bradford, 2001). We can't be sure in some cases whether a paraphilia is due to neural and hormonal abnormalities or if the brain changed because of the sexual activities pursued. However, paraphilias have been shown to develop in men with previously mainstream sexual interests who sustained a traumatic brain injury, frontal lobe lesions, brain tumors, or temporal lobe epilepsy (Bradford, 2001; Joyal, Black, & Dassylva, 2007; Kreuter, Dahllof, Gudjonsson, Sullivan, & Siosteen, 1998), suggesting that neurological foundations affect our sexual expression.

Sociological Theories

The society in which we live also influences our sexual desires and behaviors. For instance, every day we see images associating high-heeled shoes with sex appeal; Birkenstocks are not usually portrayed as particularly sexy footwear. Perhaps it is not surprising that more people develop sexual fetishes regarding stiletto heels than sandals. Additionally, in the United States we are exposed to hundreds of sexualized images each day. If a child or adolescent continually sees media images in which people have numerous sexual partners, or in which women are viewed as sex objects, he or she may incorporate this worldview. Many paraphilic rituals mirror the gender roles and sexual mores that we absorb from society.

As we've learned, complex behaviors such as sexuality are almost never caused by one single, simple factor. Most likely, the development of paraphilias is due to a combination of biological, developmental, psychological, and societal forces, all interacting with a person's unique experiences and environment.

Noncoercive Paraphilias

After completion of this section, you will be able to . . .

○ Define *fetishism, partialism, transvestic fetishism, autogynephilia, BDSM,* and *sadomasochism* as well as other noncoercive paraphilias.

○ Identify the typical behaviors and characteristics of those with noncoercive paraphilias.

Many paraphilias are harmless and are practiced by individuals privately or with other willing, adult partners. These are called **noncoercive paraphilias,** and they include fetishism, transvestism, sadism, and masochism.

Common fetishistic objects include leather boots and stiletto heels.

© Ocean/Corbis

Fetishism

Many men may find themselves aroused at the sight of a woman wearing a leather corset or stockings with a garter belt. For some, however, the woman is superfluous; the stockings or leather alone are necessary and sufficient for sexual arousal. **Fetishism** is when a person has sexually arousing fantasies, urges, and behaviors regarding a nonliving object. Common fetishistic objects include clothing such as lingerie, stockings, shoes or boots; and fabrics such as silk, leather, or rubber (Darcangelo, 2008). When a fetish involves particular body parts such as feet, hair, or breasts, it is called **partialism**.

As with most aspects of sexuality, there is a wide variation in the expression of fetishism: for some, the fetish object increases their sexual arousal, others can't get sexually aroused without it. Some only need the object for sexual gratification during times of stress, whereas others require it for all sexual satisfaction. Some men share their fetish with their partners; others keep it secret. Most fetishes are harmless, although some men resort to burglary to obtain their fetish objects. It is unknown how many people have a sexual fetish, as most are not troubled by their desires and don't seek treatment.

Fetishes often develop during childhood or adolescence. Fetishistic behavior is most easily explained by classical and operant conditioning theory. In a classic study, Rachman and Hodgson (1969) showed subjects slides of a sexual nature paired with images of women's boots. Eventually, the subjects became aroused to the pictures of the boots, without the sexually seductive items. This phenomenon may frequently occur outside of the laboratory; for example: a young man repeatedly sees a naked woman in stiletto heels. He becomes sexually aroused and associates the arousal with the fetish object. Eventually, the shoes become more important to his sexual arousal than the original sexually stimulating image. Under operant conditioning, as the young man incorporates the object into his fantasy while masturbating, he reinforces the association of the object with pleasure and orgasm. These theories do not explain why the fetishist eventually shows no interest in the original unconditioned stimulus—the woman—and instead requires the conditioned stimulus—the shoes—for his sexual arousal (Aggrawal, 2009). It is likely that there is more than one factor involved in the development of a fetish. Biological factors may also influence the

Selective serotonin reuptake inhibitors (SSRIs) A class of drugs that increase the amount of serotonin available to bind to receptors.

Noncoercive paraphilias Paraphilias that are practiced by individuals privately, or by willing, adult participants.

Fetishism (FET-ish-izm) A paraphilia in which a person has sexually arousing fantasies and behaviors regarding an inanimate object. The word *fetish* derives from the Portuguese word *feitiço,* meaning "charm," or "sorcery."

Partialism A fetish that involves a particular body part, such as breasts, hair, or feet.

Comedian Eddie Izzard, pictured, is a transvestite, as was Ed Wood, considered to be the worst director of all time.

Cross-dressing is often used in movies and TV as a point of humor. Milton Berle often dressed in drag, and Tom Hanks (pictured) got his start playing off the comedic foundation of a man wearing a dress.

development of a fetish, as fetishism has been linked to lesions in the frontal and temporal lobes of the brain (Baird, Wilson, Bladin, Saling, & Reutens, 2007).

Transvestic Fetishism

Cross-dressers enjoy wearing the clothing of the opposite sex. When this is done for sexual pleasure, it may be considered **transvestic fetishism**. This paraphilia is similar to fetishism in that the sexual arousal is dependent on an article of clothing, but for men with transvestic fetishism, the clothes must be worn, not just held or fantasized about. Some paraphilic transvestites wear women's clothing only in secret, some wear a bra and panties under their male clothes, and others go out in full dress and makeup (although this is more unusual). It is estimated that perhaps 3–6% of men have some personal experience with transvestism, although due to its mostly secret nature, this may be an underestimation (Janus & Janus, 1993; Långström & Zucker, 2005).

It is important to differentiate transvestites from drag queens and transsexuals. Transvestites are men, usually heterosexual, who usually have no desire to be women, but who derive sexual pleasure from dressing as a woman. Drag queens are men who dress as women to entertain, act out, or attract other men. Transsexuals usually cross-dress because they identify as the other sex, not for sexual arousal. Some transvestites and transsexuals may have **autogynephilia**, a paraphilia in which a man is sexually aroused by the thought or image of himself as a woman.

Transvestites are almost always heterosexual males; in fact, the diagnostic definition in the *DSM* is limited to heterosexual males (APA, 2000). Although women routinely dress in "male" clothing such as jeans, suits, and ties, men in women's apparel often provokes humor and disgust. However, there are few to no reports of women deriving sexual pleasure from wearing traditionally male attire. Most transvestites have been married at some time in their lives. Married men often try to keep their cross-dressing secret from their wives, who may respond with shock, anger, or confusion when they find out. Most wives, however, eventually become aware of their husbands' cross-dressing and learn to live with it (Docter & Prince, 1997).

Docter and Prince (1997) surveyed more than 1,000 cross-dressers and found they fit into two categories. The majority of the men were heterosexual, and they cross-dressed to express their feminine side. Some of the men in this group reported that they felt closer to women by wearing their clothing. Seventeen percent of men were more transsexually inclined and more committed to living as a woman; subjects in this group expressed less sexual arousal with cross-dressing, had lower sexual interest in women, and were more likely to identify themselves as "a woman trapped in a man's body."

Two thirds of transvestites begin cross-dressing before puberty (Docter & Prince, 1997; Wheeler, Newring, & Draper, 2008). Most cross-dressers come from middle-class households, raised by both parents, with a father who provided a masculine image. They may be more likely to be the oldest or only child in the family. Cross-dressing may begin due to an early experience in which sexual arousal is associated with women's clothing, such as masturbating with lingerie.

BDSM

Many couples enjoy **BDSM**, an acronym derived from the terms bondage and discipline, dominance and submission, and sadism and masochism. The BDSM relationship is based on the concept of partners voluntarily taking on deliberately unequal yet complementary roles. The **top**, or dominant partner, is more physically or emotionally controlling, whereas the **bottom**, or submissive partner, is controlled (although the bottom may use previously agreed upon code words to either slow down or stop the behavior). The dominant partner may **discipline** the submissive partner, by using rules or punishment to control his or her behavior during sex play.

A **dominatrix** is a woman who is paid to act as a dominant partner. There is usually no intercourse between the dominatrix and her client. Many powerful men, including CEOs and politicians, are clients of dominatrices; it may be sexually arousing for

Aren't all transvestites gay?

Transvestic fetishism A paraphilia in which a man becomes sexually aroused by wearing women's clothing.

Autogynephilia A paraphilia in which a man becomes sexually aroused at the thought of or image of himself as a woman.

BDSM An acronym derived from the terms bondage and discipline, dominance and submission, and sadism and masochism.

Top The dominant or controlling partner in a BDSM relationship.

Bottom The submissive partner in a BDSM relationship.

Discipline The use of rules or punishment to control another's behavior.

Dominatrix A woman who plays the dominant role in a BDSM relationship.

them to play the submissive role in fantasy, as they rarely play this role in real life.

Bondage refers to the use of restraints during sexual play. One partner is voluntarily bound, often with handcuffs or ties, while the other partner sexually stimulates the restrained partner. Bondage is a fairly common practice; one survey of almost 1,000 heterosexual men and women found that one quarter of the respondents said that they had engaged in sexual bondage during some of their erotic encounters (Rubin, 1990). In a more recent survey of more than 19,000 men and women, 1.8% of sexually active respondents said that they had been involved in BDSM in the previous year (Richters, de Visser, Rissel, Grulich, & Smith, 2008).

© Doug Stevens/Shutterstock

A dominatrix.

Sadism and masochism (referred to as **sadomasochism** or **S&M**) are two sides of the same coin, in which sexual pleasure is associated with physical or psychological pain. **Masochism** is named after Leopold Baron von Sacher-Masoch, an Austrian who wrote a novel in which the principal male character desires to be dominated and ill-treated by his mistress. Masochists derive sexual pleasure from being humiliated, beaten, tied up, or made to suffer in some way. A masochist is not aroused by pain alone—a headache would not be an orgasmic experience—rather, pain is part of the sexual ritual that enhances arousal. **Sadism** is a paraphilia in which a man derives sexual pleasure from intentionally hurting or humiliating others. The word is derived from the Marquis de Sade, a French aristocrat who was sent to prison for imprisoning and sexually and physically abusing a woman. De Sade spent much of his life in prison, where he wrote novels involving descriptions of physical torture.

For most people, BDSM is simply a sexual interest and not a symptom of past abuse or difficulty with "normal" sex (Richters et al., 2008). BDSM is not uncommon; many people occasionally play at mild S&M with a partner, perhaps enjoying love bites or gentle spanking. Kinsey found that 24% of men and 12% of women had at least some erotic response to stories involving S&M imagery, and 50% of men and 54% of women reported some sexual arousal to being bitten (Kinsey, Pomeroy, Martin, & Gebhard, 1953). More recent surveys found that 14% of men and 11% of women reported some S&M experience (Janus & Janus, 1993). S&M may be considered a paraphilia when the sadomasochistic activities are the sole sexual outlet for 6 months or more, when they are necessary for sexual arousal, and when these actions cause physical, psychological, or social problems to the participant.

The typical person who engages in sadomasochistic activities is a well-educated, heterosexual male, although these behav-

iors, especially masochism, are also found in women (Hucker, 2008; Moser & Levitt, 1987). Most people first experience S&M in their 20s, although they may first begin to have sadomasochistic fantasies at an earlier age.

Although S&M involves pain and humiliation, it is a noncoercive paraphilia because consenting adults, who both receive sexual pleasure from their interaction, engage in it. Common sadomasochistic activities include spanking and whipping, bondage, the use of blindfolds, or activities designed to humiliate the masochistic partner, including having him or her crawl or act like a dog, lick the dominant partner's boots, or be verbally insulted (Moser & Levitt, 1987). Sexual interactions often follow a carefully scripted ritual, or **scene**, in which one partner plays a dominant role (such as master or prison guard) and the other plays the submissive role (such as slave or prisoner) (Hucker, 2008; Moser & Levitt, 1987). The submissive partner can end the scene at any time by saying a previously agreed upon "safe word." Participants often switch between the dominant and submissive role; in one study of men and women who attended S&M support groups, only 16% felt themselves to be exclusively dominant or submissive (Moser & Levitt, 1987).

Bondage A sexual practice that involves physically restraining one of the partners.

Sadomasochism (SAY-doh-ma-suh-kizm) or **S&M** The consensual use of pain or humiliation for sexual pleasure.

Masochism (MA-suh-kizm) A paraphilia in which one derives sexual pleasure from being hurt or humiliated as part of a sexual ritual.

Sadism (SAY-dizm) A paraphilia in which one derives sexual pleasure from intentionally hurting or humiliating others.

Scene An erotic encounter between dominant and submissive partners.

As with all sexual behavior, BDSM activities exist on a continuum. Some have rules against activities that leave marks or bruises, while others do not. Some participate in "edgeplay," activities that include knives, suffocation, or electricity. Many BDSM participants establish a rule not to engage in sex play that would result in medical intervention, such as broken bones or stitches.

It is unknown exactly why some people enjoy BDSM behaviors. Biologically, pain or stress may cause the release of substances such as endorphins or norepinephrine that are associated with pleasure or excitement. The neurotransmitter dopamine, which is associated with reward and addiction, may also be released during stressful activities. Those who enjoy inflicting pain on others may have abnormalities in their brain waves (Eliseev & Kunikovskiy, 1997). Psychologically, some may enjoy these behaviors as a departure from their everyday lives. Submissives may relax and let others take control; dominants may enjoy the feeling of power. Events from early childhood often influence later sexual development. Associations may be made between sexual pleasure and early punishment. Others may develop their sadomasochistic desires later in life.

Most people don't seek treatment for BDSM; in fact, most practitioners don't technically suffer from a paraphilia because diagnosis requires that the participant suffer distress from his or her actions. In reality, most dominants and submissives happily engage in mutually satisfying, consensual sex. One study found that fewer than than 6% of those who participate in S&M were distressed by their activities (Moser & Levitt, 1987).

Other Noncoercive Paraphilias

There are many other paraphilias that involve consenting partners. People who are sexually aroused by contact with urine have **urophilia**. These people participate in "watersports" or "golden showers," in which one partner urinates on the other. It is believed that sexologist Havelock Ellis was a urophiliac (Grosskurth, 1980). Having wet and messy substances like whipped cream, pudding, or paint smeared on their body sexually arouse **sploshers**, and **furries** are turned on by having sex with stuffed animals or with people dressed as stuffed animals. Adults with **infantalism** (also called **autonepiophilia**) experience sexual pleasure from dressing and acting the role of an infant. These "adult babies" enjoy having their partner feed them a bottle or put them to sleep in a crib. Others derive sexual pleasure from wearing diapers. Men with infantalism don't have a sexual preference for children; they enjoy being treated as children. They may want to be free of responsibility or control, or they may desire to feel mothered. Other noncoercive paraphilias are listed in the Sex Actually feature on this page.

A couple at the Folsom Street Fair, an annual event for the BDSM and leather subculture in San Francisco

Urophilia Sexual arousal by contact with urine.

Sploshers Those who are sexually excited by having wet and messy substances smeared on their body.

Furries People who are turned on by having sex with stuffed animals or people dressed as stuffed animals.

Infantalism A paraphilia in which a person experiences sexual pleasure from dressing and acting as an infant. Also called **autonepiophilia**.

Autoerotic asphyxiation Also called "**breath play**" or "**scarfing**." The intentional restriction of oxygen flow to the brain to intensify the orgasm, often while masturbating.

sex actually

Other Noncoercive Paraphilias

- **Klismaphilia**: Sexual arousal from use of enemas.
- **Mysophilia**: Sexual arousal by dirt, mud, or filthy objects such as soiled underwear. Includes **coprophilia**, a sexual arousal from contact with feces.
- **Acrotomophilia**: Sexual arousal from partner who is amputee.
- **Formicophilia**: Having insects crawl on one's body enhances sexual arousal.
- **Stigmatophilia**: Arousal is dependent on being with partner who is pierced or tattooed.
- **Dacryphilia**: When someone derives sexual pleasure from making his or her partner cry.
- **Menophilia**: A sexual arousal to menstruation.
- **Narratophila**: When one's sexual arousal depends on reading or listening to erotic narratives.
- **Emetophilia**: A sexual attraction to vomiting.
- **Nyotaimori**: A Japanese term for sexual arousal from eating sushi off a woman's naked body.
- **Clinical Vampirism**: A disorder in which the affected person is obsessed with and erotically aroused by the drinking of blood, preferably of human beings.

Some people masturbate while hanging or strangling themselves for the rush that the oxygen deprivation gives. This activity, called **autoerotic asphyxiation**, "**breath play**," or "**scarfing**," can cause brain damage or death. Although it is hard to determine the actual incidence of autoerotic asphyxiation, some estimate that at least 10,000 people or more, mostly males aged 13 to 40, experiment with breath play. Perhaps 500 to 1,000 people die each year in the United States from this activity, although the exact numbers are hard to gauge because many of these deaths are called suicide or are hushed up (Jenkins, 2000). It is thought that actor David Carradine died while engaging in autoerotic asphyxiation.

Coercive Paraphilias

After completion of this section, you will be able to . . .

○ Distinguish between coercive and noncoercive paraphilias.

○ Define *exhibitionism, telephone scatologia, frotteurism, voyeurism,* and *pedophilia,* as well as other coercive paraphilias.

○ Identify the typical behaviors and characteristics of those with coercive paraphilias.

Coercive paraphilias are considered more problematic because they involve the unwilling participation of others. These kinds of paraphilias include exhibitionism, telephone scatologia, voyeurism, frotteurism, biastophilia, and pedophilia.

Exhibitionism

Exhibitionism is paraphilia in which a person—usually male—is sexually aroused by exposing his genitals to an unsuspecting stranger—usually female. Most men with exhibitionist behaviors show only the penis although about 15% show their whole nude body (Freund, Watson, & Rienzo, 1988). Most of these men will masturbate during exposure or shortly afterward (de Silva, 1999).

> **Is mooning exhibitionism? What about streaking?**

It is not the nudity, per se, that is exciting to the exhibitionist; an exhibitionist would not be sexually aroused being naked in a situation in which nudity was expected or accepted, such as at a nude beach. Similarly, **mooning** or **streaking** is usually not a paraphilic event because most people do these things for fun or shock value, rather than sexual arousal. Instead, *flashers* (as they are sometimes called) are excited in part by the power they have by frightening or surprising their victims. If you are exposed to a flasher, your best response is to ignore him and not give him the response he wants—your shock and horror.

Exhibitionism is one of the most common paraphilias in the United States (Långström, 2010; Murphy & Page, 2008). By definition, exhibitionism involves a witness, so it may be that the high rate of exhibitionism is related to a higher incidence of being caught. Children, adolescents, and women are frequent targets of exhibitionists (Murphy & Page, 2008). About 50% of women have been victims of indecent exposure, and most were below the age of 16 at the time of exposure (Riordan, 1999). Exhibitionism is against the law and accounts for up to one third of all sex convictions in the United States, Canada, and Europe (Langevin & Lang, 1987; Murphy & Page, 2008). Still, only about 15–30% of incidents are reported to the police (Cox, 1988; Murphy & Page, 2008).

The onset of exhibitionism is usually before age 18 (Aggrawal, 2009). In early reports, exhibitionists were described as shy, unassertive, and sexually repressed men in their late teens to early 40s (Freund et al., 1988). It was believed that flashers often felt dominated by women and resented them because of it. However, some of the measurements used for these early studies were not standardized; more recent measures suggest that in many ways, exhibitionists as a group do not differ greatly from controls (Murphy & Page, 2008). Furthermore, most exhibitionists' primary sexual release does not come from exposing themselves. In other words, there is no evidence that men who show exhibitionistic behavior have a preference for exposing themselves; instead, it may be that exhibitionists are hypersexual because they often also exhibit activities such as compulsive masturbation, promiscuous behavior, and a dependence on porn or telephone sex (Murphy & Page, 2008).

Some men expose themselves hoping for admiration, anger, or disgust from their victims. Many flashers claim that they hope their victims will similarly show their genitals or will want to have sexual intercourse, but it may be that these statements are geared to create the appearance of a more "normal" motivation. Instead, many flashers admit that they would be frightened and flee if their victim approached them (Murphy & Page, 2008). Other men who have exhibitionistic behaviors may have a narcissistic need for admiration, and they hope that their victim will admire the size of their penises; others enjoy the rush of the risk of exhibiting their bodies to strangers (Murphy & Page, 2008). Most flashers don't physically assault their victims, but some might eventually escalate to more sexually aggressive crimes; many men who commit rape or sexually abuse children were first charged with exhibitionism or voyeurism.

Exhibitionism may be caused by a courtship disorder (described earlier in the chapter). According to this theory, exhibitionists spend all their energy during the pre-tactile interaction stage of courtship and short-circuit the other stages (Aggrawal, 2009; Freund et al., 1983). Early conditioning may also influence their behavior.

> **I am made very uncomfortable by a fellow (female) student in my class. I think she dresses very provocatively. Her shirts are very low cut and her thong shows over the top of her jeans. Now since I don't want to be exposed to that when I'm trying to pay attention in class, does that make her an exhibitionist?**

Some women may be exhibitionists. In one study, just more than 2% of women in a national study done in Sweden answered yes to the question "Have you ever exposed your genitals to a stranger and became sexually aroused by this?" (Långström & Seto, 2006). Women who meet the diagnostic criteria for exhibitionism may

Exhibitionism The act of exposing one's genitals to an unsuspecting and nonconsenting person for the purpose of sexual arousal.

Mooning The act of displaying one's bare buttocks, usually by lowering the pants and bending over.

Streaking The act of taking off one's clothes and running naked through a public place.

derive a sense of sexual power from men's admiration of their bodies. But generally in Western society it is usually not considered a crime when a woman shows her body to the public. Low-slung jeans and cleavage-exposing shirts are often met with approval rather than law enforcement agents. Why do *you* think this double standard exists?

Telephone Scatologia

© Vibe Images RF/Alamy

Telephone scatologia is thought to be a form of exhibitionism, but whereas those with exhibitionist behaviors have direct contact with their victims, scatolophiliacs prefer more anonymous contact. An obscene phone caller is a person—usually a man—who phones his victim (almost always a woman) and uses sexually explicit language. This does not include consensual sexually explicit phone calls between partners (phone sex) or between a customer and a paid sex worker. Also, not all obscene phone callers are classified as telephone scatophiliacs; it is necessary that the caller experience sexual excitation and gratification. The sexual gratification comes not from the call and not from the obscenities but from the response of the listener (Pakhomou, 2006).

Paraphilic obscene phone callers are typically heterosexual men with an average or elevated sex drive, with limited social interactions but no significant psychopathology, who have attempted and failed in a committed long-term relationship (Pakhomou, 2006). A significant percentage of obscene phone callers, who may have feelings of inadequacy, especially toward women, are also exhibitionists and voyeurs (Price, Kafka, Commons, Gutheil, & Simpson, 2002).

The etiology of telephone scatology is not clear. Obscene phone calls may be a form of sexual terrorism against women. Men with telephone scatologia become aroused by the woman's fear or disgust and often masturbate during or after the call. Men who feel angry or victimized may strike out at defenseless women who can be safely attacked without fear of reprisal. Or perhaps, scatophiliacs have a courtship disorder and are frozen in the pre-tactile interaction state.

There are different types of paraphilic obscene phone callers. One way to classify them is by the victim's perception of threat, from least threatening to most threatening (Aggrawal, 2009). The least alarming to the victim are *telephone masturbators*. These men call telephone crisis centers and masturbate while talking to female volunteers. The victim usually has no idea that she is talking to an obscene phone caller. *Tricksters* will try to convince the listener to reveal intimate details of her sexual behavior. He may claim to be conducting a survey of sexuality and manipulate the victim into sharing personal information (Aggrawal, 2009; Bullough & Bullough, 1994). The trickster may or may not masturbate while talking, and the victim usually doesn't know she's talking to a scatophiliac. In the remaining four classes of obscene phone callers, the victim does discover that she had been talking to a scatophiliac: *Ingratiating seducers* have a non-threatening conversation with their victim at first, during which they gain their victim's confidence, and then utter obscenities (Mead, 1975). The most common type of obscene phone caller is the *shock caller,* who may breathe heavily, or describe his genitalia or desired sexual activities in explicit detail, often while masturbating (Bullough & Bullough, 1994). The victim knows from the beginning that she's talking to an obscene phone caller, and she can control the situation by hanging up. Still more threatening are the *annoyance creators* who phone their victims, speak obscenities, then hang up, thus controlling the call. These scatophiliacs often call the same woman again and again, increasing her agitation and perception of threat. The most threatening type of obscene phone callers are *panic creators.* These men may falsely inform the victim that he has someone close to her as his hostage, and if she wants the hostage freed, she should undress and do something sexual, such as masturbating or describing a sexual act.

Obscene phone calls are among the most common sexual offenses. Between 47% and 83% of American women have received at least one obscene phone call in their lives; perhaps 16%—or more than 24 million women—have received an obscene phone call in the previous 6 months (Katz, 1994; Price et al., 2002; Smith & Morra, 1994). If you get an obscene phone call, try not to panic. Simply hang up—the caller is less likely to call back if he gets no response. If the harassment continues, or if you feel threatened, report the calls to the phone company and to the police. Most obscene calls go unreported; one study found that only 7–20% of obscene calls are reported to the phone company (Price et al., 2002).

Voyeurism

Many people enjoy looking at naked people or at others having sex—the success of the pornography industry shows that. A tendency to engage in this behavior is not surprising, as both men and women rate visual cues as important elements of mate selection (Rye & Meaney, 2007). Indeed, in our society, we

---

Telephone scatologia Also called **scatolophilia**, or **obscene phone calling**, this paraphilia is characterized by sexual arousal through the use of obscene language to unsuspecting victims on the phone. The term scatologia comes from the Greek words *skato* for "dung" and *logos* for "speech."

Voyeurism (VOI-yer-izm) A paraphilia characterized by the urge to observe an unsuspecting person or persons while they are naked or engaged in sexual activities.

Scopophilia Similar to voyeurism, but in scopophilia the other party consents to being watched.

© DreamWorks/Photofest

Voyeurism has been portrayed in such movies as *Disturbia, Porky's,* and *Sliver.*

Frotteurism usually occurs on a crowded place such as an elevator or a subway.

often see images of sexually active or of nude or partially nude people. A person who meets the diagnostic criteria for clinical **voyeurism** (sometimes called a voyeur, or a Peeping Tom) derives compulsive sexual pleasure from observing strangers—without their knowledge or consent—as they undress or engage in sexual relations; in fact, he would rather watch others have sex than have sex himself. This is different from a **scopophiliac**, who enjoys watching others—*who have consented to being watched*—have sex. Some men who have voyeuristic behaviors go to peep shows or nude beaches, but this does not satisfy most, as their excitement comes from the non-consent of others. Voyeurs may peek into windows, or drill holes in the walls of public bathrooms, locker rooms, or dressing rooms. Others hide small video devices in locker rooms or elsewhere. Some even design cameras to film up women's skirts. These videos can then be used for the voyeur's own personal enjoyment or can be sold to others.

It is difficult to know the true incidence of voyeurism because most cases go undetected; voyeurism itself is not illegal, and viewers are typically arrested for differently named offenses such as trespassing or indecency (Rye & Meaney, 2007). Most voyeurs have similar characteristics of exhibitionists and frotteurs: they are almost always insecure males with feelings of social inadequacy. Also like exhibitionists and frotteurs, a courtship disorder may underlie the formation of this paraphilia. Their voyeurism usually begins in their early teens or 20s, and most voyeurs also have other paraphilias (Lavin, 2008).

gropes a woman with his hands, it's known as **toucherism**. Frotteurism and toucherism usually happen in a crowded place such as a subway or an elevator, where the man can easily escape or claim his actions were accidental. If he does not have an orgasm during the act, he may masturbate later on to images of his actions. Frotteurism is not uncommon; approximately 30–35% of women have reported unwanted or uninvited sexual touch, and 30–35% of the general population of adult males has committed at least one act that would qualify as frotteurism (Lussier & Piché, 2008). Frotteurism is strongly reinforced behaviorally by immediate sexual gratification with very little cost and investment (Långström, 2010).

It is most common in men between the ages of 15 and 25, and it becomes less common as men age (Seligman & Hardenburg, 2000). Men may exhibit frotteurism due to a courtship disorder.

Frotteurism/Toucherism

Some men become aroused by touching or rubbing against an unsuspecting person. A **frotteur** may rub his clothed penis against a woman's buttocks or thighs. When a man fondles and

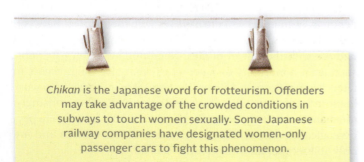

Chikan is the Japanese word for frotteurism. Offenders may take advantage of the crowded conditions in subways to touch women sexually. Some Japanese railway companies have designated women-only passenger cars to fight this phenomenon.

Pedophilia

Derived from the Greek words for love *(philia)* and young child *(pedeiktos)*, **pedophilia** is a paraphilia in which an adult is preferentially or sometimes exclusively sexually attracted to prepubescent children. To be classified as a pedophile, the individual needs to have had, over a period of at least 6 months, recurrent sexually arousing fantasies, urges, or behavior involving sexual activity with a

Frotteurism (FRAW-ter-izm) Recurrent or intense sexual urges or fantasies that involve rubbing against a nonconsenting person.

Toucherism Also called groping, this is when the offender touches intimate parts of a nonconsenting person with his hands.

Pedophilia A paraphilia in which an adult is preferentially or sometimes exclusively sexually attracted to prepubescent children.

prepubescent child (APA, 2000). The individual must be at least 16 years old and be at least 5 years older than the child or children to which he is sexually attracted. It is important to note that pedophilia is not synonymous with sexually offending against children (Seto, 2008). Some pedophiles never sexually abuse a child, and some sexual offenders against children are not pedophiles.

The vast majority of pedophiles are heterosexual men (Jenny, Roesler, & Poyer, 1994; Seto, 2008). Some pedophiles are attracted to girls, some to boys, and others are attracted to both, although twice as many girls than boys are victims of pedophiles. Ninety percent of the time, the molester is known to the child, and at least 15% are relatives (de Silva, 1999). Some pedophiles are only attracted to children; others are sometimes attracted to adults as well. It is important to distinguish among pedophilia, which is the sexual preference for prepubescent children (usually 11 or younger); **hebephilia**, a sexual preference for boys and girls in the early years of puberty; and **ephebophilia**, the sexual preference for mid- to late-adolescents and teens who have undergone puberty, usually those age 15 and older. Ephebophilia is not considered a mental disorder, and it is not considered unusual in our society for adults to be attracted to sexually mature (if legally minor) adolescents.

The pedophilic symbol for "child-love"

Pedophilia is considered the most common paraphilia, but this may be because it is most likely for those suspected of pedophilic behaviors to come under the attention of medical or legal professionals. Some estimate that 3–4% of the population are pedophiles, although the number may in fact be higher; this means there are well over 1 million pedophiles in the United States alone (Cloud, 2004; Seto, 2008). In one survey of male college students, 5–9% expressed an interest in or fantasies about having sex with young children (Seto, 2004); in another study of 193 male undergraduates, 21% reported some sexual attraction to small children, and 7% indicated some likelihood of having sex with a child if they would not be caught (Briere & Runtz, 1989). A person's sexual interest in children usually begins while he is an adolescent (Seto, 2008).

It is hard to make generalizations about pedophiles because most of what we know of them has come from clinical samples—those who are distressed about their desires and are seeking help, or those who have been convicted of criminal charges. From these samples, however, it has been shown that most pedophiles are heterosexual males in their 30s and 40s, with lower IQ scores and poorer self-esteem than normal (Blanchard et al., 2007). There may be a biological foundation for pedophilia. Pedophiles may have atypical hormonal and neurotransmitter levels (Maes et al., 2001), as well as neuroanatomical abnormalities. After one patient developed a tumor in his frontal lobe, he became unable to inhibit sexual urges and started exhibiting pedophilia. Once the tumor was removed, the inappropriate behavior ceased (Burns & Swerdlow, 2003). Pedophiles have also been shown to have less myelin in certain regions of the cortex (Cantor et al., 2008). There may also be psychological factors underlying pedophilia. These men may be socially inept and relate better to children than to adults (Seto, 2004).

The Internet has opened up a world of possibilities for pedophiles. Child molesters seek community on the web boards and chat rooms where they can exchange pictures of sexual abuse, share tips for getting near children, swap stories of their experiences, and, most frightening, find and stalk their victims (Eichenwald, 2006). The members of one website for pedophiles have created a booklet entitled "straight talk for boys," which they leave at locations likely to be found by young boys. The booklet promotes sexual encounters between children and adults. Children are encouraged to never tell their parents or therapists about sex with adults and are told of all the terrible things that will happen to them if they tell. Fellatio is described as "much like eating an ice cream cone." Parents should carefully monitor their children's computer use and consider using parental controls to filter certain websites. The sexual abuse of children will be covered in more depth in the next chapter.

Other Coercive Paraphilias

Biastophilia is a paraphilia in which a man can only become sexually aroused by the act of sexually assaulting an unconsenting person, usually a stranger, but without a preference for inflicting physical pain or injury on the victim (Thornton, 2010). It is thought that biastophilia may be the result of a courtship disorder.

Zoophilia is a persistent fantasy about or urge toward sexual contact with animals. Kinsey found that 1 out of every 13 men and 1 in 25 women admitted to sexual contact with animals at some time in their lives, most commonly with sheep, goats, dogs, and cats. Zoophilia is more frequently seen in men who were raised on farms and may sometimes be a transitory experience, if human partners are unavailable.

A **necrophiliac** is a person who is sexually attracted to dead bodies, usually in order to possess an unresisting partner who can't reject them. Rosman and Resnick (1989) described three types of necrophilias: Necrophiliac fantasy involves those who fantasize about having sex with dead people, but who don't actually act on their desires. A regular necrophiliac has sex with bodies that are already dead. Necrophiliac homicide occurs when a person kills others in order to have sex with their corpse. Between 1989 and 1991, serial killer Jeffrey Dahmer murdered 17 men and had sex with their dead bodies. Necrophiliacs often have jobs, such as in a mortuary or a cemetery, that give them access to dead bodies (Rosman & Resnick, 1989). Most people who work in these fields, however, do not have necrophilia. Unsurprisingly, men who want to have sex with corpses usually have severe psychological problems. They may hate and fear women and are only able to interact with one who is dead.

Hebephilia A sexual attraction and preference for boys and girls in the early years of puberty, typically ages 11–14.

Ephebophilia A sexual attraction and preference for adolescents who have gone through puberty.

Biastophilia A paraphilia in which sexual arousal is dependent on sexually assaulting or raping a nonconsenting victim.

Zoophilia (zoh-oh-FILL-ee-uh) Fantasies or urges to have sexual contact with animals. When actual sexual contact occurs, it is called **bestiality**.

Necrophilia A paraphilia in which a person wants to have sex with corpses.

Paraphilias in the Bible

There are a number of paraphilias mentioned in the Bible.

Bestiality: According to the Bible, sexual contact with animals is forbidden. The penalty for bestiality is death for both the offender and the animal.

Transvestism: In Deuteronomy 22:5 it states, "the woman shall not wear that which pertaineth unto a man, neither shall a man put on a woman's garment: for all that do so are abomination unto the Lord thy God."

Exhibitionism: When David "danced before the Lord with all his might," he was wearing a garment that was meager in size, and others saw his nakedness. He "uncovered himself today in the eyes of the handmaids of his servants."

Voyeurism: Noah got drunk and lay naked in his tent. His youngest son Ham, father of Canaan, saw his father's nakedness and told his other brothers, who covered Noah's nakedness. When Noah awoke, he cursed Ham's son Canaan. In another instance of voyeurism, David

watched Bathsheba taking a bath. She so sexually aroused him that David sent his messengers to bring her to him so he could have sexual intercourse with her, although she was married to another. In order to keep having sex with her, David sent Bathsheba's husband away to fight in the wars, where he was killed.

In addition, the Bible is chock-full of rape and incest, although in many of these instances these behaviors are not forbidden at all.

SOURCE: Aggrawal, 2009.

Treatment of the Paraphilias

After completion of this section, you will be able to . . .

○ Identify the factors that influence the likelihood that treatment for paraphilia will be successful.

○ Describe common medical, psychological, and behavioral treatments for paraphilias.

People with paraphilias usually don't want to refrain from the behaviors that give them sexual pleasure. And it is easy to see how a man with a noncoercive paraphilia might not need treatment—if someone is turned on by rubber or enjoys wearing women's clothing, who is he hurting? A man with noncoercive paraphilic behaviors may seek treatment if his sexual outlet causes him distress or negatively impacts his personal or professional life. Coercive paraphilias, on the other hand, violate others, and these behaviors need to be addressed.

People with paraphilias seek treatment for different reasons. Some are self-motivated to change behaviors they can't seem to control or concerned about the negative impact their behaviors are having on their intimate relationship. Others are ordered by the court to seek treatment; success for these men is variable because they may not be inwardly motivated to change (de Silva, 1999). Treatment of the paraphilia is more successful when the patient enters therapy voluntarily, is highly motivated to change, and believes that change is possible. Treatment is less successful when the paraphilia had an early onset or when it is the patient's only sexual outlet. Success is also less likely if the patient has coexisting mental disorders. The behavior of the therapist can also affect the success of the treatment. The therapist's empathy, warmth, and encouragement are predictive of the success of sexual offender treatment (Marshall, Marshall, & Serran, 2006).

There is no "cure" for paraphilias; instead, treatment aims to change the patient's behavior by reducing symptoms and preventing relapse. Therapists should start by assessing the nature

and scope of the paraphilia. They may gain information from self-reports, patient observations and interviews, personality tests, or physiological tests such as penile plethysmography, polygraph tests, or visual reaction time tests that indicate how long a subject spends looking at a particular image. Once a diagnosis has been made, treatment is often multifaceted and may involve group and individual therapy, medications, and behavior modification.

During individual therapy sessions, therapists may help their patients to understand the root cause of their paraphilia by exploring childhood experiences. Simply discussing issues from a patient's youth is not very successful at eliminating coercive paraphilias, however, because these powerful urges have been maintained by years of conditioning. Patients may also schedule therapy sessions with their partners to improve their communication skills. Cognitive behavioral therapy may help the patient to understand the distortions in his thinking and guide him in shifting to more acceptable behavior. Patients may also participate in group therapy with others who share their paraphilia. In these sessions, patients are confronted and encouraged by those with similar issues and can also reduce their isolation. Patients can improve their conversational techniques, learn to empathize with others, and enhance their self-esteem through **social skills training**.

Some therapists guide their paraphilic patients through **aversion therapy**, in which the patient links the previously arousing thoughts (exhibiting themselves to others, fantasies of sexual activity with a child) to aversive stimuli, with the hopes that the unacceptable behaviors will be newly linked to negative associations. The aversive stimuli might be physical or imaginary.

Social skills training A form of behavioral therapy designed to help people who have difficulties relating to other people.

Aversion therapy A form of behavior modification therapy, now uncommon, that uses unpleasant stimuli in a controlled fashion in order to change a patient's behavior in a therapeutic way.

Table 15.2 Worldwide Laws on Paraphilias

	CANADA	CHINA	GERMANY	INDIA	UNITED STATES
Exhibitionism	Indecent exposure is illegal. The courts determine the exact definition of terms such as "indecent act," and "clad so as to offend against public decency or order."	"Whoever acts indecently against or insults a woman by violence, coercion, or any other forcible means shall be sentenced to fixed term imprisonment of not more than 5 years." Heavier punishments are given to those who act indecently against a child.	"A man who annoys another person by an exhibitionist act shall be punished with imprisonment for not more than one year or a fine." Exhibitionism is treated more as a psychiatric disease than as a criminal act, in that if an offender can be cured after treatment, the court may suspend imprisonment.	"Whoever, intending to insult the modesty of any woman, utters any word, makes any sound or gesture, or exhibits any object, intending that such word or sound shall be heard, or that such gesture or object shall be seen by such woman, or intrudes upon the privacy of such woman, shall be punished with simple imprisonment for a term which may extend to one year, with fine, or both." Prosecution can be difficult, as prosecutors must prove the *intent* of the offender, and the victim must be a woman.	No federal law allows or prohibits exhibitionism. The legality of various forms of undress is left to the individual states to decide.
Zoophilia/ Bestiality	Bestiality is a crime in Canada. Punishable by imprisonment for a term not exceeding 10 years.	Bestiality not specifically outlawed. However, if injury results to an animal as a result of bestiality, person may be sentenced to not less than 3 years and not more than 7 years in prison.	There is no specific punishment for having sex with animals. However, pornography that shows sexual acts of human beings with animals is illegal. So having sex with an animal is not against the law, but watching someone else do it, is.	"Whoever voluntarily has carnal intercourse against the order of nature with any man, woman, or animal, shall be punished with imprisonment for life, or with imprisonment of either description for a term which my extend to 10 years and shall also be liable to fine."	There are no laws against bestiality in Arkansas, Montana, and North Carolina. Bestiality is officially illegal in 30 states. However, even if no bestiality laws exist, offenders can still be charged under animal cruelty laws.
Necrophilia	Anyone who improperly or indecently interferes with a dead human body or human remains may be liable to imprisonment for a term not exceeding 5 years.	N/A	A person who, without authorization, takes away parts of the body of a deceased person (which includes a dead fetus or ashes of a deceased person) and commits "insulting mischief thereon" may be imprisoned for not more than 3 years or receive a fine.	There is no explicit law against necrophilia. But it is a crime to trespass in a funeral home or depository for remains of the dead, or to cause any indignity to any human corpse. This crime may be punished with up to 1 year's imprisonment, a fine, or both.	There is no federal legislation specifically barring sex with a corpse. Many states have laws against it, and penalties range from misdemeanor to felony.

© Cengage Learning 2013. SOURCE: Aggrawal, 2009.

Orgasmic reconditioning aims to reinforce acceptable sexual behavior with the pleasure of an orgasm. The patient is instructed to masturbate while fantasizing about his paraphilic object or behavior but to switch to a more acceptable image as orgasm approaches. With time, the patient switches to the acceptable fantasy earlier and earlier in the fantasy.

Some therapists prescribe pharmacological treatments for their more recalcitrant patients. Selective serotonin reuptake inhibitors (SSRIs) such as Prozac have been used successfully to treat paraphilias such as exhibitionism, voyeurism, and fetishism (Bradford, 2001). SSRIs may work through a general reduction in sex drive or by controlling compulsive behaviors. Anti-androgen drugs that reduce the patient's circulating testosterone levels reduce sexual desire and behaviors. Men taking Depo-Provera show less response to erotic stimuli when measured by plethysmograph (Bradford, 2001). Depo-Provera can be given orally or by injection, and its side effects include weight gain, headache, and breast growth. Its success rate is limited because many men elect to stop taking the drug. Other anti-

Orgasmic reconditioning A behavioral therapy technique designed to reinforce acceptable sexual behaviors, in which a client is instructed to switch from a paraphilic fantasy to a fantasy of a conventional sexual stimulus or behavior as orgasm approaches.

androgen drugs include cyproterone acetate (CPA) and drugs that increase the effects of gonadotropin-releasing hormone (GnRH).

Variations in Sexual Frequency

After completion of this section, you will be able to . . .

○ Define *asexuality* and *hypersexuality*.

○ Evaluate whether variations in sexual frequency such as asexuality or hypersexuality should be pathologized.

ASK YOURSELF

Is asexuality a separate sexual identity—a "fourth" sexual orientation, if you will? Is it a disorder that needs treatment? Why do you think so?

Just as people engage in a wide variety of sexual activities, there is also a world of difference in the frequency with which people have sex. Is there a "normal" level of sexual activity? Should deviations from the statistical mean be treated as a disorder?

Many things can change a person's level of sexual desire over the course of his or her life. And in many cases, these conditions can be reversed—with medical intervention, psychological counseling, or a new lover. But some people may be born with a sex drive outside of "normal" parameters.

Asexuality

Sexual desire can wax and wane over the course of a person's life (Berin, 2009). It can change based on the status of one's relationship, a person's physical condition, or his or her drug use. Chromosomal abnormalities (such as Turner's syndrome) can lower sexual desire, and traumatic events in childhood such as sexual abuse may lead to an aversion to sex. Sometimes these conditions can be changed, or a person may seek treatment to regain his or her sexual appetite. But when a lack of desire is not due to drugs, disease, or life experience and is just an essential part of one's makeup, a person may be considered **asexual**.

Asexuality is not celibacy—a behavioral choice to not have sex—nor is it a temporarily diminished sexual desire such as hypoactive sexual desire. It is more properly considered a sexual orientation, in that an asexual person has no sexual desire for either men or women.

Asexuality may be expressed in various ways. For the most part, asexuals are not averse to or afraid of sex, and they may have sex out of curiosity or to please a partner (Prause & Graham, 2007). Some asexuals have no sex, whereas others have friendships that include cuddling and affectionate physical encounters (Bogaert, 2004). Some asexuals masturbate but report that it doesn't feel sexual when they do so (Prause & Graham, 2007).

In a sample of more than 18,000 British residents, approximately 1% of the population of adults reported that they never felt sexual attraction to anyone at all (Bogaert, 2004). However, it may be difficult to establish the true incidence of asexuality. Just as men and those with more sexual partners are over-represented in most surveys of sexuality, asexuals may be less likely to participate and thus be under-represented in this sample. Also, this study involved face-to-face interviews with subjects; asexuals might be less likely to admit their lack of sexual desire to a researcher (indeed, the incidence of homosexuality in the Bogaert study was similarly lower than in other surveys).

There may be biological causes underlying asexuality. Asexual women were found to be shorter than sexual women and to have a later onset of menarche, perhaps suggesting that a low sex drive is indicative of a hormone imbalance. People with adverse health were more likely to report a lack of sexual attraction; however, it is important not to confuse correlation with causation. Although poor health may dampen one's sex drive, it may also be that a lack of sex hurts one's health! Psychological factors such as a history of sexual abuse may predispose one to be asexual. Also, factors such as socioeconomic status (SES) and religion may come into play; asexuals tended to have lower SES and greater attendance at religious services (Bogaert, 2004). Again, religiosity does not necessarily cause a lack of sex drive. Although it may be that being raised with strong religious values dampens one's libido, it could also be that asexuals are drawn to religions because their strictures suit their asexual lifestyle.

Hypersexuality

Many people can have a drink at the end of the day with no ill effects. But when the obsessive need for alcohol negatively affects a person's work, relationships, and health, he or she may have a problem. Just as with alcohol, drugs, or gambling, people may also compulsively pursue sex, and their obsessive need for sex may harm their health, their personal or work relationships, their finances, or even get them in trouble with the law. Incidentally, when those with sexual behavior disorders come afoul of the law, they cannot legally claim that their "disease made them do it" because paraphilias are currently excluded from the Americans with Disabilities Act (Orzack & Ross, 2000).

Alfred Kinsey once joked that "most guys define a nymphomaniac as any woman who wants to have sex more than they do" (cited in Groneman, 2001, p. 158). **Nymphomania** and **satyrism** are psychological terms describing women and men, respectively, with an obsessive and uncontrollable sexual desire. Today, people often use the terms *sexual addiction* or *sexual compulsion* to describe **hypersexuality**. (Whether sexual addiction exists is a topic of hot debate among those who study sexuality. This issue is considered on page 401.)

Most people enjoy sex, many people have experienced sexual guilt at some time, and some have participated in sexual activities such as unsafe sex that could hurt them in some way. What differentiates these people from sexual compulsives? Hypersexual behavior often shares many characteristics with **obsessive-compulsive disorder (OCD)**, addictive behaviors, or impulse control disorders. Sexual compulsives spend much of their

Asexuality When a person does not experience any sexual attraction to either sex.

Hypersexuality An excessive interest in sex, to the point where it can cause problems in one's life.

Nymphomania (NIM-foe-MAY-nee-uh) and **satyrism (SAY-ter-ism)** Women and men, respectively, with obsessive and uncontrollable sexual desire.

Obsessive-compulsive disorder (OCD) An anxiety disorder characterized by intrusive, unwanted thoughts and repetitive, compulsive acts.

In 2008 actor David Duchovny entered treatment for sex addiction. Golfer Tiger Woods (pictured) sought treatment in 2010.

time obsessively thinking about sex, pursuing it, and then recovering from it (Miner, Coleman, Center, Ross, & Rosser, 2006). Their sexual pleasure is intensified by the ritualized behaviors with which they prepare for their erotic experiences. Often, sexual compulsives keep their actions secret; their closest friends and loved ones may have no idea of their actions. The sex itself is often harmful or abusive to themselves or to others. After sex, the sexual compulsive may experience depression, anxiety, and shame and vow to change his or her behavior. Some who describe themselves as "addicted" to sex often feel that they lack control over their actions, whereas others minimize the impact that sex is having on their lives, telling themselves that they could "quit any time" (Carnes, 2003; Earle & Crowe, 1990). Although a sexual compulsive's behaviors are harmful, his or her actions continue despite the adverse consequences. He or she may hit bottom when "the cycles of sex addiction become so expensive spiritually, emotionally, vocationally, martially, physically, and, sometimes, legally (when they involve criminal activities such as obscene telephone calls, voyeurism, exhibitionism, rape, incest, and child molestation) that the pain of the addiction outweighs the euphoria" (Earle & Crow, 1990, p. 93).

Hypersexuality may be manifested in many ways, including compulsive masturbation; lots of anonymous sex with multiple partners; having many extramarital affairs; exhibitionism, voyeurism, or other coercive sexual offenses; or dependence on pornography, phone sex, or cybersex. With so many new sex-related sites added to the web each day, the Internet gives sexual compulsives access to many of their sexual desires in one place (Carnes, 2003). Cybersex is available, anonymous, and affordable. It allows for instant accessibility and an endless variety of

new sexual material. On the Internet, the sexual compulsive can act out fantasies, find sex partners, join chat rooms, access porn sites, watch others having sex, or be watched themselves (Cooper, Scherer, Boies & Gordon, 1999). However, many millions of Americans access porn on the Internet, and most say that their online behavior doesn't interfere with or jeopardize any area of their lives. In one study, only 8% of those who access sexual sites on the web reported spending more than 11 hours per week accessing pornography online (Cooper et al., 1999).

As with all sexual disorders, it is difficult to ascertain the true incidence of hypersexuality, but it is usually estimated to affect from 3–6% of the population, although it is not clear what criteria were used to make these estimates (Kaplan & Krueger, 2010). Eighty percent of those who seek treatment for sexual compulsion are male (Carnes, 2009). In one study of men and women who self-identified as sexual compulsives, men reported a mean of 59.3 sexual partners over the previous 5 years, and women reported a mean of 8.0 partners in the same time period (Black, Kehrberg, Flumerfelt, & Shlosser, 1997). Many other studies also find a discrepancy in the reports of sexual behavior in male and female compulsives (Winters, Christoff, & Gorzalka, 2010). The fact that the women in the study—who had one eighth as many sexual partners as the men—defined themselves as sexual compulsives says a lot about the sexual double standard placed on men and women in our society (Kaplan & Krueger, 2010).

Sexual compulsives often have poor self-esteem, trouble dealing with stress, and hold unrealistic beliefs about themselves and their relationships with others. They may overestimate the power or importance of sex and continuously try to reclaim the "high" they got from a previous sexual experience. They also may want to escape from unpleasant emotions and use sex as an outlet to relieve their depression or anxiety (Earle & Crowe, 1990).

Both biological and environmental factors may cause compulsive sexuality. Hypersexuality's similarities to OCD and addictive behavior have suggested that comparable neural mechanisms may underlie these conditions. However, consistent findings regarding sex addicts' endocrine or neural functioning are lacking. Those who engage in "excessive" sexuality may have underlying feelings of depression, poor self-esteem, and anxiety, which are temporarily relieved by sexual behaviors that release the "reward" neurotransmitter dopamine (Carnes, 2003). Sexual compulsivity may begin in childhood or adolescence. Sexual compulsives may grow up in a home where they were neglected and starved for love, such that sex becomes the replacement for other forms of human contact. They may have been raised to think that sex is sinful and should be hidden (Earle & Crow, 1990).

Sexual compulsion encompasses many issues—sexuality, childhood fears, poor self-image, and underdeveloped social skills—so it may require a variety of treatment options (Earle & Crow, 1990). Usually, it is the addict's family members who encourage him or her to enter treatment; loved ones who are affected by the sexual compulsive's behavior can also benefit from counseling.

Patients may undergo individualized therapy to explore the root causes and to learn to deal with the mental processes of addiction or compulsion. Group therapy can help patients address their issues with others who share the problem. Pharmaceuticals may help to reduce obsessive behaviors or sex drive.

critical evaluation

Is there such a thing as sexual addiction?

> ## What is a "normal" amount of sex?

"Normal" and "deviance" are ambiguous terms. "Normal" sexual behavior is socially relative and changes greatly from place to place, from time to time, and from person to person. Does a person necessarily have a mental disorder just because he or she participates in activities that society considers atypical?

By what standards are the "normal" rates of sexual frequency determined? Do the standards depend on a person's age or gender? If so, could a person have the same behavior each day and then suddenly reach an age when that behavior is now considered deviant?

What values underlie the impulse to label someone with a mental disorder if his or her sexual activities are different from ours?

> ## How is sexual addiction defined?

At what point does compulsive sexual behavior become an addiction? When a person feels too much guilt? When their family, work, or friends are affected? If no one is harmed or upset by the activity, does that mean it's not a problem?

Sexual addiction is currently not included in the *DSM*, the handbook that provides diagnostic criteria for mental disorders. Does that necessarily mean it's not a valid diagnosis?

> ## How is sexual addiction diagnosed?

Is sexual addiction diagnosed with a definitive test? By the patient's own identification? By others' assessment of one's behavior?

One of the major diagnostic tools for sexual addiction is the "sexual addiction screening test," which is extremely ambiguous at best. Some of the questions on the test include, "Did your parents have trouble with sexual behavior?" "Do you often find yourself preoccupied with sexual thoughts?" and "Do you ever feel bad about your sexual behavior?" Such open-ended and indistinct terminology has the potential to lead to over-diagnosis.

Another question on the test is "Do you feel guilt or shame after having sex?" If a person answers "yes," does that necessarily mean his or her behavior is addictive, or could it mean that someone feels shame because of a normal, healthy activity?

> ## Where do we get our data on sex addiction?

Most of our information about sexually compulsive behavior comes from patients who are unhappy with their actions, or who are forced to seek treatment. How much can we generalize their behavior?

> ## How do sexually compulsive behaviors compare to addiction to drugs or alcohol?

Not all health professionals agree on the definition of addiction. Some limit the term to those substances that lead to physical dependence, neurological changes, and **withdrawal** symptoms when the substance is removed. By this definition, sex is not addictive because people don't go through physical withdrawal when they are not engaged in sex. However, many others broaden the definition of addiction to include substances or behaviors to which one can become psychologically dependent. Psychological addiction can cause a person to pursue a behavior compulsively and show a lack of control over his actions. He may try—unsuccessfully—to stop the behavior, but it continues despite adverse consequences. In this way,

sexual compulsivity does fit a definition of addiction. Which definition of addiction has the most validity? Why do you think so?

For recovering alcoholics or drug addicts, even one drink is too much and they live the rest of their lives—albeit one day at a time—without ever indulging again. Can the same be said about sex?

> ## Should we consider social and personal ramifications?

By recognizing sexual addiction as a disease, do we negate personal responsibility? Are people who act in ways that might hurt their family, friends, or career more likely to say, "My addiction made me do it and it's not my fault"?

By encouraging people to "admit" that they are powerless, the concept of sexual addiction prevents people from examining how they came to feel powerless—and what they can do about that feeling (Klein, 1998). This careful examination, ultimately, is the source of personality growth and behavior change.

If a person calls himself a "sex addict," he has not differentiated between what he did and who he is. To what degree are we defined by our actions?

Social skills training and self-help groups such as **Sexaholics Anonymous (SA)** or Sex Addicts Anonymous may help. In SA, "sobriety" is limited to sex between a man or woman and his or her legally married spouse. Masturbation is prohibited at all times. This can be problematic on a number of levels. In most of the United States, this condemns many gays and lesbians who define themselves as sexually compulsive to a life of celibacy because in most states they can't legally wed. For those who are able to marry, it puts a person's entire sexual destiny into the hands (so to speak) of his or her spouse. If their spouse decides that they don't want any more sexual contact, then the sex addict must also live a life of celibacy. Finally, this "just say no" policy doesn't teach the sexual compulsive decision-making skills or help him to evaluate sexual situations (Klein, 1998).

Sexologists don't universally agree whether hypersexuality should be classified as an addiction. Those who believe it does cite the similar behaviors of sexual compulsives to those who are addicted to alcohol or drugs. Others think hypersexuality is not a disease, but rather a way to pathologize unconventional sexual

behaviors and enforce conservative values. The Critical Evaluation box addresses some of these issues.

• • •

One of the quotations that began this chapter states, "There is hardly anyone whose sexual life, if it were broadcast, would not fill the world at large with surprise and horror." Most people have at one time engaged in sexual activity that would appall and disgust someone else. The concepts of sexual normalcy and deviance are largely defined by sociocultural standards, and are therefore a moving target. However, when one's sexual proclivities infringe on the rights of another, the behavior needs to stop.

Withdrawal A group of symptoms that occurs after abrupt discontinuation of a drug. These symptoms are usually the opposite of the drug itself. For instance, heroin use causes relaxation, analgesia, and constipation, and withdrawal from the drug causes agitation, pain, and diarrhea.

Sexaholics Anonymous (SA) A 12-step program designed to help people recover from sex addiction.

Chapter Summary

Introduction

- Views of sexual normalcy and deviance are dependent on societal norms, which change from time to time, and from culture to culture.

- Paraphilias are a strong sexual urge toward nonhuman objects, the suffering or humiliation of one's self or others, or children or other nonconsenting people. Paraphilias can be divided into noncoercive or coercive. Noncoercive paraphilias include fetishism, transvestic fetishism, and sexual sadomasochism. Coercive paraphilias include pedophilia, exhibitionism, voyeurism, and frotteurism.

- Like other sexual behaviors, paraphilias exist on a continuum. Some people use their paraphilic object or behavior to occasionally enhance the sexual experience, whereas others cannot function sexually without the object or behavior.

- It is almost impossible to definitively assess the prevalence of paraphilias because most people keep their actions secret and don't seek help. Almost all paraphiliacs are male. Most paraphiliacs have more than one paraphilia. They may have emotional problems, impulse control disorders, or other compulsive behaviors. Others function well in their day-to-day lives.

- Paraphilias probably have a combination of biological, psychological, and sociological causes.

Noncoercive Paraphilias

- Fetishism is a paraphilia in which a person has sexually arousing fantasies and behaviors regarding an inanimate object. Common fetishistic objects include lingerie, shoes, silk, rubber, leather, feet, or hair.

- Heterosexual men who derive sexual pleasure from wearing women's clothes are said to have transvestic fetishism. Transvestites are not to be confused with drag queens, who are men, usually gay, who wear women's clothes for entertainment, and male-to-female (MTF) transsexuals, who identify as women and are more comfortable in women's clothing.

- BDSM is an acronym that stands for bondage and discipline, dominance and submission, and sadomasochism. The BDSM relationship is based on the concept of partners voluntarily taking on deliberately unequal yet complementary roles. The top—or dominant partner—is more physically or emotionally controlling, while the bottom—or submissive partner—is controlled.

- In sadomasochism, physical and psychological pain enhances a person's sexual pleasure. Masochists derive pleasure from being hurt or humiliated, and sadists enjoy hurting or humiliating others. Most of those who practice S&M can switch between being the dominant and the submissive partner.

- Other noncoercive paraphilias include urophilia, sexual arousal from contact with urine; sploshing, sexual enjoyment from having wet and messy substance smeared on one's body; and infantalism, the desire to dress as and be treated like an infant.

Coercive Paraphilias

- An exhibitionist is a person, usually male, who is sexually aroused by exposing his genitals to an unsuspecting stranger. Most victims of exhibitionism are girls and women between the ages of 10 and 19. Exhibitionists may enjoy their victim's shock and fear.

- Men who prefer to shock women with their words are obscene phone callers, who have telephone scatologia. Types of obscene phone calls may be classified based on the perceived threat level of the victim. Most women have received an obscene phone call at least once in their lives. The best course of action upon receiving a call is not to show shock or distress, but to simply hang up, and contact the phone company or police if the calls continue or seem threatening.

- A voyeur is a man who is sexually aroused by watching unsuspecting strangers in the act of undressing or having sexual activities. Voyeurs may peek through windows or drill holes in bathroom or dressing room walls, but new technology allows them to install small cameras in public places to view and record their unknowing victims.

- Frotteurism is sexual arousal that comes from touching or rubbing against an unsuspecting person. Frotteurs often act in crowded places such as elevators or subways.

- An adult who is preferentially or exclusively attracted to prepubescent children is a pedophile. Those who are attracted to adolescents who have gone through puberty are ephebophiles, and hebephiles have a sexual preference for boys and girls in the early years of puberty. Pedophilia is reported to be the most common of paraphilias, but this may be because it is most likely for those suspected of pedophilic behaviors to come under the attention of medical or legal professionals. Most pedophiles are heterosexual men. The Internet allows pedophiles to share pictures, tell of their experiences, and find victims.

- Other coercive paraphilias include zoophilia, a persistent urge toward sexual contact with animals, and necrophilia, the desire to have sex with corpses.

Treatment of the Paraphilias

- Most people with paraphilia don't want to be "cured" because their predilections are sometimes their sole source of sexual pleasure. Although the noncoercive paraphilias are generally harmless, they may cause stress in a relationship. The coercive paraphilias involve unsuspecting victims, and coercive paraphiliacs need to learn to modify their behavior.

- Because paraphilias often have biological, psychological, and sociological roots, their treatment is similarly multifaceted. Paraphiliacs may undergo individual and group therapy, social skills training, aversion therapy, orgasmic reconditioning, and pharmaceutical interventions.

Variations in Sexual Frequency

- Just as people engage in a wide variety of sexual activities, there is also a world of difference in the frequency in which people have sex. It is hard to determine what a "normal" level of sexual activity is.

- Asexuals have no desire for sex with men or women. Although some asexuals are not in an intimate relationship, others are, and may engage in sexual behaviors to please their partners. Perhaps 1% of the population may be asexual.

- Hypersexuals have a compulsive need for sex, to the degree that it may harm their health, personal, or work relationships; cause financial crises; or get them in trouble with the law. As with other paraphilias, hypersexuality shares many characteristics with other compulsive behaviors.

- Both asexuality and hypersexuality may have biological or psychological foundations.

What is normal sexual behavior? That which is done most frequently by most people? Many people have at some point taken part in sexual activities that others might consider "deviant."

evaluate and *decide*

Consider the following situations:

> Alice has been married for 15 years to Charlie. For the past few months, she's noticed that her sweaters are stretched out and her bras are rearranged in her drawer. Last week she came home from work unexpectedly and found Charlie in their bedroom, wearing her clothing.

> It has been discovered that the manager of Aniko's gym has installed a small video camera in the women's locker room. Aniko now frantically tries to remember where she usually stands in the locker room to think if she's been observed getting undressed.

What factors will you consider in advising these people? Consider the issues and questions below to make your decision.

SITUATION	ISSUES TO CONSIDER
TRANSVESTISM	Assuming that Alice insists Charlie's behavior stop immediately, what does she risk losing? What might she gain? If she accepts his behavior, what are her potential gains and losses? Based on this information, what do you think Alice should do? What are your underlying value assumptions that supported your decision?
	Which is worse—the fact that Charlie is wearing Alice's clothes, or the fact that he has kept this from her for 15 years? Why?
	Alice routinely wears Charlie's T-shirts when lounging around the house. When Charlie points this out, she says, "That's different." Do you agree? Why or why not?
VOYEURISM	Aniko hasn't been physically touched in any way, but she feels violated. Can being observed without his or her knowledge hurt a person? In what way?
	What should the legal ramifications be for the manager's actions?
	How does voyeurism compare to other coercive paraphilias?
	Many people paid to download the Paris Hilton sex tapes, which may have been recorded without Paris's knowledge. Are the thousands of people who watched this tape voyeurs? Why or why not?

Additional Resources

Log in to CengageBrain to access the resources your instructor requires. For this book, you can access:

 **CourseMate** brings course concepts to life with interactive learning, study, and exam preparation tools that support the printed textbook. A textbook-specific website, Psychology CourseMate includes an integrated interactive eBook and other interactive learning tools including quizzes, flashcards, videos, and more.

CENGAGENOW **CengageNOW** is an easy-to-use online resource that helps you study in less time to get the grade you want—NOW. Take a pre-test for this chapter and receive a personalized study plan based on your results that will identify the topics you need to review and direct you to online resources to help you master those topics. Then take a post-test to help you determine the concepts you have mastered and what you will need to work on. If your textbook does not include an access code card, go to CengageBrain.com to gain access. Visit www.cengagebrain.com anytime to access your account and purchase materials.Current links

to all of the following websites and videos can be found on the Psychology CourseMate for this text at www.cengagebrain.com/

Web Resources
What Are Paraphilias?
A site that defines and describes many of the common paraphilias.

Sex Education Links
Educational information about the paraphilias. Includes resources, FAQs, research, etc.

Human Sexuality: An Encyclopedia
Lists and defines many various paraphilias.

Straight Talk on Sex, Love, and Intimacy
"Why there's no such thing as sexual addiction—and why it really matters," by Marty Klein.

SexHelp.com
Patrick Carnes's site for those affected by sex addiction.

Print Resources
Aggrawal, A. (2009). *Forensic and Medico-Legal Aspects of Sexual Crimes and Unusual Sexual Practices*. Boca Raton, FL: CRC Press.

Carnes, P.J. (2009). Can sex be addictive? In W.J. Taverner (Ed.), *Taking Sides: Clashing Views on Controversial Issues in Human Sexuality* (11th ed.). Dubuque, IA: McGraw-Hill/Dushkin.

Siegel, L.A., & Siegel, R.M. (2009). Can sex be addictive? In W.J. Taverner (Ed.), *Taking Sides: Clashing Views on Controversial Issues in Human Sexuality* (11th ed.). Dubuque, IA: McGraw-Hill/Dushkin.

Video Resources
Glen or Glenda. (1953). 67 minutes. Ed Wood's (voted the worst director of all time) film of cross-dressing. So awful it's funny.

Happiness. (1998). 134 minutes. Film by Todd Solenz. Chock full of paraphilias such as obscene phone calls, masochism, and voyeurism, as well as child molestation. A happy tale of a normal American family.

Secretary. (2002). 104 minutes. A young woman, recently released from a mental hospital, gets a job as a secretary to a demanding lawyer, where their employer-employee relationship turns into a mutually satisfying, sexual, sadomasochistic one.

16

Sexual Coercion and Violence

"Daddy they'll know
I'll walk funny and they'll know I've been bad
Daddy please don't please don't please don't
I'm shaking all over
I squeeze my legs together just as tight as I can
You can't you can't you can okay okay okay
Tracing the truth through the tangle of lies
Forgiving myself what I did to survive
I am living I am living"

—Fred Small and Jayne Habe
© Fred Small. All rights reserved.

© Marja Airio/Age fotostock

© Corbis RF

© Colin Anderson/Getty Images

/ 405

Power plays a role in all human interactions, including sexual ones. Sexual coercion occurs when this power—be it physical, emotional, or occupational—is used against another to force her or him into unwanted sexual activity. The abuse of sexual power can include sexual harassment or sexual assault and rape against adults or children. Anyone—man, woman, or child—may be a victim of sexual coercion, although women and children are particularly at risk. Most sexually coercive behaviors are done by men, but perpetrators are not usually, as many people believe, the suspicious stranger in the shadows. It is a grim reality that most of these crimes are committed by victims' relatives, partners, and neighbors. Although this chapter may be the most painful part of this book to read (and it was indeed the most painful to write), all people need to be informed about rape, child sexual abuse, intimate partner violence, and sexual harassment in order to better prevent these events from occurring.

Rape

After completion of this section, you will be able to . . .

- O   Define *sexual assault, rape,* and *age of consent.*

- O   Report the incidence and prevalence of rape, and understand the difficulties in getting an accurate assessment of its scope.

- O   Understand some theories as to why rape occurs.

- O   List some popular myths about rape.

- O   Characterize and define *stranger rape, acquaintance and date rape, partner rape, gang rape, statutory rape,* and *prison rape.*

- O   Consider the issue of rape on campus, and the role of alcohol in these sexual assaults.

- O   Describe some typical characteristics of rapists.

- O   Explain the effect of rape on survivors.

- O   Understand ways to protect yourself from rape.

- O   Consider the role of rape through history, and the effect of societal forces on rape.

Sexual assault is a term that encompasses a number of crimes, from unwanted sexual contact to forced intercourse. It can include unwanted touch of sexual body parts or the penetration of the vagina, mouth, or anus. It occurs without the victim's consent; sexual assault may take place with the use of threats or force, or if the victim is unable to give consent due to intoxication, mental impairment, or being below the age of consent. Sexual assault is a more general term than **rape**. In the past, rape was defined as the unwanted penetration of a woman's vagina by a man's penis. Recently, however, the definition of rape has been expanded and refers to nonconsensual sexual penetration of a man or woman's body by physical force or the

---

Sexual assault Sexual contact or activity that occurs without consent.

Rape (from the Latin *rapere,* meaning "to seize") The unwanted sexual penetration of the vagina, mouth, or anus by use of force or threat.

---

threat of harm. Rape can include forced penetration by objects other than the penis, and penetration of the mouth or anus as well as the vagina. The exact legal definition of rape varies from country to country and from state to state.

Incidence and Prevalence of Rape

In 2009, 89,000 women reported being raped in the United States (Leinwand, 2009). However, most rapes are never reported. The actual number of women who are raped each year in the United States is estimated to be between 300,000 and 683,000, which would mean that a woman is raped every 6 minutes in the United States (Tjaden & Thoennes, 2000, 2006). The National Institute of Justice, together with the Centers for Disease Control (CDC), surveyed more than 16,000 men and women, and found that 1 of every 6 women (17.6%) and 1 of every 33 men (3%) have experienced a completed or attempted rape in their lifetimes (Tjaden & Thoennes, 2000, 2006). Many believe these numbers underestimate the scope of rape in America, and that as many as 27% of women in the United States experience a completed or attempted rape during their lifetimes, making rape more common than left-handedness or alcoholism (Gannon & Ward, 2008; Wolf, 1992). Although the prevalence is horrifying, the good news is that the frequency of rape appears to be declining and has decreased by more than 85% since the 1970s (National Crime Victimization Survey [NCVS], 2004). The decrease may be attributed to greater education and awareness, as well as increased punishments for rapists. On the other hand, the decline may not represent an actual decrease in the incidence of rape but instead be due to a change in the way that the Justice Department gathers statistics about rape.

It is hard to accurately assess the occurrence of rape because of under-reporting and because of variations in the way relevant data are gathered. Experts believe that 61–95% of rapes are never reported to police and are thus not a part of the government's estimates of the crime (Koss, 1988; NCVS, 2004; Warshaw, 1994; Wolitzky-Taylor et al., 2010). Victims might not report sexual assaults because they think that no one will believe them or because they mistrust the criminal justice system. Some fear reprisals from the rapist, and others just try to block out and deny their experience. As many as 73% of victims of date rape don't identify their experience as rape, even when it meets the legal criteria for sexual assault (Szymanski, Devlin, Chrisler, & Vyse, 1993; Wolitzky-Taylor et al., 2010). Additionally, women are less likely to report a date rape if alcohol or drugs were involved (Wolitzky-Taylor et al., 2010). Others don't report their assault due to feelings of shame because rape victims are still stigmatized in this society. Men who have been raped by men are especially unlikely to report their attack; doing so would mean they'd have to confront the additional stigma of being considered homosexual.

Rape estimates also vary due to differences in data gathering, such as the operational definition, the sample used, and even the wording of the survey. For example, according to the FBI's description, rape is narrowly defined as forced vaginal intercourse with a woman. Based on this definition, only women can be raped, thus negating the experience of 93,000 men a year (Tjaden & Thoennes, 2006). The FBI also does not consider forced oral or anal sex, statutory rape, or the use of drugs to subdue a victim to be rape.

Whether a report gives the "incidence" or the "prevalence" of sexual assault can also change the estimation. The *incidence* is the number of new cases that occur in a given time period, whereas the *prevalence* is the percentage of people who have been sexually assaulted in a specified time period; "lifetime" and "in the past year" are common time frames used in the assessment of prevalence. *Incidence* may better reflect the scope of rape because 39% of women who have been raped have been raped more than once Kilpatrick, Edwards, & Seymour, 1992). Finally, the wording of the survey can greatly affect the results. Fewer people will answer yes to the question "Have you ever been raped?" than to the question "Have you ever had sexual intercourse when you didn't want to because a man threatened or used some degree of physical force to make you do so?" (Koss, Gidycz, & Wisniewski, 1987).

Theories About Rape

What drives one person to rape another? Two of the most prominent theories about rape are discussed below.

Feminist Theory

According to feminist theory, rape is a tool used by men in our society to keep women submissive and powerless (Brownmiller, 1993). Feminist theorists believe that rapists are primarily motivated not by a desire for sex but by the need to dominate and control women in an attempt to preserve a system of male supremacy. Men and women in Western society are taught to act in ways that support this hierarchy; men are conditioned to be dominant, aggressive, and sexually charged, and women are taught to be dependent, submissive, and passive. According to this theory, the goal of rape is power, dominance, and control over women; violence and sex are the means and tactics used to assert that power (Archer & Vaughn, 2001).

There is evidence to support the idea that rape is due to gender inequality and power differentials between men and women in society; rape is more prevalent in societies where women occupy a lower status than men and are treated as property (Whaley, 2001). Power and sex are closely associated in our society. Sex is commonly described as a conquest or surrender. Additionally, when people describe being taken advantage of, they describe it as being "screwed" (Chapleau & Oswald, 2010). Sex and power may be more strongly associated in the minds of sexually aggressive men. For these men, being in positions of power may automatically activate thoughts of sex, and sex may activate thoughts of domination.

Feminist theory leaves several points unanswered. For example, forced copulation is widespread in the animal kingdom (Clutton-Brock & Parker, 1995), and presumably male orangutans and ducks aren't motivated by maintaining the power differential in their society. Also, rape occurs to some degree in all known human cultures, even in those cultures that honor and respect women.

Evolutionary Theory

Rape can be viewed as an evolutionary strategy to increase the reproductive success of low-status men who would otherwise have little chance of mating; in other words, some men are drawn to rape in order to spread their genes (Thornhill & Palmer, 2000). This theory is based on the reproductive differences between males and females—the fact that females have only one egg and males have many sperm. Females must invest a huge amount of

time and energy on each offspring in order to reproduce and are therefore sexually choosy, whereas it's adaptive for males to be more indiscriminate when it comes to sexual partners. Evolutionary theory suggests that rape is inherent in men's nature and not simply a consequence of patriarchal societal structures. It posits that the motivation behind rape is primarily sexual, rather than a means of establishing and maintaining power over women (Archer & Vaughn, 2001). Supporting this theory is the fact that rapists may target more attractive women and that most rape victims are of childbearing age; in fact, almost 62% are between the ages of 12 and 24 (McKibbin, Shackelford, Miner, Bates, & Liddle, 2011; Tjaden & Thoennes, 2000).

There are flaws with this theory. First, almost a third (29%) of rape victims are under the age of 11 and presumably not yet able to get pregnant. Second, if rape is a strategy for passing on one's genes, it is a particularly ineffective one because it most likely results in pregnancy only 1–5% of the time—a poor benefit-to-risk ratio. In fact, women are less likely to be raped near ovulation than at other times in their cycle (Bröder & Hohmann, 2003), a point that is discussed further in the From Cells to Society feature on page 408. Additionally,

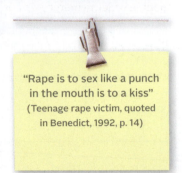

"Rape is to sex like a punch in the mouth is to a kiss" (Teenage rape victim, quoted in Benedict, 1992, p. 14)

if rape is indeed a biological drive, it would suggest that the incidence of rape would be constant worldwide, although in reality it varies greatly from society to society. Finally, a sociobiological explanation does not account for the almost 100,000 males who are raped by other heterosexual men each year (Coyne & Berry, 2000; Wertheim, 2000).

To summarize: according to feminist theory, the goal of rape is to exercise patriarchal power, and the means to this end is for a man to force a woman to have sex. According to evolutionary theory, the goal of rape is to have sex with a nonconsenting woman, and the means to achieve this is to exercise physical power over her. In both explanations, the act of rape involves motives of both sex and power, but the emphasis is different in the two cases. The nature of the power is also different: In the feminist view, the power stems from the role of men in society; according to the evolutionary view, the power comes from the relative physical strength of men compared to women (Archer & Vaughan, 2001).

In a way, these conflicting theories present the idea of rape as a question of nature versus nurture. But as we've learned, almost no behaviors are driven by solely biological or solely societal influences. Rape is not one single type of behavior, and different types of rape may have different causes. Rape may have evolutionary foundations and also be affected by societal influences (Vanderassen, 2011).

Some scientists have tried to integrate the feminist and evolutionary explanations of rape. According to Neil Malamuth's *confluence model* of sexual aggression, there are two main interacting pathways that can lead to sexual aggression (Malamuth, 1996). The first characteristic is a tendency to emphasize sexuality and sexual conquest as a source of peer status and self-esteem. Men who do so might have a tendency to engage in impersonal sex and to have a game-playing attitude toward sexual conquests.

Evolutionary Protections Against Rape

Some believe that rape evolved as an evolutionary strategy to improve some men's reproductive success (Thornhill & Palmer, 2000). In fact, some suggest that an incidence of rape may be more likely to result in a pregnancy than an incidence of consensual sex (Gottschall & Gottschall, 2003). And although some women become pregnant as a result of rape, it appears as though women have evolved a number of adaptive protections against being raped, especially during their most fertile times of their cycle.

When threatened by sexual assault, ovulating women display a measurable increase in physical strength (Petralia & Gallup, 2002). Female college students completed a questionnaire about the regularity of their menstrual cycle and then read one of two brief essays: one that depicted a woman walking to her car late at night while being pursued by a strange man, and the control essay, which portrayed a woman walking to her car on a bright sunny day with other people in the vicinity. Researchers measured the women's handgrip strength before and after the story. Only ovulating women who read the sexual assault scenario showed an increase in handgrip strength.

Ovulating women overestimate strange males' probability of being rapists (Garver-Apgar, Gangestad, & Simpson, 2007). Women were shown videotaped interviews with various men and rated them on several dimensions, including tendencies toward sexual aggression. Women who were ovulating were more likely to describe men as sexually coercive.

When women are at the most fertile times in their cycle, they are less likely to put themselves into potentially dangerous situations; for example, they are less likely to walk alone in a park or let a stranger into the house (Bröder & Hohmann, 2003). On four occasions at 1-week intervals, women were asked to report which of a number of activities—some risky, some benign—that they had participated in during the preceding 24 hours. Ovulating women reported fewer risky behaviors and more nonrisky behaviors; women on oral contraceptives did not show this effect.

The second characteristic is one of hostile masculinity—of feeling insecure, defensive, and distrustful toward women and experiencing gratification from controlling or dominating them. Singly, the paths don't lead to rape, but together they produce a man prone to sexual aggression (Malamuth, 1996).

Rape Myths

There are a number of attitudes and beliefs about rape that are "generally false but are widely and persistently held, and that serve to deny and justify male sexual aggression against women" (Lonsway & Fitzgerald, 1994, p. 134). **Rape myths** deny the existence or gravity of rape, blame the victim, assume that rapists are overwhelmed by sexual desires, and give a false impression of the typical perpetrator (Burt, 1981; Chapleau & Oswald, 2010).

- *Myth: Women really want to be raped.*

This myth suggests that when a woman says "no" she really means "yes," and her token resistance is all part of sex play. The fact that most convicted rapists do not believe they committed rape underscores the acceptance of this idea (Polaschek & Gannon, 2004; Scully & Marolla, 1985). Some people express the opinion that if a woman's vagina becomes lubricated during the assault, she is sexually excited and must secretly want to have intercourse. However, a woman's body can become sexually aroused or even experience a reflexive orgasm during genital contact. This does not indicate that the woman desired the attack or that she enjoyed it in any way (Levin & Van Berlo, 2004). Some may think that women only "cry rape" when they've been jilted or want attention. In one study, males expressed the belief that half the women who report being raped were lying (Szymanski et al., 1993). Others think that women could resist rape if they really wanted to, disregarding the reality that most men are physically stronger than most women, and rapists, who plan the time and place of their attack, have the advantages of control and surprise. Some men believe that all women secretly want to be raped; even some women ascribe to the idea that *other women* (not themselves, of course) enjoy rape (Corne, Briere, & Esses, 1992). Although some women do have rape fantasies, actual rape is very different than a rape fantasy in which the woman retains total control and is completely safe.

- *Myth: Women bring rape upon themselves.*

This widespread myth advocates that a rape victim "asked for it" and provoked the rape by her appearance, behavior, or manner. People are more likely to blame the victim for her own attack if she deviates from the traditional female role; if, for example, she is at a bar or a party rather than being home with her family. A woman is more likely to be blamed for a rape if she knows her assailant, if no weapon was used, or if, on a date, she went to the man's home or let him pay for everything (Basow & Minieri, 2011; Muehlenhard, Friedman, & Thomas, 1985). If a woman is young, thin, and attractive, she is seen as more responsible for her rape (although attractive assailants are held to be less responsible for their crimes) (Clarke & Lawson, 2009; Gerdes, Dammann, & Heilig, 1988).

Men are more likely than women to hold the victim responsible for the attack, although women may blame female victims

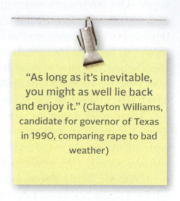

"As long as it's inevitable, you might as well lie back and enjoy it." (Clayton Williams, candidate for governor of Texas in 1990, comparing rape to bad weather)

Rape myths Commonly held beliefs about rape that are false and which deny and justify male sexual aggression against women.

as a way to make themselves feel safer (Szymanski et al., 1993). The **"just world" hypothesis** (Lerner & Simmons, 1966) suggests that people have a strong need to believe the world is fair, that good things happen to good people and bad people get their just deserts. When we encounter evidence that the world is unfair, we quickly develop a justification for the contradiction. When a woman is raped, observers may rationalize her misfortune by attributing responsibility to the victim. In this way, they protect their own sense of vulnerability.

The "blame the victim" myth suggests that rape is due to a woman's failure to protect herself, rather than the man's responsibility to not rape. More than 25% of 11- to 14-year-olds and more than 20% of college students thought if a woman was drinking, it was acceptable for a man to force her into having sex with him (Abbey, 2002; White & Humphrey, 1991). The widespread acceptance of the "blame the victim" myth forces women to live half a life, perpetually fearful, forever checking their behavior so as not to incite males.

- *Myth: Men who rape do so because they can't control their sexual desires.*

There is a persistent idea that rapists are overwhelmed with lust and can't rein in their sexual urges. Some people feel that men's biological need for sex exceeds that of women so that men require sex, even if it is not consensual. However, most men experience sexual desire, yet the majority would never rape someone. Even if men have an evolutionary drive for impersonal sex, there is a big leap from sexual desire to actually forcing oneself onto an unwilling, struggling victim (Vandermassen, 2011). Nevertheless, the idea of the sexually voracious man who cannot control his urges is endemic. A survey of teens aged 14 to 18 found that if a woman got a man sexually excited, 51% of boys and 42% of girls felt that it was all right for the man to then force the woman to have sex (Goodchilds, Zellman, Johnson & Giarrusso, 1988; cited in Warshaw, 1994). This myth once again puts the burden of preventing rape on women, suggesting that if men can't control themselves, women are responsible for preventing rape.

- *Myth: Rape is committed by psychopathic strangers.*

There is a perception that the only men who rape are knife-brandishing psychopaths who hide in the bushes; in fact, most women are raped by people they know. This myth's danger is that it suggests that "normal" men don't rape, supporting the "it can't happen to me" fallacy. In one study, however, the reality was far more frightening: one third of "normal" college men reported that they were at least somewhat likely to rape a woman if there was no possibility they would be caught or punished (Malamuth, 1981). Although this study is more than 30 years

When read an eroticized story of a rape, intoxicated female subjects are more likely than sober subjects to accept rape myths (Davis, Norris, George, Martell, & Heiman, 2006).

old, a recent study still found that more than 1 in 6 men thought it was acceptable for a man to physically force a woman to have sex under some circumstances, such as if the man felt that the woman was promiscuous, or that she teased him or led him on (Abbey, 2002). In fact, 15–25% of male college students report committing some form of sexual coercion (Chapleau & Oswald, 2010).

- *Myth: Only women can be raped.*

Although most people think of rape as something that happens only to women (as mentioned, the FBI doesn't recognize male rape in their definition of rape), men are also subject to sexual assault. It is estimated that 3–12% of men have been raped, and it is thought that male rape is even more under-reported than female rape (Chapleau, Oswald, & Russell, 2008; Male Victims of Sexual Abuse, 2007; Spitzberg & Rhea, 1999; Tjaden & Thoennes, 2000). Most assailants are heterosexual men, although some gay men and heterosexual women do rape males. Like female rape, male rape is in part motivated by power and is an act of domination and degradation, conquest and control, retaliation, and revenge (Groth & Burgess, 1980). Rape survivor Fred Pelka describes the way that rape affected his view of the world:

> While women tell me that the possibility of rape is never far from their minds, most men never give it a first, let alone a second, thought. This may explain why they react so negatively to accounts by male survivors. To see rape as "a woman's issue" is a form of male privilege most men would prefer not to surrender. They would rather believe that they can move with immunity through the toxic atmosphere of violence and fear they and their compatriots create . . . being a male rape survivor means I no longer fit our culture's neat but specious definition of masculinity, as one empowered, one always in control. (Pelka, 2003, pp. 580, 582)

Rape myths are still held by a significant proportion of Americans who feel that there are circumstances that justify rape (Lonsway & Fitzgerald, 1994; Mori, Bernat, Glenn, Selle, & Zarate, 1995; Szymanski et al., 1993). Males are generally more accepting of rape myths than women are. These myths are more accepted by those who believe in traditional gender roles, by those who are more accepting of interpersonal violence (especially sexual violence), and by those who hold sex role stereotypes (especially negative beliefs about women) and sexually conservative views. As a group, police officers are more likely than average to accept rape myths (Campbell & Johnson, 1997; Lonsway & Fitzgerald, 1994). Even some victims of sexual assault accept rape myths; those that do are more likely to blame themselves for the attack and to exhibit more depression and poorer psychological adjustment. It is important that people are educated as to the reality of rape, to reveal the inaccuracy of these beliefs.

Types of Rape

The depth of the relationship between assailant and victim is one way to distinguish the type of rape. In **stranger rape**, the assailant is unknown to the victim. When the victim

"Just world" hypothesis The tendency for people to rationalize and excuse inexplicable injustices so as to maintain the idea that the world is fair.

Stranger rape Forced sexual contact by someone unknown to the victim.

knows the rapist, this is **acquaintance rape**; **date rape** occurs when the sexual assault happens on a date. Finally, marital or **partner rape** is nonconsensual sexual activity in which the assailant is the victim's spouse or partner.

Stranger Rape

Although the typical image of rape is that of an armed stranger attacking a woman, perhaps as few as 17% of rapes against women and 23% of rapes against men are committed by strangers (Tjaden & Thoennes, 2006). Rapists who assault strangers are the most likely to reoffend, most likely to be tried and convicted, and generally receive harsher punishments than those who are acquainted with the victim.

Acquaintance Rape and Date Rape

Most women who are raped—up to 86%—are raped by someone they know (Cowan, 2000; Criminal Victimization, 2000; Tjaden & Thoennes, 2006; Warshaw, 1994). The vast majority of date and acquaintance rapes are not reported to the police (Tjaden & Thoennes, 2006).

Date rape is seen as a "lesser" crime than stranger rape (Campbell, 2008); some even deny that it is wrong. The use of sexually coercive behaviors might, to some degree, be considered a social norm on college campuses. College students don't view sexually coercive strategies as particularly aggressive, and those against whom the strategies are used are often not seen as victims, even when use of physical force on a date leads to unwanted intercourse (Oswald & Russell, 2006). A significant proportion of both male and female college students report being pressured into sexual activity. Date rape does not necessarily involve the use of physical force or violence; someone may be coerced into sexual activity with an acquaintance who uses continual arguments, verbal pressure, or threats to end the relationship.

What is sexual consent? Ted and Carly are college students who have been dating for 6 weeks. They return from a movie and settle in on the couch in Carly's apartment. "May I kiss you?" Ted asks. "Yes," Carly replies. After a while, Ted says, "I would like to touch your breasts. Is this acceptable to you?" Carly nods in assent, but Ted asks her to please express her consent verbally. Carly does so, and later asks permission from Ted to perform fellatio on him, to which he readily agrees.

The above scenario seems both awkward and absurd because sexual consent is usually not given so directly; instead, signals of sexual consent are often nonverbal, vague, and ambiguous. In one study, more than a third of participants said that they indicated sexual consent by smiling and showed their assent by just letting events unfold (Hickman & Muehlenhard, 1999). However, nonverbal signals may be misinterpreted. Women often

© Scott Griessel/Age fotostock

smile when they are uncomfortable, and men often perceive women's behaviors to be more indicative of their desire to have sex than women intend those signals to be (Hickman & Muehlenhard, 1999; Kowalski, 1992). Men may also think that if a woman accepts a date, or if she agrees to come into his home, that this is a sign that she consents to intercourse. Direct expressions of consent can prevent tragic misunderstandings.

Sometimes women do say "no" when they mean "yes" (Muehlenhard & Hollabaugh, 1988). This is confusing to men and potentially dangerous to women. Men may learn to assume that when a woman says "no," it is part of the sexual script, so women can maintain a pretense of purity. It is especially confusing when a woman's verbal refusal does not match her nonverbal signals, such as if she says no while smiling or flirting. In order to avoid date rape, women are advised to clearly indicate their desires, and men must get clear consent from their partners before proceeding.

Imagine the following scenario:

> Ramon is sitting in his dorm room and listening to his iPod. There is a knock on the door, and he recognizes Mark, a classmate from his chemistry class. Ramon invites him in, and Mark asks if he can borrow his textbook for a little while. When Ramon turns to find the book, Mark grabs him from behind and rips the iPod from his ears, pushing him down to the floor. Mark leaves, taking the iPod with him. Ramon goes to the police to report this crime. Officer Peters takes his report.
>
> "Ramon, first we'll need you to prove that you had an iPod. Can you show us the receipt?"
>
> "Well, no, officer, I don't have that anymore."
>
> "Hmm. You'd think that if this iPod was so important to you you'd have kept the receipt. So there's no proof that a crime even occurred, is there? Now Ramon, weren't you asking for it, by advertising your wealth and flaunting your possessions?"
>
> "I was sitting in my dorm room, minding my own business!" Ramon exclaims.
>
> "But you invited him into your room, didn't you? Be honest, Ramon, have you ever shared music with anyone?"
>
> "Of course, but what does that have to do with anything?"
>
> "So, you've given away music before, have you? So there's really no crime, here, is there? You haven't been hurt in any way. Maybe in the future you'll be more careful who you show off your possessions to."

Sounds ridiculous, doesn't it? Yet many women receive a similar response when reporting an acquaintance rape. Both men and

Does "no" ever mean "yes"? When? How is someone supposed to know in which situations it does?

Acquaintance rape Forced sexual contact by someone known to the victim.

Date rape Forced sexual contact that occurs on a date or social engagement.

Partner rape Forced sexual contact by one's spouse, boyfriend/girlfriend, or partner.

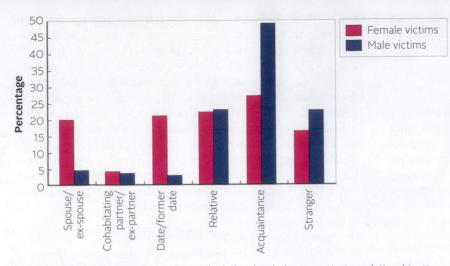

FIGURE 16.1 Distribution of sexual assault victims by victim–perpetrator relationship. (From U.S. Department of Justice, 2006.)

women are more likely to blame the victim when she is raped by someone she knows. Compared to stranger rape, date and acquaintance rapes are less likely to be reported and prosecuted, and these rapists are given less severe punishments (Oswald & Russell, 2006). This may be because of the persistence of rape myths and because it is harder to prove a lack of consent in court.

Partner Rape

Until 1993, it was legal in some U.S. states for a man to demand that his wife have sex with him whenever he wanted it, regardless of her wishes. In 1978, Greta and John Rideout set into motion a sequence of events that would bring the issue of partner rape into the nation's consciousness. Greta and John's short marriage was characterized by numerous fights. After one physical brawl, Greta maintained that John raped her, and John claimed the sex was consensual. Mrs. Rideout filed rape charges against her husband. The press attacked Greta and assailed her character and honesty. The president of the Oregon state bar declared, "It's a waste of the court's time to get into that area . . . a woman who's still in a marriage is presumably consenting to sex. Maybe this is the risk of being married, you know" (Berry, 1980, p. 1090). The jury found John not guilty of rape. Eventually, the couple divorced. John continued to threaten and harass Greta after their divorce and was eventually sentenced to jail for this behavior, where he served 40 days.

Partner rape, also called marital rape or spousal rape, accounts for 25% of all rapes in the United States (Bergen, 1999). It is estimated that 8–14% of women are raped by their husbands or ex-husbands (Ferro, Cermele, & Saltzman, 2008; Russell, 1990; Finkelhor & Yllo, 1985), usually when the husband has been drinking. Rather than sex, the man's motives for marital rape include domination and degradation. Of all rapes, spousal rape is least likely to be reported and draws the least response from law enforcement and support groups. Police sometimes won't respond to or file reports against domestic rape, clergy may tell the woman that she vowed to "obey" her husband, and even rape shelters aren't always trained to provide support for women who are victims of marital rape. Even victims often don't recognize their experience as being rape.

Most people view marital rape as an insignificant offense. A traditional husband may believe that he is entitled to sex with his wife any time he wishes and that it is his wife's duty to satisfy his sexual needs regardless of her own. A survey of 11- to 14-year-olds found that 87% of boys and 79% of girls said rape was acceptable if the man and woman were married (White & Humphrey, 1991). More recent studies show that people today may be more likely to acknowledge that forced sex is rape but are less likely to acknowledge it as such when the couple is married (Ferro et al., 2008).

Women of all ages and demographics are victims of partner rape, although women of lower socioeconomic status are more limited in their ability to leave an abusive relationship. Women are at particular risk of marital rape if their husband views them as property, if their relationship is already violent, if they are pregnant or ill, and if they are separated or divorced (Bergen, 1999). Although many people deny the problem of marital rape, victims of partner rape actually suffer longer-lasting trauma than those who are raped by strangers, perhaps because the person they loved and trusted most has hurt them.

> "When a woman is raped by a stranger, she has to live with a frightening memory. When she is raped by her husband, she has to live with the rapist."
>
> —*Abuse Counseling and Treatment, Inc. (ACT), a private, nonprofit agency that serves victims of domestic violence, sexual assault, and human trafficking*

Other Types of Rape

Gang Rape

Gang rape is the rape of a single victim by a group of assailants. Gang rapes tend to be more violent than sexual assaults committed by one attacker. Individuals who commit gang rape often know each other and share a group identity, such as members of an athletic team or gang (Kittleson, Kane, & Rennagarbe, 2005). Fifty-five percent of gang rapes of college students are committed by fraternity members, and 40% by members of a college athletic team (Sawyer, Thompson & Chicorelli, 2002). Gang rape is more likely to occur when group members are aggressive and competitive and view women as sex objects. Men may commit group rape to bond with each other and prove their masculinity and to show their power over and anger against women. More than 20% of women who are raped and more than 16% of men who are raped have more than one assailant (Tjaden & Thoennes, 2006).

> "No simple conquest of man over woman, group rape is the conquest of men over Woman."
>
> —*Susan Brownmiller (1993, p. 187)*

In 1983, a 21-year-old mother of two was gang-raped on a pool table at Big Dan's Tavern in New Bedford, Massachusetts, as a group of men stood by and cheered. The trial got national exposure and the press kept interest high with sensational headlines. Published opinions expressed the view that the victim wasn't raped, she *got herself* raped (Cuklanz, 1994) and that she got what she deserved by being in a bar and flirting. The newspapers published

Gang rape The rape of a single victim by a group of assailants.

comments such as "A decent woman would not go into any bar . . ." "What was she doing there in the first place?" and "If she had been home with her children this would not have happened" (Benedict, 1992, pp. 129, 131). The assailants were eventually found guilty. The movie *The Accused,* starring Jodie Foster, was based on this case.

In 2009, a 15-year-old girl was gang-raped outside of her high school homecoming dance in Richmond, California. As many as 20 people watched or took part in her assault, which lasted for more than 2 hours. Witnesses did not report the crime to the police; in fact, some onlookers laughed or took photos of the assault. Psychologists cite the **bystander effect**, which explains that witnesses are less likely to offer help in an emergency situation when others are present.

Statutory Rape

Statutory rape is sexual intercourse that occurs with someone who is not a child but who is below the age of consent, even if the sex was not physically forced. (The age at which someone is not considered a child differs among states, but it is usually around age 14. The age of consent also varies from state to state but typically ranges from 14 to 18.) Statutory rape is sometimes called "unlawful sexual intercourse" to differentiate it from forcible sexual abuse. Statutory rape is a morally problematic topic, especially considering that as the legal age of consent has been raised, puberty and sexual maturity occur earlier.

Rape in Prison

Prison rape refers to the rape of inmates by other prisoners or by penitentiary staff. Whereas male prisoners are most likely to be sexually assaulted by other male convicts, female inmates are most often raped by prison employees. Although high-ranking prison officials estimate that 1 in 8 male prisoners are coerced into sex, correctional officers put the estimate at 1 in 5, and estimates from prisoners themselves are even higher. Twenty-one percent of prisoners reported being victims of coerced or forced sexual contact since being incarcerated (Struckman-Johnson & Struckman-Johnson, 2000). Even using the low estimates from the corrections industry, there are more rapes in prison than all reported rapes in Los Angeles, Chicago, and New York combined (Brook, 2003). Prison rape is thought to be greatly under-reported because of the victims' shame and fear of retaliation not only from their assailants but also from prison officials—all sexual activity between prisoners is prohibited and those who report sexual assault may receive punitive sanctions.

© AP Images/Gregory Smith

Genarlow Wilson was a 17-year-old Georgia high school student who had consensual oral sex with a 15-year-old girl at a party. He was arrested on charges of rape, contributing to the delinquency of a minor, and aggravated child molestation and was sentenced to 10 years in prison. (Incidentally, if he and the girl had had intercourse instead of oral sex, under Georgia law, Wilson would have been charged with a misdemeanor instead of a felony.) In 2007 a judge voided his sentence after Wilson had served 27 months in prison.

Although it occurs between two men, most prison rape is not, in fact, perpetrated by gay men. Prison rape is usually about power, not sex. Smaller, younger, and weaker heterosexual men may pair up with a man for protection from gang rape. Although prison rape is a reality, in most prisons condoms are banned. Most administrators "refuse to allow them on the grounds that this would be 'condoning homosexuality,' something they apparently consider worse than the death of prisoners" (Donaldson, 1993).

Rape on Campus

As you're sitting in your college library or dorm, look around at your classmates. Choose 40 random women. On average, 10 of these 40 will be raped during her years in college, and 9 of the 10 will be raped by someone they know (Fisher, Cullen, & Turner, 2000; Koss et al., 1987; Tjaden & Thoennes, 2006; Warshaw, 1994). A woman runs the greatest risk of rape during her first semester in college, and 50% of the assaults are associated with alcohol (Abbey, 2002). Between 7% and 25% of college men admit to forcing sexual intercourse on a woman, and although their behavior fits the legal criteria of rape, the vast majority of these men don't view their actions as rape (Koss et al., 1987; Mori et al, 1995; Warshaw, 1994).

Many of these rapes are committed by fraternity members or athletes. Although only one quarter of male college students are members of a fraternity, fraternity members commit 48–63% of sexual assaults on campuses that have fraternities (Frintner & Rubinson, 1993; Sawyer et al., 2002). Some fraternity men share attitudes that are conducive to rape: competition, dominance, and sexual aggressiveness are valued, and women are viewed as a commodity to fulfill men's needs. Some fraternity members are encouraged to drink heavily, act in an uninhibited manner, and engage in casual sex (Abbey, 2002). The large, noisy, drunken bacchanalia of a typical fraternity party, unsupervised and full of strangers, is an environment that promotes rape. College athletes are also disproportionately reported for acquaintance rape (Sampson, 2002). College athletes, who may see themselves as a privileged class, deserving of celebrity and prestige, live in a world in which competition and aggression are valued, and physical skills are used to achieve their goals. As a group, college athletes—especially those who play team sports rather than individual sports—are more likely to believe rape myths (Sawyer et al., 2002).

Drugs and Alcohol and Rape

When your author was at college, there was a sick joke around the fraternities that went like this:

"What's the mating call of a sorority girl?"

"I'm soooo drunk!"

Alcohol is one of the strongest predictors of acquaintance rape and sexual aggression. Of those involved in acquaintance rape, up to 74% of perpetrators and 55% of victims had been

Bystander effect A social psychological phenomenon in which individuals are less likely to respond to another person's distress when others are present.

Statutory rape Sexual intercourse with someone who is not a child, but who is below the age of consent.

drinking alcohol at the time of the attack (Abbey, 2002; Warshaw, 1994).

Alcohol sexualizes an environment. Men expect to feel more powerful, sexual, and aggressive after drinking alcohol and are more likely to interpret a woman's flirtation or even normal conversation in a sexual way. Communication about sexual intentions is also impaired, as "alcohol myopia" causes men to disregard some signals and focus only on signals they read as sexual. Men also perceive women who drink alcohol as more promiscuous and sexually available. Alcohol increases risky behaviors and limits one's ability to consider the negative consequences of his or her actions. People may be more likely to take risks and end up in situations they would normally avoid. With its effects on motor skills, alcohol also diminishes a victim's ability to resist. Alcohol is often thought to excuse behavior—but only in the assailant. Whereas intoxicated rapists are held *less* responsible for their actions than sober ones, intoxicated victims are *more* likely to be held personally responsible (Oswald & Russell, 2006).

The exact causal relationship between alcohol and sexual assault is unknown. It may be that alcohol use itself increases the chance of rape. Alternatively, people who are consciously or subconsciously planning a sexual assault may drink alcohol beforehand to give an excuse for their behavior. Finally, alcohol and sexual assault could be related to a third factor, such as risk taking, impulsivity, or peer pressure.

Date rape drugs are drugs that are used to help commit a sexual assault. These drugs commonly have *amnesiac* (causing memory impairment), *disinhibiting* (leads to a loss of inhibition), and *dissociative* (may produce hallucinations and feelings of unreality) properties. *Rohypnol,* or "roofies," is similar to Valium but approximately 10 times more potent. A central nervous system depressant and sleeping pill used in Europe, Rohypnol is not approved for use in the United States. Rohypnol's effects—sedation, amnesia, poor judgments, and blackouts—typically last 6 to 8 hours or more. Tasteless and colorless, roofies may be slipped into the drink of an unsuspecting person, who may then black out and be vulnerable to sexual attack. Hoffman-La Roche, the manufacturer of Rohypnol, has recently changed its formulation so that it dissolves more slowly and turns blue in solution. Other date rape drugs include GHB, ketamine, Klonipin, and Xanax. In 1996 the Drug-Induced Rape Prevention and Punishment Act (21 U.S.C. Sec. 841[b][7]) established penalties of up to 20 years in prison for giving a date rape drug with the intent to commit a crime of violence, including rape.

You can protect yourself from date rape drugs in a number of ways, including the following:

- Don't accept a drink from a stranger.
- Don't leave your drink unattended.
- Don't drink from a punch bowl or an open container (unless you opened it).

Who Are the Rapists?

In addition to usually knowing their victims, the vast majority of rapists are single men, mostly under the age of 30. It is, however, difficult to make generalizations about rapists because most data that's gathered is about those who are *convicted* of rape; men in this group are more likely to be unknown to their victims. Also, rapists are generally similar to nonsexual offenders on a variety of variables (Gannon & Ward, 2008).

Still, it has been found that most rapists have raped more than one victim, although most of these crimes are unconfessed and unpunished. Anna Salter (2003) tells of a study in which 23 offenders, admitting to an average of 3 victims each, entered a treatment program. When faced with a lie detector test, the rapists then admitted to an average of *175* victims each. In other studies, the threat of a polygraph caused the rapists to admit to raping 4 to 6 times as many victims as previously acknowledged (Abel et al., 1987; Hindman & Peters, 2001). When considering their other transgressions, it is probably no surprise to learn that sex offenders lie about their crimes.

There is no single cause of rape. Rapists vary in their motivations, personalities, backgrounds, and psychological characteristics (Gannon & Ward, 2008; Groth, Burgess, & Holstrom, 1977; Prentky, Burgess, & Carter, 1986). As mentioned, many rapists want to gain power and control and use sex as their weapon to do so. They often feel that men have the right to demand sex from women and may use violence and force to humiliate and dominate their victims. Some use sexual violence as an expression of their anger toward women. Others are socially inadequate and have low self-esteem. For them, rape is an expression of their fantasies. They may even believe that their victim will enjoy the experience and the attack could be a start of a relationship.

Rapists are more likely to express certain characteristics and attitudes (Drieschner & Lange, 1999; Murnen, Wright, & Kaluzny, 2002). It should come as no surprise that rapists feel less empathy toward others. They are more likely to hold a sense of entitlement and exploit others for their personal gain (Polaschek & Gannon, 2004). Rapists are more likely to accept traditional gender roles, to believe that women are fundamentally different from men, and to believe that the male sex drive is uncontrollable (Polaschek & Gannon, 2004; Truman, Tokar, & Fischer, 1996). They believe that masculinity means power and aggression and may feel dominant over or anger toward women. They are more likely to accept rape myths and are more accepting of violence toward women (Chapleau & Oswald, 2010). In social situations, they may misperceive women's cues. Rapists are more likely to be sexually aroused by images of rape; their concepts of sex and power may be closely linked, and sex may be a way for them to express dominance. Sexual offenders are more likely to be politically conservative and to treat outsiders (such as gays, the physically disabled, and refugees) aggressively. Finally, environmental forces—the use of alcohol or drugs, a family history of physical violence, and sexually aggressive peers—can increase one's propensity to rape (Gannon & Ward, 2008).

Can Rapists Be "Cured"?

Rapists may be treated with psychotherapy and medications. They may be required to attend group sessions at which they own up to their wrongdoings, learn the truth about rape myths, and try to deal with day-to-day temptations (Foubert, 2000; Szymanski et al., 1993). Although this is helpful, it is unclear to what degree a change in attitude corresponds to a change in behavior. Sex offenders may get regular injections of Depo-Provera, which temporarily "castrates" the offenders by diminishing their production of testoster-

Date rape drug A drug, such as Rohypnol and GHB, that can be used to assist in the commission of a sexual assault.

one. It can be hard to ensure that sex offenders continue taking the injections, and this chemical response doesn't deal with any underlying psychological issues that may be driving their behavior. Antidepressant drugs are also being investigated as a potential treatment because they tend to decrease sex drive and can curb compulsive behavior. These treatments may help, but they are not a "cure." It is also unclear whether any success is due to the treatment itself or because those who are willing to undergo the treatment may be more motivated to change.

Who Are the Victims?

Victims of sexual assault and rape occupy all strata of the population: young and old, rich and poor, gay and straight, male and female. When socioeconomic status is controlled, the incidence of rape is similar across ethnic groups, although Native Americans are significantly more likely than whites, African Americans, Asians, or Hispanics to report a rape in their lifetime (Koss et al., 1987; Tjaden & Thoennes, 2006).

Young people are particularly likely to be victims of sexual assault (Tjaden & Thoennes, 2006). Between 54% and 63% of rape victims are under age 18; in fact, 29% are under age 11. Only 13–16.6% of victims are over age 25 (Kilpatrick et al., 1992; Tjaden & Thoennes, 2000, 2006).

Effects of Rape on Survivors

Rape is physically, emotionally, and psychologically shattering. After the attack, the survivor may have bruises and contusions. Although these fade, other physical problems such as gastrointestinal irritability, cystitis, headaches, and sleep disturbances can persist. Rapists may infect their victims with an STI, and it is estimated that approximately 32,000 women become pregnant each year as a result of rape (Holmes, Resnick, Kirkpatrick, & Best, 1996; Reynolds, Peipert, & Collins, 2000). Rape survivors also experience psychological problems: rape victims are 3 times more likely to suffer from depression, 6 times more likely to develop post-traumatic stress disorder (PTSD), and 13 times more likely to have ever attempted suicide in their lives or to have alcohol or drug dependency problems (Gidycz, Orchowski, King, & Rich, 2008; Kilpatrick, Whalley, & Edmunds, 2000; Martin & Macy, 2009).

If Someone You Know Is a Rape Survivor

There is no single "rape syndrome" any more than there is one "correct" way to respond to rape. Be patient and understanding as your friend or loved one processes his or her trauma. Often, men and women who have been raped first experience disbelief, shock, anger, and fear. They may feel humiliated and powerless and may even blame themselves for the attack, especially when they know their assailant. Some victims may be afraid to be alone; others may shut out their friends and family. While some express their emotions, others shut down and appear outwardly calm and controlled. Some victims may change their behaviors—they may change their appearance or job, they may stop engaging in behaviors such as going for walks that they previously enjoyed, or they may become reluctant to socialize. Rape can put severe stress on an intimate relationship because some

rape survivors have difficulty trusting others. Some victims suffer from sexual dysfunctions, including anorgasmia and decreased desire and arousal.

Partners of rape survivors may feel angry, frustrated, or jealous. They may be upset that they were unable to protect their partner, or the may want revenge upon the assailant. Partners may even be angry at the rape victim and question whether they somehow provoked their attack. Therapy and a strong support system will often help rape survivors deal with their psychological burden, regain their sense of control, and recreate their lives (Burgess & Holstrom, 1974).

> "My vagina a live wet water village
> They invaded it. Butchered it
> And burned it down.
> I do not touch now
> Do not visit.
> I love some place else now.
> I don't know where that is."
>
> —From *The Vagina Monologues* (Ensler, 2000)

Are you still a virgin if you have been raped?

According to Andrea Parrot (1999), virginity can be defined in three ways—physically, by the presence or absence of the hymen in women; behaviorally, by whether you have had sexual intercourse; and emotionally, if you have freely given yourself to someone else. As we remember from Chapter 4, the absence of a hymen is not an accurate indication of virginity because the hymen can be broken through exercise or by using tampons. We can therefore look at behavioral and emotional descriptors. Someone who has had consensual sexual intercourse is not a virgin. A virgin who is raped did not have consensual intercourse; she did not freely give herself to another. Therefore we can consider her a virgin.

What to Do if You Have Been Raped

First of all, don't blame yourself. The rapist is the only guilty party. Victims that blame themselves for being in a potentially dangerous situation should remember that "bad judgment is not a rape-able offense" (Warshaw, 1994, p. 21). Try to remember everything that happened and write down all you can about the assailant and his physical appearance, the location, and other details. Don't change the environment until evidence has been gathered: that means you shouldn't shower yet or disturb the area where the rape occurred, even though you might want to. Ask a friend or relative to take you to a hospital for examination. You don't have to have physical injuries in order to go to the hospital; in fact, most rapes don't result in noticeable physical injuries, but at the hospital they can gather evidence, treat wounds, and check for infections. Rape kits allow health care professionals to gather the rapist's DNA, which can make conviction of your assailant more likely.

At the hospital, they can also test your blood for evidence of a date rape drug, administer drugs for possible infection with STIs, and give emergency contraception. Hospitals don't always do all they can for rape victims. Most rape victims are not advised about pregnancy, told about emergency contraception, or given information about STI/HIV risks (Campbell, 2008; Kilpatrick, Whalley, & Edmunds, 2000). Your companion can advocate on your behalf. Although many rape victims don't want to talk about their traumatic incident, speaking to a rape crisis counselor or a therapist can help you to work through your feelings about the experience.

You will need to decide if you want to file a police report and press charges against your assailant. It is important that you make the decision that is best for you, with all the available facts at hand. Many women choose not to report sexual assaults to the police due to apprehension about others' responses, fear of retaliation, or shame. Some fear that no one will believe them or think that pressing charges would be fruitless. Though the FBI ranks rape as the second most violent crime after murder, some women still don't report rapes, downplaying what happened to themselves. You should strongly consider pressing charges against your assailant. Not only should rapists be punished for their crime, but every rapist who remains free has the potential to rape another person. Reporting your rape also gives those in authority a more accurate picture of the scope of the problem of sexual assault and may allow agencies to better address the problem. If you choose to report the rape, it is best if you do so as soon as possible. Timely reporting may not only give you a sense of power and control, but it also gives the police a better chance of catching the assailant. If you choose not to report your attack, as most women do, it does not mean that it was not traumatic or that it was not rape.

The legal system may need to investigate acquaintance rapes differently than stranger rapes. For example, unlike stranger rapes, the key to the investigation is not in identifying the perpetrator, who is already known to the victim. Instead, it is necessary to prove that intercourse occurred and that it was not consensual. Most victims of acquaintance rapes don't sustain major injuries, so the use of a **colposcope**—a tool used by gynecologists that shows damage to the vagina not visible to the naked eye—can facilitate acquaintance rape cases. Whereas rape exams without colposcopes find genital injuries in only 19–28% of rape cases, the use of a colposcope finds injuries in up to 87% of rape cases but not in cases of consensual intercourse (Kilpatrick, 2000).

If you do press charges, it won't be easy. Rape prosecution is a complex, multistage process, and few cases make it all the way through the criminal justice system. If you report your case to the police, you will be questioned many times by law enforcement personnel, who may ask questions that you find emotionally unsettling. Most reported rape cases are dropped by law enforcement and not referred to prosecutors. This may be because law enforcement officials don't think that a rape occurred or because they actively discouraged the victim from pursuing prosecution. A suspect is less likely to be charged with rape if there is a prior relationship of any kind between the victim and the suspect, if a weapon was not used, if the victim delayed in filing a report, or if victim misconduct was perceived to be involved—such "misconduct" might include behaviors such as drinking or willingly

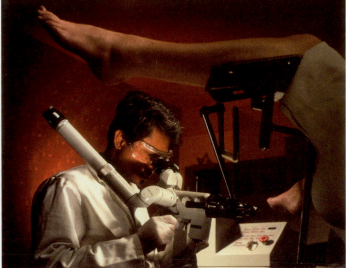

An examination with a colposcope may be part of the exam after a woman is raped.

© DEEP LIGHT PRODUCTIONS/SCIENCE PHOTO LIBRARY/Photo Researchers, Inc.

For every 100 cases reported to law enforcement, on average, 33 would be referred to prosecutors, 16 would be charged and moved into the court system, 12 would end in successful conviction, and 7 would end in a prison sentence (Campbell, 2008).

entering the suspect's house or car (Bryden & Lengnick, 1997). Most cases that are referred to prosecutors do not go to court, as prosecutors may only choose to try cases they consider "winnable" (Campbell, 2008).

If the case goes to court, you may endure a difficult ordeal because you might be put on trial. The defense attorney may attack your character, insinuating the rape was your fault. Rape shield laws limit the use of a victim's prior sex history, but these laws vary from state to state. Some rape victims try their assailants in a civil rather than a criminal court; civil cases may be easier to win because they require a lesser burden of proof, and the jury's decision does not have to be unanimous. However, in a civil trial you must pay for your own court cost and attorneys.

Once in the court system, successful prosecution is most likely for Caucasian women of a privileged background whose experiences fit the stereotyped (but actually rarer) notion of what constitutes rape: a violent attack by a stranger in which a weapon was used (Campbell, 2008). Juries are much more likely to be lenient in favor of rapists than for those who committed any other crime of equivalent severity (Bryden & Lengnick, 1997). Rape tends to be viewed as less serious and less physically and emotionally damaging than other violent crimes. Rape has the lowest conviction rate of all violent crimes (Ferro et al., 2008), although the use of DNA gathered as evidence has improved the rate of rape prosecutions and convictions (Leinwand, 2009). Only 7% of rapists whose crimes have been reported to law enforcement

Colposcope A device used to give a magnified and illuminated view of the vagina and cervix.

will spend time in prison (Campbell, 2008). When there, the average sentence for rapists is 128 days in jail, a rate that has tripled since 1980 (Reynolds, 1999).

You may consider asking at a rape crisis center for the help of a rape victim advocate. These advocates are trained paraprofessionals who help victims navigate their contacts with the criminal justice system. They can explain the legal process and can sometimes be present for interviews. Rape victim advocates watch, witness, and advocate on the victim's behalf (Campbell, 2008).

How to Protect Yourself from Rape

There are many things you can do to decrease your chances of being raped:

- *Avoid dangerous situations.* Keep away from isolated areas, and be sure to check the backseat of your car before you get in. Lock your house and car, and don't open the door to strangers. Don't keep your personal information such as name and address on your key chain. If you're meeting someone for a first date, meet in a public place, and try not to drive with someone you don't know.

- *Trust your instincts and don't be nice.* If someone calls you over to his vehicle and asks for help, overcome your socially ingrained female instinct to be nice, and take precautions. Women are more likely to avoid rape when they're being attacked by a stranger because they are less worried about hurting his feelings (Bart, 1981).

- *Maintain control.* If on a date, cover some of the expenses. Avoid drugs and alcohol: among college women who were date-raped, 72% were so drunk they couldn't give or refuse consent (Abbey, 2002).

- *Avoid people who treat you badly.* Avoid men who don't respect you or who talk negatively about women. Stay away from men who are physically violent in any way or who intimidate you.

- *Be confident in yourself and recognize your value.* Give clear messages: say what you mean, and mean what you say. If a date's physical advances are more than you like, make sure your feelings are plain. Directly refuse his advances, in no uncertain terms: say "No! This is rape!" Stating this clearly may cause the rapist to reconsider his actions, especially if he's intoxicated. Get physical if necessary—bite, scratch, and claw.

- *Attend a rape awareness seminar or self-defense classes.* Learn to recognize and avoid dangerous situations and develop techniques to protect yourself.

If you do find yourself in a dangerous situation, use multiple strategies. No single strategy works in all cases. But when rape victims were compared with those who successfully avoided rape, a larger percentage of the rape avoiders had screamed, fought physically, and escaped (Prentky et al., 1986). Make it difficult for your attacker, and don't be afraid to cause a scene. You may feel like you

Some female ducks and geese have evolved genitalia designed to thwart unwanted sexual attempts from males. Males of some waterfowl species have penises large enough to insert into the female without her consent; females of these species have evolved vaginal features to deter unwanted copulation. For example, the males of one species have penises that spiral counterclockwise; the vaginas of the females have evolved to spiral clockwise, which prevents copulation unless the female cooperates. The female of other waterfowl species have evolved a vagina that has a series of pouches that can capture unwanted sperm and prevent fertilization (Brennan et al., 2007).

are vulnerable and defenseless, but you actually have many weapons at your disposal:

- *Your mind.* Recognize dangerous situations, and respond quickly.

- *Your gut.* Trust your instincts, and remove yourself from any situation that makes you uncomfortable.

- *Your voice.* Talk your way out of the situation, if possible. If not, scream! Don't worry about being embarrassed. If you do yell, shout "fire!" instead of "rape!" because people are more likely to run toward a fire but away from violence.

- *Your body.* Go after your attacker's vulnerable spots: his eyes, knees, groin, neck, and nose. Use your powerful legs to kick at your assailant. Use your body to destroy his idea of seduction: pick your nose, urinate, defecate, or vomit on him.

- *Your heart.* Act as if you are protecting your sister, your mother, or your child. Women tend to fight harder to protect a loved one than they will to protect themselves.

Societal Factors and Rape

Rape Throughout History

Although rape is now considered one of the most serious crimes, it was not always so. Although the Ten Commandments prohibit murder, theft, and lying, "thou shall not rape" is not included. The first rape laws were not seen as criminal acts against women but as if a man's property had been damaged (Brownmiller, 1993). Among the ancient Hebrews, if a woman was raped within the walls of the city, she, along with her attacker, was stoned to death. The idea was that she would have been heard if she yelled, so she must have wanted it. If she was attacked outside of the city, then the attacker was ordered to pay the victim's family 50 silver pieces and was forced to marry her. If she was already betrothed to someone else, then her fiancé's property was damaged and her rapist was put to death. The woman was sold as damaged goods (Brownmiller, 1993).

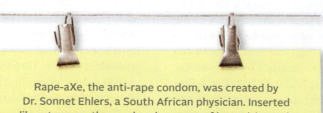

Rape-aXe, the anti-rape condom, was created by Dr. Sonnet Ehlers, a South African physician. Inserted like a tampon, the condom has rows of jagged, inward-facing teeth that grab hold of the penis upon penetration by a man. When the man withdraws, usually screaming in pain, the condom remains attached and must be removed by a physician.

Rape is seen as both a spoil of war and as an act of aggression designed to dominate and humiliate the enemy (Nagel, 2003). In the Old Testament, women of conquered tribes were kidnapped and raped and forced to marry their captors. Even today, women are seen as prizes to be taken from the enemy, just as land or property. When Japan invaded China in late 1937, the Japanese raped as many as 80,000 Chinese women and girls. American soldiers raped Vietnamese women and girls as a means of terror and domination (Brownmiller, 1993). In the 1990s there was widespread rape of Croatian women by Serbian men in Bosnia, and as many as 500,000 women and girls were sexually assaulted during the civil war in Rwanda (UNICEF, 1996). Today, rape is used as a systematic weapon of ethnic cleansing in the Darfur region of western Sudan.

Rape and Society

Rape is not universal; although it may be related to biological drives, it is also an expression of cultural forces. Peggy Reeves Sanday described the differences between "rape-free" societies and "rape-prone" societies (Sanday, 1981). In cultures where rape is rare, women are treated with respect, and there is little interpersonal violence. Women's contributions to society are admired and valued. In contrast, rape-prone societies are characterized by male dominance and interpersonal violence, especially toward women. Women are afforded a lower status and may be treated as property. Also, in these societies the natural environment is more likely to be exploited rather than treated with reverence; it's as though if one is willing to rape the land, they are more willing to rape women.

The United States is a rape-prone society. According to the U.S. Department of Justice (which only considers *reported* rapes—actual rates are much higher), the rate of rape in America is 3 times higher than Germany's, almost twice that seen in France, and 20 times higher than Japan's (Harrendorf, Heiskanen, & Malby, 2010). Gender roles in America match those of rape-prone cultures. The cultural ideal is one of a dominant and assertive man attaining his dreams no matter what the cost. That includes sex; American men receive the message that most males are in a constant state of sexual desire, and that sex is an achievement to which they are entitled. In contrast, women in our society learn to be passive and accommodating and to smile when they mean "no." Women learn that they should look sexy without actually being sexual and that they are the sexual "gatekeepers."

> "... in a culture where the dominant definition of sex is the taking of pleasure from women by men, rape is an expression of the sexual norms of the culture, not violations of those norms."
>
> —*Professor and author Robert Jensen, 2004, p. 168*

The United States is also a violent society, with comparatively weak sanctions against sexually violent men. All of these factors combine to give America one of the highest rape rates among industrialized countries (Harrendorf et al., 2010; Murnen et al., 2002).

Women in countries around the world are vulnerable. Women in South Africa have a greater chance of being raped than of learning to read; 1 in 4 South African girls will be raped before the age of 16 (Dempster, 2002). In Islamic countries, where women are seen as subordinate to men, a woman who reports a rape can be accused of the serious crime of *zina*, or extramarital sex. The only way a woman can prove that a rape occurred is if four Muslim male witnesses testify on her behalf. Without this, she will be punished: 100 lashes if she is unmarried and death by stoning if she is married.

Rape is not viewed the same in all parts of the world. In some places, rape is an initiation rite into adulthood. Among the Kikuyu tribe of East Africa, a man was not considered a man until he raped a girl, and a girl of the Aruntra tribe of Australia could not marry until after her ritual rape (Sanday, 1981). Rape is used as a punishment in some Islamic countries; in 2002 a 12-year-old

The Rape of the Daughters of Leucippus by Peter Paul Rubens.

Rape of the Daughters of Leucippus (oil on canvas), Rubens, Peter Paul (1577-1640)/Alte Pinakothek, Munich, Germany/Giraudon/The Bridgeman Art Library

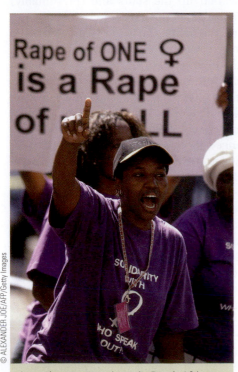

An anti-rape campaigner in South Africa.

© ALEXANDER JOE/AFP/Getty Images

In 1991, William Kennedy Smith, nephew to President John F. Kennedy, was accused of rape by Patricia Bowman. Due to rape shield laws, most accounts of the trial did not publish her name, and videos covered her face with a blue dot. Bowman, who passed two polygraph tests and a voice stress analysis, was presented by the defense as a liar. Her life was exposed in the press, which even revealed her academic record and the number of speeding tickets she had received (Benedict, 1992). After a 77-minute deliberation, the jury found Smith not guilty. In the years since his acquittal, Smith has been accused of sexual assault by at least two other women.

Also in 1991, boxer Mike Tyson was accused of raping and sodomizing Desireé Washington, Miss Black Rhode Island. His defense attorneys presented the argument that Tyson's reputation as a violent womanizer was so well known that any woman should know that going on a date with him meant agreeing to sex. Tyson was convicted and served 3 years of a 6-year sentence.

Images of rape are often eroticized in the media. This Dolce & Gabbana ad, which was banned in 2007, seems to glorify gang rape.

boy in Pakistan walked unchaperoned with a girl from a different tribe. His punishment: his teenaged *sister* was gang-raped while hundreds of people watched and cheered, in order to shame his family (Eltahawy, 2002).

Rape in the Media

Images of sexual violence are prevalent in the media (Yang & Linz, 1990). Rape is a common theme in books, music, television, and film. Unfortunately, many of the presentations of rape support rape myths.

In Ayn Rand's novel *The Fountainhead*, which has been voted one of the top 20 most influential books of all time, the hero, Howard Roark, rapes the heroine. In this book, rape is presented as love, and as a strong woman's wish for humiliation at the hands of a man. In rap music, especially **gangsta rap**, women are often reduced to objects that are only good for sex and abuse (Adams & Fuller, 2006). Twenty-two percent of gangsta rap songs contain violent and misogynistic lyrics (Armstrong, 2001). On *General Hospital,* America's longest-running daytime soap opera, Luke Spencer raped Laura Webber. Soon afterward, in the most watched event in soap opera history, Laura married Luke, and female viewers sighed at how romantic it all was. Television often associates violence with passion.

On *Cheers,* before Sam and Diane finally hook up after years of sexual tension, they call each other names and

Gangsta rap A genre of hip-hop music characterized by violent and often degrading lyrics.

ASK YOURSELF
Should rape victims be identified in the press? Why or why not?

slap each other. In films, rape is often eroticized and presented as though women enjoy it. In what many describe as film's most romantic scene, Rhett Butler carries Scarlett up the stairs and (presumably) rapes her. In the morning, Scarlett is singing and happy and in love. Contrary to the many movie rape scenes in which sexual assault is portrayed as arousing and erotic, the rape scene in *Deliverance*—a scene of *male* rape—is shown as brutal and horrifying.

Exposure to the media influences our views. After viewing scenes from R-rated films that objectified or degraded women, male subjects were more likely to feel that a woman who was raped by an acquaintance "got what she wanted" and more likely to perceive her suffering as less compared to what non-viewers perceived (Milburn, Mather, & Conrad, 2000).

Network news also presents a skewed view of rape. Most crime reporters and editors are men; men are more likely to believe rape myths, which may color their reporting on the crime (Benedict, 1992). Also, news organizations tend to ignore the average to focus on the sensational. So although most women are raped by someone they know, most news reports focus on stranger rape (unless of course, a celebrity is involved). In many publicized rape cases, the female victim is at least as vilified as the assailant.

Rape is brutal, destructive, and pervasive. Yet it is an unfortunate reality that adults are not the only ones who are sexually assaulted. Our youngest and most vulnerable are often the ones who are most callously abused by sexual predators.

Rape is seen as both a spoil of war and as an act of aggression designed to dominate and humiliate the enemy (Nagel, 2003). In the Old Testament, women of conquered tribes were kidnapped and raped and forced to marry their captors. Even today, women are seen as prizes to be taken from the enemy, just as land or property. When Japan invaded China in late 1937, the Japanese raped as many as 80,000 Chinese women and girls. American soldiers raped Vietnamese women and girls as a means of terror and domination (Brownmiller, 1993). In the 1990s there was widespread rape of Croatian women by Serbian men in Bosnia, and as many as 500,000 women and girls were sexually assaulted during the civil war in Rwanda (UNICEF, 1996). Today, rape is used as a systematic weapon of ethnic cleansing in the Darfur region of western Sudan.

Rape and Society

Rape is not universal; although it may be related to biological drives, it is also an expression of cultural forces. Peggy Reeves Sanday described the differences between "rape-free" societies and "rape-prone" societies (Sanday, 1981). In cultures where rape is rare, women are treated with respect, and there is little interpersonal violence. Women's contributions to society are admired and valued. In contrast, rape-prone societies are characterized by male dominance and interpersonal violence, especially toward women. Women are afforded a lower status and may be treated as property. Also, in these societies the natural environment is more likely to be exploited rather than treated with reverence; it's as though if one is willing to rape the land, they are more willing to rape women.

The United States is a rape-prone society. According to the U.S. Department of Justice (which only considers *reported* rapes—actual rates are much higher), the rate of rape in America is 3 times higher than Germany's, almost twice that seen in France, and 20 times higher than Japan's (Harrendorf, Heiskanen, & Malby, 2010). Gender roles in America match those of rape-prone cultures. The cultural ideal is one of a dominant and assertive man attaining his dreams no matter what the cost. That includes sex; American men receive the message that most males are in a constant state of sexual desire, and that sex is an achievement to which they are entitled. In contrast,

The Rape of the Daughters of Leucippus by Peter Paul Rubens.

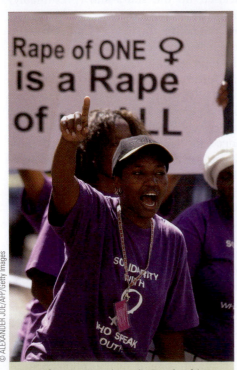

An anti-rape campaigner in South Africa.

women in our society learn to be passive and accommodating and to smile when they mean "no." Women learn that they should look sexy without actually being sexual and that they are the sexual "gatekeepers."

> "... in a culture where the dominant definition of sex is the taking of pleasure from women by men, rape is an expression of the sexual norms of the culture, not violations of those norms."
>
> —*Professor and author Robert Jensen, 2004, p. 168*

The United States is also a violent society, with comparatively weak sanctions against sexually violent men. All of these factors combine to give America one of the highest rape rates among industrialized countries (Harrendorf et al., 2010; Murnen et al., 2002).

Women in countries around the world are vulnerable. Women in South Africa have a greater chance of being raped than of learning to read; 1 in 4 South African girls will be raped before the age of 16 (Dempster, 2002). In Islamic countries, where women are seen as subordinate to men, a woman who reports a rape can be accused of the serious crime of *zina,* or extramarital sex. The only way a woman can prove that a rape occurred is if four Muslim male witnesses testify on her behalf. Without this, she will be punished: 100 lashes if she is unmarried and death by stoning if she is married.

Rape is not viewed the same in all parts of the world. In some places, rape is an initiation rite into adulthood. Among the Kikuyu tribe of East Africa, a man was not considered a man until he raped a girl, and a girl of the Aruntra tribe of Australia could not marry until after her ritual rape (Sanday, 1981). Rape is used as a punishment in some Islamic countries; in 2002 a 12-year-old

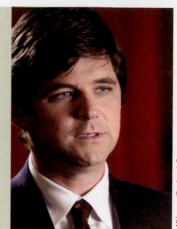

In 1991, William Kennedy Smith, nephew to President John F. Kennedy, was accused of rape by Patricia Bowman. Due to rape shield laws, most accounts of the trial did not publish her name, and videos covered her face with a blue dot. Bowman, who passed two polygraph tests and a voice stress analysis, was presented by the defense as a liar. Her life was exposed in the press, which even revealed her academic record and the number of speeding tickets she had received (Benedict, 1992). After a 77-minute deliberation, the jury found Smith not guilty. In the years since his acquittal, Smith has been accused of sexual assault by at least two other women.

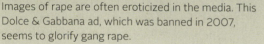

Images of rape are often eroticized in the media. This Dolce & Gabbana ad, which was banned in 2007, seems to glorify gang rape.

Also in 1991, boxer Mike Tyson was accused of raping and sodomizing Desireé Washington, Miss Black Rhode Island. His defense attorneys presented the argument that Tyson's reputation as a violent womanizer was so well known that any woman should know that going on a date with him meant agreeing to sex. Tyson was convicted and served 3 years of a 6-year sentence.

boy in Pakistan walked unchaperoned with a girl from a different tribe. His punishment: his teenaged *sister* was gang-raped while hundreds of people watched and cheered, in order to shame his family (Eltahawy, 2002).

Rape in the Media

Images of sexual violence are prevalent in the media (Yang & Linz, 1990). Rape is a common theme in books, music, television, and film. Unfortunately, many of the presentations of rape support rape myths.

In Ayn Rand's novel *The Fountainhead,* which has been voted one of the top 20 most influential books of all time, the hero, Howard Roark, rapes the heroine. In this book, rape is presented as love, and as a strong woman's wish for humiliation at the hands of a man. In rap music, especially **gangsta rap**, women are often reduced to objects that are only good for sex and abuse (Adams & Fuller, 2006). Twenty-two percent of gangsta rap songs contain violent and misogynistic lyrics (Armstrong, 2001). On *General Hospital,* America's longest-running daytime soap opera, Luke Spencer raped Laura Webber. Soon afterward, in the most watched event in soap opera history, Laura married Luke, and female viewers sighed at how romantic it all was. Television often associates violence with passion.

On *Cheers,* before Sam and Diane finally hook up after years of sexual tension, they call each other names and

Gangsta rap A genre of hip-hop music characterized by violent and often degrading lyrics.

ASK YOURSELF

Should rape victims be identified in the press? Why or why not?

slap each other. In films, rape is often eroticized and presented as though women enjoy it. In what many describe as film's most romantic scene, Rhett Butler carries Scarlett up the stairs and (presumably) rapes her. In the morning, Scarlett is singing and happy and in love. Contrary to the many movie rape scenes in which sexual assault is portrayed as arousing and erotic, the rape scene in *Deliverance*—a scene of *male* rape—is shown as brutal and horrifying.

Exposure to the media influences our views. After viewing scenes from R-rated films that objectified or degraded women, male subjects were more likely to feel that a woman who was raped by an acquaintance "got what she wanted" and more likely to perceive her suffering as less compared to what non-viewers perceived (Milburn, Mather, & Conrad, 2000).

Network news also presents a skewed view of rape. Most crime reporters and editors are men; men are more likely to believe rape myths, which may color their reporting on the crime (Benedict, 1992). Also, news organizations tend to ignore the average to focus on the sensational. So although most women are raped by someone they know, most news reports focus on stranger rape (unless of course, a celebrity is involved). In many publicized rape cases, the female victim is at least as vilified as the assailant.

Rape is brutal, destructive, and pervasive. Yet it is an unfortunate reality that adults are not the only ones who are sexually assaulted. Our youngest and most vulnerable are often the ones who are most callously abused by sexual predators.

Sexual Abuse of Children

After completion of this section, you will be able to . . .

○ Define *childhood sexual abuse* and *incest*.

○ Consider the prevalence of CSA, and understand the difficulties in getting an accurate assessment of its scope.

○ Describe some typical characteristics of child sex abusers.

○ Describe the effects of sexual abuse on children and on adult survivors.

○ Critically evaluate studies on the effects of CSA on psychological health.

○ List the types of treatment for child molesters and ways to prevent CSA.

> On average, there is one child molester per square mile in the United States. The average child molester victimizes between 50 and 150 children before ever being arrested. A child molester has a 3% chance of being caught for sexual offenses (Salter, 2003).

Child sexual abuse (CSA) is inappropriate sexual behavior between a child and an adult. It may include exhibitionism, sexual touching, and oral, anal, and vaginal intercourse. When children are sexually abused it is usually by someone they know. Because of the power disparity between adults and children, adult–child sex is seen as coercive, even if the child does not resist. Voluntary sexual contact between children of a similar age is not considered CSA.

Prevalence of Abuse

Childhood sexual abuse is widespread. Estimates for CSA range from 7% to 36% of girls and 3% to 29% of boys, but it is most likely that approximately 20% to 25% of women and one of every six men were sexually abused as children (Finkelhor, Hotaling, Lewis, & Smith, 1990; Hindman & Peters, 2001; Pereda, Guilera, Forns, & Gomez-Benito, 2009; Salter, 2003).

The exact prevalence of CSA is hard to determine because it is the most under-reported form of child abuse, with as many as 88% of cases going unreported (Hanson & Bussière, 1998). There are many reasons why children do not report their abuse. First of all, children are taught to defer to their elders, and CSA is usually committed by a trusted adult, who instructs the child not to tell. Children may think that the abuse is their own fault or that no one will believe them. They may fear possible punishment or consequences to loved ones if the abuse is reported. Sexual abuse of boys is particularly under-reported. Most sexual abusers of boys are male, and boys may be loath to tell due to the additional stigma of perceived homosexuality. As with adult rape, childhood victims of sexual abuse are most likely to report their assault if it was committed by a stranger or if it involved physical injury.

Incest is sexual contact between people who are related by blood or adoption, or who have a caregiving relationship, such as stepparents and stepchildren. In the context of CSA it is sexual contact between a child and an adult who is related to him or her or who is a stepparent. Kinsey and colleagues (Kinsey, Pomeroy, Martin, & Gebhard, 1953) reported that 24% of their sample experienced incest; more recent studies similarly show that at least 20% of women have experienced childhood sexual contact with an adult relative (Atwood, 2007). Father–daughter incest is the most reported form of incest, followed by uncle–niece, stepfather–stepdaughter, brother–sister, and incest between cousins (Atwood, 2007). Incest generally occurs in families that already have serious dysfunctions, such as physical violence or alcohol or drug abuse. Incest may also be more common in conservative fundamentalist religious families (Gil, 1988).

Typical Characteristics of Child Sex Abusers

Most of those who sexually abuse children are trusted relatives, friends, or neighbors. Some who sexually abuse children are pedophiles and are predominantly sexually attracted to children. It is important to note that not all child molesters are pedophiles; some have other motives for sexual contact with children. Also, not all pedophiles have committed sexual offenses against children.

Child molesters tend to have lower IQs, poorer social skills, and lower self-esteem than normal (Blanchard et al., 2007). They are often more religious and conservative than average, and less knowledgeable about sexuality. It is important to remember, though, that most of our information about sexual abusers comes from those who have been caught and prosecuted. Those who are not caught do not necessarily fit this profile, and may in fact be educated, socially adept, and successful.

Up to 96% of sexual abusers of children are male, and perhaps 98% of these are heterosexual (Holmes & Slap, 1998; Jenny, Roesler, & Poyer, 1994). Some people find it hard to accept that heterosexual men molest boys—wouldn't that mean the men are actually homosexual? Imagine that you are a straight male who currently doesn't have a girlfriend. You are lonely and somewhat sexually frustrated. A 6-year-old girl walks by you—would you be interested in having a sexual relationship with the child? No! You would find this idea repulsive. It is the same with gay men; they are no more interested in having a sexual relationship with a young boy than straight males are interested in young girls (Cantor, 2002).

> "To ask 'how many gay men are pedophiles' is to ask 'how many of the men with a primary interest in adults have a primary interest in non-adults.' The answer is none. . . . if one's primary interest is in adults, it is not in children, regardless of the child's sex."
>
> —*Psychologist James Cantor, 2002*

It is difficult to accept that a human being would sexually abuse a child. To reconcile this reality, people often look for ways to excuse the molester's behavior. Some people assume that molesters

Childhood sexual abuse (CSA) Inappropriate sexual behavior between a child and an adult.

Incest Sexual contact between people who are related by blood or adoption, or stepparents and stepchildren.

In the 1950s, celebrities Sandra Dee and Marilyn Van Derbur Atler (Miss America of 1958) were both victims of sexual molestation by their father, but neither spoke up for many years because they most likely would not have been believed. Experts at the time thought that incest was a one in a million occurrence. They also felt that women who reported it were expressing their Oedipal fantasies, as described by Freud. It is now thought that Freud's patients were actually incest victims, but Freud interpreted their descriptions of incest as fantasies. We now know that incest is not uncommon. Celebrities Teri Hatcher and Oprah Winfrey have come forward to talk about their own experiences with childhood incest.

etration (Kendall-Tackett, Williams, & Finkelhor, 1993; Noll, Trickett, & Putnam, 2003).

Childhood sexual abuse does not need to be violent or painful to be traumatic. In fact, when there is less physical trauma, childhood victims often feel more guilt and are more likely to see the abuse as their "fault"—that they "let it happen" (Clancy, 2010). Many adult survivors of CSA didn't experience the abuse as traumatic when it occurred and only came to regard it as such years later. As children, they may not have clearly understood the meaning or significance of the behaviors they were engaging in, but as adults they were able to reconceptualize the event. In many cases, when the abuse was not as physically traumatic at the time, the betrayal the adult victims felt later could be even more intense (Clancy, 2010). It's often presented in the media that CSA involves force, fear, and threat and is immediately traumatic for the victims. But many abusers use love and trust, not fists and fear, as weapons against the child, so adult survivors compare their own experience to these cultural scripts and feel even more guilt and shame (Clancy, 2010).

In general, the lifetime prevalence of psychiatric problems is higher in those with a history of CSA than in those without (Molnar, Buka, & Kessler, 2001). Survivors of CSA are more likely to suffer from PTSD, depression, and drug or alcohol problems than non-victims are. They may show aggressive or self-destructive behaviors and are more likely to experience low self-esteem, anxiety, fear, and a need to please others (Hindman & Peters, 2001). These problems can continue into adulthood. Boys who have been sexually abused are more likely to externalize their suffering by acting aggressively with others, whereas girls internalize and become depressed (Finkelhor, 1990).

Children who have been sexually abused have been "groomed for silence and betrayal" (Veldhuis & Freyd, 1999). Survivors may therefore have problems forming adult intimate relationships and can have difficulty trusting those who are close to them. CSA can also lead to sexual problems (Hindman & Peters, 2001; Noll et al., 2003). Although some adult survivors of CSA are more preoccupied with sex, others experience sexual aversion or ambivalence. Girls who are sexually assaulted as children or adolescents also have a greater risk of being sexually assaulted as adults (Tjaden & Thoennes, 2000). Some studies suggest that gay, lesbian, and bisexual adults were more likely to have been sexually abused as children (Balsam, Rothblum, & Beauchaine, 2005; Beitchman et al., 1992), but there is certainly no evidence that CSA *causes* homosexuality. Because most sexual assailants of children are men, this supposition would suggest that being molested by a man would cause boys to grow up to desire men but cause girls to grow up to be sexually indifferent toward them.

Not every child who has been a victim of CSA—indeed, not all who have been victims of *any* traumatic experience—has psychological problems; perhaps a third of adult survivors of sexual

were themselves abused and that this somehow justifies their actions (although it doesn't explain the majority of CSA survivors who do not go on to abuse others). The reality is that most child molesters probably were not themselves victims of CSA. In one study, 61% to 67% of child molesters said that they had been abused as children. But when the molesters were told that they would be hooked up to a lie detector, less than half—29% to 32%—reported that they had been childhood victims (Hindman & Peters, 2001).

Child molesters get close to their victims by taking advantage of a child's innocence and trusting nature. The abuser often gives the child special favors and attention. He moves slowly from normal physical affection, such as hugs, to sexual attention. The molester may tell the child that such behavior is normal and that is how people learn, or that it is how people who love each other act. Children are threatened with harm if they tell of their activities; although physical harm is sometimes threatened, more often the threat of punishment, withdrawn love, or abandonment is sufficient.

Effects of Sexual Abuse on Children and Adult Survivors

There are no specific symptoms associated with CSA; some children suffer psychological, emotional, social, and sexual problems that persist into adulthood, and others seem to experience little to no harm (Paolucci, Genuis, & Violato, 2001). In general, the consequences of CSA tend to be more serious if the abuse goes on for a long period, if it involved a close relation such as a father or stepfather, if there was violence, and if it involved pen-

critical evaluation

The effects of CSA on psychological health

Although most people take for granted that children who have been sexually abused will suffer from long-term psychological damage, not everyone agrees. Bruce Rind, Philip Tromovitch, and Robert Bauserman (1998) analyzed 59 studies involving 35,000 college students who had been abused as minors. They determined that although victims of CSA were more psychologically maladjusted in 17 out of 18 categories, this disturbance was only slight, and mostly a result of family dysfunction. The researchers thought that not all adult–child sexual interactions should be called "abuse," a term that should be reserved for cases in which "a young person felt that he or she did not willingly participate in the encounter and he or she experienced negative reactions to it." This research created great controversy among scientists and also in the media. Many scientists thought the study was poorly designed and statistically flawed. Soon after the article was published, Dr. Laura, a conservative talk show host, railed against the research on her radio program, calling it "junk science." This led to a firestorm of debate about the research, and the report was eventually condemned by the U.S. Congress, which passed a unanimous resolution that renounced the study's findings.

Consider the following issues regarding the study by Rind, Tromovitch, and Bauserman (1998):

> ### What was the research design?

Sample group. Many studies of CSA survivors use a clinical sample— patients in therapy. Because these subjects are by definition dealing with psychological issues of some type, using a clinical sample may overestimate the harm of CSA. Rind and colleagues used samples of college students, which may underestimate the harm of CSA: because childhood sexual abuse can hurt academic performance, those who have been less hurt by its effects are more likely to be in college than those who show more serious psychological harm. Can either of these samples be generalized to the entire population? What sample would you choose?

Meta-analysis. Rind and colleagues used meta-analysis to arrive at their results. An advantage of this process is that it combines data from many studies; however, the findings are only as strong as the data included (Dallam et al., 2001). How would you evaluate whether the articles chosen are a true representation of the field and whether they were accurately presented?

> ### What operational definitions were used?

An ambiguous or undefined term can lead to great variations in results. If two researchers define "sexual abuse" or "harm" differently, they may get widely dissimilar results.

Childhood sexual abuse. In Rind et al. (1998), CSA was more broadly defined than in other studies and included exhibitionism, coercive sexual contact between two adolescent peers, and consensual sexual contact between a teenager and an older partner. Although these situations fit the legal definition of CSA, Rind and colleagues combined all data and did not discriminate between, for example, an adult forcing a 5-year-old into intercourse, and a 16-year-old having willing sex with a 21-year-old. Including consensual teenage sex in the data would lessen the perceived severity of sexual contact involving children. What do you think should be included in a study of CSA? What experiences does CSA include—physical contact only, or should exhibitionism be included? Does the age of both parties matter? Is any sexual experience a child has by definition abuse (Tavris, 2000)? Why or why not?

Consent. Rind, Tromovitch, and Bauserman (1998) thought that if a child is not forced into sexual contact through violence, then they have consented to the contact. Must sexual abuse involve violence? If a child is not physically forced then does that imply consent? What do you consider consent to be?

Harm. Is what society calls harmful necessarily bad? Remember that masturbation was called "self-abuse" and was once considered to lead to blindness, disease, and death (Ericksen, 2000). How should scientists measure harm? Rind and colleagues relied on self-reports of perceived harm experienced by college students, a measurement that may minimize the potential damage of CSA. Students may not recognize nor admit to psychological harm. In the Rind study, PTSD was not measured, and 11 different measurements of depression were compressed into one score (Ericksen, 2000). Even with these manipulations, 33% of men and 75% of women experienced what the authors describe as at least a "minimal" degree of harm. What do you feel is an acceptable level of harm?

> ### What fallacies of reasoning may have come into play?

Appeal to emotion. The language used on a questionnaire can greatly influence the results. Subjects might respond differently to a survey question that asks "were you ever sexually molested as a child" compared to one that asks "as a child, did you ever experience sexual intimacy with an adult?"

Searching for perfect solutions. Must a scientific article be perfect in order for us to accept its findings? If one aspect of a study (an operational definition or a statistical analysis) is faulty, does that necessarily mean that every aspect of the data is false?

Correlation and causality. If adult survivors of CSA are in fact less psychologically healthy than those who were not molested, is it the sexual abuse or other familial factors (such as violence or emotional neglect) that caused the negative effects? Some researchers (Melchert, 2000; Rind et al., 1998) think dysfunctional family factors are more responsible for psychological maladjustment than adult–child sexual contact; others disagree (Molnar et al., 2001; Paolucci et al., 2001). It is always difficult to separate intertwined factors such as CSA and family dysfunction.

Bias. Opponents of the Rind study claim that the study is sullied by the authors' biases—because one of the authors has published articles in a pro-pedophile journal. Rind and colleagues maintain that their detractors are biased and are letting society's preconceived notions override their acceptance of a scientific finding (Rind, Bauserman, & Tromovitch, 2001). Should the personal or political views of scientists be considered when evaluating their research?

It is clear that not everyone is affected by CSA the same way. Some may experience no harm, whereas others suffer devastating effects. (It is important to note that just because some abuse victims may survive relatively unscathed, the problem of CSA should not be minimized. Some people may walk away from a car accident without severe trauma, but that doesn't mean that car accidents are something to take lightly.) Also, all adult–child sexual contact is not equivalent. Studies of CSA require—as do all studies— clear operational definitions, a strong and appropriate research design, and a mindful approach in evaluating results.

abuse have no symptoms (Kendall-Tackett et al., 1993; Putnam, 2003). It is unknown why some walk away seemingly unscathed, but it is thought that this resilience may be related to environmental as well as genetic factors. Children who have supportive adults in their lives are less likely to experience psychological problems later in life. It may also be that having two copies of a certain protective gene (called 5-HTT) predisposes someone to resilience (Caspi et al., 2003).

Attitudes About Adult–Child Sexual Abuse

"Child molester" is one of the most stigmatized labels a person can have. Even in prison, among a population of those who have broken the legal and social contract with society, child molesters are reviled (Mullis & Baunach, 2003). It was not always this way. In ancient Greece, it was typical and accepted for an older man to have a sexual relationship with an adolescent boy that he would mentor. The young boy was expected to be the passive sexual partner, and it wasn't necessary that he enjoy the sexual acts. In the Sambia tribe of Papua New Guinea, boys as young as 7 fellate older boys as a rite of passage, and children of the Mangaia tribe of Polynesia are instructed in ways of sexuality by older men and women. During colonial times in the United States, the age of consent was 10 (except in Delaware, where the age of consent was 7).

Child–adult sexual contact is no longer viewed as a normal expression of sexuality. This shift has occurred in part due to the changing status of childhood. In the past, children began work at a young age to help support the family. Today, child labor laws and compulsory education have lengthened childhood until at least the age of 16 (Mullis & Baunach, 2003). It is ironic that as the age of consent has increased, puberty occurs earlier and earlier,

creating a generation of "sexually mature legal minors." For most people, views about adult–child sexuality differ based on the age of the child. Many are not as upset by the thought of a 16-year-old engaging in sex with an adult as they are by the thought of an 8-year-old engaging in sex with an adult. Many also hold a double standard concerning adult–child sex when the minor is a boy.

Response to Adult–Child Sex

Legal and societal responses to adult–child sex offenders include punishment (in both criminal and civil courts), treatment, and prevention (Mullis & Baunach, 2003).

Punishment

There are many criminal laws by which a child molester can be punished, including those related to statutory rape, sexual assault, crimes against nature, and defilement of a minor. The maximum penalty is life imprisonment without the possibility of parole, but the average sentence for those who sexually abuse children is 11 years (Cloud, 2004). The passage of the Adam Walsh Child Protection and Safety Act of 2006 eliminated the statute of limitations for prosecution of felony sex offenses involving a minor. Victims can also sue their assailants in a civil court to be financially compensated for their suffering. The Roman Catholic Church has had to pay out up to $1 billion as a result of lawsuits brought by people who were sexually abused by priests (see the From Cells to Society feature on page 423).

Treatment

Child molesters are seen as having psychological problems that must be treated, more for the good of society than due to any concern for the individuals. Because there is no single cause of CSA, there is no one treatment. Some offenders choose to attend sup-

When 23-year-old teacher Debra LaFave (left) slept with her 14-year-old student, some people felt that the student was "lucky," although it is unlikely they would express the same view if a 14-year-old girl was involved with an adult man. The TV program *South Park* (right) parodied this situation. When it was reported to the police that the 5-year-old Ike character was having an intimate relationship with his kindergarten teacher, the officer's response was "nice."

The Catholic Church and Child Sexual Abuse

A study done by the John Jay College of Criminal Justice found that 4% of U.S. priests ministering from 1950 to 2002 were accused of sexual abuse with a minor; this represents 4,392 clergymen and almost 11,000 victims. Most of the abused were male adolescents and teenagers.

Americans were angered by the fact that nearly all of the accused priests retained their positions, and others were simply reassigned to another parish; only 6% were removed from the priesthood altogether. Also, senior Church officials who knew of the accusations did not report these crimes to the police. The U.S. Council of Catholic Bishops subsequently voted to approve a

policy that would permanently remove from the ministry any priest who committed a single act of sexual abuse; the Vatican rejected this policy because elements of it conflicted with Church law. Since the scandal broke, there have been numerous lawsuits and hundreds of millions of dollars have been paid out to accusers (Terry et al., 2004).

port groups, where they are encouraged to admit their urges and learn to restructure their lives to avoid children. Through psychotherapy, offenders may be trained for social skills and get aversion or cognitive-behavioral therapy. Others may receive pharmaceutical treatments, including antidepressants and anti-androgen treatments to reversibly reduce testosterone (Stone, Winslade, & Klugman, 2000). Although treatments do not "cure" child molesters, they are effective; out of every 100 that would reoffend without treatment, only 60 would reoffend with treatment (Hanson et al., 2002; Losel & Schmucker, 2005; Salter, 2003).

The **recidivism rate**, or incidence of repeated offense, for sex offenders is not as high as some believe, but the true extent of recidivism may be difficult to determine. Hanson and colleagues determined that 12.3% to 13.4% of sex offenders were rearrested for sexual offenses within 5 years (Hanson & Bussière, 1998; Hanson et al., 2002). However, when evaluating this finding, one must consider a number of things. First, the vast majority of sex offenses go unreported, and these studies only considered those who had been arrested and reconvicted for their crimes, which would considerably underestimate the actual recidivism rate. Also, Hanson's studies only considered reconvictions within a 4- to 5-year span, whereas others (Prentky, Lee, Knight, & Cerce, 2001) found that only half of reconvictions occur within the first 5 years. Other studies find the reoffend rate for sexual crimes to be closer to 39% for rapists and 52% for child molesters (Salter, 2003). In general, sexual offense recidivism is higher when offenders select victims much younger than themselves, victimize strangers, and fail to complete treatment.

NAMBLA, or the North American Man-Boy Love Association, is dedicated to justifying and normalizing adult men having sex with children. They claim that preventing children from exploring their sexuality with adults infringes on children's rights. A similar group, the Rene Guyon Society, has as its motto: "Sex by 8 or else it's too late."

Prevention

Society attempts to prevent child abuse by identifying convicted child molesters and educating parents and children about potential offenders. **Megan's Law** is named after Megan Kanka, a 7-year-old New Jersey girl who was raped and murdered by a convicted sex offender who moved in across the street from her family. This law requires each state to have a procedure for notifying people about convicted sex offenders who live in the community. Within 30 days of release from prison, sex offenders must register their name, address, photo, and other information with the state. This information is available to the community, although the means of community notification differs from state to state. Some states have a website of registered offenders, and others identify offenders with mailed flyers. In some states, offenders are required to go door to door to identify themselves to neighbors. Registered sex offenders may also have their freedom of movement restricted by electronic monitoring devices.

More than 674,000 Americans are on sex-offender registries—more than the population of Vermont, the District of Columbia, North Dakota, or Wyoming. At least 5 states require sex-offender registration for adults who visit a prostitute, at least 13 states require registration for public urination, and 32 states require registration for those who expose their genitals in public, such as flashers or streakers. At least 29 states require registration for teenagers who have consensual sex with another teenager under the age of consent. In some states, "Romeo and Juliet" exceptions lessen or eliminate criminal penalties for young people who have noncoercive sex with each other, but in 11 states there are no exceptions: anyone having sex with a person below the age of consent could be required to register as a sex offender (Human Rights Watch, 2007).

Upon registering, sex offenders often have trouble finding a job or buying a house; in many communities, they are forbidden to live within 2,000 feet of a school, child-care center, library, pool, or park. This

Recidivism rate The incidence of a person repeating a crime or other antisocial behavior patterns after he or she has been punished for or treated to stop the behavior.

Megan's Law The informal name for the laws in the United States regarding registration and public notification about sex offenders.

A community is notified that a registered sex offender lives in their neighborhood. The nature and severity of the crime is not described.

In April of 2006, Stephen Marshall, a 20-year-old Canadian man, got a list of 29 names and addresses from Maine's sex offender registry. He went to the homes of two registered sex offenders, who were both strangers to him. Marshall shot and killed both men. One offender had raped a child. The other had been convicted of statutory rape—when he was 19 he had sex with his girlfriend, who was 2 weeks shy of her 16th birthday.

_____

_____

_____

_____

_____

sexactually

Communicating with Your Child About Child Sexual Abuse

Although it can feel uncomfortable, it is important to talk to your children about appropriate and inappropriate sexual touch. Here are some suggestions regarding how to approach the topic.

- From an early age, talk to your child about sex. If you are open and honest, your child is more likely to be comfortable bringing questions and concerns to you.
- Speak calmly when talking about sexual abuse. Don't instill the idea that all strangers are dangerous or that danger *only* comes from strangers. Most people in the world are not child molesters, and most children who are sexually abused are molested by someone they know.
- Most parents want to teach their children to respect adults. Let your children know that this does not mean blind obedience to everything that any adult says. Let your child know that if an adult tells him to do something that he's uncomfortable with, your child should talk it over with you.
- Don't just teach your child about "good touch" and "bad touch." This is too limited and leaves too much to a child's responsibility to discern the differences. Instead teach about good touch, bad touch, and private touch. Stress to your child that if someone were to suggest private touch ("This is our secret"), your child should immediately discuss it with you (at the time of puberty, the discussion should change to focus on appropriate touch for a young adult and eventually an adult) (Hertz, 2009).
- Talk about the tricks that child molesters can use. Those who sexually abuse children may tell the child that it is her fault, that no one will believe her if she tells, or that if she tells, someone close to her will be hurt. Let your child know that you will always love and always be there for her, no matter what.
- It's not all about talking. Listen when your child tries to tell you something, especially when it seems hard for him or her to talk about it.

greatly reduces the available housing choices for these people, which may have the unfortunate effect of causing some offenders to go "underground," giving them greater freedom to reoffend. As of 2007, approximately 100,000 registered sex offenders were unaccounted for.

Prevention programs can educate both parents and children about what sexual abuse is and how to avoid it. It is important for parents to communicate with their children about child sexual abuse (see the Sex Actually feature on this page). Education should start early, as many instances of CSA begin on children younger than 3. Children should learn that their body belongs only to them, and they have the right to say "no" to unwanted contact. Parents need to respect children's boundaries: don't force them to kiss smelly old Aunt Ethel or sit on weird Cousin Bruce's lap. Be knowledgeable about who is watching your children—check your babysitter's references and drop in unexpectedly. Know your children, and talk to them if there is a sudden change in their personality. Always keep lines of communication open: let your children know that there are no secrets and they can tell you anything without judgment or shame. Trust your children, and teach them to trust themselves. If they know something is wrong or bad, encourage them to listen to their gut. Finally, parents should establish and uphold rules; for instance, tell your children that they can never go off alone with any adult without your permission.

The good news is that the incidence of child sexual abuse does appear to be declining; the 1990s saw a 39% decline in substantiated cases of CSA (Jones & Finkelhor, 2003). With the continuation of effective treatment programs, incarceration of offenders, and successful education and prevention campaigns, we can hope to eradicate this offense from our society.

Intimate Partner Violence

After completion of this section, you will be able to . . .

- Define *physical, psychological,* and *economic abuse.*

- Understand that men and women of all ages, races, socio-economic statuses, and sexual orientations experience intimate partner violence.

- Compare the incidence of intimate partner violence around the world, and consider the factors that increase the likelihood of its occurrence.

Domestic violence is the leading cause of injury to women between the ages of 15 and 44. Battering is thought to cause more injuries to women than muggings and car accidents combined (Barrier, 1998; Randell, 1990).

More than 10% of the U.S. population—more than 30 million men, women, and children—are physically and emotionally hurt in the place where they should be safest: the home (Tjaden & Thoennes, 2000). In fact, women are 6 times more likely to experience violence from an intimate partner or ex-partner than from a stranger (Bachman & Saltzman, 1995). **Intimate partner violence (IPV)**, also called domestic abuse, is a pattern of abusive behaviors by one or both partners in an intimate relationship such as marriage, cohabitation, or dating. It can happen in any partnership, no matter the gender of the partner and no matter the relationship's length or its legally recognized status. IPV includes not only the criminal acts of **physical abuse** and **sexual violence**. It also includes **psychological abuse**, which may include threats and intimidation, humiliation, or preventing the victim from seeing friends and relatives, and **economic abuse**, such as denial of funds or basic needs. Usually, physical violence against a partner is accompanied by psychological abuse, and in one third to one half of cases physical violence against a partner is accompanied by sexual assault (Krug, Pahlberg, Mercy, Zwi, & Lozano, 2002).

In the past, domestic violence against women was ignored or accepted. A report from Scotland Yard in 1954 read, "There are only about twenty murders a year in London and not all are serious—some are just husbands killing their wives" (Coontz, 2005, p. 241).

Prevalence of Intimate Partner Violence

Estimates suggest that intimate partners commit 20% of all nonfatal violent crimes against women and 3% of violent crimes against men (Rennison, 2003). However, official figures of the incidence of domestic violence are always underestimated because many victims are unwilling to report or even admit to their abuse. Men may be particularly unwilling to report abuse at the hands of their partners. Some think that although women are much more likely to be hurt by their husbands, both men and women exhibit equal overall violent behavior toward each other (Dutton & Nicholls, 2005; Gove, Stile, & Hughes, 1990).

It is a common misconception that the phrase "rule of thumb" refers to an ancient law that decreed a man could beat his wife with a stick, as long as the stick was less than the diameter of his thumb. Although it was true that husbands could legally beat their wives—the size of the stick was never specified.

The number of women killed by spouses, boyfriends, or girlfriends fell by 22% between 1976 and 2000. During this time, the number of men killed by their intimate partner dropped by 68% (Rennison, 2003). Many attribute this decline to the increased availability of women's shelters. When wives kill their husbands it is usually in response to the man's violence against her. When women have realistic options for escaping a violent relationship, they are less likely to kill their abusive spouses (Daly & Wilson, 2006). Some think that women's shelters have actually saved the lives of more men than women (van Wormer & Roberts, 2009).

Forms of Intimate Partner Violence

Why do people physically and emotionally abuse those that they should love the most? There are different forms of violence in relationships. During one form, a conflict escalates out of control and both partners make threatening and violent actions. Violence may occur without thought as to the consequences.

In the other form of relationship violence, one person in the relationship consciously uses violence to control and intimidate the other. Males more often commit this type of violence. Psychological problems and social factors such as stress, alcohol and drug abuse, and a family history of violence can exacerbate the situation. Certain factors that characterize family life may even escalate violence. For example, family members spend a substantial amount of time interacting with each other, which can lead to stress and anger. They know each other so well that they know which "buttons" to push to attack each other.

Intimate partner violence (IPV) A pattern of abusive behaviors by one or more partners in an intimate relationship.

Physical abuse Includes slapping, beating, kicking, threats with an object or weapon, and murder.

Sexual violence Sexual actions or words that are unwanted by and/or harmful to another person.

Psychological abuse Includes behavior that is intended to humiliate or intimidate one's partner, and may take the form of verbal aggression or humiliation, threats of abandonment or abuse, isolation or confinement to the home, and destruction of objects.

Economic abuse Includes such acts as denial of funds, food, or basic needs, or controlling access to health care or employment.

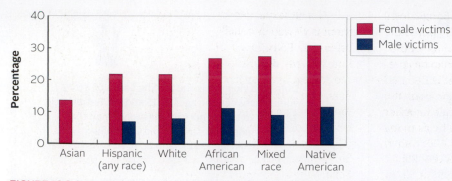

FIGURE 16.2 Comparative rates by race (in percentages) of lifetime physical assault by an intimate partner. (From U.S. Department of Justice, 2000.)

Victims of Intimate Partner Violence

Why would someone stay in an abusive relationship? Abusive relationships often start off wonderfully, and when violence occurs, the victim may believe it was a one-time occurrence. The abuser is often remorseful and apologetic as he or she promises to never again hurt the victim. When the behavior continues, the abuser slowly makes the victim believe it is his or her fault, asking, "Why do you make me do this to you?" It is often hard for people, especially women, to leave abusive relationships. They may not have the financial security to leave, especially if they have children. Also, it's sad but true that women are often safer staying in abusive relationships than leaving—women who leave violent partners are at greater risk of being killed by their partners than those who stay (Jewkes, 2002; Wilson & Daly, 1993).

Men and women of all races, socioeconomic statuses, ages, and sexual orientations may be victims of domestic abuse. Native Americans and African Americans suffer intimate partner violence at higher rates than whites and Asians (although it is thought that the low rate in Asians is due to under-reporting) (Figure 16.2). It is also thought that the incidence of domestic violence in higher income families is under-reported. Low-income women who are victims of domestic abuse are more likely than their more well off counterparts to enter domestic violence shelters or apply for social services. More economically privileged women have the option of staying in a hotel or traveling to be with distant family. These cases may be more frequently filed as divorce rather than as domestic violence.

Although 18- to 24-year-olds comprise only about 12% of the population, they represent the majority of victims of violence committed by a boyfriend or girlfriend (Durose et al., 2005). About 20% of female high school students report being physically or sexually abused by a dating parter (Silverman, Raj, Mucci, & Hathaway, 2001). Women between the ages of 20 and 24 are especially vulnerable to intimate partner violence (Catalano, 2007).

Same-sex domestic abuse may be particularly under-reported. Police officers taking reports might not know that two men or two women are a couple, or couples may be reluctant to expose the nature of their relationship, so same-sex domestic abuse may be reported as assault or battery rather than domestic violence.

Consequences of Intimate Partner Violence

Victims of domestic aggression suffer from the immediate effects of the violence, including bruises, welts, burns, and fractures. The effects of domestic abuse go deeper than the cuts and contusions, however. Domestic abuse also increases a person's risk of future ill health. Men and women who are abused by an intimate partner often suffer from irritable bowel syndrome and other gastrointestinal disorders, chronic pain syndromes such as fibromyalgia, and long-term disability. Sexual and reproductive problems such as pelvic inflammatory disease, sexual dysfunction, and STIs can occur. Victims often also suffer from psychological and behavioral problems, such as alcohol and drug abuse, depression and anxiety, eating disorders, and post-traumatic stress disorder. The consequences of domestic violence can be fatal due to AIDS-related mortality, homicide, or suicide (Krug et al., 2002).

Intimate Partner Violence Around the World

Even though most societies forbid violence against women, the reality is that violations against women's human rights are often sanctioned through cultural practices and norms or through misinterpretation of religious tenets (Kapoor, 2000). Many societies believe that men are inherently superior to women. Therefore, in many developing nations, both men and women agree with the idea that a man has the right to physically discipline his wife; in Egypt, more than 80% of rural women share the view that men are sometimes justified in beating their wives (Krug et al., 2002). Because of these beliefs, in these cultures men often have rights over women and girls. Women are often economically dependent on men, which limits their access to employment and education (Kapoor, 2000).

It can be very difficult to determine the prevalence of domestic violence in other nations because cultural mores may limit a woman's ability to report the abuse. Intimate partner violence occurs in every country on earth; its incidence ranges from about 10% to 15% of the population affected to greater than 70% (Garcia-Moreno, Jansen, Ellsberg, Heise, & Watts, 2006; Krug et al., 2002). Domestic abuse seems to be more prevalent in rural areas than in cities (Garcia-Moreno et al., 2006). For a summary of domestic violence worldwide, see Figure 16.3.

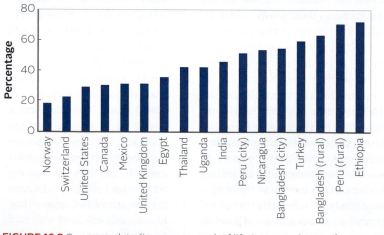

FIGURE 16.3 Summary data (in percentages) of lifetime prevalence of domestic violence around the world. (© Cengage Learning 2013. SOURCE: Garcia-Moreno et al., 2006; Kapoor, 2000; Krug et al., 2002.)

In Egypt, Jordan, Lebanon, Pakistan, Turkey, Bangladesh, and other countries, women may be killed in order to uphold the "honor" of the family. These **honor killings** can occur for a number of reasons: if there is an alleged adultery, if a woman has pre-marital sexual relations, if she dresses in a way that is deemed unacceptable to the family, if she falls in love with someone the family disapproves of, or if she is raped. Usually, a male member of the family kills the female. Worldwide, there may be as many as 5,000 honor killings each year. In 1999 more than 1,000 women were victims of honor killings in Pakistan alone (UNFPA, 2000). Perpetrators of honor killings are either not punished at all, or are served with very lenient punishments.

Sexual Harassment

After completion of this section, you will be able to . . .

○ Define *sexual harassment,* and differentiate between *quid pro quo* and *hostile environment* harassment.

○ Describe the incidence of sexual harassment and explain why most incidents are not reported.

○ List the three main types of harassment in education.

○ Describe the effects of sexual harassment on victims.

What Is Sexual Harassment?

The most widespread of all sexually coercive behavior, **sexual harassment** is unwanted attention of a sexual nature that interferes with an individual's basic right to employment or education. Sexual harassment may include unwanted and unsolicited comments, inappropriate jokes, undesired touch of a sexual nature, sexual pressure, and sexual force. Sexual harassment differs from simple flirting in that choice and mutuality are lacking. It differs from sexual assault in that it doesn't necessarily involve contact or physical force. Like other forms of sexual coercion, sexual harassment may have more to do with power than sexual desire. Some harassers get a sexual thrill or ego boost from humiliating others, whereas others try to establish a mentor-like relationship with the victim and take advantage of that relationship. Some harassers are not even aware that their actions are offensive or unlawful. Both men and women commit sexual harassment and are victims of harassment, although males are much more likely to be offenders and most victims of sexual harassment are women. Same-sex sexual harassment is also a crime—the U.S. Supreme Court has ruled that the sexual orientation of either party should not be an issue.

There are two main types of sexual harassment described by the Equal Employment Opportunity Commission (EEOC). **Quid pro quo** harassment is when compliance with unwanted sexual advances is required as a condition of employment or advancement. Quid pro quo involves individuals with differences in power or authority. A **hostile environment** occurs when persistent and inappropriate behaviors make the workplace offensive or unbearable; this may occur between individuals of equal power or authority. Although many feel as though sexual jokes or obscenities are "just for fun," women in hostile environments are more likely to be treated as sexual objects and to be subject to harassment.

Not all sexual harassment is viewed as equally offensive. Perceptions of harassment depend on the context in which it occurs, who is involved, how long it goes on for, and the severity of the incident (Charney & Russell, 1994; Terpstra & Baker, 2001). Sexual remarks, requests for dates, and repeated comments about one's appearance are generally considered among the mildest of harassing behaviors. Unwanted physical contact of a nonsexual nature and sexual propositions not linked to one's employment are seen as more hostile. Most severe of all are sexual propositions linked to one's employment, unwanted sexual contact, and sexual assault. Different people will view the same offense in different ways. For example, compared to college women, working women (who may have more experience with sexual harassment) are more likely to consider off-color jokes, graffiti, and unwanted physical contact to be sexually harassing (Terpstra & Baker, 2001). Women and men may also perceive the same actions differently: women are more likely to view less obviously threatening situations as harassment (Fitzgerald & Ormerod, 1991). This difference led to a Supreme Court decision and the implementation of the "reasonable woman" standard, in which the typical victim's sensibilities are considered rather than those of the typical offenders.

© Fuse RF/Jupiter Images

Incidence

Sexual harassment is pervasive; between 40% and 60% of women have been affected by it. Harassment is more likely to occur against those who are in a job that is nontraditional for their gender, such as female firefighters or male nurses. Harassment also occurs when one gender, usually men, holds most of the positions of power over the other gender.

Harassment occurs in the workplace, the armed forces, and in schools. In a survey of more than 24,000 federal employees, 44% of women and 19% of men reported experiencing sexual harassment in the past 24 months (U.S. Merit Systems Protection Board, 1996). At least half of the women in the armed services have experienced sexual harassment. The problem may be even worse in our

Honor killing The murder of a (usually female) member of the family where the murderers (usually a male member of the family) believe the victim to have brought dishonor upon the family).

Sexual harassment Unwanted sexual attention that interferes with an individual's basic right to employment or education.

Quid pro quo When compliance with unwanted sexual advances is required as a condition of employment or advancement.

Hostile environment When persistent and inappropriate behaviors make the workplace offensive or unbearable.

Anita Hill and Clarence Thomas.

high schools; 81% of students in eighth through eleventh grades report experiencing some form of sexual harassment in school, including having clothing pulled off or down, being spied on as they dressed or showered, or being forced to do something sexual (American Association of University Women [AAUW], 2001). University students fare only slightly better. In surveys of undergraduates, 20% to 62% of women and 9% to 61% of men report being sexually harassed at their college or university (AAUW, 2006; Charney & Russell, 1994; Kalof, Eby, Matheson, & Kroska, 2001); these numbers are widely variable because they differ based on subjects, survey methods used, and on the definition of sexual harassment.

The vast majority of cases of sexual harassment are not reported; fewer than 10% of victims file formal complaints or initiate legal proceedings (AAUW, 2006; Charney & Russsell, 1994). There are a number of reasons why victims don't report the crime. Many don't recognize their experience as sexual harassment. In addition, men and women resolve conflicts differently. Women, who are socialized to put the needs of others above their own, want to maintain relationships and keep peace. Men are more likely to force a confrontation and seek justice; women just want the behavior to stop. Finally, a fear of reprisal may force sufferers to keep quiet. As with many cases of sexual coercion, the public tends to blame the victim. The whistle-blower may lose his or her job, fail a course, be denied grants, and gain a reputation as a whiner who is unable to play with the "big boys." According to Naomi Wolf, victims are justified in their unwillingness to risk years of work or education, and wrote "not one of the women I have heard from had an outcome that was not worse for her than silence" (Wolf, 2004).

Anita Hill was a professor of law who claimed that Clarence Thomas, then a nominee for the U.S. Supreme Court, sexually harassed her. The U.S. Senate Judiciary Committee's investigation of these charges captivated the nation; in fact, more Americans tuned in to watch the Hill–Thomas hearings than the third game of baseball's American League playoffs (Charney & Russell, 1994). Hill was excoriated in the press and described as "a little bit nutty and a little bit slutty." During Thomas's senate confirmation hearing, few Americans believed her accusations, but once Thomas was confirmed, the tide shifted, and more people believed that Hill was telling the truth. The hearings helped raise national awareness about the problem of sexual harassment; in the 3 months following the hearing, the EEOC received 70% more sexual harassment charges (Charney & Russell, 1994).

"There was a man I worked with a few years ago, who used to tell me every day how nice I looked. Then he started saying how much he wanted to sleep with me. When he started saying he wished that my husband would die so I would have sex with him I started to get scared. Finally, he pushed me up against the wall in the elevator and tried to kiss me. When I went to my (female) supervisor, she told me I should be flattered."

—From the author's files

Sexual Harassment on Campus

Although about 80% of incidents of sexual harassment at a university are peer-to-peer, professors or instructors can also give unwanted sexual attention (AAUW, 2006). Male and female students are both victims of sexual harassment, but their abuse takes different forms. Women are most likely to be the target of sexual jokes or physical contact, whereas men are more likely to be called homophobic names. Those in graduate or medical schools may be particularly vulnerable to harassment; 64% of female graduate students and 73% of women undergoing medical training report being harassed (Kalof et al., 2001; Komaromy, Bindman, Haber, & Sande, 1993). This may be because graduate students often work one-on-one with someone who holds ultimate power over their career. Lesbian, gay, bisexual, and transgendered students are also more likely to experience sexual harassment than are heterosexual students (AAUW, 2006). Sexual harassment is not limited to students; there are cases in which professors report being sexually harassed by students.

There are three main types of harassment that typically occur in the academic setting: **gender harassment**, which includes sexually degrading, hostile, and sexist remarks and behaviors; **unwanted sexual attention**, such as inappropriate and offensive sexual comments, behaviors, and advances; and **sexual bribery and imposition**, including the promise of reward in return for sex or the threat of punishment for withholding sex, and forceful physical attempts at sexual contact (Fitzgerald &

Gender harassment A form of sexual harassment in education that involves sexually degrading or sexist remarks and behaviors.

Unwanted sexual attention Inappropriate and offensive sexual comments, behaviors, and advances.

Sexual bribery and imposition The promise of reward in return for sex or the threat of punishment for withholding sex, and forceful physical attempts at sexual contact.

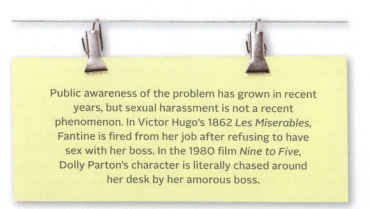

Public awareness of the problem has grown in recent years, but sexual harassment is not a recent phenomenon. In Victor Hugo's 1862 *Les Miserables*, Fantine is fired from her job after refusing to have sex with her boss. In the 1980 film *Nine to Five*, Dolly Parton's character is literally chased around her desk by her amorous boss.

Ormerod, 1991). Gender harassment is the most common reported type of sexual harassment on campus (Kalof et al., 2001). Many students don't recognize that they have been sexually harassed; most of the college students who reported behavior that fit the criteria of sexual harassment answered "no" to the question "have you ever been sexually harassed by a college professor or instructor?" (AAUW, 2006).

Effects of Sexual Harassment on Victims

Although charges of sexual harassment are often ignored or trivialized, harassment is a serious matter: it can adversely affect one's health, relationships, finances, and education or career. Victims of sexual harassment may experience both physical and psychological symptoms such as headaches, sleeplessness, depression, or PTSD. Victims may feel angry, anxious, insecure, guilty, or betrayed. Some victims blame themselves and wonder what they did to encourage the behavior. Some find it hard to keep their mind on their job or their studies and may try to avoid areas where the harasser is likely to be found, which can negatively affect their performance at work or in school. Those who report the offense may suffer from retaliation from the harasser or from others; they may lose their job, or be given a poor evaluation or grade.

There are many ways to deal with sexual harassment. You can submit, ignore the behaviors, avoid the perpetrator, confront the harasser, change jobs or classes, report the harassment, or seek legal assistance (Charney & Russell, 1994). If you choose to be proactive about the situation, you should document the episodes, making note of what happened, when and where the incidents occurred, and the names of any witnesses. If you confront your harasser, you should clearly state your position and describe what you will do if the behavior continues. If there is no change, then you should report the behavior to your supervisor. Victims of sexual harassment can also file formal actions, including filing suit with the Human Rights Commission, the Fair Employment Practices Agency, or the EEOC, or pursuing legal action. Unfortunately, seeking formal actions doesn't always improve a situation. Although 47% thought that pursuing actions did make things better, 33% thought the complaint process made things worse because they incurred retaliation from the perpetrator and/or blame from those who were supposed to help (Charney & Russell, 1994).

• • •

Sex and power are often intertwined in our society. Unfortunately, this can sometimes lead to abuse and violence. Recognizing risk factors and knowing how to best protect yourself from these situations can help to reduce your risk of sexual violence.

Chapter Summary

Rape

- Sexual assault includes many crimes, from unwanted sexual contact to forced intercourse. Rape is the unwanted sexual penetration of the vagina, mouth, or anus by use of force or threat. It is estimated that between 17% and 25% of women and 3% of men have experienced a completed or attempted rape during their lifetimes, although the incidence is underestimated, as most attacks remain unreported. It is hard to assess accurately the occurrence of rape due to under-reporting and to variations in the way relevant data is gathered.
- There are a number of theories as to why rape occurs. Feminist theorists believe that rapists are primarily motivated not by sex, but by a desire to dominate and control women. Evolutionary theory states that rape is a reproductive strategy engaged in by low-status males who would otherwise have little chance at reproductive success. There is some truth in both of these theories, as both biological and societal forces can affect sexual aggression.
- There are many false beliefs about rape, including the idea that when a woman says "no," she really means "yes"; the victim in some way provokes the rape; rape occurs because men are overwhelmed by sexual urges; rape is committed by strangers; and only women can be raped.
- The depth of relationship between assailant and victim may distinguish types of rape, including stranger rape, acquaintance and date rape, and partner rape. Other types of rape include gang rape, statutory rape, and prison rape.
- Approximately 25% of women will be raped during their years in college, most often by someone she knows. Alcohol or date rape drugs are often involved.
- Most people are raped by someone they know. Rapists tend to feel a sense of entitlement and less empathy toward others. They are more likely to accept traditional gender roles and to believe rape myths. Victims of sexual assault occupy all strata of the population, although young people are the most likely victims of sexual assault.

- Rape is physically, emotionally, and psychologically shattering. There are some habits that may help a woman protect herself from sexual assault.
- The values of a society may encourage or discourage rape. Images in the media often support rape myths.

Sexual Abuse of Children

- Child sexual abuse (CSA) includes inappropriate sexual behavior between a child and an adult. Its exact prevalence is hard to determine, as most cases go unreported, although it is estimated that approximately 20% to 25% of women and 16% of men were sexually abused as children.
- Most of those who sexually abuse children are trusted relatives, friends, or neighbors. Almost all sexual abusers of children are heterosexual males. Not all child molesters are pedophiles, and not all pedophiles have committed sexual offenses against children.
- There are no specific symptoms associated with CSA; whereas some children suffer psychological, emotional, social, and sexual problems that persist into adulthood, others seem to experience little to no harm. Some adult victims of CSA have emotional, psychological, and relationship problems.
- Child molesters are among the most reviled people in our society, although the degree of revulsion against them depends on the age and gender of both the child and the assaulter. There are treatments for child molesters with varying degrees of success. Prevention programs and educating our young can help to keep children safe.

Intimate Partner Violence

- More than 10% of the U.S. population is physically and emotionally abused at home. Intimate partners commit 20% of all non-fatal violent crimes against women, and 3% of violent crimes against men. Domestic abuse can include physical abuse, sexual violence, psychological abuse, and economic abuse.

- Men and women of all races, socioeconomic statuses, ages, and sexual orientations may be victims of domestic abuse. Native American women, African American women, and young women are particularly vulnerable to acts of violence committed at the hands of an intimate male partner.
- Victims of intimate partner abuse suffer the immediate effects of the violence, as well as long-lasting physical, reproductive, and psychological harm.
- Domestic abuse happens in all societies. IPV may be particularly rife in societies that hold the belief that men are inherently superior to women.

Sexual Harassment

- The most widespread of all sexually coercive behaviors, sexual harassment is unwanted attention of a sexual nature that interferes with an individual's basic right to employment or education.
- At the workplace, sexual harassment can take the form of quid pro quo—when compliance with unwanted sexual advances is required as a condition of employment or advancement—or a hostile environment—when persistent and inappropriate behaviors make the workplace offensive or unbearable.
- It is estimated that 40% to 60% of women have been affected by sexual harassment. However, most cases are not reported. Some don't recognize their experience as sexual harassment, some may want to avoid a confrontation, and others are afraid of possible reprisals.
- On campus, the common forms are gender harassment, unwanted sexual attention, or sexual bribery and imposition.
- Sexual harassment can have an adverse effect on one's health, relationships, finances, and education or career. There are a number of ways a victim can choose to deal with the harassment.

Sexual expression often crosses the line into violence and coercion. Sexual violence can be one of the most devastating events that can happen in a person's life.

evaluate *and decide*

Imagine the following situations:

> Mark and Natalie are on their fourth date. They have not yet had intercourse. Although Mark doesn't like to drink, when they return to Natalie's apartment, she serves him alcohol and teases him until he drinks four beers. She becomes sexually assertive and when Mark doesn't physically respond, she asks him, "So are you gay, or what? I thought you liked me. We should just break up." Although Mark's not sure he's ready, Mark and Natalie end up having intercourse that night.

> Megan's Law requires that people are notified of convicted sex offenders living in their community. Some states' laws are also written so that convicted sex offenders are forbidden to live within 2,000 feet of a school or day-care center. In fact, most childhood sexual abuse is committed by someone known to the child, not by strangers. Jacob is a politician on a committee tasked with reconsidering and reevaluating this law.

What factors will you consider in advising these people? Consider the issues and questions below to make your decision.

SITUATION	ISSUES TO CONSIDER
MARK AND NATALIE	Do you feel that Natalie raped Mark? Why or why not? Would your answer have been different if Mark coerced Natalie into having sex?
	Mark doesn't consider that he was raped. Can someone still be raped even if they don't feel themselves a victim of sexual assault?
	Do you think that physical force has to be used to make it rape? Do you think it is rape if someone agrees to sex but he or she is intoxicated?
	What is consent? Is it a decision that someone makes, or is it an expression of agreement? If it is expressed, is it expressed verbally or nonverbally? Do both expressions hold equal weight? In your personal experience, do you use one form more than others?
	Should it always be assumed that someone does not agree to sex, and that they must give their consent before sex occurs? Or is consent assumed, and one must clearly indicate their desire not to have sex (Hickman & Muehlenhard, 1999)? Are there situations where someone does not consent to sex but does not (or cannot) indicate that the sex is unwanted?
MEGAN'S LAW	Community members are not informed if a murderer or armed robber moves into their neighborhood. Should members of a community be informed of *all* crimes committed by their neighbors? If not, why are sex crimes given a different status?
	Is a sex offender's right to privacy less important than public safety? Are laws in place to punish offenders or to protect public safety? What values underlie your decision?
	What are the risks and benefits of this law?
	Registered sex offenders forfeit their Fourth Amendment protections against unreasonable search and seizure (Andriette, 2006); their houses, cars, and computers can be searched by the police without cause. Do you believe that all criminals forfeit their constitutional rights? Why or why not?
	As more communities make it a crime to live within a certain distance of schools, and as neighbors become aware of an offender's status and perhaps respond harshly, more offenders may go "underground" and not register, thus giving them greater freedom to reoffend. What would be your response to this possibility?

Additional Resources

Log in to CengageBrain to access the resources your instructor requires. For this book, you can access:

 **CourseMate** brings course concepts to life with interactive learning, study, and exam preparation tools that support the printed textbook. A textbook-specific website, Psychology CourseMate includes an integrated interactive eBook and other interactive learning tools including quizzes, flashcards, videos, and more.

CENGAGENOW **CengageNOW** is an easy-to-use online resource that helps you study in less time to get the grade you want—NOW. Take a pre-test for this chapter and receive a personalized study plan based on your results that will identify the topics you need to review and direct you to online resources to help you master those topics. Then take a post-test to help you determine the concepts you have mastered and what you will need to work on. If your textbook does not include an access code card, go to CengageBrain.com to gain access. Visit www.cengagebrain.com anytime to access your account and purchase materials.

Current links to all of the following websites and videos can be found on the Psychology CourseMate for this text at www.cengage-brain.com/

Web Resources

Domestic Violence Relationship Quiz
Are you a victim of domestic violence? Take this quiz to get more information.

ChildAbuse.com
ChildAbuse.com is a one-stop Internet resource for information on child abuse and related issues.

Rape, Abuse, and Incest National Network
This site provides visitors with news, listings of crisis centers, and statistics on the incidence of rape and sexual abuse.

Sexual Assault Care Center
Provides information on sexual assault, rape, myths and facts, and sexual assault law.

Print Resources

Adams, C. and Fay, J. (1984). *Nobody Told Me It Was Rape.* Santa Cruz, CA: Network Publications.

Brownmiller, S. (1993). *Against Our Will: Men, Women, and Rape.* New York: Ballantine Books.

Warshaw, R. (1988). *I Never Called It Rape.* New York: Harper Collins.

Video Resources

The Accused. (1988). 111 minutes. Based on actual events, *The Accused* tells the story of a rape victim whose attackers received a light sentence based on the victim's "questionable character." The victim and attorney then prosecute the men who cheered on the attack.

Against Her Will: Rape on Campus. (1990). 46 minutes. Hosted by actress Kelly McGillis, this candid documentary explores the "whys" of this widespread problem. Designed to raise student awareness about how they can protect themselves and each other, this program also details educational and security measures colleges and universities can take to stop the epidemic of acquaintance rape. The video also analyzes male rapists' attitudes, explores the often ambivalent reaction of universities, views higher education rape-awareness programs, and offers suggestions for avoiding date rape. From Coronet/MTI.

Oleanna. (1994). 89 minutes. A two-character movie based on a David Mamet play that deals with issues of sexual harassment and power differentials on campus. The film is claustrophobic, disturbing, and powerful.

Portraits in Human Sexuality: Nonconsensual Sexuality. (2006). 40 minutes. This program offers insights into sexual victimization through interviews with a young woman who was raped in her own home by an armed assailant and a young man who was expelled from college on a charge of acquaintance rape. Also, a rehabilitation service for sexual offenders is profiled, with an emphasis on the treatment of deviant sexual arousal and the cognitive restructuring, victim impact awareness, and empathy skills development that goes into it. Contains mature themes and explicit language. From Films for the Humanities and Sciences.

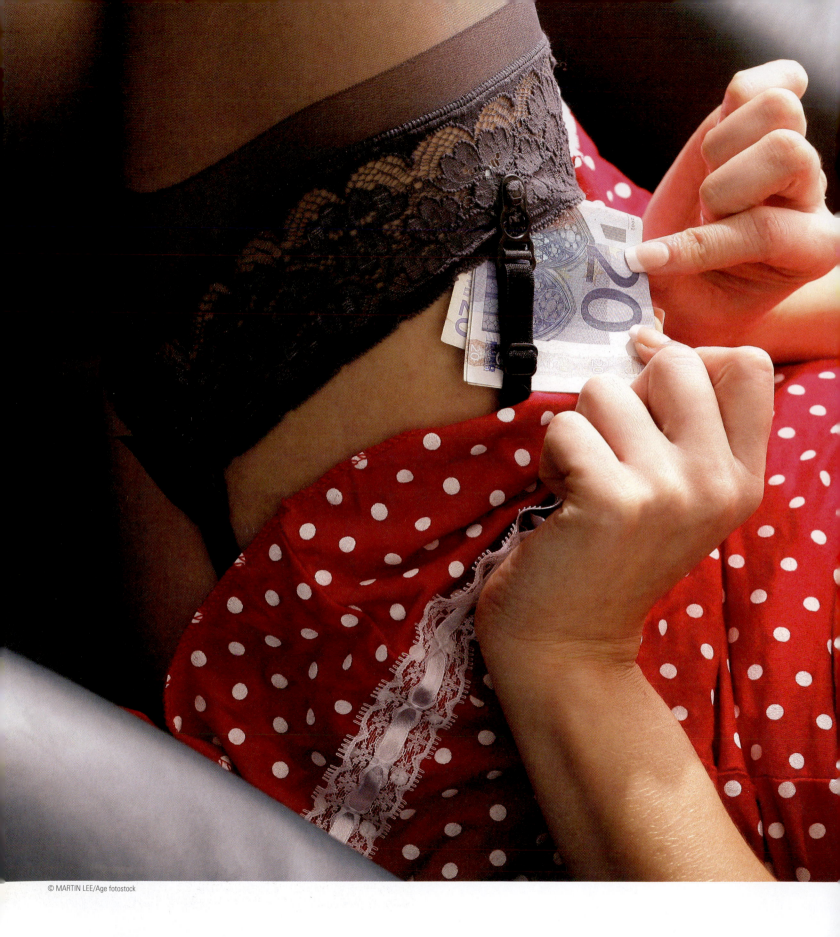

17 Sex for Sale

"Pornography is literature designed to be read with one hand."

—Angela Lambert, British writer and journalist

Man: Madam, would you sleep with me for a million pounds?
Socialite: My goodness, sir. . . . Well, I suppose I would consider it.
Man: Would you sleep with me for five pounds?
Socialite: What kind of woman do you think I am?!
Man: Madam, we've already established that. Now we are haggling about the price.

—An old anecdote, often attributed to Winston Churchill

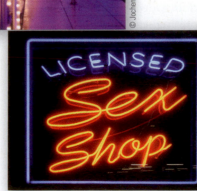

© Jochem Wijnands/Age fotostock

© Anthony Baggett/iStockphoto

© i love images/Getty Images

/ 435

Sex work is a sweeping term used to describe sexual services, performances, or the creation and distribution of sexual products given in exchange for material compensation. Sex work includes pornography, prostitution, exotic dancing, commercial phone sex, and other occupations. Pornography may account for as much as $97 billion a year in revenue worldwide. Increasingly more mainstream, some Internet porn companies are traded on the Nasdaq stock exchange (Rich, 2001). Americans pay between $9 billion and $14 billion a year for sexually explicit materials, including pornographic videos and magazines, live sex shows, adult cable, Internet porn, and commercial phone sex—more than they spend on movie tickets and the performing arts combined (Bridges, Wisnitzer, Scharrer, Sun, & Lieberman, 2010; Diamond, 2009; Edelman, 2009; Rich, 2001). Obviously, the sex industry is a thriving enterprise with many consumers, yet it is regarded by some as deviant and immoral. There are ongoing debates regarding the legal status, acceptability, and accessibility of sex work.

Pornography

After completion of this section, you will be able to . . .

○ Define *pornography* and consider its prevalence.

○ Catalogue the different genres and media forms of pornography.

○ Consider the role of changing attitudes on the acceptance of pornography.

○ Assess the legal status of pornography in the United States today, and compare it to other countries' pornography laws.

○ List the possible benefits and harmful aspects of pornography.

○ Evaluate the role of pornography on sexual aggression toward women.

The word **pornography** is derived from the Greek word *pornographia*, which literally means "to write about prostitutes." Today, pornography is considered to be any sexually explicit material—be it written, spoken, or visual—that is designed to elicit sexual arousal or interest. This may include many different media: printed books and magazines, video, photos, drawings or paintings, animation, sound recording, and video games. Acts performed for a live audience are not considered pornography because the term refers to the depiction or representation of the act. People may view pornography to enhance their lovemaking with a partner or their sexual arousal during masturbation.

Men consume more pornography than women. Compared to women, men are exposed to porn at a younger age and are more likely to watch porn while masturbating (Hald, 2006). Physiologically, both men and women are sexually aroused by pornographic images, although

women are less likely to admit or recognize their arousal. Men and women may also have a different neurological response to porn: when brain scans were performed on men and women watching porn, men showed more activity in the emotional areas of their brains than women did (Hamann, Herman, Nolan, & Wallen, 2004).

Many people have seen some form of pornography before they are adults. In one study, 93% of boys and 62% of girls in the United States had viewed online porn before the age of 18 (Sabina, Wolak, & Finkelhor, 2008). Boys were more likely to be exposed to Internet porn at an earlier age, to see more images, to see more extreme images (such as rape or child pornography), and to view pornography more often, whereas girls reported more involuntary exposure to online porn.

According to the National Health and Social Life Survey of 1994, 23% of men and 11% of women had watched an X-rated movie in the past year, and 16% of men and 4% of women had read a sexually explicit book or magazine (Laumann et al., 1994). There are more than 4.2 million pornographic websites, representing about 12% of all websites on the Internet (Grov, Gillespie, Royce, & Lever, 2011). As many as 40 million Americans regularly visit porn websites (Diamond, 2009). The minority of the population who *admit* to using pornography must be very busy because Americans shell out up to $14 billion a year on pornographic material, including 2.4 billion sex-oriented magazines, at least 60,000 pay-per-view pornographic websites, and more than 950 million rentals of "adult" videos (Bridges et al., 2010; Weitzer, 2000a). Although the United States produces much of the world's pornography, according to various surveys (cited in Weitzer, 2000a), 72% of Americans believe porn degrades women by portraying them as sex objects, and 77% say laws against pornography in books and movies should be more severe.

What Is Pornography?

The definition of pornography is subjective; different people define it different ways. If three people view the same image, one may become sexually aroused, another may squirm in disgust, and a third may yawn in boredom. There is no exact formula to differentiate pornography from other images; one can't simply count the number of nipples and multiply by the magnitude of moans to elicit its sex score. Instead, the creator's *intention* in composing a work designed to arouse sexual desire as well as the collective community's standards in viewing the porn are considered when the legal system seeks to classify whether or not a work is pornographic. This makes for an ever-shifting target and makes

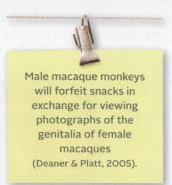

Male macaque monkeys will forfeit snacks in exchange for viewing photographs of the genitalia of female macaques (Deaner & Platt, 2005).

Around the world, more than $3,000 is spent on porn every second. The porn industry takes in more money than the combined revenues of Microsoft, Google, Amazon, eBay, Yahoo!, Netflix, and Earthlink (Top Ten Reviews, 2006).

Sex work Describes services, performances, or the production of products given in exchange for material compensation. Sex work includes pornography, prostitution, exotic dancing, commercial phone sex, and other occupations.

Pornography Any sexually explicit material that is designed to elicit sexual arousal or interest.

it very difficult to classify what is porn and what is not. Even the Supreme Court can be stymied. In an often-quoted 1964 case on obscenity, Justice Potter Stewart admitted that he could not define hard-core pornography, but "he knew it when he saw it" (*Jacobellis v. Ohio*, 378 U.S. 184 [1964]).

As if defining pornography weren't difficult enough, people also differentiate between pornography and **erotica**. Some, including political activist and writer Gloria Steinem, think that pornography is about violence, domination, and conquest, and erotica is about mutually pleasurable activities between consenting adults. Others think that the goal of pornography is solely for sexual arousal, but erotica has artistic or historical merit. Obviously, these views depend on one's personal values and culture.

> "The difference between pornography and erotica is lighting."
>
> —*Former porn star Gloria Leonard*

Categories of Pornography

Pornography can be categorized in many ways—hard core and soft core, by its genre, or by the media in which it's presented. **Hard-core pornography** includes graphic and actual images of genitalia or sexual acts, including penetration. **Soft-core pornography** depicts nudity but not always genitalia; it shows limited sexual activity that does not include penetration (Jensen, 2004a).

Genres of Pornography

For every sexual desire on the planet, somewhere, there is a magazine, movie, or website to cater to it. Sexually explicit material is produced for those who enjoy heterosexual, bisexual, and gay sex; in fact, some estimate that between one third and one half of video pornography is aimed at gay men (Thomas, 2000). Sexual interactions between women are common in heterosexual porn, but these images are typically aimed at straight men. Porn for women tends to be less explicitly visual and have more emotional context for the sexual acts. Patrons may choose their pornography based on the physical characteristics of the participants (age, race, body size, organ size), by the number of participants (single, double, group), or by the specific acts performed (oral, anal, vaginal). Consumers can find pornography that appeals to almost any fetish, including S&M, pregnant participants, and golden showers. **Voyeur pornography** involves shots taken of people without their knowledge in bathroom stalls, or with cam-

Short, hairy, and overweight, Ron Jeremy has appeared in more than 1,900 adult films.

© AP Images/Jennifer Graylock

ASK YOURSELF

Why are many paintings that depict nude forms not considered pornography, but modern photographs are? Are the drawings or photographs of genitalia or naked figures used in this textbook pornographic? Why or why not?

eras that look up skirts or down blouses. Of all the varied types of porn, most pornography is aimed at men, who consume at least 3 times more sexually explicit material than women (Bogaert, 2001).

For all the variety in pornography, some basic themes persist in most heterosexual porn. Straight porn usually involves six to eight scenes of oral, anal, and vaginal intercourse. The camera angle is designed to give the viewer the fullest shot of the woman, and usually shows the man ejaculating outside of the woman, otherwise known as the "cum shot" (Bridges et al., 2010). In the porn world, penises are always erect and sexually insatiable women are vocal and enthusiastic about any and all sexual acts; in fact, they often initiate sexual contact. If they don't want sex at first, after being forced, they generally enjoy it. If a woman in a porn film gets caught masturbating by a strange man, she will not scream with embarrassment, but rather insist he have sex with her. Women in pornographic films are usually thin with surgically enlarged breasts. They have long fake nails and wear high heels in bed. Men, on the other hand, are (at best) average looking, and are often the recipients rather than the initiators of sexual behavior (Yang & Linz, 1990).

Sexual Media

If people read it, look at it, or listen to it, there are pornographic varieties of it. There are pornographic books, magazines, movies, songs, and websites. You can download porn directly onto your iPod or cell phone for portability and easy access.

Magazines. Pornographic or "adult" magazines contain sexual content, including photos or illustrations of nudity or sexual acts. Some of these magazines are intended for a general audience; others are aimed at specific interests, such as large breasts or spanking. Some magazines, such as *Penthouse* and *Hustler,* are more hard core and explicit and contain little more than photos and writings of a sexual nature. Others, such as *Playboy,* include short fiction by top writers, interviews with public figures, and articles about fashion, celebrities, sports, consumer goods, culture, and politics. "Lad mags" such as *Maxim, FHM,* and *Stuff* usually contain nonpornographic images of scantily clad women, as well as articles of interest to men. Most pornographic magazines (indeed, most pornography) are aimed at men. Even one third to one half of *Playgirl*'s readership was thought to be gay men (Buckley, 2008). (*Playgirl* magazine is no longer being published; the website is still running, but it is aimed largely at gay men [Buckley, 2008].)

Playboy, the largest selling men's magazine, is published monthly with a total circulation of more than 3

Erotica Works of art that are sexually stimulating. In contrast to pornography, erotica is considered to have aspirations other than sexual arousal.

Hard-core pornography A form of pornography that features explicit sexual acts.

Soft-core pornography Less sexually explicit than hard-core pornography, soft-core pornography may depict nudity, but not penetration or other explicit sexual acts.

Voyeur pornography Sexual images taken of people who are unaware they are being filmed.

© Rick Maiman/Sygma/Corbis

Playboy founder Hugh Hefner holding a copy of the first issue of Playboy magazine.

million copies. Playboy was founded by Hugh Hefner, who produced the first issue (at a cost of $600) in 1953 in his kitchen. The first centerfold was Marilyn Monroe, and the issue sold for 50 cents. Fifty-thousand copies were sold. Playboy enterprises have expanded from magazines, and the company is now one of the nation's largest producers of pornography, through videos and the Internet.

Manga. Manga is the Japanese word for comics. It is directed at all ages and interests and is very popular with children and young adults. One popular genre, seijin manga ("adult manga," also called **hentai**), is sexually explicit. In Japan, 50% of male and 20% of female high school students regularly read pornographic comics (Diamond & Uchiyama, 1999). Some comics show heterosexual interactions, yaoi (or BL) focuses on love between men, and yuri shows girls in sexual and romantic interactions (Nagaike, 2010).

Video. Pornographic movies are available on cable or pay-per-view, in hotel rooms (where about half of all films rented are pornographic), or on video to rent or buy (Egan, 2000). Just as in mainstream Hollywood films, several genres are available, including period pieces, science fiction, and action adventure.

In 2005 Hollywood released 549 films. That same year, 13,588 pornographic films were released (Bridges et al., 2010). This does not include the "amateur" sex videos released, such as those by Paris Hilton, Pamela Anderson, and Kim Kardashian. More than 950 million pornographic videos are rented each year (Bridges et al., 2010), and Americans spend more than $4 billion on video porn rentals, more than the annual revenue of the NFL, the NBA, and major league baseball. Nearly 20% of all video and DVD rentals are X-rated. Twenty-two percent of Americans reported seeing an X-rated video in the last year (Davis, Smith, & Marsden, 2006).

The introduction of videotape greatly increased the availability of porn. Whereas film was cost-prohibitive and limited the production of adult motion pictures, the ease and economy of videotape allowed pornographic movies to proliferate. In 1975 approximately 100 pornographic movies were produced, at a cost of $320,000 per film. But by 2001, 11,000 videos were made for about $5,000 each. Some even suggest the reverse relationship—that videotape flourished because of porn—in 1979, 75% of all videotapes sold in the United States were hard-core adult films (Schlosser, 2003).

Why does someone enter the world of pornographic films? Some are drawn to the freedom and independence offered by porn. The hours are flexible and may provide a better salary for those who are otherwise restricted in their opportunities due to a lack of education or skills. Some enjoy the prospect of getting paid to violate social norms. Still others believe that porn is their path to fame and fortune. The reality is that while top porn stars—who are few and far between—can make up to $300,000 per year including personal appearances, most porn actors make a modest to meager living. Those who star in amateur films, which make up about one fifth of the videos and DVDs in the United States, often make no money at all (Abbott, 2000). In addition, actors may spend a lot on cosmetic surgery and mandatory monthly HIV testing. Incidentally, pornography is one of the few fields in which women are paid more than men (Rich, 2001).

© FocusJapan/Alamy

Manga are Japanese comics. Some, hentai, are sexually explicit.

According to the 2003 Protect Act (Prosecutorial Remedies and Other Tools to End the Exploitation of Children Today), it's a crime to create, purchase, or own sexually explicit images of children, including cartoons. In 2009 Christopher Handley, a 39-year-old collector of manga, pled guilty to owning manga with drawings of children being sexual. He was sentenced to 6 months in prison. There is no allegation that he ever touched a child or viewed any pornographic images of actual children.

Internet. It is thought that perhaps one third of all Internet use is related to some form of sexual activity. Surfers may visit sites to view live sex acts, chat with those who share their sexual proclivities, or look for romance. **Online sexual activity (OSA)** is the use of the Internet for any activity that involves sexuality, such as information, entertainment, arousal, or the search for sexual partners (Cooper, Morahan-Martin, Mathy, & Maheu, 2002). **Cybersex** is a subcategory of OSA that involves the use of computerized content for sexual stimulation and gratification, usually involving two or more persons (Cooper et al., 2002; Daneback, Cooper, & Mansson, 2005). Both men and women engage in online sexual activities. Women may be more interested in

Hentai Also called **seijin manga** ("adult manga"), hentai is sexually explicit Japanese comics.

Online sexual activity (OSA) The use of the Internet for any activity that involves sexuality, such as entertainment, arousal, education, or the search for sexual partners.

Cybersex Sexual activity or arousal that occurs through communication on the computer.

educational sites and interactive OSA such as chat rooms, whereas men are more drawn to visually oriented online sexual activity (Daneback et al., 2005; Shaughnessy, Byers, & Walsh, 2011).

There are several reasons why pornography is so popular on the Internet (Ross, 2005). The Internet is convenient and easily available: anyone with a web connection can view sexually explicit material and engage in cybersex with people across the globe in the privacy of their own home. Those with a digital camera can post images of themselves or friends engaging in sexually explicit acts. On the Internet, everyone is free to change his or her gender, appearance, and identity. People can hide less socially desirable characteristics and can assume any identity they desire. Internet sex is also physically safer than actual sex. Participants cannot be physically assaulted and cannot contract an STI or become pregnant. Sex surfers are also freed from embarrassment and may explore fantasies without fear of rejection from their partners (McKenna, Green, & Smith, 2001). Cybersexuality is a sexual space midway between fantasy and action (Ross, 2005). Users can experiment with a sexual behavior without actually partaking in the sexual behavior. They can have others read and respond to their fantasies, which is not as lonely as masturbation but is safer than sex with a partner (Ross, 2005). People may also use the Internet to find others who have similar sexual proclivities and to first enter into a sexual community, be it gay or lesbian, swingers, or B&D. Surfers can learn the language and make contacts in the safety and privacy of their own home. Those who are in a relationship that is unsatisfying in some way may partake in Internet sex and not consider it cheating.

Intimacy often occurs faster on the Internet than in person; the anonymity and lack of social cues allow some to reveal more personal information about themselves than they would to a casual acquaintance. Of course, the Internet can also diminish intimacy because people can easily lie about themselves or avoid answering questions that would be difficult to ignore in a face-to-face encounter.

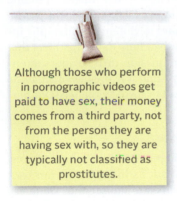

Although those who perform in pornographic videos get paid to have sex, their money comes from a third party, not from the person they are having sex with, so they are typically not classified as prostitutes.

The Internet may hold special appeal for GLBTQ individuals seeking romantic or sexual partners. Gay men are 4 times more likely to have cybersex than straight men (Daneback et al., 2005). The Internet's anonymity provides a measure of safety against the real and perceived stigma against homosexuality, and the expansive network provides wider opportunities for GLBTQ youth and adults than might otherwise be available in their community (Garofalo, Herrick, Mustanski, & Donenberg, 2007). Young white and Hispanic men who have sex with men are more likely than black youth to seek or meet sexual partners online, which may be due to differences in the accessibility and confidentiality of available computer access (Garofalo et al., 2007).

In 1996, the U.S. Congress passed the Communications Decency Act (CDA), which would have made it a crime to post "indecent" or "patently offensive" material on the Internet. This would have included everything from educational material and text from *The Catcher in the Rye* to information about breast or testicular cancer and George Carlin's "seven dirty words" comedy routine. The U.S. Supreme Court struck down the CDA as unconstitutional and therefore gave the Internet the same free speech protection as print (Communications Decency Act, 2007).

Videogames. According to the International Game Developers Association, there are more than 300 sex-themed video games, as well as a number of multiplayer online virtual sex games that support virtual sex between players. Female characters in these games are often hypersexualized and scantily dressed. Although relatively few games have sexual conquests as their main purpose, many games include sexual content in their storyline. *Grand Theft Auto: San Andreas* had a bit of software secretly embedded into the game. Named "hot coffee," this sexual minigame allowed players to have sex with their virtual "girlfriends." In *The Sims,* a series of life simulation video games, players can have sex (or "woohoo") with another sim of either sex; this can occur in a number of locations and may be accompanied by fireworks or a burst of confetti.

Cultural Considerations of Pornography

History of Pornography

When our ancestors first began to scribble on cave walls, they scribbled images of sexuality. The walls of the orgy rooms in the ruins of ancient Roman cities were adorned with *pornographos,* or "the depiction of prostitutes" (Morris, 2004). The *Kama Sutra,* an ancient Indian text about love and sex, dates as early as the 2nd century A.D. Before Johannes Gutenberg invented the movable type printing press, most books were handwritten by monks. After Gutenberg's invention, more books were printed, and pornography began to be mass produced. One could even make the argument that pornography helped to spread literacy. Pornography flourished in the outwardly sexually repressed Victorian era. At one point, the studio of pornography producer Henry Hayler had more than 130,000 obscene photographs (Sweet, 2001).

No obscenity laws existed in the United States until the middle of the 19th century, when Anthony Comstock led America's first anti-pornography crusade. Under his lead, it became a crime to send obscene, lewd, or lascivious material through the mail. This included anatomy textbooks and information about contraception.

Today, people have greater—and more private—access to pornography than ever before. Whereas in the past, viewers would have to go to X-rated theaters or peep shows in seedy parts of town to see porn, they can now watch videos, visit explicit websites, and subscribe to adult channels on cable or satellite in the privacy of their own homes.

In the 1968 ruling of *Stanley v. Georgia,* the U.S. Supreme Court allowed for the private possession of obscene material. Many members of Congress were upset by this ruling and authorized President Johnson to appoint a Presidential Commission to investigate the harm of pornography. The commission, made up of scientists, legal experts, religious authorities, and others, spent 2 years and $2 million on original research on pornography. To Congress's dismay, the commission's finding was that exposure to pornography did not lead to rape or sexual assault and that "there was insufficient evidence that exposure to explicit sexual materials played a significant role in the causation of delinquent or criminal behavior" (President's Commission on Obscenity and Pornography (PCOP), 1970) Furthermore, the commission thought that legislation "should not seek to interfere with the right of adults who wish to do so to read, obtain, or view explicit sexual materials" (Edwards, 1992; PCOP, 1970) Congress voted to reject the commission's findings.

In 1985, President Ronald Reagan appointed his attorney general, Edwin Meese, to head an 11-member committee whose charge was to overturn the 1970 findings and to find "more effective ways in which the spread of pornography could

Edwin Meese, presenting the 1986 commission report, in front of the bare-breasted "spirit of justice" statue.

© Arthur Grace/ZUMA Press/Newscom

be contained" (Attorney General's Commission on Pornography, 1987, p. 215). Most members of the committee were non-scientists who were politically appointed—many were anti-pornography campaigners. The committee met for less than a year and had a budget just one sixteenth the size of the 1970 Presidential Commission. The Meese commission funded no original research: most of their findings came from a weekend retreat during which the committee members shared their opinions about pornography. The committee also looked at previously completed research on pornography, although many of the scientists whose research they studied said the commission misinterpreted their work (Donnerstein & Linz, 1986). Their findings were released in 1986, and, as charged, they declared that "although the evidence may be slim, we nevertheless know enough to conclude that pornography does present a clear and present danger to the American public health" (Koop, 1986, p. 944). The Meese commission asserted that exposure to violent pornography increases sexual violence. Some researchers in the field feel that the statements of the Meese commission turn society's attention away from the real problem—that it is images of *violence,* rather than pornography, that lead to sexual violence (Donnerstein & Linz, 1986).

Pornography in Other Cultures

When we look at the effects pornography has on other cultures, we can sometimes learn more about its influence on our own culture. We will specifically consider Japan and Denmark because pornography in these countries has been studied extensively; we will revisit these countries and their relationship with pornography later in the chapter.

Japan. After World War II, Japan was under military occupation by the United States, who imposed their values on Japanese culture; hence, the depiction of sex acts, frontal nudity, pubic hair, or genitals was prohibited until the late 1980s (Diamond & Uchiyama, 1999). Since then, though the laws have not changed, the interpretation of them has become increasingly liberal, and much less material is now considered obscene. In addition, sexually explicit material available in Japan is typically more violent than that seen in the United States (Diamond & Uchiyama, 1999), although Japan has the lowest reported sex crime rates in the industrialized world.

Denmark. In 1967 legal restrictions on pornography were lifted in Denmark, making pornography much more accessible to the general public (Kutchinsky, 1973). At first, there was a great increase in sales of sexually explicit materials, followed by a slow steady decline; in fact, it is mostly tourists that are the major mar-

ASK YOURSELF

How much can we compare the effect of pornography in other cultures to its effect on American culture?

ket for pornography in Denmark. Following the decriminalization of pornography, the rates of sexual offenses declined. Similar results were seen in other countries that lifted restrictions on pornography (Kutchinsky, 1991). Some believe that pornography may act as a "safety valve" to relieve sexual impulses in a more socially acceptable way (Kutchinsky, 1991).

Pornography and the Law

Today, the legal status of pornography varies from country to country. In some countries, producing, distributing, and owning pornography is not a criminal act; in others, penalties are severe. Most countries allow at least some form of pornography. Almost all countries have laws against child porn. Until the mid-19th century, the United States had no laws against producing or owning pornography. In 1842 the U.S. Congress passed the first anti-obscenity law, whereby custom officials could seize "obscene or immoral prints and pictures." Printed materials were added to the list in 1865.

The first amendment of the U.S. Constitution ("Congress shall make no law . . . abridging the freedom of speech or of the press") does not apply to material considered obscene; distribution of obscene material is considered a crime. But what is obscene? The U.S. Supreme Court case *Miller v. California* (413 U.S. 15 [1973]) gave us the legal definition of **obscenity** that is in effect today. Material is considered obscene if the average person, applying contemporary community standards, would find that the work appeals to **prurient** interests, depicts sexual conduct in a way that is patently offensive, and is utterly lacking in serious literary, artistic, political, or scientific value. Some interesting questions are raised by this definition. Who is the "average person"? What are "community standards"? Consider your community: Is there one standard that all would agree on? Who gets to decide what the community standards are? Community standards change, so what is considered obscene will vary from person to person, from community to community, and from time to time. Finally, who judges a product's literary, artistic, political, or scientific value? Are all members of the community equally able to judge the merits of a work?

"Community standards" have declared many books, some of them classics of literature, to be obscene. Some of the books that have been banned for obscenity include *Ulysses*;

Fanny Hill; The Catcher in the Rye; Flowers for Algernon; Are You There God? It's Me, Margaret; and *Heather Has Two Mommies.* Even the Bible has been targeted because some believe that some sections are too explicit.

In 1990 the Cincinnati Contemporary Arts Center presented an exhibit of the works of Robert Mapplethorpe, some of which included homoerotic photographs. The Arts Center and its director were charged with pandering obscenity, but were later acquitted in a much-publicized trial. The Mapplethorpe case had widespread implications on the government funding of artistic works.

Laws vary based on different aspects of pornography. For instance, there are different laws for adults and minors concerning possession of pornography; different laws related to production, distribution, or ownership of pornography; and different laws related to what sorts of sexual acts can be shown. In *Stanley v. Georgia* (394 U.S. 557 [1969]), the U.S. Supreme Court ruled that it is not a crime to own pornography, but its dissemination is regulated.

Child pornography. Pornography that is made using children is illegal (*New York v. Ferber,* 458 U.S. 747 [1982]). According to the 2003 Protect Act, it is also illegal to use technologies that make it *appear* as though children are engaged in sexually explicit acts (U.S. code § 1466A). This applies to computer-generated images, or digitally altered photos that are transmitted through a common carrier, such as the mail or Internet, or transported across state lines. So even if no children were involved at all in creation of the images, it still constitutes child porn.

In 2008, A. J. and Lisa Demaree snapped some photos of their young daughters

A photograph by Robert Mapplethorpe

© usana Vera /Reuters/Corbis

ASK YOURSELF

What determines whether something is "art" or "obscene"? Should singers of rap lyrics considered offensive or obscene be charged with a crime? Why or why not? Is there a difference between this case and the case of the Mapplethorpe photographs?

Obscenity A legal term that describes material that appeals to prurient interests; depicts sexual conduct in a way that is patently offensive according to contemporary community standards; and is utterly lacking in serious literary, artistic, political, or scientific value.

Prurient Having or encouraging an excessive interest in sexual matters. According to the U.S. Court of Appeals, a prurient interest is "a shameful and morbid interest in nudity, sex, or excretion."

in the bathtub. A photo developer at Walmart alerted the police of the existence of "obscene" photos, and their home was searched. Their three daughters, aged 5, 4, and 18 months, were taken from their house for more than a month and subject to physical and emotional examinations, and A. J. and Lisa were placed on the sex offender registry. These charges were eventually dropped, but the family spent more than $75,000 on legal fees, and Lisa Demaree was suspended from her teaching job for a year.

> ### ASK YOURSELF
>
> Is a photo of a naked child necessarily child pornography? Did the photo developer at Walmart act improperly? Did the police? Did the parents? Is it more important to be extra vigilant to catch potential crimes or to protect potentially innocent people? How would you design a policy to balance these two necessities?

Attitudes About Pornography

Easily available, affordable, and anonymous pornography has become part of our contemporary lifestyle (Stulhofer, Busko, & Landripet, 2010). Exposure to sexually explicit material (SEM) can affect both our attitudes and our behaviors. But exactly how does SEM contribute to the construction of people's internalized working models of sexuality, and our fantasies, experiences, and sexual satisfaction? There are three main schools of thought about pornography and its effects on us: anti-porn, anti-censorship, and pro-sexuality (McElroy, 1995).

The **anti-pornography** viewpoint has both religious and feminist foundations. Some with fundamentalist religious views see sexual pleasure and immodesty as immoral. Radical feminists Andrea Dworkin and Catharine MacKinnon wrote that all pornography is demeaning to women because it portrays them as sexual objects to be used at the desire of men. They feel that pornography eroticizes the domination, objectification, and humiliation of women.

The **anti-censorship** camp feels that everyone has the right to free speech. Proponents of this point of view may not personally like pornography, but they believe that censorship is the first step on a dangerous slippery slope: if people are not allowed to write about sex, what is next? Censorship of textbooks with photos of genitalia? Restrictions on descriptions of STIs? History may support this viewpoint; laws against pornography have often been used to hinder women's rights, as the Comstock laws were used against contraception.

Pro-sexuality proponents defend the right of all adults to participate in and consume pornography (McElroy, 1995). They believe that pornography has potential benefits for both men and women. They also argue that making pornography illegal will further alienate sex workers and reduce their protections and rights.

There is some truth to each of these positions. Let's look at some of the arguments regarding the beneficial and harmful aspects of pornography.

Anti-pornography The view that pornography is immoral or demeaning to women.

Anti-censorship The view that repressing pornography is the first step on a slippery slope to censorship.

Pro-sexuality The view that pornography has potential benefits.

Possible Benefits of Pornography

- *Enhancement of sexual pleasure and relaxation:* Couples may use pornography to energize their sexual fulfillment, either alone or with a partner. Couples who view sexually explicit sites together report enhanced sexual arousal, a higher frequency of sex, increased openness to new sexual activities, and easier sexual communication (Grov et al., 2011). Pornography can also normalize sexual desire. In our culture, many people (especially women) receive the message that their sexual fantasies are wrong. By watching pornography, people may see that they are not alone in their erotic predilections.

- *Sexual education and information:* Pornography can show viewers the range of sexual possibilities that exist and open up their sexual world (Lofgren-Martenson & Mansson, 2010; Luder et al., 2011). Viewers can also get information in a more "real world" form than what they would get from textbooks or discussion. By viewing pornography, women can learn how to masturbate, an activity that doesn't come as naturally to some women as it does to men.

- *Safety:* Pornography allows viewers to satisfy their sexual curiosity in a safe way. It may offer its viewers an alternative to acting out their desires in the real world, where there is the chance of danger or infection. Some suggest that pornography reduces sexual violence by providing potential offenders with a more convenient, safer, harmless substitute (Diamond & Uchiyama, 1999).

Possible Harmful Aspects of Pornography

- *Degradation and objectification of women:* Many opponents of pornography think that it supports the idea that women are anonymous playthings that exist solely for the pleasure of men. "In pornography, women are not really people; they are three holes and two hands. Women in pornography have no hopes, no dreams, and no value apart from the friction those holes and hands can produce on a man's penis" (Jensen, 2004b, p. 169). Images in pornography are often of male domination and the humiliation of females. In fact, females in these images often look as if they are in pain. Even if they were just acting, you must ask yourself, why were the images of pain not edited out? Is the perception that the woman is in pain important to the viewer's pleasure? Or is her pain so inconsequential that it is not even noticed?

- *Produces skewed views of reality:* Those who watch pornography may get skewed ideas about relationships and appearance. Just as seeing airbrushed models all day leads to a distorted perception of what real people look like, viewing airbrushed models in *Playboy* leads to a skewed idea of what a normal naked body looks like. After viewing porn, subjects viewed average women as less attractive. In one study, men even reported loving their wives less after viewing porn (Kenrick, Gutierres, & Goldberg, 1989). In more recent studies, young women reported being influenced by the physical ideals displayed in pornographic videos, and expressed some insecurity about own bodies and whether their partners would be satisfied with them (Grov et al., 2011; Lofgren-Martenson, & Mansson, 2010). It is true that most of the images we view in the media don't accurately represent reality, but after exposure to images of beautiful women on TV, one only has to leave one's house and be exposed to hundreds of average-looking faces to reset the standards. Most people, however, don't view hundreds of average naked bodies every day. Viewers of porn may also expect their partners to react as women do in the videos, and may be hurt or angry when their women are not multi-orgasmic and sexually eager at all times. They may also get the message that women are more enthusiastic about certain sexual behaviors that are "dear to men but not necessarily to women" (Bridges et al., 2010; Grov et al., 2011; Lofgren-Martenson & Mansson, 2010; Zillmann & Bryant, 1982).

"Pornographers subvert this last, vital privacy: they do our imagining for us. They take away the words that were of the night and shout them over the roof-tops, making them hollow."

—*George Steiner, author and critic*

Sex on television can't hurt you unless you fall off.
(Anonymous)

- *Promotes violence against women:* Some opponents of pornography promote the view that sexually explicit material, especially violent sexually explicit material, will increase violence toward women.

The Critical Evaluation feature on the next page looks at arguments related to whether pornography increases sexual aggression toward women. To address this question, we must first define some terms: *Violent pornography* shows sexual images of explicit violence of varying degrees perpetrated against one individual by another (Kingston et al., 2009). *Nonviolent but degrading pornography* puts individuals (often women) in humiliating or submissive positions. *Sexually explicit but not violent or degrading pornography* shows adults engaged in sexual activities that are not coerced, violent, or degrading.

So how much aggression is in the typical pornographic film? Ana Bridges and colleagues recently analyzed the content of best-selling pornographic videos (Bridges et al., 2010). They found that nearly 90% of scenes contained at least one aggressive act, including verbal as well as physical aggression. More than 94% of acts of aggression were directed toward women and most were committed by men. When aggressed against, 95% of the victims responded either with expressions of pleasure or neutrally; men were 4 times more likely to show displeasure when aggressed against.

Some studies suggest that after viewing pornography, viewers are less sympathetic to female rape victims, show increased hostility and aggression toward women, and are more inclined to agree with rape myths (e.g., provocatively dressed women are "asking for it"; all women secretly want it) (Donnerstein & Berkowitz, 1981; Donnerstein, Linz, & Penrod, 1987; Kingston et al., 1981; Zillman & Bryant, 1982). It is important to note that most proponents of this position do not believe that pornography directly *causes* rape; instead they question whether pornography is ever a factor that contributes to rape (Jensen, 2004a).

Others disagree and think that not only does pornography not promote violence against women (Barak, Fisher, Belfry, & Lashambe, 1999; Fisher & Grenier, 1994), but it may even decrease violence by providing a "safety valve" (D'Amato, 2006; Kutchinsky, 1973, 1991; Diamond & Uchiyama, 1999). In countries that have either legalized pornography or increased its availability in the last few decades, rates of sexual violence have either stayed the same or decreased. Proponents of this position also think that human behavior is more complex than simply mirroring behaviors we see on video. Finally, some cite design problems with experiments that show an increase in aggression after viewing pornography.

No clear answer exists; the relationship between pornography and violence toward women is still being investigated. For most men, exposure to porn doesn't lead to sexual aggression, but it may be that porn, especially sexually violent porn, is one of many factors that could be involved in developing aggressive inclinations toward women, which may have an effect on those who are already predisposed to act violently. Those with violent inclinations might be more aroused than nonviolent men to sexually violent images. It may be that the way in which the violence is portrayed has an effect, and sexually violent porn in which women are shown to be enjoying their rape increases acceptance of rape myths (Barak et al., 1999).

critical evaluation

Let's evaluate some pertinent factors related to experiments that try to answer the question of whether pornography increases sexual aggression toward women.

> ## What was the experimental design?

Large-scale population studies look at the availability of porn in different societies and compare it to the rates of sexual violence (Diamond, Jozifkova, & Weiss, 2010; Diamond and Uchiyama, 1999; Kutchinsky, 1991). This method has the advantage of studying a large number of subjects over a long period of time. However, scientists can't control for other effects, such as viewing of violence or changes in the way sexual crimes are reported. In Denmark, Japan, and the Czech Republic, when the availability of pornography increased there was either no change or a decrease in sexual violence rates. However, when comparing these cultures to that of the United States, we learn that Denmark has more egalitarian relationships between the sexes and that they are much more lenient about public nudity (Malamuth, Addison, & Koss, 2000). Japan's collectivist tradition allows for public shame as a strong social force. These factors have a significant effect on sexual violence rates. Also, we must consider other changes that have occurred in the society over time. For instance, perhaps the number of rapes has decreased due to greater rape prevention, which means that the inverse relationship between porn and sexual violence is not as robust. Or perhaps rapes are *more* likely to be reported than in the past, suggesting a stronger inverse relationship between violent porn and rape.

Survey studies can reach large numbers of subjects, but it can be difficult to ascertain cause and effect relationships from them. Also, one must beware of ambiguous terms. If subjects are asked "how often do you view pornography?" their answers may vary based on the ambiguity of the survey: one person's "seldom" may be another person's "frequently," and there is no clear-cut definition of "pornography." Also remember that subjects lie, even on anonymous surveys.

Laboratory experiments have their own strengths and weaknesses. They are the best way to determine a true cause and effect relationship. In most of these studies, subjects are shown pornography, and then their aggression toward women is measured. Unfortunately, a laboratory is not a real-world experience, and asking men about their attitudes toward women doesn't necessarily tell us anything about their likelihood to rape. In many of these experiments, male subjects are instructed to watch pornography and then forced to make a violent response. In reality, many of the subjects would never choose to watch pornography (especially violent pornography), and would find nonviolent responses to situations (Bogaert, 2001; Fisher & Grenier, 1994). These studies are also not designed to measure subtle effects that occur over time and instead try to illustrate an immediate response to short exposure to porn.

> ## Do volunteer bias and selective attrition play a role?

Most laboratory studies consist of small convenience samples of volunteers. Subjects who volunteer for and stay in experiments in which they view porn (especially violent porn) may not be representative of the population as a whole.

Because subjects are told they can leave the study at any time, perhaps subjects who are more accepting of violence are less likely to leave the study, thus overestimating the effects of porn on violence (Fisher & Grenier, 1994).

> ## Does subject awareness affect outcome? As with any research design, subjects are often deceived about the nature of the study. For instance, students watching violent pornography are sometimes told that they are there to consider the aesthetics of the film. It is likely that most college students who are shown porn are going to know they aren't there to check out the lighting and sound quality but are being tested on the effects of the porn on their attitudes or behaviors.

> ## Does subject veracity affect outcome? In some studies, men watched a sexually violent video and were then asked to create a sexual fantasy. Subjects may not be comfortable describing their true fantasies to researchers or they may give responses they feel are more "politically correct." This may underestimate the effects of pornography on violence.

> ## Should positive relationships be attributed to correlation or causation?

If there is indeed a positive relationship between violent pornography and aggression toward women, does violent porn actually *cause* sexual violence? Or are sexually aggressive men more drawn to violent porn? Perhaps there is a bidirectional relationship. It may be that men who are prone to sexual violence are more drawn to sexually violent porn, and may be more likely to be influenced by it (Malamuth et al., 2000).

If men do show increased aggression toward women after viewing violent pornography, is it due to the film or to other factors? Perhaps the men are physiologically aroused, which could occur with many different stimuli, and this arousal is expressed as anger given the experimental design.

> ## What societal factors are involved? People don't view porn in a vacuum—they are exposed to violent and sexual images every day. Some feel that viewing porn increases violence against women, but that assumes that the only sexual violence people are exposed to is in pornographic films. Yang and Linz (1990) found that as a percentage, R-rated movies—which are freely available to all ages 24 hours a day on cable, satellite, and DVD— have more violence (and more sexual violence) than X- and XXX-rated movies. In fact, violence accounts for approximately 35% of *all behavior* in R-rated videos. Only 3.33% of all R-rated videos viewed had no violence or sexual violence. This is highly significant because many think that ". . . it is violence, whether or not accompanied by sex, that has the most damaging effect" (Donnerstein & Linz, 1986, p. 57).

> ## What personal factors are involved? Other factors may affect your response to porn. Your cultural background and views on gender equality could influence your response, as could your home environment; childhood exposure to violence or abuse could certainly influence your response to pornography. Emotional state and personality affect a person's response to pornography: men who are less intelligent, more sexually aggressive, and more hostile are more likely to choose to watch sexually violent films and also to exhibit the most negative effects of exposure to sexual violence (Bogaert, 2001; Malamuth et al., 2000). Drug or alcohol use can influence one's response; in one study, intoxicated female subjects were less likely to view an eroticized account of a rape as rape and were more likely to agree with rape myths (Davis, Norris, George, Martell, & Heiman, 2006).

Prostitution

After completion of this section, you will be able to . . .

○ Define *prostitution* and recognize the difficulty in ascertaining the incidence and prevalence of prostitution.

○ Compare and contrast the different types of prostitution.

○ Identify characteristics of prostitutes and pimps.

○ Compare customers with those in the general population, and consider reasons why people visit prostitutes.

○ List some of the physical and emotional health risks faced by prostitutes.

○ Define *sex trafficking.*

○ Describe the history of prostitution.

○ Evaluate issues regarding the abolition, legalization, and decriminalization of prostitution.

○ Define *phone sex* and *sexting.*

○ Explain the popularity of strip clubs.

"What's the difference between a prostitute and a politician? There are some things a prostitute won't do for money."

—*Norma Jean Almodovar, American prostitute, writer, and activist*

Consider the following situations:

- Kiri has a number of wealthy boyfriends. She sees each one about once a week, where they go out to dinner or a show, and then go back to her house to have sex. Kiri has no other job and supports herself by the "gifts" left by her paramours.
- Linda is in high school and has been using cocaine for about 6 months. Every Friday night, Linda performs oral sex on a coworker in exchange for half a gram of cocaine.
- Ira is up for a promotion at work. Greg, his competition, has been with the company longer and has a slightly better track record. Ira knows that Richard, his boss, has a bit of a crush on him, so he sleeps with Richard to help make his promotion certain.
- Tiffany is one of the finalists in the Miss Zucchini Patch beauty pageant. She has sex with one of the judges the night before the winner is announced to ensure her win.
- Malik is paid $50 to go into a room alone with pornographic magazines, masturbate into a cup, and leave.
- Luisa has been married to Jim for 14 years. Although she is fond of him, she mostly married him because he is a good provider and pays for her every whim. She doesn't really enjoy being physically intimate with him, but she has sex with him a couple of times a week to make sure he stays happy with her.

Which of these situations meets the definition of prostitution? What about Linda? No money changes hands—does prostitution necessarily involve the exchange of money for intercourse? What about Luisa? Does marriage, which some say exchanges sexual intercourse for financial security, constitute (legal) prostitution? And what about Malik? Is sperm donation sex work? Although most aspects of the sex industry promote the recreational and pleasurable aspects of sex for the client, should we neglect the procreative side (Porter, 2000)?

Prostitution describes the exchange of sexual access to one's body for something of value, be it money, drugs, or other commodities (Monto, 2004). Most prostitutes are women, although some prostitutes are male. Women are more often socioeconomically dependent and more likely to be forced into prostitution for financial reasons. Males are much more likely than women to be customers of prostitutes, not due to any differences in sexual enjoyment between men and women, but largely because of societal mores that suggest that males need and enjoy sex more than women do.

Slang terms meaning "prostitute" include *hooker, ho, hoochie, tramp, tart, harlot, lady of the evening,* and *working girl.* The word *whore* comes from the Old Norse word *hora,* meaning "adulteress." The word *slut* is more often applied to women who perform sexual behaviors outside of socially acceptable norms but who don't get paid for them. All slang terms for "prostitute" have negative connotations, whereas slang terms for the customers of prostitutes—*john, trick, client*—are more benign. This language reflects the cultural norm that prostitutes are typically more stigmatized than their customers. As Ronald Weitzer says, "you may be a bit surprised to learn that a male friend has visited a prostitute, but shocked to learn that a female friend *is* a prostitute" (Weitzer, 2000a, p. 7). Why do you think this double standard exists?

People hold a wide array of views about prostitution. Some think it is immoral and harmful to the family, while others think it is natural and necessary. Some think that prostitution oppresses women; others think it empowers women. Feminists have weighed in on both sides of the argument. Some condemn prostitution as the quintessential form of male exploitation of and domination over women, and others support women's freedom of choice, including the choice to do with their bodies as they decide. Most Americans think that prostitution is morally wrong (Weitzer, 2000a). In a May 1996 Gallup Poll, 77% of women and 63% of men thought prostitution should be illegal. More recently, 1,528 registered voters of New York State were polled regarding their thoughts on prostitution following the resignation of New York governor Eliot Spitzer, who left his position after it was revealed that he had patronized a high-priced prostitution service. In this poll, 68% of women and 54% of men opposed legalizing prostitution. Although, overall, 73% of people thought that prostitutes and customers should face the same penalties, the gender difference on this issue was significant: 76% of women favored equal penalties, but only 58% of men thought prostitutes and customers should be subject to the same legal punishments (Quinnipiac University Poll, 2008).

"Why are we so upset about sex workers selling sexual acts to consenting adults? We say that they are selling their bodies, but how different is that from what athletes do? They're selling their bodies. Models? They're selling their bodies."

—*Joycelyn Elders, former U.S. Surgeon General (Elders, 1998, p. 18)*

Prostitution From the Latin *prostituere,* meaning "to expose publicly, to set up for sale," prostitution is the exchange of sex for money or items of value.

Not surprisingly, portrayals of prostitution in the media give unrealistic and subjective views of "the life." Prostitutes in film are often portrayed as the whore with the heart of gold (*Gone with the Wind, Leaving Las Vegas*), the sharp business woman (*Risky Business, Trading Places*), or the young innocent (*Taxi Driver, Pretty Baby*). Perhaps no other portrayal is as erroneous (or as beloved) as *Pretty Woman,* in which Julia Roberts plays Vivian, a prostitute. Handsome millionaire Edward, played by Richard Gere, finds her, introduces her to high society, falls in love, and rescues her from a life on the streets. In the original version of the film, Edward dumps Vivian back on the street after he was done with her. The fairy tale ending was added after the more realistic ending tested poorly with preliminary audiences.

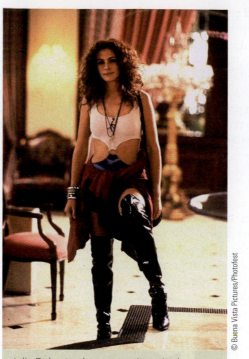

Julia Roberts plays a prostitute in the movie *Pretty Woman.*

© Buena Vista Pictures/Photofest

Incidence and Prevalence of Prostitution

It is difficult to estimate the number of people working as prostitutes in the United States. One survey found that 0.023% of the total population of Colorado Springs in the 1980s were full-time prostitutes (Potterat, Woodhouse, Muth, & Muth, 1990), although others think that number is closer to 1% of American women (Alexander, 1987). Four percent of women in the Janus and Janus survey (1993) answered "yes" to the question "Have you ever had sex for money?" According to Laumann and colleagues (1994), 16% of men admitted visiting a prostitute, although some think that men underestimate their visits to prostitutes on national sex surveys and that prostitutes are underrepresented in national sex surveys (Brewer et al., 2000). More recent data for North America are lacking (Vandepitte et al., 2006).

Although it is called "the oldest profession," prostitution is not present in every society. There are some cultural factors that increase the prevalence of prostitution (Monto, 2004). Prostitution is more common in countries characterized by "poverty, gender inequality, and cultural norms that limit women's legitimate employment opportunities" (Monto, 2004, p. 166). If given fewer opportunities, poor women lacking education and skills are more likely to enter prostitution. Strong religious prohibitions against prostitution might reduce its incidence, as might a fear of AIDS or changing sexual mores. When discussing prostitution, it is important to avoid both outright condemnation and romanticizing and look at the reality (Monto, 2004; Weitzer, 2000a, 2005).

Outdoor sex worker Prostitutes, such as streetwalkers, who establish contact with their clients in outdoor settings.

Indoor sex worker Sex workers who establish contact with their clients in an indoor setting or over the phone or Internet.

Streetwalkers/Streetworkers The low-status prostitute who attracts customers by working on the street.

Participants

Who Works as a Prostitute?

There are many reasons that women become prostitutes: Some women are trafficked into the life against their will, some think they have no other options and enter it unwillingly, and others freely choose prostitution for the independence and flexibility it affords (Bullough & Bullough, 1996). An economically deprived upbringing is the most common factor for women entering prostitution, especially streetwalking (call girls—a higher status sex worker who usually works out of her home—are more likely to come from a middle-class or upper-class background). Women may be forced into prostitution to pay for household expenses or drugs (Church, Henderson, Barnard, & Hart, 2001).

Many sex workers have a history of childhood sexual abuse (Dalla, 2000; Romans, Potter, Martin, & Herbison, 2000). This may be because those who are physically or sexually abused are more likely to be runaways and may enter the life on the street due to a lack of other options. These women have learned to treat sex as a commodity and to separate their emotions from sexual activity. Women who were sexually abused as children may also enter prostitution as a way to reclaim control over sex, where they had none as children (Dalla, 2000).

Types of Prostitution

Outdoor sex workers. Prostitutes are often classified as **outdoor** or **indoor sex workers**. In street prostitution, the sex worker solicits customers from a public place, such as a street, park, or beach, often while wearing revealing clothing. **Streetwalkers** (also called **streetworkers**) have the lowest status of prostitutes and suffer the greatest risk of physical abuse and arrest. Most research on prostitution is done on street prostitutes, even though they only represent 15% to 20% of prostitutes. Men might choose to visit streetwalkers rather than other prostitutes because of their easy access, anonymity, and low cost. Streetworkers charge less money than indoor sex workers (perhaps $15–$50 per **trick**) but have a much higher volume, having sex with four to five men each day. Sex—usually oral or vaginal intercourse—typically takes place in the customer's car, in an alley, or in a rent-by-the-hour motel (Freund, Lee, & Leonard, 1991; Monto, 2001).

Certainly, some prostitutes enjoy sex with their clients (Kontula, 2008). Savitz and Rosen (1988) surveyed a group of

When capuchin monkeys were taught about the concept of money with the use of tokens, some were found to exchange sexual activities for tokens (Chen, Lakshminarayanan, & Santos, 2006).

Do prostitutes enjoy sex?

female street prostitutes about their sexual response with both customers and with their partners. Seventy percent of the prostitutes reported enjoying intercourse with customers, and 63.5% reported having orgasms with customers at least some of the time. However, another study found that while 45% of *male* prostitutes had an orgasm with their clients most or all of the time, only 5% of female and 7% of transgendered prostitutes regularly orgasmed with clients (Weinberg, Shaver, & Williams, 1999). Sexual pleasure with a client may depend on the time spent with a client; one study found that call girls are most likely to have orgasms with their customers, followed by brothel workers, and finally streetwalkers (Prince, 1986).

Indoor sex workers. B-girls work in bars or hotels, usually with approval of management, who take a cut of the profits. As an agreement with the bar owner, B-girls try to get their customers to buy as much alcohol as possible before they leave for their sexual encounter. Some indoor sex workers are employed by **massage parlors** that are aimed at sexual gratification rather than therapeutic massage. (It is important to note that most massage therapists are trained health professionals!) Working in a bar or massage parlor may offer the sex workers more protection from customers and police.

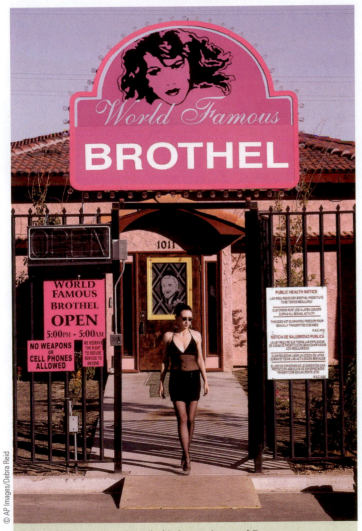

Nevada's first licensed brothel is located east of Reno.

A **brothel** (also called a whorehouse, cathouse, or bordello) is an establishment specifically intended for prostitution. Men typically can choose from a lineup of women. Brothel prostitutes generally have a higher status than streetwalkers. Although in the past brothels were a major social gathering point for men, they are rare today, except in certain parts of Nevada, where they are legal but heavily regulated. Prostitution became legal in Nevada in 1971; there are 35 licensed brothels in 10 counties in that state. Prostitution is illegal in Las Vegas and Reno, which house most of Nevada's residents. It is a state law that in brothels, condoms must be used during all oral, anal, and vaginal intercourse. Nevada state law requires brothel prostitutes to be checked weekly for STIs and monthly for HIV (Hausbeck & Brents, 2000).

The lives of the women who live in Nevada brothels are strictly controlled. They usually work three weeks in a row, during which time they must stay in the house. Some brothels forbid the women from entering a bar, dining in a restaurant after 7 p.m., or loitering around any business or public function (Hausbeck and Brents, 2000). Brothel workers typically negotiate a price with the customer. Typical prices average $300 for 30 minutes, and generally include intercourse and oral sex. The management normally gets half of the negotiated amount. Brothel workers receive no health benefits, no retirement plans, no unemployment insurance, and they pay their own taxes.

Prostitutes who work for **escort** services may work independently or with an agency. Agencies advertise their services in magazines and on the Internet. The client calls and describes his needs and the type of escort he is looking for. The escorts typically receive a flat fee or a percentage of the fee. Some escorts work independently, and are free to set their own rates, usually from $200 to over $5,000 for exclusive services. Fees may differ depending on the service sought, the length of time of the visit, and whether a customer is a regular. The escort usually meets the client at the customer's home or hotel room, or at the escort's home or hotel room.

Call girls occupy the highest status in the hierarchy of prostitution. They tend to be the most attractive and well-educated of prostitutes, and their services are the most expensive. When a call girl meets her client, it is more like a "real date," and often includes social events and conversation. Call girls may also meet their clients in their own apartments or in the customer's hotel room or home.

The characteristics of prostitutes, their clients, and the activities they engage in vary depending on the type of prostitution (Figure 17.1). Some differences include the following:

- *Demographics.* Outdoor sex workers tend to be younger, to have gotten involved in prostitution at a younger age, and to

Trick An act of prostitution. Also, a customer to a prostitute.

B-girls A prostitute who works in a bar or hotel, usually with the approval of the manager.

Massage parlors A place where illicit sex is available under the guise of therapeutic massage.

Brothel Also called a whorehouse, it is an establishment specifically intended for prostitution.

Escort A prostitute who meets with clients by appointment.

Call girl A sex worker who can be hired over the phone or the Internet to engage in intimate interactions.

© AP Images/G. Paul Burnett

Sydney Biddle Barrows, called the "Mayflower Madam," was a member of a wealthy family and a Mayflower descendant who achieved notoriety in the 1980s after it came to light that she had been running Cachet, an upscale escort service in New York from 1979 to 1984. Cachet catered to the wealthy and powerful and the escorts were well-spoken, well-dressed, and educated young women.

engage in more illegal drug use (Church et al., 2001). African Americans are disproportionately represented in streetwalking, which is the lowest paid, most dangerous, most stigmatized level of prostitution.

- *Victimization and violence.* Violence is an ever-present reality for prostitutes. Forty-eight percent of indoor workers and 81% of streetworkers have experienced client violence (Church et al., 2001), although only about a third of prostitutes report their attack. Streetwalkers are 3 times more likely than call girls to experience assault, and 11 times more likely to have been raped, although indoor sex workers are more likely to *report* attempted rape (Church et al., 2001). This may be because street prostitutes deal with more men per year, and are therefore more likely to encounter violent ones. Also, men who are violent may be more likely to seek out prostitutes to victimize.

- *Sexually transmitted infections.* Streetwalkers who inject drugs have the highest rates of STI infection; rates are lower in indoor sex workers.

- *Control over working conditions.* Freedom of choice in clients and in sex acts performed differs for different strata of sex workers. Brothel workers may be the most limited in their choice of clients and in their personal lives; streetworkers and escorts may generally choose their clients and refuse those who are intoxicated or who appear violent.

- *Psychological adjustment.* Streetwalkers have more psychological problems than indoor sex workers, but it is unclear whether the work leads to the emotional problems, or whether those with emotional problems are more likely to pursue outdoor sex work. In a survey of mostly indoor sex workers in New Zealand, researchers found no differences between prostitutes and age-matched controls for self-

Gigolos (JIG-uh-lows) Male prostitutes who service female clients. Also called escorts or call boys.

Hustlers Male prostitutes who solicit their male clients on the street or in other public places.

esteem, physical health, or mental health (Romans et al., 2001).

- *Emotion work.* Clients expect and receive more emotional intimacy from call girls and escorts than from streetwalkers (Lever and Dolnick, 2000). Escorts and call girls are more likely to have "girlfriend experiences"—to meet at personal locations, to engage in conversation, and to kiss, caress, and receive oral sex from customers.

ASK YOURSELF

Street prostitutes, particularly "crack whores" (a person who finances her habit for crack cocaine through prostitution), are generally held in lowest esteem, whereas call girls are held in highest. Are our opinions about these women based solely on the fees received for their services? Why or why not?

Male prostitutes. Male prostitutes may have male or female clients. Male prostitutes who service female clients are usually called **gigolos**, escorts, or call boys. Their clients are typically older, wealthy women who need a companion. Gigolos may or may not provide sexual services.

Male prostitutes who have sex with male clients are called **hustlers**. Hustlers often solicit their clients on streets, in bars, on the Internet, in parks, or in public restrooms. Not all hustlers are gay, although it is difficult to get precise data on the sexual orientation of male prostitutes (Vandiver & Krienert, 2007). It is clear that a significant percentage of hustlers who have sex with men identify as heterosexual (Miller, Klotz, & Eckholdt, 1998; Pleak & Meyer-Bahlburg, 1990; Vandiver & Krienert, 2007). Likewise, some male clients of hustlers identify as heterosexual. Typically, hustlers service men who want to give or receive oral or anal sex, or who want the hustler to masturbate for (or with) the client. Hand jobs and fellatio are the sexual activity most commonly performed by hustlers, either alone or with other sexual activities (Morse, Simon, Balson, & Osofsky, 1992; Weinberg et al., 1999). Unfortunately, safe sex is not practiced with any regularity, even though male prostitutes have a par-

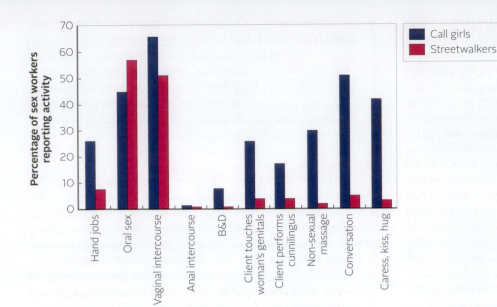

FIGURE 17.1 Acts of intimacy engaged in with last client for call girls and streetwalkers. (© Cengage Learning 2013. SOURCE: Lever & Dolnick, 2000.)

ticularly high HIV infection rate (Miller et al., 1998; Mimiaga et al., 2008; Morse et al., 1992). Male prostitutes often engage in other high-risk behaviors with their clients, such as S&M and drug use.

Like female streetwalkers, hustlers usually enter "the life" at a young age and have little education or marketable skills. Compared to male non-prostitutes, hustlers are more likely to identify themselves as addicted to drugs or alcohol (Cates & Markley, 1992). Compared to female prostitutes, male prostitutes are slightly older, less dependent on prostitution as a source of income, and more likely to move between indoor and outdoor prostitution (Vandiver & Krienert, 2007). They are less subject to violence from customers, less likely to have pimps, less susceptible to arrest or harassment by police, less likely to use hard drugs, and more likely to derive satisfaction from sex with customers (Weinberg et al., 1999; Weitzer, 2005).

Transgendered prostitutes occupy the lowest rung on the hierarchy. These male-to-female sex workers are most stigmatized and make the least money. They tend to get the least desirable locations, have higher HIV infection rates, and get exposed to more violence than male prostitutes (but less than women). Oral sex, hand jobs, and receptive anal intercourse are the most common sexual acts performed by transgendered prostitutes (Weinberg et al., 1999).

> If the otherwise manly man wishes, perhaps, to experience passive anal intercourse, a female prostitute will be somewhat limited in the task; a male prostitute will rather too directly confront the client with his own sexual ambivalence. The transsexual prostitute fills these niches just so. (Rowland, 2000, p. 126)

Pimps, Panderers, and Madams

Pimps are those who organize and benefit from prostitution. They are usually males, and **madams** are usually females who manage massage parlors or brothels. Pimps sometimes provide room and board, bail money, or some protection to their stable of women, and usually control their girls through violence and

emotional manipulation. Street prostitutes are most likely to be controlled by a pimp and generally receive little benefit from this association. Pimps often physically assault the women and take some or all of their earnings. Madams may treat their workers better; in general, Nevada brothel workers expressed "very positive feelings about their madams" (Prince, 1986, cited in Weitzer, 2005). **Procurers** or **panderers** find customers for streetworkers. As an example, this could be a bartender who helps a client and prostitute hook up.

Customers, Clients, and Johns

> "When I was a call girl, men were not paying for sex. They were paying for something else. They were either paying to act out a fantasy or they were paying for companionship or they were paying to be seen with a well-dressed young woman. Or they were paying for someone to listen to them. . . . What I did was no different from what ninety-nine percent of American women are taught to do. I took the money from under the lamp instead of in Arpege."

> —*Roberta Victor, American prostitute (quoted in Terkel, 1975)*

It is difficult to ascertain the percentage of men who patronize prostitutes. Many men won't admit to visiting prostitutes, and customers represent only about 10% of prostitution-related arrests. According to Kinsey and colleagues (1948), 69% of men visited a prostitute some time in their lives. It is important to remember, though, that the world has changed since Kinsey surveyed his subjects; that was a time when "good girls" were much less likely to engage in intercourse. During the 1950s, 7% of men had their first sexual experience with a prostitute; compared to only 1.5% in the 1990s (Bullough & Bullough, 1996). In the National Health and Social Life Survey, 16% of men admitted to visiting a prostitute (Laumann et al., 1994).

Some men travel from one country (often rich) to another (usually poor) in search of sexual services that may be illegal or expensive in their home country. Popular destination sites of **sex tourism** are Thailand, Brazil, and Russia.

So who are the men who visit prostitutes? Although these customers, also called tricks, johns, and clients, outnumber the prostitutes, there is less research about them than about the women they frequent (Earle & Sharp, 2008). Many studies suggest that customers of prostitutes are not significantly different than other men—not more likely to have sexual problems or sexually deviant—yet most men don't visit prostitutes. Compared to the subjects in the General Social Survey, cli-

Transgendered prostitutes Male-to-female sex workers.

Pimp A person, usually male, who finds and manages customers for prostitutes.

Madam A woman who runs a brothel, or a house of prostitution.

Procurer or **panderer** One who procures customers for prostitutes.

Sex tourism Travel undertaken with the specific motivation of engaging in sexual activity.

ents were less likely to be married, and if married, were less likely to be *happily* married (Brewer, Muth, & Potterat, 2008; Davis, Smith, et al., 2006; Monto & McRee, 2005). Prostitute clients were more likely to have had more sexual partners in the past year (but not more sex) compared to the national sample, and they were more likely to have seen an X-rated movie in the past year (Monto & McRee, 2005). Prostitute customers were also more accepting of sex before marriage, homosexual sex, and extramarital sex (Monto, 2000, 2004). Men who visit prostitutes are also more apt to view sex as a commodity or a service to be exchanged. They are more likely to have a sense of entitlement to sexual access to women, and they are more likely to believe that sexual desire is an essential part of manhood and that women are obligated to provide that release. One study that compared men who were arrested for soliciting a prostitute with men in the general population found that clients were less educated than the general population and that Hispanic men were consistently and strongly overrepresented in arrest data, blacks were moderately overrepresented, and whites were moderately underrepresented (Brewer et al., 2008). But does this mean that Hispanics and blacks are more likely to go to prostitutes, or that they are more likely to be *arrested* for soliciting a prostitute?

Why do people visit prostitutes? In the past, it was thought that prostitution helped keep "good" women safe from men's sexual needs. However, not all men go to prostitutes, so fulfilling a biological need can't be the only answer. Whether men go to prostitutes is also driven by personal and cultural forces (Monto, 2000; Queen, 2000; Weitzer, 2005). Some reasons that men visit prostitutes include the following:

- *Desire for a certain type of sexual experience.* Prostitute customers may want sex with a certain physical type of partner, or they may want a certain sexual experience than they have with their partner. More than half of the men in a sample of johns agreed with the statement "I like to be with a woman who likes to get nasty" (Monto, 2000). They may also desire a greater number of partners.
- *Social inhibition.* Some men, whether due to shyness or physical characteristics, feel inadequate with regard to women. Visiting a prostitute may seem like an easier way to have sexual contact with women than risking rejection in the dating world or sexual harassment charges.
- *Convenience.* When visiting a prostitute, a man can experience "McSex"—immediate, convenient, and with a variety of choices (Blanchard, as cited in Monto, 2000).
- *Emotional boundaries.* When visiting a prostitute, a man can sit back and not have to worry about fulfilling her sexual or emotional needs. There is no assumption of a relationship, and the man can reveal as much or as little about himself as he chooses.

> "When a guy goes to a hooker, he's not paying her for sex, he's paying her to leave."
>
> —Author unknown

- *Risk and illicitness.* Some men are thrilled by the illicit nature of the act (which may also carry less risk to a relationship than an affair).
- *Out of town.* Some men may be looking for sexual release while they are separated from their regular partner.

- *Companionship, conversation, intimacy, and love.* Some men visit prostitutes because they are seeking personal comfort and closeness with women. "The men . . . are seeking absolution, acceptance, understanding, compassion, kindness, and caring from a willing, friendly woman . . . granting these men acceptance and understanding instead of disgust and ridicule is the single most profound aspect of sex work" (Hartley, 2000, p. 73).

Prostitution and Health

Prostitutes face many physical and emotional health risks. Exhaustion, frequent viruses, STIs, backaches, headaches, eating disorders, and depression are common among streetwalkers (Farley, 2004). Prostitutes, who learn to disengage and separate sex from emotions, may have difficulty maintaining relationships. In one study, 68% of prostitutes in nine countries suffered from post-traumatic stress disorder, a rate comparable to that of battered women and rape survivors (Farley, 2004). Female prostitutes are also at heightened risk of cervical cancer because of their high number of sexual partners.

In the United States, prostitution is not a major vector for HIV transmission; when an STI is passed, it is much more likely to be passed from customer to prostitute. In Africa, however, sex with prostitutes is a major factor in HIV transmission. This may be because in the United States, streetworkers are most likely to perform oral sex and more likely than their African counterparts to use condoms during intercourse. Obviously, condom use greatly protects both prostitutes and their clients from STI transmission. In Nevada's legal brothels, where condoms are required by state law, none of the brothel workers has tested positive for HIV since 1985, when mandatory testing was implemented (Hausbeck & Brents, 2000). Unfortunately, although prostitutes may require that their customers use condoms, customers don't always agree. The power differential between prostitute and client—be it physical or financial—means that customers can coerce the women into unprotected sex. One study showed that customers of streetwalkers use condoms only 58% of the time: 72% for vaginal intercourse and 33% for oral sex (Freund et al., 1991). Among male sex workers who have sex with men, 69% reported at least one episode of unprotected anal sex with a client who had a different or unknown HIV status (Mimiaga et al., 2008).

Prostitutes have the highest risk of occupational mortality of any group of women. The homicide rate for prostitutes is 204 for every 100,000 women. Compare this to the next highest occupa-

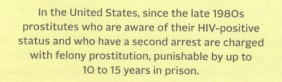

In the United States, since the late 1980s prostitutes who are aware of their HIV-positive status and who have a second arrest are charged with felony prostitution, punishable by up to 10 to 15 years in prison.

tional mortality rate, that of male taxi drivers, which have a 27 out of 100,000 work-related homicide rate, and female liquor store workers, with a rate of 4 out of 100,000 (Castillo & Jenkins, 1994; Potterat et al., 2004). Active prostitutes are 18 times more likely to be murdered than women of a similar age and race. Streetwalkers experience the most violence on the job and are at risk from brutality from pimps, customers, and even police. Serial killers can target streetwalkers due to moral indignation or the women's availability. Jack the Ripper killed at least five prostitutes in 1888 London. In 2006, Steve Wright murdered five prostitutes in Ipswich, England.

Most prostitutes have been victims of assault and rape (Farley, 2004). Legal recourse for these women, however, is lacking. In Venezuela, El Salvador, and Paraguay, the penalty for rape is reduced by one fifth if the victim is a prostitute (Farley, 2004). In California, a judge dismissed charges against a man accused of raping a prostitute, as he believed that "a whore . . . opens herself up to anybody" and is "outside the protection of the law" (quoted in Arax, 1986, p. 1).

If you believe a prostitute cannot be raped, ask yourself this: If a professional boxer was walking down the street and someone jumped him and bashed him in the face, could you charge the assailant with assault?

Can a prostitute be raped?

Sex Trafficking

Siri is a 14-year-old Thai girl, living in extreme poverty with her family. One day, they are approached by a well-dressed woman who offers Siri a good job and advances her family a year's wages (about $2,000) against her future earnings. Siri is then sold to a brothel for $4,000, where she is told she must "work off" this cost, as well as that of her room and board. Paid approximately $4 per customer, Siri must have intercourse 10 times per day just to pay her rent. Medical expenses, including contraception, are an extra expense she must shoulder. Many customers resist wearing condoms, and Siri stands a 40% chance of getting HIV. Siri's pimps take advantage of her cultural upbringing and reinforce her idea that she is unworthy and has done something to deserve this life. Siri becomes a prisoner, not only physically, but also financially and emotionally. Her best case scenario: Siri works as a sex slave for 5 years until she becomes too sick to work and is forced into the street (story cited in Leuchtag, 2003).

According to the UN, a trafficked person is "someone who is transferred or transported across national or international borders, by means of threat or coercion, for the purposes of economic exploitation in prostitution, forced labor, slavery, or the removal of organs" (Cwikel & Hoban, 2005, p. 307). Interpol calls **sex trafficking** the fastest-growing crime category today (Cwikel & Hoban, 2005). Trafficking of men, women, and children for sexual purposes is especially prevalent in Thailand, Indonesia, Malaysia, the Philippines, Sri Lanka, Vietnam, Cambodia, Russia, and India.

There are as many as 200,000 sex slaves worldwide, bringing slaveholders a profit of many billions of dollars (Leuchtag, 2003). It is difficult to gauge the exact number of sex slaves because the illegal nature of the trafficking keeps the activity hidden. The vast majority of sex slaves don't come to the attention of the police,

immigration, or health care workers, and victims don't always report abuse due to fear of reprisal. The physical and psychological costs to those trafficked into the sex industry are substantial, including rape, battery, STIs, broken bones, depression, panic attacks, and post-traumatic stress disorder (Hughes, 2008; Raymond & Hughes 2001).

Cultural Considerations of Prostitution

History

Is prostitution indeed "the oldest profession"? Probably not, but it has been around for many thousands of years. In a male-dominated world, women have had limited means of economic survival. In the distant past, women basically had three life options: they could marry, they could join a convent, or they could become a prostitute. (Another possibility opened up in the 13th century with the invention of the spinning wheel: women could become "spinsters," those who spun thread [Alexander, 1987]). Prostitution seems to thrive in periods of social change. At times when women are confined and treated as personal property, prostitutes are allowed to work without official harassment. As women's independence increases, prostitution is subject to more restrictions (Alexander, 1987).

Throughout history, prostitution has had many different incarnations. By having sex with temple prostitutes, worshipers in ancient Sumer could reach communion with the gods. In ancient Greece and Rome, prostitution flourished, and men had their choice of different types of women. The Greek *hetaerae* were sophisticated courtesans, sought after for conversation and companionship. In Rome, the *delicatae* were well-educated mistresses kept by wealthy men. Also in Rome, *famosae*—"soiled doves"—were the wives or daughters of respectable families who had sex for pleasure. *Dorae* remained naked at all times as they roamed the streets, and *busturiae* looked for customers in graveyards. Roman men would be wise to avoid the *gallinae*, who would rob men after having sex with them. *Fellatrix* specialized in using their mouths for sexual pleasure. *Lupae* attracted clients by shouted banter and would have sex with anyone for a price and would generally engage in intercourse in darkened arches or fornices (from which we get the term *fornication*) (Ringdal, 2004; Sherman, 1973).

In the Middle Ages, prostitution was common, in part due to the teachings of St. Augustine, who felt that although all extramarital sex was sinful, prostitution was a necessary evil to prevent the greater sins of rape and masturbation. As towns grew, certain streets were set aside for prostitution, and eventually, brothels were established. This changed with the Protestant Reformation of the 16th century, when prostitution was outlawed and attitudes about prostitution hardened.

Still, it was during this time that **courtesans** reached the height of their popularity. Courtesans were high-ranking prostitutes whose clients were royalty or men of high social

Sex trafficking The recruitment, harboring, transportation, or obtaining of a person for the purpose of a commercial sex act.

Courtesan A high-status prostitute with wealthy and/or powerful clients; courtesans were often known for their beauty and sophistication.

Mata Hari (pictured) was a famous Dutch courtesan and WWI spy. Madame du Barry was also a famous courtesan and mistress of King Louis XV.

A Japanese geisha is an entertainer, not a prostitute.

standing. These women were not only beautiful, but also well-educated, sophisticated, talented, and skilled in the arts as well. A courtesan "used her brains and her body to enjoy the benefits of marriage—companionship, property and financial stability—without the stifling social constraints" (Valhouli, 2000).

Japanese *geishas* are traditional female entertainers, skilled in the arts of conversation, song, and dance. Geishas are *not* prostitutes. There are high-class Japanese courtesans called **oiran**. Whereas geishas tie their obi, or sashes, at the back, oiran tie them in the front, for easier removal.

With the industrial revolution of the 19th century, prostitution thrived as people moved to the cities. It is estimated that at least 5% of women aged 15 to 25 in Paris were registered prostitutes. Not to be outdone, New York City during the 19th century also boasted a thriving prostitution trade: it is estimated that up to 15% of all young women in New York City were prostitutes (Bullough & Bullough, 1996). Brothels were popular then as a social gathering place, as well as the major source of sexual release for men.

Prostitution was legal in the United States until the early 20th century, when the Woman's Christian Temperance Union, influential in banning alcohol and drug use, fought against prostitution. Congress passed the Mann Act of 1910, also known as the White Slave Traffic Act, which prohibited the transport of women across state lines for immoral purposes.

Prostitution and the Military

Prostitution has always boomed around military posts; consequently, there are often high rates of sexually transmitted infections in those locations. During the mid-19th century, one third of the armed forces in Britain were infected with a venereal disease (Contagious Diseases Act, 2004). A number of possible solutions could have been implemented: condoms could have been distributed, or licensed and regulated brothels could have been established. At the very least, soldiers could have been inspected by physicians and treated, but this was considered demoralizing to the men. Instead, the Contagious Diseases Act, which was passed by the parliament of the United Kingdom in 1864, stated that police could arrest suspected prostitutes—or indeed any woman in a port town or army base—and make them submit to a pelvic exam for venereal disease. If infected, they were locked in a hospital until cured. Many of these women who were not previously infected with a venereal disease got one when examined with the unsterile speculum used to examine all the women. The Contagious Diseases Act mobilized the actions of early feminists, and the act was repealed in 1886 (Contagious Diseases Act, 2004).

During the American Civil War, many women who had lost their husbands, homes, loved ones, and means of support, turned to prostitution. During World War II, the Japanese army kidnapped as many as 50,000 to 200,000 young girls from surrounding countries and forced them into sexual slavery to service the men in the Japanese army. Called "comfort women," these girls were repeatedly beaten, tortured, and raped. It is estimated that only 25% survived and that those who did were infertile as a result of the multiple rapes they endured and the diseases they contracted (de Brouwer, 2005).

Prostitution and the Law

> "Why should prostitution be illegal? Selling is legal. F*cking is legal. Why isn't it legal to sell f*cking? Why should it be illegal to sell something that's legal to give away? I can't follow the logic. Of all the things you can do to a person, giving them an orgasm is hardly the worst. In the army they give you a medal for killing people; in civilian life, you go to jail for giving them orgasms. Am I missing something?"
>
> —*George Carlin, comedian*

About 90,000 people are arrested each year in the United States for violation of prostitution laws. Each arrest is estimated to cost taxpayers between $2,000 and $3,000. Penalties for prostitution usually involve small fines or short jail terms. Of these arrests, about 90% are prostitutes and 10% are customers (Weitzer, 2000a). Of all prostitutes arrested, the vast majority are streetworkers, although they represent a minority of sex workers (Alexander, 1987; Cunningham & Kendall, 2010). Police officers may demand sex from prostitutes in return for avoiding arrest. For streetwalkers who do not work with a pimp, approximately 3% of all their tricks are freebies given to the police to avoid arrest (Levitt & Venkatesh, 2007). African American street prostitutes are arrested more than white street prostitutes, and they are more likely to be jailed. In one study, 69% of prostitutes who were charged were subsequently convicted; only 9% of customers who were charged were later convicted (Weitzer, 2000a).

A high-status Japanese [...]te.

Some explanations given for why streetwalkers make up the vast majority of prostitution-related arrests include the following: most sex workers are repeat offenders, the sex workers profit from the transaction, and the plying of their trade creates a public nuisance. Each of these arguments, though, could just as well be applied to the johns.

Laws against prostitution vary greatly from place to place. There are three main positions on prostitution: *abolition*—which seeks to eliminate prostitution through legal penalties; *legalization*—in which the state controls prostitution through licenses, registration, and mandatory medical exams; and *decriminalization*—whereby all criminal penalties and regulation are removed from sex work.

Prostitution is illegal in most of the United States, where penalties (applied mostly against the sex workers) include fines or jail time. In the Sudan, Afghanistan, and Iraq, prostitution is subject to the death penalty. Prostitution is legal, with restrictions and regulations, in Canada, Israel, most of Europe, and parts of South America and Australia. The Netherlands legalized prostitution in 2000; prostitutes there are in a union and pay taxes. Prostitution was decriminalized in New Zealand in May 2003 by a one-vote majority of its Parliament. Anyone over the age of 18 may have sex for money in New South Wales, Australia.

Laws may regulate where prostitution takes place or the activities that occur. In Turkey, it is illegal for a prostitute to work the streets, but government-regulated and licensed brothels are legal. In Japan, only vaginal intercourse for pay is considered prostitution, so a person may legally receive money for performing oral or anal sex. Prostitution used to be legal in Sweden, but in 1999 the law was changed. In Sweden it is legal to *sell* sex, but it is a crime to *buy* sex. This law was made in the hopes of not further punishing the already downtrodden and exploited sex workers. Since the law has been passed, Sweden has seen a huge decrease in prostitution.

In the United States, prostitution is legal only in some states. Brothels are legal and heavily regulated in most counties in Nevada. They are prohibited in counties of more than 400,000 people, and within 400 yards of a school, religious building, or on a principal business street. Pimps and streetwalking are illegal. In Rhode Island, due to a legal loophole, the exchange of sex for money is not illegal, although it is illegal to solicit sex on the street or to operate a brothel.

What are the pros and cons of legalization of prostitution? See Table 17.1 for a summary.

Commercial Phone Sex

> "When a man talks dirty to a woman, it's sexual harassment. When a woman talks dirty to a man, it's $3.95 a minute."
>
> —*Author unknown*

Phone sex is a sexually explicit conversation that occurs between two people over the telephone. This can take place between two people involved in a romantic relationship, or it may involve a person calling a commercial phone sex business. In some of

> **Why are sex workers arrested more than their customers? Are prostitutes more "at fault" than the customers? Are they easier to catch or easier to prosecute?**

these organizations, a group of women are working together in an office, but more often there is a dispatcher that sends calls to the sex worker's home. Some phone actors work independently and advertise on the Internet or in magazines. Phone sex workers generally make between $10 and $25 per hour, depending on where they work and how many calls they take per hour (Rich & Guidroz, 2000). The commercial phone sex industry is worth as much as $1 billion a year in the United States (Diamond, 2009; Weitzer, 2000a).

During the call, a woman may guide the listener through a fantasy, narrate a sexual experience, or participate in sexual role play. Callers may desire to experience fantasies that they cannot partake of in real life, due to embarrassment or legal ramifications. Other callers may be seeking to share intimate thoughts and desires. Often, the listener masturbates during the conversation.

Sexting

When people use their cell phones to send sexually explicit messages or images, it is called **sexting**. Sexting has become fairly common: a convenience sample survey conducted by the National Campaign to Prevent Teen and Unplanned Pregnancies (NCPTUP) found that 20% of teens and 33% of young adults aged 20 to 26 had posted or texted nude or semi-nude photos or videos of themselves online, and 39% of teens and 59% of young adults had sent sexually suggestive texts, emails, or instant messages (NCPTUP, 2008). Another study using a nationally representative sample of teens aged 12 to 17 estimated that 4% of youth had created and sent "sexually suggestive nude or nearly nude" images (Lenhart, 2009; Wokak & Finkelhor, 2011).

Sexting can be classified as *aggravated* or *experimental*. Aggravated incidents involve criminal or abusive elements beyond the creation, sending, or possession of youth-produced sexual images, such as adult involvement and criminal or abusive behavior such as extortion, threats, or malicious conduct (Wolak & Finkelhor, 2011). In experimental incidents, teens take and send pictures of themselves in order to seek attention, flirt, or create romantic interest; there is no criminal behavior beyond the creating or sending of the images (Wolak & Finkelhor, 2011).

Even if the intention is not malicious or criminal, teens who send or receive nude pictures of themselves or others risk felony child pornography charges and being listed on a sex offender registry for decades. In Florida, a 16-year-old girl and 17-year-old boy took pictures of themselves engaged in sexual activity and emailed each other the pictures (McCullagh, 2007). They were charged with production and possession of child pornography. Irony abounds in this case: The teens did not break the law by *having sex*—under Florida law they're of age—but they did break the law by *documenting* the sex because they're minors. The teens were therefore charged as both adults and minors for the same act. One of the

Phone sex A sexually explicit conversation that occurs between two people over the telephone.

Sexting Sending sexually explicit messages or images by cell phone or other electronic media.

ISSUE	PROS	CONS	ISSUES TO CONSIDER
Abolition	Many believe prostitution to be immoral.	Other behaviors, such as adultery, that are considered immoral are no longer illegal.	Are laws designed to protect our safety or to legislate morality? Who is the ultimate authority? Religious leaders? Health officials? Government? Why?
	Prostitution exploits women by justifying the sale of all women, and reduces all women to sex objects.	Sex work isn't inherently exploitative. If conditions were controlled, the negative effects would be diminished.	Who would be most hurt by harsher laws against prostitution? Prostitutes? Customers? Pimps?
	Harsher laws will decrease prostitution.	Current laws have not eliminated prostitution. Abolition would just drive prostitution more underground.	What is the effect of prohibition on other illegal actions? Can you compare those to prostitution? Why or why not?
	Men will always visit prostitutes, and need harsher penalties to keep them from their basic natures.	Is this a stereotype or a reality about men?	Should laws be enacted against natural instincts? Which instincts should be controlled, and why?
	Prostitution causes crime. It augments the power of the mafia, and increases robbery, assault, and drug use.	Prostitution is no longer attractive for organized crime—it is hard to control, visible, and provides harsh penalties for a relatively small financial return.	Should you make one activity illegal in order to control another activity?
	Prostitution increases STIs.	Only a small percentage of STIs in U.S. are due to prostitution. Deaths from AIDS in the U.S. occurred exclusively among prostitutes who admitted to injected drug use (Potterat et al., 2004).	If prostitution is responsible for only a small percentage of STIs in the U.S., how much of a decrease in STI rates justifies legal action against prostitution?
	Prostitution negatively impacts the community in which it occurs through disorderly conduct, public health risks, harassment of women, and costs to merchants (Weitzer, 2000b).	Most of these effects are due to outdoor sex work. Indoor sex work is more discreet and less in the public awareness.	If prostitution were decriminalized, where should it occur? Would you want it in your neighborhood? Why or why not?
Legalization with restrictions	With licensing, background checks, and registration of prostitutes, we can better monitor the effects of prostitution on sex workers and on society.	Registration makes a permanent record and increases stigma for prostitutes. Registration makes it harder for sex workers to get out of "the life."	How can this law be enforced?
	With restrictions, we can better regulate and test for STIs.	Forcing women to register and get mandatory health exams is even more demeaning to the sex workers.	Whose rights are more important—the sex workers' or their customers'? Why?
	With federal registration, the working conditions for prostitutes can be regulated and controlled.	In legal brothels in Nevada, brothel workers generally have little influence over their working conditions and little freedom over their actions. Women may be more physically and socially isolated.	Are these rules designed to protect the customers more than the prostitutes?
	Customers can be required to wear condoms.	Some customers still refuse to wear condoms, or offer more money to financially strapped sex workers for condom-less sex.	Ultimately, who is more responsible for condom use? Why?
	Prostitution is inevitable, so why not regulate it?	Legalization normalizes and trivializes prostitution and relieves customers of guilt. Legalizing it might actually increase demand. What message would legalization send to young people?	Do you feel that prostitution is a crime? Why or why not?

Table 17.1 Issues Regarding Abolition, Legalization, and Decriminalization of Prostitution—cont'd

ISSUE	PROS	CONS	ISSUES TO CONSIDER
Decriminalization	Decriminalization would decrease the stigma of prostitution.	Prostitution will always be stigmatized, whether legal or not.	Is the stigma of prostitution related to the illegal nature of the act or of the act itself?
	Prostitution is a victimless crime; decriminalization frees the police to focus on more serious or violent crimes.	Prostitution is not a victimless crime; it "legalizes the right to buy, sexually use, and profit from sexual exploitation of someone else's body" (Leuchtag, 2003).	What constitutes a victimless crime? Is there a victim in prostitution? How would laws against it help those victims?
	Legalization of prostitution would be a source of revenue for the state. Five percent of the gross domestic product of the Netherlands comes from the sex industry (Farley, 2004).	Legalization of drugs would also provide revenue for the government, but the government should not be involved in such things.	Should prostitution be treated like any other business? Why or why not?
	Consenting adults have the right to do as they choose with their bodies.	Many of our laws—such as laws against drug or alcohol use—are designed to keep people from harming themselves.	What role should the government play in controlling our bodies?
	Legalization gives sex workers more access to police protection.	Can't sex workers press charges for assault and rape now?	The legal system is less likely to punish those who commit violence or rape against a prostitute. Would this change with decriminalization?
	Decriminalization would cut down on illegal prostitution.	In Nevada, where brothels are legal, illegal streetwalkers still exist. Amsterdam has many illegal and unregistered prostitutes who were trafficked in from outer countries, and after prostitution was legalized in Victoria, Australia, there was a 300% growth in illegal brothels (Farley, 2004).	Are we "searching for a perfect solution"? Is there any law that *completely* eliminates the action it rules against? How much can we compare what occurs in other countries to the U.S.? How much do factors such as poverty, health care, gender relationships, and religion affect prostitution?

© Chris Rout/Alamy

judges who ruled for the charges in the case did so because "if these pictures are ultimately released, future damage may be done to these minors' careers or personal lives" (Elgin, 2009). Perhaps he didn't consider that charging them with child pornography might also damage their lives.

Before you press "send," remember a few important points. Don't assume that anything you send or post is going to remain private; it is common for sexually explicit texts or images to be shared between peers (NCPTUP, 2008). Also remember that even if you delete a text, it is never truly gone. Consider the recipient's reaction. Just because something is meant to be fun doesn't mean the person who receives it will see it that way. And finally, don't give in to the pressure to do anything that makes you uncomfortable—the consequences may be widespread and devastating (NCPTUP, 2008).

Strip Clubs

Strip clubs are bars or clubs that feature erotic dancing and entertainment. Dancers, often wearing fantasy-fulfilling costumes, gradually undress in time to music. The dancers move suggestively, often using a pole as an erotic prop. There are generally two categories of strip clubs: topless, in which dancers usually wear a G-string or thong and sometimes pasties that cover their nipples, and all-nude clubs. Dancers collect tips from men while on stage dancing or afterward during private dances or lap dances. During a lap dance, the entertainer either sits on the customer's lap or moves between his legs, pressing against his genitals and moving so as to arouse him.

A century before modern-day strippers wrapped their surgically-enhanced breasts around a pole, the striptease gained popularity at the Moulin Rouge and Folies Bergère in Paris, and in burlesque shows in the United States. Witty and grace-

Strip club A bar or nightclub that offers erotic dancing, striptease, and possibly other related services such as lap dances.

ful, stripper Gypsy Rose Lee became famous in burlesque for her striptease that focused more on the tease rather than the strip. Entertainer and civil rights activist Josephine Baker gained fame in the 1920s and 1930s by dancing in the Folies Bergère wearing only high heels and a skirt made out of bananas. The Pussycat Dolls got their start as New Burlesque dancers in an act that focused on (clothed) dancing, teasing, humor, and innuendo.

Today, the more than 2,300 strip clubs in the United States are a $5 billion industry (Schlosser, 2003). Americans spend more money at strip clubs than at Broadway theaters, regional and non-profit theaters, and symphony performances combined (Schlosser, 2003). Most of this money goes to the club owners; exotic dancers are often considered independent contractors and consequently receive no wages, only tips. Some even have to pay a "stage

Men at a strip club.

fee" of up to $100 and more to dance. Most clubs now consider the dancers as employees and pay them a wage, but the women have to pay a commission to the club owners for each dance. Because the owners don't know how many dances the women perform, they often set a minimum amount that dancers must pay the house each night, which is often more than their wages. Therefore, dancers must work harder for tips and sometimes go outside the law and perform "extras" for better tips (Chapkis, 2000).

Strip clubs have a number of rules, both for the customers and the dancers. Some clubs don't allow alcohol or the touching of dancers. In others, there are rules on what part of the woman a client can touch. This is not so much to protect the women but to protect the business from pandering charges because lap dances are a gray area between performance (legal) and prostitution (illegal). There are a number of rules for the women as well. Dancers must often follow regulations regarding their weight and hair length and may be limited regarding their piercings and tattoos (Chapkis, 2000).

According to a national survey, 22% of men and 4% of women visited a strip club "in the past year" (Laumann et al., 1994). Why do men visit strip clubs? The obvious answer seems to be "to see women's bodies." However, there are many ways that men can achieve that end: they can buy pornography, visit lingerie modeling shops, or even have an actual relationship with a woman. There must be other aspects to strip clubs that make them so popular. While pursuing her doctorate in cultural anthropology, Katherine Frank interviewed a number of patrons at strip clubs to learn their views. The fact that Dr. Frank was a dancer at many of these clubs adds an insider's view to this research (Frank, 2003). Many men visit strip clubs as a means of relaxation, a way to escape from the pressures of work and home. These men feel pressured by the sometimes confusing and contradictory rules of interaction with women. They also feel that strip clubs give them the opportunity to partake in traditionally masculine activities that may not be accepted in other realms of their world, such as drinking, smoking, and acting vulgar or aggressive. Other men long to break with the established routines of everyday life, especially with regard to interactions with women. In strip clubs, women *want* to be looked at naked, and it is women who approach men and face the possibility of rejection. Men in strip clubs can receive social acceptance from women, with no emotional involvement, no requirement to pleasure the women, and no pressure for sexual performance. Finally, strip clubs are seen as both safe and exciting. Strip clubs may give the sensation of danger and excitement, but they actually have clear and rigorously enforced rules—about what one can touch and what types of interactions are allowed—that allow men to maintain their monogamy and safe lives.

Chapter Summary

Introduction

- *Sex work* is a sweeping term used to describe services, performances, or the production of products given in exchange for material compensation. Sex work includes pornography, prostitution, exotic dancing, commercial phone sex, and other occupations.

Pornography

- Pornography is any sexually explicit material that is designed to elicit sexual arousal or interest. Men consume more pornography than women. People in the United States spend up to $14 billion each year on pornographic material.
- Pornography exists in many different media, including books, magazines, video, photos, drawings or paintings, animation, sound recording, and video games. Cybersex is a type of online sexual activity that involves the use of computerized content for sexual stimulation and gratification, usually involving two or more persons. There are many genres of pornography; patrons may choose their pornography based on sexual orientation, explicitness, the physical characteristics or number of participants, or the specific acts performed.
- Pornography has existed since humans could communicate, but the laws and attitudes about pornography change from time to time and from place to place. There are no legal restrictions against pornography in Denmark. In Japan, sexually explicit material is typically more violent than that seen in the United States.
- Pornography has both beneficial and harmful consequences. Some people feel that pornography increases sexual aggression toward women, while others feel that not only does pornography not increase sexual violence, it may decrease it.

Prostitution

- *Prostitution* describes the exchange of sexual access to one's body for something of value, be it money, drugs, or other commodities. It is difficult to ascertain the scope of prostitution in the United States, because of its illegality and questionable moral standing.
- There are many different types of prostitutes, from streetwalkers, who hold the lowest status, to girls who work in bars, massage parlors, or brothels, to the higher status and better-paid escorts and call girls.
- The characteristics of prostitutes, their clients, and the activities they engage in vary depending on the type of prostitution. Men and MTF transgendered individuals also work as prostitutes. Prostitutes face many physical and emotional health risks.
- The average customer of a prostitute is probably not significantly different than other men, although there are some other differences between prostitute customers and the rest of the population. Customers may visit prostitutes due to their desire for a certain type of sexual experience; convenience; feelings of shyness or social inhibition; the thrill of the risk or illicit nature of the act; or because they are seeking companionship or intimacy.
- Prostitutes face many physical and emotional health risks, including violence at the hands of their pimps or customers, exposure to STIs, depression, and PTSD.

- Sex trafficking is the recruitment, harboring, transportation, or obtaining of a person for the purpose of a commercial sex act. There may be as many as 200,000 people worldwide who have been forced into sexual slavery.
- Prostitution has been around for many thousands of years, and attitudes and laws about prostitution vary across time and across cultures.
- About 90,000 arrests are made each year in the United States for violation of prostitution laws; of these arrests, about 90% are prostitutes and 10% are customers. There are three main positions on prostitution: abolition, legalization, and decriminalization.
- During professional phone sex, the worker (almost always a woman) may guide the listener through a fantasy, narrate a sexual experience, or participate in sexual role play. The listener often masturbates during the conversation.
- Sexting—using a cell phone to send sexually explicit messages or images—has become popular, especially among teens and young adults. There can be harsh legal consequences for sexting.
- Strip clubs are bars or clubs that feature erotic dancing. Some have topless dancers; others have nude dancers. Strip clubs generally enforce rules for both dancers and customers.

Anokhin, A. P., Golosheykin, S., Sirevaag, E., Kristjansson, S., Rohrbaugh, J. W., & Heath, A. C. (2006). Rapid discrimination of visual scene content in the human brain. *Brain Research, 1093*(1), 167-177.

Arax, M. (1986, April 24). Judge says law doesn't protect prostitutes, drops rape count. *Los Angeles Times,* pp. 1-2.

Archer, J. (2006). Testosterone and human aggression: An evaluation of the challenge hypothesis. *Neuroscience and Biobehavioral Reviews, 30*(3), 319-345.

Arck, P. C., Rose, M., Hertwig, K., Hagen, E., Hildebrandt, M., & Klapp, B. F. (2001). Stress and immune mediators in miscarriage. *Human Reproduction, 16*(7), 1505-1511.

Areton, L. W. (2002). Factors in the sexual satisfaction of obese women in relationships. *Electronic Journal of Human Sexuality, 5.* Retrieved from http://www.ejhs.org/volume5/Areton/TOC.htm

Armesto, J. C., & Weisman, A. G. (2001). Attributions and emotional reactions to the identity disclosure ("coming out") of a homosexual child. *Family Process, 40*(2), 145-161.

Armstrong, E. G. (2001). Gangsta misogyny: A content analysis of the portrayals of violence against women in rap music, 1987-1993. *Journal of Criminal Justice and Popular Culture, 8*(2), 96-126.

Armsworth, M. W. (1991). Psychological responses to abortion. *Journal of Counseling and Development, 69*(4), 377-379.

Arnold, C. B. (1978). Public health aspects of contraceptive sterilization. In S. Newman (Ed.), *Behavioral-social aspects of contraceptive sterilization.* New York: Lexington Books.

Aron, A., Fisher, H., Mashek, D. J., Strong, G., Li, J., & Brown, L. L. (2005). Reward, motivation, and emotion systems associated with early-stage intense romantic love. *Journal of Neurophysiology, 94,* 327-337.

Aronson, D. D. (2006). Should health insurers be forced to pay for infertility treatments? In W. J. Taverner (Ed.), *Taking sides: Clashing views on controversial issues in human sexuality* (9th ed., pp. 46-50). Dubuque, IA: McGraw-Hill/Dushkin.

Aronson, E. (2003). *The social animal* (9th ed., p. 243). New York: Worth.

ArtsReformation.com. (2006). The motion picture production code of 1930 (Hays code). Retrieved from http://www.artsreformation.com/a001/hays-code.html

Associated Press. (2010, July 27). Army dismisses gay Arabic linguist. Retrieved from http://www.msnbc.msn.com/id/14052513/ns/us_news-military

Astin, S., Redston, P., & Campbell, A. (2003). Sex differences in social representations of aggression: Men justify, women excuse? *Aggressive Behavior, 29*(3), 128-133.

Attorney General's Commission on Pornography. (1986). *Final report.* Washington, DC: U.S. Government Printing Office.

Atwood, J. D. (2005). Cyber affairs: "What's the big deal?" Therapeutic considerations. In F. P Piercy, K. M. Hertlein, & J. L. Wetchler (Eds.), *Handbook of the clinical treatment of infidelity* (pp. 116-134). New York: Haworth Press.

Atwood, J. D. (2007). When love hurts: Preadolescents girls' reports of incest. *American Journal of Family Therapy, 35,* 287-313.

Aubrey, J. S., Harrison, K., Kramer, L., & Yellin, J. (2003). Variety versus timing: Gender differences in college students' sexual expectations as predicted by exposure to sexually oriented television. *Communication Research, 30*(4), 432-460.

Auger, J., Kuntsmann, J. M., Czyglik, F., & Jouannet, P. (1995). Decline in semen quality among fertile men in Paris during the past 20 years. *The New England Journal of Medicine, 332*(5), 281-285.

Aunos, M., & Feldman, M. A. (2002). Attitudes towards sexuality, sterilization, and parenting rights of persons with intellectual disabilities. *Journal of Applied Research in Intellectual Disabilities, 15,* 285-296.

Auster, C. J., & Ohm, S. C. (2000). Masculinity and femininity in contemporary American society: A reevaluation using the Bem sex-role inventory. *Sex Roles, 43*(7/8), 499-528.

Auvert, B., Bure, A., Lagarde, E., Kahindo, M., Chege, J., & Rutenberg, N., et al. (2001). Male circumcision and HIV infection in four cities in sub-Saharan Africa. *AIDS, 15*(Suppl. 4), 531-540.

Auvert, B., Taljaard, D., Lagarde, E., Sobngwi-Tambekou, J., Sitta, R., & Puren, A. (2005). Randomized, controlled intervention trial of male circumcision for reduction of HIV infection risk: The ANRS 1265 trial. *PLoS Medicine, 2*(11), e298.

Axinn, W. G., & Thornton A. (1992). The relationship between cohabitation and divorce: Selectivity or causal influence? *Demography, 29*(3), 357-374.

Bachman, J. G., Johnston, L. D., & O'Malley, P. M. (2000). *Monitoring the future: Responses from the nation's high school seniors.* Ann Arbor, MI: Institute for Social Research, University of Michigan.

Bachman, R., & Saltzman, L. E. (1995). *Violence against women: Estimates from the Redesigned National Crime Victimization Survey* (NCJ-154348). Bureau of Justice Statistics, U.S. Department of Justice.

Baden, L. R., Curfman, G. D., Morrissey, S., & Drazen, J. M. (2007). Human papillomavirus vaccine opportunity and challenge. *New England Journal of Medicine, 356*(19), 1990.

Baertlein, L., & Dabrowski, W. (2006, October 28). Gamemaker courts new controversy—boys kissing. *The Washington Post.* Retrieved from http://www.reuters.com/article/2006/10/28/us-media-videogames-bully-idUSNAP35926720061028.

Bailey, J. M., Dunne, M. P., & Martin, N. (2000). Genetic and environmental influences on sexual orientation and its correlates in an Australian twin sample. *Journal of Personality and Social Psychology, 78,* 524-536.

Bailey, J. M., & Pillard, R. C. (1991). A genetic study of male sexual orientation. *Archives of General Psychiatry, 48*(December), 1089-1096.

Bailey, J. M., Pillard, R. C., Neale, M. C., & Agyei, Y. (1993). Heritable factors influence sexual orientation in women. *Archives of General Psychiatry, 50*(March), 217-223.

Bailey, N. W. & Zuk, M. (2009). Same-sex sexual behavior and evolution. *Trends in Ecological Evolution, 24*(8), 439-446.

Bailey, R. C., Muga, R., Poulusse, R., & Abicht, H. (2002). The acceptability of male circumcision to reduce HIV infections in Nyanza Province Kenya. *AIDS Care, 14*(1), 27-40.

Baird, A. D., Wilson, S. J., Bladin, P. F., Saling, M. M., & Reutens, D. C. (2007). Neurological control of human sexual behavior: Insights from lesion studies. *Journal of Neurology, Neurosurgery and Psychiatry, 78,* 1042-1049.

Balsam, K. F., Rothblum, E. D. & Beauchaine, T. P. (2005). Victimization over the life span: A comparison of lesbian, gay, bisexual and heterosexual siblings. *Journal of Counseling and Clinical Psychology, 73*(3), 477-487.

Bancroft, J. (2004). Alfred C. Kinsey and the politics of sex research. *Annual Review of Sex Research, 15,* 1-39.

Bancroft, J. (2009). *Human sexuality and its problems* (3rd ed.). New York: Churchill Livingstone.

Banis, R. J. (2006). *Sexually transmitted diseases, a practical guide: Symptoms, diagnosis, treatment, prevention.* Chesterfield, MO: Science and Humanities Press.

Banks, E., Beral, V., Bull, D., Reeves, G., & Million Women Study collaborators. (2003). Breast cancer and hormone-replacement therapy in the Million Women Study. *Lancet, 362*(9382), 419-427.

Banks, E., Meirik, O., Farley, T., Akande, O., Bathija, J. & Ali, M. (2006). Female genital mutilation and obstetric outcome: WHO collaborative prospective study in six African countries. *Lancet, 367*(9525), 1835-1841.

Barak, A., Fisher, W. A., Belfry, S., & Lashambe, D. R. (1999). Sex, guys, and cyberspace: Effects of Internet pornography and individual differences on men's attitudes toward women. *Journal of Psychology and Human Sexuality, 11,* 63-92.

Baron-Cohen, S. (2003). *The essential difference: The truth about the male and female brain.* New York: Perseus Books.

Barrett-Connor, E., & Grady, D. (1998). Hormone replacement therapy, heart disease, and other considerations. *Annual Review of Public Health, 19,* 55-72.

Barrier, P. A. (1998). Domestic violence. *Mayo Clinic Proceedings, 73,* 271-274.

Bart, P. B. (1981). A study of women who both were raped and avoided rape. *Journal of Social Issues, 37*(4), 123-137.

Bartels, A., & Zeki, S. (2000). The neural basis of romantic love. *NeuroReport, 11,* 1-6.

Bartels, A., & Zeki, S. (2004). The neural correlates of maternal and romantic love. *Neuroimage, 21,* 1155-1166.

Baskin, Y. (1999). Birds, bees, and STDs: Sexually transmitted diseases in flowers. *Natural History, 108*(10), 52-55.

Bassham, G., Irwin, W., Nardone, H., & Wallace, J. M. (2002). *Critical thinking: A student's introduction.* New York: McGraw-Hill.

Basson, R. (2000). The female sexual response: A different mode. *Journal of Sex and Marital Therapy, 26,* 51-65.

Bassow, S. A., & Minieri, A. (2011). "You owe me": Who pays, participant gender, and rape myth beliefs on perceptions of rape. *Journal of Interpersonal Violence, 26*(3), 479-497.

Bauerle, S. Y., Amirkhan, J. H., & Hupka, R. B. (2002). An attribution theory analysis of romantic jealousy. *Motivation and Emotion, 26*(4), 297-319.

Baumeister, R. F. (2007, August). *Is there anything good about men?* Invited address to the American Psychological Association. San Francisco, California.

Baumeister, R. F., Wotman, S. R., & Stillwell, A. M. (1993). Unrequited love: On heartbreak, anger, guilt, scriptlessness, and humiliation. *Journal of Personality and Social Psychology, 64,* 377-394.

Bazzini, D. G., McIntosh, W. D., Smith, S. M., Cook, S., & Harris, C. (1997). The aging woman in popular film: Underrepresented, unattractive, unfriendly, and unintelligent. *Sex Roles, 36,* 531-543.

Beh, H. G., & Diamond, M. (2006). The failure of abstinence-only education: Minors have a right to honest talk about sex [Sexuality and the Law Symposium]. *Columbia Journal of Gender and Law, 15*(1), 12-62.

Beilock, S. L. (2007, February). *Interplay of emotion and cognition: Implication for learning and high stakes testing.* Presentation at the American Association for the Advancement of Science (AAAS) annual meeting, San Francisco, CA.

Beilock, S. L., Gunderson, E. A., & Levine, S. C. (2010). Female teachers' math anxiety impacts girls' math achievement. *Proceedings of the National Academy of Sciences, 107*(5), 1860-1863.

Beitchman, J. H., Zucker, K. J., Hood, J. E., daCosta, G. A., Akman, D., & Cassavia, E. (1992). A review of the long-term effects of child sexual abuse. *Child Abuse and Neglect, 16*(1), 101-108.

Bell, D. M. (1997). Occupational risk of human immunodeficiency virus infection in healthcare workers: An overview. *American Journal of Medicine, 103*(5B), 9-15.

Bem, D. J. (1996a). Exotic becomes erotic: A developmental theory of sexual orientation. *Psychological Review, 103*(2), 320-335.

Bem, D. J. (1996b). Exotic becomes erotic: A political postscript. Retrieved from http://dbem.ws/ebe_politics.html

Bem, S. L. (1974). The measurement of psychological androgyny. *Journal of Consulting and Clinical Psychology, 42,* 155-162.

Bem, S. L. (1981). Gender schema theory: A cognitive account of sex typing. *Psychology Reviews, 88*(4), 354-364.

Ben Zion, I., Tessler, T., Cohen, L., Lerer, E., Raz, Y., Bachner-Melman, R., ... Ebstein, R. P. (2006). Polymorphisms in the dopamine D4 receptor gene (DRD4) contribute to individual differences in human sexual behavior: Desire, arousal, and sexual function. *Molecular Psychiatry, 11*(8), 782-786.

Benedict, H. (1992). *Virgin or vamp: How the press covers sex crimes.* New York: Oxford University Press.

Benevento, B. T., & Sipski, M. L. (2002). Neurogenic bladder, neurogenic bowel, and sexual dysfunction in people with spinal cord injury. *Physical Therapy, 82*(6), 601-612.

Bennett., L., & Gates, G. J. (2004). The cost of marriage inequality to children and their same-sex parents. Retrieved from http:// www.hrc.org/Content/ContentGroups/ Publications1/kids_doc_final.pdf

Ben-Ze'ev, A. (2003). Privacy, emotional closeness, and openness in cyberspace. *Computers in Human Behavior, 19,* 451-467.

Beren, S. E., Hayden, H. A., Wilfley, D. E., Grilo, C. M. (1996). The influence of sexual orientation on body dissatisfaction in adult men and women. *International Journal of Eating Disorders, 20*(2), 135-141.

Berg, S. J., & Wynne-Edwards, K. E. (2001). Changes in testosterone, cortisol, and estradiol levels in men becoming fathers. *Mayo Clinic Proceedings 76*(6), 582-592.

Bergen, R. K. (1999). *Marital rape.* Applied research forum of the National Electronic Network on Violence Against Women. Retrieved from www.vawnet.org/ DomesticViolence/Research/ VAWnetDocs/AR_mrape.pdf

Berger, J. S., Roncaglioni, M. C., Avanzini, F., Pangrazzi, I., Tognoni, G., & Brown, D. L. (2006). Aspirin for the primary prevention of cardiovascular events in women and men: A sex-specific meta-analysis of randomized controlled trials. *Journal of the American Medical Association, 295*(3), 306-313.

Berglund, H., Lindstrom, P., & Savic, I. (2006). Brain response to putative pheromones in lesbian women. *Proceedings of the National Academy of Sciences, 103*(29), 8269-8274.

Bergman, K., Rubio, R. J., Green, R-J., & Padron, E. (2010). Gay men who become fathers via surrogacy: The transition to parenthood. *Journal of GLBT Family Studies, 6*(2), 111-141.

Bergstrand, C., & Williams, J. B. (2000). Today's alternative marriage styles: The case of swingers. *The Electronic Journal of Human Sexuality, 3*(Oct. 10). Retrieved from http://ejhs.org/volume3/swing/ body.htm

Berin, J. (2009, October 29). Are there asexuals among us? On the possibility of a "fourth" sexual orientation. *Scientific American.* Retrieved from http://www .scientificamerican.com/blog/post .cfm?id5are-there-asexuals-among- us-on-the-2009-10-29

Bernstein, K. T., Kai-Lih, L., Begier, E. M., Koblin, B., Karpati, A., & Murrill, C. (2008). Same-sex attraction disclosure to health care providers among New York city men who have sex with men: Implications for HIV testing approaches. *Archives of Internal Medicine, 168*(13), 1458-1464.

Berrin, K., & Seligman, T. K. (1978). *The art of the Huichol Indians.* New York: Harry N. Adams.

Berry, S., (1980). Spousal rape: The uncommon law. *American Bar Association Journal, 66,* 1088-1091.

Besen, W. (2006, June 10). Love won out slithers into the nation's capitol. Retrieved from http://www.waynebesen.com

Besharov, D. J., & West, A. (2001). *African American marriage patterns.* Stanford University: Hoover Press. Retrieved from http://media.hoover.org/documents/0817998721_95.pdf

Bhugra, D. (2000). Disturbances in objects of desire: Cross-cultural issues. *Sexual and Relationship Therapy, 15*(1), 67-78.

Bhugra, D., Popelyuk, D., & McMullen, I. (2010). Paraphilias across cultures: Contexts and controversies. *Journal of Sex Research, 47*(2-3), 242-256.

Bisson, M. A., & Levine, T. R. (2009). Negotiating a friends with benefits relationship. *Archives of Sexual Behavior, 38*(1), 66-73.

Bivona, J., & Critelli, J. (2009). The nature of women's rape fantasies: An analysis of prevalence, frequency, and contents. *Journal of Sex Research, 46*(1), 33-45.

Bjorkqvist, K., Nygren, T., Bjorklund, A.-C., & Bjorkqvist, S.-E. (1994). Testosterone intake and aggressiveness: Real effect or anticipation? *Aggressive Behavior, 20,* 17-26.

Bjorndahl, L., & Barratt, C. L. R. (2002). Sex selection: A survey of laboratory methods and clinical results. Retrieved from www.hfea.gov.uk/docs/Appendix_C_-_Scientific_and_Technical_Literature_Review.pdf

Black, D. W., Kehrberg, L. L. D., Flumerfelt, D .L., & Schlosser, S. S. (1997). Characteristics of 36 subjects reporting compulsive sexual behavior. *American Journal of Psychiatry, 154*(2), 243-249.

Blackless, M., Charuvastra, A., Derryck, A., Fausto-Sterling, A., Lauzanne, K., & Lee, E. (2000). How sexually dimorphic are we? Review and synthesis. *American Journal of Human Biology, 12,* 151-166.

Blackwell, D., & Lichter, D. (2000). Mate selection among married and cohabiting couples. *Journal of Family Issues, 12,* 275-302.

Blackwell, R. E., & the William Mercer Actuarial Team. (2000). Hidden costs of infertility treatment in employee health benefits plans. *American Journal of Obstetrics and Gynecology, 182*(4), 891-895.

Blair, S. L., & Johnson, M. P. (1992). Wives' perceptions of the fairness of the division of household labor: The intersection of housework and ideology. *Journal of Marriage and the Family, 54*(3), 570-581.

Blake, S. M., Ledsky, R., Goodenow, C., Sawyer, R., Lohrmann, D., & Windsor, R. (2003). Condom availability programs in Massachusetts high schools: Relationships with condom use and sexual behavior. *American Journal of Public Health, 93*(6), 955-962.

Blanch, D. C., Hall, J. A., Roter, D. L., & Frankel, R. M. (2008). Medical student gender and issues of confidence. *Patient Education and Counseling, 72*(3), 374-381.

Blanchard, R., & Bogaert, A. F. (1996). Homosexuality in men and number of older brothers. *The American Journal of Psychiatry, 153*(1), 27-31.

Blanchard, R., Cantor, J. M., Bogaert, A. F., Breedlove, S. M., Ellis, L. (2006). Interaction of fraternal birth order and handedness in the development of male homosexuality. *Hormones and Behavior, 49,* 405-414.

Blanchard, R., Kolla, N. J., Cantor, J. M., Klassen, P. E., Dickey, R., Kuban, M. E., & Blak, T. (2007). IQ, handedness, and pedophilia in adult male patients stratified by referral source. *Sexual Abuse: A Journal of Research and Treatment, 19*(3). doi:10.1007/s11194-007-9049-0

Blitstein, R. (2008, June 29). I think I love you. *Chicago Tribune Magazine.* Retrieved from http://ryanblitstein.com/?p5461

Bloom, Amy. (2002). *Normal: Transsexual CEOs, cross dressing cops, and hermaphrodites with attitude.* New York: Random House.

Blow, C. M. (2008, September 6). Let's talk about sex. *New York Times.* Retrieved from http://www.nytimes.com/2008/09/06/opinion/06blow.html?_r51

Blum, R. W., Resnick, M. D., Nelson, R., & St. Germaine, A. (1991). Family and peer issues among adolescents with spina bifida and cerebral palsy. *Pediatrics, 20,* 280-285.

Blythe, M. J., Fortenberry, J. D., Temkit, M. H., Tu, W., & Orr, D. P. (2006). Incidence and correlates of unwanted sex in relationships of middle and late adolescent women. *Archives of Pediatric and Adolescent Medicine, 160,* 591-595.

Boekeloo, B. O., & Howard, D. E. (2002). Oral sexual experience among young adolescents receiving general health examinations. *American Journal of Health and Behavior, 26*(4), 306-314.

Bogaert, A. F. (2001). Personality, individual differences, and preferences for the sexual media. *Archives of Sexual Behavior, 30,* 29-53

Bogaert, A. F. (2004). Asexuality: Prevalence and associated factors in a national probability sample. *Journal of Sex Research, 41*(3), 279-287.

Bogaert, A. F. (2005, July). *Biological versus nonbiological older brothers and sexual orientation in men.* Paper presented at the meeting of the International Academy of Sex Research. Ottawa, Ontario.

Bogaert, A. F., & Hershberger, S. (1999). The relation between sexual orientation and penile size. *Archives of Sexual Behavior, 28,* 213-221.

Bogle, K. A. (2008). *Hooking up: Sex, dating, and relationships on campus.* New York: New York University Press.

Bollinger, C. (2004, August). Access denied. *Prevention,* 151-159, 184-185.

Bond, S., & Cash, T. F. (1992). Black beauty: Skin color and body image among African American college women. *Journal of Applied Social Psychology, 22*(11), 874.

Bondurant S., Ernster, V., & Herdman, R. (Eds.). (1999). *Safety of silicone breast implants.* Washington, DC: National Academy Press.

Bone, J. (2008, March 26). Thomas Beatie, a married man who used to be a woman, is pregnant with a baby girl. *New York Times.* Retrieved from http://www.timesonline.co.uk/tol/news/world/us_and_americas/article3628860.ece

Boodman, S. G. (2005, August 16). Vowing to set the world straight: Proponents of reparative therapy say they can help gay patients become heterosexual. Experts call that a prescription for harm. *Washington Post.* Retrieved from http://www.washingtonpost.com/wp-dyn/content/article/2005/08/15/AR2005081501022.html?sub5AR

Boonstra, H. D. (2008). Making HIV tests "routine": Concerns and implications. *Guttmacher Policy Review, 11*(2), 13-18.

Boonstra, H. D., Gold, R. B., Richards, C. L., & Finer, L. B. (2006). *Abortion in women's lives.* New York: Guttmacher Institute.

Booth, A., & Dabbs, J. (1993). Testosterone and men's marriages. *Social Forces, 72,* 463-477.

Bosarge, P. M. (2006). Effectiveness of barrier methods for sexually transmitted infection prevention. In A. L. Nelson & J. A. Woodward (Eds.), *Current clinical practice: Sexually transmitted diseases: A practical guide for primary care* (pp. 305-319). Totowa, NJ: Humana Press.

Bradbury, T. N., & Fincham, F. B. (1990). Attributions in marriage: Review and critique. *Psychological Bulletin, 107*(1), 3-33.

Bradford, J. M. W. (2001). The neurobiology, neuropharmacology, and pharmacological treatment of the paraphilias and compulsive sexual behaviour. *Canadian Journal of Psychiatry, 46,* 26-33.

Bradshaw, C., Kahn, A. S., & Saville, B. K. (2010). To hook up or date: Which gender benefits? *Sex Roles, 62,* 661-669.

Braithwaite, L. W. (1981). Ecological studies of the black swan: III. Behavior and social organization. *Australian Wildlife Research, 9,* 135-146.

Brand, J. M., & Galask, R. P. (1986). Trimethylamine: The substance mainly responsible for the fishy odor often associated with bacterial vaginosis. *Obstetrics and Gynecology 68*(5), 682-685.

Brandt, A.M. (1985). *No magic bullet: A social history of venereal disease in the United States since 1880.* New York: Oxford University Press.

Braun, M. F., & Bryan, A. (2006). Female waist-to-hip and male waist-to-shoulder ratios as determinants of romantic partner desirability. *Journal of Social and Personal Relationships, 23,* 805-819.

Braunstein, S., & van de Wijgert, J. (2003). Cultural norms and behavior regarding vaginal lubrication during sex: Implications for the acceptability of vaginal microbicides for the prevention of HIV/STIs. *The Robert H. Ebert Program on Critical Issues in Reproductive Health.* New York: Population Council.

Brennan, P. L., Prum, R. O., McCracken, K. G., Sorenson, M. D., Wilson, R. E., & Birkhead, T.R. (2007). Coevolution of male and female genital morphology in waterfowl. *PLoS ONE, 2*(5), e418.

Bressler, E. R., Martin, R. A., & Balshine, S. (2006). Production and appreciation of humor as sexually selected traits. *Evolution and Human Behavior, 27*(2), 121-130.

Brewer, D. D., Muth, S. Q., & Potterat, J. J. (2008). Demographic, biometric, and geographic comparison of clients of prostitutes and men in the U.S. general population. *Electronic Journal of Human Sexuality, 11.* Retrieved from http://www.interscientific.net/EJHS2008.html

Brewer, D. D., Potterat, J. J., Barrett, S. B., Muth, S. Q., Roberts, J. M., Kasprzyk, D., Montano, D. E., & Darrow, W. W. (2000). Prostitution and the sex discrepancy in reported number of sexual partners. *Proceedings of the National Academy of Sciences, 97*(22), 12385-12388.

Brewer, G., & Hendrie, C. (2011). Evidence to suggest that copulatory vocalizations in women are not a reflexive consequence of orgasm. *Archives of Sexual Behavior, 40*(3), 559-564.

Bridges, A. J., Wisnitzer, R., Scharrer, E., Sun C., & Lieberman, R. (2010). Aggression and sexual behavior in best selling pornography videos: A content analysis update. *Violence against Women, 16*(10), 1065-1085.

Briere, J., & Runtz, M. (1989). University males' sexual interest in children: Predicting potential indices of "pedophilia" in a nonforensic sample. *Child Abuse and Neglect, 13*(1), 65-75.

Brines, J. (1994). Economic dependency, gender, and the division of labor at home. *American Journal of Sociology, 100*(3), 652-688.

Bröder, A., & Hohmann, N. (2003). Variations in risk taking behavior over the menstrual cycle: An improved replication. *Evolution and Human Behavior, 24,* 391-398.

Broder, M. S., Kanouse, D. E., Mittman, B. S., & Bernstein, S. J. (2000). The appropriateness of recommendations for hysterectomy. *Obstetrics and Gynecology, 95*(2), 199-205.

Brody, L. (2009, May 7). The O/Seventeen Sex Survey. *Oprah Magazine,* 181-191, 220-223.

Brook, D. (2003). The problem of prison rape. In M. Stombler, D. M. Baunach, E. O. Burgess, D. Donnelly, & W. Simonds (Eds.), *Sex matters: The sexuality and society reader* (2nd ed.). New York: Pearson Education, 584-587.

Brosco, J. P. (1999). The early history of the infant mortality rate in America: "A reflection upon the past and a prophecy of the future." *Pediatrics, 103*(2), 478-485.

Brown, D. L., & Frank, J. E. (2003). Diagnosis and management of syphilis. *American Family Physician, 68*(2), 283-290.

Brown, J. D. (2002). Mass media influences on sexuality—Statistical data included. *The Journal of Sex Research, 39*(1), 42-46.

Brown, J. R. W. C. (1983). Paraphilias: Sadomasochism, fetishism, transvestism, and transsexuality. *British Journal of Psychiatry, 143,* 227-2231.

Brown, N. R., & Sinclair, R. C. (1999). Estimating lifetime sexual partners: Men and women do it differently. *The Journal of Sex Research, 36,* 292-297.

Brown, S. L. (2000). The effect of union type of psychological well-being: Depression among cohabitors versus marrieds. *Journal of Health and Social Behavior, 41*(3), 241-255.

Brown, S. L., & Booth, A. (1996). Cohabitation versus marriage: A comparison of relationship quality. *Journal of Marriage and the Family, 58*(3), 668-678.

Brown, S. L., Pennello, G., Berg, W. A., Soo, M. S., & Middleton, M. S. (2001). Silicone gel breast implant rupture, extracapsular silicone, and health status in a population of women. *Journal of Rheumatology, 28,* 996-1003.

Brown, W. M., Hines, M., Fane, B., & Breedlove, S. M. (2002). Masculinized finger length ratios in humans with congenital adrenal hyperplasia (CAH). *Hormones and Behavior, 42*(4), 380-386.

Browne, M. N., & Keeley, S. (2000). *Asking the right questions: A guide to critical thinking* (6th ed.). Saddle River, NJ: Prentice Hall.

Brownmiller, S. (1993). *Against our will: Men, women, and rape.* New York: Ballantine Books.

Bruckner, J., & Bearman, P. (2005). After the promise, the STD consequences of adolescent virginity pledges. *Journal of Adolescent Health, 36*(4), 271-278.

Bryant J., & Rockwell, S. C. (1994). Effects of massive exposure to sexually oriented prime-time television programming on adolescents' moral judgment. In D. Zillman, J. Bryant, & A. C. Huston (Eds.), *Media, children and the family: Social, scientific, psychological dynamics and clinical perspectives* (pp. 183-195). Hillsdale, NJ: Lawrence Erlbaum.

Bryant, A. S., & Demian. (1994). Relationship characteristics of American gay and lesbian couples: Findings from a national survey. *Journal of Gay and Lesbian Social Services, 1*(2), 101-117.

Bryden, D. P., & Lengnick, S. (1997). Rape in the criminal justice system. *Journal of Criminal Law and Criminology, 87,* 1283-1294.

Buckley, C. (2008, November 14). They couldn't get past the "mimbos." *New York Times.* Retrieved from http://www.nytimes.com/2008/11/16/fashion/16playgirl.html

Bullivant, S. B., Sellergren, S. A., Stern, K., Spencer, N. A., Jacob, S., Mennella, J. A. & McClintock, M. K. (2004). Women's sexual experience during the menstrual cycle: Identification of the sexual phase by noninvasive measurement of luteinizing hormone. *Journal of Sex Research, 41*(1), 82-93.

Bullough, B., & Bullough, V. L. (1996). Female prostitution: Current research and changing interpretations. *Annual Review of Sex Research, 7,* 158-180.

Bullough, V. L. (1994). *Science in the bedroom: A history of sex research.* New York: Basic Books.

Bullough, V. L., & Bullough, B. (1994). *Human sexuality: An encyclopedia.* New York: Routledge.

Bumpass, L. L., & Lu, H. H. (2000). Trends in cohabitation and implications for children's family contexts in the United States. *Population Studies, 54,* 29-41.

Bureau of Labor Statistics. (2007, June). Washington, DC: United States Department of Labor.

Burgess, A. W., & Holmstrom, L. L. (1974). Rape trauma syndrome. *American Journal of Psychiatry, 131*(9), 981-986.

Chavarro, J. E., Toth, T. L., Sadio, S. M. & Hauser, R. (2008). Soy food and isoflavone intake in relation to semen quality parameters among men from an infertility clinic. *Human Reproduction, 23*(11), 2584-2590.

Chehab, F. F., Mounzih, K., Lu, R., & Lim, M. E. (1997). Early onset of reproductive function in normal female mice treated with leptin. *Science, 275*(5296), 88-90.

Chen, M. K., Lakshminarayanan, V., & Santos, L. R. (2006). How basic are behavioral biases? Evidence from capuchin monkey trading behavior. *Journal of Political Economy, 114*(3), 517-537.

Chesson, H. W., Blandford, J. M., Gift, T. L., Tao, G., & Irwin, K. L. (2004). The estimated direct medical cost of sexually transmitted diseases among American youth, 2000. *Perspectives on Sexual and Reproductive Health, 36*(1), 6-10.

Chivers, M. L. (2005). A brief review and discussion of sex differences in the specificity of sexual arousal. *Sexual and Relationship Therapy, 20*(4), 377-390.

Chivers, M. L., Rieger, G., Latty, E., & Bailey, J. M. (2004). A sex difference in the specificity of sexual arousal. *Psychological Science, 15*(11), 736-744.

Chivers, M. L., Seto, M. C., Lalumiere, M. L., Laan, E., & Grimbos, T. (2010). Agreement of self-reported and genital measures of sexual arousal in men and women: A meta-analysis. *Archives of Sexual Behavior, 39,* 55-56.

Cho, E., Chen W. Y., Hunter, D. J., Stampfer, M. J., Colditz, G. A., et al. (2006). Red meat intake and risk of breast cancer among premenopausal women. *Archives of Internal Medicine, 166,* 2253-2259.

Chrisler, J. C., & Caplan, P. (2002). The strange case of Dr. Jekyll and Ms. Hyde: How PMS became a cultural phenomenon and a psychiatric disorder. *Annual Review of Sex Research, 13,* 274-306.

Chrisler, J. C., Johnston, I. K., Champagne, N. M., & Preston, K. E. (1994). Menstrual joy: The construct and its consequences. *Psychology of Women Quarterly, 18*(3), 375-387.

Chumlea, W. C., Schubert, C. M., Roche, A. F., Kulin, H. E., Lee, P.A., Himes, J. H., & Sun, S. S. (2003). Age at menarche and racial comparisons in U.S. girls. *Pediatrics, 111*(1), 110-113.

Chung, Y. B., & Katayama, M. (1996). Assessment of sexual orientation in lesbian/gay/bisexual studies. *Journal of Homosexuality, 30*(4), 49-62.

Church, S., Henderson, M., Barnard, M., & Hart, G. (2001). Violence by clients towards female prostitutes in different work settings: Questionnaire survey.

British Medical Journal, 322(7285), 524-525.

CIA World Factbook. (2007). Rank order: Infant mortality rank. Retrieved from https://www.cia.gov/library/publications/the-world-factbook/rankorder/2091rank.html

CIA World Factbook. (2008). South Africa. Retrieved from https://www.cia.gov/library/publications/the-world-factbook/

Clancy, S. A. (2010). *The trauma myth: The truth about the sexual abuse of children—and its aftermath.* New York: Basic Books.

Clarke, A. K., & Lawson, K. L. (2009). Women's judgments of sexual assault scenario: The role of prejudicial attitudes and victim weight. *Violence and Victims, 24*(2), 248-254.

Clarke, R. N., Klock, S. C., Geoghegan, A., & Travossos, D. E. (1999). Relationship between psychological stress and semen quality among in-vitro fertilization patients. *Human Reproduction 14*(3), 753-758.

Clements, M. (1994, August 7). Sex in America today: A new national survey reveals how our attitudes are changing. *Parade Magazine,* pp. 4-6.

Cleveland, A. (2000). Vaginitis: Finding the cause prevents treatment failure. *Cleveland Clinic Journal of Medicine 67*(9), 634-646.

Cloud, J. (2004). Pe-do-phil-ia. In S. J. Bunting (Ed.), *Annual editions human sexuality* (28th ed., pp. 178-183). Dubuque, IA: McGraw Hill.

Cloud, J. (2008, October 3). If women were more like men: Why females earn less. *Time Magazine.* Retrieved from http://www.time.com/time/nation/article/0,8599,1847194,00.html

CNN Opinion Research. (2010, August). Retrieved from i2.cdn.turner.com/cnn/2010/images/08/11/rel11a.pdf

Coates, J. M., Gurnell, M., & Rustichini, A. (2009). A second-to-fourth digit ratio predicts success among high-frequency financial traders. *Proceedings of the National Academy of Sciences, 106*(2), 623-628.

Cohen, A. B., & Tannenbaum, J. (2001). Lesbian and bisexual women's judgments of the attractiveness of different body types. *Journal of Sex Research, 38*(3), 226-232.

Cohen, C., Evans, A. A., London, W. T., Block, J., Conti, M., & Block, T. (2008). Underestimation of chronic hepatitis B virus infection in the United States of America. *Journal of Viral Hepatitis, 15*(1), 12-13.

Cohen, C. J., Celestine-Michener, J., Holmes, C., Merseth, J. L., & Ralph, L. (2007). The attitudes and behavior of young black

Americans: Research summary. Chicago, Illinois: Black Youth Project.

Cohen, M. S., Chen, Y. Q., McCauley, M., Gamble, T., Hosseinipour, M. C., ... HPTN 052 Study Team. (2011). Prevention of HIV-1 with early retroviral therapy. *New England Journal of Medicine.* doi: 10.1056.NEJMoa1105243.

Cohen-Kettenis, P. T., Mellenberg, G. J., Poll, N., Koppe, J. G., & Boer, K. (1999). Prenatal exposure to anticonvulsants and psychosexual development. *Archives of Sexual Behavior, 28*(1), 31-44.

Cohn, L. D., & Adler, N. E. (1992). Female and male perceptions of ideal body shapes: Distorted views among Caucasian college students. *Psychology of Women Quarterly, 16*(1), 65-79.

Colapinto, J. (2001). *As nature made him: The boy who was raised as a girl.* New York: Perennial Books.

Coleman, E. (1987). Assessment of sexual orientation. *Journal of Homosexuality, 14*(1/2), 9-24.

Colgate, E., Miranda, C., Stevens, J., Bray, T., & Ho, E. (2006). Xanthohumol, a prenylflavonoid derived from hops, induces apoptosis, and inhibits NF-kappaB activation in prostate epithelial cells. *Cancer Letters, 246*(1-2), 201-209.

Collins, R. L., Elliott, M. N., Berry, S. H., Kanouse, D. E., Kunkel, S. B., Hunter, S. B., & Miu, A. (2004). Watching sex on television predicts adolescent initiation of sexual behavior. *Pediatrics, 114,* 280-289.

Communications Decency Act. (2007). Center for Democracy and Technology. Retrieved from http://www.cdt.org/speech/cda

Compete.com. (2009). Social networks: Facebook takes over top spot. Retrieved from http://blog.compete.com/2009/02/09/facebook-myspace-twitter-social-network

Confavreux, C., Hutchinson, M., Hours, M. M., Cortinovis-Tourniaire, P., & Moreau, T. (1998). Rate of pregnancy-related relapse in multiple sclerosis. *New England Journal of Medicine, 339*(5), 285-291.

Conkright, L., Flannagan, D., & Dykes, J. (2000). Effects of pronoun type and gender role consistency on children's recall and interpretation of stories. *Sex Roles, 43*(4/3), 481-497.

Connell, E. B. (2002). *The contraception sourcebook.* New York: Contemporary Books.

Connolly, C. (2006, March 1). Unintended pregnancy linked to state funding cuts. *Washington Post.* Retrieved from http://www.washingtonpost.com/wp-dyn/content/article/2006/02/28/AR2006022801450.html

Contagious Diseases Act. (2004). *The Victorian Web*. Retrieved from http://www.victorianweb.org/gender/contagious.html

Cooke, L. P. (2006). "Doing" gender in context: Household bargaining and risk of divorce in Germany and the United States. *American Journal of Sociology 112*(2), 442-472.

Coontz, S. (2005). *Marriage: A history. From obedience to intimacy or how love conquered marriage*. New York: Viking.

Coontz, S. (2007, March 19). Traditional marriage isn't so traditional. *Hartford Courant*. Retrieved from http://articles.courant.com/2007-03-18/news/0703180240_1_same-sex-marriage-man-and-one-woman-claim

Cooper, A. (2000). *Cybersex: The dark side of the force*. New York: Brunner-Routledge.

Cooper, A., Morahan-Martin, J., Mathy, R. M., & Maheu, M. (2002). Toward an increased understanding of user demographics in online sexual activities. *Journal of Sex and Marital Therapy, 28*, 105-129.

Cooper, A., Scherer, C. R., Boies, S. C., & Gordon, B. L. (1999). Sexuality on the Internet: From sexual exploration to pathological expression. *Professional Psychology: Research and Practice, 30*(2), 154-164.

Corne, S., Briere, J., & Esses, L. (1992). Women's attitudes and fantasies about rape as a function of early exposure to pornography. *Journal of Interpersonal Violence, 4*, 454-461.

Cornog, M. (2003). *The big book of masturbation: From angst to zeal*. San Francisco, CA: Down There Press.

Cosby, W. H. (1983). *Bill Cosby: Himself*. United States: CBS/Fox.

Cowan, G. (2000). Beliefs about the causes of four types of rape. *Sex Roles, 42*(9/10), 807-823.

Cox, D. J. (1988). Incidence and nature of male genital exposure behavior as reported by college women. *Journal of Sex Research, 24*, 227-234.

Coyne, J. A., & Berry, A. (2000). Rape as an adaptation. *Nature, 404*(9), 121-122.

Cramer, D., Xu, H., & Harlow, B. (1995). Does "incessant" ovulation increase risk for early menopause? *American Journal Obstetrics and Gynecology, 172*(2; Pt. 1), 568-573.

Criminal Victimization 2000: Changes 1999–2000 with trends 1993–2000. (2001). Bureau of Justice Statistics, U.S. Department of Justice.

Crosby, R., Milhausen, R., Yarber, W. L., Sanders, S. A., & Graham, C. A. (2008). Condom "turn offs" among adults: An exploratory study. *International Journal of STD and AIDS, 19*, 590-594.

Crosby, R., Yarber, W. L., Sanders, S. A., Graham, C. A., & Arno, J. N. (2008). Slips, breaks, and "falls": Condom errors and problems reported by men attending an STD clinic. *International Journal of STD and AIDS, 19*(2), 90-93.

Croxatto, H. B., Brache, V., Pavez, M., Cochon, L., Forcelledo, M. L., Alvarez, F., … Salvatierra, A. M. (2004). Pituitary-ovarian function following the standard levonorgestrel emergency contraceptive dose or a single 0.75-mg dose given on the days preceding ovulation. *Contraception, 70*(6), 442-450.

Croxatto, H. B., Urbancsek, J., Massai, R., Bennink, H. C., van Beek, A., et al. (1999). A multicentre efficacy and safety study of the single contraceptive implant Implanon. *Human Reproduction, 14*(4), 976-981.

Cui, K. H. (1997). Size differences between human X and Y spermatozoa and prefertilization diagnosis. *Molecular Human Reproduction, 3*(1), 61-67.

Cuklanz, L. M. (1994). Public expressions of "progress" in discourses of the Big Dan's rape. *Women and Language, 17*(1), 1-11.

Cunningham, M. R. (1986). Measuring the physical in physical attractiveness: Quasi-experiments on the sociobiology of female facial beauty. *Journal of Personality and Social Psychology, 50*(5), 925-935.

Cunningham, M. R., Barbee, A. P., & Pike, C. L. (1990). What do women want? Facialmetric assessment of multiple motives in the perception of male facial physical attractiveness. *Journal of Personality and Social Psychology, 59*(1), 61-72.

Cunningham, S., & Kendall, T. D. (2010). Prostitution, technology, and the law: New data and directions. *Handbook on family law and economics*. Retrieved from http://www.toddkendall.net/ProsTechLaw.pdf

Curlin, F. A., Lawrence, R. E., Chin, M. H., & Lantos, J. D. (2007). Religion, conscience, and controversial clinical practices. *The New England Journal of Medicine, 356*(6), 593-600.

Cutler, W. B., Friedmann, E., & McCoy, N. L. (1998). Pheromonal influences on sociosexual behavior in men. *Archives of Sexual Behavior, 27*(1), 1-13.

Cwikel, J., & Hoban, E. (2005). Contentious issues in research on trafficked women working in the sex industry: Study design, ethics, and methodology. *Journal of Sex Research, 42*(4), 306-316.

Dabbs, J. M., Carr, R. S., Frady, R. L., & Riad, J. K. (1995). Testosterone, crime, and misbehavior among 692 male prison inmates. *Personality and Individual Differences, 18*, 627-633.

Dabbs, J. M., Carr, R. S., Frady, R. L., & Riad, J. K. (1997). Age, testosterone, and behavior among female prison inmates. *Psychosomatic Medicine, 59*, 477-480.

Dailard, C. (2002). Abstinence promotion and teen family planning: The misguided drive for equal funding. *The Guttmacher Report on Public Policy, 5*(1), 1-3.

Daling, J. R., Doody, D. R., Sun, X., Trabert, B. L., Weiss, N. S., Chen, C., Biggs, M. L., Starr, J. R., Dey, S. K., & Schwartz, S. M. (2009). Association of marijuana use and the incidence of testicular germ cell tumors. *Cancer, 115*(6), 1215-1223.

Dalla, R. L. (2000). Exposing the "pretty woman" myth: A qualitative examination of the lives of female streetwalking prostitutes. *Journal of Sex Research, 37*, 344-353.

Dallam, S. J., Gleaves, D. H., Cepeda-Benito, A., Silberg, J. L., Kraemer, H. C., & Spiegel, D. (2001). The effects of child sexual abuse: Comment on Rind, Tromovitch, and Bauserman (1998). *Psychological Bulletin, 127*(6), 715-733.

Daly, M., & Wilson, M. (2006, April 29). If I can't have you. *New Scientist*, 41.

Daly, M., Wilson, M., & Weghorst, S. J. (1982). Male sexual jealousy. *Ethology and Sociobiology, 3*, 11-27.

Daly, M., & Wilson, M. I. (1982). Whom are newborn babies said to resemble. *Ethology and Sociobiology, 3*, 69-78.

D'Amato, A. (2006). Porn up, rape down. *Public Law and Legal Theory Research Paper Series*. Chicago, IL: Northwestern University School of Law.

Danaher, K., & Crandall, C. S. (2008). Stereotype threat in applied settings re-examined. *Journal of Applied Social Psychology, 38*(6), 1639-1655.

Daneback, K., Cooper, A., & Mansson, S. A. (2005). An Internet study of cybersex participants. *Archives of Sexual Behavior, 34*, 321-328.

Darcangelo, S. (2008). Fetishism: Psychopathology and theory. In D. R. Laws & W. T. O'Donohue (Eds.), *Sexual deviance: Theory, assessment, and treatment* (2nd ed.). New York: The Guilford Press, 108-118.

Darling, C. A., Davidson, J. K., Conway-Welch, C. (1990). Female ejaculation: Perceived origins, the Grafenberg spot/area, and sexual responsiveness. *Archives of Sexual Behavior, 19*(6), 607-611.

Darroch, J. E., Frost, J. J., Singh, S., & The Study Team. (2001). Teenage sexual and reproductive behavior in developed countries. *Occasional Report 3*. New York: Alan Guttmacher Institute.

D'Augelli, A. R., & Hershberger, S. L. (1993). Lesbian, gay, and bisexual youth in community settings: Personal challenges and mental health problems. *American Journal of Community Psychology, 21*(4), 421-448.

Davidson, J. K., Darling, C. A., & Conway-Welch, C. (1989). The role of the Grafenberg spot and female ejaculation in the female orgasmic response: An empirical analysis. *Journal of Sex and Marital Therapy 15*(2), 102-120.

Davies, K. R., & Weller, S. C. (1999). The effectiveness of condoms in reducing heterosexual transmission of HIV. *Family Planning Perspectives, 31*(6), 272-279.

Davies, P. G., Spencer, S. J., Quinn, D. M., & Gerhardstein, R. (2002). Consuming images: How television commercials that elicit stereotype threat can restrain women academically and professionally. *Personality and Social Psychology Bulletin, 28*(12), 1615-1628.

Davies, P. G., Spencer, S. J., & Steele, C.M. (2005). Clearing the air: Identity safety moderates the effects of stereotype threat on women's leadership aspirations. *Journal of Personality and Social Psychology, 85*(2), 276-287.

Davis, J. A., Smith, T. W., & Marsden, P. V. (2006). *General social survey: Cumulative codebook: 1972–2006.* Chicago, IL: NORC.

Davis, K. C., Norris, J., George, W. H., Martell, J., & Heiman, J. R. (2006). Rape-myth congruent beliefs in women resulting from exposure to violent pornography: Effects of alcohol and sexual arousal. *Journal of Interpersonal Violence, 21*(9), 1208-1223.

Dawkins, R. (2006). *The selfish gene.* New York: Oxford University Press.

Day Baird, D., Dunson, D. B., Hill, M. C., Cousins, D., & Schectman, H. M. (2003). High cumulative incidence of uterine leiomyoma in black and white women: Ultrasound evidence. *American Journal of Obstetrics and Gynecology, 188*(1), 100-107.

De Brouwer, A-M. (2005). *Supranational criminal prosecution of sexual violence: The ICC and the Practice of the ICTY and the ICTR.* Mortsel, Belgium: Intersentia Publishing.

de La Rochebrochard, E., de Mouzon, J., Thepot, F., Thonneau, P., & the French National IVF Registry Association. (2006). Fathers over 40 and increased failure to conceive: The lessons of in vitro fertilization in France. *Fertility and Sterility, 85*(5), 1420-1424.

de Silva, W. (1999). Sexual variations. *British Medical Journal, 318*(7184), 654-656.

Dean, M., Carrington, M., Winkler, C., Huttley, G. A., Smith, M. W., Allikmets, R., ... O'Brien, S. J. (1996). Genetic restriction of HIV-1 infection and progression to AIDS by a deletion allele of the CKR5 structural gene. Hemophilia Growth and Development Study, Multicenter AIDS Cohort Study, Multicenter Hemophilia Cohort Study, San Francisco City Cohort, ALIVE Study. *Science 273,* 1856-1862.

Deaner, R. O., & Platt, M. L. (2005). Monkeys pay per view: Adaptive valuation of social images by rhesus macaques. *Current Biology, 15,* 543-548.

Deaux, K., & Hanna, R. (1984). Courtship in the personals column: The influence of gender and sexual orientation. *Sex Roles, 11*(5/6), 363-375.

Declercq, E. R., Paine, L. L., & Winter, M. R. (1995). Home birth in the United States, 1989–1992—A longitudinal descriptive report of national birth certificate data. *Journal of Nurse-Midwifery, 40*(6), 474-482.

DeForge, D., Blackmer, J., Moher, D., Garritty, C., Cronin, V., Yazdi, F., ... Sampson, M. (2004). Sexuality and reproductive health following spinal cord injury. *Summary, Evidence Report/Technology Assessment no. 109.* Rockville, MD: Agency for Healthcare Research and Quality.

DeGeneres, E. (2003). *The funny thing is...* New York: Simon & Schuster.

DeLamater, J., & Friedrich, W. N. (2002). Human sexual development. *Journal of Sex Research, 39*(1), 10-14.

DeLamater, J. D., & Sill, M. (2005). Sexual desire in later life. *Journal of Sex Research, 42*(2), 138-149.

DeLange, J. (1995). Gender and communication in social work education: A cross-cultural perspective. *Journal of Social Work Education, 31*(1), 75-82.

DeMaris, A. (2009). Distal and proximal influences on the risk of extramarital sex: A prospective study of longer duration marriages. *Journal of Sex Research, 46*(6), 597-607.

DeMaris, A., & MacDonald, W. (1993). Premarital cohabitation and marital instability: A test of the unconventionality hypothesis. *Journal of Marriage and the Family, 55*(2), 399-407.

DeMaris, A., & Rao, K. V. (1992). Premarital cohabitation and subsequent marital stability in the United States: A reassessment. *Journal of Marriage and the Family, 54*(1), 178-190.

D'Emilio, J. (1983). *Sexual politics, sexual communities: The making of a homosexual minority in the United States, 1940–1970* (pp. 44-47). Chicago, IL: University of Chicago Press.

Dempster, C. (2002, April 9). Rape—Silent war on South African women. *BBC News.* Retrieved from http://news.bbc.co.uk/1/hi/world/africa/1909220.stm

Denizet-Lewis, B. (2009, September 27). Coming out in middle school. *New York Times.* Retrieved from http://www.nytimes.com/2009/09/27/magazine/27out-t.html?_r=1&ref=magazine

DeRosa, M., Zarrilli, S., Paesano L., Carbone, U., Boggia, B., et al. (2003). Traffic pollutants affect fertility in men. *Human Reproduction, 18*(5), 1055-1061.

Desiderato, L. L., & Crawford, H. J. (1995). Risky sexual behavior in college students: Relationships between number of sexual partners, disclosure of previous risky behavior, and alcohol use. *Journal of Youth and Adolescence, 24*(1), 55-68.

DeSteno, D., Bartlett, M. Y., Braverman, J., & Salovey, P. (2002). Sex differences in jealousy: Evolutionary mechanism or artifact of measurement? *Journal of Personality and Social Psychology, 83*(5), 1103-1116.

DeVaus, D., Qu, L. & Weston, R. (2005). The disappearing link between premarital cohabitation and subsequent marital stability, 1970–2001. *Journal of Population Research, 22*(2), 1443-2447.

DeVivo, M. J., & Fine, P. R. (1985). Spinal cord injury: Its short-term impact on marital status. *Archives of Physical Medicine and Rehabilitation, 66*(8), 501-504.

Diamond, L. (2003b). Was it a phase? Young women's relinquishment of lesbian/bisexual identities over a 5-year period. *Journal of Personality and Social Psychology, 84,* 352-364.

Diamond, L. (2003a). What does sexual orientation orient? A biobehavioral model distinguishing romantic love and sexual desire. *Psychological Review, 110,* 173-192.

Diamond, L. (2008). *Sexual fluidity: Understanding women's love and desire.* Cambridge, MA: Harvard University Press.

Diamond, M. (1993). Homosexuality and bisexuality in different populations. *Archives of Sexual Behavior, 22*(4), 291-310.

Diamond, M. (1997). Sexual identity and sexual orientation in children with traumatized or ambiguous genitalia. *The Journal of Sex Research, 34*(2), 199-211.

Diamond, M. (2005). Interview with Professor Milton Diamond: Transsexuality, intersexuality, and ethics. In L. May, (Ed.), *Everything you ever wanted to know but couldn't think of the question* (pp. 72-94). Bowden, Australia: East Street Publications.

Diamond, M. (2009). Pornography, public acceptance, and sex-related crime: A review. *International Journal of Law and Psychiatry, 32,* 304-314.

Diamond, M., Jozifkova, E., & Weiss, P. (2010). Pornography and sex crimes in the Czech Republic. *Archives of Sexual Behavior.* doi:10.1007/s10508-010-9696-y

Diamond, M., & Uchiyama, A. (1999). Pornography, rape, and sex crimes in Japan. *International Journal of Law and Psychiatry, 22*(1), 1-22.

Dibble, S. L., Roberts, S. A., & Nussey, B. (2004). Comparing breast cancer risk between lesbians and their heterosexual sisters. *Women's Health Issues, 14*(2), 60-68.

DiBisceglie, A. M. (2009). Hepatitis B and hepatocellular carcinoma. *Hepatology, 49*(S5), S56-S60.

Dickinson, R. L. (1949). *Atlas of human sex anatomy.* Baltimore, MD: Williams and Wilkins.

DiClemente, R. J., Sales, J. M., Danner, F., & Crosby, R. A. (2011). Association between sexually transmitted diseases and young adults' self-reported abstinence. *Pediatrics, 127*(2), 208-213.

Diener, E., Gohn, C. L., Suh, E., & Oishi, S. (2000). Similarity of the relations between marital status and subjective well-being across cultures. *Journal of Cross-Cultural Psychology, 31*(4), 419-436.

Dijk, C., de Jong, P. J., & Peters, M. L. (2009). The remedial value of blushing in the context of transgressions and mishaps. *Emotion, 9*(2), 287-291.

Dinh, T-H., Sternberg, M., Dunne, E. F., & Markowitz, L. E. (2008). Genital warts among 18- to 59-year-olds in the United States, National Health and Nutrition Examination Survey, 1999–2004. *Sexually Transmitted Diseases, 35*(4), 357-360.

Dion, K. L., & Dion, K. K. (1993). Gender and ethnocultural comparisons in styles of love. *Psychology of Women Quarterly, 17,* 463-473.

Dittman, R. W., Kappes, M. E., & Kappes, M. H. (1992). Sexual behavior in adolescent and adult females with congenital adrenal hyperplasia. *Psychoneuroendocrinology, 17*(2-3), 153-170.

Ditzen, B., Schaer, M., Gabriel, B., Bodenmann, G., Ehlert, U., & Heinrichs, M. (2009). Intranasal oxytocin increases positive communication and reduces cortisol levels during couple conflict. *Biological Psychiatry, 65*(9), 728-731.

Dizon, D., Partridge, A., Amsterdam, A., & Krychman, M. L. (2009). Sexual pain and cancer. In A. T. Goldstein, C. F. Pukall, & I. Goldstein (Eds.), *Female sexual pain disorders: Evaluation and management.* New York: Wiley-Blackwell, 218-223.

Docter, R. F., & Prince, V. (1997). Transvestism: A survey of 1032 cross-dressers. *Archives of Sexual Behavior, 26*(6), 589-605.

Dodge, B., Reece, M., Herbenick, D., Schick, V., Sanders, S. A., & Fortenberry, J. D. (2010). Sexual health among U.S. black and Hispanic men and women: A nationally representative study. *Journal of Sexual Medicine, 7*(Suppl. 5), 330-345.

Dohnt, H. K. & Tiggemann, M. (2006). Body image concerns in young girls: The role of peers and media prior to adolesence. *Journal of Youth and Adolescence, 35*(2), 141-151.

Domar, A., Zuttermeister, P., Friedman, R. (1993). The psychological impact of infertility: A comparison with patients with other medical conditions. *Journal of Psychosomatic Obstetric Gynaecology, 14,* 45-52.

Dominguez-Bello, M. G., Costello, E. K., Contreras, M., Magris, M., Hidalgo, G., Fierer, N., & Knight, R. (2010). Delivery mode shapes the acquisition and structure of the initial microbiota across multiple body habitats in newborns. *Proceedings of the National Academy of Sciences, 107*(26), 11971-11975.

Donaldson, S. (1993). A million jockers, punks, and queens: Sex among American male prisoners and its implications for concepts of sexual orientation. *Stop Prisoner Rape.* Retrieved from http://www.spr.org/en/docs/doc_01_lecture.asp

Donnerstein, E., & Berkowitz, L. (1981). Victim reactions in aggressive erotic films as a factor in violence against women. *Journal of Personality and Social Psychology, 41*(7), 10-24.

Donnerstein, E., Linz, D., & Penrod, S. (1987). *The question of pornography.* New York: Free Press.

Donnerstein, E. I., & Linz, D. G. (1986, December). The question of pornography: It is not sex, but violence that is an obscenity in our society. *Psychology Today, 20*(12), 56-59.

Doty, R. L., Shaman, P., Applebaum, S. L., Giberson, R., Sikorski, L., & Rosenberg, L. (1984). Smell identification ability: changes with age. *Science, 226,* 1441-1443.

Dover, K. J. (1989). *Greek homosexuality.* Cambridge, MA: Harvard University Press.

Downey, J. L., & Damhave K. W. (1991). The effects of place, type of comment, and effort expended on the perception of flirtation. *Journal of Social Behavior and Personality, 6,* 35-43.

Dreher, J-C., Schmidt, P. J., Kohn, P., Furman, D., Rubinow, D., & Berman, K. F. (2007). Menstrual cycle phase modulates reward-related neural function in women. *Proceedings of the National Academy of Sciences, 104*(7), 2465-2470.

Drieschner, K., & Lange, A. (1999). A review of cognitive factors in the etiology of rape: Theories, empirical studies, and implications. *Clinical Psychology Review, 19*(1), 57-77.

Druckerman, P. (2007). *Lust in translation: The rules of infidelity from Tokyo to Tennessee.* New York: Penguin Press.

D'Souza, G., Kreimer, A. R., Viscidi, R., Pawlita, M., et al. (2007). Case-control study of human papillomavirus and oropharyngeal cancer. *New England Journal of Medicine, 356*(19), 1944.

Duffy, S., Marsh, F., Rogerson, L., Hudson, J., Cooper, K., et al. (2005). Female sterilization: A cohort controlled comparative study of ESSURE versus laparoscopic sterilization. *British Journal of Obstetrics and Gynaecology, 112*(11), 1522-1528.

Dunbar, E. (2006). The importance of race and gender membership in sexual orientation. Hate crime victimization and reportage: Identity politics or identity risk. *Violence and Victims, 21*(3), 323-337.

Duncan, S. R., Scott, S., & Duncan, C. J. (2005). Reappraisal of the historical selective pressures for the CCR5-D32 mutation. *Journal of Medical Genetics, 42,* 205-208.

Dunn, K. M., Cherkas, L. F., & Spector, T. D. (2005). Genetic influences in variation in female orgasmic function: A twin study. *Biology Letters, 1*(3), 260-263.

Dunn, M. E., & Cutler, N. (2000). Sexual issues in older adults. *AIDS patient care and STDs, 14*(2), 67-69.

Dunne, E. F., Unger, E. R., Sternberg, M., McQuillan, G., Swan, D. C., Patel, S. S., & Markowitz, L. E. (2007). Prevalence of HPV infection among females in the United States. *Journal of the American Medical Association, 297*(8), 813-819.

Durand, A. M. (1992). The safety of home birth: The farm study. *American Journal of Public Health, 82*(3), 450-453.

Durante, K. M., & Li, N. P. (2009). Oestadiol level and opportunistic mating in women. *Biology Letters, 5*(2), 179-182.

Durante, K. M., Li, N. P., & Haselton, M. G. (2008). Changes in women's choice of dress across the ovulatory cycle: Naturalistic and laboratory task-based evidence. *Personality and Social Psychology Bulletin, 34*(11), 1451-1460.

Durose, M. R., Harlow, C. W., Langan, P. A., Motivans, M., Rantala, R. R., & Smith, E. L. (2005). *Family violence statistics: Including statistics on strangers and acquaintances.* U.S. Department of

Iodice, S., Barile, M., Rotmensz, N., Feroce, I., Bonanni, B., Radice, P., ... Gandini, S. (2010). Oral contraceptive use and breast or ovarian cancer risk in BRCA1/2 carriers: A meta-analysis. *European Journal of Cancer, 46*(12), 2275-2294.

Ismail, H., Mansour, D., & Singh, M. (2006). Migration of Implanon. *Journal of Family Planning and Reproductive Health Care, 32*(3), 157-159.

Jackson, G. (2009). Sexual response in cardiovascular disease. *Journal of Sex Research, 46*(2-3), 233-236.

Jacob, J. A. (1981). The Mosher report. *American Heritage Magazine*, June/July, 56-64.

Jacob, S., & McClintock, M. K. (2000). Psychological state and mood effects of steroidal chemosignals in women and men. *Hormones and Behavior, 37*, 57-78.

Jankowiak, W.R., & Fischer, E. F. (1992). A cross-cultural perspective on romantic love. *Ethnology, 31*, 149-155.

Janus, S., & Janus, C. (1993). *The Janus report on sexual behavior*. New York: John Wiley & Sons.

Jenkins, A. P. (2000). When self-pleasuring becomes self-destruction: Autoerotic asphyxiation paraphilia. *International Electronic Journal of Health Education, 3*(3), 208-216.

Jenkins, M., Lambert, E. G., & Baker, D. N. (2009). The attitudes of black and white college students toward gay and lesbians. *Journal of Black Studies, 39*(4), 589-613.

Jenny, C., Roesler, T. A., & Poyer, K. L. (1994). Are children at risk for sexual abuse by homosexuals? *Pediatrics, 94*(1), 41-44.

Jensen, R. (2004b). A cruel edge. In S. J. Bunting (Ed.), *Annual editions human sexuality* (30th ed., pp. 167-169). Dubuque, IA: McGraw Hill.

Jensen, R. (2004a, July). Pornography and sexual violence. Retrieved from http://www.vawnet.org/SexualViolence/Research/VAWnetDocuments/AR_PornAndSV.pdf

Jewkes, R. (2002). Intimate partner violence: Causes and prevention. *Lancet, 359*(9315), 1423-1429.

Jha, P., Kumar, R., Vasa, P., Dhingra, N., Thiruchelvam, D., & Moineddin, R. (2006). Low male-to-female sex ratio of children born in India: National survey of 1.1 million households. *Lancet, 367*(9506), 211-218.

Joannides, P. (2006). The HSRC—Is everything better in black and white? In W. J. Taverner, (Ed.), *Taking sides: Clashing views on controversial issues in human sexuality* (9th ed., pp. 46-50). Dubuque, IA: McGraw-Hill/Dushkin.

Johnson, D. R., & Wu, J. (2002). An empirical test of crisis, social selection, and role explanations of the relationship between marital disruption and psychological distress: A pooled time-series analysis of four-wave panel data. *Journal of Marriage and the Family, 64*(1), 211-224.

Johnson, L. A., Welch, G. A., Keyvanfar, K., Dorfmann, A., Fugger, E. F., & Schulman, J. D. (1993). Gender preselection in humans? Flow cytometric separation of X and Y spermatozoa for the prevention of X-linked diseases. *Human Reproduction, 8*, 1733-1739.

Johnson, S. M., & O'Connor, E. (2002). *The gay baby boom: The psychology of gay parenthood*. New York: New York University Press.

Johnston, M. V., & Hagberg, H. (2007). Sex and the pathogenesis of cerebral palsy. *Developmental Medicine and Child Neurolology, 49*(1), 74-78.

Johnston, V. S., & Franklin, M. (1993). Is beauty in the eye of the beholder? *Ethology and Sociobiology, 14*, 183-199.

Jonason, P. K., Li, N. P., & Cason, M. J. (2009). The "booty call": A compromise between men's and women's ideal mating strategies. *Journal of Sex Research, 46*(5), 460-470.

Jones, I. R., & Higgs, P. F. (2010). The natural, the normal, and the normative: Contested terrains in ageing and old age. *Social Science and Medicine, 71*(8), 1513-1519.

Jones, L. M., & Finkelhor, D. (2003). Putting together evidence on declining trends in sexual abuse: A complex puzzle. *Child Abuse and Neglect, 27*, 133-135.

Jones, R. E. (1997). *Human reproductive biology* (2nd ed.). San Diego, CA: Academic Press.

Jones, R. K., Fennell, J., Higgins, J. A., & Blanchard, K. (2009). Better than nothing or savvy risk-reduction practice? The importance of withdrawal. *Contraception, 79*, 407-410.

Jones, R. K., Finer, L. B., & Singh, S. (2010). *Characteristics of U.S. abortion patients, 2008*. New York: Guttmacher Institute.

Jones, R. K., Zolna, M. R.S., Henshaw, S. K, & Finer, L. B. (2008). Abortion in the United States: Incidence and access to services, 2005. *Perspectives on Sexual and Reproductive Health, 40*(1), 6-16.

Jong, E. (2006). *Seducing the demon*. New York: Tarcher/Penguin.

Joyal, C. C., Black, D. N., & Dassylva, B. (2007). The neuropsychology and neurology of sexual deviance: A review and pilot study. *Sex Abuse, 19*(2), 155-172.

Kahlenborn, C., Modugno, F., Potter, D. M., & Severs, W. B. (2006). Oral contraceptive use as a risk facto for premenopausal breast cancer: A meta-analysis. *Mayo Clinic Proceedings, 81*(10), 1290-1302.

Kahn, A. S., Fricker, K., Hoffman, J., Lambert, T., Tripp, M., & Childress, K. (2000, August). Hooking up: Dangerous new dating methods? In A. S. Kahn (Chair), *Sex, unwanted sex, and sexual assault on college campuses*. Symposium conducted at the annual meeting of the American Psychological Association, Washington, D.C.

Kailey, M. (2005). *Just add hormones: An insider's guide to the transsexual experience*. Boston, MA: Beacon Press.

Kaiser Family Foundation. (1997). *Doctors don't ask, and women don't tell: New survey finds STDs are rarely discussed as part of routine gynecological care*. Retrieved from http://www.kff.org/womenshealth/1313-experiencer.cfm

Kaiser Family Foundation. (2001). *Teens and sex: The role of popular TV*. Menlo Park, CA: Author.

Kaiser Family Foundation. (2002). Relationships: A series of national surveys of teens about sex. Retrieved from http://www.kff.org/entpartnerships/upload/Relationships-Summary-of-Findings.pdf

Kaiser Family Foundation. (2006). *The Global HIV/AIDS timeline*. Retrieved from http://www.kff.org/hivaids/timeline/hivtimeline.cfm

Kalb, C., & Murr, A. (2006, May 15). Battling a black epidemic. *Newsweek*, pp. 42-48.

Kalick, S. M., & Hamilton, T. E. (1986). The matching hypothesis reexamined. *Journal of Personal and Social Psychology, 51*, 673-682.

Kalof, L., Eby, K. K., Matheson, J. L., & Kroska, R. J. (2001). The influence of race and gender on student self-reports of sexual harassment by college professors. *Gender and Society, 15*(2), 282-302.

Kamarck, T. W. (1990). Social support reduces cardiovascular reactivity to psychological challenge: A laboratory model. *Psychsomatic Medicine, 52*, 42-58.

Kamp Dush, C. M., Cohan, C. L., & Amato, P. R. (2003). The relationship between cohabitation and marital quality and stability: Change across cohorts? *Journal of Marriage and Family, 65*, 539-549.

Kaplan, M. S., & Krueger, R. B. (2010). Diagnosis, assessment, and treatment of hypersexuality. *Journal of Sex Research, 47*(2-3), 181-198.

Kapoor, S. (2000). *Domestic violence against women and girls*. UNICEF: Innocenti Research Center. Retrieved from http://www.unicef-icdc.org

Karama, S., Lecours, A. R., Leroux, J. M., Bourgoiun, P., Beaudoin, G., Joubert, S., & Beauregard, M. (2002). Areas of brain activation in males and females during viewing of erotic film excerpts. *Human Brain Mapping, 16*, 1-13.

Karim, Q. A., Karim, S. S. A., Frohlich, J.A., Gobler, A. C., Baxter, C.B., Mansoor, L. E.,

... on behalf of the CAPRISA 004 Trial Group. (2010). Effectiveness and safety of Tenofovir Gel, an antiretroviral microbicide, for the prevention of HIV infection in women. *Science, 329*(5996), 1168-1174.

Katz, A. (2007). *Breaking the silence on cancer and sexuality: A handbook for healthcare providers.* Pittsburgh, PA: Oncology Nursing Society.

Katz, J. E. (1994). Empirical and theoretical dimensions of obscene phone calls to women in the United States. *Human Communication Research, 21*(2), 155-182.

Kauth, M. R. (2002). Much ado about homosexuality: Assumptions underlying current research on sexual orientation. *Journal of Psychology and Human Sexuality, 14*(1), 1-23.

Kauth, M. R. (2005). Revealing assumptions: Explicating sexual orientation and promoting conceptual integrity. *Journal of Bisexuality, 5*(4), 81-105.

Kellogg, S., Kingsberg, S., & Krychman, M. (2009). REVEAL: Revealing vaginal effects at mid-life. Wyeth Pharmaceuticals.

Kelly, J. (2007). Ovary removal boosts risks for cognitive impairment, dementia, and Parkinson's. *Neurology Reviews, 15,* 10.

Kelly, M. P., Strassberg, D. S. & Kircher, J. R. (1990). Attitudinal and experiential correlates of anorgasmia. *Archives of Sexual Behavior, 19*(2), 165-177.

Kendall-Tackett, K. A., Williams, L. M., & Finkelhor, D. (1993). Impact of sexual abuse on children: A review and synthesis of recent empirical studies. *Psychological Bulletin, 113*(1), 164-180.

Kennamer, J. D., Honnold, J., Bradford, J. & Hendricks, M. (2000). Differences in disclosure of sexuality among African American and white gay/bisexual men: Implications for HIV/AIDS prevention. *AIDS Education and Prevention, 12*(6), 519-531.

Kenrick, D. T., Gutierres, S. E., & Goldberg, L. L. (1989). Influence of popular erotica on judgments of strangers and mates. *Journal of Experimental Social Psychology, 25,* 159-167.

Keshavarz, H., Hillis, S. D., Kieke, B. A., & Marchbanks, P. A. (2002). Hysterectomy surveillance—United States, 1994–1999. In *Surveillance Summaries* (MMWR No. 51[SS05]). Atlanta, GA: Centers for Disease Control and Prevention.

Kessler, S. (1995, November). *Meanings of genital variability.* Paper presented at the Society for the Scientific Study of Sexuality, San Francisco, CA.

Kidd, S. A., Eskenazi, B., & Wyrobek, A.J. (2001). Effects of male age on semen quality and fertility: A review of the literature. *Fertility and Sterility, 75*(2), 237-248.

Kiecolt-Glaser, J. K., Glaser, R., Cacioppo, J. T., & Malarkey, W. B. (1998). Marital stress: Immunologic, neuroendocrine, and autonomic correlates. *Annals of the New York Academy of Sciences, 840,* 656-663.

Kiecolt-Glaser, J. K., Loving, T. J., Stowell, J. R., Malarkey, W. B., Lemeshow, S., Dickinson, S. L., & Glaser, R. (2005). Hostile marital interactions, proinflammatory cytokine production, and wound healing. *Archives of General Psychiatry, 62,* 1377-1384.

Kilbourne, J. (1999). *Can't buy my love: How advertising changes the way we think and feel.* New York: Touchstone.

Kilpatrick, D. G. (2000). Rape and sexual assault. Retrieved from http://www.musc.edu/vawprevention/research/sa.shtml

Kilpatrick, D. G., Edwards, C. N., & Seymour, A. E. (1992). *Rape in America: A report to the nation.* Arlington, VA: National Crime Victims Center.

Kilpatrick, D. G., Whalley, A., & Edmunds, C. (2000). Sexual assault. In A. Seymour, M. Murray, J. Sigmon, M. Hook, C. Edmunds, M. Gaboury, & G. Coleman (Eds.), *2000 National Victim Assistance Academy.* Retrieved from http://www.ojp.usdoj.gov/ovc/assist/nvaa2002/chapter10.html

Kim, N. N. (2003). Phosphodiesterase type 5 inhibitors: A biochemical and clinical correlation survey. *International Journal of Impotence Research, 15*(Suppl. 5), S13-S19.

Kimmel, M. (2001, March). *Gender equality: Not for women only.* Lecture prepared for International Women's Day seminar, European Parliament, Brussels, Belgium.

Kimura, D. (1992). Sex differences in the brain. *Scientific American, 267,* 118-125.

Kimura, D. (2002). Sex hormones influence human cognitive pattern, *Neuroendocrinology Letters. 23*(Suppl.), 67-77.

Kingston, D. A., Malamuth, N. M., Federoff, P., & Marshall, W. L. (2009). The importance of individual differences in pornography use: Theoretical perspectives and implications for treating sexual offenders. *Journal of Sex Research, 46*(2-3), 216-232.

Kinnish, K. K., Strassberg, D. S., & Turner, C.M. (2005). Sex differences in the flexibility of sexual orientation: A multidimensional retrospective assessment. *Archives of Sexual Behavior, 35*(2), 173-183.

Kinsey, A. C., Pomeroy, W. B., Martin, C. E., & Gebhard, P. H. (1948). *Sexual behavior in the human male.* Philadelphia, PA: Saunders.

Kinsey, A. C., Pomeroy, W. B., Martin, C. E., & Gebhard, P. H. (1953). *Sexual behavior in the human female.* Philadelphia, PA: Saunders.

Kirby, D. (2001). *Emerging answers: Research findings on programs to reduce teen pregnancy.* Washington, DC: National Campaign to Prevent Teen Pregnancy.

Kirby, D. B., & Brown, N. L. (1996). Condom availability programs in U.S. schools. *Family Planning Perspectives, 28*(5), 196-202.

Kirchengast, S., & Gartner, M. (2002). Changes in fat distribution (WHR) and body weight across the menstrual cycle. *Collegium Anthropologicum, 26,* S47-S57.

Kirkpatrick, M., Smith, C., & Roy, R. (1981). Lesbian mothers and their children: A comparative survey. *American Journal of Orthopsychiatry, 51,* 545-551.

Kirk-Smith, M., Booth, D. A., Caroll, D., & Davies, P. (1978). Human social attitudes affected by androstenol. *Research Communications in Psychology, Psychiatry, and Behavior, 3*(4), 379-384.

Kittleson, M. J., Kane, W., & Rennagarbe, R. (2005). *The truth about rape.* New York: Facts on File.

Klebanoff, S. J., Hillier, S. L., Eschenbach, D. A., & Waltersdorph, A. M. (1991). Control of the microbial flora of the vagina by H_2O_2-generating lactobacilli. *Journal of Infectious Diseases, 164*(1), 94-100.

Klein, F. (1990). The need to view sexual orientation as a multivariable dynamic process: A theoretical perspective. In D. McWhirter, S. Sanders, & J. Reinisch (Eds.), *Homosexuality/heterosexuality: Concepts of sexual orientation* (pp. 277-282). New York: Oxford University Press.

Klein, F., Sepekoff, B., & Wolf, T. J. (1985). Sexual orientation: A multivariable dynamic process. *Journal of Homosexuality, 11,* 35-49.

Klein, M. (1998, March). Why there's no such thing as sexual addiction—And why it really matters. Retrieved from http://www.sexed.org/archive/article08.html

Klein, R. (1999). Penile augmentation surgery. *Electronic Journal of Human Sexuality, 2.* Retrieved from http://www.ejhs.org

Kleinfeld, J. (1998). *The myth that schools shortchange girls: Social science in the service of deception.* Washington, DC: The Women's Freedom Network.

Kleinplatz, P. J., Menard, A. D., Paquet, M.-P., Paradis, N., Campbell, M., Zuccarino, D., & Mehak, L. (2009b). The components of optimal sexuality: A portrait of "great sex." *The Canadian Journal of Human Sexuality, 18*(1-2), 1-13.

Kleinplatz, P. J., Menard, A. D., Paradis, N., Campbell, M., Dalgleish, T., Segovia, A., & Davis, K. (2009a). From closet to reality: Optimal sexuality among the elderly. *The Irish Psychiatrist, 10,* 15-18.

Delayed ejaculation When a man is unable to reach orgasm within a satisfactory amount of time.

Dependent variable The variable that is observed and measured and that may change as a result of manipulations to the independent variable.

Depo-Provera The hormonal contraceptive injection, given every 3 months.

Desire A drive or motivation to seek out sexual objects or to engage in sexual activities.

Developed country A country with financial, educational, and health standards that allow for higher levels of human well-being, as measured by the economic factors, life expectancy, and educational opportunities of the country. Developed countries include the United States, Canada, Australia, the countries of Western Europe, Israel, Kuwait, Japan, Hong Kong, and others.

Diabetes A metabolic disease in which the body is unable to produce or is resistant to insulin, leading to abnormally high levels of blood sugar.

Diagnostic and Statistical Manual of Mental Disorders (DSM) The manual that describes mental health disorders in children and adults.

Diaphragm, cervical cap, Lea's shield, and Today contraceptive sponge Contraceptive devices that cover the cervix and act as a barrier to prevent sperm from entering the uterus.

Dihydrotestosterone (DHT) A potent male hormone involved in prenatal development of the penis and scrotum.

Dilation When the diameter of the cervix widens.

Dilation and curettage (D&C) An abortion method in which the uterine contents are scraped out with a metal loop.

Dilation and evacuation (D&E) A method of surgical abortion most commonly used during the second trimester, which combines vacuum aspiration with forceps and a curette.

Dildo A penis-shaped object, usually made of rubber, silicone, or plastic, that is inserted into the vagina or anus for sexual pleasure.

Direct observation A study in which the investigators do not manipulate the conditions, but only observe subjects in a particular situation and record and interpret the outcome.

Discipline The use of rules or punishment to control another's behavior.

Discrepancy in desire When partners routinely experience different levels of sexual desire to the point where it has a negative impact on their relationship.

Disorders of sex development Congenital conditions in which development of chromosomal, gonadal, or anatomic sex is atypical.

Disseminated gonococcal infection (DGI) When the gonorrhea bacterium spreads throughout the body, often to the joints.

Divorce The legal dissolution of a marriage.

Dizygotic twins Twins that result from the fertilization of two separate eggs from two separate sperm.

DOMA (Defense of Marriage Act) A U.S. law, passed in 1996, that limits the federal government's definition of marriage as a legal union between one man and one woman.

Domestic partnership A relationship between two people, sometimes of the same gender, who live together and mutually support each other as spouses.

Dominatrix A woman who plays the dominant role in a BDSM relationship.

Don't ask, don't tell The policy which prohibited anyone who "demonstrates a propensity or intent to engage in homosexual acts" from serving in the U.S. military.

Dopamine (DOH-pah-mean ; DA), serotonin (ser-oh-TOE-nin), and norepinephrine (nor-ep-ih-NEF-rine; NE) Substances released from neurons that affect mood, motivation, and excitement.

Double blind study An experimental procedure in which neither the investigator nor the subjects know who is in the experimental group and who is in the control group.

Douche (DOOSH) A device or procedure in which water, vinegar, or other solutions are gently sprayed into the vagina.

Doula An experienced labor companion who provides physical and emotional support to laboring women.

Dower The money or property that a man brings to his bride at marriage. A *dowry* is the money or property that a woman brings to her husband at marriage.

Drag kings, drag queens A person who dresses (often flamboyantly) as the opposite sex for the purpose of entertainment or performance. Gender stereotypes are often exaggerated in drag performances.

Dysmenorrhea (dis-men-or-REE-ah) Pain or discomfort during menstruation.

Dyspareunia (dis-puh-ROO-nee-ah) Difficult or painful sexual intercourse.

Early labor The first, longest, and least intense phase of labor.

Eclampsia A potentially life-threatening complication of pregnancy brought about by severe hypertension.

Economic abuse Includes such acts as denial of funds, food, or basic needs, or controlling access to health care or employment.

Ectoparasites Any parasitic organism that lives on the outside of a body, such as fleas or lice.

Ectopic pregnancy When the fertilized egg implants outside of the uterus, usually in the fallopian tube.

Effacement Softening and thinning of the cervix.

Egalitarian marriage A marriage characterized by shared roles and responsibilities, regardless of gender.

Ego The part of the psyche that mediates the drives of the id and superego.

Egocentrism The practice of regarding one's own experiences or opinions as most important.

Ejaculate When used as a noun, it is another word for semen.

Ejaculation The ejection of sperm and semen from the penis, usually accompanied by orgasm.

Ejaculatory duct The part of the ejaculatory pathway that passes through the prostate and connects the vas deferens and the urethra.

Ejaculatory inevitability The feeling of a "point of no return" when an orgasm is coming and can't be prevented.

Electra complex The psychoanalytic term used to describe a girl's romantic or sexual feelings toward her father.

Embryo A fertilized egg before it becomes a fetus, from conception to 8 weeks of pregnancy.

Emergency contraception Measures that protect against pregnancy after unprotected sex has already occurred.

Emission The first stage of orgasm, when seminal fluids move into the upper urethra.

Empiricism (em-PEER-uh-sizm) The view that knowledge comes through experience and observation.

Endocrine system A glandular system that produces hormones.

Endometriosis (END-oh-me-tree-OH-sis) The presence of endometrial tissue outside of the uterus.

Endometrium (end-oh-MEE-tree- um) The inner lining of the uterus, consisting of epithelial cells, blood vessels, and glands.

Endorphins (en-DORE-fins) Chemicals released in the brain that reduce pain and promote feelings of well-being.

Ephebophilia A sexual attraction and preference for adolescents who have gone through puberty.

Epididymis (ep-uh-DID-ih-mus) The portion of the ejaculatory pathway where sperm mature and learn to swim.

Epididymitis Inflammation of the epididymis.

Epidural Injection of an anesthetic into the space of the spinal cord where spinal fluid circulates, resulting in decreased sensation from the waist down.

Episiotomy An incision made to the perineum during childbirth.

Erectile dysfunction The persistent inability of a man to obtain or sustain an erection.

Erection The enlarged and firm state of the penis, clitoris, or nipple.

Erogenous zones Areas of the body that are particularly sensitive to touch, and that may lead to sexual arousal when stimulated.

Eros Romantic or passionate love.

Erotic Relating to or tending to arouse sexual desire or excitement.

Erotic dreams Dreams with an erotic content.

Erotic plasticity The degree to which a person's sexual expression can change as a result of social, cultural, and situational forces.

Erotic stimulus pathway theory David Reed's model of sexual arousal that includes seduction, sensation, surrender, and reflection.

Erotica Works of art that are sexually stimulating. In contrast to pornography, erotica is considered to have aspirations other than sexual arousal.

Error management theory The theory that suggests that when making a decision, a subject can make two types of errors, a false positive or a false negative. It is more adaptive to err on the side that is less evolutionarily risky or that allows for a possible sexual encounter.

Escort A prostitute who meets with clients by appointment.

Estradiol One of the "female" hormones responsible for female sex characteristics, as well as reproductive, bone, and brain development in both sexes.

Estrogen A generic term for a group of female sex hormones that affect secondary sexual characteristics and regulate the menstrual cycle.

Ethnicity A group of people with common racial, national, religious, or cultural ties.

Ethnocentric The tendency to look at the world from the perspective of one's own ethnic group or culture, which you believe to be superior.

Evidence-based An approach to decision-making that is based on data and scientific studies to determine the best practices.

Excitement The body's initial physical response to sexual arousal.

Exhibitionism The act of exposing one's genitals to an unsuspecting and non-consenting person for the purpose of sexual arousal.

Experiment A controlled test or investigation, designed to examine the validity of a hypothesis. Also, the act of conducting an investigation. An experiment is the only way in which a cause-and-effect relationship can be determined.

Extramarital A sexual relationship outside of marriage without the consent of one's spouse.

Eyebrow flash A very brief lift of the eyebrows that designates recognition or an invitation for interaction.

Fallacy of insufficient evidence An argument that doesn't provide sufficient evidence to support its conclusion.

Fallacy of relevance An argument that focuses on matters unrelated to the facts of the issue.

Fallopian tubes These tubes lead from the ovaries to the uterus, and carry the egg on its way to the uterus. Also called *uterine tubes or oviducts.*

Fecundity The state of being fertile; the ability to produce offspring.

Fellatio Oral stimulation of the male genitals.

Feminine Qualities and behaviors judged by a particular culture to be ideally associated with or especially appropriate to women and girls.

Femoral coitus When the penis is thrust between a partner's thighs.

Fertilization or conception The joining of the nucleus of the egg with the nucleus of the sperm.

Fertility awareness–based methods (FABM) A set of practices used to determine the most fertile times of a woman's cycle. Abstinence or barrier methods of contraception may be used during these fertile times.

Fetal alcohol syndrome A medical condition that causes developmental problems in an unborn child; it results from excessive alcohol consumption by the mother during pregnancy.

Fetishism (FET-ish-izm) A paraphilia in which a person has sexually arousing fantasies and behaviors regarding an inanimate object. The word *fetish* derives from the Portuguese word *feitiço,* meaning "charm," or "sorcery."

Fetus The unborn baby from the end of the 8th week after conception until it is born.

Fibroid tumors A benign tumor that commonly grows in the uterus.

"Fight or flight" Long considered to be the instinctual response of humans when survival is threatened, this is now thought to better characterize a male's behavioral response to danger.

Fimbriae (FIM-bree-ah) Fingerlike projections of the fallopian tube.

Fisting The insertion of the fist or hand into the rectum or vagina. Typically, the clenched fist is not inserted; instead, the fingers are kept flat and as close together as possible. This is more often practiced among lesbians and gay male couples.

Flirtation Behaviors meant to arouse romantic or sexual interest. In the 16th century, the word "flirt" meant "to sneer or scoff at" (Morris, 2004).

Fluctuating asymmetry Small, subtle differences in the size of one of a bilateral feature, such as arms, legs, or breasts.

fMRI (functional magnetic resonance imaging) A specialized form of MRI, fMRI is a medical imaging technique that shows the neural activity of the brain.

Folkways Patterns of conventional behavior within a group.

Follicles Fluid-filled sacs in the ovaries that contain the primary oocytes and hormone-secreting cells.

Follicle-stimulating hormone (FSH) A hormone that stimulates the development of eggs during a woman's ovulatory cycle.

Intimate partner violence A pattern of abusive behaviors by one or more partners in an intimate relationship.

Intracytoplasmic sperm injection (ICSI) An in vitro fertilization procedure in which a single sperm is injected directly into an egg for fertilization.

Intrauterine device (IUD) A small device that is placed in the uterus to prevent pregnancy.

Jaundice The yellowing of the skin and whites of the eyes due to accumulation of bilirubin in the blood.

Jealousy A state of envy, fear, or suspicion caused by a real or imagined threat to an existing situation or relationship.

"Just world" hypothesis The tendency for people to rationalize and excuse inexplicable injustices so as to maintain the idea that the world is fair.

Kama Sutra An ancient Indian text, made up of poetry, prose, and illustrations, which contains practical advice for sexual pleasure, love, and marriage.

Kegel (KAY-gill) exercises Exercises that involve clenching and unclenching of the muscles of the pelvic floor.

Kinsey scale A classification system to gauge a person's sexual orientation at a given time.

Klein sexual orientation grid (KSOG) A multidimensional measurement of sexual orientation.

Klinefelter's syndrome A condition in which males have an extra X chromosome.

Labia majora (LAY-bee-ah ma-JORE-ah) Large outer folds of skin on both sides of the vulva.

Labia minora The inner hairless lips that surround the vaginal opening.

Labiaplasty A surgical alteration in the size and/or appearance of the labia.

Lactation consultant A health care professional who provides support and information about breastfeeding to new mothers.

Lactation The production and secretion of milk from the breast by the mammary glands.

Lactobacteria Beneficial bacteria that help prevent the growth of harmful microorganisms in the vagina.

Laws A written collection of enforceable rules that govern a community.

Leptin A hormone that plays a key role in appetite regulation and fat metabolism.

Lesbian A term used to describe a woman whose sexual and romantic attractions are toward women.

Lesbian bed death (LBD) The slang term for the diminishment of sexual activity between two long-term lesbian partners.

Lesser vestibular glands Also called *Skene's glands* (SKEENZ) or the female prostate, these glands may be involved with female ejaculation.

Libido (li-BEE-doh) Sexual desire or drive.

Lightening When the baby drops into the pelvic cavity in preparation for delivery.

Limbic system A set of structures in the brain that controls emotions, instinctive behavior, and motivation. The hypothalamus is part of the limbic system.

Liminal The threshold between two different states or stages.

Linea nigra The dark vertical line that runs down the belly button to the pubic area during pregnancy.

Longitudinal study A research study that involves repeated observations of the same group of subjects over a long period of time. This usually involves surveys or observations rather than experiments that determine causal relationships.

Lovemap A theory developed by psychologist John Money that describes a person's template for his or her ideal romantic partner.

Ludus A game-playing style of love.

Luteal (LOO-tee-al) phase Typically from days 15 to 28; during this stage the hormones released from the corpus luteum prepare the body for possible pregnancy.

Luteinizing hormone (LH) A pituitary hormone that causes the production and release of testosterone in males and stimulates ovulation in females.

Lymphocyte A type of white blood cell that fights infection.

Madam A woman who runs a brothel, or a house of prostitution.

Magic ratio A relationship is more likely to be successful if there are at least five positive interactions for each negative interaction.

Mammary coitus The man rubs his penis between his partner's breasts.

Mammogram An X-ray of the soft tissue of the breast, used to detect abnormalities such as tumors.

Mania Obsessive jealous love that combines eros and ludus.

Masculine Qualities and behaviors judged by a particular culture to be ideally associated with or especially appropriate to men and boys.

Masochism (MA-suh-kizm) A paraphilia in which one derives sexual pleasure from being hurt or humiliated as part of a sexual ritual.

Massage parlors A place where illicit sex is available under the guise of therapeutic massage.

Masturbation The stimulation of one's own genitals, which produces feelings of pleasure and often results in orgasm.

Matching hypothesis The idea that people are most likely to form long-term relationships with those who are equally as attractive as they are.

Maternal immune hypothesis The theory that a man's sexual orientation is related to the number of older brothers he has; prenatal factors in the mother's womb play a role.

Meatus (me-ATE-us) The opening at the tip of the glans.

Media The tools used to deliver information; often referred to as "mass media" because they are designed to reach a very large audience.

Megan's Law The informal name for the laws in the United States regarding registration and public notification about sex offenders.

Meiosis (my-OH-sis) The process of cell division in the egg and sperm.

Menarche (MEN-are-key) A woman's first menstrual cycle.

Menopause (MEN-oh-paws) The time of life when a woman's menstrual cycles permanently end, usually around age 51.

Menstrual phase (also called *menses*) The shedding of the endometrium on days 1 through 5 of the cycle.

Menstrual synchrony The theory that the menstrual cycles of women who live together tend to become synchronized over time.

Menstruation The shedding of the uterine lining that occurs approximately once a month.

Mere exposure effect The phenomenon in which people prefer things they are familiar with.

Meta-analysis A statistical method of combining and evaluating a large body of research on a related issue.

Methodology The methods, procedures, and techniques used to gather information.

Methotrexate (meth-oh-TREKS-ate) Ends a pregnancy by stopping cell division and interfering with the implantation of the embryo.

Midwife A professional trained to assist in normal labor and birth.

Mifepristone (mih-FEH-prih-stone) Also called *RU-486,* this drug ends a pregnancy by blocking the actions of progesterone.

Miscarriage A pregnancy that terminates on its own before the embryo or fetus can survive outside of the womb.

Miscegenation Marrying, cohabiting, or having sexual relations with a partner of a different race.

Misoprostol (mye-so-PRAH -stole) Aids mifepristone by increasing the effects of prostaglandins.

Missionary position Vaginal intercourse with the man on top and the woman lying on her back.

Monogamy From the Greek words *monos,* meaning "one," and *gamos,* meaning "marriage," monogamy is the practice of having one spouse at a time.

Monozygotic twins Genetically identical twins derived from a single fertilized egg.

Mons pubis (mahns PYOO-bis) The pad of fat that covers, cushions, and protects the pubic joint. It is also called the *mons veneris* ("mound of Venus"), named for the Roman goddess of love.

Mooning The act of displaying one's bare buttocks, usually by lowering the pants and bending over.

Mores (MORE-ayz) Social norms or customs that embody the fundamental values of a group. Mores are more strongly enforced than folkways.

Morning sickness Nausea, vomiting, and food aversions associated with pregnancy, perhaps related to high hCG levels.

Morula A solid mass of 16 to 64 cells.

Müllerian duct system The prenatal duct system that will become the female uterus, fallopian tubes, and upper vagina.

Multiphasic pills Oral contraceptives in which the level of hormones change throughout the month. These pills more closely mimic the body's natural hormonal cycle than monophasic pills, in which all the pills in the pack have the same amount of hormone.

Multiple orgasm When a person has an orgasm, and then has one or more additional orgasms without his or her body first going through resolution.

Multiple pregnancy When a woman is pregnant with more than one fetus.

Mutation A random change in the DNA sequence of a gene.

Myometrium The thick middle layer of the uterus, made up of smooth muscle.

Natural family planning Avoidance of sex during a woman's fertile time of her cycle, without the use of any other contraceptive method.

Natural selection A process by which organisms that are best suited to their environment are most likely to survive. Traits that confer a reproductive advantage tend to be passed on, whereas maladaptive traits are lost.

Necrophilia A paraphilia in which a person wants to have sex with corpses.

Negative feedback A control mechanism by which a change sets off a response that counteracts the initial change.

Neurotransmitter A chemical substance released from a nerve cell that carries signals between neurons and other cells.

Nipple The pigmented erectile tissue in the center of the surface of the breast from which milk is secreted.

Nocturnal emissions Also called a "wet dream," this is an ejaculation that occurs during sleep, usually during a dream.

Noncoercive paraphilias Paraphilias that are practiced by individuals privately, or by willing, adult participants.

Nonconsensual sex Also called "non-con," nonconsensual sex involves sexual acts that occur without mutual consent and against the will of one participant.

Nonverbal leakage Cues in a person's body language that indicate their true emotional state or intentions.

Nonviolent but degrading pornography Sexual images with no explicitly violent content, but which may portray acts of submission or humiliation.

NuvaRing The hormonal contraceptive ring.

Nymphomania (NIM-foe-MAY-nee-uh) and satyrism (SAY-ter-ism) Women and men, respectively, with obsessive and uncontrollable sexual desire.

Obscenity A legal term that describes material that appeals to prurient interests; depicts sexual conduct in a way that is patently offensive according to contemporary community standards; and is utterly lacking in serious literary, artistic, political, or scientific value.

Observer effects The effect that the presence of the observer has on a subject's behavior.

Obsessive relational intrusion Similar to stalking, it is the willful and continued intrusion into the personal life of a former partner.

Obsessive-compulsive disorder (OCD) An anxiety disorder characterized by intrusive, unwanted thoughts and repetitive, compulsive acts.

Oedipal complex The idea that men unconsciously want to eliminate or replace their fathers and have sex with their mothers.

Oiran A high-status Japanese prostitute.

On the down-low (DL) An African American slang phrase often used to describe men who have sex with men but who identify as heterosexual.

Oncogenic That which gives rise to tumors or cancer.

Online sexual activity (OSA) The use of the Internet for any activity that involves sexuality, such as entertainment, arousal, education, or the search for sexual partners.

Oogenesis (OH-uh-GEN-ih-sis) The production of eggs.

Oogonia (OH-uh-GO-nee-ah) A stem cell that will become a primary oocyte.

Open marriage A marriage in which partners, with each other's permission and without guilt or jealousy, have intimate relationships with others outside the primary relationship.

Operant conditioning The use of reinforcement and punishment to increase or decrease the likelihood of certain behaviors.

Opportunistic infections An infection by a microorganism that doesn't usually cause disease in a person with a healthy immune system.

Oral contraceptives Chemicals that are taken by mouth to prevent pregnancy.

Orgasm Waves of intense pleasure, an orgasm is often associated with vaginal contractions in females and ejaculation in males.

Orgasmic disorder When there is a delay in or absence of orgasm following sexual stimulation, or if orgasm occurs more quickly than desired.

Orgasmic platform The swelling of the walls of the outer third of the vagina, which occurs during the plateau stage.

Orgasmic reconditioning A behavioral therapy technique designed to reinforce acceptable sexual behaviors, in which a client is instructed to switch from a paraphilic fantasy to a fantasy of a conventional sexual stimulus or behavior as orgasm approaches.

Oropharyngeal cancer Cancer that affects the middle part of the throat.

Ortho Evra The hormonal contraceptive patch.

Os (ahss) The opening of the cervix.

Osteoporosis A disease in which bones become porous and easily fractured. This can often occur in postmenopausal women.

Outdoor sex worker Prostitutes, such as streetwalkers, who establish contact with their clients in outdoor settings.

Outercourse Sexual activity that does not include the insertion of the penis into the vagina, mouth, or anus.

Ovaries The female gonads that produce eggs, estrogen, and progesterone.

Ovulation Release of the ovum into the fallopian tube; the release of the secondary oocyte, usually around day 14 of the cycle.

Ovulation predictor kits Allow a woman to test her urine daily for the presence of luteinizing hormone (LH), which increases prior to ovulation.

Oxytocin (ox-ee-TOE-sin) Hormone involved in uterine contractions, love, and bonding.

Pap smear Developed by Dr. George Papanicolaou, this procedure involves a physician taking a sample of cells from the cervix to test for cellular changes that may indicate infection or cancer.

Paraphilia (pair-uh-FILL-ee-uh) From the Greek words *para,* meaning "deviation," and *philia,* meaning "love or attraction," a paraphilia is a persistent and atypical sexual interest in nonhuman objects, physically or emotionally painful experiences, or nonconsenting or sexually immature individuals.

Parasites Creatures that depend upon a host organism to survive.

Parasympathetic nervous system Nerve pathways involved with maintaining "business as usual" processes in the body, as well as erections.

Partial birth abortion A rarely performed procedure in which an intact fetus is removed from the uterus during the second trimester. Also called *intact dilation and extraction.*

Partialism A fetish that involves a particular body part, such as breasts, hair, or feet.

Participant observation The researcher participates in the events being studied.

Partner rape Forced sexual contact by one's spouse, boyfriend/girlfriend, or partner.

Pedophilia A paraphilia in which an adult is preferentially or sometimes exclusively sexually attracted to prepubescent children.

Peer review process The means by which experts in the field check the quality of a research study.

Pelvic inflammatory disease (PID) An infection of the upper reproductive system in women that can lead to scarring and infertility if untreated; inflammation of the uterus, fallopian tubes, and/or ovaries usually caused by any infection with a microorganism.

Penile implant A surgical implant that creates an artificial erection.

Penile plethysmograph (pluh-THIZ-moh-graf) A device that indirectly measures blood flow in the penis.

Penis From the Latin word for "tail," the penis is the external male genitalia.

Perimenopause The time from the onset of menopausal symptoms until 1 year after a woman's last period.

Perimetrium The outermost layer of the uterus.

Perineum (per-ih-NEE-um) The sensitive skin between the genitals and the anus.

Peyronie's (pay-ra-NEEZ) disease Curvature of the penis caused by the growth of fibrous scar tissue.

PFLAG (Parents and Friends of Lesbians and Gays) A support group for gays, lesbians, bisexuals, as well as transgendered and intersex individuals and their friends and family.

Phenylethylamine (FEN-el-ETH-el-a-mean; PEA) A neurochemical released during infatuation and excitement.

Pheromones (FAIR-uh-mone) A chemical released by one individual that changes the physiology or behavior of another individual of the same species.

Phimosis (fye-MOE-sus) A tight, nonretractable foreskin.

Phone sex A sexually explicit conversation that occurs between two people over the telephone.

Phosphodiesterase-5 (PDE-5) The enzyme inhibited by Viagra.

Physical abuse Includes slapping, beating, kicking, threats with an object or weapon, and murder.

Pill period The bleeding that occurs upon withdrawal from the hormone-containing oral contraceptive pills.

Pimp A person, usually male, who finds and manages customers for prostitutes.

Pituitary gland Also called the "master gland," the pituitary gland produces hormones that control other glands and many bodily functions including growth, metabolism, and reproduction.

Placebo (plu-SEE-bo) An inactive substance that resembles the treatment you are testing.

Placenta The organ that supplies the developing fetus with nutrients and oxygen.

Plasticity The characteristic of the brain that allows it to change and reorganize with experience.

Plateau The period of sexual excitement prior to orgasm, characterized by intensification of the changes begun during excitement.

Pluralistic ignorance A situation where most members of a group privately reject a norm, but secretly and incorrectly assume that most others accept it.

Polar body A by-product of meiosis, this cell contains 23 chromosomes but is nonfunctional.

Polyamory The practice, desire, or acceptance of having more than one loving and sexual relationship at a time, in a context of honesty, openness, and negotiation.

Polyandry The system in which one woman has more than one husband.

Polycystic ovarian syndrome An endocrine disorder in which the ovaries are prevented from releasing an egg; cysts form instead. PCOS is associated with obesity, irregular menstruation, and excessive amounts of androgenic hormones.

Polygamy The practice of having more than one spouse at a time.

Polygyny The system in which one man has more than one wife.

Population The group of individuals being studied.

Pornography Any sexually explicit material that is designed to elicit sexual arousal or interest.

Positive feedback A control mechanism by which a change sets off a response that increases the initial change.

Postpartum depression A form of clinical depression that can affect women after childbirth. Symptoms can be moderate or severe enough to require hospitalization.

Postpartum psychosis A serious mental illness that affects new mothers. It can include severe anxiety, hallucinations, and delusions.

Pragma Pragmatic love that combines storge and ludus.

Preeclampsia A complication of pregnancy, characterized by hypertension, protein in the urine, and fluid retention, which can lead to organ failure, seizures, coma, and death.

Prejudice A hostile or negative attitude toward a distinguishable group.

Premature birth Also called *preterm,* a baby is premature if it is born between 20 and 37 weeks. Babies born at less than 32 weeks of gestation are "very preterm."

Premature ejaculation Ejaculation that occurs too rapidly for one's partner to fully enjoy sexual relations.

Premenstrual dysphoric disorder (PMDD) A severe and debilitating form of PMS.

Premenstrual syndrome (PMS) The physical and/or emotional difficulties that some women experience in the days before menstruation.

Prepared childbirth The mother and her birth partner learn what occurs during labor and delivery, and practice breathing and relaxation techniques.

Prevalence The number or percentage of people in a group that have a particular condition.

Priapism (PRY-uh-pizm) A prolonged and often painful erection.

Primary erogenous zones Sensitive areas of the body, often located around body openings, that lead to sexual arousal when stimulated.

Primary oocyte (OH-uh-site) An immature female germ cell containing 46 chromosomes.

Primary source The original publication of a scientist's data, results, and theories.

Primary spermatocyte (sper-MAT-oh-site) An immature male germ cell containing 46 chromosomes.

Proceptivity An automatic, hormonally driven, situation-independent sexual response.

Procurer or panderer One who procures customers for prostitutes.

Prodromal A set of symptoms that occur before the onset of an attack or disease.

Progesterone Secreted by the ovaries, progesterone is very important in the maintenance of pregnancy.

Progestin A synthetic or externally derived form of progesterone.

Progestin-only pills Also called *mini-pills,* these are oral contraceptives that contain only progestin.

Pro-sexuality The view that pornography has potential benefits.

Prostate gland A gland that surrounds the urethra, which produces a fluid that is added to semen.

Prostate specific antigen (PSA) A protein produced by the prostate; PSA levels are elevated with prostate cancer and BPH.

Prostatitis (PROS-ta-TIE-tis) An inflammation of the prostate gland, usually caused by bacteria.

Prostitution From the Latin *prostituere* meaning "to expose publicly, to set up for sale," prostitution is the exchange of sex for money or items of value.

Protozoa Single-celled animals that are more complex than bacteria.

Proximity Being around another person frequently.

Prurient Having or encouraging an excessive interest in sexual matters. According to the U.S. Court of Appeals, a prurient interest is "a shameful and morbid interest in nudity, sex, or excretion."

Pseudohermaphrodite An obsolete term describing an individual whose internal reproductive organs are of one sex, and whose external genitalia resemble that of the other sex, or are ambiguous.

Psychological abuse Includes behavior that is intended to humiliate or intimidate one's partner, and may take the form of verbal aggression or humiliation, threats of abandonment or abuse, isolation or confinement to the home, and destruction of objects.

Psychology The science of mind, emotions, and behavior.

PTSD (post-traumatic stress disorder) An anxiety disorder that occurs in reaction to a traumatic event. Sufferers can experience flashbacks, emotional numbness, and physical symptoms.

Puberty The stage of life during which physical growth and sexual maturation occur.

Pubic hair (PYOO-bic hair) The hair, often somewhat coarse and stiff, that grows in the pubic region just above the external genitals.

Pubic lice A parasitic insect that infests human genitals.

Pubococcygeus (PU-bo-coc-see- GEE-us; PC) muscles The sling of muscles that form the pelvic floor.

Purity pledge A promise to refrain from sexual activity until marriage.

Queer An umbrella term to describe people with a sexual orientation or gender expression that does not conform to heteronormative society.

Quickening The initial movements of the fetus as felt by the pregnant woman.

Quid pro quo When compliance with unwanted sexual advances is required as a condition of employment or advancement.

Race A group of people who are believed to have the same genetic background based on physical characteristics.

Random sample (also called a *probability sample*) A sample in which each member of the population has an equal probability of participating.

Rape (from the Latin *rapere,* meaning "to seize") The unwanted sexual penetration of the vagina, mouth, or anus by use of force or threat.

Rape myths Commonly held beliefs about rape that are false and which deny and justify male sexual aggression against women.

Recidivism rate The incidence of a person repeating a crime or other antisocial behavior patterns after he or she has been punished for or treated to stop the behavior.

Reciprocity A mutual give and take, generally used to describe the idea that we like someone better if they like us.

Refractory period The period after an orgasm during which a male is physiologically incapable of having another orgasm.

Reliability The extent to which the measurement of a test is consistent and accurate over time.

Religious marriage A religious rite, sacrament, or solemnization of the union of two people.

REM sleep The stage of sleep associated with rapid eye movements, dreams, erections, and a lack of skeletal muscle tone.

Representative sample A sample that has similar characteristics (such as age, sex, ethnicity, education) as the population from which it was drawn.

Research methods A systematic approach to gathering information and evaluating the findings.

Resolution The last stage in Masters and Johnson's sexual response cycle, when the body returns to its non-excited state.

Retrograde ejaculation When ejaculated fluid enters a man's bladder rather than leaving the body.

Retrovirus An RNA virus that requires reverse transcriptase to convert RNA into DNA, which can be incorporated into the host cell's genes.

Rh factor An antigen found on the surface of the red blood cells of most people.

RhoGAM A drug that can prevent an Rh-negative mother's antibodies from reacting to the fetus's Rh-positive cells.

Rhythm method Also known as the calendar method, this is a way to determine a woman's most fertile times by charting her menstrual cycle.

Roe v. Wade The 1973 U.S. Supreme Court decision that stated that most laws against abortion violated a woman's constitutional right to privacy, thus overturning many laws that restricted abortion.

Sadism (SAY-dizm) A paraphilia in which one derives sexual pleasure from intentionally hurting or humiliating others.

Sadomasochism (SAY-doh-ma-suh-kizm) or S&M The consensual use of pain or humiliation for sexual pleasure.

Sample A subset of individuals in the population.

Sampling bias The tendency for some members of the population to be over-represented and others to be excluded from a sample.

Scabies (SKAY-bees) An infestation by mites that burrow into the skin.

Scene An erotic encounter between dominant and submissive partners.

Scopophilia Similar to voyeurism, but in scopophilia the other party consents to being watched.

Scrotum (SKROH-tum) The pouch of skin that holds the testicles.

Sebum A waxy secretion that helps to protect the vulva.

Secondary erogenous zones Areas of the body that become sensitized through personal experience.

Secondary oocyte Also called the *ovum,* this is a female germ cell containing 23 chromosomes that is released from the ovary during ovulation.

Secondary sexual characteristics Traits (other than those that are part of the reproductive system) that distinguish males and females.

Secondary spermatocyte A male germ cell that has gone through its first meiotic division.

Secure attachment Infants show some distress upon caregiver's departure, and are comforted by his or her return.

Selective serotonin reuptake inhibitors (SSRIs) A class of drugs that increase the amount of serotonin available to bind to receptors.

Self-objectification The process by which people regard themselves superficially, by their physical appearance, measurements, or weight, rather than by their health, character, or intelligence.

Semen (SEE-men) The fluid released during ejaculation, which is made up of sperm and seminal fluid.

Seminal fluid The white milky substance produced by the seminal vesicles, prostate gland, and Cowper's glad that provides nutrition and protection for the sperm.

Seminal vesicles Two glands that produce a thick, alkaline secretion that makes up most of semen.

Seminiferous tubules (sem-ih-NIFF-er-us—from Latin roots meaning "seed bearing") Long, convoluted tubes in the testes where sperm is produced.

Sensate focus Designed to reduce anxiety, these exercises help participants focus on the sensory experience, rather than viewing orgasm as the sole goal of sex.

Separation In a liminal experience, the stage where a person is separated from his or her previous situation in anticipation of taking on a new role or identity.

Seroconversion The point at which antibodies to an illness such as HIV are detectable.

Sertoli cells (sir-TOLE-ee) Supportive cells that secrete hormones, nurture developing sperm, and form the blood–testes barrier.

Sex The classification of an individual as male or female, based on a biological foundation.

Sex chromosome The X and Y chromosomes.

Sex flush A reddening of the skin of the chest and upper abdomen that can spread to other parts of the body.

Sex hormone–binding globulin (SHBG) A substance that binds testosterone and keeps it from binding to body cells.

Sex reassignment The process by which transsexuals change their physical and legal status to better align with their gender identity. This process may include psychological counseling, hormone therapy, and surgery.

Sex tourism Travel undertaken with the specific motivation of engaging in sexual activity.

Sex trafficking The recruitment, harboring, transportation, or obtaining of a person for the purpose of a commercial sex act.

Sex work Describes services, performances, or the production of products given in exchange for material compensation. Sex work includes pornography, prostitution, exotic dancing, commercial phone sex, and other occupations.

Sexaholics Anonymous (SA) A 12-step program designed to help people recover from sex addiction.

Sexism A belief that one sex is inferior to the other, often characterized by discriminatory or abusive behavior toward the other sex.

Sexologist One who studies human sexuality. Sexologists may come from various disciplines, including biology, medicine, psychology, sociology, anthropology, and criminology. Many sexologists are also therapists or educators.

Sexting Sending sexually explicit messages or images by cell phone or other electronic media.

Sexual arousal disorders The persistent or recurrent inability to attain or maintain sufficient sexual excitement necessary for satisfactory sexual encounters.

Sexual assault Sexual contact or activity that occurs without consent.

Sexual aversion disorder Aversion to or avoidance of sexual activity.

Sexual bribery and imposition The promise of reward in return for sex or the threat of punishment for withholding sex, and forceful physical attempts at sexual contact.

Sexual disorder An inability to react physically or emotionally to sexual stimulation compared to an average healthy person or according to one's own standards.

Sexual fantasies Mental imagery that is sexually arousing to the individual.

Sexual fluidity The idea that a person may change from other-sex attractions to same-sex attractions throughout his or her life.

Sexual harassment Unwanted sexual attention that interferes with an individual's basic right to employment or education.

Sexual health The World Health Organization defines sexual health as ". . . a state of physical, emotional, mental, and social well-being related to sexuality . . . [that] requires a positive and respectful approach to sexuality and sexual responses, as well as the possibility of having pleasurable and safe sexual experiences."

Sexual orientation A person's predisposition or inclination regarding sexual behavior, emotional attachment, or physical attraction to one or both sexes.

Sexual reproduction The creation of new generations by the fusion of egg and sperm.

Sexual response The physical and emotional ways a person may respond to sexual stimulation.

Sexual script The socially learned idea of "proper" sexual behavior. Men and women often have different sexual scripts; traditionally, men are seen as the sexual initiators, and women as the "gatekeepers" who decide how much sexual activity will occur.

Sexual violence Sexual actions or words that are unwanted by and/or harmful to another person.

Sexuality A broad term that includes many facets of the way we experience our lives as sexual beings. Sexuality encompasses our sexual behaviors, feelings, gender identities and roles, sexual orientation, and reproduction. It is influenced by physical, psychological, spiritual, and cultural factors.

Sexuality education A broad term to describe education about human sexuality, which may include information about physical, emotional, and social aspects of sexual health and disease; as well as rights and responsibilities; identity; values and attitudes; and many other aspects of sexual behavior.

Sexualization To make sexual (usually inappropriately), or to hold a person to a standard that equates a narrowly defined physical attractiveness with being sexy.

Sexually dimorphic An anatomical area that has a different form in males and females.

Sexually explicit but not violent or degrading pornography Sexual images that are not coerced, violent, or degrading.

Sexually transmitted infection (STI) An infection that is most commonly transmitted through sexual contact, such as chlamydia, genital herpes, or HIV.

Shared focus An external subject that both participants can see, hear, or experience.

Single blind study An experimental procedure in which the subjects do not know if they have received the treatment being tested.

Sixty-nine Simultaneous oral-genital stimulation.

Smegma A thick and malodorous substance that can accumulate under the foreskin in uncircumcised men.

Social aggression Also called *relational aggression*, this type of aggression involves the causing of harm by intentionally damaging one's relationship with others.

Social expectancy theory The theory that suggests that our expectations about how we'll be treated become a self-fulfilling prophecy.

Social skills training A form of behavioral therapy designed to help people who have difficulties relating to other people.

Socialization The way people learn and adopt the behavior patterns of their culture.

Society A group of people that share cultural aspects such as language, dress, and norms of behavior.

Sociobiology/evolutionary psychology The study of how evolutionary forces affect our behavior.

Sodomy Any sexual act that is not penile-vaginal penetration although it usually refers to oral or anal intercourse.

Soft-core pornography Less sexually explicit than hard-core pornography, soft-core pornography may depict nudity, but not penetration or other explicit sexual acts.

Spectatoring Mentally stepping outside of oneself during sexual activity with a partner and monitoring the experience.

Speed dating A dating event in which people meet a large number of people through a series of short one-on-one encounters.

Sperm The male gamete.

Sperm washing A procedure in which sperm cells are separated from semen, to facilitate the removal of dead or slow moving sperm, as well as prostaglandins, which might impair fertilization.

Spermatic cord The cord-like structure containing blood vessels, nerves, and the vas deferens that runs from the abdomen down to each testicle.

Spermatid (SPERM-ma-tid) An immature sperm cell with 23 chromosomes.

Spermatogenesis (sper-mat-o-GEN-i-sis) The production of sperm.

Spermatogonia (sper-mat-o-GO-nee-ah) A stem cell that will become a sperm.

Spermatozoa (sper-mat-o-ZO-ah) A mature sperm cell.

Spermicide A contraceptive agent that kills sperm.

Spina bifida A congenital defect in which the spinal cord is exposed and imperfectly fused.

Spirochete (SPY-ro-keet) A spiral-shaped bacterium.

Sploshers Those who are sexually excited by having wet and messy substances smeared on their body.

Statutory rape Sexual intercourse with someone who is not a child, but who is below the age of consent.

Stereotype An oversimplified, preconceived idea about a group of individuals.

Stereotype threat The fear that one will perform negatively on a task and that this will confirm an existing stereotype of a group with which one identifies.

Sterility The complete inability to conceive.

Sterilization The act of making a man or woman unable to reproduce.

Steroid A type of lipid molecule with a multiple-ring structure.

Stillbirth The death of a fetus more than 20 weeks after conception but before birth.

Stonewalling Emotionally or physically removing yourself from the conflict by not responding to your partner.

Stop-start technique A method of overcoming premature ejaculation in which a man and his partner learn to recognize when he is approaching orgasm, temporarily stop sexual stimulation, and restart when he has regained some control.

Storge Companionate attachment or nonsexual affection.

Straight A slang term for a heterosexual.

Stranger rape Forced sexual contact by someone unknown to the victim.

Streaking The act of taking off one's clothes and running naked through a public place.

Streetwalkers/Streetworkers The low-status prostitute who attracts customers by working on the street.

Strip club A bar or nightclub that offers erotic dancing, striptease, and possibly other related services such as lap dances.

Superego Our sense of morality, or conscience.

Surfactant A substance that prevents the collapse of the lungs.

Surrogate mother A woman who is artificially inseminated and carries a baby to term for another woman or couple.

Surveys A scientific collection of data from people regarding their attitudes, beliefs, and behaviors.

Swinging Non-monogamous, consensual sexual activity that is experienced together as a couple.

Sympathetic nervous system The branch of the autonomic nervous system that prepares the body for emergency, stress, activity, and excitement; a series of nerves that are involved with "fight or flight" responses, the sympathetic nervous system also diminishes erection and is more active during orgasm.

Symptomatic HIV infection A person's T-cell count has fallen enough to start producing symptoms.

Symptothermal method A combination of fertility awareness based methods used to determine a woman's most fertile time.

Syphilis (SIH-fi-lis) A bacterial STI that has progressive stages.

Telephone scatologia Also called *scatolophilia,* or *obscene phone calling,* this paraphilia is characterized by sexual arousal through the use of obscene language to unsuspecting victims on the phone. The term scatologia comes from the Greek words *skato* for "dung" and *logos* for speech.

"Tend and befriend" A behavioral pattern in response to stress that involves tending offspring and seeking out others for joint protection. This better characterizes the female response to threat or stress.

Teratogen An agent that can cause physical defects in the developing embryo or fetus.

Testes (TEST-ease, singular: testis or testicle) The male gonad that produces sperm and testosterone.

Testosterone Produced by the testes and in small amounts by the ovaries, this hormone stimulates development of male sexual characteristics, bone and muscle growth, and libido.

The attachment phase A long-term bond between partners.

The attraction phase The period of time during which couples are infatuated and pursue a relationship.

The lust phase An intense craving for sexual contact.

T-lymphocytes A group of white blood cells involved in cell-mediated immunity.

Top The dominant or controlling partner in a BDSM relationship.

Toucherism Also called *groping,* this is when the offender touches intimate parts of a nonconsenting person with his hands.

Toxemia A potentially dangerous condition of pregnancy characterized by hypertension, edema, and protein in the urine.

Toxic shock syndrome (TSS) A rare but potentially fatal pattern of symptoms caused by bacteria. The use of very absorbent tampons can increase the risk of TSS.

Trachoma A bacterial infection of the eye caused by infection with the bacterium *Chlamydia trachomatis.*

Traditional marriage A marriage in which spouses assume traditional gender roles.

Transgendered A general term for variations of gender expression, including female and male impersonators, transsexuals, and drag kings and queens.

Transgendered prostitutes Male-to-female sex workers.

Transition The actual liminal stage, when the person is not in one state or another, but is "betwixt and between."

Transitional labor The shortest and hardest stage of labor, during which the cervix dilates to its full 10 centimeters and the head of the fetus moves into the birth canal.

Transman and transwoman A person who is born male but identifies as female can be called male-to-female (MTF) or a transwoman. One who is born female but identifies as male is called female-to-male (FTM) or transman.

Transsexual A more specific term, referring to people who feel that their biological sex doesn't represent their true identity.

Transverse The birth position in which the baby's shoulders or arms are presented first.

Transvestic fetishism A paraphilia in which a man becomes sexually aroused by wearing woman's clothing.

Transvestite A person, usually male, who derives sexual gratification from dressing in the clothing of the opposite sex.

Tribadism A form of non-penetrative sex in which two women rub their vulvas together.

Trichomoniasis (trick-oh-moe-NYE-uh-sis) Also called "trich" (pronounced *trick*), this is a common STI caused by a single-celled protozoan parasite.

Trick An act of prostitution. Also, a customer to a prostitute.

Triphasic model Helen Singer Kaplan's model of sexual response that includes desire, excitement, and orgasm.

True hermaphrodite An obsolete term describing a congenital condition in which a person has both testes and ovaries.

Tubal sterilization A procedure in which the fallopian tubes are cut or blocked, thus preventing the egg and sperm from meeting.

Twin concordance rate The extent to

which each twin shares similar characteristics such as height, weight, or sexual orientation.

Ultrasound A procedure in which sound waves are bounced off internal tissues in order to visualize the fetus.

Ultraviolet (UV) light A component of sunlight that is beneficial in small amounts, but can damage the skin cells and cause premature aging and skin cancer.

Umbilical cord The cord that connects the placenta to the fetus.

Unrequited love (un-ree-KWHY-ted) Love that is not reciprocated.

Unwanted sex Sex that is willingly consented to, although at least one participant may have no sexual interest or motivation to take part in the sexual activity.

Unwanted sexual attention Inappropriate and offensive sexual comments, behaviors, and advances.

Urethra (you-REE-thra) Tubular structure that serves as a passageway for both urine and semen.

Urophilia Sexual arousal by contact with urine.

Uterus The pear-shaped organ in which a fertilized egg is implanted and a fetus develops.

Vacuum aspiration A surgical method of abortion, in which the uterine contents are removed by suction.

Vacuum pressure pump A manual or battery-operated pump that draws blood into the penis to create an erection.

Vagina From the Latin word meaning "sheath" or "scabbard," the vagina is the muscular passage into which the penis is inserted during heterosexual intercourse and through which the baby passes during birth.

Vaginal photoplethysmograph A device that uses light to indirectly measure blood flow to the vagina.

Vaginismus A painful involuntary spasm of the muscles of the vagina.

Vaginitis An inflammation of the vagina.

Validity The extent to which findings accurately reflect the concept that they are intended to measure.

Variable Anything that can vary or change, such as an attitude or a behavior.

Varicocele (VAIR-ih-ko-seel) A dilated vein in the spermatic cord.

Vas deferens (Vas DEAF-er-enz, plural: vas deferentia) The tube that carries sperm from each epididymis to the ejaculatory duct.

Vascular surgery An operation to improve blood flow to the penis to improve erection.

Vasectomy A method of sterilization in which the vas deferentia are cut, preventing sperm from being added to the ejaculate.

Vasocongestion Accumulation of blood in the genitals caused by sexual excitement.

Vasopressin (vay-zo-PRESS-in) Hormone that affects water levels in the body, as well as bonding and parenting behaviors.

Vernix A white waxy substance that coats and protects the skin of the fetus.

Vestibule The cavity between the labia minora that contains the openings of the urethra and vagina.

Viagra One of a number of drugs used to treat erectile dysfunction.

Vibrator A dildo powered by batteries or electricity to vibrate, thus intensifying genital stimulation.

Violent pornography Images of sexual violence or sexual coercion against an individual.

Viral load The amount of virus present in the blood. This gives an idea of the severity of a viral infection.

Viruses Submicroscopic infectious agents that need a host to grow and reproduce.

Volunteer bias The tendency for those who volunteer for research to be different in some way from those who refuse to participate.

Vomeronasal organ (VNO) The organ that detects pheromones in many species. Its function in humans is controversial.

Voyeur pornography Sexual images taken of people who are unaware they are being filmed.

Voyeurism (VOI-yer-izm) A paraphilia characterized by the urge to observe an unsuspecting person or persons while they are naked or engaged in sexual activities.

Vulva (VUL-vah) The external female genitalia. Another word for vulva is *pudendum,* which regrettably derives from the Latin word meaning "something to be ashamed of."

Waist-to-hip ratio (WHR) The ratio of a person's waist measurement to his or her hip measurement. Someone with a 28-inch waist and 40-inch hips would have a WHR of 0.7.

Widow A woman whose partner has died.

Widower A man whose partner has died.

Window period The period between exposure to HIV and the time at which antibodies are evident in a blood test.

Withdrawal Also called *coitus interruptus,* the withdrawal method of contraception is when a man removes his penis from the vagina and ejaculates outside of the woman's body.

Withdrawal A group of symptoms that occurs after abrupt discontinuation of a drug. These symptoms are usually the opposite of the drug itself. For instance, heroin use causes relaxation, analgesia, and constipation, and withdrawal from the drug causes agitation, pain, and diarrhea.

Wolffian duct system The prenatal duct system that will become the male epididymis, vas deferens, and seminal vesicles.

Zona pellucida The thick protective coating around the egg.

Zoophilia (zoh-oh-FILL-ee-uh) Fantasies or urges to have sexual contact with animals. When actual sexual contact occurs, it is called bestiality.

Zygote A fertilized egg.

subject index

Phenylethylamine (PEA)
  chemical structure of, 191
  explanation of, 191
Pheromones, 144
Phi, 164
Phimosis, 65
Phone sex, 453
Phosphodiesterase-5 (PDE-5), 147
Physical abuse, 425
Physical attractiveness, 194
PID. *See* Pelvic inflammatory disease (PID)
Pill period, 294
Pimp, 449
Pituitary gland (master gland)
  definition of, 58
  oxytocin and, 191
Placebo
  explanation of, 38
  oxytocin, 191
Placenta
  abnormalities, 344
  explanation of, 331
  expulsion of, 341, 342
Plan B, 307, 308, 309
Planned Parenthood of Southeastern Pennsylvania v. Casey, 313, 314
Plasticity, 107
Plateau
  effects of, 138
  explanation of, 132, 133
  HSRC phase and, 130
Playboy (magazine), 72, 437, 438, 443
Playgirl (magazine), 437
Plural marriages, 217
Pluralistic ignorance, 179
PMS. *See* Premenstrual syndrome (PMS)
Pocket pussies, 271
"Point of no return," 135, 136
Polar body, 82
Polyamory, 216
Polyandry, 216
Polycystic ovarian syndrome, 295
Polygamy
  explanation of, 216
  Mormons and, 217
Polygyny, 12
  common culture and, 224
  explanation of, 216
"Poppers," 155
Population, 33
Porky's (movie), 396
Pornography
  attitudes and, 442
  benefits of, 442, 443
  categories of, 437–439, 440
  Denmark and, 440–441
  explanation of, 436
  genres of, 437
  harmful aspects of, 443
  history of, 440
  Internet and, 400, 439
  Japan and, 440
  nonviolent, 443
  other cultures and, 440, 441
  sexuality and, 111
Positive feedback, 58
Post-abortion syndrome (PAS), 313, 314
Post-exposure prophylaxis (PEP), 375
Postpartum depression, 347
Postpartum period, 347
Postpartum psychosis, 347
Pragma, 187
Preeclampsia, 327
Preemies, 345

Pregnancy
  abortions and, 311–313
  abstinence and, 301
  anandamide and, 77
  breast size and, 80
  chances of, 291
  Depo-Provera and, 296
  first trimester of, 330–332, 333
  intercourse positions and, 334, 335
  IUDs and, 303
  length of, 329
  maternal death and, 330
  miscarriage and second trimester of, 336
  mythical causes of, 290
  oral contraceptives and, 295
  problems during, 335–338, 339
  rabbit test and, 330
  rape and, 414
  second trimester and, 333, 334
  teen, 5, 6, 339
  teen rates of, 17, 25
  television sexual content and, 20
  tests, 329, 330
  third trimester and, 334, 335
  trichomoniasis and, 376
  twins and, 330, 331
  unplanned, 338, 339, 340
  woman's body and, 329, 333
  yeast infection and, 375
Prejudice, 254, 255
Premature birth
  explanation of, 345
  low birth weight and, 345
Premature ejaculation (PE), 149
Premenstrual dysphoric disorder (PMDD), 93
Premenstrual syndrome (PMS)
  explanation of, 92, 93
  symptomatic causes of, 93
Prenatal development
  embryonic stage of, 331, 332
  germinal stage and, 330
  organ development and, 333
  physical development and, 333, 334
Prepared childbirth, 343
Prepuce, 51
Pretty Baby (movie), 446
Pretty Woman (movie), 200, 446
Prevalence, 356
Priapism
  explanation of, 65
  older adults and, 146
  PDE5 and, 147
Primary erogenous zones, 143, 272, 273
Primary oocyte, 82
Primary source, 44
Primary spermatocyte, 64
Prison rape, 412
Probability sample, 34
Proceptivity, 130
Procreation, 12
Procurer, 449
Prodromal, 366
Progesterone
  explanation of, 81
  functions of, 59, 81
  hormone replacement therapy and, 89
  luteal phase and, 85
  PMS symptoms and, 93
  sex offenders and, 142
  testosterone and, 61
Progestin
  definition of, 89
  Depo-Provera and, 296
  luteinizing hormone (LH) and, 294

Progestin-only pills, 294
Prolactin
  functions of, 59
  orgasm and, 133
  refractory period and, 135
Propecia, 65
Pro-sexuality, 442
Prostaglandins
  prenatal drugs and, 156
  sperm washing and, 326
  uterus and, 77
Prostate cancer
  masturbation and, 265
  symptoms of, 66, 67
Prostate gland
  definition of, 57
  ejaculatory pathway and, 57
  health issues and, 65–67
  orgasms and, 135
  Skene's glands and, 75
Prostate specific antigen (PSA), 67
Prostatitis, 66
Prostitution
  characteristics of prostitutes and, 447, 448
  customers of, 449, 450
  explanation of, 445
  health and, 450, 451
  history of, 451, 452
  law and, 452, 453
  legalization of, 454, 455
  male, 448, 449
  military and, 452
  occupational mortality and, 451
  participants in, 446–449, 450
  prevalence of, 446
  pros/cons of, 454, 455
  reasons for male visitations and, 450
  sex trafficking and, 451
  types of, 446, 447
Protect Act (Prosecutorial Remedies and Other Tools to End the Exploitation of Children Today), 438
Protectaid, 297
Protestant Reformation, 11
Protestantism
  contraception and, 290
  view of sexuality and, 11
Protozoa, 356
Protozoal infections, 376
Proximity, 194
Prozac, 156, 389, 398
Prurient, 441
PSA. *See* Prostate specific antigen (PSA)
Pseudohermaphrodite, 119
PsychINFO database, 74
Psychoanalytic theory, 237, 388
Psychological abuse, 425
Psychology
  behavioral theories and, 10
  cognitive learning theories and, 10
  explanation of, 9
  sexuality theories and, 9, 10
  social learning theories and, 10
  theories of love, 193
Psychopathia Sexualis (Krafft-Ebing), 30, 386
PTSD (post-traumatic stress disorder), 254
Puberty
  body image and, 171
  breasts and, 79, 80
  circumcision and, 51
  explanation of, 79
  genital phase and, 9
  hormones and, 61
  oocytes and, 82

steroids and, 62
    WHR and, 166
    women and, 82, 143
Theories of love, 193
There's Something about Mary (movie), 267
Third trimester, 334, 335
Thirtysomething (TV show), 252
T-lymphocytes, 372
Tobacco
    penile cancer and, 65
    testicular cancer and, 65
Today sponge, 297
Top, 390
Touch, 143
Toucher and toucherism, 388, 396
Toxemia, 336
Toxic shock syndrome (TSS), 94
Trachoma, 358
Trading Places (movie), 446
Traditional marriage, 212
Transcutaneous electrical nerve stimulation
    (TENS), 344
Transgendered prostitutes, 449
Transgenders/Transsexuals
    congenital adrenal hyperplasia (CAH) and,
        121, 122
    cross-dressing and, 390
    discrimination and, 117, 118
    explanation of, 116
    gender origins of, 116
    Klinefelter's syndrome and, 121
    legal issues and, 119
    salaries and, 106
    sex reassignment and, 116
    sexual harassment and, 428
    treatment path for, 32
Transition, 216, 217
Transitional labor, 340, 341
Transman/transwoman, 116
Transverse position, 341
Transvestic fetishism, 390
Transvestites
    Bible and, 397
    explanation of, 18
Triangular theory of love, 188
Tribadism, 271
Trichomoniasis
    explanation of, 376
    protozoa and, 356
    STI and, 357, 380
Trick, 446
Tricksters, 394
Trimethylamine, 76
Triphasic model, 137
True hermaphrodite, 119
Trust, pro-relationship and, 206
TSS. *See* Toxic shock syndrome (TSS)
Tubal sterilization, 304, 305
Tuskegee Syphilis Study, 362
Twins, 330, 331
2D:4D ratio, 240

Ultrasound, 336, 338
Ultraviolet (UV) light, 164
Ulysses (Joyce), 441
Umbilical cord
    birthing and, 342
    explanation of, 331
Unitarian Universalist
    homosexual behavior and, 252
    human sexuality and, 13
United Methodist, human sexuality and, 13
Unrequited love, 196

Unwanted sex, 175
Unwanted sexual attention, 428
Urethra
    definition of, 52
    explanation of, 75
    female, 73, 75
    sperm and, 58
Urinary tract infections (UTI), 75
Urophilia, 392
U.S. Supreme Court
    pornography and, 437
    sexual harassment and, 428
Uterine tubes, 77
Uterus
    explanation of, 77
    follicular phase and, 84
    labeled parts of, 76
    PID and, 359
    sexual response and, 131

Vaccine
    Gardasil, 365
    hepatitis B, 368
Vacuum aspiration, 312
Vacuum pressure pumps, 148
Vagina
    bacterial vaginosis and, 362, 363
    birth canal and, 76
    childbirth and, 341, 342, 343
    contraceptive ring and, 296
    dilators and, 151
    explanation of, 75
    fibrogenase and, 58
    function of, 76
    resolution phase and, 137
    sexual practices and, 268–274
    sexual response and, 131
    uterus and, 76
    vaginal photoplethysmograph and, 37
    vulva and, 73
    yeast infection and, 375
Vaginal intercourse
    adolescents and, 277
    HIV and, 371
    outercourse and, 301
    positions of, 273–274
Vaginal photoplethysmograph
    explanation of, 37
    sexual arousal and, 130
Vaginal rejuvenation, 73
Vaginismus
    explanation of, 150
    lesbian community and, 151
Vaginitis, 362
Vaginosis, 76
Validity, 33
Values
    abstinence-only education and, 24
    forming, 15
Variables, 38
Varicocele, 66
Vas deferens, 57
Vascular surgery, 148
Vasectomy, 57
Vasocongestion, 131
Vasomax, 148
Vasopressin
    explanation of, 191
    orgasm and, 133
    pair bonding and, 191
Venereal diseases. *See* Sexually transmitted
    infections (STI)
Vernix, 334

Vestibule, 75
Viagra
    Brazil program and, 146
    delayed ejaculation and, 151
    effects of, 147
    explanation of, 147
    premature ejaculation and, 149
    priapism and, 65
    sex attitudes and, 36
    sexuality study and, 39–40
    side effects of, 147
    spinal cord injuries and, 281
    working process of, 147
Vibrators
    explanation of, 264, 265
    types of, 271
Victorian Era, sexuality and, 11
Video pornography, 438
Videogames
    Bully, 253
    Grand Theft Auto, 253
    Grand Theft Auto: San Andreas, 440
    SaGa Frontier, 253
    sexual media and, 439, 440
    Sims, The, 440
Viral infections
    herpes and, 365–366, 367
    HIV/AIDS, 368–374, 375
    HPV, 363–364, 365
    viral hepatitis, 367, 368
Viral load
    explanation of, 372
    HIV progression and, 373
    HIV-positive and, 374
Virginity, 414
Viruses, 356
Vision
    sexual response and, 143
    Viagra and, 147
Volunteer bias, 35
Vomeronasal organ (VNO), 144
Voyeur and voyeurism
    Bible and, 397
    exhibitionist and, 394
    explanation of, 388, 394, 395
    Peeping Tom, 396
Voyeur pornography, 437
Vulva
    anatomy of, 73
    components of the, 72–74, 75
    definition of, 72

Waist-to-hip ratio (WHR), 166
Web sites
    ArtsReformation.com, 21
    gaygamer.net, 253
    gaysingles.come, 253
    peteralsop.com, 101
    social networks and, 20
Weight
    appearances and, 170
    diets and, 169
    physiological differences and, 105
Wet dreams, 267
White Slave Traffic Act, 452
Whites
    abortions and, 310
    body image and, 171
    breast cancer and, 90
    cervical cancer and, 364, 365
    children and households of, 211
    chlamydia and, 358
    chlamydia/gonorrhea rates and, 360